Your Office

PREMIUM MEDIA SITE

Improve your grade with hands-on tools and resources!

- Master *Key Terms* to expand your vocabulary.
- Prepare for exams by taking practice quizzes in the *Online Chapter Review*.
- Download *Student Data Files* for the applications projects in each chapter.

And for even more tools, you can access the following Premium Resources using your Access Code. Register now to get the most out of ***Your Office!***

- *Blue Box Videos* are brief videos that accompany each active blue box in the workshop. These videos demonstrate the steps as well as the concepts to accomplish the individual skills of each workshop.*
- *Real World Interview Videos* feature real business professionals from a variety of backgrounds discussing how they use the skills and objectives of each workshop to be successful in their careers.*

*Access code required for these premium resources

Your Access Code is:

Note: If there is no silver foil covering the access code, it may already have been redeemed, and therefore may no longer be valid. In that case, you can purchase online access using a major credit card or PayPal account. To do so, go to **www.pearsonhighered.com/youroffice**, select your book cover, click on "Buy Access" and follow the on-screen instructions.

To Register:

- To start you will need a valid email address and this access code.
- Go to **www.pearsonhighered.com/youroffice** and scroll to find your text book.
- Once you've selected your text, on the Home Page, click the link to access the Student Premium Content.
- Click the Register button and follow the on-screen instructions.
- After you register, you can sign in any time via the log-in area on the same screen.

System Requirements

Windows 7 Ultimate Edition; IE 8
Windows Vista Ultimate Edition SP1; IE 8
Windows XP Professional SP3; IE 7
Windows XP Professional SP3; Firefox 3.6.4
Mac OS 10.5.7; Firefox 3.6.4
Mac OS 10.6; Safari 5

Technical Support

http://247pearsoned.custhelp.com

Microsoft Office® 2013

VOLUME 1

Amy Kinser

KINSER | LENDING | MORIARITY

O'KEEFE | POPE | SHAH

PEARSON

Boston Columbus Indianapolis New York San Francisco Upper Saddle River
Amsterdam Cape Town Dubai London Madrid Milan Munich Paris Montréal Toronto
Delhi Mexico City São Paulo Sydney Hong Kong Seoul Singapore Taipei Tokyo

Editor in Chief: Michael Payne
Acquisitions Editor: Samantha McAfee Lewis
Product Development Manager: Laura Burgess
Editorial Project Manager: Anne Garcia
Development Editor: Nancy Lamm
Editorial Assistant: Laura Karahalis
Director of Digital Development: Taylor Ragan
VP Director of Digital Strategy: Paul Gentile
Digital Media Editor: Eric Hakanson
Production Media Project Manager: John Cassar
Director of Marketing: Maggie Moylan Leen
Marketing Manager: Brad Forrester
Marketing Coordinator: Susan Osterlitz
Marketing Assistant: Darshika Vyas
Managing Editor: Camille Trentacoste
Sr. Production Project Manager/IT Procurement Lead: Natacha Moore
Senior Art Director: Jonathan Boylan
Manager, Cover Visual Research & Permissions: Karen Sanatar
Manager of Rights & Permissions: Michelle McKenna
Cover and Interior Design: Jonathan Boylan
Composition: GEX Publishing Services
Full-Service Project Management: GEX Publishing Services

Credits and acknowledgments borrowed from other sources and reproduced, with permission, in this textbook appear on appropriate page within text.

Pearson Education Ltd., London
Pearson Education Singapore, Pte. Ltd
Pearson Education, Canada, Inc.
Pearson Education–Japan
Pearson Education Australia PTY, Limited
Pearson Education North Asia Ltd., Hong Kong
Pearson Educación de Mexico, S.A. de C.V.
Pearson Education Malaysia, Pte. Ltd.
Pearson Education, Upper Saddle River, New Jersey

Library of Congress Cataloging-in-Publication Data available upon request

10 9 8 7 6 5 4 3 2 1
ISBN-13: 978-0-13-314269-3
ISBN-10: 0-13-314269-8

Dedications

I dedicate this series to my Kinser Boyz for their unwavering love, support, and patience; to my family; to my students for inspiring me; to Sam for believing in me; and to the instructors I hope this series will inspire!

Amy Kinser

For my wife, Amy, and our two boys, Matt and Aidan. I cannot thank them enough for their support, love, and endless inspiration.

J. Eric Kinser

I dedicate this book to my mother, Dagmar, for inspiring my love of books. And to Art, for keeping life going while I work too much and for making life so much fun when I'm not working.

Diane Lending

I dedicate this book to my amazing wife, April. Without her support and understanding this would not have been possible.

Brant Moriarity

This book is a product of the unselfish support and patience of my wife and daughters, Bonnie, Kelsie, and Maggie, and of the values instilled by my parents, Paul and Carol. They are the authors—I am just a writer.

Timothy O'Keefe

For my wife, Laura, and for my children Sophie, Richard, and Anna Grace, who all tolerated my absence while writing, and to my dad, who always loved my books.

Charles Pope

I dedicate this book to my family and friends for all their support and love through the years. To Shila, for always being there. And last, but always most, to Fred and Maya for their amazing faith, patience, and love!

Ancelin Shah

My work is dedicated to those who taught me all I ever wanted to know and answered all the questions I was never afraid to ask.

Hilda Wirth Federico

I dedicate this book to my fiancée, Anny, for generously sacrificing her time to provide feedback and support me through the writing process; to my network of friends; to the administrators at Passaic County Community College who supported me in pursuing my dream of writing, specifically, President Steve Rose, Vice President Jackie Kineavy, and Dean Bill Morrison; and to my students, who make this all worthwhile.

Eric Cameron

About the Authors

Amy S. Kinser, Esq., Series Editor

Amy holds a B.A. degree in Chemistry with a Business minor from Indiana University, and a J.D. from the Maurer School of Law, also at Indiana University. After working as an environmental chemist, starting her own technology consulting company, and practicing intellectual property law, she has spent the past 12 years teaching technology at the Kelley School of Business in Bloomington, Indiana—#1-ranked school for undergraduate program performance in the specialty of Information Systems according to 2012 *Bloomberg Businessweek*. Currently, she serves as the Director of Computer Skills and Senior Lecturer at the Kelley School of Business at Indiana University. She also loves spending time with her two sons, Aidan and J. Matthew, and her husband J. Eric.

J. Eric Kinser, Mobile Computing and Excel Author

Eric Kinser received his B.S. degree in Biology from Indiana University and his M.S. in Counseling and Education from the Indiana School of Education. He has worked in the medical field and in higher education as a technology and decision support specialist. He is currently a lecturer in the Operations and Decision Technology Department at the Kelley School of Business at Indiana University. When not teaching he enjoys experimenting with new technologies, traveling, and hiking with his family.

Dr. Diane Lending, Access Author

Diane Lending is a Professor at James Madison University where she has taught Computer Information Systems since 2000. She received a Ph.D. in Management Information Systems from the University of Minnesota and a B.A. degree in Mathematics from the University of Virginia. Her research interests are in adoption of information technology and information systems education. She enjoys traveling; playing card and board games; and living in the country with her husband, daughter, and numerous pets.

Brant Moriarity, PowerPoint Author

Brant Moriarity earned a B.A. in Religious Studies/Philosophy and an M.S. in Information Systems at Indiana University. He is a full-time lecturer at the Indiana University Kelley School of Business where he teaches "The Computer in Business." In addition to teaching, he also builds and maintains websites, databases, and several web-based information systems. He is currently researching ways to use mobile technologies to enhance the classroom for both students and faculty.

Dr. Timothy P. O'Keefe, Excel Author

Tim is Professor of Information Systems and Chair of the Department of Information Systems and Business Communication at the University of North Dakota. He is an Information Technology consultant, cofounder of a successful Internet services company, and has taught in higher education for 30 years. Tim is married to his high school sweetheart, Bonnie; they have two beautiful daughters, Kelsie and Maggie. His life is greatly enriched by family, cherished friends and colleagues, and his dogs. In his spare time he enjoys traveling, cooking, and archery.

Charles Pope, PowerPoint Author

Charles is a Senior Lecturer in the Computer Science Department of the School of Informatics and Computing at Indiana University, Bloomington. He has been teaching a very large, multisection service course, "Introduction to Computers and Computing," since 2003. Prior to teaching, he worked in the Technology Industry as a project manager and client executive for major accounts. He received a B.A. in Religious Studies/Theology, a B.S. in Management Information Systems, and a B.S. in Business Administration from Ambassador University.

Ancelin Shah, Word Author

Anci received a B.S. degree in Computer Science and a Masters of Computer Science from Texas A&M University. After working as a UNIX systems administrator, and then as a UNIX and Perl training consultant, she has spent the last 13 years as an instructor in the Computer Science Technology Department at Houston Community College where she earned the NISOD Excellence Award in teaching twice. When not working she enjoys spending time with her family, Fred, Chris, Katie, Maya, and their cat Napawleon.

Hilda Wirth Federico, Integrated Projects Author

Hilda has taught computer literacy and applications courses at Jacksonville University in Jacksonville, Florida, for over 20 years. She recently retired to have more time for writing and traveling. She enjoys visiting new countries and learning about different cultures. Her current goal is to see the sites recently declared the New Seven Wonders of the World. So far, she has visited six of the seven destinations and is planning to check the last one off her list very soon.

Eric Cameron, Windows 8 Author

Eric holds an M.S. in Computer Science and a B.S. degree in Computer Science with minors in Mathematics and Physics, both from Montclair State University. He is an Assistant Professor at Passaic County Community College, where he has taught in the Computer and Information Sciences Department since 2001. He maintains a professional blog at profcameron.blogspot.com. He is also occasionally an adjunct professor at Bergen Community College.

Brief Contents

Windows 8

Common Features

Cloud Mobile Computing

Word

Excel

Access

PowerPoint

Integrated Projects

Appendix

Contents

WINDOWS 8

WORD MODULE 2

EXCEL MODULE 1

ACCESS MODULE 1

POWERPOINT MODULE 1

POWERPOINT MODULE 2

INTEGRATED PROJECTS

Acknowledgments

The ***Your Office*** team would like to thank the following reviewers who have invested time and energy to help shape this series from the very beginning, providing us with invaluable feedback through their comments, suggestions, and constructive criticism.

We'd like to especially thank our Focus Group attendees and User Diary Reviewers:

Heather Albinger
Waukesha County Technical College

Melody Alexander
Ball State University

Mazhar Anik
Owens Community College

David Antol
Hartford Community College

Cheryl Brown
Delgado Community College

Janet Campbell
Dixie State College

Kuan Chen
Purdue Calumet

Jennifer Day
Sinclair Community College

Joseph F. Domagala
Duquesne University

Christa Fairman
Arizona Western University

Denise Farley
Sussex County Community College

Drew Foster
Miami University of Ohio

Lorie Goodgine
Tennessee Technology Center in Paris

Jane L. Hammer
Valley City State University

Kay Johnson
Community College of Rhode Island

Susumu Kasai
Salt Lake Community College

Linda Kavanaugh
Robert Morris University

Jennifer Krou
Texas State University, San Marcos

Michelle Mallon
Ohio State University

Sandra McCormack
Monroe Community College

Melissa Nemeth
Indiana University – Purdue University Indianapolis

Janet Olfert
North Dakota State University

Patsy Ann Parker
Southwestern Oklahoma State University

Cheryl Reindl-Johnson
Sinclair Community College

Jennifer Robinson
Trident Technical College

Tony Rose
Miami University of Ohio

Cindi Smatt
North Georgia College & State University

Jenny Lee Svelund
University of Utah

William VanderClock
Bentley University

Jill Weiss
Florida International University

Lin Zhao
Purdue Calumet

We'd like to thank all of our conscientious reviewers, including those who contributed to our previous editions:

Sven Aelterman
Troy University

Nitin Aggarwal
San Jose State University

Angel Alexander
Piedmont Technical College

Melody Alexander
Ball State University

Karen Allen
Community College of Rhode Island

Maureen Allen
Elon University

Wilma Andrews
Virginia Commonwealth University

Mazhar Anik
Owens Community College

David Antol
Harford Community College

Kirk Atkinson
Western Kentucky University

Barbara Baker
Indiana Wesleyan University

Kristi Berg
Minot State University

Kavuri Bharath
Old Dominion University

Ann Blackman
Parkland College

Jeanann Boyce
Montgomery College

Lynn Brooks
Tyler Junior College

Cheryl Brown
Delgado Community College West Bank Campus

Bonnie Buchanan
Central Ohio Technical College

Peggy Burrus
Red Rocks Community College

Richard Cacace
Pensacola State College

Margo Chaney
Carroll Community College

Shanan Chappell
College of the Albemarle, North Carolina

Kuan Chen
Purdue Calumet

David Childress
Ashland Community and Technical College

Keh-Wen Chuang
Purdue University, North Central

Suzanne Clayton
Drake University

Amy Clubb
Portland Community College

Bruce Collins
Davenport University

Margaret Cooksey
Tallahassee Community College

Charmayne Cullom
University of Northern Colorado

Christy Culver
Marion Technical College

Juliana Cypert
Tarrant County College

Harold Davis
Southeastern Louisiana University

Jeff Davis
Jamestown Community College

Jennifer Day
Sinclair Community College

Anna Degtyareva
Mt. San Antonio College

Beth Deinert
Southeast Community College

Kathleen DeNisco
Erie Community College

Donald Dershem
Mountain View College

Bambi Edwards
Craven Community College

Elaine Emanuel
Mt. San Antonio College

Diane Endres
Ancilla College

Nancy Evans
Indiana University – Purdue University Indianapolis

Christa Fairman
Arizona Western College

Marni Ferner
University of North Carolina, Wilmington

Paula Fisher
Central New Mexico Community College

Linda Fried
University of Colorado, Denver

Diana Friedman
Riverside Community College

Susan Fry
Boise State University

Virginia Fullwood
Texas A&M University, Commerce

Janos Fustos
Metropolitan State College of Denver

John Fyfe
University of Illinois at Chicago

Saiid Ganjalizadeh
The Catholic University of America

Randolph Garvin
Tyler Junior College

Diane Glowacki
Tarrant County College

Jerome Gonnella
Northern Kentucky University

Connie Grimes
Morehead State University

Debbie Gross
Ohio State University

Babita Gupta
California State University, Monterey Bay

Lewis Hall
Riverside City College

Jane Hammer
Valley City State University

Marie Hartlein
Montgomery County Community College

Darren Hayes
Pace University

Paul Hayes
Eastern New Mexico University

Mary Hedberg
Johnson County Community College

Lynda Henrie
LDS Business College

Deedee Herrera
Dodge City Community College

Marilyn Hibbert
Salt Lake Community College

Jan Hime
University of Nebraska, Lincoln

Cheryl Hinds
Norfolk State University

Mary Kay Hinkson
Fox Valley Technical College

Margaret Hohly
Cerritos College

Brian Holbert
Spring Hill College

Susan Holland
Southeast Community College

Anita Hollander
University of Tennessee, Knoxville

Emily Holliday
Campbell University

Stacy Hollins
St. Louis Community College
Florissant Valley

Mike Horn
State University of New York, Geneseo

Christie Hovey
Lincoln Land Community College

Margaret Hvatum
St. Louis Community College Meramec

Jean Insinga
Middlesex Community College

Jon (Sean) Jasperson
Texas A&M University

Glen Jenewein
Kaplan University

Gina Jerry
Santa Monica College

Dana Johnson
North Dakota State University

Mary Johnson
Mt. San Antonio College

Linda Johnsonius
Murray State University

Carla Jones
Middle Tennessee State University

Susan Jones
Utah State University

Nenad Jukic
Loyola University, Chicago

Sali Kaceli
Philadelphia Biblical University

Sue Kanda
Baker College of Auburn Hills

Robert Kansa
Macomb Community College

Susumu Kasai
Salt Lake Community College

Linda Kavanaugh
Robert Morris University

Debby Keen
University of Kentucky

Mike Kelly
Community College of Rhode Island

Melody Kiang
California State University, Long Beach

Lori Kielty
College of Central Florida

Richard Kirk
Pensacola State College

Dawn Konicek
Blackhawk Tech

John Kucharczuk
Centennial College

David Largent
Ball State University

Frank Lee
Fairmont State University

Luis Leon
The University of Tennessee at Chattanooga

Freda Leonard
Delgado Community College

Julie Lewis
Baker College, Allen Park

Suhong Li
Bryant Unversity

Renee Lightner
Florida State College

John Lombardi
South University

Rhonda Lucas
Spring Hill College

Adriana Lumpkin
Midland College

Lynne Lyon
Durham College

Nicole Lytle
California State University, San Bernardino

Donna Madsen
Kirkwood Community College

Susan Maggio
Community College of Baltimore County

Kim Manning
Tallahassee Community College

Paul Martin
Harrisburg Area Community College

Cheryl Martucci
Diablo Valley College

Sebena Masline
Florida State College of Jacksonville

Sherry Massoni
Harford Community College

Lee McClain
Western Washington University

Sandra McCormack
Monroe Community College

Sue McCrory
Missouri State University

Barbara Miller
University of Notre Dame

Michael O. Moorman
Saint Leo University

Kathleen Morris
University of Alabama

Alysse Morton
Westminster College

Elobaid Muna
University of Maryland Eastern Shore

Jackie Myers
Sinclair Community College

Russell Myers
El Paso Community College

Bernie Negrete
Cerritos College

Melissa Nemeth
Indiana University – Purdue University Indianapolis

Jennifer Nightingale
Duquesne University

Kathie O'Brien
North Idaho College

Michael Ogawa
University of Hawaii

Rene Pack
Arizona Western College

Patsy Parker
Southwest Oklahoma State Unversity

Laurie Patterson
University of North Carolina, Wilmington

Alicia Pearlman
Baker College

Diane Perreault
Sierra College and California State University, Sacramento

Theresa Phinney
Texas A&M University

Vickie Pickett
Midland College

Marcia Polanis
Forsyth Technical Community College

Rose Pollard
Southeast Community College

Stephen Pomeroy
Norwich University

Leonard Presby
William Paterson University

Donna Reavis
Delta Career Education

Eris Reddoch
Pensacola State College

James Reddoch
Pensacola State College

Michael Redmond
La Salle University

Terri Rentfro
John A. Logan College

Vicki Robertson
Southwest Tennessee Community College

Dianne Ross
University of Louisiana at Lafayette

Ann Rowlette
Liberty University

Amy Rutledge
Oakland University

Candace Ryder
Colorado State University

Joann Segovia
Winona State University

Eileen Shifflett
James Madison University

Sandeep Shiva
Old Dominion University

Robert Sindt
Johnson County Community College

Cindi Smatt
Texas A&M University

Edward Souza
Hawaii Pacific University

Nora Spencer
Fullerton College

Alicia Stonesifer
La Salle University

Cheryl Sypniewski
Macomb Community College

Arta Szathmary
Bucks County Community College

Nasser Tadayon
Southern Utah University

Asela Thomason
California State University Long Beach

Nicole Thompson
Carteret Community College

Terri Tiedema
Southeast Community College, Nebraska

Lewis Todd
Belhaven University

Barb Tollinger
Sinclair Community College

Allen Truell
Ball State University

Erhan Uskup
Houston Community College

Lucia Vanderpool
Baptist College of Health Sciences

Michelle Vlaich-Lee
Greenville Technical College

Barry Walker
Monroe Community College

Rosalyn Warren
Enterprise State Community College

Sonia Washington
Prince George's Community College

Eric Weinstein
Suffolk County Community College

Jill Weiss
Florida International University

Lorna Wells
Salt Lake Community College

Rosalie Westerberg
Clover Park Technical College

Clemetee Whaley
Southwest Tennessee Community College

Kenneth Whitten
Florida State College of Jacksonville

MaryLou Wilson
Piedmont Technical College

John Windsor
University of North Texas

Kathy Winters
University of Tennessee, Chattanooga

Nancy Woolridge
Fullerton College

Jensen Zhao
Ball State University

Martha Zimmer
University of Evansville

Molly Zimmer
University of Evansville

Mary Anne Zlotow
College of DuPage

Matthew Zullo
Wake Technical Community College

Additionally, we'd like to thank our MyITLab team for their review and collaboration with our text authors:

LeeAnn Bates

Jennifer Hurley

Ralph Moore

Jerri Williams

Jaimie Noy
Media Producer

Preface

The ***Your Office*** series focuses first and foremost on preparing students to use both technical and soft skills in the real world. Our goal is to provide this to both instructors and students through a modern approach to teaching and learning Microsoft Office applications, an approach that weaves in the technical content using a realistic business scenario and focuses on using Office as a decision-making tool.

The process of developing this unique series for you, the modern student or instructor, requires innovative ideas regarding the pedagogy and organization of the text. You learn best when doing—so you will be active from Page 1. Your learning goes to the next level when you are challenged to do more with less—your hand will be held at first, but progressively, the case exercises require more from you. Since you care about how things work in the real world—in your classes, your future jobs, your personal life—Real World Advice, Videos, and Success Stories are woven throughout the text. These innovative features will help you progress from a basic understanding of Office to mastery of each application, empowering you to perform with confidence in Windows 8, Word, Excel, Access, and PowerPoint, including on mobile devices.

No matter what career you may choose to pursue in life, this series will give you the foundation to succeed. ***Your Office*** uses cases that will enable you to be immersed in a realistic business as you learn Office in the context of a running business scenario—the Painted Paradise Resort and Spa. You will immediately delve into the many interesting, smaller businesses in this resort (golf course, spa, restaurants, hotel, etc.) to learn how a larger organization actually uses Office. You will learn how to make Office work for you now, as a student, and in your future career.

Today, the experience of working with Office is not isolated to working in a job in a cubicle. Your physical office is wherever you are with a laptop or a mobile device. Office has changed. It's modern. It's mobile. It's personal. And when you learn these valuable skills and master Office, you are able to make Office your own. The title of this series is a promise to you, the student: Our goal is to make Microsoft Office ***Your Office***.

Key Features

- **Starting and Ending Files:** These appear before every case in the text. Starting Files identify exactly which Student Data Files are needed to complete each case. Ending Files are provided to show students the naming conventions they should use when saving their files. Each file icon is color coded by application.
- **Workshop Objectives List:** The learning objectives to be achieved as students work through the workshop. Page numbers are included for easy reference. These are revisited in the Concepts Check at the end of the workshop.
- **Real World Success:** A boxed feature in the workshop opener that shares an anecdote from a real former student, describing how knowledge of Office has helped him or her to get ahead or be successful in his or her life.
- **Active Text Box:** Represents the active portion of the workshop and is easily distinguishable from explanatory text by the blue shaded background. Active Text helps students quickly identify what steps they need to follow to complete the workshop Prepare Case.
- **Quick Reference Box:** A boxed feature in the workshop, summarizing generic or alternative instructions on how to accomplish a task. This feature enables students to quickly find important skills.
- **Real World Advice Box:** A boxed feature in the workshop, offering advice and best practices for general use of important Office skills. The goal is to advise students as a manager might in a future job.
- **Side Note:** A brief tip or piece of information aligned visually with a step in the workshop, quickly providing key information to students completing that particular step.
- **Consider This:** In-text critical thinking questions and topics for discussion, set apart as a boxed feature, allowing students to step back from the project and think about the application of what they are learning and how these concepts might be used in the future.
- **Concept Check:** Review questions appearing at the end of the workshop, which require students to demonstrate their understanding of the objectives in that workshop.
- **Visual Summary:** A visual review of the objectives learned in the workshop using images from the completed solution file, mapped to the workshop objectives using callouts and page references so students can easily find the section of text to refer to for a refresher.
- **Business Application Icons:** Appear with every case in the text and clearly identify which business application students are being exposed to, i.e., Finance, Marketing, Operations, etc.
- **MyITLab™ Icons:** Identify which cases from the book match those in MyITLab™.
- **Real World Interview Video Icon:** This icon appears with the Real World Success Story in the workshop opener and features an interview of a real business person discussing how he or she actually uses the skills in the workshop on a day-to-day basis.
- **Blue Box Video Icons:** These icons appear with each Active Text box and identify the brief video demonstrating how students should complete that portion of the Prepare Case.
- **Soft Skills Icons:** These appear with other boxed features and identify specific places where students are being exposed to lessons on soft skills.

Business Application Icons

Customer Service

Finance & Accounting

General Business

Human Resources

Information Technology

Production & Operations

Sales & Marketing

Research & Development

MyITLab Icons

MyITLab®

Video Icons

Real World Success Story

Workshop Videos

Soft Skills

Instructor Resources

The Instructor's Resource Center, available at www.pearsonhighered.com, includes the following:

- AACSB mapping that identifies which cases and exercises in the text prepare for AACSB certification.
- Business application mapping, which provides an easy-to-filter way of finding the cases and examples to help highlight whichever business application is of most interest.
- Annotated Solution Files with Scorecards assist with grading the Prepare, Practice, Problem Solve, and Perform Cases.
- Data and Solution Files
- Rubrics for Perform Cases in Microsoft Word format enable instructors to easily grade open-ended assignments with no definite solution.
- PowerPoint Presentations with notes for each chapter.
- Audio PowerPoints which serve as great refreshers for students
- Instructor's Manual that provides detailed blueprints to achieve workshop learning objectives and outcomes and best use the unique structure of the modules.
- Complete Test Bank, also available in TestGen format
- Syllabus templates for 8-week, 12-week, and 16-week courses
- Additional Practice, Problem Solve, and Perform Cases to provide you with variety and choice in exercises both on the workshop and module levels.
- Scripted Lectures provide instructors with a lecture outline that mirrors the Workshop Prepare Case.
- Flexible, robust, and customizable content is available for all major online course platforms that include everything instructors need in one place. Please contact your sales representative for information on accessing course cartridges for WebCT or Blackboard.

Student Resources

- Student Data Files
- Blue Box videos walk students through each Blue Active Text box in the Workshop, showing and explaining the concepts and how to achieve the skills in the workshop. There is one video per Active Text box.
- Real World Interview videos introduce students to real professionals talking about how they use Microsoft Office on a daily basis in their work. These videos provide the relevance students seek while learning this material. There is one video per workshop.
- Soft Skills videos introduce students to important non-technical skills such as etiquette, managing priorities, proper interview preparation, etc.

Pearson's Companion Website

www.pearsonhighered.com/youroffice offers expanded IT resources and downloadable supplements. Students can find the following self-study tools for each workshop:

- Online Workshop Review
- Workshop Objectives
- Additional Cases
- Glossary
- MOS Certification Mapping
- Student Data Files
- Blue Box videos*
- Real World Interview videos*
- Soft Skills videos*

* Access code required for these premium resources

MyITLab®

My**IT**Lab for Office 2013 is a solution designed by professors for professors that allows easy delivery of Office courses with defensible assessment and outcomes-based training. The new **Your Office 2013** system will seamlessly integrate online assessment, training, and projects with My**IT**Lab for Microsoft Office 2013!

My**IT**Lab for Office 2013 features…

- **Assessment and training built to match Your Office 2013** instructional content so that my**it**lab works with Your Office to help students make Office their own.
- **Both project-based and skill-based assessment and training** allow instructors to test and train students on complete exercises or individual Office application skills.

Dear Students,

If you want an edge over the competition, make it personal. Whether you love sports, travel, the stock market, or ballet, your passion is personal to you. Capitalizing on your passion leads to success. You live in a global marketplace, and your competition is global. The honors students in China exceed the total number of students in North America. Skills can help set you apart, but passion will make you stand above. ***Your Office*** is the tool to harness your passion's true potential.

In prior generations, personalization in a professional setting was discouraged. You had a "work" life and a "home" life. As the Series Editor, I write to you about the vision for ***Your Office*** from my laptop, on my couch, in the middle of the night when inspiration strikes me. My classroom and living room are my office. Life has changed from generations before us.

So, let's get personal. My degrees are not in technology, but chemistry and law. I helped put myself through school by working full time in various jobs, including a successful technology consulting business that continues today. My generation did not grow up with computers, but I did. My father was a network administrator for the military. So, I was learning to program in Basic before anyone had played Nintendo's Duck Hunt or Tetris. Technology has always been one of my passions from a young age. In fact, I now tell my husband: don't buy me jewelry for my birthday, buy me the latest gadget on the market!

In my first law position, I was known as the Office guru to the extent that no one gave me a law assignment for the first two months. Once I submitted the assignment, my supervisor remarked, "Wow, you don't just know how to leverage technology, but you really know the law too." I can tell you novel-sized stories from countless prior students in countless industries who gained an edge from using Office as a tool. Bringing technology to your passion makes you well-rounded and a cut above the rest, no matter the industry or position.

I am most passionate about teaching, in particular teaching technology. I come from many generations of teachers, including my mother who is a kindergarten teacher. For over 12 years, I have found my dream job passing on my passion for teaching, technology, law, science, music, and life in general at the Kelley School of Business at Indiana University. I have tried to pass on the key to engaging passion to my students. I have helped them see what differentiates them from all the other bright students vying for the same jobs.

Microsoft Office is a tool. All of your competition will have learned Microsoft Office to some degree or another. Some will have learned it to an advanced level. Knowing Microsoft Office is important, but it is also fundamental. Without it, you will not be considered for a position.

Today, you step into your first of many future roles bringing Microsoft Office to your dream job working for Painted Paradise Resort and Spa. You will delve into the business side of the resort and learn how to use ***Your Office*** to maximum benefit.

Don't let the context of a business fool you. If you don't think of yourself as a business person, you have no need to worry. Whether you realize it or not, everything is business. If you want to be a nurse, you are entering the health care industry. If you want to be a football player in the NFL, you are entering the business of sports as entertainment. In fact, if you want to be a stay-at-home parent, you are entering the business of a family household where ***Your Office*** still gives you an advantage. For example, you will be able to prepare a budget in Excel and analyze what you need to do to afford a trip to Disney World!

At Painted Paradise Resort and Spa, you will learn how to make Office yours through four learning levels designed to maximize your understanding. You will Prepare, Practice, and Problem Solve your tasks. Then, you will astound when you Perform your new talents. You will be challenged through Consider This questions and gain insight through Real World Advice.

There is something more. You want success in what you are passionate about in your life. It is personal for you. In this position at Painted Paradise Resort and Spa, you will gain your personal competitive advantage that will stay with you for the rest of your life—***Your Office***.

Sincerely,

Amy Kinser

Series Editor

Painted Paradise

RESORT & SPA

Welcome to the Team!

Welcome to your new office at Painted Paradise Resort and Spa, where we specialize in painting perfect getaways. As the Chief Technology Officer, I am excited to have staff dedicated to the Microsoft Office integration between all the areas of the resort. Our team is passionate about our paradise, and I hope you find this to be your dream position here!

Painted Paradise is a resort and spa in New Mexico catering to business people, romantics, families, and anyone who just needs to get away. Inside our resort are many distinct areas. Many of these areas operate as businesses in their own right but must integrate with the other areas of the resort. The main areas of the resort are as follows.

- The **Hotel** is overseen by our Chief Executive Officer, William Mattingly, and is at the core of our business. The hotel offers a variety of accommodations, ranging from individual rooms to a grand villa suite. Further, the hotel offers packages including spa, golf, and special events.

  Room rates vary according to size, season, demand, and discount. The hotel has discounts for typical groups, such as AARP. The hotel also has a loyalty program where guests can earn free nights based on frequency of visits. Guests may charge anything from the resort to the room.

- **Red Bluff Golf Course** is a private world-class golf course and pro shop. The golf course has services such as golf lessons from the famous golf pro John Schilling and playing packages. Also, the golf course attracts local residents. This requires variety in pricing schemes to accommodate both local and hotel guests. The pro shop sells many retail items online.

  The golf course can also be reserved for special events and tournaments. These special events can be in conjunction with a wedding, conference, meetings, or other event covered by the event planning and catering area of the resort.

- **Turquoise Oasis Spa** is a full-service spa. Spa services include haircuts, pedicures, massages, facials, body wraps, waxing, and various other spa services—typical to exotic. Further, the spa offers private consultation, weight training (in the fitness center), a water bar, meditation areas, and steam rooms. Spa services are offered both in the spa and in the resort guest's room.

  Turquoise Oasis Spa uses top-of-the-line products and some house-brand products. The retail side offers products ranging from candles to age-defying home treatments. These products can also be purchased online. Many of the hotel guests who fall in love with the house-brand soaps, lotions, candles, and other items appreciate being able to buy more at any time.

  The spa offers a multitude of packages including special hotel room packages that include spa treatments. Local residents also use the spa. So, the spa guests are not limited to hotel guests. Thus, the packages also include pricing attractive to the local community.

- **Painted Treasures Gift Shop** has an array of items available for purchase, from toiletries to clothes to presents for loved ones back home including a healthy section of kids' toys for traveling business people. The gift shop sells a small sampling from the spa, golf course pro shop, and local New Mexico culture. The gift shop also has a small section of snacks and drinks. The gift shop has numerous part-time employees including students from the local college.

- **The Event Planning & Catering** area is central to attracting customers to the resort. From weddings to conferences, the resort is a popular destination. The resort has a substantial number of staff dedicated to planning, coordinating, setting up, catering, and maintaining these events. The resort has several facilities that can accommodate large groups. Packages and prices vary by size, room, and other services such as catering. Further, the Event Planning & Catering team works closely with local vendors for floral decorations, photography, and other event or wedding typical needs. However, all catering must go through the resort (no outside catering permitted). Lastly, the resort stocks several choices of decorations, table arrangements, and centerpieces. These range from professional, simple, themed, and luxurious.
- **Indigo5** and the **Silver Moon Lounge**, a world-class restaurant and lounge that is overseen by the well-known Chef Robin Sanchez. The cuisine is balanced and modern. From steaks to pasta to local southwestern meals, Indigo5 attracts local patrons in addition to resort guests. While the catering function is separate from the restaurant—though menu items may be shared—the restaurant does support all room service for the resort. The resort also has smaller food venues onsite such as the Terra Cotta Brew coffee shop in the lobby.

Currently, these areas are using Office to various degrees. In some areas, paper and pencil are still used for most business functions. Others have been lucky enough to have some technology savvy team members start Microsoft Office Solutions.

Using your skills, I am confident that you can help us integrate and use Microsoft Office on a whole new level! I hope you are excited to call Painted Paradise Resort and Spa ***Your Office***.

Looking forward to working with you more closely!

Aidan Matthews

Aidan Matthews
Chief Technology Officer

WORKSHOP 1 | UNDERSTAND THE WINDOWS 8 INTERFACE

OBJECTIVES

1. Explore the Windows 8 Start screen p. 10
2. Use the Snipping Tool p. 14
3. Use WordPad p. 16
4. Switch between programs p. 17
5. Open and close programs p. 20
6. Log in using a Microsoft account p. 29
7. Use picture passwords p. 33
8. Add a PIN login p. 36
9. Log in using PINs and picture passwords p. 36
10. Add a trusted PC p. 37

Prepare Case

Painted Paradise Golf Resort and Spa—Employee Introduction to Microsoft Windows 8

Information Technology

Robert Kneschke/Shutterstock

Aidan Matthews, Chief Technology Officer of the Painted Paradise Golf Resort and Spa, has decided to upgrade computers from Windows 7 to the brand new Windows 8 operating system. The vendor who supplies the hotel's software has a new version optimized for Windows 8. This version will fix some of the problems the company has had with the software.

There is a considerable difference between Windows 7 and Windows 8, and Painted Paradise employees have asked for help in making the transition. You have been asked to plan a workshop to train personnel in all departments to use their new operating system efficiently. Aidan has asked that you start by learning the Windows 8 interface. He wants you to focus on fundamental skills but would also like you to introduce new features that will enhance productivity, such as the enhanced search functionality. Making the transition to Windows 8 will not only require employees to learn the new version of the hotel's software; it will also require them being comfortable with the operating system on a daily basis. In this workshop, you will focus on demonstrating new features in Windows 8.

Student data file needed for this workshop:

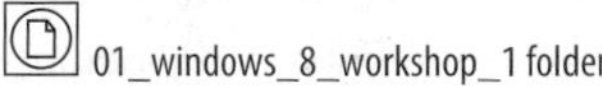
01_windows_8_workshop_1 folder

You will save your files as:

 w801ws01WordPad_LastFirst.jpg

 w801ws01StartSnip_LastFirst.jpg

 w801ws01Experience_LastFirst.rtf

 w801ws01Search_LastFirst.rtf

Understanding Windows 8

Microsoft Windows 8 is the latest version of the Windows **operating system**. The operating system is **system software**, which controls and coordinates computer hardware operations so other programs can run efficiently. The operating system acts as an intermediary between **application software**—programs that help you perform specific tasks, such as word processing—and the computer hardware. It also helps you perform essential tasks such as displaying information on the computer screen, saving data on a storage device, and sending documents to a printer. You can have multiple programs open at the same time and switch between programs easily using several different methods. A good operating system is like a good thief. You can tell a thief is good at their job by how little you notice them. The same idea applies to an operating system. Most people notice Windows only when problems arise.

Microsoft releases a new version of Windows every few years to take advantage of improvements made to hardware and to add new features. Windows 8 replaces Windows 7, which was released in late 2009. Like previous versions of Windows, Windows 8 uses a **graphical user interface (GUI)**, an interface that uses **icons**, which are small pictures representing commands, programs, and documents. This type of interface helps you interact with the hardware and software in a simpler fashion. However, Windows 8 introduces a number of new features that will leave even an experienced user in need of some retraining. Since the release of Windows 95, the center of the Windows experience has been the Start button. Windows 8 has moved away from the Start button and moved towards a touch-screen type of interface, similar to what you may have become accustomed to with smartphones. Windows 8 also supports **gesture recognition**, which allows you to control the computer with gestures instead of mouse clicks, if you have a touch-screen device. **Gestures** allow you to perform actions like zooming and switching programs by performing certain movements. If you have an eBook reader or iPad, this may already be second nature.

Windows 8 is introducing other new features to this version of the operating system, including support for **ARM devices**. An ARM device uses a different processor than personal computers. Devices with ARM chips use less power than a traditional PC processor. By supporting ARM processors for the first time, Windows 8 allows for new innovations in computing. Smaller, more power efficient laptops may now be feasible in a way never before available. Some vendors anticipate battery lives of 10 hours or more for devices running an ARM processor. ARM processors are also less susceptible to viruses, at the moment. Most computer viruses affect the traditional PC CPU, and do not affect ARM chips. This is why there are fewer viruses found on mobile devices. They are not impossible to create, but virus writers currently focus on Windows PCs.

Windows RT is Microsoft's alternative to the Android and Apple devices. What sets this apart may be the integration of standard desktop applications, such as Microsoft Office. This new version of Microsoft Office includes not only keyboard and mouse support, but also touch-screen support. By combining work functions with the functions casual users like, Microsoft presents some stiff competition for rivals. Microsoft has released a tablet computer called Microsoft Surface that is designed to compete with other tablets like the iPad.

The fundamental changes to the Windows operating system will lead to exciting changes in the way we use computers. Most home users do not have touch-screen monitors on their desktop or laptop computers, primarily because the operating system and applications were not designed to take advantage of touch-screen features. Because the demand has been low, prices have remained high for touch-screen devices on personal computers. If this version of Windows is well-received, touch-screen monitors will become the standard for home users. As demand goes up, supply goes up, and prices fall.

Starting and Shutting Down Windows 8

Windows 8 starts automatically when your computer is switched on unless you are more technical and have configured your computer to do otherwise. Several different things might occur, depending on where you are using your computer. You may be brought directly to the Windows **Start screen**—the working area of the Windows 8 screen (see Figure 1). If user accounts are set up, you may be required to login before you see the Start screen. You may be required to **click**—press the left mouse button one time—your user icon, and then you may be asked to enter a password. This prevents other users from accessing your documents or other personal data. Your school or business may have a different logon procedure because many people may be sharing a network.

Figure 1 Windows 8 Start screen

Windows 8 starts up more quickly than previous versions of the operating system, due to a new feature called **hybrid boot**. In previous versions of the operating system, users tended to shut down completely rather than use the sleep and hibernate options. When the computer was idle, it often went into sleep mode to minimize power consumption. Hibernate was similar to sleep. Hibernate was a good option for laptops, allowing users to decrease startup times and use even less battery power than sleep. However, it would often take longer to go into hibernate mode than it would to fully shut down the machine, as it often had to save large amounts of information to the hard drive before hibernating. Many users, not realizing the advantage of hibernation, would shut down instead.

Hybrid boot is the new default shutdown option for Windows 8. As its name implies, it provides the best of both worlds. You will experience faster startups than with previous versions of Windows, while not having to wait long for the system to shut down.

After starting the machine, you may be confused when it is time to shut down. Shutting down is now done from **Charms**, which are buttons appearing on the right side of the screen. Charms were introduced in Windows 8. Charms are hidden from view, so you will need to point the mouse to the bottom-right corner of the screen. This will bring up a menu including a button labeled Settings. From Settings, there is a power icon, which allows you to select either Shut down or Restart. You may occasionally see an option labeled Update and restart, which will appear if your computer has downloaded updates to Windows 8.

You will begin your workshop by showing the participants how to start and shut down the machine.

W801.00

To Start and Shut Down Windows

a. Switch on your computer, and then wait a few moments. If necessary, follow any logon instructions required for the computer you are using. The Windows Start screen is displayed.

b. Move your mouse to the bottom-right corner of the screen to display the Charms, and then click **Settings**.

Figure 2 Windows 8 Charms

c. Click the **Power** icon, and select **Shut down**.

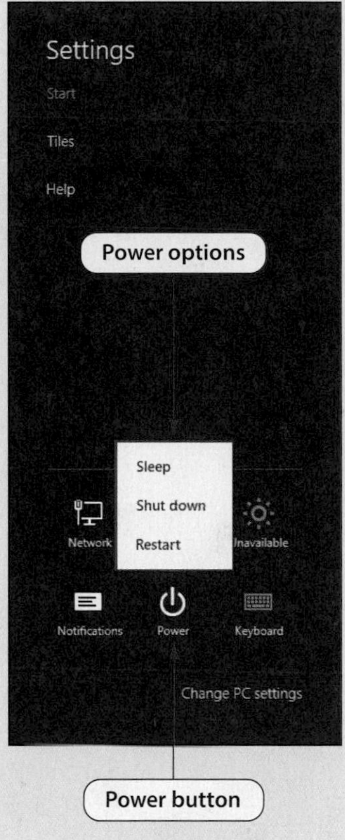

Figure 3 Power button options

Exploring the Windows 8 Interface

The Windows 8 operating system has replaced the standard desktop interface with a new interface. The idea behind this redesign was to make the operating system simpler to use, relying on easy to read commands instead of small icons.

In addition to this, Microsoft is attempting to minimize the clutter around the screen (such as the taskbar). Instead of active tasks using screen space, you will be able to access these by pointing to the edge of the screen or performing certain gestures on a touch-screen device, such as swiping. If this sounds familiar, it is similar to the way many touch-screen devices such as the iPad and some mobile phones interact with users. Though the idea is similar to the iPad, the implementation is a bit different. Users with iPad experience will still need to do some retraining due to the differences.

The default screen for the operating system is now the Start screen. The Start screen can be identified by the word "Start" in the upper-left area of the screen, and a number of colored **tiles** on the rest of the screen. The tiles represent programs that can be opened. These are similar to shortcut icons found on the desktop or taskbar in previous versions of Windows. Much like icons in previous versions of Windows, they can be manipulated. You can change the placement and size of the tiles, as well as add and delete tiles.

Tiles designed for Windows 8 may be **Live Tiles** (see Figure 4). These tiles give you a constant stream of information. For example, the Weather tile shows the current weather for your location, updated frequently. Some Internet connections, including some cell phone networks and satellites, do not include unlimited data. In such a case, a user may wish to switch the option off.

Figure 4 Windows 8 Start screen tiles

In order to find installed applications not shown on the Start screen, you can right-click in any blank area of the Start screen. This will bring up a menu at the bottom of the screen allowing you to click "All apps".

The original Windows desktop is still available. By default, the Start screen will have a tile labeled Desktop. The **desktop** is the interface you are familiar with from previous versions of Windows. The **taskbar** is the bar at the bottom of the desktop showing all open programs. All programs not specifically written for Windows 8 will use the desktop interface (see Figure 5). However, the Start button has been removed, and you will need to get comfortable with the Windows 8 interface for greater efficiency. The Start button is no longer the center of the Windows experience.

Figure 5 Windows 8 Desktop

Existing applications will run under the Windows 8 interface. However, touch-screen functionality may not work as well with older applications as it will on applications designed for Windows 8. Expect many companies to release new versions of their software as Windows 8 gains acceptance.

REAL WORLD ADVICE **Reluctant to Retrain?**

Users are often reluctant to retrain, and converting to Windows 8 will likely be met with resistance. A company named Stardock has already released a program to bring back the Start menu in Windows 8, called Start8. This is not a new phenomenon. When Microsoft released Office 2007, users were used to the Office 2003 style menus, and did not want to move to the Office 2007 Ribbon interface. A company named Addintools released a tool called Classic Menu that restored the older interface for users uninterested in retraining. However, business users will likely find their employers uninterested in purchasing and deploying these tools. A user who has retrained is more valuable to a company than a user who has not. In any career involving technology, retraining is going to be a fact of life.

The next part of your workshop will focus on showing Painted Paradise Resort employees how to use the Start screen. You will also show users how to launch, interact with, switch between, and close programs. You will demonstrate the Snipping Tool and WordPad. As the Painted Paradise Resort computers do not yet have touch screens, you will focus on showing the employees how to interact with the operating system using a mouse.

Explore the Windows 8 Start Screen

You will ask Painted Paradise Resort employees to explore the Windows 8 Start screen. They will examine various elements on the Start screen and learn correct terminology. Additionally, they should learn how to interact with elements of the Start screen and manipulate icons. Again, because the Painted Paradise Resort computers do not yet have touch screens, you will focus on showing the employees how to interact with the operating system using a mouse.

W801.01

To Explore the Windows 8 Start Screen

a. If your computer is not already started, switch the computer on and log in, if necessary.

b. Notice the new Windows Start screen. Somewhere on the screen you will see a **mouse pointer**—an arrow that shows the position of the mouse. A mouse or other pointing device is used to interact with objects on the screen, to open programs, or select commands. **Right-clicking**—pressing the right mouse button—opens a **shortcut menu**—a group or list of commands—containing commands related to the right-clicked item. These menus may also be referred to as contextual menus.

c. If the entire Start screen does not fit on your screen, you will see a **scroll bar** at the bottom of the page. The scroll bar allows you to access parts of the screen which are otherwise hidden from view due to screen size issues. You can also zoom out to see more of the screen. You can do this by clicking the Zoom button in the bottom-right corner of the screen. If the screen (as shown in Figure 6) has already been zoomed out, you can click this button to zoom in.

Figure 6 Start screen zoom button

d. If the Weather tile does not display your current weather conditions, click on the tile, click **Unblock** to display current weather, and then return to the Start screen. Right-click the **Weather** tile, which displays the current weather conditions. Four options are displayed at the bottom of the screen. Unpin from Start allows users to remove the tile from the Start screen. Uninstall removes the Weather application from your computer completely. Smaller allows you to make an icon smaller. If this icon is already small, you may instead be able to click Larger. As the Weather tile also includes live content (updated weather), it is considered a Live Tile. On this specific contextual menu, you can also click Turn live tile off. Please note other tiles may have different options available. Select the option **Smaller** from the contextual menu to make the Weather appear in a smaller tile.

Figure 7 Right-click menu for Weather

e. Tiles can be moved. To do so, **drag** the icon to a new location. To drag, click and hold the left mouse button down on a tile. Move the pointer where you want the item to appear, and then release the mouse button. Drag **Weather** to a different location (any location will do).

f. You can also add new tiles to the Start screen. To add a new tile, **right-click** in a blank area of the Start screen. You are presented with the option to click **All Apps**. If you do not see this, ensure you are pointing to a blank area on the Start screen. Click **All Apps**.

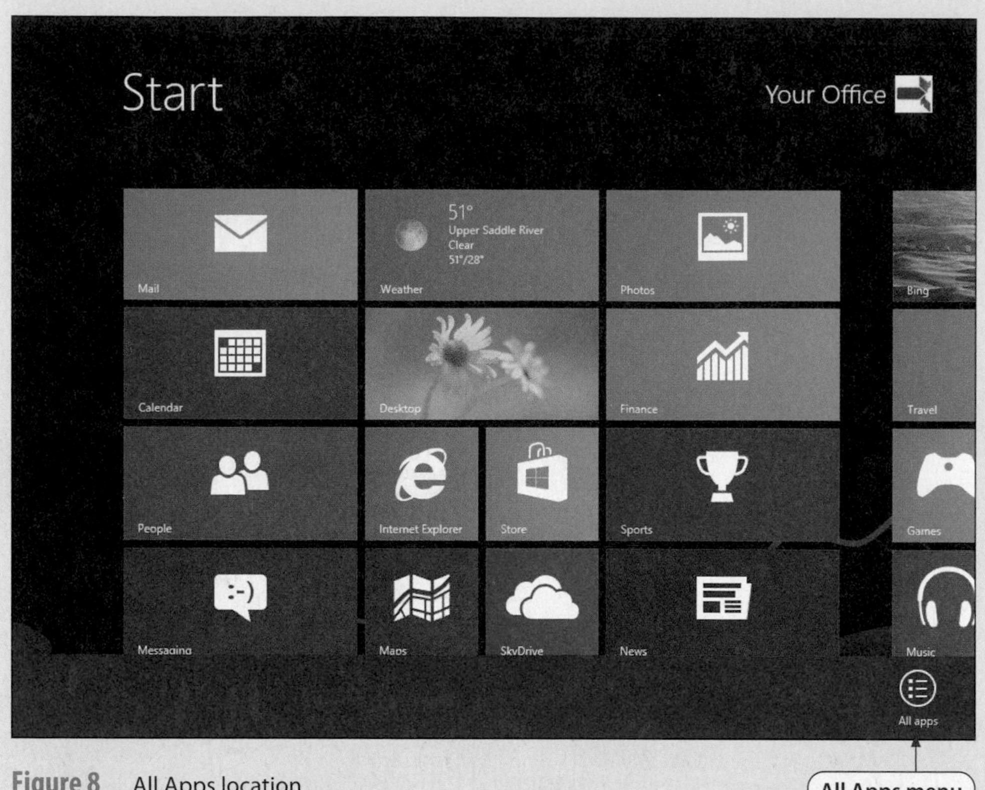

Figure 8 All Apps location

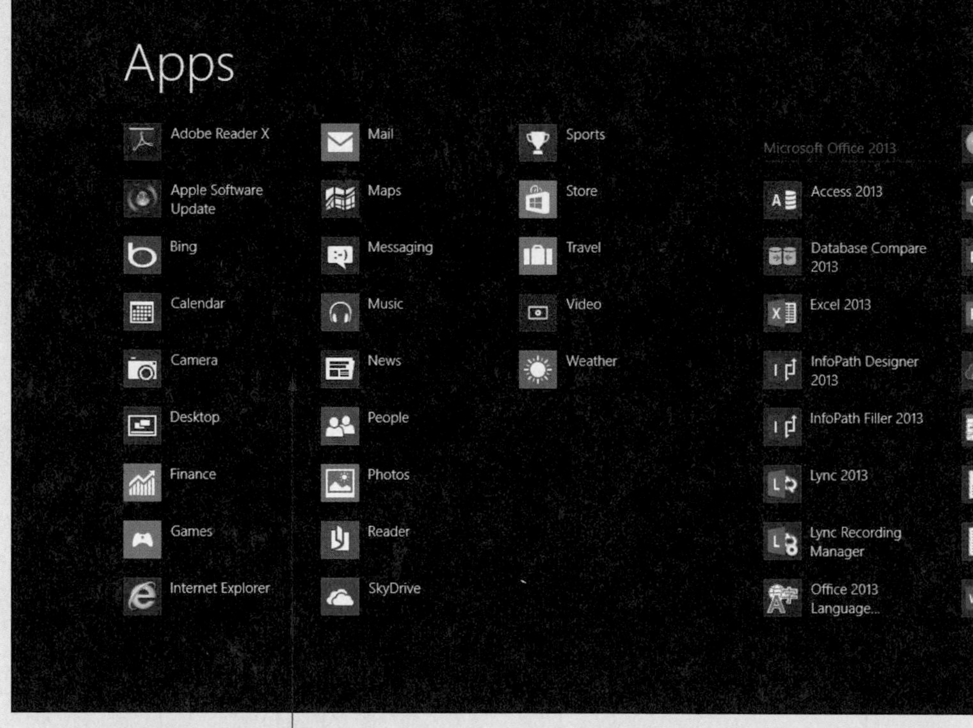

Figure 9 All Apps list

g. Locate the icon for the **Snipping Tool**. Note: If you cannot find the Snipping Tool, you can also type Snipping Tool on the Start screen. Right-click **Snipping Tool**, and then select **Pin to Start**. This will make this tool available on the Start screen.

MODULE 1

h. Point to the bottom-left corner of the screen, and then select **Start** to return to the main Start screen. Note when you are switching to the Start screen in this fashion, you need to move the pointer on to the Start screen thumbnail and click. This can be tricky. Verify that a link to the Snipping Tool now appears on your Start screen. Note: you may need to scroll if your screen resolution does not show the entirety of the Start screen.

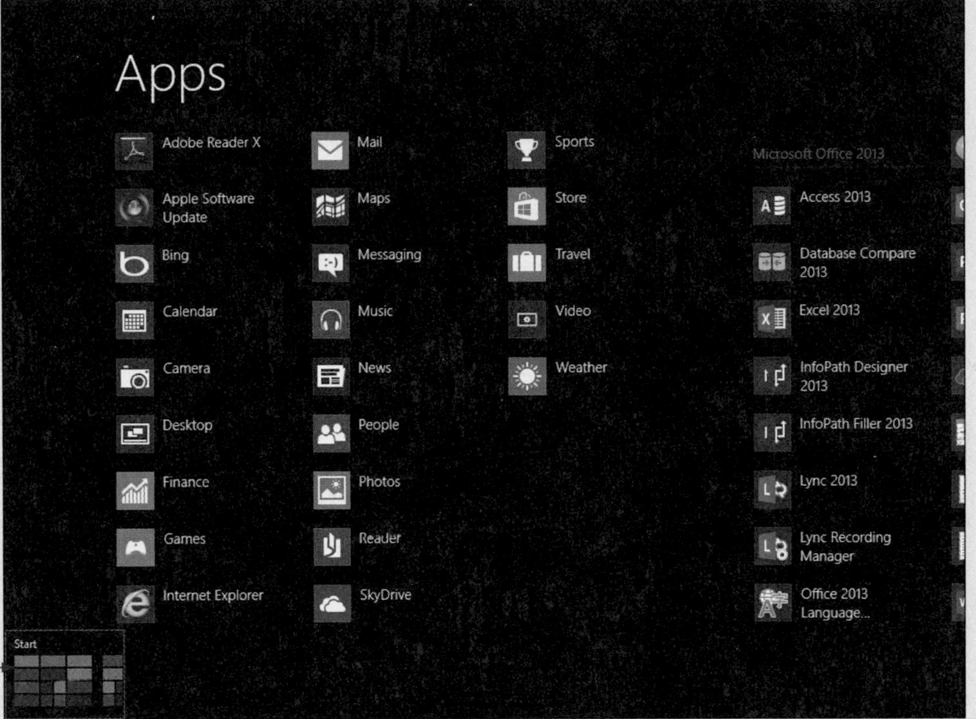

Figure 10 Start screen thumbnail

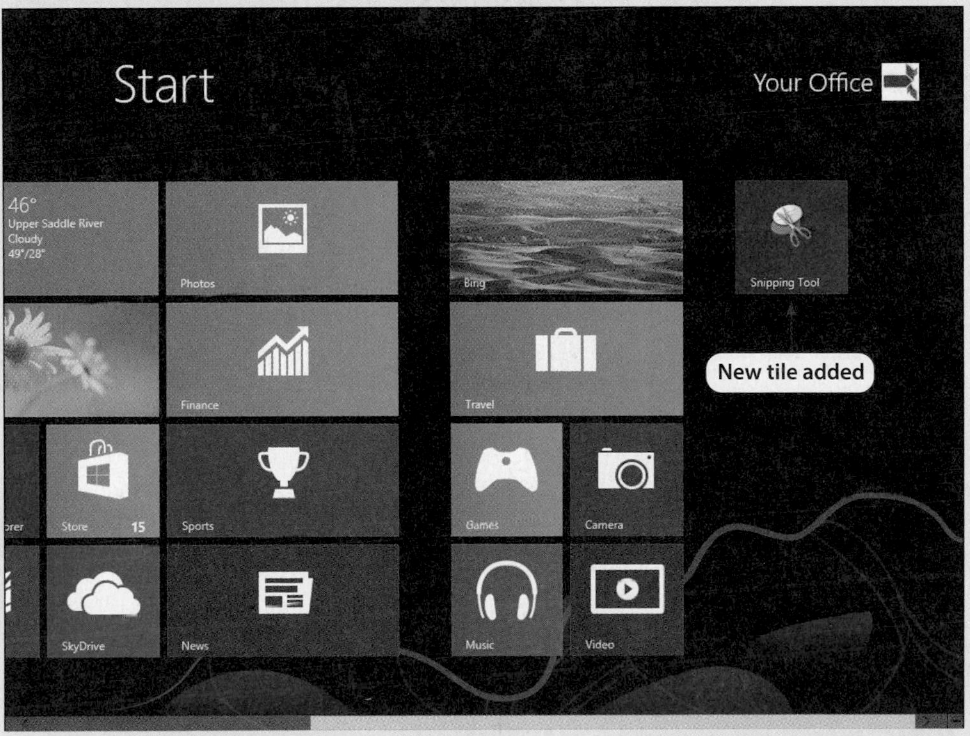

Figure 11 Snipping Tool added to Start screen

i. If the tile for the Reader app is not on your Start screen, **right-click** a blank area of your screen, and then locate the icon for Reader. Right-click **Reader**, and then select **Pin to Start**.

j. If the tile for the Photos app is not on your Start screen, **right-click** a blank area of your screen, and then locate the icon for Photos. Right-click **Photos**, and then select **Pin to Start**.

Use the Snipping Tool

In order to have your workshop attendees take before and after images of their screen, you will use the **Snipping Tool**. The Snipping Tool allows you to take a **snip**—a picture of your current screen. For many years, people have been able to take pictures of their screen using the Print Screen key on their keyboard, but that required pasting the image into a photo-editing tool to save it. The Snipping Tool was introduced to personal computers in Windows Vista to streamline this process.

This tool can be used in any area that requires taking snips of what is on a screen. Authors can use the Snipping Tool to take pictures of their screens to add to a textbook. People creating manuals for software can take snips to help users understand how to use their product. The tool can be used to show a technical support person what an error on the screen looks like. Any time you need an image of screen contents, you can create one using this program, which comes with Windows 8.

One drawback to the Snipping Tool is that it does not allow you to take snips of the Start screen. In order to do so, you will need to press the Print Screen key on your keyboard, open the Paint program, and then paste. You can then save your image.

W801.02

To Use the Snipping Tool and Print Screen Tool

a. Locate the program WordPad using the All apps method discussed earlier. Start **WordPad**.

b. Return to the Start screen, and then click **Snipping Tool**. The Snipping Tool window opens.

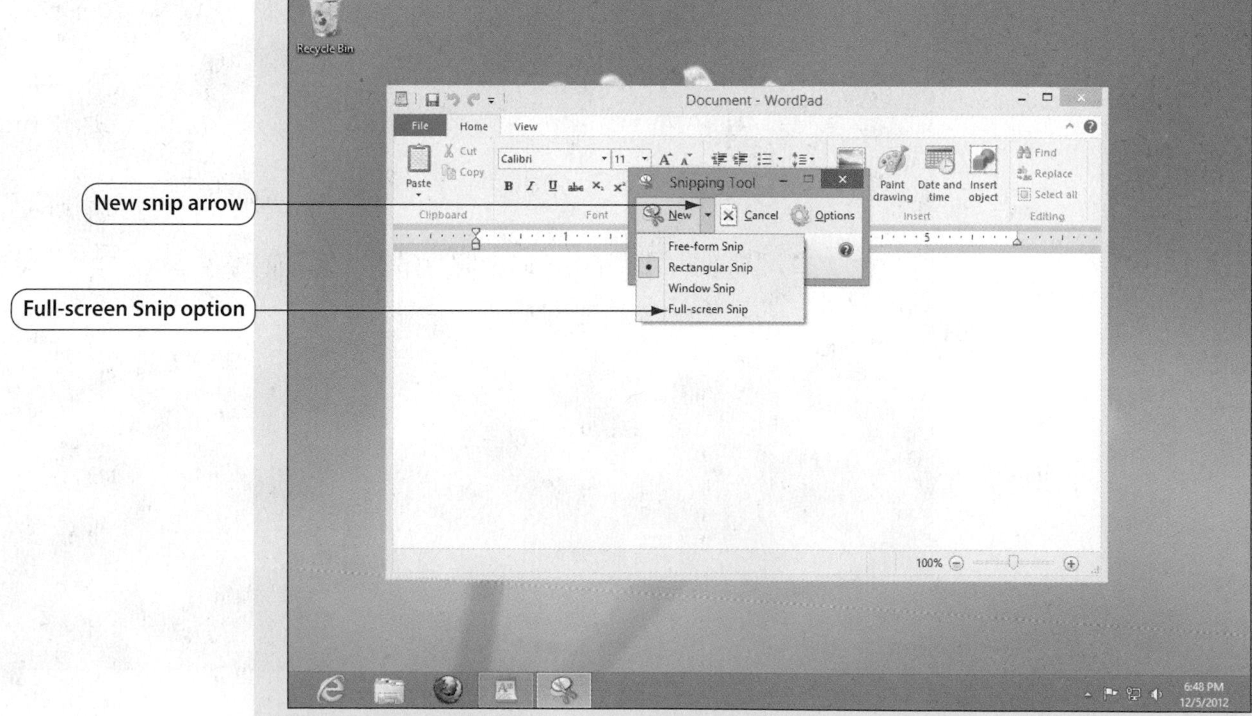

Figure 12 Snipping Tool options

c. Click **New Snip arrow**, and then click **Full-screen Snip**. The Snipping Tool window opens and the snip is displayed.

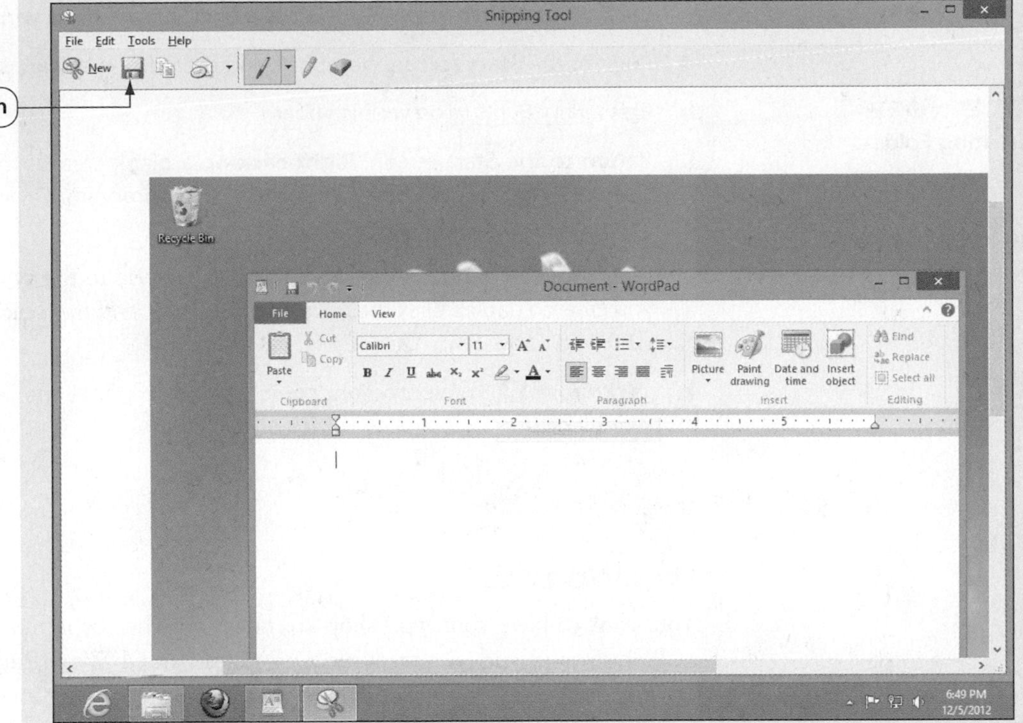

Figure 13 Snip of WordPad

d. On the menu bar, click **File**, and then click **Save As**. Browse to the location of your data files. Click the **New folder** button to create a new subfolder. Name this subfolder Windows 8 Workshop 1. Press Enter. Double-click the **Windows 8 Workshop 1** folder.

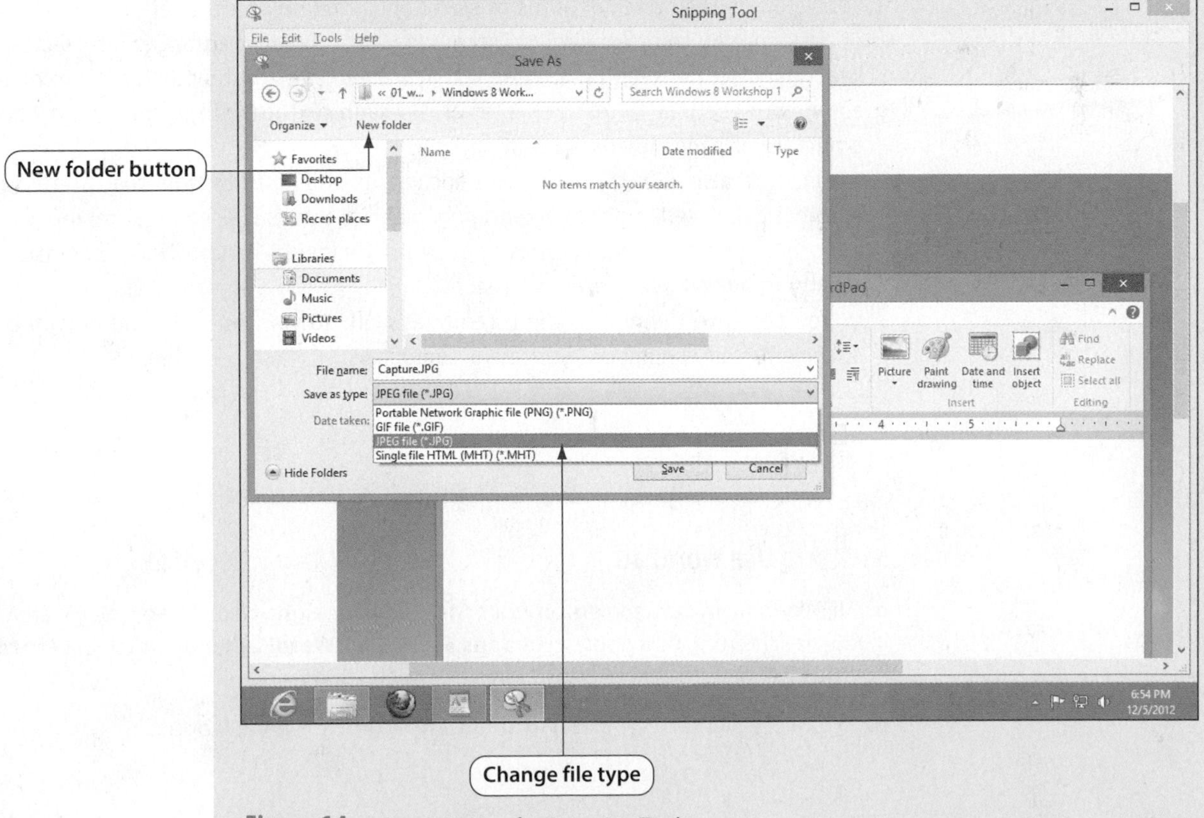

Figure 14 Save options for Snipping Tool

e. Click the **Save as type** arrow, and then click **JPEG file**. In the File name box, type w801ws01WordPad_LastFirst, using your last and first name, and then click **Save**.

f. Click **Close** in the top-right corner of the Snipping Tool window to close it.

g. Point to the **Start screen** thumbnail, and then click the **Start screen**.

h. Press Print Screen on your keyboard.

i. Return to the Start screen. **Right-click** on a blank area of the Start screen, and then select **All Apps**. Click **Paint** to launch the Paint program. Click **Paste**. The image of your Start screen displays in Paint.

j. Click the **File** menu, and then select **Save**. Browse to the Windows 8 Appendix folder you created earlier. Click the **Save as type** arrow, and then click **JPEG file**. Name the file w801ws01StartSnip_LastFirst.

k. Click **Close** in the top-right corner of Paint to close the program. Do the same for WordPad.

SIDE NOTE

Creating Folders

There are other ways to create folders. These will be further discussed in Windows 8 Workshop 2.

Use WordPad

You want to have your workshop attendees use the computer to take notes. All versions of Windows include a text-editing program named **WordPad**. Though not as powerful as word processing programs (such as Microsoft Word or OpenOffice Writer), WordPad is free and pre-installed.

REAL WORLD ADVICE | **Note-Taking Software**

Certain versions of Microsoft Office include the OneNote tool. OneNote is designed to allow you to keep track of notes in electronic notebook files. OneNote features the options for you to type anywhere on a page, organize related pages into sections, and keep many sections within a notebook. You may have a notebook for their computer class, with sections for each chapter of the main textbook. Each section may contain a number of pages related to that section.

OneNote also allows you to paste documents and pictures from the Internet, and automatically keeps track of the original website address. Users with tablets can use a digitizer pen and handwrite notes as well. Windows 8 handwriting recognition has greatly improved over previous versions.

You can save the files to the Internet as well, so you can open and modify the document from a number of different computers.

W801.03

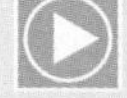

To Use WordPad

a. If WordPad is not shown on your Start screen, **right-click** in any blank area of the Start screen, and then select **All apps**. Right-click **WordPad**, and then select **Pin to Start**. This will make this application available on the Start screen.

b. From the Start screen, click **WordPad**. The WordPad window opens.

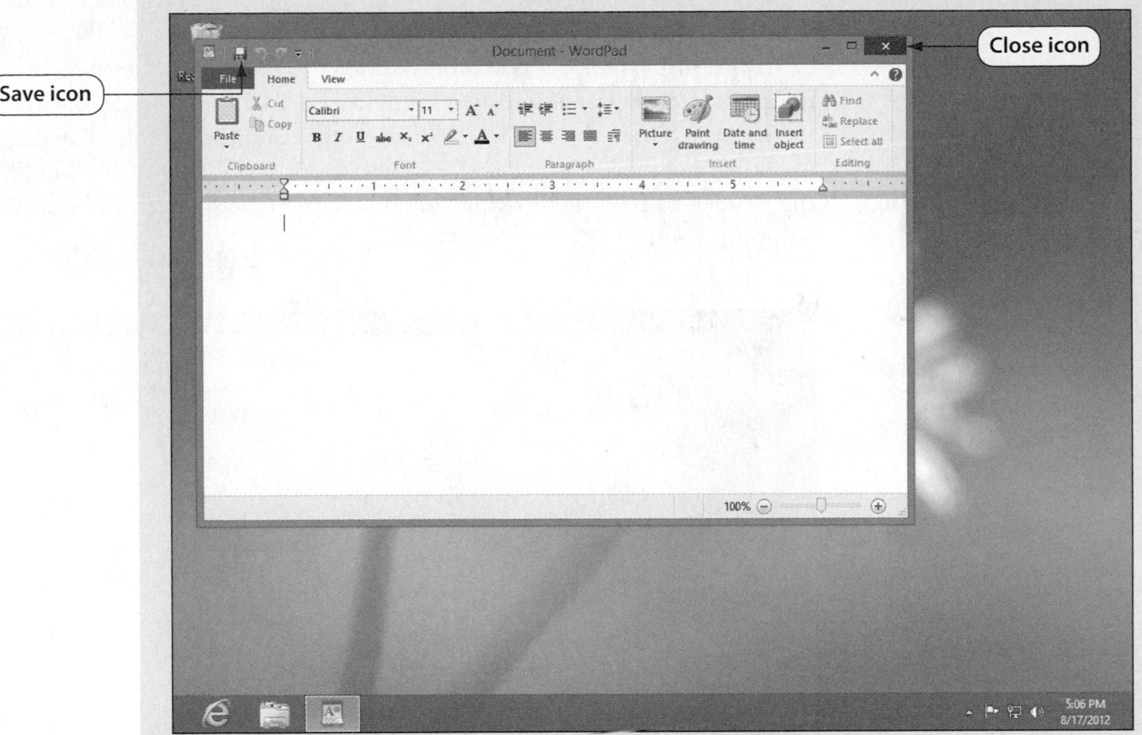

Figure 15 WordPad interface

c. Type a paragraph describing your experience so far with Windows 8. Click **Save** at the top of the screen.

d. Navigate to your Windows 8 Workshop 1 folder. In the **File name** box, type w801ws01Experience_LastFirst.

e. Click **Close** in the top-right corner of the WordPad window to close the program.

f. Point to the **Start screen** thumbnail, and then click **Start screen.**

Switch Between Programs

The Windows operating system supports **multitasking**, or the ability to run more than one program at once. Many users take full advantage of this feature. You may be running Internet Explorer to log on to Facebook while you type a document in Microsoft Word, listen to music in iTunes, and play World of Warcraft. You may not realize that while you are running these programs, other applications like your antivirus software are also open. The ability to multitask presents great advantages over older operating systems like Microsoft's DOS, but can also slow down the computer. Just because a computer can run 10 applications at once does not necessarily mean it should. If you find your computer is running slow, a quick fix might be to do less multitasking. Windows 8 will also attempt to manage some of this for the user with better management of open programs.

Windows 8 has changed switching between programs. You can access open programs through the **task switcher** by pointing to the top-left corner of the screen. The task switcher displays a thumbnail for the most recent application (other than the current one). So, for example, if you open Internet Explorer and then open the Snipping Tool, when you point to the top-left corner of the screen, the Internet Explorer thumbnail displays. If you want to see all open applications, you would point to the top-left corner of the screen and wait for the thumbnail to display. You would then move the mouse along the left side of the screen to bring up thumbnails of all running software. If you have experience using the Alt+Tab key combination in older versions of Windows, you will recognize this type of interface.

Applications not designed for Windows 8 allow you to switch using the taskbar at the bottom of the screen. All non-Windows 8 programs will be shown on the taskbar of the desktop. So, if you open WordPad and the Snipping Tool, as well as the Windows 8 Reader App, the only two options at the top-left of the screen would be to switch to the Reader App or the desktop containing the taskbar with links to WordPad and the Snipping Tool.

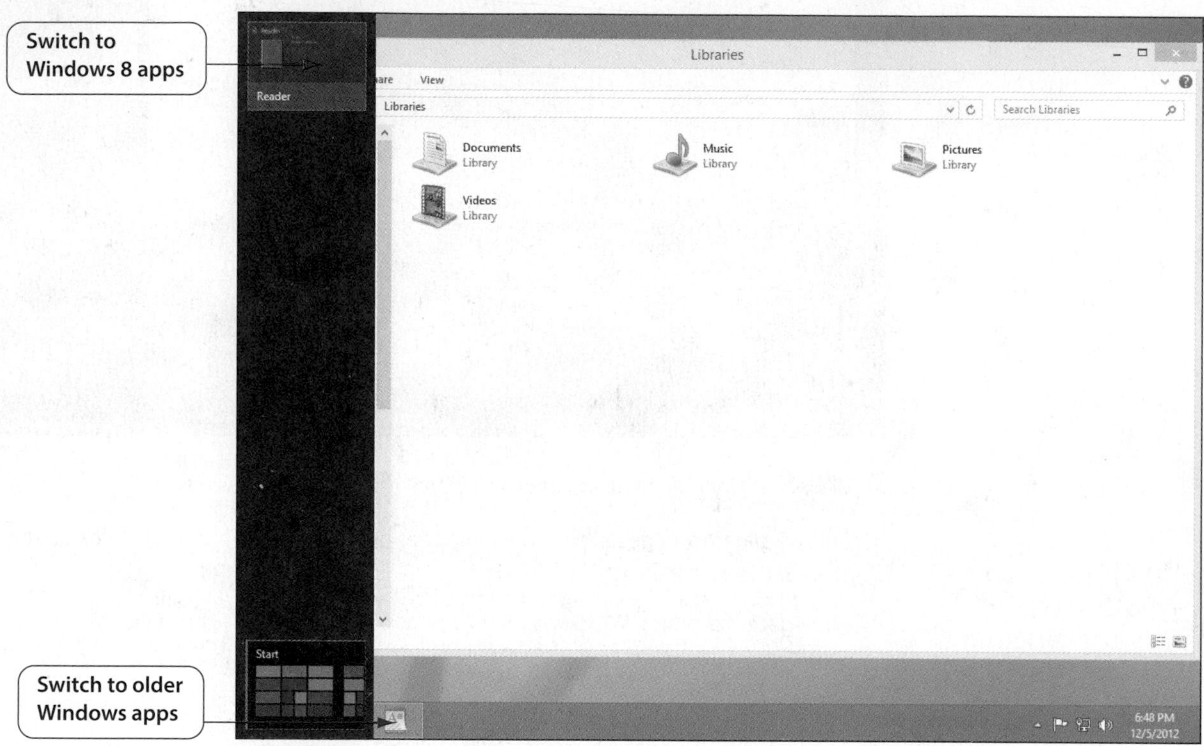

Figure 16 Switching program comparison

W801.04

To Switch Between Open Applications

a. From the Start screen, click **Snipping Tool**. The Snipping Tool window opens.

b. Click the **Start screen** thumbnail to return to the Start screen.

c. From the Start screen, **right-click** a blank area of the screen, and then click **All Apps** at the bottom of the screen. Locate and click **WordPad** to open the program.

d. Notice the taskbar at the bottom of the screen shows two programs open. One is WordPad and the other is the Snipping Tool. Click the **buttons** at the bottom of the screen to switch between the open programs.

Most recently used application

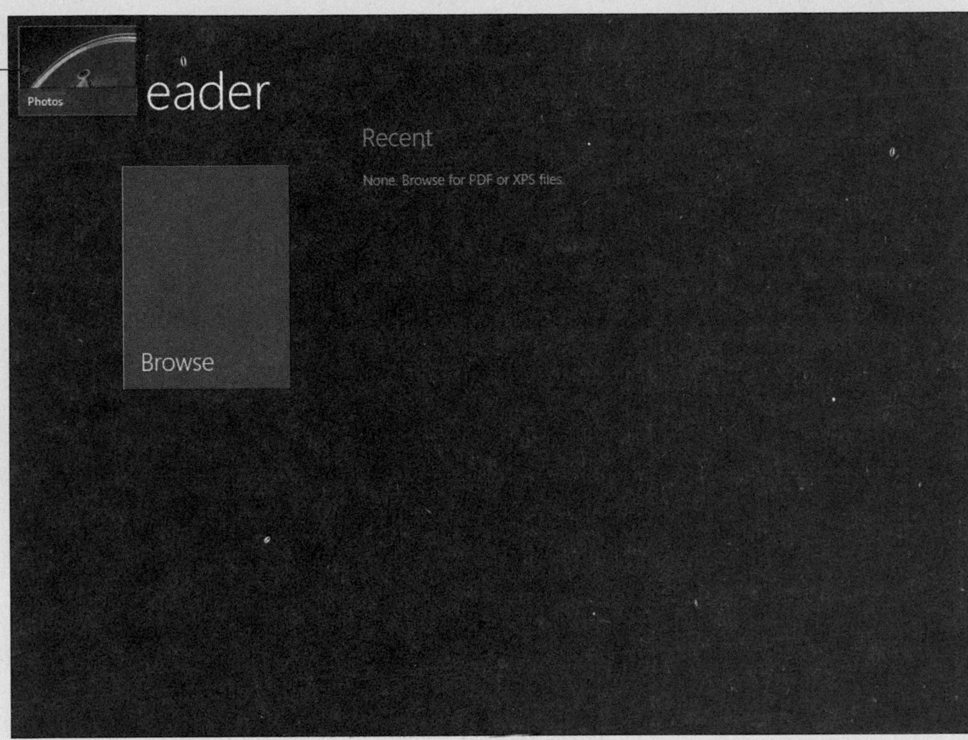

Figure 17 Switching to most recently used application

e. Click the **Start screen thumbnail** to return to the Start screen. Click the **Photos** tile on the Start screen. The Photos tool will open.

f. Click the **Start screen thumbnail** to return to the Start screen. Click the **Reader** tile on the Start screen. The Reader tool will open. You now have two Windows 8 programs open: Photos and Reader. You also have the desktop open, with WordPad and the Snipping Tool open.

g. Point to the **top-left** of the screen to display the task switcher, and notice a preview of Photos will appear. This is because Photos was the most recently used application aside from the current Reader application.

h. Move the mouse pointer along the **left edge** of the screen. Notice all other open programs appear on the left side of the screen. Click **Photos** to switch to it.

i. Display the **task switcher**, and then move the mouse pointer along the **left edge** of the screen. All open programs will display. Click **Reader** to switch back.

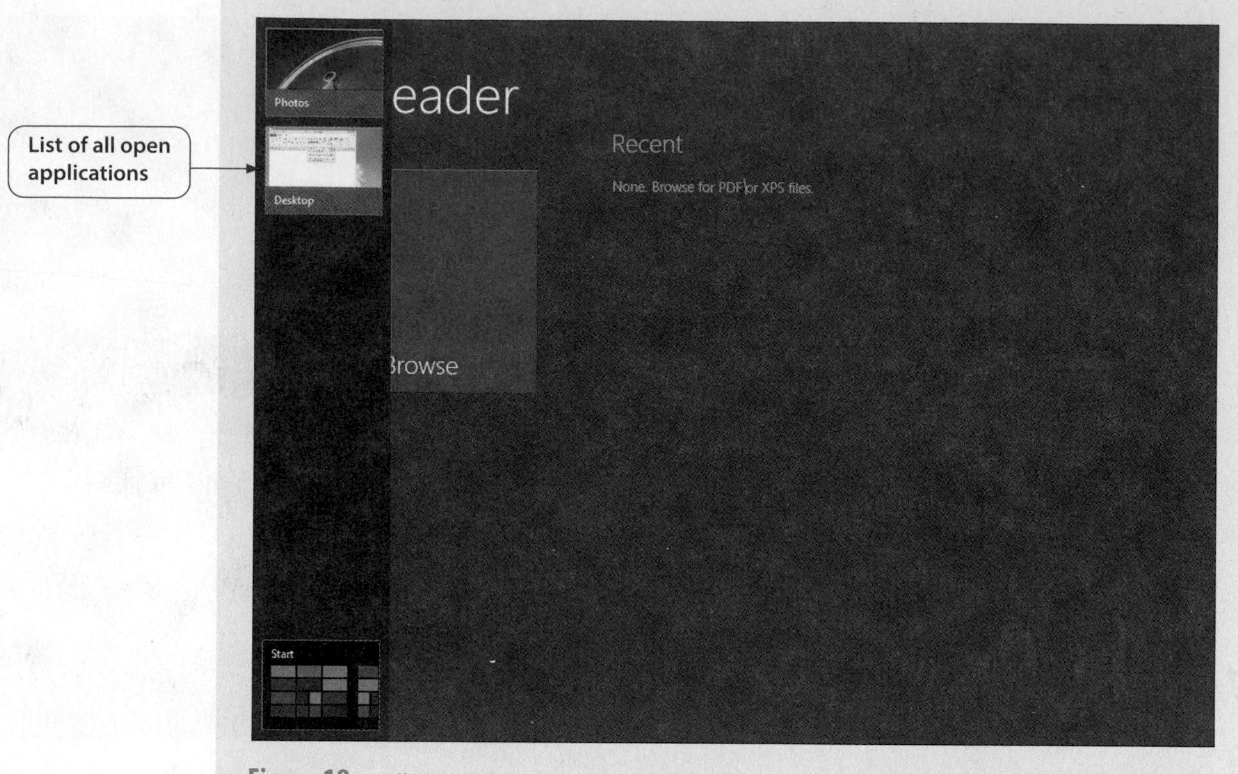

Figure 18 All open applications

Open and Close Programs

You will find Windows 8 is very different than previous versions of Windows when dealing with programs. You likely are used to a taskbar at the bottom of the screen that showed all running programs, and a set of icons in the top-right corner of each window to close programs. Applications designed for earlier versions of Windows will open up in the Windows desktop view. These applications will include the standard Close button in the top-right corner of the window to allow you to close them. All applications not designed for Windows 8 will open in the desktop view.

Applications designed for Windows 8 will not include the close buttons you have become accustomed to. Instead, you are expected to trust the operating system to manage the computer's resources. If you do not wish to trust Windows you can also close an application manually by pointing to the task switcher, and moving the mouse pointer down the left side of the screen. Any application shown there can be right-clicked and closed. You can also use gestures to do so on a touch-screen device. A list of gestures is shown in the Using Gestures section of this workshop.

One of the reasons the Close option was removed from Windows 8 is because the operating system **suspends** programs when they are not being used. A suspended application will not use any processing power, and thus leads to Windows 8 devices being more energy-efficient than previous versions of Windows. Instead of expecting you to manage applications, the operating system is attempting to handle application management. This is similar to how cell phones work.

You will find applications designed for Windows 8 have a different interface than applications not designed for this operating system. You will demonstrate both of these to your workshop.

W801.05

To Open and Close a Program

a. Most programs can be started either from the Start screen or from All Apps. If it is not already started from the previous section, click the **Photos** tile on the Start screen. The Photos application opens.

b. If it is not already started from the previous section, return to the Start screen, and then click the **Reader** tile. The Reader application opens.

c. As Reader is designed for Windows 8, it does not have the options you may be used to in earlier versions of Windows. Point to the **task switcher**, and then move the mouse pointer **down** the left side of the screen. A list of open programs will appear.

Right-click menu for Windows 8 application

Figure 19 Closing an application designed for Windows 8

d. Right-click the **Photos** application, and then select **Close**. The program has been closed.

e. Return to the Start screen, and then click the **Snipping Tool**, if it is not already open from the previous section. Notice this program opens in the Windows 7 style desktop.

f. Return to the Start screen, and then click **WordPad**, if it is not already open from the previous section. This program also opens in the Windows 7 style desktop.

g. Click **Close** in the top-right corner of the Snipping Tool. The program has been closed.

h. Click **Close** in the top-right corner of WordPad. The program has been closed.

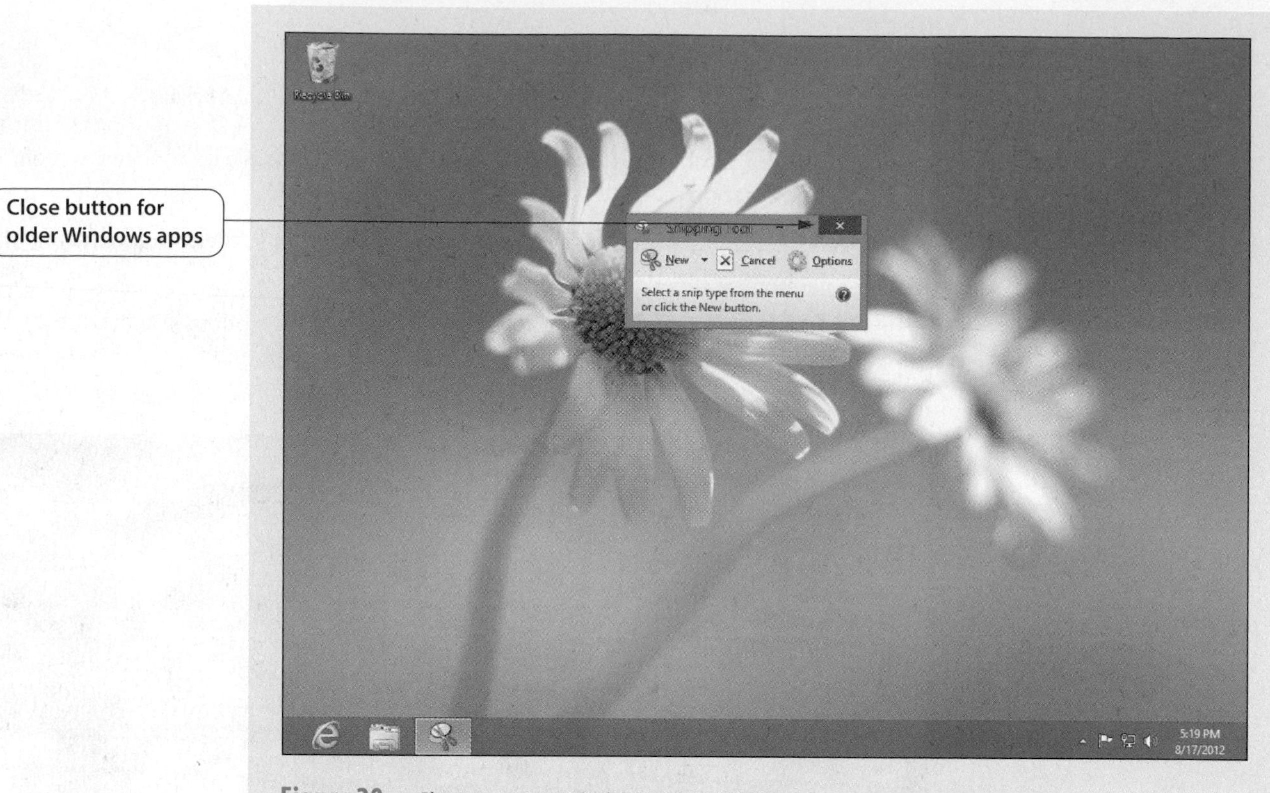

Figure 20 Closing a non-Windows 8 application

Using Charms and Windows Search

Charms are buttons which provide quick access to a number of useful functions. Charms bring together some functions that were found in different places. From this menu, you have five options to choose from. You can access the new Search charm, which has greatly improved Windows search functionality. You can access the Share charm to send information to social networking sites (such as Facebook or Twitter), blogging sites, and e-mail. The Start charm will bring you back to the main Start screen. The Devices charm allows you to access hardware such as display devices. The Settings charm allows you the chance to shut down the machine. In addition, it provides access to settings related to the program you are using. For example, when you click Settings from the Desktop, you will be provided with options such as Control Panel. However, if you click Settings from the Start screen, you are given options related to tiles.

Microsoft Windows has always included a search tool. However, in earlier versions of Windows, users did not always use this functionality due to a confusing interface. Windows 7 improved search functionality, but users still had to go to two different places to search effectively. The search on the Start menu was easy to use, but did not offer advanced options. The search in Windows Explorer (now called File Explorer) was more powerful to use, but was not as obvious. Windows 8 has added a search Charm, which will allow you to search applications, settings, and files by default. If you log in to a Microsoft account, you will also have the option to search many other areas, including Mail, Maps, People, and Photos. Search will find results not only for file names, but also for contents of files. The only requirement for the advanced find is that the file be on an **indexed** folder. Indexed folders are locations the Windows search tool has already searched and produced a keyword list for. Common indexed locations include the My Documents folder on the hard drive. Removable media, such as USB flash drives and CDs, cannot be indexed by the Windows search tool. You can also search by simply typing from the Start screen. This is a quick way to find applications not shown on the Start screen.

You will demonstrate Charms and the Windows search function to your workshop (see Figure 21). As your users will need to search files, you will have them copy files to the hard drive for your demonstration.

Figure 21 Charms

W801.06

To Use Charms and Search for Files

a. If you have not already done so, copy the **01_windows_8_workshop_1** folder to the My Documents folder.

b. From the Start screen, point to the **bottom-right corner** of the screen. The Charms will display on the right side of the screen.

c. Note the labels underneath each of the charms. Click the **Search** charm.

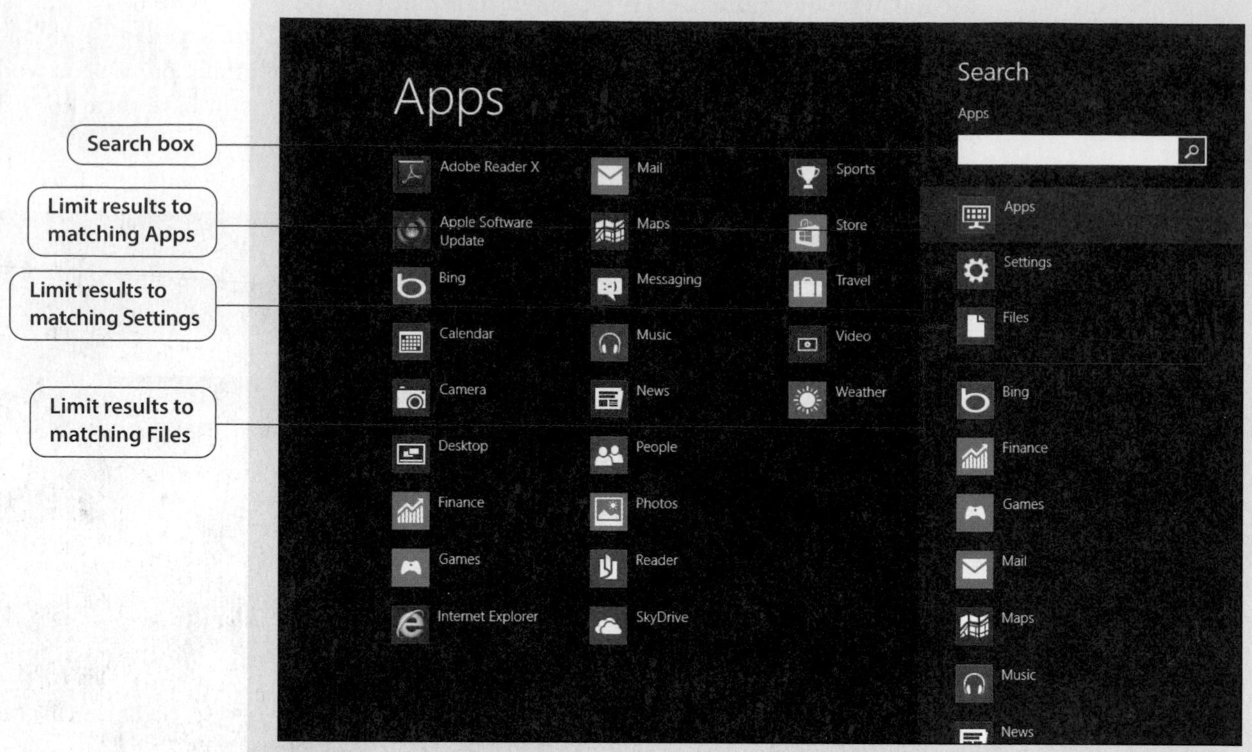

Figure 22 Search charm

d. Click inside the **Search** box at the top of the page. Your data files contain a list of workshop attendees. You will search for a name in the files. Type **Abdelfattah** and then click **Search**. The first results shown will be for apps, not files.

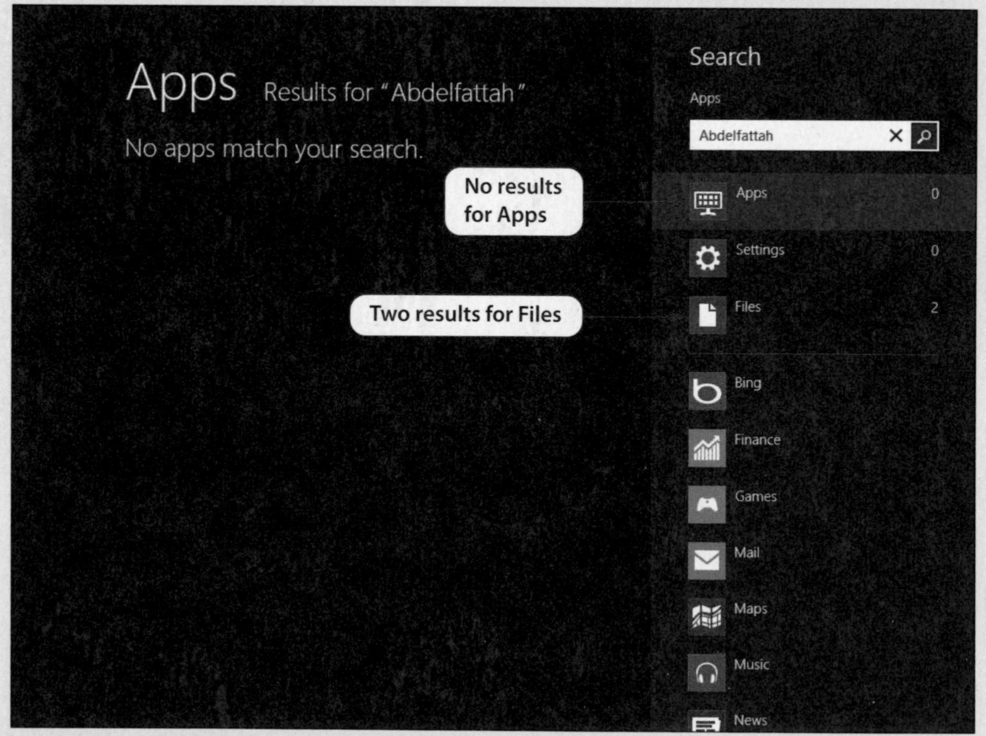

Figure 23 Search results for Abdelfattah

e. Notice you are given three sets of results by default. Apps will show you all applications matching the phrase. Settings will match settings on the computer matching the phrase. Files will show you a list of all files matching the phrase. As you wish to see results from files, click **Files**. If your data files are set up correctly, the number 2 will follow the Files icon.

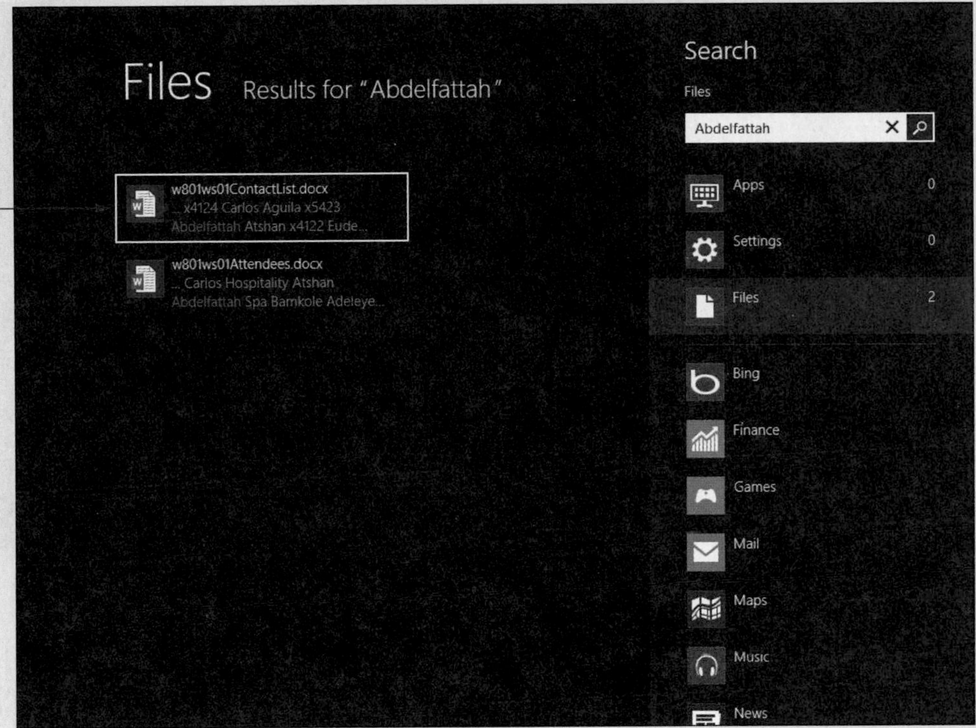

Figure 24 Search results for Abdelfattah in Files

f. The search results will show a list of files matching the search criteria. Your results should have a minimum of one result. Make a note of how many files match the search criteria.

g. Click the **Start screen thumbnail**.

h. Locate and click **WordPad** to open a new document.

i. Type Search Results for Abdelfattah and then follow this with the number of files found. Save the document as w801ws01Search_LastFirst in your Windows 8 Workshop 1 folder.

j. Display the Charms, and then select the **Search charm**.

k. If necessary, click the X next to the Search button to clear the search box. Type Internet Explorer in the search box, and then click .

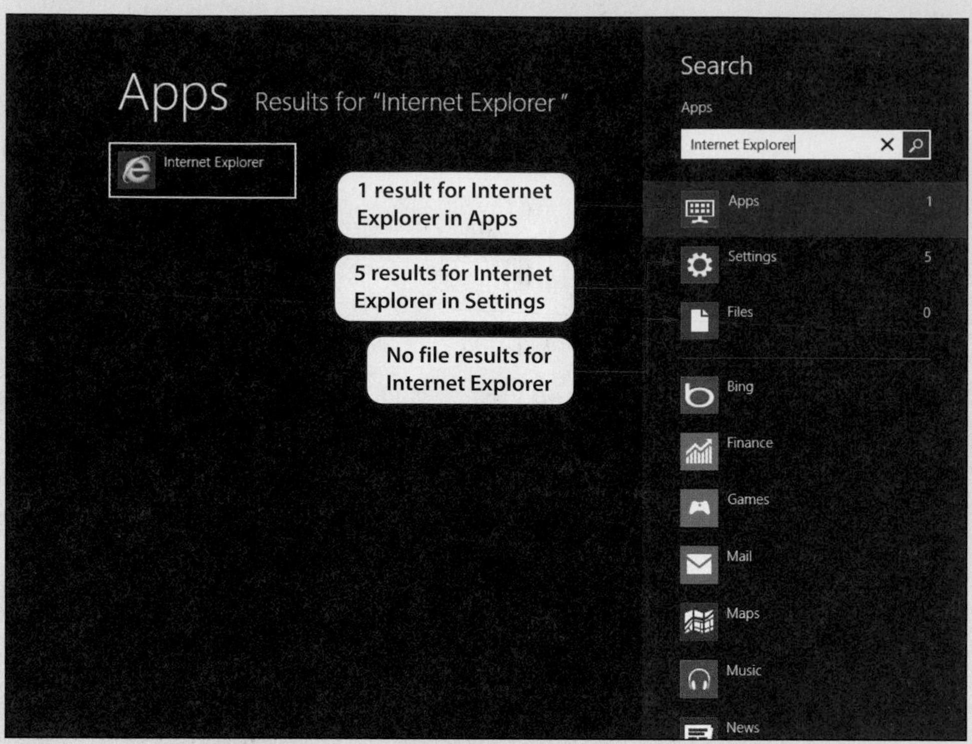

Figure 25 Search results for Internet Explorer

l. Notice your results include **Apps**, **Settings**, and **Files** matching this criteria. Make a note of how many files match the search criteria for each of these three categories. Your results may not match Figure 25.

m. Display the **task switcher**, and then select the **desktop** icon to switch back to WordPad.

n. Press Enter. Type Search Results for Internet Explorer in Apps and then follow this with the number of files found for Apps. Press Enter. Type Search Results for Internet Explorer in Settings and then follow this with the number of files found for Settings. Press Enter. Type Search Results for Internet Explorer in Files and then follow this with the number of files found. Press Enter. **Save** the document, and then close **WordPad**.

o. Click the **Start screen thumbnail**.

Using Gestures

As mentioned earlier, one of the key features that sets Windows 8 apart from previous versions is the built-in touch-screen recognition. At first, this functionality will likely be for mobile devices, but it would be a surprise if this technology is not embraced by home users to replace some mouse clicking. Many gestures are available from the bezel, or the edge of the screen. You can swipe from off-screen on to the screen to make certain actions happen, as you will see in the table below.

You will provide your workshop attendees with a list of Windows 8 gestures, so when the touch-screen devices become available at the Resort, they have a reference.

Desired Action	Gesture	Gesture
Bring up additional menu options	Swipe down from the top bezel, or swipe up from the bottom bezel	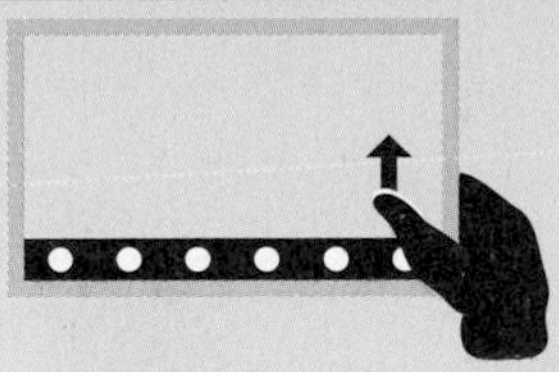
Bring up tile options on the Start screen	Swipe down on the tile	
Close the current application	Swipe down from the top bezel to the bottom	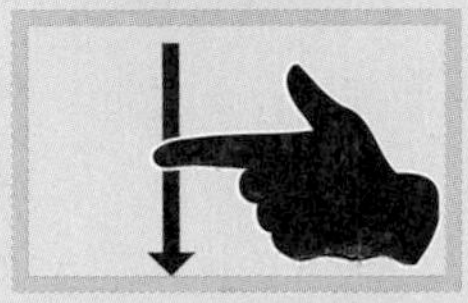
Display Charms	Swipe from the right bezel towards the left	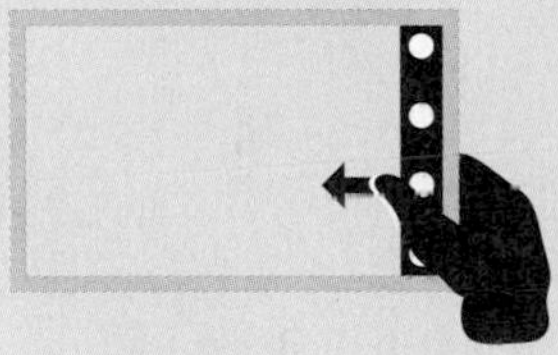
Show all open applications	Swipe out from the left bezel a little, and then swipe back to the left bezel	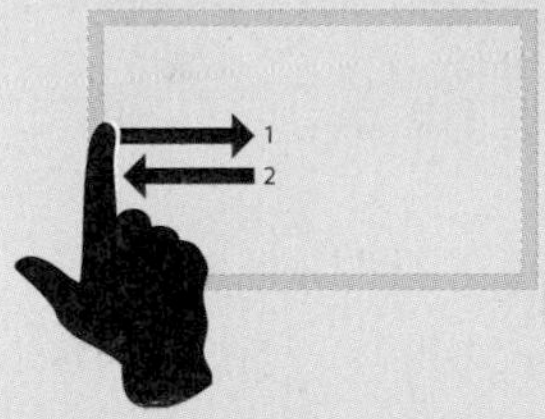
Switch between applications	Swipe from the left bezel towards the right	
Zoom in	Pinch	
Zoom out	Stretch—start two fingers pinched and spread fingers apart	

Figure 26 Windows 8 Gestures

Protecting Windows 8

Windows 8 has added a number of security features. In an effort to give the desktop operating system features that users enjoy from mobile devices, Microsoft has introduced multiple login methods. You can add security by pointing to the bottom-right side of the screen and selecting the Settings charm. From the menu, you can select Personalization and then click Users. There are four options here. You can switch to a Microsoft account, which will allow you to take your settings with you from machine to machine, change your password, create a picture password, or create a PIN. Many of these setups will be done using a **wizard**. Wizards are used to guide you through complex tasks. Wizards present you with questions, and based on your responses, may ask you more questions after you click next.

REAL WORLD ADVICE Security Versus Ease of Use

Users have a tendency to use the same password everywhere. You might have many accounts compromised at once if someone gets ahold of your password to one site. Many users tend to choose ease of use over security. Security expert Bruce Schneier explained this as follows in his 2000 book, *Secrets and Lies*: "If J. Random websurfer clicks on a button that promises dancing pigs on his computer monitor, and instead gets a hortatory (strong) message describing the potential dangers of the applet—he's going to choose dancing pigs over computer security any day."

There is no reason you cannot have both security and ease of use. For example, you can create a more secure password by using words not found in the dictionary, or just making a password longer. Mixing in capital letters, symbols, and numbers will make your password more complex, and therefore harder to hack.

You can add even more complexity by creating some sort of mnemonic device. You may still remember the order of operations as "please excuse my dear aunt Sally", which helps people remember to first perform operations in parentheses, then exponentiation, then multiplication and division, and finally addition and subtraction. You can do something similar for your password. For example, you could use the following lyrics from the Lynyrd Skynyrd song "Free Bird":

For I'm as free as a bird now. And this bird you cannot change.

If you take the first letter of each word, you would get the following password: fiafaabnatbycc

This is a tough password for a hacker to find due to the length and complexity, but one you can recall simply by recalling a song lyric.

However, if you use the same password everywhere, you are still open to risk. You can vary the password by site; for example, you can add the first letter of the website you are visiting to your password, so your password to Amazon.com might be afiafaabnatbycc, and your password to eBay would be efiafaabnatbycc. Adding numbers or capitalization would make this even more secure. For example, you could capitalize the first letter, and add a sequence of numbers to the end.

If you have some sort of pattern to your passwords, it adds security but still makes them easy to remember. That is, of course, if you want to be more secure.

You can visit the Microsoft Password Strength Calculator at www.microsoft.com/security to check the strength of your passwords. Click on **Create strong passwords**, and click **Check your password**.

Password	Security Rating	Rationale
password	Weak	Though it may seem clever to choose a password so simple, this is one of the first passwords hackers guess.
abc123	Weak	Though it involves letters and numbers, this is a short password.
qwerty	Weak	Though not in the dictionary, this is a common password.
123456789	Weak	Though nine characters long and numeric, this is an easily guessed password.
prenticehall	Medium	Password length is good, but if you work for Prentice Hall, this would be too obvious.
poptart8675309	Strong	Length of password and combination of letters and numbers makes this a stronger password.
efiafaabnatbycc	Strong	Length of password and randomness of letters makes this difficult to guess.
Efiafaabnatbycc@8675309	Best	Capital letters, symbols, numbers, and password length make this nearly impossible to guess—if protected correctly.

Figure 27 Security of Passwords

Log in Using a Microsoft Account

Microsoft allows you to sign into Windows 8 using a Microsoft account. The term "Microsoft account" refers in this context to what was previously known as a Windows Live ID. You can use a free live.com or hotmail.com account to sign in, or create a Microsoft account for another e-mail address. In other words, Gmail and Yahoo users can use your regular e-mail accounts as your login. You will be able to choose logging on to a local account, which exists only on one single machine, or a Microsoft account.

Signing in using a Microsoft account is an example of **cloud computing**. Cloud computing allows you to keep files on the Internet rather than on the client computer. The advantage here is that even if the client computer fails, files and settings are still safe. You do not have to use a Microsoft account in this version of Windows, but Microsoft has introduced a number of features that make it attractive. Personal settings, photos, and documents can be saved to a Microsoft account rather than to the local machine. Favorites for Internet Explorer and installed apps will follow you to any machine. This will reduce the need for home users to set up a home network, as they can simply log on to each machine with their Microsoft account.

Your college or work policy may not allow you to log in this way, but if it does, you will have access to the same files at school and work that you do at home. Using this type of account will reduce the problems associated with forgetting or losing a USB flash drive.

Note this can be undone at any point by going back to PC Settings, selecting Users, and selecting Switch to a local account. You will demonstrate to your workshop how they can switch to a Microsoft account.

W801.07

To Set Up a Microsoft Account

a. Display the Charms, and then click the **Settings charm**.

b. Click **Change PC Settings**.

Figure 28 Personalization options

c. Click **Users**.

d. Click **Switch to a Microsoft account**. You will be prompted to enter your current password for security.

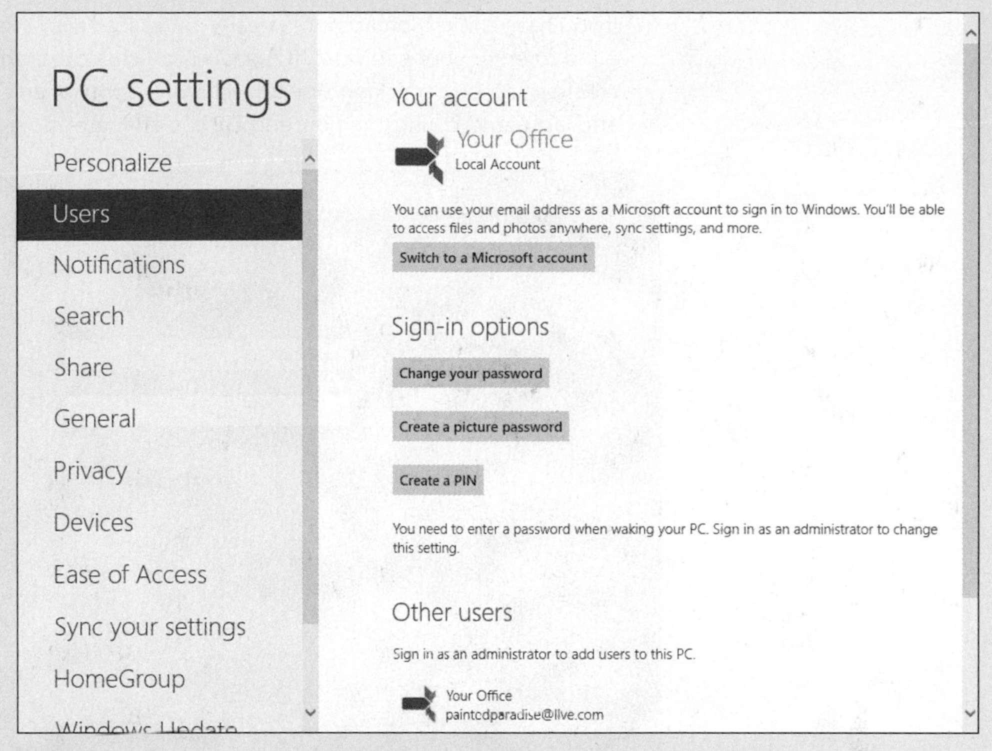

Figure 29 User settings

e. Type your **e-mail address** in the box provided. This does not have to be a Microsoft account.

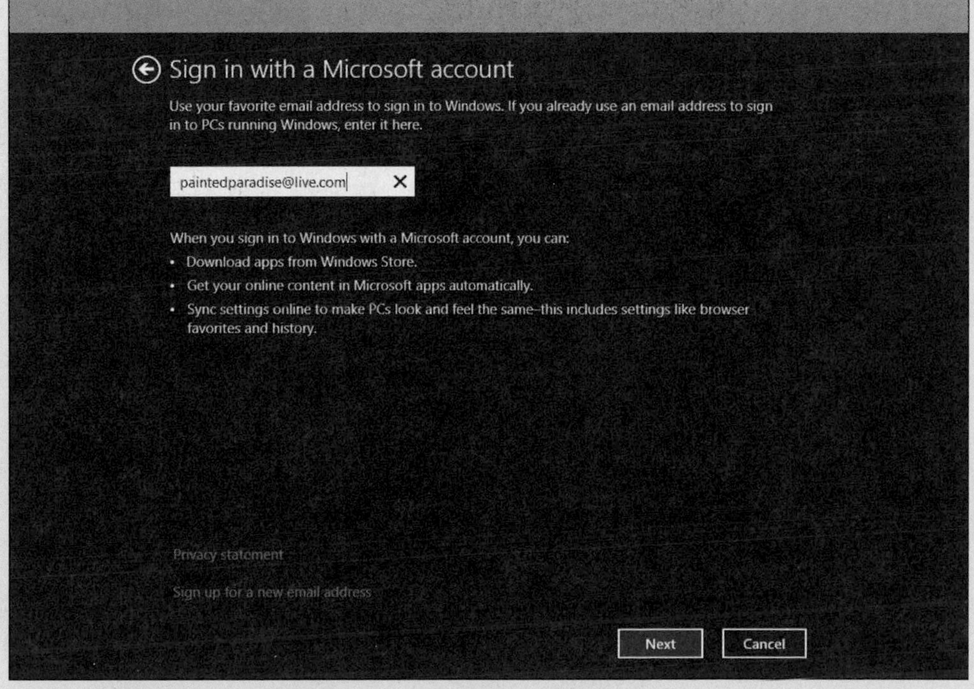

Figure 30 Sign in with a Microsoft account

f. If you have a Microsoft account already associated with this e-mail address, you will just need to enter your password. If not, you can click **Sign up for a Microsoft account** to create an account. Clicking Sign up will prompt you for an e-mail address, password, first and last name, country/region, and ZIP code (where applicable).

Figure 31 Entering a Microsoft account password

g. Existing users may be prompted to enter security verification information if they have not already set that up. If you are prompted, enter this information, and then click **Next**.

Figure 32 Successful Microsoft account setup

h. The final step of the wizard will confirm the information you have entered. Click **Finish**. You return to PC Settings. Return to the Start screen, and your Microsoft account will be displayed at the top of the screen.

Figure 33 Windows Start screen with new account

At this point, any other Windows 8 machines you logged into using your e-mail address would have access to the same applications, files, and settings.

Use Picture Passwords

For some users, a combination of a picture and gestures is more intuitive than remembering a password. **Picture passwords** allow you to select a picture and define a series of patterns that need to be "drawn" in order to unlock the system. This will be more commonly used on mobile devices and home devices, as public computer labs will likely not utilize this feature.

Before setting up this picture password, you will first be prompted to confirm your password to prevent another user from adding a picture password to your account. You will use a wizard that allows you to select the picture and the gestures you want to make up your picture password. You will demonstrate to your workshop how they can use picture passwords.

W801.08

To Set Up a Picture Password

a. Display the Charms, and then click the **Settings charm**.

b. Click **Change PC Settings**.

c. Click **Users**.

d. Click **Create a picture password**. You will be prompted to verify your current password. Type your password, and then click **OK**.

e. You will be given a choice of pictures to use. You can click any picture you may have on the PC, or choose from the pictures provided in your data files. Select any **photo**, and then click **Open**.

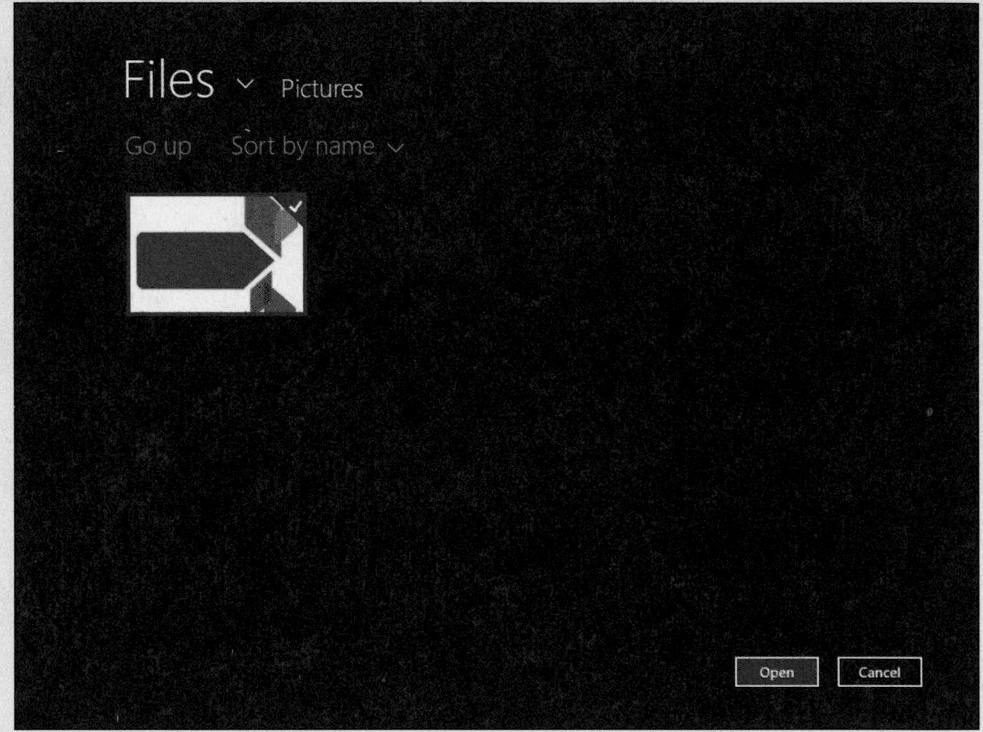

Figure 34 Choosing a source picture

f. You will move the picture to position it the way you want. Smaller pictures may not be centered on the screen, so you can position the picture to your liking. Click **Use this picture**.

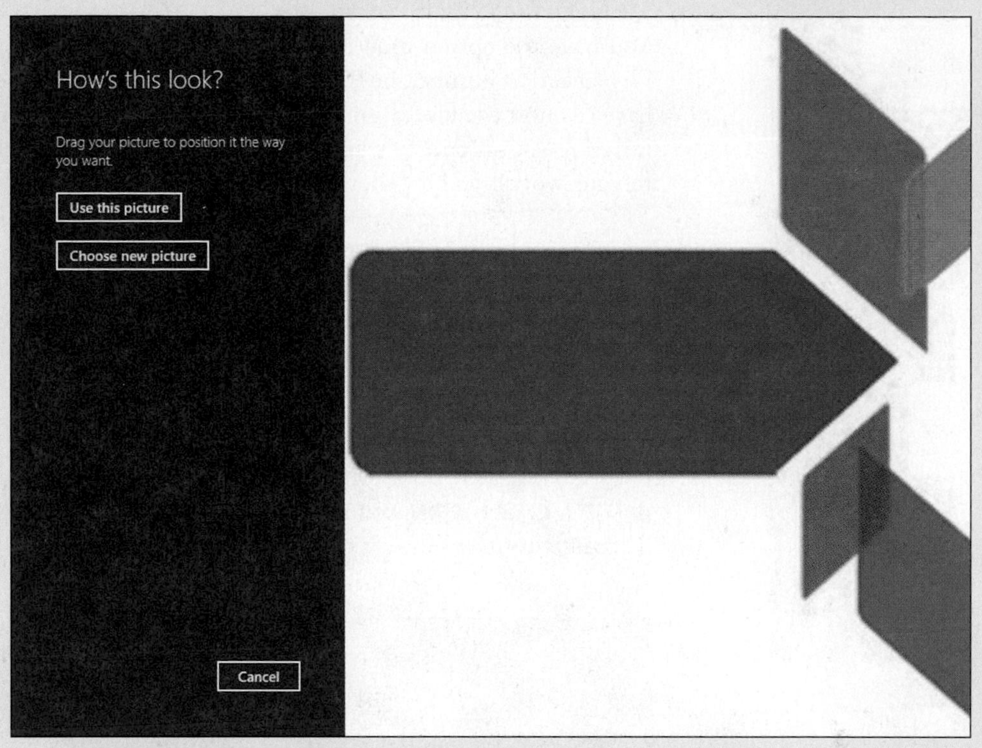

Figure 35 Positioning your picture password

g. Picture passwords require a combination of three gestures. The gestures can be a tap, a straight line, or a circle. Direction matters, so a circle drawn clockwise is not the same as one drawn counterclockwise. Set up a set of **three gestures** you will remember.

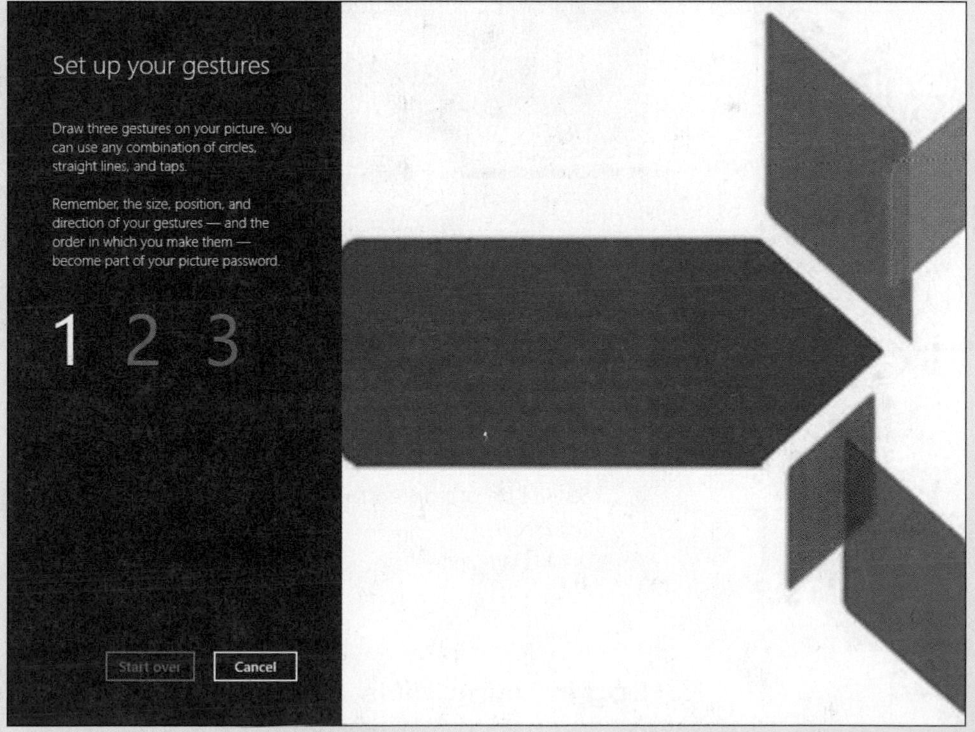

Figure 36 Gesture Setup

h. Re-enter the **gestures** to verify.

i. Click **Finish**. You now have added a picture password to the system.

Add a PIN Login

You have the option in Windows 8 to add an alternative to a password with a personal identification number, or **PIN**. A PIN is a four-digit numeric pass code. You will simply have to enter the four digits of the PIN to login to Windows. The system will automatically log you in once you have entered the four digits of the code. You will demonstrate to your workshop how they can set up PIN logins.

W801.09

To Set Up a PIN

a. Display the Charms, and then click the **Settings** charm.

b. Click **Change PC Settings**.

c. Click **Users**.

d. Click **Create a PIN**. You will be prompted to verify your current password. Type your password, and then click **OK**.

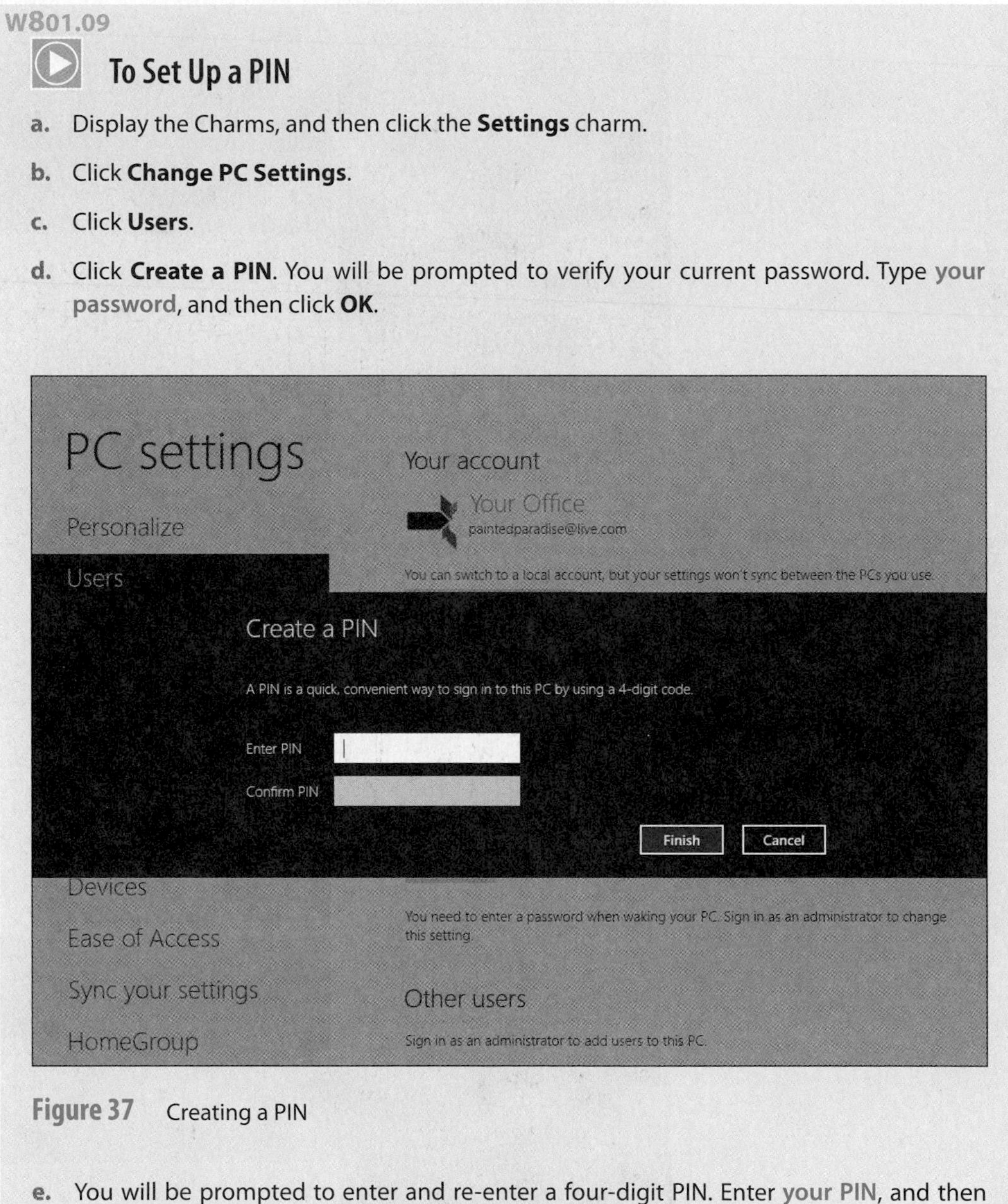

Figure 37 Creating a PIN

e. You will be prompted to enter and re-enter a four-digit PIN. Enter your PIN, and then click **Finish**.

Log in Using PINs and Picture Passwords

Once you have set up a PIN and/or a picture password, you can use it to log in from the main screen. You can click Sign-in options to access any of the alternate login methods discussed here. You will demonstrate to your workshop how they can use some of the alternate login methods.

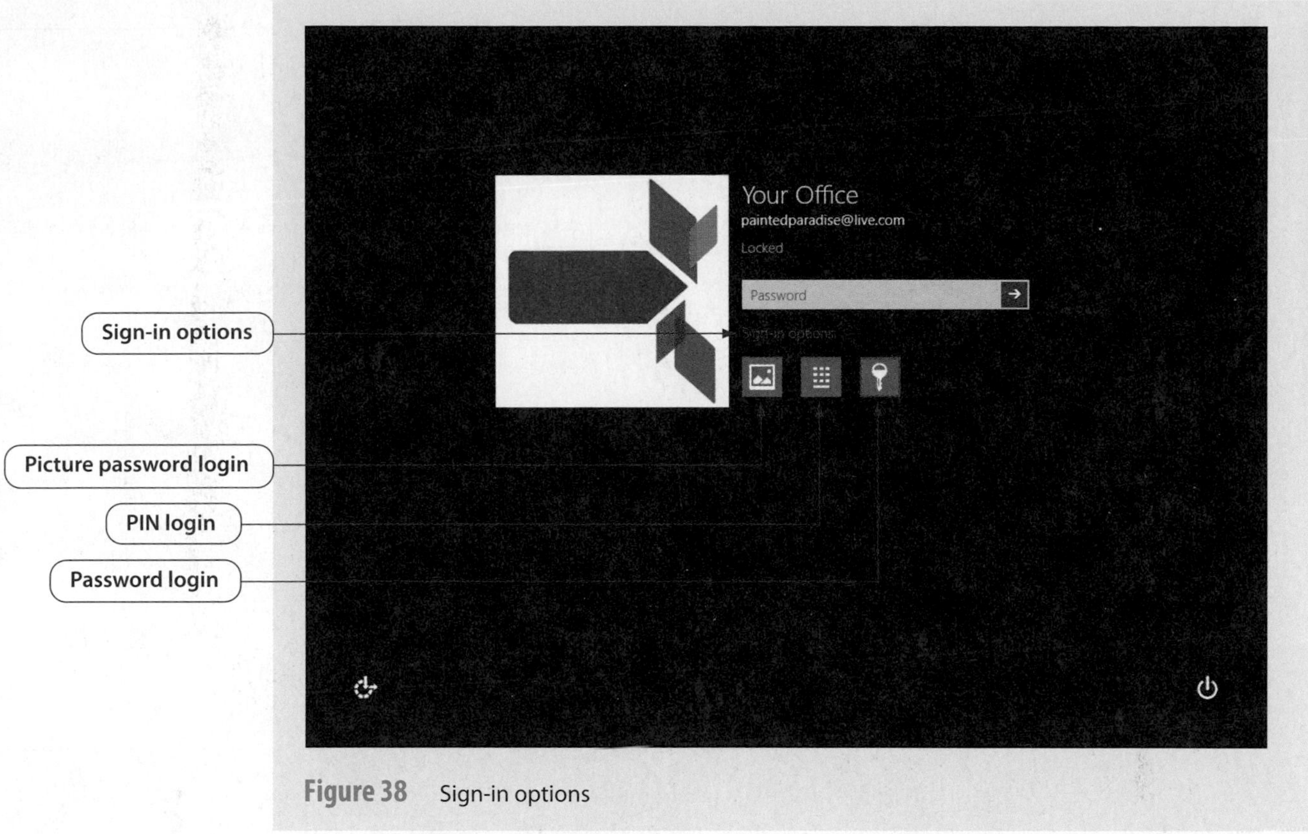

Figure 38 Sign-in options

Add a Trusted PC

A **trusted PC** is a computer that users have associated with a Microsoft account. This functionality has been in place for a few years to assist with password resets for online accounts, but has expanded use with the Windows 8 operating system. Trusted PCs need to be set up in order for users to take full advantage of the cloud computing functions within Windows 8.

Your college's policy may prevent you from setting this up, but home users may want to set this up as soon as possible to take advantage of the cloud features of Windows 8. You should consider whether you want to do this on a public machine, such as a computer lab machine. You will demonstrate to your workshop how they can trust PCs.

W801.10

To Trust a PC

a. Display the Charms, and then click the **Settings** charm.

b. Click **Change PC Settings**.

c. Click **Users**.

d. Click **Trust this PC**. Internet Explorer will launch and open the Microsoft account page.

SIDE NOTE
Available for Microsoft Account Users Only
Users who have not switched to a Microsoft account will not see this option.

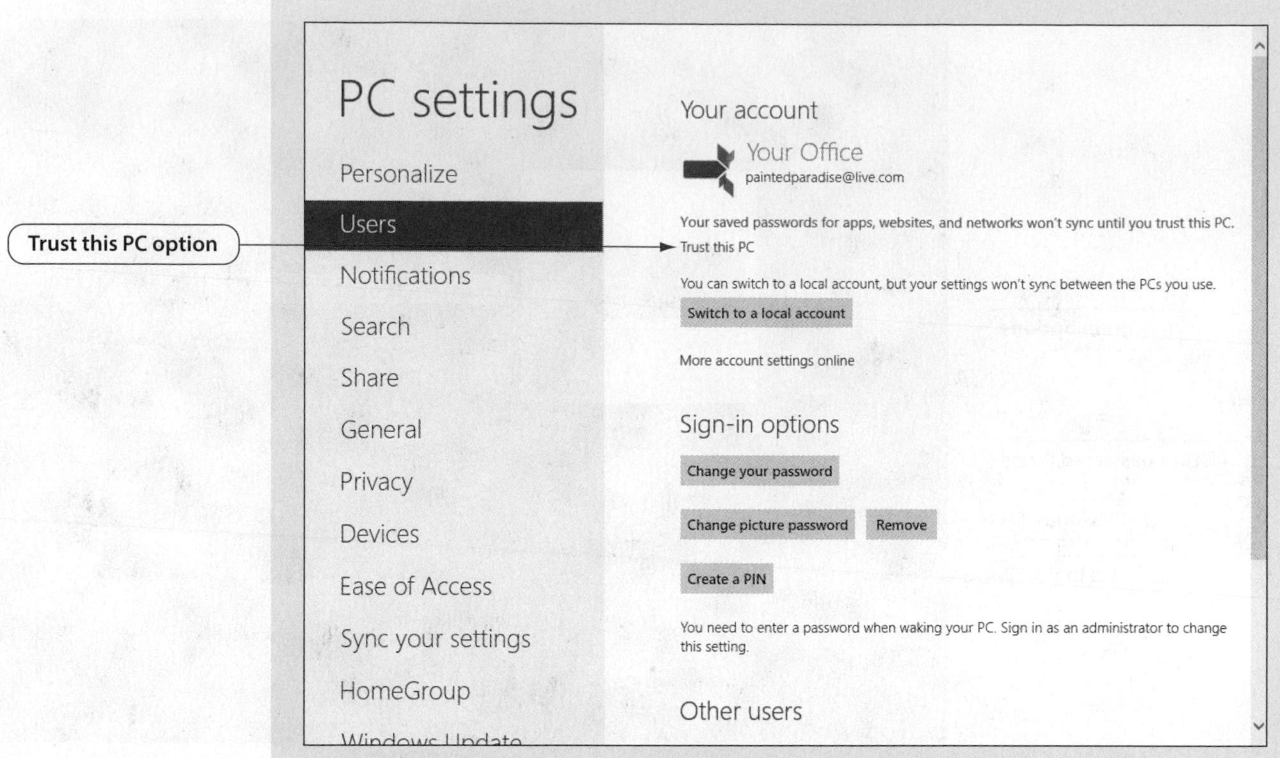

Figure 39 Trusting a PC from Users Menu

e. Click **Confirm** located next to the PC name of your current machine.

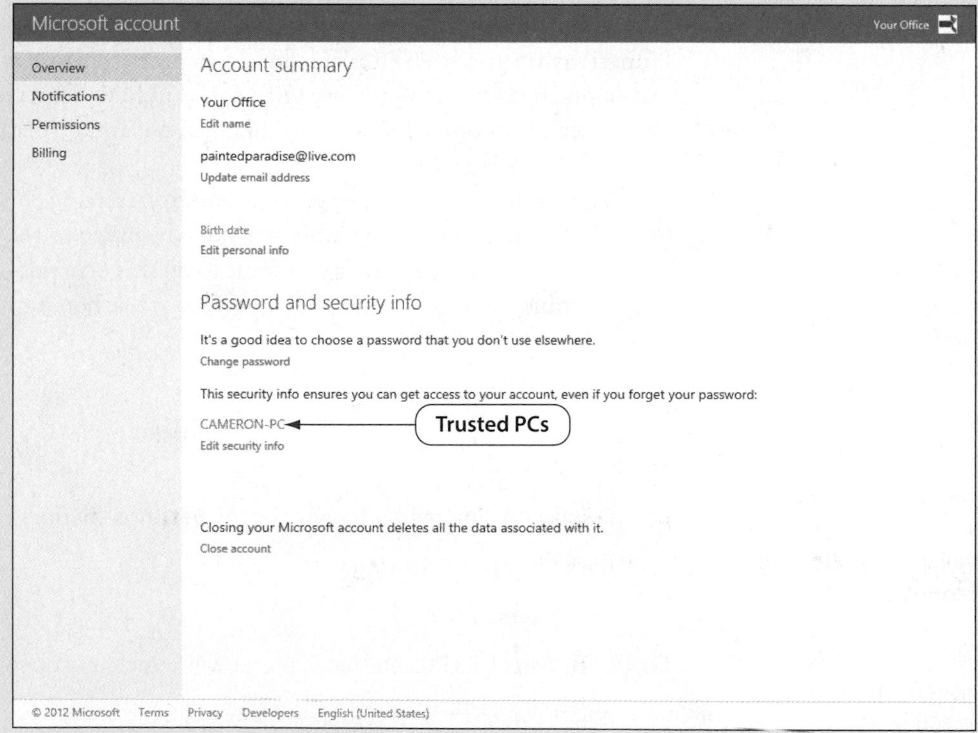

Figure 40 Trusted PCs Associated with an Account

f. Click **Done**, and then close **Internet Explorer** and the **Users** window.

Using Internet Explorer 10

Microsoft's web browser, Internet Explorer, has gone through some major changes for Windows 8. Internet Explorer 10 includes a Windows 8 style interface. The Windows 8 style application fully supports touch-screen functionality and will also allow you to add specific websites to your Start screen.

One of the major changes you will notice is the Windows 8 style application does not support **plug-ins**. Plug-ins are programs that extend the capabilities of the web browser. For example, you may be familiar with plug-ins such as Adobe Flash Player. Plug-ins will likely become obsolete with the introduction of new web standards. You can still view web pages requiring plug-ins, but they must be viewed through the traditional desktop interface.

One advantage of the Windows 8 style browser application is that it reduces security risks. As the browser does not open a second program, you can be less concerned about the security risks plug-ins have traditionally presented.

Users with Windows 7 can also download Internet Explorer 10, though they will not be able to use the Windows 8 application functionality. You will demonstrate the Internet Explorer 10 app to your workshop.

W801.11

To Use the Internet Explorer 10 App

a. If the Internet Explorer app is not shown on your Start screen, **right-click** a blank area of the Start screen, and then click **All Apps** at the bottom of the screen. Locate **Internet Explorer**. Right-click **Internet Explorer**, and then select **Pin to Start**.

b. Point to the **bottom-left** of the screen, and then select **Start** to return to the main Start screen. Verify that a link to Internet Explorer now appears on your Start screen. Move this tile to an appropriate location.

c. Click the **Internet Explorer** tile to open the app. Type www.google.com to visit Google.

Figure 41 Internet Explorer 10 app interface

d. At the bottom of the screen, click the **Pin to Start** button, the button that resembles a push pin. A small box will open allowing you to name the link. Accept the default name of **Google**, and then click **Pin to Start**.

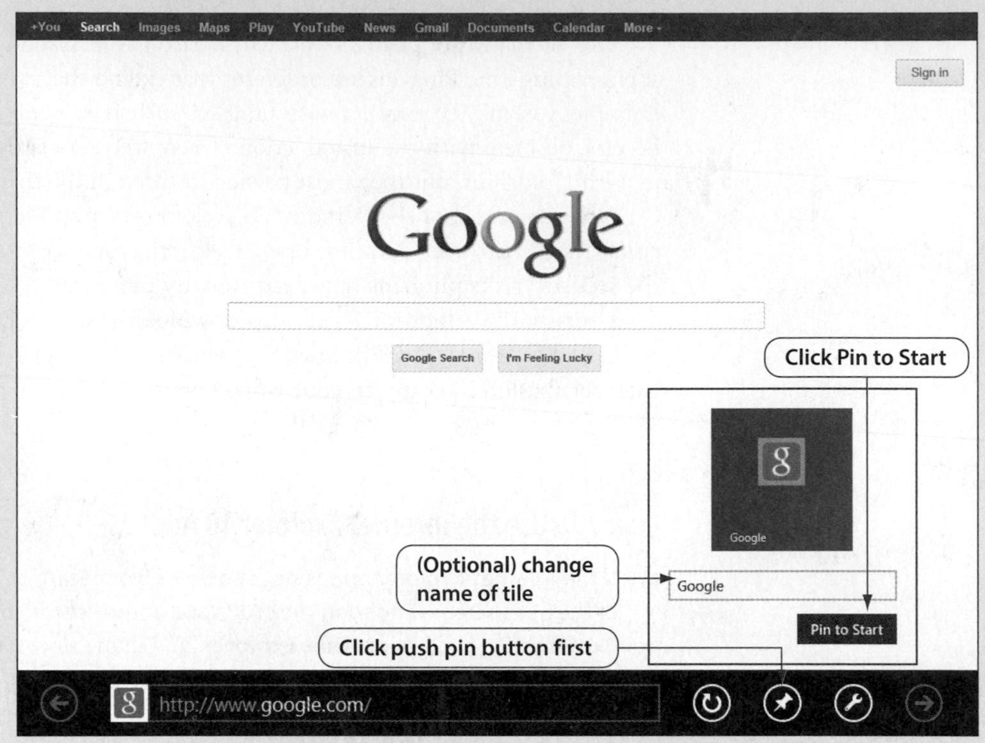

Figure 42 Pinning Google to Start screen

e. Point to the **bottom-left** of the screen, and then select **Start** to return to the main Start screen. Verify that a link to Google now appears on your Start screen. Move this tile to an appropriate location.

Figure 43 Start screen with Google and Internet Explorer tiles

f. Click the **Internet Explorer** tile, and then visit **www.flash.com**. Notice there are no plug-ins available to display the contents of the website.

g. Click the **Start screen thumbnail** to return to the Start screen. Click the **Desktop** tile.

h. Start the desktop version of Internet Explorer by clicking [IE icon] found on the taskbar.

i. Visit **www.flash.com** and notice the site loads properly, assuming you have Adobe Flash Player installed on the system.

Concept Check

1. Discuss navigating the Windows 8 Start screen including mouse pointer, right-click, shortcut menu, and scroll bar. p. 10
2. What is the purpose of the Snipping Tool? p. 14
3. What text-editing program is on all versions of Windows? p. 16
4. Discuss multitasking. Describe the task switcher. p. 17
5. Why was the Close option removed from Windows 8? p. 20
6. What is a Microsoft account? How do you sign in to a Microsoft account? p. 29
7. What is a picture password? p. 33
8. What is a PIN? p. 36
9. What are your sign-in options? p. 36–37
10. Define trusted PC and why this functionality is in place. p. 37

Key Terms

Application software 4
ARM device 4
Charm 5
Click 5
Cloud computing 29
Desktop 8
Drag 11
Gesture 4
Gesture recognition 4
Graphical user interface (GUI) 4
Hybrid boot 5
Icons 4
Indexed 22
Live Tile 7
Mouse pointer 10
Multitasking 17
Operating system 4
Picture password 33
PIN 36
Plug-in 39
Right-click 10
Scroll bar 10
Shortcut menu 10
Snip 14
Snipping Tool 14
Start screen 5
Suspend 20
System software 4
Taskbar 8
Task switcher 17
Tiles 7
Trusted PC 37
Windows RT 4
Wizard 28
WordPad 16

Visual Summary

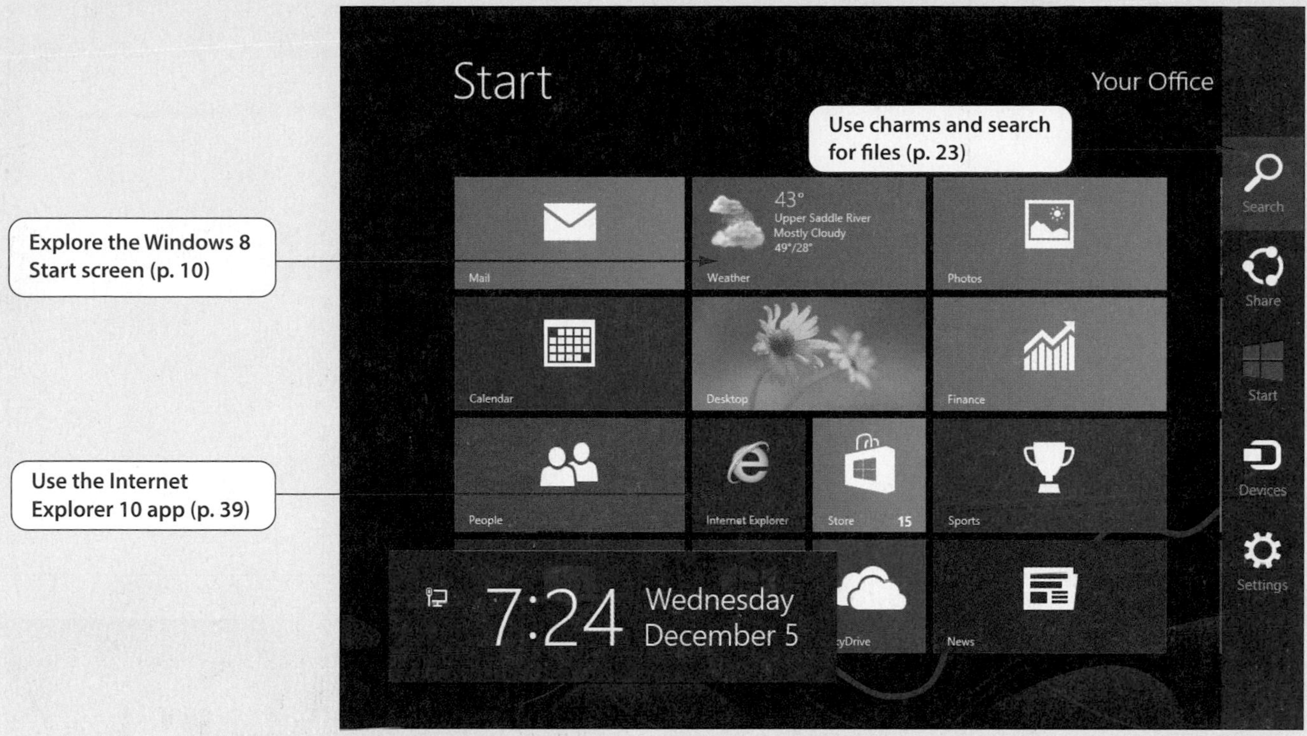

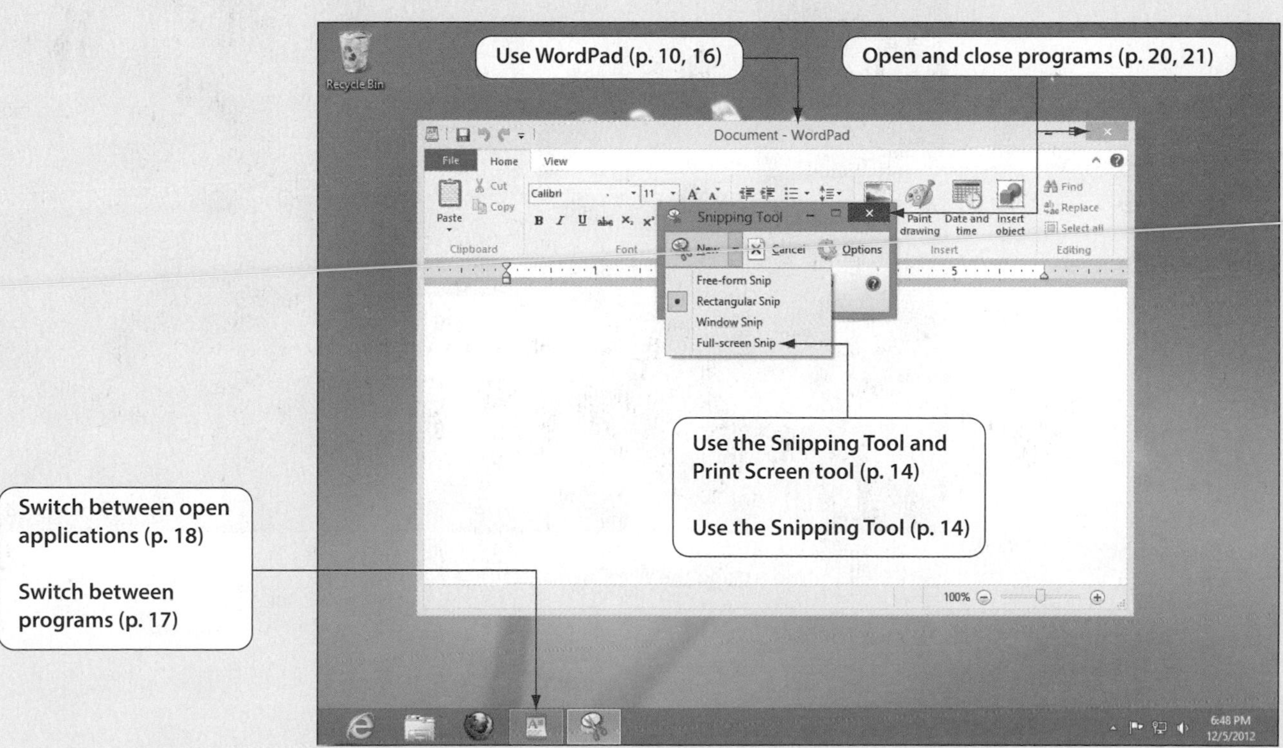

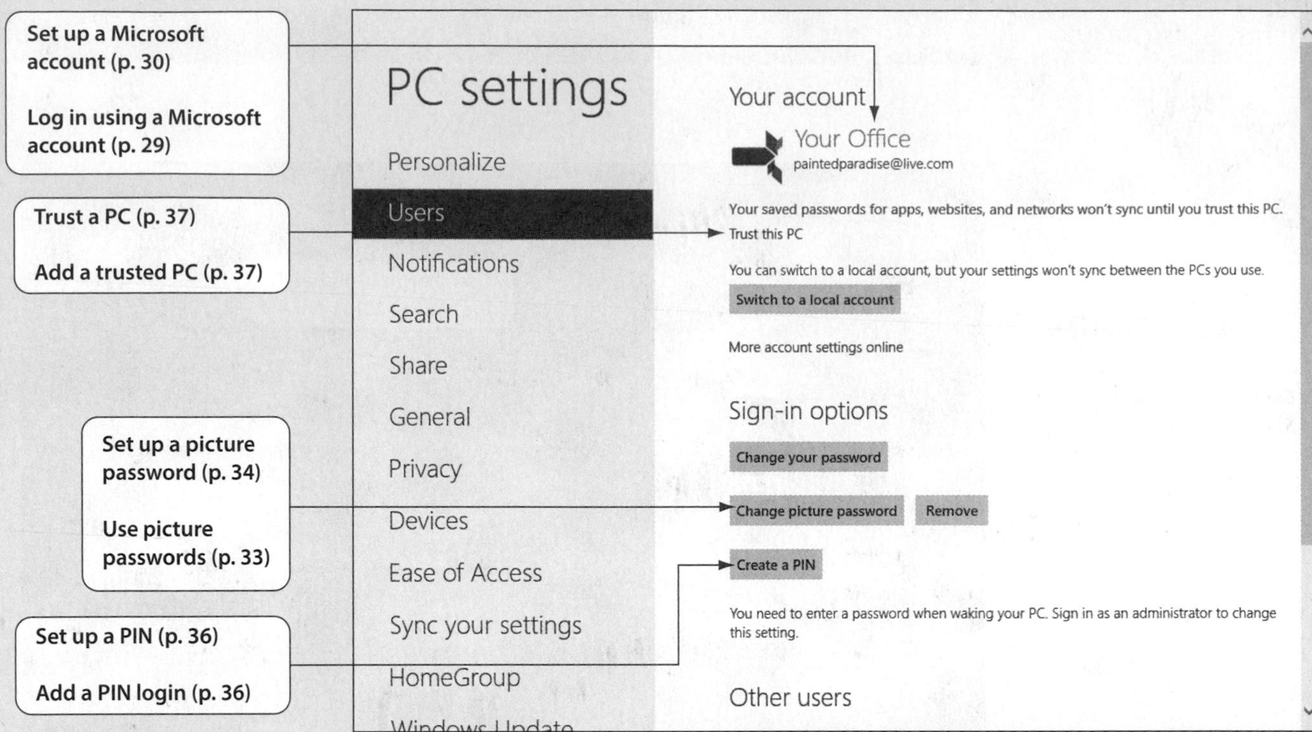

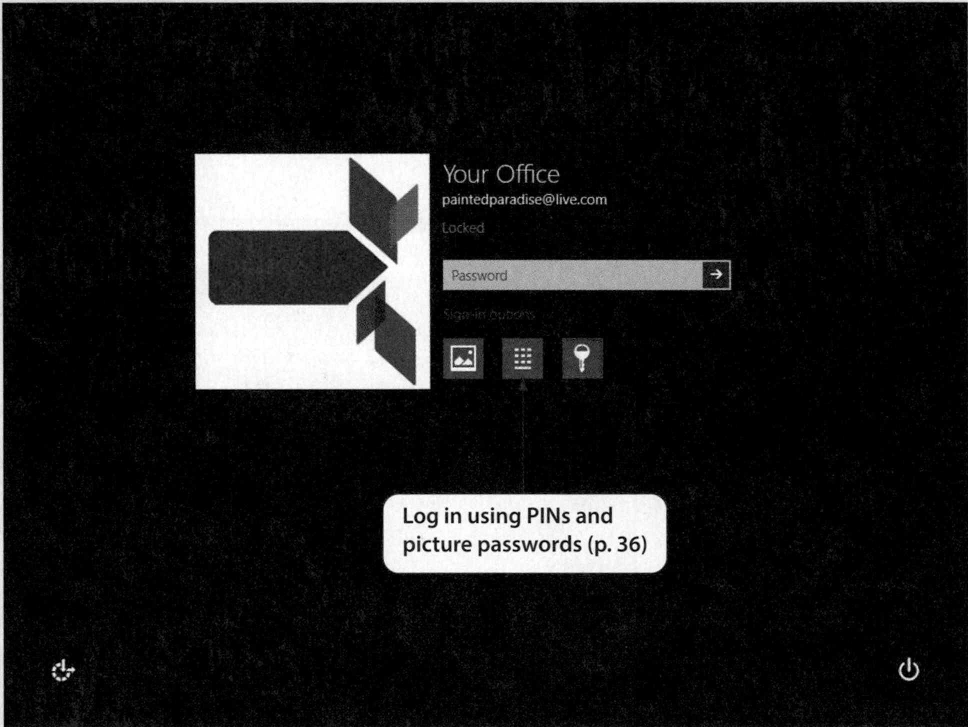

Figure 44 Understand the Windows 8 Interface Final

Practice 1

Student data file needed:

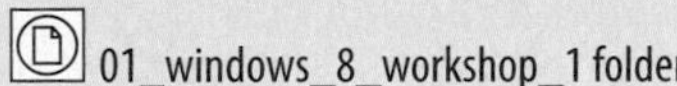
01_windows_8_workshop_1 folder

You will save your files as:

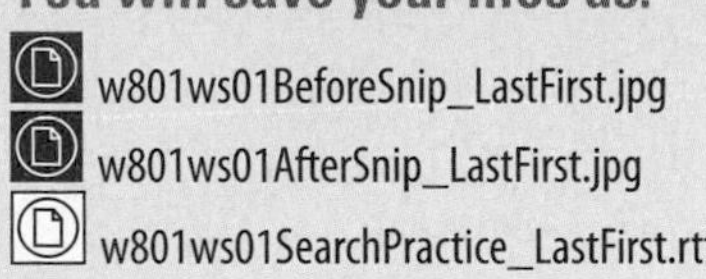
w801ws01BeforeSnip_LastFirst.jpg
w801ws01AfterSnip_LastFirst.jpg
w801ws01SearchPractice_LastFirst.rtf

Using New Features in Windows 8

Information Technology

Patti Rochelle, corporate event planner at Painted Paradise Golf Resort and Spa, would like you to work with her staff to help them customize their new Windows 8 computers and become comfortable with the new Search feature. In order to assess your workshop, you are going to have workshop attendees take before and after snips of their screens, and perform and record search results.

a. Switch on your computer and, if necessary, follow any logon instructions required for the computer you are using.

b. Use the Print Screen key on your keyboard to create a screenshot of your Start screen. Paste this image into **Paint**, and then save it as a JPG file named w801ws01BeforeSnip_LastFirst in your **01_windows_8_workshop_1** folder, using your last and first name. Close the Snipping Tool.

c. If the Snipping Tool is not on your Start screen, right-click a blank area of the screen, click **All Apps**, and then right-click **Snipping Tool**. Click **Pin to Start**.

d. Right-click **Weather** or any other large tile. Select **Smaller** to make the icon appear as a smaller tile.

e. Locate the **Snipping Tool** tile. Move the tile near the **Weather** tile.

f. Right-click a blank area on the Start screen, click **All Apps**, and then select any other tool to pin to the Start screen.

g. Locate the tile for the program you added to your Start screen. Move the tile near the **Weather** tile.

h. Use the Print Screen key on your keyboard to create a screenshot of your Start screen. Paste this image into Paint, and then save the snip as a JPG file named w801ws01AfterSnip_LastFirst in your **01_windows_8_workshop_1** folder. Close Paint.

i. Return to the Start screen, and then click the **Internet Explorer** tile. Visit **www.golfsmith.com**, and then pin this site to the Start screen. Close Internet Explorer. Move the new Start tile so it is on the same screen as the Weather and Snipping Tool tiles.

j. Click the bottom right area of the screen to make the **Charms** visible. Click the **Search** charm.

k. Right-click a blank area on the Start screen, and then select **All Apps**. Locate and click **WordPad** to open a new document. Save the created file as w801ws01SearchPractice_LastFirst in your **01_windows_8_workshop_1** folder.

l. Use the Search charm to locate the name **Ishaaya** in your data files. Switch to WordPad, add the text Number of files containing Ishaaya, and then follow that text with the number of files your search found.

m. Use the Search charm to locate the text **series of sensors** in your data files. Switch to WordPad, add the text Number of files containing series of sensors and then follow that text with the number of files your search found.

n. Save your WordPad document, and then close the program.

o. Submit the three files as directed by your instructor.

Problem Solve 1

Student data file needed:

01_windows_8_workshop_1 folder

You will save your files as:

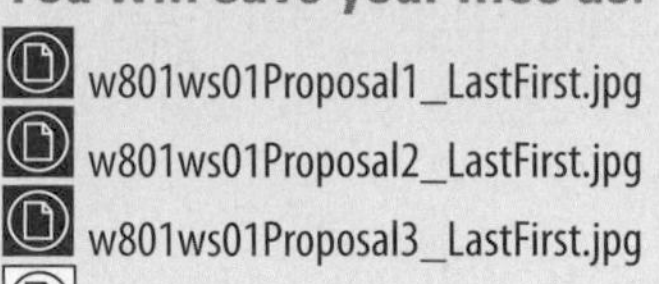

w801ws01Proposal1_LastFirst.jpg

w801ws01Proposal2_LastFirst.jpg

w801ws01Proposal3_LastFirst.jpg

w801ws01SampleSearch_LastFirst.rtf

Presenting Windows 8 to Management

Information Technology

Kathleen Lordelo, manager of Painted Paradise Resort and Spa's Information Technology services, is hoping to enlist your assistance in creating model Start screens. She has asked you to move some icons around and add tools and links to websites you think most users need, and remove any you think they would not. She would like you to create three different snips of your ideas, from which she would allow management to choose the best one. She has also asked for your assistance in demonstrating the Search charm. Members of the management team saw a demonstration of Windows 8 and noticed the ability to search for programs is gone. She has asked you to take screen shots of a few searches that demonstrate that search still works.

a. As you cannot find information within files through the Search charm unless the files are in an indexed location such as your My Documents folder, ensure that your 01_windows_8_workshop_1 folder has been downloaded and copied to your computer's Documents folder.

b. Think about applications and tools you think would fit well on a Start screen. Add and remove tiles as necessary. Include at least one link to a website using Internet Explorer 10. Use the Print Screen key on your keyboard to create a screenshot of your Start screen. Paste this image into Paint, and save it as a JPG file named **w801ws01Proposal1_LastFirst** in your 01_windows_8_workshop_1 folder, replacing last and first with your last name and first name.

c. Create a second arrangement by adding and removing tiles as necessary. Include at least one link to a website using Internet Explorer 10. Use the Print Screen key on your keyboard to create a screenshot of your Start screen. Paste this image into Paint, and save it as a JPG file named **w801ws01Proposal2_LastFirst** in your 01_windows_8_workshop_1 folder.

d. Create a third arrangement by adding and removing tiles as necessary. Include at least one link to a website using Internet Explorer 10. Use the Print Screen key on your keyboard to create a screenshot of your Start screen. Paste this image into Paint, and save it as a JPG file named **w801ws01Proposal3_LastFirst** in your 01_windows_8_workshop_1 folder.

e. Perform a search for any Windows application you know is installed on the system. Make a note of how many apps, settings, and files match the results for this search. Create a WordPad document named **w801ws01SampleSearch_LastFirst** in your 01_windows_8_workshop_1 folder, and summarize how many results match each criterion.

f. Browse the contents of w801ws01Attendees, found in your 01_windows_8_workshop_1 folder. Find a distinctive name and perform a search for the name. If you get no results, ensure your data files are stored in the Documents folder. Summarize how many apps, settings, and files match the criteria inside the file you created in the previous step. Save the file and close WordPad.

g. Submit the files as directed.

Additional Cases

Additional Workshop Cases are available on the companion website and in the instructor resources.

WORKSHOP 2 | MANAGE FILES, FOLDERS, AND THE WINDOWS DESKTOP

OBJECTIVES

Prepare Case

Painted Paradise Golf Resort and Spa Updates to Microsoft Windows 8

IT
Information Technology

StockLite / Shutterstock

Aidan Matthews, Chief Technology Officer of the Painted Paradise Golf Resort and Spa, has decided to upgrade computers from Windows 7 to the brand new Windows 8 operating system. The vendor who supplies the hotel's software has a new version optimized for Windows 8. This version will fix some of the problems the company has had with the software.

Most resort employees are familiar with File (formerly Windows) Explorer. However, Aidan would like a workshop reinforcing basic concepts within Windows 8, as the look of the new operating system has confused employees. Aiden would like you to do a workshop similar to one you gave a few years ago. He's asked you to focus on folders and files, libraries, zipping files, switching between windows, and personalizing the desktop. As the resort's computers do not have touch-screen monitors yet, he's asked that you focus on using the keyboard and mouse.

Student data file needed for this workshop:

01_windows_8_workshop_2 folder

You will save your files as:

w801ws02Library_LastFirst.jpg

w801ws02ZippedPresentations_LastFirst.zip

w801ws02Zipped_LastFirst.jpg

w801ws02Search_LastFirst.jpg

Using File Explorer

File Explorer—formerly known as Windows Explorer—is a program used to create and manage folders and files. It uses a storage system similar to what you would use in a file cabinet. A file cabinet has drawers to divide files, and each drawer contains folders, which can contain files and more folders. The same idea applies to the way computers store data. A computer storage device might be a hard drive or USB flash drive. The storage device may contain a number of folders, subfolders, and files. In this way, a storage device is similar to a file cabinet. A file cabinet has drawers which contain folders and subfolders, which contain files.

As the word "windows" implies, almost everything you view on your computer screen is displayed in a **window**—a rectangular frame that displays a program, folder, or file. Windows contain common elements such as the address bar, title bar, and status bar.

File Explorer can be accessed in Windows 8 by clicking on the Desktop icon found on the Start screen, and then clicking on the File Explorer icon on the taskbar. Though the interface will look somewhat familiar to experienced users, Microsoft has made some major changes. The familiar menus at the top of the screen, such as File, are gone. The new interface is similar to that found in Office 2007 through Office 2013. This interface, known as the **Ribbon**, allows users to interact with the operating system using tabs at the top of the screen instead of menus. This is part of the Windows 8 interface introduced in Workshop 1.

Microsoft's redesign of the interface was based on usage data reported anonymously by users. If you have ever installed a Microsoft program, you may have noticed an option to provide Microsoft anonymous usage data. This data has been used to determine how people use their programs, including File Explorer. Microsoft used this information to redesign the interface based on the most widely used features.

The new File Explorer Ribbon has four tabs: File, Home, Share, and View. Additionally, when you click certain objects, a contextual menu will appear. The contextual menu expands the Ribbon to display commands specific to the selected item. Within each tab on the Ribbon, there are a number of commands. These commands are divided into **groups**, which are collections of related commands on a Ribbon tab.

In addition to the tabs found on the Ribbon, users will notice there is also a **title bar** at the top of the window. The title bar contains the typical control buttons that let you minimize, maximize (or restore down), and close the window. The **address bar** (which may be hidden by default) is the toolbar immediately below the Ribbon. It includes Back and Forward buttons, which allow users to browse folders like they would in a web browser. This also displays the current file path and allows users to perform searches for files. Below this toolbar, Windows displays two **panes**, or divisions, similar to window panes in a house. The left pane, also called the **Navigation Pane**, displays common locations where users can find files: Favorites, Libraries, Computer, and Network (you may have other locations based on your computer's configuration). The right pane, also called the **file list**, will show files and folders. The **status bar** is located at the bottom of a window. It provides information about the selected window or object.

Selecting **Favorites** allows users to browse through locations they have previously marked as important. For example, users may add a Favorite to a folder on their USB flash drive they access frequently. **Libraries**, introduced in Windows 7, allow users to view multiple folders at the same time. Generally, libraries consist of related folders. **Computer** allows the user to view the contents of the computer's storage devices, including the hard drive, CD/DVD drive, and USB flash drives. A **USB flash drive** is a small storage device that plugs into your computer's USB port, and usually holds large amounts of information. **Network** allows users to browse files found on network drives rather than on local drives. The Network location is more commonly used in a business environment.

You will demonstrate the new File Explorer interface to your workshop.

Open and Navigate File Explorer

You can view all the drives, folders, and files that are part of your computer's storage system using File Explorer. File Explorer opens with Libraries selected in the Navigation Pane. By default, the Windows 8 installation includes four standard libraries: Documents, Music,

Pictures, and Videos. Each contains two folders, a personal folder and a public folder that can be shared with others. In addition to the pre-defined libraries, users can also create their own.

W802.00

To Open File Explorer

a. From the Start screen, click **Desktop**, and then click the File Explorer icon on the taskbar. The File Explorer window opens.

Figure 1 Desktop

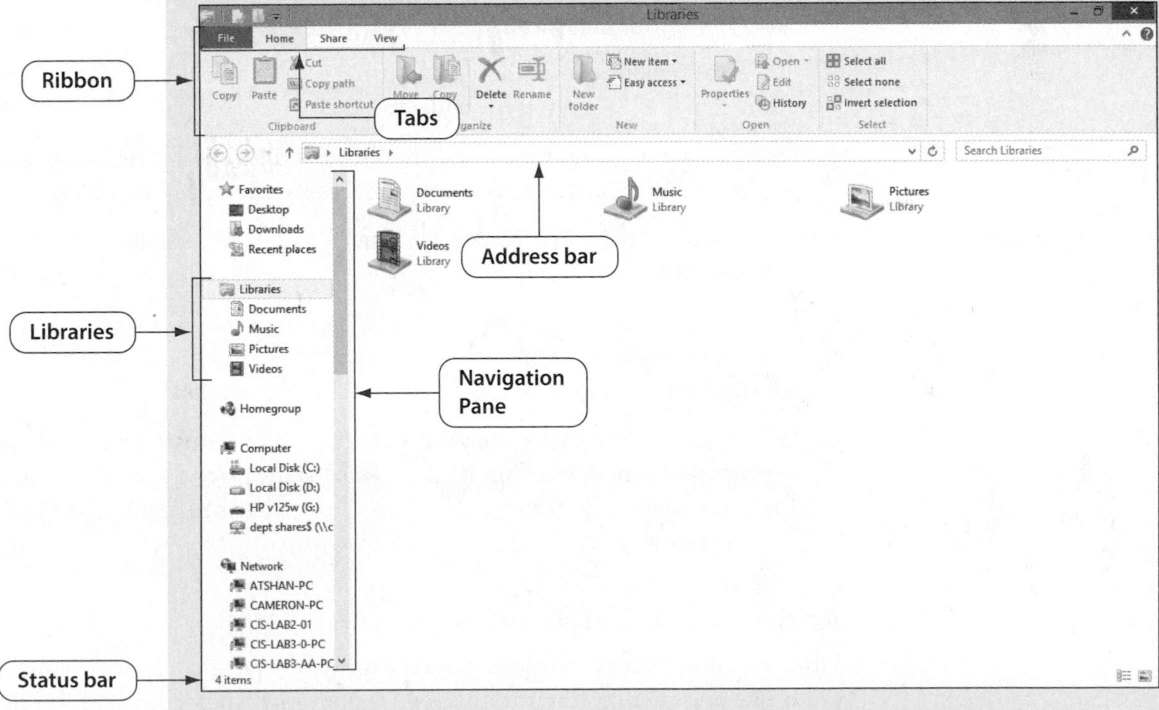

Figure 2 File Explorer

b. Double-click the **View** tab. This will ensure the full contents of the Ribbon are shown.

c. On the View tab, in the Layout group, click **Large icons**.

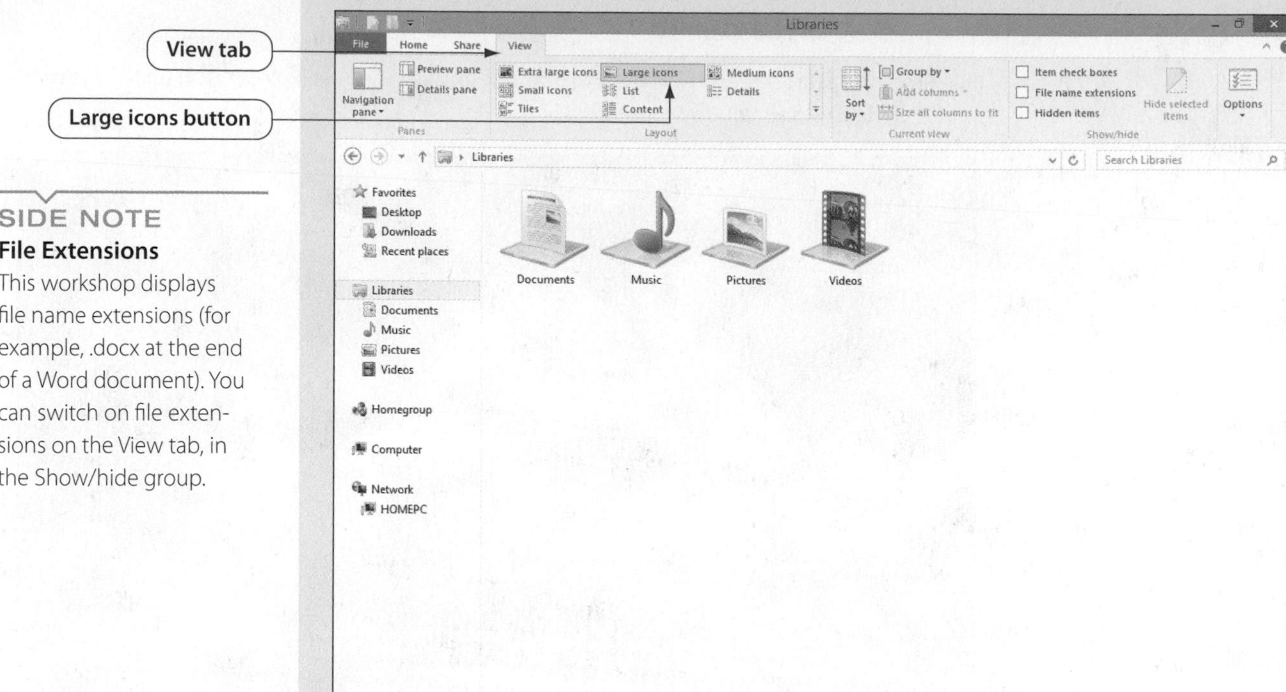

Figure 3 File Explorer View tab

File Extensions

This workshop displays file name extensions (for example, .docx at the end of a Word document). You can switch on file extensions on the View tab, in the Show/hide group.

d. In the Navigation Pane, if necessary, click the **arrow** ▷ to the left of **Libraries** to expand the folder. The arrow changes to ◢, and a list of Libraries is displayed that correspond to the libraries shown in the file list.

e. In the Navigation Pane, click **Music**. The file list displays all folders in the Music library no matter where they are located.

f. In the Navigation Pane, to the left of **Music**, click the **arrow** ▷. The My Music and Public Music subfolders are displayed under the Music folder.

g. Click the **arrow** ▷ to the left of **My Music** and **Public Music**. More subfolders are displayed, and a Sample Music subfolder is displayed under Public Music.

h. Click **Sample Music**. The file list will display any music files installed by default with Windows 8.

i. Look at the address bar near the top of the File Explorer window. The address bar displays the path to the folder whose contents are currently displayed. You can use the address bar to navigate back to any of the folders in the path.

j. On the address bar, click the **arrow** ▶ to the right of **Music**. The folders under Music are displayed with Public Music in bold. Point to the **arrow** ▶ to the right of **Libraries**. The folders under **Libraries** are displayed. Click Libraries to return to the Libraries folder.

SIDE NOTE

Expanding and Collapsing Folders

You can also expand and collapse folders by double-clicking the folder name in the Navigation Pane.

Add Folders to Libraries

Libraries allow users to access a number of folders at once, as mentioned earlier. Users can create and modify libraries to keep track of important folders. Libraries can include folders on the hard drive, but cannot include folders on removable storage, such as USB flash drives or CDs.

Aidan downloads many documents during the course of his workday, and they end up in a folder on his computer named Downloads. He would like you to show the workshop attendees how to modify the library to include the Downloads folder.

SIDE NOTE

Maximizing the Ribbon

The Ribbon requires you to click on it to see options by default. You can double-click Home or any Ribbon tab to change this.

W802.01

To Add a Folder to a Library

a. If File Explorer is not displayed, from the Start screen, click **Desktop**, and click the **File Explorer** icon on the taskbar. The File Explorer window opens.

b. Click **Libraries**. The Ribbon will display the Library Tools contextual tab.

c. Right-click **Documents** in the Navigation Pane, and select **Properties** from the menu to open the Document Properties dialog box.

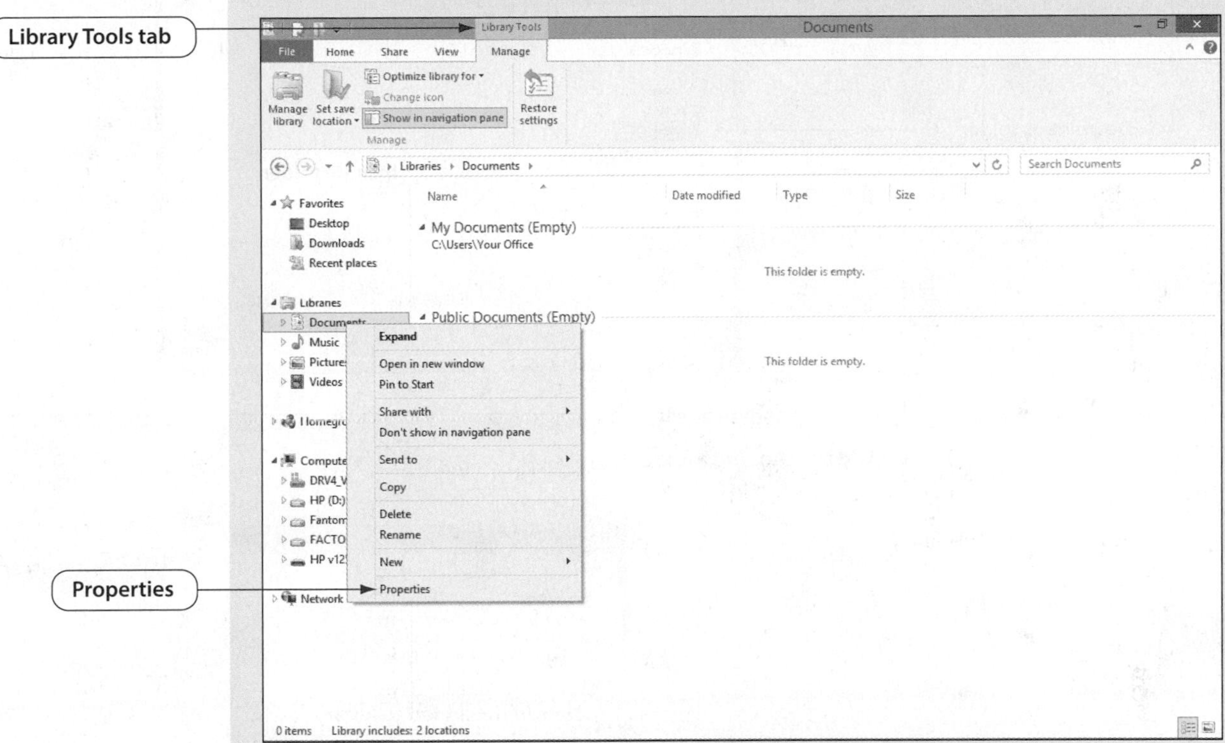

Figure 4 File Explorer Library Tools

d. Click **Add**. This allows you to add locations to your library.

Figure 5 Document Library Properties

MODULE 1

e. In the file list, click the folder labeled **Downloads**, and then click **Include folder**. Click **OK**. You will see the Downloads added to the Documents properties as shown in Figure 7.

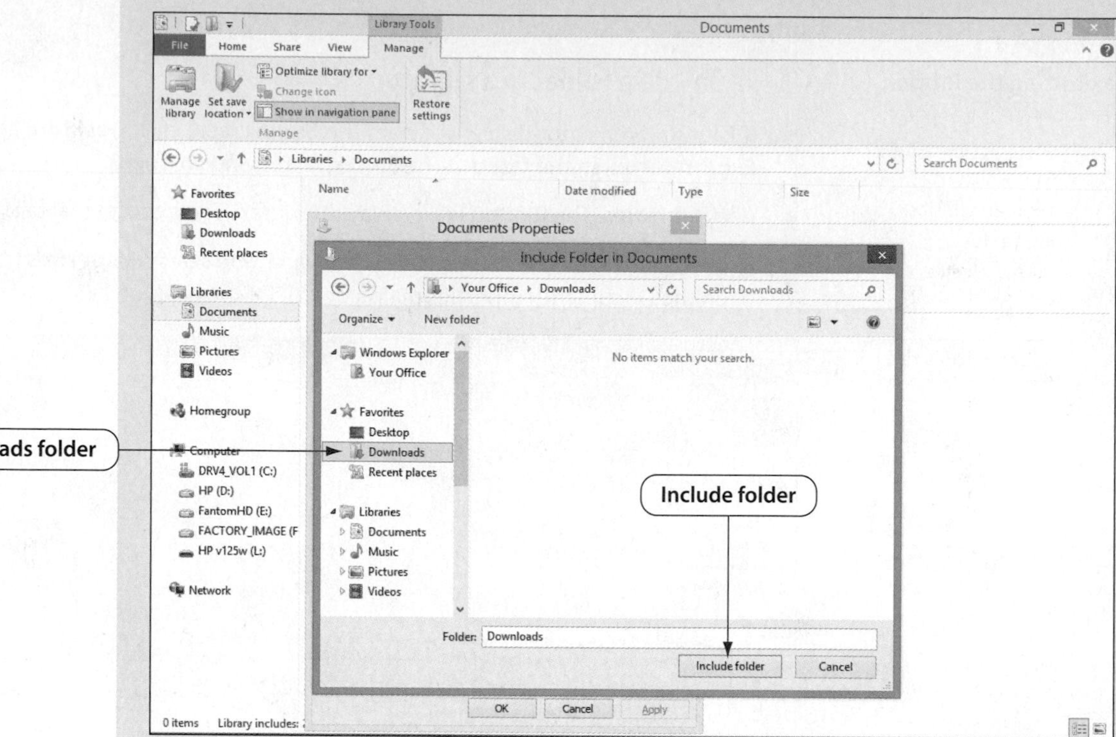

Figure 6 Adding a folder to a library

Figure 7 Folder added to library

f. Click the arrow ▷ next to **Documents** in the Navigation Pane, if necessary, to show the folders associated with the Documents library. The Downloads folder has been added to the Documents library.

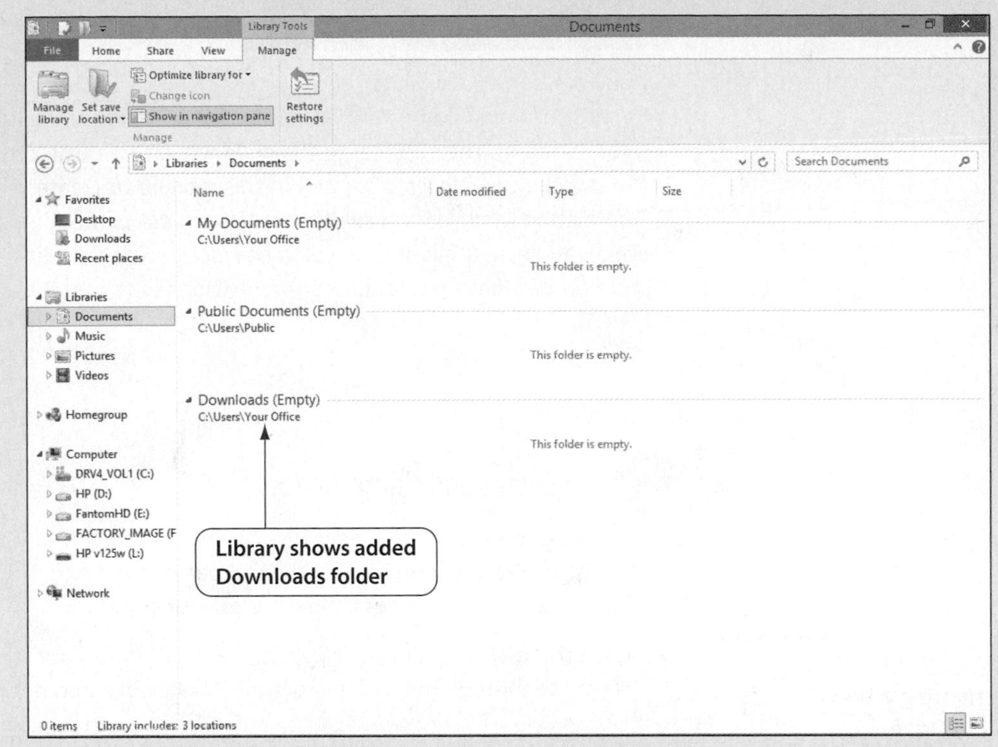

Figure 8 Documents library with new folder added

g. Right-click the Downloads folder, and then select **Properties**. The Document Properties dialog box opens.

h. Open the **Snipping Tool**, and then use the skills you practiced to create a Full-screen Snip of the window. Save it as a JPEG file in the folder with your data files. Name the file w801ws02Library_LastFirst, using your last and first name, and then **Close** ☒ the Snipping Tool window.

Working with Folders

Folders and files on your computer are similar to folders in a filing cabinet. **Folders** are commonly used to store related documents. They keep related files together so they are easier to find when you need them. If you still receive paper statements, you might place your cell phone bills in one folder and your utility bills in another. Just as you use paper folders to hold related documents, you can create folders on your computer to contain related files. Files types include documents, spreadsheets, images, songs, and more. You can also create folders within folders, also known as **subfolders**. Program and system files are also stored in folders, but you will be concerned primarily with organizing the files you create. In this section of your workshop, you will demonstrate how to create, name, move, rename, and delete folders.

Create and Name a New Folder

Aidan has already collected numerous files that all employees need. He has put some of these files in folders but wants help to better organize them. He asks you to use his files as an example when demonstrating how to create folders and organize files.

You suggest creating folders to hold specific types of files, such as documents, pictures, and presentations. The first folder you will create will be on a USB flash drive or on the computer's hard drive. This is the location where you will store all the files for this workshop.

It is always a good idea to organize related files. You will create a folder called Windows 8 Practice to hold the files used for the exercises in this workshop.

REAL WORLD ADVICE | **Contact Information**

Many places with computer labs, such as libraries, colleges, and schools, have a lost and found containing dozens of USB flash drives. Often users do not include any contact information on their device, so the drive will sit in a lost and found, unclaimed. You can use the techniques discussed in this module to create a folder named Contact Information, and add a small WordPad document containing a cell phone number or an e-mail address. It might save you a headache someday. With all the information users store on USB flash drives, losing information is often more costly than losing hardware.

W802.02

To Create and Name Folders

a. If File Explorer is not displayed, display the Start screen, and then click the **Desktop** icon. Click the **File Explorer** icon on the taskbar. In the Navigation Pane, click **Computer**. The file list displays the drives connected to your computer.

b. Click the **disk drive** in the Navigation Pane where your student data files are located. Navigate through the folder structure, if necessary, and notice the file structure.

c. On the Home tab, browse to the location you plan on storing your files, and then in the New group, click **New folder** to create a new, empty subfolder. A New folder appears in the file list with the words "New folder" highlighted.

d. Type Windows 8 Practice, and then press Enter to name the new folder. Click anywhere on a blank area to deselect the new folder.

SIDE NOTE
Renaming a USB Flash Drive
In the Navigation Pane, right-click the name of your USB flash drive, and then click Rename. Type the new name and press Enter to rename the drive.

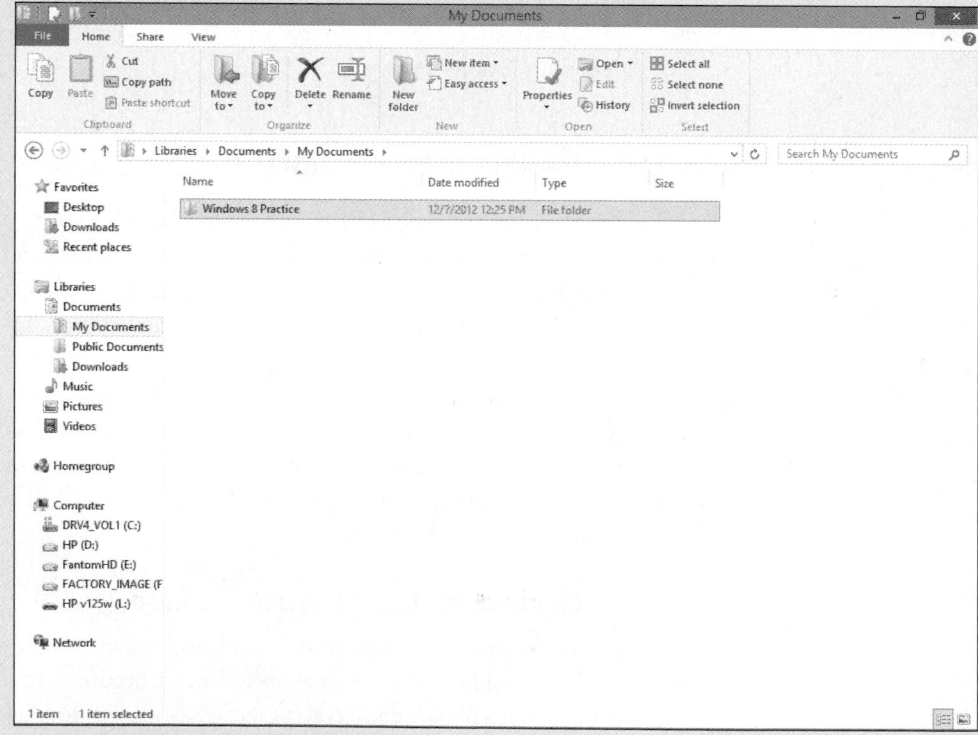

Figure 9 New Windows 8 Practice folder

e. Double-click the **Windows 8 Practice** folder you just created. The file list will be empty.

MODULE 1

f. To add a subfolder inside the Windows 8 Practice folder, click the **New folder** button, type **Resort Documents**, and then press Enter. Deselect the new folder. Click the **arrow** ▷ to the left of **Windows 8 Practice** in the Navigation Pane. Notice that the Resort Documents folder appears in the Navigation Pane and the file list.

g. Use the same method to create two more subfolders named **Resort Pictures** and **Resort Presentations**.

h. Create one more folder named **Lastname Snips**, using your last name. For example, student Megan Musall would create a folder named Musall Snips. This folder will be used to store snips that can be submitted to your instructor.

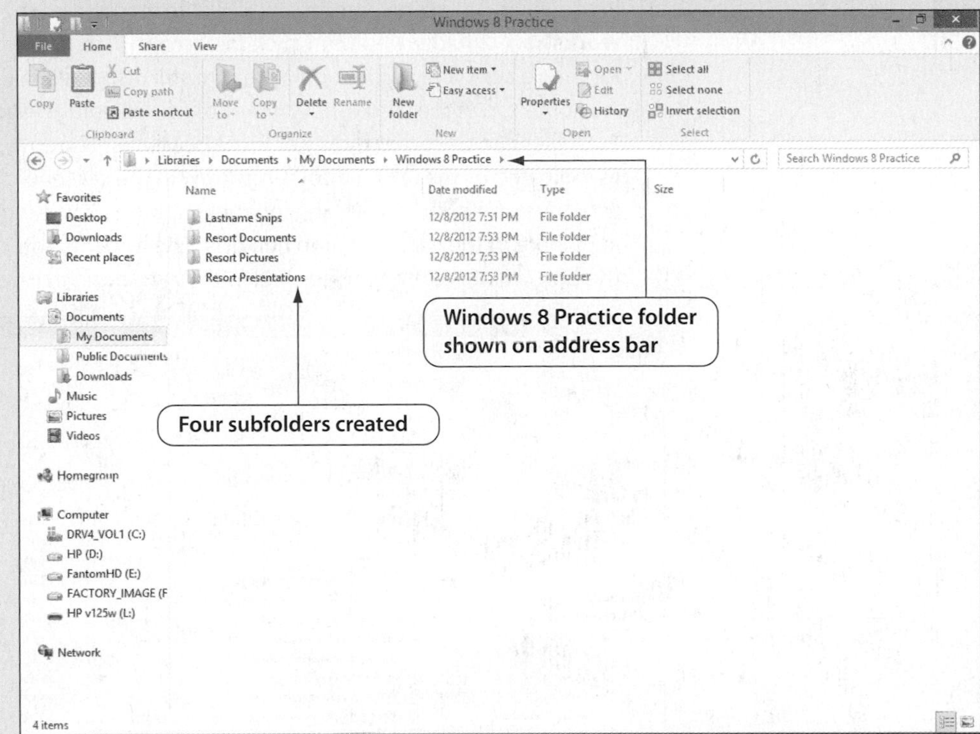

Figure 10 Windows 8 Practice folder with subfolders

i. Scroll to the bottom of the Navigation Pane, as necessary, so the four subfolders are visible under the Windows 8 Practice folder.

Copy, Move, Rename, and Delete Folders

As you create more and more files, the original folders that you created may no longer meet your needs. You can move folders to a new location, or copy them so they exist in two or more locations. You can also rename folders if the original name no longer fits, and you can delete folders when they are no longer needed.

In the following exercises you will copy, move, rename, and delete folders.

Copying Folders

The files that Aidan has already accumulated are on your student data disk. You will help organize these files by copying them into the corresponding folders that you just created in your Windows 8 Practice folder.

W802.03

To Copy Folders from Student Data Files to a Storage Device

a. If you have not already done so, download the Windows 8 Module 1 Workshop 2 Data Files from **http://www.pearsonhighered.com/youroffice/** and then extract the files.

b. In the Navigation Pane, browse to the location of your student data files. In the Navigation Pane, select the **01_windows_8_workshop_2** folder. Three folders and numerous files are displayed in the file list.

c. If your file list looks different than Figure 11, click the **View** tab, and then in the Layout group, click **Details**.

d. In the Navigation Pane, if necessary, click the **arrow** ▷ to the left of your **01_windows_8_workshop_2** folder, and then click the **arrow** ▷ to the left of the **Windows 8 Practice** folder. Be sure your student data files are still displayed in the file list.

At the top of the file list, notice the column headings: Name, Date modified, Type, and Size. Files can be sorted by any of these headings. Currently, the files are sorted by Name as indicated by the upward pointing arrow in the center of the Name column. Folders are listed first, followed by files in alphabetical order. You can reverse this order by clicking anywhere in the Name column heading. The arrow points downward and folders are at the bottom of the list with files and folders arranged in reverse alphabetical order.

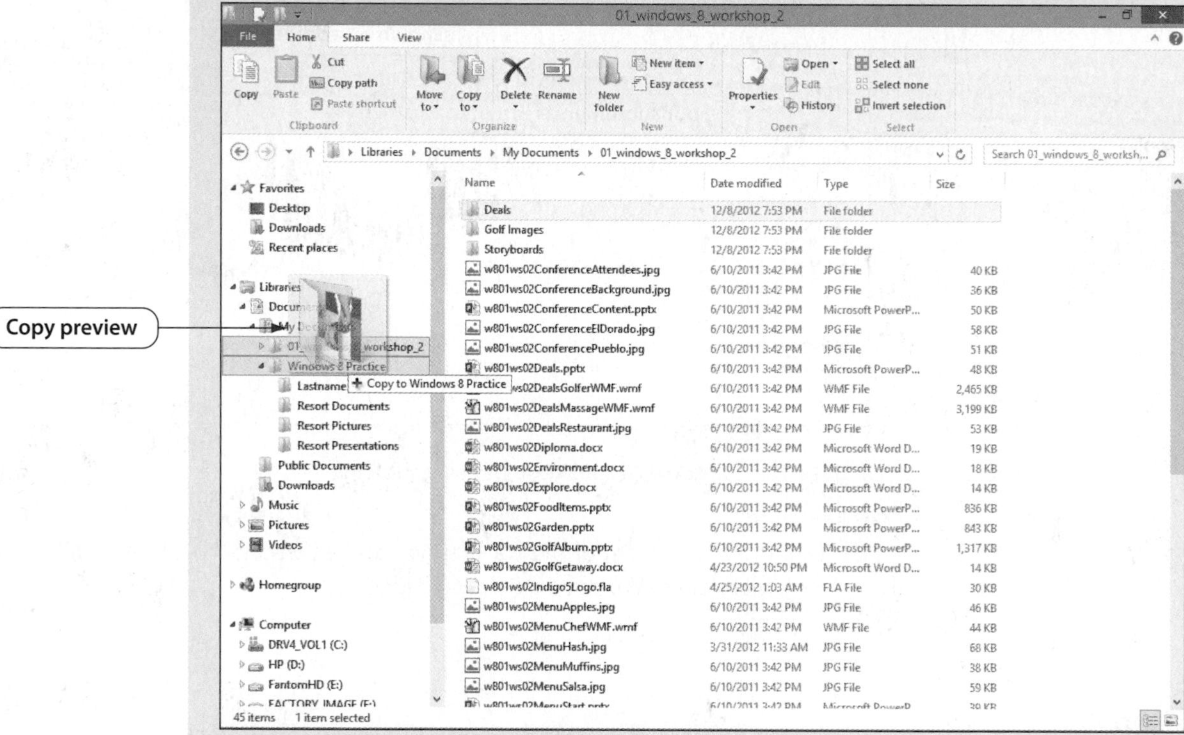

Figure 11 Copying folders

e. You want to make sure you copy the **Deals** folder to the **Windows 8 Practice** folder. Drag the **Deals** folder on top of the Windows 8 Practice folder in the Navigation Pane, but before you release the mouse button, ensure the preview says **Copy to Windows 8 Practice**. If this message is not displayed, hold down the Ctrl key on your keyboard to direct Windows to copy instead of move, and then release the mouse button. The Deals folder now appears under the Windows 8 Practice folder.

f. Copy the **Golf Images** folder to the **Windows 8 Practice** folder, holding down Ctrl, if necessary. Repeat this process to copy the **Storyboards** folder to the **Windows 8 Practice** folder. The three folders that were copied appear under Windows 8 Practice in the Navigation Pane. You now have seven folders—the four you created and the three that were just copied.

SIDE NOTE

Copying or Moving?

Dragging files from one location to another on the same storage device results in a move. Dragging to a different device results in a copy.

Moving Folders

You have two folders related to pictures—Golf Images and Resort Pictures. Since both folders contain pictures, it would be logical to move the Golf Images folder to the Resort Pictures folder so all picture files will be in the same place.

W802.04

To Move Folders

SIDE NOTE

Forcing a Move

Since you are dragging to a folder on the same device, it results in a move. If you were dragging to a different disk and want to force a move, hold down the Shift key on your keyboard, and then release the mouse button.

a. In the Navigation Pane, in the Windows 8 Practice folder, drag **Golf Images** on top of the **Resort Pictures** folder, but before you release the mouse button, ensure the preview says **Move to Windows 8 Practice**. The Golf Images folder is moved to the Resort Pictures folder and is no longer visible in the Navigation Pane.

b. In the Navigation Pane, under the Windows 8 Practice folder, click the **arrow** ▷ to the left of **Resort Pictures**, and then verify that the Golf Images folder is under the Resort Pictures folder in the Navigation Pane.

c. In the Navigation Pane, click **Resort Pictures** to see the Golf Images folder in the file list.

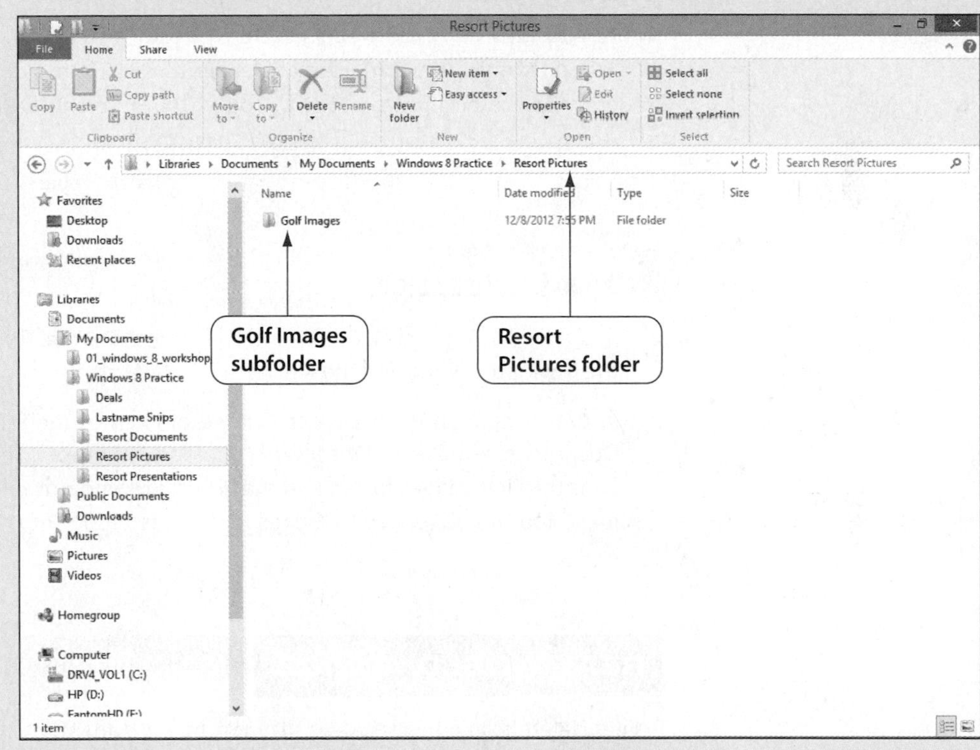

Figure 12 Golf Images subfolder moved to Resort Pictures folder

d. Click the **arrow** ◢ to close the Resort Pictures folder.

Renaming Folders

As you work with folders you will often find that the name you first assigned to a folder does not work anymore. You can easily rename a folder to maintain the organization that you want. In the next exercise, you will rename the Storyboards folder to match the names of the other folders.

SIDE NOTE
Renaming a Folder
You can rename a folder by right-clicking the name in either the Navigation Pane or the file list and then clicking Rename.

To Rename a Folder

a. In the Navigation Pane, click the **Windows 8 Practice** folder. Six folders should be displayed in the file list.

b. In the file list, right-click **Storyboards**, and then select **Rename**. The folder name is highlighted and is in Edit mode. Type Resort Storyboards and then press Enter. The folder is renamed.

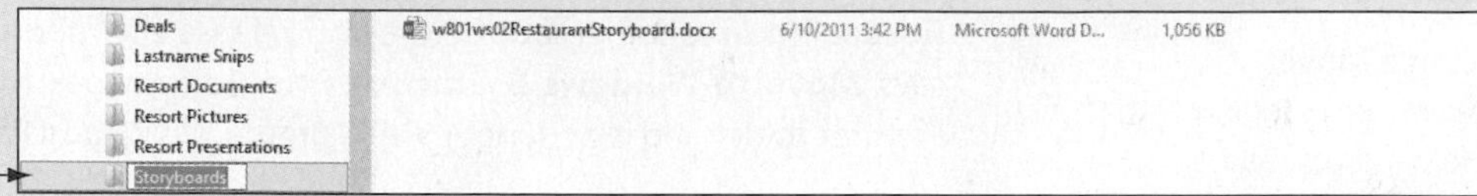

Figure 13 Renaming a folder

Deleting Folders

There will also be times when you have a folder that contains files you no longer need. Just as you would shred and discard paper files that are outdated, you will want to delete folders that are no longer needed. You will delete the Deals folder that contains image files for special resort promotions that have expired.

W802.06

To Delete a Folder

a. In the file list, right-click **Deals**, and then select **Delete**. Five folders should be visible in the Navigation Pane and the file list.

b. In the Navigation Pane, click the **name** of each of the folders. Notice that the Resort Documents and Resort Presentations folders are empty. The Resort Pictures folder contains the Golf Images folder, and the Resort Storyboards folder contains storyboard files for various topics related to the resort. The Lastname Snips folder will be empty for now.

REAL WORLD ADVICE **How Can Deletions Not Be Permanent?**

Files deleted from your devices may not be permanently deleted. Data recovery specialists can often recover information from storage devices. This is often done as part of police criminal investigations. Throwing out a hard drive can lead to people recovering your personal information from it, even if you have deleted and formatted the drive. You can physically destroy the device, but even that might not be enough. A free program named Darik's Boot and Nuke, downloadable at www.dban.org, is a free utility that will wipe the contents of your hard drive to conform to United States Department of Defense standards.

Working with Files

Many different types of files are stored on your computer. There are operating system files that make Windows run, application files that run the programs you use, and data files that store the information used by those programs. Most of your work will be done with data files such as Word documents, Excel workbooks, PowerPoint presentations, various types of image and sound files, and other types of data files. In this section, you will copy, move, rename, preview, and delete files. You will also compress and extract files and add tags to make searching more efficient.

REAL WORLD ADVICE | **Working with Others**

When several people work on the same document, they often add their initials and a date before saving a file and sending it to someone else on the team. That way everyone always knows who made the most recent revision and when it was made. Meaningful document names can be extremely useful and make finding files easier.

MODULE 1

Copy, Move, Rename, and Delete Files

The same procedures that you just practiced with folders can also be applied to files. As you create more documents, you will often find that you did not anticipate how your files would need to be organized. Files can be copied or moved to new locations. They can also be renamed or deleted when no longer needed.

Copying a Single File

In the following exercise, you will copy files from your student data files to appropriate folders in the Windows 8 Practice folder. You will begin by copying one file. You will notice these steps are nearly identical to moving.

W802.07

To Copy One File

a. In the Navigation Pane, click the **01_windows_8_workshop_2** folder. If necessary, click the **arrow** ▷ to the left of the Windows 8 Practice folder you created earlier, to display the five subfolders.

b. In the file list, click **w801ws02GolfGetaway**, and then drag the file to the **Resort Documents** folder in the Navigation Pane. A thumbnail, showing this as a Word document, is attached to the pointer. Before you release the mouse button, ensure the preview says **Copy to Resort Documents**. If this message is not displayed, hold down the Ctrl key on your keyboard to direct Windows to copy instead of move, and then release the mouse button.

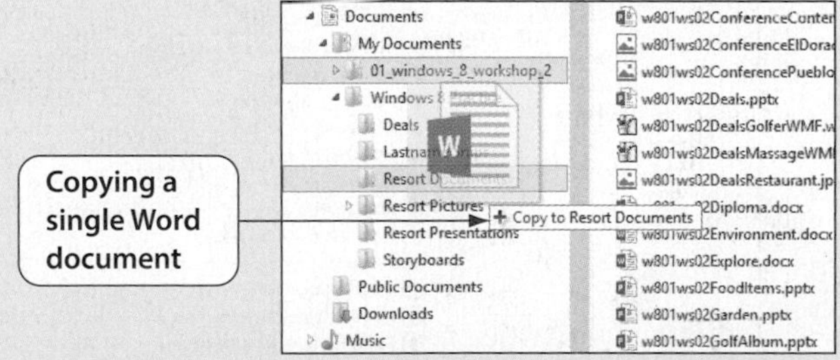

Figure 14 Copying a document to Resort Documents folder

c. In the Navigation Pane, click the **01_windows_8_workshop_2** folder.

d. In the file list, click **w801ws02DealsGolferWMF**, and then drag the file to the **Golf Images** folder in the Navigation Pane. Before you release the mouse button, ensure the preview says **Copy to Golf Images**. If this message is not displayed, hold down the Ctrl key on your keyboard to direct Windows to copy instead of move, and then release the mouse button.

Copying a Group of Files

Currently the folders and files in the 01_windows_8_workshop_2 folder are arranged by name. When you want to copy several files of the same type, it is more useful to arrange the files by type.

W802.08

To Copy Adjacent Files at the Same Time

a. Click the **Type** heading at the top of the column. The upward pointing arrow is now in the Type column, and files are sorted alphabetically by the type of file. Use the scroll bar to see the different types of files in the folder.

b. Move the pointer to the right side of the Type column heading until you see a ✛ pointer. Double-click to widen the column so all text is visible.

c. Scroll until you see all Microsoft Word documents. Click **w801ws02Diploma**. Press and hold Shift, and then click **w801ws02Putts**. All Microsoft Word document files are selected. You can select any number of adjacent files by using this method.

d. Point anywhere in the selection. Press and hold the left mouse button, and then drag the thumbnails on top of the **Resort Documents** folder. Notice the number 8 on the thumbnail indicating that you are copying eight files. Before you release the mouse button, ensure the preview says **Copy to Resort Documents**. If this message is not displayed, hold down the Ctrl key on your keyboard to direct Windows to copy instead of move, and then release the mouse button.

> **SIDE NOTE**
> **No Word? No Problem.**
> If you do not have Microsoft Word installed, you may see these files listed as WordPad documents.

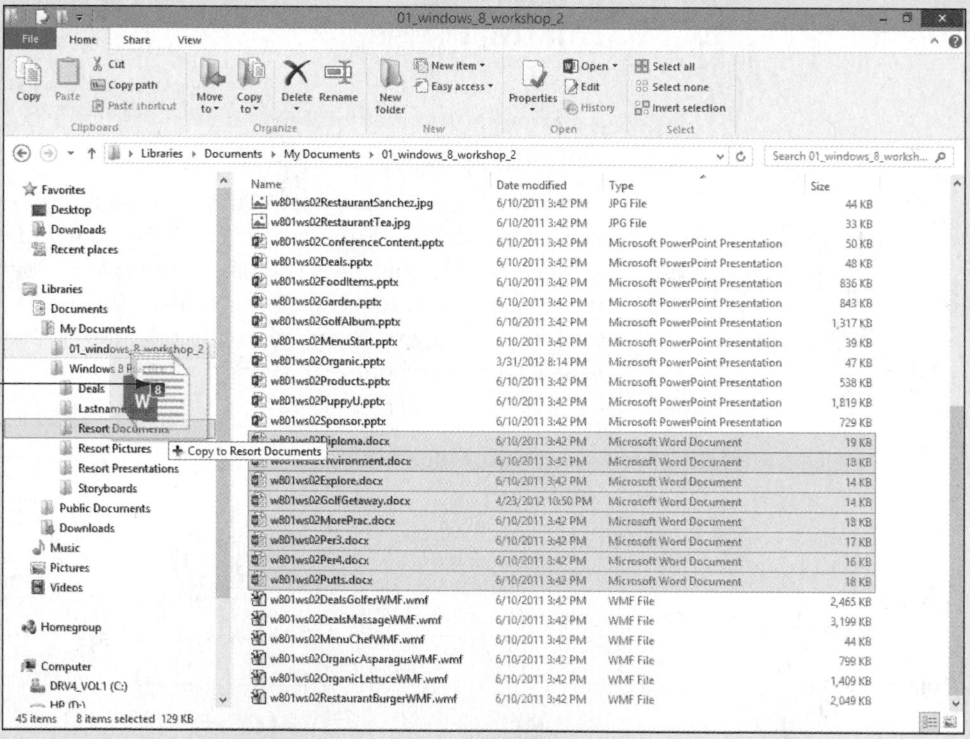

Small 8 indicates eight files being copied

Figure 15 Copying 8 Word documents

e. Since you already copied the w801ws02GolfGetaway file to this folder, a dialog box labeled Replace or Skip appears asking you to decide if you want to copy this file again. Since you know the files are identical, click **Skip this file**.

> **SIDE NOTE**
> **To Replace or To Skip?**
> When copying a file to a folder containing a file with the same name, details—such as size and date modified—of both files are displayed. You can replace or skip the file.

f. Scroll until you see all the files for the type Microsoft PowerPoint Presentation. Click **w801ws02ConferenceContent**. Press and hold Shift, and then click **w801ws02Sponsor**. All presentation files are selected. Drag these files to the **Resort Presentations** folder in the Navigation Pane. Notice the number 10 on the thumbnail indicating that you are copying ten files. Before you release the mouse button, ensure the preview says **Copy to Resort Presentations**. If this message is not displayed, hold down the Ctrl key on your keyboard to direct Windows to copy instead of move, and then release the mouse button.

Copying a Nonadjacent Group of Files

There are times when you will want to copy several files that are not adjacent in the file list. You can do this by selecting files using Ctrl instead of Shift. If you accidentally click on an incorrect file, you can simply click it again to deselect it.

W802.09

To Copy Nonadjacent Files at the Same Time

a. Scroll until all files of the WMF File type are visible in the file list.

b. Click **w801ws02MenuChefWMF**. Hold down the Ctrl key and click **w801ws02RestaurantBurgerWMF**, **w801ws02MenuMuffins**, and **w801ws02RestaurantCoffee**. Four files that are not adjacent are selected.

c. Point to any of the selected files. Press and hold the left mouse button, and then drag the thumbnail on top of the **Resort Pictures** folder in the Navigation Pane. The number **4** appears on the thumbnail showing you are copying four files. Before you release the mouse button, ensure the preview says **Copy to Resort Pictures.** If this message is not displayed, hold down the Ctrl key on your keyboard to direct Windows to copy instead of move, and then release the mouse button.

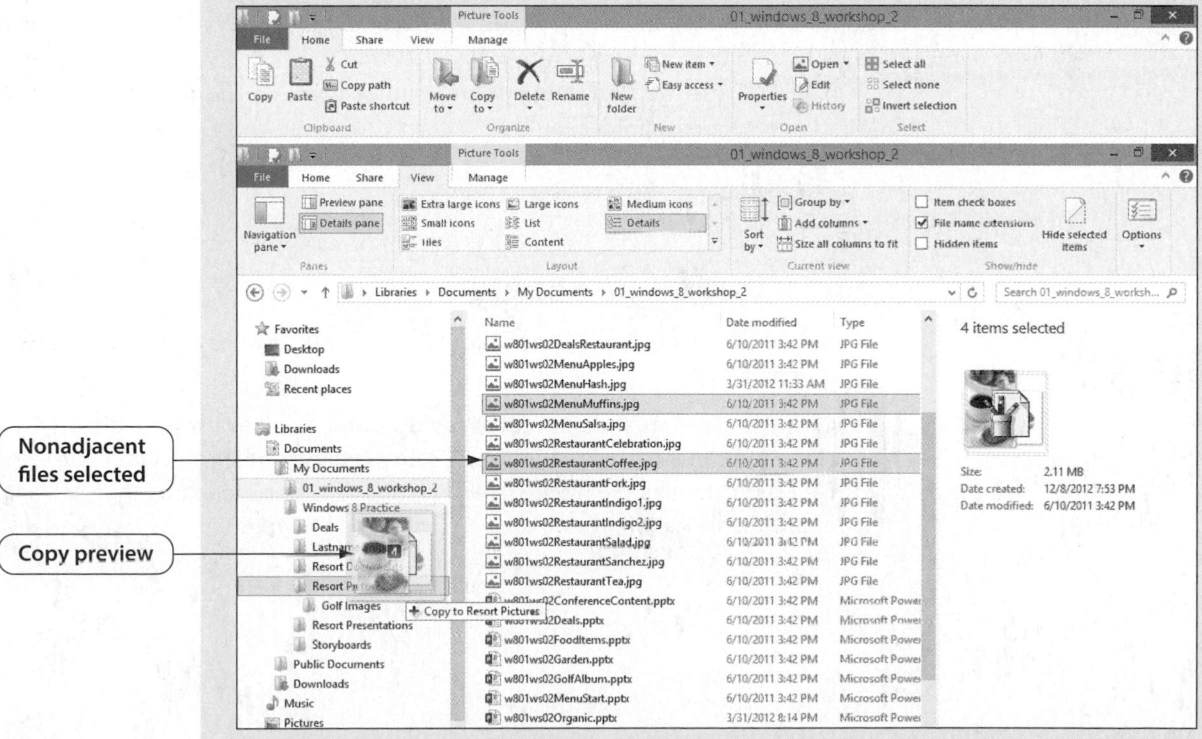

Figure 16 Copying four files that are not adjacent

CONSIDER THIS | USB or Cloud?

Today, you have many options for moving your files from computer to computer. USB Flash Drives are one popular choice. However, cloud technologies such as SkyDrive or DropBox are gaining in popularity. What are the pros and cons of using a USB versus using a cloud technology? What about the security of your files in both choices?

Moving a Single File

Files can easily be moved from one folder to another. Using the drag method is a quick and easy way to accomplish this.

W802.10

To Move a File

a. In the Navigation Pane, ensure the **Lastname Snips** folder is visible.

b. Browse to your **Windows 8 Practice** folder. Drag **w801ws02Library_LastFirst** to the **Lastname Snips** folder.

c. In the Navigation Pane, click **Lastname Snips**, and then verify that the w801ws02Library_LastFirst file is now in that folder.

Previewing Files

The Preview pane in File Explorer is turned off by default. When it is open on the right side of the window, it displays a preview of the file selected in the file list. The Preview pane can display the contents of documents, workbooks, presentations, many image files, and other common file types. Using the Preview pane is very helpful when you just want to look at a file without opening it.

You will use the Preview pane to examine some of the files that you copied to the Windows 8 Practice folder.

W802.11

To Use the Preview Pane

a. In the Navigation Pane, if necessary, click the **Golf Images** folder. The file list displays four files.

b. Click the **View** tab, and then click **Preview pane**. The Preview pane opens. If necessary, resize the Preview pane so the Name, Date modified, and Type columns are visible in the file list by bringing the mouse over the pane divider, clicking and then draging it to an appropriate location. The pane divider is shown in Figure 17.

c. In the file list, click **w801ws02CaddyBackground**. The image is displayed in the Preview pane.

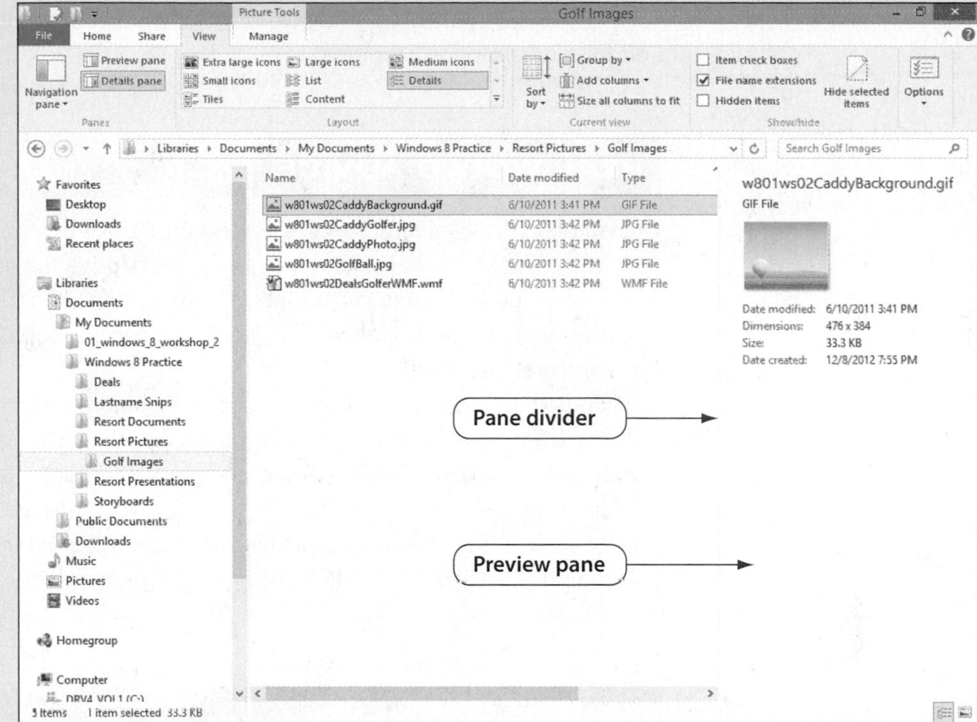

Figure 17 Preview pane

d. Click each of the remaining files. Notice that a preview of each JPG file is displayed but the WMF file has no preview. This type of file is not supported in the Preview pane.

e. Browse to the Resort Pictures folder. Double-click the **w801ws02DealsGolferWMF** file. The Paint program opens. Maximize the Paint window so you can view the .wmf image. Close the Paint window.

f. In the Navigation Pane, click **Resort Presentations**. In the file list, click **w801ws02 GolfAlbum**. The first slide of the presentation is displayed in the Preview pane.

SIDE NOTE

Changing Your View

You can also preview thumbnails of images and presentations as Extra Large, Large, or Medium icons on the View tab.

SIDE NOTE

Programs Other Than Paint

If you have another image editing tool installed, such as Adobe Photoshop, Windows may use that instead of Paint to open image files.

REAL WORLD ADVICE — How Does Windows Know My Word Document Is a Word Document?

The Windows operating system uses a file extension to determine which programs are used to open a file. The file extension is usually the three or four characters listed after a period in the file name. For example, Document1.docx would be associated with Microsoft Word, if you have Word installed. If the file extension is changed, the file may no longer open properly. By default, the operating system hides file extensions to prevent accidental renaming. If your installation of Windows shows file extensions, you can click the **View** tab of File Explorer and clear the box labeled **File name extensions** to hide extensions.

Renaming and Deleting Files

There will be times when you will want to rename files to keep your files organized. Sometimes, the name you chose for a file no longer applies. For example, a file named Term Paper may need renaming when you create a term paper for a different class. This way, you avoid confusion. The goal of deleting files is to remove the file from the device and free up computer storage.

REAL WORLD ADVICE | **Naming Files**

Giving files a meaningful name is essential to efficiently locating your files and sharing files with others. Many years ago, descriptive file names were difficult to create due to naming constraints. Names could only be eight characters long. Spaces were not permitted. Today, file names can be much longer and can include many more characters.

Does that mean you should give your files long file names? A long name can distract from being meaningful as much as one that is too short. Further, some web systems will still remove any characters after eight and replace spaces with an underscore when uploaded. Thus, best practice is to make the name just long enough to be meaningful. Meaningful document names can be extremely useful and make finding files easier.

QUICK REFERENCE

	Old File Naming Constraints	Windows 8 File Naming Constraints
Maximum Characters	8	255
Acceptable Characters	Letters, numbers, spaces, and some symbols	Letters, numbers, spaces, and some symbols
Characters to avoid	Spaces \ / ? : * " > < | [ ]	\ / ? : * " > < |

W802.12

To Rename and Delete a File

a. In the Navigation Pane, click the **Golf Images** folder. Right-click the **w801ws02DealsGolferWMF** file. Select **Rename** on the shortcut menu. The file name is highlighted.

b. You do not want to change the name completely. Click in the highlighted area to the left of the **D** in **Deals**. Press Delete five times to delete the word "Deals". Press Enter. The file now shows the new name—**w801ws02GolferWMF**.

c. Right-click the **w801ws02GolfBall** file, and then select **Delete**. The file is removed from the list, and three files remain.

QUICK REFERENCE

There are often a number of ways to perform an action in any software program. There can literally be dozens of ways to accomplish the same task. Of course, whichever way is comfortable for you is fine, but it can be instructive to look at other ways.

Home tab: Many file commands can be performed by using commands on the Home tab. Commands such as Move To, Copy, Delete, and New folder all appear on the Home tab in File Explorer.

Right-click: When you right-click on a file or a folder, a shortcut menu appears with options related to the current object.

Right-drag: You are probably used to dragging by holding down the left mouse button. If you drag a file or folder while holding down the right mouse button, Windows will give you the option to Move or Copy.

Key Combinations: There are a number of key combinations you can use to replace mouse operations.

- **Rename:** Select a file, and press [F2]
- **Select all files:** Hold down the [Ctrl] key and press [a] ([Ctrl] + [a])

You can also perform a move by cutting files and then pasting them, or a copy by copying files and then pasting them.

- **Copy:** Hold down the [Ctrl] key and press [c] ([Ctrl] + [c])
- **Cut:** Hold down the [Ctrl] key and press [x] ([Ctrl] + [x])
- **Paste:** Hold down the [Ctrl] key and press [v] ([Ctrl] + [v])

Zip Files

If you have ever had to e-mail multiple files to someone at once, you realize many e-mail programs make it tedious to attach many files simultaneously. Some will also limit the number of attachments, so sending fifteen small files would require multiple e-mail messages, and you would risk accidentally missing a file or attaching the same file twice.

In addition, when attaching files to an e-mail message, it also is impossible to maintain folder structure. For example, if you wanted to e-mail some files from a subfolder named 2014 and some files from a subfolder named 2015, you would not be able to distinguish which files were in which folder. Windows provides a solution for this. Users can create a **zip file** containing a number of files and folders.

Files containing graphics, video, or sound are often too large to transfer easily. Windows 8 allows users to compress one or more files into a single zipped folder with a .zip extension. Files stored in a zip file take up less storage space and are easier to transfer via e-mail or uploading.

The ability to create zipped files is not new. In previous versions of Windows, this function was often referred to as compressed folders. Many professionals used the term "zipped" instead of "compressed", and Microsoft seems to have made the term "zip" more prominent, perhaps to match terminology used by many professionals.

You will zip the files in the Resort Presentations folder. The Details pane will display the size of the files before and after compressing. Some files show little savings while others may show a savings of as much as 80% or more.

To Zip Files

a. Click the **View** tab, and then in the Panes group, click **Details pane**. The button should be highlighted, indicating it has been selected. If it does not, click **Details pane** in the Panes group to display it.

b. In the Navigation Pane, click the **Resort Presentations** folder. Click the **Home** tab, and then in the Select group, click **Select all**. The Details pane indicates that 10 items are selected. Notice the total size of the files on the status bar.

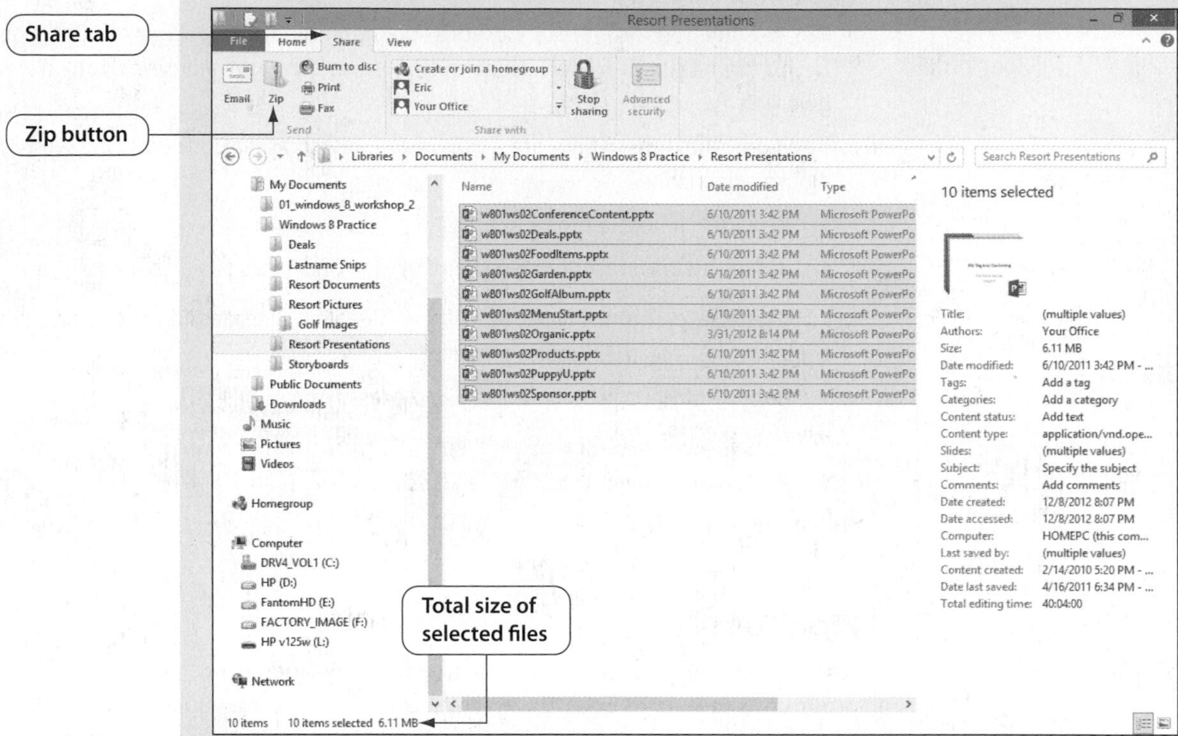

Figure 18 Share tab

c. Click the **Share** tab, and then in the Send group, click **Zip**. After a few moments, during which time the files are compressed, a new folder with a zipper icon appears in the file list. The default name reflects the first file in the folder. Type w801ws02ZippedPresentations_LastFirst and then press Enter. The folder is renamed. Move this file to your Windows 8 Practice folder.

d. Look at the **Details pane**. Notice the size of the zipped folder. This should reflect a savings in space. Other files may show a much greater compression rate.

e. In the file list, double-click **w801ws02ZippedPresentations_LastFirst**. Scroll to the far right and then notice that the files are listed with the original sizes and compressed sizes. The compression ratio for each file is also listed and shows a range from as low as 1% to a high of 25%.

Troubleshooting

This exercise shows how to zip and unzip using Windows. Other compression tools, such as WinZip, WinRAR, and 7Zip, may be installed on your machine. If double-clicking launches one of these programs, you can right-click on **w801ws02ZippedPresentations_LastFirst** and select **Open with**. From there, select **Windows Explorer**. Oddly enough, even though Microsoft has renamed the tool File Explorer, it appears in this location as Windows Explorer.

f. Make sure the horizontal scroll bar is to the far right of the screen.

g. Open the **Snipping Tool**, and then use the skills you practiced to create a Full-screen Snip of the window. Save it as a JPEG file in the **Lastname Snips** folder as w801ws02Zipped_LastFirst, and then **Close** the Snipping Tool window.

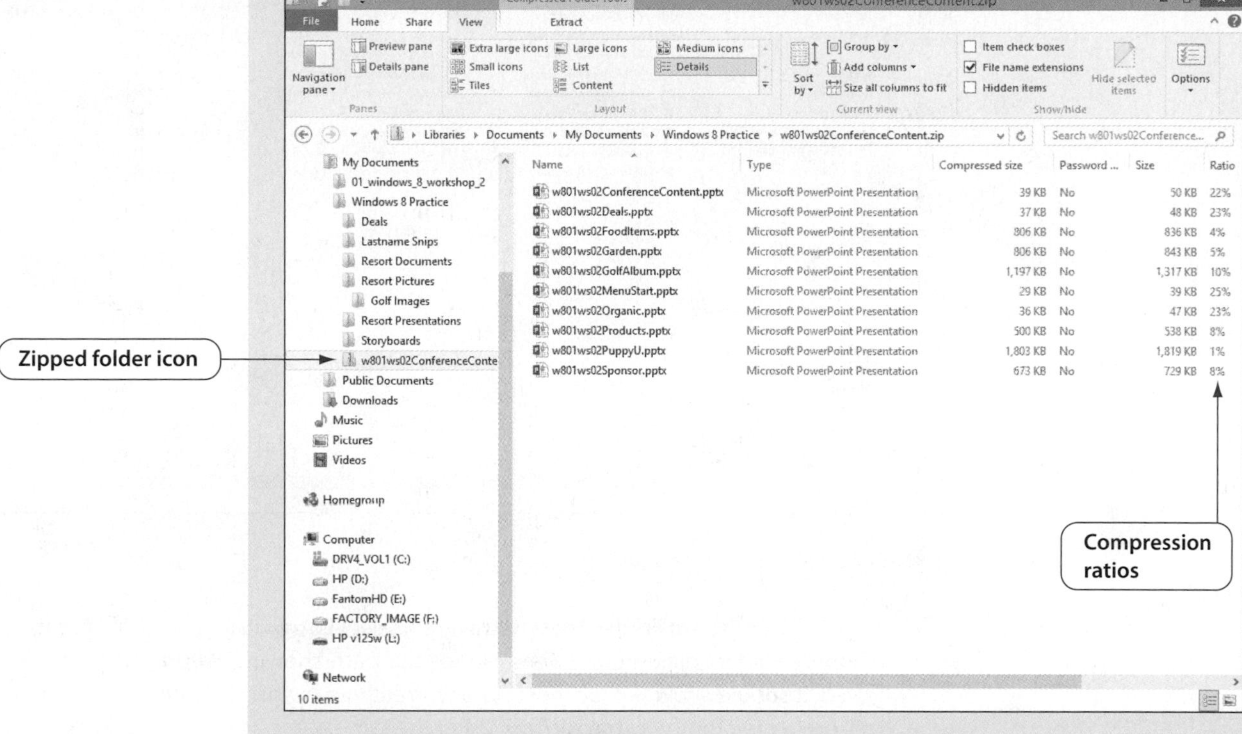

Figure 19 Compression example

> **Troubleshooting**
> If you cannot see the ratios, hide the Details pane by clicking on the **View** tab and clicking **Details pane.**

h. Close File Explorer.

Extract Files

If you receive a zipped folder from someone, you will need to extract the files in order to view them. When you select a zipped folder in the Navigation Pane, a contextual menu appears on the Ribbon. This contextual menu is named **Compressed Folder Tools** and has a tab named **Extract**. On the Extract tab, in the Extract To group, users can click **Extract all** to browse to a location, or select a location from the list in the **Extract To** area of the tab.

W802.14

To Extract Zipped Files

a. In the Navigation Pane, if necessary, click Windows 8 Practice. Click **w801ws02 ZippedPresentations_LastFirst**. On the Extract tab, in the Extract To group, click **Extract all**. The Extract Compressed (Zipped) Folders dialog box opens.

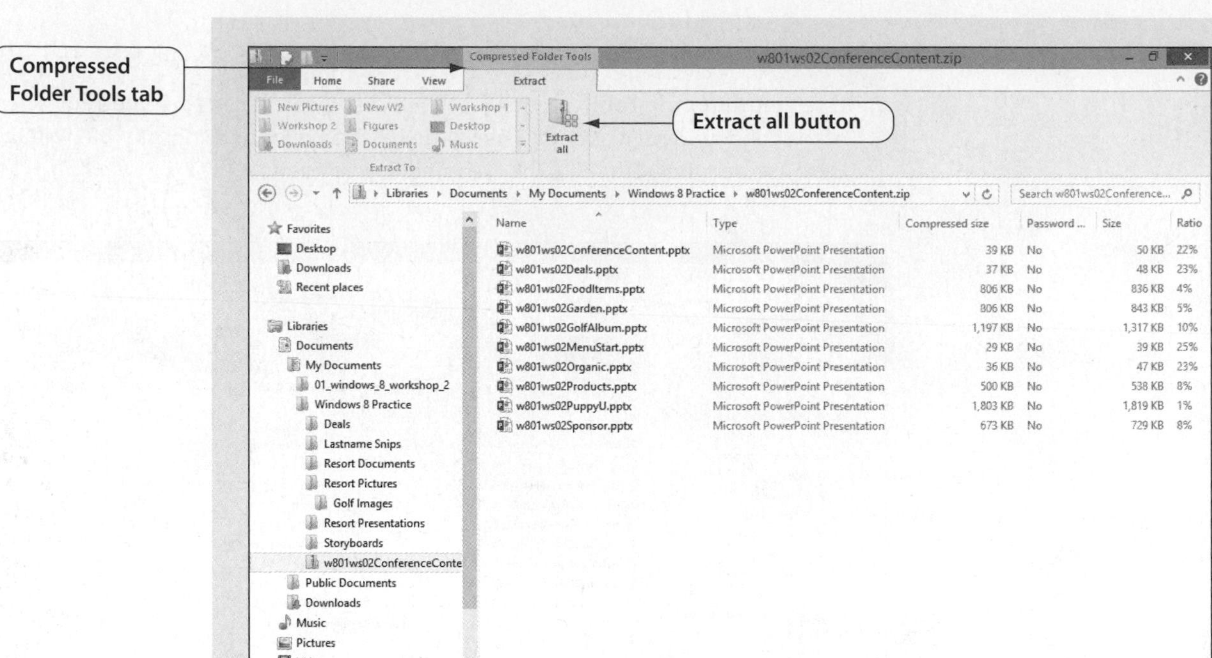

Figure 20 Compressed Folder Tools tab

b. On the **Compressed Folder Tools Extract** tab, select **Extract all**. The Extract Compressed (Zipped) Folders dialog box opens. Notice the path showing where the folder will be saved. It should show the location of the current folder. This indicates that a new folder will be created for the extracted files using the same name as the zipped folder.

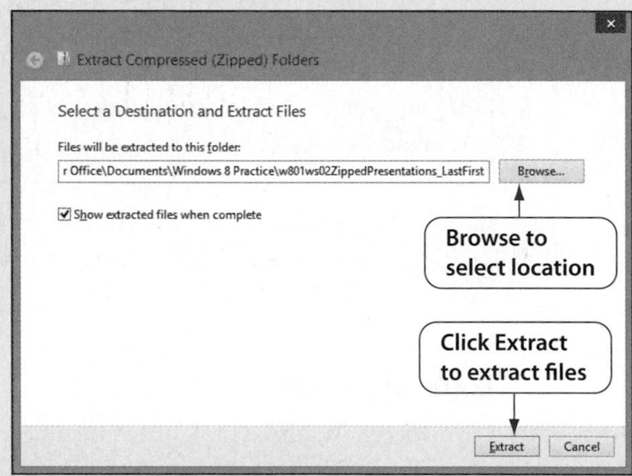

Figure 21 Extract Compressed (Zipped) Folders tool

SIDE NOTE

Compressing and Extracting Files

This exercise showed the process of compressing and extracting files. You would not normally compress files and then extract them immediately.

c. Make sure the **Show extracted files when complete** check box is checked. Click the **Extract** button. When the extraction process is complete, the contents of **w801ws02ZippedPresentations_LastFirst** are displayed in a new File Explorer window.

Add Tags to Files

A **tag** is a custom file property that allows you to add keywords to files to categorize and organize them. Tags also help you find the files you need more quickly. Sometimes, users may want to specify categories for a file. Most image file types and all Microsoft Office file types will support tags. However, certain file types such as .wmf do not support them.

Tags prove to be especially useful for images. Unlike Office documents, Windows cannot search inside image files for information. This makes finding images that match certain criteria difficult. For example, the data files from this textbook contain a number of image files. You may have noticed there are a number of food-related images. However, searching for "food" would only find one image file. Even though other files such as the w801ws02RestaurantSalad image in your data files obviously contain food images, Windows cannot interpret this. Users can add tags to help make files easier to find.

Adding tags allows a user to search for files on their hard drive much like they might search for Clip Art in Microsoft Office programs.

You will show your workshop attendees how to add tags to files so they can better organize and locate images.

W802.15

To Add Tags to Files

a. Click the **View** tab, and then ensure that the **Details pane** is selected. If it is not, you will not be able to see file tags. If necessary, on the View tab, in the Panes group, click **Details pane**.

b. Navigate to the **Resort Pictures** folder.

c. Click the **w801ws02MenuMuffins** file. In the Details pane, click **Add a tag**. A box opens in which you can enter your keywords as tags to help locate related files.

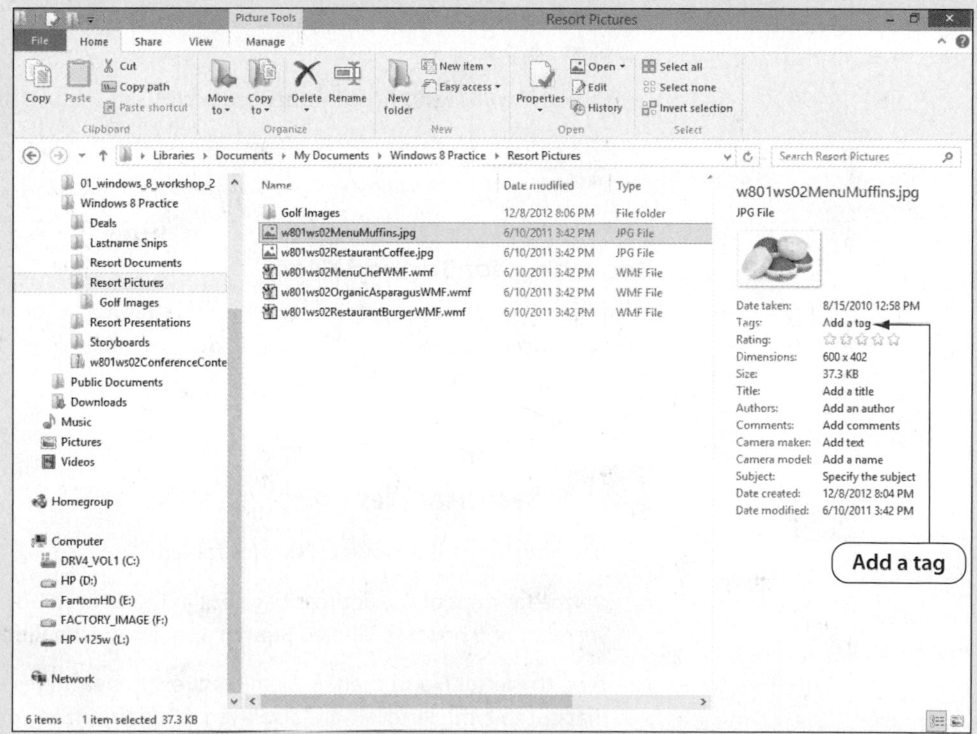

Figure 22 File tag location

d. In the Tags box, type Muffin, press ⇥, type Breakfast, press ⇥, and then type Food. Click **Save**.

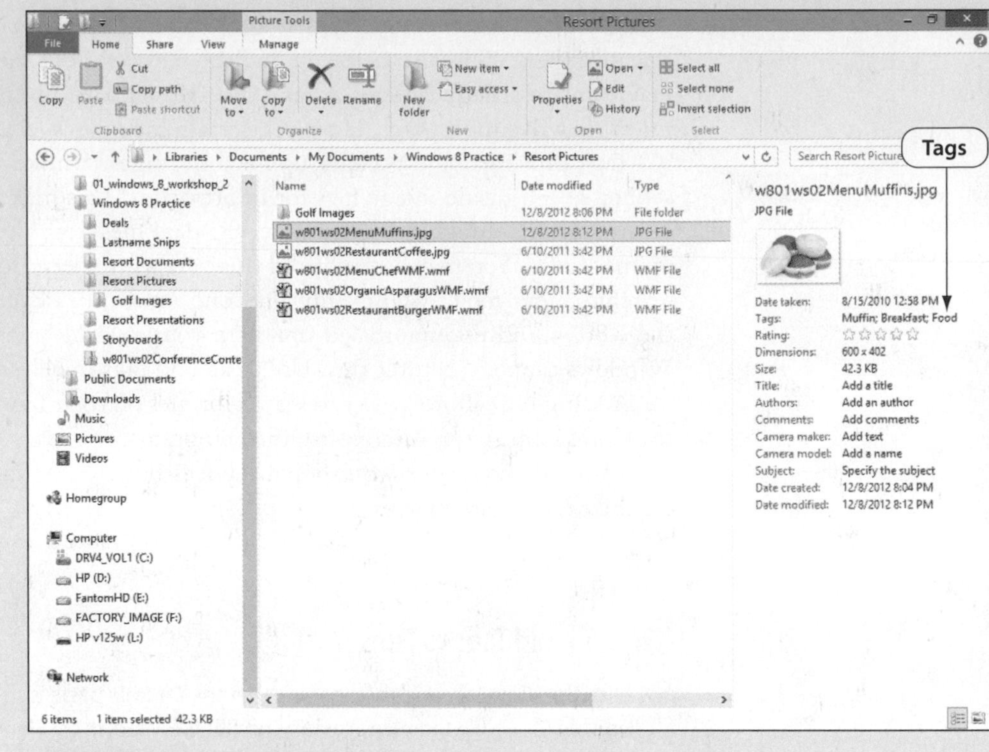

Figure 23 Tagged file

e. In the file list, click **w801ws02RestaurantCoffee**. In the Details pane, click **Add a tag**, type Coffee, press [→], type Breakfast, press [→], and then type Food. Click **Save**. Notice small windows will show up when you start to type Breakfast and Food, since these are existing tags.

f. Click the **w801ws02RestaurantBurgerWMF** file. Notice this file does not allow users to add tags to it.

Searching for Tagged Files

Windows 8 includes powerful search tools that make locating files easy. In Workshop 1, you explored the Search Charm. You will use File Explorer Search to see how tags work.

W802.16

To Search for Files

a. Navigate to the **Windows 8 Practice** folder.

b. On the far right of the address bar, click in the **Search** box. Notice when you click in the Search box, a new tab labeled **Search** appears on the Ribbon.

c. Type the letter F and then in the file list, examine the results of your search. File names that contain the letter "F" are displayed. In addition, any file extensions starting with "F" are displayed.

d. In the Search box, continue typing ood so your Search box displays **Food**. Notice the search results include files where you added tags for Food.

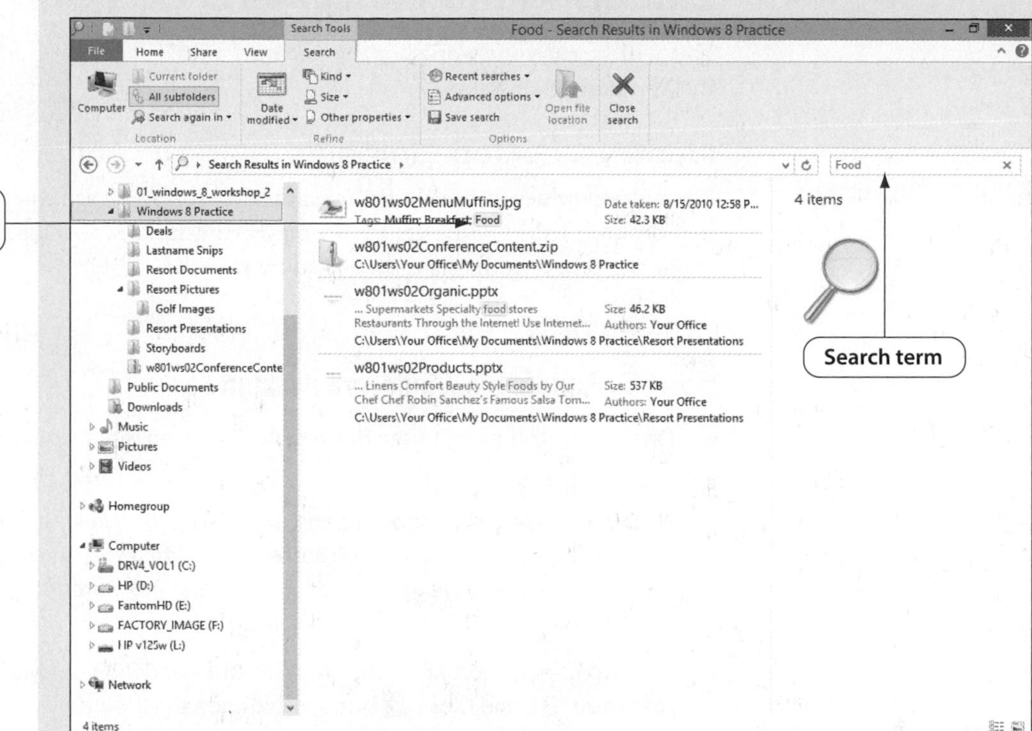

Figure 24 Search results for Food

> **Troubleshooting**
> If you do not see any results, the options on your machine may be set to not search inside files. To fix this, click the Search tab and click **Other properties**. Ensure **File contents** is selected.

e. Open the **Snipping Tool**, and then use the skills you practiced to create a Full-screen Snip of the window. Save it as a JPEG file in the **Lastname Snips** folder as w801ws02Search_LastFirst, and then **Close** the Snipping Tool window.

f. Submit all files as directed by your instructor. **Close** File Explorer.

REAL WORLD ADVICE — Does Improved Searching Replace Organization?

Given the power of search, it may seem folders are no longer necessary. However, search and folders are more powerful when they work in tandem. Recall from previous discussions that you can only search within files on indexed locations, which does not include removable storage. In addition, in a business environment, many files will be kept on a network, which will take much longer to search than a typical hard drive. Organizing files into folders is still an important task.

Exploring the Windows 8 Desktop

You will begin your workshop by asking Painted Paradise Resort employees to explore the Windows 8 desktop.

Identify Desktop Elements

You will examine various elements on the desktop and learn correct terminology. Pointing to a desktop icon highlights it and may bring up a ScreenTip. Double-clicking an icon opens the program that is represented by the icon.

W802.17

To Explore the Windows 8 Desktop

a. On the desktop, point to the **Recycle Bin**. The icon is highlighted.

b. Double-click the **Recycle Bin**.

The Recycle Bin window opens, showing any files that have been deleted. Your window may fill the screen or some of the **desktop background**—the picture or pattern that is displayed on the desktop—may show around the edges of the Recycle Bin window.

c. In the top-right corner of the **Recycle Bin** window, you will see the Minimize, Maximize, and Close buttons common to all windows. Click **Close**.

d. Point to the **Recycle Bin** again, and then **right-click**.

A shortcut menu is displayed, showing context-sensitive commands or commands that can be performed relating to the Recycle Bin. Note that you can also open the Recycle Bin by clicking Open on the shortcut menu.

Figure 25 Recycle Bin context menu

e. Point to a blank area on the desktop, and then **right-click**. A different shortcut menu appears, listing options that can be performed relating to the desktop.

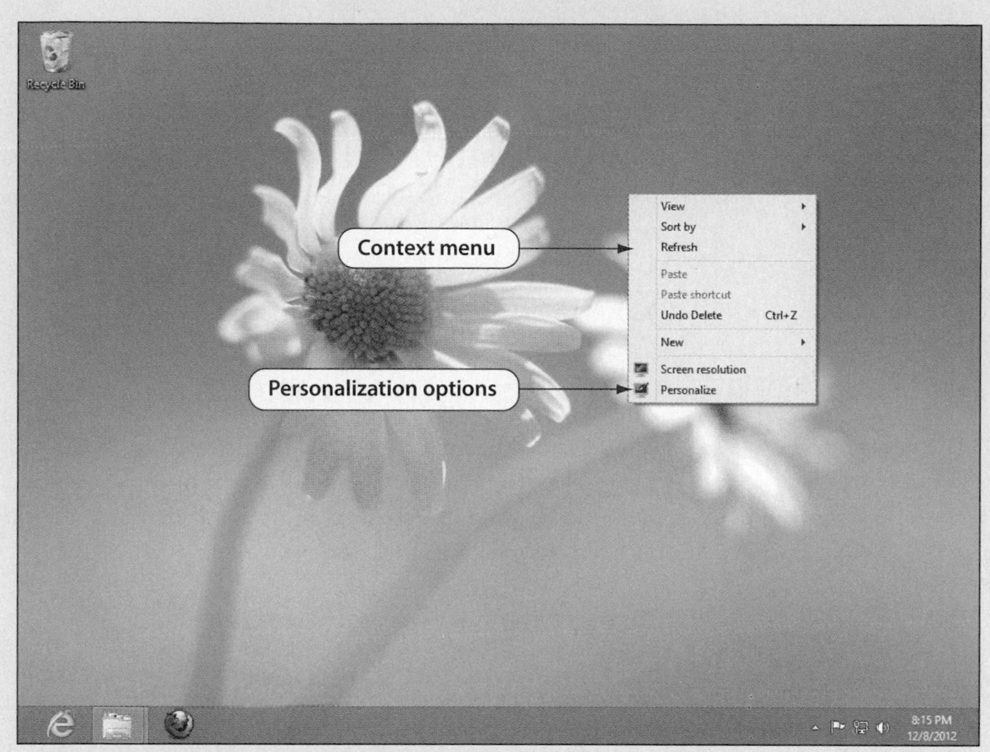

Figure 26 Desktop context menu

f. Click a blank area of the desktop to close the shortcut menu without making a selection.

REAL WORLD ADVICE Using the Recycle Bin

Files sent to the Recycle Bin remain on the computer's **hard drive**—a disk drive inside your computer, also called the local drive—until the Recycle Bin is emptied. As long as a file is in the Recycle Bin, it can be restored to its original location. This is similar to putting a piece of paper in a trash can. As long as the trash has not been emptied, you can still retrieve the piece of paper. However, once the Recycle Bin has been emptied, the file is extremely difficult to recover.

Do not expect files on USB Flash drives or other auxiliary storage devices to appear in the Recycle Bin. Only files deleted from your hard drive are placed in the Recycle Bin, so be extra careful when deleting from removable devices.

Understand the Taskbar

The taskbar is the long horizontal bar at the bottom of your screen. The taskbar is visible most of the time and consists of three main sections:

- The Pinned taskbar buttons let you start programs with one click. In Windows 8, programs eligible to be pinned to the taskbar will have the option to Pin to Taskbar on the contextual menu of the Start screen.
- The middle section displays temporary buttons for programs and documents that are open.
- The **notification area**, which displays information about the status of programs running in the background, also includes a clock and the option to safely remove devices such as USB flash drives.

REAL WORLD ADVICE | **Removing a USB Flash Drive**

A USB flash drive may end up damaged if it is not properly ejected. To eject properly in Windows 8, enter the desktop. Locate and click the **Safely Remove Hardware and Eject Media** icon on the taskbar in the Notification Area. Note you may need to click the Show hidden icons option. Click the command that begins with **Eject** followed by your USB flash drive name. The **Safe to Remove Hardware** message appears, indicating you may remove the USB flash drive.

Working with Windows

Windows can be moved, resized, **minimized** to a taskbar button, and **maximized** to fill the entire screen. Several windows can be open at the same time and can be manipulated in the same way. In this section, you will demonstrate how to move, size, and manage both single and multiple windows.

Open and Manage Windows

There are several ways to open windows. You have already opened windows using icons on the Start screen and Search box in the Start screen. Programs not designed for Windows 8 will open in Desktop view. When a window is open, a temporary program button is added to the middle area on the taskbar.

All windows have similar components. The bar at the top of a window is the title bar. On the right side of the title bar are three control buttons that let you minimize, maximize or restore down, and close a window. If a window is maximized, the center button changes to the Restore Down button. Clicking this button when the window is maximized **restores** the window to its previous size and location. Most windows display these three control buttons. If a window cannot be resized, the center button is usually dimmed. **Dialog boxes**—boxes that present information or require a response from the user—may display only a Close button.

The title bar can be used to move a window that is not maximized to another location on the desktop. Double-clicking the title bar maximizes a window or restores a window. Many windows also display icons on the left side of the title bar that represent the program which is open. Clicking the icon opens a menu of commonly used commands. To the right of this icon, many Microsoft programs display a Quick Access Toolbar with Save, Undo, and Redo buttons. Additional buttons can be added to the Quick Access Toolbar. Program windows also display the name of the document or file that is open and the name of the program you are using.

W802.18

To Understand the Elements of a Window

a. From the Start screen, click the **Desktop** icon, and select the **File Explorer** icon on the taskbar. The File Explorer window opens.

b. If the File Explorer window does not fill the screen, click **Maximize** near the top-right of the title bar. The Maximize button is in the center of the three control buttons if the window is not maximized. When the window is maximized, the button becomes the Restore Down button.

c. The Ribbon displays above the address bar. Notice the different tabs available.

d. Locate the **address bar** under the Ribbon. This shows the path to wherever you are currently located. The address bar indicates that you are viewing the libraries on the computer.

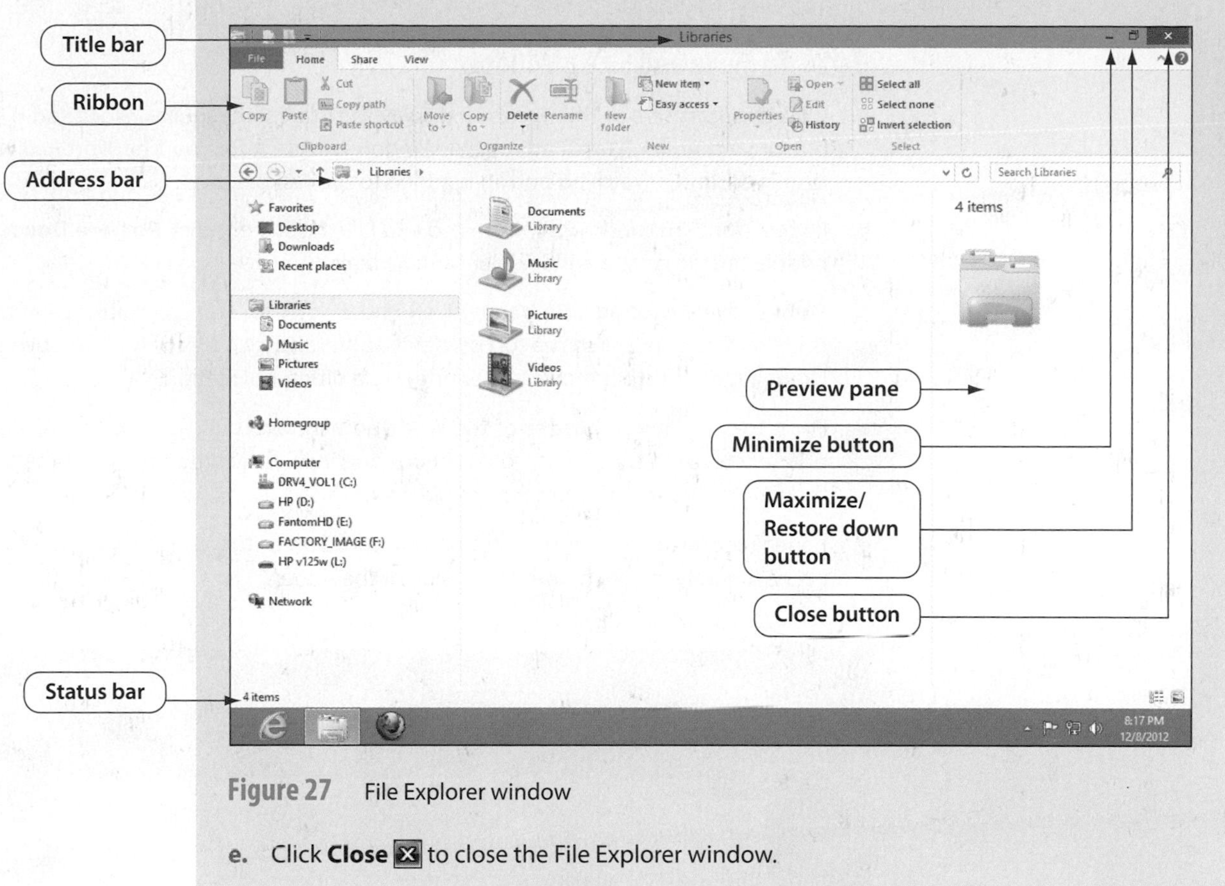

Figure 27 File Explorer window

e. Click **Close** ☒ to close the File Explorer window.

Moving and Sizing a Window

You can move a window that is not maximized by clicking its title bar, holding down the left mouse button, and then dragging the window to a new location.

The borders of a window contain options that let you resize the window, as long as the window is not maximized. Point to any corner until you see a diagonal resize pointer, and then drag the corner in or out to resize the window both vertically and horizontally. Pointing to the top or bottom border displays a vertical resize pointer; pointing to the left or right border displays a horizontal resize pointer. Use these pointers to resize the window as you like.

You will use the WordPad program in the following exercise to practice moving and resizing a window. Notice that the WordPad title bar is slightly different than the File Explorer title bar. It displays an icon representing the program on the far left. Click this icon to display a menu of options. To the right of this icon, the Quick Access Toolbar contains three buttons that are displayed by default: Save, Undo, and Redo. Clicking the arrow to the right of these buttons displays the Customize Quick Access Toolbar menu that lets you add other buttons to the Quick Access Toolbar. The title bar also displays Document, which is the current file name, and WordPad, the name of the open program. The word "Document" will be replaced with the name of the file once it is created and saved. WordPad also displays a Ribbon, which is common to many Microsoft applications.

W802.19

To Move and Size a Window

a. Click the Start screen thumbnail to display the Start screen. Click **WordPad** if it is present, or start typing WordPad to have Windows locate it for you. The WordPad window is displayed, and a WordPad button is added to the taskbar.

b. If your WordPad window is maximized and fills the screen, click **Restore Down** , the middle button on the right side of the title bar.

c. Point to the **WordPad title bar**, click and hold down the mouse button, and then drag the WordPad window so the top border is about one inch below the top of your screen. Dragging the title bar moves the window to a different location.

d. Point to the **bottom border** of the WordPad window until you see the Vertical Resize pointer . Drag the border so it is about one inch above the taskbar at the bottom of the screen. Dragging a border resizes the window.

e. Repeat this process with the left and right borders of the WordPad window so each is approximately one inch from either side of the screen.

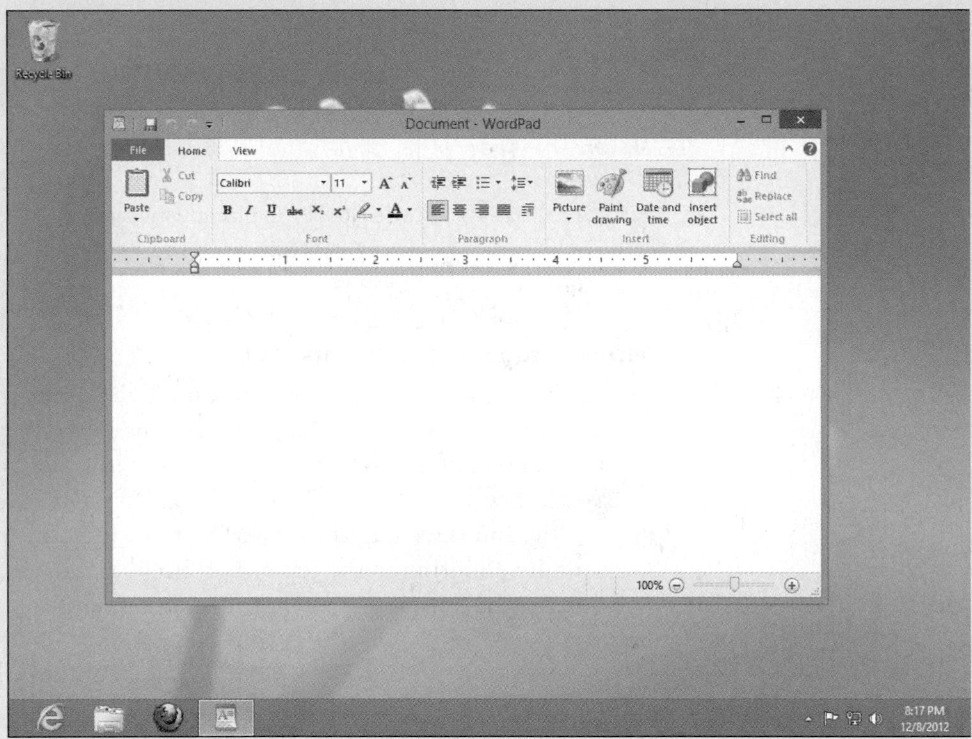

Figure 28 WordPad open on Desktop

> **Troubleshooting**
> If one of your borders is off the screen so you cannot see the resize pointer, use the title bar to drag the window so the border is visible. Then resize as necessary.

f. Point to the **bottom-right corner** of the WordPad window until you see the Diagonal Resize pointer . Drag the corner of the window up and to the left until the window is about three-fourths the original size.

Figure 29 Resized WordPad

Minimizing and Restoring a Window

Minimizing and closing a window appear to do the same thing. However, it is important to understand that the two procedures are quite different. When you minimize a program, the window is removed from the screen, but the program is still running on the computer. The program button on the taskbar shows that it is still available but not active. When you close a program, the window is removed from the screen, and the program closes and is removed from computer memory. When a program is closed, the program button is removed from the taskbar, unless it has been pinned there.

W802.20

To Minimize and Restore a Window

a. On the right side of the WordPad title bar, click **Minimize** [-]. The window is removed from the screen, but notice that the WordPad icon is still displayed on the taskbar.

b. Point to **WordPad** on the taskbar. A preview window is displayed, giving you a chance to see what the window looks like. Click **WordPad**. The WordPad window is the same size and in the same location where it was before it was minimized.

Maximizing, Snapping, and Closing a Window

You can maximize a window by using the Maximize button on the right side of the title bar. You can also double-click the title bar of a window to maximize it or to restore it. If a window fills the screen, double-clicking the title bar restores the window to its former size and location. If the window does not fill the screen, double-clicking the title bar maximizes the window. Dragging the title bar so the pointer touches the top of the screen also maximizes the window. Note that a maximized window cannot be moved or resized. **Snap** is a quick way to arrange open windows by dragging them to the edges of your screen. When the window snaps to the edge of the screen, it will take up exactly half of the current screen.

W802.21

To Maximize, Snap, and Close a Window

a. On the right side of the WordPad title bar, click **Maximize** ▣. The WordPad window fills the entire screen.

b. Double-click the **WordPad title bar**. The window is restored down to its previous size.

c. Point to the **WordPad title bar**, and then drag it to the top of the screen until the mouse pointer touches the top of the screen. You will see a translucent image that fills the screen. Release the mouse button and the WordPad window is maximized.

Figure 30 WordPad Maximize option

d. Point to the **title bar** of the WordPad window and drag to the left until the mouse pointer touches the left edge of the screen. When you see a translucent image filling the left half of the screen, release the mouse button. The WordPad window is arranged on the left half of your screen.

e. Click **Close** ☒ on the right side of the WordPad title bar. If a dialog box appears asking if you want to save changes to the document, click **Don't Save**. The window closes. The WordPad button no longer is displayed on the taskbar, and the program is removed from memory.

Work with Multiple Windows

Often you will want to work with several programs at the same time in order to move data between them. Or, you may want to have several windows open in the same program so you can compare different documents. Learning to manage multiple windows makes it easy to quickly access a window you want to use. You can also arrange open windows in ways that help you work more productively. Windows 8 makes it very easy to work with several programs and windows at the same time.

W802.22

To Open Multiple Windows

a. If necessary, display the Start screen. Click the **WordPad** icon if it is present, or start typing WordPad to have Windows locate it for you. If necessary, maximize the WordPad window.

b. Click the **Start screen thumbnail** to display the Start screen. Click the **Paint** icon if it is present, or start typing Paint to have Windows locate it for you. If necessary, maximize the Paint window.

c. Click the **File Explorer** icon on the taskbar.

d. If necessary, maximize the File Explorer window.

Even though multiple programs are open, you can only work in the **active window**—the window in which you can move the mouse pointer, type text, or perform other tasks. This is the window that is on top or in front of any other window. Only one window can be active at a time. Several methods are available for switching between programs. You will demonstrate these features and encourage Painted Paradise Resort staff to try them all. After experimenting with all of the methods, most people settle on the one or two methods they prefer.

Switch Option	Method
Gesture	Swipe from the left bezel towards the right.
Key combination	Press and hold Alt and then press Tab repeatedly to cycle through all open windows. When the program you want is highlighted, release Alt.
Taskbar buttons	On the taskbar, click the button for the program on which you want to work to switch to that program. The program appears in front of the other windows and becomes the active window.

Figure 31 Switching between programs

Switching Between Windows Using Taskbar Buttons

Using taskbar icons to switch between windows is familiar to most users. If you like using the mouse to control the operating system, this is a good way to switch between programs.

W802.23

To Switch Between Windows Using Taskbar Buttons

a. Point to **WordPad** on the taskbar. A preview window appears showing a thumbnail of a blank document in the WordPad window.

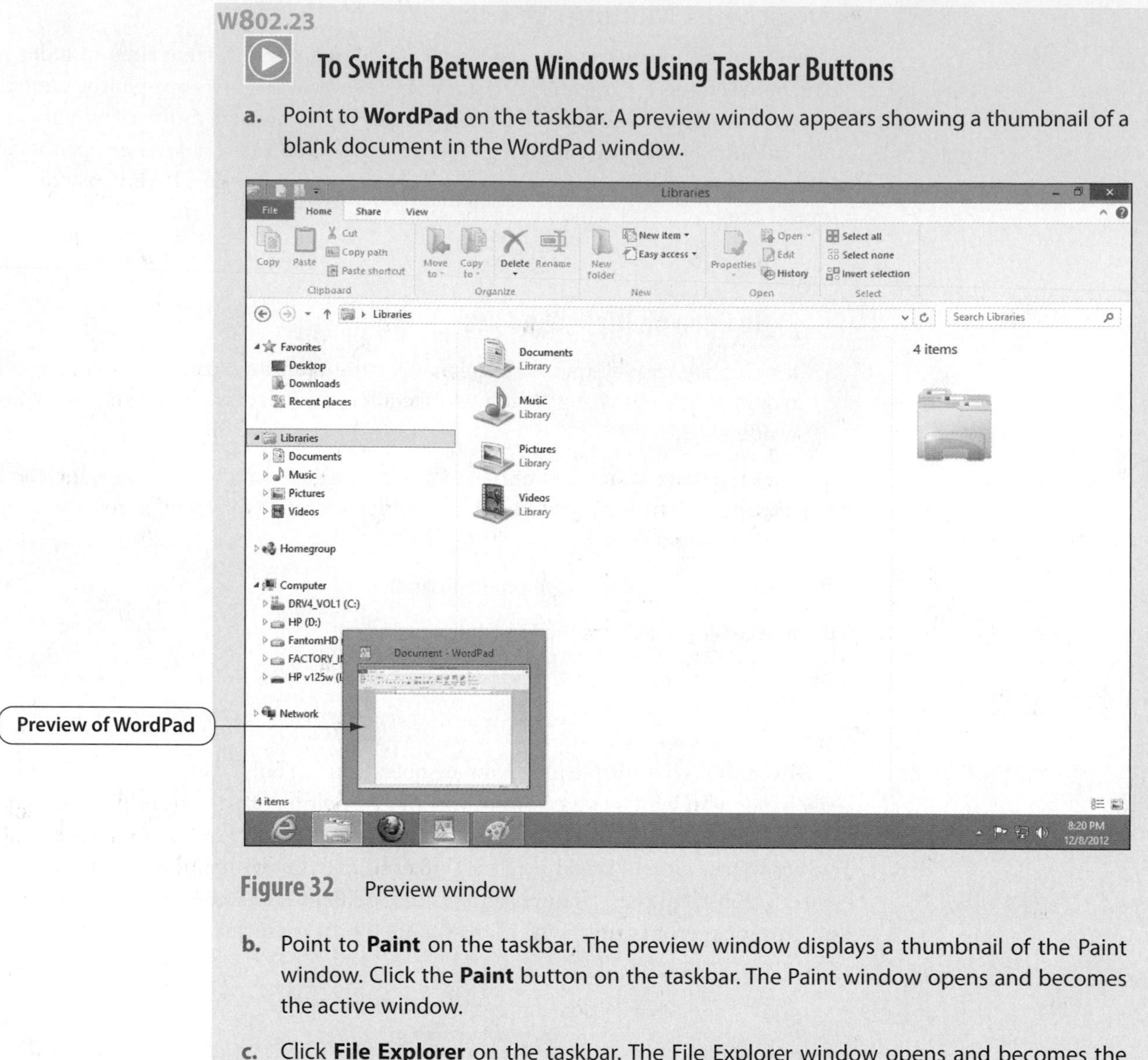

Figure 32 Preview window

b. Point to **Paint** on the taskbar. The preview window displays a thumbnail of the Paint window. Click the **Paint** button on the taskbar. The Paint window opens and becomes the active window.

c. Click **File Explorer** on the taskbar. The File Explorer window opens and becomes the active window.

Switching Between Windows Using a Key Combination

Key combinations, also known as keyboard shortcuts, are a set of keys pressed together to perform some sort of action. Key combinations can help you become more efficient as a user. If you become fluent with key combinations, you save time you might otherwise spend searching for commands. You can switch between windows by using a key combination, by holding down the Alt key on your keyboard and pressing the Tab key. Holding down Alt and hitting Tab multiple times will allow you to flip through the open windows. Once you have reached the program you wish to use, you can release the Tab key. A variation of the Alt + Tab key combination is to hold down the Windows key and press the Tab key. This technique, known as Aero Flip 3D, will perform the same function, with a different graphical display, though it may not be available in all installations of Windows 8.

 CONSIDER THIS | **Why Use Key Combinations?**

There are literally hundreds of key combinations. Users will not take the time to memorize all possible key combinations. However, if there is a command you use frequently, it might be worth looking up the key combination on the Internet or in Help. What are some common commands you perform frequently that might be worth finding key combinations for?

MODULE 1

W802.24

To Switch Between Windows Using Alt+Tab

a. Press and hold down [Alt], and then press [Tab]. A window appears in the center of the screen with thumbnails representing each of the open programs. The program name at the top of the window indicates the program that will be active when you release [Alt].

Figure 33 [Alt] + [Tab] switching

b. Hold down [Alt], and then press the [Tab] key repeatedly, until the Paint thumbnail is highlighted and Untitled - Paint appears at the top of the window. Release [Alt]. The Paint window fills the screen and becomes the active window.

Using Shake

When multiple windows are open you can minimize all but the active window by using **Shake**—shaking the title bar to minimize all other windows. This method will leave the user with only one window displayed, and is a good way to minimize many programs at once.

W802.25

To Use Shake to Minimize Windows

a. Point to the **File Explorer** title bar. Click and hold the **mouse button** and then shake the title bar back and forth. All other program windows are minimized to the taskbar, and the File Explorer window is the only window visible on the screen.

Arranging Windows Using Cascade

You can control how windows are arranged and displayed on your screen. Cascading windows places open windows on top of each other with just the title bar and a small portion of the border visible. The active window is on top. To make a different window active, click any portion of the window which is visible.

W802.26

To Cascade Windows

a. Make sure that the **WordPad**, **Paint**, and **File Explorer** windows are open and that corresponding buttons are displayed on the taskbar. If necessary, click the WordPad and Paint buttons on the taskbar so they are no longer minimized.

b. Point to a blank area on the taskbar and right-click. A shortcut menu appears. Click **Cascade windows**. All open windows are cascaded one on top of the other with the title bar and a small portion of the left border visible. The window on top is the active window.

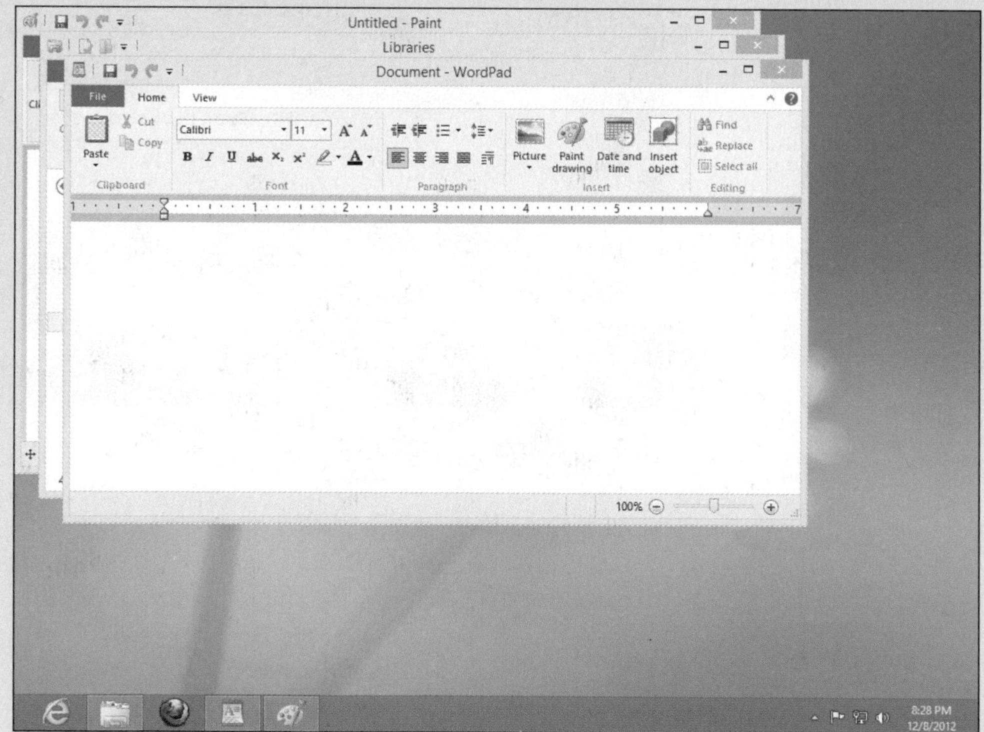

Figure 34 Cascaded windows

c. Click anywhere on the edge of a window that is not active to bring it to the front and to make it the active window.

Stacking Windows

Open windows can be stacked vertically on the screen. This works best when only two or three windows are open. If you have more than three windows open, it will become unmanageable.

W802.27

To Show Windows Stacked

a. Make sure that the **WordPad**, **Paint**, and **File Explorer** windows are open.

b. Point to a blank area on the taskbar and right-click. A shortcut menu appears. Click **Show windows stacked**. All open windows are stacked vertically on the screen.

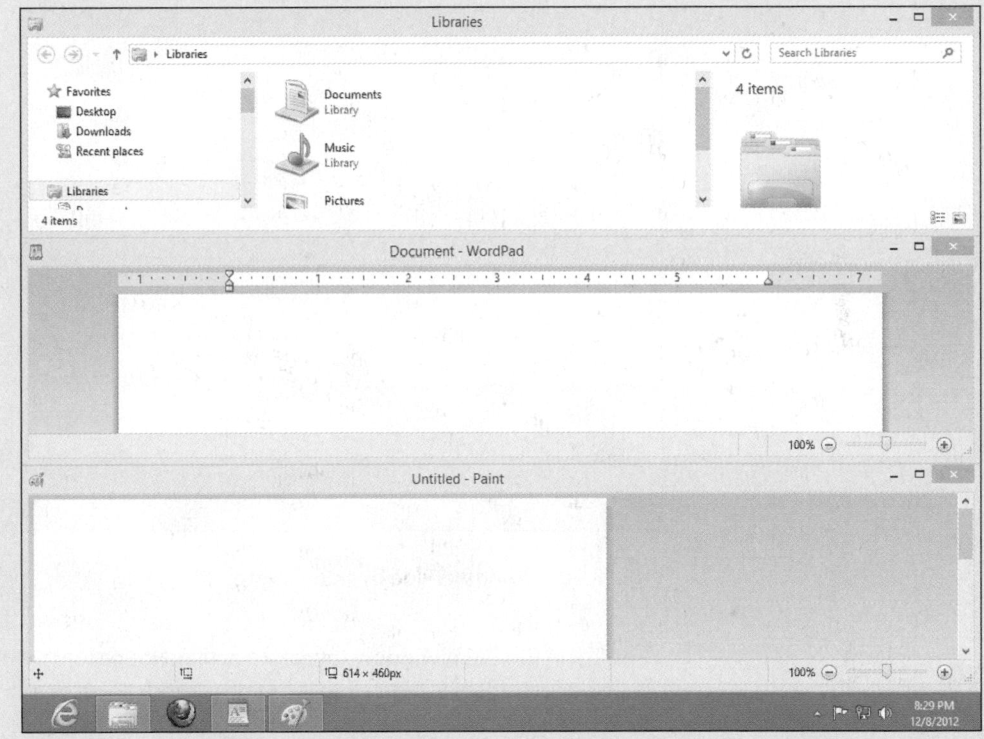

Figure 35 Windows stacked vertically

c. Click in the **WordPad** window to make it active. Notice that the Close button in the active window turns red, indicating it can be clicked.

Arranging Windows Side By Side

Open windows can also be displayed side by side. This can be useful if you are working between two open programs, and want to switch between them. This can be done manually, but this shortcut will make this process quicker.

W802.28

To Show Windows Side by Side

a. Make sure that the **WordPad**, **Paint**, and **File Explorer** windows are open.

b. Point to a blank area on the taskbar and right-click. A shortcut menu appears. Click **Show windows side by side.** All open windows are displayed side by side.

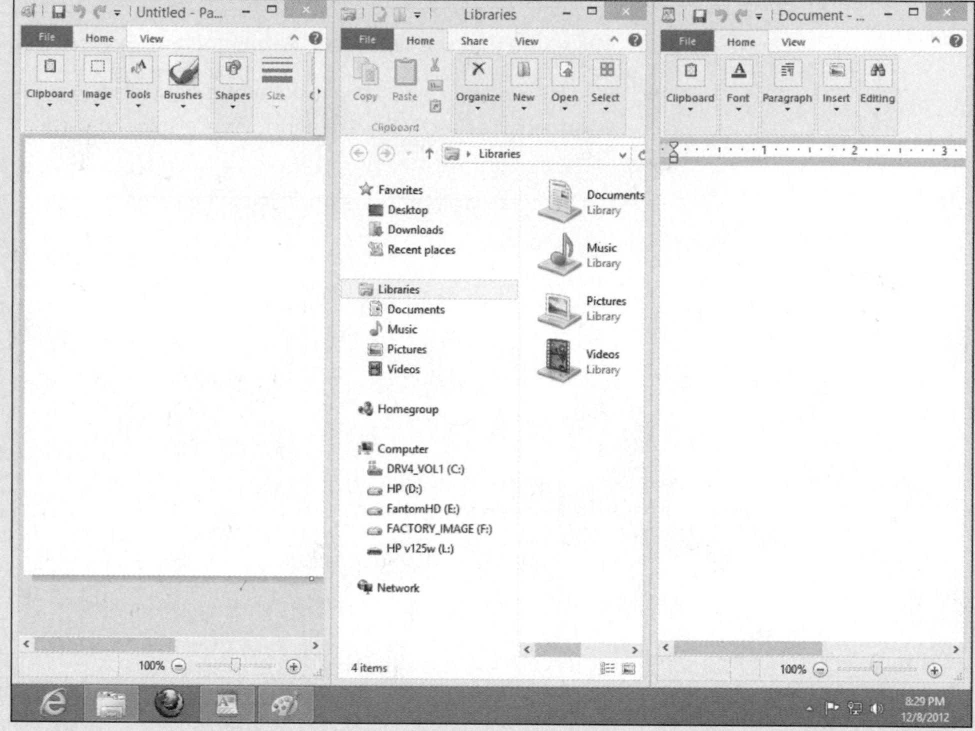

Figure 36 Windows side by side

c. Click in the **Paint** window to make it active. Notice that the Close button in the active window turns red, indicating it can be clicked.

d. **Close** Paint, File Explorer and WordPad.

Personalizing the Desktop

Windows 8 offers many ways to personalize and customize the desktop. Some personalization leads to higher efficiency and more productivity. Other customization is just for fun and might become distracting if overdone.

Since the Painted Paradise Resort personnel are now familiar with Windows 8 basics, in this section you will show them a few ways to personalize their computers.

Change the Appearance of the Desktop

Resort employees have been anxious to personalize their new computers. You will show them several ways to do this. Windows 8 comes with a number of different desktop backgrounds that can be used instead of the default background. Other desktop backgrounds can be downloaded from the Internet. Some people may even choose to use their own personal photos as the desktop background.

Screen savers are another way of changing the appearance of your desktop. A **screen saver** is a moving graphic that starts when a computer sits idle for a specified amount of time, such as 10 minutes. It prevents others from seeing work on your screen if you walk away from your computer. Users can also require a password after the screen saver is stopped, allowing further protection from wandering eyes.

Changing the Desktop Background

The desktop background is the first thing you see when you open the desktop from the Start screen. Most people want to change the background from the default background that is installed with Windows to something more pleasing to them. The background is definitely a personal choice, but it should not make it more difficult to perform tasks. Further, in a business setting the background should be professional and inoffensive. You will choose a background where desktop icons will still be easy to see.

W802.29

To Change the Desktop Background

a. Point to a blank area on the desktop and **right-click** to display a shortcut menu. Select **Personalize**. The Personalization window opens.

b. On the bottom left of the window, the Desktop Background thumbnail shows the current background picture. Make a note of this background so you will be able to return to it later.

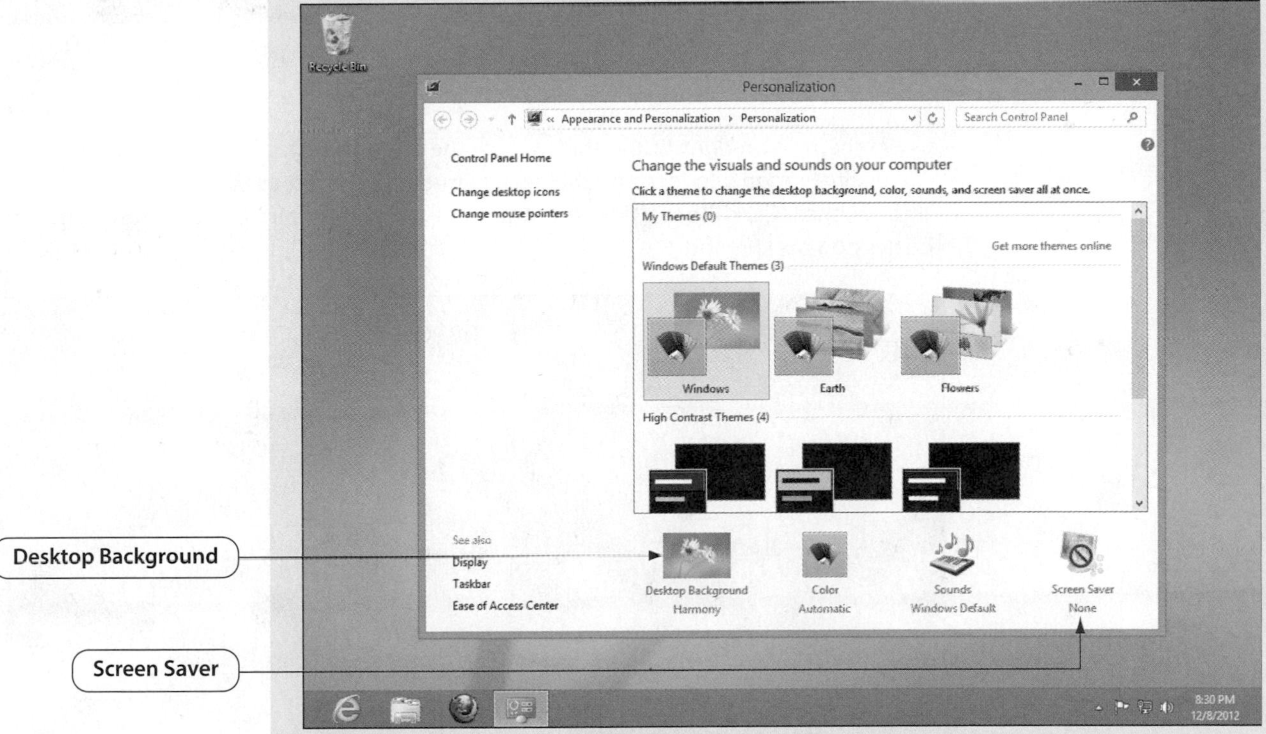

Figure 37 Personalization window

c. Click **Desktop Background**. If necessary, **Maximize** ▢ the window. A gallery of backgrounds opens, arranged by categories.

d Select an appropriate desktop background from the list. Clicking on a picture will make it the background. A check appears in the top-left corner and a highlighted frame is displayed around the picture. Select the **desert background** under Earth. If that is not available, choose another, similar background.

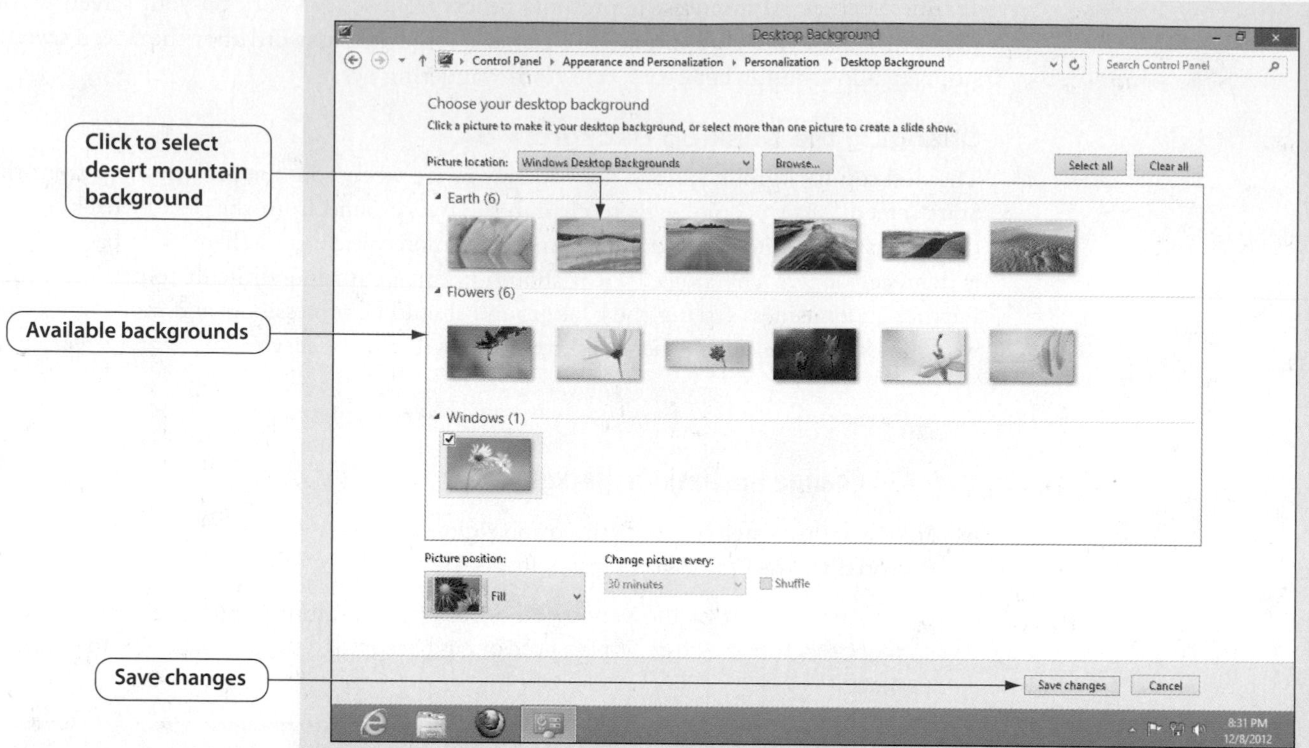

Figure 38 Selecting a new background

e. On the bottom-right of the screen, click the **Save changes** button. You return to the Personalization window, and the new picture is displayed as the Desktop Background thumbnail. Click **Close** to return to the desktop. The picture you chose is now the desktop background.

Figure 39 New desktop background

MODULE 1

Selecting a Screen Saver

A screen saver begins after your computer is idle for a predefined period, hiding the contents of your desktop. Several screen savers are installed with Windows 8. The **Wait time**—the time before the screen saver starts—default is 10 minutes, but this can be adjusted. You will ask staff members to shorten the wait time to just one minute so they can observe the effect of setting a screen saver without having to wait a long time. The screen saver provides extra security as well. Users can check an option to require a password after the screen saver is deactivated. This ensures people cannot use your machine if you walk away from it.

W802.30

To Set a Screen Saver

a. Point to a blank area on the desktop and **right-click** to display a shortcut menu. Select **Personalize**. The Personalization window opens.

b. On the bottom right of the window, click **Screen Saver.** The Screen Saver Settings dialog box is displayed.

c. Under Screen saver, click the **Screen saver** arrow, click **3D Text**, and then observe the preview in the screen at the top of the dialog box. If the default text has not been replaced with another message, you will see Windows 8 revolving in the center of the Preview window.

d. Under Screen saver, click the **Screen saver** arrow, click **Mystify**, and then observe the preview.

e. Make note of the current Wait time. Click the **arrow** until the Wait time box displays **1 minutes**. Click **OK**, and then **Close** the Personalization window to return to the desktop.

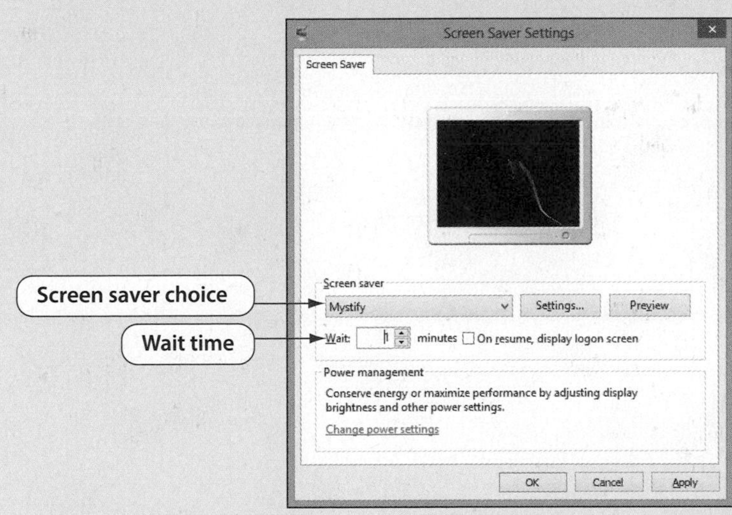

Figure 40 Selecting a screen saver

SIDE NOTE

Setting Screen Saver Wait Time

Using a wait time of one minute is for demonstration purposes only. A much more reasonable wait interval would be the 10 minute default.

f. Wait approximately **one minute** without touching the mouse or keyboard. The Mystify screen saver will start. Move the mouse or press any key to return to the screen that was active before the screen saver started.

g. Repeat Steps a, b, and e, but set the Wait time to **10 minutes** or to the time that was set before. **Close** the Personalization window.

Undoing Changes

During your training at Painted Paradise, you will want to return everything to its original state after your demonstration. Then, employees can add their own personalization and practice the skills you demonstrated. The following steps will return to the former desktop background and screen saver.

W802.31

To Return to the Original Desktop

a. Right-click the desktop, select **Personalize**, and then click **Desktop Background**. Click the original background, and then click **Save changes**. You will return to the Personalization window.

b. Click **Screen Saver**. In the Screen Saver Settings dialog box, click the **arrow**, and then select the original screen saver. Check to make sure the Wait time was adjusted to the former time. Click **OK**. **Close** the Personalization window.

c. Start **File Explorer**. In the Navigation Pane, click the **arrow** in front of Documents, and then right-click on **Documents**. Click **Remove location from library**. **Close** File Explorer.

Concept Check

1. How has File Explorer changed in Windows 8? p. 48
2. Can libraries contain folders on USB drives? p. 50
3. Why should a user create folders? p. 53
4. What is the difference between copying a folder and moving a folder? p. 55
5. Describe two reasons you would zip a folder. p. 65
6. What is the purpose of adding a tag to an image file? p. 69
7. What is the taskbar? p. 73
8. If you were switching between multiple programs frequently, how would you arrange your windows? p. 75
9. List two reasons to personalize your desktop with a screen saver. p. 87

Key Terms

Active window 79
Address bar 48
Computer 48
Dialog boxes 74
Favorites 48
File Explorer 48
File list 48
Folder 53
Group 48
Hard drive 73
Key combination 80
Libraries 48
Maximize 74
Minimize 74
Navigation Pane 48
Network 48
Notification area 73
Pane 48
Restore 74
Ribbon 48
Screen saver 84
Shake 81
Snap 77
Status bar 48
Subfolder 53
Tag 69
Title bar 48
USB flash drive 48
Wait time 87
Window 48
Zip file 65

Visual Summary

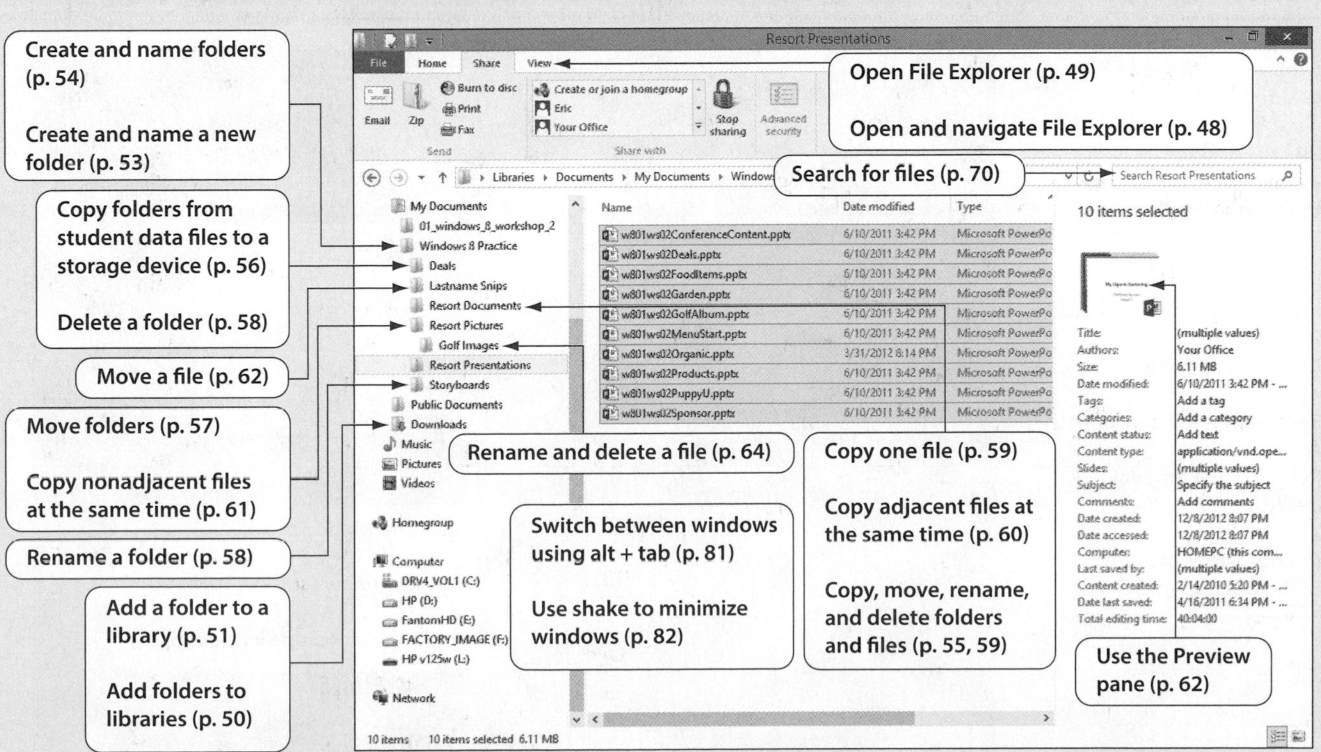

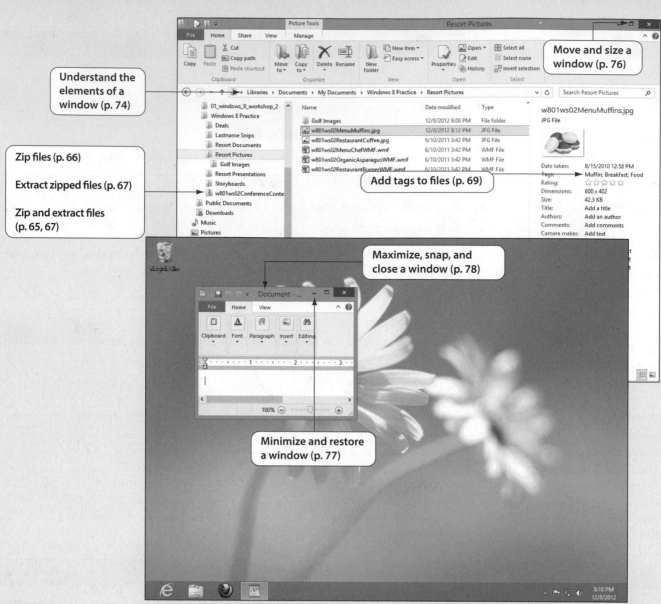

Understand the elements of a window (p. 74)

Zip files (p. 66)

Extract zipped files (p. 67)

Zip and extract files (p. 65, 67)

Move and size a window (p. 76)

Add tags to files (p. 69)

Maximize, snap, and close a window (p. 78)

Minimize and restore a window (p. 77)

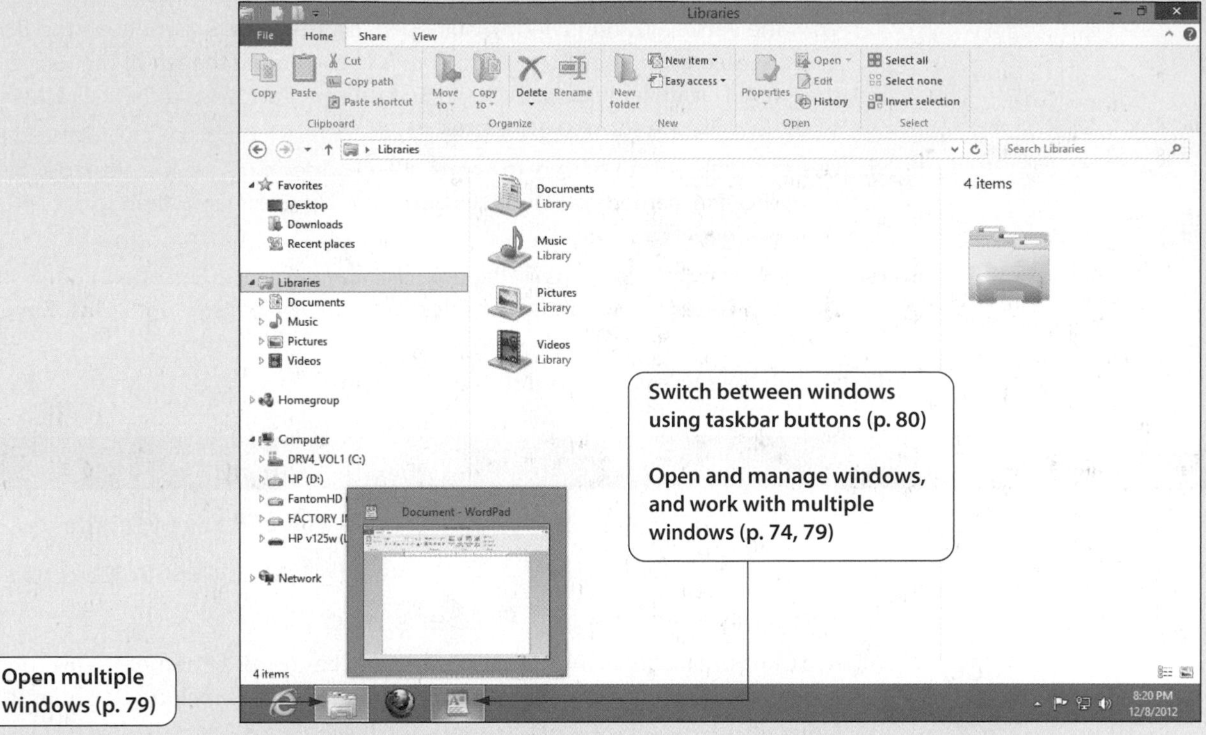

Figure 41 Managing Files, Folders, and the Windows Desktop Final

Practice 1

Student data file needed:

None

You will save your files as:

w801ws02Desktop_LastFirst.jpg

w801ws02Background_LastFirst.jpg

Personalizing Event Planning Department Computers

Information Technology

Patti Rochelle, corporate event planner at Painted Paradise Golf Resort and Spa, would like you to work with her staff to help them customize their new Windows 8 computers. Because computer screens are sometimes visible to guests, Patti would like to have the desktop background reflect the ambience of the resort. To better meet the needs of her department, she has also asked you to show her staff how to add useful gadgets to the desktop and to add shortcuts for frequently used programs.

a. Turn on your computer and, if necessary, follow any logon instructions required for the computer you are using.

b. From the Start screen, click **Snipping Tool**. If the Snipping Tool is not available on your Start screen, type Snipping Tool and click it to start the program.

c. Use the skills you practiced to create a Full-screen Snip of the desktop. Save the file as a JPG file named w801ws02Desktop_LastFirst, and then close the Snipping Tool window.

d. Point to an open area of the desktop, and then right-click. From the shortcut menu, select **Personalize**. Resize the Personalization window so it is centered on the screen with about an inch of the desktop showing on all four sides. Make note of the current background as you will return to this background at the end of this practice exercise.

e. At the bottom left of the Personalization window, click **Desktop Background**. Locate the Earth desktop backgrounds, and then click the picture of the desert. If your background is already the desert choose another appropriate background. Click **Save changes** to apply the new background.

f. With the Personalization window still open, click **Screen Saver**. Move the Screen Saver Settings dialog box so the top-left corner is above and to the left of the top-left corner of the Personalization window. Click the **Screen saver** arrow, and then click **Mystify**. Make sure the Wait time shows **10 minutes**.

g. Use the skills you practiced to create a Full-screen Snip of the desktop. Save the file as a JPG file named w801ws02Background_LastFirst, and then close the Snipping Tool window.

h. In the Screen Saver Settings dialog box, click **Cancel**. In the Personalization window, click **Desktop Background**, and then select the original background. Click **Save changes**, and then close the Personalization window.

i. Submit the two snip files as directed by your instructor.

Problem Solve 1

Student data file needed:	You will save your file as:
 01_windows_8_workshop_2 folder	w801ws02RestaurantZipped_LastFirst.zip

Managing Restaurant Folders and Files

Sales & Marketing

Alberto Dimas, manager of the Indigo5 Restaurant, has received numerous files related to the Painted Paradise Resort from the resort manager. These files include documents, presentations, and images for all areas of the resort. You have been asked to review all files and select and organize those that would be useful for promotional materials for the restaurant. To do this as efficiently as possible, you will preview the files instead of opening each one.

a. Open **File Explorer**. In your Windows 8 Practice folder, create a new folder named Restaurant.

b. In the Restaurant folder, create two subfolders for Documents and Pictures.

c. Locate your 01_windows_8_workshop_2 files. Sort the files by **Type**. In File Explorer, turn on the Preview pane. In the file list, click each file, and then examine its preview. If the file is food related, copy it to the appropriate folder. Food pictures will be copied to the Pictures folder, and all other food-related files will be copied to the Documents folder. Note that the WMF files are not displayed in the Preview pane. You can double-click each WMF file to open it in Paint.

d. Compress the Restaurant folder to a zipped folder named w801ws02RestaurantZipped_LastFirst replacing last and first with your last name and first name.

e. Submit the compressed file as directed by your instructor.

Additional Cases

Additional Workshop Cases are available on the companion website and in the instructor resources.

MODULE CAPSTONE

More Practice 1

Student data file needed:

01_windows_8_capstone folder

You will save your file as:

w801mpEvents_LastFirst.zip

Organizing Folders and Files for the Event Planning Department

Production & Operations

Patti Rochelle would like you to continue working with the events planning staff to help them develop strategies for organizing folders and files. Because employees must often fill in for one another, Patti thinks it would be helpful if her staff could develop a common folder hierarchy. She has asked you to show them how to set up folders that will be useful for the various events that take place at the Painted Paradise Resort.

a. Switch on your computer and, if necessary, follow any login instructions required for the computer you are using.

b. Open **File Explorer**, and then, if necessary, maximize the window. Ensure the Details pane is showing, as shown in Workshop 2. In the Navigation Pane, under Libraries, click **Documents**, and then create a new subfolder named Windows 8 More Practice.

c. Create two subfolders in the Windows 8 More Practice folder named Conferences and Weddings. In the Navigation Pane, click the **arrow** to the left of the Windows 8 More Practice folder so both subfolders are visible.

d. In the File Explorer window, navigate to the location where your student data files are stored. Click the **arrow** in front of **01_windows_8_capstone**, and then click the **01_windows_8_capstone** folder in the Navigation Pane to display the contents in the file list.

e. In the file list, in the Name column, make sure the arrow is pointing up and the files are sorted in ascending order, from "a" to "z." Click **w801mpConferenceAttendees**, hold down **Shift**, and then click **w801mpConferencePueblo**. Copy the five selected files to the **Conferences** folder inside the Windows 8 More Practice folder. Select the six files with the word **Menu** in the file name, and then copy these files to the **Weddings** folder inside your Windows 8 More Practice folder.

f. In the Navigation Pane, click the **Weddings** folder. In the file list, right-click the file **w801mpMenuStart**, and then from the shortcut menu, select **Rename**. Change the file name to w801mpMenuPresentation.

g. Right-click **w801mpMenuChefWMF**, and then select **Delete**.

h. With the **Weddings** folder still selected, in the file list, click the **w801mpMenuPresentation** file. In the Details pane, click in the box to the right of the word **Tags**. Type Appetizers, press [→], and then type Lunch. Click **Save**.

i. Zip the **Windows 8 More Practice** folder. Name the folder w801mpEvents_LastFirst.

j. Submit the zip folder as requested by your instructor.

Problem Solve 1

Student data file needed:

None

You will save your file as:

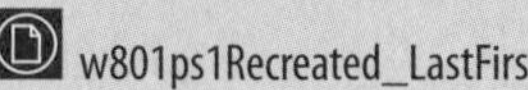
w801ps1Recreated_LastFirst.jpg

IT
Information Technology

Recreating a Desktop

Recreate the Start screen shown in Figure 1.

Desktop background

Figure 1 Target Start screen

a. Remove any tiles on your Start screen not shown in Figure 1.

b. Add links to **costco.com** and **sodexo.com** on the Start screen.

c. Add any other tiles shown in Figure 1 that are not shown on your Start screen.

d. Change the Desktop background to match the one shown in the Figure 1 preview. The background should be desert sands.

e. Resize tiles and move tiles so they match the order shown in Figure 1. Note your Weather tile may show a different location.

f. Create a screen shot of your Start screen. Save it as a JPEG file named w801ps1Recreated_LastFirst, and then submit the file as requested by your instructor.

Problem Solve 2

Student data file needed:

w801ps2Sonny.zip

You will save your file as:

w801ps2Organized_LastFirst.zip

Uncompressing and Organizing Old Files

Production & Operations

The head concierge for the Painted Paradise Resort and Spa, Sonny Fuller, recently retired. The information technology department for the resort created a zip folder containing the files from the Documents folder on Sonny's computer. You have been asked to sort through his files and organize them.

a. Extract the contents of the w801ps2Sonny file into a new folder named Windows8_PS2. Because you will be searching, ensure this folder is created on the computer's hard drive in your Documents folder.

b. Delete any files referencing **ElDorado**, as these are no longer needed. Use the Windows search to find and delete these files.

c. Delete all **JPG** files.

d. Inside the **Windows8_PS2** folder, create a new subfolder named WMFs.

e. Perform a search for **WMF** in the Windows8_PS2 folder. Move all matching files to the WMFs folder.

f. Rename w801ps2Sonny to w801ps2Putts.

g. Find any files with the tag **Sonny**. Click each file, and then on the Details pane, delete the tag Sonny. Save your changes. Note: Do not delete the files.

h. Inside the **Windows8_PS2** folder, create a new subfolder named Documents.

i. Move all of the remaining files except for **w801ps2Indigo5Logo** to the Documents folder.

j. Zip the **Windows8_PS2** folder. Save the zip folder as w801ps2Organized_LastFirst, and then submit the file as requested by your instructor.

Perform 1: How Others Perform

Student data file needed:

Blank WordPad document

You will save your files as:

w801pf1Evaluation_LastFirst.rtf

w801pf1Background_LastFirst.jpg

w801pf1StartScreen_LastFirst.jpg

w801pf1Solution_LastFirst.zip

Evaluating a Windows 8 Setup

Information Technology

Locate a computer with Windows 8 installed on it, other than your own. This can be a computer in your school lab, a public library, or a friend or relative's computer.

a. Restart the computer, and note the login procedure. Note whether passwords are required, or if the system logs in automatically. Can you log in using a PIN or picture password?

b. Log in to the computer, if necessary. Open WordPad. Create a new document and save it as w801pf1Evaluation_LastFirst.

c. Summarize the login options, as you noted in Step a. Do you feel this is too restrictive, or not restrictive enough?

d. Minimize your document, and notice the background. Take a screen shot of the background and save it as a JPG file named w801pf1Background_LastFirst.

e. Switch back to **w801pf1Evaluation_LastFirst**. In a new paragraph, describe whether you feel the background is appropriate or not.

f. Minimize your document, and display the screen saver options. Take note of which screen saver is selected, and how long of a delay there is before the screen saver activates.

g. Switch back to **w801pf1Evaluation_LastFirst**. In a new paragraph, describe whether you feel the screen saver timer is appropriate or not, and which screen saver was selected.

h. Display the Start screen. Take a screen shot of the Start screen and save it as a JPG file named w801pf1StartScreen_LastFirst.

i. Switch back to **w801pf1Evaluation_LastFirst**. In a new paragraph, describe the positives and negatives about the way the Start screen is set up on this computer. Save the document and exit WordPad.

j. Open File Explorer. Create a zip file containing w801pf1Evaluation_LastFirst, w801pf1Background_LastFirst, and w801pf1StartScreen_LastFirst. Save the zip file as w801pf1Solution_LastFirst. Submit the file as requested by your instructor.

Perform 2: Perform in Your Career

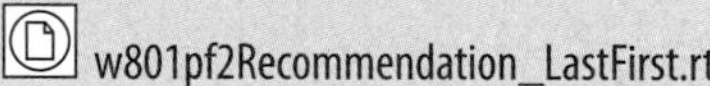

Student data file needed:

Blank WordPad document

You will save your file as:

w801pf2Recommendation_LastFirst.rtf

Should We Upgrade?

Information Technology

You have recently been hired as a consultant for Passaic County Convalescent Care, a small company that routes nurses and home aides to the community. Part of your job is to evaluate and recommend software upgrades. The company is currently running Windows Vista on all its desktop computers, and would like you to evaluate the pros and cons of upgrading to Windows 8, and make a recommendation on whether to upgrade or not.

a. Open WordPad. Create a new document and save it as w801pf2Recommendation_LastFirst.

b. Write approximately 150 words in sentence form describing advantages of the new operating system you feel the company's employees would benefit from.

c. Write approximately 150 words in sentence form describing disadvantages of the new operating system. Make sure to include a cost estimate for upgrading, and whether you feel the employees would need training or not.

d. Write approximately 100 words in sentence form recommending whether you feel the company should upgrade to Windows 8. Be persuasive in your argument.

e. Save the document, and submit the file as requested by your instructor.

Common Features of Microsoft Office 2013

Understanding the Common Features of Microsoft Office

OBJECTIVES

Prepare Case

Painted Paradise Resort and Spa Employee Training Preparation

Sales & Marketing

The gift shop at the Painted Paradise Resort and Spa has an array of items available for purchase from toiletries to clothes to souvenirs for loved ones back home. There are numerous part-time employees including students from the local college. Frequently, the gift shop holds training luncheons for new employees. Your first assignment will be to start two documents for a meeting with your manager, Susan Brock—the beginning of meeting minutes and an Excel budget. To complete this task, you need to understand and work with the common features within the Microsoft Office Suite.

DOC RABE Media / Fotolia

REAL WORLD SUCCESS

"I am a returning student and the thought of having to use a computer for anything other than e-mail and social networking scared me. It was not as bad as I anticipated by taking it one step at a time. Now, I feel comfortable typing a research paper and creating a budget on a spreadsheet. It is a welcoming feeling that all the Microsoft applications share the same look! Knowing the common elements gave me a jump-start for learning each additional Microsoft application."

- Esther, current student

Student data files needed for this workshop:

 Blank Word document

 Blank Excel workbook

 Blank Word document in SkyDrive

 cf01ws01Logo.jpg

You will save your files as:

 cf01ws01Minutes_LastFirst.docx

 cf01ws01Budget_LastFirst.docx

 cf01ws01Minutes_LastFirst.pdf

 cf01ws01SkyDrive_LastFirst.docx

Working with the Office Interface

When you walk into a grocery store, you usually know what you are going to find and that items will be in approximately the same location, regardless of which store you are visiting. The first items you usually see are the fresh fruit and vegetables while the frozen foods are near the end of the store. This similarity among stores creates a comfortable and welcoming experience for the shopper—even if the shopper has never been in that particular store. The brands may be different, but the food types are the same. That is, canned corn is canned corn.

Microsoft Office 2013 creates that same level of welcoming feeling and comfort with its Ribbons, features, and functions. Each application has a similar appearance or user interface. The interface for Microsoft Office 2013 is called Modern because of its sleek appearance. The new look is minimalist, mimicking the tiles on the Windows 8 Start screen. There is now a more two-dimensional appearance. There is no more shading or shadows and if you choose a background, there is only a hint of a watermark. In this section, you will learn to navigate and use the Microsoft Office interface.

Understand Office Applications and Accounts

Microsoft Word is a word-processing program. This application can be used to create, edit, and format **documents** such as letters, memos, reports, brochures, resumes, and flyers. Word also provides tools for creating **tables**, which organize information into rows and columns. Using Word, you can add **graphics**, which consist of pictures, online pictures, SmartArt, shapes, and charts that can enhance the look of your documents.

Microsoft Excel is a spreadsheet program. Excel is a two-dimensional grid that can be used to model quantitative data and perform accurate and rapid calculations with results ranging from simple budgets to financial and statistical analyses. Data entered into Excel can be used to generate a variety of charts such as pie charts, bar charts, line charts, or scatter charts, to name a few, to enhance spreadsheet data. Excel files are known as **workbooks**, which contain one or more worksheets. Excel makes it possible to analyze, manage, and share information, which can also help you make better and smarter decisions. New analysis and visualization tools help you track and highlight important data trends.

Microsoft PowerPoint is a presentation and slide program. This application can be used to create slide shows for a presentation, as part of a website, or as a stand-alone application on a computer kiosk. These presentations can also be printed as handouts.

Microsoft OneNote is a planner and note-taking program. OneNote can be used to collect information in one easy-to-find place. With OneNote, you can capture text and images, as well as video and audio. By sharing your notebooks, you can simultaneously take and edit notes with other people in other locations, or just keep everyone in sync and up to date. You can also take your OneNote notebooks with you and then view and edit your notes from virtually any computer with an Internet connection or your Windows 8 phone device.

Microsoft Outlook is an e-mail, contact, and information management program. Outlook allows you to stay connected to the world with the most up-to-date e-mail and calendaring tools. You can manage and print schedules, task lists, phone directories, and other documents. Outlook's ability to manage scheduled events and contact information is why Outlook is sometimes referred to as an **information management program**.

Microsoft Access is a relational database management program. Access is a three-dimensional database program that allows you to make the most of your data. Access is known as **relational database** software—or three-dimensional database software—because it is able to connect data in separate tables. Access connects the data through relationships formed from common fields that exist in both tables. For example, a business might have one table that lists all the employees—their employee ID, first name, last name, address, hire date, and job title. Another table might track data for each shift they are working—their employee ID, date, start time, and end time. Since the common field of employee ID is in both database tables, you could create a report of which employees are working on Thursday at noon along with their name and job title. Thus, Access is used primarily to compile, store, query, and report data. Best practice is to use Access to store data and Excel to model and analyze data by creating charts.

Microsoft Publisher is a desktop publishing program that offers professional tools and templates to help easily communicate a message in a variety of publication types, saving time and money while creating a more polished and finished look. Whether you are designing brochures, newsletters, postcards, greeting cards, or e-mail newsletters, Publisher aids in delivering high-quality results without the user having graphic design experience. Publisher helps you to create, personalize, and share a wide range of professional-quality publications and marketing materials with ease.

Microsoft Lync is a unified communication platform. With Lync, which is able to be fully integrated with Microsoft Office, users can keep track of their contacts' availability; send an instant message; start or join an audio, video, or web conference; or make a phone call—all through a consistent, familiar interface.

InfoPath is used to design sophisticated electronic forms, which enables you to gather information quickly and easily.

Understanding Versions of Microsoft Office 2013

Microsoft Office 2013 is a suite of productivity applications or programs. You can purchase the each application separately or as a package. The exact applications available depends on the package installed. Office 2013 is available in greater variety and flexibility than ever before.

People use different devices for different purposes. You may use your tablet for information consumption and entertainment. Likewise, you may prefer your desktop computer to write a paper. Office 2013 has embraced the concept of every device has its purpose with more flexible versions for platforms such as **Windows Phone** and **Windows Run Time (RT)** and a revised interface to better make use of a touch interface and ARM chip devices. Advanced RISC Machine (ARM) chips are designed for low energy embedded systems, such as in an iPad. The Windows Phone and Windows RT versions of Office 2013 contain substantively similar functionality for Word, PowerPoint, Excel, and OneNote as the Windows version of Office 2013. Visually, Windows RT even looks the same as the full Office 2013 for Windows. However, applications that run on Windows Phone and RT do not support some of the more sophisticated Office features or back-end Visual Basic programming. The advantage is that these versions are optimized for phones and tablets—Office for every device or purpose. This text is written to the full version of Office 2013 for Windows, not Windows Phone or RT.

Office 2013 will be available in two different ways. You can purchase Office 2013 the traditional way from a retailer for a one-time fee that can be installed on exactly one computer. In addition, Office 2013 can also be purchased on a subscription, cloud basis called Office 365. The **Office 365** version is the same product that comes with more frequent updates, the ability to install on more than one computer, more SkyDrive storage space, tight integration with SkyDrive, and several other additional perks. However, the subscription version requires a yearly fee instead of a one-time fee. At the time of this writing, the Office 365 version is competitively priced to be cheaper for many people despite the yearly fee. Furthermore, many different packages for Office 2013 exist from Home to Enterprise for both the traditional and Office 365 versions. Each package contains a different combination of the applications and options available in Office 2013. Ultimately, the decision on which version to purchase depends on your needs and personal situation. For the latest in pricing and options, you can visit **http://office.microsoft.com**.

Using Office 2013 on a Mac

Traditionally, Office is available in different suites for Macs and also came later in time than the PC version. For example, Office 2010 (PC version) was followed by Office 2011 (Mac version). Typically, Access has not been supported on Mac versions of Office. According to the Microsoft website at the time of writing this text, Microsoft stated that the Office 365 Home Premium version of Office will support a Mac installation when the full version is available. Importantly, the Office 365 Home Premium includes Access.

Two other popular options exist for using Office 2013 on a Mac—virtualization and dual boot. Virtualization of Office on a Mac is software that mimics Windows. Many different applications provide virtualization. In any major search engine, search for "PC virtualization on Mac" and you will find many software options for emulating a PC on a Mac. While many virtualization programs promise to mimic entirely, there can be some—usually minor—differences.

Dual boot is the ability to choose the operating system on startup. **Bootcamp** is the Mac software that allows the user to decide which operating system to launch on Intel chip-based Macs. The computer has both the Mac operating system and Windows installed. When the computer is turned on, the user is given the choice of operating system. Thus, the user can be running Windows. If Office is installed on the Windows partition, then Office can run the same as it does on any PC.

You should consult your instructor about the policy in your course. Policies on the usage of the Mac operating system and the Mac versions of Office vary greatly from course to course and school to school. Your instructor will be best able to advise you on what is acceptable for you.

Obtaining a Microsoft Account

Before you get started, Office 2013 requires users to sign in with a Microsoft account that comes with a free SkyDrive account, as shown in Figure 1. This typically will be an account for either the Microsoft Hotmail or Live domain. The Microsoft account gives you free e-mail and tracks your licenses for Microsoft applications. If you have used

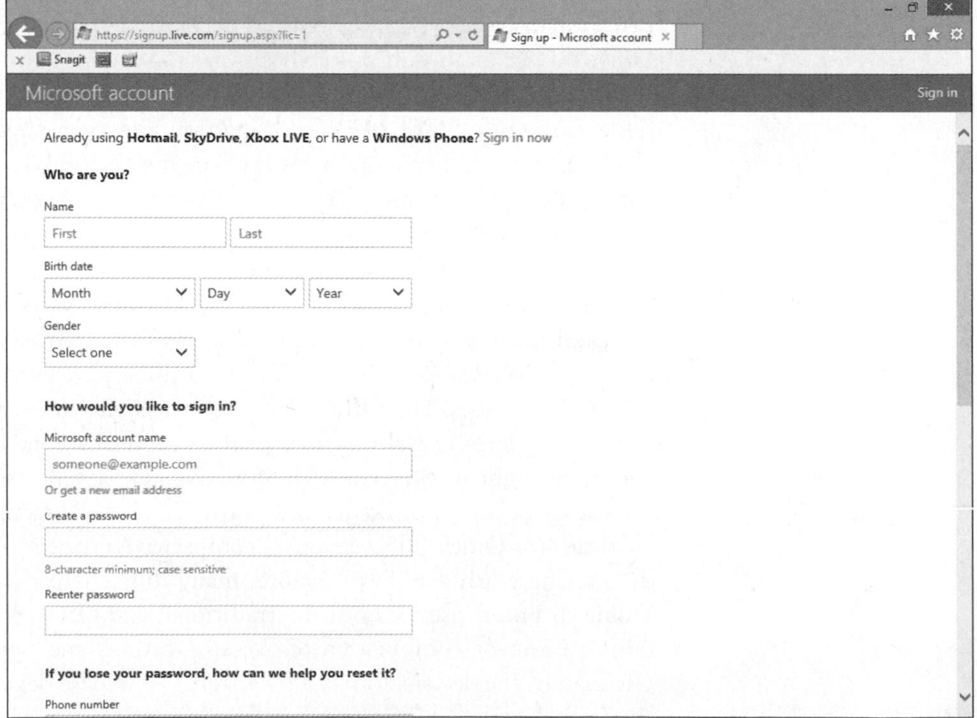

Figure 1 Microsoft account sign up page

Hotmail, SkyDrive, Xbox Live, or Windows phone in the past, you may already have a Microsoft account. The SkyDrive portion of the account is an online storage and collaboration cloud space. As of this writing, you are provided with 7+ GB of online cloud file storage on SkyDrive, additional storage is available for purchase. Microsoft has designed Office 2013 and SkyDrive to complement one another and is discussed in more detail later in this workshop.

If you are working in a computer lab or enterprise version of Windows 8, you may not need to sign into a Microsoft account to run Office or Windows 8. If you are running it on a personal computer, you will need to have a Microsoft account. You can create the account when you install Windows 8. If you install Office 2013 on an earlier version of Windows, you may need to sign up for an account. To sign up for an account, go to **https://signup.live.com** and follow the on-screen instructions. Your first name, last name, and profile image for your Microsoft account will appear in various screens of Windows and Microsoft Office.

Start Office Programs and Manipulate Windows

Office programs can start from the Windows 8 Start screen, as shown in Figure 2, or from search results. Windows 8 contains robust searching capabilities from the Search charm. The **Windows Start screen** is the main interface to launch applications, and it replaces the Windows 7 start button. The Windows **charms** are a specific and consistent set of buttons to users in every application: search, share, connect, settings, and start. Additionally, the procedure for opening an application via searching is the same no matter the configuration of the computer you are using. If you launch the application from the Windows 8 Start screen, the location of the application tile is dependent on the other applications installed on the computer and the applications pinned to the Start screen. On a personal computer you may prefer to use the Windows Start screen, but in a computer lab or unfamiliar computer the search method may be preferable.

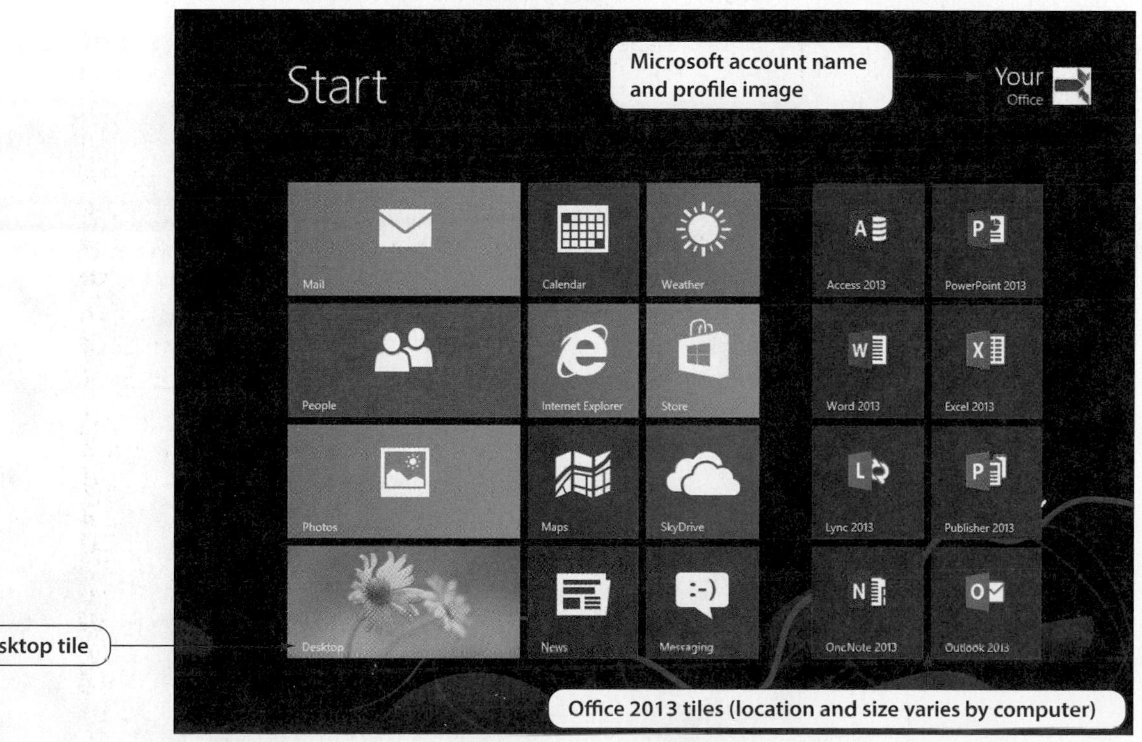

Figure 2 Windows Start screen

In addition to the Windows Start screen, each application has its own specific application Start screen, as shown in Figure 3. From the **Application Start screen**, you can select a blank document, workbook, presentation, database, or one of many application specific templates. Files that have already been created can also be opened from this screen. When existing files are double-clicked from a File Explorer window, the Start screen is not needed and does not open.

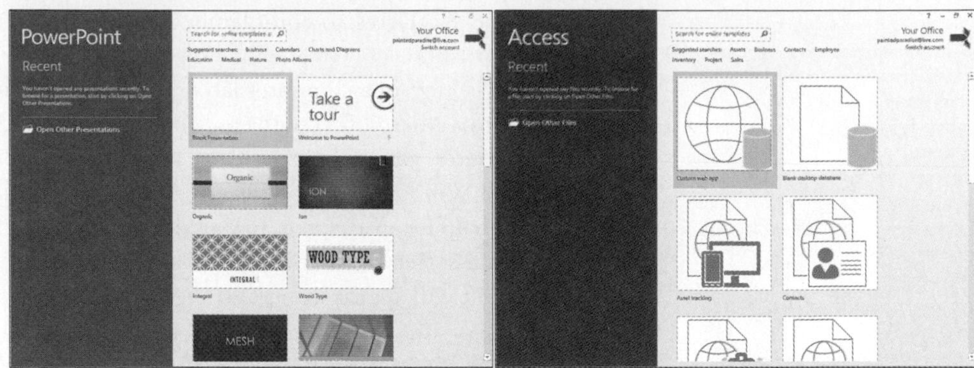

Figure 3 Application Start screens—PowerPoint and Access

Opening the Microsoft Word Start Screen

In the next exercise, you will use the search method to open the Word Start screen and start a new Word document. You will use this new document to start a template for meeting minutes with Susan Brock, the gift shop manager.

MyITLab®
Workshop 1 Training

CF01.01

To Open the Word Start Screen and Start a New Document

a. Click the **Start screen** or desktop, point to the **bottom-right corner** of the screen. The charms will be displayed on the right side of the screen.

b. Note the labels underneath each of the charms. Click the **Search** charm.

SIDE NOTE
Alternate Method
Clicking a tile on the Windows Start screen will also open the application. Whereas, searching also finds unpinned applications.

Figure 4 Windows Start screen with Charms

c. Click the **Search** box at the top of the page. Type Word.

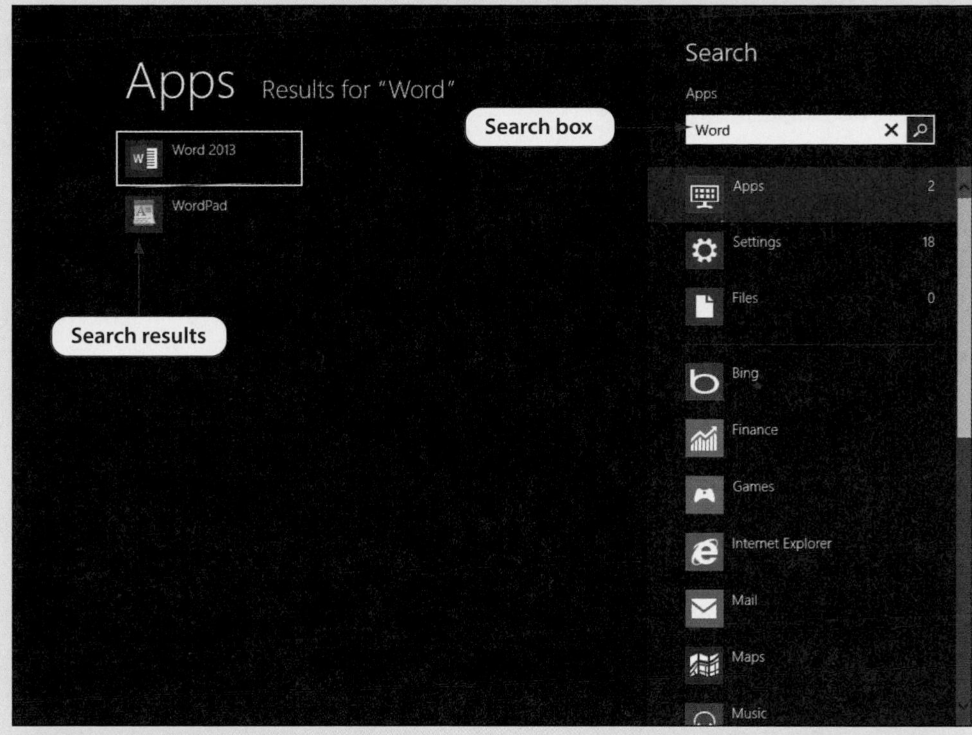

Figure 5 Windows Search screen

d. Click **Word 2013** in the search results. The Word Start screen is displayed when Word is launched.

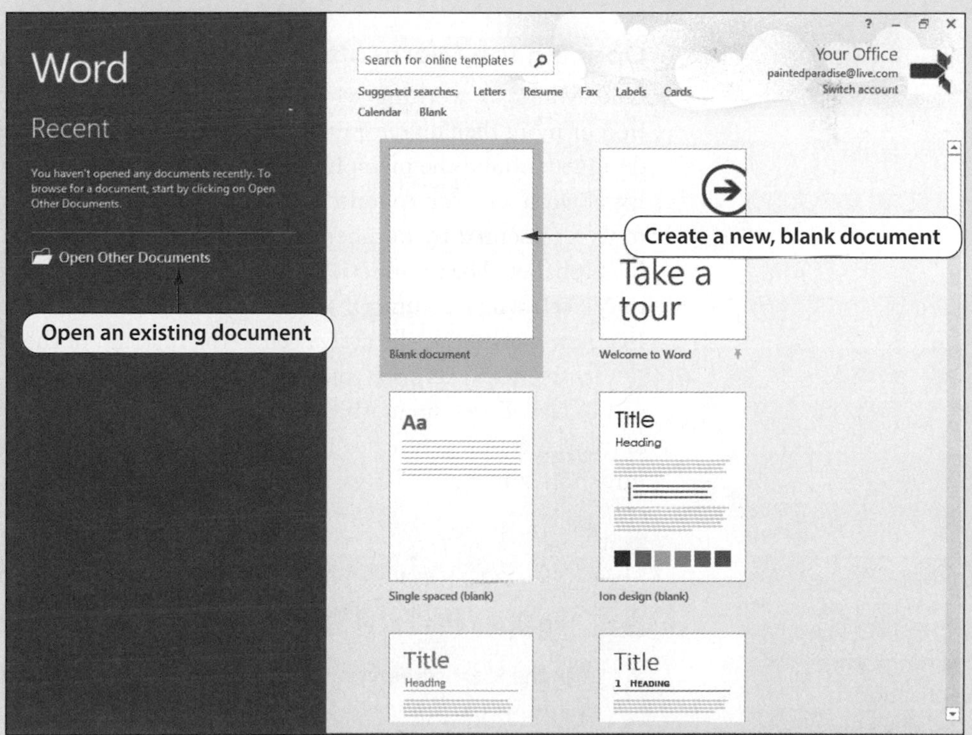

Figure 6 Word Start screen

e. Click **Blank document**.

Notice this opens a blank document—a blank piece of paper. The insertion point is at the first character of the first line.

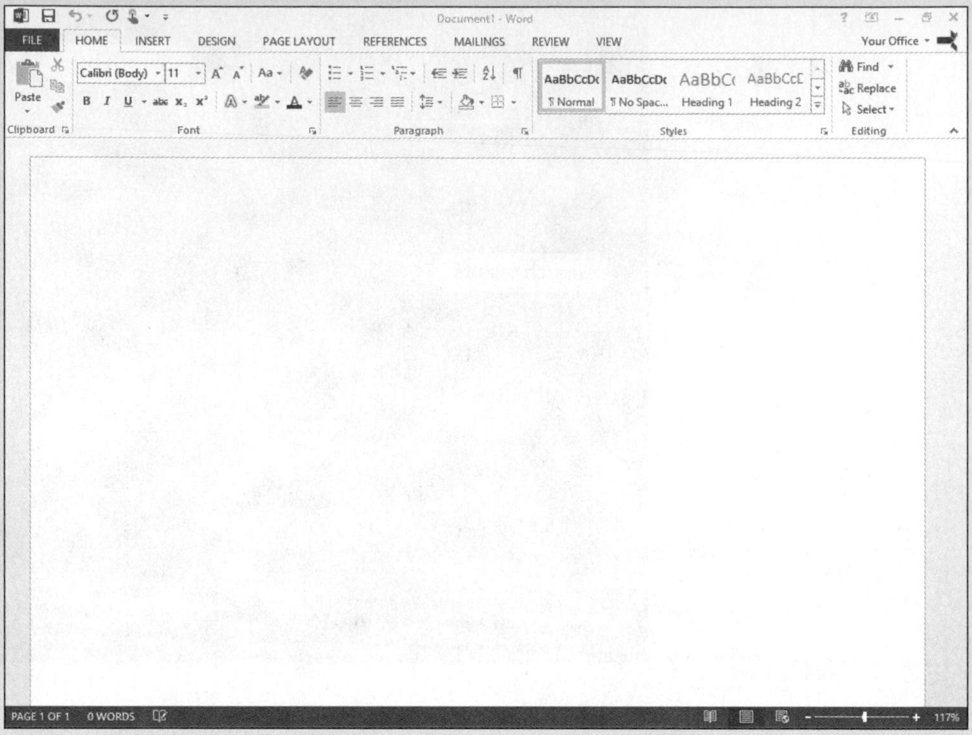

Figure 7 Blank Word document

Opening the Microsoft Excel Start Screen

Once you start working with these applications, you can have more than one application or more than one instance of the same application open at a time. Microsoft Excel is designed around the metaphor of a book. An Excel file is referred to as a workbook. Each Excel workbook can contain many different worksheets—pages in a book. Each sheet has rows represented by numbers. Further, each sheet has columns represented by letters of the alphabet. The intersection of any row and column is a cell. For example, cell B2 refers to the cell where column B and row 2 cross. The active cell is the currently selected cell. In a new worksheet, the active cell is the first cell of the first row, cell A1.

In the next exercise, you will use the search method to open the Excel Start screen and a new Excel spreadsheet. You will use this new document to start a budget for employee training lunches that you will finish in your meeting with Susan Brock, the gift shop manager.

SIDE NOTE
Opening Other Applications
In Windows 8, you can open any of the other Office 2013 application with this search method.

CF01.02

To Open the Excel Start Screen and Start a New Spreadsheet

a. Click the **Start screen** or desktop, point to the **bottom-right corner** of the screen. The charms will be displayed on the right side of the screen.

b. Point your mouse over the **charms** and note the labels that appear. Click the **Search** charm.

c. Click the **Search** box at the top of the page. Type Excel.

d. Click **Excel 2013** in the search results.

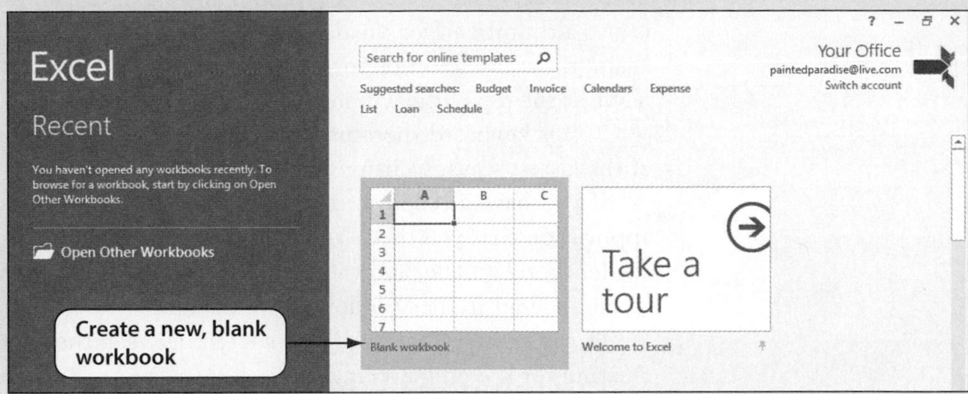

Figure 8 Excel Start screen

e. Click **Blank workbook**.

Notice this opens a blank workbook with one worksheet named Sheet1. The active cell is A1.

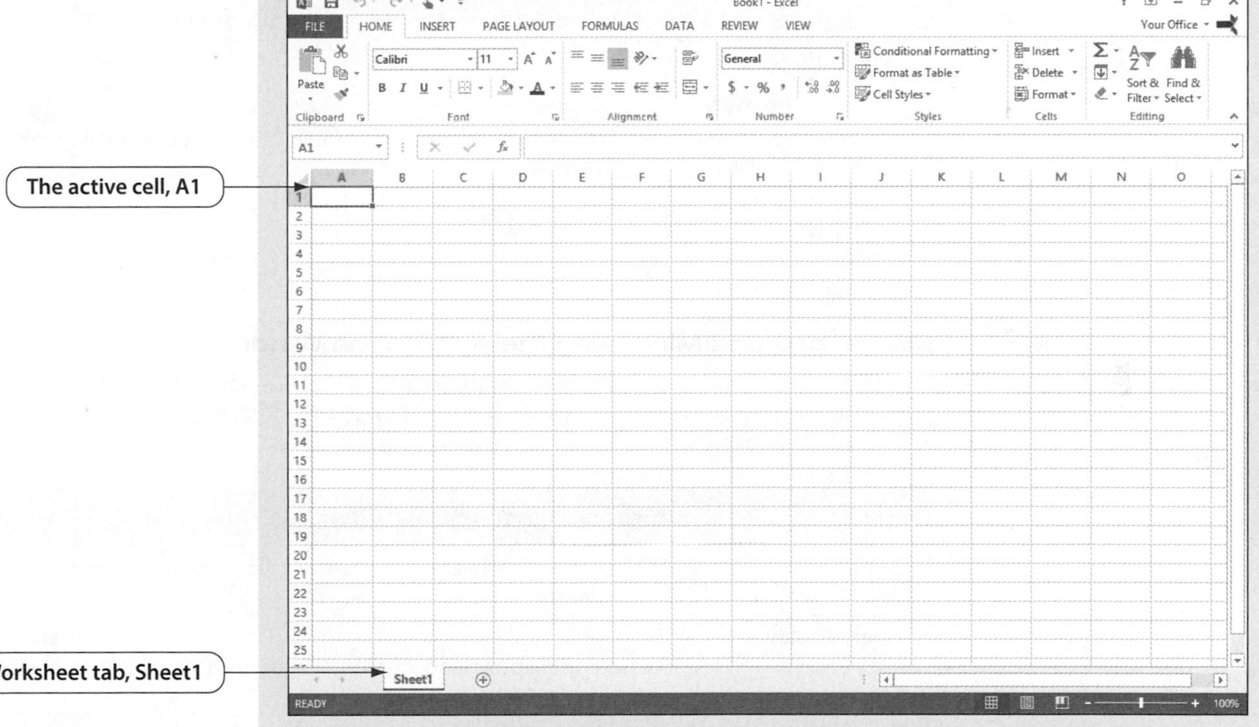

Figure 9 Blank Excel workbook

Switching Between Open Programs and Files

When two or more programs are running at the same time, you can also access them through the taskbar buttons. When moving your mouse pointer over a taskbar icon for an open program, a **thumbnail** or small picture of the open application file is displayed. This is a useful feature when two or more files are open for the same application. A thumbnail of each open file for that application is displayed, and you simply click the file thumbnail that you want to make the active application.

As an alternative to using the thumbnails, you can use the keyboard shortcut to move between applications by holding down Alt and pressing Tab. A small window appears in the center of the screen with thumbnails representing each of the open programs. There is also a thumbnail for the desktop. If you keep Alt pressed down, and then press Tab again, the active selection toggles and previews the selected open application. The program name at the top of the window indicates the program that will be active when you release Alt. This keyboard shortcut is particularly useful when giving presentations as it is one of the fastest ways to change the active application.

If you have a touch screen, you can also use a left bezel swipe to switch to the last application that you used. You can also show all open applications by swiping out from the left bezel a little, and then swipe back to the left bezel. Touch gestures are explained in more detail in the Windows 8 workshop.

In the next exercise, you will switch between the document and spreadsheet you are creating for the gift shop manager.

CF01.03

To Switch Between Open Programs and Files

a. Press Alt + Tab at the same time. Notice the active application changes to Word.

b. On the taskbar, point to **Excel**, and then observe the thumbnail of the Excel file.

c. Click the **Book1 - Excel** thumbnail to make sure the Book1 workbook is the current active program.

d. Click cell **A6**, type Budget and then press Tab.

Later, you intend to add the gift shop logo. Thus, you left the first five rows blank and started in cell A6. Notice the active cell is now A7.

e. In cell **B6**, type 500, and then press Enter.

Maximizing and Minimizing the Application Window

One feature common among all of the application's Ribbon is the five buttons that appear in the top-right corner of an application's title bar as shown in Table 1.

Button	Keyboard Shortcut	Action
Help	F1 (specific to active cursor location)	Opens Microsoft Help
Ribbon Display Options	Ctrl+F1 (toggles between collapsing and showing the Ribbon)	Auto-Hide Ribbon, Display Tabs, and Display Tabs and Commands
Minimize	Alt+Spacebar	Hides a window so it is only visible on the taskbar
Restore Down and **Maximize**	Alt+Spacebar	When the window is at its maximum size, the button will restore the window to a previous, smaller size. When a window is in the Restore Down mode, the button expands the window to its full size.
Close	Alt+F4	Closes a file. Closes all files and **exits** the program if no other files are open for that program.

Table 1 Top-right Ribbon buttons

These buttons offer you the flexibility to size and arrange the windows to suit your purpose or to minimize a window and remove it from view. The largest workspace is when the window is maximized. If several applications are opened, the windows can be arranged using the Restore Down button so several windows can be viewed at the same time. If you are not working on an application and want to have it remain open, the Minimize button will hide the application on the taskbar.

In the next exercise, you will manipulate the sizing of the document and spreadsheet you are creating for the gift shop manager.

CF01.04

To Minimize, Maximize, and Restore Down the Windows

a. On the **Excel** title bar, click **Minimize** to reduce the program window to an icon on the taskbar. The Word window will now be the active window in view.

b. On the **Word** title bar, click the **Restore Down** button. Notice the window becomes smaller and can be resized by clicking and dragging at the corners.

c. Click **Maximize** to expand the Word program window to fill the screen.

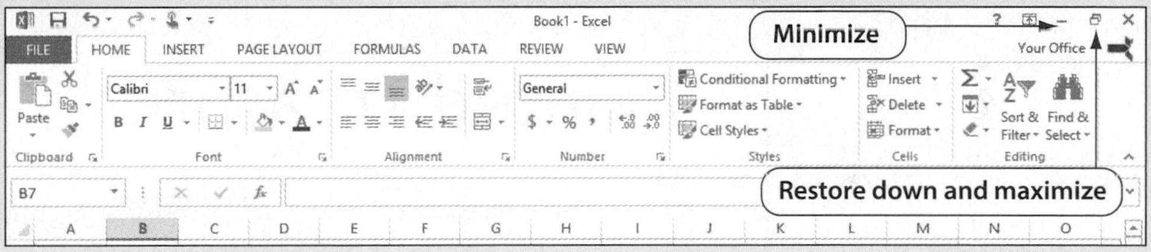

Minimize

Restore down and maximize

Figure 10 Minimize, Maximize, and Restore Down buttons

d. Click **Excel** on the taskbar to make Excel the active program. Notice the workbook is maximized.

Zooming and Scrolling

To get a closer look at the content within the program, you can zoom in. Alternatively, if you would like to see more of the contents, you can zoom out. Keep in mind that the Zoom level only affects your view of the document on the monitor and does not affect the printed output of the document, similarly to using a magnifying glass to see something bigger—the print on the page is still the same size. Therefore, the zoom level should not be confused with how big the text will print—it only affects your view of the document on the screen.

On the right side of the status bar is a slide control that permits zooming in Word from 10% to 500%. The plus and minus propose an easy method, or you can drag the Zoom Slider. In Excel and PowerPoint the zoom range is from 10% to 400%. When using zoom, sometimes text is shifted off the viewing screen. Depending on the program and the Zoom level, you might see the vertical or horizontal scroll bars, or both scroll bars, which can be used to adjust what is displayed in the window. The scroll bars have arrows that can be clicked to shift the workspace in small increments in a specific direction and a scroll box that can be dragged to move a workspace in larger increments. Lastly, touch screens allow you to zoom in and out using pinch and stretch gestures.

In the next exercise, you will zoom in and out on the document you are creating for the gift shop manager.

CF01.05

To Zoom and Scroll in Office Applications

a. On the taskbar, click **Word**. On the Word title bar, if necessary, click **Maximize** to expand the Word program window to fill the screen.

b. The insertion point should be at the beginning of the blank document and the cursor should be blinking. Type Painted Treasures.

> **Troubleshooting**
> If you made any typing errors, you can press Backspace to remove the typing errors and then retype the text.

SIDE NOTE
Methods for Zooming
Several ways exist to zoom Office applications: Zoom Slider, View tab in the Zoom group, Ctrl and a mouse wheel, and touch gestures.

c. On the Word status bar, drag the **Zoom Slider** to the right until it reaches 500%. The document is enlarged to its largest size. This makes the text appear larger. Scroll to see the words **Painted Treasures**, if necessary.

d. On the Word status bar, click **500%**. Notice, this percentage is the Zoom level button that opens the Zoom dialog box. This dialog box provides options for custom and preset settings.

Figure 11 Zoom controls and dialog box

e. Click **Page width**, and then click **OK**.
The Word document zooms to its page width. Notice that this zoom level will give you the maximum size without creating a horizontal scroll bar.

Use the Office Ribbon, Contextual Tools, and Other Menus

Office has a consistent design and layout that helps make it welcoming and comfortable to the user. Once you learn to use one Office 2013 program, you can use many of those skills when working with other Office programs. The **Ribbon** is the row of tabs with buttons across the top of the application. The Ribbon may be open as shown in Figure 12 or hidden. Your Ribbon may look different than as shown in Figure 12. The Ribbon will change based on the screen resolution of your monitor. This text shows all figures with a 1024×768 screen resolution.

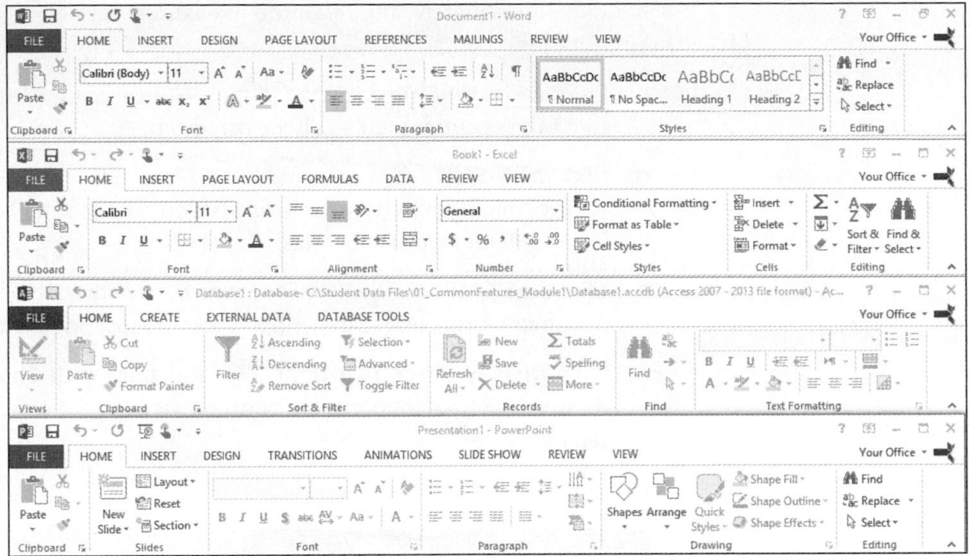

Figure 12 Ribbons of Word, Excel, Access, and PowerPoint

Each Office application's Ribbon has two tabs in common: the File tab and the Home tab. The File tab is the first tab on the Ribbon and is used for file management needs. When clicked, it opens a menu that provides access to the file-level features, such as saving a file, creating a new file, opening an existing file, printing a file, and closing a file, as well as program options. The Home tab is the second tab and contains the commands for the most frequently performed activities, including copying, cutting, and pasting; changing fonts and styles; and other various editing and formatting tools. The commands on these tabs may differ from program to program. Other tabs are program specific, such as the Formulas tab in Excel, the Design tab in PowerPoint, and the Database Tools tab in Access.

Using the Ribbon Tabs

You can enlarge your workspace by collapsing the Ribbon. The Ribbon Display Options button is located in the top-right corner of the window. In the next exercise, you will change the Ribbon display options and format the meeting minutes document using the Home tab.

CF01.06

To Change Ribbon Display Options

a. In Word, click the **Ribbon Display Options** button, and then click **Show Tabs**. Notice that the Ribbon collapses, but the tabs are still visible.

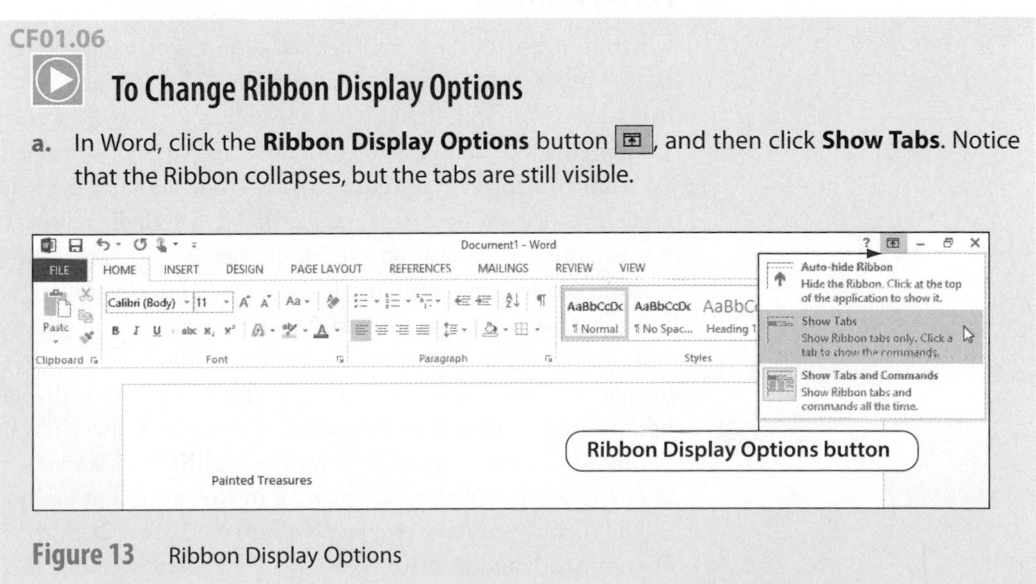

Figure 13 Ribbon Display Options

b. Click immediately after **Painted Treasures**, and then press Enter. Type Meeting Minutes.

c. Point to the **INSERT** tab on the Ribbon. Notice that the INSERT tab is in a different color font but the current tab is still the active tab.

d. Click the **INSERT** tab.
   The INSERT tab is now the active tab on the Ribbon. This tab provides easy access to insert different types of objects.

e. Click the **HOME** tab. The HOME tab is now the active tab on the Ribbon. If you click in the document again, notice that Ribbon commands toggle out of view again.

f. Click **Display Ribbon Options**, and then click **Show Tabs and Commands** to return the Ribbon options into constant view—or alternatively, double-click any of the tab names.

REAL WORLD ADVICE | **How Buttons and Groups Appear on the Ribbon**

If you noticed that your Ribbon appears differently from one computer to the next—the buttons and groups might seem condensed in size—there could be a few factors at play. The most common causes could be monitor size, lower screen resolution, or a reduced program window. Since the Ribbon changes to accommodate the size of the window or screen, buttons can appear as icons without labels and a group can be condensed into a button that must be clicked to display the group options. So, do not worry! All of the same features are on the Ribbon and in the same general area.

CONSIDER THIS | **Advantages of a Common Interface**

The Ribbon provides a common user interface. This common interface can help you learn additional applications quickly. What elements have you noticed that are common? What elements have you noticed that are different? Of the elements that are different, how are they still presented in a common way?

Using Buttons

Clicking a button will produce an action. For example, the Font group on the Home tab includes buttons for bold and italic. Clicking any of these buttons will produce an intended action. So, if you have selected text that you want to apply bold formatting to, simply click the Bold button and bold formatting is applied to the selected text.

Some buttons are **toggle buttons**—one click turns the feature on and a second click turns the feature off. When a feature is toggled on, the button remains highlighted. For example, in Word, on the Home tab in the Paragraph group, click the Show/Hide button. Notice paragraph marks appear in your document, and the button is highlighted to show that the feature is turned on. This feature displays characters that do not print. This allows you to see items in the document that can help to troubleshoot a document's formatting, such as when Tab is pressed an arrow is displayed, or when Spacebar is pressed dots appear between words. Click the Show/Hide button again, and the feature is turned off. The button is no longer highlighted, and the paragraph characters, as well as any other nonprinting characters, in the document are no longer displayed.

Some buttons have two parts: a button that accesses the most commonly used setting or command, and an arrow that opens a gallery menu of all related commands or options for that particular task or button. For example, on the Home tab in the Font group, the Font Color button includes the different colors that are available for fonts. If you click the button, the default is to apply the last color used. Notice the last used color is also displayed on the icon. To access the gallery menu for other color options, click the arrow next to the Font Color button. Whenever you see an arrow next to a button, this is an indicator that more options are available.

The two buttons on your mouse operate in a similar fashion. The left mouse click performs an action. The right-click—or right mouse button—will never perform an action, but rather provides more options. The options that appear on the shortcut menu when you right-click change depending on the location of the mouse pointer.

In the next exercise, you will format the gift shop meeting minutes using bold and font color.

CF01.07

To Use Buttons

SIDE NOTE
Text Selection
To select a single word, you can double-click the word to select it or triple-click for the entire paragraph. You can also use Shift and arrow keys to select text.

a. In Word, click immediately before **Meeting Minutes** to position the insertion point to the left of the word **Meeting**, and then press and hold the left mouse button and drag to the right to select the words **Meeting Minutes**.

b. On the HOME tab, in the Font group, click **Bold** B. This will toggle on the Bold command. Notice that the bold button is now highlighted and the selected text is displayed in bold format.

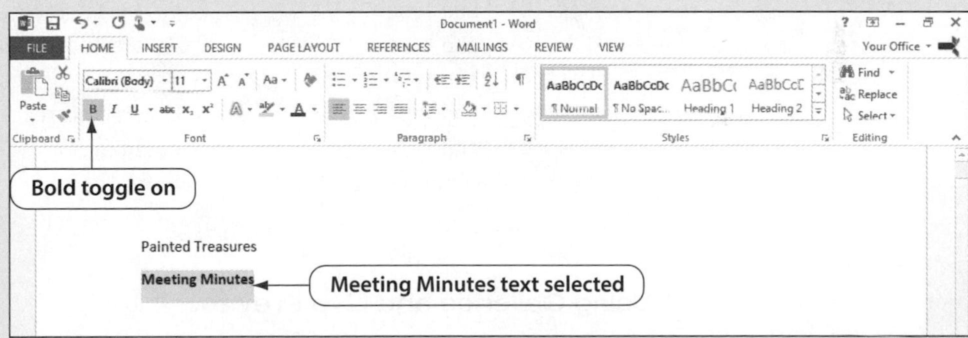

Figure 14 Bold toggled on with text highlighted

SIDE NOTE
Live Preview
Live Preview shows how formatting looks before you apply it. This feature is available for many of the gallery libraries.

c. With the text selected, on the HOME tab, in the Font group, click the **Font Color** arrow A. Under Standard Colors, point to, but do not click, **Dark Red**—under standard colors it is the first one. Notice the Live Preview feature that shows how the selected document text will change color. As the mouse pointer hovers over a color, a ScreenTip appears to show the color name.

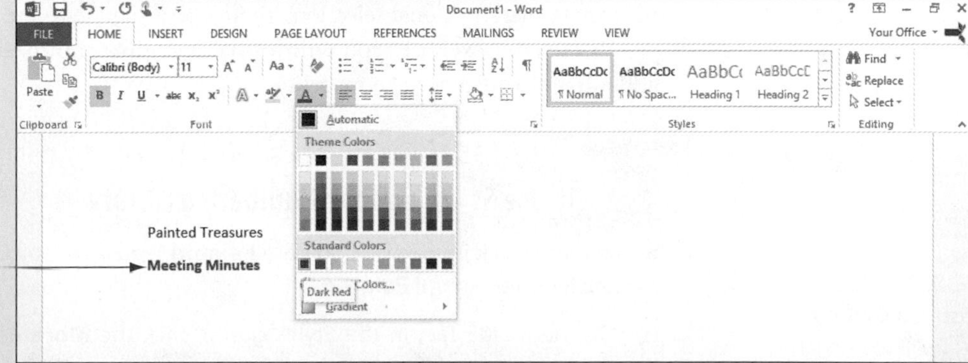

Figure 15 Live Preview of font color

d. Click **Dark Red**. The selected text should now be bold and dark red.

e. Click after **Meeting Minutes** to place your cursor after the end of the word **Minutes**. Notice that the Bold button is still highlighted and the Font Color button is shows Dark Red. Thus, any text you type right now will be bold and dark red.

f. In the Font group, click **Bold** [B] to toggle Bold off. Then, click the **Font Color** arrow [A▾], and then select **Automatic**.

g. Press [Enter]. Type your first name and last name.

REAL WORLD ADVICE Using Keyboard Shortcuts and Key Tips

Keyboard shortcuts are extremely useful, and some are universal to all Windows programs. They keep your hands on the keyboard instead of reaching for the mouse —increasing efficiency and saving time.

Pressing [Alt] will toggle the display of **key tips**—or **keyboard shortcuts**—for items on the Ribbon and Quick Access Toolbar. After displaying the key tips, you can press the letter or number corresponding to request the action from the keyboard.

For multiple key shortcuts, you hold down the first key listed and press the second key once. Some common keyboard shortcuts are listed below.

Press [Ctrl] and type C	Copy the selected item
Press [Ctrl] and type V	Paste a copied item
Press [Ctrl] and type A	Select all the items in a document or window
Press [Ctrl] and type B	Bold selected text
Press [Ctrl] and type Z	Undo an action
Press [Ctrl]+[Home]	Move to the top of the document
Press [Ctrl]+[End]	Move to the end of the document

Using Galleries and Live Preview

Live Preview lets you see the effects of menu selections on your document file or selected item before making a commitment to a particular menu choice. A **gallery** is a set of menu options that appear when you click the arrow next to a button which, in some cases, may be referred to as a More arrow [▿]. The menu or grid shows samples of the available options.

When you point to an option in a gallery, Live Preview shows the results that would occur in your file if you were to click that particular option. Using Live Preview, you can experiment with settings before making a final choice. When you point to a text style in the Styles gallery, the selected text or the paragraph in which the insertion point is located appears with that text style. Moving the pointer from option to option results in quickly seeing what your text will look like before making a final selection. To finalize a change to the selected option, click the style.

In the next exercise, you will format the gift shop meeting minutes using styles and add a list of topics for the meeting.

CF01.08

To Use Styles and the Numbering Library

a. In Word, click immediately before **Painted Treasures** to position the insertion point to the left of the word **Painted**.

b. On the HOME tab, in the Styles group, click the **More** arrow [▿]. This will show all of the options for different styles. Point your mouse to **Title** to see the Live Preview. Then, select **Title** to change the words "Painted Treasures" to Title style. Notice that the style changed the whole line even though you did not select the text.

SIDE NOTE

Closing a Gallery

[Esc] will close a gallery without making a selection. Alternatively, you can click outside the gallery menu.

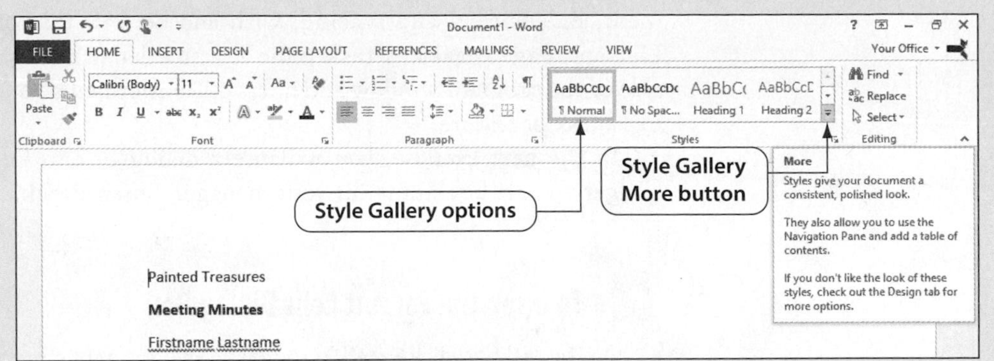

Figure 16 Styles gallery

c. Click immediately after your **last name**, press Enter twice, type Topics, and then press Enter one time.

d. On the HOME tab, in the Paragraph group, click the **Numbering** arrow. The Numbering Library gallery opens. Point to, but do not click, the **third option** in the first row, the number one followed by a closing parenthesis.

e. Select the **Number Alignment: Left** style with **1)**—the third button in the first row.

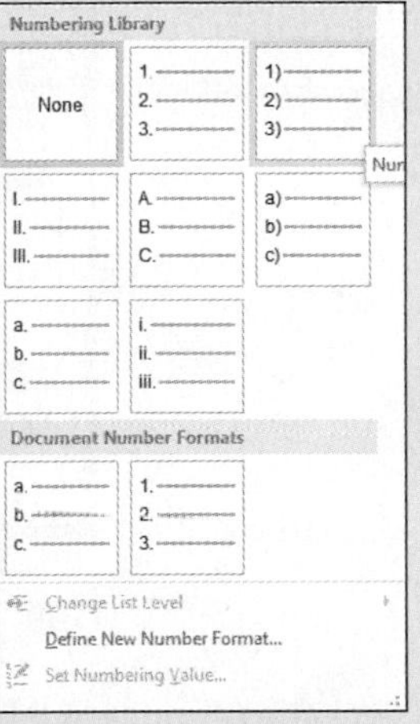

Figure 17 Numbering Library

f. Type Training Lunch Budget - and then press Enter. After the meeting, you intend to type the notes after the dash.

g. Type New Products - and then press Enter twice to end the numbered list.

Opening Dialog Boxes and Task Panes

Some Ribbon groups include a diagonal arrow in the bottom-right corner of the group section, called a **Dialog Box Launcher** that opens a corresponding dialog box or task pane. Hovering the mouse pointer over the Dialog Box Launcher will display a ScreenTip to indicate more information. Click the Dialog Box Launcher to open a **dialog box**, which is a window that provides more options or settings beyond those provided on the Ribbon. It often provides access to more precise or less frequently used commands along with the commands offered on the Ribbon; thus using a dialog box offers the ability to apply many related options at the same time and located in one place. As shown in Figure 18, many dialog boxes organize related information into tabs. In the Paragraph dialog box shown in the figure, the active Indents and Spacing tab shows options to change alignment, indentation, and spacing, with another tab that offers options and settings for Line and Page Breaks. A **task pane** is a smaller window pane that often appears to the side of the program window and offers options or helps you to navigate through completing a task or feature.

In the next exercise, you will use a dialog box to format some of the cells in the budget you are beginning for your manager, Susan Brock.

CF01.09

To Open the Format Cells Dialog Box

a. On the taskbar, click **Excel** to make Excel the active program.

b. Click cell **B6**, the second cell in the sixth row.

c. On the HOME tab, in the Number group, click the **Number Dialog Box Launcher**. The Format Cells dialog box opens with the Number tab displayed.

d. On the Number tab under Category, click **Currency**. Click in the **Decimal places** box, delete the 2, and then type 0.

SIDE NOTE

Check Box and Radio Options

Check boxes allow you to select more than one option in the group. Radio options only allow you to select one.

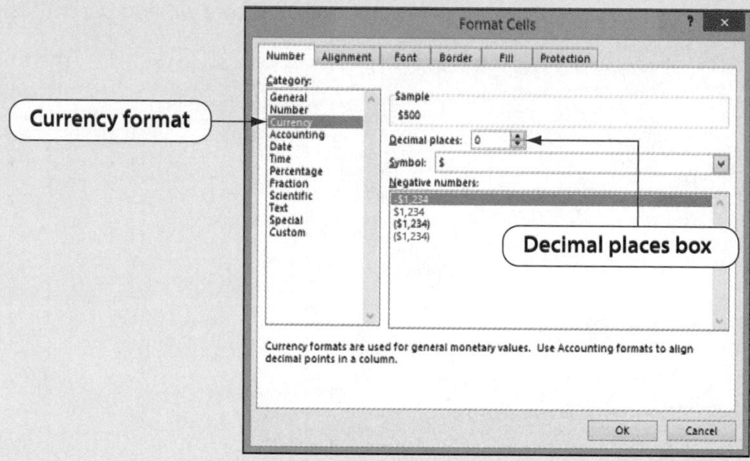

Figure 18 Format Cells Dialog Box

e. Click the **Alignment** tab, click the **Font** tab, and then click the **Border** tab to explore the available options.

f. Click the **Fill** tab. In the second row of colors, click the last **Light Green** color. The light green color will be shown in the Sample box.

g. Click **OK**. The format changes are made to the number, and the fill color is applied.

Inserting Images and Using Contextual Tools

In Word, Excel, PowerPoint, and Publisher, you can insert pictures from a file, a screen shot, or various online sources. The online options include inserting images within the Office Online Pictures collection, via a Bing search, or from your own SkyDrive. The Insert tab contains all of the options for using images in Word, PowerPoint, and Excel.

The term **contextual tools** refers to tools that only appear when needed for specific tasks. Some tabs, toolbars, and menus are displayed as you work and only appear if a particular object is selected. Because these tools become available only as you need them, the workspace remains less cluttered.

A **contextual tab** is a Ribbon tab that contains commands related to selected objects so you can manipulate, edit, and format the objects. Examples of objects that can be selected to produce contextual tabs include a table, a picture, a shape, or a chart. A contextual tab appears to the right of the standard Ribbon tabs. The contextual tab disappears when you click outside the target object—in the file—to deselect the object. In some instances, contextual tabs can also appear as you switch views.

In the next exercise, you will insert a Painted Treasures Gift Shop logo into the budget you are beginning for your manager, Susan Brock. This budget will become a part of Susan's larger budget that she must present to the CEO of Painted Paradise in an internal memo once a year. Logos are an excellent way to brand both internal and external communications.

CF01.10

To Insert an Image

a. In **Excel**, click cell **A1**.

b. Click the **INSERT** tab, and then in the Illustrations group, click **Pictures**. The Insert Picture dialog box opens.

c. Navigate to your student data files, and then click **cf01ws01Logo**. Click the **Insert** button. The Painted Treasures Gift Shop logo is inserted on the worksheet and actively selected. Notice the logo is too large and covers the cells you created in row 6. Also, notice that the FORMAT contextual tab in the PICTURE TOOLS contextual tab group is now the active tab.

d. On the **FORMAT** tab, in the Size group, click in the **Shape Height** box. Delete **2.19**, type 1, and then press Enter. Notice the width automatically adjusts to keep the original image proportions.

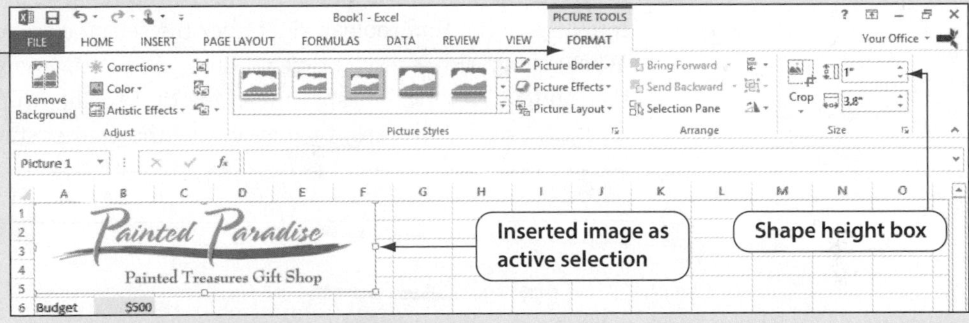

Figure 19 Picture Tools Format contextual tab and shape height

> **Troubleshooting**
> To see a contextual tab, the object relating to the tab must be selected. If you do not see it, click the image to reselect the image.

e. Click cell **A7**. Notice that the contextual tab disappears.

Accessing the Mini Toolbar

The **Mini toolbar** appears after text is selected and contains buttons for the most commonly used formatting commands, such as font, font size, font color, center alignment, bold, and italic. The Mini toolbar button commands vary for each Office program. The toolbar disappears if you move the pointer away from the toolbar, press a key, or click the workspace. All the commands on the Mini toolbar are available on the Ribbon; however, the Mini toolbar offers quicker access to common commands since you do not have to move the mouse pointer far away from the selected text for these commands.

In the next exercise, you will add some additional information to the budget you are beginning for your manager. You will also edit some of the cells with the Mini toolbar.

CF01.11

To Access the Mini Toolbar

a. Click cell **A8**, the first cell in the eighth row of the worksheet. Type Expenses and then press Enter.

b. In cell **A9**, type Food and then press Enter.

c. In cell **A10**, type Drinks and then press Enter.

d. Click cell **B9**, type 450 and then press Enter. In cell **B10**, type 50.

e. Double-click cell **A8** to place the insertion point in the cell. Double-clicking a cell enables you to enter edit mode for the cell text.

f. Double-click cell **A8** again to select the text. The Mini toolbar appears and comes into view directly above the selected text. If you were to move the pointer off the cell, the Mini toolbar becomes transparent or disappears entirely. When you move the pointer back over the Mini toolbar it may become visible again or you may need to repeat the text selection.

Troubleshooting

If you are having a problem with the Mini toolbar disappearing, you may have inadvertently moved the mouse pointer to another part of the document. If you need to redisplay the Mini toolbar, right-click the selected text and the Mini toolbar will appear along with a shortcut menu. Once you select an option on the Mini toolbar, the shortcut menu will disappear and the Mini toolbar will remain while in use—or repeat the prior two steps, then make sure the pointer stays over the toolbar.

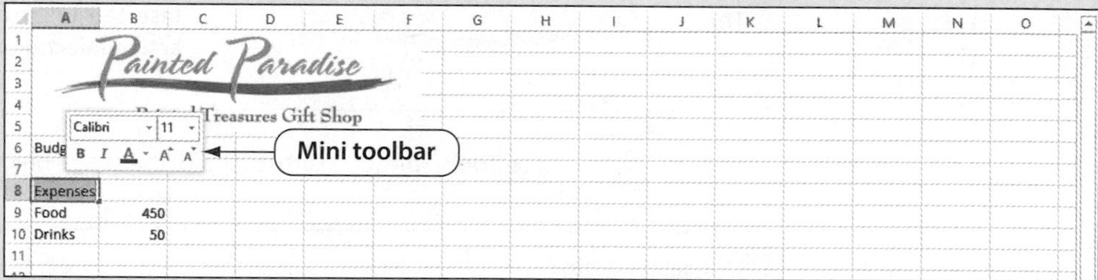

Figure 20 Mini toolbar

g. On the Mini toolbar, click **Italic** *I*.

h. Press Enter. Cell A9 is now selected.

The Mini toolbar is particularly helpful with the touch interface. When Office recognizes that you are using touch instead of a mouse or digitizer pen, it creates Mini toolbars that are larger and designed to work with fingers more easily. An example of a touch Mini toolbar in Excel touch mode is shown in Figure 21.

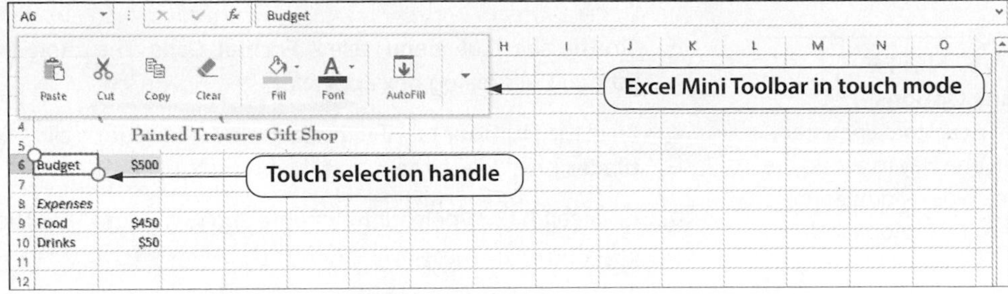

Figure 21 Excel Mini toolbar in touch mode

Using Shortcut Menus

Shortcut menus are also context sensitive and enable you to quickly access commands that are most likely needed in the context of the task being performed. A **shortcut menu** is a list of commands related to a selection that appears when you right-click—click the right mouse button. This means you can access popular commands without using the Ribbon. Included are commands that perform actions, commands that open dialog boxes, and galleries of options that provide Live Preview. As noted previously, the Mini toolbar opens when you click the right mouse button. If you click a button on the Mini toolbar, the shortcut menu closes, and the Mini toolbar remains open allowing you to continue formatting your selection.

In the next exercise, you will add some additional information to the budget you are beginning for your manager. You will also edit some of the cells with a shortcut menu.

CF01.12

To Use the Shortcut Menu to Add Currency Formatting

a. Click cell **B9**, hold down your left mouse button, and then drag down to cell **B10** to select both B9 and B10. Right-click the selected range, **B9:B10**. A shortcut menu opens with commands related to common tasks you can perform in a cell, along with the Mini toolbar.

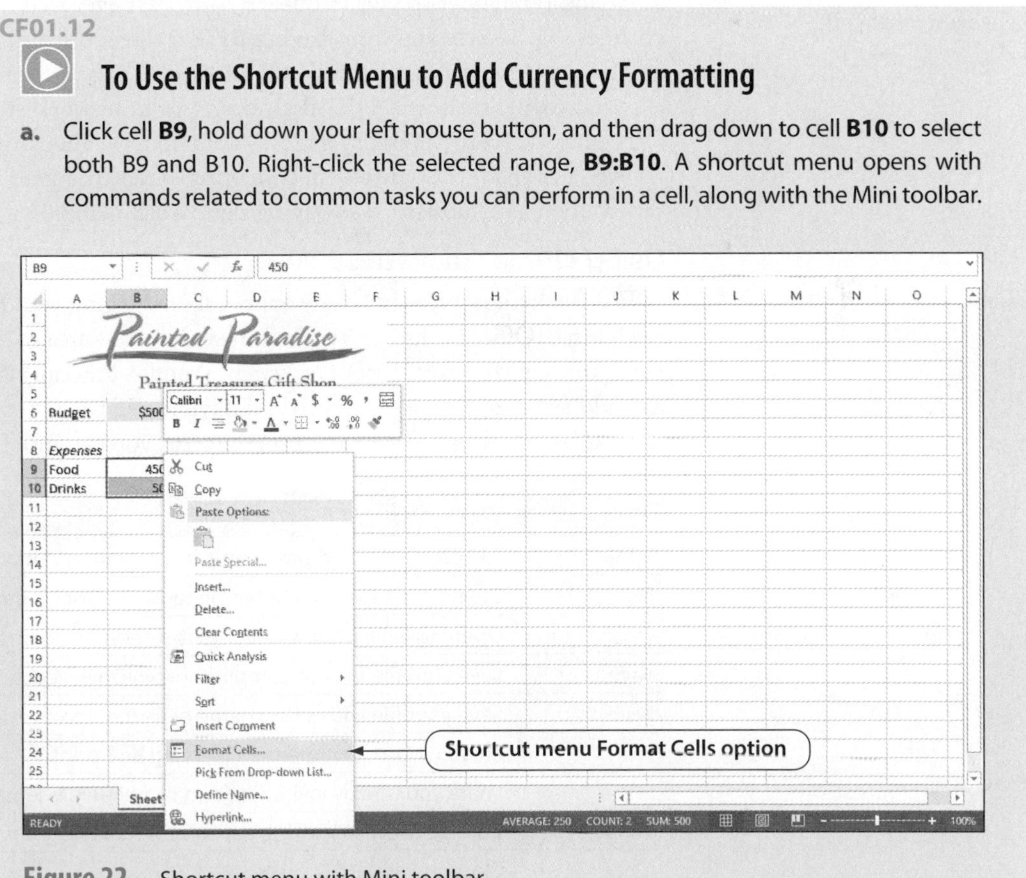

Figure 22 Shortcut menu with Mini toolbar

SIDE NOTE
Many Options!
Office can contain more than one way to access the same type of formatting, dialog box, or options.

b. On the shortcut menu, select **Format Cells**. The shortcut menu closes, and then the Format Cells dialog box appears.

c. Click the **Number** tab, if necessary. Under Category, click **Currency**. Click in the **Decimal places** box, delete the 2, and then type 0. Click **OK**.

d. Click cell **A13**, type your first name and last name, and then press Enter.

Manipulating Files and Finding Help in Office

Creating, opening, saving, closing, troubleshooting, and printing files are common everyday tasks performed in any Office program. Most of these tasks can all be accessed from the File tab. These processes are basically the same for all the Office programs. When you start a program, you either have to create a new file or open an existing one. Since Office has a common interface, learning a new Office application is easy as long as you can find help when needed. In this section, you will use Office Help, making it easy to learn more.

Manage Files in Office

While working on an Office file, whether creating a new file or modifying an existing file, your work is stored in the temporary memory on your computer, not on the hard drive or your USB flash drive. Any work done will be lost if you were to exit the program, turn off the computer, or experience a power failure without saving your work or the program automatically saving your work. To prevent losing your work, you need to save your work and remember to save frequently—at least every 10 minutes or after adding several changes. That saves you from having to re-create any work you did prior to the last save.

You can save files to the hard drive, which is located inside the computer; to an external drive, such as a USB flash drive; to a network storage device; or to SkyDrive. Office has an **AutoRecovery** feature—previously called AutoSave—that will attempt to recover any changes made to a document if something goes wrong, but this should not be relied upon as a substitute for saving your work manually.

Using Office Backstage View

Office Backstage View has many options for managing your files in Office and is accessed via the File tab. Office Backstage View now includes a new area called Account. This enables you to log in to your Microsoft account or switch accounts. You can also see a list of connected services and add services, such as LinkedIn and SkyDrive. Save & Send has been replaced by Export and has been downsized. Table 2 lists the areas you can modify in Office Backstage View.

Area	Description
Info	File properties and protecting, inspecting, and managing versions of the file
New	Creating a new blank or template-based document
Open	Opening a file from your computer, recent documents list, or SkyDrive account
Save	Save your file to your computer or SkyDrive account
Save As	Save your file with a new name or format to your computer or SkyDrive account
Print	Preview your document for printing and print
Share	Share your file by invitation, e-mail, online presentation, or blog post
Export	Change the file type or create a PDF/XPS document
Close	Close the file
Account	User and Production information including connected services
Options	Launches the Application Options dialog box with many options including advanced options

Table 2 Office Backstage View

Saving a File

In addition to Office Backstage View, Office provides several ways to save a file. To quickly save a file, simply click Save [icon] on the Quick Access Toolbar or use the keyboard shortcut of pressing Ctrl and then pressing S. The **Quick Access Toolbar** is the series of small icons in the top-left corner that can be customized to offer commonly used buttons. There are two different Save icons to show whether you are saving to your computer or to SkyDrive. When saving to SkyDrive, the Save icon looks more like a syncing icon.

The first time you save a new file, it behaves the same as the Save As command where the Save As dialog box opens. This allows you to specify the save options. In the Save As dialog box, you can name the file and specify the location to save it, similar to the first time you save a file. Once you save a file, the simple shortcut methods to save any changes to the file work fine to update the existing file. No dialog box will open to save after the first time—as long as you do not need to change the file name or location as with the Save As command.

A file name includes the name you specify and a **file extension** assigned by the Office program to indicate the file type. The file extension may or may not be visible depending on your computer settings. You can check your computer's setting in the File Explorer window under the View tab in the Show/hide group. The check box for File name extensions should be checked to see file extension as shown in Figure 23. Each Office program adds a period and a file extension after the file name to identify the program in which that file was created. Table 3 shows the common default file extensions for Office 2013.

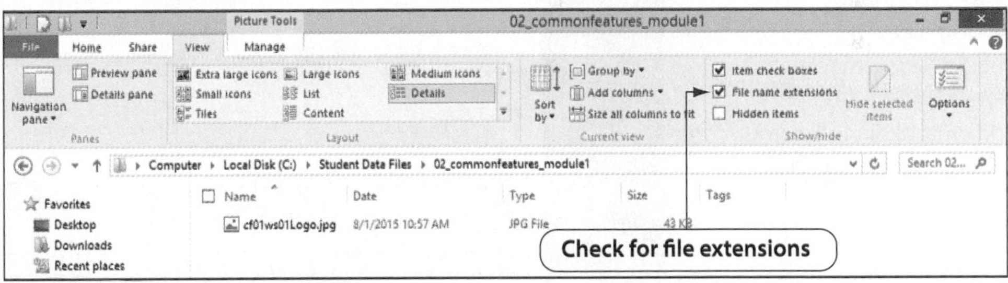

Figure 23 File Explorer file extension setting

Application	Extension
Word 2013	.docx
Excel 2013	.xlsx
PowerPoint 2013	.pptx
Access 2013	.accdb

Table 3 Office 2013 default file extensions

REAL WORLD ADVICE **Sharing Files Between Office Versions**

Different Office versions are not always compatible. The general rule is that files created in an older version can always be opened in a newer version, but not the other way around—a 2013 Office file is not easily opened in versions of Office prior to Office 2007. Sharing files with Office 2003 users is a concern because different file extensions were used. For example, .doc was used for Word files instead of docx, .xls instead of .xlsx for Excel, and so on.

It is still possible to save the Office 2013 files in a previous format version. To save in one of these formats, use the Save As command, and click the 97-2003 format option. If the file is already in the previous format, it will open in Office 2013 and be saved with the same format in which it was created. If a file is saved with a previous version's extension, it may not save all the new formatting features.

Name your file with a descriptive name that accurately reflects the content of the document, workbook, presentation, or database, such as "January 2014 Budget" or "012014 Minutes". The descriptive name can include uppercase and lowercase letters, numbers, hyphens, spaces, and some special characters—excluding ? "/ | < > * :—in any combination. File names can include a maximum of 255 characters including the extension—this includes the number of characters for the folder names to get to the file location known as the file path. Even though Windows 8 can handle a long file name, some systems cannot. Thus, shorter names can prevent complications when transferring files between different systems.

In the next exercise, you will name and save the files you have been creating for your meeting with your manager.

CF01.13

To Save a File

a. In Excel, click the **FILE** tab. Office Backstage View opens with command options and tabs for managing files, opening existing files, saving, printing, and exiting. Click **Save As**.

SIDE NOTE

Saving a File

The default save location is your SkyDrive account—you must be signed in. You can also save to Computer or Add a Place.

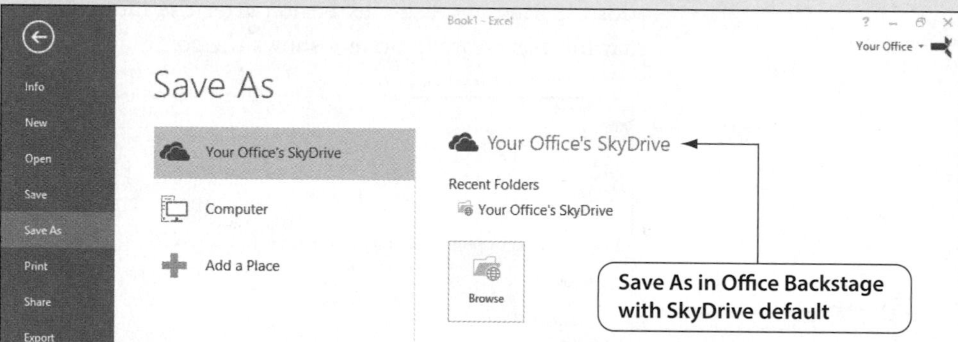

Figure 24 Save As with SkyDrive as default

b. Click **Computer**. Click **Browse**.

This will enable you to select the location on your computer where you are saving your files. The Save As dialog box opens. This provides the opportunity to enter a file-name and a storage location. The default storage location is the Documents folder and the suggested file name is the first few words of the first line of the document.

c. Click the **location** in the left pane, and then navigate through the folder structure to where your student data files are located. Click in the **File name** box, and then select the current suggested file name, if necessary. Navigate to where you are storing your files, and then type cf01ws01Budget_LastFirst using your last and first name in the File name box. Change the Save as type to **Excel Workbook**, if necessary.

This file name describes both the content of the file and the portion of this book that the file is associated. The "Budget" part describes the content. The "cf01ws01" describes Common Features workshop 1.

d. Click the **Save** button. The Save As dialog box closes, Excel returns to the HOME tab, and the name of your file appears in the Excel window title bar.

e. On the taskbar, click **Word** to make Word the active program. Repeat Steps b through d, and then save the file as cf01ws01Minutes_LastFirst using your last and first name.

Modifying Saved Files

Saved files only contain what was in the file the last time it was saved. Any changes made after the file was saved are only stored in the computer's memory and are not saved with the file. It is important to remember to save often—after making changes—so the file is updated to reflect its current contents. One of the most useful shortcuts is the keyboard shortcut for saving, which can be utilized by pressing Ctrl, and then pressing S.

Remember that it is not necessary to use the Save As dialog box once the file has been saved unless you want to save a copy of the file with a different name or you want to store it in a different location.

In the next exercise, you will modify and save the files that you have been creating for your meeting with your manager. You will save them to the same location you saved them to in the last exercise.

CF01.14

To Modify and Save a File to the Previously Saved Location

a. In Word, click below the numbered list to make sure the insertion point is on the last line. Type today's date and then press Enter.

b. Press Ctrl + S. The changes you made to the document have just been saved to the file stored in the location you selected earlier. Recall that no dialog boxes will open for the Save after the first time the document has been saved.

SIDE NOTE
Customize Quick Access
You can customize the Quick Access Toolbar for favorite or common commands such as Print, Spelling & Grammar, or New.

REAL WORLD ADVICE Saving Files

Most programs have an added safeguard or warning dialog box to remind you to save if you attempt to close a file without saving your changes first. Despite that warning, best practice dictates you save files before closing them or exiting a program. If you press the wrong answer on the warning by accident, you will lose work. Remembering to save before you close prevents this kind of accident.

Best practice also dictates saving often. The more often you save the less work you can lose in the event of an unexpected closing of the application. Pressing Ctrl and S only takes a few seconds. Train yourself now to use this keyboard shortcut regularly and often. If you do, it will become second nature and save you from losing work in the future!

Closing a File and Exiting an Application

When you are ready to close a file, you can click the Close command in Office Backstage View. If the file you close is the only file open for that particular program, the program window remains open with no file in the window. You can also close a file by using the Close button ☒ in the top-right corner of the window. However, if that is the only file open, the file and program will close when using that method of closing. If you exit the window, it will close both the file and the program. Exiting programs when you are finished with them helps save system resources and keeps your Windows desktop and taskbar uncluttered, as well as prevents data from being accidentally lost.

In the next exercise, you will modify, save, and close the Meeting Minutes document that you have been creating for your meeting with your manager. You are also finished with Excel. Thus, you will save and exit the budget you prepared.

CF01.15

To Modify and Close a Document

a. In Word, with the insertion point on the line under the date, type your course number and section and then press Enter. The text you typed should appear below the date.

b. Click the **FILE** tab, and then click **Close**. A warning dialog box opens, asking if you want to save the changes made to the document.

c. Click **Save**.

The document closes after saving changes, but the Word program window remains open. You are able to create new files or open previously saved files. If multiple Word documents are open, the document window of the file you just closed will remain open with the other documents that are currently still open in the window.

d. On the taskbar, click **Excel** to make Excel the active program.

e. Press Ctrl + S to save the file to the previous location. Click **Close** X in the top-right corner. Notice that the file closes and you exit the Excel application.

SIDE NOTE

Best Practice

Best practice is to save the file before closing instead of allowing the warning dialog box to prompt for the save.

Opening a File from the Recent Documents List

You create a new file when you open a blank document, workbook, presentation, or database. If you want to work on a previously created file, you must first open it. When you open a file, it copies the file from the file's storage location to the computer's temporary memory and displays it on the monitor's screen. When you save a file, it updates the storage location with the changes. Until then, the file only exists in your computer's memory. If you want to open a second file, while one is open, the keyboard shortcut of pressing Ctrl and then pressing O will open the Open tab of Office Backstage View. If you use the keyboard shortcut of Ctrl+F12 you will launch the Open dialog window without taking you to Office Backstage View.

In Office Backstage View, Office keeps a list of your most recently modified files—**Most Recently Used list**. As the list grows, older files are removed to make room for more recently modified files. You can also pin a frequently used file to always remain at the top of the list. To clear the recent files, right-click any file in the recent files list and select the option to clear unpinned files.

When opening files downloaded from the Internet, accessed from a shared network, or received as an attachment in e-mail, the file usually opens in a read-only format called **Protected View** in Reading Mode, as shown in Figure 25. In Protected View, the file contents can be seen and read, but you are not able to edit, save, or print the contents until you enable editing. If you see the information bar shown in Figure 25, and you trust the source of the file, simply click the Enable Editing button on the information bar.

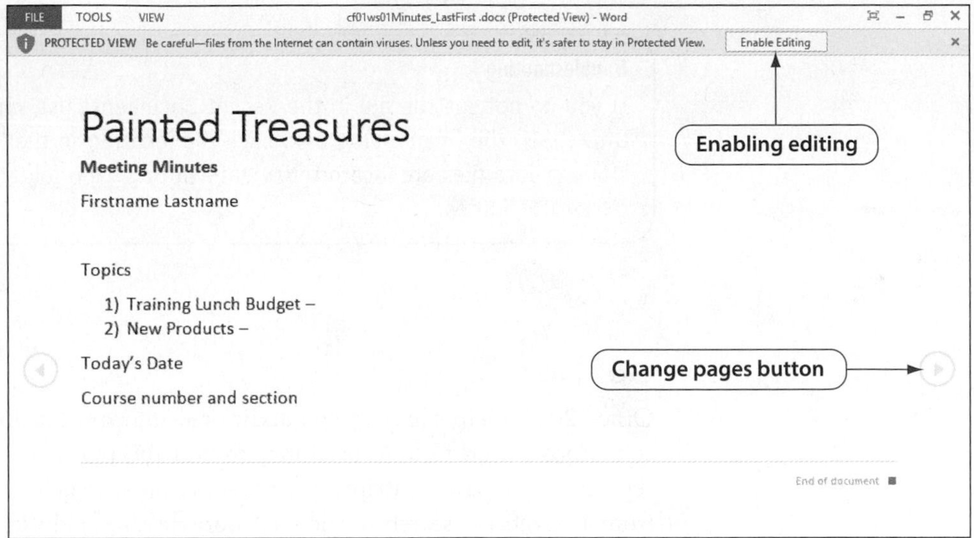

Figure 25 File opened in Protected View

CF01.16

To Reopen a Document from the Recent Documents List

a. In Word, click the **FILE** tab. Notice the Recent Documents list.

b. Point to **cf01ws01Minutes_LastFirst**. Notice the Pin icon . If you want the document to always remain at the top of this list, you would click the Pin icon.

cf01ws01Minutes_LastFirst.docx - Word
Your Office
Info
New
Open
Save
Save As
Print
Share
Export
Close
Account
Options
Open
Recent Documents
Your Office's SkyDrive
Computer
Add a Place
Recent Documents
cf01ws01Minutes_LastFirst.docx
C: » YourOffice » Student Data Files » 02_commonfeatures_module1
C:\YourOffice\Student Data Files\02_commonfeatures_module1\cf01ws01Minutes_LastFirst.docx
Pin icon
Recent Documents list
Recover documents with unsaved work
Recover Unsaved Documents

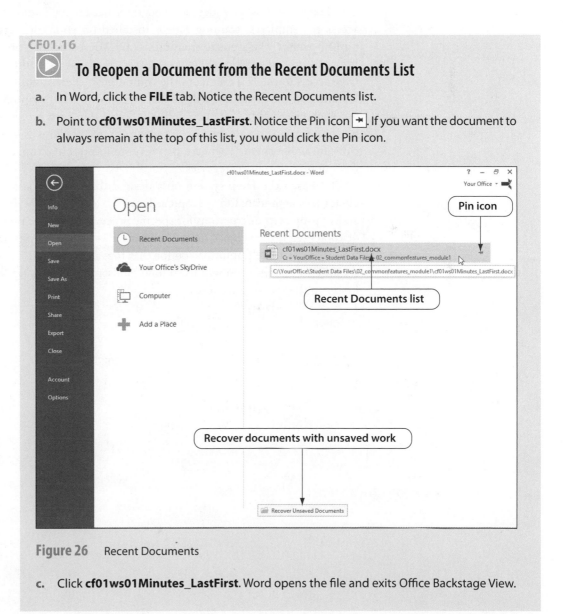

Figure 26 Recent Documents

c. Click **cf01ws01Minutes_LastFirst**. Word opens the file and exits Office Backstage View.

Troubleshooting

If you do not see the file in the Recent Documents list, click Computer and then Browse. In the Open dialog box, click the location in the left pane where your student data files are located. Navigate through the folder structure, and then click cf01ws01Minutes.

Get Help

Office 2013 Help can give you additional information about a feature or steps for how to perform a new task. Your ability to find and use help can greatly increase your Office repertoire and save you time from seeking outside help. Office has several levels of help from a searchable search window to more directed help such as ScreenTips.

Using the Help Window

The **Help** window provides detailed information on a multitude of topics, as well as access to templates, training videos installed on your computer, and content available on Office.com, the website maintained by Microsoft that provides access to the latest information and additional Help resources. To access the contents at Office.com you must have access to the Internet from the computer. If there is no Internet access, only the files installed on the computer will be displayed in the Help window.

Each program has its own Help window. From each program's Help window you can find information about the Office commands and features as well as step-by-step instructions for using them. There are two ways to locate Help topics—the search function and the Popular searches categories.

To search the Help system on a desired topic, type the topic in the search box and click the Search icon. Once a topic is located, you can click a link to open it. Explanations and step-by-step instructions for specific procedures will be presented. To access a subject or topic, click the subject links to display the subtopic links, and then click a subtopic link to display Help information for that topic.

In this exercise, you will learn how to insert a footer using Word help and then add a footer to the meeting minutes.

CF01.17

To Search Help for Information about the Ribbon in Word

SIDE NOTE
Help Shortcut
For those who prefer keyboard shortcuts, pressing F1 is the shortcut to access Help.

a. On the Word title bar, click **Microsoft Word Help** ?. The Word Help window opens.

Figure 27 Word Help window

b. Click in the **Search** box or if you are online, the box will display **Search online help**. Type add a footer and then press Enter.

c. The Help window displays a list of the topics related to the keyword "footer". Scroll through the list to review the Help topics. Click the **Add a header or footer** from the list of results, and then read the information.

d. On the Help window title bar, click **Close** ✕ to close the window. Now that you know how to add a footer, you will add a footer to your Word document.

e. Click the **INSERT** tab, and then in the Header & Footer group, click **Footer**. Click **Blank**. Notice a footer is added at the bottom of your document.

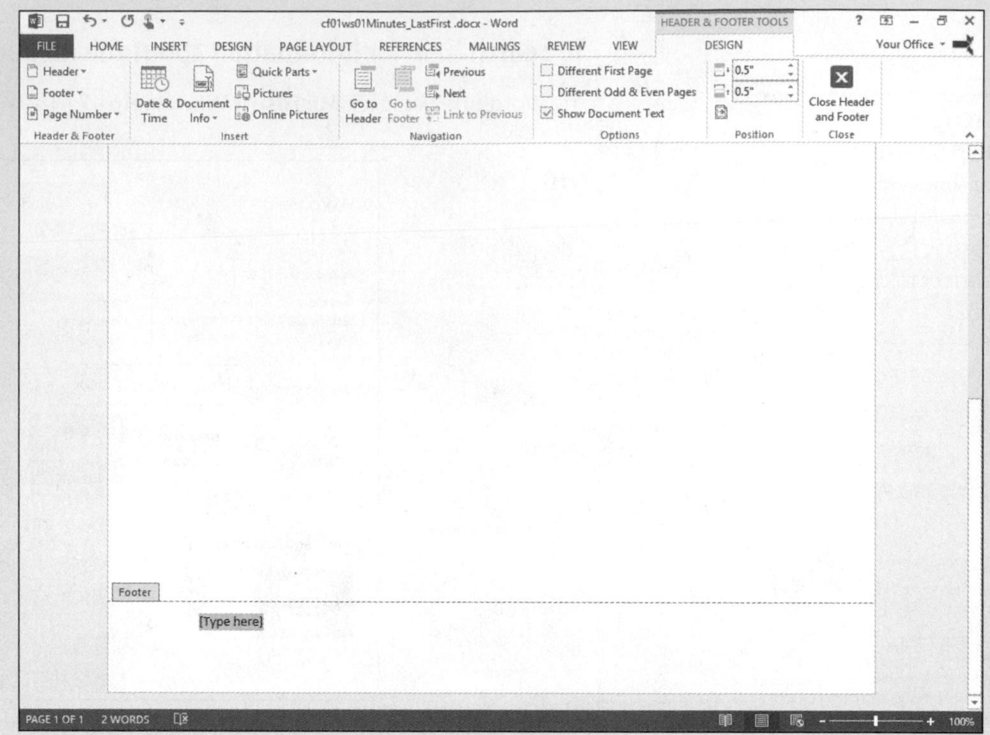

Figure 28 Document with blank footer inserted

f. On the HEADER & FOOTER TOOLS DESIGN tab, in the Insert group, click the **Document Info** button, and then select **File Name**. Notice Word inserts the name of the file.

g. On the HEADER & FOOTER DESIGN tab, in the Close group, click **Close Header and Footer**.

Using ScreenTips

ScreenTips are small windows that display descriptive text when you rest the mouse pointer over an object or button. You can point to a button or object in one of the Office applications to display its ScreenTip. In addition to the button's name, a ScreenTip might include the keyboard shortcut if one is available, a description of the command's function, and possibly more information.

In this exercise, you will use a ScreenTip to center the title of the meeting minutes.

CF01.18

To Open ScreenTips and Topic-Specific Help

a. Press Ctrl + Home to place the insertion point right before **Painted Treasures**.

b. On the HOME tab, in the Paragraph group, hover the mouse over the **Center** button. The ScreenTip is displayed with the button's name, its keyboard shortcut, and a brief description.

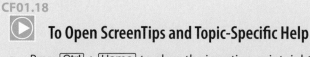

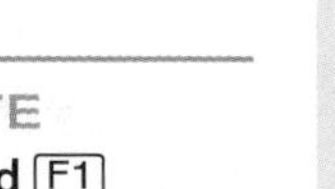

SIDE NOTE

ScreenTip and F1

If a topic for a ScreenTip does not exist in Help, the window will open to the starting search page.

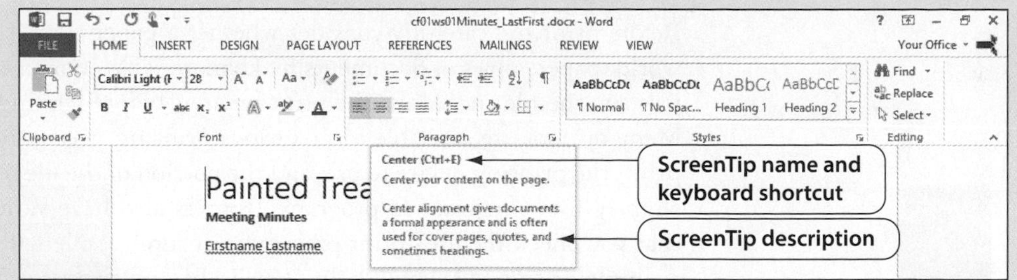

Figure 29 Center button Screen tip

c. Click the **Center** button [≡] to center the Painted Treasures title.

d. On the HOME tab, in the Clipboard group, point to the **Format Painter** to display the ScreenTip. With the mouse pointer still over the **Format Painter** and the ScreenTip showing, press F1 and notice that the Help window opens with information on how to use the Format Painter. Scroll down and read through the information.

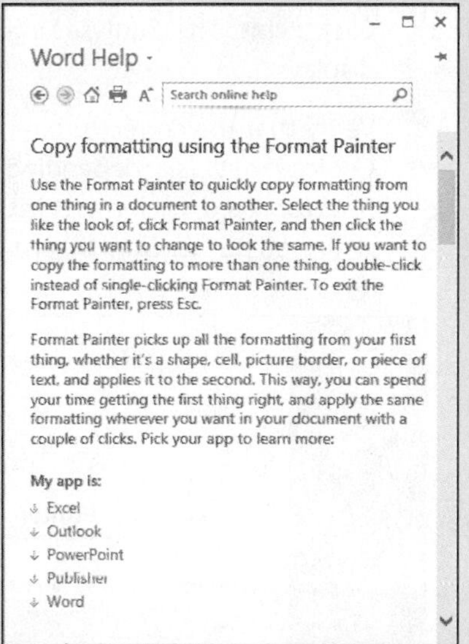

Figure 30 Format Painter Word Help

e. When you are finished reading, click the **Close** [×] button in the top-right corner of the Word Help window. You do not need to use the Format Painter at this time.

f. Press Ctrl+S to save the document.

Print and Share Files

In Office 2013, many ways exist for sharing files. There are times you will need a paper copy, also known as a hard copy, of an Office document, spreadsheet, or presentation. When a printed version is not needed, a digital copy will save paper and costs. Office 2013 provides many ways to share your document. You can use traditional ways of sharing by printing or exporting a PDF. You can also save it to SkyDrive, invite others to share the document, and specify whether others are allowed to edit the document. From inside of Office Backstage View, the document can be e-mailed to others, transformed into an online, browser-not-required presentation, or posted to a blog.

Printing a File

Before printing, carefully consider whether a paper copy is necessary. Even in the digital world, paper copies of documents make more sense in many situations. Always review and preview the file and adjust the print settings before sending the document to the printer. Many options are available to fit various printing needs, such as the number of copies to print, the printing device to use, and the portion of the file to print. The print settings vary slightly from program to program. Printers also have varied capabilities. It is advisable that you check the file's print preview to ensure the file will print as you intended. Doing a simple print preview will help to avoid having to reprint your document, workbook, or presentation, which requires additional paper, ink, and energy resources.

In this exercise, you will print the start of the meeting minutes document to handwrite notes on during the meeting.

CF01.19

To Print a File

a. In Word, click the **FILE** tab to open Office Backstage View.

b. Click **Print**. The Print settings and Print Preview appear. Verify that the Copies box displays **1**.

c. Verify that the correct printer—as directed by your instructor—appears as the Printer. Choices may vary depending on the computer you are using. If the correct printer is not displayed, click the **Printer** button arrow, and then click to choose the correct or preferred printer from the list of available printers.

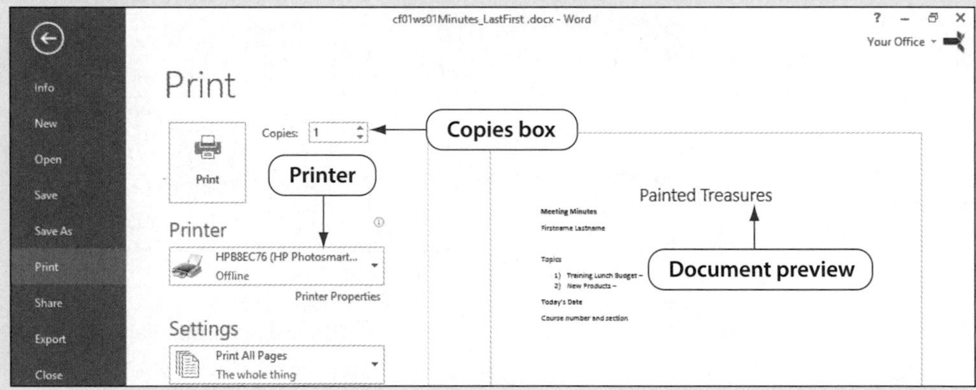

Figure 31 Printing settings

d. If your instructor asks you to print the document, click **Print**.

Exporting a PDF

When you want to give someone else a document, consider whether an electronic version of the file is better than a printed copy. A **portable document format—PDF**— is a type of document that ensures the document will look the same on someone else's computer. For example, different computers may have different fonts installed. A PDF maintains the font. Even if the computer viewing the file does not have the same fonts as the computer used to create the file, the viewer will see the correct font. Further, PDFs are a common file format used in business to share documents because of the readily available free readers.

In this exercise, you will export a PDF of the meeting minutes and e-mail a copy to a colleague who is also attending the meeting.

WORKSHOP 1

CF01.20

To Export a PDF

a. Click the **FILE** tab to open Office Backstage View.

b. Click **Export**, and then click **Create PDF/XPS**.

c. Navigate to the location where your student files are stored. Verify the file name selected is **cf01ws01Minutes_LastFirst**. Notice settings in the Publish as PDF or XPS dialog box for optimizing for online verses printing publishing. Since your colleague will print this document, the default setting of Standard is appropriate.

d. Click **Publish**. Close the **PDF** file.

CONSIDER THIS | Sending Files Electronically

Sending an electronic file can be easier and cheaper than sending a printed copy to someone. What should you consider when deciding the type of file to send? When you send an application specific file, such as Word or Excel, what happens if the recipient does not have the application installed? When you send a PDF, how easy is it for a recipient to edit a document? How does the file type affect the quality of a recipient's printout?

Understanding the Cloud and Touch Integration

Over the past few years, cloud networks and touch screens started to proliferate the market. Thus, Office 2013 made many changes to allow Office to work better with these technologies. If you have never used any cloud technology, Office 2013 makes SkyDrive easy to use and provides some free storage space. If you do not have a touch screen, you can still take advantage of touch technology with a Windows 8 mouse that accepts touch gestures. Over the next several years, these technologies will become standard for most computers and devices. In this next section, you will learn about using SkyDrive and touch features.

Use Windows SkyDrive

When you use computing resources—either hardware or software—of another computer over a network, you are using **cloud computing**. The cloud uses economies of scale by combining the power of many computers. One example of cloud computing is online file storage and syncing—services such as SkyDrive, DropBox, or Box. Some services, such as SkyDrive, also allow you to edit the document online through a browser or to collaborate with simultaneous document editing. Specifically, **SkyDrive** is an online cloud computing technology that offers a certain amount of collaborative storage space free that is integrated with Office 2013.

Traditionally for file storage, files are saved locally on a hard drive or external storage device like a USB drive. A **USB drive** is a small and portable storage device—popular for moving files back and forth between a lab, office, and/or home computer. However, USBs are also easily lost. Further, file versions and backups are usually manually maintained causing versioning problems.

File storage cloud technologies are made possible through Apps that sync all the files for all of your devices. When you edit a file, your computer or device automatically updates the file in the online storage location. All of the other computers and devices check the online storage for changes and update as needed. Thus, when saving your file, you automatically place a copy online and in all of your synced computers. This creates an online backup if your computer crashes. Additionally, there is no USB drive to lose. File-versioning problems are also minimized. Once all applications are properly set up, you have your files everywhere you want them and shared with exactly who needs them without having copies of files around or e-mailing attachments.

REAL WORLD ADVICE **Backing Up the Cloud**

Best practice still dictates bringing files to important meetings on a physical drive such as a USB drive as backup. Cloud technologies are dependent on an Internet connection. Nothing is worse than showing up for a presentation and you cannot get to your files because of a poor Internet connection.

The Save As option in Office Backstage View gives you direct access to SkyDrive, which you can access with the same Microsoft account discussed earlier in the workshop—except Access, which requires you to save locally. With SkyDrive Apps or SkyDrive Pro, you have a local folder directly accessible from the File Explorer that automatically syncs with SkyDrive. Thus, you can sync Access files in the local syncing SkyDrive folder.

Microsoft has designed Office 2013 and SkyDrive to complement one another. When Office 2013 is not available on the computer you are using, you can even view, download, upload, and perform some limited revision via a browser at SkyDrive.com.

Creating a Document on SkyDrive

To use SkyDrive, you need your Microsoft account. After you sign in, you can create new folders and save files into the folders. You will need to have Internet access to complete this exercise.

CF01.21

To Create a New Document at SkyDrive

a. On the taskbar, click **Internet Explorer**  to open Internet Explorer; or alternatively, from the search screen, search for Internet Explorer to open the program.

b. In the address bar type skydrive.live.com.

c. If prompted, log in with your Microsoft account created earlier in the workshop.

d. Click **Create**, and then click **Word document** to create a new document.

e. Type cf01ws01SkyDrive_LastFirst using your last and first name, and then click **Create**.

f. Type your first name and last name, and then press Enter.

g. Type List of New Gift Shop Products. You intend to edit the list and share it will all employees after the meeting.

h. Click the **FILE** tab, and then click **Save**.

i. To return to your SkyDrive folders, click **Exit** x in the top-right corner of the document.

j. Explore the SkyDrive browser interface. To add a file you previously saved, click **Upload**. To delete a file from the folder, select the check box in the top-right corner of the file's tile, click **Manage** from the menu across the top, and then click **Delete**. To share a file, select the check box in the top-right corner of the file's tile, and then click **Share**. Follow the prompts for sharing.

k. Click your **name or picture**—located in the top-right corner—and then click **Sign Out** to exit SkyDrive. Close Internet Explorer.

Roaming Settings

Office 2013's **roaming settings** are a group of settings that offer easy remotely synced user-specific data that affects the Office experience. Across logins these settings remain the same. When signing into Office 2013, the user will experience Office the same way, no matter whether they are on a desktop, a laptop, or a mobile device.

Office 2013 includes the following roaming settings: Most Recently Used List (MRU) Documents and Places, MRU Templates, Office Personalization, Custom Dictionary, List of Connected Services, Word Resume Reading Position, OneNote—custom name a notebook view, and in PowerPoint the Last Viewed Slide.

Word Resume reading appears when you reopen a document. You are given a choice to keep reading where you left off. Word remembers where you were—even when you reopen an online document from a different computer.

Inserting Apps for Office

To enhance the features of Office, Office 2013 is the first version of Office to allow you to install apps from Microsoft's Office Store—**Apps for Office**, as shown in Figures 32 and 33. These apps run in the side pane to provide extra features like web search, dictionary, and maps. You will have to create an account to take advantage of them. You must be running Office 2013, and you must be signed into Office with your Microsoft Account.

1. Open up any Office applications in which you want to use apps.
2. Go to the Insert tab, and then select Apps for Office. Select See All from the menu.
3. The Apps for Office window appears showing all the apps you have installed to your Microsoft account under My Apps. If you see the app you want, select the app, and then click Insert.
4. If you do not see the app you want, click the Find more apps at the Office Store link.
5. Search for the app you want, and then follow the steps online to install the app to your account. You may have to sign into your Microsoft account.
6. Once installed, return to the Office application and repeat steps 2 and 3.

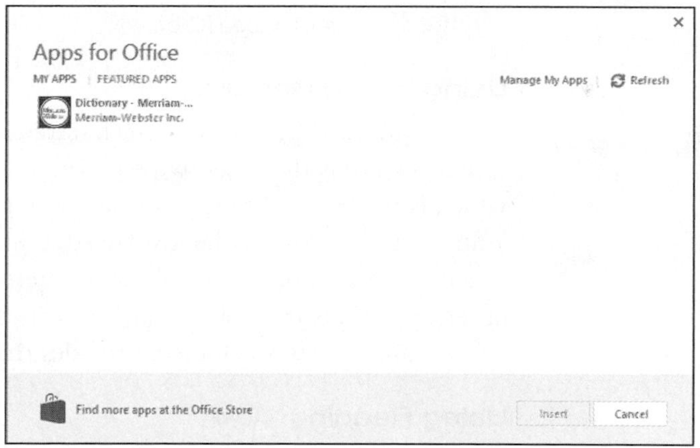

Figure 32 Apps for Office window with one app installed

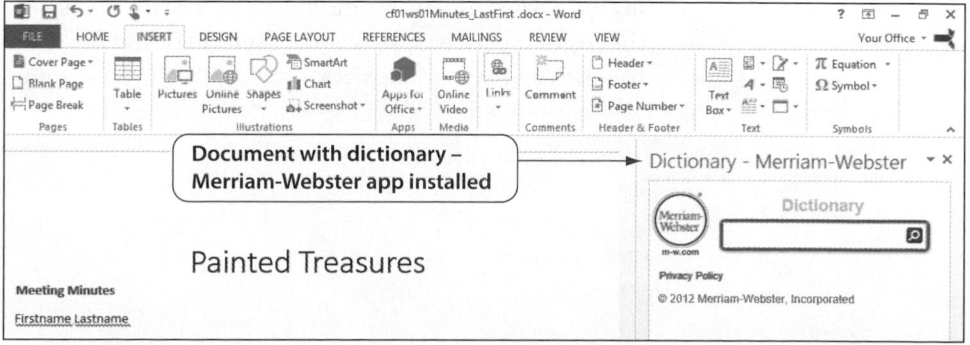

Figure 33 Dictionary - Merriam-Webster app

Use Touch Mode, Gestures, and Reading Mode

Office touch integration is based on the gestures underlying Windows 8 **touch gestures**. Microsoft provides an Office Touch Guide on the website and in Help by searching for Gesture Guide. The main gestures used are: tap, pinch, stretch, slide, and swipe. On a desktop with a touch-screen monitor, you can change this behavior back to the more traditional page navigation mode if you wish.

Using Touch Mode

Touch mode switches Office into a version that makes a touch screen easy to use. Click the Touch Mode button on the Quick Access Toolbar, and the Ribbon toolbar spreads its icons further apart for easier access to fingers. When you toggle this display mode, the on-screen controls space out a bit from each other to make them more accessible to users via touch. Figure 34 displays the normal Word 2013 Ribbon. Figure 35 displays the Ribbon in touch mode.

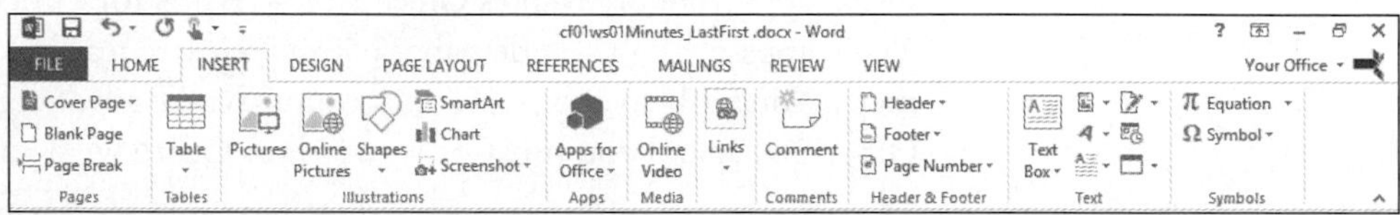

Figure 34 Normal Ribbon

Figure 35 Touch mode Ribbon

Using Touch Gestures

In addition to the main tap, pinch, stretch, slide, and swipe gestures, another common touch gesture is the bezel swipe gesture. A **bezel swipe gesture** is started on the bezel, which is the physical touch-insensitive frame that surrounds the display. The user swipes a finger from a part of the display edge into the display. Depending upon the device, a bezel swipe supports multiple object selection such as cutting, copying, pasting, and other operations on mobile touch-screen devices without conflicting with the panning and zooming gestures. Table 4 provides the Microsoft touch gestures guide.

Using Reading View

The new Reading View in Word 2013 is optimized for touch screens. By swiping your finger horizontally, you can navigate through the document. If you are reading, not writing or editing, **Read Mode** hides the writing tools and menus to leave more room for the pages themselves. Read Mode automatically fits the page layout to your device, using columns and larger font sizes, both of which you can adjust.

To	Gestures Steps
Enter full screen	1. Tap the Ribbon Display Options button in the top-right corner. 2. Tap Auto-hide Ribbon.
Enter standard view	1. Tap the Ribbon Display Options button. 2. Tap Show Tabs and Commands.
Show or hide touch keyboard	1. Tap the Touch Keyboard button to show. 2. Tap the Close button on the Touch keyboard to hide.
Scroll	1. Touch the document. 2. Move finger up and down while maintaining contact.
Zoom in and out	1. Stretch two fingers to zoom in. 2. Pinch two fingers to zoom out.
Place the cursor insertion point	1. Tap the location for the cursor.
Select and format text	1. Tap. 2. Drag the selection handle to desired selection. 3. Tap the selection to show and use the Mini toolbar.
Edit an Excel cell	1. Double-tap.
Change PowerPoint slides in Normal view	1. Make a quick vertical flick.

Table 4 Microsoft's Touch Gestures Guide

CF01.22

To Use and Close Read Mode

a. Click the **VIEW** tab, and then in the Views group, click **Read Mode**. Notice this is the same view that protected documents are in when opened.

SIDE NOTE
Alternative Method
On the status bar, click the Read Mode icon. Click Print Layout View to exit Read Mode.

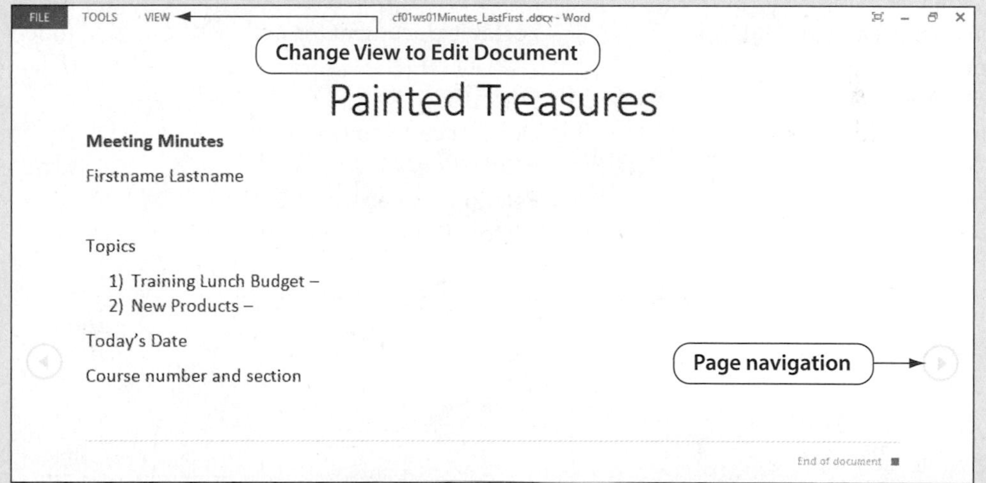

Figure 36 Meeting Minutes in Read Mode

b. Click the **VIEW** menu, and then select **Edit Document** to exit reading mode.

c. Press Ctrl+S. Then, click **Close** ✕ in the top-right corner. Notice that the file closes and you exit the Word application.

Concept Check

1. What kind of Microsoft account and program do you need to create a budget? p. 98–100
2. What is the difference between the Windows and Word Start screens? p. 101–102
3. Which tab on the Ribbon would you use to change the margins in a Word document? p. 109
4. Explain the main purpose of Office Backstage View. p. 118
5. Describe ways to obtain help in Office 2013. p. 124–127
6. How could you share a newsletter with all the members of your business fraternity without printing? p. 127–129
7. What are the advantages of using SkyDrive instead of a USB flash drive? p. 129–130
8. What features in Office 2013 make using a touch screen easier? p. 132

Key Terms

Application Start screen 101
Apps for Office 131
AutoRecovery 118
Bezel swipe gesture 132
Bootcamp 100
Charms 101
Close 106
Cloud computing 129
Contextual tab 114
Contextual tools 114
Dialog box 113
Dialog Box Launcher 113
Document 98
Exit 106
File extension 119
Gallery 112
Graphic 98
Help 124
Information management program 98
Key tip 112
Keyboard shortcut 112
Live Preview 112
Maximize 106
Mini toolbar 115
Minimize 106
Most Recently Used list 122
Office 365 99
Office Backstage View 118
Portable document format (PDF) 128
Protected View 122
Quick Access Toolbar 119
Read Mode 132
Relational database 98
Restore Down 106
Ribbon 108
Ribbon display options 106
Roaming settings 131
ScreenTip 126
Shortcut menu 117
SkyDrive 129
Table 98
Task pane 114
Thumbnail 105
Toggle buttons 110
Touch gestures 132
Touch mode 132
USB drive 129
Windows Phone 99
Windows Run Time (RT) 99
Windows Start screen 101
Workbook 98

Visual Summary

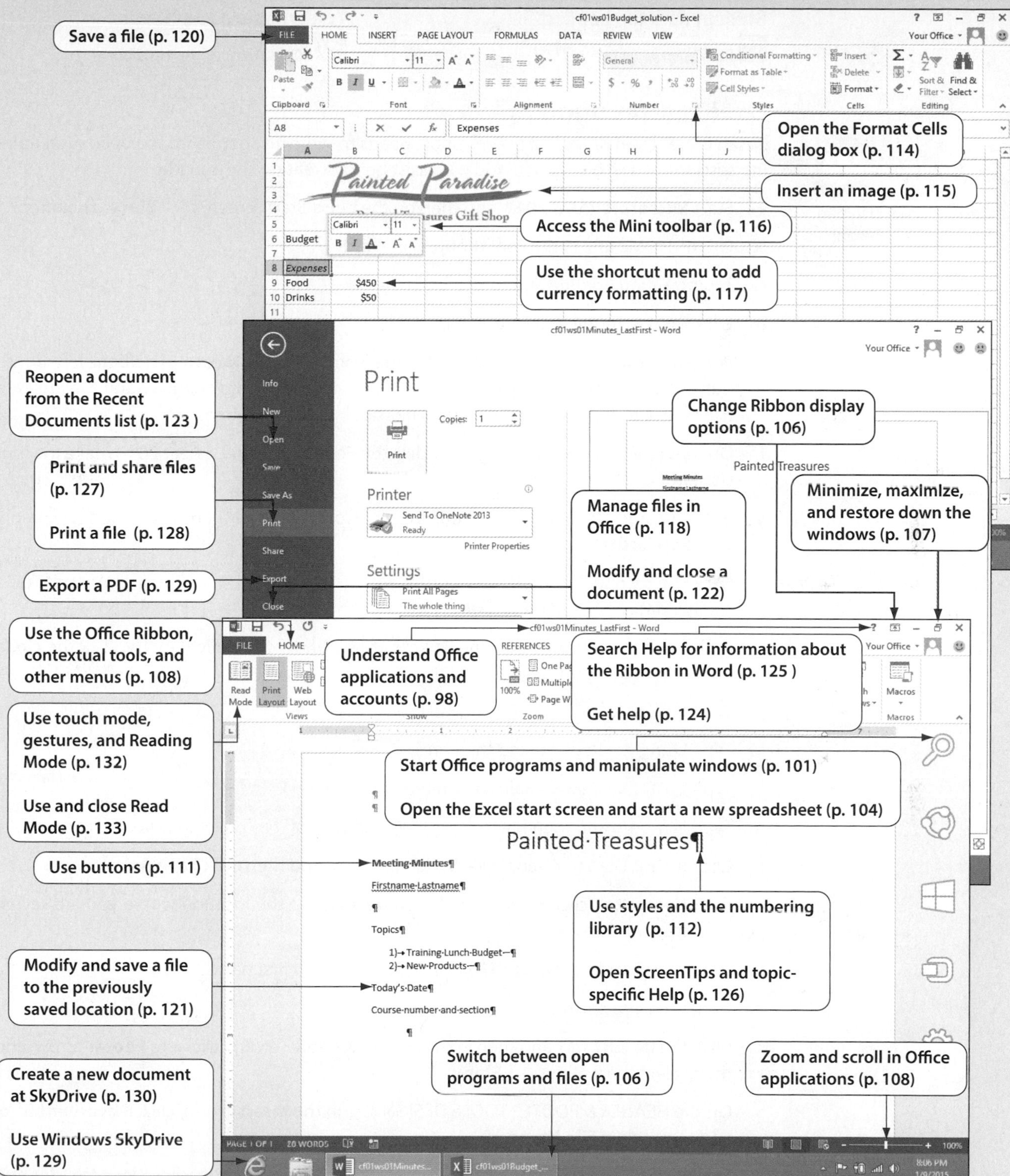

Save a file (p. 120)
Open the Format Cells dialog box (p. 114)
Insert an image (p. 115)
Access the Mini toolbar (p. 116)
Use the shortcut menu to add currency formatting (p. 117)
Reopen a document from the Recent Documents list (p. 123)
Print and share files (p. 127)
Print a file (p. 128)
Export a PDF (p. 129)
Change Ribbon display options (p. 106)
Manage files in Office (p. 118)
Modify and close a document (p. 122)
Minimize, maximize, and restore down the windows (p. 107)
Use the Office Ribbon, contextual tools, and other menus (p. 108)
Understand Office applications and accounts (p. 98)
Search Help for information about the Ribbon in Word (p. 125)
Get help (p. 124)
Use touch mode, gestures, and Reading Mode (p. 132)
Use and close Read Mode (p. 133)
Start Office programs and manipulate windows (p. 101)
Open the Excel start screen and start a new spreadsheet (p. 104)
Use buttons (p. 111)
Use styles and the numbering library (p. 112)
Open ScreenTips and topic-specific Help (p. 126)
Modify and save a file to the previously saved location (p. 121)
Create a new document at SkyDrive (p. 130)
Use Windows SkyDrive (p. 129)
Switch between open programs and files (p. 106)
Zoom and scroll in Office applications (p. 108)
Painted Treasures¶
Meeting-Minutes¶
Firstname-Lastname¶
Topics¶
1)→Training-Lunch-Budget—¶
2)→New-Products—¶
Today's-Date¶
Course-number-and-section¶

Figure 37 Painted Paradise Resort and Spa Employee Training Preparation Complete

Practice 1

Student data file needed:

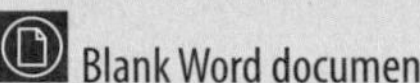

Blank Word document

You will save your file as:

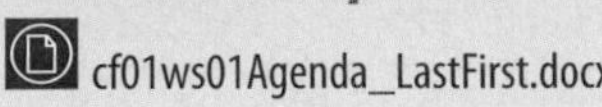

cf01ws01Agenda_LastFirst.docx

Creating an Agenda

Human Resources

Susan Brock, the manager of the gift shop, needs to write an agenda for the upcoming training session she will be holding. You will assist her by creating the agenda.

a. Start **Microsoft Word 2013**, and then on the Word Start screen, click **Blank document**.

b. On the HOME tab, in the Font group, click **Bold**.

c. Type Training Agenda and then press Enter.

d. Click **Bold** to toggle the feature off.

e. Position the insertion point to the left of the word **Training**, press and hold the left mouse button, drag the cursor across the text to the end of the word **Agenda**, and then release the mouse button. All the text in the line should be highlighted.

f. On the HOME tab, in the Font group, click the **Font Size** arrow. Select **20** to make the font size larger.

g. In the Paragraph group, click the **Borders** arrow, and then select the first option, **Bottom Border**.

h. Click the second line under the border you just inserted. Under Training Agenda, type today's date and then press Enter twice.

i. In the Paragraph group, click the **Bullets** arrow. Under the Bullet Library, click the **circle** bullet—the third option in the gallery.

j. Type Welcome trainees 2:00 pm and then press Enter.

k. Type Using the Register and then press Enter.

l. Type Customer Service Policies and then press Enter.

m. Type Wrap-Up and then press Enter twice to turn off the bullet feature.

n. Click the **FILE** tab to open Office Backstage View, and then click **Save As**.

o. Click **Computer**, click **Browse**, and then Navigate to the location where you are saving your student data files.

p. Type cf01ws01Agenda_LastFirst, using your last and first name.

q. Click the **Save** button.

r. Click the **INSERT** tab, and then in the Header & Footer group, click the **Footer** arrow, and then select the first option, **Blank**.

s. On the HEADER & FOOTER TOOLS DESIGN tab, in the Insert group, click **Document Info**, and then select **File Name**.

t. On the HEADER & FOOTER TOOLS DESIGN tab, in the Close group, click **Close Header and Footer** to exit the footer.

u. Press Ctrl + S to save your changes.

v. Close the cf01ws01Agenda_LastFirst document, and then exit Word.

w. Submit your file as directed by your instructor.

Problem Solve 1

Student data files needed:

 cf01ps1Expense.xlsx

cf01ps1Cookies.jpg

You will save your file as:

 cf01ps1Expense_LastFirst.xlsx

Formatting an Expense Report

Finance & Accounting

Recently, you opened a business with a few partners called Midnight Sweetness. With the slogan "No more starving late-night studies," the business specializes in delivering freshly baked cookies, brownies, and other sweet treats to local college students. Midnight Sweetness has been a huge success. Currently, you rent a small building that includes major kitchen appliances. Now, you and your partners are looking for a bank loan to expand your business. You are responsible for putting together an expense report from last month to include in the bank application.

a. Open the **cf01ps1Expense** workbook. Save it as cf01ps1Expense_LastFirst. Click **Enable Content** if necessary.

b. Click cell **A1**, and then change the font to **bold**, **20** point, and the standard color **Blue**.

c. Click cell **A2**, and then change the font to **bold**.

d. Click cell **B3**, and then type your first and last name.

e. Click cell **A5**, and then right-align the text.

f. Click cell **A6**, and then right-align the text.

g. Click cell **A16**, and then right-align the text.

h. Click cell **A8**, and then change the font to italic.

i. Select the range **B9:B16**, and then format the cells as **Currency** with **0** decimals.

j. Click cell **B15**, and then add a **double bottom border**.

k. Click cell **D1**, insert the image **cf01ps1Cookies**, and then set the image height to **3.5**.

l. Save and close the cf01ps1Expense_LastFirst workbook, and then exit Excel.

m. Submit your file as directed by your instructor.

Perform 1: Perform in Your Career

Student data file needed:

 Blank Excel workbook

You will save your file as:

 cf01pf1OfficeTraining_LastFirst.xlsx

Creating a Training Schedule

Information Technology

One of the managers you work for at a local real estate company—Hope Properties—has asked you to create a training schedule in Excel for several of the trainings he is planning to schedule. The trainings include Windows 8, Word 2013, Excel 2013, and PowerPoint 2013. The trainings will be offered on Mondays: January 13, January 27, February 10, and February 24, 2014. Each training is three hours in length with one hour between sessions. The first session starts at 9:00 am. There are two trainings per day. You will create an attractive schedule using features you worked with in this workshop.

a. Start **Excel**. Using the features of Excel, create a training spreadsheet that is attractive and easy to read. Some suggestions include the following.
   - Create column headings for the application and date of training.
   - Enter the session times in the cells where the application and date meet.
   - Format the date as a long date.
   - Format the column headings.
   - Format a title for the workbook.
   - Use bold, italics, and colors.

b. Save and Close the cf01pf1OfficeTraining_LastFirst workbook, and then exit Excel.

c. Submit your file as directed by your instructor.

Perform 2: Perform in Your Life

Student data files needed:

Blank Word document

cf01pf2Vintage.docx

cf01pf2Dinner.xlsx

You will save your file as:

cf01pf2Critique_LastFirst.docx

Improving the Appearance of Files

Finance & Accounting

Human Resources

Your boss at a local vintage clothing store has asked you to review a spreadsheet and a document—made by a prior employee—and make suggestions on what to do to improve the appearance of the document and spreadsheet. Examine the two files cf01pf2Vintage and cf01pf2Dinner. Answer the questions below.

a. Open a new blank document in Word, and then save the file as cf01pf2Critique_LastFirst.

b. List five items you would change in the document and why?

c. List five items you would change in the spreadsheet and why?

d. Exit Word, and then submit your file as directed by your instructor.

Additional Cases

Additional Workshop Cases are available on the companion website and in the instructor resources.

Accessing Office Documents from Mobile Devices

WORKSHOP 1 | MOBILE COMPUTING

OBJECTIVES

Prepare Case

Women's Golf Getaway Collaboration

Sales & Marketing

Several employees of Painted Paradise are collaborating on the Women's Golf Getaway event at the Red Bluff Golf Course and Pro Shop. Three members of the team are traveling and need to share documents related to the event. Timothy Smith, the marketing manager, is using a Microsoft Surface device to take notes in Word while also editing a related Excel document. He contacts two other members of his team and asks them to review and edit the documents.

Vatika / Shutterstock.com

REAL WORLD SUCCESS

"The ability to work on Office documents while being mobile has been an incredible asset while traveling. Using Microsoft SkyDrive I have been able to save files in the cloud and then access them both from my laptop and my tablet computer. Using apps on my tablet computer, I can make changes to the documents and have them synchronized back to my laptop by the time I get back to the office."

- Roger, alumnus

Student data files needed for this workshop:

 ms01ws01GolfGetaway.docx

 ms01ws01Registration.xlsx

 ms01ws01GolfGetaway_Android.docx

 ms01ws01Registration_Android.xlsx

ms01ws01GolfGetaway_iPad.docx

 ms01ws01Registration_iPad.xlsx

 ms01ws01TurquoiseOasis.jpg

You will save your files as:

 ms01ws01GolfGetaway_LastFirst.docx

 ms01ws01Registration_LastFirst.xlsx

Understanding Mobile Computing

With the growing popularity of tablet computing and increasingly powerful smartphones, mobile computing has experienced significant growth. **Tablet computers** are alternatives to traditional desktop or laptop computers. Tablet computers are lightweight, portable, wireless computing devices that use a touch-screen interface. Instead of clicking or double-clicking on icons or files, users tap or double-tap on a tablet. To scroll, you tap and hold on a screen and swipe your finger in the direction that you want the screen to move. The speed and length of the swipe often control the amount of movement on screen.

Some tablets also use a stylus. A **stylus** is a pointing device that simulates using a pen on a tablet computer. The functionality of the stylus depends on the device and the software being used. A stylus can serve as an alternative to a mouse, simulating clicking and right-clicking. A stylus can also allow for digital inking, allowing the user to write within an application on the tablet. The digital ink is then saved as an image or can be converted to text.

Tablet computers vary in their size and features. Some have screens as small as 7" measured diagonally, while others have screens closer to 14". Most are capable of connecting to wireless networks, and some are able to access data via cellular network connections. Since they are designed to be lightweight and have long battery lives, tablet computers are traditionally not as powerful as traditional PCs. Many of the functions that a laptop can perform cannot be accomplished on a tablet. Tablets are capable of Internet browsing, e-mail, light gaming, and some productivity work. As the devices become more powerful, while maintaining low weights and long battery life, these capabilities will undoubtedly expand.

Due to their reduced computing power, tablet computers primarily run operating systems and applications different from their desktop counterparts. Using a device with a different operating system than your desktop computer can lead to problems accessing and sharing files. A tablet may not have compatible applications for opening and editing your documents, and not all tablet computers are designed for productivity. For example, some tablet computers do not feature a file storage interface the way desktop and laptop computers do.

The tablet computer market is a competitive and quickly evolving environment. While new devices enter the market regularly, existing devices are constantly upgraded with new features and technologies. This rapidly changing environment means the list of available tablet computers and their respective prices is constantly changing. The information contained below was accurate as of the printing date of the text.

CONSIDER THIS | Purchasing a Tablet Computer

There is a great deal of variety in tablet computing on both the hardware and software aspect of the devices. If you have purchased, or are thinking of purchasing a tablet computer, what considerations would you make? How would you decide which operating system was right for you? Which hardware option is the right one? How does file compatibility factor into your decision?

Cloud computing has become a popular way to cope with the increasing amount of mobility and diversity in computing. **Cloud computing** is the concept of storing, accessing, and editing files that are stored in another physical location. Files can be accessed "in the cloud" from a variety of devices. The files are stored on a server that is maintained by the service provider. The server, which acts as the "cloud," is never physically seen by the user. Rather, the user's device or devices connect to the server and save changes to the documents on that server.

Some services allow for copies of the files to be stored on the local device for offline editing. Any files modified while offline are then synchronized, or copied to the service provider's server, once an Internet connection is established. The process of **synchronization** updates changes made to a document on one computing device to all devices attached to the service. Table 1 describes some popular cloud services.

Cloud Computing Option	Free Storage	Subscription Service
SkyDrive	7 GB	20, 50, or 100 GB starting at $10 per year
DropBox	2 GB	100, 200, or 500 GB starting at $9.99 per month
Google Drive	5 GB	25 or 100 GB starting at $2.49 per month
iCloud	5 GB	10, 20, or 50 GB starting at $20.00 per year
SugarSync	5 GB	30, 60, or 100 GB starting at $4.99 per month

Table 1 Cloud computing options (as of publication date)

The synchronization process is managed by an application that can be installed on your mobile device or PC. The files stored in the cloud service can generally be accessed via a website as well. This process has several simultaneous benefits. Backup copies of your files are created by default as a result of the synchronization process. If a device crashes or is damaged, the files stored in the cloud service will be safe.

The files and folders that exist within the cloud services can be easily shared with users of the same service. This creates a collaboration tool where the most recent version of files are easily accessible. Some services also allow for simultaneous editing of documents. Lastly, your files are always accessible. Even if your desktop is turned off, you can access your files from your tablet computer. Figure 1 demonstrates the process of synchronizing documents between multiple devices.

Figure 1 The cloud computing environment

CONSIDER THIS | Privacy in Your Company

Smartphone and tablet computers are in widespread use today. These devices make it easy for employees to view their corporate e-mail accounts and documents on their personal mobile devices. What privacy concerns might there be with viewing corporate data on a personal mobile device? What policies might be put in place to protect employees and companies that allow the use of mobile devices?

Cloud services help with synchronizing documents between mobile devices. Opening and editing those documents on mobile devices can be a significant problem. While most mobile operating systems will allow you to view basic word-processing, spreadsheet, or presentation files, you will not be able to edit them on the device.

REAL WORLD ADVICE | **What About Access?**

Access databases have not been easily accessible via mobile devices. Microsoft, with Access 2013, has now introduced the ability to publish Access databases as apps via the Windows Store or with SharePoint. This means that your Access databases can now be used on a wide array of devices. SharePoint will allow you to publish your database for use in a web browser. The Windows Store will allow your Windows 8 device to download and install your database as an app directly to your device. This allows for much greater mobile access to your databases.

Desktop and laptop computers use applications, such as those that come with Microsoft Office, for creating and editing these types of documents. An **application** is software that is written for an operating system that users interact with to accomplish a given task. These applications are generally purchased on a CD, DVD, or downloaded from a website. Mobile devices, similar to desktop and laptop PCs, also require specific software for creating and editing these types of documents. Applications on mobile devices are called apps. An **app** is an abbreviation for application and is commonly used as a term for programs that are installed on both smartphones and tablet computers. The amount of functionality within the app to view, create, or edit a document depends upon the device and the app. It also depends on whether the app is free to use or is a paid app. Apps are downloaded from specialized stores that are maintained by the operating system manufacturer. In this section, you will compare tablet computers from different manufactures.

CONSIDER THIS | **Applications and Apps**

Applications and apps both allow users to perform tasks on computing devices. How are applications different from apps? What differences are there in the purchasing and installations of the two?

Understand Different Tablet Computers

There are many types of tablet computers in terms of both hardware and software. This workshop will discuss three of these devices: the Microsoft Surface, Apple iPad, and the Android tablet computer. Each device runs a different operating system and has different features and capabilities.

In October 2012, Microsoft released the Surface tablet. This tablet comes in two versions, the Surface and Surface Pro. The Surface tablet, as shown in Figure 2, uses the Windows RT operating system, a mobile version of Windows 8. Since the Surface runs on tablet-specific hardware, its feature set is slightly different than laptop or desktop computers. The Surface uses the Windows Store for installing apps to the device. These apps can be created in a number of programming languages, including Visual Basic, C++, and JavaScript. A key distinction with the Windows RT operating system is that is has been designed to perform and look just like Windows 8 on other Windows 8 computers. Microsoft Word, Excel, and PowerPoint are included with Windows RT.

CONSIDER THIS | Building Apps

Many companies build customized software to fit their specific business needs. Microsoft Office provides a platform on which to build these customized applications. Since Office 2013 will run on both the Surface and Surface Pro, applications built with Office could be deployed to corporate devices via the Windows Store. How could companies benefit from this combination of Windows and Office?

Figure 2 The Microsoft Surface tablet

The Surface Pro tablet runs Windows 8 Pro and is built with hardware that lets it perform like a traditional PC. The Surface Pro tablet will be able to run full versions of any Windows applications and Office 2013. Applications for the Surface Pro can be downloaded from the Windows Store or installed directly from the hard drive. The Surface Pro will also be able to run legacy software, or software built for previous versions of Windows.

While Microsoft manufactures the Surface tablet, other hardware vendors make tablet computers that run Windows 8 and Windows RT. For example Lenovo, Dell, and ASUS make tablet computers that run Windows RT. Lenovo and ASUS, among others, make tablet computers that run Windows 8.

Apple manufactures a series of tablet computers called iPads. iPads run the iOS operating system which is similar to the Macintosh operating system. iPads are tightly integrated with Apple's iTunes software, an online multimedia and app store. Software for iPads can be downloaded through the Apple App Store. Apple is the only manufacturer of iPads and currently maintains two sizes for iPads. The iPad, as seen in Figure 3, has a screen that measures 9.7" diagonally while the iPad Mini is a 7" device.

Figure 3 An Apple iPad with on-screen keyboard

Several manufacturers make tablets that run the Android operating system. Asus, Samsung, Dell, HTC, and Google are among some of the companies that sell tablet computers running the Android operating system. Figure 4 shows an ASUS model Android tablet. The Android operating system is owned and maintained by Google. It also has an app store called the Google Play Store. Books, music, movies, and apps can be downloaded through the Google Play Store. The Android operating system is an open source operating system, meaning that developers can easily create apps and code for the devices.

All three operating systems are also available on smartphones. This makes the difference between small tablets and larger smartphones difficult to distinguish. From a consumer perspective it also means that having one similar operating system on all of your devices is appealing. Having similar operating systems across devices creates a more efficient experience when working with documents and interacting with apps.

View Documents on Mobile Devices

Timothy has e-mailed Patti Rochelle, the event planning manager at Painted Paradise. He would like Patti to review a Word document. The document concerns the Women's Golf Getaway. This was a past event that was very successful. Painted Paradise plans to make the Women's Golf Getaway an annual event.

Timothy has suggested some changes to the document. He has also added an image into the document and a comment related to the image. Figures 5 and 6 show the original document that Timothy edited in Word 2013. Patti is currently out of her office on a business trip, but she has taken her personal iPad with her. Her iPad is connected to her Painted Paradise e-mail account. Timothy has attached the document to the e-mail he has sent to Patti. The document was last edited on Timothy's Microsoft Surface RT tablet using Microsoft Word 2013.

Taipei
Partly Sunny
25°C

Figure 4 A tablet with the Android operating system

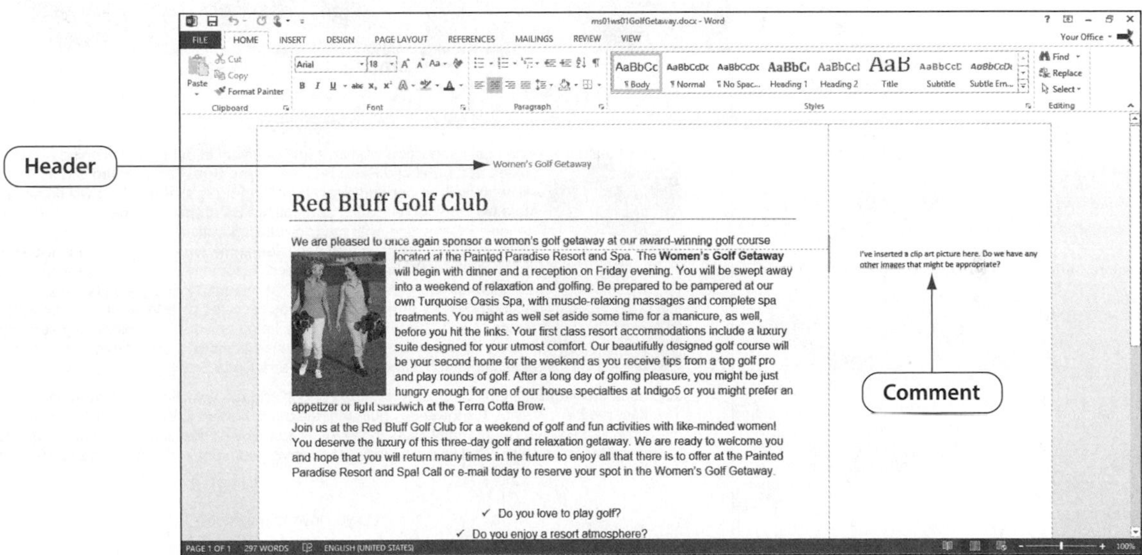
ms01ws01GolfGetaway.docx - Word
FILE HOME INSERT DESIGN PAGE LAYOUT REFERENCES MAILINGS REVIEW VIEW
Header
Women's Golf Getaway
Red Bluff Golf Club
We are pleased to once again sponsor a women's golf getaway at our award-winning golf course located at the Painted Paradise Resort and Spa. The Women's Golf Getaway will begin with dinner and a reception on Friday evening. You will be swept away into a weekend of relaxation and golfing. Be prepared to be pampered at our own Turquoise Oasis Spa, with muscle-relaxing massages and complete spa treatments. You might as well set aside some time for a manicure, as well, before you hit the links. Your first class resort accommodations include a luxury suite designed for your utmost comfort. Our beautifully designed golf course will be your second home for the weekend as you receive tips from a top golf pro and play rounds of golf. After a long day of golfing pleasure, you might be just hungry enough for one of our house specialties at Indigo5 or you might prefer an appetizer or light sandwich at the Terra Cotta Brew.
Join us at the Red Bluff Golf Club for a weekend of golf and fun activities with like-minded women! You deserve the luxury of this three-day golf and relaxation getaway. We are ready to welcome you and hope that you will return many times in the future to enjoy all that there is to offer at the Painted Paradise Resort and Spa! Call or e-mail today to reserve your spot in the Women's Golf Getaway.
✓ Do you love to play golf?
✓ Do you enjoy a resort atmosphere?
I've inserted a clip art picture here. Do we have any other images that might be appropriate?
Comment
PAGE 1 OF 1 297 WORDS ENGLISH (UNITED STATES)

Figure 5 The header and comment in the ms01ws01GolfGetway document viewed in Word 2013

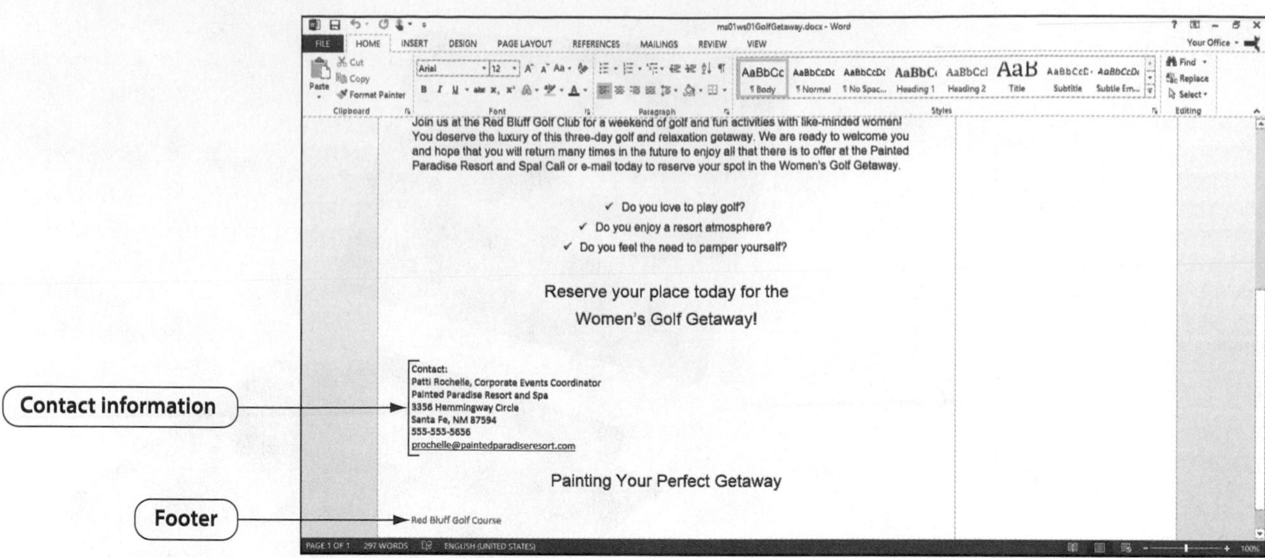

Figure 6 The footer and contact information in the ms01ws01GolfGetaway document viewed in Word 2013

Patti receives the e-mail from Timothy on her iPad and reads the message. Seeing that Timothy would like her feedback on some changes he made to the document she opens the attachment directly from the e-mail app on her iPad. Figure 7 shows the heading and top portion of the document as it appears when opened via the iPad e-mail app.

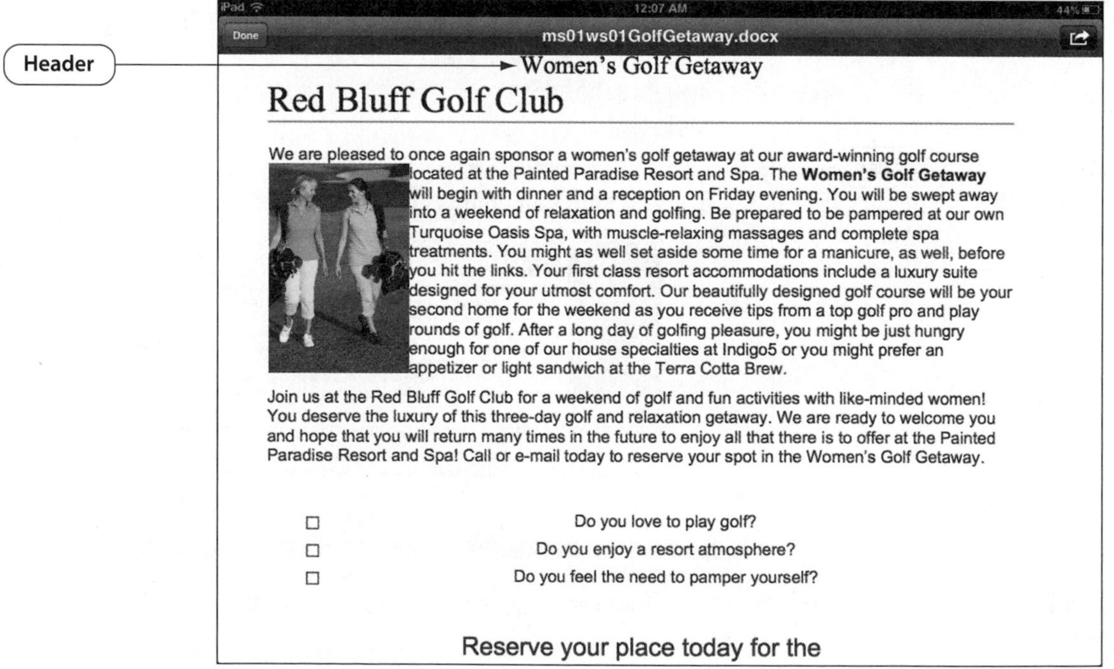

Figure 7 The header and top portion of the ms01ws01GolfGetaway document viewed in the iPad e-mail app

There are notable differences between the document Timothy sent—Figures 5 and 6—and the view of the document that Patti has—Figure 7. On the iPad the header text appears in a different format than in the original document. Additionally, the header text is not distinguished from the rest of the document as it would appear in Word. The bullet points are also displayed in a different format. In Word they appear as checkmarks while on the iPad they appear as squares. In Figure 5, a comment can be seen attached to the image in the document that was inserted into the text of the first paragraph. This comment is not visible in the iPad view.

Figure 6 shows Patti Rochelle's contact information at the bottom of the Word 2013 document. Only the e-mail address, which appears as a hyperlink, is formatted differently from the rest of the text. In Figure 8, the iPad view formats the telephone number at the bottom of the document as a hyperlink. If you tap the phone number, two options are presented to you. One is to copy the number and the other is to add the number to the Contacts app. Similar to the header of the document, the text in the footer of the document is not distinguished from the rest of the document text.

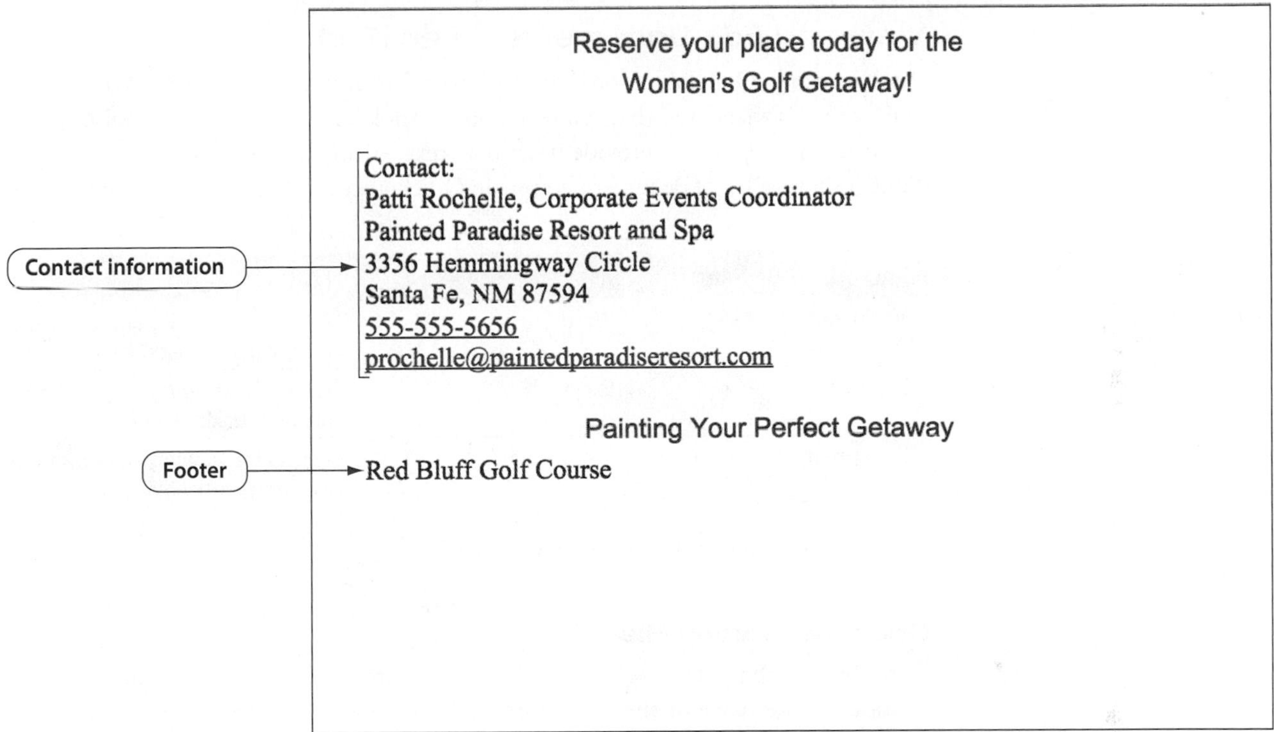

Figure 8 The footer and contact information in the ms01ws01GolfGetaway document

The differences discussed above are due to how the iPad app is interpreting the document being viewed. They are not permanent changes to the document. In fact, the document cannot be edited from this view. To make changes to this document it would need to be saved to the device and opened with an app that has the ability to edit Office documents.

QUICK REFERENCE | **Common Office Apps**

Each mobile operating system (see Table 2) has apps designed for accessing Microsoft Office documents. Each app is different. Some allow for full editing while others only allow for viewing. Additionally, free versions have different features than their paid counterparts. The most popular apps are compatible with Word, Excel, and PowerPoint documents.

Mobile Operating System	App Name	Price
iOS	Quickoffice Pro HD	$14.99
iOS	Documents To Go	$9.99 and $16.99 versions
Android	Kingsoft Office	Free
Android	Quickoffice Pro	$14.99
Windows	Microsoft Office 2013	Bundled with Windows RT or purchased on Windows 8 Pro tablets

Table 2 Apps that can edit Microsoft Office documents

View and Edit Documents on an iPad

Patti is using Quickoffice on her iPad to open and edit Microsoft Word documents. Quickoffice is a paid app that can be found in Apple's App Store. At the publication date of this text, most apps that provide functional text editing of Word documents are paid apps. Table 3 shows a list of document editors in Quickoffice and their supported document types.

Quickoffice App Name	Related Office App	Features
Quickword	Word	Allows for viewing and editing of .doc, .docx, and .txt files
Quicksheet	Excel	Allows for viewing and editing of .xls and .xlsx files
Quickpoint	PowerPoint	Allows for viewing and editing of .ppt and .pptx files

Table 3 Description of Quickoffice applications

Open the Starting File

Timothy has requested that Patti change two items in this document. First, the title containing the name of the golf course is inconsistent with the name of the golf course. The title should match the terminology used in the footer of the document. Additionally, the golf outing will become an annual event. To distinguish each event the year should be added to the end of each instance of the name of the event. In this exercise, you will open a Word document in Quickoffice.

M01.00

To Open the Word Document

a. Open your preferred e-mail application, attach the **ms01ws01GolfGetaway** and **ms01ws01Registration** documents to an e-mail message, and then send the e-mail to your preferred e-mail account.

b. On an iPad, tap the **Mail** icon to open the Mail app. From the e-mail containing the attached Word file, tap and hold the **ms01ws01GolfGetaway** icon. A submenu will appear presenting different options for opening or saving the file.

Troubleshooting

You may not have access to an iPad device for parts of this workshop. Alternate documents are provided on the student resource CD for completed versions of the iPad documents. You should consult with your instructor about how to proceed with the workshop.

SIDE NOTE

Cloud Service

If you are using a cloud service to access files, you may open the file in a slightly different manner.

SIDE NOTE
iPad Shortcut
Frequently used apps may appear in the Open In box when you initially tap and hold on the file icon.

c. Tap **Open In**, and then tap **Quickoffice**. The document will now open in the Quickoffice app.

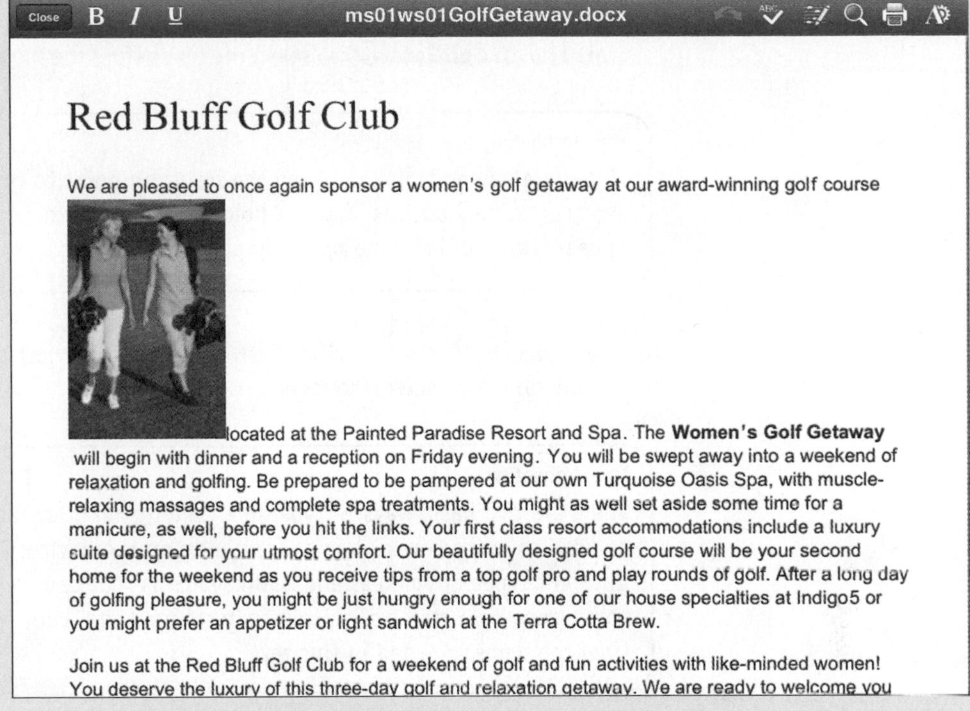
Close
ms01ws01GolfGetaway.docx
Red Bluff Golf Club
We are pleased to once again sponsor a women's golf getaway at our award-winning golf course located at the Painted Paradise Resort and Spa. The Women's Golf Getaway will begin with dinner and a reception on Friday evening. You will be swept away into a weekend of relaxation and golfing. Be prepared to be pampered at our own Turquoise Oasis Spa, with muscle-relaxing massages and complete spa treatments. You might as well set aside some time for a manicure, as well, before you hit the links. Your first class resort accommodations include a luxury suite designed for your utmost comfort. Our beautifully designed golf course will be your second home for the weekend as you receive tips from a top golf pro and play rounds of golf. After a long day of golfing pleasure, you might be just hungry enough for one of our house specialties at Indigo5 or you might prefer an appetizer or light sandwich at the Terra Cotta Brew.
Join us at the Red Bluff Golf Club for a weekend of golf and fun activities with like-minded women! You deserve the luxury of this three-day golf and relaxation getaway. We are ready to welcome you

Figure 9 The ms01ws01GolfGetaway document viewed in Quickoffice

d. Tap **Close** in the top-left corner of the screen. Opening the file in Quickoffice will automatically save it to your iPad within the Quickoffice app. By default, Quickoffice will place the document in the Inbox folder. It cannot be edited in that folder.

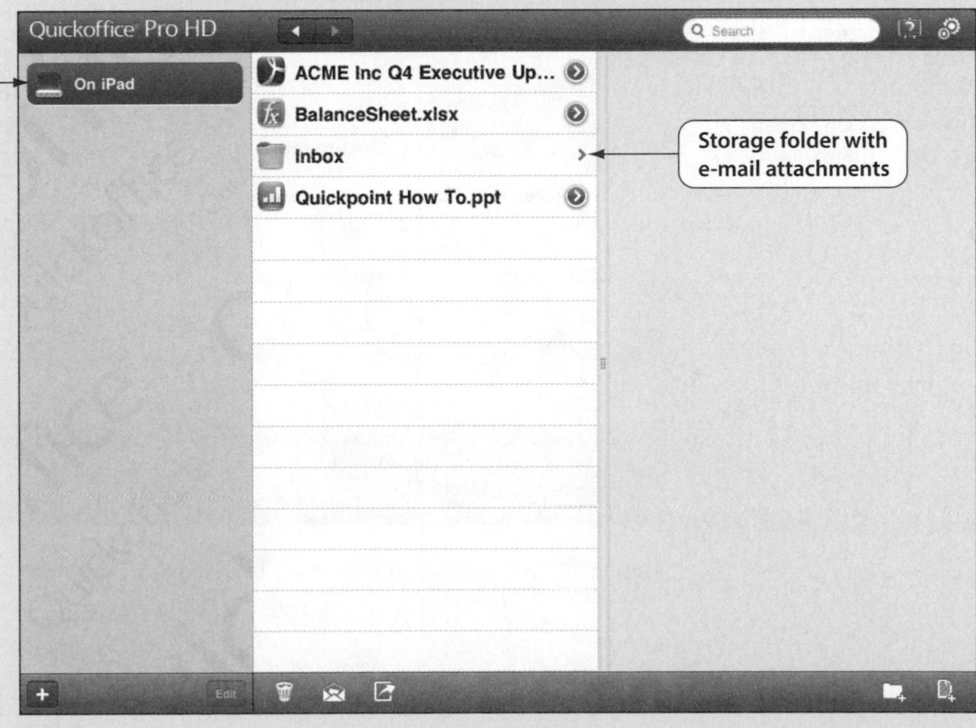
Available storage devices and cloud services
Quickoffice Pro HD
Search
On iPad
ACME Inc Q4 Executive Up...
BalanceSheet.xlsx
Inbox
Quickpoint How To.ppt
Storage folder with e-mail attachments
Edit

Figure 10 The Quickoffice file management screen

e. Tap the **Inbox** folder, tap and hold the **ms01ws01GolfGetaway** document, and then drag it to the middle column of Quickoffice.

f. Tap the **arrow** next to the document name to view the document properties. Tap the box that contains the file name **ms01ws01GolfGetaway**, and then double-tap the text **ms01ws01GolfGetaway** to select the text before the file extension.

> **Troubleshooting**
> If you are having trouble placing the insertion point to type on an iPad there is a shortcut to help do this. Tap and hold on any text and a magnifying glass view will appear. This will help you precisely place the insertion point.

g. Type ms01ws01GolfGetaway_LastFirst, using your last and first name, and then tap **Done** on the on-screen keyboard.

> **Troubleshooting**
> There are two basic ways to type on a tablet computer. Tablet operating systems come with on-screen keyboards for typing on the device. There are also many different types of wireless and USB keyboards that can be attached to tablet computers. As a result of this diversity of products, your specific keyboard may vary from the icons included in this text.

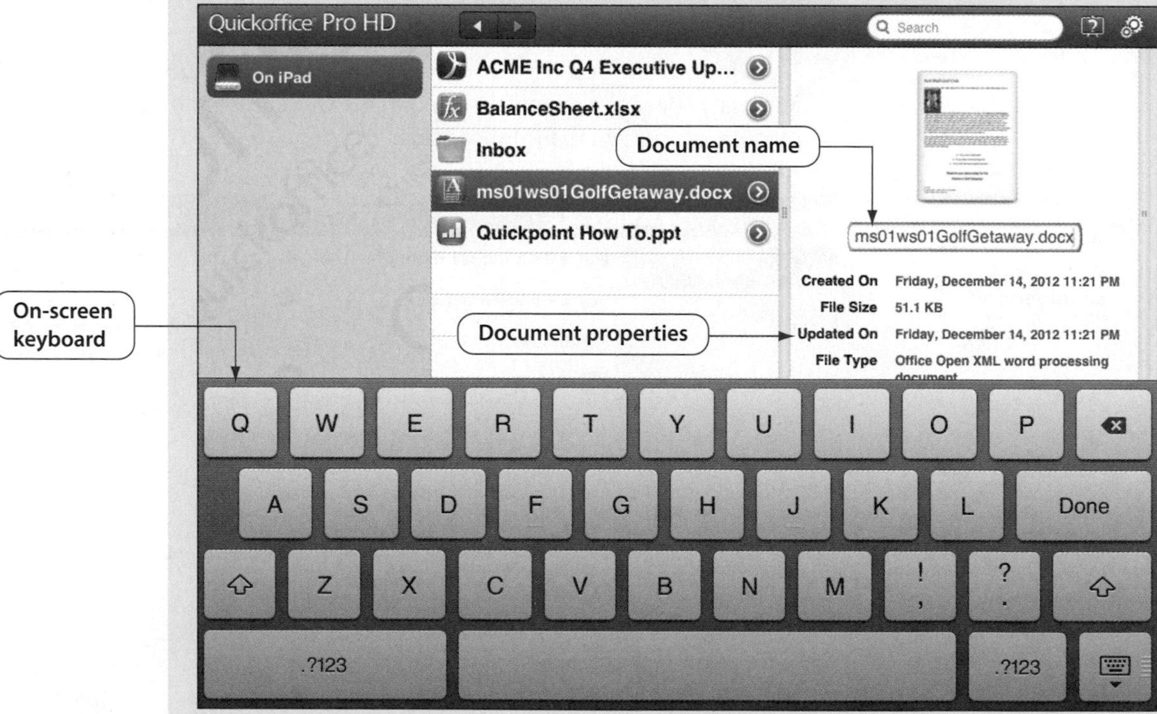

Figure 11 Editing the properties of a document in Quickoffice

REAL WORLD ADVICE Microsoft OneNote

Microsoft OneNote is an application that is included in all versions of Microsoft Office 2013. OneNote also has apps available for iOS and Android devices. It allows for syncing and editing of OneNote notebooks across all connected devices via Microsoft's SkyDrive service. The apps have limited functionality on their respective mobile devices. The OneNote app is free in both the Apple App Store and the Google Play Store. This provides a quick and easy method of synchronizing text and multimedia documents across multiple devices and operating systems.

Editing Word Documents with Quickoffice

There are several distinctions to make between the view of the original document in Word 2013 and the view of the document in Quickoffice. Notice that the headers and footers, images, and comments that exist in this document are not available for viewing or editing in Quickoffice. Any edits to these items would need to take place in another app or on another device. Also notice that the bulleted list items appear differently.

You can edit the text in the document body and make basic formatting changes such as bold and italic with Quickoffice. In this exercise you will edit the Word document in Quickoffice. The name of the Red Bluff Golf Course and Pro Shop will need to be updated in the document. The year 2015 will also need to be added to references of the event title.

M01.01

To Edit the Document with Quickoffice

a. Tap the **ms01ws01GolfGetaway_LastFirst** document to open it for editing.

SIDE NOTE
Alternate Method
An alternative to replacing text in a document is to place the insertion point after a word and use the Delete button on the keyboard.

> **Troubleshooting**
> If you are using a different app for editing the ms01ws01GolfGetaway document, the steps outlined below may vary. Additionally, the editing capabilities of the app may vary.

b. Tap and hold the text **Club** in the title of the document. When the pop-up screen appears, tap **Select.** This will select the word "Club."

c. Type Course and Pro Shop to complete the name of the Red Bluff Golf Course and Pro Shop.

d. In the second sentence, tap at the end of the text **Women's Golf Getaway**, tap the [Spacebar], and then type 2015 to change the title to "Women's Golf Getaway 2015." Bold [B] the **2015** text, if necessary.

e. At the beginning of the second paragraph, tap at the end of the text **Red Bluff Golf Club**, and then tap [Delete] to delete the text **Club**. Type Course and Pro Shop to complete the name of the Red Bluff Golf Course and Pro Shop.

f. At the end of the second paragraph, tap at the end of the text **Women's Golf Getaway**, tap the [Spacebar], and then type 2015 to change the title to "Women's Golf Getaway 2015." Bold [B] the text **Women's Golf Getaway 2015**.

g. Tap **Close**, and then tap **Save** to close and save your changes to the document.

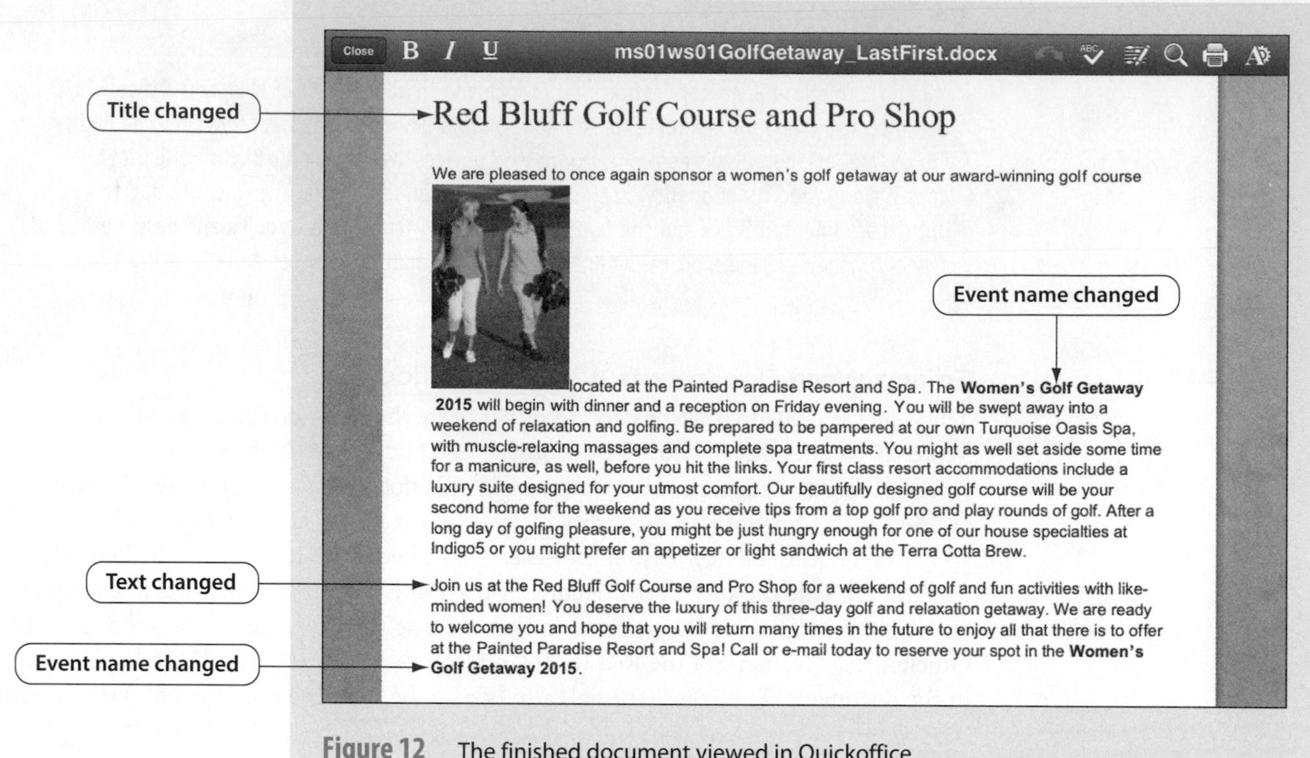

Close
B I U
ms01ws01GolfGetaway_LastFirst.docx
Title changed
Red Bluff Golf Course and Pro Shop
We are pleased to once again sponsor a women's golf getaway at our award-winning golf course
Event name changed
located at the Painted Paradise Resort and Spa. The Women's Golf Getaway 2015 will begin with dinner and a reception on Friday evening. You will be swept away into a weekend of relaxation and golfing. Be prepared to be pampered at our own Turquoise Oasis Spa, with muscle-relaxing massages and complete spa treatments. You might as well set aside some time for a manicure, as well, before you hit the links. Your first class resort accommodations include a luxury suite designed for your utmost comfort. Our beautifully designed golf course will be your second home for the weekend as you receive tips from a top golf pro and play rounds of golf. After a long day of golfing pleasure, you might be just hungry enough for one of our house specialties at Indigo5 or you might prefer an appetizer or light sandwich at the Terra Cotta Brew.
Text changed
Join us at the Red Bluff Golf Course and Pro Shop for a weekend of golf and fun activities with like-minded women! You deserve the luxury of this three-day golf and relaxation getaway. We are ready to welcome you and hope that you will return many times in the future to enjoy all that there is to offer at the Painted Paradise Resort and Spa! Call or e-mail today to reserve your spot in the Women's Golf Getaway 2015.
Event name changed

Figure 12 The finished document viewed in Quickoffice

REAL WORLD ADVICE **Landscape vs. Portrait View**

Most tablet computers are equipped to rotate their views between landscape and portrait modes. Depending upon your device, accessories, and preferences, you may choose one view over the other when viewing or editing documents. The type of document and placement of the on-screen keyboard may also influence your choices.

Editing Excel Documents with Quickoffice

Before leaving her office, Patti was working on an Excel document related to the Women's Golf Getaway event. The document contains registration information and budget data concerning the event. Given the past success of the event, some new features have been added for future events.

In this exercise you will open, rename, and edit an Excel document using Quickoffice. You will also ensure that the correct name of the Red Bluff Golf Course and Pro Shop is used throughout the document.

M01.02

To Open and Edit an Excel Document in Quickoffice

a. From the e-mail containing the attached Excel file, tap and hold the **ms01ws01Registration** icon. A submenu will appear presenting different options for opening or saving the file.

b. Tap **Open In**, and then tap **Quickoffice**.

	A	B	C	D	E	F
1	Red Bluff Golf Club					
2	*Women's Golf Getaway*					
3						
4	Fees					
5	Non-Member Registration	$250.00				
6	Member Registration	$200.00				
7	Meal Plan	$100.00				
8						
9	Number Of Expected Guests					
10	Non-Members	2				
11	Members	3				
12	Number of Meal Plans Ordered	3				
13						
14	FirstName	LastName	Address	City	State	ZipCo
15	Missy	Malone	2500 Red Oak Court	Santa Fe	NM	87594
16	Courtney	Miller	2503 Disse Avenue	Santa Fe	NM	87594
17	Fiona	Britt	1199 Suspendisse Road	Santa Fe	NM	87594
18	Maggie	Gibbons	1857 32nd Street	Santa Fe	NM	87594
19	Lacey	Hannigan	3016 Apple Road	Santa Fe	NM	87594
20						

Figure 13 The ms01ws01Registration document viewed in the Quickoffice app

c. Tap **Close** in the top-right corner of the screen.

d. If necessary, tap the **Inbox** folder. Tap and hold the **ms01ws01Registration** document, and then drag it to the middle column of Quickoffice.

e. Tap the **blue arrow** to view the document properties, and then double-tap the **name** of the document to select the text before the file extension.

f. Type ms01ws01Registration_LastFirst, using your last and first name. Tap **Done**.

g. Tap the **ms01ws01Registration_LastFirst** document to open it for editing.

> **Troubleshooting**
> To change the zoom level of the document use two fingers to pinch the screen. This will decrease the zoom and show more of the spreadsheet. To increase the zoom, use two fingers and move them apart diagonally.

h. The Budget Items worksheet contains the names of individuals currently signed up for the event. Tap cell **A1** to select it, and then tap at the **end of the text** in the formula bar to place the insertion point.

i. Delete the text **Club**, and then type Course and Pro Shop to change the text in cell A1 to "Red Bluff Golf Course and Pro Shop".

j. Tap cell **A2** to select it, and then tap at the **end of the text** in the formula bar to place the insertion point.

k. Type 2015 to change the text to "Women's Golf Getaway 2015", and then tap Enter.

Entering Formulas with Quickoffice

The Quickoffice spreadsheet editor, Quicksheet, offers some of the same functionality as Excel. You can enter text and simple formulas into cells and use a variety of functions such as SUM, COUNT, IF, and DATE and TIME functions. Quicksheet also allows for adding and removing worksheets, rows, and columns.

In this exercise you will insert rows into the spreadsheet and add special meal plan pricing for members and total registration fees for members and "non-member" You will then add calculations for registration and meal plan fees.

M01.03

To Add Formulas to the Spreadsheet

a. Tap cell **A7** to select it. Tap in the **formula bar**, and then place the insertion point at the beginning of the cell text. Type Non-Member and then add a **space** character to change the text in cell A7 to read Non-Member Meal Plan.

b. Tap row **8** to select the entire row, tap , and then tap **Insert rows – below**.

c. Tap cell **A8** to select it, and then type Member Meal Plan in the formula bar.

d. Tap , and then tap **Color**. Tap **Cell Color**, tap **Gray** (the option in the fourth row and third column), and then tap .

e. Tap cell **B8** to select it, type 90 to enter the price of a member meal plan, and then tap Enter. Ensure the formatting is currency. If it is not, tap , and then tap **Currency**.

f. Tap cell **C10**, type Registration Fees, and then tap **Return**. Tap cell **D10**, type Meal Plan Fees, and then tap **Return**.

g. Tap cell **C11**, and then type =B5*B11. Tap , tap **Currency**, and then tap to close the Number Format menu.

h. Tap cell **C12**, and then type =B6*B12. Tap , tap **Currency**, and then tap.

i. Tap cell **D11**, and then type =B7*B11. Tap , tap **Currency**, and then tap.

j. Tap cell **D12**, and then type =B8*B12. Tap , tap **Currency**, and then tap.

k. Tap **Close** and then tap **Save**.

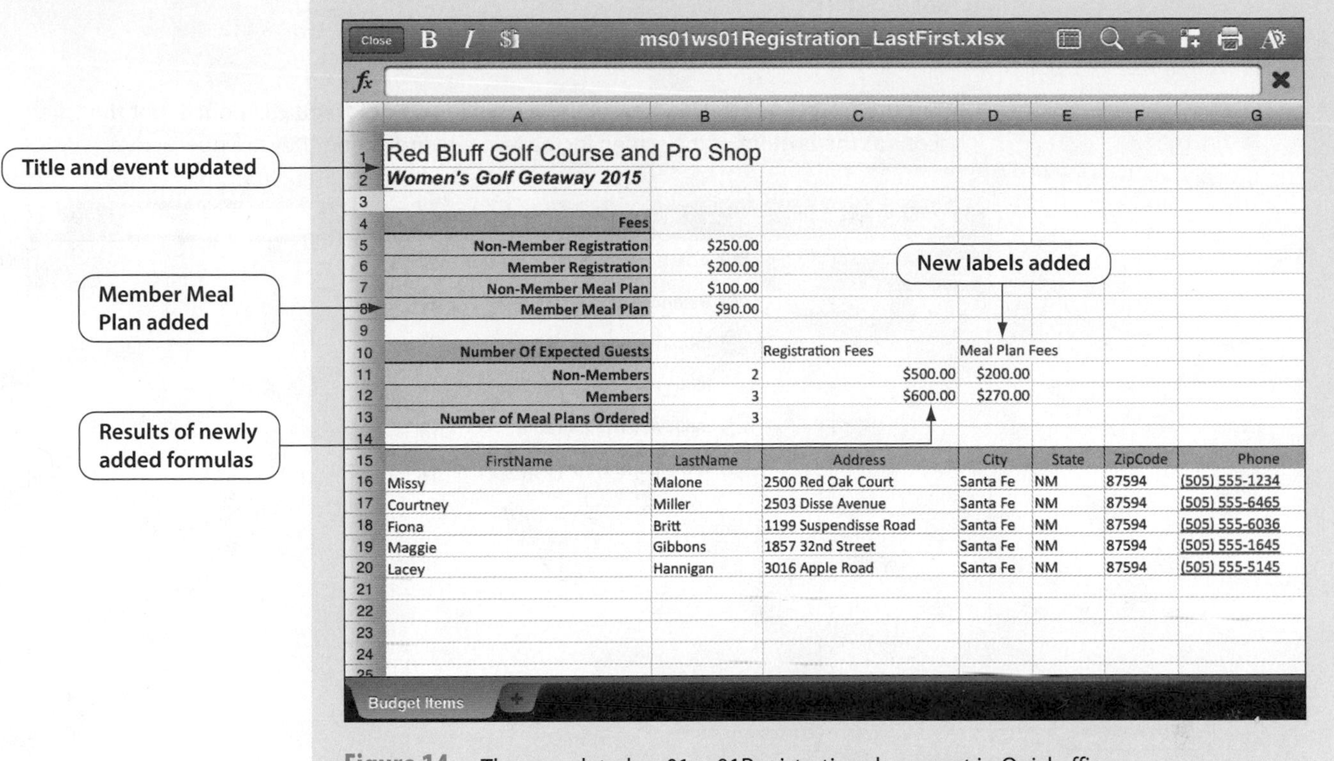

Figure 14 The completed ms01ws01Registration document in Quickoffice

Share Documents with Mobile Devices

Now that the documents have been updated and saved, they can be sent to Barry Cheney for a final review. If the documents are stored in a cloud service app such as SkyDrive, they will be automatically synchronized to all computers connected to the account. This includes desktop computers, laptops, and most types of mobile devices. Some organizations use web-based collaboration tools like Microsoft SharePoint. If no cloud technology is available, the files can be e-mailed as attachments to the next reviewer.

Sharing Documents with Quickoffice

If the tablet computer has the capability to store files locally, they can be attached to an e-mail with an e-mail app. Some productivity apps have this capability built into their interface. Quickoffice offers the ability to e-mail a document in the file manager using the default e-mail app. In this example, Quickoffice will use the iPad e-mail app.

M01.04

To Attach the Documents to an E-Mail

a. Tap the **ms01ws01GolfGetaway_LastFirst** file and hold. You will notice that the three icons at the bottom of the screen increase in size indicating they are now active.

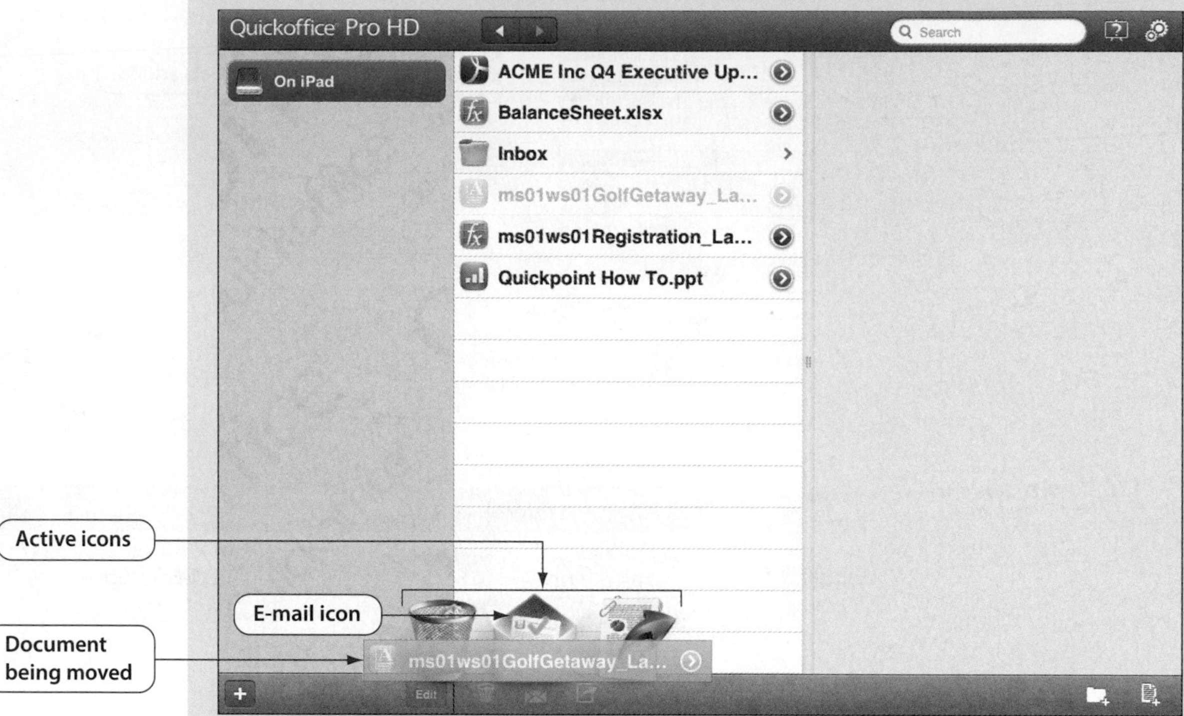

Figure 15 Dragging the ms01ws01GolfGetaway document to the e-mail icon

SIDE NOTE
File Options in the Quickoffice File Manager
The other icons represent the ability to delete a file (the wastebasket) or share a file (the document with a blue arrow).

b. Drag the **ms01ws01GolfGetaway_LastFirst** document to the e-mail icon, and then release the document when it is over the **e-mail** icon to attach it to an e-mail.

c. Type your e-mail address in the To: field of the e-mail, and then tap **Send** to send the e-mail with the attached file.

d. Only one file may be attached at a time to an e-mail with Quickoffice. Repeat this process, attaching the **ms01ws01Registration_LastFirst** spreadsheet to an e-mail.

CONSIDER THIS | **When to Share and When to E-Mail**

Attaching files to e-mails is a common practice. With the growing popularity and ease of use of cloud services, however, this practice deserves more consideration. When might it be more practical to share a file via a cloud service as opposed to attaching it to an e-mail?

View and Edit Documents on an Android Tablet

Patti has made the necessary changes to both documents that were originally sent by Timothy. Now Barry Cheney must review the documents before forwarding them back to Timothy. In reviewing the documents some changes will still need to be made. Barry is currently traveling and does not have access to his office computer. Instead, he is using a tablet computer that is running the Android 4 operating system. To view and edit Microsoft Office documents while he is away from the office, he has installed an app titled Kingsoft Office. As of the publication date of this text, Kingsoft Office was a free app in the Google Play Store.

Kingsoft Office is compatible with Word, Excel, and PowerPoint files. Each editor carries a different name. Table 4 contains a list of Kingsoft Office applications and a description of their features.

Kingsoft Office App Name	Related Office App	Features
Writer	Word	Allows for editing of .doc, .docx, and .txt files
Spreadsheets	Excel	Allows for editing of .xls and .xlsx files
Presentation	PowerPoint	Allows for viewing and running presentations of .ppt and .pptx files

Table 4 Description of Kingsoft Office applications

Editing Documents with Kingsoft Writer

Kingsoft Office has the capability to perform a wide variety of edits to Word documents. The Writer app can view and edit headers and footers, view and create comments, and insert a variety of objects into a document.

In this exercise you will update the header and footer of the document. You will also view an existing comment and create a new comment about the image in the document.

M01.05

To Edit the Document in Kingsoft Writer

a. On an Android tablet, open the e-mail containing the attached Word file. Tap **Attachment 1**. Next to the ms01ws01GolfGetaway attachment, tap **View**. In the Complete action using dialog box, tap **Kingsoft Office**.

> **Troubleshooting**
> If you did not have access to an iPad to complete prior work on the documents, use the document ms01ws01GolfGetaway_iPad as your starting file. The changes made in the iPad portion of this workshop have already been completed in this file.

b. Before opening the document, at the bottom of the Complete action using dialog box, you will be prompted to specify how frequently you want to open files of this type with Kingsoft. You may specify Always or Just once. Tap **Just once**. Notice that the header of the document is clearly differentiated from the body. Overall, the formatting of the document is very close to how it appears in Word 2013.

> **Troubleshooting**
> Choosing Always from this menu will not affect how the document opens. It will omit this step in the future however. If Always is selected, in the future, tapping a Word document will automatically open Kingsoft.

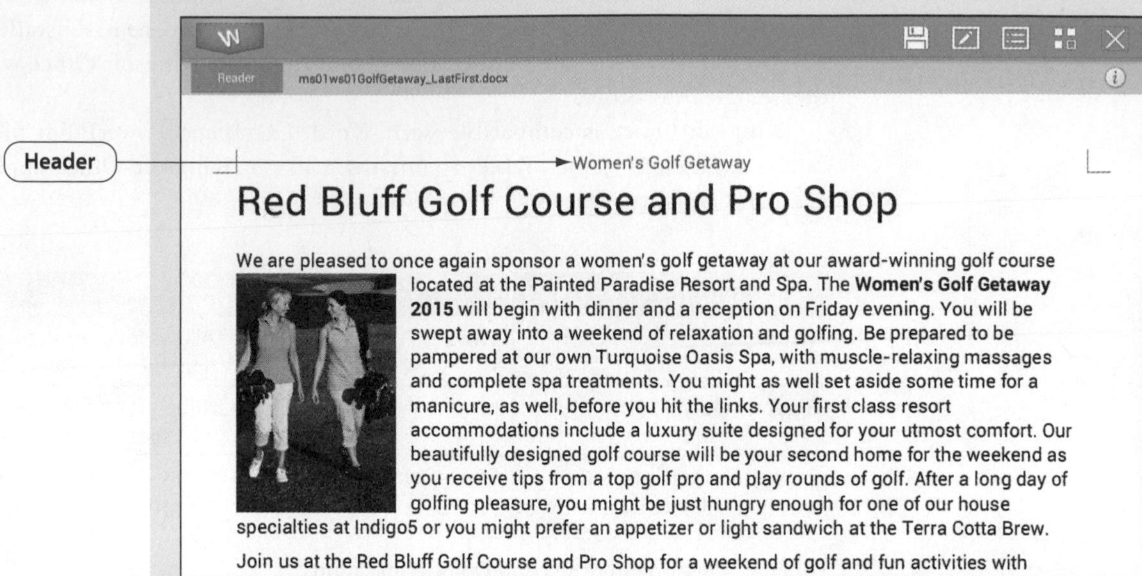

W
Reader
ms01ws01GolfGetaway_LastFirst.docx
Header
Women's Golf Getaway
Red Bluff Golf Course and Pro Shop
We are pleased to once again sponsor a women's golf getaway at our award-winning golf course located at the Painted Paradise Resort and Spa. The Women's Golf Getaway 2015 will begin with dinner and a reception on Friday evening. You will be swept away into a weekend of relaxation and golfing. Be prepared to be pampered at our own Turquoise Oasis Spa, with muscle-relaxing massages and complete spa treatments. You might as well set aside some time for a manicure, as well, before you hit the links. Your first class resort accommodations include a luxury suite designed for your utmost comfort. Our beautifully designed golf course will be your second home for the weekend as you receive tips from a top golf pro and play rounds of golf. After a long day of golfing pleasure, you might be just hungry enough for one of our house specialties at Indigo5 or you might prefer an appetizer or light sandwich at the Terra Cotta Brew.
Join us at the Red Bluff Golf Course and Pro Shop for a weekend of golf and fun activities with

Figure 16 The ms01ws01GolfGetaway document viewed in Kingsoft Writer

c. Double-tap the **header** of the document to edit the name of the event. Tap at the **end of the first line** of text, tap the Spacebar, and then type 2015 to change header to "Women's Golf Getaway 2015".

> **SIDE NOTE**
> **Increasing Screen Size**
> You can hide and show the context menu by tapping the icon in the top-left corner of the screen.

> **Troubleshooting**
> If you are having trouble placing the insertion point to type in Kingsoft, there is a shortcut to help do this. Tap and hold on any text and a magnifying glass view will appear. This will help you precisely place the insertion point.

d. Double-tap the **footer** of the document to edit the name of the golf course. Tap to place the insertion point at the end of the footer text, tap the Spacebar, and then type and Pro Shop to change the text in the footer to "Red Bluff Golf Course and Pro Shop".

> **SIDE NOTE**
> **On-screen Typing**
> Many tablet operating systems will attempt to AutoComplete words as you type. This can greatly speed up the typing process on a tablet.

e. Tap **Comment & Revise** in the context menu at the top of the screen, and then tap **Show comment & revise.** Any comments made that have been placed in the document will now be visible. Notice the comment by Timothy concerning the picture that has been inserted.

f. Tap the **picture** to select it, tap **Insert**, and then tap **Comment**. Type LastFirst to set your user name, using your first and last name.

g. Tap the **Contents** box to activate the on-screen keyboard. Type Should we add the Red Bluff logo to this document also? in the comment box, and then tap **OK** to return to the main document and view your comment.

> **Troubleshooting**
> Accessing special characters, such as a question mark, with on-screen keyboards requires switching keyboard views. Most on-screen keyboards have a button to the left of the spacebar button that provides access to one or more views of special characters.

h. Tap **Close**, and then tap **Save**.

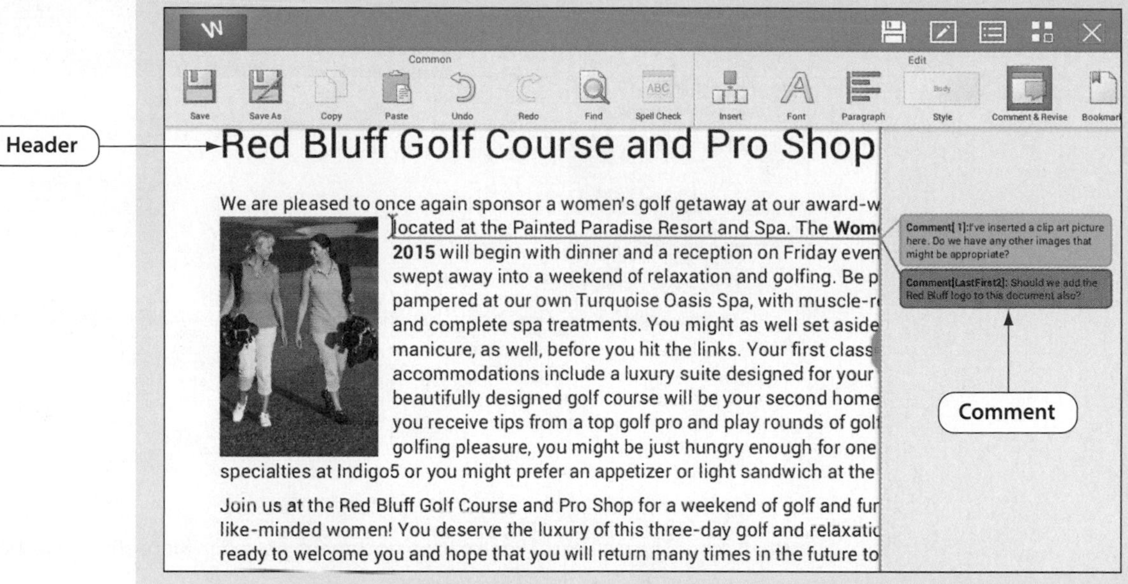

Figure 17 The completed ms01ws01GolfGetaway document

Entering Formulas with Kingsoft Spreadsheets

Barry must now review the registration spreadsheet Excel file that Patti forwarded to him. Currently, the values in cells B11:B13 of the spreadsheet are numbers and not formulas. Instead, these values should be replaced with formulas that will be updated automatically if the data changes. Kingsoft's Spreadsheet app allows for text and formulas to be added to cells in the spreadsheets. Kingsoft Spreadsheets has a wide variety of statistical, logical, text, and date and time functions. The software also includes an embedded on-screen keyboard for easier spreadsheet editing.

In this exercise, you will update the document to be more dynamic. Cell B11 should display the number of non-members that have registered by counting all registered guests and subtracting the number of registered members. Cell B12 should display the number of members that have registered by counting the number of "Yes"s that occur in column H. Cell B13 should display the number of meal plans that have been ordered by counting the number of "Yes"s that occur in column I.

M01.06

To Edit a Spreadsheet in Kingsoft Spreadsheets

a. On an Android tablet, open the e-mail containing the attached Excel file. Tap **Attachment 1**. Next to the attachment titled **ms01ws01Registration_LastFirst**, tap **View**. In the Complete action using dialog box, tap **Kingsoft Office**. If necessary, tap **Just once**.

Troubleshooting

If you did not have access to an iPad to complete prior work on the documents, use the document ms01ws01Registration_iPad as your starting file. The changes made in the iPad portion of this workshop have already been completed in this file.

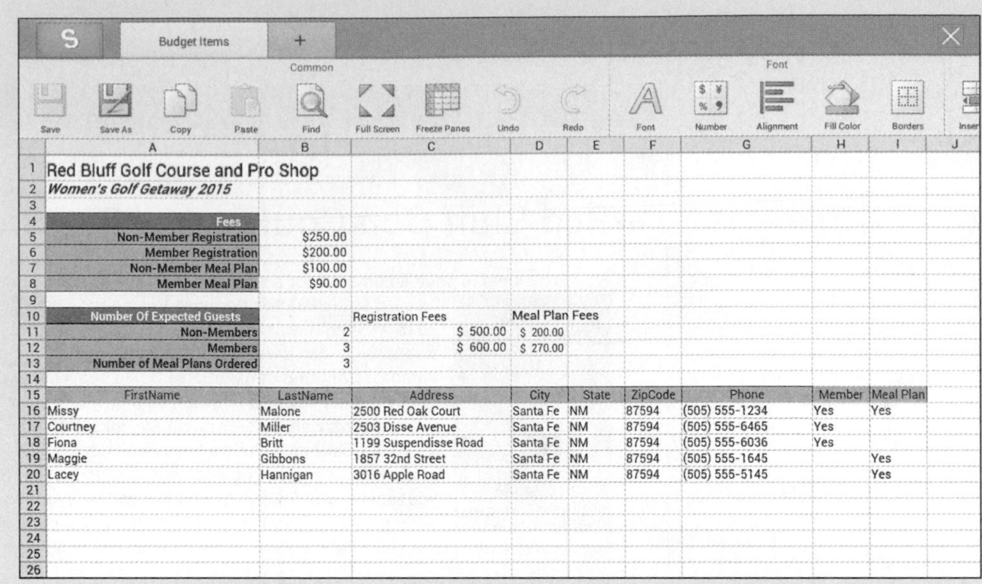

	A	B	C	D	E	F	G	H	I
1	Red Bluff Golf Course and Pro Shop								
2	*Women's Golf Getaway 2015*								
3									
4	Fees								
5	Non-Member Registration	$250.00							
6	Member Registration	$200.00							
7	Non-Member Meal Plan	$100.00							
8	Member Meal Plan	$90.00							
9									
10	Number Of Expected Guests		Registration Fees	Meal Plan Fees					
11	Non-Members	2	$ 500.00	$ 200.00					
12	Members	3	$ 600.00	$ 270.00					
13	Number of Meal Plans Ordered	3							
14									
15	FirstName	LastName	Address	City	State	ZipCode	Phone	Member	Meal Plan
16	Missy	Malone	2500 Red Oak Court	Santa Fe	NM	87594	(505) 555-1234	Yes	Yes
17	Courtney	Miller	2503 Disse Avenue	Santa Fe	NM	87594	(505) 555-6465	Yes	
18	Fiona	Britt	1199 Suspendisse Road	Santa Fe	NM	87594	(505) 555-6036	Yes	
19	Maggie	Gibbons	1857 32nd Street	Santa Fe	NM	87594	(505) 555-1645		Yes
20	Lacey	Hannigan	3016 Apple Road	Santa Fe	NM	87594	(505) 555-5145		Yes

Figure 18 The ms01ws01Registration document viewed in Kingsoft Spreadsheets

b. Double-tap cell **B11** to select and edit it. Tap in the **Edit bar**, and then tap Delete to delete the 2.

c. Tap the **Function** button *fx*, tap **Statistical**, and then tap **COUNTA()**. Swipe down to scroll to cell **A16**. Tap cell **A16**, tap the **right selection handle**, and then drag it to cell **A20**.

d. Tap after the **COUNTA** function. Type a minus sign, -, and then tap the **Function** button. Tap **Statistical**, and then tap **COUNTA()**. Swipe left to scroll to cell **H16**. Tap cell **H16**, tap the **right selection handle**, and then drag it to cell **H20**. Tap Enter to create a formula to count the registered non-members. This formula counts the number of attendees and subtracts the number of members attending. The result is the number of non-members attending.

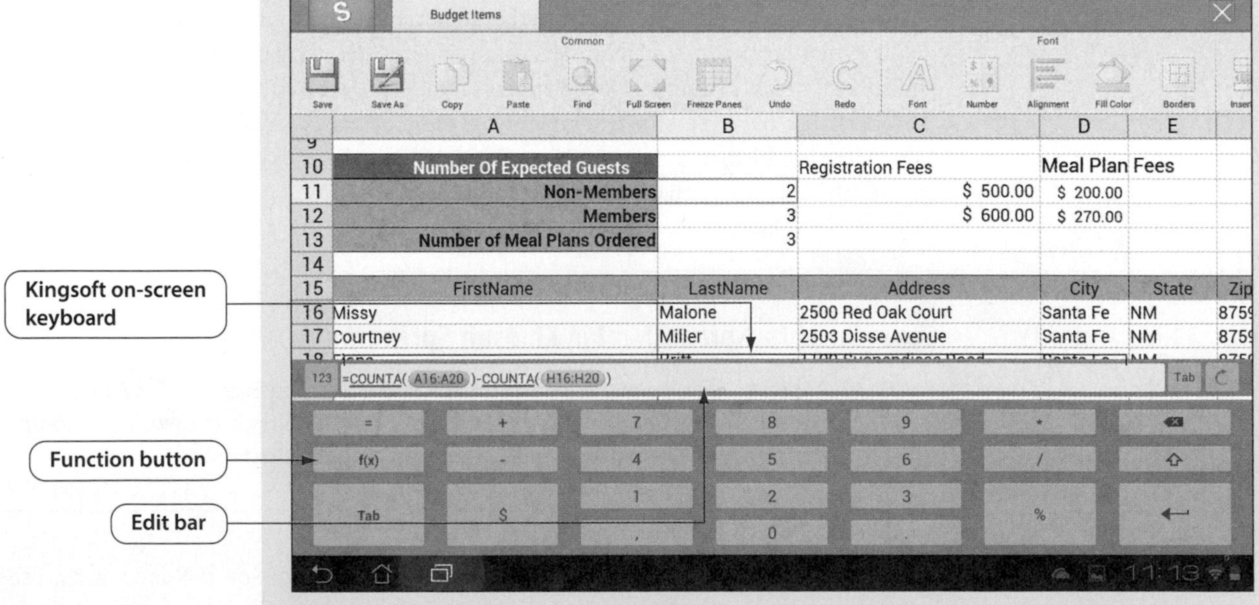

Figure 19 Editing a formula in Kingsoft Spreadsheets

Troubleshooting

Spreadsheet functions require a combination of text and numeric characters. This generally is not a problem with traditional keyboards. On-screen keyboards, due to space constraints, have a limited set of keys available. In Kingsoft Spreadsheets, tap the button on the left of the Edit bar to switch between the text, numeric, and symbol characters as you type.

e. Tap cell **B12** to select it, tap in the **Edit bar**, and then tap Delete to delete the 3.

f. Tap the **Function** button, tap **Statistical**, and then tap **COUNTA()**. Swipe left to scroll to cell **H16**. Tap cell **H16**, and then tap the **selection handle**, and then drag it to cell **H20**. Tap Enter to create a formula to count the registered members.

Troubleshooting

In Microsoft Excel, formulas using relative cell references will be appropriately modified if copied and pasted to another cell. In Kingsoft Spreadsheets, the formula will not be updated.

g. Tap cell **B12** to select it, and then tap and hold the text in the **Edit bar** to select it. From the contextual menu at the top of the screen, tap **Copy**, and then tap **Done**.

h. Tap Enter to go to cell B13. Tap after the **3** in the Edit bar, tap Delete, and then tap in the **Edit bar** and hold until Paste appears. Tap **Paste**, tap after the **H20**, and then tap Delete.

i. Swipe left to view columns **H** and **I**. Tap **I16**, tap the **left selection handle**, and then drag the left selection handle to cell **I20**. Tap Enter to create a formula to count the number of meal plans that have been ordered.

j. Tap **Save**.

Freezing Panes with Kingsoft Spreadsheets

If the event is as popular as anticipated, the list of attendees will become quite long. To increase the readability of the document it would be helpful to freeze the panes on the spreadsheet. In this exercise you will freeze the panes on the spreadsheet to allow a user to scroll through the attendees without losing sight of the registration information.

M01.07

To Freeze Panes in Kingsoft Spreadsheets

a. Tap cell **B16** to select it.

b. In the Context Menu, tap **Freeze Panes**. Notice that the Freeze Panes icon now has a filled background.

c. Tap **below** row 16 in the spreadsheet, and then swipe your finger **up**. This will scroll the worksheet rows. Notice that rows 1 through 15 are frozen, while rows 16 and below scrolled up with your swipe.

d. Tap to the **right** of column A, and then swipe your finger to the **left**. This will scroll the worksheet columns to the left. Notice that column A is frozen, while the columns to the right scrolled to the left with your swipe.

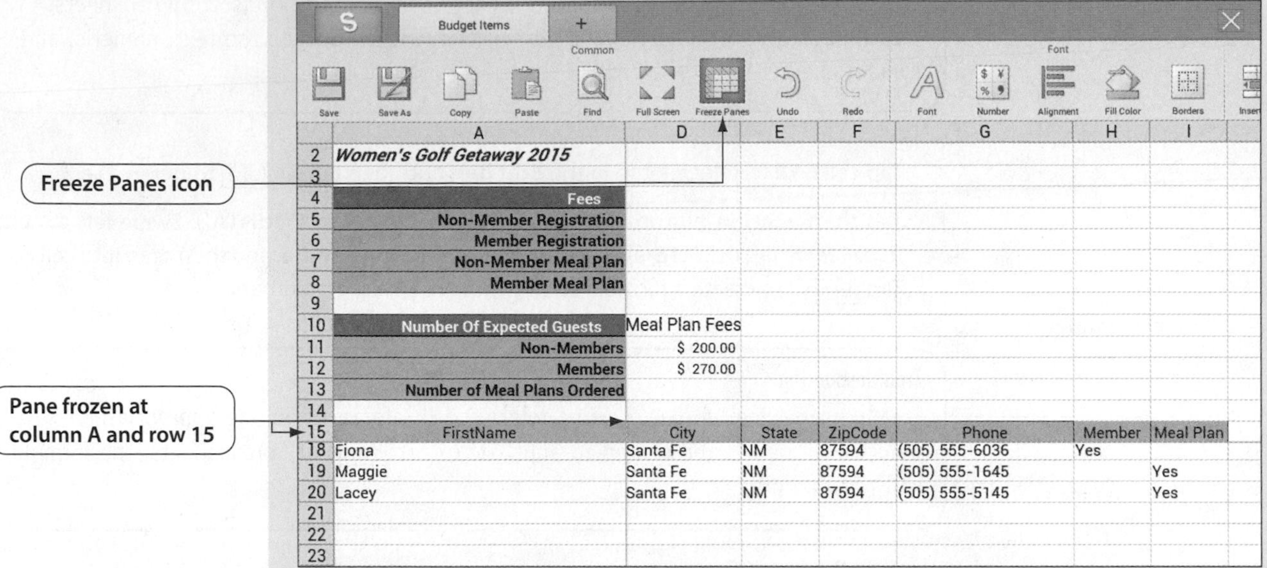

Figure 20 Freeze Panes in Kingsoft Spreadsheets

e. Tap to the **right** of column A, and then swipe your finger to the **right**. Scroll the worksheet columns so that column B is again visible.

f. Tap **below** row 16 in the spreadsheet, and then swipe your finger **down**. Scroll the worksheet rows so that row 16 is again visible.

Sharing Documents with Kingsoft

The spreadsheet is now finished and needs to be saved and sent on to Timothy.

M01.08

To Save and Forward the Documents

a. Tap **Save As** in the context menu. By default Kingsoft may be set to save Excel documents as .xls files. This results in the loss of several Excel 2013 features and possibly formatting changes to the document. Ensure that the file extension is .xlsx.

b. Tap **Save,** and then tap **Close** to close the document.

c. Be sure that the **ms01ws01Registration_LastFirst** file is currently centered on the screen.

d. Tap the **E-mail** icon in the upper-right corner of the screen. In the context menu that appears, tap **E-mail** in the Share group.

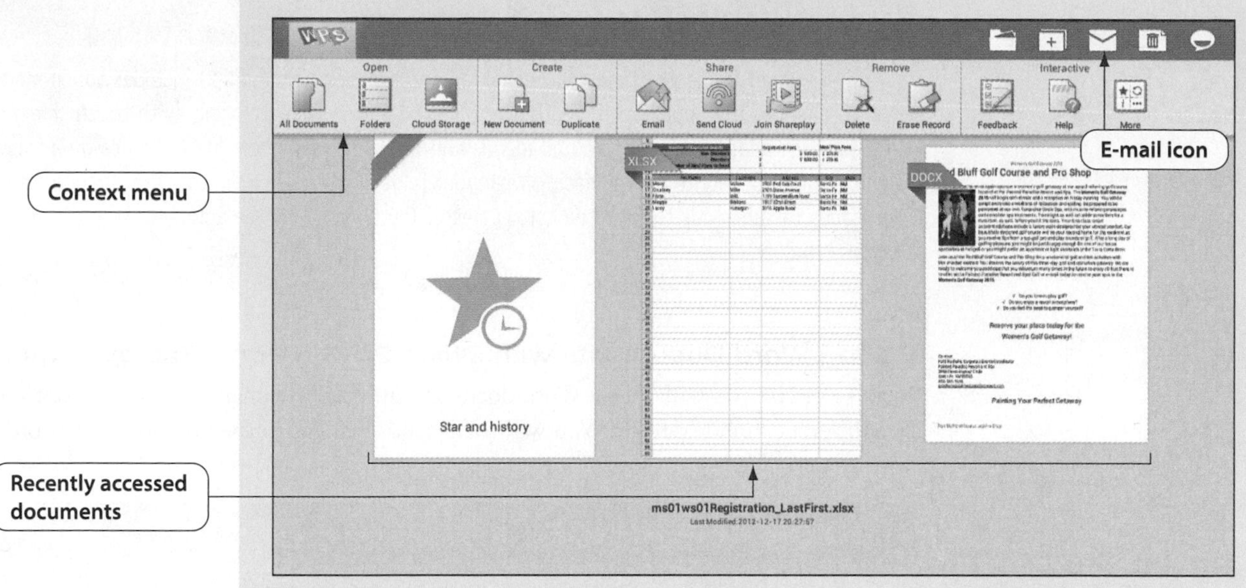

Figure 21 Managing files with Kingsoft

SIDE NOTE
Cloud Option
You also have a "Send Cloud" option that allows for file share via several cloud storage services.

e. If presented with a choice of e-mail apps, choose your preferred app, and then tap **Compose**.

f. In the To: field, type the e-mail address. In the Subject: field, type Please review, and then tap the **Paperclip** icon to attach a second document.

g. From the Choose attachment menu that appears, tap **File Manager**. Locate the **ms01ws01Registration_LastFirst** and **ms01ws01GolfGetaway_LastFirst** files on your tablet, and then tap the **file name** to attach the document.

h. Tap **Send**.

View and Edit Documents on a Surface Tablet

When Timothy receives the documents on his Surface RT tablet, he will have access to Microsoft Office 2013 RT. Timothy would like the document to more closely match other informational flyers that have been sent out. This would mean putting the Red Bluff Golf Course and Pro Shop logo into the header of the document, adjusting the font size and style of the document, and changing the document margins. Timothy has his Surface tablet with him but does not have access to a wireless keyboard or mouse. He will be making all changes to the documents with touch gestures and the on-screen keyboard. To make this easier he has entered touch mode in Word 2013.

QUICK REFERENCE | **Common Windows 8 Gestures**

1. Swipe from the right edge of the screen to activate the Charms bar.
2. Swipe from the left edge of the screen to change apps.
3. Swipe from the bottom edge of the screen to activate app commands.
4. Tap and hold to activate menus.

REAL WORLD ADVICE | **Touch Mode**

Windows 8 and Office 2013 are touch-enabled applications. Office 2013 includes touch mode, which changes the appearance of Office applications to work more easily with touch screens. Touch mode adds more space around menus and icons to make them easier to use on a tablet where you are likely to be navigating with your finger instead of a mouse. This change also cascades to submenus such as the color palette. Touch mode can be activated from the Quick Access toolbar.

Editing Word Documents with Office 2013 RT on a Tablet Computer

In this exercise you will open a Word document and observe changes that have been made on two different mobile devices. You will then make changes to the document in Word 2013.

QUICK REFERENCE | **Common Office 2013 Gestures**

1. Pinch to zoom in on a document.
2. Stretch to zoom out on a document.
3. Swipe to scroll through the document.
4. Tap objects to select them.
5. Tap and move your finger to move objects in a document.

M01.09

To Open and Edit the Document

a. Start **Word**, and then open the file ms01ws01**GolfGetaway_LastFirst**.

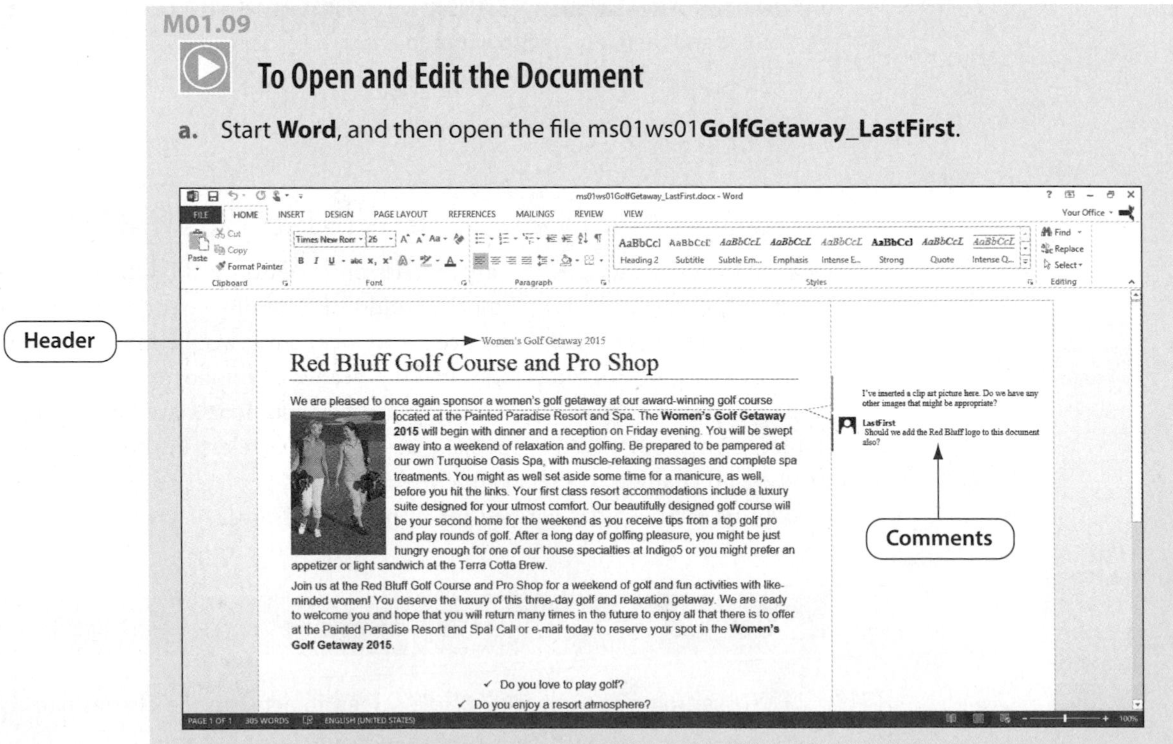

Figure 22 The document viewed in Word on a Surface tablet

SIDE NOTE

The Mouse vs. Your Finger

Windows 8 and Office 2013 recognize the difference between your finger, the stylus pen, and the insertion point.

b. Double-tap the **header** of the document to edit it, select the **text** in the header, and then tap Delete.

c. Tap the **INSERT** tab, and then in the Illustrations group, tap **Pictures**. Click **Browse**, select the **ms01ws01TurquoiseOasis** image, and then click **Insert** to insert the new image.

d. Tap the **FORMAT** tab, and then tap in the **Shape Height** [Height: 0.19"] box. Type 1, and then tap Enter to change the height of the image.

Troubleshooting

The width of the image should change to 3.8" by default. If it remains at 6.25", tap in the Shape Width box and type 3.8.

e. Tap the **FORMAT** tab, and then in the Arrange group, tap **Position**, and then tap **More Layout Options**.

f. Tap the **Position** tab, and then in the Horizontal category, tap **Alignment**. Tap the **selection arrow**, tap **Centered**, and then tap **OK**.

g. Tap the **PAGE LAYOUT** tab, and then in the Page Setup group, tap **Margins**, and then tap **Normal** to set the page margins to 1".

h. Double-tap the **body** of the document to exit the header, and then double-tap the first word of the body of the document, **We**.

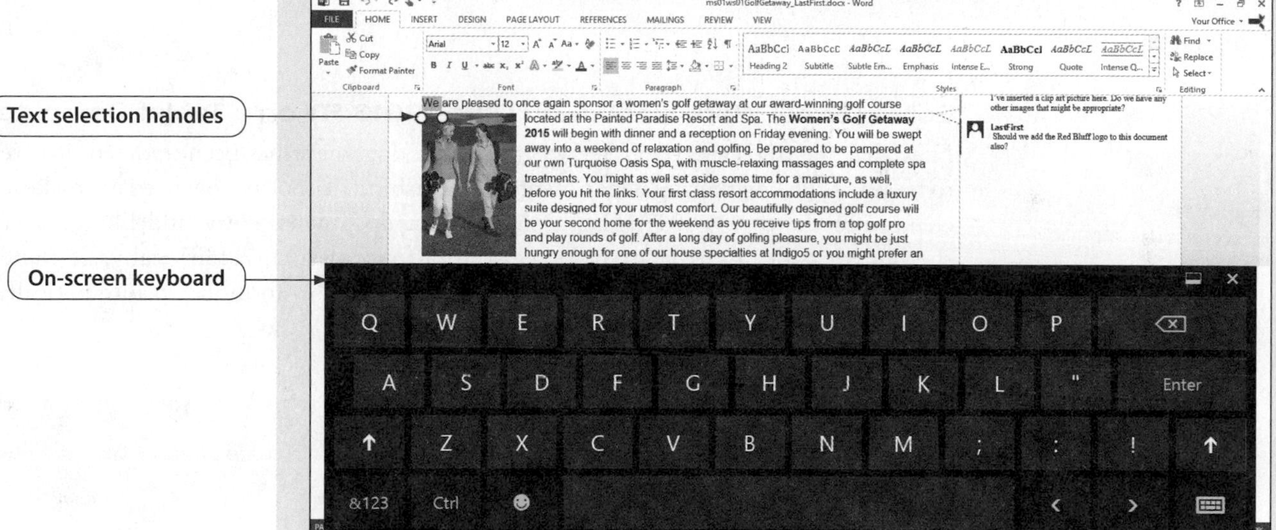

Figure 23 The text selection handles and on-screen keyboard

i. Tap and hold the right **text selection handle**, and then drag it to the end of the document, including the text **Painting Your Perfect Getaway**. Tap the **HOME** tab, tap the **Font** arrow, and then choose **Times New Roman** from the available font styles. Tap the **Font Size** arrow, and then select **11** from the available font sizes.

j. Save and close the document. Close Word.

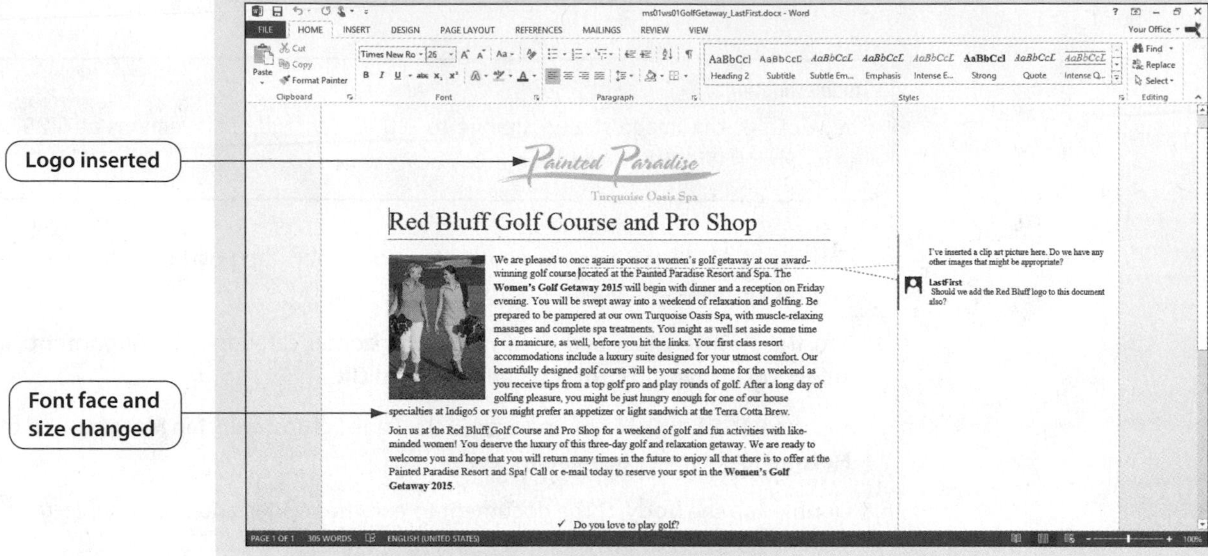

Figure 24 The finished document in Word 2013

Editing Excel Worksheets with Office 2013 RT on a Tablet Computer

Now that the ms01ws01GolfGetaway_LastFirst document has been updated, it is ready to be sent to the marketing department for publishing. Timothy now needs to make a few changes to the ms01ws01Registration_LastFirst document. He would like to separate the budget data from the attendee registration information. Additionally, he wants to make the attendee registration data a table. This will allow formulas to automatically be updated if new data are added.

QUICK REFERENCE | **Excel 2013 Gestures**

1. Double-tap a cell to edit it.
2. Tap a cell, and use the selection handles to select a range of cells.
3. Tap and hold to activate the MiniBar.

In this exercise, you will move the portion of the spreadsheet that contains the registration information to a new worksheet. You will also insert a chart in the main worksheet.

M01.10

To Open and Edit the Spreadsheet

a. Start **Excel**, and then open the data file **ms01ws01Registration_LastFirst**.

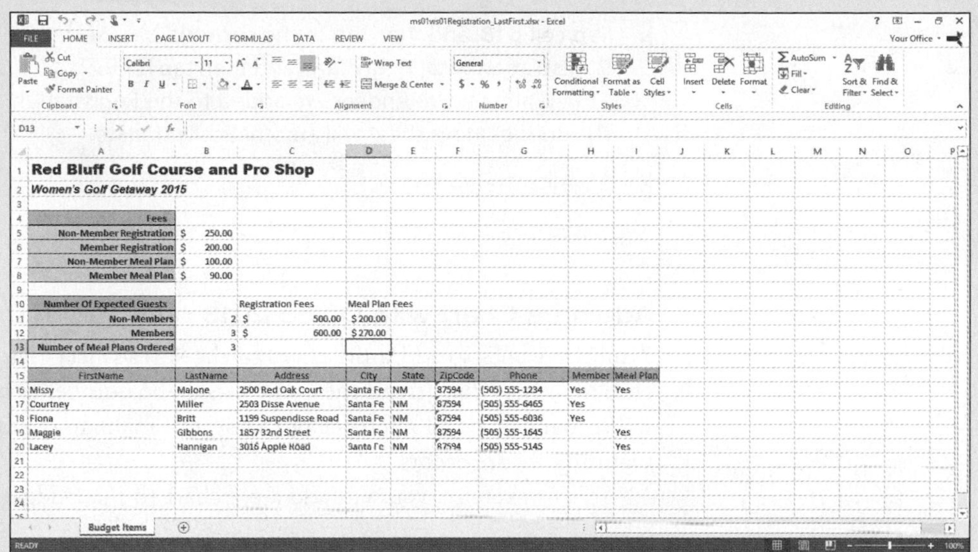

	A	B	C	D	E	F	G	H	I
1	**Red Bluff Golf Course and Pro Shop**								
2	*Women's Golf Getaway 2015*								
3									
4	Fees								
5	Non-Member Registration	$ 250.00							
6	Member Registration	$ 200.00							
7	Non-Member Meal Plan	$ 100.00							
8	Member Meal Plan	$ 90.00							
9									
10	Number Of Expected Guests		Registration Fees	Meal Plan Fees					
11	Non-Members	2	$ 500.00	$ 200.00					
12	Members	3	$ 600.00	$ 270.00					
13	Number of Meal Plans Ordered	3							
14									
15	FirstName	LastName	Address	City	State	ZipCode	Phone	Member	Meal Plan
16	Missy	Malone	2500 Red Oak Court	Santa Fe	NM	87594	(505) 555-1234	Yes	Yes
17	Courtney	Miller	2503 Disse Avenue	Santa Fe	NM	87594	(505) 555-6465	Yes	
18	Fiona	Britt	1199 Suspendisse Road	Santa Fe	NM	87594	(505) 555-6036	Yes	
19	Maggie	Gibbons	1857 32nd Street	Santa Fe	NM	87594	(505) 555-1645		Yes
20	Lacey	Hannigan	3016 Apple Road	Santa Fe	NM	87594	(505) 555-5145		Yes

Figure 25 The document viewed in Excel on a Surface tablet

b. Tap **New Sheet** ⊕ to add a new worksheet. Double-tap the **Sheet1** tab to rename it, and then type Registration for the name of the worksheet.

c. Tap the **Budget Items** worksheet, tap cell **A15**, and then tap the **right text selection handle** and drag it to cell **I20**.

d. Tap the **selected cells** to display the MiniBar. Tap **Cut**, and then tap the **Registration** worksheet. Tap in cell **A1**, tap the **HOME** tab, and then tap **Paste**.

> **Troubleshooting**
> The text that is being moved is connected to formulas on the Budget Items worksheet. Excel will automatically adjust the formulas connected to these cells when they are moved. Apps on other tablet computers may not be able to carry out that function, resulting in broken formulas.

e. Tap the **INSERT** tab, and then in the Tables group, tap **Table**. Confirm that the table data box contains the range $A$1:$I$6, and the My table has headers check box is selected, and then tap **OK**.

f. Tap the **DESIGN** tab**,** and then in the Properties group, tap **Table Name**, and then type RegistrationData to replace the default table name.

g. Tap the **Budget Items** worksheet, and then tap cell **B11**. Tap in the **formula bar**, and then select the text **Registration!A2:A6** in the first COUNTA function. Type RegistrationData[FirstName] to replace the original cell reference.

h. Select the text **Registration!H2:H6** in the second COUNTA function. Type RegistrationData[Member], and then tap Enter to replace the original cell reference.

i. Tap cell **B12**, and then tap in the **formula bar**. Select the text **Registration!H2:H6**, type RegistrationData[Member], and then tap Enter to replace the original cell reference.

j. Tap cell **B13**, and then tap in the **formula bar**. Select the text **Registration!I2:I6**, type RegistrationData[Meal Plan], and then tap Enter to replace the original cell reference.

When new attendees are added to the Registration spreadsheet, the formulas on the Budget Items sheet will automatically update.

k. Save the workbook.

Adding a Chart with Office 2013 on a Tablet Computer

Timothy wants to add a pie chart to the spreadsheet that compares the number of golf club members that attend the event versus the number of non-members that attend. This will provide a visual reference of the overall makeup of attendees to the event and aid in planning future events.

In this exercise, you will add a pie chart to the Budget Items worksheet.

M01.11

To Add a Chart

a. Tap cell **A11** to select it, tap the **right text selection handle**, and then drag it to cell **B12**.

b. Tap the **INSERT** tab, and then in the Charts group, tap **Recommended Charts**. Tap the **Pie** chart, and then tap **OK** to insert the pie chart.

c. Tap the **chart** to select it, and then double-tap the **chart title** box to edit the chart title.

d. Tap the **right text selection handle**, and then drag it to the end of the default chart title. Type Member versus Non-Member Attendees to replace the default chart title.

e. Tap the **chart** to select it. Position the chart to begin in cell **E2**, and then if necessary, adjust the size of the chart so that the bottom-right corner covers cell **H13**.

f. Save and close the document.

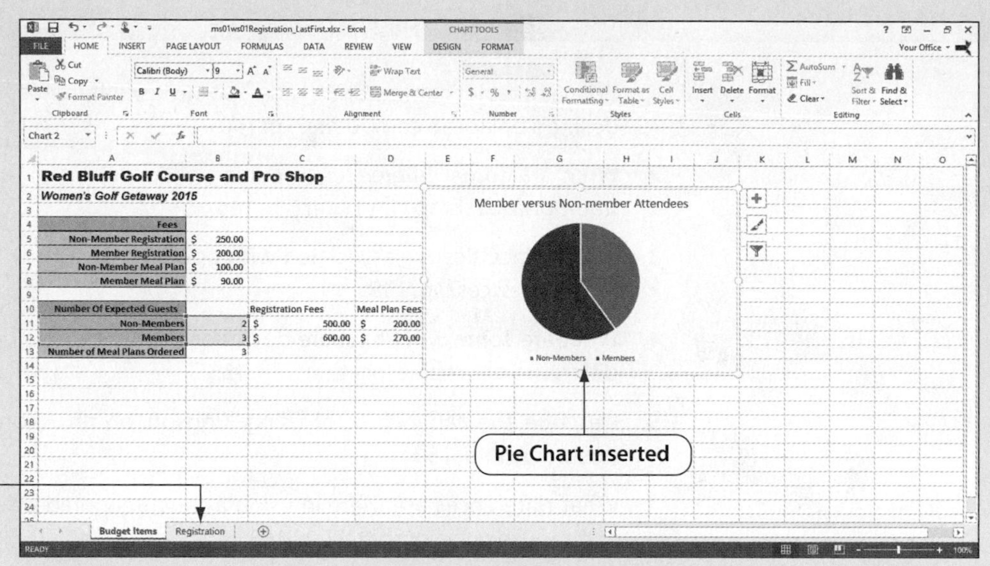

Figure 26 The finished worksheet

CONSIDER THIS | **Touch vs. Mouse vs. Digitizer Pen?**

All tablets use touch screens in place of a traditional mouse. Office 2013 was designed with this in mind. If you have used a tablet computer to modify Word or Excel documents, how was the experience different than using a traditional mouse? Were there advantages or disadvantages?

Concept Check

1. What is a tablet computer? What are some key differences between tablet computers and desktop or laptop computers? p. 140
2. What are some differences in editing a document on a tablet computer versus on a traditional desktop computer? p. 144
3. What difficulties are associated with opening Office 2013 documents on non-Windows mobile devices? p. 148
4. What are some ways to share documents from mobile devices if team members are in different geographic locations? p. 155
5. Describe the capabilities of using Kingsoft on an Android tablet to edit Office 2013 documents. p. 156
6. What differences are there in using a touch-enabled device as opposed to a keyboard and mouse on a computer? p. 163

Key Terms

App 142
Application 142
Cloud computing 140
Stylus 140
Synchronization 141
Tablet computer 140

Visual Summary

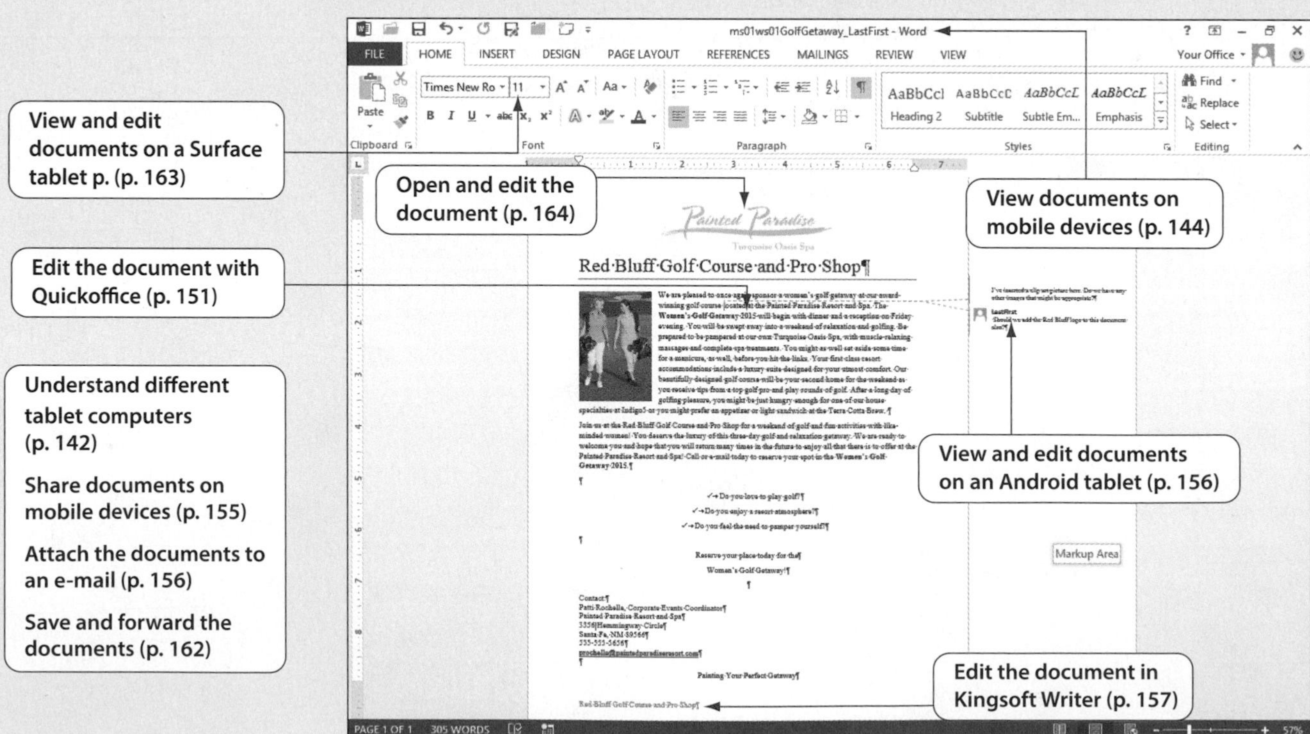

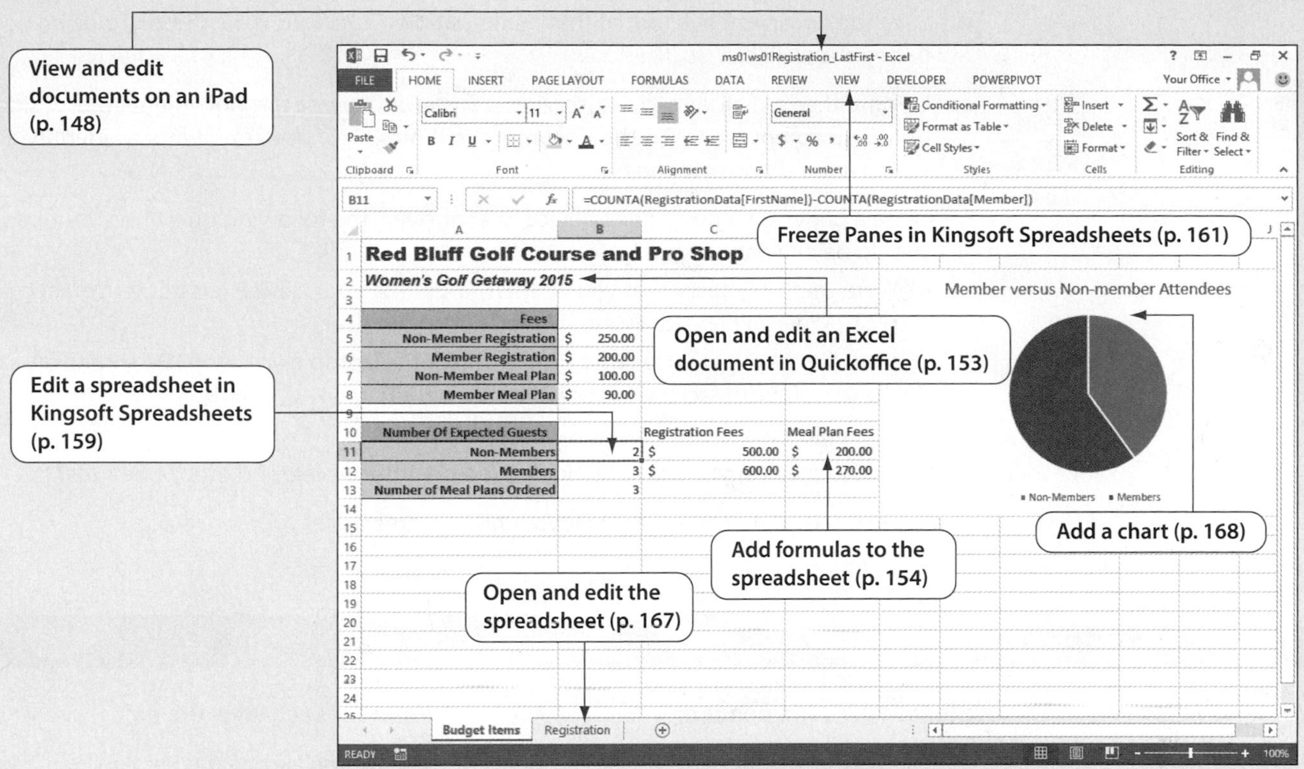

Figure 27 Women's Golf Getaway Collaboration Final Document

Perform 1: Perform in Your Life

Using New Features in Windows 8

Student data file needed:

 Blank Word document

You will save your files as:

 ms01ws01StudentOrg_LastFirst.docx

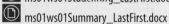

 ms01ws01Summary_LastFirst.docx

Promoting Your Organization

Sales & Marketing

Using a tablet computer or smartphone, create a Word document advertising an organization of which you are a member. This could be a student organization or a community organization. This document could be shared directly from your mobile device through social networking sites. It could also be shared through e-mail or printed and distributed by hand. Your document should meet the following requirements.

a. Start your preferred Office app, create a new document, and then save the document as ms01ws01StudentOrg_LastFirst, using your last and first name.

b. The document must contain the name of your organization and a brief summary of the purpose of the organization.

c. The document should contain several of the following features. The number of features you include in the document may depend upon the device and app combination you are using and any specific instructions by your instructor.
   - Header and footer in the document
   - A bulleted list
   - The logo of your organization or other related image
   - An example of a font that has been bolded, italicized, highlighted, or otherwise styled differently than the default text

d. Save the document in a format that is compatible with Word 2013. Choose .doc or .docx if they are available.

e. Using either e-mail or a cloud service, transfer a copy of the document to a desktop or laptop computer. Open the document in Word 2013. Use comments to identify any unexpected changes to the file.

f. Write a paper, on a nonmobile device, that answers the following questions. Your paper should be one page or less.
   - Were there any tasks that you wanted to do that your device did not let you accomplish? Were you able to insert an image into your flyer?
   - How did the experience differ from a traditional laptop or desktop? Be sure to discuss the use of the on-screen keyboard versus a traditional keyboard.
   - What did your device do well?
   - Would the flyer you produced look good on other tablets and mobile devices?

g. Save your documents, and submit your files as directed by your instructor.

Perform 2: Perform in Your Career

Student data file needed:

ms01ws01Inventory.xlsx

You will save your file as:

ms01ws01Inventory_LastFirst.xlsx

Managing Video Game Inventory

Production & Operations

Information Technology

You have been tasked with updating an inventory spreadsheet. This spreadsheet contains items that have been stored in a large warehouse. While the warehouse has wireless Internet access, there are few means of tracking the inventory using technology. You have been given a spreadsheet to begin with. You have also been asked to perform several tasks in the spreadsheet to update the inventory and improve the usability of the document. A list of these tasks is provided below. You may not be able to perform all of these tasks on your mobile device. When you are finished with the tasks that you can complete, compose a memo in Word 2013 outlining the tasks that remain to be completed in the spreadsheet. Include in your memo a brief explanation of why the tasks on the list could not be completed in the app you were using.

a. Start the spreadsheet app on your mobile device, open **ms01ws01Inventory**, and then save the spreadsheet as ms01ws01Inventory_LastFirst.

b. The Inventory worksheet contains a list of items currently in the store's inventory room. Enter new records for the following:
   - 50 new copies of ZombieZone arrived on 1/15/2015.
   - 12 copies of the racing game Life in the Fast Lane were sold on 1/13/2015 for $15.99.
   - 25 new copies of the racing game Hamster Behind the Wheel arrived on 2/1/2015 and will be sold for $39.99.

c. Two records that were previously entered need to be changed as they were incorrect.
   - On 1/9/2015, 20 copies of SuperNatural Heroes were sold.
   - On 3/15/2015, 15 copies of Racing Mayhem arrived.

d. The worksheet Dashboard contains a summary of the inventory. The values for each game genre in cells B7:B9 are values in the worksheet, not formulas. Construct formulas that will complete these calculations.

e. On the Dashboard worksheet, cell B5 should calculate the total number of transactions listed on the Inventory worksheet.

f. On the Dashboard worksheet, cell B1 should calculate the total number of units sold on the Inventory worksheet.

g. On the Inventory sheet, ensure that the following formatting options are made.
   - Cells D2:D12 should be formatted to appear as currency.
   - The headers in row 1 should be bolded with a grey background and white text.

h. On the Dashboard sheet, the summary data from A7 to B9 should have a solid border around the outside of the cells.

i. Create a pie chart that displays the transactions by genre displayed in A7 to B9 of the Dashboard sheet. Type Transactions by Genre for the chart title.

j. On the Inventory sheet, apply a filter to the inventory data, and then set the filter so that only Racing games are visible.

k. Save your documents, and then submit your files as directed by your instructor.

Perform 3: Perform in Your Team

Student data file needed:

Blank Word document

You will save your files as:

ms01ws01Proposal_TeamName.docx

ms01ws01Proposal_TeamName.xlsx

Proposing a New Course

Research & Development

Information Technology

Form a team as directed by your instructor. Develop a proposal for a new course at your institution. Each team member will complete a different aspect of the project. One team member will compose a single-page proposal for the course in a word-processing app. The other team member will build an outline of the class in a spreadsheet app.

a. Select one team member to set up the database by completing Steps b–f.

b. Create a Word document, and then name it ms01ws01Proposal_TeamName. Replace TeamName with the name assigned to your team by your instructor.

c. Create an Excel document, and then name it ms01ws01Proposal_TeamName. Replace TeamName with the name assigned to your team by your instructor.

d. Rename Sheet1 as Contributors, list the names of each of the team members on the worksheet, and then add a heading above the name to read Team Members. Include any additional information on this worksheet required by your instructor.

e. Point your browser to **www.skydrive.live.com**, **www.drive.google.com**, or any other instructor-assigned tool. Be sure all members of the team have an account on the chosen system—Microsoft or Google. Create a new folder, and then name it TeamName_Assignment, replacing Name with the name assigned to your team by your instructor.

f. Share the documents with the other members of your team. Make sure that each team member has the appropriate permission to edit both documents.

g. You will need to meet the following requirements in the proposal document:

- Assume the instructor of your course is the dean, and address the proposal as such.
- Include a course title and description.
- Include hyperlinks to websites that contain content related to your course proposal.
- Include at least one image in your proposal. This could be your institution's logo or a logo for your course specifically.
- The proposal must contain a header and footer. Include all team member names and the current date in your footer.
- Include at least one bulleted list in your proposal.

h. You will need to meet the following requirements in the spreadsheet outline of your proposal:

- Using your institution's semester structure, create a timeline of classes. Each day of class must contain a class title and have one row each for a reading assignment and a homework assignment.
- In one of the first three rows of your worksheet, use the appropriate formula to document the number of weeks in the semester.
- In one of the first three rows of your worksheet, use the appropriate formula to count the number of class meetings in the semester.
- Arrange individual classes vertically and class details horizontally.
- Freeze the panes of the spreadsheet so that the rows containing the headings will not move if the view of the sheet is scrolled vertically.

i. Once the assignment is complete, share the spreadsheet with your instructor or turn it in as your instructor directs. Make sure that your instructor has permission to edit the contents of the folder.

Additional Cases

Additional Workshop Cases are available on the companion website and in the instructor resources.

WORKSHOP 1 | REVIEW AND MODIFY A DOCUMENT

OBJECTIVES

Prepare Case

Putts for Paws Golf Tournament Memo

Customer Service   Sales & Marketing

photofriday / Shutterstock.com

Painted Paradise Resort and Spa sponsors an annual charity golf tournament, with proceeds benefiting a different organization each year. This year, the tournament spotlights the Santa Fe Animal Center. The goal is to raise money for the center as well as to facilitate the adoption of as many animals as possible to loving homes. Your assignment is to review and edit a memorandum to the employees of the hotel's event-planning staff. The memo provides a summary of tournament activities and sponsorship opportunities so the staff can answer questions and encourage participation.

REAL WORLD SUCCESS

"During my job search, I was having a difficult time getting called in for an interview. I realized that with so many applicants out there, having a resume that stands out is an exceedingly important aspect of getting to the next step. Thankfully, I was able to take advantage of Word's formatting to make my resume look much more professional and help me land the interviews I had been striving for."

-Chris, recent graduate

Student data files needed for this workshop:

 w01ws01Putts.docx

w01ws01PuttsPDF.pdf

You will save your files as:

 w01ws01Putts_LastFirst.docx

 w01ws01Putts_LastFirst.pdf

 w01ws01PuttsPDF_LastFirst.pdf

Understanding Business Communication

Communication is a regular part of daily life, both verbally and in writing. As you converse with others, you want your listeners to understand your meaning and to become engaged in the topic. It is equally important that written communication reflect your objectives and convey your messages exactly as you intend. Excellent communication skills are crucial in the success of a business—so much so that American businesses spend $3.1 billion annually training people to communicate effectively.

Business communication is defined as communication between members of an organization for the purpose of carrying out business activities. Always remember that the way you communicate verbally, and in writing, is often the first and most lasting impression that others have of you. In fact, communication skills are often the factor that sets you apart from others in a company. Its importance cannot be overstated. Often referred to as a *soft skill,* excellent written and oral communication abilities can identify you as one of the most valued employees in a business.

Communication is not a one-way street. It is not a monologue but is, instead, a dialogue. If your message is not interpreted by your audience exactly as you intended, then the communication has failed. Students often spend an inordinate amount of time developing technical skills in software and business operations, but they give too little credence to the importance of understanding the target audience and communicating on a level where both the sender and receiver can understand each other. Regardless of the message topic, always take time to identify and understand your audience. In this section, you will explore the topic of business communication, identifying standard business letter styles, standard memo styles, and effective methods of communication.

Use Word-Processing Software

Word processing is often cited as one of the main reasons to use a computer. People in businesses, schools, and homes use word-processing software on a daily basis to create, edit, and print documents. It is used to create reports, letters, memos, newsletters, flyers, business cards, and many other documents. Within documents, you can format text, adjust margins, insert graphics, organize data into tables, create charts, and easily make revisions. Clearly, it is a versatile tool that enables you to efficiently create effective documents for written communication.

Although you can select from several word-processing software packages with a wide range of capabilities and cost, Microsoft Word is the leading word-processing program in terms of usage and sales. This textbook provides information on **Microsoft Word 2013**, Microsoft's most current version of word-processing software.

Opening a File

When you open Microsoft Word 2013, the **Word Start screen** is displayed so that you can easily begin to work with new or existing files. A list of recent documents is displayed in the left pane, along with an option to open other documents from your hard drive, SkyDrive, or other web locations. The right pane enables you to select a new blank document or choose from a variety of templates.

You are ready to begin work on your memorandum. You will start Word 2013, open the memorandum file, and save it to a new name.

REAL WORLD ADVICE **Minimize Distractions**

Word gives you the ability to open multiple documents. Each opened document is shown as an overlapped Word icon on the Windows taskbar. Unless there is a specific need to have several documents open, perhaps because you need to copy text from one to another, it is best to keep the number of open documents to a minimum. This will enable you to focus on your current project.

W01.00

To Open a Document

a. From the Start screen or desktop, point to the **bottom-right corner** of the screen. The Charms will be displayed on the right side of the screen.

b. Note the labels underneath each of the charms. Click the **Search** charm.

c. Click inside the **search** box at the top of the page. Type Word.

d. Click **Word 2013** in the search results. The Word Start screen displays.

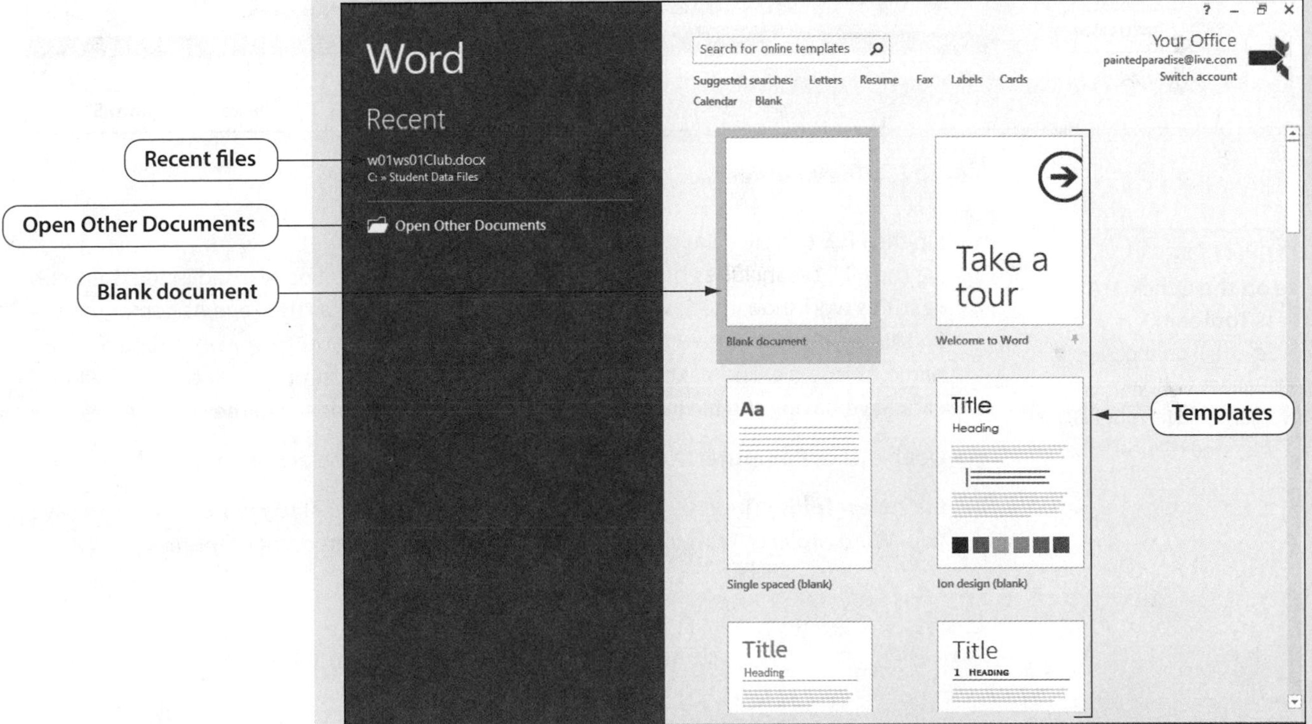

Figure 1 The Word Start screen interface

e. The Word Start screen is displayed when Word is launched. Click **Open Other Documents** in the left pane. Double-click **Computer**. Navigate through the folder structure to the location of your student data files. Double-click **w01ws01Putts**. A memorandum providing information on the upcoming Putts for Paws golf tournament opens.

Read through the memorandum, noting the various elements of a memo, such as the header and body. You will address the grammatical and typographical errors later in this workshop.

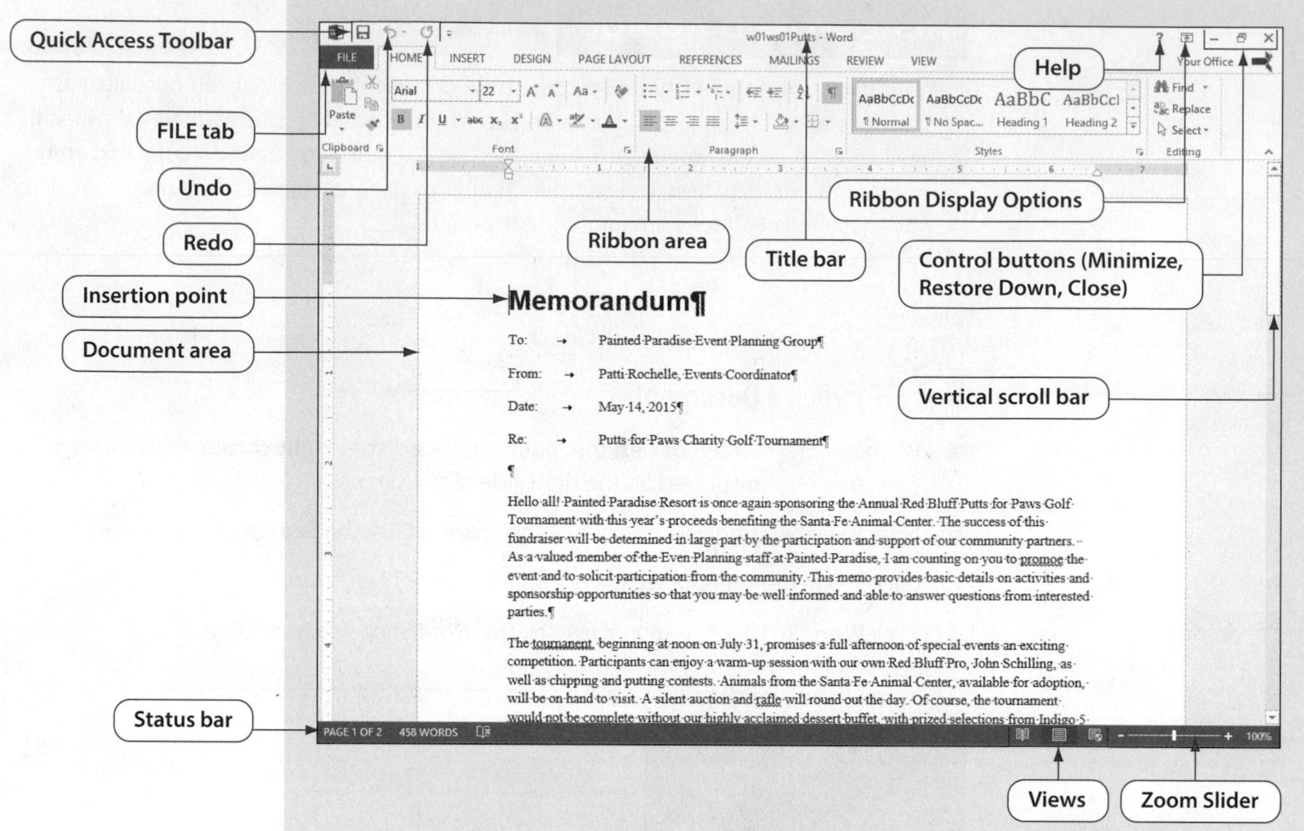

Figure 2 The Word interface

SIDE NOTE
Save on the Quick Access Toolbar
Click Save on the Quick Access Toolbar to conveniently save your file with the same name, in the same location.

f. On the **FILE** tab, click **Save As**.

The FILE tab includes both Save and Save As options. As you learned in the Common Features workshop, the Save command behaves the same as the Save As command the first time you save a new file—both commands will ask you to specify a location and name for the file. The next time you save the file, you can simply click the FILE tab and click Save, saving the file in the same location with the same file name.

g. Double-click **Computer**. Navigate to the location where you are saving your files.

h. Click **New folder**. Type WordProjects and then press Enter to create a folder to save your Word projects. With the WordProjects folder still selected, click **Open**.

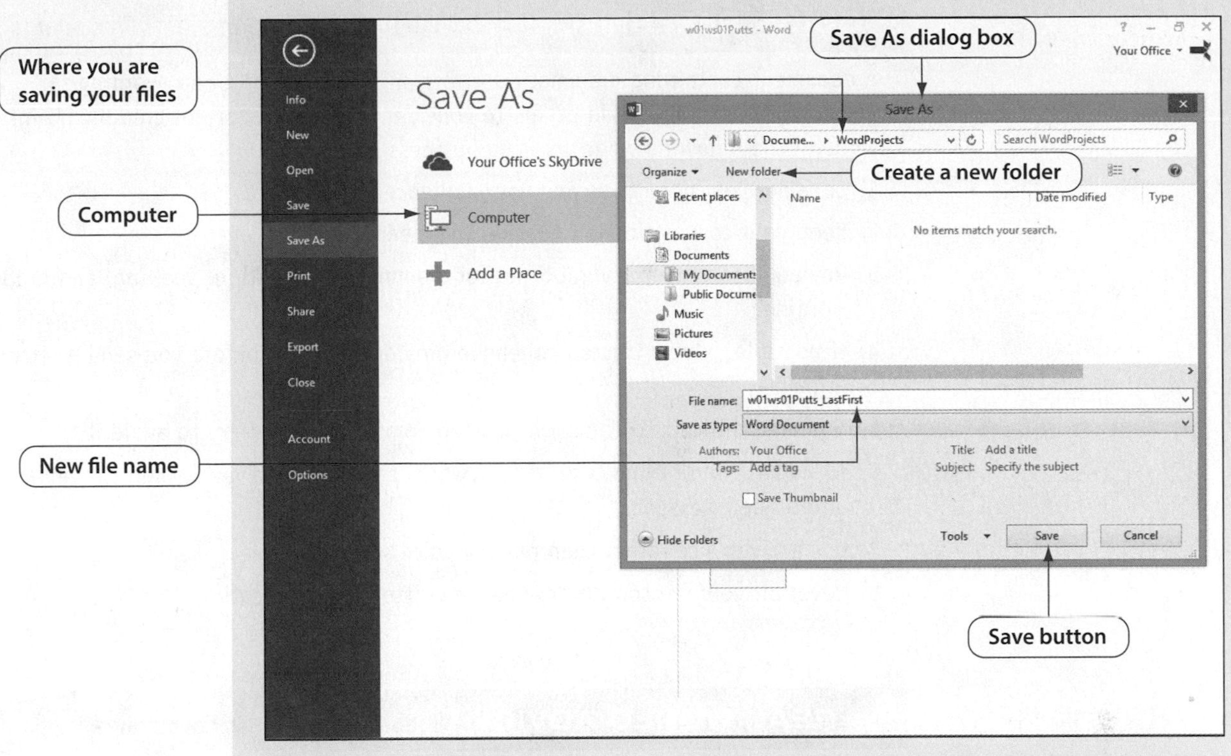

Figure 3 Save As dialog box

i. Click in the **File name** box, and then change the file name to w01ws01Putts_LastFirst, using your last and first name.

j. Click **Save** to save your file.

> **Troubleshooting**
> If the Your document will be upgraded to the newest file format message appears, click OK. If you do not want to see this warning again, click the Do not ask me again check box before clicking OK. This occurs the first time you use Save As to save a file that was originally created in a previous version of Word.

Develop Effective Business Documents

When you talk with others, you get immediate feedback in the form of body language and conversation. Usually, you have an accurate feel for how your message is received, and you are able to elicit responses from your target audience. However, once a word is spoken, it cannot be retracted. On the contrary, you can give much more forethought to the selection of words included in written communication. In the absence of body language, however, it can be difficult for a reader to understand your tone. By carefully considering your objectives and your audience, you can craft a well-worded document that achieves your purpose.

QUICK REFERENCE | **Developing Effective Business Documents**

A document containing grammatical errors, misspellings, informal wording, or inaccurate facts might lead others to consider you careless or not credible. Think through the following when creating business documents:

1. Consider your objectives and your audience.
2. Keep your communication concise and clear.
3. Review a document several times for grammar, punctuation, spelling, and proper wording.
4. If possible, have a trusted colleague provide feedback before you send a letter or memo.
5. Humor is difficult to convey in written communication—try to avoid it.
6. Avoid the use of uppercase letters, which can mislead a reader and convey an unintended message.
7. Use active voice rather than passive voice when possible.
8. Never air your frustration or anger in written communication.

SS REAL WORLD ADVICE | **Preparing Business Correspondence**

Before writing any document, allow ample time for planning. Ask yourself these questions first. Who is my target audience? Do I understand the audience and what they are looking for in my communication? What is the purpose of my document? How can I build support for my message? What information do I need to include? Answering these questions will enable you to effectively communicate your message.

Work with Business Correspondence

Business documents include many forms of written communication. Some are considered internal communication, while others are external communication. Examples of written internal communication are memos, in-house newsletters, and e-mail. Effective internal communication can create a better work atmosphere and increase productivity as employees are more likely to understand and support the goals and objectives of the company. Effective external communication, through letters, brochures, reports, and newsletters, can encourage a healthy corporate image and serve to attract and retain customers.

At this point, you should understand the importance of planning a document and understanding your target audience. This section of the workshop focuses on the technical aspects of letters and memos—how to structure a memo and letter, and exactly what elements to include.

REAL WORLD ADVICE | **Document Formats**

Although you may be familiar with generally accepted styles for letters, memos, and even e-mail, always check with your place of employment when creating business documents. Some businesses require employees to adhere to a specific format. For example, a company might require that the company logo be included in all correspondence, or that a specific letterhead be used. There may be rules regarding the use of headings, enclosures, or attachments. Become familiar with the specifics related to your workplace.

Working with Memos and Business Letters

The main difference between a memo and a letter is the target audience. Much less prescriptive than a letter, a memorandum is intended for internal distribution. The typical audience for a memo is your coworkers and colleagues. A memo generally includes the word "Memo" or "Memorandum," followed by a heading area, the body of the memo, and end notations, if necessary (see Figure 4).

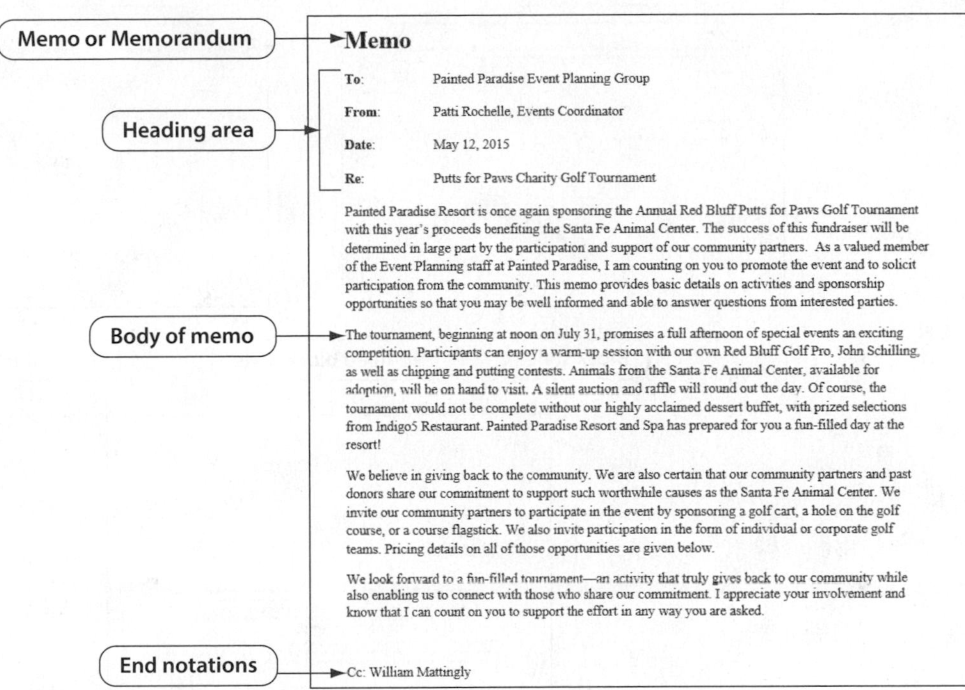

Memo

To: Painted Paradise Event Planning Group

From: Patti Rochelle, Events Coordinator

Date: May 12, 2015

Re: Putts for Paws Charity Golf Tournament

Painted Paradise Resort is once again sponsoring the Annual Red Bluff Putts for Paws Golf Tournament with this year's proceeds benefiting the Santa Fe Animal Center. The success of this fundraiser will be determined in large part by the participation and support of our community partners. As a valued member of the Event Planning staff at Painted Paradise, I am counting on you to promote the event and to solicit participation from the community. This memo provides basic details on activities and sponsorship opportunities so that you may be well informed and able to answer questions from interested parties.

The tournament, beginning at noon on July 31, promises a full afternoon of special events an exciting competition. Participants can enjoy a warm-up session with our own Red Bluff Golf Pro, John Schilling, as well as chipping and putting contests. Animals from the Santa Fe Animal Center, available for adoption, will be on hand to visit. A silent auction and raffle will round out the day. Of course, the tournament would not be complete without our highly acclaimed dessert buffet, with prized selections from Indigo5 Restaurant. Painted Paradise Resort and Spa has prepared for you a fun-filled day at the resort!

We believe in giving back to the community. We are also certain that our community partners and past donors share our commitment to support such worthwhile causes as the Santa Fe Animal Center. We invite our community partners to participate in the event by sponsoring a golf cart, a hole on the golf course, or a course flagstick. We also invite participation in the form of individual or corporate golf teams. Pricing details on all of those opportunities are given below.

We look forward to a fun-filled tournament—an activity that truly gives back to our community while also enabling us to connect with those who share our commitment. I appreciate your involvement and know that I can count on you to support the effort in any way you are asked.

Cc: William Mattingly

Figure 4 Memo style

Business letters are generally intended for external distribution between two businesses, or a business and its clients. Because of this, business letters tend to be more formal and longer than memos. The three accepted letter styles are shown in Table 1 and Figure 5.

Letter Style	Description
Block	Entire letter is left-aligned, single-spaced, and includes double-spacing between paragraphs
Modified block	Body of the letter is left-aligned, single-spaced, and includes double-spacing between paragraphs; the date and closing are left-aligned slightly to the right of center
Semi-block	Identical to modified block style except that each body paragraph is indented by ½"

Table 1 Letter styles

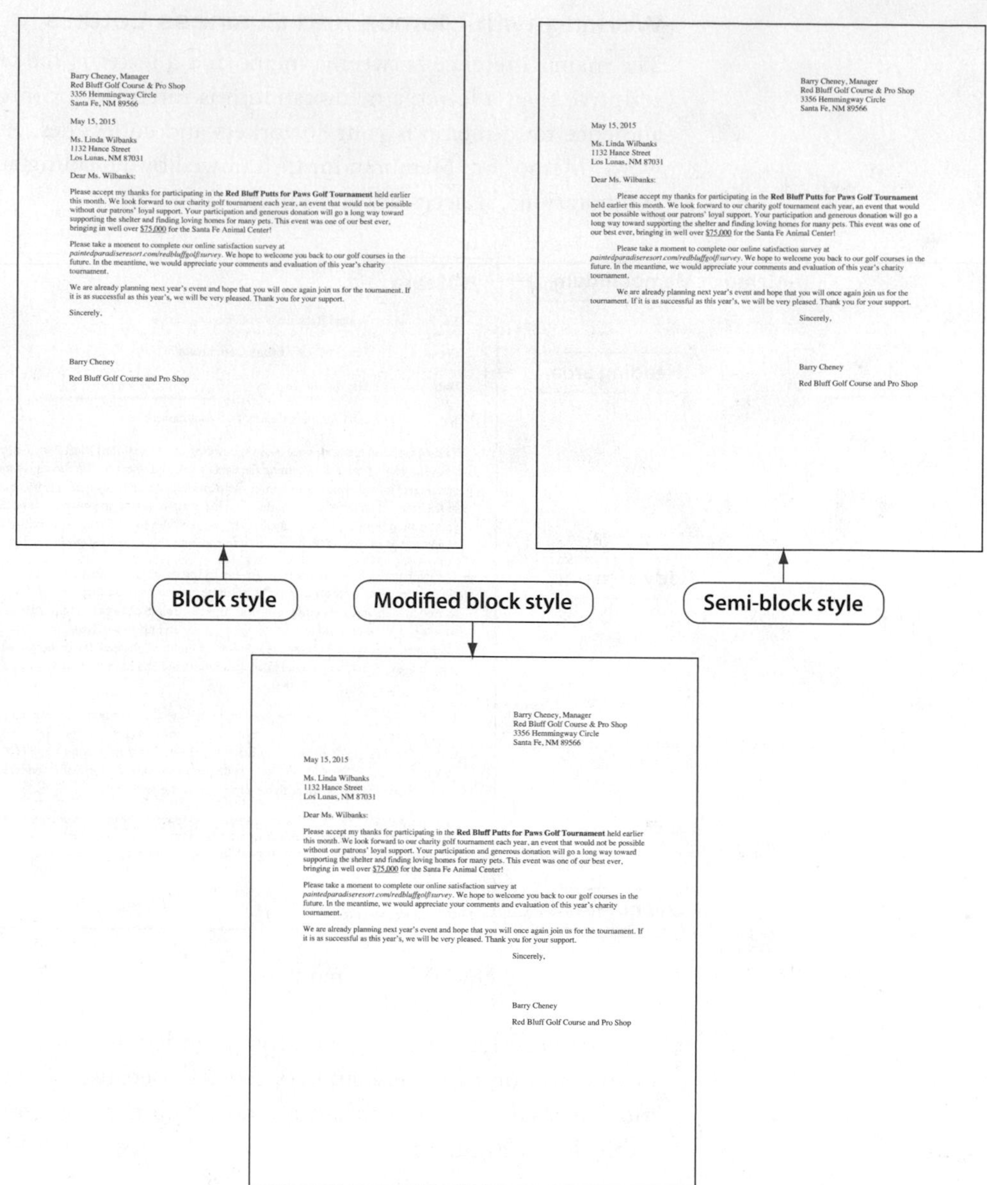

Barry Cheney, Manager
Red Bluff Golf Course & Pro Shop
3356 Hemmingway Circle
Santa Fe, NM 89566

May 15, 2015

Ms. Linda Wilbanks
1132 Hance Street
Los Lunas, NM 87031

Dear Ms. Wilbanks:

Please accept my thanks for participating in the **Red Bluff Putts for Paws Golf Tournament** held earlier this month. We look forward to our charity golf tournament each year, an event that would not be possible without our patrons' loyal support. Your participation and generous donation will go a long way toward supporting the shelter and finding loving homes for many pets. This event was one of our best ever, bringing in well over $75,000 for the Santa Fe Animal Center!

Please take a moment to complete our online satisfaction survey at *paintedparadiseresort.com/redbluffgolf/survey*. We hope to welcome you back to our golf courses in the future. In the meantime, we would appreciate your comments and evaluation of this year's charity tournament.

We are already planning next year's event and hope that you will once again join us for the tournament. If it is as successful as this year's, we will be very pleased. Thank you for your support.

Sincerely,

Barry Cheney

Red Bluff Golf Course and Pro Shop

Barry Cheney, Manager
Red Bluff Golf Course & Pro Shop
3356 Hemmingway Circle
Santa Fe, NM 89566

May 15, 2015

Ms. Linda Wilbanks
1132 Hance Street
Los Lunas, NM 87031

Dear Ms. Wilbanks:

Please accept my thanks for participating in the **Red Bluff Putts for Paws Golf Tournament** held earlier this month. We look forward to our charity golf tournament each year, an event that would not be possible without our patrons' loyal support. Your participation and generous donation will go a long way toward supporting the shelter and finding loving homes for many pets. This event was one of our best ever, bringing in well over $75,000 for the Santa Fe Animal Center!

Please take a moment to complete our online satisfaction survey at *paintedparadiseresort.com/redbluffgolf/survey*. We hope to welcome you back to our golf courses in the future. In the meantime, we would appreciate your comments and evaluation of this year's charity tournament.

We are already planning next year's event and hope that you will once again join us for the tournament. If it is as successful as this year's, we will be very pleased. Thank you for your support.

Sincerely,

Barry Cheney

Red Bluff Golf Course and Pro Shop

Barry Cheney, Manager
Red Bluff Golf Course & Pro Shop
3356 Hemmingway Circle
Santa Fe, NM 89566

May 15, 2015

Ms. Linda Wilbanks
1132 Hance Street
Los Lunas, NM 87031

Dear Ms. Wilbanks:

Please accept my thanks for participating in the **Red Bluff Putts for Paws Golf Tournament** held earlier this month. We look forward to our charity golf tournament each year, an event that would not be possible without our patrons' loyal support. Your participation and generous donation will go a long way toward supporting the shelter and finding loving homes for many pets. This event was one of our best ever, bringing in well over $75,000 for the Santa Fe Animal Center!

Please take a moment to complete our online satisfaction survey at *paintedparadiseresort.com/redbluffgolf/survey*. We hope to welcome you back to our golf courses in the future. In the meantime, we would appreciate your comments and evaluation of this year's charity tournament.

We are already planning next year's event and hope that you will once again join us for the tournament. If it is as successful as this year's, we will be very pleased. Thank you for your support.

Sincerely,

Barry Cheney

Red Bluff Golf Course and Pro Shop

Figure 5 Letter styles

CONSIDER THIS | Be Careful with Written Words

Experts have suggested that e-mail messages are like postcards, in that they can be read by anyone involved in their delivery. Letters, memos, and any other form of written communication are not much more private. With that in mind, do you have any suggestions for composing written communication so that as much privacy as possible is maintained?

QUICK REFERENCE | **Business Letter Components**

Some business letter components are required and some are optional, as you will see in the following description. Refer to Figure 6 for a visual summary of letter components.

1. Heading—Includes the writer's address and the date of the letter; if you are using letterhead, you may not need to include an address.
2. Inside address—Shows the name and address of the recipient of the letter.
3. Salutation—Directly addresses the recipient by title and last name; follow the salutation with a colon as in "Dear Mr. Durham:".
4. Reference or subject line—May replace the salutation if you are not sure who will be receiving the letter; may also be used in addition to a salutation.
5. Body—The message area.
6. Complimentary close—The letter ending, always followed by a comma; usually in the form of "Sincerely yours," although other possibilities include "Respectfully," "Respectfully yours," and "Sincerely."
7. Signature block—Most often two to four blank lines after the complimentary close, followed by your typed name, and whenever possible, your position. The blank space is for your written signature.
8. End notations—One or more abbreviations or phrases that have important functions. They include *initials* (capital letters for the writer and lowercase letters beneath for the typist), *enclosures* (usually abbreviated "Enc" or "Encl" and followed by a very brief summary of the enclosure), and *copies* (an indication of any other recipients of the letter, such as "Cc: Ms. Jane Clemmons").

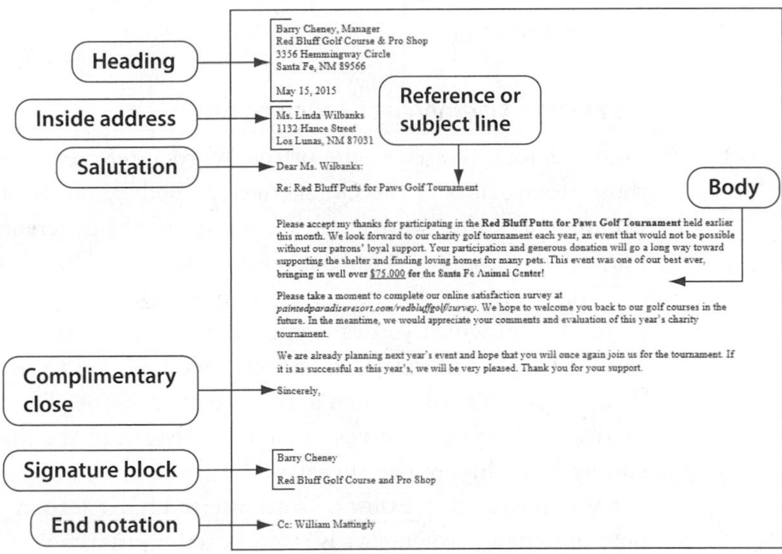

Barry Cheney, Manager
Red Bluff Golf Course & Pro Shop
3356 Hemmingway Circle
Santa Fe, NM 89566

May 15, 2015

Ms. Linda Wilbanks
1132 Hance Street
Los Lunas, NM 87031

Dear Ms. Wilbanks:

Re: Red Bluff Putts for Paws Golf Tournament

Please accept my thanks for participating in the **Red Bluff Putts for Paws Golf Tournament** held earlier this month. We look forward to our charity golf tournament each year, an event that would not be possible without our patrons' loyal support. Your participation and generous donation will go a long way toward supporting the shelter and finding loving homes for many pets. This event was one of our best ever, **bringing in well over $75,000 for the Santa Fe Animal Center!**

Please take a moment to complete our online satisfaction survey at *paintedparadiseresort.com/redbluffgolf/survey*. We hope to welcome you back to our golf courses in the future. In the meantime, we would appreciate your comments and evaluation of this year's charity tournament.

We are already planning next year's event and hope that you will once again join us for the tournament. If it is as successful as this year's, we will be very pleased. Thank you for your support.

Sincerely,

Barry Cheney

Red Bluff Golf Course and Pro Shop

Cc: William Mattingly

Figure 6 Components of a letter

Editing a Document

Word-processing software, such as Word 2013, can facilitate the creation of your business communication. Word enables you to easily revise or update your text to effectively reach your audience. For example, as you look back over a project, you might want to change wording, add emphasis effects—such as italics and boldfacing—or adjust line spacing. This section begins with an overview of the Word interface, and then reviews character formatting and paragraph formatting. In addition, you will learn to use Word's proofreading tools to help you find and correct errors.

REAL WORLD ADVICE Saving Time with KeyTips

KeyTips enable you to access Ribbon commands without ever taking your hands off the keyboard. Press Alt on the keyboard to display KeyTips for each Ribbon tab or Quick Access Toolbar command, as shown in Figure 7, and then press a corresponding key to select a Ribbon item. Additional key tips will be displayed if necessary. Press Alt to remove key tips. By using KeyTips, most Ribbon commands can be accessed by pressing only three keys.

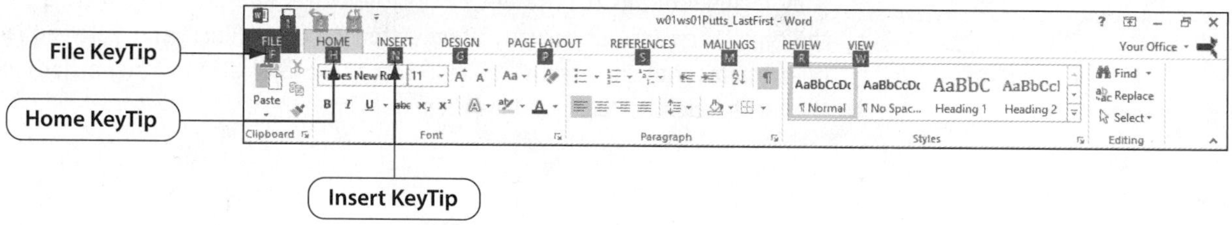

Figure 7 KeyTips

Explore the Word Interface

Figure 2 identifies elements of the Word interface. You were introduced to several of those items, such as the Quick Access Toolbar, the Ribbon, and the status bar, in the Common Features workshop. With only slight differences, these items serve a similar purpose in each of the Office applications: Access, Excel, PowerPoint, and Word.

The Word interface is unique to other Office applications because of its large document area on which you can type. As you type, text automatically wraps from one line to the next. **Word wrap**, the feature enabling you to continue typing without pressing Enter, places a **soft return** at the end of each line. The placement of a soft return automatically changes when you change the length of the line by modifying the margins or simply by adding or deleting words.

When you press Enter, Word inserts a **hard return**. The placement of a hard return does not change when text is reformatted. Only the user can change the placement of a hard return. Hard returns are commonly used at the end of a paragraph or a distinct line, such as a date or salutation (see Figure 8).

Changing the View

Word provides a number of ways to view your document. New to Word 2013 is the Read Mode. Each view serves a different purpose, displaying its own unique features and elements, as shown in Table 2. The default view in Word 2013 is Print Layout. A **default** setting is one that is automatically in place until you specify otherwise.

Also new to Word 2013 are the Ribbon Display Options. The Ribbon Display Options button is on the title bar, to the left of the window control buttons. These options enable you to configure the Ribbon interface regardless of the current view. You can auto-hide the Ribbon, show Ribbon tabs only, or show the full Ribbon, with both tabs and commands, which is the default.

MODULE 1

View	Description of View
Print Layout	Shows all margins, headers, footers, graphics, and other features that will be displayed when a document is printed; provides a close approximation to the way a document will look when printed
Web Layout	Shows how a document will appear in a web browser
Outline view	Shows the structure of a document in a hierarchical fashion; expand or collapse details to show only what is necessary
Draft view	Includes the Ribbon, but does not show margins, headers, footers, columns, tables, or other graphical objects; used to edit and format in a text-only environment
Read Mode	Provides an interactive, screen-reading experience; define your column width, page color, and preferred layout; zoom in and out of graphical objects, translate words, and search on Bing; the user interface is minimized to avoid reading distractions

Table 2 Document views

Showing Nonprinting Characters

Many keys, such as Spacebar, Enter, and Tab, insert **nonprinting characters** in a document. For example, when you press Tab, text is indented and a tab "character" is inserted. Sometimes called **formatting marks**, nonprinting characters are not displayed on the screen by default. These formatting marks are not shown when the document is printed, even when they are displayed on the screen. Figure 8 shows a document with nonprinting characters displayed.

You will experiment with different views of the memo. You will also work with the nonprinting characters. As you continue working with the memorandum, you realize that choosing to show or hide nonprinting characters is ultimately a matter of preference. Many experienced Word users, however, find that displaying nonprinting characters is helpful when trying to fix formatting errors caused by hard returns, tabs, spaces, or page breaks.

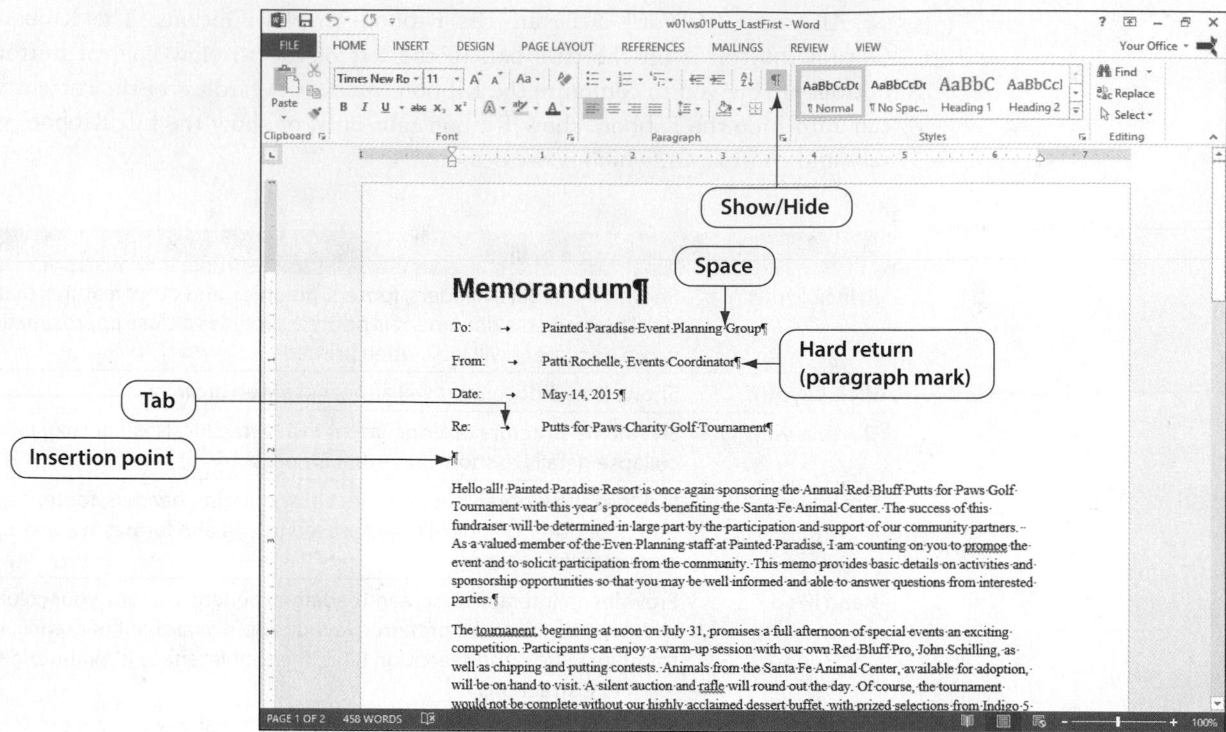

Figure 8 Nonprinting characters displayed

MyITLab® Workshop 1 Training

W01.01

To Change the View and Show Nonprinting Characters

a. Click the **VIEW** tab, and then in the Views group, click **Read Mode**.

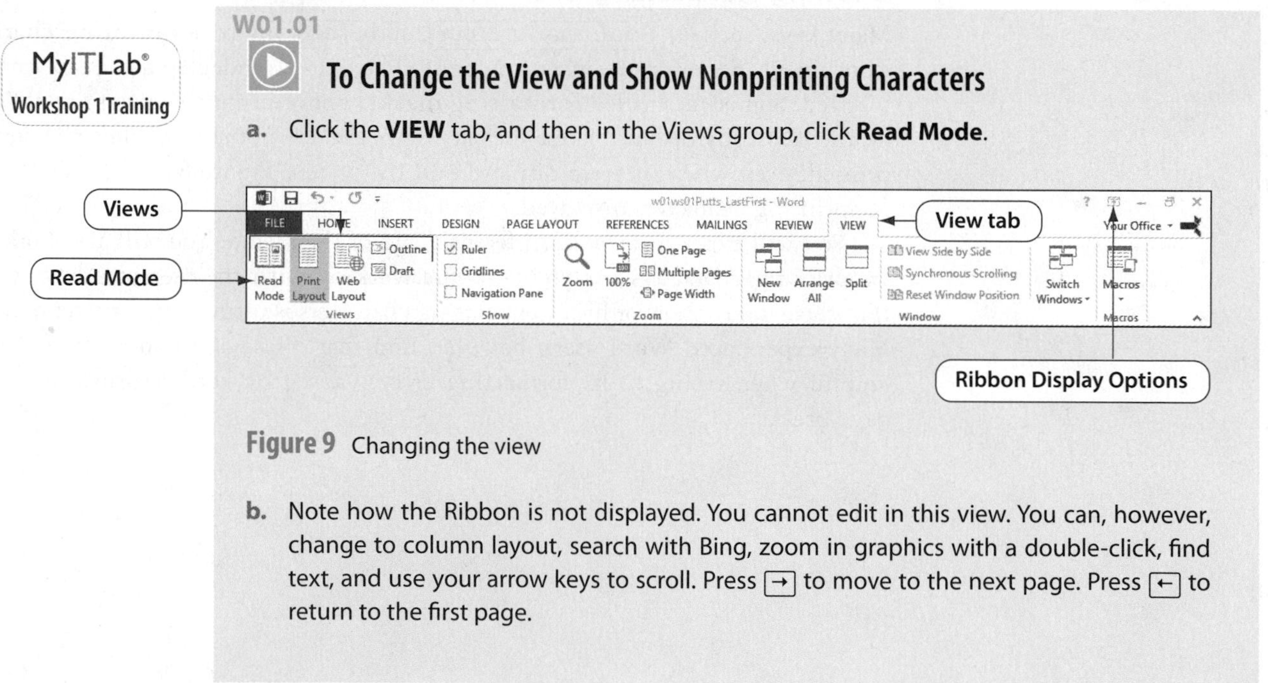

Figure 9 Changing the view

b. Note how the Ribbon is not displayed. You cannot edit in this view. You can, however, change to column layout, search with Bing, zoom in graphics with a double-click, find text, and use your arrow keys to scroll. Press → to move to the next page. Press ← to return to the first page.

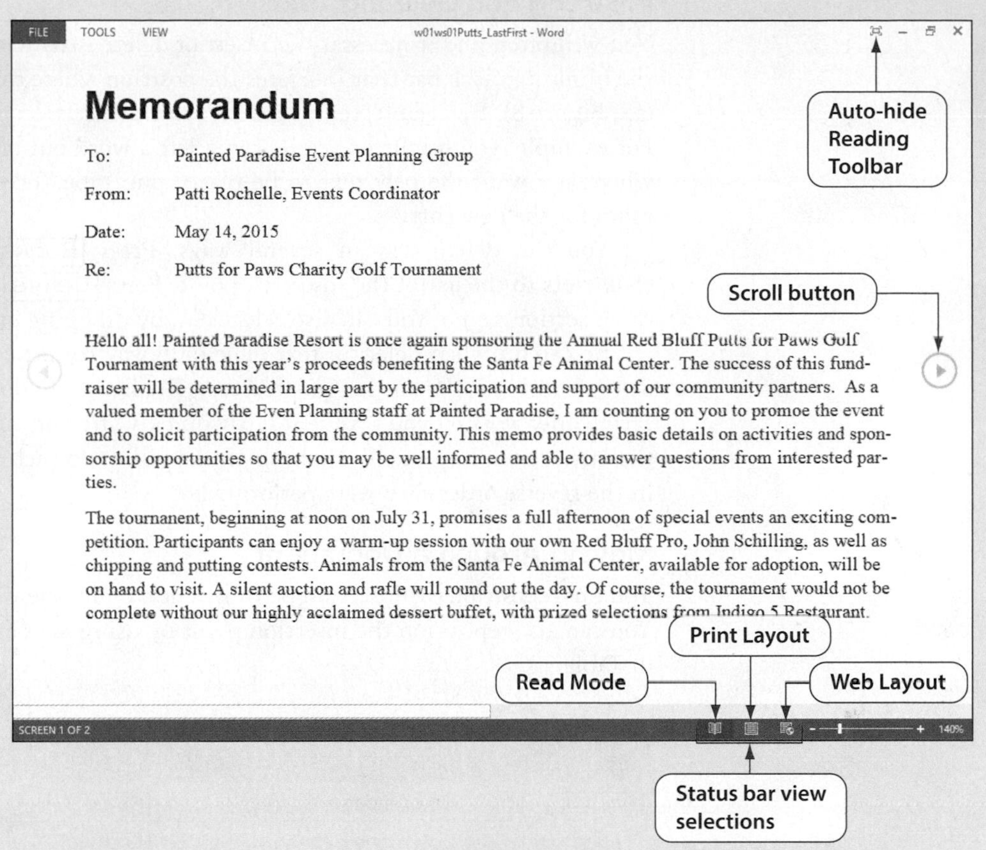

Figure 10 Read Mode

c. Click **Print Layout** on the status bar to return to Print Layout.

Print Layout, along with Read Mode and Web Layout, is available on both the VIEW tab and the right side of the status bar. The view options on the status bar are always available, regardless of which Ribbon tab is selected.

d. Click the **HOME** tab, and then in the Paragraph group, click **Show/Hide** ¶, if necessary, to show nonprinting characters (see Figure 8).

> **SIDE NOTE**
> **What Is a Toggle?**
> A command that switches between an on and off state each time it is clicked is called a **toggle**.

> **Troubleshooting**
> If nonprinting characters are already displayed, the display will be toggled off when you click Show/Hide. In that case, click Show/Hide once again to display them.

e. Click to place the insertion point before the paragraph mark ¶ that is displayed just beneath the **Re:** line. Press Delete. The paragraph mark is deleted, and the text moves up.

The insertion point is the blinking black bar that indicates the position where the next character will be placed.

f. Click **Save** on the Quick Access Toolbar to save the document.

Inserting and Deleting Text

You will often find it necessary to insert or delete text. Recall that an **insertion point** is the blinking black bar that indicates the position where the next character will be placed (see Figure 8). By default, text is inserted at the insertion point, within the existing text. For example, you might notice that you left a word out of a sentence. In that case, click where you want the new text to be placed and type. Text automatically shifts to make room for the new entry.

You can delete text in several ways. Press Backspace repeatedly to remove characters to the left of the insertion point. Press Delete to remove text to the right of the insertion point. You can also select text by dragging and then press Delete.

Be careful when deleting text. The only way to retrieve deleted text is to retype it, or to click Undo ↶ on the Quick Access Toolbar—if you are quick enough! The Undo action only works if you invoke it fairly quickly after the unwanted deletion. It will undo the last action. Repeatedly clicking Undo will undo each action performed, one by one, in the reverse order they were performed.

Moving Around a Document

You can reposition the insertion point by clicking in a new location within the document. You can also reposition the insertion point by using keys and key combinations as shown in Table 3.

Keys	Resulting Insertion Point	Keys	Resulting Insertion Point
Page Up	Up one page	Home	Beginning of the current line
Page Down	Down one page	End	End of the current line
←	Left one character	Ctrl + Home	Beginning of the document
→	Right one character	Ctrl + End	End of the document
↑	Up one line	Ctrl + ←	Left one word
↓	Down one line	Ctrl + →	Right one word

Table 3 To reposition the insertion point

As you will notice when making your next set of changes to the memorandum, scrolling does not change the position of the insertion point, but rather it changes the section of the document currently in view. Even after scrolling to another location in a document, newly typed text will be inserted back at the position of the insertion point. To avoid this common error, always make a habit of noting the position of the insertion point before you begin to type. When text is inserted in the wrong location, click Undo ↶ on the Quick Access Toolbar. You will position the insertion point to insert and delete text in the memo.

W01.02

To Move Around a Document and Change Zoom Level

a. Press Ctrl+End to position the insertion point at the end of the document.

b. Press Ctrl+← to place the insertion point before the exclamation point. Continue pressing Ctrl+← until the insertion point is before the word **effort** on the last line. Type the, and then press the Spacebar once.

c. Press [Ctrl]+[Home] to move the insertion point to the beginning of the document. The date is incorrect. It should be "May 12, 2015." Click to place the insertion point after the number **4** in the date. Press [Backspace], and then type 2.

When removing text or nonprinting characters, press [Backspace] to remove characters to the left of the insertion point, or press [Delete] to remove characters to the right.

d. Click the **VIEW** tab, and then in the Zoom group, click **Zoom**. Click **200%**, and then click **OK**. Drag the vertical and horizontal scroll bars to view the document.

Dragging the scroll bar changes the area of the document that is displayed, but it does not physically reposition the insertion point. Note that the insertion point remains in the same position as where you placed it in Step c. You can only move the insertion point by clicking in another location in the document, or by using a keyboard shortcut—several of which are described in Table 3.

e. On the status bar, drag the **Zoom Slider** to the left to reduce the size of the document to **100%**.

f. Click **Save** on the Quick Access Toolbar.

MODULE 1

Viewing Backstage and Working with Word Options

As you learned in the Common Features workshop, Microsoft Office **Backstage view** is a collection of common actions and settings that apply to the current document. For example, the Print menu enables you to preview the document, set print options, and print. The Options menu enables you to customize Word according to your preference, such as customizing the Ribbon, changing the default location where files are saved, or automatically displaying paragraph marks. You will examine Backstage view in the following exercise.

QUICK REFERENCE | **Backstage View**

Backstage view is best defined as a collection of common actions, properties, and settings related to an open file. Below is a brief summary of the commands found in Backstage view.

1. Info—View and set document properties and security permissions, inspect your document for hidden content, and manage versions.
2. New—Open a new blank document or use a template to create a new document.
3. Open—Open an existing document.
4. Save—Save a file.
5. Save As—Save a file with a new name, location, or file type.
6. Print—Print an open document.
7. Share—Send an open document through e-mail, publish it as a blog post, or save to a SkyDrive for others to view.
8. Export—Save an open document in a different format, including PDF/XPS.
9. Close—Close an open document.
10. Account—Gain access to product information and your Office account.
11. Options—Customize Word preferences.

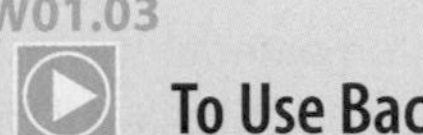

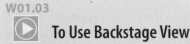

W01.03

To Use Backstage View

a. Click the **FILE** tab. Backstage view appears.

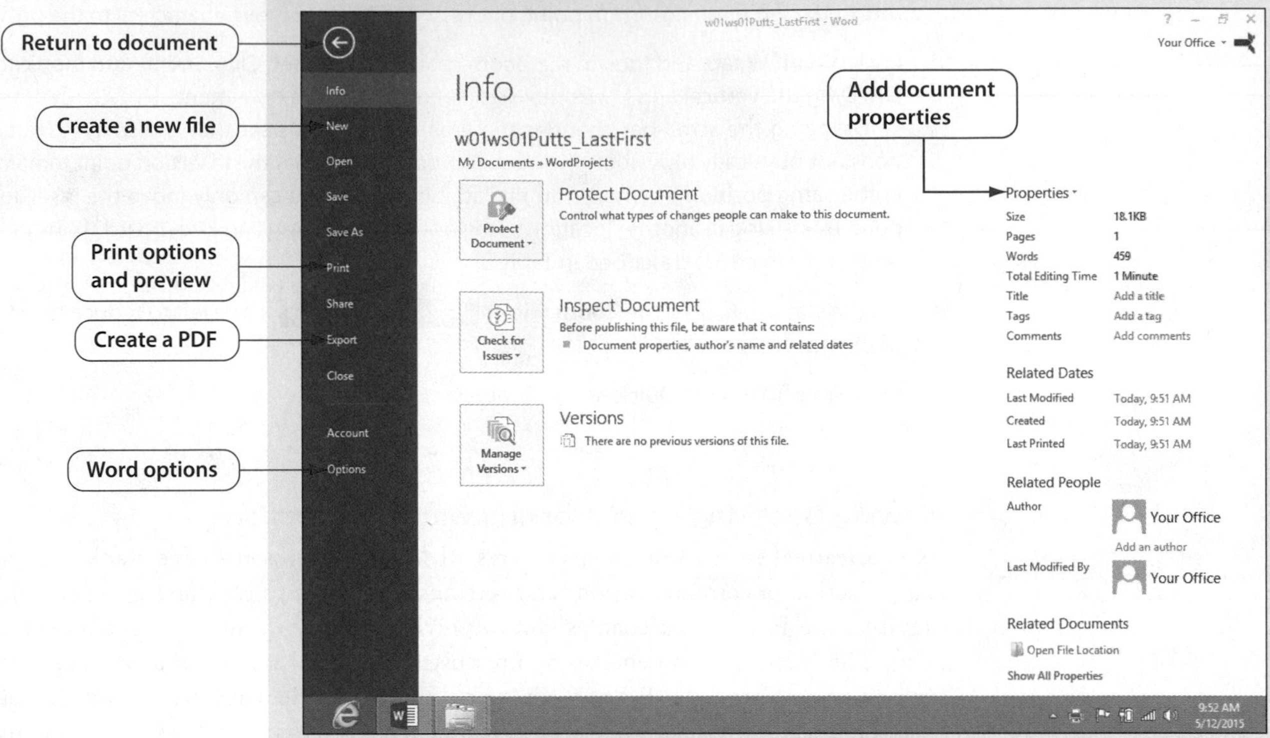

Figure 11 Backstage view

b. Click **Print** to preview your document.

Selecting the Print option displays the document as it will appear when printed. It also enables you to select print options, such as the number of copies to print, and to change the margins and page orientation. You will explore print settings later in the workshop.

> **SIDE NOTE**
> **Adding Document Properties**
> Click Properties, select Advanced Properties, and then click the Summary tab to add document properties.

c. Taking a moment to review some of the other Backstage commands. Click **New**, **Share**, and **Export**.

Notice the options available within each of these areas. You will explore Open, Save As, Print, and Options later in this workshop.

d. Click the **back** arrow in the top-left corner to exit Backstage view and return to the document.

> **SIDE NOTE**
> **Exit Backstage View**
> Alternatively, you can press Esc to return to your document from Backstage view.

e. Click the **FILE** tab, click **Options**. The Word Options dialog box opens.

Note the categories on the left side, such as General, Display, and Proofing. Click a category to view related settings that you can confirm or change. Keep in mind these changes are global, not local. For example, if you change the way Word corrects spelling errors, the change applies to the current document and to all future documents. In effect, you are modifying the Word installation, not just the current Word document. For that reason, you may not be allowed to change these options if you are working in a computer lab.

f. Click **Proofing** in the Word Options dialog box.

Word Options in the Proofing group change how spelling and grammatical errors are corrected.

g. Click **Customize Ribbon** in the Word Options dialog box.

You can select or deselect tabs that you want to include on the Ribbon, as well as indicate commands to be included in groups. Click the Customize button to create your own keyboard shortcuts.

h. Click **General** in the Word Options dialog box. General options enable you to change global settings, such as your user name and initials.

i. Click **Cancel**.

When you click Cancel, you return all settings to their previous state, even if you have made changes, and you are returned to the document. If you click OK, all changes that you have made are accepted, and you are also returned to the document.

j. **Save** [Save] the document.

Format Characters

Character formatting is used to change the physical appearance of your text. For example, you may want to bold a word, underline a sentence, or apply a blue color to an entire paragraph. Many of these formats are available on the Home tab in the Font group. For example, to bold a sentence, select the sentence, and then click Bold [B]. If you change your mind, select the same sentence, and then click Bold [B] to reverse the effect. Regardless of the change, however, always keep the purpose of the document in mind. While you might have fun experimenting with color and unique fonts in a newsletter, you will need to take a more conservative approach when editing a business document.

Selecting Text

You must first select text before applying character formats. Selecting text is easy: Simply position the pointer before the text, press and hold the mouse button, drag to highlight the text, and then release the mouse button. This textbook will refer to such an action as "dragging," not "clicking and dragging." To deselect text, simply click anywhere outside of the selection.

Using this method to select text, however, can present challenges when the area of selection is too small or too large. Imagine trying to select a 200-page document solely by dragging. Although possible, it would take some time and patience to drag through 200 pages. Similarly, it can be difficult to select a single word without including the surrounding spaces. Table 4 presents some keyboard shortcuts to selecting blocks of text. You will experiment with some of these shortcuts when making your next set of changes.

To Select	Do This
One word	Double-click the word
One sentence	Press and hold [Ctrl] while you click in the sentence
One paragraph	Triple-click the paragraph
Entire document	Press [Ctrl]+[A]
One line	Position the pointer in the left margin beside the line to select; when the pointer becomes a white arrow, click to select the line
One character to the left of the insertion point	Press [Shift]+[←]
One character to the right of the insertion point	Press [Shift]+[→]
One block of text	Click where the selection is to begin, hold down [Shift], and then click where the selection is to end
Two nonadjacent blocks of text	Select the first block of text, hold down [Ctrl], and then select the second block of text

Table 4 Shortcuts to selection

W01.04

To Edit a Document

a. Press [Ctrl]+[Home]. Move the pointer into the left margin, just to the left of the word **Memorandum**, to change the pointer to [pointer]. Click to select the line of text. When you click in the left margin—the selection area—the entire line to the right of the pointer is selected. Type Memo.

Once a word is selected you can add character formatting, such as bold, italic, or font size. You can delete a selected word by pressing [Delete]. Alternatively, you can double-click the word Memorandum to select it.

b. Triple-click in the **third paragraph** of the memo body—the paragraph beginning with **This year**—to select it. Press [Delete] to delete the paragraph.

> **Troubleshooting**
>
> If only one word is selected, you double-clicked instead of triple-clicked. Click anywhere to deselect the current selection, and then triple-click the paragraph once more.

c. In the first paragraph of the body of the memo, drag to select the first sentence **Hello all!** making sure to include the space after the exclamation point. Scroll to the bottom of the document, press and hold [Ctrl], and then drag to select the last sentence, **Hope to see you there!** After both sentences are selected, release [Ctrl], and then press [Delete] to delete both sentences simultaneously.

When selecting a word, the space following the word is also selected. If necessary, use [Shift]+[→] or [Shift]+[←] to select only the characters you desire.

> **Troubleshooting**
>
> If the first paragraph does not align with the left margin, then you did not select the space after Hello all! Place your insertion point in front of the blank space at the beginning of the first paragraph, and then press [Delete].
>
> If the first sentence is still there, you clicked in the document before selecting the second sentence. Scroll to the top of the memo, and then delete the sentence.

d. **Save** [Save] the document.

Changing Font Type, Size, and Color

An essential feature of word processing is its ability to easily manipulate text—characters, words, sentences, and paragraphs. One such way is through the use of fonts. A **font** is a character design, including qualities such as typeface, size, and spacing. A typeface is a style of printed characters. Typeface, combined with character size and the amount of spacing between characters, makes up a font. You can choose to use the default font—Calibri, 11pt—which is the specified font when you begin a new document in Word 2013, or you can select from a number of additional fonts. With experience, you will develop font preferences and will understand that some font selections are better suited for certain document types than are others.

The Font group on the Home tab shows the current font and font size. When you click the Font arrow, a list of fonts is displayed, with each font shown as a sample of the actual font. Theme fonts—described later in this workshop—are shown first, followed by recently used fonts. The remaining fonts are listed in alphabetical order.

The **Live Preview** feature enables you to preview the change to your selected text. Simply select the text and hover the mouse over any font selection. If you like the change, click the font to select it.

Typefaces are divided into two categories: serif and sans serif. A **serif font**, such as Times New Roman, has small, thin lines, or hooks, that end the main stroke of each letter, often referred to as feet. Because a serif font is easy to read in large amounts of text, it is a good choice for printed material, such as reports and lengthy documents. Newspapers and books almost always use serif fonts for body text. In addition to Times New Roman, other serif fonts include Bodoni and Century Schoolbook.

The word "sans" means "without" in Latin. A **sans serif font**, then, is *without* the ending strokes typical of a serif font. The clean, simple lines of a sans serif font lend itself to titles, logos, and headings. Because the decorative strokes of serif fonts can often appear blurred on a computer screen, web developers prefer sans serif fonts for web page readability. Common sans serif fonts include Arial, Helvetica, Verdana, and Geneva. Figure 12 compares serif and sans serif fonts.

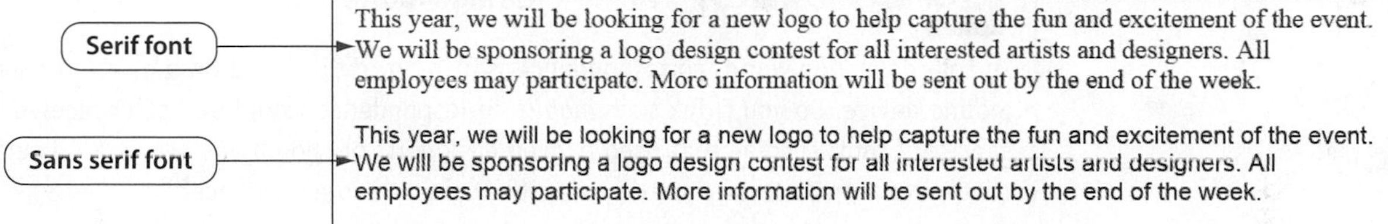

Figure 12 Sans serif and serif fonts

Another characteristic of a font is its spacing. A font's spacing is either **monospaced** or **proportional**. If you consider the way that you would print words, you can envision giving more space to some characters than to others. For example, printing the letter "w" typically requires more space than the letter "l." Giving more horizontal space to some letters and less to others is an example of proportional spacing. Alternatively, all the characters in a monospaced font, such as Courier New, take up the same amount of horizontal space. Monospaced text, sometimes referred to as fixed-width, is appropriate for tables and financial reports where text must line up neatly in columns and rows. Figure 13 compares monospaced and proportional fonts.

This is an example of a monospaced font. Each character requires the same amount of space.

This is an example of a proportional font. Each character requires only the space that is necessary for display. For example, the letter *m* requires more space than the letter *i*.

Figure 13 Monospaced and proportional fonts

Regardless of which font type you select, you can apply additional attributes, including reducing or increasing the font size and changing the color. All of these options are located in the Font group on the Home tab. Font size is measured in points (abbreviated "pt"), with each point equivalent to 1/72 of an inch. A typical font size for the body of a document is 11-pt or 12-pt. Report titles and headings typically use a larger font size. You can also change font color, apply highlighting, and add text effects. Text effects enable you to enhance text by adding a shadow, outline, reflection, or glow. Such effects can be very effective in certain documents as you draw attention to headers or text blocks.

Although you can quickly learn the mechanics of how to select a typeface, or font, you will want to develop skills in preparing business documents—selecting an appropriate font and text style for the project under development. As you progress through this module, you will be presented with tips for creating well-designed business documents.

REAL WORLD ADVICE | **Selecting an Appropriate Font for Business Correspondence**

If you do not conform to typical business standards, your boss will most likely notice! Do not risk your professional image to make a document look a little longer or shorter. A serif font at 11-pt to 12-pt size is a good choice for printed material, such as letters, memos, and reports. The accepted standard is Times New Roman 12-pt. Avoid overly ornate or abnormal fonts, such as Comic Sans.

Longer documents, such as reports, will often use more than one font. Be consistent with your use of fonts in these cases. For example, use one font style for all headings, one font style for all captions, and one font style for the main body of the document.

CONSIDER THIS | **Going Mobile**

In today's mobile world, correspondence is also often displayed on a computer screen or mobile device. Do you think such *mobile* correspondence would be better received in a sans serif font, such as that used by web designers, or should you stay with a serif font that is more traditionally associated with business correspondence?

W01.05

To Change Character Formatting

SIDE NOTE
Shortcut to Change Font Size
Select the text, and then press Ctrl+[to decrease the font size. Press Ctrl+] to increase the font size.

a. Scroll to the top of the document. Double-click the word **Memo** to select it.

b. On the **HOME** tab, in the Font group, click the **Font** arrow, and then select **Times New Roman**.

c. With Memo still selected, click the **Font Size** arrow, and then select **20**. Click anywhere in the document to deselect the text.

The heading is now consistent with the Painted Paradise Resort and Spa style guide, the standard for all business documents produced within the organization.

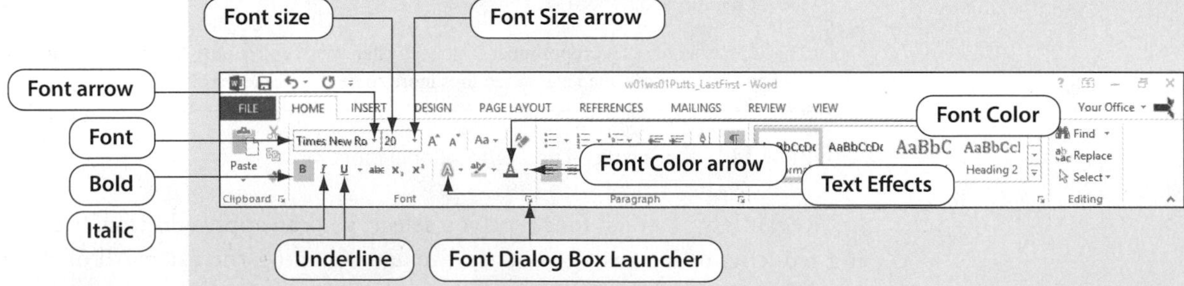

Figure 14 The Font group

SIDE NOTE
Formatting Shortcuts
Press Ctrl+B for bold.
Press Ctrl+I for italics.
Press Ctrl+U for underline.

d. Double-click **To** on the second line of the memo. Notice that the colon is not selected. Move the pointer near the selected area to reveal the Mini toolbar. Click **Bold** B on the Mini toolbar. Similarly, select and bold the words **From**, **Date**, and **Re**.

Figure 15 The Mini toolbar

SIDE NOTE
Removing the Mini Toolbar
Press [Esc] to temporarily remove the Mini toolbar when it appears beside a selection.

> **Troubleshooting**
> If you do not see the Mini toolbar when the pointer is near the selection, right-click the selected text to reveal the Mini toolbar along with shortcut menu options. Once you click an option on the Mini toolbar, the shortcut menu disappears and the toolbar remains available for the selected text.

e. Select **July 31** in the second paragraph of the body of the memo.

f. On the HOME tab, in the Font group, click the **Font Dialog Box Launcher**. Under Font style, select **Bold**. Click the **Underline style** arrow, and then select the **third line selection**—a thick dark line. Click the **Font color** arrow, and then under Standard Colors, select **Dark Red**. Click **OK**. The date is now bold, dark red, and with a thick underline.

After clicking the Font Color arrow, point to a color to display its name.

SIDE NOTE
Changing Font Color
Select text, and then click the Home tab. Click the Font Color arrow and select a color. Point to a color to display its name.

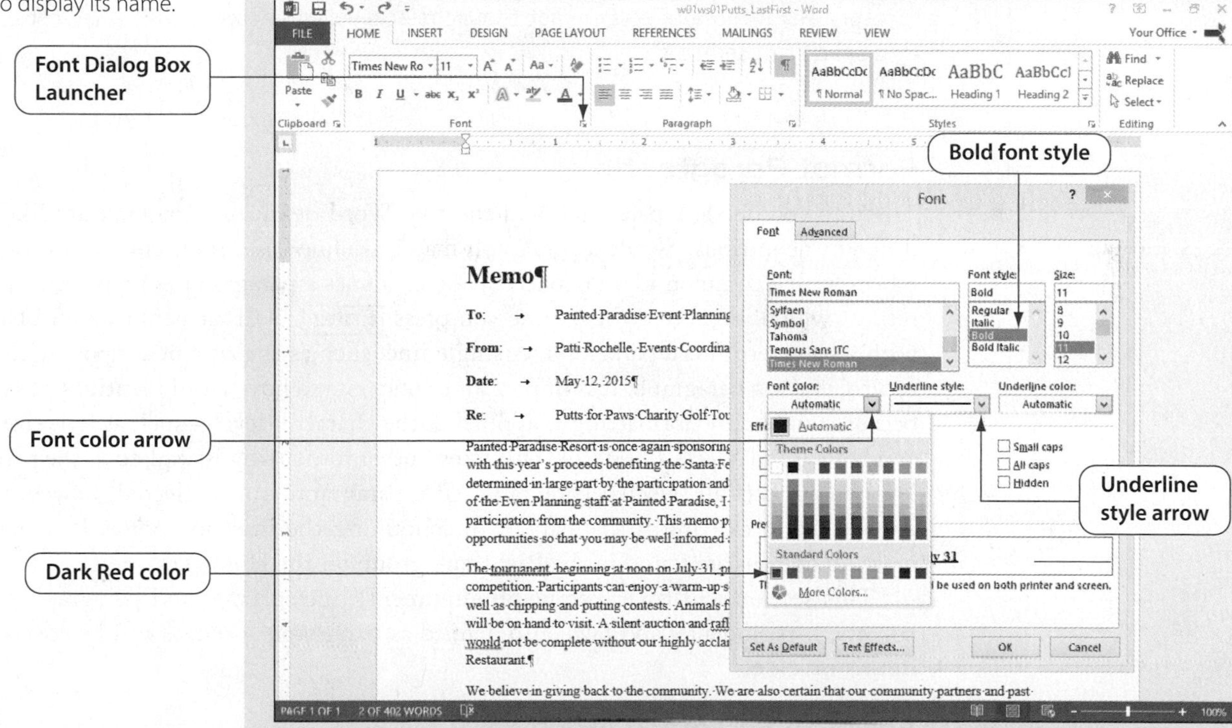

Figure 16 Font dialog box

g. Click **Undo** on the Quick Access Toolbar to undo the bold, underline, and font color change.

When you click Undo once, it enables you to undo the most recent action. If the action that you want to reverse is not the most recent, you can still undo it by clicking Undo repeatedly. Each time you click Undo, an action is reversed, in the order that you

SIDE NOTE
[Ctrl]+[Z] to Undo
Alternatively, you can press [Ctrl]+[Z] to undo a change.

performed the steps. You can also select an action to undo when you click the Undo arrow and select the action.

h. Click **Redo** on the Quick Access Toolbar to reapply the formatting.
   When you click Redo, the most recent "undone" action is redone.

i. **Save** the document.

QUICK REFERENCE	Four Different Methods to Change Character Formatting

Assume the text is selected.

1. Click a formatting option in the Font group.
2. Move the pointer to reveal the Mini toolbar, and then specify formatting.
3. Press Ctrl+Shift+P to open the Font dialog box, and then specify formatting.
4. Click the Dialog Box Launcher in the Font group, and then specify formatting.

REAL WORLD ADVICE	Why Use the Font Dialog Box?

Use the Font dialog box when applying several formatting effects at one time, especially if those effects are not commonplace—such as superscript, small caps, or a specific underline style.

Format Paragraphs

The way you define a paragraph and the way Word defines a paragraph are likely very different definitions. While a paragraph may be defined as a group of two or more sentences with a common idea or concept, Word defines a paragraph as identified by a hard return, which is inserted every time you press Enter. By that definition, a blank line with a hard return is a paragraph. A single line, such as the title of a report with a hard return, is also a paragraph. It is important to understand how Word identifies paragraphs, because while some formatting is applied at the character level—such as font size, color, and bold—and affects all selected characters, other formatting is applied at the paragraph level and affects all selected paragraphs. If a paragraph is not selected, however, Word applies the formatting to the paragraph containing the insertion point. Paragraph formatting options are found in the Paragraph group on the Home tab.

This section will cover paragraph alignment, line spacing, and paragraph spacing. Bullets, lists, indents, and tabs, also defined as paragraph spacing, will be covered later in this module.

Adjusting Paragraph Alignment

Alignment determines how the edges of a paragraph align with the left and right margins (see Figure 17). Alignment settings apply to all text within a paragraph. By default, paragraphs in a Word document are **left-aligned**, which means that lines of text begin evenly on the left, but include an uneven, or ragged, right edge. Left-aligned text is easy to read; therefore, it is the primary form of alignment of paragraphs in letters, reports, and memos. Text that is **right-aligned** is the reverse: Text is aligned on the right with a ragged left edge. Right-aligned text is often used for short lines such as dates, figure captions, and headers. Text that is **centered** places the middle of each line precisely in the center of the page, between the left and right margins. Report titles and major headings are usually centered. **Justified** (sometimes called *fully justified*) is an alignment style that spreads text evenly between the right and left margins so that lines begin on the left margin and end uniformly on the right margin. Such alignment can cause awkward spacing as text is stretched to fit evenly between the margins, as you will see when you try to justify the memorandum. Newspaper articles and textbooks are often formatted in justified alignment.

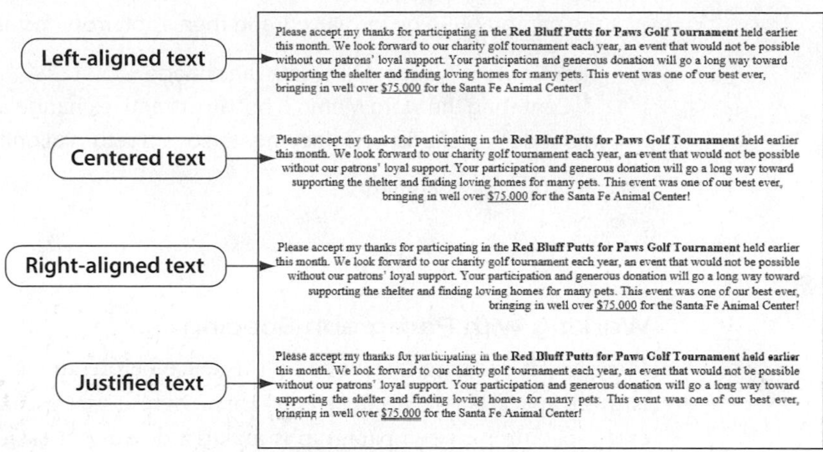

Figure 17 Alignment examples

CONSIDER THIS | **Using Mixed Formatting**

The main text in this textbook is fully justified, but the Quick Reference, Consider This, Side Note, and Real World Advice sections are left-aligned. Which alignment is used for the hands-on exercises? Why do you think the authors made these choices?

W01.06

To Adjust Alignment

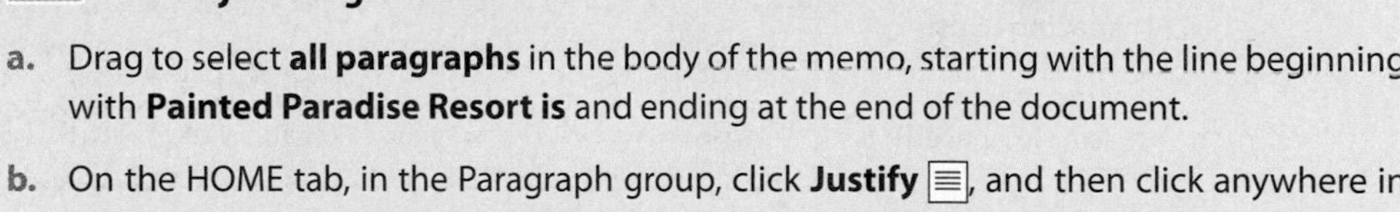

a. Drag to select **all paragraphs** in the body of the memo, starting with the line beginning with **Painted Paradise Resort is** and ending at the end of the document.

b. On the HOME tab, in the Paragraph group, click **Justify**, and then click anywhere in the document to deselect the selection. All paragraphs are evenly aligned on both the left and right margins.

SIDE NOTE
Empty Field Boxes
The Font Size box is empty when the selected text has multiple font sizes. Similarly, the Font box will be empty if the selected text contains multiple fonts.

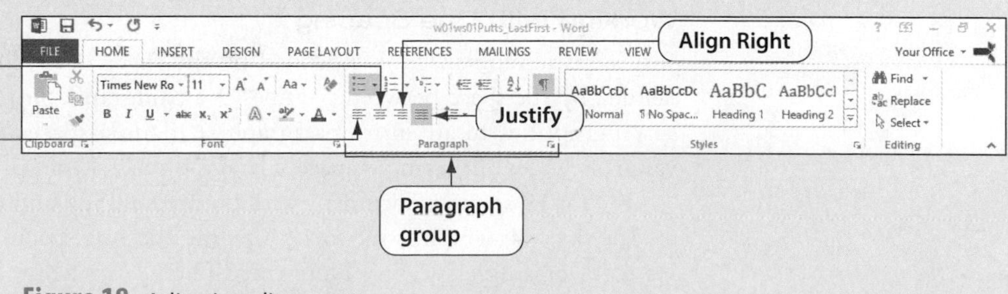

Figure 18 Adjusting alignment

SIDE NOTE

Common Alignment Shortcuts

Ctrl+L left-aligns
Ctrl+R right-aligns
Ctrl+E centers
Ctrl+J justifies

c. Click **Undo** on the Quick Access Toolbar to undo paragraph alignment.

Justify is an alignment that is often used in published documents, such as newspapers and magazines, but it is not suitable for a memo.

d. Scroll to the top of the document. Click anywhere in the line containing the word **Memo**, and then in the Paragraph group, click **Center**.

As you recall, alignment applies to an entire paragraph—text ending with a hard return. To apply paragraph formatting, simply click within the line of text that identifies the paragraph to be formatted, and then apply your formatting.

e. Click **Center** again to reverse the change.

Centering the word Memo is not an attractive change and is not an accepted practice in the design of business documents, so you return alignment to left-align.

f. **Save** the document.

Working with Paragraph Spacing

Paragraph spacing is defined by the space before and after paragraphs. Generally, there is more space between paragraphs than there is within paragraphs (see Figure 19). The extra spacing between paragraphs makes a document easier to read.

Paragraph spacing is measured in terms of points, with a point equal to 1/72". Settings are generally specified in units of six—0 pt, 6 pt, 12 pt, 18 pt—though you can set it to any value in the Paragraph dialog box. The default paragraph after spacing for a new, blank document is 8 pt. Set it to 0 to remove paragraph spacing.

You can identify paragraph spacing *before* or *after*, and making that choice is much like the old adage "Which came first—the chicken or the egg?" Most often, it does not make a difference how you interpret the spacing because either way you are creating space between paragraphs. As a general rule, most spacing is specified *after* a paragraph.

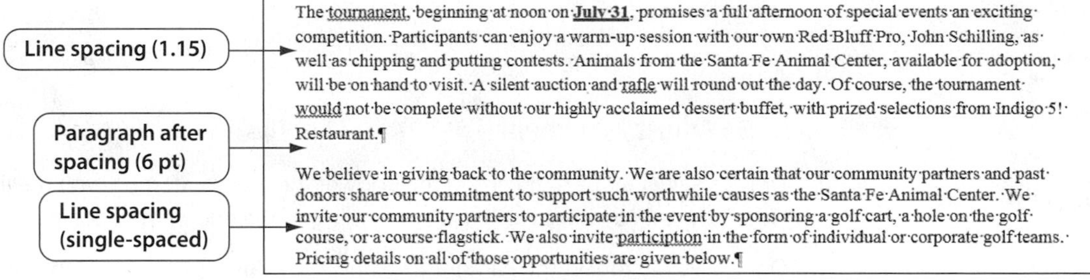
The·tournanent,·beginning·at·noon·on·July·31,·promises·a·full·afternoon·of·special·events·an·exciting·competition.·Participants·can·enjoy·a·warm-up·session·with·our·own·Red·Bluff·Pro,·John·Schilling,·as·well·as·chipping·and·putting·contests.·Animals·from·the·Santa·Fe·Animal·Center,·available·for·adoption,·will·be·on·hand·to·visit.·A·silent·auction·and·rafle·will·round·out·the·day.·Of·course,·the·tournament·would·not·be·complete·without·our·highly·acclaimed·dessert·buffet,·with·prized·selections·from·Indigo·5!·Restaurant.¶

We·believe·in·giving·back·to·the·community.·We·are·also·certain·that·our·community·partners·and·past·donors·share·our·commitment·to·support·such·worthwhile·causes·as·the·Santa·Fe·Animal·Center.·We·invite·our·community·partners·to·participate·in·the·event·by·sponsoring·a·golf·cart,·a·hole·on·the·golf·course,·or·a·course·flagstick.·We·also·invite·particiption·in·the·form·of·individual·or·corporate·golf·teams.·Pricing·details·on·all·of·those·opportunities·are·given·below.¶

Figure 19 Paragraph and line spacing

Working with Line Spacing

Just as paragraph spacing is defined by the space between paragraphs, **line spacing** is defined by the space between the lines of a paragraph. Similar to paragraph spacing, line spacing applies to an entire paragraph. A double-spaced paragraph has a line spacing value of two, while a single-spaced paragraph has a line spacing value of one.

Figure 19 shows a document with both paragraph and line spacing. The line spacing for the first paragraph is set to 1.15, while the line spacing for the second paragraph is set to 1, or single-spacing. Note the difference in white space between the lines. The paragraph spacing is set to 6pt. Notice that there is more space between the paragraphs than there is between the lines. The default line spacing in Word 2013 is 1.08, though this can be changed by going to the Home tab, and then clicking Line and Paragraph Spacing in the Paragraph group.

W01.07

To Work with Paragraph and Line Spacing

a. Press Ctrl+Home to move the insertion point to the beginning of the document.

b. Select the four lines in the heading area of the memo beginning with the text **To:** and ending with **Charity Golf Tournament**. In the Paragraph group, click the **Paragraph Dialog Box Launcher**. The Paragraph dialog box opens, enabling you to adjust both paragraph and line spacing.

> SIDE NOTE
> **Page Layout Tab**
> Alternatively, you can change the paragraph spacing from the Page Layout tab.

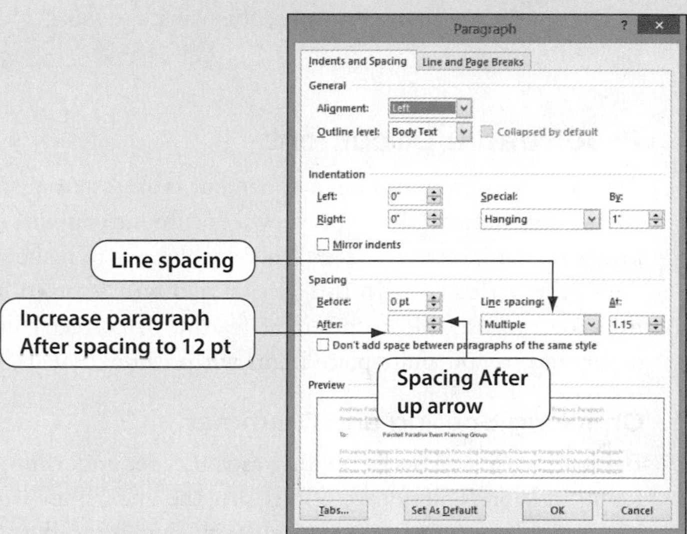

Figure 20 Spacing in Paragraph dialog box

c. In the Paragraph dialog box, under Spacing, click the **After** up arrow three times to increase it to **12 pt**. This will add a little more white space in the heading area. Each time you click the arrow, the spacing value is adjusted by 6, starting with 0. Click **OK**.

Instead of clicking the arrow, you can simply click in the Spacing Before or Spacing After box and type a value, such as 12. The value that you type does not have to be a multiple of 6.

d. Click anywhere in the third paragraph of the body memo, beginning with **We believe**. In the Paragraph group, click **Line and Paragraph Spacing**. Notice the current setting is 1.0, single-spacing. Select **1.15** to change the line spacing to be unified with the rest of the document.

The extra white space makes the document easier to read.

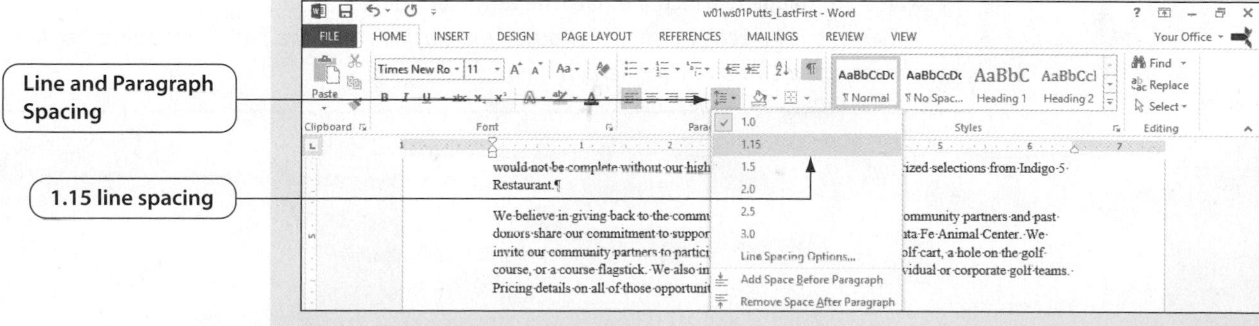

Figure 21 Spacing options in the Paragraph group

e. **Save** the document.

REAL WORLD ADVICE | **How and When to Choose Line Spacing**

When you use the Paragraph dialog box to select line spacing, you have more choices than simply single and double spacing. You can also select Exactly, At Least, or Multiple. *Exactly* enables you to choose a highly precise line spacing that remains fixed at a specified point size. *At Least* lets you specify a minimum line spacing while allowing Word to adjust the height if necessary to accommodate such items as drop caps, which are oversized letters that sometimes begin paragraphs. The At Least setting is more commonly used in desktop publishing. *Multiple* enables you to set line spacing at an interval other than single, double, or 1.5.

Proofread a Document

Reviewing, or proofreading, a document is an essential step in the process of creating an effective document. As you review a document you will most likely identify text that is misspelled or incorrectly used. Word enables you to make sweeping changes to a document with very little effort. In this section you will learn to how to quickly correct spelling mistakes, to use the AutoCorrect feature to correct common typing mistakes as they occur, and to find and replace items within a document.

Checking Spelling and Grammar

By default, Word checks spelling as you type, underlining in red any words that are not found in Word's dictionary. Sometimes the underlined words are not actually misspelled, but instead are names or technical terms that Word does not recognize. In that case, you can ignore the flagged text. Grammatical, capitalization, and spacing errors are underlined in green. Word-usage errors, such as using "lose" instead of "loose," are underlined in blue. Occasionally, the underlined text is not an error at all but is instead part of the document formatting or wording that you prefer to leave as is. Often, the "grammatical error" is simply too many spaces between words. Display nonprinting characters to quickly identify and remove any extra spaces. Word's **Spelling & Grammar** tool may not catch every occurrence of a word-usage, grammatical, or spelling error, as you will discover in the following exercise. Therefore, always proofread the document yourself.

CONSIDER THIS | **The Importance of Proofreading**

Should you rely solely on a spelling checker for your proofreading needs? Before answering that question, try typing the following paragraph into a Word document. Which words are flagged? Which are not? Are any even flagged at all?

Eye enjoyed meeting u the other day. After further revue, we feel Ur resume is per fict. Peas call me with any farther questions.

W01.08

To Check Spelling and Grammar

a. Right-click the wavy red underlined word in the first paragraph of the body of the memo, **promoe**. Select **promote** in the shortcut menu of suggested correct spellings.

When you right-click a flagged spelling mistake, a shortcut menu is displayed. You can then choose to accept a suggestion or to ignore the error. If none of Word's suggested corrections are appropriate, you can edit the document to correct the misspelling or grammatical mistake.

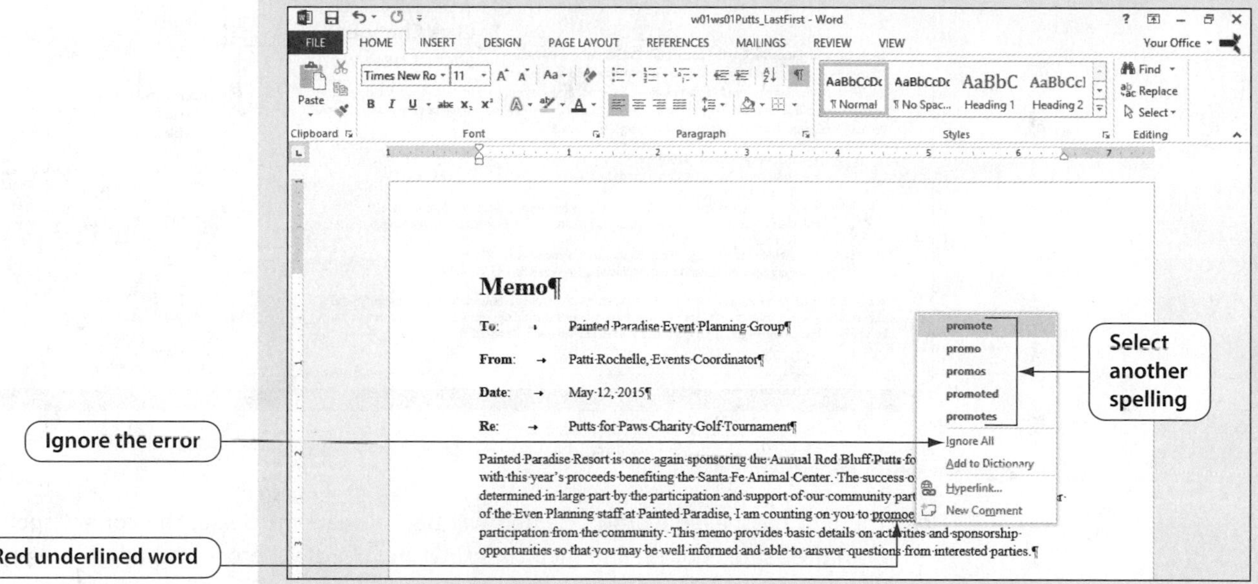

Figure 22 Correcting spelling

> **Troubleshooting**
>
> If you right-click outside the underlined area, the displayed shortcut menu will not include the appropriate selections.

b. Click the **REVIEW** tab, and then in the Proofing group, click **Spelling & Grammar**. The Spelling pane appears. Position the pointer in the title area of the Spelling pane until it changes to a four-headed arrow, and then double-click to dock it to the side of the window (make it stationary). If the pane was already docked before you double-clicked, you will see no change.

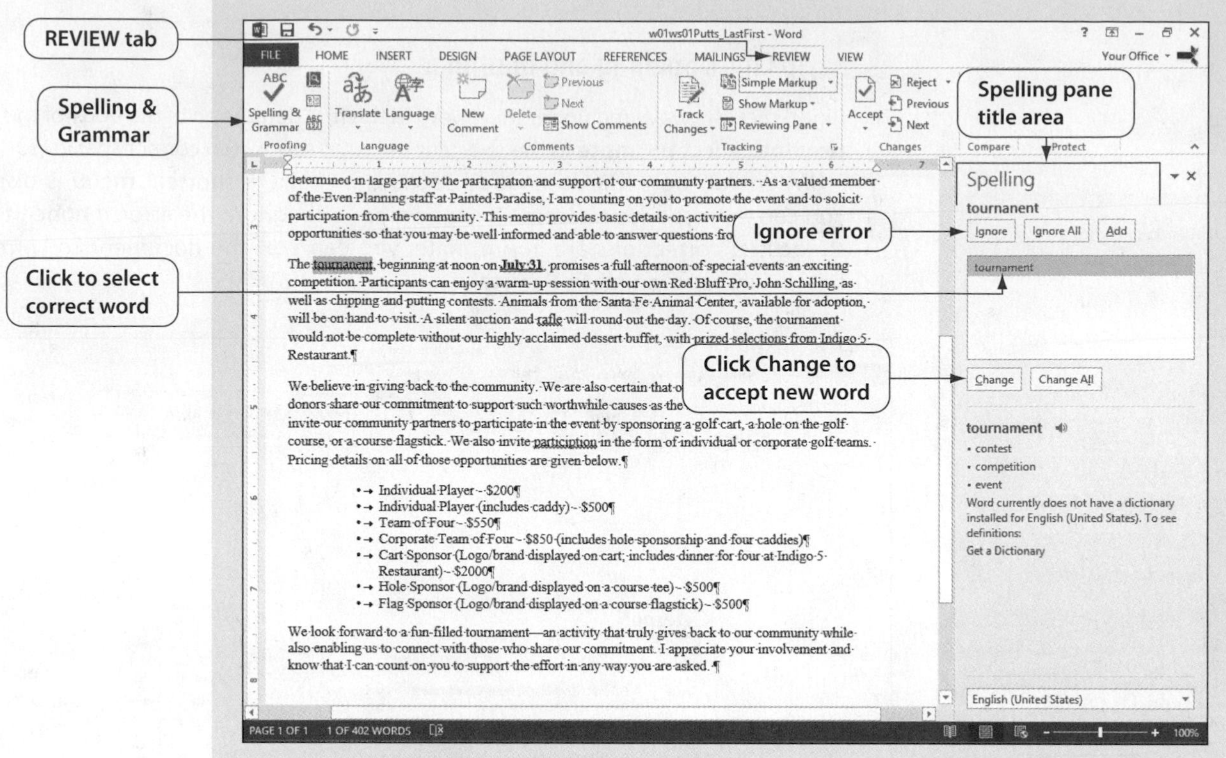

Figure 23 Spelling pane

c. The first misspelled word presented will be "tournanent". Select the correct spelling from the list of choices, and then click **Change**. Word will proceed through the entire document, presenting each error for your consideration. Repeat this process for the remaining errors (raffle and participation). Click **OK** when the spelling and grammar check is complete.

d. Drag the vertical scroll bar to view the first two body paragraphs. Locate the word-usage error in the first paragraph of the body of the memorandum. The word "Even" should be "Event." The word is not flagged as a spelling error because it is not misspelled. Click after the word **Even**, and then type t.

e. **Save** the document.

Using AutoCorrect

Have you ever noticed when you begin a new line or sentence with a lowercase word, Word automatically changes the first letter to uppercase? **AutoCorrect** is a feature that automatically corrects common typing mistakes as they occur. For example, you might notice that you sometimes type "adn" when you meant to type "and". Similarly, the word "the" is often typed "teh". AutoCorrect automatically fixes these errors. You can also create AutoCorrect entries to correct words you often misspell.

AutoCorrect can also be customized to expand frequently used abbreviations, or to apply special formatting, such as replacing (c) with ©. For example, you will configure AutoCorrect to replace "pp" with "Painted Paradise Resort and Spa".

W01.09

To Use AutoCorrect

a. Click the **FILE** tab, click **Options**. The Word Options dialog box opens. Click **Proofing**, and then under the AutoCorrect options section, click **AutoCorrect Options**.

You will often use the phrase "Painted Paradise Resort and Spa" in documents that you prepare for the resort. You will create an AutoCorrect entry to simplify that entry. When you create an AutoCorrect entry, the replacement will not only apply to text that you type in the current document, but to all Word documents that you create on your computer.

b. Type pp in the **Replace** box.

c. Type Painted Paradise Resort and Spa in the **With** box.

> **Troubleshooting**
>
> If the words "Painted Paradise Resort and Spa" are displayed in the With box before you type them, another student might have worked with this exercise before you at the same computer. In that case, the AutoCorrect entry has already been created. Verify that the "pp" entry is in the list of AutoCorrect entries, and if so, then skip to step e.

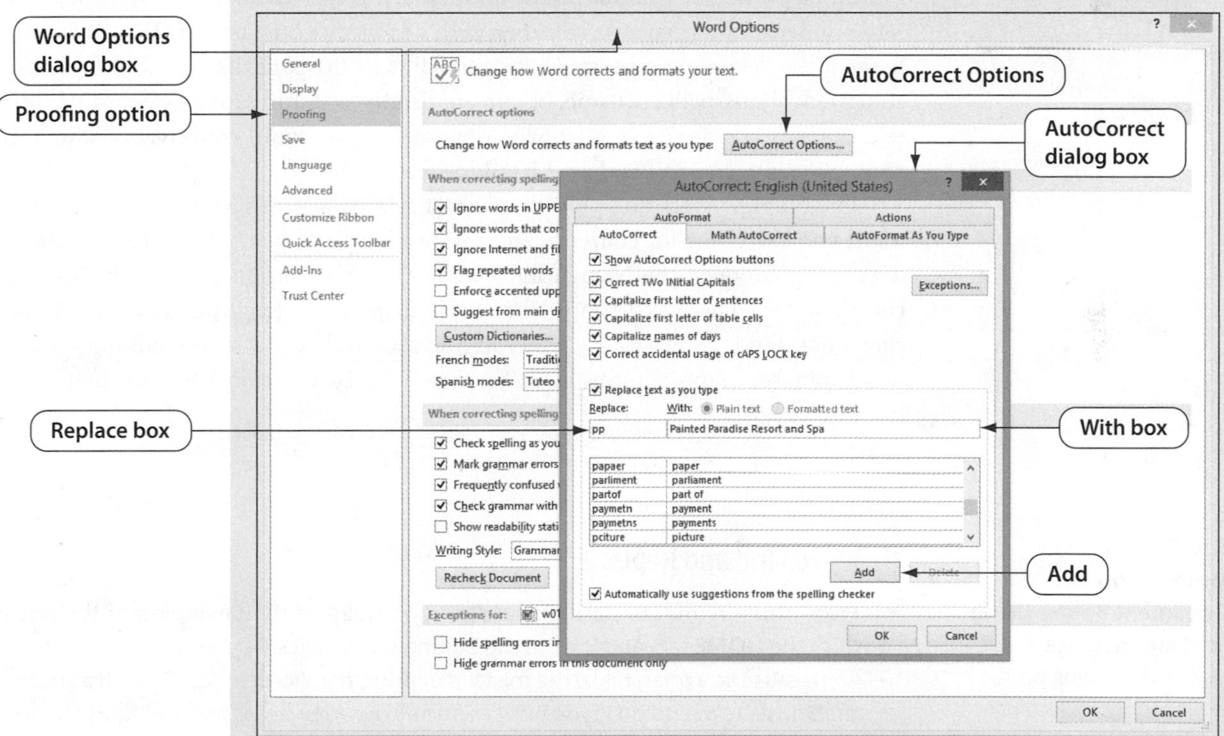

Figure 24 AutoCorrect

d. Click **Add**.

You know that you will often use the word "resort" in the documents that you prepare. However, you tend to type quickly, sometimes reversing the order of letters resulting in "resrot."

e. Scroll through the list of replacements to see if the text "resrot" has been added to the list. If you do not see "resrot" in the replacement list, click in the **Replace** box, delete the text **pp**, and then type resrot. Click in the **With** box, delete any existing text, and then type resort. Click **Add**, click **OK**, and then click **OK** again to close the Word Options dialog box.

f. Click at the end of the second paragraph of the memo body, after the text **Indigo 5 Restaurant**. (Click after the period.) Press Spacebar. Type **pp has prepared for you a fun-filled day at the resrot!** (Type the word "resrot" misspelled as shown.)

   As you type the letters "pp" and press Spacebar, the text will adjust to show "Painted Paradise Resort and Spa." As you type "resrot!" the text will automatically adjust to show the word "resort."

g. Because you are most likely in a computer lab, you will remove the two AutoCorrect entries created in this exercise. Click the **FILE** tab, click **Options**, click **Proofing**, and then click **AutoCorrect Options**. Scroll through the list of AutoCorrect entries, click **pp**, and then click **Delete**. Scroll through the list, click **resrot**, click **Delete**, click **OK**, and then click **OK** again to close the Word Options dialog box.

h. **Save**  the document.

SIDE NOTE

Undo an AutoCorrect Change

You can undo an AutoCorrect change by pressing Ctrl+Z immediately after the change takes effect.

Finding and Replacing Text

Finding a particular word or phrase and replacing it with another might not seem to be a huge undertaking if you are working with a very short document. But consider the challenge if the document were much longer—like a 400-page dissertation! Perhaps you have consistently misspelled a name, or you are simply searching for a keyword. If the incorrect text appears repeatedly in a lengthy document, you could conceivably save a great deal time by using Word's **Find and Replace** feature.

The **Navigation Pane** provides a set of related features for getting around in a document and searching for content. The Navigation Pane is displayed to the left of an open document. To open the Navigation Pane, select Navigation Pane in the Show group on the View tab. The Navigation Pane is also displayed when you click the Home tab and then click Find. Alternatively, you can press Ctrl+F. If you are looking for a particular word, phrase, graphic, formula, or footnote, the Navigation Pane can help you find the item quickly.

W01.10

To Find and Replace

a. Press Ctrl+Home to position the insertion point at the beginning of the document. Click the **HOME** tab, and then in the Editing group, click **Replace**.

   Because you often make the mistake of using the word "Indigo 5", with a space before the 5, instead of "Indigo5", you want to find all occurrences of "Indigo 5" and replace them.

SIDE NOTE

Move to Top of Document Before Using Find and Replace

Move the insertion point to the top of the document before finding and replacing text in order to start the search at the top of the document.

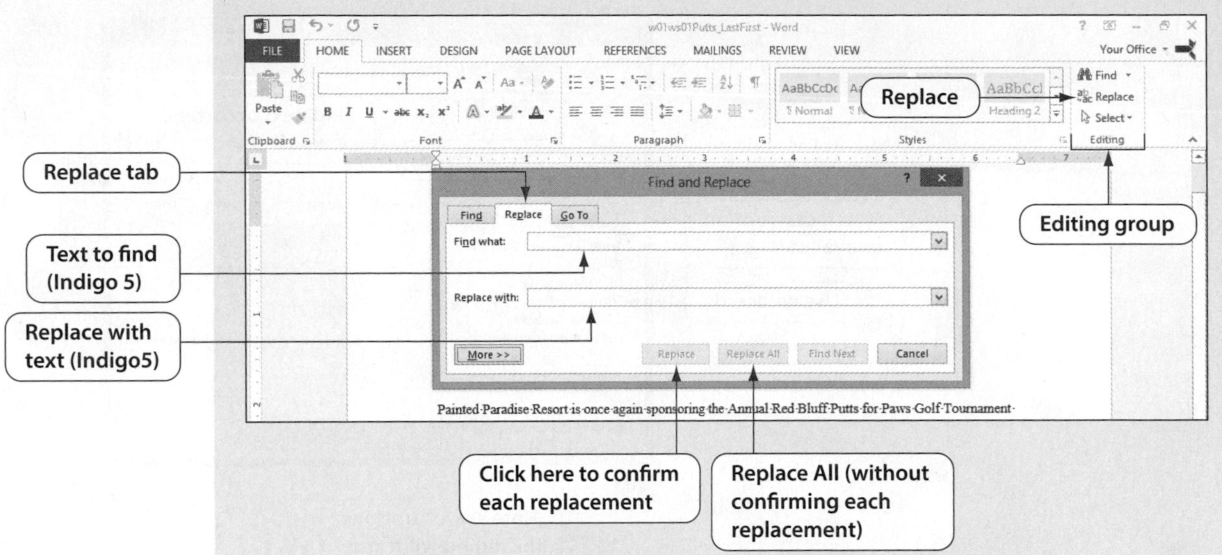

Figure 25 Replace tab in the Find and Replace dialog box

b. Click in the **Find what** box, delete any text if necessary, and then type Indigo 5 with a space before the 5. Press Tab. In the **Replace with** box, type Indigo5 with no space.

c. Click **Replace All** so that you will not be asked to confirm every replacement. Two replacements are made. Click **OK**, and then click **Close** to close the Find and Replace dialog box.

> **SIDE NOTE**
> **Use Caution with Find and Replace**
> Replace All does not ask for your confirmation, so it can be a dangerous activity if you have not carefully thought through the possible changes.

d. Press Ctrl+Home. In the Editing group, click **Replace**, and then in the Find and Replace dialog box, click the **Find** tab.

The words "caddy" and "caddies" appear at various places throughout the flyer. You will use a **wildcard** to find each occurrence of words beginning with "cad," that should identify each of these words. Because you only care that a search result begins with "cad" and you know what follows those letters is irrelevant to your search, you will use the asterisk (*) wildcard.

Wildcard Symbol	Represents
*	Any number of characters, including none
?	One character
#	One number

Table 5 Find and Replace wildcards

> **SIDE NOTE**
> **To Go To a Page Number**
> On the Home tab, in the Editing group, click the Find arrow, and then select Go To. Enter a page number, and then click Next.

You will use the asterisk wildcard because the number of letters following "cad" varies in the search previously described. For example, the word "caddy" includes two additional letters following "cad", while the word "caddies" includes four additional letters. Because wildcard searches are case sensitive (the option to deselect Match Case is unavailable) results will only display words beginning with "cad," not "Cad."

e. Click in the **Find what** box, and then remove any existing text if necessary. Type cad* (with no spaces) and then click **More**. Click **Use wildcards**, and then click **Find Next**. The first word containing the text "cad" is displayed.

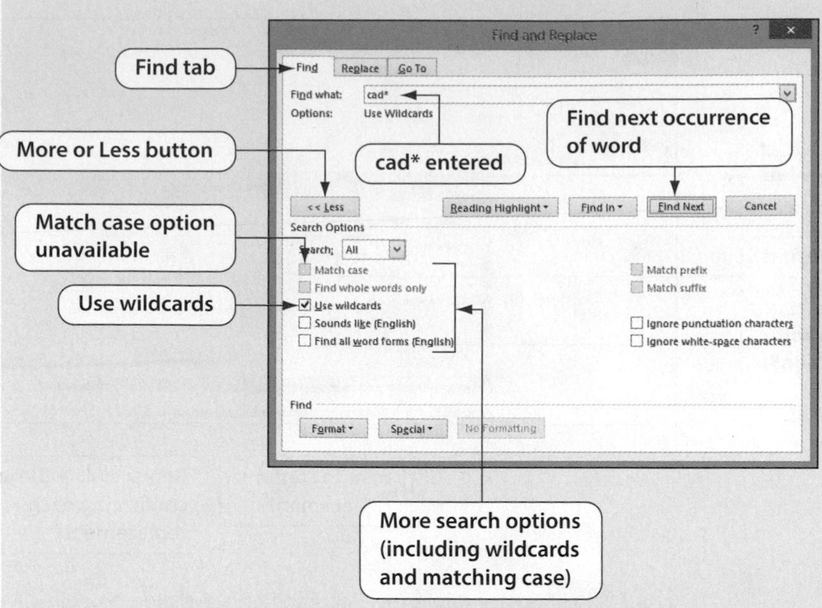

Figure 26 Find tab in the Find and Replace dialog box

> **Troubleshooting**
> If the Find and Replace dialog box hides the search result, click the dialog box title bar, and drag the dialog box out of the way.

SIDE NOTE
Navigation Pane Shortcut
Press Ctrl+F to quickly open the Navigation Pane.

f. Click **Find Next** to view another word beginning with "cad." Continue clicking **Find Next** until the search is complete, click **OK**, and then click **Close** × to close the Find and Replace dialog box.

g. In the Editing group, click **Find**. The Navigation Pane appears to the left of the document. Be sure any text in the **Search** box is highlighted, type **tournament**, and then press Enter.

All occurrences of the word "tournament" are temporarily highlighted in the flyer. Because the flyer is a one-page document it is easy to see all the matches, but if the document were lengthier, you could scroll through pages to view the results.

Tabs in the Navigation Pane provide even quicker access to search results. If a document includes sections with titles formatted in a heading style (Heading 1, Heading 2, etc.), click HEADINGS in the Navigation Pane to see search results organized by section. You can see resulting pages when you click PAGES, and all resulting text when you click RESULTS.

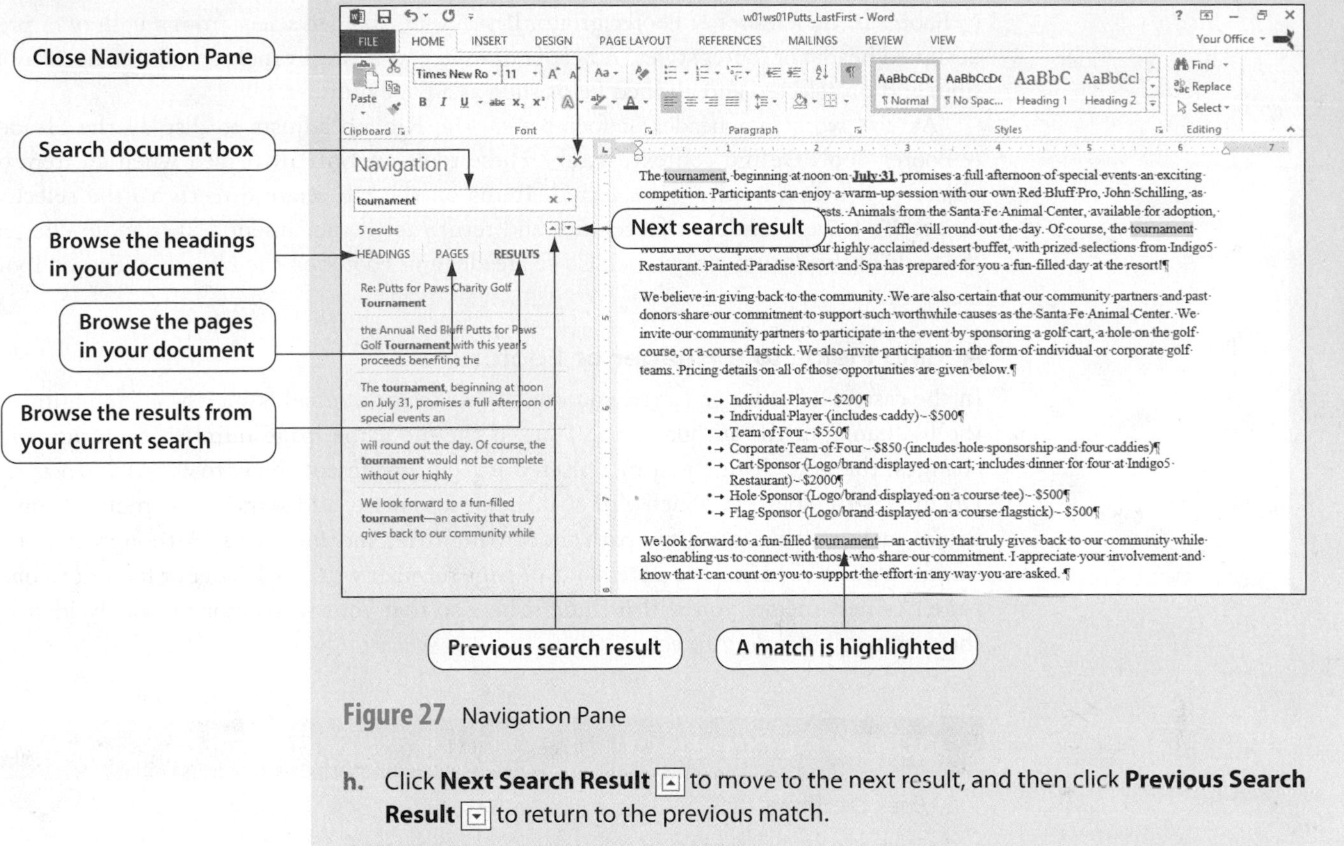

Figure 27 Navigation Pane

h. Click **Next Search Result** [▲] to move to the next result, and then click **Previous Search Result** [▼] to return to the previous match.

i. Click **Close** [×] in the Navigation Pane to remove highlights and close the Navigation Pane.

j. **Save** [💾] the document.

Insert a Header and Footer

A **header** or **footer** consists of one or more lines of text or graphics printed in the top or bottom margin of a document. A header appears in the top margin; a footer is in the bottom margin. Headers and footers are not included in a document by default.

The most commonly used footer is a page number. A page number footer automatically increases in increments so that all pages are properly numbered. When you specify a header or footer, the item appears on all pages unless you specify otherwise. For example, you can indicate that a header or footer is only to appear on odd or even pages. You can set a header or footer on all pages except the first page, which would be handy if the first page is a cover page or the title page of a report. You can also include headers or footers in only one section of a document. You will learn to create sections in Workshop 2.

You can insert a header or footer by simply double-clicking in the top or bottom margin of a document. The insertion point is displayed in the header or footer area, with the rest of the document grayed out. At that point, you can type text, such as your name, and align it using the alignment options on the Home tab. You can also use Tab to position text. A header, or footer, has three sections—left, center and right. Press Tab to go from one section to the other. For example, enter your name in the left section, then press Tab to move to the center and insert a company name.

You can also insert a header or footer when you click the Insert tab and select Header or Footer in the Header & Footer group. If you like, you can select from a gallery of predesigned header or footer styles. A header or footer style might include colored horizontal lines and preselected and aligned fields such as a page number.

As you work in a header or footer area, the Ribbon adjusts to display the Header & Footer Tools Design contextual tab. These tools are only displayed when an item or object—such as a header—is selected. Items on the tab relate directly to the selected object. To leave a header or footer area and return to the document text, double-click in the body of the document, or click Close Header and Footer on the Header & Footer Tools Design tab.

Adding Fields to a Header or Footer

In the case of a header or footer, you can choose to include fields such as a page number, the file name, or the author name. Thus, if the file name, page number, or author ever changes, the new change will be reflected in your document. New to Word 2013 is the Document Info button, which will enable you to quickly add some of the more common fields, such as the author, file path, document title, and file name. Although it is not common practice to include a file name or page number within a header or footer of a one-page business memo, you will include it here so that your instructor can easily identify the memo as belonging to you.

QUICK REFERENCE | **Insert a Header or Footer**

1. Click the Insert tab.
2. Click Header (or Footer) in the Header & Footer group.
3. Click Edit Header (or Edit Footer).
4. Type a header or footer, or select a predefined item such as Date & Time, File Name, or Page Number.
5. Click Close Header and Footer to return to the document, or double-click in the document.

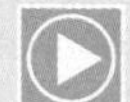

To Insert Headers and Footers

a. Click the **INSERT** tab, and then in the Header & Footer group, click **Footer**. Although you can select from a gallery of footer designs, select **Edit Footer** to create your own.

The document text appears grayed out, and the insertion point is displayed in the footer area. The Ribbon is expanded to include the HEADER & FOOTER TOOLS DESIGN tab. These tools contain commands related to the currently selected item, which is a footer.

SIDE NOTE
To Open a Header or Footer
Alternatively, you can double-click in the header or footer area.

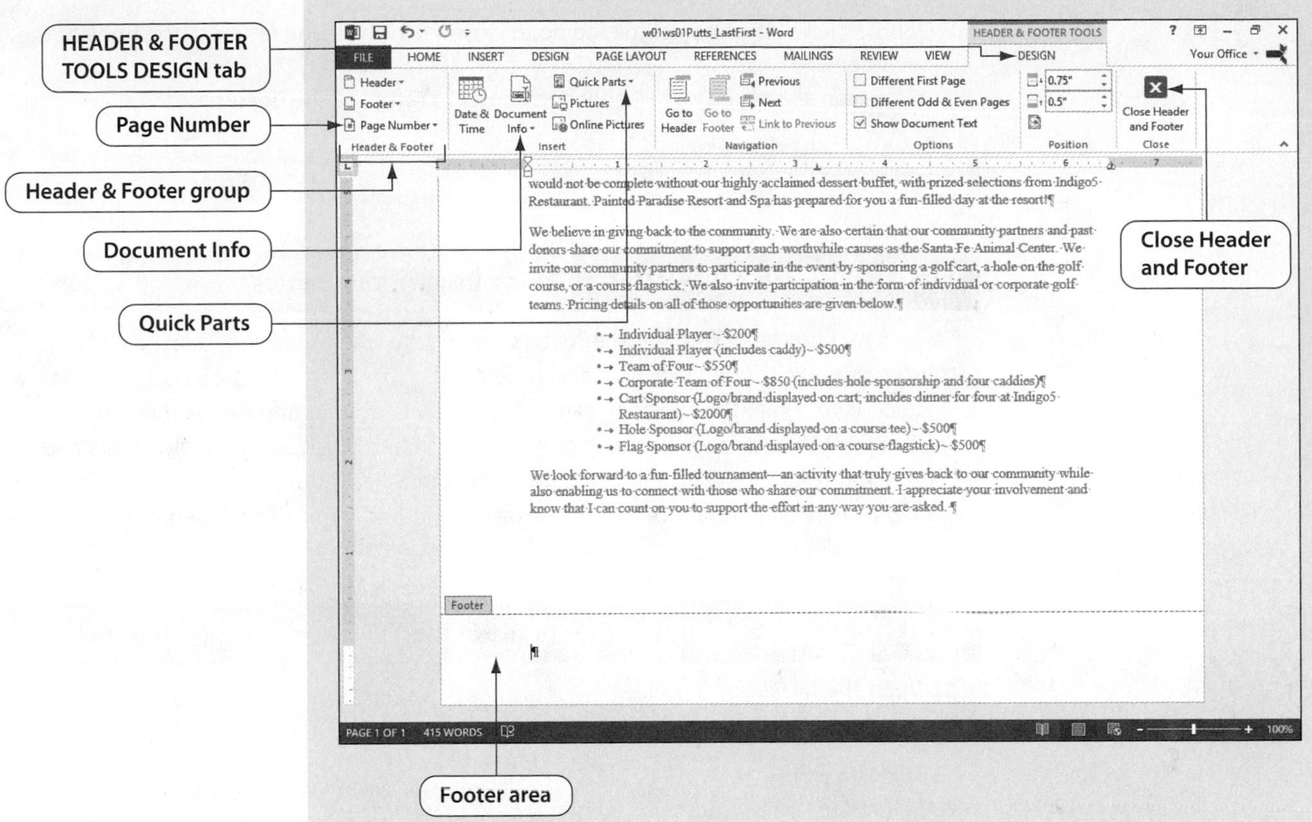

Figure 28 Inserting headers and footers

b. Type Painted Paradise Resort and Spa, and then press Tab.

c. Under HEADER & FOOTER TOOLS, on the DESIGN tab, in the Header & Footer group, click **Page Number**. Point to **Current Position**, select **Plain Number**, press Tab, and then type Internal Communication.

You have included a page number as part of the footer. Choose Current Position so that you can control where the page number field is placed.

d. Drag to select the entire line of the footer. Click the **HOME** tab, and then in the Font group, click the **Font** arrow, and then select **Times New Roman**. While the text is still selected, click the **Font Size** arrow, and then select **10**.

e. Double-click in the body of the memo to close the footer and return to the body of the document.

The footer will now appear grayed out to indicate that you are working in the main body of the document.

f. Click the **INSERT** tab, and then in the Header & Footer group, click **Header**. Although you can select from a gallery of header designs, select **Edit Header** to create your own.

g. Under HEADER & FOOTER TOOLS, on the DESIGN tab, in the Insert group, click **Quick Parts**. Select **Field**. The Field dialog box opens. Scroll down the Field names list, select **FileName**, and then click **OK**. Click the **HOME** tab, and then in the Paragraph group, click **Center**.

You have included the file name as part of the header, making it convenient to identify the source of the document. As previously mentioned, you will not often include a file name header in a business memo. You are including it here so that your instructor can easily identify the memo as belonging to you.

SIDE NOTE

Use Document Info Button to Insert the File Name

Alternatively, on the Header & Footer Tools Design tab, in the Insert group, click Document Info, and then select File Name.

h. Double-click in the body of the memo to close the header and return to the body of the document.

   You can also click Close Header and Footer to return to the document.

i. **Save** [icon] the document.

REAL WORLD ADVICE | **Using Headers and Footers**

A primary purpose of headers and footers, especially when used in academic and business reports, is to identify pages as belonging to a particular project. If you include your name, the company name, or a project name in a footer, you will be reminded with each page of the document's origin and purpose. Research papers and books might include page and chapter numbers in a header or footer. Use headers and footers where appropriate to add organization and professionalism to a document.

QUICK REFERENCE | **To Insert Page Numbers in a Header or Footer**

1. Open the header or footer.
2. On the Header & Footer Tools Design tab, click Page Number in the Header & Footer group.
3. Select Current Position.
4. Select Plain Number, or any other desired format.
5. Align the text in the header or footer as necessary.

Save and Close a Document

You will often need to save and close your work in order to reopen it at a later time. By default, Word 2013 saves files in a .docx format, which is different from the .doc format used in Word 97-2003. Word still enables you, though, to save your file in the previous Word 97-2003 format, if necessary, or in a variety of other formats. In the following sections you will also learn that you can save your file as a PDF file, or directly to the cloud, an Internet storage concept. Regardless of how you save your file, do not forget to save your work often. Saving often will prevent you from losing your work in the event of a system failure, formatting error, or other unexpected disruption.

Saving a Document to SkyDrive

When you save a file, you must specify a location. That location is usually a flash drive, or perhaps a hard drive. Recognizing the mobile lifestyle of most people today, Microsoft built functionality into Word 2013 that enables you to save files directly to the cloud, and open them on any computer, even if that computer does not have Word 2013 installed.

Cloud computing allows users to keep files on the Internet rather than on a client computer. When you save files to the cloud you are actually saving the files to an internet storage concept, such as a **SkyDrive** account. SkyDrive is web storage space that Microsoft makes available to you at no cost. When you sign up for SkyDrive storage, you are given access of up to 7 GB of space in which you can create folders and upload documents, spreadsheets, presentations, and other files. In addition, with the release of Office 2010, Microsoft introduced Office Web Apps, a web-based version of Word, PowerPoint, Excel, and OneNote. Despite the fact that Office Web Apps has limited functionality, missing many of the features that you find in a locally installed Office suite, core editing and formatting commands are still included.

MODULE 1

QUICK REFERENCE | **Creating a Strong Password**

Passwords should be easy to remember but difficult for anyone to guess. Whether you are Internet shopping, managing your work e-mails, or creating a SkyDrive account, here are some tips that can help you create a strong password:

1. Include at least 14 characters, including numbers and letters—both uppercase and lowercase.
2. Do not use real words, as software used by ill-intentioned hackers can quickly check every word in the dictionary.
3. Use a passphrase, such as the first letter of every word in a favorite song, poem, or phrase, combined with numbers that are easily remembered.
4. Do not use personal information, such as your pet's name or a middle name.
5. Use the entire keyboard, including special characters.
6. Do not use the same password for all of your online activity.
7. Do not use your username as the password.

Saving a Document to a PDF File

PDF (Portable Document Format) is a file type that preserves most formatting attributes of a source document, regardless of the software in which it was created. It is a format that can easily be viewed on multiple platforms. The only software required to read or print a PDF file is Adobe Reader, which is available as a free download at www.adobe.com/products/reader/. For example, if you create a .docx file using Word, Microsoft Word will be required in order to view the file. However, if you create a PDF file, a user can easily view the file using Adobe Reader without having to purchase any additional software. Word has long been able to save a document as a PDF file; however, Word 2013 now has the ability to edit PDF documents, discussed later in this workshop. You will create a PDF format of your memorandum in the following exercise.

REAL WORLD ADVICE | **Why Save a Document as a PDF?**

Saving a document as a PDF file will ensure accessibility by others, regardless of how the file was created or the type of computer the recipient is using.

- A PDF format will preserve the appearance of your document—the font size, the spacing, and the placement of graphics will remain the same, regardless of who is viewing the document.
- A PDF format is secure, not easily altered, and it cannot be modified without leaving an "electronic footprint"— a trail of modifications.

W01.12

To Save a Document

a. Click to place the insertion point just before the word **Pro** in the second body paragraph. Type Golf, and then press Spacebar. You have now specifically identified the type of professional by changing "Pro" to "Golf Pro."

Troubleshooting

If you see any unnecessary spaces, click to the right of the unnecessary space and press Backspace to remove it—or click to the left of the space and press Delete to remove it. If a space is needed, click where the space is to be placed, and press Spacebar as necessary to add a space or spaces.

b. **Save** the document.

Because you made changes to the file, you will save it before creating a PDF file.

c. Click the **FILE** tab, and then click **Export**. Verify that Create PDF/XPS Document is selected under Export, and then click the **Create PDF/XPS** button. Navigate to the location where you are saving your files.

Note the Save as type box displays PDF to indicate that the document will be saved as a PDF file.

d. Because you do not want the PDF file to open after publishing, if necessary, click to deselect the **Open file after publishing check box**.

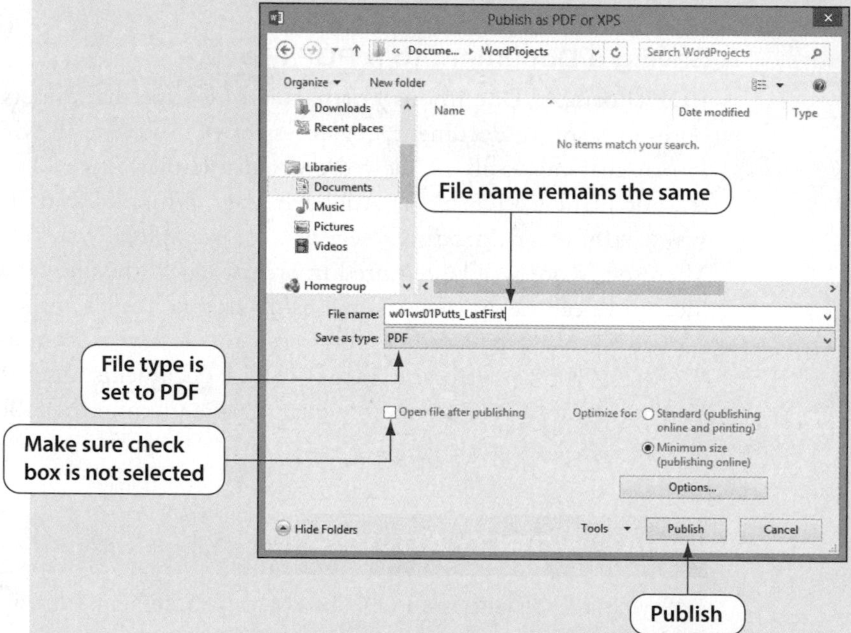

Figure 29 Publish as PDF or XPS dialog box

e. Click **Publish** to save the file as w01ws01Putts_LastFirst.

Troubleshooting

If a PDF version of the file opens in a reader, you did not deselect the Open file after publishing check box. Simply close the reader and continue with the next step.

f. Click **Close** to close this file and exit Word. If the "Want to save your changes to w01ws01Putts_LastFirst?" message appears, click **Save**.

Editing a PDF File

A PDF file is not easily modified. In the past, the source file and the purchase of a PDF editor had been required in order to alter a PDF file. Word 2013 has a new feature called PDF Reflow, which enables you to easily convert PDF files into Word documents. PDF Reflow is not intended to replace a PDF reader, but rather it allows you to make changes to an existing PDF file. Any PDF file can be modified, though text-based files are preferred. A copy of the PDF file is converted into a Word document, and then placed into Word, so the original PDF file will remain intact. As you will see in the following exercise, converting a PDF file is not always a seamless process, but with a few simple changes you will successfully alter the PDF file without having to edit the original source file. Your boss has made a copy of the PDF file. You notice that the date is wrong, so to save time you open the PDF file in Word as a Word document, make the necessary changes, and then save the file as a PDF file again.

W01.13

To Edit a PDF File

a. Start **Word**, click **Open Other Documents**, and then double-click **Computer**. Navigate to the location of your student data files, and then click **w01ws01PuttsPDF**.

Make sure to select the PDF file, and not the .docx file. Look for the icons in front of the file to help you distinguish between .docx files and PDF files. The PDF file will have the PDF icon in front of its name.

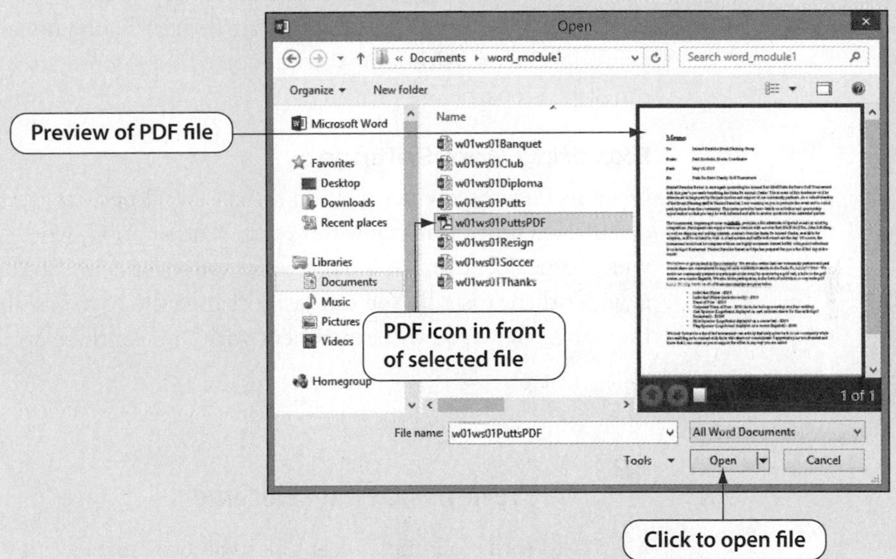

Figure 30 Open the PDF file

b. Click **Open** to open the file. If the "Word will now convert your PDF" message appears, wait until the pointer appears, and then click **OK**.

c. Press CTRL+END. After converting the PDF to a Word document, the footer is now part of the main body of the file. Triple-click the last line of the file, beginning with **Painted Paradise**, and then press Delete.

You remove the line that was originally intended to be the footer.

d. Double-click in the **footer area** to insert a new footer. Under HEADER & FOOTER TOOLS, on the DESIGN tab, in the Insert group, click **Document Info**, and then select **File Name**. On the **HOME** tab, in the Paragraph group, click **Center**. Press Enter. Type Firstname Lastname, using your first and last name. Double-click in the main body of the memo to close the footer.

e. Scroll to the top of the document. On the **Date:** line, change the date from May 12, 2015 to May 13, 2015.

f. Click the **FILE** tab, click **Export**, and then click **Create PDF/XPS**. If necessary, click to deselect the **Open file after publishing check box** so the PDF file does not open. Navigate to the location where you are saving your files, click in the **File name** box, and then change the filename to w01ws01PuttsPDF_LastFirst, using your last and first name. Click **Publish**.

g. Click **Close** to close this file and exit Word. The Want to save your changes to w01ws01PuttsPDF? message will appear. Click **Don't Save** because you do not want to create another Word document from the PDF file.

Print a Document

Printing and previewing commands are accessed via Backstage view. In earlier versions of Word, it was a bit cumbersome to preview a document before printing because the Print and Preview actions were located in separate areas of the Word command structure. Backstage view brings those actions together, displaying a preview of the document when you click Print. Although you cannot edit a document in print preview, you can take a quick last look before printing.

Exploring Print Settings

Once in Backstage view, you can select several options related to printing a document. By default, documents are shown in portrait orientation, where the document is taller than it is wide. Some documents might be better suited for landscape orientation—when the document is wider than it is tall. You can easily change the page orientation and other print settings in Backstage view. You will experiment with some of these options in the next exercise.

W01.14

To Preview and Print a Document

a. Start **Word**. Your most recent files will be displayed on the left. Click **w01ws01Putts_LastFirst** from the Recent list. Recall that your last name and your first name will be shown instead of LastFirst.

Make sure to open the w01ws01Putts_LastFirst file and not the w01ws01PuttsPDF_LastFirst file. You can point to the file name to reveal a ScreenTip to verify that the full file name is w01ws01Putts_LastFirst.

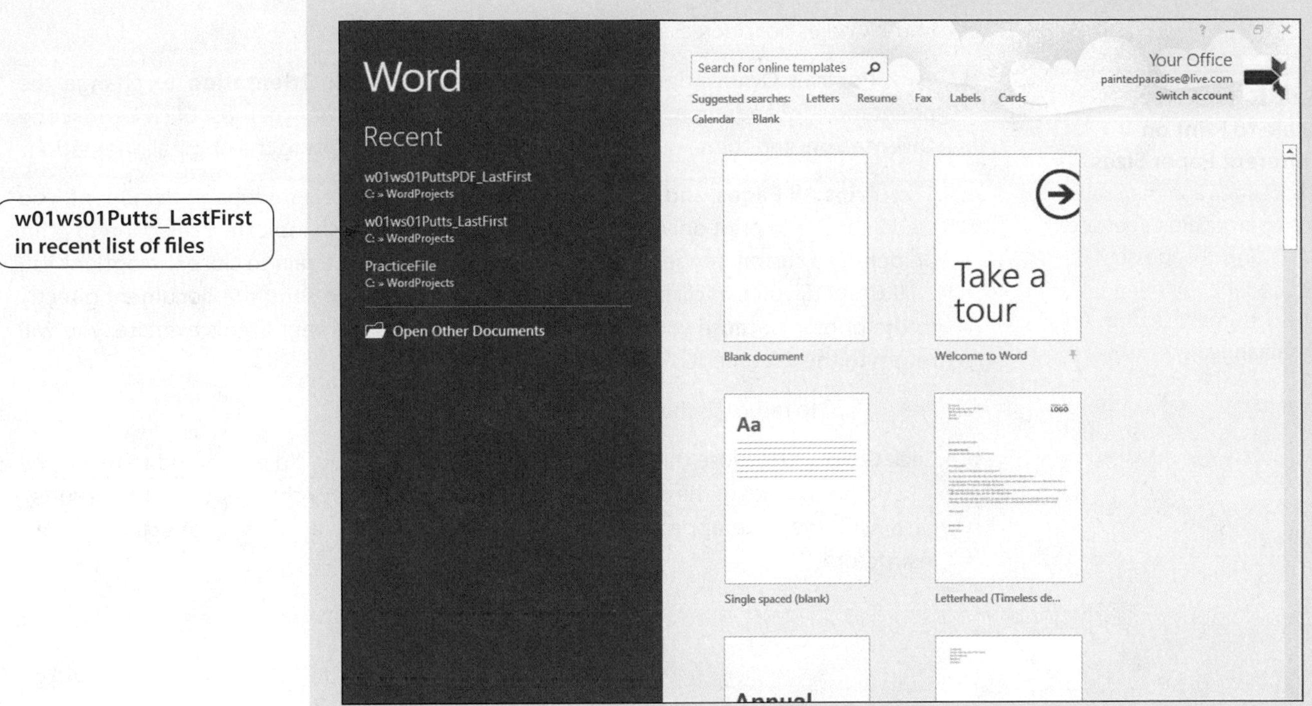

Figure 31 Recent file

b. Click the **FILE** tab, and then click **Print**.

Note the preview of the memorandum that is displayed on the right. Options, such as number of copies, orientation, and printer selection, are available in the center section.

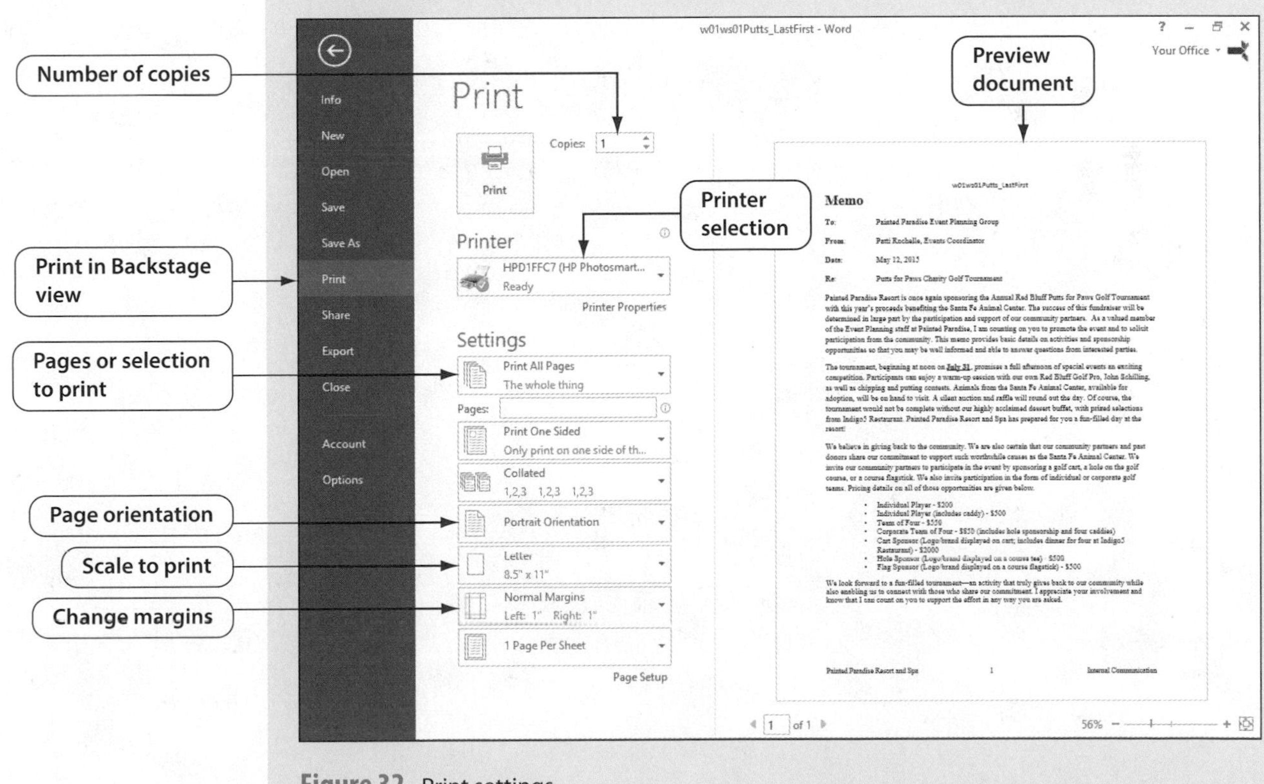

Figure 32 Print settings

c. In the Copies box, increase the number of copies to **2**.

d. Click **Portrait Orientation**, and then select **Landscape Orientation** to change the orientation to landscape. This is not an accepted format for memos. Click **Landscape Orientation**, and then select **Portrait Orientation** to return to the original orientation.

e. Click **Print All Pages**, and note that if the document were a multipage document, you could choose to print only the current page. You could also indicate a selection to print or identify a custom range of pages. Click **Print All Pages** again to close the options list.

   If desired, you can click the Print button at this time to send the document directly to the printer. Because you will not be printing the document in this exercise, you will return to the document.

f. Press Esc to return to the document.

g. Click **Close** × to close this file and exit Word. Because you did not intend to make any additional changes to the document, if the "Want to save your changes to w01ws01Putts_LastFirst?" message appears, click **Don't Save**. Submit your files as directed by your instructor.

SIDE NOTE

Scale to Print on Different Paper Sizes

Click Letter, and then select the appropriate paper size. The sizing change only occurs when printing. The document settings do not change.

MODULE 1

Concept Check

1. Which version of Microsoft Word is used in this textbook? Word enables you to easily format text in a document. What are some other features available in Word? p. 176
2. When you write business communication it can be difficult for a reader to understand your tone. Always keep your communication brief and concise. What are some other do's and don'ts when writing business communication? p. 180
3. What is the difference between a memo and business letter? What is the difference between a block, modified block, and semi-block letter? p. 181–183
4. Show/Hide is referred to as a toggle. What is a toggle, and what are some examples of other toggles? What purpose does Show/Hide serve? There are five ways to view your document—Print Layout, Web Layout, Outline view, Draft view, and Read Mode. Which view does not display hard returns, and why? p. 185–187
5. What is the first thing you must do before formatting characters? What are some examples of character formatting? p. 191
6. What is the difference between paragraph spacing and line spacing? What is a specific example of when you would decrease paragraph spacing in a business letter? p. 198
7. What is the difference between the Spelling & Grammar tool and the AutoCorrect feature? p. 200–202
8. What can you add into a header or footer? What is the difference between typing the page number in a footer and inserting the page number field? p. 207
9. What is a PDF file, and why would you use it? Can you edit a PDF file in Word? p. 211
10. You can select several options related to printing a document in Backstage view. Explain why you might use these options, even if you are not planning to send your document to a printer. p. 214

Key Terms

AutoCorrect 202
Backstage view 189
Block 181
Business communication 176
Centered 196
Cloud computing 210
Default 184
Draft view 185
Find and Replace 204
Font 192
Footer 207
Formatting marks 185
Hard return 184
Header 207
Insertion point 188
Justified 197
KeyTips 184
Left-aligned 196
Line spacing 198
Live Preview 193
Microsoft Word 2013 176
Modified block 181
Monospaced font 193
Navigation Pane 204
Nonprinting characters 185
Outline view 185
Paragraph spacing 198
PDF (Portable Document Format) 211
Print Layout 185
Proportional font 193
Read Mode 185
Right-aligned 196
Sans serif font 193
Semi-block 181
Serif font 193
SkyDrive 210
Soft return 184
Spelling & Grammar 200
Toggle 187
Web Layout 185
Wildcard 205
Word processing 176
Word Start screen 176
Word wrap 184

Visual Summary

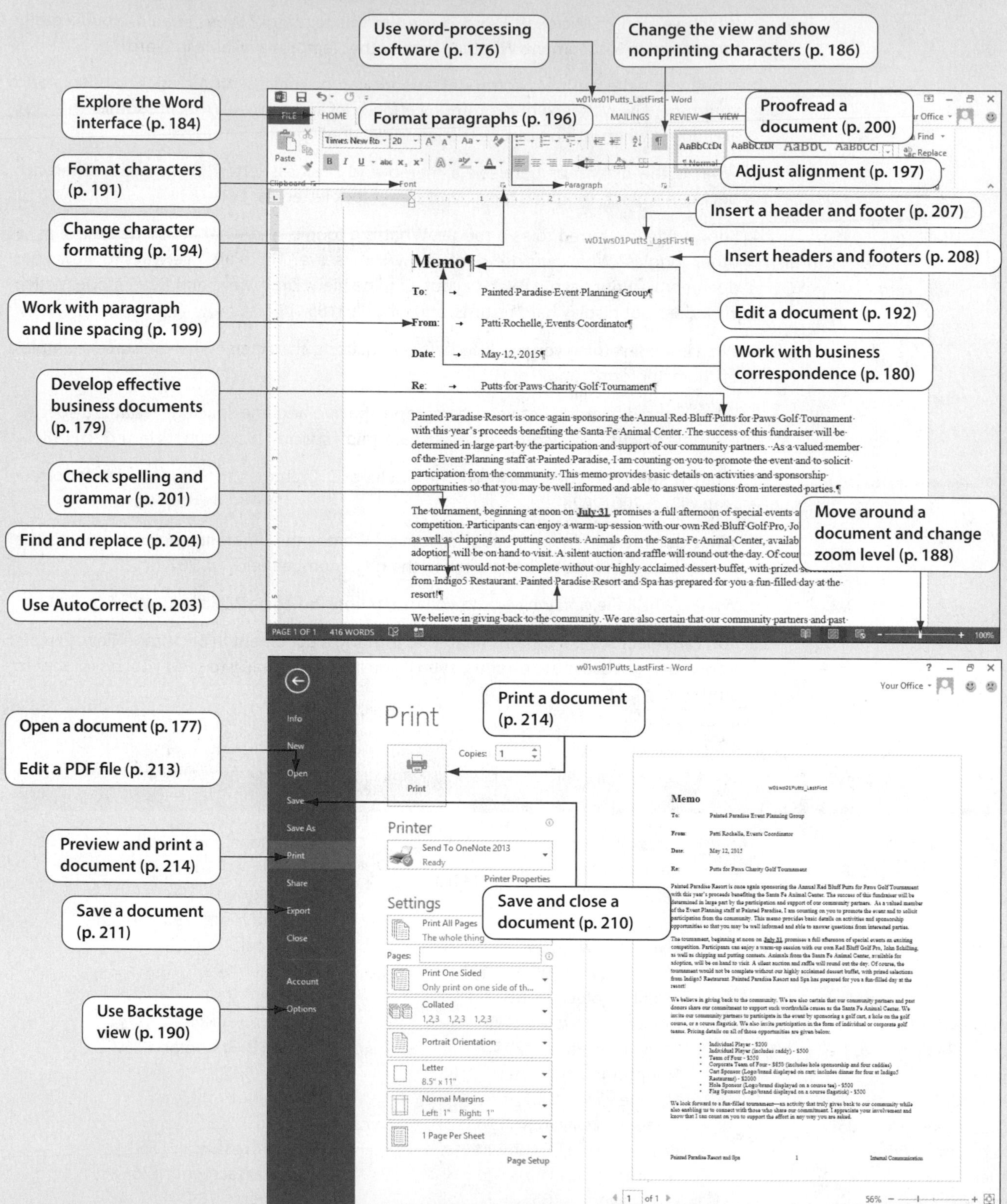

Figure 33 Putts for Paws Golf Tournament Memo Final Document

Practice 1

Student data file needed:

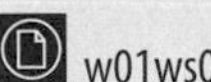

w01ws01Thanks.docx

You will save your files as:

w01ws01Thanks_LastFirst.docx

w01ws01Thanks_LastFirst.pdf

Thank You Letter

Customer Service

Sales & Marketing

The Putts for Paws Golf Tournament was a tremendous success! Over 80 golfers enjoyed a day on the greens putting for the Santa Fe Animal Center. You plan to send a thank-you letter to each participant. Your first step is to create a standard letter that will be used as a template once you are ready to create the remaining letters. For this exercise you will use a standard business format to create a single, professionally formatted letter, free of spelling and grammatical mistakes.

a. Start **Word**, click **Open Other Documents**, double-click **Computer**, navigate to the location of your student files, and then double-click **w01ws01Thanks**. A draft of a thank-you letter is displayed. Click the **FILE** tab, click **Save As**, double-click **Computer**, and then navigate to the location where you are saving your files. Change the File name to w01ws01Thanks_LastFirst, using your last and first name, and then click **Save**.

b. If necessary, click **Show/Hide** in the Paragraph group to display formatting marks.

c. Select the first nine paragraphs, starting from the line beginning with **Barry Cheney, Manager** and ending with the line **1132 Hance Street**. On the HOME tab, in the Paragraph group, click the **Paragraph Dialog Box Launcher**. In the Paragraph dialog box, under Spacing, click the **After** down arrow twice to set the spacing to **0 pt** and remove the After spacing completely. Click **OK**, and then click anywhere to deselect the text.

d. Drag to select **$75,000** in the first paragraph in the body of the letter. Do not select the space following the dollar amount. With **$75,000** selected, in the Font group, click **Underline**.

   The easiest way to select a word without including the following space is to move the insertion point to the beginning of the word, and then use Shift+→ to select only the characters you need. The space after "$75,000" should not be underlined. If it is, select the single space and click Underline in the Font group to remove the underline.

e. Press Ctrl+A to select the entire document. In the Font group, click the **Font** arrow, and then scroll to select **Times New Roman**. With the text still selected, click the **Font Size** arrow, and then select **11**. Click anywhere to deselect the text.

f. Press Ctrl+Home to place the insertion point at the beginning of the document. Change the date from **May 10, 2015** to May 15, 2015. Locate the word **often** in the second paragraph in the body of the letter. Double-click the word to select it, and then press Delete.

g. Click the **REVIEW** tab, and then in the Proofing group, click **Spelling & Grammar**. Change any misspelled words as they are presented by selecting the correct word and clicking Change. If a flagged word is not actually misspelled, as in a last name, street name, or a city name, ignore the error by clicking Ignore. Click **OK**.

h. Proofread the document to make sure you did not overlook any misspellings or incorrect word usage. Correct anything that is out of order.

   You will find two word-usage errors that Word did not identify in the first and last paragraphs of the memo body.

i. Click the **FILE** tab, click **Options**, click **Proofing**, and then click **AutoCorrect Options**.

j. Click in the **Replace** box, and then type bc. Click in the **With** box, and then type Barry Cheney. Click **Add**, click **OK**, and then click **OK** again.

   Because you often type the manager's name, Barry Cheney, you create an AutoCorrect entry so that the letters "bc" automatically convert to "Barry Cheney."

k. Press Ctrl+End to place the insertion point at the end of the document. Type bc, and then press Spacebar. The words "Barry Cheney" are displayed. Press Enter, and then type Red Bluff Golf Club and Pro Shop. Do not press Enter.

l. Press ↑ once to position the cursor in the above line, **Barry Cheney**. Click the **HOME** tab, and then in the Paragraph group, click the **Paragraph Dialog Box Launcher**. Remove the paragraph **After** spacing by changing the spacing to **0 pt**. Click OK to close the Paragraph dialog box.

m. Scroll to the top of the document. Drag to select **Red Bluff Putts for Paws Golf Tournament** in the first paragraph in the body of the letter. On the HOME tab, in the Font group, click **Bold**.

n. Drag to select the **URL** (**web address**) in the second paragraph in the body of the letter, starting with **http** and ending with **survey**. In the Font group, click **Italic**, and then on the Quick Access Toolbar, click **Undo** to remove the italic. You decide that you do want italic, so on the Quick Access Toolbar, click **Redo** to italicize the web address.

o. Select the **first four lines** of the letter, starting with the line **Barry Cheney, Manager**, and ending with the line **Santa Fe, NM 89566**. On the HOME tab, in the Paragraph group, click **Align Left**. Click anywhere to deselect the text.

p. Click the **FILE** tab, and then click **Print** to see a preview of the document. Press Esc to return to the document.

After viewing the preview, you realize that you forgot to add a header and footer.

q. Click the **INSERT** tab, and then in the Header & Footer group, click **Footer**, and then select **Edit Footer**. You will include your name and the file name in the footer so that your instructor can identify your submission. Type Firstname Lastname, using your first and last name, and then press Enter. Under HEADER & FOOTER TOOLS, on the DESIGN tab, in the Insert group, click **Document Info**, and then select **File Name**.

r. In the Close group, click **Close Header and Footer**.

s. Click the **INSERT** tab, and then in the Header & Footer group, click **Header**, and then select **Edit Header**. Type Painted Paradise Resort and Spa. Select the **text** in the header. Click the **HOME** tab, and then in the Font group, click the **Font Color** arrow. Select **Dark Red**, the first color under Standard Colors. With the text still selected, click the **Font Size** arrow, and then select **14**. In the Paragraph group, click **Center**. Close the header and the footer.

t. Click the **FILE** tab, and then click **Options**. You will remove the AutoCorrect entry that you created in this exercise. Click **Proofing**, and then click **AutoCorrect Options**. Scroll through the list, select **bc**, click **Delete**, click **OK**, and then click **OK** again.

u. Press Ctrl+Home to place the insertion point at the top of the document. On the HOME tab, in the Editing group, click **Replace**. Click in the **Find what** box, delete any text if necessary, and then type Club. Press Tab. In the **Replace with** box, type Course. Click **Replace All**. Two replacements are made. Click **OK**, and then click **Close**.

v. **Save** the document.

w. Click the **FILE** tab, and then click **Export**. Click **Create PDF/XPS**, navigate to the location where you are saving your files, make sure the **Open file after publishing check box** is **not selected**, and then click **Publish** to create a PDF file with the same name.

x. Click **Close** to exit Word. Click **Save** if the Want to save your changes to w01ws01Thanks_LastFirst message appears. Submit your files as directed by your instructor.

Student data file needed:

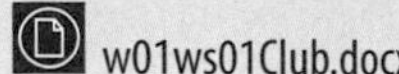

You will save your files as:

Club Memorandum

Production & Operations

You have recently been elected secretary of Covington Club, a college service organization. Your primary responsibility is to make sure members are kept informed about club-supported volunteer activities. Covington Club is coordinating with the campus Women's Center to participate in Caps for Cancer, an effort to provide hats to cancer patients who are dealing with hair loss as a side effect of cancer treatment. You will finish editing a memorandum to club members encouraging them to participate in the program. You will proofread the memo, make formatting changes, and correct any spelling and grammatical errors.

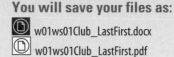

a. Start **Word**, and then open **w01ws01Club**. A draft of the memorandum is displayed. Click the **FILE** tab, click **Save As**, double-click **Computer**, and then navigate to where you are saving your files. Change the File name to w01ws01Club_LastFirst, using your last and first name.

b. If necessary, click **Show/Hide** in the Paragraph group to display formatting marks.

c. Select the entire document, and then change the paragraph After spacing to **12 pt**.

d. Double-click **To** in the second line of the memorandum, and apply **Bold**. The colon will not be bolded. Similarly, apply bold to **From**, **Date**, and **Re**.

e. Select the lines of the agenda, starting from the line Call to Order and ending with the line Closing. Change the paragraph After spacing to **6 pt**. Click anywhere to deselect the text.

f. Create an AutoCorrect entry so that the letters cc automatically convert to Covington Club.

g. Scroll to the top of the document, and then place the insertion point at the end of the **To** line, after the colon. Press Tab, and then type cc Members.

h. Locate the sentence beginning **As you are aware** in the first body paragraph, click to place the insertion point immediately before the word As, and then press Enter.

i. Underline the words **room 213C** in the second body paragraph.

j. Replace the word **Monday** in that same sentence, with Thursday, February 5. (Include a space after the comma.)

k. Select the entire document, change the font to **Franklin Gothic Book**, and then with the text still selected, change the font size to **12**.

l. Scroll to the top of the document, select the word **Memorandum**, and then change the font to **Arial Black** and the font size to **22**.

m. Correct all the spelling and grammar errors, and then proofread the document yourself to identify any mistakes Word might have missed. (Hint: The phrase "side affect" needs to be changed to "side effect.")

   You will find one word-usage error that was overlooked by the spelling checker, in the second body paragraph.

n. Insert a footer. Under the HEADER & FOOTERS TOOL DESIGN tab, click **Page Number** in the Header & Footer group, point to **Current Position**, select **Plain Number**, and then press Enter. Insert the **File Name** field, and then center all the text in the footer. Close the footer.

o. Insert a header, and then type cc Meeting Notes. Select all the **text** in the header, change the font color to **Blue, Accent 1** (column 5, row 1), change the font size to **14**, center the text in the header, and then close the header.

p. Remove the **AutoCorrect** entry for **cc**.

q. Apply a **12 pt** paragraph **Before** spacing to the paragraph at the bottom of the document.

r. Because some members of the club may request a copy via e-mail, create a PDF document with the same name. Make sure to deselect the Open file after publishing check box before clicking **Publish**.

s. Save the document and then exit Word. Submit your files as directed by your instructor.

Perform 1: Perform in Your Life

Student data file needed:

w01ws01Resign.docx

You will save your files as:

w01ws01Resign_LastFirst.docx

w01ws01Resign_LastFirst.pdf

Resignation Letter

Human Resources

You have accepted a new job that is due to begin in four weeks. You need to send your current employer a letter of resignation in order to notify them of your intent to resign, and when you will be leaving. Keep it brief, focused, and most of all, positive.

You have already started writing the letter. You will need to add a heading, inside address, salutation, and closing. You do not need to include the company name in the heading area or signature block. Format the letter using the modified block style. Because your employer may request an e-mail version, you will save the file as both a Word document and a PDF.

a. Start **Word**, and then open **w01ws01Resign**. A draft of the letter is displayed. Save the file as w01ws01Resign_LastFirst, using your last and first name.

b. Using the **Modified block style**, add your information—your name and address—into the heading area. Press Tab, or create tabs, to move to the desired location when inserting your name and address.

c. Type May 15, 2015 as the current date.

d. Include an inside address with your employer's information:

   Martha Nguyen, Manager
   Old Apothecary Pharmacy
   3014 West Main Street
   Cranberry, AZ 12349

e. Adjust the paragraph spacing for the addresses accordingly, and then adjust paragraph spacing for the body of the letter accordingly. Add a salutation.

f. You are ready to add the complimentary close and signature block. Use Pharmacy Technician as your title. Tab as necessary. Select an appropriate font and font size for the letter.

g. Check the spelling. If you are not certain of whether a word is misspelled, you need to look it up online or in a dictionary. Make sure and check for any word-usage errors that Word might have overlooked.

h. Make any changes you feel necessary.

i. Because your employer may request a copy sent via e-mail, save the letter as a PDF file, with the same name.

j. Save the document and exit Word. Submit your files as directed by your instructor.

Additional cases

Additional Workshop Cases are available on the companion website and in the instructor resources.

Microsoft Office Word 2013

Module 1

Understanding Business Documents

WORKSHOP 2 | CREATE AND EDIT A DOCUMENT

OBJECTIVES

1. Create a new document p. 224
2. Understand Word styles p. 230
3. Copy and clear formats p. 237
4. Add bullets, numbers, and symbols p. 239
5. Set line and paragraph indents p. 241
6. Work with templates p. 244
7. Change page setup p. 247
8. Change page background p. 250
9. Use themes p. 255

Prepare Case

Red Bluff Caddy School Flyer

Sales & Marketing

Each spring, Painted Paradise Resort and Spa sponsors a caddy school that is open to current and aspiring caddies. The four-day event teaches the basics of caddying and provides an opportunity for participants to caddy for a golf tournament. A prize of a $25 gift certificate from the Red Bluff Bistro, located between the 9th and 18th greens, will be given away on the last day of the caddy school. Your assignment is to create, edit, and format a flyer providing information on the caddy school. You will copy most of the information for the flyer from a memo that the golf course manager sent you. In addition, you will create the $25 gift certificate to the Red Bluff Bistro using an existing template.

Denise Kappa / Shutterstock

REAL WORLD SUCCESS

"I work as a systems technician at an IT company. I am in charge of creating the agendas and writing the minutes for our weekly group meetings. Using Word's built-in templates has saved me a considerable amount of time. I download the template, click in the fields, make my changes, and I am done. I am able to produce a professional-looking document in a very short amount of time."

- Nikil, recent graduate

Student data files needed for this workshop:

 w01ws02Memo.docx

 Blank Word document

You will save your files as:

 w01ws02School_LastFirst.docx

 w01ws02Gift_LastFirst.docx

Creating and Styling a Document

Written communication is the most common form of correspondence used in business, with its ultimate goal being to effectively deliver a message. Microsoft Word's extensive formatting capabilities can help you achieve this goal. Because the reader's first impression will be the visual layout of the document, its appearance can have as great of an impact as the actual words used. Formatting can emphasize important points, help organize data, and ultimately make it easier to read. In this section, you will create, format, and design a document using styles, themes, indents, bullets, and numbering. You will also learn to create a new document based on an existing format—a template.

Create a New Document

Word enables you to start a new project by either using a template or opening a new blank document. Templates, covered later in this workshop, enable you to create a new document based on an existing design and layout. Most often, though, you will start a new blank document in order to create your own layout and structure. Many refer to this as "starting a document from scratch." There are two ways to start a new document. When Word is launched, choose Blank document from the Word Start screen to display a blank workspace and begin typing. If you are currently in Word, click New in Backstage view.

Opening a New Blank Document

You will open a new blank document so that you can start work on the caddy flyer. You will start Word and create a blank document.

W02.00

To Create a New Document

a. Start **Word**. The Word Start screen is displayed. Click **Blank document** in the right pane.

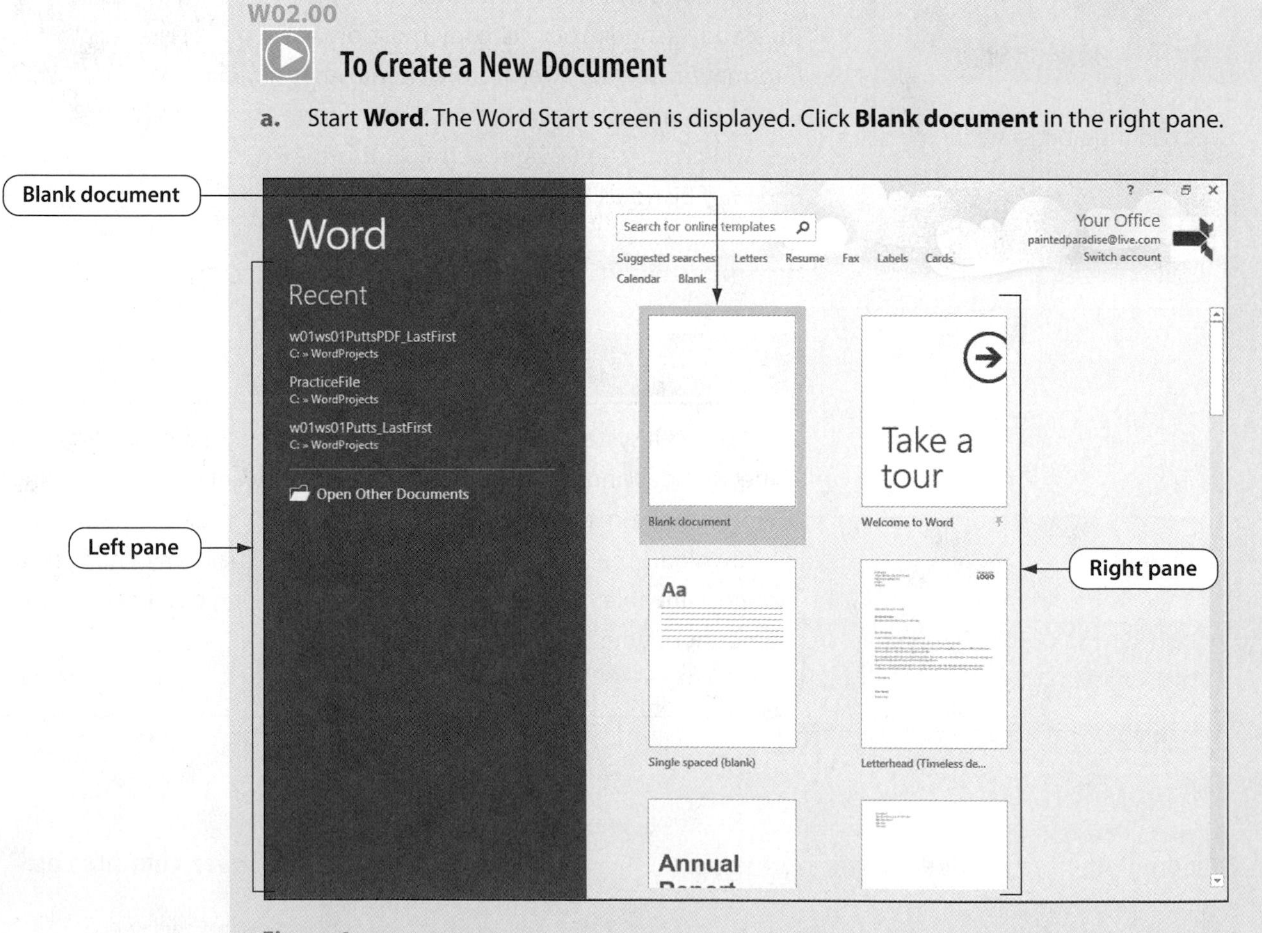

Figure 1 Creating a blank document

b. Click the **FILE** tab, and then click **Save As**. Double-click **Computer**. In the Save As dialog box, navigate to where you are saving your project files, and then change the file name to w01ws02School_LastFirst, using your last and first name. Click **Save**.

Displaying the Ruler

When you work with indents and margins, you need to specify placement in terms of inches. For example, you might want to indent a quote for a research paper 1" from both the left and right margins. In addition, measurements are needed when trying to align graphics, tabs, tables, and charts. The use of a **ruler** can simplify those settings by providing a visual guide of the measurements. Word provides both a vertical and horizontal ruler. You are now ready to begin adding text to the flyer. If you do not see the ruler in your flyer, you will turn it on and begin entering the introduction text.

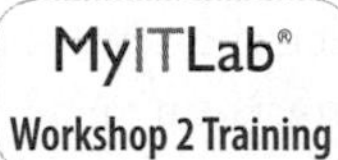

W02.01

To Display the Rulers and Begin Editing

a. On the HOME tab, in the Paragraph group, click **Show/Hide** ¶ to show nonprinting characters, if necessary.

b. If the horizontal and vertical rulers are not visible at the top and left sides of the new document, click the **VIEW** tab, and then in the Show group, click **Ruler**.

c. Type the following four lines, pressing Enter after each line, including after the last line.

Painted Paradise Resort and Spa
Invites you to participate in a
Caddy School
Sponsored by

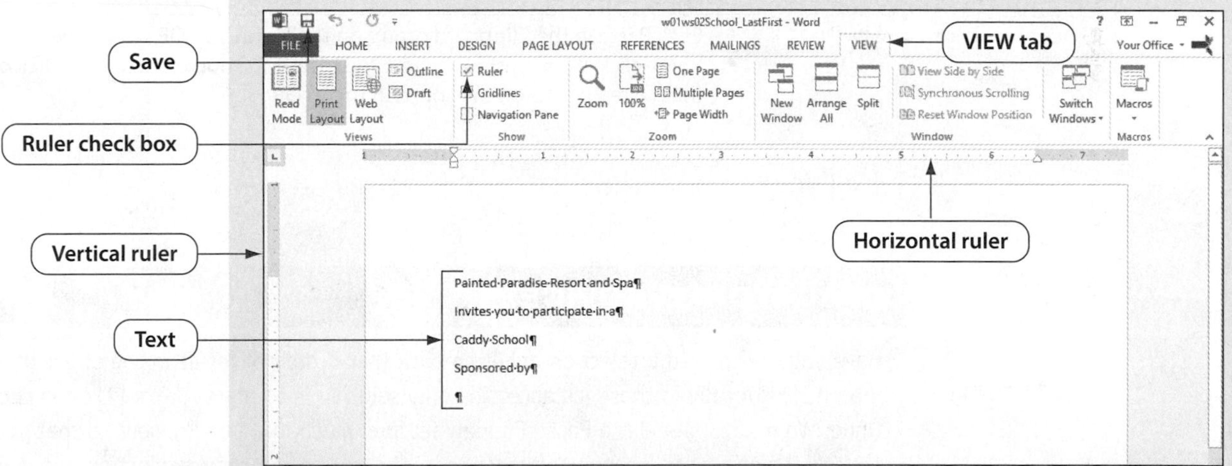

Figure 2 Showing the ruler

d. On the Quick Access Toolbar, click **Save** to save the document.

Cutting, Copying, and Pasting Text

You will seldom create a document that you do not change later. Often, those changes involve moving or copying text from one location to another. Using Microsoft Office, you are not limited to copying within only one document. You can copy text from a

Word document, and *paste* it in an Excel worksheet, a PowerPoint presentation, or even another Word document.

The *Windows* **Clipboard** is an area of memory reserved to temporarily hold text that has been cut or copied. When you **copy** text, you place a copy of the selected text in the Clipboard. The original text remains in your document. When you **cut** text, the text is removed from its original location and placed in the Clipboard. You can then **paste** the text from the Clipboard into a document at the insertion point. However, the Windows Clipboard can only hold one item at a time. When you cut or copy another selection, the new item overrides the current contents of the Clipboard. For this reason, you usually cut or copy text, and then immediately paste it into a new location.

If you need to work with multiple selections, you can open the *Office* Clipboard by clicking the Dialog Box Launcher in the Clipboard group. With the Clipboard pane open, the Office Clipboard can hold up to 24 selections. The **Clipboard pane** shows the most recently cut or copied item first. You can select any selection in the Clipboard pane and paste it in another location. Keep in mind, the Clipboard pane *must* be open in order to work with multiple selections.

Table 1 identifies several methods of cutting, copying, and pasting a selection. Regardless of which method you prefer, the first step is to select the text you want to copy or cut. Because the process of cutting, copying, and pasting is universal, you will want to remember shortcuts for those operations—shortcuts that are applicable to many other applications, including other Office components. The methods described in Table 1 assume that you intend to paste immediately after cutting or copying.

To	Select Text and Then Do This
Copy	• Click Copy in the Clipboard group on the Home tab OR • Right-click the selection, and click Copy on the shortcut menu OR • Press Ctrl + C
Cut	• Click Cut in the Clipboard group on the Home tab OR • Right-click the selection, and click Cut on the shortcut menu OR • Press Ctrl + X
Paste	• Click Paste in the Clipboard group on the Home tab OR • Right-click in the position where the insertion should occur, and click one of the paste options on the shortcut menu OR • Press Ctrl + V

Table 1 Copy, cut, and paste

REAL WORLD ADVICE **Paste Preview**

Have you ever pasted a selection only to realize that it did not result in the effect that you intended? Normally in these instances the only solution is to press Ctrl + Z or to click Undo. Word 2013 provides a **Paste Preview** feature, much like Live Preview, so that you can *preview* the effect of a change before you accept it. After you copy a selection, move your insertion point to where you intend to paste the text. Click the Paste arrow in the Clipboard group and point to one of the Paste Options preview buttons to preview the change. Keep Source Formatting retains the formatting from the *source,* or original document. Merge Formatting maintains most of the formatting from the *destination* document, which is the document into which a cut or copied item is pasted. It does, however, retain the emphasis formatting options from the source document, such as bold and italics. Keep Text Only discards certain things that were present in the source such as images and formatting. Click the preview button to accept the change. Other preview options are available depending on the data you are copying, such as Use Destination Styles or Picture.

CONSIDER THIS | Avoid Plagiarism

When completing a paper or a homework assignment, you might be tempted to copy and paste text from the Internet. When do you think such activity is permissible, and when is it considered plagiarism? How might you detect plagiarism in a document given to you? If you revise a document and fail to recognize plagiarism, should you be held accountable?

Your manager has sent you a memo with specific information that he would like you to include in the flyer. You will open the memo, copy the necessary information, and paste it into your flyer. You will format the information later in the workshop.

SIDE NOTE
To Open a Pre-existing Word File from File Explorer
Open File Explorer and navigate to your student data files. Double-click the Word file to open it directly into Word.

SIDE NOTE
Copying and Pasting Text
Remember, in addition to clicking Copy or Paste in the Clipboard group, you can also press Ctrl + C to copy, and Ctrl + V to paste.

W02.02

To Copy Text from One File into Another

a. Click the **FILE** tab, and then click **Open**. Double-click **Computer**, navigate to the location of your student files, and then open **w01ws02Memo**.

   You will now have two Word documents open at the same time—the flyer, w01ws02School_LastFirst, and the memo file you just opened, w01ws02Memo.

Troubleshooting

If you see only one document, it is probably because one document is *hiding* behind the other. Click in the title bar of the Word document displayed, and then drag it to the side to reveal the other document. Move and resize both documents as desired.

b. Click the title bar of the **ws01ws02Memo** file to make the document active. Select the lines beginning with **The Red Bluff Golf Course and Pro Shop Staff**, and ending at the end of the document.

c. With the text still selected, on the HOME tab, in the Clipboard group, click **Copy**.

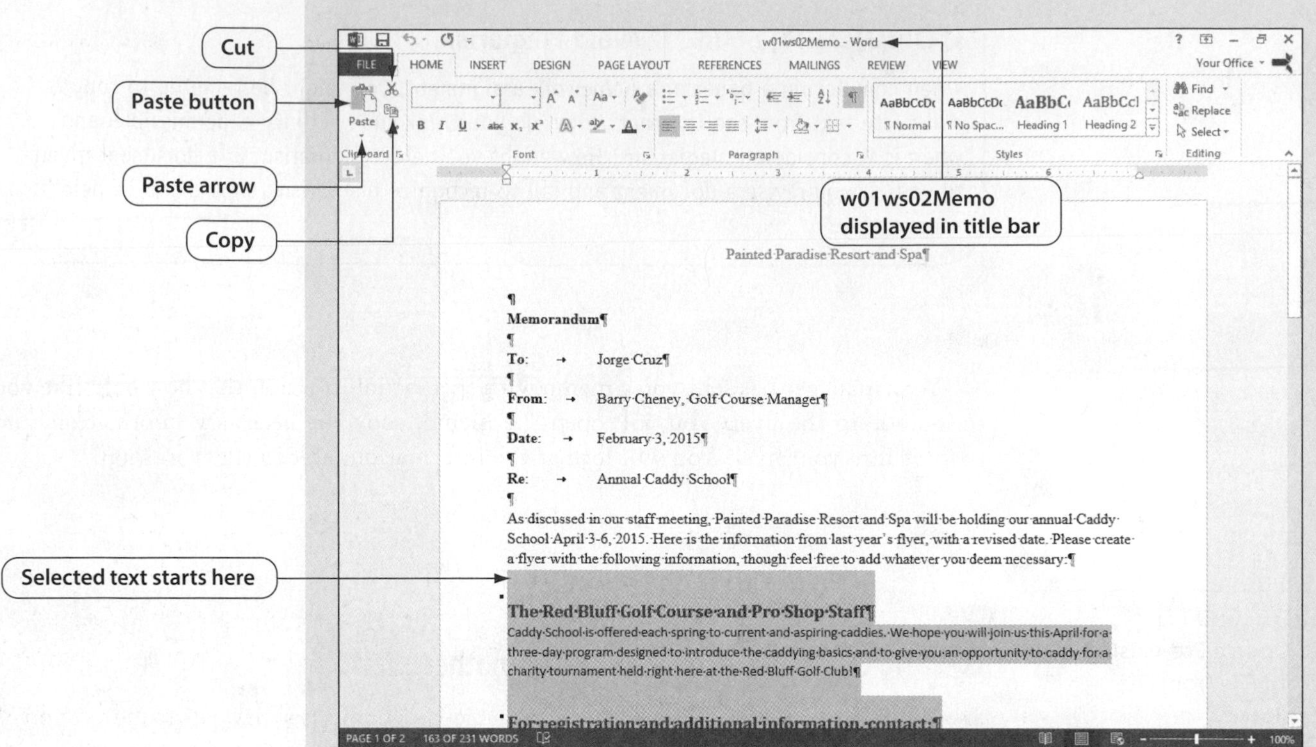

Cut
Paste button
Paste arrow
Copy
w01ws02Memo displayed in title bar
Selected text starts here
Painted Paradise Resort and Spa
Memorandum
To: Jorge Cruz
From: Barry Cheney, Golf Course Manager
Date: February 3, 2015
Re: Annual Caddy School
As discussed in our staff meeting, Painted Paradise Resort and Spa will be holding our annual Caddy School April 3-6, 2015. Here is the information from last year's flyer, with a revised date. Please create a flyer with the following information, though feel free to add whatever you deem necessary:
The Red Bluff Golf Course and Pro Shop Staff
Caddy School is offered each spring to current and aspiring caddies. We hope you will join us this April for a three-day program designed to introduce the caddying basics and to give you an opportunity to caddy for a charity tournament held right here at the Red Bluff Golf Club!
For registration and additional information, contact:

Figure 3 Clipboard group

SIDE NOTE

Paste Options Button

A Paste Options button appears just below the pasted text, enabling you to easily format the text. Press Esc to clear it from the display.

d. If necessary, click in the title bar of the **w01ws02memo** document, and then drag it to the side to reveal the other document. Click in the title bar of the **w01ws02School_LastFirst** document to make it the active document. Press Ctrl+End to move to the end of the document. Click the **HOME** tab, and then in the Clipboard group, click **Paste**.

Click the Paste button instead of the Paste arrow. The Paste button is actually a combination of the Paste command and the Paste arrow. When you click the Paste command, the most recently cut or copied item is immediately pasted at the position of the insertion point. When you click the Paste arrow, you can then choose a Paste option or use the Paste preview.

e. **Save** the **w01ws02School_LastFirst** document.

f. Click in the **title bar** of the w01ws02Memo document to make it the active document. **Close** the **w01ws02Memo** document. Because you may have accidentally made changes to the memo document, you may be asked to save the changes. If this happens, click **Don't Save**.

> **Troubleshooting**
>
> If you accidentally closed the w01ws02School_LastFirst document, go to Backstage view, and then click Open. Click the file in the Recent Documents list to open it, and then redo Step f, if necessary.

Dragging and Dropping Text

If you plan to copy (or cut) and paste text within the same document, and if the beginning and ending locations are within a short distance of each other, you can simply drag text to paste a selection. First select the text to copy or cut, and then position the pointer over the selection to display the pointer as a white arrow. Drag the selected text to another location to move it, or press and hold Ctrl while you drag the selection to copy it. Before you release the mouse button, a small vertical bar will appear, indicating the position where the text will be placed. You are ready to make revisions in the flyer. You will use various copy, cut, and paste techniques to make the changes.

W02.03

To Work with the Clipboard

SIDE NOTE
Why Use the Clipboard Pane?
The real value of working with the Clipboard pane is that you can paste any item—even if it is not the most recently collected.

a. On the HOME tab, in the Clipboard group, click the **Dialog Box Launcher**. Position the pointer in the **title area** of the Clipboard pane until it changes to a four-headed arrow, and then double-click to dock it to the side of the window (make it stationary). If the pane was already docked before you double-clicked, you will see no change.

The Clipboard pane is displayed on the left. Although it is not necessary to open the Clipboard pane unless you plan to cut or copy multiple items, you view it here simply to illustrate the concept of the Clipboard. As you continue to cut or copy text, the text will be shown in the Clipboard pane. Until you turn off the computer or otherwise lose power, you can paste any item shown in the Clipboard pane, regardless of its order.

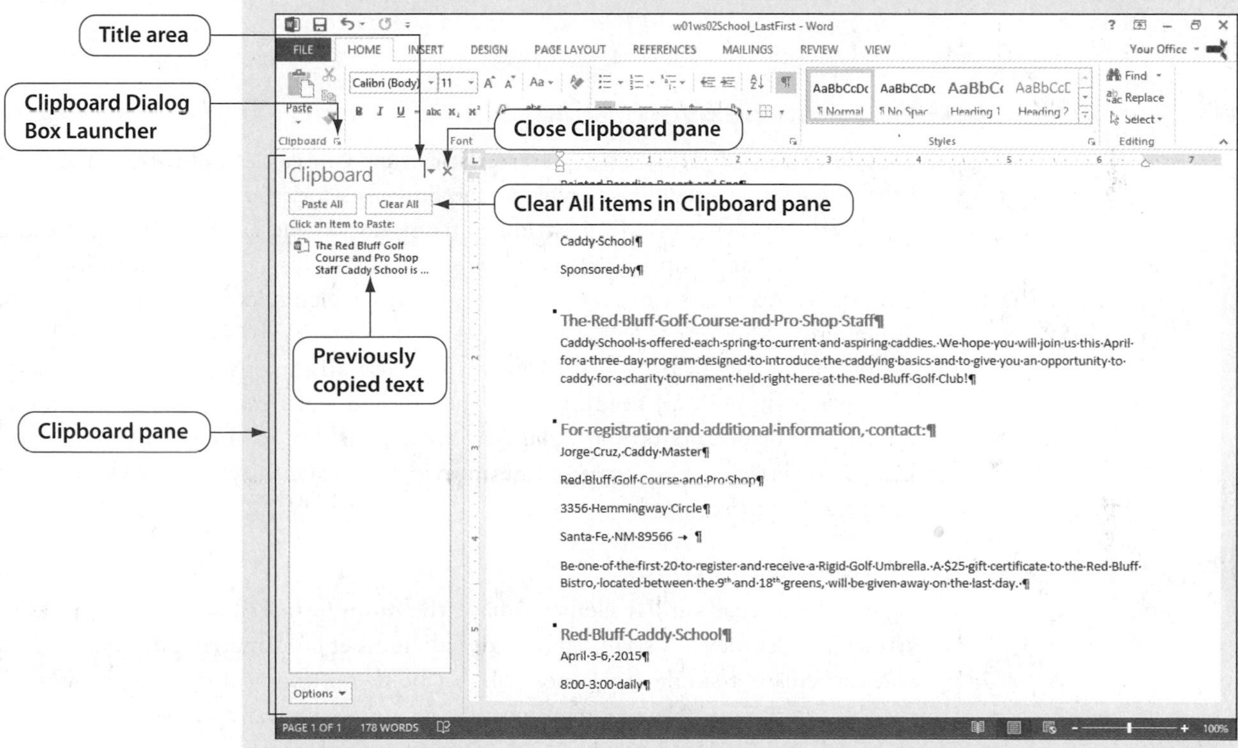

Figure 4 Clipboard pane

b. In the paragraph under the heading **The Red Bluff Golf Course and Pro Shop Staff**, double-click the word **basics** to select it. With the pointer, drag the selection to the left until a small vertical line shows just before the word **caddying**. Release the mouse button.

c. Click to place the insertion point just before the word **caddying**, type of, and then press Spacebar.

SIDE NOTE
Alternate Way to Copy
Select the word, right-click the selection, and then select Copy on the shortcut menu.

d. If necessary, scroll down to view the **For registration and additional information, contact** section. Select the two words **Jorge Cruz**. In the Clipboard group, click **Copy**. The selection is displayed as the first item in the Clipboard pane. Scroll to the end of the document, and then select the words **a Golf Pro** in the second to last line of the document.

SIDE NOTE

Alternate Way to Paste the Last Copied Item

Copy text, right-click in the location where you want the new text to appear, and then click one of the Paste Options on the shortcut menu.

e. At the top of the Clipboard pane, click **Jorge Cruz** to paste the text.

   The selected text is replaced by the pasted text.

f. In the Clipboard pane, click **Clear All**.

   All items are removed from the Clipboard. If you want to remove only one selection, point to the selection, click the arrow that appears beside the item, and then click Delete.

g. **Save** [icon] the document.

h. In the top-right corner of the Clipboard pane, click **Close** [×]. The Clipboard pane closes, and the file remains open.

> **Troubleshooting**
>
> If you closed the w01ws02School_LastFirst document instead of the Clipboard pane, then you clicked the window Close button, instead of the Close button on the Clipboard pane. If this is the case, reopen the w01ws02School_LastFirst file.

Understand Word Styles

A **style** is a *set* of formatting characteristics that you can apply to selected text. Word provides a set of predefined styles in the Styles gallery that can be found in the Style group on the Home tab. In addition to using one of the existing styles, Word enables you to create and apply your own styles. Using styles, you can simplify the task of formatting text, and you can be sure that similar elements have the same formatting. When creating a report, for example, you will most likely want all major headings to be formatted identically, with the same font and alignment settings. Simply apply an appropriate style to all headings, and the job is done! Because a style can include any number of formatting options, you can save a great deal of time when you apply a style instead of setting each format option individually, especially if the style includes many complex format settings.

Working with Styles

Styles ensure that similar elements have the same formatting, resulting in a cohesive, attractive document. A style can include any number of formatting options. For example, you can create a single style consisting of bold, red font color, 12 pt paragraph After spacing, and Times New Roman font. This single style can be saved, and then applied to any element of your document, as often as desired. Simply select your text, and then under the Home tab, click the desired style from the Styles gallery.

Most styles are considered to be either a *character style* or a *paragraph style.* Character styles set the formatting of font, font size, color, and emphasis—underline, bold, or italic—to individual characters or selections. You can apply a character style to any area of selected text. If text is not selected, Word will apply the character format to the current word—the word containing the insertion point. A paragraph style sets the alignment, spacing, and indentation formatting. Paragraph styles are applied to entire paragraphs. Therefore, to apply a paragraph style to a single paragraph, simply position the insertion point within a paragraph and select the style. To apply a style to multiple paragraphs, you must first select the paragraphs.

A few styles are neither character nor paragraph, but are instead *linked styles.* A linked style behaves as either a character style or paragraph style, depending on what you select. For example, if you click within a paragraph without selecting any specific text, and then select the Heading 1 style, the entire paragraph is formatted with both font and paragraph characteristics, such as color and alignment. However, if you select only one word, or a limited amount of text within the paragraph, and then apply the Heading 1 style, only the font characteristics are applied. For example, the font color may change, but alignment does not.

Using the Normal Style

The default style for all new documents is called Normal. Normal style is a paragraph style with specific spacing and formatting characteristics. Although that style might be appropriate for some documents, it will not be the best choice for all documents. You can easily select another style that is more appropriate for either the entire document or for selected text or paragraphs. Normal style formats text as 11-pt Calibri font, left-aligned, with 1.08 line spacing, and 8 pt after paragraph spacing. You will use various existing styles from the Styles gallery to format the text in the caddy flyer.

To Apply Styles

SIDE NOTE

Pointing

Recall that "point to" refers to hovering—not clicking—the mouse over text in order to view a ScreenTip or activate Live Preview.

a. Press Ctrl+Home to move to the top of the document. Click anywhere in the first line of the document, **Painted Paradise Resort and Spa**. On the HOME tab, in the Styles group, click **More** to display the Styles gallery. In the Styles gallery, point to **Heading 1**. Live Preview shows the effect that the style will have on the selected text. Without clicking, point to another **heading style**, and then move back to **Heading 1** and click. The Heading 1 style is applied to the selected line.

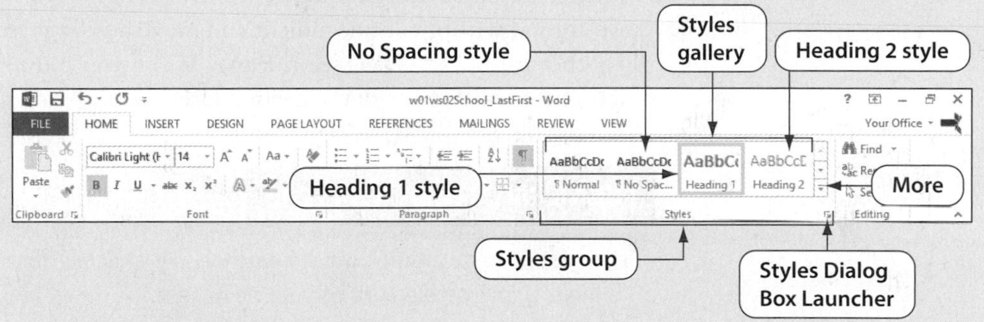

Figure 5 Styles group

b. Click in the third line of the document, **Caddy School**, and then in the Styles gallery, click **Heading 1**.

Notice the extra white spacing that appears above the line when you apply the Heading 1 style. You will fix this later in the workshop.

c. Apply the **Heading 2** style to the second and fourth lines of the document, **Invites you to participate in a** and **Sponsored by**.

d. Press Ctrl+End to move to the end of the document. Select the three lines, starting with line **Day 1 – Indoor lecture on basics of caddying** and ending with line **Day 4 – Caddying for a tournament**. In Styles group, in the Styles gallery, click **No Spacing**. The lines are now set to single-spacing, with no before or after paragraph spacing.

e. **Save** the document.

QUICK REFERENCE	Adding the Current Style to the Quick Access Toolbar

To determine the current style, simply click in the text area and look in the Styles gallery. The Styles gallery, however, does not always contain a list of all the styles. In this case, either open the Styles pane or add a Styles list to the Quick Access Toolbar. Do the following to add a Styles list to the Quick Access Toolbar.

1. Click the File tab.
2. Click Options.
3. Click Quick Access Toolbar.
4. Click the Choose commands from arrow, and then select Commands Not in the Ribbon.
5. Scroll through the list, and then click Style.
6. Click Add, and then click OK.
7. You can now click in any paragraph within the document and the current style will be displayed in the Styles list on the Quick Access Toolbar.

Using the Navigation Pane

Related styles in the Styles gallery (Styles group) are designed to work together. For example, the Heading 2 style is designed to color coordinate with and to look subordinate to the Heading 1 style. Additionally, if you use built-in heading styles, Word can automatically generate a table of contents and organize your document into a series of headings. Based on the headings applied through Styles, Word enables you to quickly move around within your document and move headings from one location of a document to another using the **Navigation Pane**. When you move headings, the heading, and all of its content will move to the desired location.

REAL WORLD ADVICE	Why Use Styles?

1. Styles provide a quick way to easily apply multiple formatting characteristics to more than one element of your document.
2. New to Word 2013, you can now collapse and expand sections of your document by clicking on the gray triangle next to a heading style.
3. You can easily generate a Table of Contents.
4. Quickly reorganize your document from within the Navigation Pane.

W02.05

To Work with the Navigation Pane

a. Press Ctrl+Home to move to the top of the document.

b. Click the **VIEW** tab, and then in the Show group, click **Navigation Pane**. If necessary, double-click the **title area** of the Navigation Pane to dock it to the side of the window.

A hierarchical outline of your document is displayed. In the Navigation Pane, click on any heading to move the insertion point to that location within the document. Notice only heading styles appear in the list.

SIDE NOTE

Alternate Way to View Navigation Pane

Alternatively, you can view the Navigation Pane by pressing Ctrl + F.

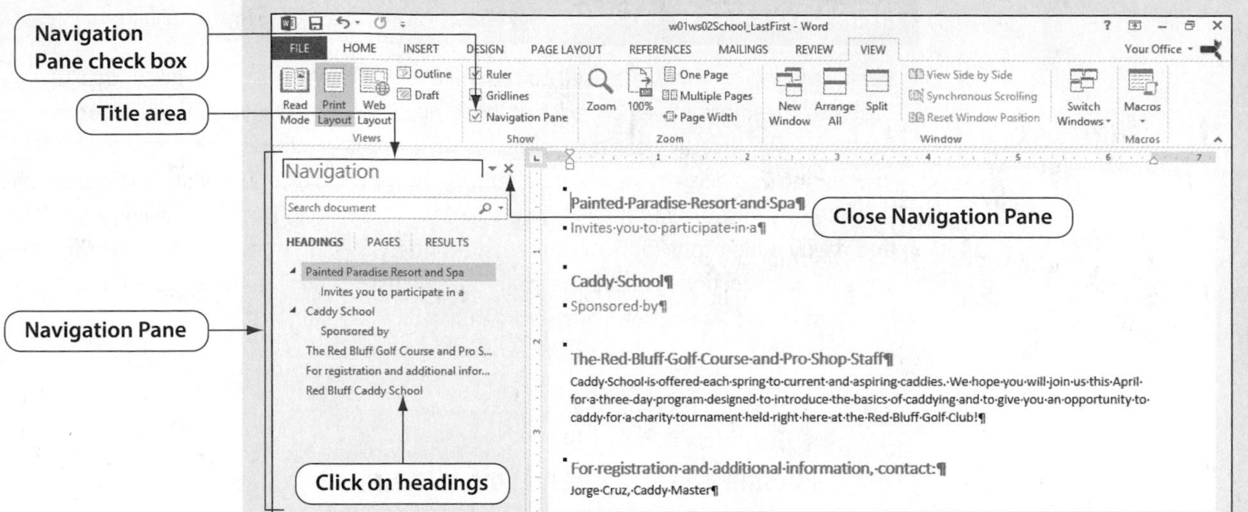

Figure 6 Navigation Pane

c. In the Navigation Pane, click the last heading line, **Red Bluff Caddy School**, and drag it up one level, so that it is above the section starting with **For registration and additional information, contact**. Notice the heading, and all of its text, is moved in the document.

   When you drag, a horizontal dark line will appear indicating where the heading will be placed. Drag the heading so that the dark line is above the heading, "For registration and additional information, contact:". Long heading names may only be partially displayed in the Navigation Pane.

d. **Save** the document.

e. In the top-right corner of the Navigation Pane, click **Close**. The Navigation Pane closes.

f. Point to the last heading of the document, **For registration and additional information, contact**. A gray triangle will appear to the left of the heading. Click the **triangle** to collapse the section. The text within this section disappears. Point to the heading **For registration and additional information, contact:** again. A white triangle appears to the left of the heading. Click the **triangle** next to the section heading to expand the section and to view the text again.

   When you point to a heading style, a triangle appears to the left of the heading name. Click the triangle to collapse or expand the section. When you collapse a section, the heading remains visible, but its text will disappear. When you expand the section, the text will reappear.

Creating a New Style

Word enables you to adjust a current style. For example, Normal is the default style when you begin a new document, but it does not single-space text. If you prefer to single-space your documents, you can simply modify the Normal style to single-spacing. Occasionally, however, you cannot find a style that contains even a few of the formatting options that you need for a selection. In that case, you can create a new style, which will then be available to use throughout the current document. When you no longer need a style, you can delete it. Be careful though—deleting a style will remove its formatting options from any text where the style has been applied. You will create a new style called Lower Paragraph and apply it to the second and fourth lines of the caddy flyer.

REAL WORLD ADVICE — Base New Styles on Similar Existing Styles

Because style headings are used to organize your document, it is a good idea to base new headings styles on existing heading styles. For example, if you need a new heading style, first set your text to any of the current heading styles, such as Heading 1 or Heading 2. Make any necessary changes, and then create a new style. Because the new style is now based on a heading style, it will be included in the Navigation Pane, and easily added to a Table of Contents. Similarly, when creating a new style for the body of your document, base the style on an existing body style. When headings are included in the Navigation Pane, reorganization is a snap!

W02.06

To Define a New Style and Edit a Document

a. Press Ctrl+Home to move to the top of the document. Select the second line, **Invites you to participate in a**. Click the **HOME** tab, and then in the Paragraph group, click **Center**.

b. With the text still selected, in the Font group, click the **Font Size** arrow, and then select **14**. Click the **Font Color** arrow, and then under Theme colors, in the fourth column and first row, select **Blue-Gray, Text 2**.

You will now create a new style based on those settings.

SIDE NOTE
To Select a Font Color
Click the Font Color arrow in the Font group to display a palette of colors, and then point to a color to display a ScreenTip identifying its name.

c. In the Styles group, click the **Dialog Box Launcher** to open the Styles pane. If necessary, double-click the **title area** of the Styles pane to dock it.

d. In the Styles pane, click **New Style**, and then in the Create New Style from Formatting dialog box, click in the **Name** box and remove any text. Type Lower Paragraph, and then make sure **Add to the Styles gallery** and **Only in this document** are selected.

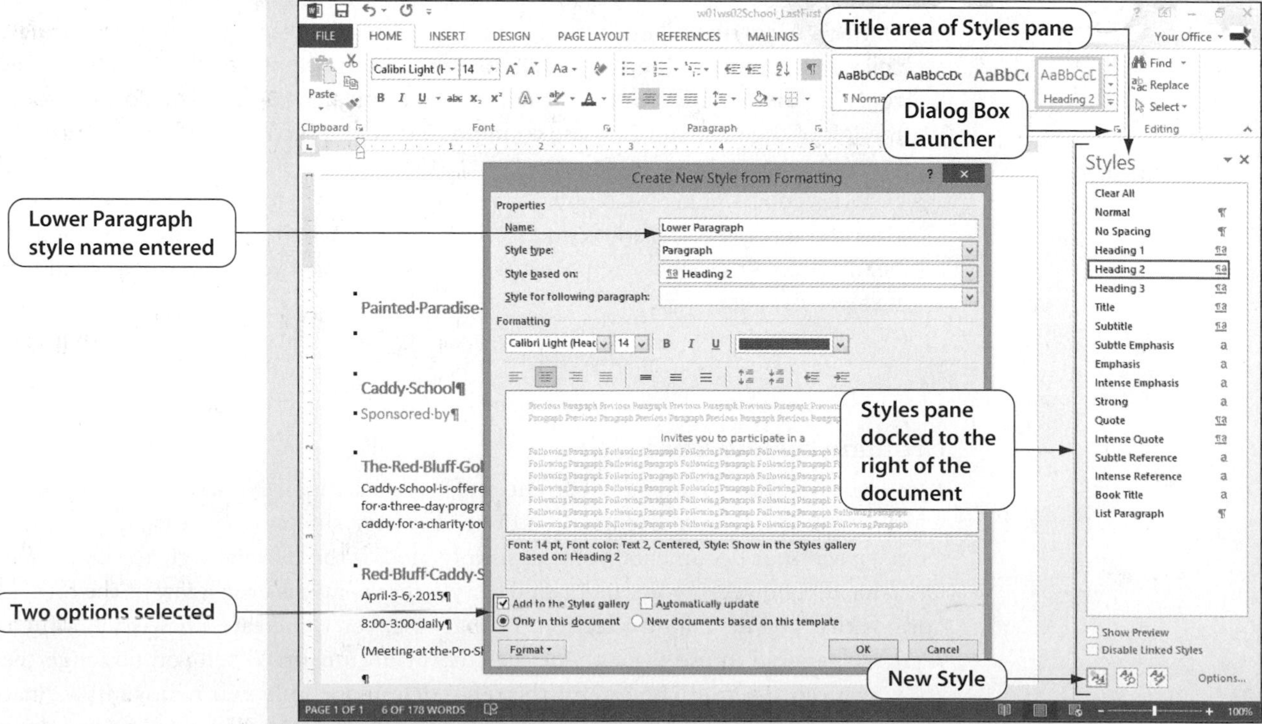

Figure 7 Creating a new style

SIDE NOTE
Selecting a Style
Alternatively, you can select the Lower Paragraph style directly from the Styles gallery, in the Styles group on the HOME tab.

e. Click **OK**. Click anywhere in the fourth line, **Sponsored by**, scroll through the Styles pane, and then click **Lower Paragraph**.
   Because the new style is based on Heading 2—a heading style—the new style will be included in the Navigation Pane.

f. **Save** the document.

Modifying a Style

Word enables you to modify current styles. A modified style is saved and then available to use throughout the current document. You can modify styles, even if you have already applied those styles to elements of your document. When you change a style's formatting options, the new options are immediately applied to all text that has been formatted in that style within the current document. That means if your research paper includes 10 major headings, all of which have been formatted in a certain style, modifying that style immediately causes all 10 headings to reflect the new settings. *Though not recommended*, you can change a setting to make the style available on all future documents. However, once you do this the original existing settings will no longer be available. You will now modify the Heading 1 and Normal styles in the caddy flyer.

W02.07

To Modify a Style

a. If the Styles pane is not already open, in the Styles group, click the **Dialog Box Launcher**.
   If you click the Styles Dialog Box Launcher when the Styles pane is open, the Styles pane will close. Just click the Dialog Box Launcher a second time to reopen the Styles pane.

b. In the Styles pane, point to **Heading 1**, and then note the style description that displays.
   Because you plan to repeat the Heading 1 style in this document, but with different font and alignment settings, you will modify the style.

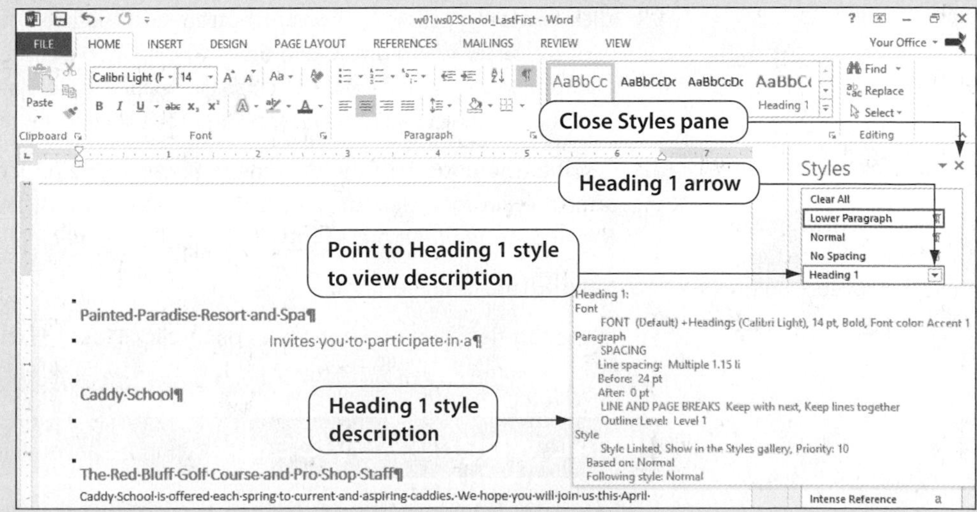

Figure 8 Styles pane

c. Click the **Heading 1** arrow, and then select **Modify**. The Modify Style dialog box opens.

Troubleshooting

If you accidentally clicked Heading 1 instead of the arrow, click Undo, and then repeat Step c.

d. Under Formatting, click **Center**. Click the **Font Size** arrow, and then select **18**.

e. Click the **Font Color** arrow, and then under Theme colors, in the fourth column and first row, select **Blue-Gray, Text 2**.

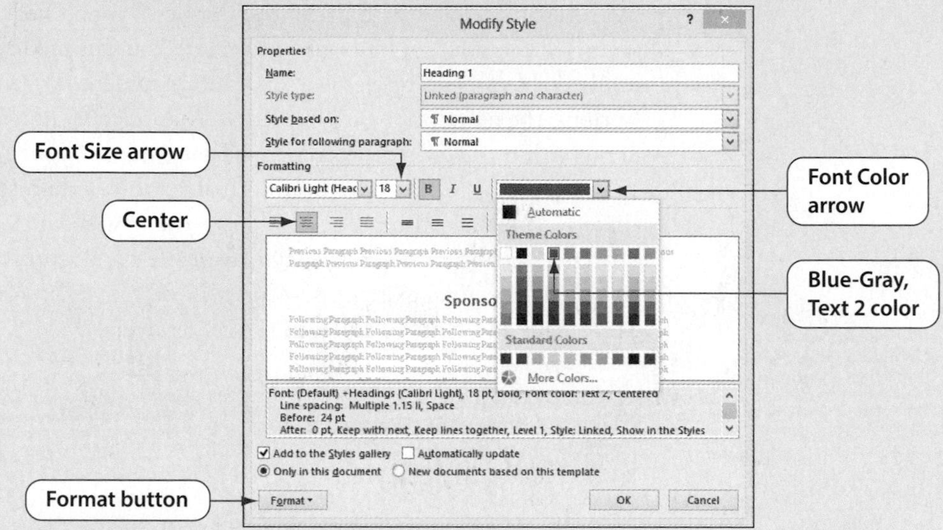

Figure 9 Modify Style dialog box

f. Click the **Format** button, and then select **Paragraph**. Under Spacing, click the **Before** down arrow to display **18 pt**, and then click the **After** up arrow three times to display **18 pt**. Click **OK** to close the Paragraph dialog box, and then click **OK** to close the Modify Style dialog box.

All previous Heading 1 styles in your document have been updated with the new formatting changes.

g. In the Styles pane, click the **Normal** arrow, and then select **Modify**. Under Formatting, click **Center**, click the **Format** button, and then select **Paragraph**. Under Spacing, click the **After** down arrow two times to display **0 pt**. Click **OK** to close the Paragraph dialog box, and then click **OK** to close the Modify Style dialog box.

This centers and adjusts the spacing of the text under the headings.

h. Scroll to the bottom of the document. Because you notice that white space is needed after the address, click to place the insertion point at the end of the line **Santa Fe, NM 89566**, and then press Enter.

SIDE NOTE

To Increase White Space

Alternatively, increase the paragraph After spacing to add more white space.

i. **Save** the document.

j. In the top-right corner of the Styles pane, click **Close** to close the Styles pane.

REAL WORLD ADVICE **Creating a Shortcut Key for a Style**

If you often apply a particular style, you might find it cumbersome to continually find and click the style on the Styles pane or in the Styles gallery. Instead, you might want to create a shortcut key combination for the style. To do this, modify the style, and then click the Format button. Select Shortcut key, and then in the Press new shortcut key box, press the keys that you want assigned to the style and then click Assign. For example, you can assign Alt + T, B to a style named Text Body.

Copy and Clear Formats

A document's visual appearance can draw attention to the content and encourage readers' interest. Achieving the right combination of format settings is not always an easy task, but once done, you will probably want to re-create the same format elsewhere in the same document. Similar to the principle of cut and paste, the **Format Painter** is a tool that enables you to quickly copy a format from one location to another. For example, perhaps you have formatted a caption to 10-pt, Blue, Times New Roman font. Because you want all captions to appear identically, simply select the first caption that is formatted correctly and use Format Painter to copy the formatting to the other sections.

MODULE 1

Using Format Painter

You will add a shadow effect to the first heading of the document. You will then use the Format Painter to copy the format to the next heading.

W02.08

To Use the Format Painter

a. Press Ctrl + Home to move to the beginning of the document. Select the first line of text, **Painted Paradise Resort and Spa**. On the HOME tab, in the Font group, click **Text Effects and Typography**, and then point to **Shadow**. Under Outer, in the first column and second row, click **Offset Right**.

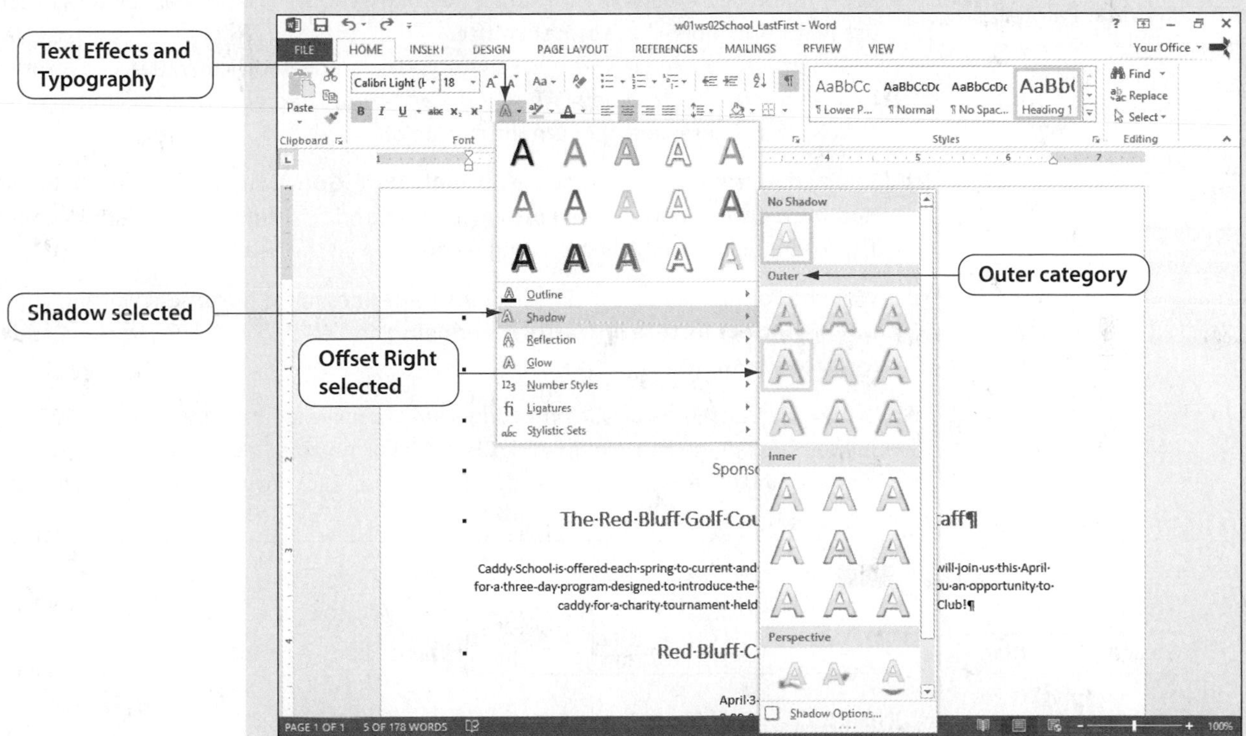

Figure 10 Text effects

b. With the text **Painted Paradise Resort and Spa** still selected, in the Clipboard group, click **Format Painter**. As you move the mouse pointer over the text in the document, note that it resembles a paintbrush

c. Select the third line of the document, **Caddy School**.
   The formatting from the first header was applied to the second header.

d. **Save** the document.

Using Clear Formatting

Too many format changes can sometimes make a document difficult to read. To remove the formatting, reverse the action by selecting the text and clicking the command again. For example, to undo a bold format, select the bolded text, and then click Bold. As you recall, a toggle key or button switches back and forth between two states (on and off) each time it is clicked. But what if the selected text has several character attributes assigned? What if you are unsure of how it was formatted? The Clear All Formatting command will clear all of the formats of the selected text, returning the format to the default style, which in most cases will be the Normal style.

Using Format Painter on Multiple Selections

As seen in the previous exercise, clicking Format Painter enables you to copy a format to a single selection. To copy a format to multiple locations, simply double-click Format Painter. Click Format Painter again to turn it off. You will now format "Day 1" in the caddy flyer, and then use the Format Painter to copy the format to the remaining days.

W02.09

To Use Format Painter on Multiple Selections and to Clear Formatting

SIDE NOTE
Turn Off Format Painter
Alternatively, you can press Esc to turn off Format Painter's multiple-use feature.

SIDE NOTE
Selecting Headings
Because the heading is a paragraph, you can triple-click the heading to select it.

a. Click anywhere in the third line of the document, **Caddy School**. Because you want to apply the same formatting to the other headings, you will use Format Painter's multiple-use feature. Double-click **Format Painter**.

   When you double-click Format Painter, you can repeatedly copy the same formatting from one selection to others. When you have completed all formatting, press Esc or click Format Painter again to turn the feature off.

b. Select the remaining headings, **The Red Bluff Golf Course and Pro Shop Staff**, **Red Bluff Caddy School**, and **For registration and additional information, contact:**. The formatting from the first heading is copied to all the headings.

c. With the Format Painter still on, select the three lines in the document starting with line **Day 1 – Indoor lecture on basics of caddying** and ending with line **Day 4 – Caddying for a tournament**.

d. You decide that this particular formatting is not attractive for three lines of text. With the text still selected, in the Font group, click **Clear All Formatting**. All character formatting is removed and the text is returned to the Normal style. Click anywhere to deselect the text.

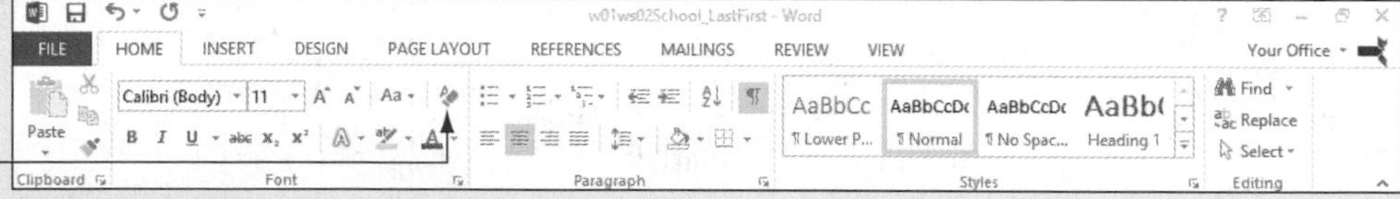

Figure 11 Clear formatting

e. Select only the text **Day 1**—not the entire line. On the HOME tab, in the Font group, click **Underline**, and then click **Bold**.

f. Double-click **Format Painter**, select the text **Days 2 and 3**, and then select **Day 4**. The formatting from the first day is copied to all the days. Click **Format Painter** again to turn the feature off.

g. **Save** the document.

MODULE 1

Add Bullets, Numbers, and Symbols

Lists can make your document easier to read and help your readers quickly hone in on major points. For example, if your document is outlining steps in a process, you could *number* those steps for better readability. You might even consider developing an itemized or *bulleted* series of summary points. Word provides three types of lists: bulleted, numbered, and multileveled. A bulleted list uses shapes and symbols. The default **bullet** is a round, filled-in, black circle. A numbered list uses numbers, roman numerals, or letters, with the default numbered list consisting of numbers followed by a period. A multilevel list is a hierarchical list, consisting of numbers, letters, or symbols. Typically, numbered lists are used to indicate sequence, while bulleted lists are used when the order of the list items is not important.

Selecting Bullets and Numbers

Lists are simply a series of paragraphs. Recall that the definition of a paragraph is any text that ends with a hard return. To list items in a document, type each item, and then press Enter. You can then select the list of items and apply bullets or numbers to the list. You can also apply a list format before you begin to type. To do this, click the Bullets, Numbering, or Multilevel List button to turn on the format, and then begin to enter the list. Click the button again to return to normal formatting. Use the Increase Indent and Decrease Indent buttons to quickly create multilevel lists. Press the Increase Indent button on a bulleted line to move the bulleted item to the right, creating a second-level list. The Decrease Indent button will move the item to the left one level.

Defining New Bullets

Typically a bulleted list is prefaced by a circle shape, though Word also provides checks, squares, or other symbols. If you prefer a bullet that is not included in Word's Bullet Library, you can create your own. You can select a symbol for your bullet, or you can modify the format of an existing bullet, such as changing its color. In addition, you can include a personal picture as a bullet, or select from Microsoft's picture gallery at Office.com.

You will list the day-by-day schedule on the caddy flyer. You will experiment with numbering and bullets to see which is the most appealing.

SIDE NOTE
Change Numbering
To change numbering in a list, right click on the number and select either Set Numbering Value, or Continue Numbering.

W02.10

To Insert Bullets or Numbers

a. Select the three lines, starting with the line **Day 1 – Indoor lecture on basics of caddying** and ending with the line **Day 4 – Caddying for a tournament**.

b. On the HOME tab, in the Paragraph group, click **Numbering**.

Figure 12 Applying bullets and numbering

c. On the Quick Access Toolbar, click **Undo** to remove Numbering.
Because the days already include numbers, you decide Numbering does not look appropriate.

SIDE NOTE
Bullets and Numbering Toggle
The lists feature is actually a toggle key, which means that you can click the command once to begin an action, and a second time to end it.

d. With the three lines still selected, click the **Bullets** arrow to view additional bullet styles. Select the **black square shape**.

   If you want to apply the default bullet style (round black bullet), you can simply click Bullets in the Paragraph group.

e. Click the **Bullets** arrow again, and then select **Define New Bullet**.

f. Click **Font** in the Define New Bullet dialog box, click the **Font color** arrow, and then under Theme colors, in the fourth column and first row, select **Blue-Gray, Text 2**. Click **OK** to close the Font dialog box, and then click **OK** again to close the Define New Bullet dialog box. Click anywhere to deselect the text.

g. **Save** the document.

SIDE NOTE
Deleting a Numbered Item
If you delete a numbered list item, Word will re-number the subsequent items so that they remain consecutive.

Inserting Symbols

Symbols are characters that do not usually appear on a keyboard, such as © or ™. Word provides a gallery of symbols that you can select from. Some frequently accessed symbols are considered special characters, such as a nonbreaking hyphen or double opening and closing quotes. You will insert the trademark symbol after the word "Rigid" in the caddy flyer.

W02.11

To Insert Symbols

a. Press Ctrl+End to move to the bottom of the document, and then in the paragraph beginning with **Be one of the first 20**, click immediately after the word **Rigid** to position the insertion point.

b. Click the **INSERT** tab and then, in the Symbols group, click **Symbol**.

   A few of the most commonly used symbols are shown when you click Symbol, but even more symbols are available when you click More Symbols.

c. Select **More Symbols**. The Symbol dialog box opens. Click the **Special Characters** tab, and then click **Trademark**. Click **Insert**, and then click **Close**.

Troubleshooting
If you have more than one trademark symbol in your document, you clicked Insert too many times. Simply delete the extra characters from the document.

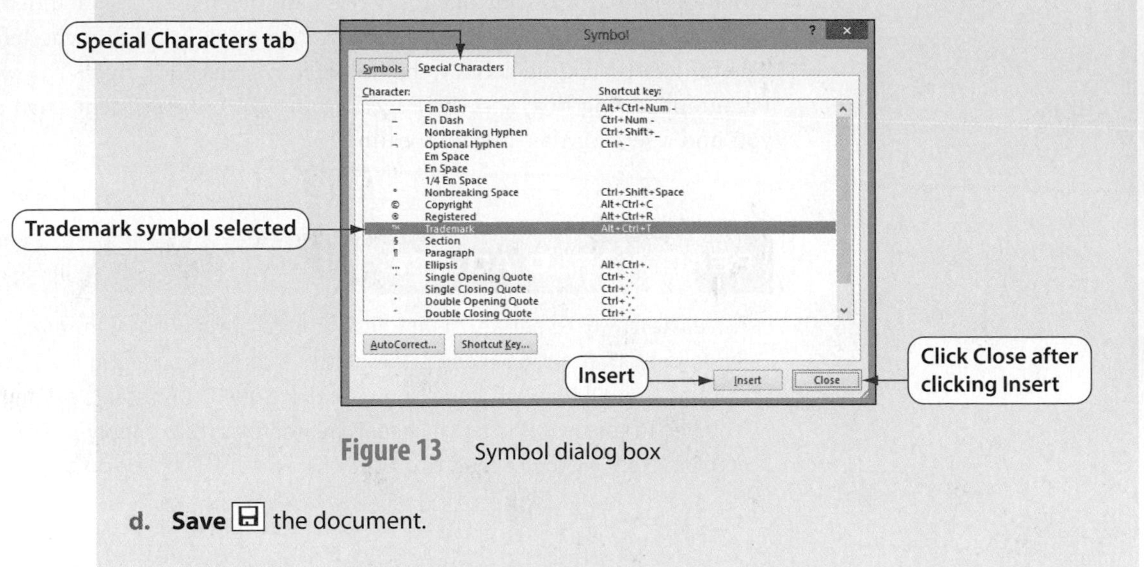

Figure 13 Symbol dialog box

d. **Save** the document.

Set Line and Paragraph Indents

As you recall, a semi-block letter style requires the first line of each paragraph to be indented from the left margin. Such an indent is called a **first-line indent**. Typically the first line of a citation in a bibliography begins at the left margin, with all other lines indented. That indent style is called a **hanging indent**. When writing a research paper, a lengthy quote is often indented an equal distance from both the left and right margins. Indenting an entire paragraph from the left margin is called a **left indent**. Similarly, indenting from the right margin is a **right indent**. You create indents in a document using either the Paragraph dialog box or the ruler. Figure 14 provides examples of indents.

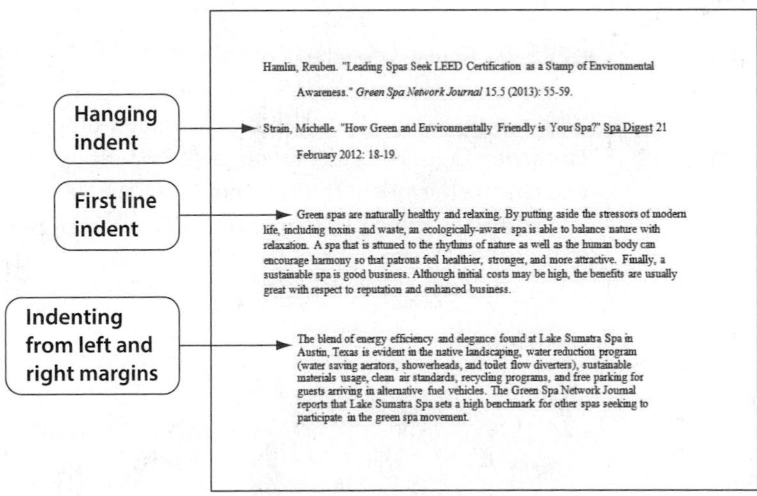

Figure 14 Examples of indents

Paragraph Indentation

Indentation is considered to be paragraph formatting. Therefore, unless you are indenting several paragraphs, you do not need to select a block of text. Simply click within the paragraph to be indented, or select an indent setting before typing a paragraph. Word provides several tools that enable you to specify indents. The Paragraph dialog box and the ruler provide access to all the indents—first-line, hanging, left, and right. The Home tab provides quick access buttons to increase and decrease the left indent, by 1/2" tab intervals, and the Page Layout tab enables you to quickly modify the left and right indents. The bulleted schedule needs to be indented in the caddy flyer. You will use the ruler, the Paragraph dialog box, and the Page Layout tab to experiment with the left indent until you find a setting that looks appealing.

REAL WORLD ADVICE | **Is There an Easier Way to Create a First-Line Indent?**

The easiest way to set a first-line indent is to press Tab before you begin to type. By default, that action indents the first line of each paragraph 0.5" from the left margin, though you will learn how to change the 0.5" default setting in the next module. To remove a first-line indent created by a tab, simply position the insertion point in front of the tabbed text, and then press Backspace.

W02.12

To Indent Paragraphs

a. Select the three lines, starting with line **Day 1 – Indoor lecture on basics of caddying** and ending with line **Day 4 – Caddying for a tournament**. Because centering the schedule does not look appealing, click the **HOME** tab, and then in the Paragraph group, click **Align Left**, and then click **Increase Indent** to move the lines to the right.

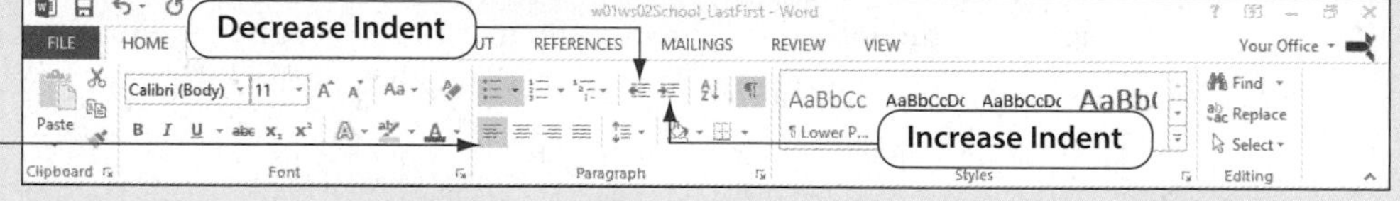

Figure 15 Indentation on the HOME tab

b. With the text still selected, in the Paragraph group, click the **Paragraph Dialog Box Launcher**. Under Indentation, click the **Left** up arrow until it displays **1"**. Make sure and change the indent to 1" and not 0.1". Click **OK** to close the Paragraph dialog box.

Because all three paragraphs are selected, each paragraph—or line in this case—is indented by 1".

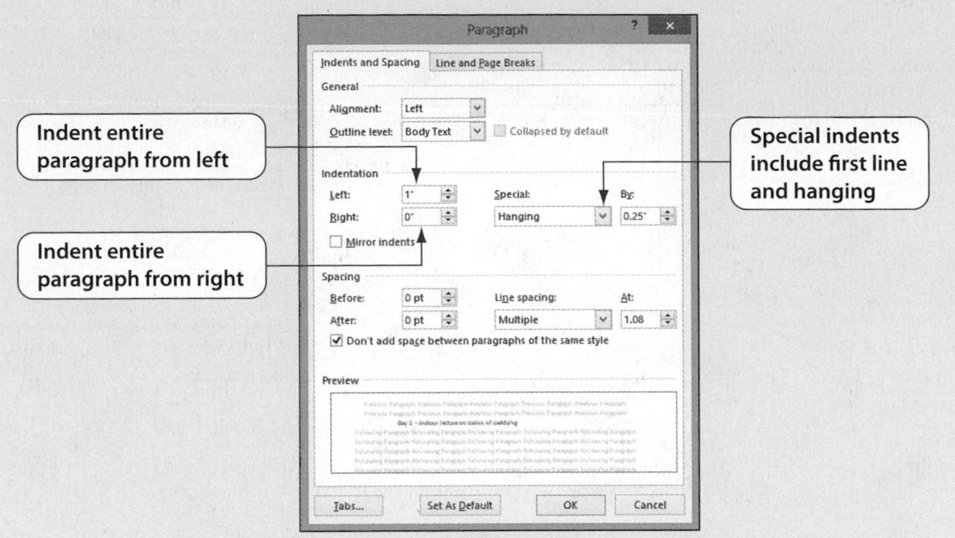

Figure 16 Indentation in the Paragraph dialog box

> **Troubleshooting**
> If only one line is indented, you did not have all three lines selected. Select the remaining lines and repeat Step b.

c. To adjust the indentation visually, you decide to use the ruler. Point to the **Left Indent** marker on the ruler.

When you point to the square on the ruler, you will see a ScreenTip indicating that the marker is for the left indent. Just above the Left Indent marker is a small marker that represents a hanging indent. On the top of the side of the ruler is a marker representing a first-line indent. On the right side of the ruler, note the small marker, similar to the hanging indent. It represents a right indent. You can drag any of those markers to set a corresponding indent.

d. Drag the **Left Indent** marker on the ruler to the **2"** ruler mark to increase the left indent. As you drag, notice the vertical guide that moves with you, giving a visual clue as to placement within the document. Keep the text selected.

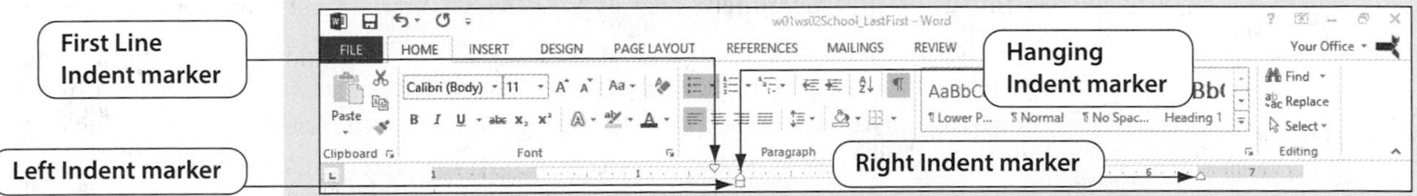

Figure 17 Indentation using the ruler

> **Troubleshooting**
> If you drag a marker other than the Left Indent marker, your text may not line up cleanly at the 2" mark. In that case, click Undo, and then repeat Steps c and d.

e. Click the **PAGE LAYOUT** tab, and then in the Paragraph group, under Indent, click the **Left** down arrow to decrease the left indent to **1.5"**. Click anywhere in the document to deselect the text.

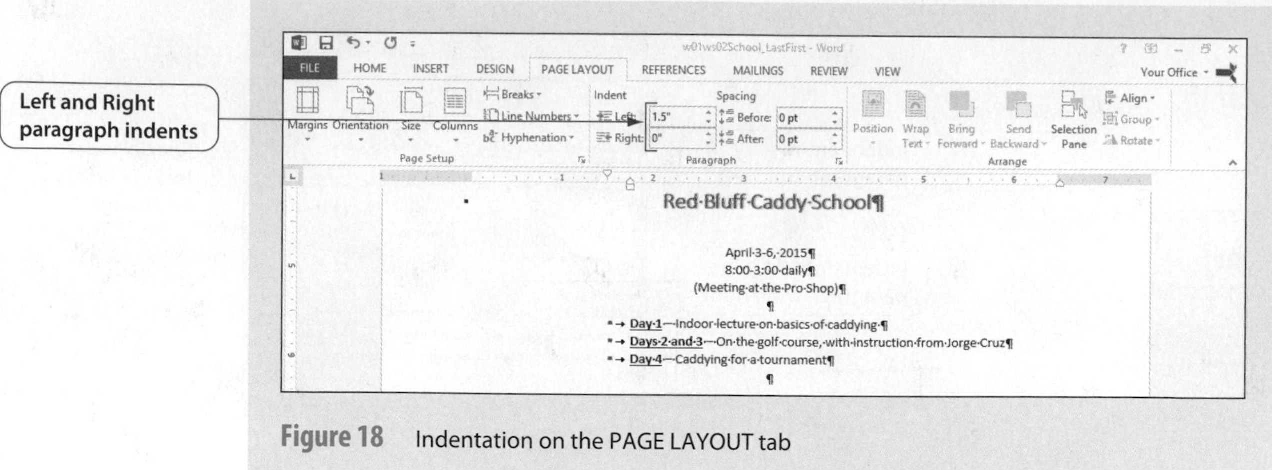

Figure 18 Indentation on the PAGE LAYOUT tab

f. **Save** the document.

g. Click the **FILE** tab, and then click **Close**. The document closes, but Word remains open.

QUICK REFERENCE | **Indents**

Word provides four types of indentation.

Indent	Icon	Description
First-line	▽	Indent only first line of paragraph from the left margin
Hanging	△	Except for the first line of paragraph, indent all lines from the left margin
Left	▭	Indent entire paragraph from the left margin
Right	△	Indent entire paragraph from the right margin

Work with Templates

A **template** is a document that is used as a starting point for another document. It has a pre-established format and layout. A template has very little content of its own, perhaps only headings, or very generic sample text. For example, a resignation letter template may contain sample text and addresses, structured in a semiblock style that you can modify to suit your own situation. Another resignation template, however, may use a block style layout. Select the template that suits your needs, and then add, delete, and modify the existing text and graphics. Some templates are stored on the local computer, from the Office installation, while others are available from Microsoft's online site, Office.com.

REAL WORLD ADVICE | **Selecting a Template**

Some businesses develop templates that are used in-house and that are preferred over certain templates provided by Microsoft. Check with your company before using a template obtained online or within an Office application.

Working with Template Placeholders

A template's sample text and headings are sometimes stored in named placeholders. To change text in a placeholder, click in the placeholder to select the text, and then format as necessary. In addition, a placeholder can be moved to a new location in the template, or deleted. A gift certificate of $25 to the Red Bluff Bistro will be given away on the last day of the Caddy School. You will download a template to create the gift certificate, and then fill in the placeholders with the necessary information.

MODULE 1

W02.13

To Work with Templates

a. Click the **FILE** tab, and then click **New**.

This is similar to the Word Start screen in that you can create a new file from either a blank document or template.

b. Click in the **Search for online templates** box, type gift certificates, and then press Enter. Point to any **gift certificate** to reveal its full name.

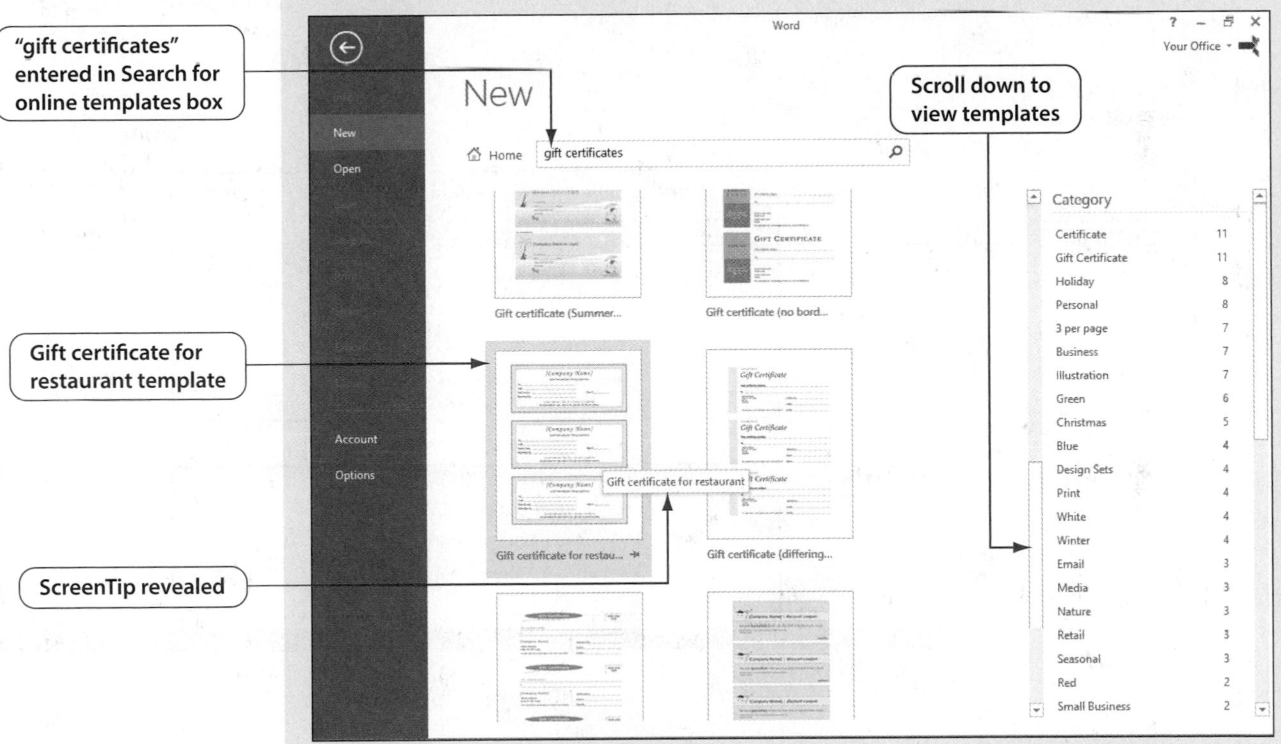

Figure 19 Searching for a template

c. Scroll down, click **Gift certificate for restaurant**, and then click **Create**.

Troubleshooting

If you have trouble locating the Gift certificate for restaurant template, click in the Search for online templates box again, and type "restaurant gift certificate". Click the picture of the Gift certificate for restaurant template, and then click Create.

d. Click **Save** [Save icon], double-click **Computer**, and then navigate to where you are saving your project files. Save the file with the file name of w01ws02Gift_LastFirst, using your last and first name. Click **Save**. If asked about saving in a new file format, click **OK**.

Because this is the first time you are saving this file, you are required to specify a name and location for the file.

e. Three gift certificates appear in the document. In the top certificate, click in the placeholder **Company Name**. The Company placeholder field is displayed, and the text in the placeholder is selected.

Troubleshooting

If the text in the placeholder is not selected, triple-click in the placeholder area to select the text.

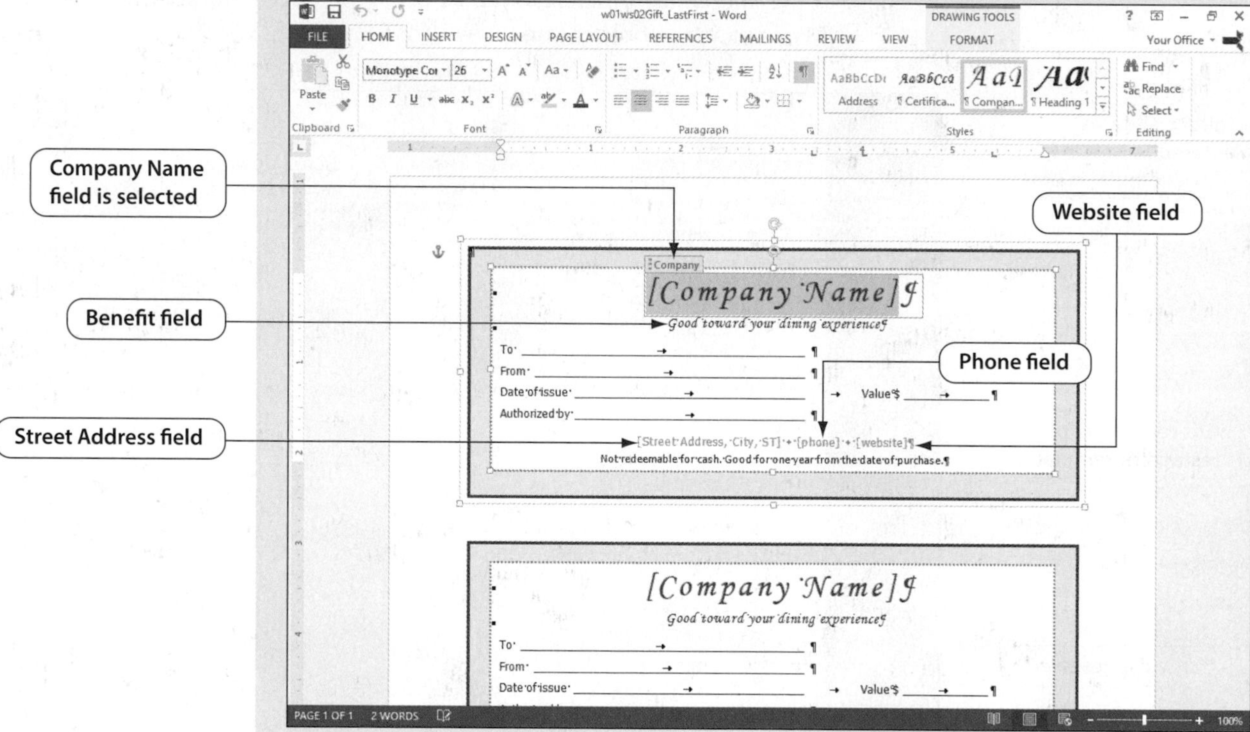

Figure 20 Restaurant template

f. Making sure not to press Enter, type Red Bluff Golf Course and Pro Shop. On the HOME tab, in the Font group, click the **Font Size** arrow [11], and then scroll down to select **20**.

g. Click anywhere in the line **Good toward your dining experience**. The Benefit placeholder field is displayed and the text is selected. Making sure not to press Enter, type $25 meal at Red Bluff Bistro.

h. Click anywhere in the field **Street Address, City, ST** to select the text. Making sure not to press Enter, type 3356 Hemmingway Cir, Santa Fe, NM.

i. Similarly, change the phone placeholder text to **505-555-1387** and the website placeholder text to **http://www.paintedparadiseresort.com**. Click outside of the certificate to deselect the text.

j. **Save** the document. Click the **FILE** tab, and then click **Close**.

Word automatically fills in the fields for the remaining two gift certificates in the template, though the formatting is not applied. Because we only need one gift certificate, we do not need to fix the formatting on the remaining certificates.

Formatting a Document

You have explored formatting at the character level and at the paragraph level. Formatting at the *document* level affects the pages in the document. For example, you may want to change the page margins or add a page border. When working with a lengthy document, knowing how to apply formats that affect an entire document can get a job done quickly and easily. In this section, you will explore page layout settings, learn to adjust margins, change page orientation, modify backgrounds, use borders, and work with themes.

Change Page Setup

The page setup of a document includes such settings as margins, orientation, and alignment. A format can be applied to the entire document, or as you will learn in a later workshop, to individual sections and pages. Selections on the Page Layout tab enable you to easily complete these tasks.

Changing Page Orientation

A document presented in **portrait orientation** is taller than it is wide, while **landscape orientation** displays a page wider than it is tall. The default orientation for a document is portrait. Use Backstage view or the Page Layout tab to change the orientation.

CONSIDER THIS | Selection of Page Orientation

Typically, documents are best suited in portrait orientation. Can you identify any documents that would be more attractive or effective in landscape orientation?

Changing Margins

The empty space at the top, bottom, left, and right side of a document is called a **margin**. If you do not specify otherwise, all margins are set at 1". Inevitably, you will find a need to change margins in some documents. For example, reducing the margins can sometimes make the difference between being able to fit all the text onto one page versus having one or two extra lines on a second page. Word provides a collection of predefined margin settings you can select from, or you can easily define custom margins if you need to be more specific.

REAL WORLD ADVICE | **Changing Default Margins**

The default margins are 1" on all sides. What if your company requires 2" top and bottom margins? Instead of modifying the margins for each document you create, Word enables you to change the default margin setting. On the Page Layout tab, click Margins in the Page Setup group. Click Custom Margins, and select the new margin settings. Then, if desired, click Set As Default to set those margin settings as the default. From now on, the new margin settings will be in effect each time you begin a new document, thus saving you time!

QUICK REFERENCE | **Setting Margins and Page Orientation**

You can set the margins and page orientation of a document in the same location.

1. Click the Page Layout tab.
2. Click Margins in the Page Setup group.
3. Click Custom Margins.
4. Change the Margins settings on the Margins tab.
5. Select an Orientation on the Margins tab.
6. Click OK.

Centering a Page Vertically

As you recall, when you click Center in the Paragraph group, text is centered between the left and right margins. Word also provides a way to center the text between the top and bottom margins. This is known as centering a page vertically, and is commonly used when creating cover pages and flyers. Unless you specify otherwise, all pages in a document are centered vertically when you apply that setting. You will change the margins and vertically align the text in the caddy flyer. You will also experiment with the orientation of the flyer.

REAL WORLD ADVICE | **A Quick Way to Design a Cover Page**

Although you can develop a cover page by centering a page vertically, you can let Word do the work for you instead. On the Insert tab, in the Pages group, click Cover Page. Select a cover style, or click More Cover Pages from Office.com for even more choices.

W02.14

To Work with Page Layout Settings

a. Click the FILE tab, and then click **Open**. In the Recent Documents list, click **w01ws02School_LastFirst**.

b. Click the **VIEW** tab, and then in the Zoom group, click **One Page**. By reducing the magnification, you are better able to see the results of changes made to the page layout.

c. Click the **PAGE LAYOUT** tab, and then in the Page Setup group, click the **Page Setup Dialog Box Launcher** . In the Page Setup dialog box, click the **Layout** tab.

d. Click the **Vertical alignment** arrow, and then select **Center**.

If you want to vertically center only a selection of text (perhaps one page) instead of the entire document, click the Apply to arrow and select Selected text. The selected text will be centered vertically on a separate page.

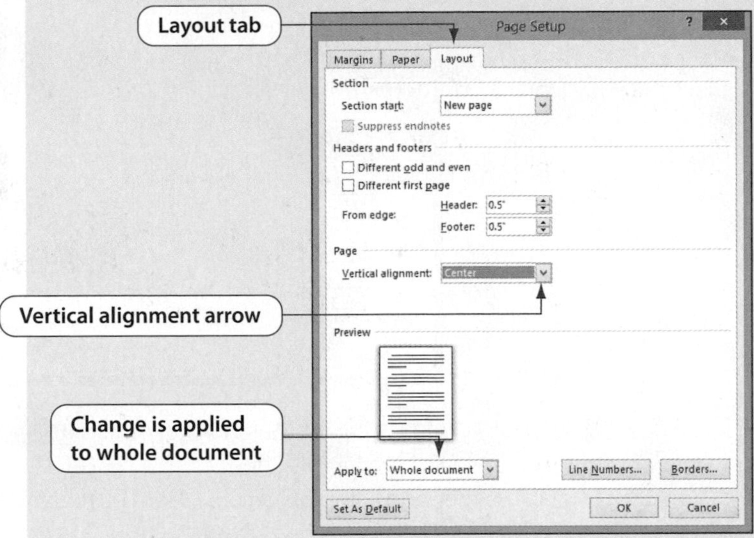

Figure 21 Centering a page vertically

SIDE NOTE

Another Way to Change the Orientation and Margins

You can set margins and orientation in Backstage view under Print. The changes are then immediately displayed in the print preview.

e. Click **OK** to close the Page Setup dialog box. In the Page Setup group, click **Orientation**, and then select **Landscape**. As you see from the resulting document layout, Landscape is not an attractive option for this document. On the Quick Access Toolbar, click **Undo** .

f. In the Page Setup group, click **Margins**, and then select **Custom Margins**.

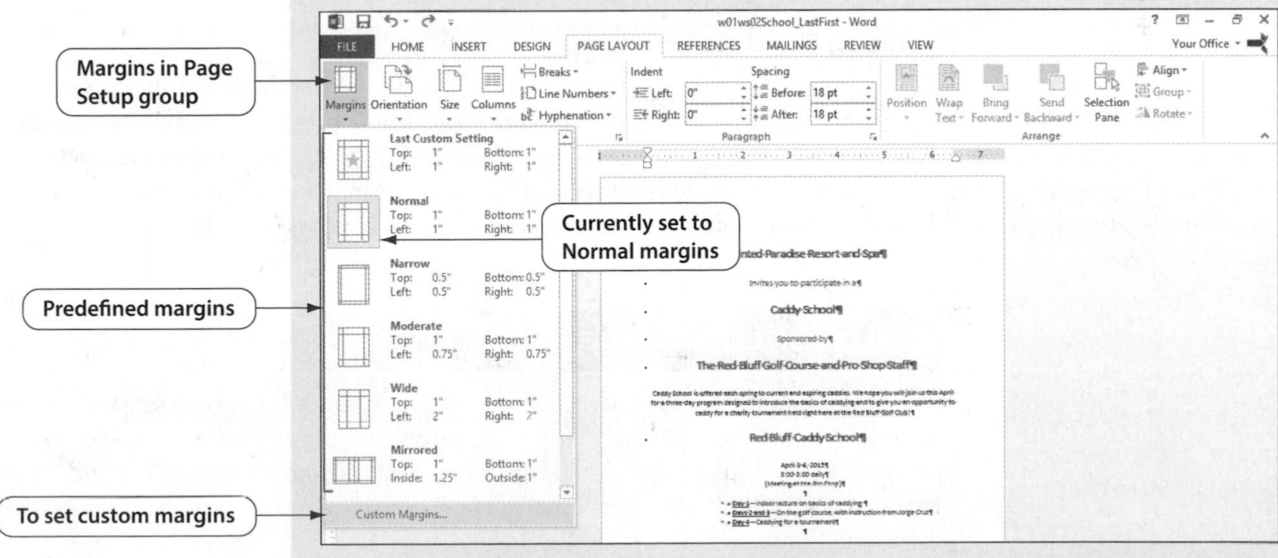

Figure 22 Selecting margins

g. With the text in the **Top** box selected, type .75 and then press Tab. Similarly, change the **Bottom**, **Left**, and **Right** margins to .75.

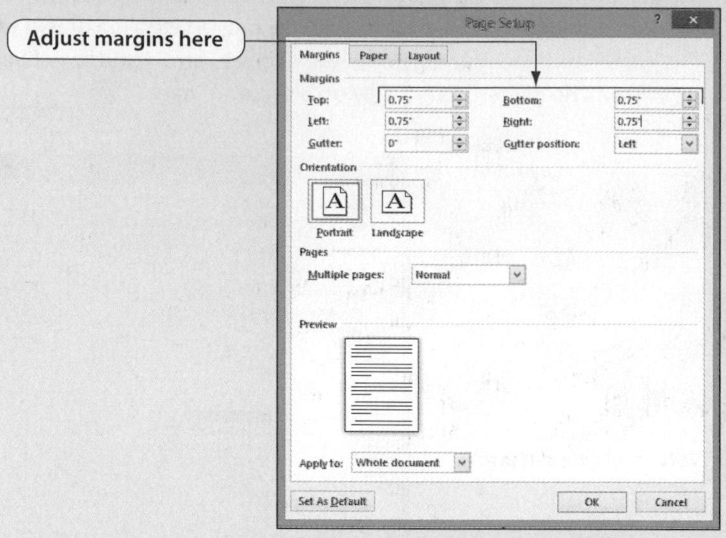

Figure 23 Define custom margins

h. Click **OK** to close the Page Setup dialog box. **Save** the document.

Change Page Background

The default page background for Word 2013 is white, with no border or graphics. Although you never want to go overboard with color or graphics, you might need to enhance a document with color, borders, or even texture. These and other page background settings are now located on the Design tab in Word 2013.

Changing Page Color

In limited cases, a change to a more colorful or textured background might better suit the document's purpose and audience. Keep in mind brightly colored documents can be expensive to print, and they are generally not necessary or appropriate for business documents. Colored backgrounds can liven up greeting cards, flyers, business cards, or personal stationery, but the background should never overwhelm the text.

REAL WORLD ADVICE **Printing a Page Background**

Changing the color of a page background is no guarantee that the colored background will print. To make sure that your newly colored pages print, on the File tab, click Options. Click Display, and then select Print background colors and images under Printing options. Always carefully scrutinize readability when using a background color.

Inserting a Watermark

A **watermark** is text or a picture that appears behind document text. A watermark can add interest or identity to a document. For example, documents often include a DRAFT watermark, indicating that they are not in their final form. Figure 24 shows a document with a watermark. If you include a watermark, it will only be displayed in Print Layout or when the document is printed. Word provides built-in text and graphics that you can select as a watermark, or you can create your own. You can lighten a watermark so that it does not interfere with the readability of the document, or you can remove the current watermark. You will now change the page background color of the caddy flyer and add a DRAFT watermark.

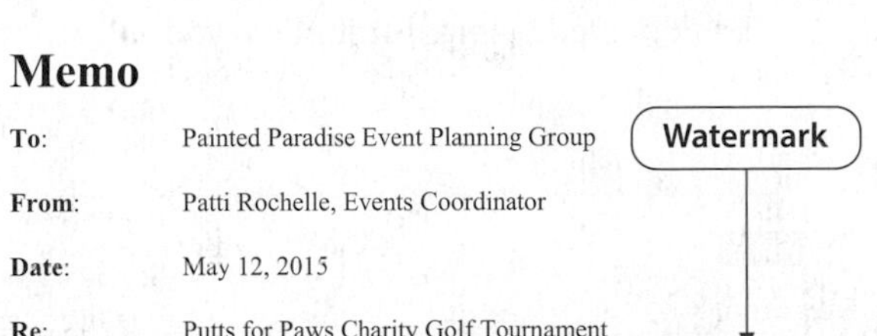

Memo

To: Painted Paradise Event Planning Group

From: Patti Rochelle, Events Coordinator

Date: May 12, 2015

Re: Putts for Paws Charity Golf Tournament

Painted Paradise Resort is once again sponsoring the Annual Red Bluff Putts for Paws Golf Tournament with this year's proceeds benefiting the Santa Fe Animal Center. The success of this fundraiser will be determined in large part by the participation and support of our community partners. As a valued member of the Event Planning staff at Painted Paradise, I am counting on you to promote the event and to solicit participation from the community. This memo provides basic details on activities and sponsorship opportunities so that you may be well informed and able to answer questions from interested parties.

The tournament, beginning at noon on July 31, promises a full afternoon of special events an exciting competition. Participants can enjoy a warm-up session with our own Red Bluff Golf, John Schilling, as well as chipping and putting contests. Animals from the Santa Fe Animal Center, available for adoption, will be on hand to visit. A silent auction and raffle will round out the day. Of course, the tournament would not be complete without our highly acclaimed dessert buffet, with prized selections from Indigo5! Restaurant. Painted Paradise Resort and Spa has prepared for you a fun-filled day at the resort!

We believe in giving back to the community. We are also certain that our community partners and past donors share our commitment to support such worthwhile causes as the Santa Fe Animal Center. We invite our community partners to participate in the event by sponsoring a golf cart, a hole on the golf course, or a course flagstick. We also invite participation in the form of individual or corporate golf teams. Pricing details on all of those opportunities are given below.

- Individual Player - $200
- Individual Player (includes caddy) - $500
- Team of Four - $550
- Corporate Team of Four - $850 (includes hole sponsorship and four caddies)
- Cart Sponsor (Logo/brand displayed on cart; includes dinner for four at Indigo5! Restaurant) - $2000
- Hole Sponsor (Logo/brand displayed on a course tee) - $500
- Flag Sponsor (Logo/brand displayed on a course flagstick) - $500

We look forward to a fun-filled tournament—an activity that truly gives back to our community while also enabling us to connect with those who share our commitment. I appreciate your involvement and know that I can count on you to support the effort in any way you are asked

Figure 24 Including a watermark

W02.15

To Change a Page Color and Add a Watermark

a. Click the **DESIGN** tab, and then in the Page Background group, click **Page Color**, and then point to any **color selection** in the color palette without clicking.
 A preview of the selection is displayed. Explore the effect of several colors. For even more color detail, you can click More Colors. If you prefer a gradient or texture fill, click Fill Effects. Other effects include patterns or even pictures.

b. Under Theme Colors, in the first column and second row, select **White, Background 1, Darker 5%**.

c. In the Page Background group, click **Watermark**.
 The gallery provides selections from a predefined list. You can also create a custom watermark with text or a picture or you can remove a watermark. Because the flyer must be approved before distribution, you will include a DRAFT watermark.

d. Scroll through the predefined watermarks, and then select **DRAFT 1**.

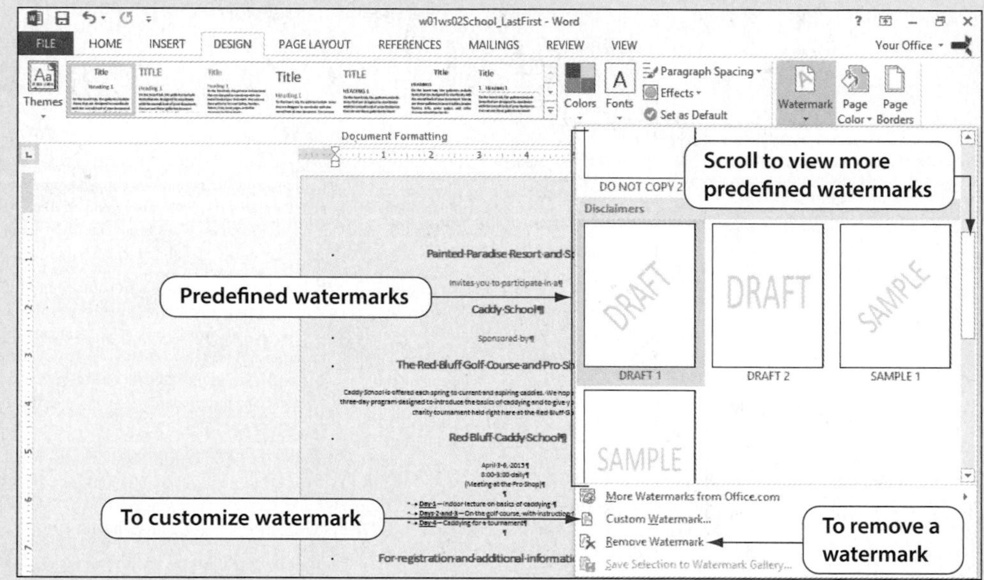

Figure 25 Creating a watermark

e. In the Page Background group, click **Watermark**, and then select **Custom Watermark**. The Printed Watermark dialog box opens. Because the watermark is a little too transparent, click to deselect the **Semitransparent** check box to make it darker, and easier to read. Click **OK** to close the dialog box.

f. **Save** the document.

Adding a Page Border

A page border, a line or graphic that surrounds a page, works especially well in flyers and customized stationery. A page border is most appropriate for one-page documents; it is seldom necessary to include one in a multiple-page document. You will add a page border to the Caddy School flyer.

W02.16

To Add a Page Border

a. On the DESIGN tab, in the Page Background group, click **Page Borders** to open the Borders and Shading dialog box. Under Setting, click **Shadow**.

   Shadow is not to be confused with Shading. The Borders and Shading dialog box has three tabs—Borders, Page Border, and Shading. Shading is another tab of the Borders and Shading dialog box. Click the Shading tab to shade, or color, selected areas of text. Shadow, on the Page Border tab, is a type of border.

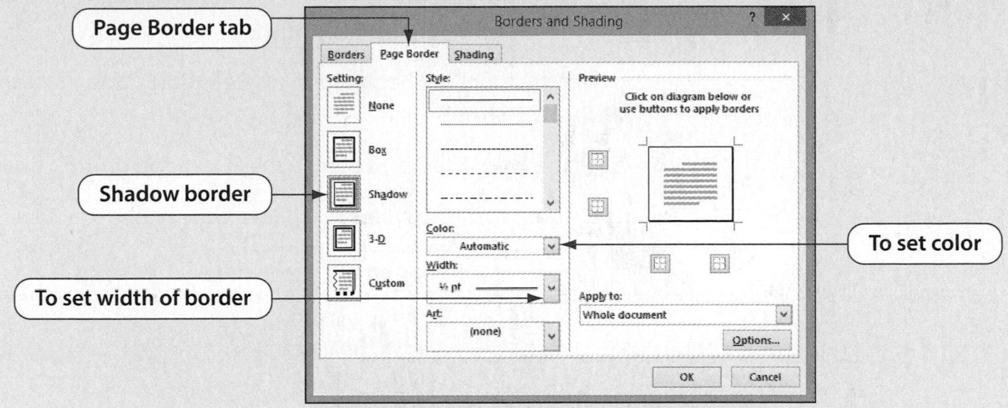

Figure 26 Adding a page border

b. While still on the Page Border tab of the Borders and Shading dialog box, click the **Color** arrow, and then under Theme Colors, in the fourth column and first row, select **Blue-Gray, Text 2**. Click the **Width** arrow, select **1 pt**, and then click **OK** to close the dialog box.

   Borders do not have to be solid lines. You can select from a variety of art borders when you click the Art arrow in the Borders and Shading dialog box.

c. Click the **VIEW** tab, and then in the Zoom group, click **100%**.

d. **Save** [Save icon] the document.

Adding Borders and Shading

The addition of borders and shading can add emphasis to one or more paragraphs or to the entire document. Although the most frequently used borders are bottom, top, left, right, or outside, Word provides a wide range of additional specialty borders. Borders are available in the Paragraph group on the Home tab, if applying borders to a paragraph. Alternatively, they are available in the Page Background group of the Design tab when applying borders to the entire document page. As you apply a border to a paragraph, you can specify line style, color, and weight. In addition, you can apply shading, or a background color to a bordered area. When used in conjunction with a border, shading can add definition and draw attention to one or more paragraphs.

Because the use of shading and borders is a type of paragraph formatting, you do not have to select a paragraph to be bordered or shaded. Instead, the selected border or shading is only applied to the paragraph in which the insertion point is positioned. Of course, to apply a border or shading to more than one paragraph, you must select all those paragraphs.

You will now add a border to the Red Bluff Caddy School section. After adding the border, you will shade it and indent it from the left and right margins.

REAL WORLD ADVICE Highlighting Text vs. Shading

Paragraph shading adds background color to one or more paragraphs. If you want to add background color to a smaller selection of text, rather than to an entire paragraph, you can add highlighting by selecting text and clicking the Text Highlight Color arrow in the Font group on the Home tab.

W02.17

To Add Borders and Shading

a. Select the four lines beginning with **Red Bluff Caddy School** and ending with **(Meeting at the Pro Shop)**.

b. Click the **HOME** tab, and then in the Paragraph group, click the **Borders** arrow .

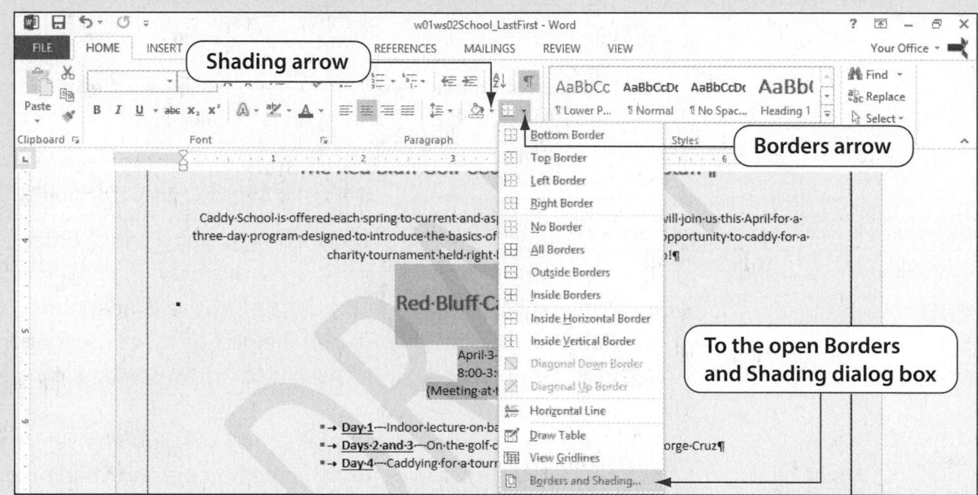

Figure 27 Selecting a border

c. Select **Borders and Shading**. The Borders and Shading dialog box opens, with the Borders tab selected. Under Setting, click **Box**, and then under Style, scroll down the list and select the **double underline** (seventh from top). Because you selected text before applying the border, the Apply to box is set to Paragraph.

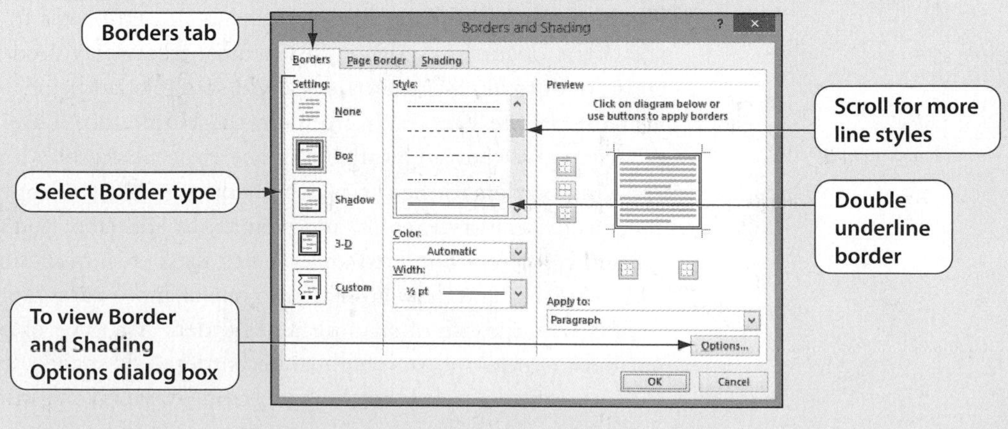

Figure 28 Borders and Shading dialog box

d. Click **Options** to open the Border and Shading Options dialog box, and then click the **Bottom** up arrow three times to display **4 pt**. Click **OK** to close the Border and Shading Options dialog box, and then click **OK** to close the Borders and Shading dialog box. Do not deselect the text.

Because the style of text had no paragraph after spacing, you increased the spacing after the last line of text to 4 pt in the Border and Shading Options dialog box. This increased the white space above the bottom border.

e. With the text still selected, in the Paragraph group, click the **Shading** arrow, and then under Theme colors, in the first column and fourth row, select **White, Background 1, Darker 25%**.

f. With the text still selected, click the **PAGE LAYOUT** tab, and then in the Paragraph group, change the **Left** and **Right** values to **1.5"** each, and then click anywhere in the document to deselect the text.

g. **Save** the document.

Use Themes

A **theme** is a set of design elements that enables you to create professional, color-coordinated documents with minimal effort. Color, fonts, and graphics can be combined to provide a unified look for a document and can even coordinate with other Office applications to create "matching" files. For example, a PowerPoint presentation that includes a certain theme can be matched to a Word document sporting the same color coordination. A company might require a certain theme so that all documents portray a unified, even branded, look.

CONSIDER THIS | Global Theme

Businesses today must think globally. The use of technology simplifies worldwide communication and facilitates global marketing. Communicating in so many diverse cultures can be quite a challenge. When creating a theme or common design to represent your business globally, what sorts of considerations are necessary to be effective in a worldwide market?

Working with a Theme

Themes are located in the Document Formatting group of the Design tab. As you point to a theme, you see a live preview of the effect of the theme on the document text. Click on the theme to accept the change.

Even a blank document is based on a theme. If you do not specify otherwise, the default theme, which is called Office, is in place when a new document is created. When you click the Font Color arrow on the Home tab, you will see colors divided into Theme Colors and Standard Colors. The Theme Colors set is a group of colors that work well together for a particular theme. A theme contains four text and background colors, six accent colors, and two hyperlink colors. Similarly, Theme Fonts is a set of fonts that coordinate with the theme. Each theme identifies one font for document headings and another for body text. Because theme colors are designed to complement one another, it is a good idea to select colors from a single theme's color palette to ensure compatibility.

If you like some elements of a theme but want to change others, you can select Theme Colors, Theme Fonts, or Theme Effects in the Document Formatting group of the Design tab. Each group of coordinated colors, fonts, or effects is identified by name. Select an existing group or if desired, you can customize the individual colors or fonts within a group.

W02.18

To Work with a Theme

a. Click the **DESIGN** tab, and then in the **Document Formatting** group, click **Themes**.

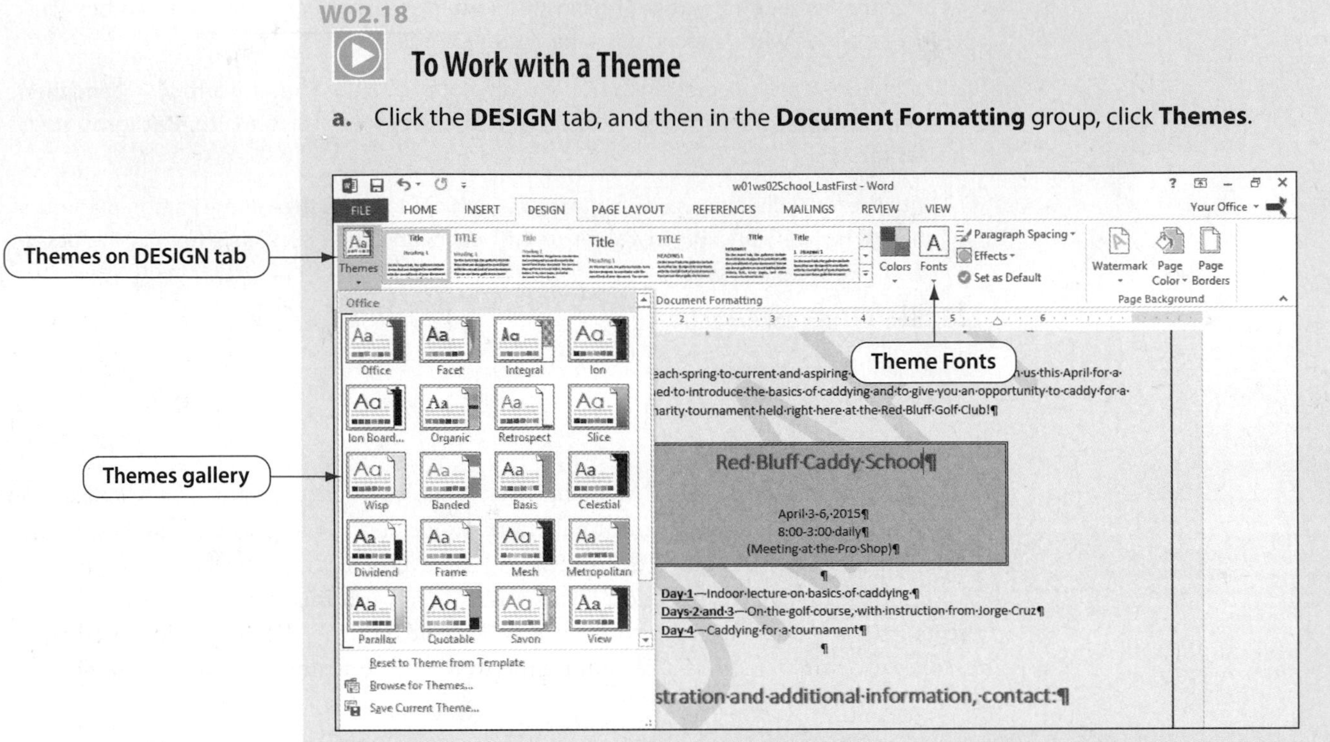

Figure 29 Selecting a theme

b. Select **Integral** to apply the theme to the entire document. Font, font color, and effects are modified.

You like the new theme but prefer it to have a different font.

c. On the DESIGN tab, in the Document Formatting group, click **Theme Fonts**. Scroll through the font selections, pausing on several to view the effect on the document's font, and then select **Times New Roman-Arial**.

You have now set Times New Roman as the font for all headings in this theme and Arial as the font for all body text.

d. Click the **HOME** tab, and then in the Font group, click the **Font Color** arrow, noting the different theme colors.

Because you have selected a different theme, the font color selections have changed. Also make note of the different fonts and font sizes.

e. **Save** the document, exit Word, and then submit your files as directed by your instructor.

QUICK REFERENCE | **Creating a Flyer**

Creating a flyer is more than simply listing a few facts. It needs to grab your audience's attention and clearly convey your message. The following tips can help you create an effective flyer.

1. Before delving into the design of the flyer, decide the message you want the flyer to convey, and create a list of the information you want to include in the flyer.
2. Keep it brief and simple. Only include the necessary information.
3. Use bold, persuasive, and descriptive words.
4. Do not use too many fonts.
5. Use pictures and graphics, if possible.
6. Proofread it!
7. Put the flyer on a wall, and then step back to take a look at it. If you are distracted by an overabundance of color, text, and graphics, your audience will be too.

Concept Check

1. What are some techniques to copy, cut, and paste text in a document? p. 226
2. Why would you use styles? When would you use a Heading 1 style versus a Heading 2 style versus the Normal style? Why would you use the Navigation Pane? When you modify an existing style, or create a style, the style is available to use throughout your document. Would you ever want the style to be available in all future documents? p. 230–235
3. Provide at least two different examples of when you might want to use the Format Painter. p. 237–238
4. What is the difference between a bulleted list and a numbered list? When should you use a numbered list? p. 239
5. What is the difference between a left, right, hanging, and first-line indent? List three different ways to change a left or right indent. p. 241–244
6. What is a template? What is the difference between creating a new file "from scratch" and creating a new file based on a template? What is a business example of when you might use a template? p. 244
7. When would you use landscape versus portrait orientation? What is the difference between center-aligned text and centering your page vertically? What is a margin? p. 247–248
8. What is a watermark? How are they used in a business environment? What is the difference between page borders and borders on text? What is the difference between shading and highlighting? p. 251–254
9. What is the default theme when you create a new document? Why would you use themes? p. 255–256

Key Terms

Bullet 239
Clipboard 226
Clipboard pane 226
Copy 226
Cut 226
First-line indent 241
Format Painter 237
Hanging indent 241
Landscape orientation 247
Left indent 241
Margin 247
Navigation Pane 232
Paste 226
Paste Preview 226
Portrait orientation 247
Right indent 241
Ruler 225
Style 230
Symbol 240
Template 244
Theme 255
Watermark 251

Visual Summary

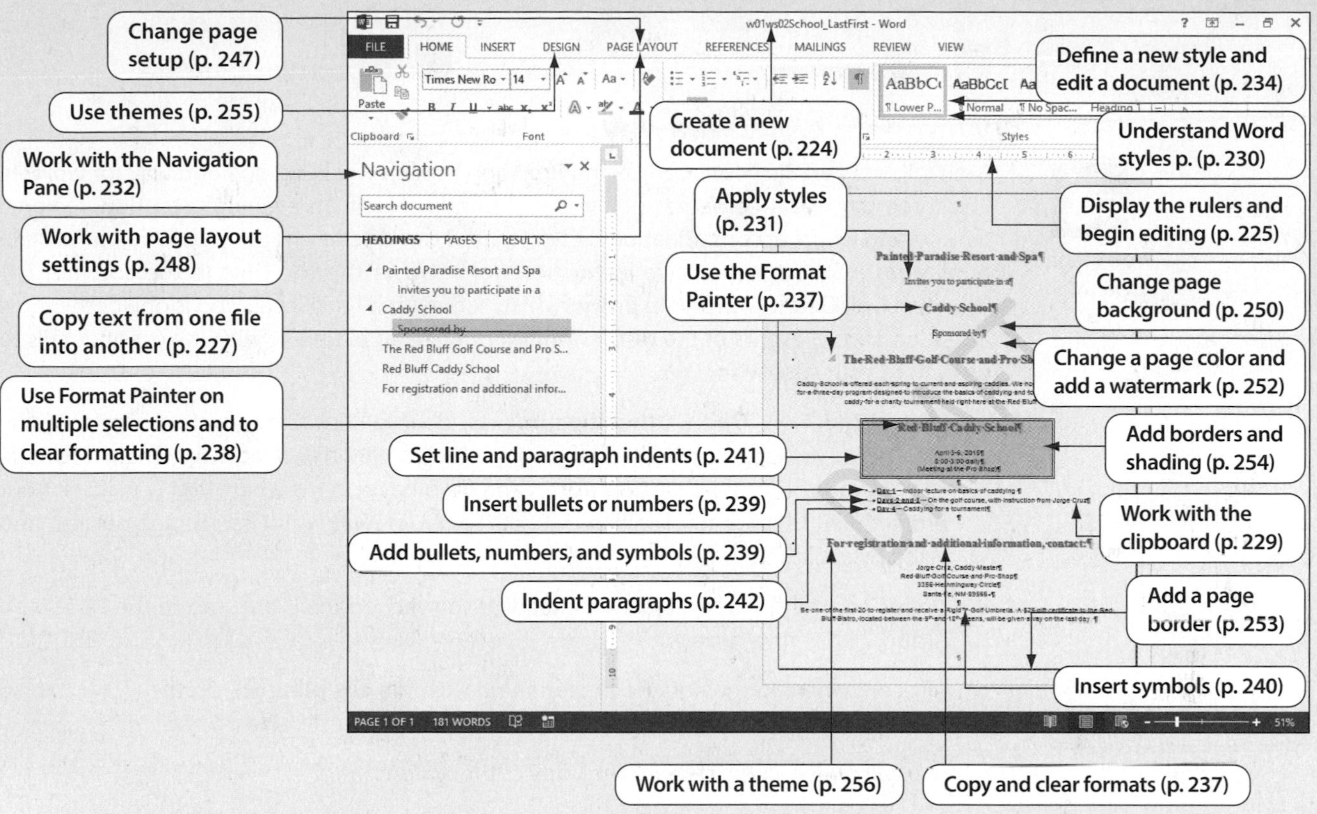

Change page setup (p. 247)
Use themes (p. 255)
Work with the Navigation Pane (p. 232)
Work with page layout settings (p. 248)
Copy text from one file into another (p. 227)
Use Format Painter on multiple selections and to clear formatting (p. 238)
Set line and paragraph indents (p. 241)
Insert bullets or numbers (p. 239)
Add bullets, numbers, and symbols (p. 239)
Indent paragraphs (p. 242)
Create a new document (p. 224)
Apply styles (p. 231)
Use the Format Painter (p. 237)
Define a new style and edit a document (p. 234)
Understand Word styles p. (p. 230)
Display the rulers and begin editing (p. 225)
Change page background (p. 250)
Change a page color and add a watermark (p. 252)
Add borders and shading (p. 254)
Work with the clipboard (p. 229)
Add a page border (p. 253)
Insert symbols (p. 240)
Work with a theme (p. 256)
Copy and clear formats (p. 237)

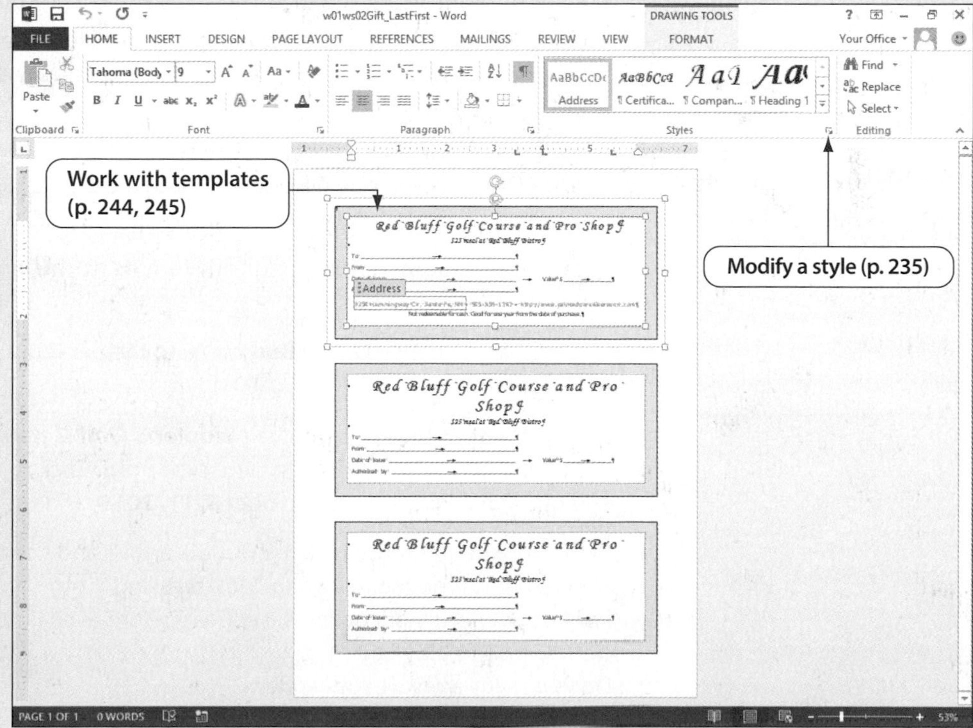

Work with templates (p. 244, 245)
Modify a style (p. 235)

Figure 30 Red Bluff Caddy School Flyer Final Document

Practice 1

Student data file needed:

 w01ws02Getaway.docx

You will save your file as:

 w01ws02Getaway_LastFirst.docx

Women's Golf Getaway

Production & Operations

Each fall, the Red Bluff Golf Course and Pro Shop hosts a weekend golf getaway for women. The three-day event combines golf lessons, rounds of golf, an evening reception, regional cuisine, and luxury accommodations at the Painted Paradise Resort and Spa. Open to women of all ages, participants receive instruction from two of the top pros in the country. The Women's Golf Getaway program provides instruction for all skill levels and is one of the most attended annual events of the resort. You will prepare a document with the event details to present to your supervisor.

a. Start **Word**, click **Open Other Documents**, double-click **Computer**, navigate to the location of your student files, and then double-click **w01ws02Getaway**. On the **FILE** tab, click **Save As**. Double-click **Computer**, and then navigate to where you are saving your project files. Change the File name to w01ws02Getaway_LastFirst, using your last and first name. Click **Save**.

b. Unless nonprinting characters are already displayed, on the HOME tab, in the Paragraph group, click **Show/Hide**.

c. Click anywhere in the paragraph beginning with **We are pleased**. On the HOME tab, in the Styles group, click the Dialog Box Launcher, and then click **New Style**.

d. You will create a new style for the body of the document.
   - In the **Name** box, type Getaway Body.
   - Click the **Font** arrow, and then select **Arial**. Click the **Font Size** arrow, and then select **12**.
   - Click **Format**, and then select **Paragraph**. Under Indentation, click the **Left** up arrow to display **0.5"**, and then click the **Right** up arrow to display **0.5"**. You have set a 0.5" left and right indent.
   - Under Spacing, change **Before** and **After** to **18 pt**.
   - Click **OK**, and then click **OK** again to close the Create New Style from Formatting dialog box and to apply the style to the paragraph beginning with **We are pleased**.

e. Click in the paragraph beginning with **Join us at the**, and then in the Styles pane, click **Getaway Body**.

f. Similarly, apply the **Getaway Body** style to the paragraph beginning with **We are ready to welcome you**.

g. Press Ctrl+Home, select the text **Women's Golf Getaway** in the first paragraph under the title, and then in the Font group, click **Bold**. Click to place the insertion point at the end of the paragraph, after **October 9-11, 2015**, and then press Enter.

h. In the Paragraph group, click the **Bullets** arrow, and then under Bullet Library, select the **check mark**. Type the following lines, pressing Enter after each line, including after the last line. A check mark bullet will appear before each line that you type.
   Do you love to play golf?
   Do you enjoy a resort atmosphere?
   Do you feel the need to pamper yourself?

i. When you pressed Enter after the last line, another check mark appeared. In the Paragraph group, click **Bullets** to turn off bullets. Make sure and click the Bullets button, and not the Bullets arrow.

j. Press Delete to remove the blank line after the bulleted list.

k. Click the **PAGE LAYOUT** tab, and then in the Page Setup group, click **Orientation**, and then select **Portrait**.

   Because you see that landscape might not be the best orientation for this document, you change the orientation to portrait.

l. Select all three bulleted lines, and then in the Paragraph group, change **Left** to **2"**.

m. Select the five lines beginning with **Luxury suite accommodations** and ending with **Saturday lunch at Red Bluff Bistro**. In the Styles pane, click **Emphasis**. With the text still selected, click the **HOME** tab, and then in the Paragraph group, click **Center**, click the **Font Size** arrow, and then select **12**.

n. Select the five lines beginning with **Patti Rochelle, Event Planning Manager** and ending with **prochelle@paintedparadiseresort.com**. In the Styles pane, click **No Spacing**. With the text still selected, in the Paragraph group, click **Center**. Close the Styles pane.

o. Press Ctrl+Home to move to the top of the document. Click anywhere in the first line of the document, **Red Bluff Golf Course and Pro Shop**. On the HOME tab, in the Clipboard group, double-click **Format Painter**. Scroll to the bottom of the document, select the lines **Reserve your place today!** and **Painting Your Perfect Getaway!**, and then in the Clipboard group, click **Format Painter** to turn off the Format Painter.

p. You decide that your document needs a little more white space. Click anywhere in the line **Luxury suite accommodations**. Click the **PAGE LAYOUT** tab, and then in the Paragraph group, change the paragraph **Before** spacing to **30 pt**. Similarly, change the paragraph **After** spacing to **30 pt** for the line **Saturday lunch at Red Bluff Bistro**.

q. Click to place the insertion point in front of the **S** in the sentence **Spaces fill up fast**. Press Backspace twice to remove the space and the period. Click the **INSERT** tab, and then in the Symbols group, click **Symbol**, and then select **More Symbols**. Click the **Special Characters** tab, click **Em Dash**, click **Insert**, and then click **Close**.

r. Click the **PAGE LAYOUT** tab, and then in the Page Setup group, click **Margins**, and then select **Narrow**.

s. Click **Margins**, select **Custom Margins**, and then in the Page Setup dialog box, click the **Layout** tab. Click the **Vertical alignment** arrow, select **Center** to center the document vertically, and then click **OK**.

t. Click the **DESIGN** tab, and then in the Page Background group, click **Page Borders** to open the Borders and Shading dialog box with the Page Border tab selected. Click **Box** under Setting, and then click **OK**.

u. In the Document Formatting group, click **Themes**, and then select **Facet**.

v. In the Page Background group, click **Page Color**, and then in the first column and second row, click **White, Background 1, Darker 5%**.

w. Select the five lines beginning with the line **Luxury suite accommodations** and ending with **Saturday lunch at Red Bluff Bistro**. Click the **HOME** tab, and then in the Paragraph group, click the **Borders** arrow, and then select **Borders and Shading**. The Borders and Shading dialog box opens with the Borders tab selected.

x. Under Setting, click **Box**, and then click **OK**.

y. Click the **PAGE LAYOUT** tab, and then in the Paragraph group, under Indent, change **Left** to **1"**, and then change **Right** to **1"**.

z. Click the **INSERT** tab, and then in the Header & Footer group, click **Footer**, and then select **Edit Footer**. In the Insert group, click **Document Info**, and then select **File Name**. Click the **HOME** tab, and then click **Center**. Double-click in the body of your document to close the footer.

aa. Click the **DESIGN** tab, and then in the Page Background group, click **Watermark**. Scroll down, and then select the **DRAFT 1** watermark.

ab. **Save** the document, and then exit Word. Submit your file as directed by your instructor.

Problem Solve 1

Production & Operations

Student data file needed: Blank Word document

You will save your file as: w01ws02Minutes_LastFirst.docx

Minutes Template

You are helping coordinate a summer children's robotics camp. The camp provides children an opportunity to design and build basic robots, with teams competing for camp awards. You recorded notes of a recent planning meeting and will organize those notes into meeting minutes for distribution. You will use a template to begin the document.

a. Start **Word**. Search for the minutes for organization meeting template. Two templates will be displayed, a long form and a short form. Point to the **templates** to display a ScreenTip, and then select the **Minutes for organization meeting (short form)** template.

b. Save the file as w01ws02Minutes_LastFirst. If a message appears asking if you want to upgrade to the latest format, click **OK**.

c. If necessary, show nonprinting characters.

d. Click in the **[Organization/Committee Name]** placeholder to select the text, and then type ACSB Robotics Camp.

e. Click in the **[Click to select date]** placeholder, and then type 01/08/15.

f. Press Tab to select the **[Attendee Names]** placeholder, and then type Christy, Suzanne, Nicolas, Your First Name. Do not include the period, and Your First Name is your actual first name. Include a space after each comma.

When you press Tab, the text in the next placeholder will be selected. You can then begin typing.

g. Similarly, press Tab twice, and then replace the **[Date, Time, Location]** placeholder with TBD.

Do not continue to press Tab. If you press Tab at the end of the table, Word will insert a new row in the table.

h. Click in the **placeholder** under the Announcements section, starting with **[List all announcements...]**, and then type Welcome to our new team member, Suzanne! Do not press Enter when you are finished. Make sure to include a space after the comma. Do not include a space after the exclamation mark.

i Replace the **[Summarize the discussion...]** placeholder with Brochures are at the printer. remembering not to press Enter when you are finished. Do not include a space after the period.

j. Replace the **[Summarize the status...]** placeholder with N/A, and then press Enter.

k. Type IV. Camp Publicity, and then press Enter.

Note: IV is the Roman numeral consisting of a capital I and a capital V. Include a space after the period. Word will automatically adjust the formatting to match the other headings.

l. Type Adhere to the following guidelines:, and then press Enter.

MODULE 1

m. Type the following, pressing Enter after each line, including after the last line:
Concise and informative
Attractive
Proofread!

n. Select the three lines, beginning with **Concise and informative** and ending with **Proofread!** Apply the **check mark bullet**, and then with the text still selected, change the left indent to **0"**.

o. Open the Styles pane, modify the Heading 2 style to have a 12-pt font size and a 12-pt paragraph After spacing.

p. Modify the Name style to have a 14-pt font size. Similarly, modify the Title style to have a 14-pt font size, and then close the Styles pane.

q. Click to place the insertion point in front of the **S** in the sentence **Welcome to our new team member, Suzanne!**, and then press Backspace twice to remove the space and the comma. Insert the **em dash** symbol.

r. Click to place the insertion point in the line **Adhere to the following guidelines:**, and then change the paragraph After spacing to 6 pt.

s. Change the top and bottom margins to **1.25"** each.

t. Apply the **Ion** theme.

u. Apply a **White, Background 1, Darker 5%** page color to the document (under Theme Colors, column 1, row 2).

v. Insert a footer with the File Name field centered, and then close the footer.

w. Insert the **CONFIDENTIAL 1** watermark and deselect the **Semitransparent** option.

x. Save the document, and then exit Word. Submit your file as directed by your instructor.

Perform 1: Perform in Your Life

Student data file needed:

Blank Word document

You will save your file as:

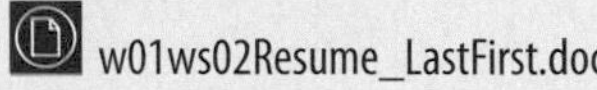

Resume Template

Human Resources

Create a new resume using a template. At a minimum, your resume should contain your name, address, school and work experience, and qualifications or job requirements.

a. Start **Word**. Click in the **Search for online templates** box, and then type resume. Under Category, click **Basic** resumes, and then select a resume of your choice.

b. Save the file as w01ws02Resume_LastFirst. If a message appears asking if you want to upgrade to the latest format, click **OK**.

c. If possible, change the theme of the template.

d. At a minimum, include the following information: your name, your address, your phone number, your e-mail address, school experience, work experience, and qualifications.

Additional information may include certifications, specific job requirements, or references.

e. Remove any unnecessary information in the template.

f. Make any other improvements you think necessary, such as bullets, spacing, or borders.

g. Check the spelling and grammar.

h. Insert a footer with the File Name field centered.

i. Add a watermark to show that the resume is a draft.

j. Save the document, and then exit Word. Submit your file as directed by your instructor.

Additional Cases

Additional Workshop Cases are available on the companion website and in the instructor resources.

MODULE CAPSTONE

More Practice 1

Student data file needed:

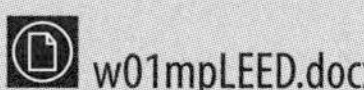
w01mpLEED.docx

You will save your files as:

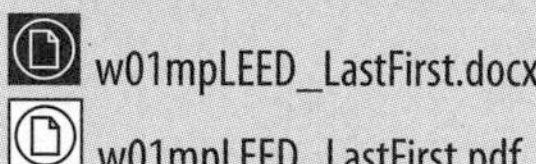
w01mpLEED_LastFirst.docx
w01mpLEED_LastFirst.pdf

Environmental Alliance Sustainable Hotel Information

Research/ Development

Sales & Marketing

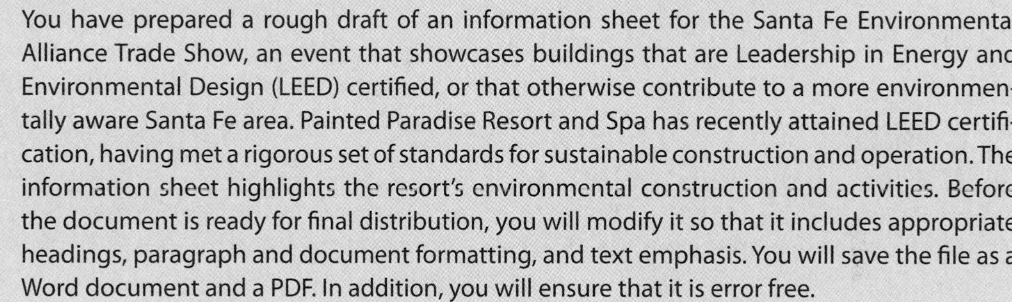
You have prepared a rough draft of an information sheet for the Santa Fe Environmental Alliance Trade Show, an event that showcases buildings that are Leadership in Energy and Environmental Design (LEED) certified, or that otherwise contribute to a more environmentally aware Santa Fe area. Painted Paradise Resort and Spa has recently attained LEED certification, having met a rigorous set of standards for sustainable construction and operation. The information sheet highlights the resort's environmental construction and activities. Before the document is ready for final distribution, you will modify it so that it includes appropriate headings, paragraph and document formatting, and text emphasis. You will save the file as a Word document and a PDF. In addition, you will ensure that it is error free.

a. Open **Word**, open **w01mpLEED**, and then save the document where you are saving your project files as w01mpLEED_LastFirst, using your last and first name. Show nonprinting characters.

b. Select the first line, **Painted Paradise Resort and Spa**. In the Styles group, click **More**, and then apply the **Title** style from the Styles gallery. Select the second line, **A Leader in Energy and Environmental Design**, and then apply the **Subtitle** style.

c. Click anywhere in the paragraph beginning with **Santa Fe is on a quest**. Open the Styles pane, and then create a new style called Body Paragraph, with the following characteristics:
   - **Verdana** font
   - Font size of **10**
   - **Justified** alignment
   - **Blue, Accent 1, Darker 25%** font color (Hint: Under Theme Colors, in the fifth column and the fifth row)

   With the Create New Style from Formatting dialog box still open, click **Format**, and then select **Paragraph**.
   - Under Line spacing, select **1.5 lines**.
   - Under Spacing, set After to **12 pt**.
   - Under Special, select a **First line** indent of 0.5".
   - Click **OK** to close the Paragraph dialog box.
   - Click **OK** to close the Create New Style from Formatting dialog box.

d. Click to place the insertion point anywhere in the paragraph beginning with **Painted Paradise Resort and Spa recently became a LEED-certified hotel**. Apply the **Body Paragraph** style.

e. In the Styles pane, point to the **Normal** style, and then click the **arrow**. Select **Modify**, set the font color to **Blue, Accent 1, Darker 25%**, and then click **OK**.

f. Select the paragraph beginning with **Conservation doesn't have to mean deprivation**. With the paragraph selected, click the **HOME** tab, and then do the following.

- In the Font group, click **Bold**.
- In the Paragraph group, click the **Borders** arrow, and then select **Borders and Shading**. Under Setting, click **Box**, and then click **OK**.
- In the Paragraph group, click the **Shading** arrow. Under Theme Colors, in the fifth column and third row, select **Blue, Accent 1, Lighter 60%**.
- In the Paragraph group, click the **Paragraph Dialog Box Launcher**, and then set a **0.5"** left and right indent. Click **OK**.

g. Under the **Guest Room Enhancements** heading, click to place the insertion point immediately after the word **Plus** in the first numbered line. Click the **INSERT** tab, and then in the Symbols group, click **Symbol**, and then select the **Trade Mark Sign** symbol(™).

h. Select the four numbered lines, beginning with the line starting with **Carpeting certified**, and ending with the line starting with **Energy-conserving**. Click the **HOME** tab, and then in the Paragraph group, click the **Bullets** arrow, and then click the **right arrowhead**.

i. Select the heading **Green Roof**, and then in the Styles gallery, apply the **Heading 2** style. Using the Styles pane, modify the **Heading 2** style to have a font size of **12**, **Arial** font, **bold** text, and a **6 pt** paragraph After spacing.

j. Apply the **Heading 2** style to all other headings: **Guest Room Enhancements, Solar Panels**, **Water Usage and Air Quality**, **Building Material**, **Kitchen**, and **Lighting**. Close the Styles pane.

k. Change the **Building Material** heading to Recycled Building Materials. Change the **Kitchen** heading to Energy-Efficient Kitchen.

l. Rearrange the headings and their content so they appear in alphabetical order. For example, the first category should be **Energy-Efficient Kitchen**, followed by **Green Roof**, and so on. (Hint: Click the **VIEW** tab, and then in the Show group, click Navigation Pane. You can then use the Navigation Pane to quickly move the headings.)

m. If necessary, close the Navigation Pane. Press Ctrl+Home to move to the beginning of the document. Place the insertion point at the start of the paragraph beginning with **Santa Fe is on a quest**, and then press Enter to add one blank paragraph after the subtitle.

n. Click the **PAGE LAYOUT** tab, and then in the Page Setup group, click **Margins**, and then select **Normal**.

o. Press Ctrl+Home to move the insertion point to the beginning of the document. Bold the words **Painted Paradise Resort and Spa** wherever they appear in the document. To do this using Find and Replace, click the **HOME** tab, and then in the Editing group, click **Replace** . In the **Find what** box, type Painted Paradise Resort and Spa, and then in the **Replace with** box type Painted Paradise Resort and Spa. If necessary, click the **More** button to display additional Search Options. Click **Format**, select **Font**, click **Bold**, and then click **OK**. Click **Replace All**. Four replacements should be made. Click **OK**, and then close the dialog box.

p. Press Ctrl+Home. Click the **REVIEW** tab, and then in the Proofing group click **Spelling & Grammar**. Correct any errors. **Plyboo** is not misspelled.

q. Proofread the document to make sure you did not overlook any misspellings or incorrect word usage. Correct anything that is out of order.

   You will find one word-usage error that Word did not identify in the second sentence under the "Green Roof" heading.

r. Click the **INSERT** tab, and then in the Header & Footer group, click **Footer**, and then select **Edit Footer**. Enter your First name and Last name separated by a space. Press Tab twice. On the HEADER & FOOTER TOOLS DESIGN tab, in the Insert group, click **Document Info** and then select **File Name**. Press Spacebar. In the Header & Footer group, click **Page Number** point to **Current Position**, and then select **Plain Number**. Double-click anywhere in the document to close the footer.

s. Click the **DESIGN** tab, and then in the Document Formatting group, click **Themes** and then select **Slice**.

t. In the Page Background group, click **Watermark**, scroll down, and then select **DRAFT 1**.

u. **Save** the document. Click the **FILE** tab, and then click **Export**. Click **Create PDF/XPS**, navigate to the location where you are saving your project files, make sure the **Open file after publishing check box** is **not selected**, and then click **Publish** to create a PDF file with the same name.

v. Save the document, exit Word, and then submit your files as directed by your instructor.

Problem Solve 1

Student data file needed:

w01ps1Romantic.docx

You will save your file as:

Sales & Marketing

Production & Operations

"Romantic Getaway" Gift Basket Welcome Note

Painted Paradise Resort and Spa offers a "Romantic Getaway" package especially designed for couples who want to celebrate their partnership by enjoying a relaxing visit to the resort. The two-night package includes a welcome amenity of champagne, fruit, and favors, delivered upon arrival. Each basket includes a note, welcoming the couple to the resort and inviting them to enjoy all that the resort has to offer them during their stay.

Your supervisor has supplied you with a draft of the welcome note, but it is incomplete. You will add and format text, include bullets where appropriate, create and apply a style, move text, and ensure that the document is error free. When complete, the document will be the perfect addition to the welcome package that is planned for those special couples!

a. Start **Word**, open **w01ps1Romantic**, and then save the document as w01ps1Romantic_LastFirst, using your last and first name. Show nonprinting characters.

b. Click the **DESIGN** tab, and then click **Watermark** and remove the current watermark.

c. Apply the **Heading 1** style to the title line, **Welcome to the Painted Paradise Resort and Spa!**, and then change the font color of the line to **Black, Text 1**.

d. Click anywhere in the paragraph beginning with **This complimentary gift basket**. Open the Styles pane, and then create a new style named **Body Paragraph**. This style should include a **12-pt** font size, **single** line spacing, **6 pt** paragraph Before spacing, and **0 pt** paragraph After spacing.

e. Apply the **Body Paragraph** style to the next two paragraphs in the document, the paragraphs beginning with **During your stay here** and **Along with this gift basket**.

f. Select the paragraph **Compliments of Indigo5:**, apply the **No Spacing** style, change the font size to **14**, and then change the font to **Lucida Handwriting**. With the paragraph still selected, **bold** and **center** the paragraph.

g. Select the next four paragraphs, beginning with the line **Fruit and champagne**, and ending with the line **Souvenir letter opener and pen set**. Apply a heart shaped bullet to those four paragraphs. (Hint: Click the **Bullets** arrow, and then select **Define New Bullet**. Click **Symbol**, verify that Symbol is the selected Font, and then select the **heart shape**.)

h. With the four bulleted lines still selected, change the font to **Lucida Handwriting**, the line spacing to **1.15**, and then set the left indent to **1.5"** and the right indent to **1.2"**.

i. With the four bulleted lines still selected, apply a **Box** border, with a **1 pt** width, and a **White, Background 1, Darker 15%** shaded fill.

j. Click immediately after the word **hope** in the second sentence of the first paragraph of the document, press Spacebar, and then insert the word that in the sentence.

k. Select the last paragraph of the document, **Thank you for letting us Paint Your Perfect Getaway**, and then apply the **Heading 1** style to the paragraph.

l. Use the spelling checker to help correct only those items that are actually misspelled or that are grammatically incorrect, if any. Note that the word "Salbarro" is not misspelled. Also note that one space is required after a comma.

m. Modify the Heading 1 style to have an **18-pt** font size, **bold** and **centered** text, and an **18 pt** paragraph After spacing.

n. Move the second paragraph so it is beneath the third paragraph. Make sure there is one blank line above the line **Compliments of Indigo5:**.

o. Set the margins to **Mirrored**.

p. Apply the **Ion** theme.

q. Insert a page border with a **Box** setting, a **double line** style, and a **1½ pt** width.

r. Center the page vertically.

s. Insert a footer with the File Name field, center-aligned. Close the footer.

t. Preview the document as it will look when printed.

u. Save the document, exit Word, and then submit your file as directed by your instructor.

Problem Solve 2

Student data file needed:

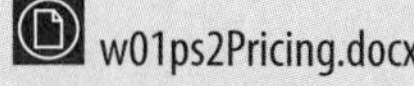

You will save your files as:

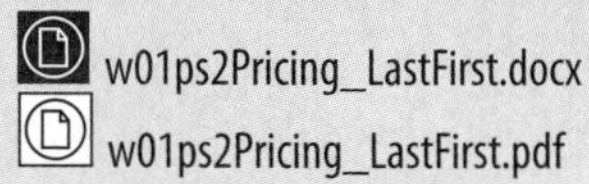

Resort Business Center New Pricing Table

Brian Paxton, the coordinator of the resort business center, wants your help in designing a memo informing resort staff of pricing changes in the business center. Given recent increases in the cost of business supplies, the center will slightly increase the amount charged for certain services. It is important that the memo accurately convey both the reasoning for the increase and the current prices. Mr. Paxton has given you a draft of a memo, but it is incomplete. He wants you to include the new pricing table and to proofread the document.

You will make improvements to the readability of the text, including the use of styles, formatting existing text, adjusting margins, and replacing text where necessary. You will save the file as a Word document and a PDF.

a. Start **Word**, open **w01ps2Pricing**, and then save the document as w01ps2Pricing_LastFirst, using your last and first name. Show nonprinting characters.

b. Place the insertion point anywhere in the line beginning with **All incoming faxes**. Create a new style named Item List. Set the new style to **Italic**, with a paragraph Before spacing of **6 pt**.

c. Apply the new style to the remaining eight lines, beginning with **All local outgoing faxes**, and ending at the bottom of the document.

d. Place the insertion point at the end of the line beginning with **Transparencies**, and then press Enter. Type the following text in the new blank line, without pressing Enter at the end of the line.
Transparencies (color) - $2.50

e. Delete the - in the line you just typed, and then insert an **en dash** symbol in its place.

f. Apply a right-facing arrowhead bullet to the 10 lines providing pricing information.

g. Bold and underline the text **October 1** in the last sentence of first body paragraph, and then change the font color for the text **October 1** to Dark Red.

h. Change the font for the text beginning with **To:** through the end of the document to **Times New Roman** with a **12-pt** font size. Do not select the word **Memo**.

i. Bold the words **To**, **From**, **Date**, and **Re** in the heading area of the memo. Do not select the colons.

j. Replace the word **photocopying** throughout the document with copying.

k. Change the left and right margins to **1"**, and then change the top and bottom margins to **0.5"**.

l. Copy the last bulleted line, **Shipping (1–5 lbs.) – $5.00**. Move the insertion point to the end of the document, press Enter to add an additional bullet, and then paste the line two times. Remove the extra bullet that appears. (Hint: Press Ctrl+V two times in a row to paste twice.)

m. Change **1-5** on the second shipping line to 6-15. On the same line, change **$5.00** to $10.00.

n. Change **1-5** on the last shipping line to 16-100. On the same line, change **$5.00** to $0.60 per pound.

o. Apply a **12 pt** paragraph Before spacing to the first bulleted line, **All incoming faxes - $1.00**.

p. Using cut and paste, alphabetize the bulleted line items.

If a blank bulleted line appears after moving text, click in the blank bulleted line and then press Delete.

q. Select all the bulleted lines, and then apply a **1"** left indent.

r. Move the insertion point to the beginning of the document, use the spelling checker to correct any mistakes, and then proofread the document.

s. Insert a footer with the File Name field, followed by a space, and then the Plain Number page number field. Center the text in the footer, and then close the footer.

t. Insert the **CONFIDENTIAL 1** watermark. Save the document.

u. Create a PDF document with the same name. Make sure the Open file after publishing check box is not selected before clicking **Publish**.

v. Save the document, exit Word, and then submit your files as directed by your instructor.

Perform 1: Perform in Your Life

Student data file needed:

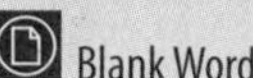

Blank Word document

You will save your files as:

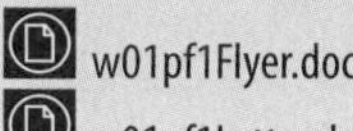

w01pf1Flyer.docx

w01pf1Letter.docx

Class Reunion Announcement

Sales & Marketing

In this project, you will create a cover letter and a flyer that will be mailed to former classmates who graduated from high school with you. The letter and flyer will include information regarding an upcoming class reunion. Assume that you have been out of high school for almost 10 years, and you are responsible for getting the word out to others about the event. The cover letter invites classmates to the event to be held at a time and location that is relevant to your high school. The letter should provide general details on the weekend event, while the flyer is much more descriptive and is designed to generate enthusiasm.

Select a modified block style, making sure to include relevant components, such as an address and salutation. Although the content is up to you, be sure to include at least two body paragraphs informing your audience of the event and encouraging interest. Design the flyer as a one-page summary, using appropriate color (think school colors!) and a tasteful design. The flyer should include contact information for the chair of the planning committee, as well as information on accommodations and any dress requirements. Be sure to mention any monetary charge. Above all, make the flyer fun, eye-catching, and informative.

a. Start **Word**, create a new blank document, and then save the document as w01pf1Letter_LastFirst, using your last and first name.

b. Using the Modified Block style, include your address in the heading area. Include a classmate's name and address in the inside address area. Use August 22, 2015 as the date. Include a salutation of subject line.

c. You will design the content, but keep your audience in mind, providing a general description of the event. Make sure to include the high school graduating year, date and cost of reunion, hotel accommodations, and contact information for any additional information.

d. In the body of the letter, provide a bulleted list with the weekend events. Select a bullet that is eye-catching and appropriate. You can use a symbol or picture for a bullet if you prefer.

e. Because the cover letter will be shared with other planning committee members before the document is finalized, insert a draft watermark.

f. Include the file name field as a footer, center-aligned.

g. Use the spelling checker, and then proofread the document. Save and close the document.

h. Create a one-page flyer, incorporating design elements that will generate enthusiasm and interest in the event. Save the flyer as w01pf1Flyer_LastFirst, using your last and first name.

i. Include a contact name, number, and e-mail address for more information. Make sure and include specific information on events, with times and locations. Add any other necessary information, such as reminders on what to bring and an appropriate introduction.

j. Define **1"** top and bottom margins and **0.75"** right and left margins on the flyer.

k. Use one or more Word styles in the flyer to provide consistency and ease of formatting.

l. Include at least two different font selections and sizes in the flyer. Use at least one instance of bold and italic formatting in the flyer.

m. Include one list in the flyer.

n. Include a border around a section of the text.

o. Include a page color on the flyer. Center the page vertically.

p. Insert a draft watermark.

q. Include the file name field as a footer, center-aligned.

r. Use the spelling checker, and then proofread the document.

s. Save the document, exit Word, and then submit your files as directed by your instructor.

Perform 2: Perform in Your Career

Student data file needed:

Blank Word document

You will save your files as:

w01pf2Agenda_LastFirst.docx

 w01pf2Minutes_LastFirst.docx

w01pf2MinutesPDF_LastFirst.pdf

Meeting Minutes

Production & Operations

You recently were appointed to chair the Ducky Derby Subcommittee at the Stone River Rotary Club. After your first meeting, you offer to develop an agenda for the next meeting. Using Word, you download an agenda template and use it as a starting point to create your agenda. After inserting the relevant data, you remove any unused fields or information from the template. You will also draft a second document containing minutes of the previous meeting, and then save the file as a PDF. You will format the documents to create professional-looking documents that are easy to read.

a. Start **Word**. In the Search for online templates box, type **meeting agenda**, and then choose an appropriate agenda template. If possible, select the Formal meeting agenda. Save the document as **w01pf2Agenda_LastFirst**, using your last and first name.

b. The following text summarizes the agenda for the upcoming meeting. At a minimum, include the following information in your template. Format the document as you see fit. Remember, a template is a guideline to help you get started. You can add to the template if it does not contain all the necessary fields. Include your first and last name where it lists "Your Name".

   It is not necessary to create a bulleted or numbered list. Use the method in the chosen template. If necessary, you can press Tab in a list to create a second-level list item. Press Shift+Tab to decrease the list, or return back to a first-level list item.
   Meeting Title/Type: **Stone River Rotary Club - Ducky Derby Subcommittee**
   Meeting Date: **August 20, 2015**
   Meeting Time: **7:30 p.m.**
   Meeting Leader (or Facilitator): **Phung Burns**
   Meeting Invitees: **Your Name, Randy King, Michael Summer, Marsha Cooper, Tucker Dodd**

   Agenda:

   - **Call to order**
   - **Approval of minutes from last meeting**
   - **Open issues**
     - **Appoint festival committee**
     - **Develop derby budget**
     - **Finalize charities**
   - **Study/Report items**
     - **Summary of 2014 festival**
     - **Financial report**
     - **Nominating committee report**
   - **Adjournment**

c. Remove any unused or unnecessary items from the agenda template.

d. Move the **Study/Report items** section so that it appears before **Open issues**.

e. Use the spelling checker on the document, and then proofread for errors.

f. Change the top, bottom, left, and right margins to **1.5"**.

g. Include a footer with your first and last name, aligned on the left margin.

h. Save and close the document. Keep Word open.

i. Open a blank document, and then save the document as w01pf2Minutes_LastFirst. You jotted down the following notes at the previous Ducky Derby Subcommittee meeting, which you will now include in the new document. Reword and format the information as you see fit. Include your first and last name where it lists "Your Name".
Stone River Rotary Club
Ducky Derby Subcommittee Meeting
Meeting Date: July 18, 2015
Meeting Time: 7:30 p.m.
Attendance: Phung Burns, Tucker Dodd, Michael Summer, Marsha Cooper, Your Name
Absent: Randy King

Topics and Discussion:
- Charity this year: Stone River Advocacy Center, a nonprofit training and development center for adults with developmental disabilities
- Duck Cost: 1 duck is $5, a quack pack is $25, a big quack pack is $50, and a flock of ducks is $100.
- Prizes are still being identified, but we already have a Honda Civic, a motor scooter, and $1,200 cash. We will continue to seek prizes through July 31.
- Plans for preliminary promotional activities:
    - Duck Tagging Party, where we will put race numbers on the bottom of 10,000 ducks
    - Kick-Off Party to begin "Duck Season"
    - Local newspaper article on partnership with the Stone River Advocacy Center and plans for the Derby
    - Development of SR Ducky Derby website and Facebook page
- Appointed Nominating Committee to develop slate of officers for next year's Ducky Derby. The Nominating Committee will report at next month's meeting.
- Ducky Derby Day will be November 9, 2015, at Flat Creek Falls. We will have a maximum of 10,000 ducks ready for purchase and float. Most ducks will be presold before Derby Day.

j. Use at least two different Word styles of your choosing.

k. Center and bold text appropriately.

l. Apply bullets and/or numbering to items, as appropriate.

To create a multilevel list, first create a bullet or numbered list, enter the first list item, and then press Enter. To create a second-level list item, simply press Tab or **Increase Indent**. Press Shift+Tab or **Decrease Indent** to decrease the list level.

m. Set margins appropriately.

n. Proofread and check the spelling of the document.

o. Format the text so the document is attractive and easy to read. Make sure to include a heading (not a header, but a heading).

p. Include a footer, with your first and last name, aligned on the left margin.

q. Place a watermark on the minutes to show that they are currently unapproved.

r. Create a PDF copy of the meeting minutes to e-mail ahead of time to committee members. This will allow them to read the minutes before a vote for approval. Name the PDF w01pf2MinutesPDF_LastFirst, using your last and first name.

s. Save the document, exit Word, and then submit your files as directed by your instructor.

Perform 3: Perform in Your Team

Student data file needed:

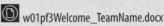

Blank Word document

You will save your file as:

w01pf3Welcome_TeamName.docx

PTO New Family Welcome Information

Customer Service

You are the current Parent Teacher Organization president for your child's school. The PTO is creating a welcome packet containing information that is often requested by new families. The packet will include PTO contact information, along with information on each of the upcoming PTO functions. The chairs for each function will edit the document with their specific information. Sit down with your team members to discuss the layout, style, and any special formatting characteristics you plan to use before you begin. Remember, only one person can edit the document at any single time, so make sure you plan ahead by determining what each team member will be responsible for contributing and when they will make their updates.

a. Select one team member to set up the document by completing steps b–e.

b. Open your browser and navigate to either www.skydrive.live.com, www.drive.google.com, or any other instructor-assigned tools. Be sure all members of the team have an account on the chosen system—Microsoft or Google.

c. Start **Word**, create a new document, and then name it w01pf3Welcome_TeamName, where TeamName is the name assigned to your team by your instructor.

d. Share the file with the other members of your team, making sure that each team member has the appropriate permissions to edit the document.

e. Type in the following text, and then save the file:
Contact Information
PTO Meeting Information
Getting Started Volunteering
Back to School Picnic
Father Daughter Dance
President's Day Walk-A-Thon
Mother Son Breakfast
Auction
Contributions

f. The team is responsible for adding the appropriate information under each of the sub-headings listed above. Divide the work evenly. *At a minimum*, include the following information:

Contact Information: Include contact information for the PTO President, PTO Vice President, PTO Treasurer, PTO Secretary, New Family Chair, Volunteer Coordinator, Auction Co-Chair, another Auction Co-Chair, Father Daughter Dance Chair, Mother Son Breakfast Chair, Walk-A-Thon Chair, and Back to School Picnic Chair.

PTO Meeting Information: Include information on when and where the PTO meeting takes place each month, how long the meeting takes, and any other necessary information.

Getting Started Volunteering: Include easy ways for a parent to volunteer, such as lunch room duty, recess monitors, and library volunteer.

Upcoming PTO Events: Include the following for each of the PTO events (Back to School Picnic, Father Daughter Dance, President's Day Walk-A-Thon, Mother Son Breakfast, Auction).

When:
Where:
Information:
Volunteers:

g. List each team member's first and last name under the Contributions heading. Include a summary of their planned contributions in this section. Include any additional information required by your instructor.
h. Enter a main heading (not a header) at the top of the document. Apply the Title style to the heading.
i. Format the document appropriately. Create a new style for the sub-headings.
j. Use lists appropriately.
k. Insert a footer, include the first and last name of the team members in the footer, and then format the footer appropriately.
l. Apply an appropriate theme. Use color appropriately.
m. Use at least two fonts and two different font sizes. Use bold and italic.
n. Make any necessary additions.
o. Proofread the document.
p. Once the assignment is complete, share the documents with your instructor or turn in as your instructor directs. Make sure that the instructor has permission to edit the contents of the folder.

Perform 4: How Others Perform

Student data file needed:

w01pf4Garden.docx

You will save your file as:

Arbor Day Business Letter

Sales & Marketing

You are the manager of the Smarty Plants Nursery in Lebanon, Texas. With Arbor Day approaching, the nursery is planning a promotion of historical plants and trees. Perfect for school field trips or history lovers, the plants are representative of various eras of American history.

You will finalize a cover letter, originally created by your assistant, informing the Ebersold Botanical Garden of the program. Working from a draft, you will make sure the paragraphs flow well and that the document is formatted using the block style. In addition, you will format paragraphs and develop appropriate styles. Your goal is to produce an attractive, well-formatted document that is informative, readable, and error free.

a. Navigate to the location of your student data files, open **w01pf4Garden**, and then save the document as w01pf4Garden_LastFirst, using your last and first name. The letter is from a local plant nursery, introducing a new program that offers seedlings from historical plants.

b. Edit the document so that it is in block style. Study the various parts of the letter (recipient address, date, return address, salutation, etc.), and then make any adjustments you find necessary.

c. Select an attractive font type and size for the document.

d. Create a new style for the paragraphs in the body of the letter using an appropriate paragraph spacing. Apply the style to all body paragraphs with the exception of the numbered items.

e. The paragraphs are not in logical order. Rearrange them so they flow well.

f. Check the spelling. If you are not certain of whether a word is misspelled, you need to look it up online or in a dictionary.

g. Because the items listed in the numbered list are not sequential items, numbers are not the best choice. Use bullets and indentation of your choice, instead.

h. Make sure the document fits on one page. If it extends over two, adjust the margins, spacing, and/or font size to reduce it.

i. Include a footer with the file name field, center-aligned.

j. Make any other improvements you think necessary. Save the document, exit Word, and then submit your file as directed by your instructor.

Microsoft Office Word 2013

Module 2

Impressing with Sophisticated Documents

WORKSHOP 3 | INCLUDE TABLES AND OBJECTS

OBJECTIVES

1. Use WordArt p. 278
2. Create SmartArt p. 286
3. Insert a text box p. 290
4. Insert graphics p. 292
5. Set tabs p. 297
6. Create a table p. 300
7. Work with page breaks p. 309
8. Work with sections p. 310
9. Insert text from another document p. 311

Prepare Case

Turquoise Oasis Spa Services Publication

Sales & Marketing

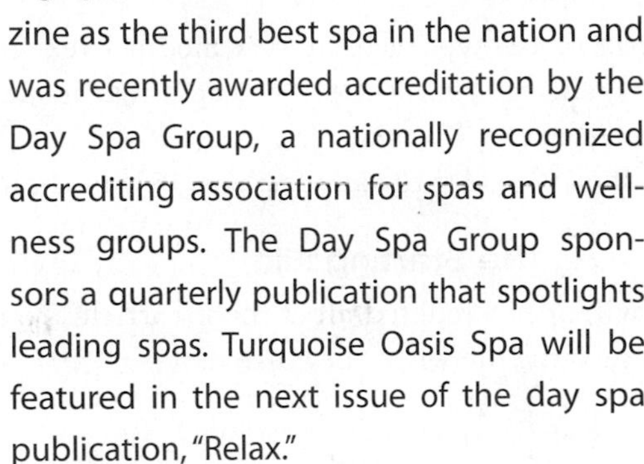

The Turquoise Oasis Spa has been recognized as one of the leading spas in the nation. It was rated by "Traveler's Choice" magazine as the third best spa in the nation and was recently awarded accreditation by the Day Spa Group, a nationally recognized accrediting association for spas and wellness groups. The Day Spa Group sponsors a quarterly publication that spotlights leading spas. Turquoise Oasis Spa will be featured in the next issue of the day spa publication, "Relax."

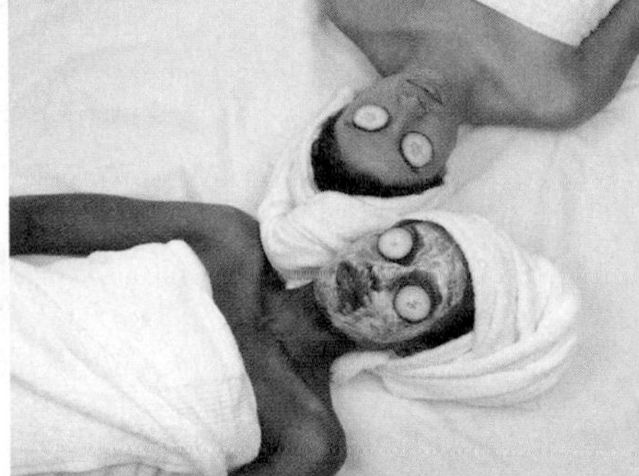

Courtesy of www.Shutterstock.com

You are responsible for collecting information and preparing the article. You want to include information on spa benefits and spa packages, highlighting the spa's unique location, facilities, and treatments. Using Word to create the document, you will include text, graphics, WordArt, and SmartArt. In the process, you will work with tabs, tables, and text from other documents.

REAL WORLD SUCCESS

"I teach first grade and use Word daily to create center activities that tie in with the concepts we're learning—worksheets to help them practice our new skills, and mini-assessments to check mastery of concepts. I'm able to easily make them fun and appealing with Clip Art, WordArt, and SmartArt so they take on more of a gamelike look, making the students more willing and excited to complete them."

- Amanda, elementary teacher and recent graduate

Student data files needed for this workshop:

 w02ws03Relax.docx

 w02ws03SpaCover.docx

 w02ws03Service.jpg

You will save your file as:

 w02ws03Relax_LastFirst.docx

Including Objects in a Document

It is important to create documents that effectively communicate your message. One approach is to use a combination of text and pictures, or graphical images. Decorative headings and graphics, for example, can add spark, drawing attention to the topic. A shaded box with text can emphasize or restate an item of interest. Charts and tables can add organization to a document, summarizing and diagramming data. All of these "objects" enhance a document if used in the right context. An **object** is an item that you can work with independently of the surrounding text. You can insert an object, resize it, format it, and even delete it without affecting document text. Word objects include pictures, clip art, WordArt, text boxes, SmartArt, charts, and screenshots. The challenge is to include objects in moderation, always keeping a document's main purpose in mind. In this section you will learn to insert and modify objects in a Word document.

Use WordArt

WordArt is a Word feature that modifies text to include shadows, outlines, colors, gradients, and 3-D effects. It also shapes text in waves, curves, and angles. You can format existing text as WordArt, or you can insert new WordArt text into a document. You can also drag WordArt to various places within the document.

Opening the Starting File

You will open a rough draft of the spa article. You will display nonprinting characters and then save the file with a new name.

W03.00

To Open the Starting File

a. Start **Word**, click **Open Other Documents** in the left pane, and then double-click **Computer**. Navigate through the folder structure to the location of your student data files, and then double-click **w02ws03Relax**. A rough draft of the article opens.

b. If necessary, on the HOME tab, in the **Paragraph** group, click **Show/Hide** ¶ to display nonprinting characters. If the ruler is not displayed, click the **VIEW** tab, in the **Show** group, click the **Ruler** check box.

c. Click the **FILE** tab, click **Save As**, and then double-click **Computer**. In the **Save As** dialog box, navigate to the location where you are saving your project files, and then change the file name to w02ws03Relax_LastFirst, using your first and last name. Click **Save**.

Creating and Selecting a WordArt Object

The Insert tab includes an Insert WordArt command that produces a gallery of WordArt styles from which you can choose. When an object is first created, a dashed border will appear around the object. Similarly, a dashed border also appears when you click in the object to select it. A dashed border indicates the text is selected—ready for you to enter text, delete text, or format portions of the text. Click the dashed border to change it to a solid border. A solid border indicates the entire WordArt object is selected and that any changes will now be applied to the entire object. Click outside the selected object to deselect it. When an object is "selected," with either a dashed or solid border, the Ribbon displays **contextual tabs**—specialized tabs containing commands related to that object. When you deselect the object the contextual tabs disappear. For example, when you select a WordArt object, Word displays the Drawing Tools contextual tab with the Format tab. Other selected objects, such as charts or SmartArt, cause other contextual tabs to be displayed, with commands related to the specific object.

You are ready to begin work on your article. Scroll through the article. You will notice the article contains a WordArt object at the bottom of the document. You will create a new WordArt object at the top of the article, and then modify the object at the bottom of the article.

MyITLab®
Workshop 3 Training

W03.01

To Create and Select WordArt

SIDE NOTE
Triple-Click
Remember, when you triple-click in a paragraph, you select all the text, including the ending paragraph mark.

a. Triple-click in the first line of the document, **Turquoise Oasis Spa**, to select the entire paragraph. Click the **INSERT** tab, and then in the Text group, click **Insert WordArt**.

The WordArt gallery presents several styles to choose from. If you position the pointer over a style, a ScreenTip displays the style name.

b. In the fourth column and third row, click **Fill - White, Outline - Accent 2, Hard Shadow - Accent 2**. The selected text now appears as a WordArt object. You will fix the spacing of the surrounding text later in the workshop.

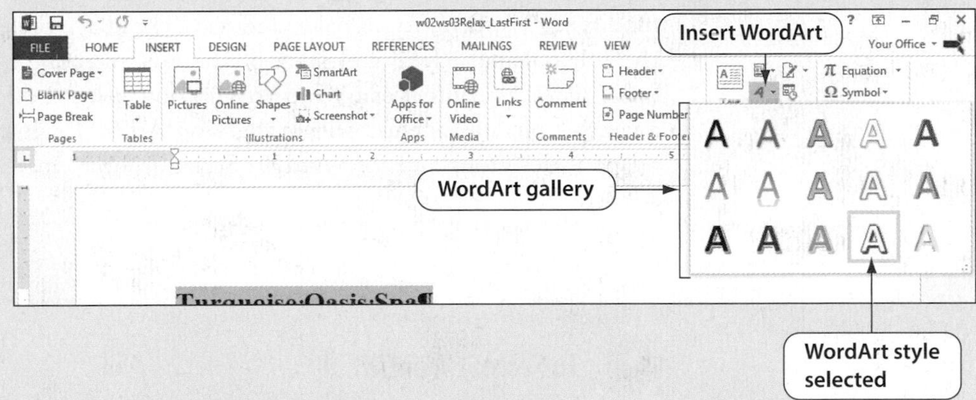

Figure 1 WordArt gallery

c. Click outside of the WordArt object to deselect it and to see the result.

SIDE NOTE
Solid Border on WordArt
A solid border indicates the entire object is selected. A format change will now affect all the text within the object.

d. Press Ctrl+End to position the insertion point at the end of the document. Notice the WordArt object at the bottom of the document with the text, **A passion for helping people relax**. Click anywhere in the **WordArt** object to select it. A dashed border appears around the WordArt object. Position the pointer on the **dashed border** until it changes to a four-headed arrow, and then click the **dashed border**. The border changes to a solid line, indicating the entire WordArt object is selected.

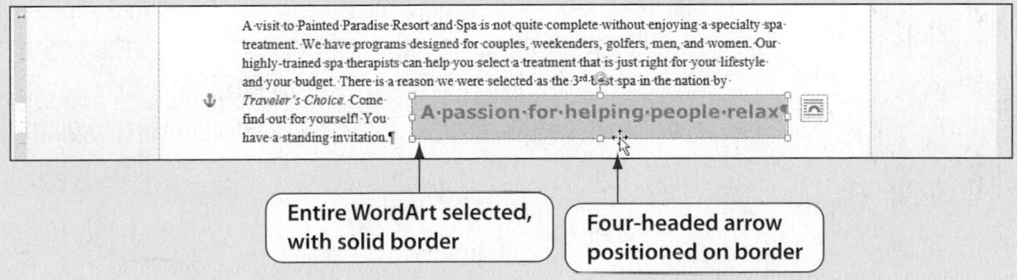

Figure 2 WordArt with solid border

e. Click the **HOME** tab, and then in the Font group, click the **Font Color** arrow, and then, under Theme Colors, in the second column and first row, select **Black, Text 1**.

Troubleshooting

If the formatting was applied to a portion of the text, the "entire" WordArt was not selected. On the Quick Access Toolbar, click Undo. Click the dashed border, changing it to a solid line, and then reapply the change.

SIDE NOTE

Three Ways to Select a Word

Drag to select all the characters in the word, double-click the word, or simply click to place the insertion point in the word.

f. In the WordArt, select the word **relax**, and then in the Font group, click **Underline** [U ▾]. Notice the dashed border when a portion of the WordArt is selected.

g. Click outside of the WordArt object to deselect it and to see the result, and then click **Save** [💾] on the Quick Access Toolbar.

Formatting a WordArt Object

The Format tab that is shown when a WordArt object is selected includes options for modifying WordArt styles, color, and text. The Shape Styles group enables you to change the fill, outline, effect, and style of the box surrounding the WordArt selection. To enhance the actual text of a WordArt selection, select a different WordArt style, or select a text fill, outline, or effect within the WordArt Styles group. You will use options in the Shape Styles group and the WordArt Styles group to modify the WordArt objects in the spa article.

W03.02

To Format WordArt

SIDE NOTE

Selecting an Object When Using Shape Styles

Because Shape Styles automatically affect the entire shape, you can either select the object with a dashed border or with a solid border.

a. Press [Ctrl]+[Home] to position the insertion point at the top of the document, and then click in the **Turquoise Oasis Spa** WordArt object to select it.

b. Click the **FORMAT** tab, in the Shapes Styles group, click **More** [▾], and then place the pointer over any style to reveal the ScreenTip. Live Preview shows the effect of each potential selection.

c. In the third column and the second row, click **Colored Fill - Red, Accent 2**.

Troubleshooting

If you do not see a FORMAT tab under DRAWING TOOLS, the WordArt is not selected. Click anywhere in the WordArt to select it and to display the FORMAT tab.

d. With the WordArt object still selected, in the Shape Styles group, click **Shape Effects**. Point to **Bevel**, and then under Bevel, in the first column and second row, click **Angle**.

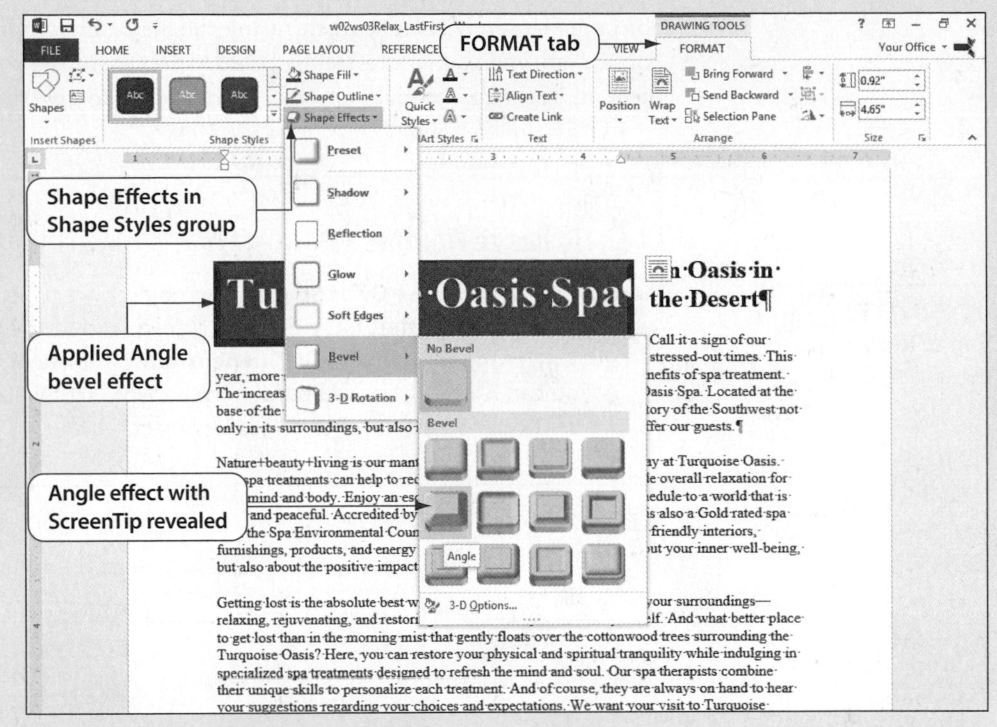

Figure 3 Shape effects

e. In the WordArt Styles group, click **Text Effects**, and then point to **Transform**.
A gallery of transform effects is displayed. As you move the pointer over each effect, you see a preview of the effect on the selected WordArt object.

f. Under **Warp**, in the first column and second row, click **Chevron Up**. The text slants upward and then down in a chevron effect.

g. Drag the **pink square**, located near the top-left border of the WordArt object, up slightly to reduce the chevron effect. You can drag the pink square up or down to reduce or increase the transform effect.

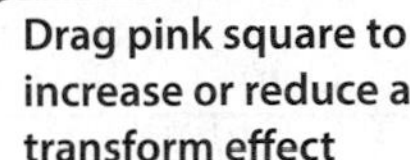

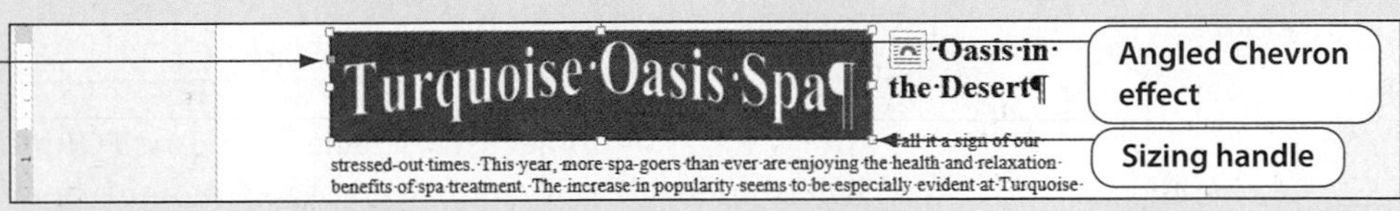

Figure 4 Modify a text effect

h. Click outside the WordArt object to see the result. **Save** the document.

Resizing a WordArt Object

When an object is selected, small boxes will appear on the dashed or solid border surrounding the object. These boxes are called **sizing handles**. Sizing handles are located in the center and corners of the border surrounding an object and can be used to resize an object. To resize an object, simply drag a sizing handle to increase or decrease the size of the object. If you drag a corner handle, both sides of the object change size simultaneously. For more precise sizing, adjust the height and width selections in the Size group on the Format tab. You can also resize a WordArt object by changing the font size. Word will resize the object, making it larger or smaller to accommodate the new font size.

The WordArt objects in the article are not sized correctly. You will resize the WordArt object at the top of the document using the Shape Height and Shape Width boxes on the Format tab, and you will resize the WordArt object at the bottom of the page by adjusting the font. You will also make a format modification to give the WordArt a little more spark.

SIDE NOTE

Drag to Resize

You can also resize an object by dragging a sizing handle. For more precise sizing adjust the height and width in the Size group.

SIDE NOTE

Chevron Effect Disappears

As you edit the WordArt, the text effect will temporarily disappear. When you click outside the object, the effect will return.

W03.03

To Resize WordArt

a. Click in the **Turquoise Oasis Spa** WordArt object once to select it. On the FORMAT tab, in the Size group, click the **Shape Height** down arrow once to change the height to **0.8"**. Similarly, change the value in the **Shape Width** box to **6.3"**.

You can leave the dashed border on the WordArt for sizing since resizing an object automatically affects the entire WordArt object.

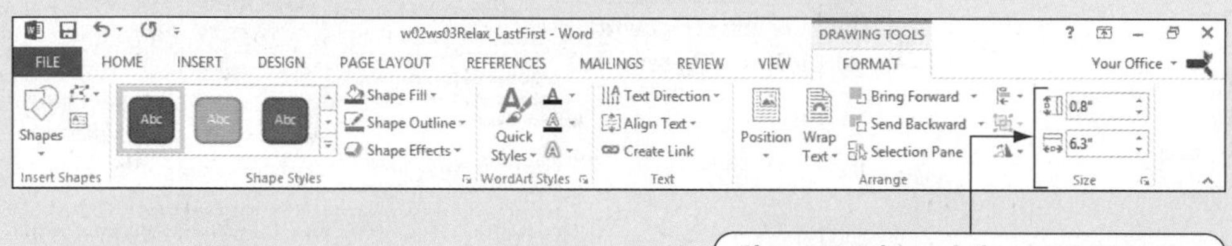

Figure 5 Resizing WordArt

b. Click outside of the WordArt object to deselect it. Press Ctrl+End to position the insertion point at the end of the document, and then click in the WordArt object containing the text, **A passion for helping people relax**, to select it.

c. If necessary, click the **dashed border** of the WordArt to select the entire WordArt and to display a solid border. Click the **HOME** tab, and then in the Font group, change the font size to **20**.

Troubleshooting

If only a portion of the text changes to a 20-pt font size, you did not select the entire WordArt. Click Undo, and then select the entire WordArt object and reapply the change.

d. With the WordArt object still selected, click the **FORMAT** tab, and then in the Shape Styles group, click **Shape Fill**. Point to **Gradient**, and then under Variations, in the second column and first row, select **Linear Down**. Click outside of the WordArt object to deselect it.

e. **Save** the document.

QUICK REFERENCE | **Dashed Borders vs. Solid Borders**

1. A solid border around an object indicates the entire object is selected. You can apply formats related to the entire object at this time—centering the object, formatting all the text in the object, and so on.
2. A dashed border around an object indicates that the text, or a portion of the text, is selected. You can add text, delete text, or format the selected text.

MODULE 2

Repositioning a WordArt Object Using Alignment Guides and Live Layout

To move a WordArt object, select the object, position the pointer on a border of the object to change the pointer to a four-headed arrow, and then drag the object to a new location. **Alignment guides** are a new feature in Word 2013. When moving an object to the top, middle, or bottom of a document, or to the top of a paragraph, Word automatically displays green alignment guides to help you place the object in the exact location. The guides disappear when the object is released or when the guides are not needed anymore.

When dragging an object, the **Live Layout** feature, also new to Word 2013, will reflow the text around the object in real time so you can see the result before actually placing the object. The way text wraps around the WordArt is determined by the object's **text wrap** setting. With a WordArt object selected, you can click the Format tab and then click Wrap Text in the Arrange group to determine the current text wrap setting or to change its setting. Text Wrap options are shown in the Quick Reference table below. The Layout Options button that appears to the top right of a selected object is also new to Word 2013 and enables you to quickly and easily select a text wrap setting.

QUICK REFERENCE | **Text Wrap Options**

The following text wrap options are available on the Format tab or by using the new Layout Options button.

Text Wrap Option	Effect
In Line with Text	A graphic or other object that is positioned directly in the text of a document at the insertion point and responds as another character in the paragraph. This is the default setting when a picture is inserted into a document.
Square	Text wraps on all sides of the object, following the border of an invisible square. This is the default setting when existing text is formatted into WordArt.
Tight	Text follows the shape, but does not overlap it. The text adheres closely to the object's shape but is always an equal distance from the edge.
Through	Text follows the shape, filling any open spaces in the object.
Top and Bottom	Text appears above and below the borders of an object.
Behind Text	The object appears behind the text. Unless the fill color exactly matches the text color, both the object and text will be visible.
In Front of Text	The object appears on top of the text, obscuring the text unless there is no shape fill or the fill is set to semitransparent. This is the default setting when a WordArt is created from scratch. Text will not wrap around the object, but rather it will stay behind the object at all times.

In addition, you can position a WordArt object within a document using the Position button, also on the Format tab in the Arrange group. The Position options enable you to place an object in a preset location within a document with Square text wrapping. You can place an object in the top, middle, or bottom of a document—situated at the top, middle, or right side horizontally. As you explore options in the Position gallery, you can see the effect of each option on a selected object.

The WordArt object at the bottom of the document needs to be repositioned. Using the alignment guides and text wrap feature, you will move the WordArt object to a better location.

W03.04

To Reposition WordArt

a. If necessary, press Ctrl+End to position the insertion point at the end of the document. Click in the WordArt object containing the text, **A passion for helping people relax**.

b. Click the **Layout Options** button to the right of the object, and then under **With Text Wrapping**, in the first column and second row, click **Top and Bottom**. Click anywhere in the document to view the result. Text will now appear above and below the WordArt object, and not to its side.

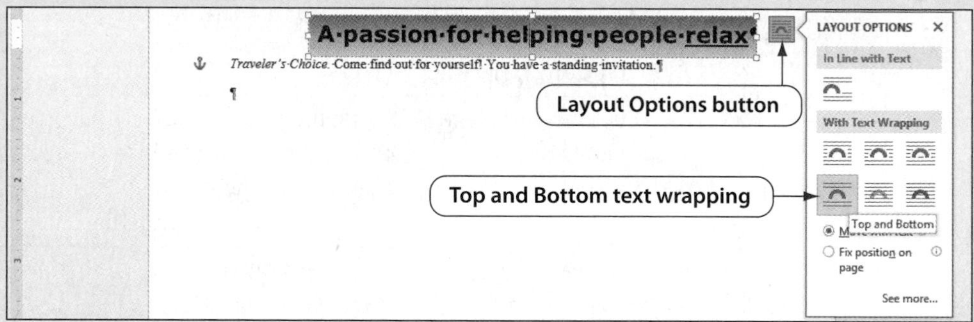

Figure 6 Layout Options button

c. Click in the **WordArt** object again. Place the pointer on a **border** of the WordArt object so that the pointer changes to a four-headed arrow. Drag the **object** just above the text, **Join Us at Turquoise Oasis Spa**, minimizing the white space above and below the object. Continue dragging it slowly to the center of the page. When the green vertical alignment guide appears in the middle of the page, release the object. The object will be center-aligned on the page.

You may need to move the WordArt object up and down slightly in order to find the location with the least amount of white space above and below it.

SIDE NOTE

Center-Align an Object on the Page

Alternatively, on the Format tab, in the Arrange group, click Align Objects, and then select Align Center.

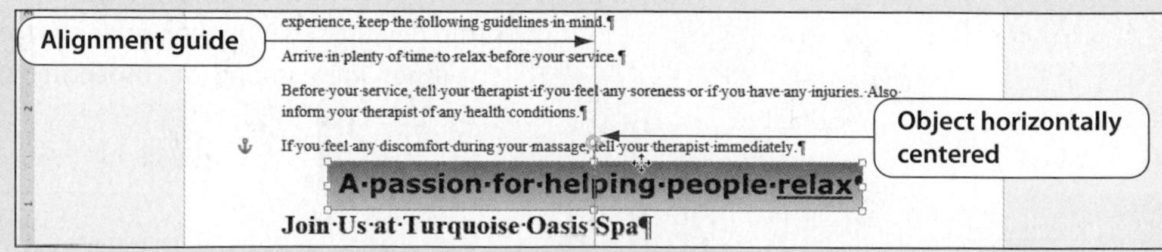

Figure 7 Repositioning WordArt

d. Click outside of the WordArt object to deselect it, and then **save** the document.

MODULE 2

Understanding Anchors

You may have noticed that an image of an **anchor** appears in the left margin when a WordArt object is selected. When text wrapping is set to something other than In Line with Text, the object will be anchored to a paragraph. Once an object is anchored to a paragraph, it stays with the paragraph. If the paragraph is moved to another location of the document, the object moves with it. When you move the WordArt object, the object anchor will move to the closest paragraph, unless the Lock Anchor option is set. You can access the Lock Anchor option when you select More Layout Options from the Wrap Text menu. To associate the object with a different paragraph, drag the anchor. To improve readability, one of the WordArt objects in the article needs a little more white space above and below it. You will use your knowledge of anchors to easily increase the white space.

W03.05

To Anchor a WordArt Object

a. Click in the **WordArt** object containing the text, **A passion for helping people relax**. Notice the anchor displayed to the left of the paragraph just above the WordArt. Point to the **anchor** so that the pointer changes to a four-headed arrow, and then drag the anchor down so that it is positioned to the left of the paragraph **Join Us at Turquoise Oasis Spa**.

New location for anchor

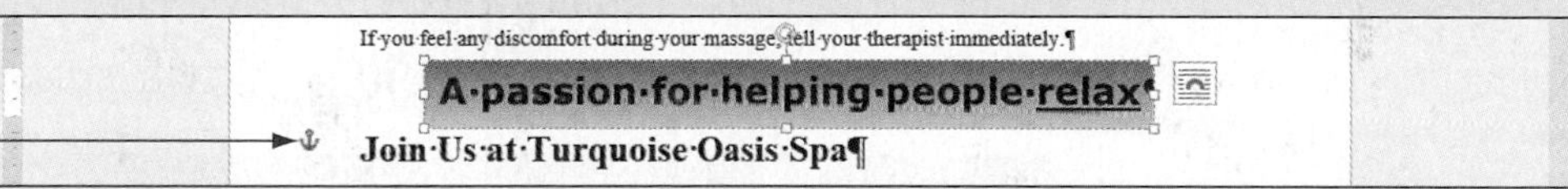

Figure 8 Anchors

b. Click before the word **Join** in the line just below the WordArt, and then press Enter to insert a blank line and open some space above the WordArt.

Because the object is anchored to the paragraph, moving the paragraph moves the WordArt.

c. Click in the **WordArt** object to view the anchor, and then drag the anchor up so that it is positioned to the left of the paragraph beginning with **If you feel any discomfort**.

d. Click before the word **Join** in the line just below the WordArt, and then press Enter to insert a blank line below the WordArt.

e. Since the object is now anchored to the above paragraph, moving this paragraph does not move the WordArt.

f. **Save** the document.

REAL WORLD ADVICE Repeating Text on Every Page of a Document

Have you ever wanted to create a header outside of the header area, or a footer outside of the footer area? For example, suppose you needed text to repeat on every page of your document in the right margin area. Insert a header or footer, and then create a text box in the header area. Drag the text box into the margin area. It is that simple. The text box will now appear on every page of the document. Since it is anchored in the header, changing text or spacing in the document will not affect the text box.

Create SmartArt

SmartArt is a visual representation used to communicate processes, concepts, or ideas that would otherwise require a great deal of text to describe. Using SmartArt, you can create diagrams such as organization charts, process flows, relationship charts, cycle diagrams, and step-by-step processes. Word 2013 includes over 200 SmartArt diagrams in nine categories. Click SmartArt in the Illustrations group of the Insert tab to select from the SmartArt categories, including one that enables you to insert your own pictures within SmartArt shapes. Once created, you can format the entire SmartArt or its individual shapes. You can include your own text in SmartArt shapes, and you can format SmartArt with color, special effects, and font selections. When a SmartArt diagram is selected, the Ribbon displays the SmartArt Tools contextual tab with the Design and Format tabs.

Identifying Types of SmartArt

Using SmartArt saves a great deal of time that would otherwise be spent describing a process or even designing a chart yourself. The built-in SmartArt diagrams enable you to quickly portray a situation or process. You can select from eight categories of SmartArt, as described in the following Quick Reference. When you select a SmartArt, consider the main points in the process or concept and the relationship between each main point. Choose the design that best describes your concept, and then create one shape per main point. You will create a two-shaped cycle SmartArt for the spa article, representing the mind and body in a continuous cycle.

QUICK REFERENCE | **Types of SmartArt**

The nine categories of SmartArt are listed below.

1. List – Nonsequential information
2. Process – Steps in a process or timeline
3. Cycle – A continual process
4. Hierarchy – Top-down relationship, or organization chart
5. Relationship – Connections
6. Matrix – How parts relate to a whole
7. Pyramid – Proportional relationship, with the smallest part on top, or bottom
8. Picture – Arrangements of pictures in a relationship
9. Office.com – Additional layouts available from Office.com

W03.06

To Create SmartArt and Add Text

SIDE NOTE
ScreenTip
Point to the different SmartArt designs to display a ScreenTip containing its name.

a. Scroll to the top of the document. Click to place the insertion point at the end of the third body paragraph, immediately after **in a very long while.** Press Enter. Click the **INSERT** tab, and then in the Illustrations group, click **SmartArt**. The Choose a SmartArt Graphic dialog box appears. Select **Cycle** from the list of categories to the left, select **Nondirectional Cycle**, and then click **OK**.

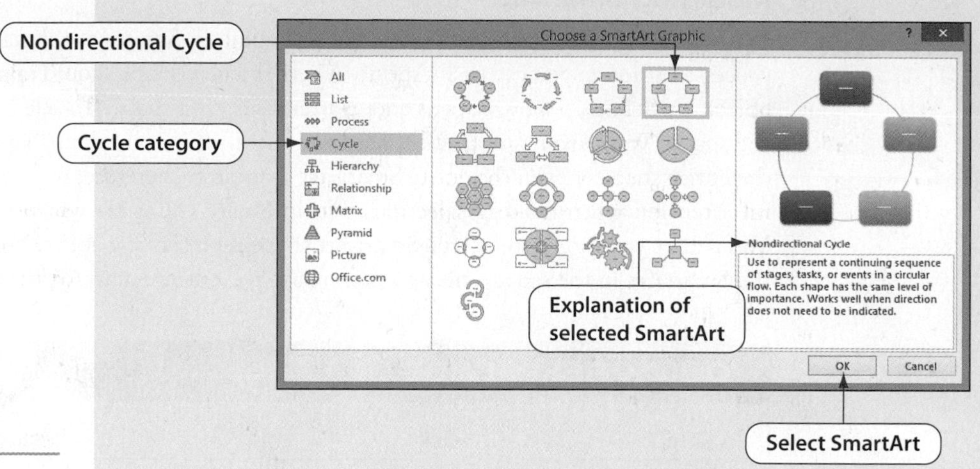

Figure 9 Inserting SmartArt

> **SIDE NOTE**
> **SmartArt Text Pane**
> The SmartArt Text pane simplifies the task of typing text in SmartArt shapes. Click or use the arrow keys to move from bullet to bullet.

b. If necessary, scroll to view the SmartArt. If you do not see a SmartArt Text pane, click the **small rectangular box containing a left arrow** on the left border of the SmartArt object. With the insertion point next to the first bullet, type Mind. Do not press Enter. Click beside the second **bullet**, and then type Body.

Alternatively, to enter text in a shape, click in the shape and type.

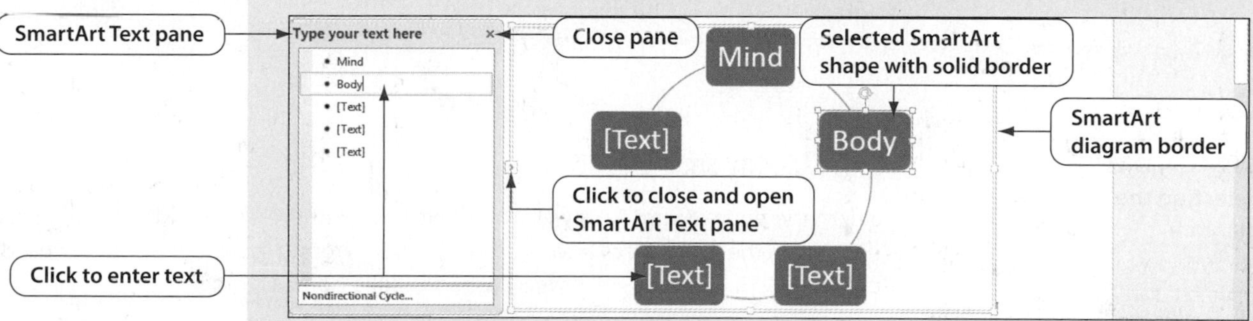

Figure 10 SmartArt Text pane

> **SIDE NOTE**
> **Delete the Entire SmartArt Diagram**
> Click the border of the SmartArt diagram to select the entire SmartArt, and then press Delete.

c. Close × the SmartArt Text pane. Click in one of the three remaining **SmartArt** shapes that are without text. If necessary, click the **dashed line** on the shape to change the border to a solid line. With the shape selected, press Delete to delete the shape, and then press Delete two more times to delete the two remaining shapes without text. Click outside the SmartArt graphic to deselect it.

> **Troubleshooting**
> If you have more than three remaining shapes without text, you pressed Enter when typing the bulleted list of data. Remove any extra shapes as discussed in Step c.

d. **Save** the document.

Modifying SmartArt

You will often find that you need to add a shape to a SmartArt diagram to better depict a process. Although you can easily specify whether a new shape should appear before or after an object, by default, a new shape is added after a selected shape. To select a shape, click inside the shape. While some tasks affect the text within the individual shapes, other tasks affect the entire shape or even the entire SmartArt diagram. Therefore, it is important to pay careful attention when making selections within SmartArt, as shown in the Quick Reference. You realize you forgot to insert a SmartArt shape representing spirit. You will add a shape to the SmartArt in the spa article, and then resize the entire SmartArt diagram.

QUICK REFERENCE | **How to Select SmartArt**

To Select	Click	Resulting Border
The text within a shape	Text within a shape	Dashed border on shape
A shape	White space within a shape, next to its text	Solid border on shape
A shape	The dashed border of a shape	Solid border on shape
The entire SmartArt diagram	The white space outside of a shape, but within the SmartArt diagram	One border appears around entire SmartArt
The entire SmartArt diagram	The outside border of the SmartArt diagram	One border appears around entire SmartArt

SIDE NOTE
Selecting the SmartArt diagram
Alternatively, click the SmartArt diagram border to select the entire SmartArt..

To Modify SmartArt

a. Select the entire **SmartArt** by clicking next to one of the shapes within the SmartArt diagram in the white space area. A box will appear around the entire SmartArt and none of the individual shapes will have a dashed or solid border.

> **Troubleshooting**
> If a dashed or solid border is displayed around any of the individual shapes, then the individual shape has been selected as opposed to the entire SmartArt. If that is the case, click in the white space just outside the shape to select the entire SmartArt.

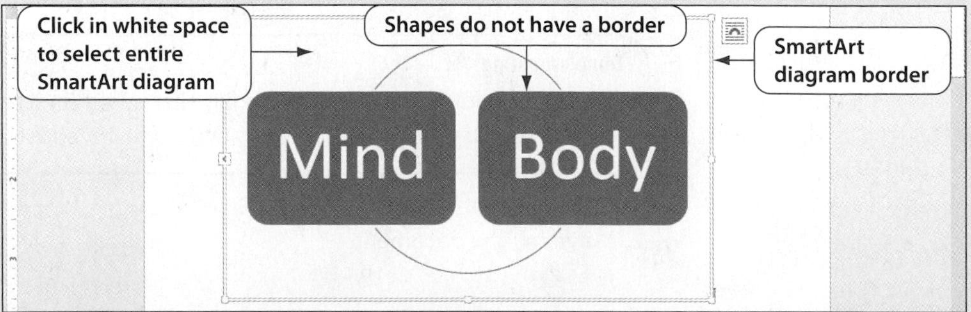

Figure 11 Selecting the entire SmartArt diagram

b. Under SMARTART TOOLS, on the DESIGN tab, in the Create Graphic group, click **Add Shape**, and then type Spirit. The font size adjusts in the shape to accommodate the new text.

Troubleshooting

If you do not see the Add Shape command you may have clicked the wrong DESIGN tab. Select the diagram, and then click the DESIGN tab under SMARTART TOOLS.

c. Because an individual shape is selected, click in the white space just outside the shape to select the entire **SmartArt diagram**. Click the **FORMAT** tab, and then in the Size group, click in the **Shape Height** box, and then type 2.5. Press Enter.

Troubleshooting

If only one shape was resized then the entire SmartArt diagram was not selected, but rather an individual shape, indicated by a dashed border around the shape. On the Quick Access Toolbar, click Undo. Click in the white space to the left or right of the individual shape to select the entire SmartArt, and then resize the diagram.

d. If necessary, scroll to view the SmartArt diagram. Click outside the SmartArt diagram to deselect it, and then **save** the document.

Formatting SmartArt

The Design tab and Format tab, found on the SmartArt Tools contextual tab, provide plenty of options for formatting SmartArt. After creating a diagram, you might want to explore other styles and color selections. The Design tab—typically used to format the entire SmartArt object—provides a SmartArt Styles gallery and a Layouts gallery, with options for enhancing and modifying a diagram. The Format tab contains many of the commands used to format the individual shapes of a diagram. You will format the layout and style of the SmartArt diagram in the spa article. You will then add a new color style to the diagram.

W03.08

To Format SmartArt

a. Select the entire **SmartArt diagram**. Under SMARTART TOOLS, click the **DESIGN** tab, and then in the Layouts group, click **More**. Point to any **selection** in the Layouts gallery and view the effect on the selected SmartArt. In the first column and first row, select **Basic Cycle**.

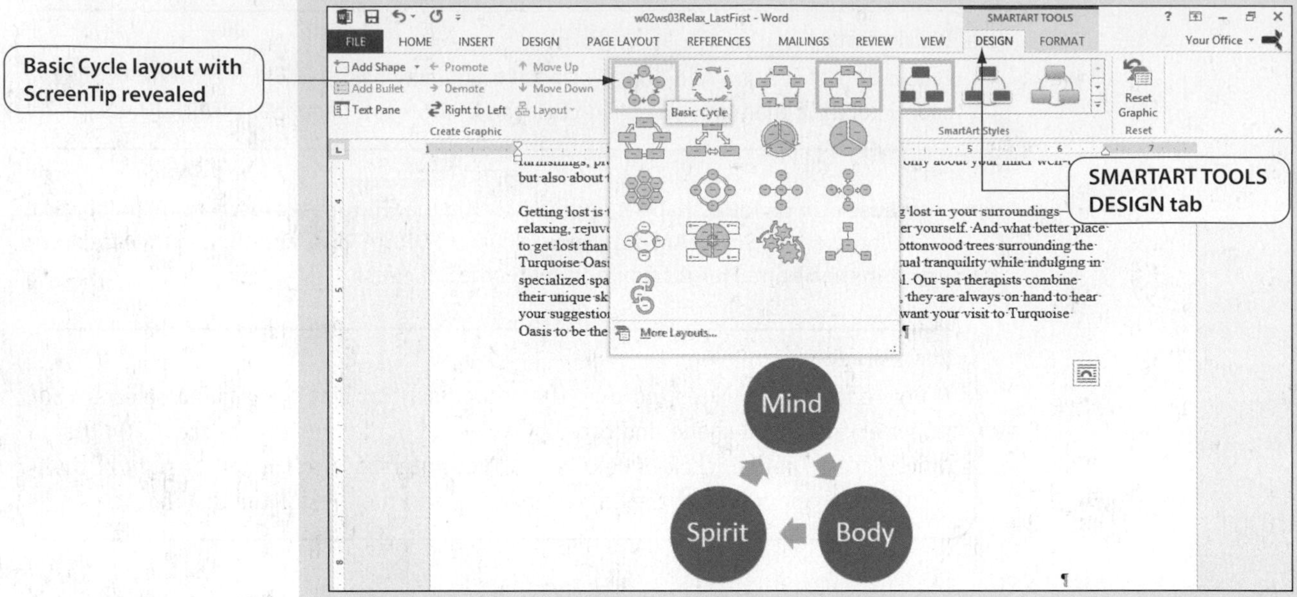

Basic Cycle layout with ScreenTip revealed

SMARTART TOOLS DESIGN tab

Figure 12 Modifying SmartArt

b. With the entire SmartArt still selected, in the SmartArt Styles group, point to any **style** in the SmartArt Styles gallery to view the effect on the SmartArt diagram. Click **More** to explore other style options, and then under 3-D, in the first column and first row, select **Polished**.

c. With the entire SmartArt still selected, in the SmartArt Styles group, click **Change Colors**. Point to any **selection** and view the effect on the SmartArt diagram. Under Accent 2, in the third column, click **Gradient Range - Accent 2**.

d. Click outside the SmartArt diagram to deselect it, and then **save** the document.

SIDE NOTE

Color an Individual Shape

To change the color of an individual shape, select the shape, and then on the Format tab, in the Shape Styles group, click Shape Fill.

Insert a Text Box

A **text box** is an object that gives you control of text placement in a document. It is literally a box of text that you can format just as you would any other drawing object. A text box can be placed anywhere on your page, without regard to the margins. It is often used for information that needs to stand out, such as in a margin or in a diagram. A text box can also help you control the layout of your document, as it limits the text to certain areas. For example, projects such as newsletters, business cards, and greeting cards are easily created by using multiple text boxes to position text in specific areas of a document. Once created, you can shade the text box, add a border to it, rotate it, and add special effects, such as shadows or special fills. When a text box in a document is selected, Word displays the Drawing Tools contextual tab with the Format tab.

Creating a Text Box

Word provides a selection of text boxes that you can insert into your document with predefined sizes, shapes, colors, fonts, and placement. Once inserted into a document a text box can be easily modified to suit your needs. You can also insert a text box from "scratch" by using the Draw Text Box option. The pointer will change to a plus sign symbol, and you can click in the document to create a narrow blank text box that you can then format and resize. You can also drag the plus sign pointer—precision select pointer—and draw a blank text box of any size. You will add a text box at the bottom of the spa article to hold the spa address. You will create a text box, add the address into the text box, and then resize the text box.

MODULE 2

W03.09

To Create and Resize a Text Box

a. Press Ctrl+End to move the insertion point to the end of the document. Click the **INSERT** tab, and then in the Text group, click **Text Box**, and then select **Simple Text Box**. A text box is inserted in your document.

b. Click the **HOME** tab, and then in the Styles group, click **No Spacing** to single-space the text.

c. Type **Turquoise Oasis Spa** and press Enter. Type **Painted Paradise Resort and Spa** and press Enter. Type **3356 Hemmingway Circle** and press Enter. Type **Santa Fe, NM 89566** but do not press Enter.

> **Troubleshooting**
> If text appeared in your document and not in the text box, then the text box was not selected. Click Undo to remove the text from the document. Click to place the insertion point in the text box, and then redo Step c.

d. Point to a **border** of the text box so the pointer appears as a four-headed arrow, and then click the **dashed border**. The border is now solid and the entire text box is selected. On the FORMAT tab, in the Size group, click the **Shape Height** up arrow two times to increase the height to **1"**.

e. Click outside the text box to deselect it, and then **save** the document.

Modifying a Text Box

Both the Text box and SmartArt graphics use the same Format tab. It includes options for modifying styles, color, and text. Because you want the address to stand out, you will color and shade the text box in the spa article. You will also vertically align and center-align the text within the text box.

W03.10

To Modify a Text Box

a. Click in the **text box** to select it, and then, if necessary, click the dashed border to select the **entire text box**. On the FORMAT tab, and then in the Shape Styles group, click **More**. Point to a **style** to view the effect on the selected text box. In the third column and second row, select **Colored Fill - Red, Accent 2**.

b. In the Shape Styles group, click **Shape Effects**, and then point to **Shadow**. Under Outer, in the first column and first row, select **Offset Diagonal Bottom Right**. A slight shadow appears to the right and bottom of the shape.

c. In the Text group, click **Align Text**, and then select **Middle**. The text is now vertically centered in the box.

SIDE NOTE
Align the Text Box Horizontally on the Page
On the Format tab, in the Arrange group, click Align Objects, and then select the alignment, Align Center, Align Left, or Align Right.

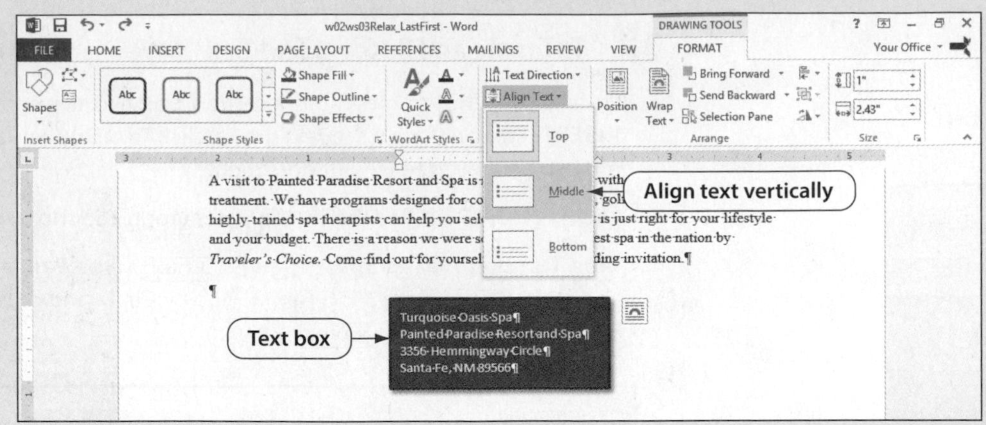

Figure 13 Vertically align text

d. With the entire text box still selected, click the **HOME** tab, and then in the Paragraph group, click **Center** to center the text horizontally within the text box.

e. Click outside the text box to deselect it, and then **save** the document.

CONSIDER THIS | **SmartArt Without Borders**

You can remove the border and fill of all the SmartArt shapes within a SmartArt diagram. When might you want to do this? How does it compare to creating a series of text boxes?

QUICK REFERENCE | **Align a Text Box**

1. To align a text box horizontally or vertically on a page, on the Format tab, in the Arrange group, click Align Objects.
2. To align text horizontally within the text box, on the Home tab, in the Paragraph group, click one of the alignment buttons.
3. To align text vertically within the text box, on the Format tab, in the Text group, click Align Text.

Insert Graphics

Newsletters, business cards, and other specialty documents can be enhanced with the addition of graphical illustrations—pictures and clip art. For example, when creating a family newsletter, you might want to include a personal picture saved on a disk drive, or when creating a flyer for a Fourth of July party, you might include a flag clip art from Office.com. You can then crop, recolor, set the text wrap, or format these graphics with outline styles and various artistic effects. To delete a picture or clip art, simply select the graphic and press Delete. Word 2013 also enables you to insert online videos using a Bing or YouTube search.

Inserting a Picture

A **picture** is a photo, or graphical image, that is saved on a storage device. You can save your photos on a CD or disk drive and then insert a photo into a document. The photo becomes a graphic object that you can manage just as you do other objects—resizing, formatting, and wrapping text as needed. If you locate a picture or graphic image online that you plan to use in a document, you can save the graphic to a CD or disk drive and then insert the image into your document. The Online Pictures command is new to Word 2013. The Online Pictures command, in the Illustrations group of the Insert tab, enables you to insert clip art from Office.com. You can even insert a picture from your SkyDrive, Flickr account, or directly from the Internet, using the Bing search engine. Keep in mind, though, when copying images from the Internet, you must take care to adhere to all copyright laws. When a picture is inserted into a document, Word displays the Picture Tools contextual tab with the Format tab.

Formatting a Picture

When a picture is inserted in a document it is surrounded by a solid border that includes sizing handles—small squares at the corners and centers of each side. To resize the photo, drag a handle. You should always drag a corner handle so the picture is resized proportionally. If you drag a center handle, the picture will be skewed. To ensure that a picture does not get skewed, on the Format tab, click the Layout Dialog Box Launcher in the Size group, and select Lock aspect ratio in order to maintain the picture's size ratio. To move a picture, point to a border—not a handle—so it appears as a four-headed arrow, and then drag to move the picture to a new location.

When a picture is selected, the Format tab is displayed on the Ribbon. The Format tab includes options for changing the picture style, adding a border, adding special effects, cropping the picture, and wrapping text. You can even apply color corrections and add artistic effects. You have a picture saved on your disk drive that you want to include in the spa article. You will insert the picture, change its text wrap setting, and adjust its color.

W03.11

To Insert and Format a Picture

a. Press Ctrl+Home, and then click at the beginning of the third body paragraph immediately before **Getting**.

b. Click the **INSERT** tab, and then in the Illustrations group, click **Pictures**, and then navigate to the location of your student data files. Click **w02ws03Service**, and then click **Insert**.

A picture of a spa service is inserted in the document at the position of the insertion point. The picture is selected, as you can tell by the border surrounding it. The border includes sizing handles.

c. On the FORMAT tab, in the Arrange group, click **Wrap Text**, and then select **Square**. Text wraps around the picture on the right, in a square fashion.

SIDE NOTE

Default Text Wrap on a Graphic

The default text wrap on a graphic is In Line with Text.

SIDE NOTE

Centering a Picture

On the Home tab, click Center to center a picture set to In Line with Text. Use Align Objects on the Format tab to center all other pictures.

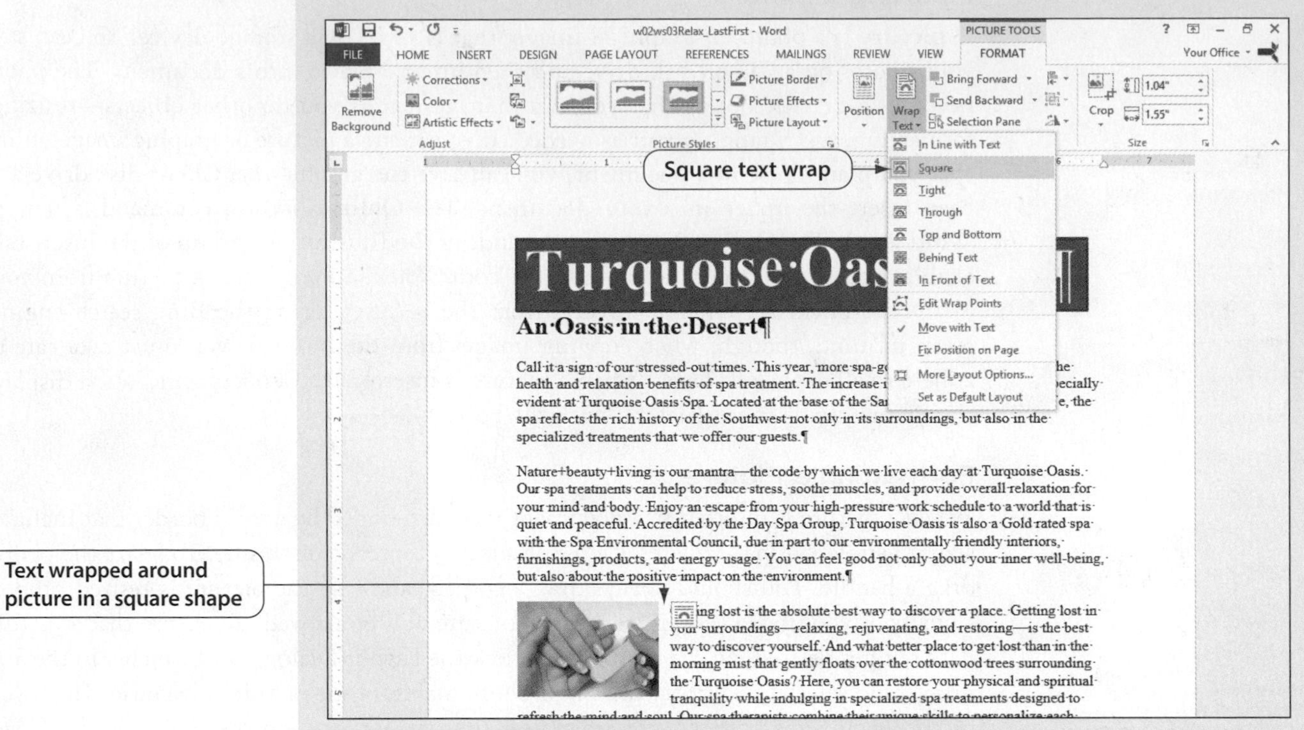

Figure 14 Picture with wrapped text

d. In the Adjust group, click **Color**, and then under Recolor, in the third column and third row, select **Red, Accent color 2 Light**.

e. Click outside the picture to deselect it, and then **save** the document.

REAL WORLD ADVICE Graphics in a Header or Footer

Companies often use logos to develop their company letterhead. Logos, however, can take up valuable space within a document. Insert small logos—or graphics— in a header to create a quick letterhead without using up space in the document.

Inserting Clip Art

Clip art is a graphic illustration that can be inserted into a Word document. Clip art images range from simple cartoonlike illustrations to photographic images. Word provides an extensive collection of clip art for you to select from when developing a document—drawings, audio, video, and photographs. Clip art is inserted as a graphic object that can be resized, recolored, and formatted. You will insert a clip art into the spa article and then resize it.

W03.12

To Insert and Resize Clip Art

a. Under the heading **Specialty Spa Massages**, click to place the insertion point at the beginning of the paragraph starting with **We offer many types of massages**.

b. Click the **INSERT** tab, and then in the Illustrations group, click **Online Pictures**. Click in the **Office.com Clip Art** box, if necessary remove any text, and then type spa woman.

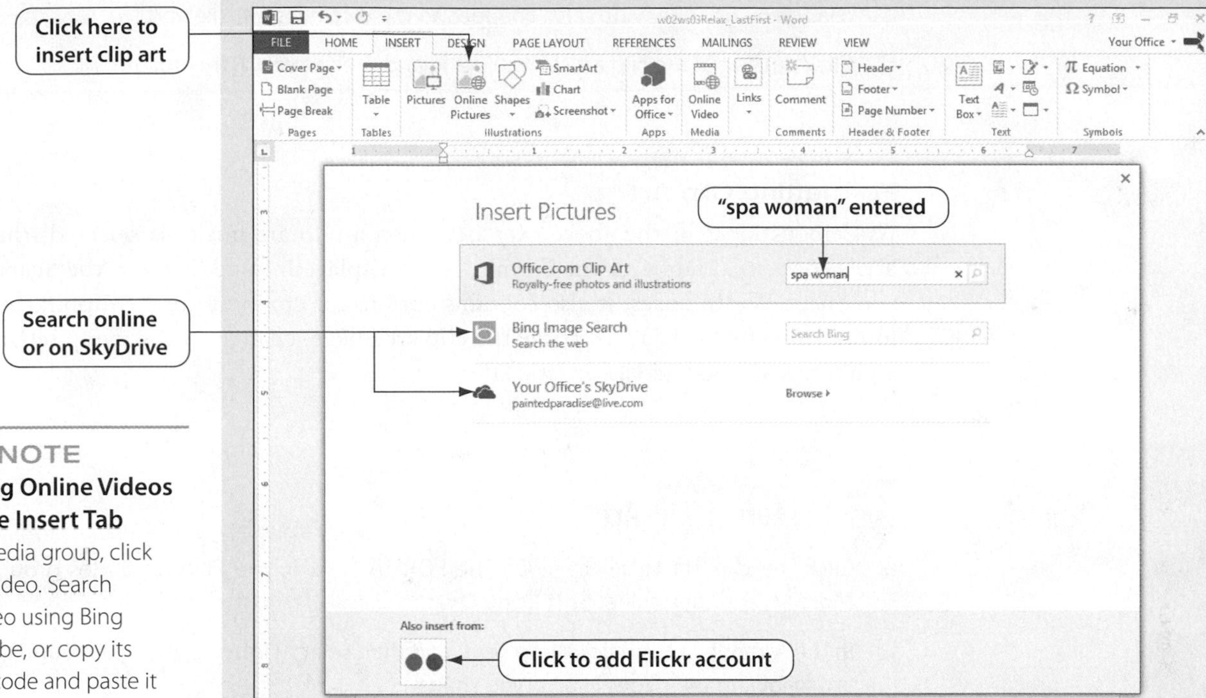

Figure 15 Searching for clip art

c. Press Enter. Click the **clip art** image described as **Woman relaxing with incense** when you point to the image, and then click **Insert**.

If you do not see that image, select a similar image. The clip art is placed in the document. The picture is likely to be too large.

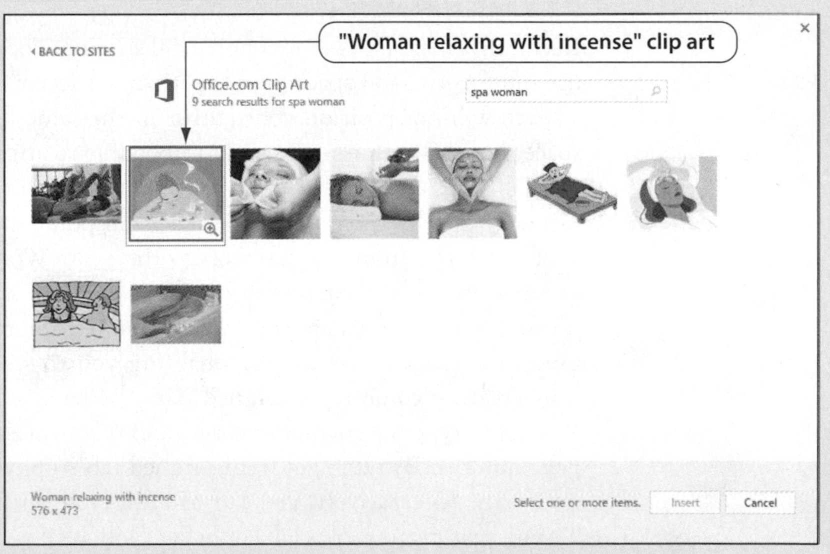

Figure 16 Selecting clip art

d. Point to the **top-right sizing handle** of the picture so the pointer appears as a diagonal two-headed arrow. Watching the horizontal ruler, drag the **corner of the picture** toward the center, reducing the picture size, so the right edge is approximately at the 1.5" mark on the ruler.

SIDE NOTE

Inserting Online Videos from the Insert Tab

In the Media group, click Online Video. Search for a video using Bing or YouTube, or copy its embed code and paste it into the box provided.

SIDE NOTE

Rotating a Clip Art or Picture

Drag the rotation handle that appears at the top center of the selected graphic to rotate it.

e. With the picture still selected, on the FORMAT tab, in the Size group, click in the **Shape Height** box, and then type 1.5, replacing the current height with the new dimension. Press Enter to resize the clip art image. If necessary, scroll to view the picture. As you change height, the width also changes so the picture is not skewed.

f. Click outside of the clip art to deselect it, and then **save** the document.

Formatting Clip Art

As demonstrated in the above exercise, when a clip art image is selected, the Picture Tools contextual tab with the Format tab is displayed. In addition to the Shape Height and Shape Width boxes, it also contains options for cropping, text wrapping, and other formatting effects. You will resize the clip art image, change its text wrap setting, apply a picture style, and add an artistic effect.

W03.13

To Format Clip Art

a. Click the **clip art** to select it. On the FORMAT tab, in the Pictures Styles group, click **More**, and then select **Soft Edge Oval**.

b. In the Arrange group, click **Wrap Text**, and then select **Tight**. Text wraps around the clip art, following the edges in a curved shape.

c. In the Adjust group, click **Color**, and then in the third column and third row, select **Red, Accent color 2 Light**.

d. Click outside of the clip art to deselect it, and then **save** the document.

Working with Tabs and Tables

Recall that most fonts use proportional spacing. For example, the letter "w" will typically use more horizontal space on a line than the letter "i". Thus, typing "wam" followed by a space will not position your cursor in the same location as typing "lit" followed by a space. For this reason, it is nearly impossible to align data in columns using spaces.

Tab stops and tables can be used to help align text and to create columns of data. A **tab stop** is a location where the insertion point will stop when you press Tab. Press Tab to move from one tab stop to the next. Word stores paragraph formatting, such as tab stops, in the paragraph marks at the end of a paragraph. Thus, when you press Enter, the tab stops are copied to the next paragraph. The same tab stops can then be used in sequential paragraphs, enabling you to start or end text in the same location, thus creating columns of aligned data. Perhaps you are preparing a table of contents. You could type the chapter or topic, and then leave a set amount of space before typing a page number. By setting a right-aligned tab stop, you can be sure all page numbers line up evenly. Alternatively, you can define a table with a set number of columns and rows. Typing text in the table cells, or boxes, will keep your rows of data aligned. You can even select a predesigned table style to draw attention to table text.

Although both methods enable you to align text in columns, each has unique features that make it appropriate for various applications. In this section, you will format documents with tabs and you will learn to summarize data in tables.

Set Tabs

Recall that a tab stop is a location where the insertion point will stop when you press Tab. If you do not specify tab stops, the default tab stop is set at each 1/2" on the ruler. If you press Tab once, the insertion point stops 1/2" from the left margin. Press Tab again to stop at 1". Most often, though, you will create your own tab stops, which will temporarily override the default settings. As mentioned earlier, tab stops are applied to the current paragraph and all subsequent paragraphs that you have yet to type from that point forward, until you decide to remove them, or reset them. You can remove the tab stops from a paragraph at any time, or even reset them to new positions.

You will frequently select from five tab types, as shown in Table 1. Tab stops you create will appear on the horizontal ruler. A **left tab** aligns text on the left, while a **right tab** aligns text on the right. A right tab stop is appropriate for a table of contents or menu, where numbers need to be aligned on the right. A **decimal tab** aligns text on a decimal point, such as a columnar list of student grades, where grades might have varying places to the right of the decimal point. A **center tab** aligns text evenly to the left and right of the tab stop. You can add **leaders** to a tab stop so that a row of dots or dashes is displayed before a tab stop, such as on restaurant menus where a line of dots precedes a menu price. Lastly, a **bar tab** inserts a vertical bar at the tab stop, creating a line, or separator, between columns of data.

Marker	Tab name	Description
	Left tab	Aligns the left edge of the text under the left tab
	Center tab	Aligns the middle of the of the text under the tab
	Right tab	Aligns the right edge of the text under the right tab
	Decimal tab	Aligns numbers by the decimal point 123.45 1.2345 1234.5
	Bar tab	Acts as a Divider | Positions a vertical bar under the tab stop

Table 1 Tab stops

Using the Ruler to Set Tabs

In most cases, the easiest way to set a tab stop is to use the ruler. The default tab stop is left, but you can easily select another tab type by clicking the tab button to the left of the horizontal ruler. Click the tab button once to select a center tab stop. Click again to select a right tab stop, and then click again to select a decimal tab stop. After selecting the tab type, simply click the location on the ruler where the tab stop is to be placed. You can move a tab stop by dragging it along the ruler. If you want to delete a tab, drag it off the ruler. Once you create a tab stop, simply press Tab to move the insertion point to that location, and then begin typing.

You decide to align the spa days and hours using tabs. The extra white space will add readability and give it a more professional look.

W03.14

To Set Tabs Using the Ruler

a. Click to place the insertion point before the paragraph mark [¶] that is displayed just beneath the **Spa Hours** heading.

b. If the ruler is not displayed, click the **VIEW** tab, and then in the Show group, click the **Ruler** check box. You will create tab stops. Point to the tab button to the left of the ruler to view the ScreenTip. Verify that a Left Tab is selected. If a Left Tab is not selected, click the tab button until a Left Tab is selected. Point to the **1.5"** mark on the horizontal ruler, and then click to set a left tab stop. Click the **4"** mark to set another left tab stop, and then click the **5"** mark to set a third left tab stop.

Figure 17 Using the ruler to set tabs

c. You realize that you need to adjust the tabs. On the ruler, click the **5"** tab stop, and then drag it down, off the ruler to remove it. Point to the left tab stop at **1.5"**, and then drag it to the **2"** mark.

You have created a 2" left tab stop and a 4" left tab stop. You will enter text at the tab stops in the next set of steps.

Troubleshooting

If you accidentally create extra tabs while trying to move a tab, simply drag the extra tabs off the ruler to remove them.

d. **Save** [💾] the document.

Using the Tabs Dialog Box

It can be difficult to create exact tab stops using a ruler. For example, if you click to place a left tab stop at the 1" mark, you might instead place it at 1.1", or perhaps at 0.9". The Tabs dialog box enables you to create precise tab stops. If you plan to use tab leaders—dots or dashes that precede a tab stop—you must make that selection in the Tabs dialog box. You can also clear tab stops and set a default tab stop measurement. Click the Tabs button in the Paragraph dialog box to open the Tabs dialog box. You will adjust the tab stops in the spa article using the Tabs dialog box.

QUICK REFERENCE	Setting Tabs Using the Tabs Dialog Box

1. On the Home tab, click the Paragraph Dialog Box Launcher.
2. Click Tabs.
3. Type a tab stop position.
4. Select an alignment and leader, if necessary.
5. Click Set.
6. Repeat Steps 3–5, if necessary.
7. Click OK when finished.

W03.15

To Set Tabs Using the Tabs Dialog Box

a. Press Tab, and then type Monday-Friday making sure not to leave a space before or after the dash. Press Tab, and then type 7:00 a.m.-11:00 p.m., making sure not to leave a space before or after the dash. Press Enter.

b. Press Tab, type Saturday and then press Tab. Without leaving a space before or after the dash, type 7:00 a.m.-Midnight and then press Enter. Press Tab, and type Sunday. Press Tab, and type Closed. Do not press Enter.

c. You realize the tab stops need to be adjusted again. Select the **three lines** containing the spa hours, starting with **Monday** and ending with **Closed**. Click the **HOME** tab, and then in the Paragraph group, click the **Paragraph Dialog Box Launcher**, and then click **Tabs** at the bottom of the dialog box.

You will replace the 2" tab stop with a 1" tab stop, and you will specify a dot leader for the space between the days and times. Leaders are attached to the tabs that follow them, so you will adjust the 4" tab stop to include a dot leader.

SIDE NOTE

Open the Tabs Dialog Box

Alternatively, double-click either of the left tabs on the ruler to open the Tabs dialog box.

d. Click in the **Tab stop position** box. If necessary, clear any text, type 1 and then click **Set** to create a 1" left tab stop.

e. In the list under the Tab stop position box, select **2"**. If you did not set the tab stop precisely at 2", you may not see that exact tab stop. In that case, select the tab stop position closest to 2", and then click **Clear**.

f. In the list under the Tab stop position box, select **4"**. If you did not set the tab stop precisely at 4", you may not see that exact tab stop. In that case, select the tab stop position closest to 4", and then in the Leader area, select option **2** (dot leader).

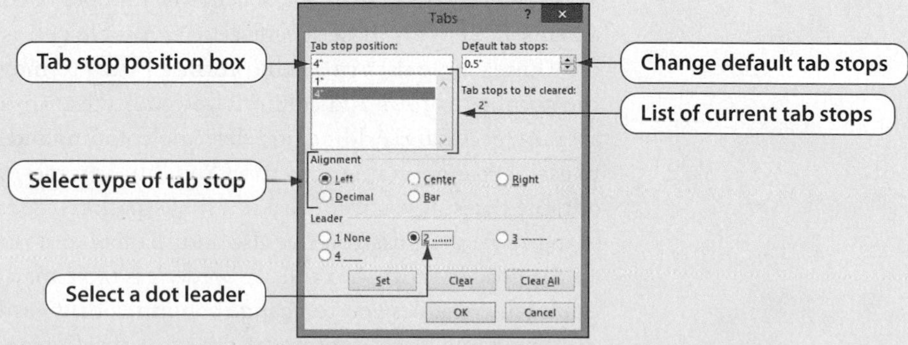

Figure 18 The Tabs dialog box

g. Click **OK**. The tabs are adjusted and the dot leader is displayed.

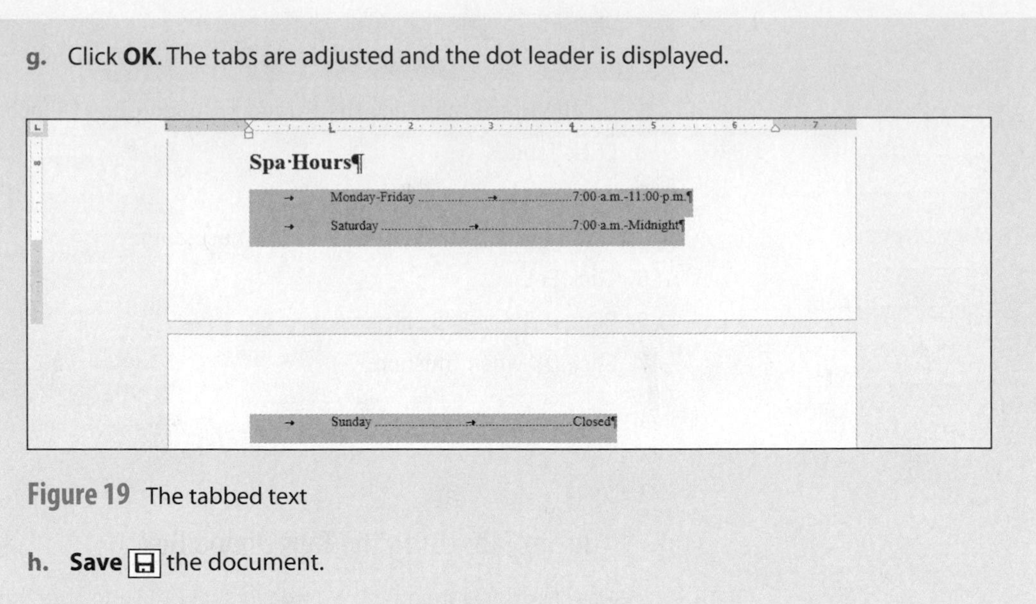

Figure 19 The tabbed text

h. **Save** the document.

Create a Table

A **table** is a grid of columns and rows. A table is often used to summarize data, such as sales totals for various divisions of a company or enrollment data for college classes. A table typically includes headings that identify each column or row that contains data. For example, if you are summarizing sales data for company divisions, the headings in row 1 could be "Division" and "Sales". Data for each division would be displayed in the subsequent rows, as shown in Figure 20. If there are four divisions in the company, the table will include five rows—one header row and four rows of data.

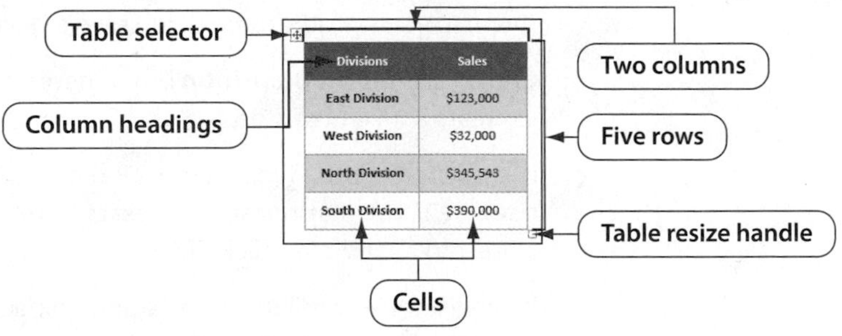

Figure 20 Sample table

When you create a table, you specify the number of columns and rows. Word then creates a blank table with those specifications. A table **cell** is the intersection of a column and a row. Enter table data in a cell, pressing Tab to move from one cell to the next. Often, the number or rows and columns you indicate turns out to be more or less than what is actually necessary. Adding and deleting columns and rows is a simple task, enabling you to easily change a table structure. You can even merge cells to accommodate long entries or table titles. If you want to add a little spark to the table, choose from a gallery of preexisting table designs. You can also add shading and modify borders. You can even remove all the borders from the table. A borderless table may appear to be similar to tabbed data, but a table enables you to change column widths easily and wrap text within a cell.

The Table Tools contextual tab with the Design tab and Layout tab enable you to change the table layout and design, insert rows and columns, merge cells, sort table data, create sums and averages, change styles, and modify table properties. Before formatting table text, however, you must first select it, as shown in the Quick Reference.

QUICK REFERENCE	Selecting Text in a Table

1. **Select all text in a cell—**Position the pointer just inside the left edge of the cell until the pointer becomes a slanted black arrow and click.
2. **Select a row—**Position the pointer in the left margin to the left of the row until the pointer becomes a white arrow, and then click.
3. **Select a column—**Position the pointer on the top border of the column until the pointer becomes a downward black arrow, and then click.
4. **Select the entire table—**Click the table selector at the top-left corner of the table.

Entering Data in a Table

When you insert a table, Word creates an empty grid of columns and rows. You can enter data in a cell by clicking in the cell and typing. To move to another cell, simply click in the cell; you can also press Tab or any of the directional arrows to move to an adjacent cell. Most often, you will press Tab to continue completing the table. As you type in a cell, Word automatically wraps text that reaches the end of the cell, increasing the cell's height—along with all other cells in the row—to accommodate the entry. If you want to add another line within a cell, you can press Enter to add a blank paragraph.

Information on the specialty spa packages needs to be added to the article. You will present the information in a 3x4 table. The table will draw attention to the data, while maintaining readability.

W03.16

To Create a Table

a. Click to place the insertion point at the end of the **first paragraph** under the heading **Specialty Spa Packages**, after the text **fancy!**, and then press Enter. Click the **INSERT** tab, and then in the Tables group, click **Table**. A table grid is presented for you to specify the number of columns and rows to include in the table.

b. As you point to the different squares in the grid, a Live Preview of the table is displayed in the document. Click to select a table with three columns and four rows, a **3x4** Table (column 3, row 4).

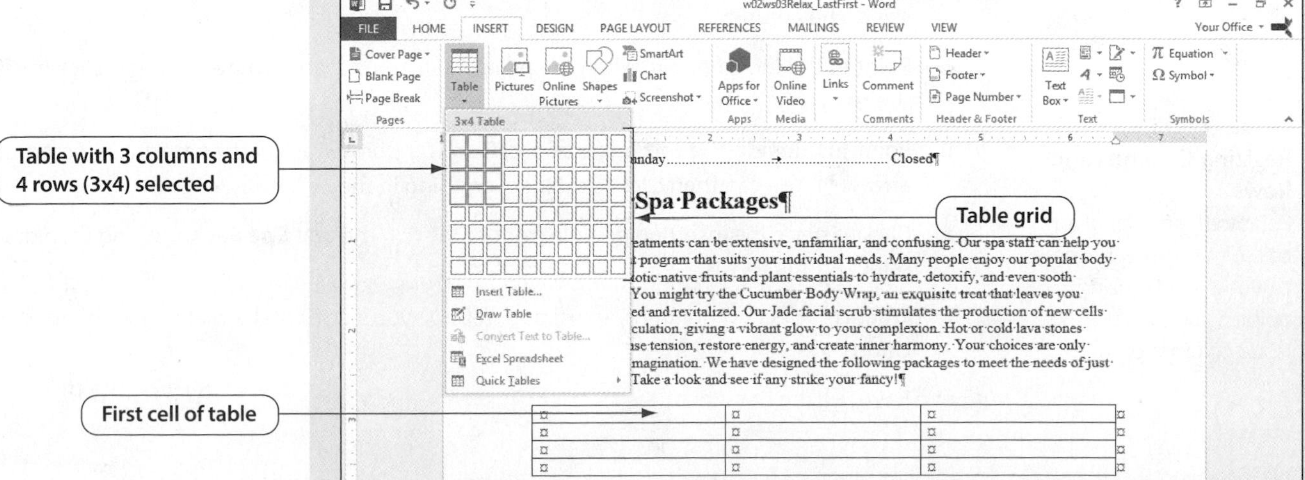

Figure 21 Creating a table

SIDE NOTE

Tabs Within a Table Cell

You can create tab stops within a cell. Simply press Ctrl+Tab to move the insertion point to the tab stop.

SIDE NOTE

Moving Back a Cell

Press Shift+Tab to move to a previous cell.

SIDE NOTE

Resizing Columns and Rows

Point to the border of any cell so the pointer becomes a two-headed resizing pointer, and then drag to resize columns or rows.

c. With the insertion point in the **top-left cell** of the table, type Spa Package and press Tab to move to the adjacent cell. Type Services and press Tab. Type Prices and press Tab to move to the first cell of the second row.

Note that all three columns are equal width and each row is the same height. If non-printing characters are shown, you will see an end-of-cell mark in each cell and an end-of-row mark at the right side of each row. The table selector at the top-left corner of the table enables you to select the entire table. You can drag the resize handle in the bottom-right corner of the table to resize the table.

d. With the insertion point in the first cell of the second row, type Body Package (2 hours) and then press Tab. Type Oasis Massage. Because two spa services are included in the Body Package, you will list them all within the same cell. Press Enter. The pointer is positioned on the next line in the same cell. Type Oasis Mani-Pedi. Do not press Enter.

The style is Normal, so there is a large space between lines. You will fix that later in the workshop.

e. Press Tab, type $135 and press Tab.

f. Type the following text in the remaining two rows of the table. Remember to press Tab to move from cell to cell, and to press Enter when listing the spa services in the second column. Do not press Tab or Enter after typing $325.

Soul Package (3 hours)	Oasis Massage Oasis Mani-Pedi Mini-Facial	$185
Mind Package (4 hours)	Oasis Massage Oasis Facial Oasis Mani-Pedi Paradise Fruit Bar	$325

Troubleshooting

If a new row appears at the bottom of the table, you pressed Tab after typing $325. Click Undo.

g. Click the **table selector** to select the entire table. Click the **HOME** tab, and then in the Styles group, click **No Spacing**, and then click outside the table to deselect it.

h. Point to the top of the second column—the **Services** column—so the pointer appears as a downward black arrow. When the pointer becomes a downward black arrow, click to select the **column**.

i. Point to the **left of a row**. When the pointer becomes a large white arrow, click to select the **row**.

j. Point just **inside the left edge of a cell** so the pointer appears as a right-directed black arrow. You can then click to select everything in the cell.

k. Click to place the insertion point in front of the **S** in the text **Spa Package**, and then drag to select multiple cells.

l. Practice selecting columns, rows, and cells. If you accidentally make any changes, click Undo.

m. **Save** the document.

Inserting and Deleting Columns and Rows

You will seldom develop a table that is perfect the first time. Most often, you will need to modify the number of rows or columns after the table is created. As you enter text in the last cell of a table, you can press Tab to insert a new row at the end of the table. That method works well for adding a row at the end of the table, but what if the new row should be inserted between two existing rows? Simply click to position the insertion point in a row or column that is to appear next to the new row or column. Click the Layout tab, and in the Rows & Columns group, select Insert Above, Insert Below, Insert Left, or Insert Right. One-click row and column insertion is new to Word 2013. To add a new row, position the pointer just to the left of a table, between two existing rows. A control with a plus sign appears outside the table (see Figure 22). Click the plus sign to add a new row above the control. Similarly, to add a new column, point to the top of the table between two existing columns, and then click the plus sign control to add a new column to the left of the control.

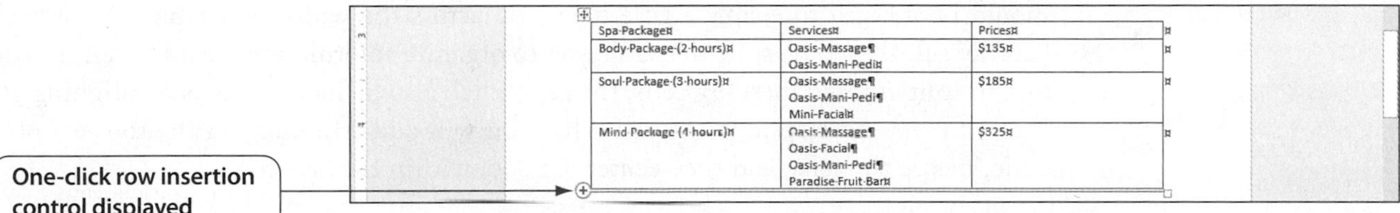

Figure 22 One-click row insertion

Deleting a column or row is not the same as deleting the contents of a column or row. To delete the contents, simply select the row or column and press Delete. The data in the row or column is deleted, but the empty row or column remains. You can then enter new data in the row (or column). When you delete a row or column, the entire row or column, and all its contents, are removed. Select the row or column and click Delete in the Rows & Columns group on the Layout tab. You can then choose to delete cells, columns, rows, or the entire table. You can delete multiple rows and columns by selecting them first. You realize you forgot to add information on the Balance Package. You will also add a row to the top of the table that you will later format as a heading. You will then delete the Soul Package row from the table since it is no longer offered by the spa and then add a row containing information on the Balance Package.

W03.17

To Insert and Delete Rows

a. Click anywhere in the **Soul Package** row. Click the **LAYOUT** tab, and then in the Rows & Columns group, click **Delete**, and then select **Delete Rows**. The Soul Package row is removed because you no longer offer that package.

b. Point to the **left of the bottom border**, just outside the table, to display a control with a plus sign . Click the **plus sign** to add a new row, click in the first cell of the new row, and then type Balance Package. Press Tab, and then type Mind Package plus a one-night hotel stay with full breakfast. Press Tab and then type $575. Do not press Enter or Tab.

c. Click in any **cell** in row 1. You will insert a top row so you can include a table heading. In the Rows & Columns group, click **Insert Above**. A new row is added at the top of the table.

SIDE NOTE

Adding a New Row at the Bottom of the Table

Position the insertion point in the last cell of the table, and then press Tab.

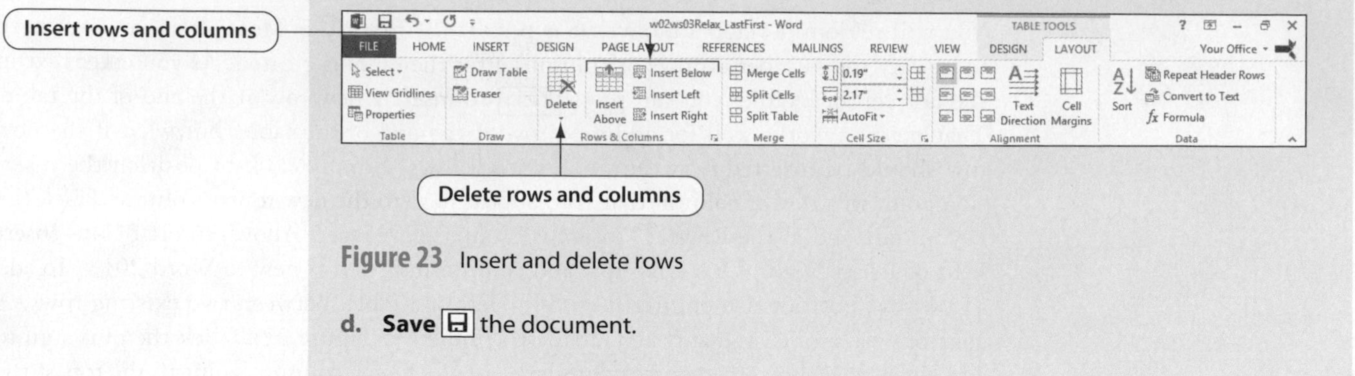

Figure 23 Insert and delete rows

d. **Save** the document.

Merging and Splitting a Row

Cells can be merged or split. Often as an afterthought, you will find that several cells should be merged to enable a title to extend across the width of a table. Or perhaps a lengthy cell should be split to enable you to organize information within a cell. In addition to splitting and merging cells, the Layout tab also includes options for aligning your data once you have split or merged cells. You will add a heading in the top row of the table, merge the cells, and then center the data within the new row.

W03.18

To Merge a Row

a. Click in the **first cell of the first row**, and then type Specialty Spa Packages.

b. Point to the **left of the first row** until a white arrow appears. Click to select the **top row** of the table. On the LAYOUT tab, in the Merge group, click **Merge Cells** to merge all cells in the row into one cell. The first row can now be used as a title row.

c. In the Alignment group, click **Align Center**.

Merge Cells

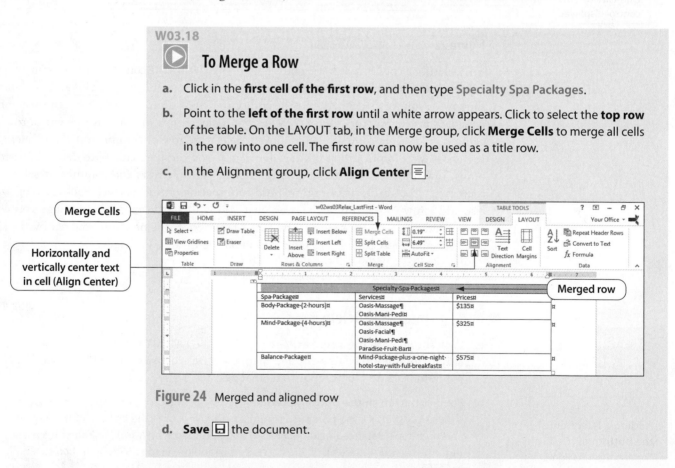

Horizontally and vertically center text in cell (Align Center)

Merged row

Specialty Spa Packages		
Spa Package	Services	Prices
Body Package (2 hours)	Oasis Massage Oasis Mani-Pedi	$135
Mind Package (4 hours)	Oasis Massage Oasis Facial Oasis Mani-Pedi Paradise Fruit Bar	$325
Balance Package	Mind Package plus a one night hotel stay with full breakfast	$575

Figure 24 Merged and aligned row

d. **Save** the document.

Formatting a Table

Once selected, text in a table can be formatted in a variety of ways. You can identify options in the Font group of the Home tab to format selected text, such as bold, shading, font, and font color. You can even apply bullets or numbers to selected text. In addition to the formatting options on the Home tab, the Table Tools Design tab provides a gallery of table styles with preexisting colors, borders, shading, and other design elements to quickly and easily format your table. You can then choose to add further shading, color, and formatting to the style. Some table styles apply a different color to the first row or to the first column to emphasize the header row or column. Others apply alternating color to rows, called banded rows. Still others apply alternating color to columns, called banded columns. Word 2013 now organizes table styles based on a plain, list, or grid design, as shown in Table 2. New to Word 2013 is the Border Painter, which enables you to quickly format borders of the table. You will now add some spark to the Specialty Spa Packages table. You will add a table style, and then modify the style by adding shading and removing bold.

Table Style Categories	Description
Plain	More black-and-white table design options
List	Tables designed to present list-oriented data (with fewer column separators)
Grid	Tables designed to present data in a grid (with column separators)

Table 2 Word 2013 table styles

W03.19

To Format a Table

a. Click the **table selector** in the top-left corner of the table to select the entire table. Under TABLE TOOLS, click the **DESIGN** tab, and then in the Table Styles group, click **More**. Scroll down to view all the styles, and then under **List Tables**, select **List Table 3 - Accent 2**. The table is formatted to include a shaded red title area and dark red borders.

b. Select the **second row** of the table containing the Spa Packages, Services, and Prices headings. In the Table Styles group, click the **Shading** arrow, and then under Theme Colors, in the sixth column and third row, select **Red, Accent 2, Lighter 60%**.

c. Click the **table selector** to select the entire table. Click the **HOME** tab, and then in the Font group, click **Bold** B to remove bold from the table.

d. Remove the extra paragraph mark after the table.

e. **Save** the document.

REAL WORLD ADVICE **Aligning Graphics in Your Document**

Have you ever tried to insert multiple graphics in a document, side by side? Aligning and spacing multiple graphics evenly can be a challenging task. Create a table with no borders to quickly align your pictures. For example, if you are inserting three pictures in a row, side by side, create a one row table, with three columns. Remove the borders and insert each picture into its own cell. It is that simple!

Resizing and Aligning a Table

The Table Tools Layout tab enables you to align text horizontally or vertically within cells, change the text direction within a cell, modify cell margins, and change heights and widths. When Word creates a table, all columns and rows are of equal width and height. As you enter text in a table cell, Word will automatically increase row height to accommodate additional text if necessary. The column width, however, will remain the same.

If you want to manually change column width or row height, you can drag a row or column border. For more precise resizing, click Properties in the Table group of the Layout tab and indicate a measurement for a selected table, column, row, or cell. The alignment buttons on the Home tab, in the Paragraph group, enable you to align a table horizontally on a page. You will resize the table width, center the table horizontally on the page, and then add vertical inside borders.

SIDE NOTE
Alternate Way to Resize a Table
Position the pointer on a border of the table until it changes to a double-headed arrow. Drag to resize.

W03.20

To Resize and Align a Table

a. Point to the table, and then click the **table selector** to select the table. Click the **LAYOUT** tab, and then in the Table group, click **Properties**. The Table Properties dialog box is displayed. On the TABLE tab, under **Size**, click the **Preferred width** check box, and then click the arrow as needed to resize the table to **5"**.

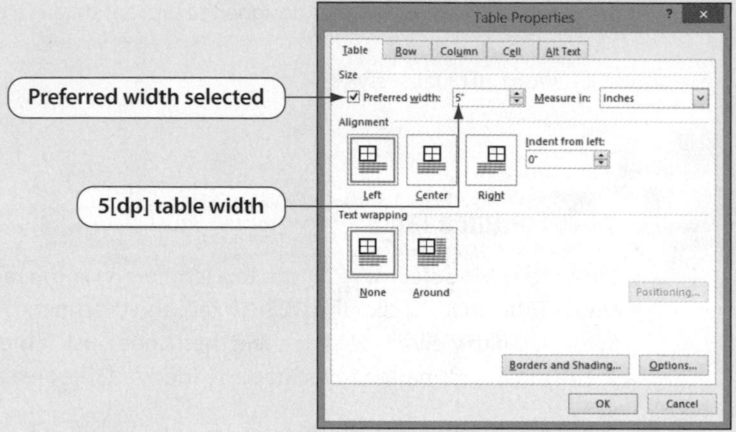

Figure 25 Table Properties dialog box

b. Click **OK**. Click the **HOME** tab, and then in the Paragraph group, click **Center** to center the table horizontally on the page.

c. Click the **LAYOUT** tab, and then in the Alignment group, click **Align Center** to center the text within each cell of the table. Because you do not find this change attractive, on the Quick Access Toolbar, click **Undo** to undo the alignment change.

d. Under TABLE TOOLS, click the **DESIGN** tab, and then in the Borders group, click **Pen Color** and then under Theme Colors, in the sixth column and first row, select **Red, Accent 2**. In the Borders group, click the **Borders** arrow, and then select **Inside Vertical Border**.

e. Click outside the table to deselect it, and then **save** the document.

Converting Text into a Table

Word also enables you to quickly convert existing text to a table. The key is indicating how the text is separated on each row—or paragraph. If your text is separated using commas, the first paragraph will be entered into the first row of the table, with text in between each comma placed into individual columns. Using existing text, you will create a one-column table based on the five benefits of massages. Since you only need one column per paragraph, you will use the paragraph mark as the separator.

W03.21

To Convert Text into a Table

a. In the **Specialty Spa Massages** section, select the five lines starting with the line **Increasing the body's energy flow** and ending with the line **Reducing insomnia, stress, and fatigue**.

b. Click the **INSERT** tab, and then in the Tables group, click **Table**, and then select **Convert Text to Table**.

The Convert Text to Table dialog box appears. Word will automatically place each line—paragraph—of data into a row. Notice "Paragraphs" is selected under the Separate text at section. This will determine how the columns are created. Since there is only one paragraph mark per row in your data, Word will only create one column in the table. You can override this by changing the Number of columns value. You will accept all the defaults.

c. In the Convert Text to Table dialog box, click **OK**. Click the **LAYOUT** tab, and then in the Cell Size group, click **AutoFit**, and then select **AutoFit Contents**. Word will automatically determine the best column width for the table data.

d. With the table still selected, under TABLE TOOLS, click the **DESIGN** tab, and then in the Borders group, click **Border Styles**, and then under **Theme Borders**, in the first column and third row, select **Double solid lines, 1/2 pt**. The pointer changes to a brush to indicate that the Border Painter is turned on. Click **each horizontal line** of the table.

SIDE NOTE

Changing the Horizontal Borders

Alternatively, in the Borders group, select the border style, and then click Borders. Select Bottom Border, Top Border, and Inside Horizontal Border.

Troubleshooting

If the Border Painter turns off while trying to create the border, simply click Border Painter in the Borders group again to turn it on.

Select borders instead of using Border Painter

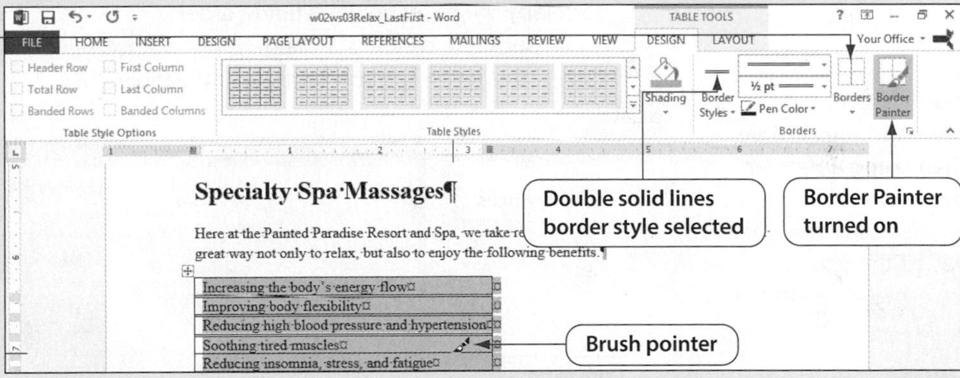

Figure 26 Border Painter

e. In the Borders group, click **Border Painter** to turn off the border painter. With the table still selected, click the **HOME** tab, and then in the Paragraph group, click **Center**.

f. Click outside the table to deselect it, and then **save** the document.

Sorting Table Data

You can sort, or rearrange, rows based on the contents of one or more columns. For example, if a table includes divisions of a company in one column and their sales in another column you can sort the table to place rows in order based on their sales. If more than one division has the same sales value, you can sort by both sales and division names, so that if their sales are identical, the matching records will then be sorted by division names.

You can sort in alphabetic, numeric, or chronological order in either ascending or descending fashion. Alphabetically, the letter "Z" is higher than the letter "A", so a descending alphabetic sort would place records in order from "Z" to "A", while an ascending sort would arrange them from "A" to "Z". You will sort the Specialty Spa Massages table in alphabetical order. You will then sort the Specialty Spa Packages table by the prices, in descending order—with the most expensive package at the top of the list.

W03.22

To Sort a Table

a. Click anywhere in the table under the **Specialty Spa Massages** heading. Click the **LAYOUT** tab, and then in the Data group, click **Sort**. The Sort dialog box opens. At the bottom of the dialog box, under My list has, verify that **No header row** is selected.

The first column (Column 1) is correctly assumed to be the sort field. If such were not the case, you could click the Sort by arrow and select another column. The field is a Text field, and the sort order is assumed to be Ascending. If any of those assumptions were not correct, you would change them in the dialog box.

b. Click **OK**, and then click outside the table to deselect it. The benefits of massages are rearranged alphabetically.

c. Scroll up to locate the Specialty Spa Packages table, and then select the **last four rows** of the table, starting with **Spa Package** and ending with **$575**. Click the **LAYOUT** tab, and then in the Data group, click **Sort**.

SIDE NOTE

Selecting Multiple Rows

Position the pointer to the left of a row and when the pointer changes to a white arrow, drag to select multiple rows.

d. Under **My list has**, click **Header row** to indicate that the selected data contains headers. Notice that Spa Package is assumed to be the sort field. Click the **arrow** next to **Spa Package**, and then select **Prices**. Under **Sort by**, on the right, click **Descending**, and then click **OK**. Click outside the table to deselect it. The Spa Service records are now sorted by the prices, in descending order.

If your table contains a merged row, do not select it when sorting data within the table, otherwise you can select the entire table.

SIDE NOTE

Column Names Visible When Using a Header Row

Because Header row was selected, the actual column names were listed in the Sort by section.

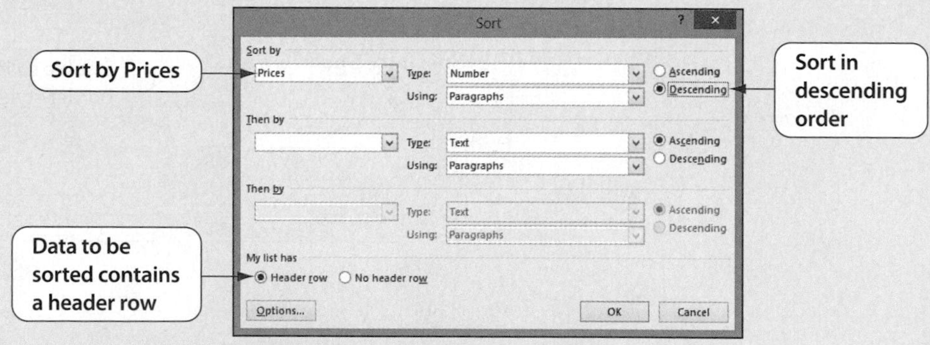

Figure 27 Sorting a table with headers

e. **Save** the document.

CONSIDER THIS | Selecting Appropriate Objects

With the multitude of objects provided by Word, including WordArt, SmartArt, charts, and tables, you should take care to include objects that are appropriate for the documents they appear in. When would you use one object over another? Does it have more to do with the type of document you are working with—school, personal, business—or more with the way you present and format the object?

Managing Pages

When a document includes more than one page of text, there is always a possibility that a page will end awkwardly. A heading may show up at the bottom of a page, with the contents of that section displayed on the next page. Or perhaps only the first line of a paragraph shows at the bottom of a page, with the remainder of the paragraph on the next page. Always be sure to preview a document before printing so you can identify and correct an unattractive page ending. You will now explore ways to manage the end of a page, making sure that each page ends attractively. You will also learn to format text in sections.

Work with Page Breaks

A **page break** is where one page ends and another one begins. Word automatically separates pages according to a standard page size, inserting a soft page break when you reach the end of a page. Word automatically adjusts the page break as you add and delete text. Occasionally, you will want to insert a page break in a different location than where Word locates it. For example, in the case where a heading shows on one page with the remainder of the section on the next page, you might want to force a page break immediately before the heading to keep the heading and its text together. When typing a report divided into sections or chapters, insert a page break at the end of each section to ensure that each section or chapter begins on a new page. You can manually insert a page break from either the Insert or Page Layout tabs.

Avoiding Orphan and Widow Lines

Orphans and widows are lines that dangle at the beginning or ending of a page. An **orphan** is the first line of a paragraph that is alone at the bottom of a page. The rest of the paragraph appears at the top of the next page. A **widow** is a paragraph's last line that is alone at the top of a page. The first part of the paragraph appears at the end of the previous page. Widows and orphans affect the readability of a document, breaking the flow of text. Because you generally want to avoid widows and orphans, Word automatically sets Widow/Orphan control to prevent their occurrence, ensuring that at least two lines of a paragraph appear together.

Working with the End of a Page

You notice that the spa hours are split apart, with some of the hours listed at the end of page two, and the rest of the hours displayed at the top of page three. You will insert a page break so that all of the spa hours are listed together at the top of page three. You will also verify that Widow/Orphan control is turned on.

W03.23

To Work with the End of a Page

SIDE NOTE

Inserting Page Breaks

Alternatively, you can press Ctrl+Enter to insert a page break.

a. Press Ctrl+Home. Click the **VIEW** tab, and then in the Zoom group, click **Multiple Pages**. Scroll to view all four pages. Note that page three begins awkwardly, with the spa hours split between pages two and three.

b. Click to place the insertion point in front of the heading **Spa Hours**. Click the **PAGE LAYOUT** tab, and then in the Page Setup group, click **Breaks**, and then select **Page**.

c. A page break is inserted. If you are in Print Layout view, with nonprinting characters displayed, you will see the page break. Click the **VIEW** tab, and then in the Zoom group, click **100%**.

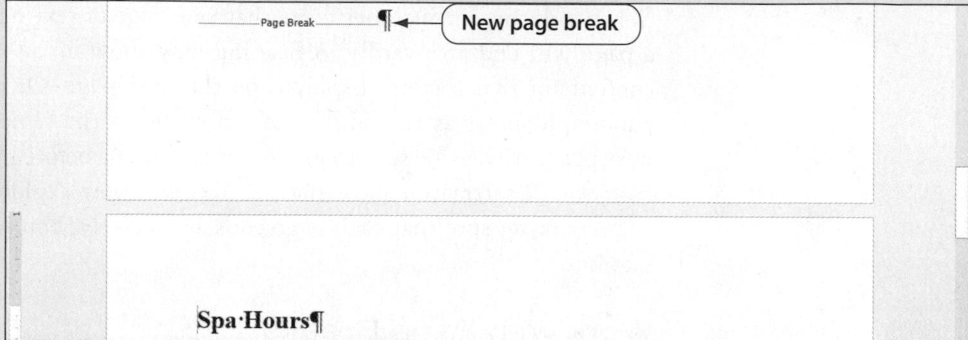

Figure 28 Inserting a page break

d. Click the **HOME** tab, and then in the Paragraph group, click the **Paragraph Dialog Box Launcher**, and then click the **Line and Page Breaks** tab. Verify the **Widow/Orphan control** check box is selected. If it is not, click to select it. Click **OK**. By default, Word is configured to avoid orphan and widow lines.

e. **Save** the document.

Work with Sections

A document can be divided into **sections**, which are areas that can be formatted differently. Each section can have its own orientation, margins, headers, footers, and any other document format. Suppose you have a document formatted in the portrait orientation, but the last page of your document contains a table that is best suited for landscape orientation. In that case, you simply define a separate section for the table and apply landscape orientation to that section. The rest of the document will remain in portrait orientation.

Inserting a New Section

Options on the Page Layout tab enable you to assign a section break, which divides a document into a new section. When you insert a section break you will see a dotted line with the words "Section Break" if nonprinting characters are displayed. You can insert a Continuous section break, which starts at the position of the insertion point but does not break the page flow. For example, if you are creating a newsletter, you might want the title of the newsletter to be centered horizontally, but all text beneath that point is to be arranged in columns. After centering the title, insert a Continuous section break so the remaining text can be formatted in columns on the same page, without affecting the title. A Next Page section break begins a section on a new page. Perhaps a report's cover sheet should appear in landscape orientation, while the body of the report is in portrait orientation. Simply insert a Next Page section break after the cover page and change the orientation, as shown in the following exercise.

SIDE NOTE

Deleting a Section Break

Display nonprinting characters, click the section break, and then press Delete.

W03.24

To Insert a New Section

a. Press Ctrl+Home. Click the **PAGE LAYOUT** tab, and then in the Page Setup group, click **Breaks**. Under the Section Breaks category, select **Next Page** (do not select Page).

Day Spa Group requires that all articles include a cover sheet in landscape orientation, with contact information related to the submission. You have just created a new blank page at the top of your document.

b. Press Ctrl+Home to place the insertion point at the top of the new page. On the PAGE LAYOUT tab, in the Page Setup group, click **Orientation**, and then select **Landscape**.

The new page is set to landscape orientation. Because the new page is in a different section, the remaining pages in the document are still set to portrait orientation.

c. Click the **DESIGN** tab, and then in the Page Background group, click **Page Borders**. The Borders and Shading dialog box opens with the Page Border tab selected. Under Setting, click **Box**. Click the **Apply to** arrow, select **This section**, and then click **OK**.

d. Click the **VIEW** tab, and then in the Zoom group, click **Multiple Pages**.

The first page should be in landscape orientation, and the second page should be portrait. The border should only be on the first page. You will insert the remaining text into the cover sheet later in the workshop.

e. In the Zoom group, click **100%**.

f. **Save** the document.

Insert Text from Another Document

Word makes it possible to insert text from another document without using copy and paste. If you need to insert an entire document into your current document, use the Object command on the Insert tab. If you have text that you often insert into various documents, save the text in a separate file, and then insert the file into your documents. Not only can you save time by reusing text, but you also minimize typing errors.

Creating a Cover Page by Inserting Text from Another Document

Because you must often include a cover page for articles, you have saved the necessary information in a separate document. You will insert the text from the saved document into the cover page.

W03.25

To Insert Text from Another Document

a. Press Ctrl+Home to place the insertion point at the top of the new page.

b. Click the **INSERT** tab, and then in the Text group, click the **Object** arrow, and then select **Text from File**.

Troubleshooting

If you click Object instead of the arrow beside it, you will see an Object dialog box. Close the dialog box, and redo Step b.

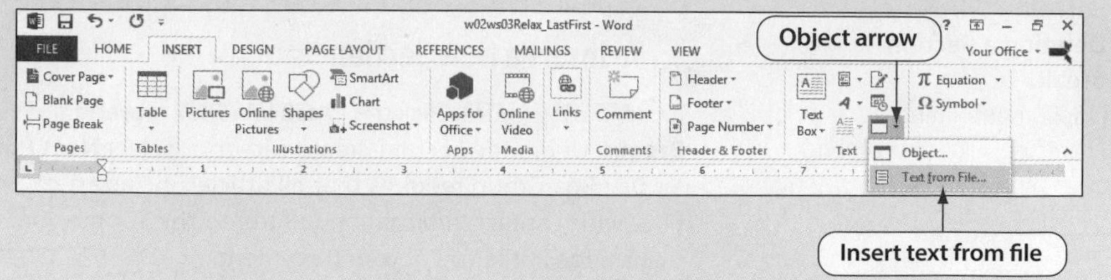

Figure 29 Inserting text from another file

c. Navigate to the location of your student data files, and then double-click **w02ws03SpaCover**.

d. Click the **VIEW** tab, and then in the Zoom group, click **Multiple Pages** to view your article.

e. Click the **PAGE LAYOUT** tab, and then in the Page Setup group, click the **Dialog Box Launcher**. In the **Page Setup** dialog box, click the **Layout** tab, click the **Vertical alignment** arrow, select **Center**, and then click **OK**. You have vertically centered text on the cover page.

SIDE NOTE
Pre-formatted Cover Pages
Word provides pre-formatted cover pages on the Insert tab, in the Pages group—which automatically insert a next page section break.

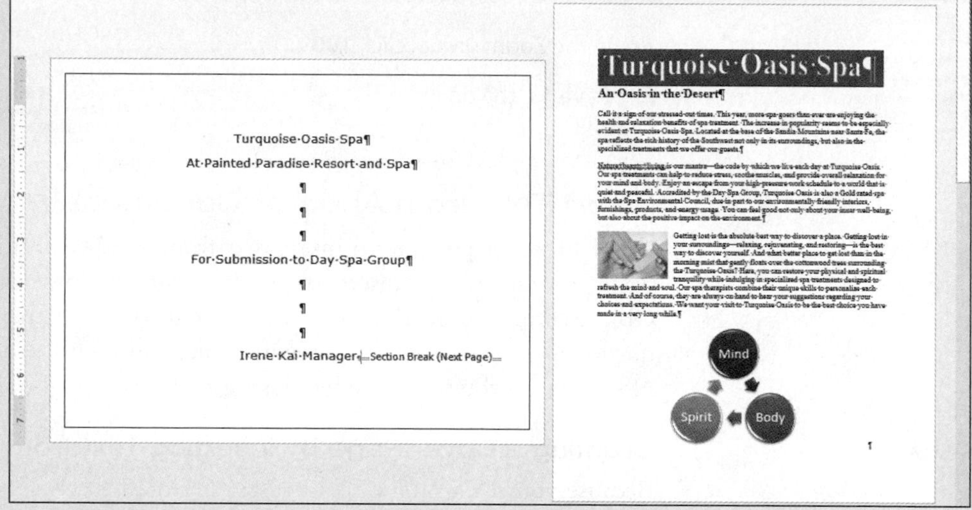

Figure 30 Cover page

f. After reviewing the article, on the VIEW tab, in the Zoom group, click **100%**.

g. **Save** the document, exit Word, and then submit the file as directed by your instructor.

Concept Check

1. What is the difference between creating WordArt and using Text Effects and Typography in the Font group? p. 278
2. What is a SmartArt graphic, and what is an example of how you could you use the Hierarchy layout in a business setting? p. 286
3. What are two ways to create a text box, and what are some examples of when you would use a text box in your document? p. 290
4. What is the difference between Pictures and Online Pictures in the Illustrations group? p. 293
5. Describe how to insert tabs using the ruler and the Tabs dialog box. p. 297–298
6. Although both tabs and tables enable you to align text in columns, each has unique features that make it appropriate for various applications. What are some examples of when you would use a table versus a tab? p. 296
7. What is a page break? What is the difference between a widow and an orphan? p. 309
8. What are some examples of when you would need to create a new section? p. 310
9. How do you insert all the text from one document into another document without using the copy and paste feature? Why would you use this feature? p. 311

Key Terms

Alignment guides 283
Anchor 285
Bar tab 297
Cell 300
Center tab 297
Clip art 294
Contextual Tab 278
Decimal tab 297
Leader 297
Left tab 297
Live Layout 283
Object 278
Orphan 309
Page break 309
Picture 293
Right tab 297
Section 310
Sizing handle 281
SmartArt 286
Tab stop 296
Table 300
Text box 290
Text wrap 283
Widow 309
WordArt 278

Visual Summary

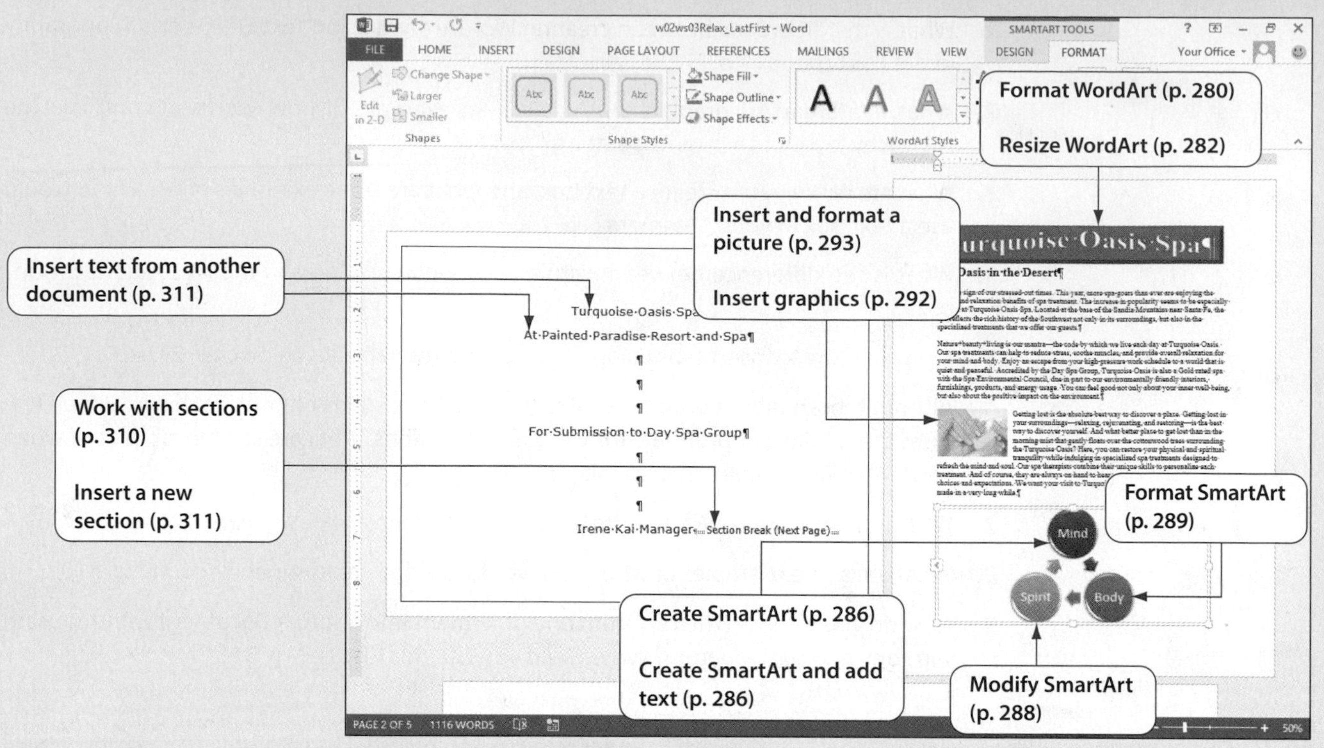

Format WordArt (p. 280)
Resize WordArt (p. 282)
Insert and format a picture (p. 293)
Insert graphics (p. 292)
Insert text from another document (p. 311)
Work with sections (p. 310)
Insert a new section (p. 311)
Format SmartArt (p. 289)
Create SmartArt (p. 286)
Create SmartArt and add text (p. 286)
Modify SmartArt (p. 288)

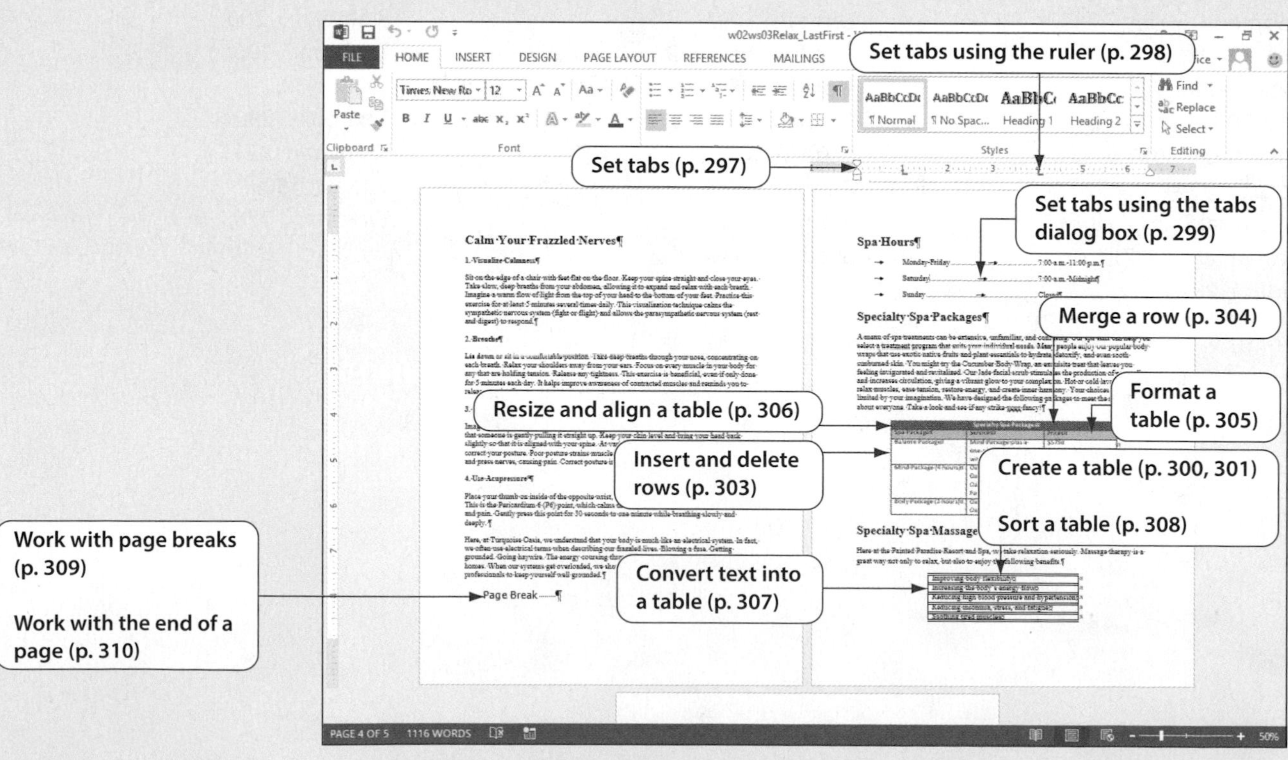

Set tabs using the ruler (p. 298)
Set tabs (p. 297)
Set tabs using the tabs dialog box (p. 299)
Merge a row (p. 304)
Resize and align a table (p. 306)
Format a table (p. 305)
Insert and delete rows (p. 303)
Create a table (p. 300, 301)
Sort a table (p. 308)
Work with page breaks (p. 309)
Work with the end of a page (p. 310)
Convert text into a table (p. 307)

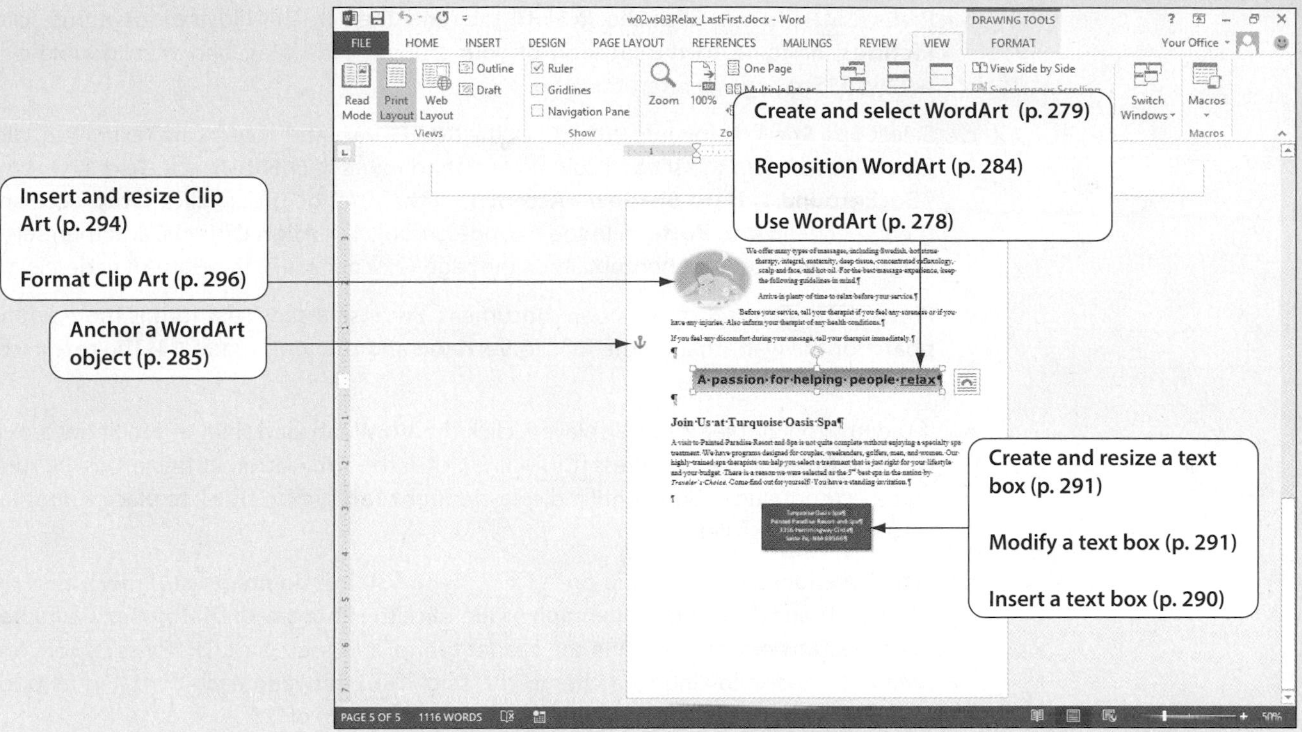

Figure 31 Turquoise Oasis Spa Services Publication Final Document

Practice 1

Student data files needed:

 w02ws03SpaExcl.docx

 w02ws03SpaTable.docx

 w02ws03SpaLogo.jpg

You will save your file as:

 w02ws03SpaExcl_LastFirst.docx

Spa Exclusives

Sales & Marketing

The website for Turquoise Oasis Spa includes a link where visitors to the site can register for Spa Exclusives, a program that e-mails reminders of spa specials and product sales. Visitors are asked to indicate an interest category—Fitness, Group Events, Spa Boutique, or Spa Treatments—and to provide an e-mail address. Each month, a targeted flyer is sent by e-mail and also made available as a link on the Spa Exclusives Member web page. This month, you are preparing a flyer that highlights items in the spa boutique. The flyer will be prepared as a Word document and sent as an e-mail attachment. It will also be available at the Painted Paradise Resort and Spa web page.

a. Start **Word**, click **Open Other Documents**, and then double-click **Computer**. Navigate to the location of your student files, and then double-click **w02ws03SpaExcl**. Click the **FILE** tab, click **Save As**, double-click **Computer**, and then navigate to where you are saving your files. Change the **File name** to w02ws03SpaExcl_LastFirst, using your first and last name, and then click **Save**.

b. Press Ctrl+Home. Click the **INSERT** tab, and then in the Illustrations group, click **Pictures**, navigate to the location of your student data files, and then double-click **w02ws03SpaLogo** to insert the logo.

c. Select **Spa Specials for July 2015**. Click the **INSERT** tab, and then in the Text group, click **Insert WordArt**. In the second column and third row, select **Fill - Black, Text 1, Outline - Background 1, Hard Shadow - Accent 1**. In the Arrange group, click **Wrap Text**, and then select **Top and Bottom**. In the Arrange group, click **Align Objects**, and then select **Align Center** to center it horizontally on the page. Click outside of the WordArt to deselect it.

d. Press Ctrl+A to select the entire document. Because a sans serif font is more appropriate for the web, change the font to **Verdana** and the font size to **14**. The text in the objects will not change.

e. If the horizontal ruler is not displayed, click the **VIEW** tab, and then in the Show group, click the **Ruler** check box. Press Ctrl+End, click the **Tab** button at the left of the ruler, and then continue clicking until it displays a **Right Tab** symbol. Click to place a right tab stop at **6"** on the ruler.

f. Type Lavender Bath Salts and press Tab. Type $30 but do not press Enter. Click the **HOME** tab, and then in the Paragraph group, click the **Paragraph Dialog Box Launcher**. Click the **Tabs** button, click **2** in the Leader group, and then click **OK**. Press Enter, and then enter the following three items, pressing Tab between each item and its price. Press Enter after each item, including after the last entry of "$8".

Lavender Shower Gel $18
Lavender Lip Balm $3
Signature Lavender Lotion $8

g. Click to place the insertion point at the beginning of the **second body paragraph**, immediately before **Each month**. Click the **INSERT** tab, and then in the Illustrations group, click **Online Pictures**. Click in the **Office.com Clip Art** box, type lavender herb and then press Enter.

h. Point to the **pictures** displayed, and then click the clip art described as "**Flowering lavender herb**". Click **Insert**. If you cannot locate the clip art, select another clip art related to lavender. The clip art is placed in the document and remains selected. On the FORMAT tab, in the Adjust group, click **Color**. Under Recolor, in the sixth column and third row, select **Aqua, Accent color 5 Light**. In the Picture Styles group, click **Picture Border**, and then select **Black, Text 1.**

i. With the clip art still selected, in the Arrange group, click **Wrap Text**, and then select **Square**. In the Size group, change the clip art height to **0.5"**.

j. Press Ctrl+End. Click the **INSERT** tab, and then in the Text group, click **Text Box**, and then select **Simple Text Box**. Click the **Shape Height** down arrow in the Size group until **0.8"** is displayed, and then click the **Shape Width** up arrow until **6"** is displayed.

k. With the text in the text box still selected, click the **Tab** button at the left of the ruler until it displays a **Left Tab** symbol. Click **2.5"** on the horizontal ruler to set a left tab stop, and then click **4.5"** to set another left tab stop.

l. With the text in the text box still selected, type Painted Paradise Resort and Spa in the box, and then press Tab. Type 3356 Hemmingway Circle and press Tab. Type (505)555-0806. Press Enter, and then type www.paintedparadiseresort.com.

m. Click the dashed line surrounding the text box to make it solid, indicating the entire text box is selected. Click the **HOME** tab, and then in the Paragraph group, click **Center**, and then change the font size to **12**. In the Paragraph group, click **Line and Paragraph Spacing**, and then select **Remove Space After Paragraph** to set a 0 pt paragraph after spacing.

n. Click the **FORMAT** tab, and then in the Shape Styles group, click **Shape Fill**. Under Theme Colors, in the ninth column and third row, select **Aqua, Accent 5, Lighter 60%**. Click **Shape Outline**, point to **Weight**, and then select **1½ pt**. In the Text group, click **Align Text**, and then select **Middle** to align the text vertically.

o. Press Ctrl+End. Click the **PAGE LAYOUT** tab, and then in the Page Setup group, click **Breaks**, and then select **Next Page**. In the Page Setup group, click **Orientation**, and then select **Landscape**.

p. Click the **INSERT** tab, and then in the Text group, click the **Object** arrow, and then select **Text from File**. Navigate to the location of your student data files, and then double-click **w02ws03SpaTable**.

q. Scroll down to view the second page. Select the six paragraphs beginning with **11-A-231, Body** and ending with the text, **Ultra Healing Lotion, $20.95**. On the INSERT tab, in the Tables group, click **Table**, and then select **Convert Text to Table**. The Convert Text to Table dialog box is displayed. Under **AutoFit behavior**, click **AutoFit to contents**, and then under **Separate text at**, click **Commas**. Click **OK**.

r. Click anywhere in the **first row** of the table. Click the **LAYOUT** tab, and then in the Rows & Columns group, click **Insert Above**. Click in the **first cell** of the first row, type Item # and then press Tab. Type the following text, pressing Tab after each entry:

   Category
   Product
   Size
   Description
   Price

s. Point to the **top border** of the first column until the pointer changes to a black downward arrow, and then click to select the **first column**. On the LAYOUT tab, in the Cell Size group, click in the **Table Column Width** box, and then change the value displayed to **1.5"**. Press Enter to view the result. Similarly, change the column width of the Size column to **0.9"**.

t. Click the **table selector** to select the entire table, and then in the Alignment group, click **Align Center Left** to align the text vertically and to the left in each cell. Select the **first row**, and then in the Alignment group, click **Align Center** to align the text horizontally and vertically in each cell of the first row.

u. Click in any **table cell**, and then in the Data group, click **Sort**. Under **My list has**, confirm **Header row** is selected. Click the **Sort by** arrow, and then select **Category**. Click the **Then by** arrow, and then select **Product**. Click **OK**.

v. Under TABLE TOOLS, click the **DESIGN** tab, and then in the Table Styles group, click **More**. Under Grid Tables, click **Grid Table 4 - Accent 5**.

w. Press Ctrl+End. Click the **INSERT** tab, and then in the Header & Footer group, click **Footer**, and then select **Edit Footer**. In the Insert group, click **Document Info**, and then select **File Name**. **Center** the text in the footer, and then double-click anywhere in the document to close the header and footer.

x. Click the **VIEW** tab, and then in the Zoom group, click **Multiple Pages** to view your document. Save the document, exit Word, and then submit the file as directed by your instructor.

Problem Solve 1

Student data files needed:

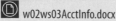

w02ws03Bank.docx

w02ws03AcctInfo.docx

You will save your file as:

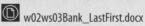

w02ws03Bank_LastFirst.docx

Bank Flyer

Sales & Marketing

As an account manager for Midfield Independent Bank, you are working with a marketing campaign to publicize the bank. In this exercise, you will create a two-page flyer to attractively display the account options and services, the bank hours, and a new bank slogan. You will work with tables, clip art, WordArt, SmartArt, tabs, and section breaks.

a. Start **Word**, and then open **w02ws03Bank**. Save the document as w02ws03Bank_LastFirst, using your first and last name. If necessary, display nonprinting characters and the rulers.

b. Select the **clip art** image, and then change the height of the clip art to **0.5"**. Change the color of the clip art to **Grayscale**.

c. Press Ctrl+A to select the entire document, and then **convert the text to a table**. Accept the default values in the dialog box.

d. Click the **TABLE TOOLS DESIGN** tab, click the **Borders** arrow in the Borders group, and then select **No Border**. Set the **Line Weight** to 2 1/4 pt, and then apply a **Bottom Border**.

e. Press Ctrl+End, press Enter, and then insert all the text from the **w02ws03AcctInfo** file into the document.

f. Delete the blank row in the table.

g. Sort the table by **Fees**, in Ascending order.

h. Insert a new row above the first row of the account information table. Type BANK ACCOUNT SUMMARY INFORMATION in the first cell of the new row, and then merge the cells in the first row of the table.

i. Apply the **Grid Table 5 Dark** table style to the table. Apply the **Black, Text 1** shading to the second row of the table, and then click **Banded Rows** in the Table Style Options group to turn off banded rows.

j. Add a row above **Min. deposit to open**. Enter the following data in the new row:

Free checks	No	No	Yes

k. Select the **first row**, change the height of the first row to **0.5"**, and then center-align the text horizontally and vertically in the row.

l. Select the **entire table**, and then AutoFit the contents of the table. Center-align the table horizontally on the page.

m. Press Ctrl+End, and then insert a **WordArt** object using the **Gradient Fill – Aqua, Accent 1, Reflection** style. Type Bank Hours. **Align Center** the WordArt horizontally on the page, and then set the text wrap to **Top and Bottom**.

n. Select the entire **WordArt**, and then apply a **Black, Text 1, Lighter 35%** text fill. Change the font size to **20**.

o. Press Ctrl+End. Set a **1"** left tab stop, and then set a **5.5"** right tab stop with a dot leader. Set the Font Color to **Black, Text 1**.

p. Press Tab, and then type Monday-Friday without typing a space before or after the dash. Press Tab, and then type 8:30a.m.-6:00p.m. without any spaces. Press Enter.

q. Press [Tab], type Saturday and then press [Tab]. Type 8:30a.m.-Noon without typing any spaces. Press [Enter], and then press [Tab]. Type Sunday and then press [Tab]. Type Closed and then press [Enter].

r. Insert a **Simple Text Box**. Type Contact us at 555-555-7323 for a comprehensive list of services and fees. in the text box. Do not use any spaces in the phone number, and include the period at the end of the sentence.

s. Change the width of the text box to **2"** and the height to **0.8"**. Apply the **Subtle Effect - Black, Dark 1** shape style. Apply the **Perspective Diagonal Upper Left** shadow shape effect.

t. **Center** the text within the text box.

u. Press [Ctrl]+[End], insert a **Next Page** section break, and then change the orientation of the new page to **Landscape**.

v. Insert the **Equation** SmartArt (Under the Process category).

w. Select the entire **SmartArt**, and then change the height of the entire SmartArt diagram to **5"** and the width to **8"**. Apply **Top and Bottom** text wrap, center-align the **SmartArt** horizontally on the page, and then vertically align the **SmartArt** to the center of the page.

x. Type Midfield Independent Bank in the first shape, type Our Savings Plans in the second shape, and then type Balance in Your Life in the third shape.

y. Select the entire **SmartArt**. Change the color of the SmartArt to **Dark 1 Outline**, and then apply the **Polished** SmartArt style.

z. Insert a **footer** with the file name field centered, and then close the header and footer.

aa. Click the **FILE** tab, and then click **Print** to preview the document. Save the document, exit Word, and then submit the file as directed by your instructor.

Perform 1: Perform in Your Life

Student data file needed:

 Blank Word document

You will save your file as:

 w02ws03Sale_LastFirst.docx

Selling Furniture

Sales & Marketing

You will be graduating from college in a month and you are hoping to sell some of your furniture for a little extra cash. Create an attractive flyer that you will post in the University Student Center with information on what you plan to sell, the price and description of each item, and your contact information. You will include WordArt, clip art, a text box, and a table.

a. Start **Word**, create a new blank document, and then save the file as **w02ws03Sale_LastFirst**, using your first and last name.

b. Using WordArt, add a title to your document. Change the text fill and text outline, and then add at least one shape effect to the WordArt.

c. Insert four pictures of furniture (clip art or photos). Apply either a picture style or border to the four pictures, and then adjust spacing and alignment as necessary.

d. Create a table with 5 rows and 3 columns. The first row of the table will contain the column headings. Each subsequent row should include information on each piece of furniture. The first column will include the type of furniture, the second column will include a brief description, and the third column will include the price. Label the columns appropriately.

e. Sort the table by the price in ascending order, and then by the type of furniture in ascending order.

f. Use a table style, and then modify the shading, borders, or other options as desired.

g. Center the table horizontally on the page.

h. Insert a text box with your contact information, and then add a shape style and shape effect to the text box.

i. Add any other necessary information.

j. Insert a footer with the file name field centered.

k. Save the document, exit Word, and then submit the file as directed by your instructor.

Additional Cases

Additional Workshop Cases are available on the companion website and in the instructor resources.

Microsoft Office Word 2013

Module 2

Impressing with Sophisticated Documents

WORKSHOP 4 | SPECIAL DOCUMENT FORMATTING AND MAIL MERGE

OBJECTIVES

1. Format a research paper p. 323
2. Develop a bibliography or works cited page p. 332
3. Work with comments p. 335
4. Track changes p. 337
5. Work with columns p. 340
6. Use a style guide to format a newsletter p. 344
7. Use mail merge p. 348
8. Create mailing labels and envelopes p. 356

Prepare Case

Turquoise Oasis Spa Newsletter

The Turquoise Oasis Spa is considering an incremental program that will phase in environmental improvements. The Spa also will start a newsletter, Solutions, to help market the new program. As a graduate class requirement, you will edit a research paper on this program and help develop the newsletter. You will use Word to develop the "happenings at the oasis" section, formatting text in columns and including graphics. You will also develop a cover letter to accompany the full-version of the newsletter. You will use Word's mail merge feature to personalize the letter and to produce mailing labels.

Sales & Marketing

Research & Development

curtis / Shutterstock

REAL WORLD SUCCESS 

"I am in charge of the quarterly and annual reporting to the Securities Exchange Commission. From our internal compilation of the report to the final sign-offs by an outside firm, the process is less than 30 days to complete. This is due mainly to the facilitation of tracked changes in MS Word, allowing the many reviewers to make comments directly on the electronic document. Without using the Track Changes feature this process could take two to three months. Thank goodness for Microsoft Word, otherwise everyone would be asking for extensions from the SEC!"

–PB, alumnus and CFO

Student data files needed for this workshop:

- w02ws04Addresses.accdb
- w02ws04Letter.docx
- w02ws04Research.docx
- w02ws04Review.docx
-  w02ws04SpaLogo.jpg
-  w02ws04SpaNews.docx
-  w02ws04Wine.jpg

You will save your files as:

- w02ws04Addresses_LastFirst.accdb
- w02ws04Labels_LastFirst.docx
- w02ws04Letter_LastFirst.docx
- w02ws04Merged_LastFirst.docx
-  w02ws04Research_LastFirst.docx
-  w02ws04Review_LastFirst.docx
-  w02ws04SpaNews_LastFirst.docx

Creating a Research Paper

Most composition classes require that you write a research paper. The very words "research paper" strike fear in the hearts of many college students. Researching a topic, however, might not be the most difficult part of the assignment. Instead, ensuring that your paper is in the correct format, according to an identified **style guide**, might be the bigger challenge.

A style guide, or style manual, is a set of standards for designing documents. A style manual is not as concerned with the selection of wording as it is with the standardized documentation of citations and general page characteristics such as margins, spacing, headers, footers, and page numbers. Although it may seem that adherence to a particular style is yet another hurdle to overcome in an already challenging chore of writing a research paper, it is really very helpful. When you follow set rules for citing works, meaning giving credit to the original author, you are less likely to inadvertently plagiarize. Adherence to a style also gives your instructor the ability to work through a paper's ideas and to judge the validity of the work in a consistent manner with other student papers.

REAL WORLD ADVICE **What Is Plagiarism?**

When writing any sort of paper, you should be very careful not to plagiarize. **Plagiarism** occurs when you present the information, ideas, or phrasing, as worded by another author, as if it were your own. In effect, you mislead others into believing that the original work is your own, when in fact you are theoretically "stealing" it from someone else. Regardless of the writing style guide that you use, you must identify the source of information, and you must identify all quoted material by quotation marks or indentation on the page. You can be charged with plagiarism for the following activities:

- Copying, paraphrasing, or quoting any person or source without giving proper credit
- Claiming another person's published or unpublished work as your own, with or without permission

There is no universally accepted style guide for all writing. Instead, different industries, academic disciplines, and even different journals within a discipline, tend to favor one or another standard style. As you progress through a field of study, you will be required to write papers that adhere to a prescribed style manual. You will find a wealth of information on the various writing style guides, both in print and online.

When assigning a research paper, your instructor will identify the preferred writing style. The major writing style guides are MLA, APA, Chicago, and CSE. The paper's subject matter is often what determines the style. Some styles are preferred by the social sciences, while others are the choice of humanities or sciences. Each style has unique requirements regarding the treatment of citation of sources, and preparation of a bibliography or title page. Some elements of a writing style even address such topics as when to spell out numerals. For example, should you write the number "thirty-one" or "31"?

MLA (Modern Language Association) style is often used in the humanities, including English, foreign languages, philosophy, religion, art, architecture, and literature. MLA is generally considered simpler and more concise than other styles. It requires brief parenthetical citations that are keyed to an alphabetical list of works cited at the end of a paper. Available for over 50 years, the style is widely followed internationally, including North America, Brazil, China, India, and Japan. The association publishes two manuals, "MLA Handbook for Writers of Research Papers" and "MLA Style Manual and Guide to Scholarly Publishing."

APA (American Psychological Association) is preferred by the social sciences, including business, economics, communication, justice, education, geography, law, political science, and sociology. Originating in 1929, the style was developed to simplify the communication of scientific ideas in a consistent manner. It focuses on the presentation of technical ideas and research, and is often the required style for the compilation of literature reviews and experiment reports. The association publishes the "Publication Manual of the American Psychological Association," containing style requirements.

Chicago (University of Chicago) style is primarily concerned with the preparation and editing of papers and books for publication. As such, it is less prescriptive with regard to such items as a title page or an abstract—a summary of the research or paper contents. Since 1906, Chicago has been the recognized standard with regard to American English style, grammar, and punctuation. Offering writers a choice of several different formats, Chicago style only requires that the result is clear and consistent. The Chicago Manual of Style" provides guidance to writers using Chicago style.

CSE (Council of Science Editors) is the primary style used in the sciences, such as biology, chemistry, computer science, engineering, environmental sciences, geology, math, health sciences, physics, and astronomy. Previously known as CBE (Council of Biology Editors), the association publishes "Scientific Style and Format: The CBE Manual for Authors, Editors, and Publishers," which provides detailed guidelines for using the CSE style.

In this section, you will create and format a research paper.

REAL WORLD ADVICE | **Style Guide Updates**

Major research style guides, including MLA, APA, Chicago, and CSE, are not static. New style manuals are published regularly, often with minor changes to style requirements. Although Word incorporates the citation, footnote, and bibliography requirements of the writing style that you indicate, it is possible that the most current style manual requirements are not included. Always refer to a current style manual when preparing a research paper. Do not depend on Word as the final authority.

CONSIDER THIS | **Plagiarism?**

In 2004, a school board member in North Carolina delivered a commencement speech that was identical to one given by Donna Shalala, former U.S. Secretary of Health and Human Services. He admitted that he had found the speech by searching the Internet for "commencement speeches." He claimed that the availability of the speech on the Internet made it open for use. What do you think?

Format a Research Paper

Regardless of the writing style in use, a research paper typically includes several standard elements. A title page, copyright page, dedication, table of contents, and a list of illustrations and tables are all possibilities for the front matter—pages preceding the actual report. Different styles require some or all of those parts. The body of the research paper is the typed text, including the report, appropriate citations, headers, and footnotes. At the end of the report is reference material, which could include appendices, a bibliography or references, a glossary, and an index. The body of the report is usually double-spaced, with the exception of indented block quotes, which are single-spaced. Footnotes should also be single-spaced.

Opening the Starting File

You will open a rough draft of the research paper. The paper is a first draft for research on the sustainable spa industry. A sustainable establishment includes building features and resources that conserve energy and protect the environment, such as low-flow water fixtures and solar lighting. You will display nonprinting characters, view the rulers, and then save the file with a new name.

W04.00

To Open the Starting File

a. Start **Word**, click **Open Other Documents** in the left pane, and then double-click **Computer**. Navigate through the folder structure to the location of your student data files, and then open **w02ws04Research**. A rough draft of the research paper opens.

b. If necessary, on the HOME tab, in the Paragraph group, click **Show/Hide** ¶ to display nonprinting characters.

c. If the horizontal and vertical rulers are not visible at the top and left sides of the document, click the **VIEW** tab, and then in the Show group, click **Ruler**.

d. Click the **FILE** tab, and then click **Save As**. Double-click **Computer**. In the Save As dialog box, navigate to where you are saving your project files, and then save the file name as w02ws04Research_LastFirst, using your last and first name.

Pages in a research paper are numbered, with a few exceptions. The title page and dedication do not display page numbers, but they are included in the page count. The front matter is numbered with consecutive lowercase Roman numerals. The remaining pages are numbered with Arabic numerals: 1, 2, 3, and so on. The exact placement of page numbers depends upon the writing style in use.

Both MLA and APA are well-accepted writing styles in college composition classes. With the exception of page numbering rules and heading alignment, both styles are very similar. Although you will use MLA style for the document in this workshop, a quick review of APA formatting guidelines would enable you to easily format the research paper in APA style. An MLA document should be formatted as follows:

- All lines are double-spaced.
- The first line of each body paragraph is indented 0.5" from the left margin.
- The font should be 10 pt to 12 pt Times New Roman or a similar font.
- A right-aligned header is included, with your last name and a page number.
- The top, bottom, right, and left margins are set to 1".
- It is recommended that you include your name, instructor name, class number, and date, left-aligned and double-spaced above the report title.

Working with Spacing and Indentation in a Research Paper

Review the document for adherence to MLA formatting rules. You will then double-space the body of your report and remove the paragraph after spacing. You will also set a 0.5" first-line indentation.

MyITLab®
Workshop 4 Training

W04.01

To Work with Spacing and Indentation in a Research Paper

a. Select all body paragraphs, beginning with **Often associated** and ending at the **end of the document**. Click the **HOME** tab, and then in the Paragraph group, click the **Paragraph Dialog Box Launcher** .

b. Under Indentation, click the **Special** arrow. Select **First line** to indent the first line of each paragraph 0.5".

c. Under Spacing, click the **After** down arrow to set a **0 pt** paragraph After spacing. Click the **Line spacing** arrow, and then select **Double**. Click **OK**.

d. Click anywhere in the document to deselect the paragraphs. Scroll to the bottom of the first page, and then select the heading **Seeking LEED Certification**.

Because the heading should be aligned on the left margin, you will move the first-line indent to the 0" mark.

e. On the ruler, drag the **First Line Indent** marker to the left to align it with the left margin at the 0" mark. Similarly, adjust the first-line indent of the heading **Living in Harmony with Nature**.

f. **Save** the document.

Working with Headers in a Research Paper

You will continue to follow the MLA formatting rules to format your research paper. With the exception of the first page, you will add a right-aligned header with your last name and the current page number.

W04.02

To Work with Headers in a Research Paper

a. Press Ctrl+Home. In the first line of the document, change **Firstname** to your first name and change **Lastname** to your last name.

b. Click the **INSERT** tab, and then in the Header & Footer group, click **Header**, and then select **Edit Header**. Click the **HOME** tab, and then in the Paragraph group, click **Align Right** .

You will insert a right-aligned header including your last name and a page number, as required by MLA style.

c. Type your last name, and then press Spacebar. Under HEADER & FOOTER TOOLS, click the **DESIGN** tab, and then in the Insert group, click **Quick Parts**, and then select **Field**. In the Field dialog box, scroll through the **Field names** list, and then select **Page**. Under Field Properties, in the Format group, select the first item in the list, **1, 2, 3**. Click **OK**.

d. In the Options group, click the **Different First Page** check box because you do not want the header to be displayed on the first page of the report. **Close** the header.

e. Click the **VIEW** tab, and then in the Zoom group, click **Multiple Pages** to view the report. Scroll through the report, noting that it includes four pages, and that the header is displayed on all pages with the exception of the first.

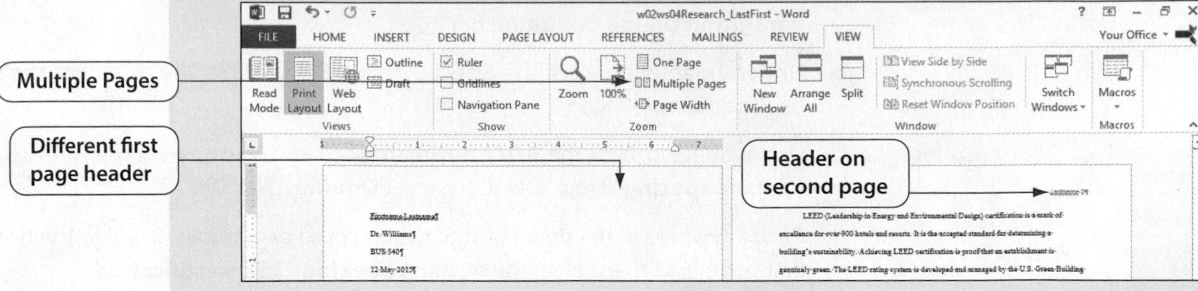

Figure 1 Research paper header

f. In the Zoom group, click **100%**. **Save** the document.

Inserting Citations

Referencing, or citing, is the act of giving credit for ideas and information in your research paper. If you quote someone, use someone else's words or ideas, or include information gleaned from another publication, you must indicate the source of your information. Including a reference to a published or unpublished source, or a **citation**, is necessary whether you use the exact words of the source or whether you paraphrase it. You must always give credit so that you are not in danger of plagiarism.

An in-text reference is information that you include beside any text to give credit to another source. For example, the information can include the author's name and page number in parentheses. This parenthetical reference should be short, in order to minimize interruption of the text itself. It should be placed at the end of a paragraph, if the entire paragraph is borrowed, or at the end of a sentence if the following sentence is your own work or is identified by another citation. The purpose of an in-text citation is to direct the reader to the correct entry in your list of works cited at the end of the research paper or to locate the source in a library. Rules for including citations vary among the writing styles, but generally you are required to list the author or publication name along with a year, with an optional page number.

You are not required to reference information that is assumed to be general knowledge in the field. Neither should you reference text that is your own summary or determination based on your research. The conclusion of a research paper is most often comprised of your thoughts and suggestions, so references are seldom included in a paper's conclusion.

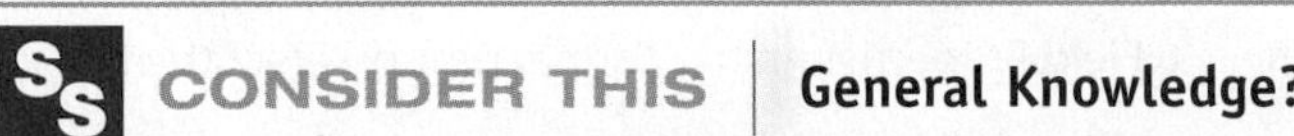

"General knowledge" is broadly defined. You do not need to cite general knowledge, but you do need to give credit for knowledge from the others' work; therefore, you should have a clear definition in mind. How would you define general knowledge?

Word includes reference tools that enable you to accurately include citations, according to one of several writing styles. Enabling Word to format the citations means that you do not have to pay as much attention to learning the minutia of a particular writing style. Although a style guide is handy, it becomes less necessary when Word assists you in the referencing task. The References tab contains several tools that you will become familiar with when formatting a research paper.

REAL WORLD ADVICE **When to Place a Citation**

Although Word simplifies the technical task of citing research, you must still remember to include citations. The task is easier if you place citations in the text as you write the paper. If you wait until the paper is finished, you must backtrack to locate material and position citations. If you have to backtrack, you risk missing a citation and plagiarizing.

You have already begun to insert citations into your research paper. You will continue this process and insert an additional journal and website citation. You will also edit one of the citations in the document and reuse a previous citation.

W04.03

To Insert Citations

a. At the top of the second page, in the first sentence of the first paragraph, place the insertion point after the word **resorts** but before the period. The information in this first sentence came from a journal that you will reference.

b. Click the **REFERENCES** tab, and then in the Citations & Bibliography group, click the **Style** arrow, and then if necessary, select **MLA Seventh Edition**. In the Citations & Bibliography group, click **Insert Citation**, and then select **Add New Source**. In the Create Source dialog box, click the **Type of Source** arrow, and then select **Journal Article**.

c. Because the MLA style requires a volume number and an issue number for a journal, you must show more areas than those currently displayed in the dialog box. Click the **Show All Bibliography Fields** check box to expand the areas shown. Insert the information shown below. You must scroll down the listing to locate the Volume and Issue fields.

Title	The Greening of the Spa Industry
Journal Name	LEED News
Year	2015
Pages	58
Volume	68
Issue	4

SIDE NOTE
Move from Field to Field
Press Tab to move to the next field.

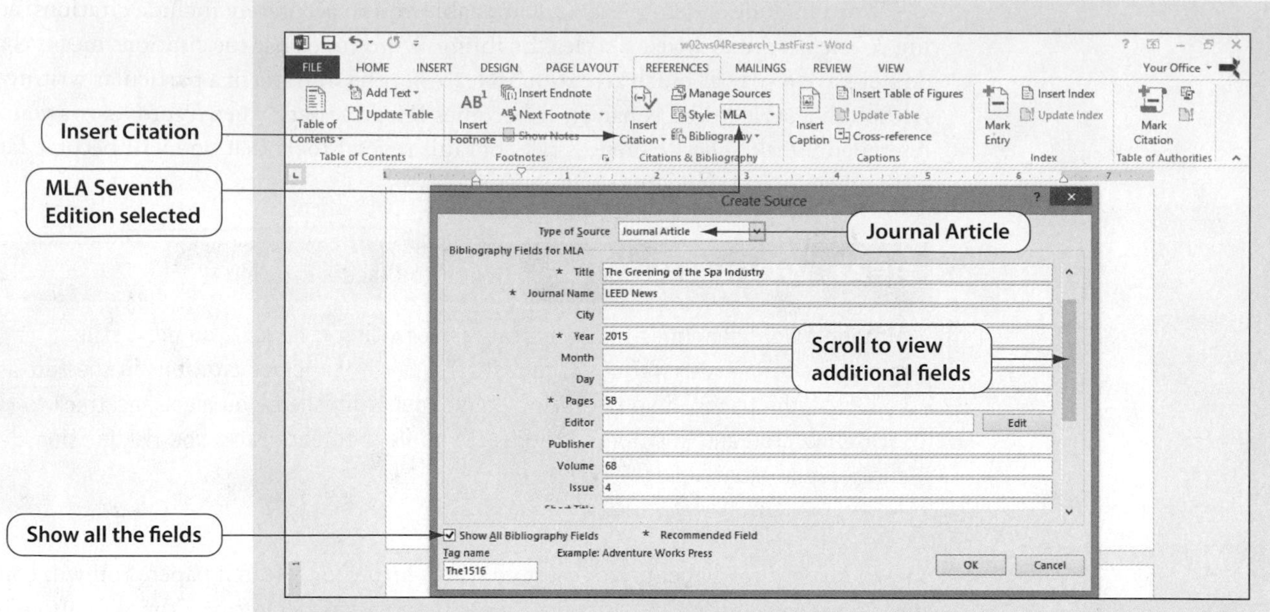

Figure 2 Adding a journal citation

d. Click **OK** when finished entering the data.

The citation (The Greening of the Spa Industry) is inserted at the end of the sentence.

e. Under the **Seeking LEED Certification** heading, toward the bottom of the second paragraph, after the word **practices**, click in the **(Clairday)** citation. A content control is displayed around the citation. Click the **arrow** on the right of the content control, and then select **Edit Citation**. Type 48 in the Pages box, and then click the **Author**, **Year**, and **Title** check boxes to suppress the display of those items within the citation.

Because the author name is mentioned in the sentence, you are revising the parenthetical citation so it includes a page number, but no author name.

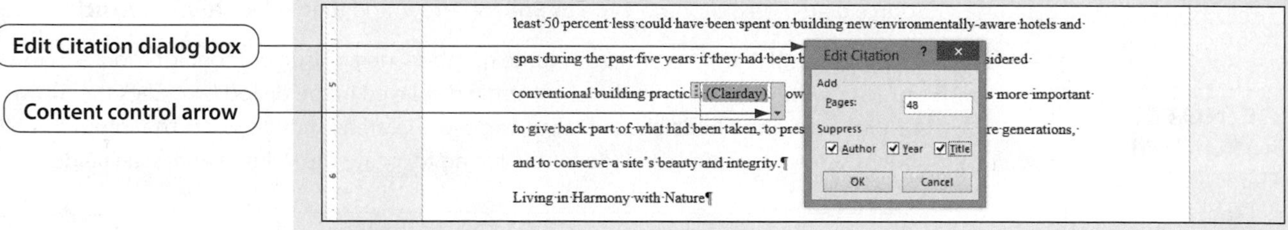

Figure 3 Editing a citation

f. Click **OK**. Scroll down to the bottom of the second page. Under the heading **Living in Harmony with Nature**, in the first sentence, click after the word **future** but before the period. On the REFERENCES tab, in the Citations & Bibliography group, click **Insert Citation**, and then select **Clairday, Steven**.

Because you are reusing a citation referring to work referenced earlier, you can simply select the citation from the list.

Select preexisting citation

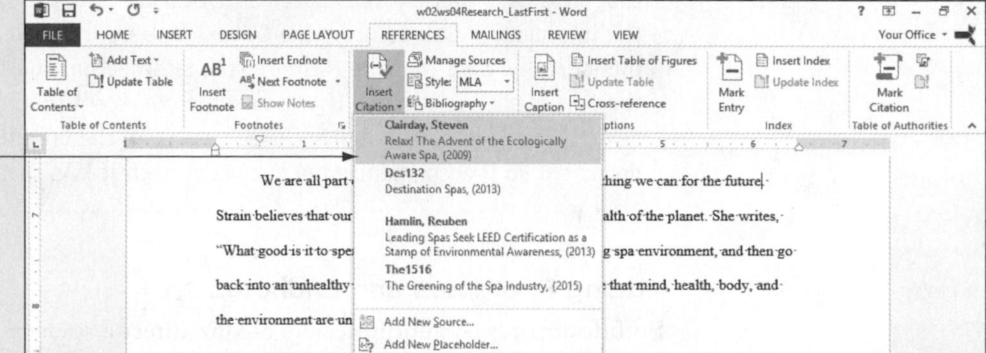

Figure 4 Reusing a citation

SIDE NOTE
Website Citations
URLs are no longer required in citations. MLA recommends a URL if the reader is not likely to find the source otherwise.

g. Near the bottom of page 3, in the sentence ending with **accountability expected of a green spa**, click after the word **spa** and before the period. In the Citations & Bibliography group, click **Insert Citation**, and then select **Add New Source**. Click the **Type of Source** arrow, scroll down the list, and then select **Web site**. Click the **Show All Bibliography Fields** check box. Type the information below:

Name of Web Page	The Green Spa Industry
Year Accessed	2015
Month Accessed	April
Day Accessed	12
URL	http://www.spanetworknews.com/green

h. Click **OK**, and then **save** the document.

QUICK REFERENCE | **Helpful Tips for Placing Citations**

1. For regular text citations, always place a citation outside a quotation and before a punctuation mark that ends a sentence.
2. For long quotations which have been set off—indented—from the main text, place a citation after the punctuation mark.
3. If possible, include reference information such as an author's name in the sentence to avoid long parenthetical information.

REAL WORLD ADVICE Managing Sources

Did you know that Word maintains two lists of sources—a Master List and a Current List? When you create a source in a research paper, the citation is added to both lists. The Current List contains cited sources for the current document. The Master List includes sources that are available for use in any document on the local computer. That means, by using the Master List, you can include sources in the current document that were used in a previous document. This prevents you from having to retype the information. Sources from the Current List are included in the document's bibliography. Note that the Master List is retained only on the computer on which the document was created. If you save the document to another computer's storage device, the Master List is not included. However, the Current List is saved with the document so it accompanies the document even if it is saved to another disk drive.

Adding Footnotes and Endnotes

Both **footnotes** and **endnotes** are used to direct a reader to a specific source of information referred to in a paper. Footnotes are placed numerically at the foot of the page where a direct reference is made, while endnotes appear in a numerical list at the end of the paper, but before a bibliography or works cited page. A footnote is required each time a document is referenced in a paper, possibly yielding several footnotes on the same source. A general rule of thumb is that if you include footnotes to identify references, you do not need endnotes. Word makes it easy to include footnotes and endnotes, with options on the References tab.

When you include a footnote or endnote, you place a number or symbol in superscript—slightly elevated from the line—to the right of the source information that you want to reference. The detailed reference is then keyed to the same number or symbol at the end of the page (footnote) or at the end of the document (endnote). If you use footnotes or endnotes, you do not need to include parenthetical information beside the source.

Footnotes and endnotes are not used as often as they once were. Since 1988, MLA has recommended parenthetical information instead of footnotes. Parenthetical references are directly tied to a works cited list, which serves as a comprehensive list of all references throughout a paper. A works cited page or a bibliography is a general requirement in university composition classes and is standard practice in the preparation of research papers.

Including parenthetical information does not mean that you cannot use footnotes to provide more detailed descriptions of statements or facts in the paper. A research paper can appear cluttered if you overuse footnotes or endnotes, but depending on the writing style used, and an instructor's preference, you might be required to include them. For example, you can use a footnote to provide an explanation of statistics. You might also define or illustrate a concept included in the report, providing a personal comment. Using a footnote is a great way to further describe a concept without having to incorporate it into the written paragraph. That way, you do not risk muddling the text with overly explanatory text, perhaps losing or diverting the attention of the reader.

If you choose to include footnotes, you should know that most writing styles limit a footnote to only one sentence. In a bibliography, however, each entry consists of three sentences. The first sentence gives the author name, the second is the title statement, and the last describes publication information including publisher and publication date. You will add a footnote to your document and then change the superscript numeral to an asterisk.

W04.04

To Add and Edit Footnotes

a. Scroll to the second page. In the first paragraph, place the insertion point immediately after the period following **Washington, DC**. You will add a footnote providing additional information on the LEED program.

b. On the REFERENCES tab, in the Footnotes group, click **Insert Footnote**.

A numeral superscript is placed at the insertion point, a divider is placed at the foot of the current page, and the same superscripted numeral begins the footnote. You will type additional text to make the comment.

c. Type **LEED is the primary internationally recognized building certification system for environmental awareness.** Include the period.

> **Troubleshooting**
> If the insertion point is displayed at the end of the document instead of the bottom margin of the current page, you clicked Insert Endnote instead of Insert Footnote. Click Undo and repeat Steps b and c.

SIDE NOTE
A Footnote is Not a Footer
A footnote provides further explanation of an item in a paper. A footer is text that appears at the bottom of every page, such as a file name.

d. Double-click the raised number **1** in the footnote to return to the reference in the document.

> **Troubleshooting**
> If double-clicking the footnote number does not advance you to the footnote in the document, you probably clicked near, but not on, the number. Double-click the footnote number in the footnote area of the report again.

SIDE NOTE
To Quickly Move to the Footnote
Double-click the footnote reference number at the end of the sentence in the document to move directly to the footnote at the end of the page.

e. Drag to select the raised number **1**—superscript—beside the words **Washington, DC**.

Because this is the only footnote you will include in the document, you decide to define a symbol instead of a number for the footnote designator. You will use an asterisk.

f. On the REFERENCES tab, in the Footnotes group, click the **Footnote and Endnote Dialog Box Launcher**, and then click the **Symbol** button.

g. Confirm that the Font box displays **Symbol**. Scroll up, if necessary, and then near the middle of the first row, click the **asterisk (*)**. If you do not see the symbol, click in the **Character code** box, and then type 42.

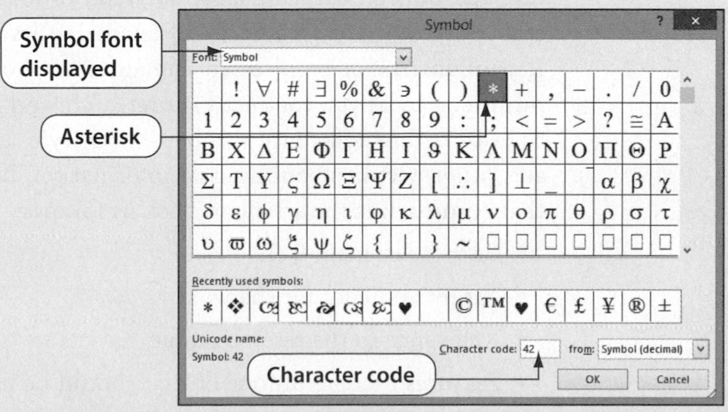

Figure 5 Selecting a footnote symbol

h. Click **OK**, and then click **Insert**. The footnote symbol is changed to an asterisk in both the document reference and in the footnote itself.

i. Select the entire **footnote line**. Click the **HOME** tab, and then in the Font group, change the font size to **9** and the font to **Times New Roman**.

j. **Save** [Save] the document.

Develop a Bibliography or Works Cited Page

A **bibliography** is an alphabetical list of all documents or sources used during the research of a paper, even if they were not specifically referenced in the paper. A bibliography can help others understand the basis for your work. In addition, they can use your bibliography as a springboard, perhaps consulting some of the same sources as they continue to study the subject of your research. Although similar to a bibliography, a **works cited** page serves a different purpose. Only those sources that you actually referenced in the paper are included as works cited. The rule is, if you place a parenthetical reference in a paper, there must be a corresponding item in the list of works cited. The major difference is that a bibliography is more inclusive, listing all sources whether they were referenced or not. A works cited page is considered part of the document, continuing the page numbering, whereas a bibliography is a separate component.

MLA style uses the term "works cited" to refer to the works cited page, whereas APA style prefers "references." Both terms are synonymous. Each is an alphabetical list of works that you have referenced in the body of a research report. Entries are placed in alphabetical order by last names of authors, editors, or by first words of titles.

Options on Word's References tab enable you to easily add citations, footnotes, endnotes, bibliographies, and works cited pages. Word prepares the bibliography or works cited page directly from the parenthetical citations that you included when you used the Insert Citation command. Having selected the writing style (MLA, APA, etc.), Word formats all citations and the works cited page appropriately. You can edit the bibliography page to include additional sources or to modify existing ones, if necessary.

Using an Annotated Bibliography

An **annotated bibliography** is a special type of bibliography that compiles references along with a short paragraph summarizing or reviewing the value of the source to the research project. Creating an annotated bibliography gives you a chance to consider several sources, evaluating each to determine its applicability and value to your project. If your instructor requires an annotated bibliography, you should begin preparing the bibliography as you conduct your research, and you should consult relevant writing style rules to ensure adherence to a particular style. For each source, include not only the title and other pertinent publication information, but also a paragraph of 150 words or less that summarizes the article or book as follows:

- Purpose or main focus
- Target audience for the work
- Relevance to the research topic
- Features that are unique or that should be helpful
- Author credibility and background
- Author conclusions and observations

Creating a Bibliography or Works Cited Page

Although a writing style manual (MLA, APA, Chicago, etc.) can be helpful as you develop various parts of a research paper, you can also rely on Word to correctly format bibliography and works cited pages. The Citations & Bibliography group on the References tab includes a Bibliography option from which you can insert a predesigned bibliography or works cited page. You can also choose to insert a bibliography page with no heading or title, so you can manage it more independently. Regardless of which approach you take, you should always confirm the resulting page meets all requirements of the particular style you are following. Just as you would proofread a document instead of relying solely on Word's spelling checker, you should also consult a writing style manual to make sure your bibliography or works cited page is correct.

When Word creates a bibliography or works cited page, it places all citations in a field, which is a unit that is recognized as a single entity. The name of the field does not change, but its contents can. The Citations field is a unit that can be updated if you add more references to the document. In fact, when you click any text on a bibliography or works cited page, a content control tab, titled Update Citations and Bibliography, appears at the top of the selected list of citations. If you have included additional citations in the body of the research paper, clicking the content control tab automatically updates the bibliography. You can also change bibliography entries into static text, which removes the field designation and enables you to treat the text as normal, editing and deleting references at will. You will create a Works Cited page in your research paper.

W04.05

To Create a Works Cited Page

a. Press Ctrl+End.

Because a bibliography or works cited must begin on a new page, you will insert a manual page break so text begins on the following page.

b. Click the **PAGE LAYOUT** tab, and then in the Page Setup group, click **Breaks**, and then select **Page**.

SIDE NOTE
Insert a Page Break
Alternatively, press Ctrl+Enter to insert a page break.

c. Click the **REFERENCES** tab, and then in the Citations & Bibliography group, click **Bibliography**, and then select **Works Cited**. The sources that you inserted as you created the research paper will be alphabetically placed under the title Works Cited.

SIDE NOTE
Insert a Bibliography
Click Bibliography and then select Bibliography, which includes all citations, but without a page title.

d. Scroll up to view the works cited page, with five entries. The Works Cited title is left-aligned above the entries. Click any **entry** to select the Works Cited field. Note that all entries are shaded, indicating they are considered a single unit. You will also see the content control tab, **Update Citations and Bibliography**, which you will use later in the workshop to update the Works Cited page.

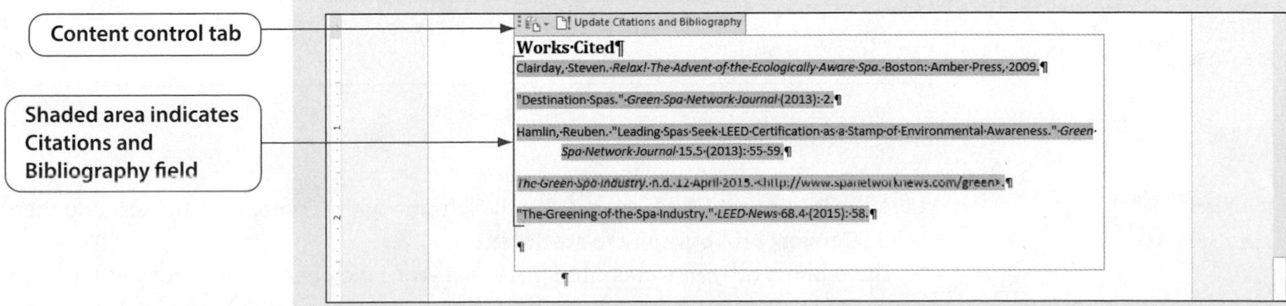

Figure 6 Works Cited page

e. **Save** the document.

Editing a Bibliography or Works Cited Page

The only distinction that Word makes between a bibliography and a works cited page is the title. All sources that you have created in the paper are included on the bibliography or works cited page. However, a bibliography actually differs from a works cited page in that it includes all resources, even those that are not cited in the paper. Therefore, the bibliography included with your research paper might not be complete after Word creates it. In that case, you will need to edit the page to include other resources that helped you develop the paper. You can add and edit sources using the Manage Sources button on the References tab. In addition, as shown in the following exercise, you can modify a source directly from the parenthetical information in your document.

In reviewing your research paper, you determine that one of the citations should be updated and corrected. Even if you have already created a works cited page, you can edit the citation source and then easily update the works cited to include the new information. You will then format the Works Cited page according to the MLA style.

W04.06

To Edit an Existing Source and to Update Works Cited

SIDE NOTE
Edit a Source
Alternatively, on the References tab, click Manage Sources. Select the source from the Current List, and click Edit.

a. Scroll to the second page and locate the **(48)** reference in the second paragraph. Click in the **(48)** citation. A content control appears around the citation. Click the **arrow** on the right, and then select **Edit Source**.

b. Click the **Show All Bibliography Fields** check box. Click in the **Year** box, and then change the year to 2015. Scroll down, click in the **Edition** box, and then type 2nd ed. including the period. Click **OK**. If you are asked to update the master source list and the current document, click **Yes**. MLA requires an edition for a book if it is a 2nd edition or later.

c. Press Ctrl+End. Scroll up slightly and note that the Clairday reference still includes 2009 as the year. Click any reference in the **Works Cited page** to display the content control. Click the **Update Citations and Bibliography** tab. The works cited list is updated with the new edition and year in the Clairday reference.

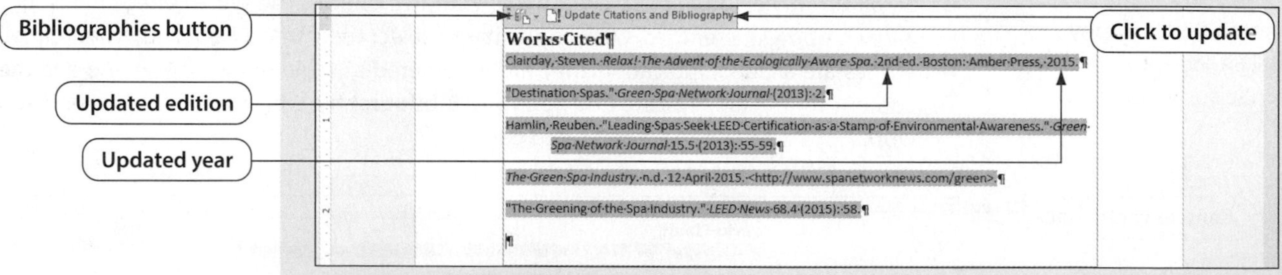

Figure 7 To update works cited

d. Click the **Bibliographies** button on the left side of the content control tab, and then select **Convert bibliography to static text**.

The bibliography or works cited page that Word includes is not exactly as required by MLA. Because you must edit the page slightly to accommodate the MLA style, you convert the field to regular, or static, text. After you convert the page, it can no longer be updated automatically if citations are changed, so only convert to static text after all updates are complete.

> **Troubleshooting**
> Even though the bibliography is converted to static text, the Update Citations and Bibliography tab will still appear, and the bibliography will still be selected as a unit when you click any entry.

e. Select all text on the works cited page, including the Works Cited title, and then change the font size to **12** and the font to **Times New Roman**. With the text still selected, change the paragraph **After** spacing to **0 pt** and the Line spacing to **Double**. Center the title **Works Cited**. If necessary, click outside the Works Cited area to deselect the text. The Works Cited page is now formatted according to the MLA style.

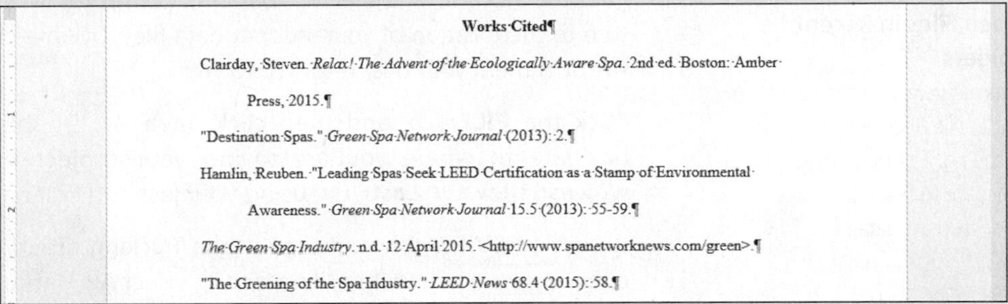

Works·Cited¶

Clairday,·Steven.·*Relax!·The·Advent·of·the·Ecologically·Aware·Spa.*·2nd·ed.·Boston:·Amber·Press,·2015.¶

"Destination·Spas."·*Green·Spa·Network·Journal*·(2013):·2.¶

Hamlin,·Reuben.·"Leading·Spas·Seek·LEED·Certification·as·a·Stamp·of·Environmental·Awareness."·*Green·Spa·Network·Journal*·15.5·(2013):·55-59.¶

The·Green·Spa·Industry.·n.d.·12·April·2015.·<http://www.spanetworknews.com/green>.¶

"The·Greening·of·the·Spa·Industry."·*LEED·News*·68.4·(2015):·58.¶

Figure 8 Works cited in MLA format

f. **Save** the document. Click the **FILE** tab, and then click **Close** to close the w02ws04Research_LastFirst file. The Word application remains open.

Reviewing a Document

Word enables multiple people to effectively collaborate on a project with the Tracking and Comment tools on the Review tab. A **comment** is a note or annotated text that can be added to a document that has been sent to you for review. You can also add comments to your own document to remind yourself, for example, to verify an address or research a topic in more depth. The **Track Changes** tool enables you to keep track of all formatting changes, additions, and deletions in your document. Typically the original author will turn on the Track Changes feature, and then send the document for review to one or more people. The reviewers in turn will make their changes and return the document to the original author. The changes are tracked with revision marks. For example, deletions are marked with strikeout lines, and additions are indicated with underlines, though the marks can vary depending on how you set up your preferences. The original author can then choose to accept or reject those changes. In this section, you will track changes, accept and reject changes, and work with comments.

Work with Comments

Comments can be displayed in the Reviewing pane or in the margin of the document. The comment will contain your user name and the time it was created. You can set how your name will appear in a comment by setting the User name in the General section of the Word Options dialog box. When reviewing comments from multiple users, Word will automatically color code the comments, one color per user. For new documents created in Word 2013, the comments will display the user's picture if he or she signs in with a Microsoft account. In addition, Word enables you to easily contact the reviewers via an e-mail, IM, or chat link. The ability to reply directly to a comment so an entire discussion is saved as one unit is a new feature in Word 2013. In addition, you can now mark a comment as done. This will shrink the comment and grey it out. It gets the comment out of the way, but keeps the information accessible if needed.

Reviewing Comments

You asked your boss to review your research paper, providing suggestions wherever possible. You will open the document he returned to you and review the comments. You will reply to a comment and mark the comment as done.

W04.07

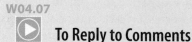

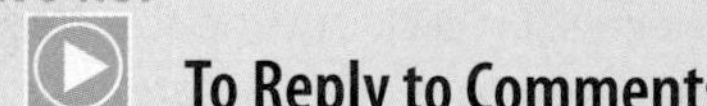

To Reply to Comments

SIDE NOTE
Open Files in Recent Folders
Alternatively, you can click under the Recent Folders list in the right-pane to quickly navigate to the location of your student data files.

a. Click the **FILE** tab, and then double-click **Computer**. Navigate through the folder structure to the location of your student data files. Double-click **w02ws04Review** to open the document your boss returned to you.

b. Click the **FILE** tab, and then click **Save As**. Double-click **Computer**, and then navigate to where you are saving your project files. Save the document as w02ws04Review_LastFirst, using your last and first name.

c. Click the **REVIEW** tab, and then in the Tracking group, click the **Display for Review** arrow Simple Markup, and then, if necessary, select **All Markup**.

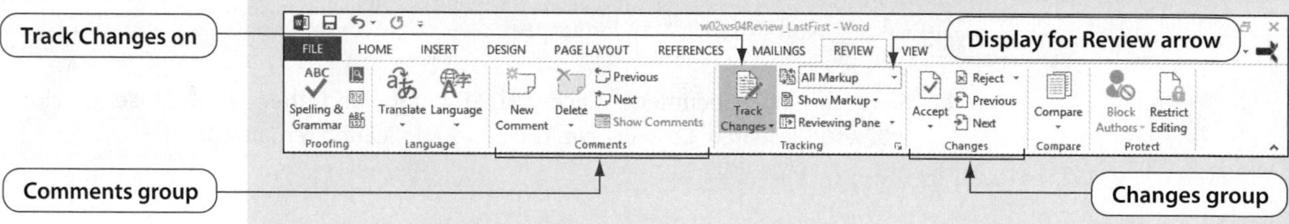

Figure 9 Review tab

SIDE NOTE
Hide All Comments in a Document
On the Review tab, in the Tracking group, click Show Markup, and then select Comments to deselect it.

d. Press Ctrl+Home. On the REVIEW tab, in the Comments group, click **Next** to view the first comment, starting with **I think they changed their name**.

Troubleshooting
If you are not viewing the comment, you might have clicked Next in the Changes group instead of the Comments group. Click Next in the Comments group.

SIDE NOTE
Reply to a Comment
Alternatively, right-click the comment, and then select Reply To Comment.

e. If necessary, scroll to the right of the document. Click the **Reply** button in the comment to reply to the comment. Type Verify name. including the period.

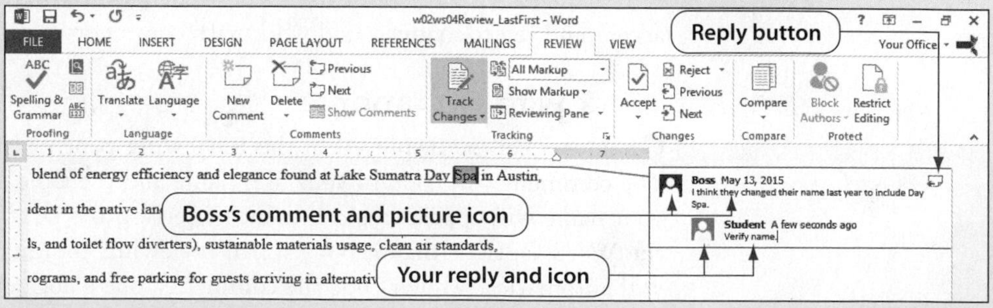

SIDE NOTE
Print Comments
On the Review tab, click Show Markup. Select Comments. In Backstage view, click Print, and then click Print All Pages. Select Print Markup.

Figure 10 Reply to a comment

MODULE 2

f. Point to the left of the boss's comment, in the picture icon, and then right-click. Select **Mark Comment Done** from the shortcut menu. The entire comment will be greyed out and the text will shrink down; yet it remains in the document for future access.

Troubleshooting

If only your comment is greyed out, you pointed to the left of your reply, instead of to the left of the boss's comment. Click Undo and redo Step f.

g. **Save** the document.

Deleting and Adding Comments

You will continue to review the comments. You will now delete the second comment and add a new comment.

SIDE NOTE

Delete All Comments in a Document

On the Review tab, in the Comments group, click the Delete arrow, and then select Delete All Comments in Document.

W04.08

To Delete and Add Comments

a. Press Ctrl+End. On the REVIEW tab, in the Comments group, click **Previous** to view the comment at the end of the document, **Great job!** In the Comments group, click **Delete**. If you clicked the Delete arrow instead of the Delete button, then simply select Delete.

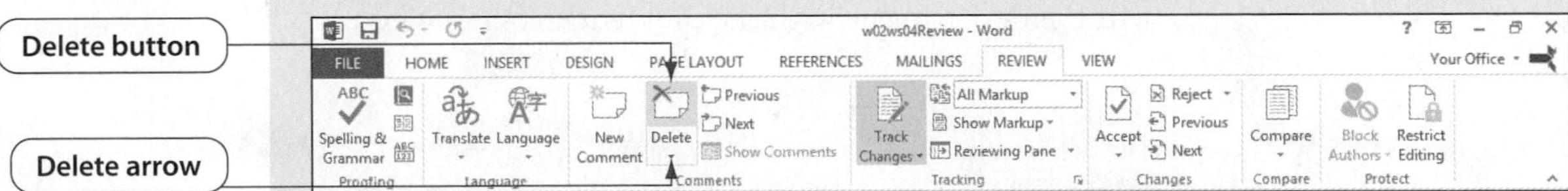

Figure 11 Delete a comment

b. Scroll to the middle of page 3. At the beginning of the second paragraph, select the word **Sarah**. In the Comments group, click **New Comment**, and then type Verify spelling. including the period.

c. **Save** the document.

Track Changes

Click the Track Changes button on the Review tab to track all changes, from that point on. Click the Track Changes button again to turn the feature off. When the feature is turned off, changes made to the document will not be monitored, though previous changes made while the feature was on will still be documented until they have been rejected or accepted. Word 2013 enables you to Lock Tracking to ensure that all changes made to a document will be monitored. A password is required to lock and unlock tracking. Once it is turned on, changes cannot be accepted or rejected, though comments can still be deleted.

REAL WORLD ADVICE Track Changes Indicator on the Status Bar

Right-click the status bar, and then select Track Changes from the shortcut menu. A Track Changes indicator will appear on the status bar set to ON or OFF depending on if the Track Changes feature is active or not. This is an easy way to determine if your changes are being tracked. You can even click the indicator for a quick and easy way to turn the feature on and off without having to click the Review tab.

Viewing a Changed Document

Word provides four ways to view tracked changes and comments. By default, in **All Markup** view, comments and formatting changes appear to the right of the document, while addition and deletion marks appear directly in the document. The Track Changes Options dialog box enables you to modify how you view these changes. New to Word 2013 is **Simple Markup**. It provides a less cluttered view of the document, using red vertical lines to indicate changes and balloons to indicate comments. Simply click the vertical red lines to view the changes in All Markup view; click again to hide the changes and return back to Simple Markup view. Similarly, click a balloon to view a single comment, and then click again to hide the comment. The Original view enables you to view the original document, without any of the changes. The No Markup view enables you to view the final document, if you were to accept all the suggested changes. The changes are still there, but only hidden from view. The next time the document is opened, the changes will be displayed. Keep in mind, the only way to permanently remove the changes from a document is to accept or reject them. You can accept or reject one change at a time or all at one time. You will now review the changes made to the document. The first thing you will do is to turn off the Track Changes feature so further changes are not tracked. You will then experiment with the different tracking views.

W04.09

To Turn Off Track Changes and to Change Tracking Views

SIDE NOTE
Turn Off Track Changes
Turn off the Track Changes feature when you do not need to track any more changes to the document.

a. Press Ctrl+Home. As you review the document you realize that you entered the wrong course number. In the third line of the document, place the insertion point immediately after **BUS 340**, and then type 1.

b. You realize the Track Changes feature is still on. On the Quick Access Toolbar, click **Undo**. On the REVIEW tab, in the Tracking group, click **Track Changes** to turn the feature off. Type 1 and notice that the text is now added without tracking.

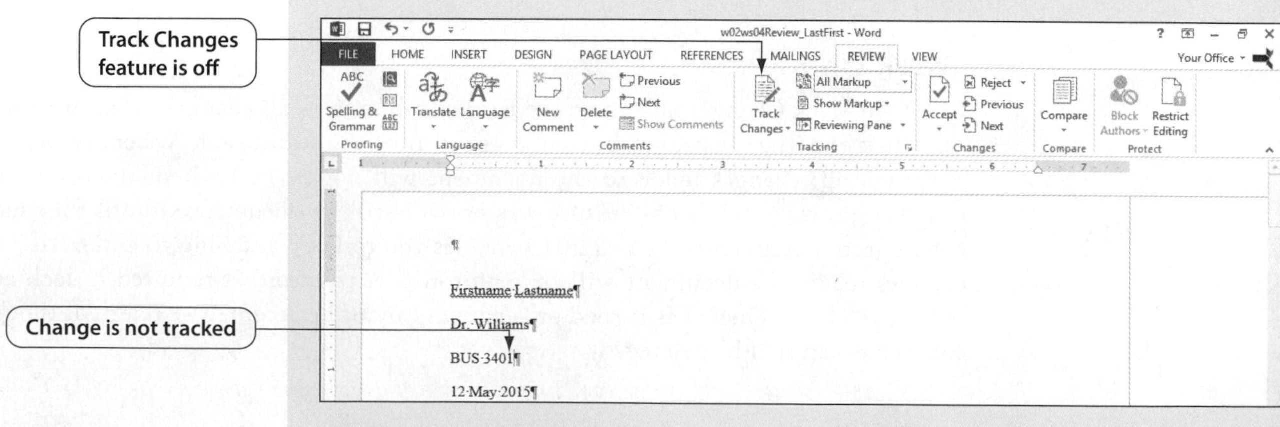

Figure 12 Tracking group

c. In the Tracking group, click the **Display for Review** arrow Simple Markup, and then select **Simple Markup**. Notice the changes to the document. Tracked changes are indicated with red vertical lines. Scroll down to view the comments at the end of the document. Comments are indicated with balloons.

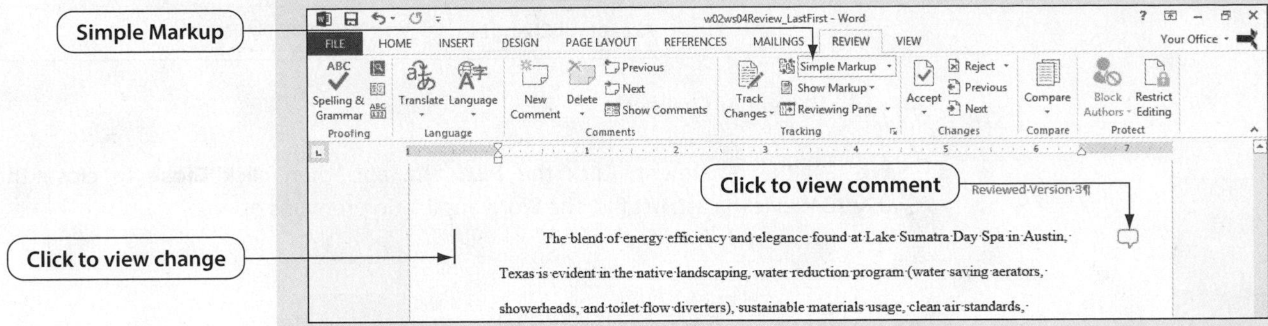

Figure 13 Simple Markup

SIDE NOTE

View Comments in Simple Markup View

Simply click the balloon to view the comment, and then click anywhere in the document to hide the comment.

d. Press Ctrl+Home. Click the **first red vertical line** in the left margin. The view changes to All Markup and the red vertical line changes to a grey color.

You can click the grey vertical line to return to Simple Markup view. Because you prefer to view all the changes at one time, you will remain in All Markup view.

e. **Save** the document.

Accepting and Rejecting Changes

You will now incorporate the changes your boss made into the document. Because the Track Changes feature was turned on when he made the changes, you are able to accept or reject the changes as you see necessary. You will reject the first change, accept the second change, and then automatically accept the remaining changes.

W04.10

To Accept and Reject Changes

a. Press Ctrl+Home. On the REVIEW tab, in the Changes group, click **Next** to view the first change. Because the MLA style does not support underlined titles, in the Changes group, click **Reject**.

Troubleshooting

If you click the Reject arrow, select Reject and Move to Next.

b. The change was rejected, and the next change is highlighted. Because the MLA does not support extra spacing before the body of the document, you will accept this change to remove the spacing. In the Changes group, click **Accept**. Make sure to click the Accept button, and not the Accept arrow.

c. Because you plan to accept the remaining changes, in the Changes group, click the **Accept** arrow, and then select **Accept All Changes**. The comments remain, but the changes have now been applied to the document.

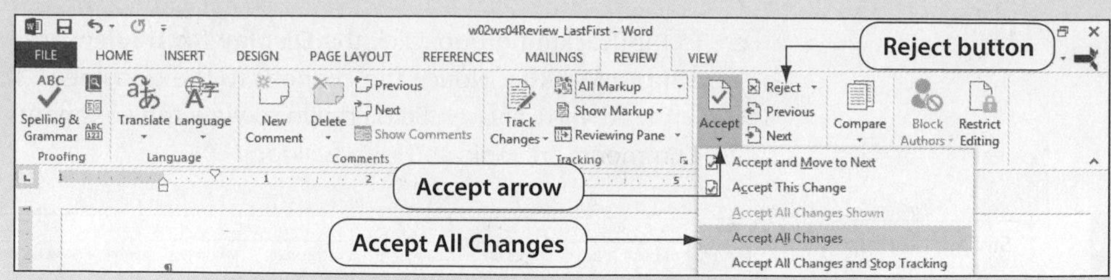

Figure 14 Accept All Changes

d. **Save** the document. Click the **FILE** tab, and then click **Close** to close the w02ws04Review_LastFirst file. The Word application remains open.

Creating a Newsletter

A **newsletter** is a regular publication that is distributed in print, through e-mail, or as a link on a web page. A newsletter is designed to provide information of interest to a defined group of people. Its main purpose is to convey information in an at-a-glance format, using design techniques that consolidate points so they are quickly understood. Catchy graphics and color add an element of entertainment and hold the interest of a reader.

Newsletters can be designed for internal distribution to employees of a company or for external communication to customers, clients, or patrons. Information included in a company newsletter could just as easily be included in a memo, but the newsletter's columnar format, the vibrancy of the text, and the eye-catching graphics is an effective way to grab a reader's attention. Clubs, churches, societies, and professional associations use newsletters to provide information of interest to their members. An organization might include news and upcoming events, as well as contact information, for general member inquiries. Often used as a marketing strategy, a regularly scheduled newsletter can be an effective way to draw attention to a company or a cause and to create enthusiasm among clients. In this section, you will create and format the newsletter.

REAL WORLD ADVICE **When Should You Use an E-Zine?**

An e-zine is an electronic magazine or newsletter, delivered via e-mail or available online. You can duplicate the same content from the electronic version to a printed newsletter, and encourage visits to your website by printing a link at the bottom of all pages of the printed newsletter. An electronic newsletter or e-zine can reach customers outside your immediate geographic area, give you greater exposure, and may even open new business channels. The ideas and strategies for both printed and online newsletters are the same. The only difference is that printed material is more expensive to generate and to distribute. PDF is often used as the format for distribution of electronic newsletters because most computers have the ability to display PDF documents, and the recipient is not able to manipulate the contents without PDF-editing software.

Work with Columns

Many newsletters are designed with text in **columns**, narrow vertical sections of text. A column draws the eye downward, enabling you to scan through information fairly quickly. Because the column widths are narrower, the lines of text are shorter.

This can give the impression that minimal reading is required, making the document more inviting to read. A section break is a common element in a Word newsletter, enabling you to format a newsletter heading or an ending line differently, so the format does not affect other text that may be presented in columns. An entire document can be formatted using columns, or with the use of section breaks, column formatting can be limited to specific sections. You can define up to three columns in each section, or page.

Formatting in Columns

The Columns option on the Page Layout tab enables you to format an entire document in columns, or to limit columns to a specific section. Word evenly spaces columns with equal width by default, but you can specify column width in inches if you need to be more prescriptive. You can even specify the width of the spacing between the columns. Word also enables you to display a line between the columns. You will open the rough draft of the newsletter excerpt. You will then format the body of the newsletter using a three-column layout, keeping the title and the picture in the original one-column layout.

QUICK REFERENCE **Formatting Columns**

1. Click the Page Layout tab.
2. Click Columns.
3. Select the number of columns, or click More Columns for additional options.

W04.11

To Format a Newsletter in Columns

a. Click the **FILE** tab to enter Backstage view. Double-click **Computer**, and then navigate to the location of your student data files. Double-click **w02ws04SpaNews** to open the rough draft of the newsletter excerpt.

b. Click the **FILE** tab, and then click **Save As**. Double-click **Computer**, and then navigate to where you are saving your project files. Save the document as w02ws04SpaNews_LastFirst, using your last and first name.

c. Place the insertion point immediately before the heading **Children at the Oasis**. Click the **PAGE LAYOUT** tab, and then in the Page Setup group, click **Columns**, and then select **Three**.

   The entire document is formatted in a three column layout. Because you prefer to keep the title and picture in a one-column layout, you will undo the format and use the Columns dialog box to specify where to begin the column.

d. On the Quick Access Toolbar, click **Undo** . If necessary, place the insertion point immediately before **Children at the Oasis**. In the Page Setup group, click **Columns**, and then select **More Columns** to open the Columns dialog box.

e. Under Presets, click **Three**. A preview shows three columns of equal width. Click the **Apply to** arrow, and then select **This point forward**.

SIDE NOTE
Apply Columns to Selected Text
Select text, click Columns, and then simply select One, Two, Three, Left, or Right.

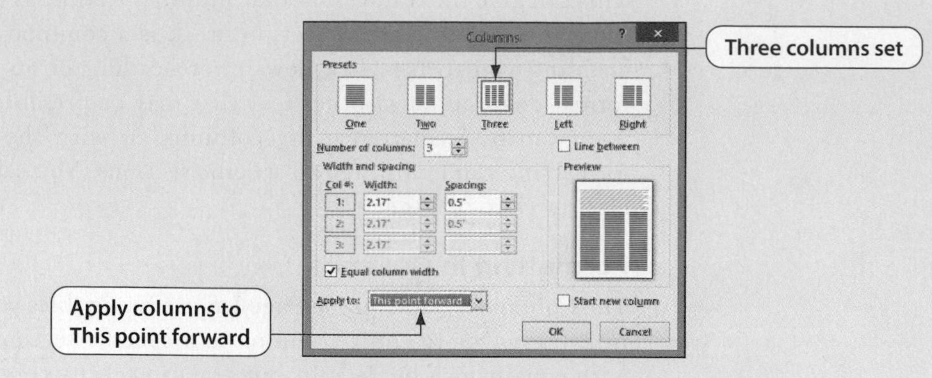

Figure 15 Columns dialog box

f. Click **OK**. Click the **VIEW** tab, and then in the Zoom group, click **One Page**.

A continuous section break is inserted, and all text following the section break is formatted in three evenly spaced columns. The columns are not balanced, however, as they end unevenly. You will address that problem later in this workshop.

g. In the Zoom group, click **100%** to return the view to normal size. **Save** the document.

Inserting a Drop Cap

A **drop cap** is a design element in which the first letter of a paragraph is shown as a large graphic representation of the character. You often see drop caps in magazines and books. They tend to draw the eye to the beginning of an article, providing interest and eye appeal. A drop cap can be placed in the margin next to the paragraph, or with text wrapped around the character. You will set a drop cap for the first letter of the first body paragraph.

W04.12

To Insert a Drop Cap

a. In the first body paragraph, place the insertion point immediately before the text **Join us for mom-and-child**.

b. Click the **INSERT** tab, and then in the Text group, click **Add a Drop Cap**, and then select **Dropped**.

If you need more precision, you can click Drop Cap Options. However, most often, the orientation of the drop cap is appropriate without any additional settings. The letter "J" appears in large print at the left of the paragraph, with text wrapped around it.

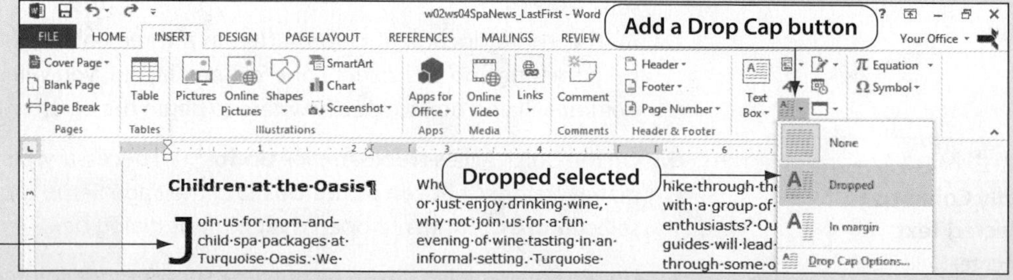

Figure 16 Inserting a drop cap

c. Click anywhere in the document to deselect the drop cap. **Save** the document.

Balancing Columns

Columns will seldom end evenly. Although columns rarely contain an identical amount of text, you will definitely want to avoid having column headings begin awkwardly at the end of a column, or having a small amount of text in a column. You will insert a column break to manually align the columns in a more even fashion.

MODULE 2

W04.13

To Insert a Column Break

a. Scroll down and place the insertion point immediately before **An Evening of Wine Tasting**.

   The first column ends unattractively, with a heading and none of its text. You will insert a column break before the wine heading to move it to a new column.

b. Click the **PAGE LAYOUT** tab, and then in the Page Setup group, click **Breaks**, and then select **Column**.

c. **Save** the document.

Using Pictures in a Columnar Layout

As you recall, newsletters, business cards, and other specialty documents can be enhanced with the addition of pictures and clip art. After inserting a graphic, you can crop, recolor, set the text wrap, or format these graphics with outline styles and various artistic effects. In addition, Word enables you to place graphics in between two columns. Insert the picture, set the text wrap and other effects, and then drag the picture into the white space. The part of the picture that overlaps with the text in the column will still maintain its text wrap setting. You will insert a graphic between the first two columns to enhance the body of the newsletter.

W04.14

To Insert a Picture in a Columnar Layout

a. Under **An Evening of Wine Tasting**, place the insertion point immediately before **Whether you are a wine buff**.

b. You will insert a picture of a wine glass to enhance the body of the newsletter. Click the **INSERT** tab, and then in the Illustrations group, click **Pictures**. Navigate to the location of your student data files, and then double-click **w02ws04Wine**.

c. On the FORMAT tab, in the Arrange group, click **Wrap Text**, and then select **Square**.

d. Drag to position the **picture** as shown. Use the alignment guide to line up the picture with the right edge of the first column.

SIDE NOTE

Clear the Layout Options Button

Press Esc to clear the Layout Options button from the screen.

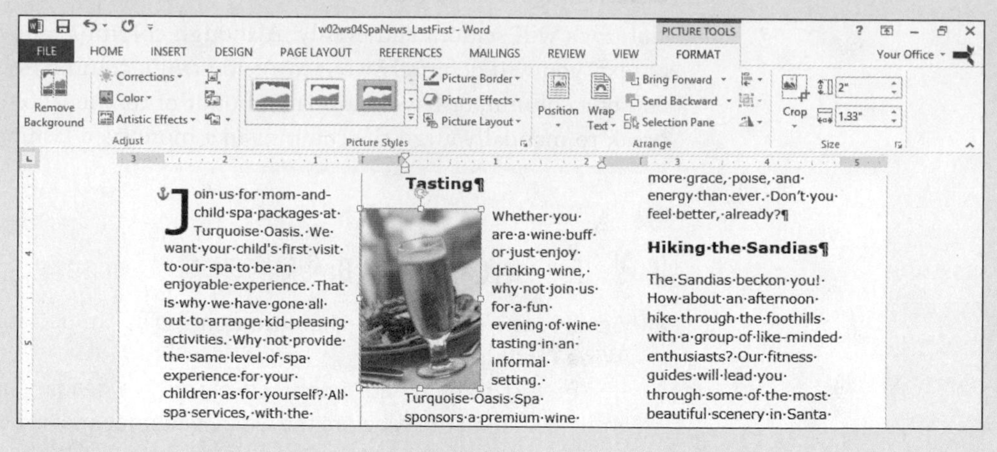

Figure 17 Positioning a picture

e. Click anywhere in the document to deselect the picture. **Save** the document.

Use a Style Guide to Format a Newsletter

As you recall, a style guide is a set of standards for the writing and design of written or edited materials. Organizations and companies use their own style guides to ensure that documents conform to corporate image and policy. Style guides help maintain uniformity and consistency to all publications written for internal or external use. Style guides vary from organization to organization, and can range anywhere from a couple of pages to even hundreds of pages. Many style guides include rules on the use of punctuation, grammar, capitalization, abbreviations, placement of logos, and font types, colors, and sizes. A style guide can even include information for conducting research. For example, the Painted Paradise Resort and Spa has recently produced a style guide that includes a section on how to format a business letter—11-pt or 12-pt Times New Roman font, 1" margins, Plain Number page numbers, resort logo centered in the header, and watermarks when appropriate.

All new written communication is expected to follow The Painted Paradise Resort and Spa style guide from this point forward. The style guide is available in your student data files. Below is an excerpt from the style guide, which includes guidelines that are applicable to the creation of any newsletter. Refer to the style guide for a complete list of guidelines.

- Your newsletter should communicate clearly, consistently, and truthfully.
- Check the newsletter for spelling and grammatical errors before distributing it.
- Provide your contact information.
- Keep the format simple.
- Avoid the use of such words as "we," "us," or "I." Instead, use "you" or "your."
- If possible, provide a simple way to navigate the newsletter, especially if it spans more than one page. A front page sidebar is a great place for navigational aids, as is a short table of contents.
- Select a short, to-the-point newsletter title. The title should be uncluttered and does not need to include the word "newsletter" or start with the word "The". Consider using words ending in "ing" whenever possible, or words with news appeal, such as "alert," "connection," "digest," and "happenings".
- Use colors and graphics to enhance the newsletter and to increase the user's interest. Incorporate the company's logo in some area of the newsletter. Use the company's colors wherever possible.

Inserting a Company Logo in a Header

The Painted Paradise Resort and Spa has recently developed a style guide. To conform to the logo rules in the style guide, you will add the company logo into the header of the document.

W04.15

To Insert a Graphic in a Header

a. Click the **INSERT** tab, and then in the Header & Footer group, click **Header**, and then select **Edit Header**.

b. Under HEADER & FOOTER TOOLS, on the DESIGN tab, in the Insert group, click **Pictures**. Navigate to the location of your student data files, and then double-click **w02ws04SpaLogo** to insert the graphic in the header. On the FORMAT tab, in the Size group, click in the **Shape Height** box, type 1", and then press Enter.

c. Click the **HOME** tab, and then in the Paragraph group, click **Center**.

Logo centered in header area

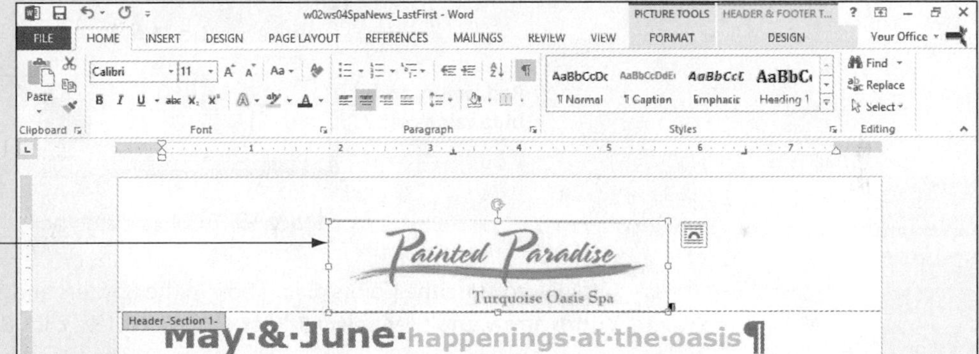

Figure 18 Logo in the header

d. Double-click anywhere in the body of the newsletter to close the header.

The logo is now placed in the document as per the Painted Paradise Resort and Spa style guide. You can find the resort style guide with your student data files.

e. **Save** the document.

Formatting a Newsletter

Word provides millions of color choices, each color represented by an **RGB** color—a color system in which red, green, and blue are combined in various proportions in order to produce other colors. In most cases, each red, green, and blue value is represented by a number range of 0 to 255. Use these three values to match a color. For example, to match the turquoise blue in the newsletter, select the turquoise text and then click the Font Color arrow. Choose More Colors, and then in the Colors dialog box that opens, look at its values, listed on the Custom tab. Use those values to recreate the color at any time.

You will add the finishing touches to the newsletter. You will modify the title of the newsletter by changing the font and applying a bottom border. You will then use the company colors, listed in the Painted Paradise Resort and Spa style guide, to precisely match the color of the border to the logo colors. Finally, you will apply a picture style to the wine graphic, and add a footer containing the company website address.

W04.16

To Format a Newsletter

a. Place the insertion point anywhere in the title of the newsletter, **May & June happenings at the oasis**. On the HOME tab, in the Paragraph group, click the **Borders** arrow, and then select **Borders and Shading**.

b. In the Borders and Shading dialog box, click the **Color** arrow, and then select **More Colors**. The Colors dialog box opens. Click the **Custom** tab, click in the **Green** box, delete the current value, and then type 167. Press Tab, and then type 157.

You have matched the border color to the turquoise blue color according to the RGB value listed in the Painted Paradise Resort and Spa style guide.

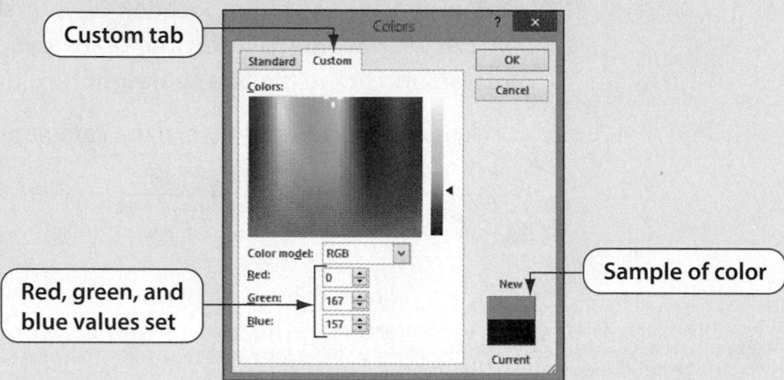

Figure 19 Colors dialog box

c. Click **OK** to close the Colors dialog box. In the Borders and Shading dialog box, click the **Width** arrow, and then select **1 ½ pt**. Under Preview, click **Bottom Border**.

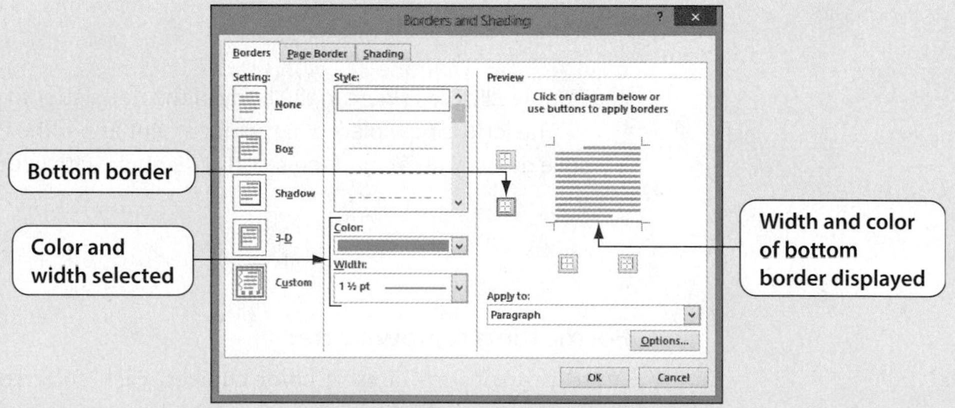

Figure 20 Creating a bottom border

d. Click **OK**. Select the words **happenings at the oasis** in the title of the newsletter. Set the font to **Lucida Handwriting**.

e. Click to select the **wine glass** graphic. Click the **FORMAT** tab, and then in the Picture Styles group, click **More**, and then select **Soft Edge Rectangle**. Click anywhere in the document to deselect the picture.

f. Click the **INSERT** tab, and then in the Header & Footer group, click **Footer**, and then select **Edit Footer**. Type http://www.paintedparadiseresort.com. Center the text in the footer, and then close the footer.

SIDE NOTE

Insert a Hyperlink into a Document

Press Enter or Spacebar after a URL to convert it to a hyperlink. Alternatively, select the text to link, click the Insert tab, and click Hyperlink. Type the URL in the Address box.

g. Click the **VIEW** tab, and then in the Zoom group, click **One Page** to view the newsletter.

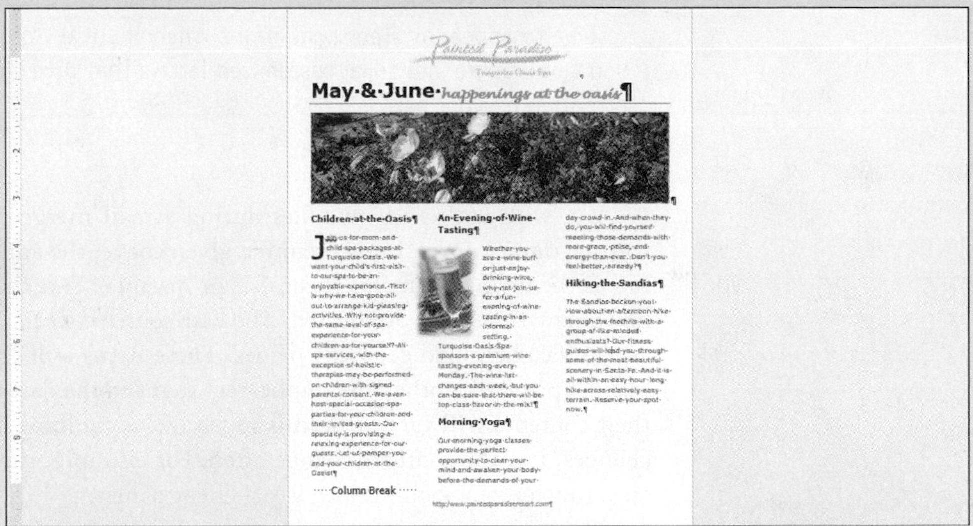

Figure 21 Final newsletter

h. In the Zoom group, click **100%. Save** the document. Click the **FILE** tab, and then click **Close** to close w02ws04SpaNews_LastFirst. The Word application remains open.

You checked Office.com for a relevant newsletter template that you could modify. To your surprise, when you open the newsletter template that you selected, the newsletter columns are organized in boxes instead of Word columns. Why do you think the template's designer chose to use boxes instead of formatting in columns? Can you identify any advantages or disadvantages to using boxes as columns?

Creating a Mail Merge Document

The term **mail merge** is a little misleading. The term suggests that the process focuses only on preparing documents for mailing, and although that is a primary application, it is not the only reason to use the feature. Actually, mail merge simplifies the task of preparing documents that contain identical formatting, layout, and text, but where only certain portions of each document vary. Perhaps you are preparing a document announcing a new product line that you plan to distribute to your client base. To personalize the announcement, you want to include the client's name and company in the body. The bulk of the announcement is text that will not vary, but the client name and company name should be inserted as if they were part of the original document. You will include a field for each bit of variable data in the document, and then simply merge, or copy, data into those fields from a master list of clients and companies.

Obviously, mail merge is the ideal vehicle for generating mailing labels, envelopes, address lists, and personalized letters and handouts. In addition to generating mailings, mail merge can be helpful in the preparation of multiple e-mails and electronic faxes. To succeed, a company needs to maintain a well-informed client base, where each customer is made to feel a part of the success.

REAL WORLD ADVICE | **Cover Letter and the Job Search**

Especially during a job search, you will want a cover letter that accompanies your resume to appear as a personal effort. When you use Word's mail merge feature, you can prepare individual customized letters that give the appearance of personal attention on your part.

You will work with two files during a mail merge process—the **main document** and the **data source**. In the example given above, the announcement of the new product line is the main document. It consists primarily of text that will not change regardless of how many times it is duplicated. The data source contains the variable information, such as specific client and company names. Those items will change each time the announcement is printed or otherwise duplicated. Items in the data source are called fields, because their contents will vary. A **field** is much like a mailbox. The name on the outside never changes, but the contents change often. For example, the client name field is a holding area, much like a mailbox, for actual client names.

The main document contains not only text that does not change, but also **merge fields**, which are references to the fields in the data source. When the two documents are merged, Word replaces each merge field with data from the data source. Ultimately, the two documents are merged into a third document that is a combination of the main document and the data source. However, if you are merging to the printer, fax, or e-mail, you will not actually create a third document. In this section you will create and complete a mail merge.

Use Mail Merge

Mail merge is a step-by-step process, achieved by using the Mailings tab in Word. You indicate the type of mail merge—letters, labels, envelopes, e-mails, or directory—the starting document, which is called the main document, will use, and the location of the data source. You can then edit the data source, and choose which fields of the data source to include in the document.

If you are creating mailing labels or envelopes, you will not have a main document. Instead, you will simply begin with a blank document. Similarly, you do not have to begin with a data source. Instead, you can create a field list during the mail merge process. Of course, it is much more common to use a data source of fields that you can call on for use in more than one merged document. Your Outlook Contacts can also serve as a data source.

Before completing the mail merge, you can preview the document and make changes, if necessary. Although the most common option is to merge to a document, you can also merge to an e-mail. Simply indicate where the text should be sent, enter a subject line, and select a format option. The document will automatically be sent to all e-mail recipients that you indicated earlier in your data source.

Creating a Mail Merge Document

You will be sending each of your spa clients a letter informing them of the regular newsletter mailings that Turquoise Oasis Spa is beginning. You will also include the first newsletter in your mailing. You will use two documents for the mail merge process—the main document and the data source. In this project, the main document is the letter that you will send to the spa clients on your mailing list. The data source is a database containing your client address list. You will copy the data source to where you are saving your project files. You will then open the form letter in Word and review it to become familiar with its content. You will format the date to be updated automatically each time the letter is opened.

W04.17

To Review the Main Document

a. Open **File Explorer**. Navigate to the location of your student data files. Right-click **w02ws04Addresses**, and then select **Copy** from the shortcut menu. Navigate to the location where you are saving your project files, right-click the folder or disk drive, and then select **Paste**. Locate the file that you pasted, right-click it, and then select **Rename** from the shortcut menu. Type w02ws04Addresses_LastFirst, using your last and first name, and then press Enter. **Close** File Explorer.

b. In Word, click the **FILE** tab to enter Backstage view. Double-click **Computer**, and navigate to the location of your student data files. Double-click **w02ws04Letter** to open the form letter that you will be mailing to your client base. If necessary, on the HOME tab, in the Paragraph group, click **Show/Hide** to display nonprinting characters.

c. Click the **FILE** tab, and then click **Save As**. Double-click **Computer**, and then navigate to where you are saving your project files. Save the document as w02ws04Letter_LastFirst, using your last and first name.

   You will personalize this letter for each of your clients. During the mail merge process, you will replace the bracketed information with data from your client address list, which is your data source.

d. Place the insertion point immediately before the **left bracket** before **[Current Date]**, and then press Delete **14 times** to remove the left bracket, the text, and the right bracket. Do NOT remove the final paragraph mark.

   You will insert the current date, in the format "August 6, 2015." When you insert the date, you can specify that it be updated automatically, which means that each time the document is opened, the date will change to reflect the current date.

Troubleshooting
If you mistakenly remove the final paragraph mark beside the date, click Undo and repeat Step d.

SIDE NOTE
Should You Always Set the Date to Automatically Update?
Do not set the date to automatically update if the date needs to reflect the date of the document creation.

e. Click the **INSERT** tab, and then in the Text group, click **Insert Date and Time**. The Date and Time dialog box opens.

f. Click the **third selection** from the top, indicating the current date is to be displayed in the format of Month Day, Year, such as August 6, 2015. If necessary, click the **Update automatically** check box to select it, and then click **OK**.

g. Click in the **current date** in the letter to select the content control, which is indicated by the shaded area and the Update tab. This indicates that the date is a field which will update automatically.

   If you had included the current time in the selected date format and wanted to update the document to reflect the current time, you could click the Update tab to automatically update the date and time.

h. Click outside the content control to deselect it. **Save** the document.

Beginning a Mail Merge

Options on the Mailings tab enable you to create a merged document, edit the data source, and create envelopes and labels. The basic process of merging a main document and data source is fairly simple, accomplished by responding to a series of prompts and indicating preferences. You will start the Mail Merge Wizard, and then select the document to use to start the mail merge. You will use a form letter that you will then personalize later for each client.

W04.18

To Begin a Mail Merge

SIDE NOTE
Dock the Mail Merge Pane
Double-click the title area in the Mail Merge pane to dock the pane in place.

a. Click the **MAILINGS** tab, and then in the Start Mail Merge group, click **Start Mail Merge**, and then select **Step-by-Step Mail Merge Wizard**. The Mail Merge pane opens, enabling you to complete the mail merge process one step at a time.

From the Start Mail Merge menu, you can work with letters, envelopes, labels, or e-mail messages. Perhaps the simplest way to begin the process is to work with the Mail Merge wizard. A wizard leads you through a process step by step. Simply respond to the prompts to produce a desired result.

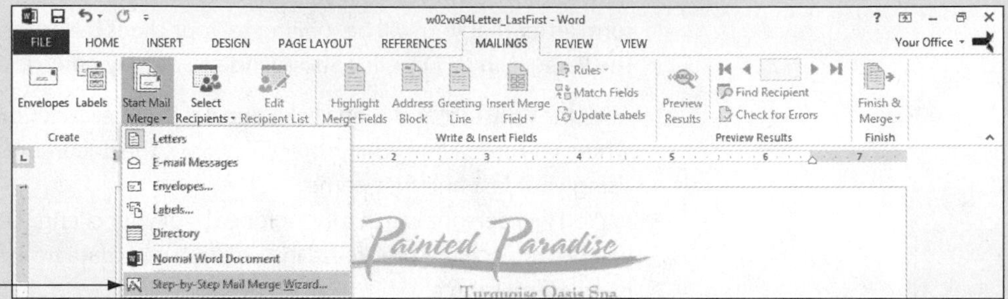

Figure 22 Start the Step-by-Step Mail Merge Wizard

b. In the Mail Merge pane, in the Select document type area, confirm that **Letters** is selected.

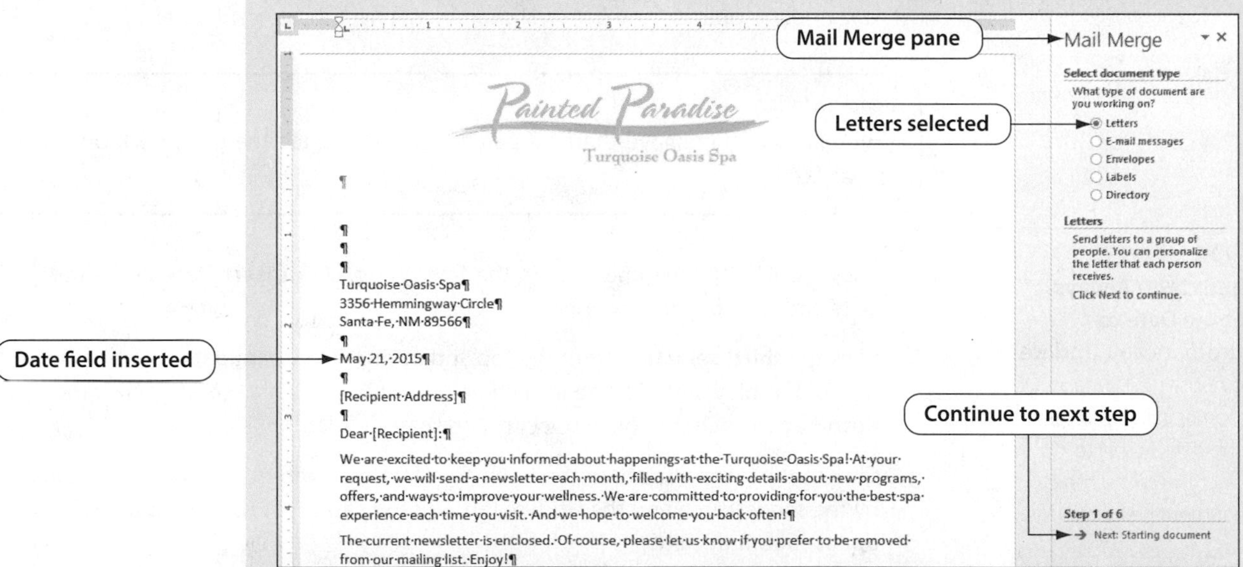

Figure 23 Selecting the document type

c. In the Mail Merge pane, click **Next: Starting document**. In the Select starting document area, confirm that **Use the current document** is selected.

The document that you choose here is the main document. Although the main document is often the currently open document—as is the case here, you could also indicate that a template is to be used or that you prefer to use a previously saved document.

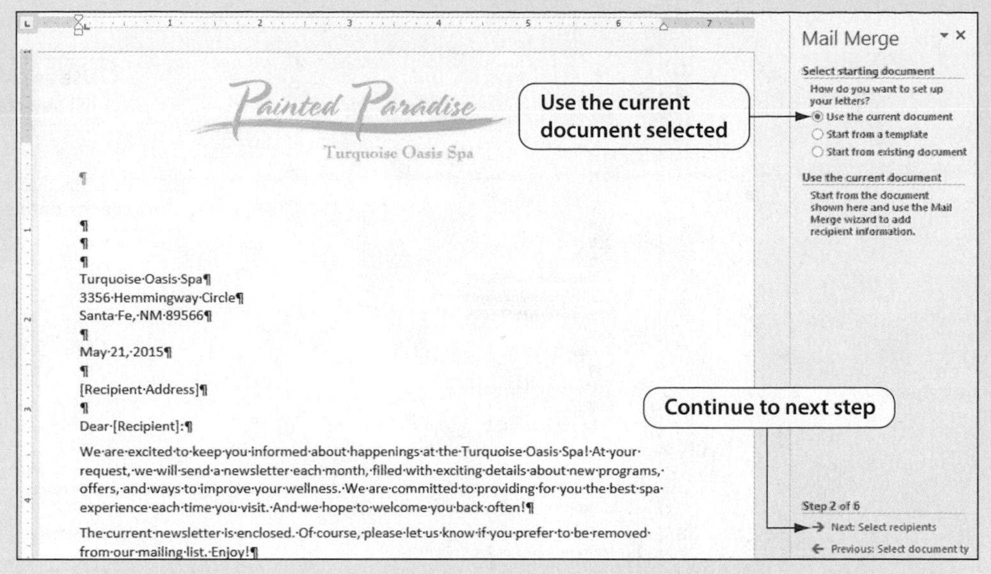

Figure 24 Selecting a starting document

Selecting a Data Source

A data source is a list of fields that contains variable data. For example, a list of mailing addresses, including names, street addresses, cities, and states, can supply data for a client mailing. A Word table, containing such data, can serve as a data source, as can an Excel worksheet, an Access database, and an Outlook contacts list. By keeping the data source current, you can reuse it countless times in the preparation of documents that require such variable data. Keep in mind, when you merge a document with a data source, formatting is not incorporated. For example, if text is bolded in a data source, the text will not carry the bold format into the merged document. Instead, you must format in the merged document as well.

You will select the data source containing your names and addresses, and then sort the data. You will also modify one of the addresses in the data source.

W04.19

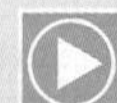

To Select a Data Source

a. In the Mail Merge pane, click **Next: Select recipients**. In the Select recipients area, confirm that **Use an existing list** is selected.

   In most cases, you will be working with a predefined list—a Word table, Excel worksheet, or Access database. If, however, you have not yet created a data source, you can select Type a new list to create a list of data. In this case, the data source is an Access database that was created earlier to include client mailing addresses.

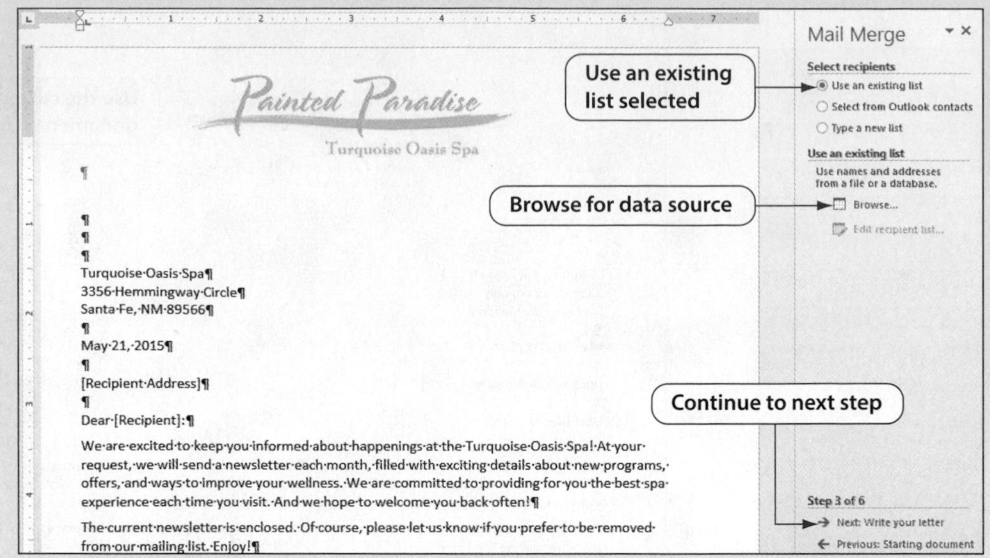

Figure 25 Selecting a data source

b. In the Use an existing list area, click **Browse**.

Earlier, you copied the Access database that will be used as your data source to the location where you save your Word projects. It is always a good idea to include the main document and the data source in the same storage location so the main document will always have the data source at hand.

c. Navigate to the location where you save your Word projects, and then double-click **w02ws04Addresses_LastFirst**. The Mail Merge Recipients dialog box opens.

Note that all of the records in the data table are checked, indicating they will each be included in a letter. You can deselect any you do not wish to include. In this case, you will include them all.

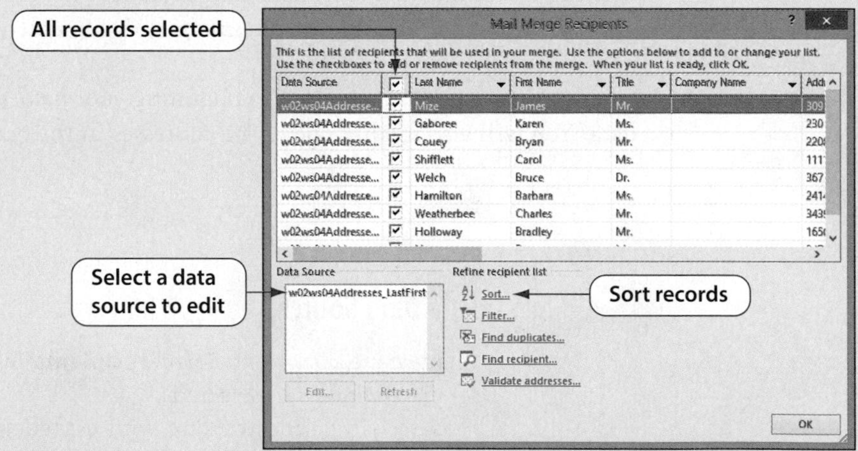

Figure 26 Mail Merge Recipients dialog box

d. Click **Sort**.

The Filter and Sort dialog box includes several selections related to sorting, filtering, and editing the recipient list. You will sort the list by last name.

e. Click the **Sort by** arrow, and then select **Last Name**. Click **OK**.

The default sort order is ascending. Although you will sort by only one field, note that you could also refine the sort to include secondary fields, in the event of duplicates in the primary sort field. For example, you could sort by Last Name and then by First Name.

f. In the Mail Merge Recipients dialog box, in the Data Source box, select the **w02ws04Addresses_LastFirst** file name, and then click **Edit**.

   You can edit records, changing data and adding new contacts. You can also remove records. Dana Nye's address has changed.

g. In the Edit Data Source dialog box, click the address, **347 Maple Drive**, delete the current address, and then type 3213 Main Street. Select the name **Dana**, and then change it to your first name. Select the name **Nye**, and then change it to your last name. Click **OK**, and then click **Yes** when asked whether to update the recipient list. Click **OK** to close the Mail Merge Recipients dialog box.

h. In the Mail Merge pane, click **Next: Write your letter**.

Completing the Letter

To complete the letter, you will identify specific data to be inserted from the data source into the main document. Since the mail merge process is commonly used for preparing mailings, Word is designed to simplify the use of mailing addresses. Although you could work with the recipient name, street address, city, state, and zip as separate fields, Word incorporates them all into a single unit called an Address block, with the fields automatically positioned in a correct mailing format. You will add the Address Block to your form letter.

W04.20

To Insert an Address Block

a. Place the insertion point immediately in front of the left bracket before **[Recipient Address]**, and then press Delete **19 times** to remove the brackets and text, but leaving the paragraph mark.

   You should see three paragraph marks between the date and the salutation. The insertion point should be displayed before the second paragraph mark.

SIDE NOTE
Manage Address Items Separately
Alternatively, you can select More Items to individually position such items as a title, street address, city, and state.

b. In the Mail Merge pane, in the Write your letter area, click **Address block**. The Insert Address Block dialog box opens. Confirm that **Insert recipient's name in this format** is checked.

c. From the address formats shown, select the second item in the list, **Joshua Randall Jr.** This will format the address block to include only the first and last name of recipients.

d. Confirm that **Insert postal address** is selected, so the entire address including street address, city, state, and zip will be included in the address block.

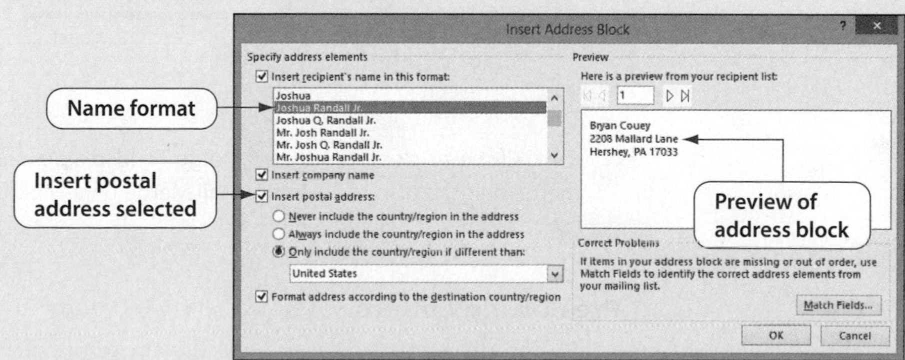

Figure 27 Selecting an address block

e. Click **OK**. A merge field, **<<AddressBlock>>**, is inserted in the letter. The field begins and ends with double characters that appear to be left and right-facing arrows.

f. Click in the **AddressBlock** field in the letter and note that the entire field is shaded, indicating that it is now considered a unit.

g. Click outside the AddressBlock field to deselect it.

Designing a Salutation Line

A salutation is included in a typical business letter. Although the format can vary slightly, it typically includes a title and a last name, followed by a colon. You can include any fields from the data source in any order, providing for appropriate spacing between each field. To finish the personalization of the letter, you will include a salutation to include the client's title and last name, followed by a colon.

W04.21

To Design a Salutation

a. Place the insertion point immediately in front of the left bracket before **[Recipient]**. Press Delete **11 times** to remove both brackets and the word **Recipient**. Do NOT delete the colon.

b. With the insertion point in front of the colon, in the Mail Merge pane, click **More items**, and then select **Title**. Click **Insert**, and then click **Close**. The Title field is inserted into the document. Press Spacebar so a space is placed between the title and the last name. Click **More items** again, click **Last Name**, and then click **Insert**.

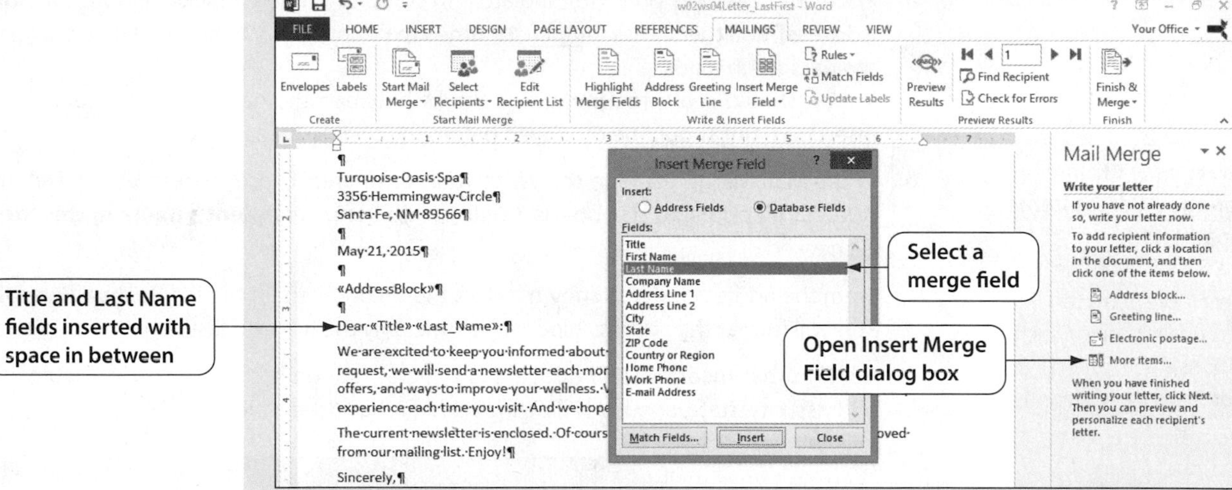

Figure 28 Selecting merge fields

c. Click **Close** to close the Insert Merge Field dialog box. The salutation line, with two merge fields, is displayed. In the Mail Merge pane, click **Next: Preview your letters**.

Previewing Letters

Before completing the merge you will want to preview the finished result. The Preview step of the mail merge process presents a document with the actual data from the data source in place of the merge fields. You will now see a letter with an address and a salutation instead of the placeholders visible earlier. Before the merge is complete, the preview enables you to check for formatting errors. You will preview the letters and then make a change to the font.

W04.22

To Preview a Merged Document

a. In the Mail Merge pane, next to **Recipient: 1**, click the **Next Recipient** button [>>] to view another letter. Click the **Next Recipient** button [>>] again. You can page forward or backward among letters, although each letter is identical with the exception of the address and salutation.

b. Press Ctrl + A to select the entire document.

   Before completing the merge, you can edit the letter, if necessary. Because the Painted Paradise Resort and Spa style guide requires business letters to use the Times New Roman font, you will change the font for the entire letter.

c. Click the **HOME** tab, and then in the Font group, change the font to **Times New Roman**. In the Mail Merge page, click the **Next Recipient** button [>>] to view another letter. You can page forward or backward among letters to confirm that the font change has been applied.

d. In the Mail Merge pane, click **Next: Complete the merge**.

Completing a Mail Merge

The last step of the Mail Merge Wizard completes the merge, resulting in a document with one page for each recipient. In this case, because you are sending letters to nine recipients, the merged document will include nine pages. The resulting document is separate from the main document and the data source, and as such, must be saved as a separate file. You will save the individual letters to the location where you are saving your files.

W04.23

To Complete the Merge

a. In the Mail Merge pane, in the Merge area, click **Edit individual letters**. The Merge to New Document dialog box opens.

   The Merge to New Document dialog box enables you to specify whether to merge all letters or a subset into a new document. In this case, you will merge all letters, so the default option All is correct as selected. Click Print instead of Edit individual letters to print the letters directly to the printer.

b. Click **OK**. Scroll through the letters, noting that each letter is in its own page section, as noted by the Next Page section break dividing each letter from the next.

   All address and salutation information is unique to the recipient, but the body of each letter is identical. Changes made at this time will be made to the individual letters. For example, if you need to fix a spelling mistake, you will need to fix the mistake on each letter individually.

c. The file name, shown in the title bar, begins with **Letters**, indicating that this is a new document. Click the **FILE** tab, and then click **Save As**. Navigate to where you are saving your project files, and then save the merged letters as w02ws04Merged_LastFirst, using your last and first name.

   The data source is not required in order to view this file.

d. Click the **FILE** tab, and then click **Close** to close w02ws04Merged_LastFirst.

   You have closed the new file containing all the merged letters. The original main document, w02ws04Letter_LastFirst, remains open as is indicated on the title bar. The original w02ws04Letter_LastFirst file requires the data source in order to view the merged letters or make changes to the mail merge. Use this file to update and regenerate the merged letters, if necessary.

e. **Save** [icon] the original main document, **w02ws04Letter_LastFirst**. Click the **FILE** tab, and then click **Close** to close the w02ws04Letter_LastFirst document. Word remains open.

REAL WORLD ADVICE | **Using an Excel Worksheet as a Data Source**

An Excel worksheet, which is a grid of columns and rows, is a logical choice when creating a table of mailing addresses to use as a data source for a mail merge. When creating the Excel worksheet, do not leave a blank row between the column headings and the mailing records. Also, give column headings recognizable titles such as First Name and Last Name, so that Word is able to connect the fields with its mail merge blocks. When working through the Mail Merge Wizard, you will select an existing list for the data source and navigate to the Excel workbook. Open the workbook, and then select the worksheet containing the data source. At that point, you can edit, filter, and sort records in the Excel data source just as you would with other data sources, such as an Access or Word table.

Create Mailing Labels and Envelopes

You use the same method to create mailing labels and address envelopes as you use to create the merged letters. You create one mailing label for each record in the data source. Using Word's Mail Merge feature, you simply select labels, specify the label type and size and then select or create the data source. Insert the fields, and then adjust the font and positioning of the data to suit the needs of your project. The mail merge process creates a layout of the label sheet. You then load the label sheets into the printer and print.

When you create envelopes, the entire envelope is fed through the printer so the address is printed directly on the envelope. To address envelopes, begin with a new blank document. Using Word's Mail Merge wizard, step through the process of creating an envelope. This process actually creates a layout of the addressed envelopes in your document, which you then print directly onto the envelopes. During this process, you select the envelope type and the data source. You then arrange the data source fields, and format the layout, if necessary. Although mailing labels are probably easier to manage than envelopes, there may be occasions when an envelope is more suitable.

Selecting Labels

When creating labels, you begin with a blank Word document. Use Mail Merge to design a sheet of labels in your document, format the labels, load the label sheets into the printer, and then print. The Mail Merge feature enables you to select from numerous label types, including mailing, folder, and even name tag labels. Although the most common type of label used is a mailing label, it is by no means the only choice. Labels are listed by manufacturer, such as Microsoft, 3M, and Avery. Avery is such a standard that you will often find other label types providing an Avery equivalent number so you can use the label in a Word mail merge process. You will use the same data source to create labels that was used to create the merged letters. You will print the labels on Avery 5160 Easy Peel Address labels.

W04.24

To Select Labels

a. Click the **FILE** tab, click **New**, and then click **Blank document**. Click the **MAILINGS** tab, and then in the Start Mail Merge group, click **Start Mail Merge**, and then select **Step-by-Step Mail Merge Wizard**.

b. In the Mail Merge pane, in the Select document type area, select **Labels**. Click **Next: Starting document**. In the Select starting document area, confirm that **Change document layout** is selected, and then in the Change document layout area, click **Label options**. You must indicate the label type in order for Word to correctly design the label sheet.

c. Click the **Label vendors** arrow, and then scroll, if necessary, to select **Avery US Letter**. Scroll through the list of product numbers to locate and select **5160 Easy Peel Address Labels**.

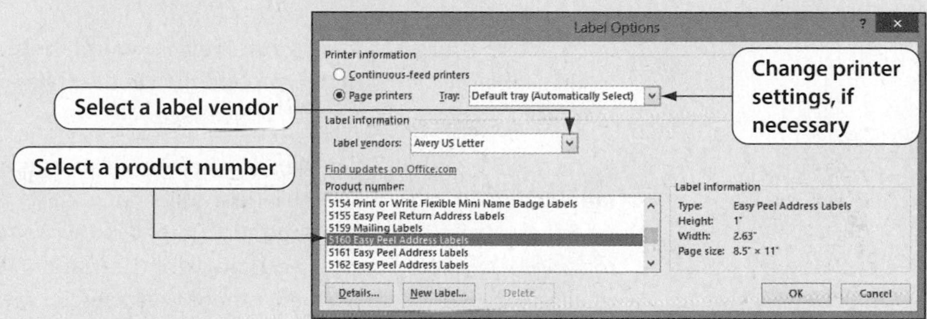

Figure 29 Selecting a label type

d. Click **OK**, and then in the Mail Merge pane, click **Next: Select recipients**.

Selecting Recipients and Arranging Labels

As you learned in the previous section, you need to select recipients from a data source. You can then filter the data, sort it, delete records, edit records, and insert records. Word will then insert fields from the data source into your document in a mailing label format, duplicating the fields for each label so each label contains a different recipient. You will select the recipients, arrange the labels, and then complete the merge.

W04.25

To Select Recipients and Arrange Labels

a. In the Mail Merge pane, in the Select recipients area, confirm that **Use an existing list** is selected, and then click **Browse**. Navigate to the location where you are saving your project files, and double-click **w02ws04Addresses_LastFirst** to select the data source.

b. Click **Sort**, click the **Sort by** arrow, and then select **Last Name**. Click **OK**. The mailing labels will be printed alphabetically by last name. Click **OK**.

c. In the Mail Merge pane, click **Next: Arrange your labels**. Confirm that the insertion point is located in the top-left label. Click **Address block** in the Arrange your labels area, select **Joshua Randall Jr.**, and then click **OK**.

d. In the Mail Merge pane, in the Replicate labels area, click **Update all labels**.

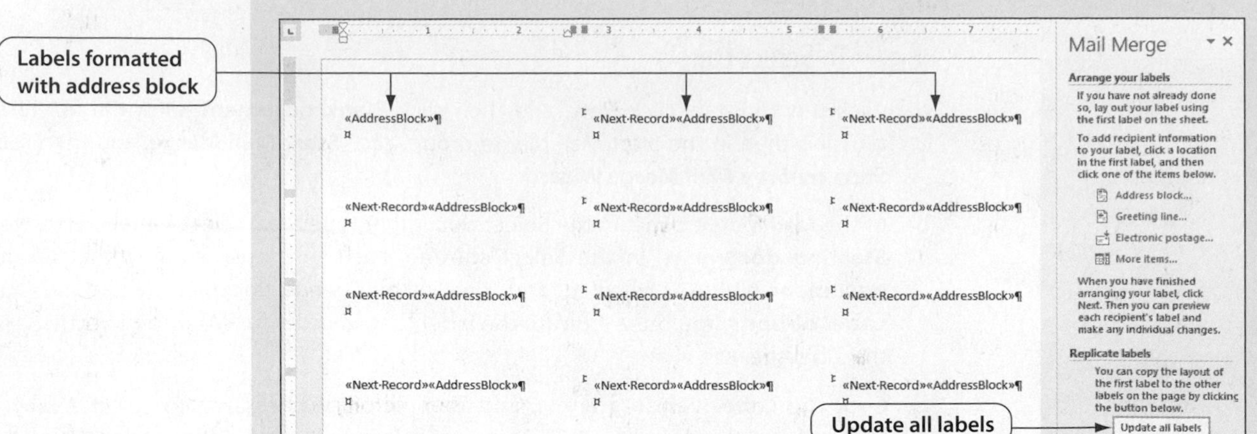

Figure 30 Arranging mailing labels

e. In the Mail Merge pane, click **Next: Preview your labels**. Press Ctrl + A to select all mailing labels. Click the **HOME** tab, and then in the Styles group, click **No Spacing** so all text fits more neatly within each label space.

f. In the Mail Merge pane, click **Next: Complete the merge**, and then click **Edit individual labels**. Click **OK** to select all the labels.

   The completed mailing label document is displayed. After loading a sheet of mailing labels in the printer, you can print the mailing labels. Note that the merged mailing labels are actually a document that you can save, if you like, and then print at a later time.

g. The file name, shown in the title bar, begins with **Labels**, indicating that this is a new document. Click the **FILE** tab, and then click **Save As**. Navigate to where you are saving your project files. Save the merged labels, calling the document w02ws04Labels_LastFirst, using your last and first name. Click the **FILE** tab, and then click **Close** to close w02ws04Labels_LastFirst.

h. You will now close the original labels document without saving the changes. Click the **FILE** tab, and then click **Close** to close the original labels document. Click **Don't Save** when asked to save the changes. Exit **Word**. Submit the files as directed by your instructor.

CONSIDER THIS | **Mailing Labels or Envelopes?**

Word allows you to create mailing labels as well as addresses on envelopes. Is there a preference for one over the other? Do you feel any differently when you receive a letter that is addressed on an envelope without a mailing label?

Concept Check

1. List six specific guidelines to follow when using the MLA style. p. 324
2. What is the difference between a bibliography and a works cited page? p. 332
3. What is a comment? Where do comments appear in your document? p. 335
4. What is the difference between the All Markup and Simple Markup views? p. 338
5. How would you create a document in which the title is positioned across the top of the document, but the text under the columns is formatted using a three-column layout? p. 340–342
6. What is a style guide and why would a company use one? p. 344
7. What is mail merge? What is an example of why you would use mail merge in a business? p. 347–348
8. What is the difference between creating labels and creating envelopes in mail merge? p. 356

Key Terms

All Markup 338
Annotated bibliography 332
APA 323
Bibliography 332
Chicago 323
Citation 326
Column 340
Comment 335
CSE 323
Data source 348
Drop cap 342
Endnote 330
Field 348
Footnote 330
Mail merge 347
Main document 348
Merge field 348
MLA 322
Newsletter 340
Plagiarism 322
RGB 345
Simple Markup 338
Style guide 322
Track Changes 335
Works cited 332

Visual Summary

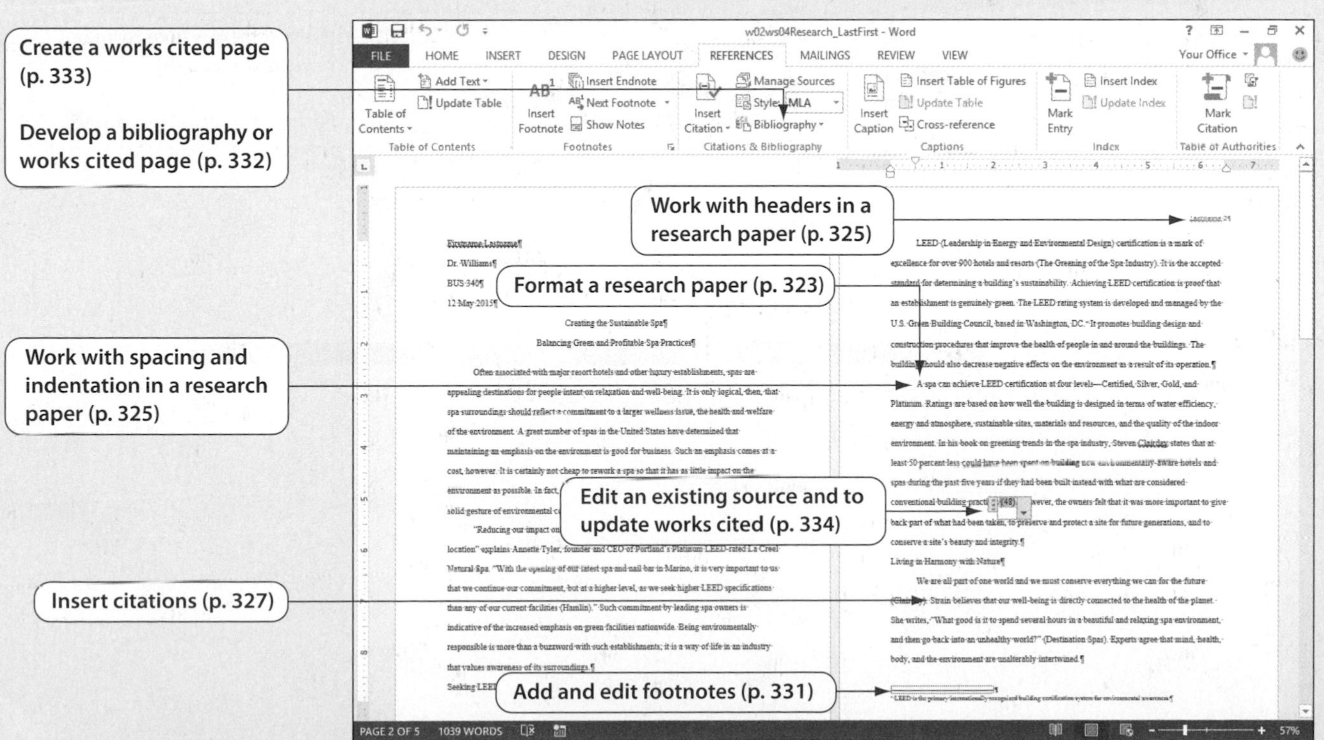

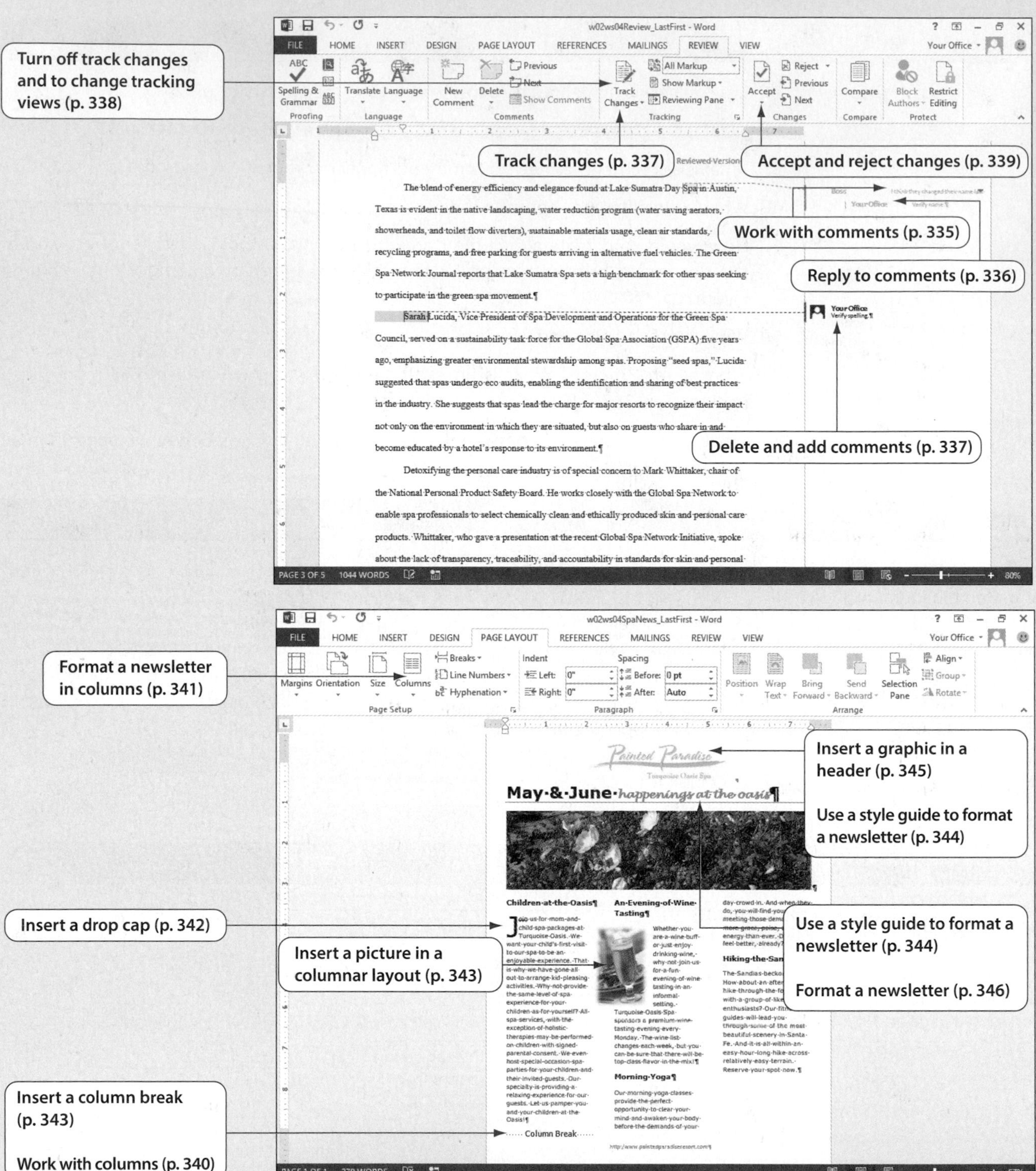
Turn off track changes and to change tracking views (p. 338)
Track changes (p. 337)
Accept and reject changes (p. 339)
Work with comments (p. 335)
Reply to comments (p. 336)
Delete and add comments (p. 337)
Format a newsletter in columns (p. 341)
Insert a graphic in a header (p. 345)
Use a style guide to format a newsletter (p. 344)
Insert a drop cap (p. 342)
Insert a picture in a columnar layout (p. 343)
Use a style guide to format a newsletter (p. 344)
Format a newsletter (p. 346)
Insert a column break (p. 343)
Work with columns (p. 340)

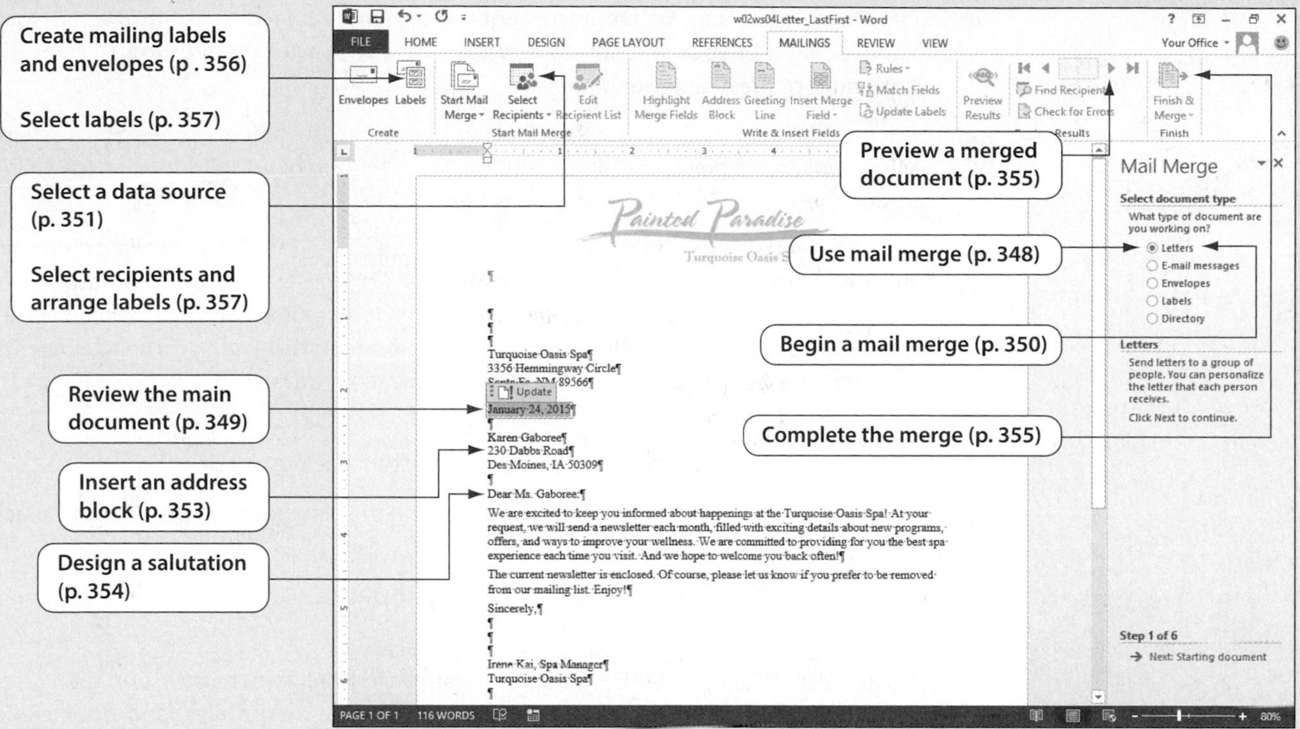

Figure 31 Turquoise Oasis Spa Newsletter and Research Final Document

Practice 1

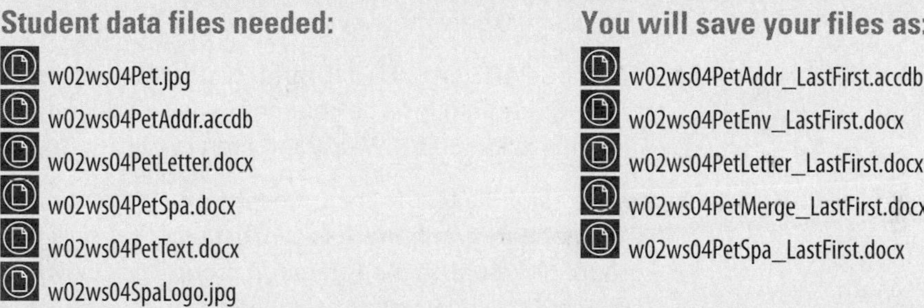

Student data files needed:

- w02ws04Pet.jpg
- w02ws04PetAddr.accdb
- w02ws04PetLetter.docx
- w02ws04PetSpa.docx
- w02ws04PetText.docx
- w02ws04SpaLogo.jpg

You will save your files as:

- w02ws04PetAddr_LastFirst.accdb
- w02ws04PetEnv_LastFirst.docx
- w02ws04PetLetter_LastFirst.docx
- w02ws04PetMerge_LastFirst.docx
- w02ws04PetSpa_LastFirst.docx

Turquoise Oasis Spa Newsletter

Sales & Marketing

Production & Operations

The Turquoise Oasis Spa has expanded to include a center for pets—Turquoise Oasis Pet Pals. Guests of the Painted Paradise Resort and Spa often place their pets in the resort's pet lodge, and the spa is capitalizing on that group by offering pet spa services. Pets can enjoy massages, baths, grooming, and pedicures. In addition, Turquoise Oasis Pet Pals offers a full line of pet clothing and grooming accessories in the on-site boutique. The pet lounge affords space for occasional seminars with pet professionals and veterinarians, and provides play space. The new pet center is spotlighted in the summer edition of Solutions, the Turquoise Oasis Spa's quarterly newsletter. You will develop the first page of the newsletter in this exercise. Your boss also requested that addressed envelopes, rather than mailing labels, be used to mail out the newsletter. You will prepare the envelopes.

a. Open **File Explorer**. Navigate to the location of your student data files, and then right-click **w02ws04PetAddr**. Select **Copy**. Navigate to the location where you are saving your project files, right-click the folder (or disk drive), and then select **Paste**. Locate the file that you pasted, right-click it, and then select **Rename**. Type w02ws04PetAddr_LastFirst, using your last and first name, and then press Enter.

b. Start **Word**, click **Open Other Documents**, and then double-click **Computer**. Navigate to the location of your student data files. Double-click **w02ws04PetSpa** to open the rough draft of the newsletter page.

c. Click the **FILE** tab, and then click **Save As**. Save the document as w02ws04PetSpa_LastFirst, using your last and first name. If nonprinting characters are not displayed, click the **HOME** tab, and then in the Paragraph group, click **Show/Hide**.

d. Press Ctrl+End. Click the **PAGE LAYOUT** tab, and then in the Page Setup group, click **Columns**, and then select **More Columns**. The Columns dialog box displays. Under Presets, click **Left** to create two columns, with the left column slightly smaller than the right column. Click the **Apply to** arrow, and then select **This point forward**. Click **OK**. Note that the horizontal ruler displays two uneven columns, with more space in the column on the right.

e. In the Paragraph group, change the paragraph **After** spacing to **0 pt**.

f. Click the **HOME** tab, change the font size to **18**, and then change the **Font Color** to **Black, Text 1**.

g. Type SUMMER 2015 and then press Enter. Type TURQUOISE OASIS SPA and then press Enter twice.

h. Click the **INSERT** tab, and then in the Text group, click the **Object** arrow, and then select **Text from File**. Navigate to the location of your student data files, and double-click **w02ws04PetText**. The text is inserted in the document. Press Delete to remove the extra paragraph mark at the end of the document.

i. Scroll to the bottom of the document, and then click to place the insertion point immediately in front of the paragraph **Experience Turquoise Pet Pals**. Click the **VIEW** tab, and then in the Zoom group, click **One Page**. With the entire page displayed, column changes that you make are more evident.

j. Click the **PAGE LAYOUT** tab, and then in the Page Setup group, click **Breaks**, and then select **Column** to insert a column break so the entire article appears to the right of the contents. Click the **VIEW** tab, and then in the Zoom group, click **100%**.

k. Select all of the text in the **first column**, beginning with **SUMMER 2015** and ending at the **final paragraph mark** in the first column. Click the **HOME** tab, and then in the Font group, click **Bold**. In the Paragraph group, click **Center** so text will be centered in the first column. Click the **Borders** arrow, and then select **Borders and Shading**. The Borders and Shading dialog box opens, with the Borders tab selected.

l. In the Borders and Shading dialog box, in the Setting area, click **Box**. Click the **Color** arrow, and then select **Black, Text 1**. Click the **Width** arrow, and then select **1½ pt**. In the Borders and Shading dialog box, click the **Shading** tab, click the **Fill** arrow, and then select **Aqua, Accent 5, Lighter 40%**. Click **OK**.

m. **Center** and **bold** the text **Experience Turquoise Pet Pals** at the top of the second column. Click before the word **Share** in the second paragraph of the second column. Click the **INSERT** tab, and then in the Illustrations group, click **Pictures**. Navigate to the location of your student data files, and then double-click **w02ws04Pet**. In the Size group, click in the **Shape Height** box, and then type 1. In the Arrange group, click **Wrap Text**, and then select **Square**.

n. Insert a **footer** with the **File Name** field centered. Close the footer. Save and close the document. Keep Word open.

o. Click the **FILE** tab. Double-click **Computer**, and then navigate to the location of your student data files. Double-click **w02ws04PetLetter**. The letter will serve as the main document for a mail merge. It is a cover letter that will accompany the newsletter, inviting spa clients to an open house for Turquoise Oasis Pet Pals. Click the **FILE** tab, and then save the document as w02ws04PetLetter_LastFirst where you are saving your files, using your last and first name.

p. Place the insertion point immediately before **[Current Date]**, and then press Delete **14 times** to delete both brackets and the text, but leaving the paragraph mark. The insertion point should be positioned before the second blank paragraph between the inside address and the **[Recipient]** line. Click the **INSERT** tab, and then in the Text group, click **Insert Date and Time**, and then select the **third date format**, showing month, day, and year, similar to **April 3, 2015**. Click **Update automatically** if necessary, and then click **OK**.

q. Click the **MAILINGS** tab, and then in the Start Mail Merge group, click **Start Mail Merge**, and then select **Step-by-Step Mail Merge Wizard**. Confirm that **Letters** is selected as the document type, and then click **Next: Starting document**.

r. Confirm that **Use the current document** is selected, and then click **Next: Select recipients**.

s. Confirm that **Use an existing list** is selected, and then click **Browse**. Navigate to the location where you are saving your project files, and double-click **w02ws04PetAddr_LastFirst**. Click **Sort**. Click the **Sort by** arrow, select **Last Name**, and then click **OK**.

t. In the Data Source box, click **w02ws04PetAddr_LastFirst.accdb**, and then click **Edit**.

u. In the First Name column, click **Barbara**, delete the name, and then type your first name. Replace the Last Name, **Alim**, with your last name. Click **OK**, click **Yes** when asked whether to update the recipient list, and then click **OK**.

v. Click **Next: Write your letter**. Click before the first bracket on the **[Recipient]** line, and then remove the entire line of text, with the exception of the final paragraph mark. In the Mail Merge pane, click **Address block**. Under Specify address elements, click **Joshua Randall Jr.,** and then click **OK**.

w. Place the insertion point immediately after the **r** in **Dear** but before the colon. With the insertion point positioned before the colon, press Spacebar. In the Mail Merge pane, click **More items**. Select **Title**, click **Insert**, and then click **Close**. Press Spacebar, and then click **More items**. Select **Last Name**, click **Insert**, and then click **Close**. Click **Next: Preview your letters**.

x. You remember that the new Painted Paradise Resort and Spa style guide requires the logo to be placed in the header of all business letters. Click the **INSERT** tab, and then in the Header & Footer group, click **Header**, and then select **Edit Header**. Under HEADER & FOOTER TOOLS, on the DESIGN tab, in the Insert group, click **Pictures**. Navigate to the location of your student data files, and then double-click **w02ws04SpaLogo** to insert the graphic in the header.

y. In the Size group, change the **Shape Height** of the logo to **1"**. Click the **HOME** tab, and then in the Paragraph group, click **Center**. Double-click the **body** of the letter to close the header.

z. Click **Next: Complete the merge**, click **Edit individual letters**, and then click **OK**. Note that the resulting merged document includes nine pages, with one letter on each page. Also note that the letters are arranged alphabetically by last name.

aa. Click the **FILE** tab, and then save the merged document as w02ws04PetMerge_LastFirst, using your last and first name. Save and close all open documents, but do not exit Word.

bb. Click the **FILE** tab, and then click **New**. Click **Blank document**, and then start the **Step-by-Step Mail Merge Wizard**.

cc. Click **Envelopes** in the Select document type area, click **Next: Starting document**, and then click **Envelope options**.

The Envelope Options dialog box appears. You can select an envelope type, and you can indicate a font size and type. Options on the Printing Options tab enable you to identify printing methods.

dd. The default envelope size is Size 10. Leave the size as is, or click the **Envelope size** arrow to select **Size 10** if it is not displayed. Click **OK**.

ee. Click **Next: Select recipients**. In the Select recipients area, confirm that **Use an existing list** is selected, and then click **Browse**. Navigate to the location where you are saving your project files, and then double-click **w02ws04PetAddr_LastFirst**. The data source is displayed, with all records selected. You will print an envelope for all recipients. Click **OK**.

ff. Click **Next: Arrange your envelope**. Click before the paragraph mark in the delivery address area in the lower middle of the **envelope**, and then in the Mail Merge pane, click **Address block**. The Insert Address Block dialog box appears. Click **Joshua Randall Jr.** to select a recipient name format, and then click **OK**.

gg. Click **Next: Preview your envelopes**. Click the left or right arrows in the **Preview your envelopes** area to view the envelopes.

hh. Click before the first paragraph mark in the top-left corner of the envelope. You will type a return address. Type Turquoise Oasis Spa and then press Enter. Type 3356 Hemmingway Circle and then press Enter. Finally, type Santa Fe, NM 89566.

ii. Click **Next: Complete the merge**, click **Edit individual envelopes**, and then click **OK**.

jj. The file name, shown in the title bar, begins with **Envelopes**, indicating that this is a new document. Click the **FILE** tab, and then save the merged envelopes as w02ws04PetEnv_LastFirst, using your last and first name. Close w02ws04PetEnv_LastFirst.

kk. Close the original envelopes document without saving it, and then exit Word. Submit the files as directed by your instructor.

Problem Solve 1

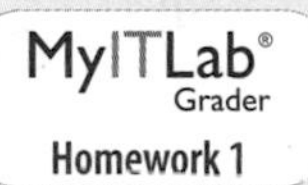

Student data file needed:

You will save your file as:

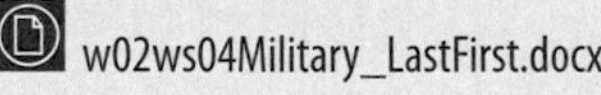

Military Research Report

Research & Development

As a project for your English class, you are required to prepare a research report on the preparedness of young adults for service in the U.S. armed forces. Based on your research, you are to take a position either in support of or in opposition to the recruitment of young adults, ages 18–21. You have developed a very rough draft of the report, in which you make the argument that young adults are not emotionally mature enough to contribute significantly to the military effort. Your report will be submitted to a university committee, which will select several student reports for inclusion in an academic journal. You sent the report to your advisor for his input. In this exercise, you will accept or reject your advisor's suggestions, and then edit the report so that it adheres to the MLA writing style.

a. Start **Word**, open **w02ws04Military**, and then save the document as w02ws04Military_LastFirst. If necessary, click **Show/Hide** to display nonprinting characters.

b. Turn the **Track Changes** feature off. Scroll through the document to view the tracked changes. Accept all changes. Delete the comment at the end of the document.

c. Select the entire document. Change the font to **Times New Roman**, and then verify the font size is set to **12**.

d. With the text still selected, set the paragraph After spacing to **0 pt** and the paragraph Before spacing to **0 pt**. Change the Line spacing to **2.0** (or Double). Set a First line indent of **0.5"**. Click to deselect the text.

e. Move to the beginning of the document, and then press Enter. Press Ctrl+Home again, and align left the new paragraph. Type your first name and last name, separated by a space. Press Enter. Type Dr. Peterson and then press Enter. Type English 112 and then press Enter. Type 19 April 2016. Do not press Enter.

f. Select the first five paragraphs of the document starting with the line containing your first and last name, and ending with the title of the document, **Young Adults in the Military**. Move the **First Line Indent** marker to the 0" mark on the ruler.

g. Scroll to the bottom of page 4. Click to place the insertion point immediately after the quotation mark, but just before the period at the end of **"a long-term reaction to war-zone exposure"**. If necessary, set the Bibliography Style to **MLA Seventh Edition**. Add a new source. Enter the following information for the journal article.

   Authors: Matthew J. Friedman, Paula P. Schnurr, and Annmarie McDonagh-Coyle
   Title: Post-Traumatic Stress Disorder in the Military Veteran
   Journal Name: Psychiatric Clinics of North America
   Year: 1994
   Pages: 265–277
   Volume: 17
   Issue: 2

h. Edit the citation to include 265 as the page number.

i. In the same paragraph, click before the period, but after the quotation mark, that ends the sentence after **childhood behavior problems"**. Insert the **Friedman, Schnurr and McDonagh-Coyle** citation. Edit the citation to include 275 as the page number, and then suppress the Author, Year, and Title.

j. Insert a **header**. Type your last name, and then press Spacebar. Insert the page number, using the 1,2,3 format. Right-align the header. Change the font size of the header to **12**. Change the font to **Times New Roman**. Close the header.

k. Move to the end of the document. Insert a page break, and then insert a Works Cited page.

l. Convert the bibliography to static text.

m. Select all text in the **Works Cited** page, including the Works Cited title. Change the line spacing to **double**, and then set the paragraph before and after spacing to **0 pt**. With the text still selected, change the font size to **12** and the font to **Times New Roman**. Center the **Works Cited** line.

n. Move to the beginning of the document. Select the word **Military** in the title of the paper, and then insert a comment with the text Can you review again?

o. Save and close the document. Exit Word. Submit the file as directed by your instructor.

Perform 1: Perform in Your Life

Student data file needed:

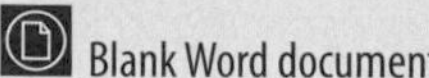

Blank Word document

You will save your files as:

w02ws04FamilyNL_LastFirst.docx

w02ws04FamilyNL_LastFirst.pdf

Family Newsletter

Sales & Marketing

You decide to create a quarterly newsletter to keep the family up to date on news and events in everyone's lives. Create a fun, well-designed, error-free newsletter. Create a catchy title and use pictures or clip art to enhance the newsletter. You will save the newsletter as a Word document and a PDF file so that you can e-mail a copy of the document to your family members.

a. Start **Word**. Create a new blank document, and then save it with the name w02ws04FamilyNL_LastFirst. Display nonprinting characters if necessary.

b. Create a catchy title across the top of the document. Format the title appropriately. Apply a bottom border to the title.

c. Create a two or three column layout, depending on your needs.

d. Insert at least one graphic. Position the graphic in between two columns, adjust the text wrap appropriately, and then apply a picture style to the graphic.

e. Include a drop cap as the first letter of the body of the newsletter.

f. Insert a column break if necessary so that topic headings are aligned at the top of each column.

g. Apply a border around one section of text, and then apply shading in the bordered area.

h. Include your contact information somewhere in the newsletter, in the form of firstname.lastname@website.com, where firstname is your actual first name, and lastname is your actual last name.

i. Format as necessary.

j. Save the document. Create a PDF file with the same name, exit Word, and then submit the files as directed by your instructor.

Additional Cases

Additional Workshop Cases are available on the companion website and in the instructor resources.

MODULE CAPSTONE

More Practice 1

Student data files needed:

w02mpChildren.docx

w02mpLogo.jpg

w02mpMovies.docx

w02mpPlay.jpg

w02mpText.docx

You will save your file as:

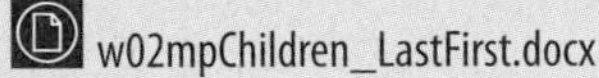

w02mpChildren_LastFirst.docx

Paradise Kids

Sales & Marketing

Production & Operations

Painted Paradise Resort and Spa is a favorite destination for many families and business travelers. Over half of those enjoying the resort's facilities are families, many with children under the age of 13. So parents can enjoy some leisure time apart from the children, Painted Paradise Resort and Spa offers activities just for children in an on-site center staffed with resort employees. Children enjoy themed afternoons, movies, crafts, and outdoor activities in the Paradise Kids Resort. A one-page flyer, listing children's activities for each week, is placed in each guest room. You will prepare the flyer for this week, in a two-column style, including graphics and WordArt. Activities will be summarized in a table within the flyer. Because you will send this to your boss for approval, you will add a watermark and a comment.

a. Start **Word**, click **Open Other Documents**, and then double-click **Computer**. Navigate to the location of your student data files, open **w02mpChildren**, and then save the document as w02mpChildren_LastFirst where you are saving your project files, using your last and first name. If necessary, click **Show/Hide** to display nonprinting characters. If necessary, click the **VIEW** tab, and then in the Show group, click **Ruler** to display the horizontal and vertical rulers.

b. Select the text **Paradise Kids**. Click the **FORMAT** tab, and then in the **WordArt Styles** group, click **Text Effects**. Point to **Shadow**, and then under Perspective, in the first column, select **Perspective Diagonal Upper Left**.

c. Place the insertion point immediately after **2015**. Click the **HOME** tab, and then in the Paragraph group, click the **Paragraph Dialog Box Launcher**, and then click **Tabs**. Click in the Tab stop position box, and then type 7.5. Select a **Right** tab with a **dot leader**. Click **Set**, and then click **OK**.

d. Press Tab. Using your first name and last name, type First Last, Director and do NOT press Enter.

e. Press Ctrl + End. Click the **PAGE LAYOUT** tab, and then in the Page Setup group, click **Columns**, and then select **More Columns**. Under Presets, click **Two**, click the **Apply to** arrow, and then select **This point forward**. Click **OK**.

   A continuous section break has been added to the document. All text below the break will be formatted in two columns. Note that the horizontal ruler displays two columns.

f. Click the **HOME** tab, and then in the Paragraph group, change the alignment to **Center**. In the Font group, change the **Font Color** to **Dark Blue, Text 2, Darker 25%**. Click **Bold**, and then type Paradise Kids Membership. Do not press Enter.

g. You will create a new style based on the text typed in Step f. In the Styles group, click the **Styles Dialog Box Launcher** to open the Styles pane, and then click **New Style**. Name the style Topic Heading, click **OK**, and then press Enter.

h. Click the **INSERT** tab, and then in the Text group, click the **Object** arrow, and then select **Text from File**. Navigate to the location of your student data files, double-click **w02mpText** to insert the text into the document, and then press Delete to remove the extra paragraph mark at the end of the document.

i. Select the newly added text, starting with **We invite your child** and ending at the bottom of the document. Click the **HOME** tab, and then in the Font group, change the **Font Color** to **Black, Text 1**, and then change the **Font Size** to **12**. Create a new style based on the existing text. Name the new style Topic Text.

j. Select the four paragraphs beginning with the line **Paradise backpack** and ending with the line **Paradise key ring or mug**. In the Paragraph group, click **Bullets**, and then click **Decrease Indent**.

k. Click anywhere to deselect the text. Select the **first three bulleted items** (making sure not to select the final bulleted item), click the **PAGE LAYOUT** tab, and then in the Paragraph group, change the paragraph **After** spacing to **0 pt** to remove the paragraph after spacing.

l. Apply the **Topic Heading** style to the text **Babysitting Services**.

m. Press Ctrl+End, and then press Enter. Click the **HOME** tab, and then in the Styles group, click **Topic Heading**. Type Check Out the September Specials and then press Enter.

n. Click the **INSERT** tab, and then in the Tables group, click **Table**, and then insert a table with two columns and six rows (**2×6 Table**).

o. Click the **Table Selector** in the top-left corner of the table to select the entire table. Click the **HOME** tab, and then in the Paragraph group, click **Center**. With the table still selected, in the Styles group, click **Normal**. Click in the **first cell** of the table, and then type 9/5. Press Tab, type Water slide and then press Tab. Complete the table as shown below, pressing Tab after each entry, including the last entry.

9/6	Star Wars movie time
9/11	Native American art
9/12	Boogie board race
9/19	Guitar Hero competition
9/26	Nature and mountain hike

p. Because you pressed Tab after Nature and mountain hike, a new blank row was added. With the insertion point in the blank row, click the **LAYOUT** tab, and then in the Rows & Columns group, click **Delete**, and then select **Delete Rows**.

q. Click in the **first row** of the table. In the Rows & Columns group, click **Insert Above**, and then type All events are scheduled from 1:00–4:00. Do not include the period.

r. Select the **first row** of the table, and then on the LAYOUT tab, in the Merge group, click **Merge Cells**. In the Alignment group, click **Align Center**. In the Cell Size group, click **AutoFit**, and then select **AutoFit Contents**.

s. Under TABLE TOOLS, click the **DESIGN** tab, and then in the Table Styles group, click **More**. Scroll down, and under List Tables, click the **List Table 6 Colorful - Accent 1** style.

t. Press Ctrl+End, and then press Enter. Type See You at the Movies and then press Enter. Insert text from the file **w02mpMovies**. Press Delete to remove the extra paragraph mark. In the Styles pane, click **Topic Text** to apply the Topic Text style to the newly inserted text.

u. In the Styles pane, click the **Topic Heading** arrow, and then select **Modify**. Click **Format**, select **Paragraph**, and then change the paragraph **After** spacing to **6 pt**. Click **OK**, click **OK**, and then close the Styles pane.

v. Place the insertion point immediately to the left of the first body paragraph, beginning with **We invite your child to be a Paradise Kid!** On the INSERT tab, in the Illustrations group, click **Pictures**. Insert the picture **w02mpPlay** from your student data files. In the Arrange group, click **Wrap Text**, select **Square**, and then in the Size group, change the picture height to **1.1"**. In the Picture Styles group, click **More**, and then apply the **Perspective Shadow, White** picture style.

w. Using the alignment guides, drag the **picture** so its top edge is aligned with the top of the text, **We invite your**, and then drag the picture all the way to the left. The picture will extend to the left of the text and the Paradise Kids Membership title will be above the picture.

x. Place the insertion point in front of the text, **Babysitting Services**. Click the **PAGE LAYOUT** tab, and then in the Page Setup group, click **Breaks**, and then select **Column**.

y. Click the **INSERT** tab, and then in the Header & Footer group, click **Footer**, and then select **Edit Footer**. In the Illustrations group, click **Pictures**, and then insert the picture **w02mpLogo** from your student data files. In the Size group, change the height of the picture to **0.6"**. In the Adjust group, click **Color**, and then under Recolor, select **Grayscale**. Because the text wrap is set to In Line with Text, click the **HOME** tab, and then in the Paragraph group, click **Center** to center the logo. Close the footer.

z. Select the word **Native** in the September specials table. Click the **REVIEW** tab, and then in the Comments group, click **New Comment**, and then type the text Is this still scheduled?

aa. Click the **DESIGN** tab, and then in the Page Background group, click **Watermark**, and then select the **DRAFT 1** watermark. Click **Watermark** again, select **Custom Watermark**, deselect the **Semitransparent** check box to darken the watermark, and then click **OK**.

bb. Preview the document to view the final result. Save the document, and then exit Word. Submit the file as directed by your instructor.

Problem Solve 1

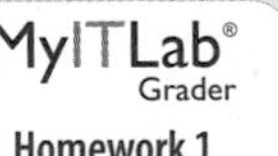

Student data files needed:

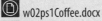

 w02ps1Coffee.docx

 w02ps1CoffeeAddr.accdb

w02ps1TerraLogo.jpg

You will save your files as:

 w02ps1Coffee_LastFirst.docx

 w02ps1CoffeeMrg_LastFirst.docx

 w02ps1CoffeeAddr_LastFirst.accdb

Terra Cotta Brew "Coffee Klatch"

Sales & Marketing

Paul Medina, the manager of the Terra Cotta Brew Coffee Shop at Painted Paradise Resort, is beginning a weekly coffee klatch and book club for hotel guests and local residents. The coffee shop has recently expanded its line of gourmet and specialty coffees, and he sees the coffee klatch as a way to introduce the new line and encourage sales. Terra Cotta Brew is located in the hotel lobby, which is an excellent location for walk-through traffic and visibility for the weekly gathering. To introduce the coffee klatch, he has asked you to edit and merge a letter that he has reviewed. You already have a mailing list, so you will simply merge the letter with the addresses. He has also asked you to design a table that can be included with the letter, providing detail on the new line of coffee carried by Terra Cotta Brew. You will include SmartArt, as well, to depict coffee klatch activity.

a. Open **File Explorer**, navigate to the location of your student data files, and then right-click **w02ps1CoffeeAddr**. Select **Copy**. Navigate to the location where you are saving your project files, right-click the folder (or disk drive), and select **Paste**. Locate the file that you pasted, right-click it, and select **Rename**. Type w02ps1CoffeeAddr_LastFirst, using your last and first name, and then press Enter.

b. Start **Word**, and then open **w02ps1Coffee**. Save the document where you are saving your project files as w02ps1Coffee_LastFirst, using your last and first name. If necessary, show nonprinting characters and display the horizontal and vertical rulers.

c. Turn off the Track Changes feature. If necessary, switch to **All Markup** view. Delete the comment beginning with **Can you verify**. Because you verified that the Coffee Klatch will be held at 3:30 instead of 4:30, reject the deletion of the **3** and the insertion of the **4**. The time in the letter should be 3:30. Accept all other changes.

d. Remove the current watermark.

e. Place the insertion point at the end of the second paragraph in the body of the letter, after the text **Terra Cotta Brew**. Make sure to place the insertion point after the period. Press Enter, and then set a **5" right tab** stop with a **dot leader**.

f. Type Thunder Blend. Press Tab, and then type Smoky, sweet tones. Press Enter.

g. Enter the following data. Press Tab between entries, and then press Enter at the end of each line. Do not press Enter after the last entry of "Tangy honey-orange."

Sumatra Roast	Creamy tropical and vanilla
Costa Rica Cerro	Citrus and fruit notes
Colombian Organic	Tangy honey-orange

h. Select the four tabbed lines. Reposition the right tab for the tabbed lines to **4.5"**.

i. With the text still selected, convert the **text** to a **table**. In the Convert Text to Table dialog box, change the Number of columns to **1**, select **AutoFit to contents**, and separate text at **Paragraphs**.

j. With the table still selected, apply a **6 pt** paragraph after spacing. Apply the **Plain Table 2** table style, remove the **bold**, and then center the table on the page.

k. Insert a **header**. With the insertion point in the header, insert the **w02ps1TerraLogo** graphic from your student data files. Change the height of the logo to **0.6"**, and then center the **logo** in the header. Close the header.

l. Select all the **text** in the document, and then change the font to **Times New Roman** and the font size to **11**.

m. Place the insertion point at the end of the last body paragraph, after the text **see you there!** Apply a **12 pt** paragraph before spacing, and then press Enter.

n. Insert the **Basic Block List** SmartArt, under the List category. Change the height of the SmartArt to **0.8"**. Type the text Bring a Book in the first shape. Type Enjoy Coffee and Pastries in the second shape. Type Have Great Conversation in the third shape. Delete the remaining blank shapes. Change the color of the SmartArt to **Dark 1 Outline**. Apply the **Flat Scene** SmartArt Style, and then save the document.

o. Use the **Step-by-Step Mail Merge Wizard** to begin a mail merge process for **letters**. Indicate that you want to use the **current document**.

p. Indicate that you will use an **existing list** for addresses, **browse** and navigate to where you are saving your project files, and then select **w02ps1CoffeeAddr_LastFirst** as the data source. Select **w02ps1CoffeeAddr_LastFirst** in the Data Source box, and then click **Edit**. Replace the name **Roger Troup** with your first and last name. Sort the recipients by last name in ascending order.

q. Replace the **[Recipient]** text in the letter with an **Address Block**. Select **Joshua Randall Jr.** as the format. Replace the **[Title]** and **[Last name]** text with the **Title** and **Last Name** merge fields. Keep a space between the two fields. Do not delete the colon. Preview your letters.

r. Complete the **merge**. Select **Edit individual letters**. Confirm that all five letters are included in the merged document, each addressed to a different recipient. Save the document as w02ps1CoffeeMrg_LastFirst, using your last and first name, and then close the document.

s. Save and close any remaining documents, and then exit Word. Submit the files as directed by your instructor.

Problem Solve 2

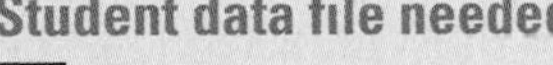

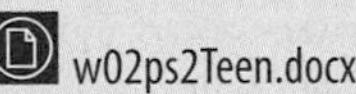

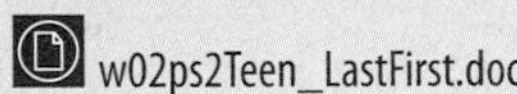

You will save your file as:

MyITLab® Grader
Homework 2

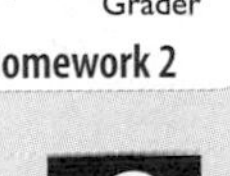

Research & Development

Teens and Smoking

Each year, the Medical Society of New Mexico sponsors a conference at the Painted Paradise Resort and Spa. Medical professionals from throughout the state attend the conference, at which time papers are presented on various health topics. Dr. Bernard Spelling, an associate of the Tobacco Awareness Center at USNM School of Medicine, is presenting a research paper on the effects of smoking on teenagers. Although your job as an assistant events coordinator does not often include providing clerical assistance for conference participants, you agree to assist Dr. Spelling in the final preparation and distribution of his report. His responsibilities at the university have caused him to arrive too late to put the final touches on the report himself. The report is complete with regard to content. However, because it is planned for publication, you will modify it to make sure it is in correct MLA style. You will also include citations where appropriate and you will develop a list of works cited. The organization that the paper will be submitted to after its presentation at the conference also requires that a cover page be included for proper identification of the sender.

a. Start **Word**, and then open **w02ps2Teen**. Save the document as w02ps2Teen_LastFirst, using your last and first name. If necessary, show nonprinting characters and display the horizontal and vertical rulers.

b. Change the font of the entire document to **12-pt Times New Roman**. Set the line spacing to **Double**, and then set a **first line indent** of 0.5" to the entire document.

c. Dr. Spelling created a style with no first line indent and centered text. Apply the **Paper Titles** style to the first two lines of the document. Bold the **first two lines** of the document.

d. Scroll through the document, and then apply the **Paper Titles** style to the headings, **The Link Between Smoking and Drinking**, **The Link Between Smoking and Illegal Drugs**, **The Link Between Smoking and Mental Health Disorders**, and **Recommended Changes**.

e. Select the last four paragraphs in the **The Link Between Smoking and Mental Health Disorders** section, beginning with the text **Twice as likely** and ending with the text **anxiety disorders**. Apply a **black square bullet** to the selected text, and then set a **0"** left indent.

f. Insert a right-aligned **header**. The header should contain the text Dr. Spelling, followed by a space, followed by the **Plain Number** page number field. Close the header.

g. Move the insertion point to the beginning of the document. Press Enter, and then move to the beginning of the document. Type Bernard Spelling, M.D. and then press Enter. Type Teen Health Medical News and then press Enter. Type July 14, 2015. Do not press Enter. Remove bold and left align the three lines just typed.

h. Click after the **last sentence** in the second body paragraph, after the word **Recovery**, but before the **period**. Make sure the Bibliography Style is set to **MLA Seventh Edition**, and then add the following new **Web site** article citation.

Name of Web Page	Bradford Center
Year	2014
Month	June
Day	18
Year Accessed	2015
Month Accessed	July
Day Accessed	10
URL	http://www.bradfordrecovery.com

i. At the end of the second sentence in the third body paragraph, click after the word **disorders**, but before the **period**. Insert the following new **Article in a Periodical** citation.

Author	Arthur Stephenson
Title	Hidden Nicotine Dangers
Periodical Title	ASA Journal
Year	2015
Month	February
Day	21
Pages	19–20

j. In the same paragraph, click at the end of the last sentence after the word **Abuse** but before the **period**. Insert a citation using the predefined source, **The National Center on Addiction and Substance Abuse**. Because there is no need to repeat the center's name in the citation, edit the citation. The page number will be sufficient. Suppress the **Author**, **Year**, and **Title**, and then type 52 for the page number.

k. At the end of the first sentence in the section, **The Link Between Smoking and Illegal Drugs**, click after the word **addiction**, but before the **period**. Insert a citation using the predefined source, **Center for Disease Identification and Control**.

l. Move the insertion point to the end of the document, and then insert a **Next Page** section break. Type Early Nicotine Addiction Effects and then press Enter. Center the **text** you just entered, and then press Ctrl+End.

m. Insert the **Diverging Radial** SmartArt, under the Cycle category. Enter Early Nicotine Use Likely to Cause in the center circle graphic. Enter Alcohol Addiction in the top graphic. Working clockwise, type the following text in the next three graphics. Do not press Enter.

Marijuana Use
Heroin Use
Cocaine Use

n. Apply **Square** text wrap to the SmartArt. Center-align the **SmartArt** diagram on the page. Change the color of the SmartArt to **Dark 1 Outline**. Apply the **Moderate Effect** SmartArt style, and then change the height of the SmartArt to **5.5"**.

o. Apply a **Hard Edge** bevel shape effect to the SmartArt, and then apply a **White, Background 1, Darker 50%** shape outline, with a **4 ½ pt** weight.

p. Move the insertion point to the end of the document, insert a **Next Page section break**, and then insert a **Works Cited** page. Double-space the **works cited page**, and then apply **0 pt** paragraph after spacing, and a **12-pt Times New Roman** font. Center the **Works Cited** title.

q. Click anywhere in page 5, the page containing the SmartArt. Because this page is in its own section, you can change its orientation. Change the orientation of the page to **Landscape**. Center the page vertically. Select the word **Effects** in the title above the SmartArt. Insert a new comment and then type, Is this OK?

r. Insert a **footnote** at the end of the first line on the first page, immediately after **Bernard Spelling, M.D.** Type Dr. Spelling is an associate of the Tobacco Awareness Center at USNM School of Medicine. (include the period).

s. Click the **INSERT** tab, and then in the Pages group, click **Cover Page**, and then select **Grid**. Click in the **DOCUMENT TITLE** placeholder to select it, and then type SMOKING AND TEENS. Similarly, change the **Document subtitle** placeholder to Structural, chemical, and health effects and then change the **Abstract** placeholder to First Last using your first and last name.

t. Save and close the document, and then exit Word. Submit the file as directed by your instructor.

Perform 1: Perform in Your Life

Student data file needed:

Blank Word document

You will save your files as:

w02pf1Resume_LastFirst.docx
w02pf1Cover_LastFirst.docx
w02pf1Companies_LastFirst.accdb
w02pf1CoverMerge_LastFirst.docx
w02pf1CoverEnv_LastFirst.docx

Resume, Cover Letter, and Envelopes

Sales & Marketing

As you prepare to seek employment, you are aware of the importance of an attractive resume and cover letter. Websites such as **www.monster.com** provide resume and cover letter tips, and Microsoft provides templates for both resumes and cover letters. Using a resume template, you will prepare your resume. You will also prepare a cover letter, providing potential employers with information on your employment goals. You will then create a data source, with addresses of employers, so you can personalize the cover letter. Finally you will create envelopes to mail your packet.

a. Start **Word**. Search the online templates for a **resume** template. Download an appropriate resume template, and then save the resume as w02pf1Resume_LastFirst.

b. Modify the resume document to include information specific to your educational and professional preparation. Enhance the resume in any way you like, keeping in mind the need to present a concise, professional document. Save and close the document, but keep the Word application open.

c. You will now create a cover letter. You can create a new blank document to start your cover letter from scratch, or you can search the online templates for an appropriate cover letter. You may even choose to search monster.com for ideas, which you can then incorporate into a new blank document. Save the document as w02pf1Cover_LastFirst.

d. Insert a date field to be automatically updated in the cover letter. Personalize the cover letter to include information specific to your job search. Because the letter will be the basis for a mail merge document, include a placeholder for the address block and for the salutation. Save the document.

e. Begin a mail merge, using the Step-by-Step Mail Merge Wizard to create letters.
   - The merge is to produce letters, using the current document.
   - You will create the data source. In Step 3 of the Mail Merge Wizard, under the Select recipients area, select **Type a new list**. Then click **Create**. Type at least 8 address records using fictional addresses, if you like. Click **New Entry** to start a new address. Click **OK** when the list is complete, navigate to where you are saving your files, and then save the data as w02pf1Companies_LastFirst.
   - Sort the recipients by last name, alphabetically.
   - Include an AddressBlock and an appropriate salutation, so each letter is individualized.
   - Preview your letters. Adjust the spacing in the address block and salutation area, if necessary.
   - Complete the merge, and then edit the individual letters. Save the file containing all the letters as w02pf1CoverMerge_LastFirst. Close the file. Save and close the **w02pf1Cover_LastFirst** file. Keep Word open.

f. Use the Step-by-Step Mail Merge Wizard to create envelopes for the employers to whom you are sending the cover letter.
   - Use a Size 10 envelope size.
   - Use the **w02pf1Companies_LastFirst** file as the data source. Sort the recipients by last name, alphabetically.
   - If necessary, show nonprinting characters in order to properly place the address block. Type in your address in the return address area, and then enter an appropriate address block in the delivery address area.
   - Preview the envelopes, and then adjust the spacing and font as necessary.
   - Complete the merge, and then edit the individual letters. Save the document containing all the envelopes as w02pf1CoverEnv_LastFirst. Close the file, and then close any remaining files without saving. Exit Word.

g. Submit the files as directed by your instructor.

Perform 2: Perform in Your Career

Student data files needed:

 w02pf2NSIDAddr.accdb

 Blank Word document

You will save your files as:

 w02pf2NSIDAddr_LastFirst.accdb

 w02pf2NSID_LastFirst.docx

 w02pf2NSIDMerge_LastFirst.docx

NSID Scholarships

Sales & Marketing

You are employed as the marketing director for the National Society of Interior Designers (NSID). Your job responsibilities include preparing marketing and educational material to promote the society and to encourage new membership. NSID has partnered with the Interior Design Educators Group to provide scholarship opportunities for interior design students. You will prepare a letter to be sent to high school guidance counselors outlining the various scholarship programs provided by NSID. You will then create a mail merge document, combining addresses from a data source with the letter.

a. Copy **w02pf2NSIDAddr** from the student data files to the location where you are saving your files, renaming it w02pf2NSIDAddr_LastFirst, using your last and first name. Start **Word**, and then begin a new document. Save the document as w02pf2NSID_LastFirst.

b. The font should be 11-pt Times New Roman. In block letter style, type your address as shown below, replacing Firstname and Lastname with your first and last names.
Firstname Lastname, Marketing Coordinator
National Society of Interior Designers
134 Greenfield Street
Fort Worth, TX 76102

c. Insert the date field, so it is updated automatically. You should not simply type the date, but insert it using the INSERT tab. The format is Month Day, Year (for example, September 2, 2016).

d. Leave space for a mailing address that will be inserted in the mail merge process. The salutation should include the word **Dear**, with space left for a recipient's name to be placed during the mail merge process.

e. Compose a letter to guidance counselors encouraging them to inform students of the exciting opportunities in the interior design field. Include in the letter that interior design is more than the knowledge of color, fabrics, and design. An interior designer must also be proficient with budgets, computers, and communication. Remind them that the field of interior design has expanded over the years to include even more specialties, such as eco-friendly and antique architectural designs. Inform them of the scholarships available through the partnership of NSID with the Interior Design Educators Group. List the scholarships in the form of a table, as shown below. You should note in your letter that additional information regarding specific requirements for each scholarship is available through the NSID website, **www.NSIDDesign.com/careers**, or at (555) 555-0088.

Scholarship	Sponsor	Award
NDFA Scholarship	National Design and Furnishings Association	$1,500/semester
Metropolis Design	In Sync Design Professionals	$1,500/semester plus all books
Student Design Award Competitions	National Society of Interior Designers	$2,000/semester

f. Apply an attractive design style to the scholarship table, or create your own, using shading and bordering. Insert a row above the first row, merge the cells, and enter the text Interior Design Scholarships. Center all the text in the table.

g. Resize columns if necessary to provide the best readability and use of space. Align and format the data appropriately. Center the table horizontally on the page.

h. Design a SmartArt diagram (perhaps a process chart) in the letter to graphically indicate the progression to a career in interior design. Include the following steps, in sequence, in the SmartArt diagram.
Practice your skills at home
Seek an industry mentor
Explore scholarships
Network and market yourself

i. End the letter with a closing paragraph and a complimentary close. Adjust the size of the table and SmartArt in order for the letter to fit on one page. If necessary, change the design layout of the SmartArt or edit the text in the letter. Save the document.

j. Begin the Step-by-Step Mail Merge Wizard, to create a Letters mail merge, using the current document. You will merge the letter with an existing data source called **w02pf2NSIDAddr_LastFirst**, which you copied and renamed in Step a. Edit the data source, and then change one of the entries to include your first and last name. Sort the data by last names, alphabetically.

k. Insert an AddressBlock. Insert the appropriate fields in the salutation. Preview the letters, and then complete the merge by editing the individual letters. Save the file containing all the letters as w02pf2NSIDMerge_LastFirst. Close the document, save **w02pf2NSID_LastFirst**, and then exit Word. Submit the files as directed by your instructor.

Perform 3: Perform in Your Team

Student data file needed:

w02pf3Millennial.docx

You will save your file as:

w02pf3Millennial_TeamName.docx

The Millennial Generation

Research & Development

You are majoring in education and have been assigned a group project by your instructor. Your team is researching the learning style of "millennials," those born between 1977 and 1998. Your team has already drafted a report, but it is still in a rough draft format. Your team will edit and modify the report, making sure it follows the MLA style. You will also make sure all sources are properly cited. Sit down with your team members to discuss the work remaining. Remember, only one person can edit the document at any single time, so make sure you plan ahead by determining what each team member will be responsible for contributing, and when they will make their updates.

a. Select one team member to set up the document by completing Steps b–d.

b. Open your browser and navigate to either **www.skydrive.live.com**, **www.drive.google.com**, or any other instructor-assigned locations. Be sure all members of the team have an account on the chosen system—Microsoft or Google.

c. Start **Word**, navigate to the location of your student data files, and then open the **w02pf3Millennial** document. Save the file as w02pf3Millennial_TeamName, where TeamName is the name assigned to your team by your instructor.

d. Share the file with the other members of your team, and then make sure that each team member has the appropriate permissions to edit the document. Divide the work evenly among the team members.

e. Format the document text appropriately, according to MLA style, and then center the subheadings.

f. Insert a right-aligned header. The header should contain your team name followed by a space, followed by the Plain Number page number field. Make sure the first page does not have a header.

g. Insert four lines, left-aligned, at the top of the document containing your team name, your instructor's name, your class name, and the current date. Format appropriately, according to MLA style.

h. Use Find and Replace to find all occurrences of **millennials** and replace them with **Millennials**.

i. Bullet the last four paragraphs of the document, under the **General Observations** heading, using the standard round bullet.

j. Create a citation in MLA style for the statistic given in the last sentence of the second paragraph under **Social and Workplace Expectations**, at the end of the sentence **Therefore, 80% of them still live at home.** The source is a book titled Generational Learning Styles by Andrew Keller. It is published by Brennan Publishers located in Boston. The publish date is 2015.

k. Insert a citation at the end of the third sentence of the report, the sentence beginning with **Millennials have been showered**. The source is a journal article, by Sarah Belknap titled What Now? How to Bridge the Digital Divide. It is located in the Teaching and Learning Digest on page 15. The journal year is 2013.

l. You mistakenly listed the year for the Belknap journal citation as 2013. It is actually 2015. Edit the source to make the correction.

m. Correct any spelling or grammatical errors. Remember, Millennials is spelled with two n's.

n. Insert a works cited page at the end of the document, and center the page heading. Format the works cited page appropriately.

o. Insert a cover page with your report title, your team member names, each member's contribution, and the current date.

p. Save and close the document. Exit Word.

q. Once the assignment is complete, share the document with your instructor or turn in as your instructor directs. Make sure that the instructor has permission to edit the file.

Perform 4: How Others Perform

Student data file needed:

w02pf4Fall.docx

You will save your file as:

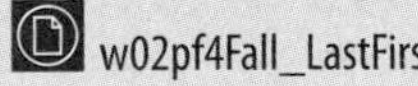

w02pf4Fall_LastFirst.docx

Gibson Elementary Fall Festival

Sales & Marketing

As a new fourth grade teacher at Gibson Elementary, you are in charge of organizing the school's fall festival. Your homeroom parent, the parent who has volunteered to help with school functions throughout the year, has begun the process of creating a flyer to send home with school children. The flyer provides details on the festival. Because your homeroom parent is unable to complete the flyer, you will edit and modify it. You want to build the flyer around a fall color scheme, and you plan to include graphics to make it fun and eye appealing.

a. Start **Word**, and then open **w02pf4Fall**. Save the document as w02pf4Fall_LastFirst.

b. Change the text **Fall Festival** into a WordArt. Format it in a color that coordinates with the fall theme. Add a Transform text effect to the WordArt. Add any other picture effects that you think necessary.

c. Add a border around the text beginning with **Join us** and ending with **11:30 am – 2:30 pm**. Shade the bordered text. Apply appropriate formatting and color schemes. Resize the box as necessary.

d. Use a left tab and a right tab to align the date and time as shown below.

Join us on the front lawn of Gibson Elementary	
Saturday, October 15	**11:30 am – 2:30 pm**

e. Remove the four lines of activities. Insert a 2×4 table below the bordered text. Enter the following text in the table. Center the text vertically and horizontally within each cell. Remove the borders on the table, and then format the table as desired.

Games	Pumpkin Painting
Face Painting	Dunking Booth
Cake Walk	Food
Crafts	Music

f. Apply a page color. Include at least one additional fall-related clip art.

g. Include contact information with your first and last name.

h. Make any other improvements you think necessary. Save the document, and then exit Word. Submit the file as directed by your instructor.

Microsoft Office Excel 2013
Module 1
Understanding the Fundamentals

WORKSHOP 1 | NAVIGATE, MANIPULATE, AND PRINT WORKSHEETS

OBJECTIVES

Prepare Case

Red Bluff Golf Course and Pro Shop Golf Cart Purchase Analysis

Finance & Accounting

The Red Bluff Golf Course and Pro Shop makes golf carts available to its members for a fee. Recently, the resort has been running out of carts. The time has come for the club to add more golf carts to its fleet of 10. Club manager, Barry Cheney, wants to use Microsoft Excel to analyze the purchase of golf carts by model, price, and financing parameters.

Laura Gangi Pond / Shutterstock

REAL WORLD SUCCESS

"My family has operated the same farm for four generations. When I graduated from college I decided to become the first woman to run the family farm. I now track all of our production inputs and outputs using Excel. The quality information I produce with Excel has made our farm more efficient and more profitable. Farming is a business—a successful business requires intelligence in handling information as much, or more, than it requires intelligence in any other critical business activity."

- Leah, recent graduate

Student data file needed for this workshop:

e01ws01GolfCarts.xlsx

You will save your files as:

 e01ws01GolfCarts_LastFirst.xlsx

 e01ws01GolfCartsP_LastFirst.pdf

 e01ws01Mowers_LastFirst.xlsx

Excel—What If Data and Information Could Speak?

Data play an integral part in supporting business. Without data, businesses are not able to determine their effectiveness in the market, let alone their profit or loss performance. In addition, as businesses grow and change, the types of data collected by a particular business is one of the few things that remain relatively static over time. Jobs change, products change, and businesses grow or evolve into different lines of business—even into different organizations—based on customer and market demands. However, the data gathered and analyzed is relatively constant. Data tracked typically only expand as new data is made available and deemed necessary for business purposes, or as new technologies easily capture data that was prohibitive to track in the past. Much of the same information is required about customers, vendors, products, services, materials, transactions, and so on regardless of the line, or type, of business. Many things may change, but the type of information remains the same.

The problem is that in all that data, there is so much information to decipher. Thus, data require processing—categorization, counting, averaging, summarization, statistical analysis, and formatting for effective communication—to reveal information that the data cannot tell you itself. With an application like Excel, it is possible to structure data and to process it in a manner that creates information for decision-making purposes. With the help of Excel, you give data a voice, a medium through which underlying trends, calculated values, predictions, decision recommendations, and other information can be revealed.

In this workshop, you will be introduced to spreadsheets, called worksheets in Excel. You will learn to create worksheets and to manipulate rows and columns, as well as to navigate in and among worksheets within a workbook. You will learn how to enter data—text, numbers, dates, and times—into a worksheet, and how to use a few powerful analysis features that enable you to give data a voice.

Understand Spreadsheet Terminology and Components

To learn the efficient and effective utilization of Excel, you must know the terminology and componentry of a spreadsheet. In this section, you will learn the basic terms that are used universally to reference spreadsheet components in Excel.

What Is a Spreadsheet?

A **spreadsheet** application is a computer program with a user interface that is made of a grid of rows and columns. The intersection of each row and column is called a **cell**. A **row** is a horizontal set of cells that encompasses all the columns in a worksheet and only one cell vertically. A **column** is a vertical set of cells that encompasses all the rows in a worksheet and only one cell horizontally. Each cell can contain text, numbers, formulas, and/or functions. A **formula** is an equation that produces a result and may contain numbers, operators, text, and/or functions. A **function** is a built-in program that performs a task such as calculating a sum or average. Both formulas and functions must always start with the equal sign (=). In Excel, each instance of a spreadsheet is referred to as a **worksheet**.

From balancing an accounting ledger to creating a financial report, many business documents use Excel spreadsheets. Excel spreadsheets are designed to support analyzing business data, representing data through charts, and modeling real-world situations.

Spreadsheets are also commonly used to perform **what-if analysis**. In what-if analysis, you change values in spreadsheet cells to investigate the effects on calculated values of interest.

Spreadsheets are used for much more than what-if analysis, however. A spreadsheet can be used as a basic collection of data where each row is a **record** and each column is a **field** in the record. Spreadsheets can be built to act as a simple accounting system. Businesses often use spreadsheets to analyze complex financial statements and information. Excel can calculate statistical values such as mean, variance, and standard deviation. Excel can even be used for advanced statistical models such as forecasting and regression analysis. Spreadsheet applications "excel" at calculations of most any kind.

What Is a Workbook?

A **workbook** is a file that contains at least one worksheet. In Microsoft Excel 2013, workbooks have a file extension of .xlsx. By default a new, blank workbook contains one worksheet, identified by a tab at the bottom of the Excel window titled Sheet1. As additional worksheets are added, they are given the default name Sheet*n* where "*n*" is an integer incremented by 1 for each new worksheet; for example, two new worksheets would be given the names Sheet2 and Sheet3. The active worksheet is denoted by a white tab with bold letters and a thick bottom border. Worksheets that are not active are denoted by gray tabs with normal letters. The number of worksheets that can be contained in a workbook is determined by the amount of available memory.

Once a workbook has been created, or opened, any changes to the workbook will need to be saved. Save and Save As accomplish the same task; however, Save As is useful for saving a copy of a file with a new name. It is also useful for creating a backup of a file or for creating a copy of a workbook when you want to use that workbook as the starting point for another workbook.

In the first exercise, you will learn how to start Excel, to open a workbook, and to save that workbook with a new name.

E01.00

To Start Excel, and Open, Save, and Rename a Workbook

a. Point to the **bottom-right corner** of the Start screen or desktop.

The Charms will appear on the right side of the screen. Move the pointer over the bottom charm. Note the labels underneath each of the charms.

b. Click **Search**.

c. Click inside the **Search** box at the top of the page, and then type Excel.

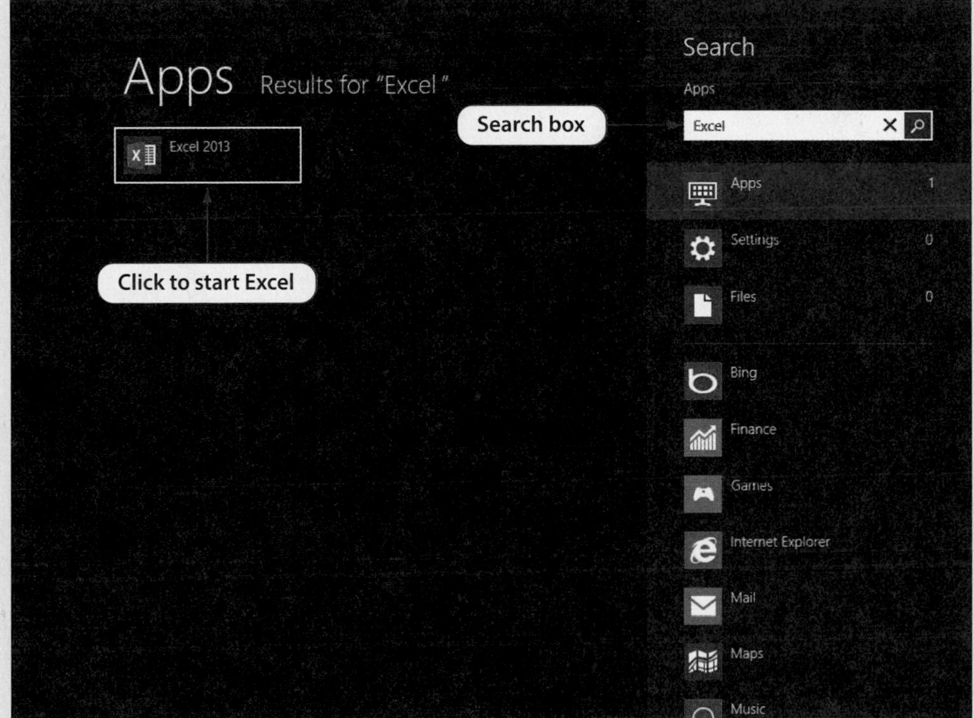

Figure 1 Starting Microsoft Excel 2013

d. Click **Excel 2013** in the search results.

e. In the lower-left corner of the Excel screen, click **Open Other Workbooks**.

f. In the **Open pane** under Places, click **Computer** and then click **Browse**.

g. Click the **disk drive** in the left pane where your student data files are located—you may have to double-click **Computer** to see the disk drive list, navigate through the folder structure, and then select **e01ws01GolfCarts**.

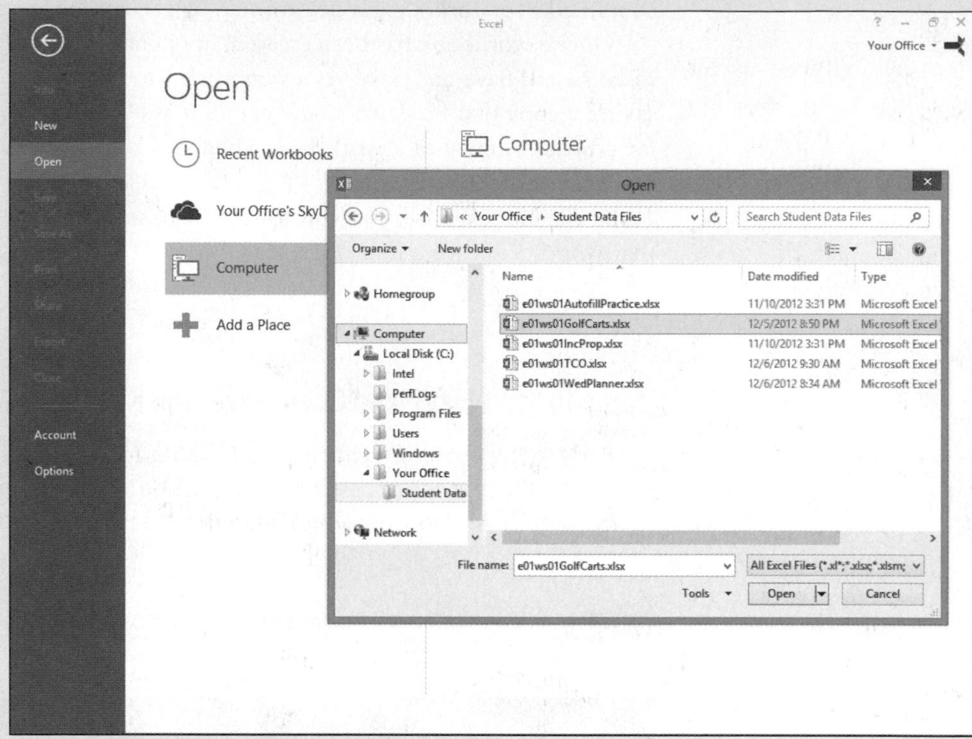

Figure 2 Open an existing workbook

h. Click **Open**.

i. Click the **FILE** tab to access Backstage view.

The Info pane is displayed. The Info pane displays document properties such as file size, create and modified dates, and author.

j. Click **Save As**, click **Browse**, and then in the Save As dialog box, navigate to the location where you are saving your files. Click in the **File name** box, type e01ws01GolfCarts_LastFirst using your last and first name. Click **Save**.

SIDE NOTE
Save As
Click Save As to save your file with a new name and/or to save it a new location.

CONSIDER THIS | Excel Can Store a Vast Amount of Data

There are 1,048,576 rows x 16,384 columns = 17,179,869,184 cells in an Excel 2013 worksheet. With so much capacity, some are tempted to use Excel as a database. What other Office application would be better for storing vast amounts of data?

REAL WORLD ADVICE — **AutoRecover and Quick Save—Outsmart Mr. Murphy!**

Computers are not perfect. While life's imperfections often make things interesting, they are also an opportunity for Murphy's Law: Anything that can go wrong, will go wrong. However, never fear, AutoRecover and Quick Save are here!

Excel automatically saves your work every 10 minutes, but you can change that interval. Click in Backstage view under Options, and then click the Save tab. In the Excel Options dialog box, change the value in the Save AutoRecover information every box. The saved copies of your work are called AutoRecover files. If your computer shuts down unexpectedly, Office will recognize that the file you were working on was not closed properly and will give you the option of opening the most recent AutoRecover file.

The Ctrl + S shortcut quickly saves your file to the same location as the last save. Whenever you make a significant change to your file, save it right away using the "quick save" keyboard shortcut.

Navigate Within Worksheets and Workbooks

Workbooks often contain more than a single worksheet, and in order to effectively develop and use workbooks and worksheets you must be able to navigate between and among worksheets in a workbook and to navigate in the worksheets. In this section you will learn to navigate within a worksheet and to navigate between worksheets.

Navigate Among Worksheets

Workbooks often contain more than one worksheet. The workbook you have opened contains four worksheets. The worksheet tabs are located in the bottom-left corner of the Excel window. Each tab represents a single worksheet in the workbook.

The **active worksheet**, the worksheet that is visible, is readily identifiable because the background color of its worksheet tab is white and it has a thick bottom border. To make a different worksheet active, click its worksheet tab.

When you open a workbook that you have not worked with before, it is a good practice to spend some time familiarizing yourself with its worksheets. In the following exercise, you navigate among worksheets to familiarize yourself with the contents of the e01ws01GolfCarts_LastFirst workbook.

MyITLab®
Workshop 1 Training

E01.01

To Change the Active Worksheet

a. Click the **May Golf Cart Usage Analysis** worksheet tab. This worksheet is an analysis of golf cart usage for the month of May that Barry Cheney built to assess whether the number of carts in the current fleet is optimal.

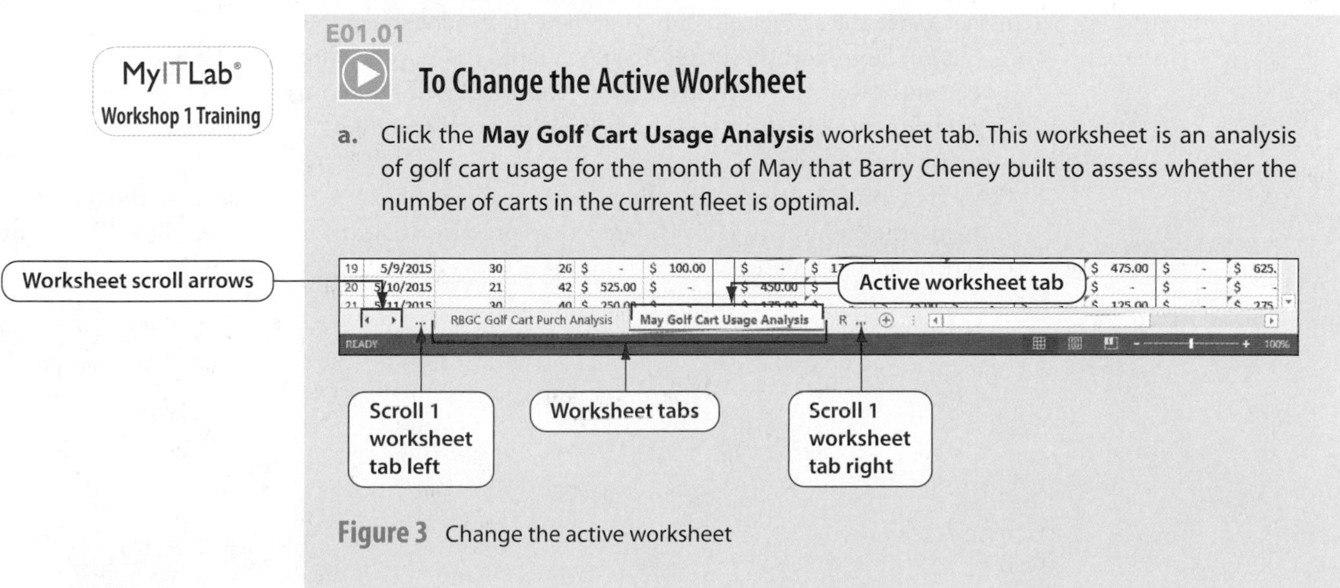

Figure 3 Change the active worksheet

SIDE NOTE

Navigate Between Sheets Using Shortcuts

Ctrl + PageUp and Ctrl + PageDown move you one worksheet to the left and right respectively.

SIDE NOTE

Navigate Quickly Among Many Worksheets

Right-click the worksheet scroll arrows and select the worksheet you want to make active in the Activate dialog box.

b. Click the **RBGC Golf Cart Purch Analysis** worksheet tab in the bottom-left corner of the worksheet window. This worksheet is the start of a purchase analysis for replacement of the Red Bluff Golf Course fleet of golf carts.

c. Click the **Documentation** worksheet tab—you may need to scroll left using the worksheet scroll arrows to see the Documentation worksheet tab.

This worksheet is used to document the contents of the workbook. Documentation is an important component in a well-structured workbook.

Troubleshooting

All the figures in this text were taken at a monitor resolution of 1024 X 768. Higher or lower resolution will affect the way Excel displays Ribbon options.

Navigating Worksheets

Whether a worksheet is small or extremely large, navigation from one cell to another is necessary to enter, or to edit, numbers, formulas, functions, or text. Navigation requires an understanding of how Excel addresses rows, columns, and cells.

Each row is identified by a number in ascending sequence from top to bottom. Each column is identified by a letter in ascending sequence from left to right. The intersection of each row and column is called a cell. Each cell has a default name, called a **cell reference**—the combination of its column letter and row number. For example, the intersection of column A and row 1 has a cell reference of A1, and the intersection of column D and row 20 is cell D20.

Navigating in a small worksheet is simple—move the mouse pointer over a cell and click to make it the active cell. The **active cell** is the recipient of an action, such as a click, calculation, or paste. The border around the cell changes to a thick, green line. Any information you enter via the keyboard is placed into the active cell. **Worksheet navigation** is simply defined as moving the location of the active cell.

When part of a document—or in the case of Excel, a worksheet—is out of view because it is too large to be displayed in the visible application window, use the vertical and horizontal scroll bars to shift other parts of the document into view. The vertical scroll bar is on the right side of the application window, and the horizontal scroll bar is at the bottom right of the application window. It is important to note that scrolling does not move the active cell, only your view in the document.

For large worksheets, Go To allows rapid navigation. Although the worksheet you are currently working with is not large, knowledge of how to use the Go To dialog box to navigate directly to any cell in the worksheet by specifying a cell reference is a skill that you will find useful.

Keyboard shortcuts allow rapid navigation in a worksheet without having to usethe mouse. It is considered best practice to learn and use keyboard shortcuts whenever possible.

QUICK REFERENCE | **Navigation with Keyboard Shortcuts**

There are several keyboard shortcuts that may be used to navigate a worksheet and move the active cell:

Keyboard Shortcuts	Moves the Active Cell
[Enter]	Down one row
[Shift] + [Enter]	Up one row
[→] [←] [↓] [↑]	One cell in the direction of the arrow key
[Home]	To column A of the current row
[Ctrl] + [Home]	To column A, row 1 (cell A1)
[Ctrl] + [End]	To the last cell, highest number row and far-right column, that contains information
[End] + [→] [End] + [←] [End] + [↓] [End] + [↑]	If the first cell in the direction of the arrow beyond the active cell contains data, to the last cell containing data in the arrow direction before an empty cell If the first cell in the direction of the arrow beyond the active cell is empty, to the next cell in the arrow direction that contains information
[Page Up] [Page Down]	Up one screen, down one screen
[Alt] + [Page Up]	Left one screen
[Alt] + [Page Down]	Right one screen
[Ctrl] + [Page Up] [Ctrl] + [Page Down]	One worksheet left One worksheet right
[Tab] [Shift] + [Tab]	One column right One column left

To Navigate Within a Worksheet

a. Click the **RBGC Golf Cart Purch Analysis** worksheet tab, and then press [Ctrl] + [Home] to make A1 the active cell. Press [↓] six times, and then press [→] four times. The active cell should be E7. Type 6495 and then press [Ctrl] + [Enter] to keep cell E7 active.

b. Press [←], and then press [↑] two times. The active cell should be D5. Type E-Z-GO and then press [Enter].

   Notice that the active cell is now D6. Pressing [Enter] moved the active cell down one row.

c. On the HOME tab, in the Editing group, click **Find & Select**, and then click **Go To**. The Go To dialog box appears. Click in the **Reference** box, type D13, and then click **OK**. The active cell is now D13. On the HOME tab, in the Font group, click **Bold** [B].

d. Press [Home]. This takes you to column A of the row with the active cell. The active cell should be A13. Type Total Interest Cost: and then press [Ctrl] + [Enter].

e. Press [Ctrl] + [Home] to return the active cell to A1, and then click **Save** [💾].

> **Troubleshooting**
> The active cell is repositioned using the mouse pointer and keyboard. Even experienced users often scroll through a worksheet and press an arrow key only to be returned to the active cell where they began scrolling.

Touch Devices

If you have a device such as a tablet PC with a touch screen, you can control Excel 2013 using your finger. The commands on the Ribbon and in shortcut menus are the same, but Excel recognizes when you have touched the screen and enables touch mode. In **touch mode**, the Ribbon and shortcut menus are enlarged to make selecting commands with your fingertip easier. Figure 4 shows the Excel interface in touch mode.

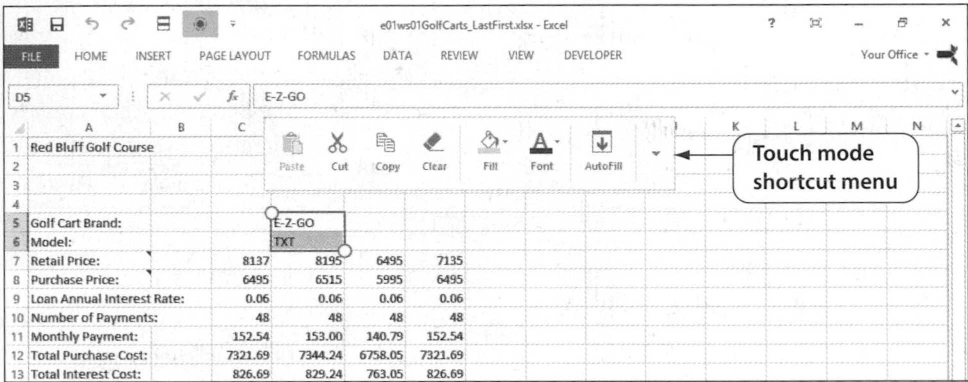

Figure 4 Touch mode in Excel 2013

Document Your Work

Worksheets are often used by people who did not develop them. Even if a worksheet will never be used by anyone other than its builder, best practice dictates that you document a workbook and its worksheets.

Documentation is vital to ensure that a worksheet remains usable. A well-documented worksheet is much easier to use and maintain, particularly for a user who did not develop the worksheet. You may use a worksheet on a regular basis, you may even have developed it, but over time you may forget how the worksheet actually operates.

Documentation takes several forms, such as descriptive file and worksheet names, worksheet titles, column and/or row titles, cell labels, cell comments, or a dedicated documentation worksheet. Many people do not take the time to document adequately because they do not feel it is time spent productively. Some do not feel it is necessary because they do not think anyone else will ever use the workbook. For a workbook to be useful, it must be accurate, easily understood, flexible, efficient, and documented. While accuracy is most important, an undocumented workbook can later create inaccurate data. Where documentation is concerned, less is not more—more is more.

Using Comments to Document a Workbook

Unlike documentation worksheets that generally include documentation for an entire workbook, comments are created specifically to add documentation to a worksheet and address individual fields, calculations, and so on and are included as content in an individual cell.

E01.03

To Document a Workbook Using Comments

a. Click the **RBGC Golf Cart Purch Analysis** worksheet tab. Notice that cell A7 has a red triangle in the upper-right corner. This indicates the existence of a comment. Point to cell **A7**. The comment that appears defines Retail Price.

b. Click cell **A9**. Click the **REVIEW** tab.

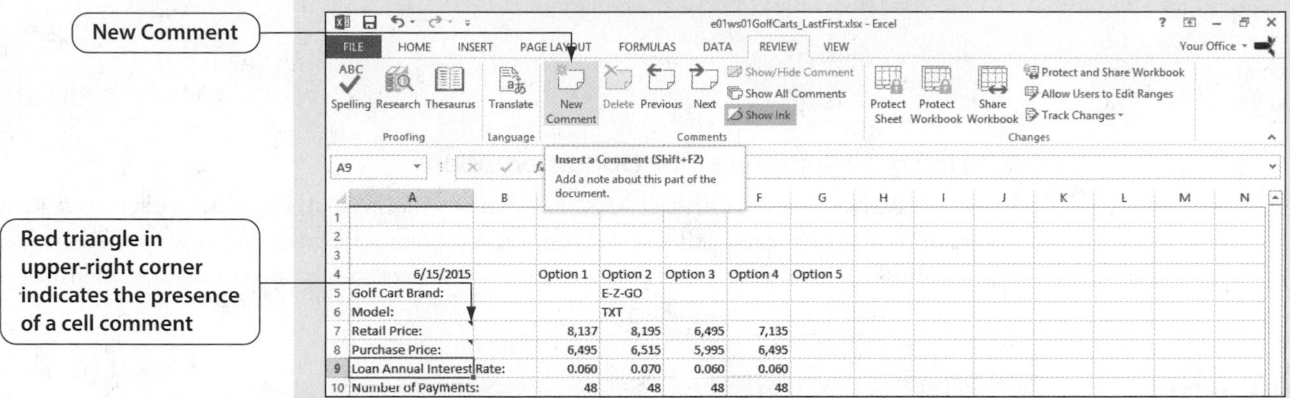

Figure 5 Insert a comment into a cell

c. In the Comments group, click **New Comment** to create a comment.

d. In the comment box, double-click the **user name** text that is automatically inserted into the comment. Press Delete to delete the user name. You may have to do this more than once if there are any spaces in the user name. Click the **HOME** tab. In the Font group, if Bold is turned off, then click **Bold** B to turn bold on. Click the **REVIEW** tab.

> **Troubleshooting**
>
> Double-clicking only selects a word. If your user name contains a space, repeat Step c until the user name is completely deleted before moving to Step d.

e. Type **Annual Interest Rate**, and then press Ctrl + B to turn off bold text. Press Enter, and then type **Annual rate of interest in decimal or percentage format, e.g., 5% is entered as 0.05 or as 5%.**

Cell A9 now has a red triangle in the top right corner to indicate the presence of a comment.

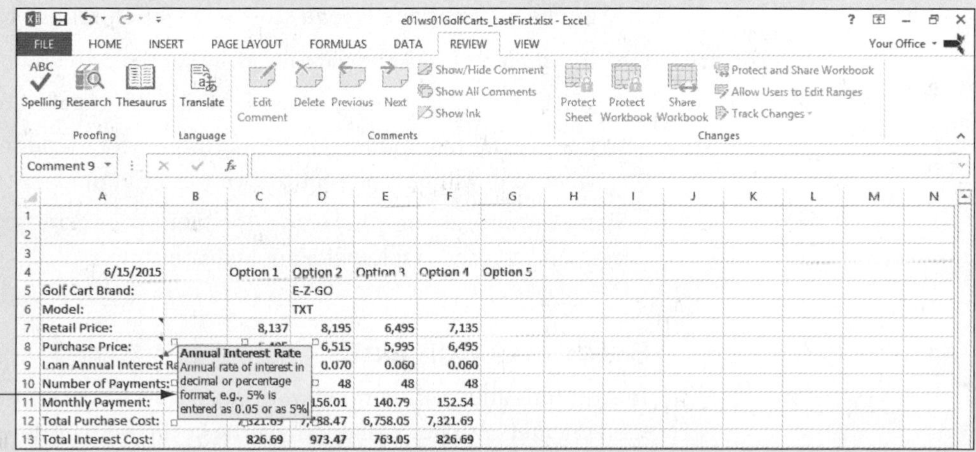

Figure 6 Documenting annual interest rate using a comment

f. Click cell **A10**, and then click **New Comment**.

g. In the comment box, double-click the **user name** text that is automatically inserted into the comment, and then press [Delete]. If necessary, repeat until the user name is completely removed. Click the **HOME** tab. In the Font group, if Bold is not turned on, click **Bold** [B].

h. Type # of Payments and then click **Bold** [B] to turn off bold text.

i. Press [Enter], type Total number of payments over the term of the loan and then press [Esc] two times to close the comment.

j. Click **Save** [H].

SIDE NOTE
Save Often
Murphy's Law for computers: The likelihood your computer will crash is proportional to the amount of time since you last saved.

Using a Worksheet for Documentation

A well-structured worksheet is self-documenting in that there are descriptive titles, column headings, and cell labels. However, a separate documentation worksheet includes information not generally specified in a worksheet, such as authorship, modification dates, and modification history.

E01.04

To Document a Workbook Using a Documentation Worksheet

a. Click the **Documentation** worksheet tab—you may have to scroll left in the worksheet tabs. Click cell **A8**, and then type the current date in mm/dd/yyyy format.

b. Click cell **B8**, and then type your last name, first name.

c. Click cell **C8**, and then type Added comments to key headings.

d. Click **Save** [H].

SIDE NOTE
Shortcut to Insert the System Date
[Ctrl] + [;] is a keyboard shortcut that inserts the computer system date into the active cell.

SS REAL WORLD ADVICE **Failing to Plan Is Planning to Fail**

Winston Churchill said, "He who fails to plan, plans to fail." The first step in building a worksheet should be planning. There are several questions that should be considered before you begin actually entering information:

- What is the objective of the worksheet? Is it to solve a problem? Is it to analyze data and recommend a course of action? Is it to summarize data and present usable information? Is it to store information for use by another application?
- Do you have all of the data necessary to build this worksheet?
- What information does your worksheet need to generate?
- How should the information in your worksheet be presented? Who is the audience? What form will best present the worksheet information?

Plan your work before you begin—the time spent planning will be saved several times over, and the end result will be of higher quality.

Enter and Edit Data

In building and maintaining worksheets, the ability to enter, edit, and format data is fundamental. As data is entered via the keyboard, the data simultaneously appears in the active cell and in the formula bar. Figure 7 shows the result when a cell is double-clicked to place the insertion point into cell contents. If you click in the formula bar, the insertion point is displayed in the formula bar.

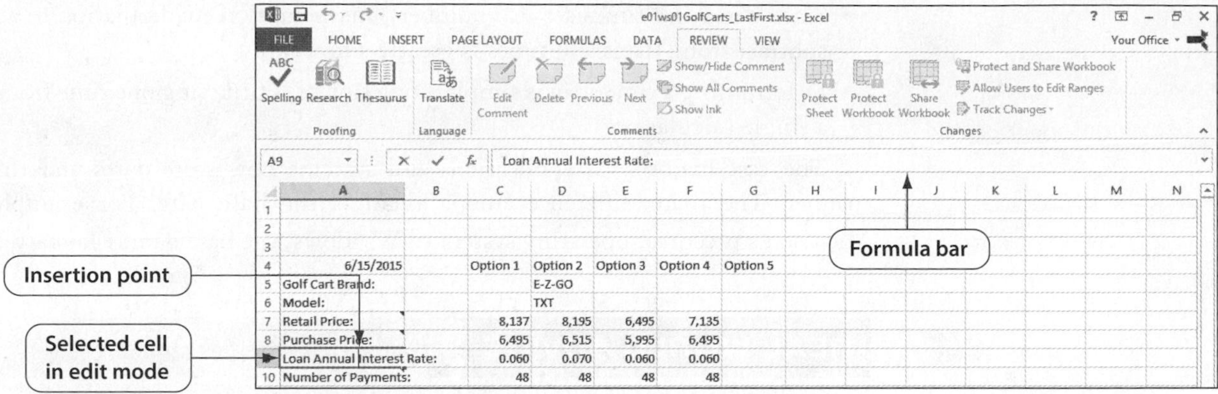

Figure 7 Editing data in a cell

Using Text, Numbers, Dates, and Times

Text data consists of any combination of printable characters including letters, numbers, and special characters available on any standard keyboard.

Numeric data consists of numbers in any form not combined with letters and special characters such as the period (decimal) and/or hyphen (to indicate negativity). Technically, special characters such as the dollar sign ($) or comma (,) are not considered numeric. They are only displayed for contextual and readability purposes and are not stored as part of a numeric cell value.

In Excel, **date data** and **time data** are a special form of numeric data. Information entered in a recognized date and/or time format will be converted automatically to an Excel date and/or time value. Table 1 includes examples of valid dates and times that can be entered into Excel and how they will be displayed by default:

Enter	Excel Displays	Enter	Excel Displays
December 21, 2012	21-Dec-12	12/21/2012	12/21/2012
December 21, 2012 10 p	12/21/2012 22:00	2012/12/21	12/21/2012
Dec 21, 2012	21-Dec-12	13:00	13:00
21 Dec 2012 10:30	12/21/2012 10:30	1:00 p	1:00 PM

Table 1 Date entry and how Excel displays dates

If Excel recognizes a value as a date/time, it will right-align the entry. If you enter a date or time that is not recognized, Excel treats the information as text and left-aligns it in the cell. By default, Excel left-aligns text data and right-aligns numeric, date, and time data.

Storing Date and Time Data

Date and time information is automatically displayed in a format easily understood by the user, but in Excel, dates and times are actually a real number where the value to the left of the decimal place is the number of days since December 31, 1899 (1 = January 1, 1900) and the value to the right of the decimal place is the proportion of one day that represents a time value (1.1 = January 1, 1900 + 144 minutes = January 1, 1900 2:24 AM). The advantages of storing dates and times in what is commonly referred to as the 1900 date system are many:

- Sorting a list of dates and/or times is as simple as putting the list in ascending or descending numerical order.

- Since dates and times are real numbers, mathematical manipulation to add to, or to subtract from, dates and times is greatly simplified.
- Determining a time span is simply a function of subtracting one time from another—a single calculation.

The vast majority of applications and systems now store dates and times in this manner. The main difference among them is the base date. For example in DOS, Microsoft's precursor operating system to Windows, the base date is January 1, 1980.

REAL WORLD ADVICE | **Balance Cost with Consequences!**

The Y2K bug was the result of a widespread practice of storing the year as two digits—1999 was stored as 99; 2000 as 00. Most information systems sort information by date, and since 1999 is greater than 2000 when stored as a 2-digit year, as of 1/1/2000 many systems would have output incorrect information; it was feared that many systems would fail entirely.

Why store a 2-digit year? Unlike today, digital storage used to be very expensive—every character consumed expensive space.

The result was a massive worldwide effort in the late 1990s to eradicate the Y2K "bug" at a cost estimated by some to have exceeded $1 trillion—far more than was ever saved by storing 2-digit year values. The lesson for technology practitioners: Money saved by "cutting corners" today will cost you way more when you have to do it right later.

Do it right the first time, as much as is possible, and you will save a lot of time and resources in the long run.

SIDE NOTE
Undo Keyboard Shortcut
Ctrl + Z is a fast and efficient method of performing an Undo.

SIDE NOTE
Use Undo History
If you need to Undo a change but have made other changes since, click the Undo arrow to see the change history.

E01.05

To Enter Information into a Worksheet

a. Click the **RBGC Golf Cart Purch Analysis** worksheet tab, click cell **A2**, type Red Bluff Golf Course & Pro Shop and then press Enter.

b. In cell **A3**, type Golf Cart Purchase Analysis and then press Enter.

c. Notice the values in cells D11, D12, and D13. Click cell **D9**, type 0.06 and then press Enter.
Notice the monthly payment in cell D11 changes to 153.00. The values in cells D11, D12, and D13 are automatically recalculated.

Troubleshooting
If the monthly payment is larger than it should be, you probably entered 0.6 or 006. That is actually 60% or 600% respectively for calculation purposes. You must enter the percentage, 6%, or enter 0.06—the decimal equivalent for 6%.

REAL WORLD ADVICE | **Back Up Your Workbook!**

It is a good idea to back up your workbook when you are about to make significant changes to it, when those changes have been made, and/or when you have finished working for the moment.

To make a backup of your workbook:

1. Click the File tab, click Save As, under Places click Computer, and then click Browse.
2. In the Save As dialog box, navigate to the location where you are saving your files. In the box, type the name of your file, such as YourFile_yyyy-mm-dd where yyyy-mm-dd is today's date. Click Save.

If possible, the best practice is to store backup files on an entirely different drive, such as a USB drive or to a cloud service like SkyDrive.

Save As not only saves a copy of your file, it changes the file Excel has open. YourFile_yyyy-mm-dd will be the open file, and the title bar at the top of the Excel application window will display the new file name. Click Close [X], and open your original file before continuing your work.

Wrapping Text and Line Breaks

Excel, by default, places all information in a single line in a cell. Text that is too long to fit in a cell is displayed over adjoining cells to the right, unless those cells contain information. If adjoining cells contain information, then lengthy text from cells to the left is not displayed.

Text truncation can be avoided by changing the alignment of a cell in order to wrap words or by placing hard returns into text to force wrapping at a particular location.

E01.06

To Wrap Text in a Cell

a. Click the **Documentation** worksheet tab, click cell **C9**, and then type **Entered a descriptive title for the cart purchase worksheet and updated the interest rate of the second golf cart**. Press Ctrl + Enter.

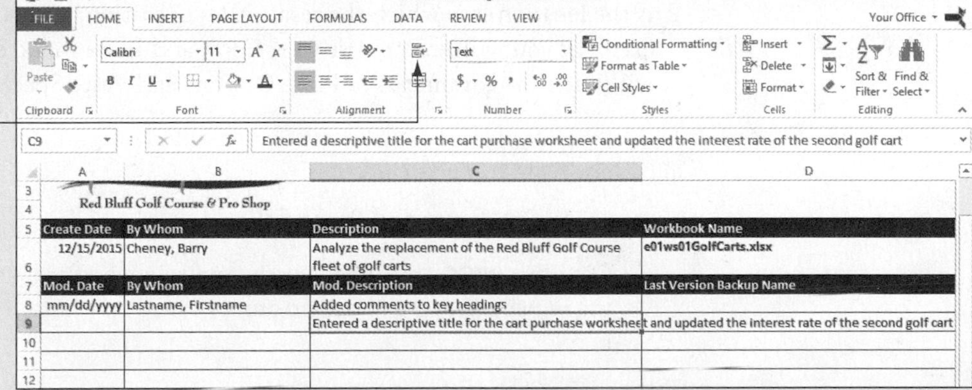

Figure 8 Wrap text

b. On the HOME tab, in the Alignment group, click **Wrap Text**. The vertical size of row 9 is increased to allow all content within the boundaries of cell C9.

c. Click the **RBGC Golf Cart Purch Analysis** worksheet tab.

d. Double-click cell **A3**. If necessary, use either ← or → to move the insertion point, or click to position the insertion point, immediately after **Cart**. Press Delete to remove the space between Cart and Purchase, and then press Alt + Enter to insert a line break—often referred to as a hard return.

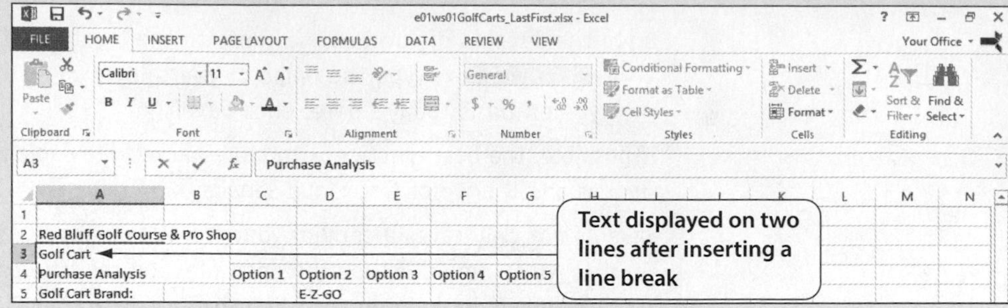

Figure 9 Insert a hard return to control text wrap location

e. Press Enter to complete the entry, and then click **Save**.

Manipulate Cells and Cell Ranges

Part of what makes a worksheet an efficient tool is the ability to perform actions that affect many cells at once. Knowing how to work with cells and cell ranges is an important part of maximizing your efficiency. **Cell range** refers to the cells in the worksheet that have been selected. A cell range can reference a single cell, several contiguous cells, or noncontiguous cells and cell ranges. A **contiguous cell range** consists of multiple selected cells, all directly adjacent to one another. A **noncontiguous cell range** consists of multiple selected cells, but at least one cell is not directly adjacent to other cells.

Cutting, Copying, and Pasting

Copy and paste copies everything in a cell, including formatting. Cut and paste moves everything in a cell, including formatting. However, through Paste Options and Paste Special, you control exactly what is placed into the destination cells. A **destination cell** is the location into which the result of an operation, such as paste, is inserted. In the next exercise, you will learn to use Cut, Copy, and Paste in Excel. Later in this workshop, you will learn the advantages of Paste Options and Paste Special.

E01.07

To Cut, Copy, and Paste Cells

a. Click the **RBGC Golf Cart Purch Analysis** worksheet tab, and then click cell **D5**. On the HOME tab, in the Clipboard group, notice that Paste is not available—it is light gray in color.

b. In the Clipboard group, click **Cut**.
   The solid border around cell D5 changes to a moving dashed border.
   Notice that once cell D5 has been cut to the Clipboard, Paste is available.

c. Click cell **C5**.

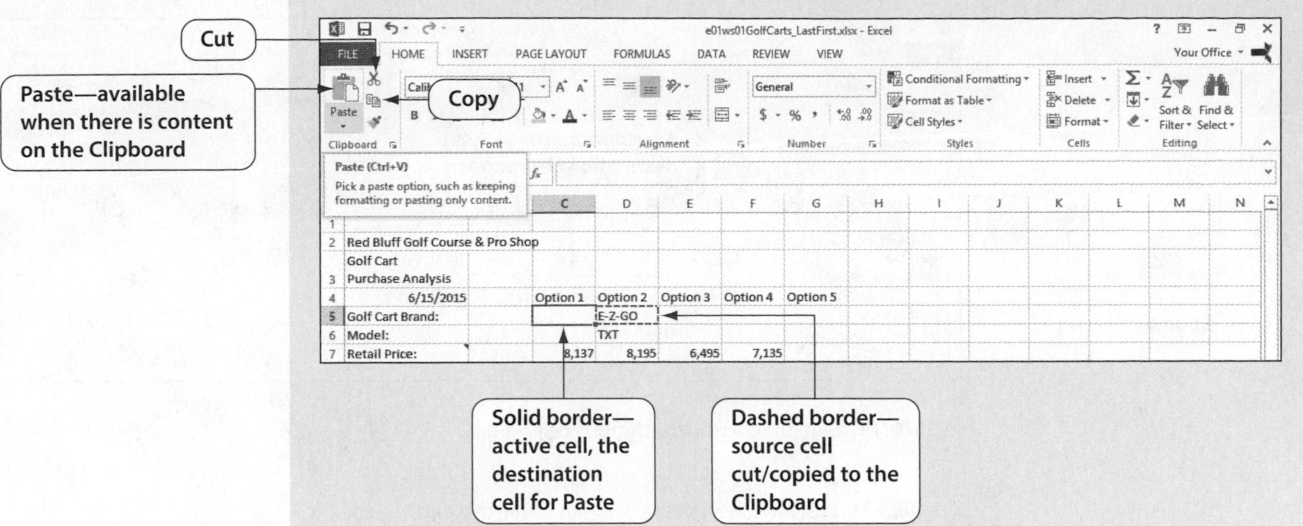

Figure 10 Cut, Copy, and Paste

d. In the Clipboard group, click **Paste**.

e. Click cell **D6**, and then in the Clipboard group, click **Copy**. The solid border around cell D6 changes to a moving dashed border. Click cell **C6**, and then in the Clipboard group, click **Paste**.

f. Press Esc to clear the Clipboard and remove the dashed border from around cell D6. Notice that once the Clipboard is cleared, the Paste icon is again unavailable.

g. Click **Save**.

Selecting Cell Ranges

Using the mouse, multiple cells can be selected simultaneously. Selected cells can be contiguous to each other or they can be noncontiguous. Once multiple cells are selected, they can be affected by actions such as clear, delete, copy, paste, formatting, and many other actions while offering the convenience of performing the desired task only once for the selected cells.

E01.08

To Select, Copy, and Paste to Contiguous and Noncontiguous Selections

a. Click the **RBGC Golf Cart Purch Analysis** worksheet tab, and then click cell **C5**. Press Shift + ↓—the active cell border expands to include C5:C6, and the background color of selected cells also changes.

Shift can be used in combination with other navigation keys and/or the mouse to select a contiguous range of cells.

b. Click the **HOME** tab, and then in the Clipboard group, click **Copy** to copy the selected cells to the Clipboard. Click cell **E5**, and then in the Clipboard group, click **Paste** to paste Clipboard contents to the selected cell.

c. Click cell **D5**, press and hold Ctrl, click cell **F5**, release Ctrl, and then press Shift + →.

Ctrl is used in combination with other navigation keys and/or the mouse to select noncontiguous cell ranges.

SIDE NOTE

Select a Range Using the Mouse

Click and hold on a cell and then drag the mouse pointer to select a cell range.

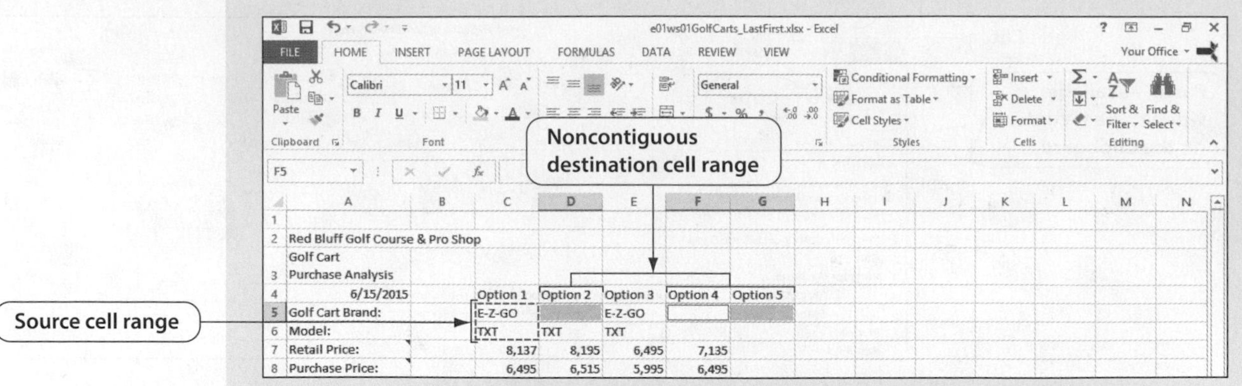

Figure 11 Selecting a noncontiguous cell range

d. Click **Paste**, and then press Esc to clear the clipboard.

e. Click **Save**.

QUICK REFERENCE — Selecting Cell Ranges

There are several ways to select a contiguous range of cells:

- Expand the active cell by dragging the mouse.
- Select the first cell in the range, press Shift, and click the last cell in the desired range.

A contiguous range of rows or columns can be selected in the following ways:

- Click a row or column header. Drag the mouse pointer across the headers to select contiguous rows or columns.
- Click a row or column header, press Shift, and then click the header of the last row or column you wish to select.

Once a cell or contiguous range of cells has been selected, you can add noncontiguous cells and ranges by pressing Ctrl and using any of the above methods for selecting ranges that do not involve Shift.

Dragging and Dropping

As worksheets are designed, built, and modified, it is often necessary to move information from one cell, or range of cells, to another. One of the most efficient ways to do this is called "drag and drop" and is accomplished with the mouse, as shown in the following exercise.

E01.09

To Drag and Drop Cells

a. Click the **RBGC Golf Cart Purch Analysis** worksheet tab, and then click cell **A2**. Press and hold Shift, and then press ↓ two times. Cell range A2:A4 is selected. Point to the **border** of the selected range. The mouse pointer changes to a move pointer.

b. Click and hold the left mouse button, and then drag the selected cells up one row to cell range **A1:A3**. A ghost range, also referred to as a destination range, and destination range ScreenTip are displayed as the pointer is moved, to show exactly where the moved cells will be placed.

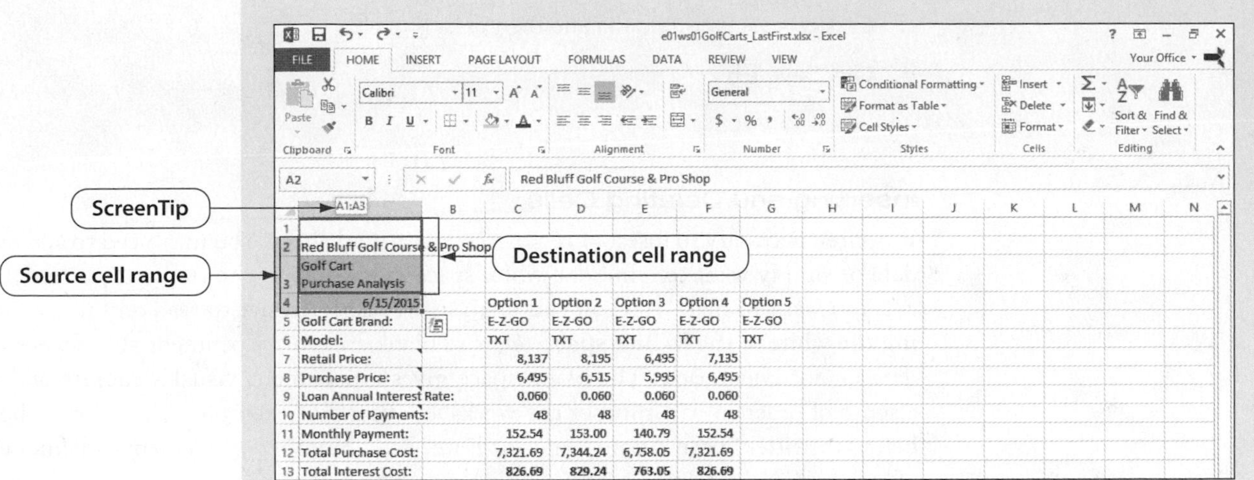

Figure 12 Drag and drop to move a cell range

c. Drop the dragged cells by releasing the mouse button.

d. Click cell **F13**. Press and hold [Shift], press [End], and then press [↑]. Cell range F4:F13 is selected. Press and hold [Shift], and then press [↓] three times. Cell range F7:F13 is selected.

e. Move the mouse pointer until it is over the border of the selected range in column **F**. The mouse pointer changes to a move pointer. Press and hold [Ctrl]. The move pointer changes to a copy pointer. Drag the selected range until the ghost range is directly to the right of column F, over range **G7:G13**. Release the mouse button, and then release [Ctrl].

   Cell range F7:F13 has been copied to cell range G7:G13.

f. Click **Save**.

Modifying Cell Information

Copying and pasting content from one range of cells to another range, or ranges, is a highly efficient way to reuse parts of a worksheet. The range you just copied into column G contains information that is calculated using formulas that you do not want to type more than once. However, once you have duplicated a cell or cell range, it is usually necessary to change some content.

To edit the contents of cells, you double-click the cell to enter edit mode. The active cell will now contain an insertion point. If you want to change part of the content, use the arrow keys or click to position the insertion point at the desired location. If all the cell content is to be replaced, click the cell once to make it the active cell. All cell content will be replaced when you begin typing to enter the new content for the selected cell.

E01.10

To Modify Worksheet Contents by Changing Copied Information

a. Click the **RBGC Golf Cart Purch Analysis** worksheet tab, click cell **D6**, type RXV, and then press [→]. Double-click cell **E6**, press [Home] to go to the left margin of the cell, type Freedom, and then press [Spacebar] once so the formula bar displays **Freedom TXT**. Press [Tab], type Freedom RXV and then press [Tab]. Type The Drive and then press [Enter].

b. In **G7**, type 6995 and then press [Enter]. In cell **G8**, type 6350 and then press [Ctrl] + [Enter].

   Notice that when you changed the value in cell G8 that Monthly Payment, Total Purchase Cost, and Total Interest Cost are recalculated.

c. Click cell **G5**. Type Yamaha and then press Enter.

d. Click **Save**.

Inserting and Deleting Cells

It is often necessary to insert or remove cells in a worksheet. You may need to add or delete data or simply want to refine the white space in a worksheet to improve its readability.

You want to make the golf cart analysis worksheet easier to read and to use by refining the white space. **White space** refers to blank areas of a document that do not contain data or documentation. The blank space gives a document visual structure and creates a sense of order in the mind of the worksheet user. For example, white space above and below the titles "Loan Annual Interest Rate" and "Number of Payments" defines the area of information associated with financing the golf carts.

E01.11

To Insert and Delete Cells and Cell Ranges in a Worksheet

a. Click the **RBGC Golf Cart Purch Analysis** worksheet tab, and then click cell **A4**. On the HOME tab, in the Cells group, click the **Insert** arrow.

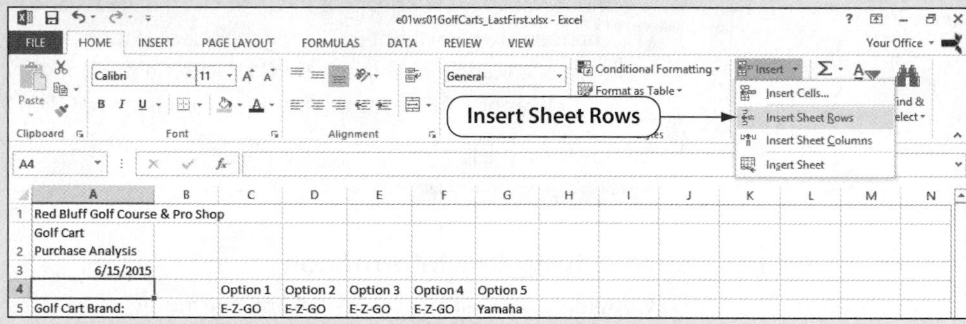

Figure 13 Home tab, Insert to insert sheet rows

b. Click **Insert Sheet Rows**. Excel inserts a row above the active cell location and moves all cells in row 4 and below down.

c. Click cell **A8**, right-click cell **A8**, and then click **Insert** on the shortcut menu. In the Insert dialog box, click **Entire row**.

SIDE NOTE

A Keyboard Shortcut to Insert

Ctrl + + will insert cells, rows, or columns depending on what is selected.

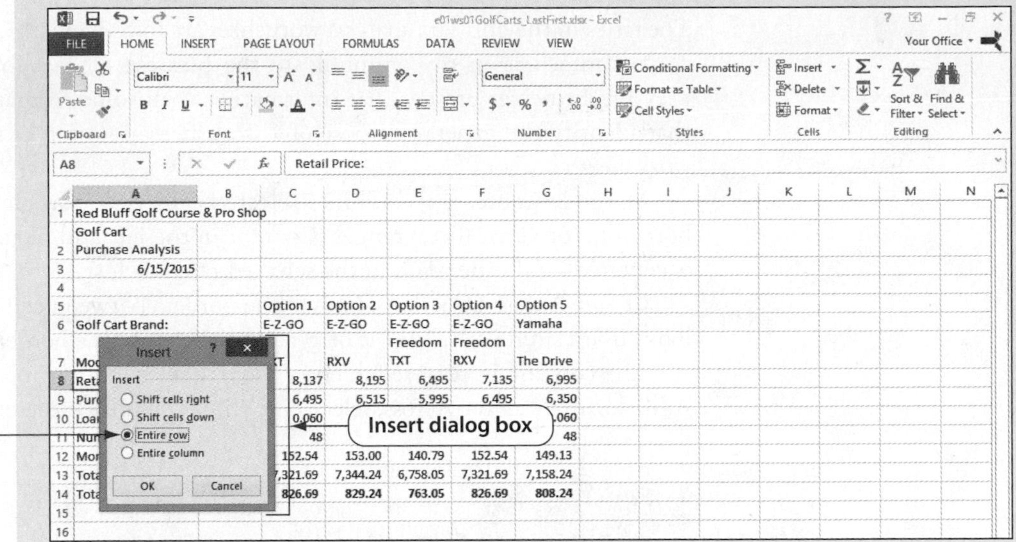

Figure 14 Insert dialog box

d. Click **OK**.

e. Click cell **A11**, and then press Shift + ↓. Cell range A11:A12 is selected. In the Cells group, click the **Insert** arrow, and then click **Insert Sheet Rows**. Excel inserts a row for each row in the selected range.

f. Click cell **A15**, and then press Shift + ↓. Right-click anywhere on the selected range, and then select **Insert** from the shortcut menu. Click **Entire row** in the Insert dialog box, and then click **OK**.

> **Troubleshooting**
> If you click the Insert button instead of the Insert arrow, Excel will default to inserting extra cells only, instead of a row. Press Ctrl + Z to undo the last change, and then repeat Step f.

g. Click cell **B5**, and then in the Cells group, click **Delete**.
Notice that the Option headings in row 5 moved left.

> **Troubleshooting**
> Click the Delete icon, not the Delete arrow. Alternatively, you can click Delete Cells in the list.

h. Click cell **B6**, press and hold the mouse button, and then drag down until the active cell expands to select the range **B6:B19**. In the Cells group, click **Delete**. The remaining cell values in rows 6:19 moved left one cell.
Inserting two rows above and below rows 13:14 appears to be too much. Often you cannot tell until you try, but the worksheet might look better if a couple of the rows of white space were removed.

i. Click a cell in row **11**, press Ctrl, and then click a cell in row **16**. In the Cells group, click the **Delete** arrow, and then click **Delete Sheet Rows**.

j. Click **Save**.

Merging and Centering vs. Centering Across

The titles in the golf cart analysis worksheet are in cells A1:A3. Although they contain the correct information to communicate the purpose of the golf cart analysis worksheet, they might better present that information with some formatting improvements. Titles that identify the general purpose of a worksheet are often at the top and centered above worksheet content.

Merge & Center combines selected cells into a single cell and can be applied to horizontal or vertical cell ranges. Content in the left and/or top cell of the selected range is centered—all other data in the selected range is lost.

Center Across Selection removes the borders between cells such that a selected range looks like a single cell, but the original cells remain, the borders between them are hidden and the content is centered. Center Across Selection can only be applied horizontally. Additionally, Center Across Selection will never replace the data in the other cells.

E01.12

To Merge & Center Headings

a. Click the **RBGC Golf Cart Purch Analysis** worksheet tab, and then press Ctrl + Home. Press and hold Shift, and then press → repeatedly until cell range **A1:F1** is selected. On the HOME tab, in the Alignment group, click **Merge & Center**.

b. Click cell **A2**. Press and hold Shift, press ↓, and then press → repeatedly until cell range **A2:F3** is selected. In the Alignment group, click **Merge & Center**.

Notice the warning message. If you Merge & Center data in more than one cell at a time, only the data in the upper-left cell of the selected range will be kept, the rest will be lost.

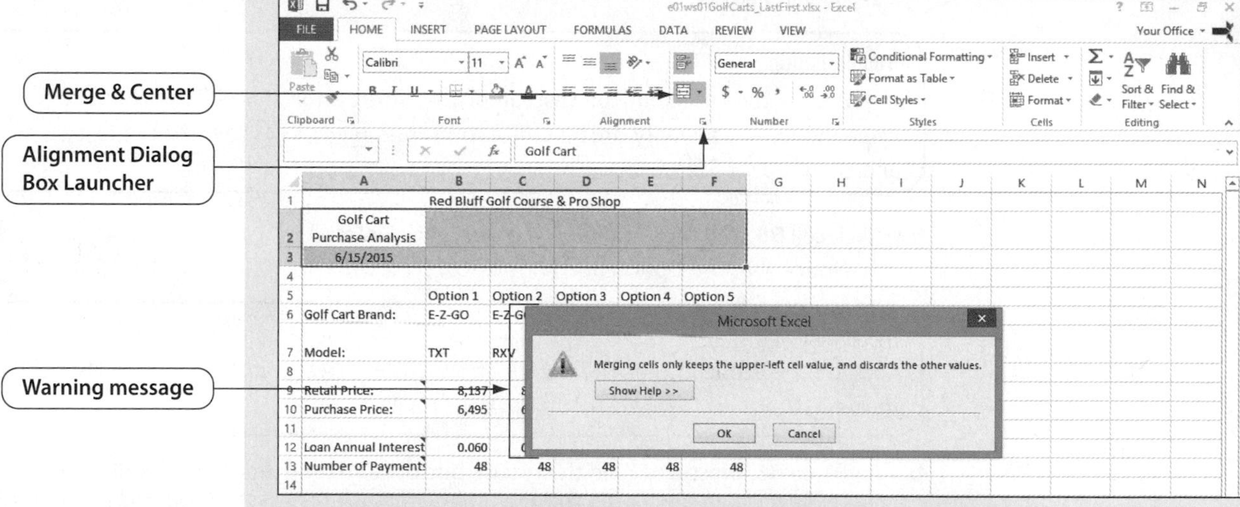

Figure 15 Merge and center a range containing multiple values and data

c. Click **Cancel**. You do not want to lose the data in cell A3.

Troubleshooting

You probably clicked OK instead of Cancel. Press Ctrl + Z to undo the last change and go back to Step b.

d. On the HOME tab, in the Alignment group, click the **Alignment Settings** Dialog Box Launcher. This opens the Format Cells dialog box. With the Alignment tab selected, click the **Horizontal** list, and then click **Center Across Selection**.

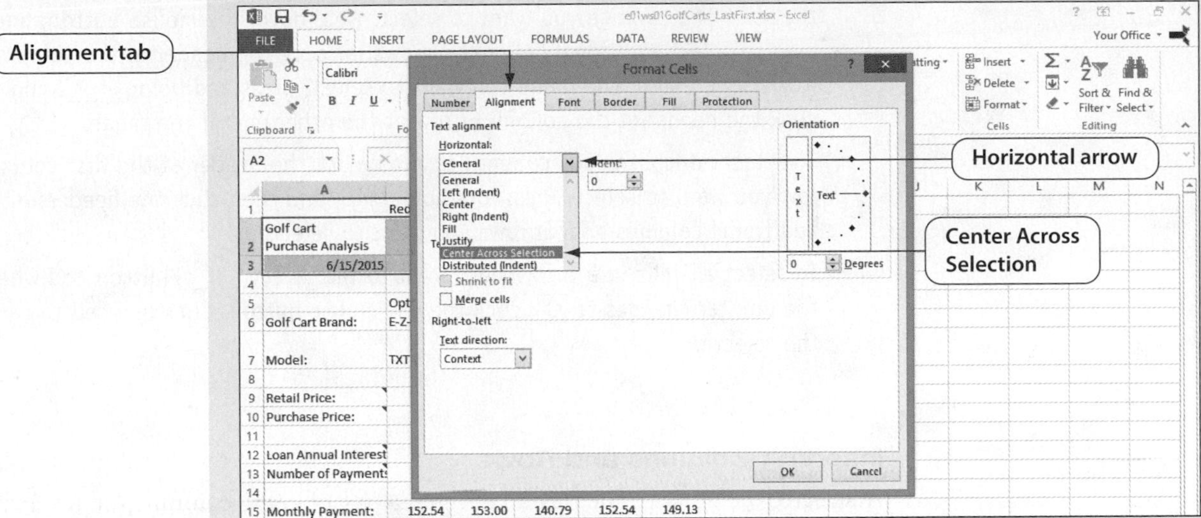

Figure 16 Center Across Selection

e. Click **OK**. Cell A2 content is centered across cell range A2:F2, and cell A3 content is centered across cell range A3:F3.

f. Click **Save**.

CONSIDER THIS | **Merge & Center and Cell Range Selection**

Try this: In the RBGC Golf Cart Purch Analysis worksheet, select cell range A1:D17. Try to select cell range A1:B9. Now select cell range A2:F16.
Merge & Center creates a single cell that can cause problems if you want to select a range of cells that includes only part of the merged cell range.
Some Excel experts feel Merge & Center should never be used. Do you agree?

Manipulate Columns and Rows

Any worksheet you create has default column widths and row heights. As you build, refine, and modify a worksheet, it is often necessary to add and/or delete columns and rows or to change column widths and/or row heights for formatting and content purposes. Fortunately, Excel makes these activities extremely easy to accomplish.

Selecting Contiguous and Noncontiguous Columns and Rows

To manipulate columns and rows, you must first indicate which of each you wish to affect by your actions. As with cells and cell ranges, you can select entire columns, rows, multiple columns, and multiple rows. You can select noncontiguous columns and rows, and even select multiple columns and multiple rows at the same time.

QUICK REFERENCE	Selecting Columns and Rows

- To select a column or row click the header—the letter or number respectively—in the header.
- To select a range of contiguous columns or rows, point to and click the header at the start of the range you want to select. Hold down the mouse button, and then drag to select additional columns or rows, or click the header of the column or row at one end of the range you want to select, press and hold Shift, and then click the header of the column or row at the other end of the range.
- To select noncontiguous columns or rows, click the header of the first column or row you want to select. Press and hold Ctrl, and then click the headers of any additional columns and/or rows you want to select.
- To select all cells in a worksheet, point to the Select All button and when the pointer changes to ✚, click the left mouse button. Click any cell to cancel the selection.

Inserting Columns and Rows

A selected range is defined as a contiguous set of cells, columns, or rows that are all part of a single contiguous selection. However, how you select cells, columns, and rows determines whether they are a single, contiguous range or are considered separate, individual selections.

If you click column C, press and hold Shift, and click column E, you have created a contiguous selection of columns C:E. All three columns are highlighted as a group. But, if you click column C, press and hold Ctrl, click column D, and then click column E, you have just selected three individual columns—three individual selections. In this situation, columns C, D, and E are treated by Excel as noncontiguous columns—there is a white border highlighted between the columns. Whether columns—or rows—are contiguous or are noncontiguous has an effect on how actions such as Insert are applied to a worksheet.

There is still a need to add some white space to the cart analysis worksheet—the columns of information for the different carts are too close together. One way to add white space is to insert a blank column between each column of cart information. Additionally, there is enough definitional difference between the Monthly Payment and the Purchase and Interest totals that some white space to separate them may be advisable. This can be accomplished by inserting a row in the appropriate locations.

SIDE NOTE

Select Several Rows or Columns Using Shift

Click the header of the first row or column, press Shift and then click the last row or column.

E01.13

To Insert a Column Between Each Column of Cart Data

a. Click the **RBGC Golf Cart Purch Analysis** worksheet tab, and then click the header for column **C** to select column C. Click the **HOME** tab, and then in the Cells group, click **Insert**.

b. Click the header for column **E**, press and hold Ctrl, and then select column **F** and column **G** by clicking on each column header individually. Notice the white line between each column selection—this is not a selected range of columns, it is three individually selected columns.

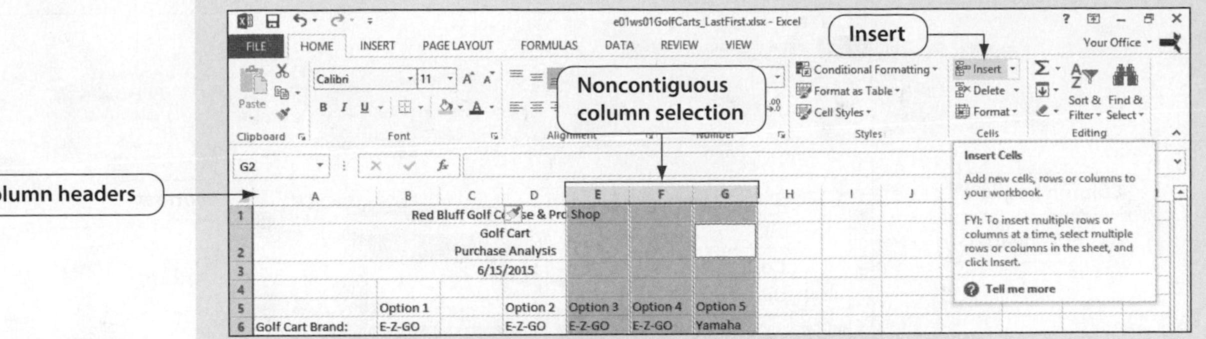

Figure 17 Use Ctrl to select individual columns, rows, cells, or ranges

SIDE NOTE
Another Way to Insert/Delete
Select the cells or columns, right-click the selection, and then click Insert or Delete in the shortcut menu.

c. On the HOME tab, in the Cells group, click **Insert**.
A column has been inserted to the left of each selected column because columns E, F, and G were selected as noncontiguous individual columns. Had you selected columns E:G as a single contiguous selection, three columns would have been inserted to the left of column E.

Troubleshooting
If you now have three blank columns to the left of column H, you selected columns E:G as a contiguous selection. Press Ctrl + Z to Undo and repeat Steps b and c.

Notice also that the merged and centered cells in rows 1:3 expanded to include the inserted columns. This ensures that the content in rows 1:3 remains centered over the columns that were in the original merged range.

d. Click **Save**.

Adjusting Column Width and Row Height

You have inserted columns and rows to add additional white space, but there is still a need to refine the amount of white space in the worksheet. At this point there is too much—the information is spread too far apart.

Column width and row height often need to be adjusted for a couple of reasons. One reason is to reduce the amount of white space a blank column or row represents in a worksheet; the other is to allow the content of cells in a row or column to be displayed properly.

Column width is defined in characters. The default width is 8.43 characters. The maximum width of a column is 255 characters.

Row height is defined in points. A point is approximately 1/72 of an inch (0.035 cm). The default row height in Excel is 15 points, or approximately 1/6 of an inch (0.4 cm). A row can be up to 409 points in height (about 5.4 inches).

E01.14

To Manually Adjust Column Width and Row Height

a. Click the **RBGC Golf Cart Purch Analysis** worksheet tab, select column **C**, press and hold Ctrl, and then select columns **E**, **G**, and **I**.

b. In the Cells group, click **Format**. In the Cell Size list, click **Column Width**, and then in the **Column Width** dialog box, type 2.

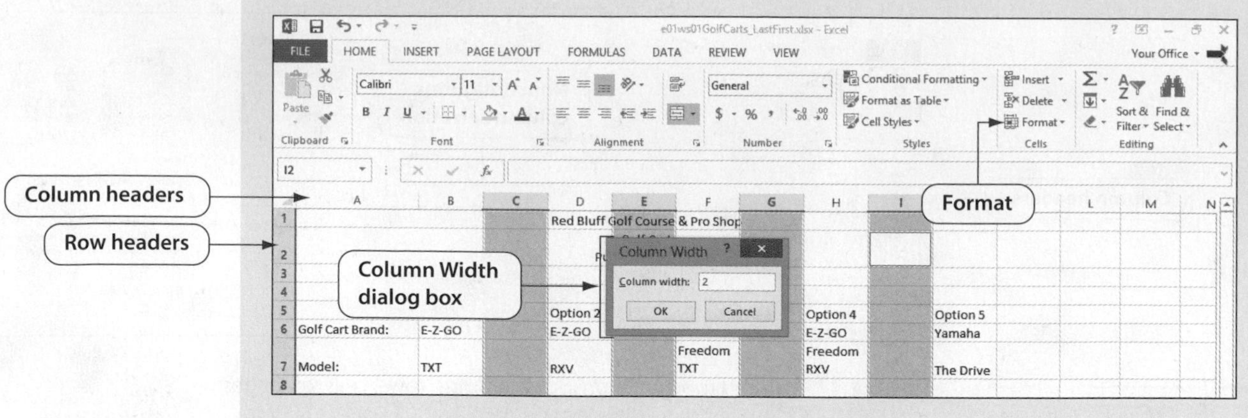

Figure 18 Column Width dialog box

c. Click **OK**.

d. Click the row **4** header, press and hold Ctrl, and then select row **8** and cells **A11** and **E14**.

e. In the Cells group, click **Format**, and then in the Cell Size list click **Row Height**. In the Row Height dialog box, type 7 and then click **OK**.

f. Click **Save**.

Changing Column Widths Using AutoFit

Column width and row height can also be adjusted automatically based on the width and height of selected content using the AutoFit feature. AutoFit adjusts the width of columns—and the height of rows—to allow selected content to fit. Care is required in that data in unselected cells not be truncated or improperly displayed.

E01.15

To Use AutoFit to Adjust Column Width

a. Click the **RBGC Golf Cart Purch Analysis** worksheet tab, click cell **A7**, press and hold Ctrl, and then select cells **B7**, **D7**, **F7**, **H7**, and **J7**.

b. Click the HOME tab, and then in the Cells group, click **Format**, and then click **AutoFit Column Width**.

Since AutoFit sizes columns to the selected content, columns B and D are too narrow to display most of their numeric information, so now the information is displayed as a series of number signs (#). Notice also that column A is too narrow to display the content of most of the cells in range A6:A17, so content is truncated on the right.

c. Select column **A** by clicking its header, press and hold Ctrl, and then select columns **B, D, F, H**, and **J**.

d. In the Cells group, click **Format**.

SIDE NOTE

AutoFit Row Height

AutoFit Row Height works in exactly the same manner as AutoFit Column Width.

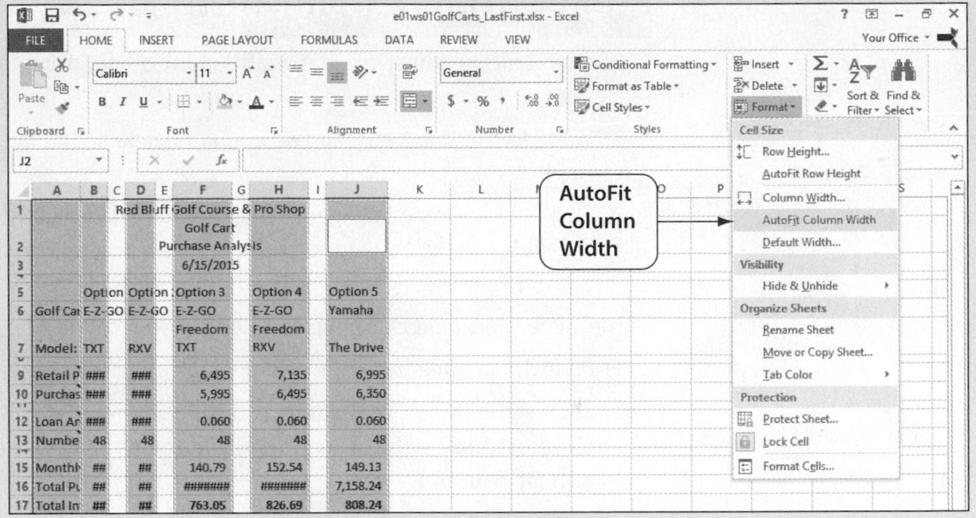

Figure 19 AutoFit Column Width results for selected cells

e. In the Cell Size menu, click **AutoFit Column Width**.

Since columns were selected instead of individual cells, the columns are automatically adjusted to the widest content in the column, resulting in no number signs.

Column width can also be set manually. Column A could be a little wider than set by AutoFit Column Width.

f. Click cell **A1** to deselect the columns. Point to the **border** between column A and column B. The pointer should change to [+]. Click and hold the left mouse button. Drag the mouse to the right until column **A** is has a width of 26.00 (187 pixels). Notice the column width Screen Tip next to the [+] pointer.

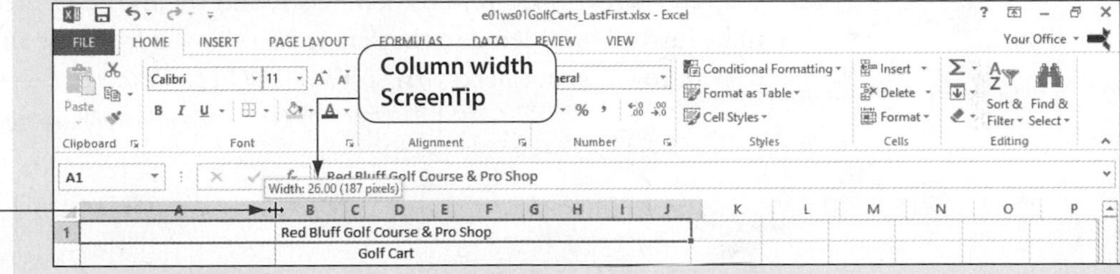

Figure 20 Manually adjust column width

g. Release the left mouse button.

h. Click **Save** [Save icon].

REAL WORLD ADVICE — Quick Ways to Adjust Column Width and Row Height

You can quickly adjust column width and row height using any of the following methods.

1. Point to the line between two column headers. The mouse pointer will change to ↔.
2. Click and hold the left mouse button, and move the mouse left or right to adjust the width of the column to the left of the pointer, or double-click to use the AutoFit feature.

The same procedure can be used to adjust row height.

1. Point to the line between two row headers; the pointer will change to ↕.
2. Click and hold the left mouse button, and then move the mouse up or down to adjust the height of the row above the pointer, or double-click to use the AutoFit feature.

If multiple columns or rows are selected, adjusting the width or height for one selected column or row adjusts the width or height for all.

Learn to use keyboard shortcuts and alternative ways to execute commands in Excel. You will save a lot of time.

Deleting vs. Clearing

Worksheet data can be either cleared or deleted—there is a difference. Clearing contents from a cell does not change the location of other cells in the worksheet. Deleting a cell shifts surrounding cells in a direction determined from a prompt. When editing a string of characters in a cell, Delete works exactly as you would expect. When you are not in edit mode, pressing Delete clears content, but it does not delete the cell(s).

The golf cart analysis worksheet is formatted well, but Barry has decided that the E-Z-GO RXV, E-Z-GO Freedom TXT, and the E-Z-GO Freedom RXV are not options to be further considered so they are to be removed from the analysis. Barry also thinks the date in row 3 is not necessary, so you have been asked to delete that as well.

E01.16

To Delete Columns and Rows

a. Click the **RBGC Golf Cart Purch Analysis** worksheet tab. Click the header for column **C**, hold down the mouse button, and then drag right until columns **C** through **H** are selected.

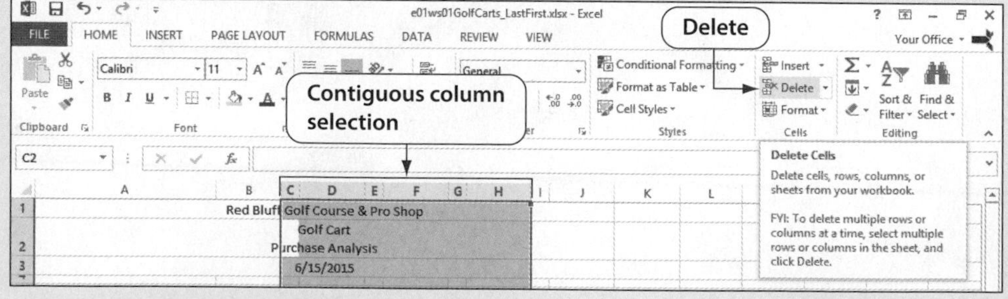

Figure 21 Contiguous columns selected for deletion

b. In the Cells group, click **Delete**.

c. Right-click cell **A3**, and then select **Delete**. In the Delete dialog box, select **Entire row**, and then click **OK**.

Now you need to fix the option headings since they are out of sequence.

d. Select cell **D4**, type Option 2 and then press Ctrl + Enter.

e. Click **Save**.

Inserting Columns That Contain Data

Barry has asked that the analysis include multiple payment schedules for 24, 36, and 48 months of interest for each of the two remaining golf carts in the analysis. The interest rate for 24-month financing is 5.0%, 36-month financing is 5.5%, and 48-month financing is 6.0%. Expanding the analysis to include additional payment schedules is easily accomplished by inserting new columns that have been copied to the Clipboard and then editing the newly inserted data.

E01.17

To Expand the Analysis by Reusing and Editing Column Data

a. Click the **RBGC Golf Cart Purch Analysis** worksheet tab.

SIDE NOTE
Rows of Copied Data Can Be Inserted, Too
Rows can be copied and inserted, too. Simply select using row headers instead of column headers.

b. Right-click the header for column **B**, and then click **Copy**. Right-click the header for column **C**.

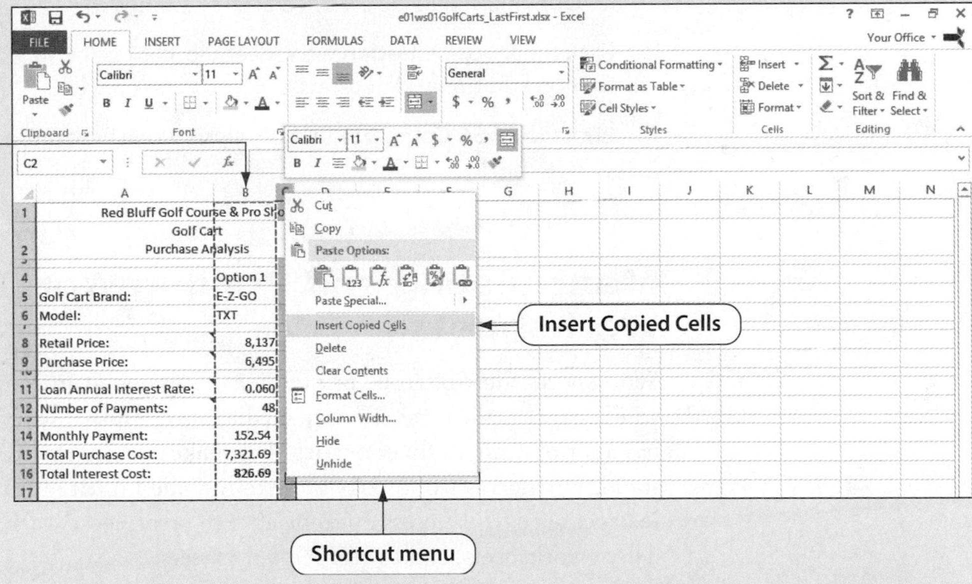

Figure 22 Insert columns that contain data

c. In the shortcut menu, select **Insert Copied Cells**.

d. Repeat Steps b–c one time. Press Esc to clear the Clipboard.

e. Click the header for column **F**. On the **HOME** tab, and then in the Clipboard group, click **Copy**. Click and hold the column **F** header, drag the pointer to the right and select columns **F:G**, right-click anywhere in the selected columns, and then select **Insert Copied Cells**.

Troubleshooting

If the heading in row 1 in not centered across columns A:H, you probably selected columns G:H in Step e rather than columns F:G. The column of copied data would have been inserted to the right of column F, and therefore would not have expanded the range across which the heading in row 1 is centered. Press [Ctrl] + [Z] to Undo, and then repeat Step e.

f. Press [Esc] to clear the Clipboard. The copied data now needs to be edited to generate the comparative loan terms Barry requested.

g. Click cell **B11**, type 0.05, press [Tab], type 0.055, and then press [Ctrl] + [Enter]. Click cell **B12**, type 24, press [Tab], type 36, and then press [Ctrl] + [Enter].

h. Click cell **B11**, press and hold [Shift], press [↓], and then press [→]. Press [Ctrl] + [C] to copy the selected range to the Clipboard. Click cell **F11**, and then press [Ctrl] + [V]. Press [Esc] to clear the Clipboard.

   Now you need to address some of the duplicate text data created when you inserted the copied columns.

i. Click cell **C4**, press and hold [Shift], press [→], and then press [↓] two times. Press [Ctrl], click cell **G4**, press and hold [Shift], press [→], and then press [↓] two times. Press [Delete].

j. Click cell **B4**, press and hold [Shift], press [↓] two times, and then press [→] two times. Press [Ctrl] and then select cell **F4**. Press and hold [Shift], press [↓] two times, and then press [→] two times. Click the **Alignment Settings** Dialog Box Launcher. In the **Horizontal** list, click **Center Across Selection**, and then click **OK**.

   The headings for Option 1 should be centered across columns B:D, and the headings for Option 2 should be centered across columns F:H.

k. Click the **Documentation** worksheet tab, click cell **C10**, and then type Added analysis for two additional loan terms.

l. Click the **RBGC Golf Cart Purch Analysis** worksheet tab, and then click **Save**.

Manipulating and Printing Workbooks and Worksheets

Worksheets must often be printed for discussion at meetings, for distribution in venues where paper is the most effective media, or to send digitally in a printed file format. Excel has a lot of built-in functionality that makes printed worksheets easy to read and understand. Further, as workbooks grow to include multiple worksheets and evolve to require maintenance, it is necessary to be able to create new worksheets, to copy worksheets, to delete worksheets, and to reorder worksheets.

In this section you will learn to create, copy, delete, and reorder worksheets in a workbook, and you will learn to use Excel's print functionality to ensure that your worksheets are usable when presented on paper.

Manipulate Worksheets and Workbooks

Worksheets can be added to a workbook, deleted from a workbook, moved/copied within a workbook, or moved/copied to other workbooks. Sheet names are displayed on each sheet's tab at the bottom of the application window, just above the status bar—see Figure 22. The white worksheet tab identifies the active worksheet. Gray worksheet tabs identify inactive worksheets.

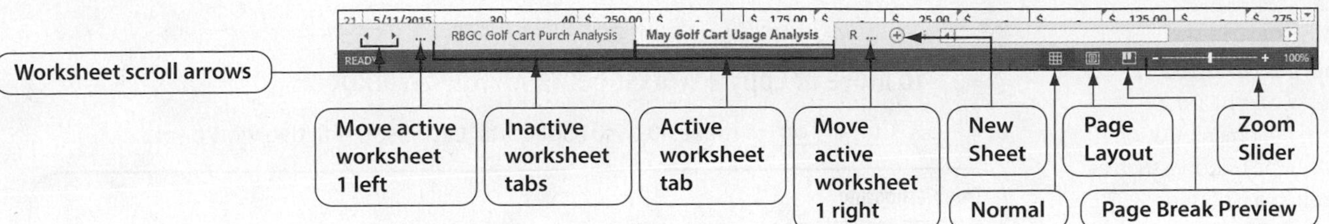

Figure 23 Worksheet tabs and controls

When a workbook contains a large number of worksheets or when worksheets have very long names, some worksheet tabs may not be visible in the application window. To bring tabs that are not visible into view, use the worksheet tab scrolling buttons to the left of the worksheet tabs.

Barry Cheney used the cart analysis to perform an analysis of lawn mowers he is considering for purchase. The RBGC Mower Purchase Analysis worksheet is located in the e01ws01GolfCarts_LastFirst workbook. Barry wants to present the mower analysis at an upcoming staff meeting. He asked you to create a separate workbook for the mower analysis. You will have to create a new workbook and move or copy the appropriate worksheets to the new workbook.

Creating a New Workbook

When you first open Excel, you can click Blank workbook to create a new, blank workbook. However, sometimes you may wish to create a blank workbook when Excel is already open. This can be accomplished in Backstage view.

E01.18

To Create a Blank Workbook

a. Click the **FILE** tab to access Backstage view.

b. Click **New**. Available templates will appear in the right pane.

c. Click **Blank workbook**. You will leave Backstage view and see the blank workbook.

d. Click the **FILE** tab, click **Save**, under **Save As**, click **Computer**, and then under Computer, click **Browse**. In the Save As dialog box, navigate to the location where you are saving your files. In the **File name** box, type e01ws01Mowers_LastFirst using your last and first name.

e. Click **Save**.

SIDE NOTE
Save As—Quickly
If a new workbook has not been saved, Ctrl + S takes you directly to the Save As dialog box.

Moving and Copying Worksheets Between Workbooks

Well-developed worksheets are often used as the starting point for new worksheets. Excel makes it easy to copy worksheets from one workbook to another. In the next exercise, you will copy the RBGC Mower Purchase Analysis and Documentation worksheets to the e01ws01Mowers_LastFirst workbook.

SIDE NOTE
There Is No Undo…
Most workbook and worksheet manipulation cannot be undone, such as deleting a worksheet.

E01.19

To Move or Copy a Worksheet to Another Workbook

a. Press [Ctrl] + [Tab] to make e01ws01GolfCarts_LastFirst the active workbook.

> **Troubleshooting**
> If [Ctrl] + [Tab] did not make e01ws01GolfCarts_LastFirst the active workbook, there are two possible explanations. One is that you have more than two workbooks open, so you need to press [Ctrl] + [Tab] more than once to cycle through open workbooks until e01ws01GolfCarts_LastFirst is active.
> The other possibility is that you closed e01ws01GolfCarts_LastFirst. In this case, you will need to open the file, at which time it will be the active workbook.

b. Right-click the **RBGC Mower Purchase Analysis** worksheet tab, and then select **Move or Copy** in the shortcut menu. In the Move or Copy dialog box, click the **To book** arrow, and then click **e01ws01Mowers_LastFirst**.

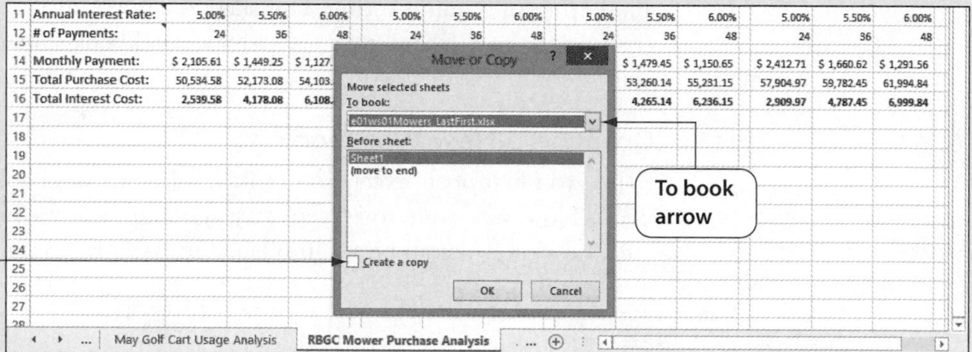

Figure 24 Move a worksheet to another workbook

SIDE NOTE
Hot Keys to Navigate Between Worksheets
Press [Ctrl]+[PgUp] to go to the prior worksheet or [Ctrl]+[PgDn] to go to the next worksheet.

c. Click **OK**.
The RBGC Mower Purchase Analysis worksheet is moved to the e01ws01Mowers_LastFirst workbook, which is now the active workbook.

d. Press [Ctrl] + [Tab] to make e01ws01GolfCarts_LastFirst the active workbook.

e. Right-click the **Documentation** worksheet tab, and then select **Move or Copy** in the shortcut menu. In the Move or Copy dialog box, click the **To book** arrow, and then click **e01ws01Mowers_LastFirst**. In the **Before sheet** box, click **Sheet1**, click the **Create a copy** check box, and then click **OK**.
The Documentation worksheet is copied to the e01ws01Mowers_LastFirst workbook, which is now the active workbook.

f. Press [Ctrl] + [Tab] to make e01ws01GolfCarts_LastFirst the active workbook. In the **Documentation** worksheet, select cell range **A22:D22**, press [Delete], and then click **Save**.

g. Press [Ctrl] + [Tab] to make e01ws01Mowers_LastFirst the active workbook. In the **Documentation** worksheet, select cell range **A20:D21**. Press and hold [Ctrl], select cell range **C8:C10**, and then press [Delete].

h. Click the header for row **20**, and then press [Shift] + [↓]. On the HOME tab, in the Clipboard group, click **Cut** [✂]. Right-click the header for row **23**, and then select **Insert Cut Cells**.
The documentation that had been in line 22 should now be in line 20.

i. Double-click cell **C6**. Position the insertion point after "carts". Press [Backspace] 19 times to delete **fleet of golf carts**. Type fairway mower and then press [Enter].

j. Click **Save** [💾].

Deleting, Inserting, and Renaming a Worksheet

Deleting a worksheet removes it from a workbook. This action cannot be undone. Unused worksheets are a form of clutter in a workbook and add unnecessary size to the stored workbook file.

Inserted worksheets are by default given a name such as "Sheet4" where the number is one larger than the last number used for a worksheet name. An inserted worksheet is automatically the active worksheet. To insert a worksheet, move to the right of the list of worksheet tabs and click New Sheet ⊕. In Excel 2013, new worksheets are always inserted to the right of the active worksheet.

The default worksheet names are not particularly descriptive and do nothing to help document the contents or purpose of a worksheet. Worksheets can be renamed by double-clicking the worksheet tab or by right-clicking the worksheet tab and clicking Rename on the shortcut menu. Worksheet names can be up to 31 characters long.

Now that you have created a separate workbook for the mower purchase analysis, Barry wants you to prepare a worksheet in the golf cart purchase analysis to extend the golf cart usage analysis to the month of June. He asked you to create a new worksheet and use the May usage analysis as a starting point. You just need to create the worksheet and get it ready for Barry to enter the data later. First, you should remove an unnecessary worksheet from the mower analysis workbook.

E01.20

To Delete, Insert, and Rename a Worksheet

a. In the e01ws01Mowers workbook, right-click the **Sheet1** worksheet tab.

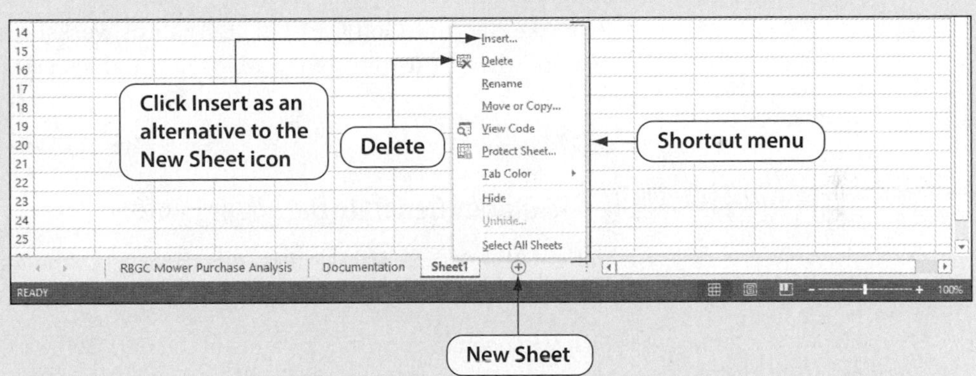

Figure 25 Delete or insert a worksheet

b. Select **Delete** in the shortcut menu. Click **Save**.

Now prepare a new golf cart usage analysis worksheet for June.

c. Press Ctrl + Tab to make e01ws01GolfCarts_LastFirst the active workbook.

d. Click the **May Golf Cart Usage Analysis** worksheet tab.

e. Click **New Sheet** ⊕ to the right of the worksheet tabs. A new Sheet1 worksheet is inserted to the right of the May Golf Cart Usage Analysis worksheet.

f. To rename Sheet1, double-click the **Sheet1** worksheet tab, and then type June Golf Cart Usage Analysis to rename the new sheet.

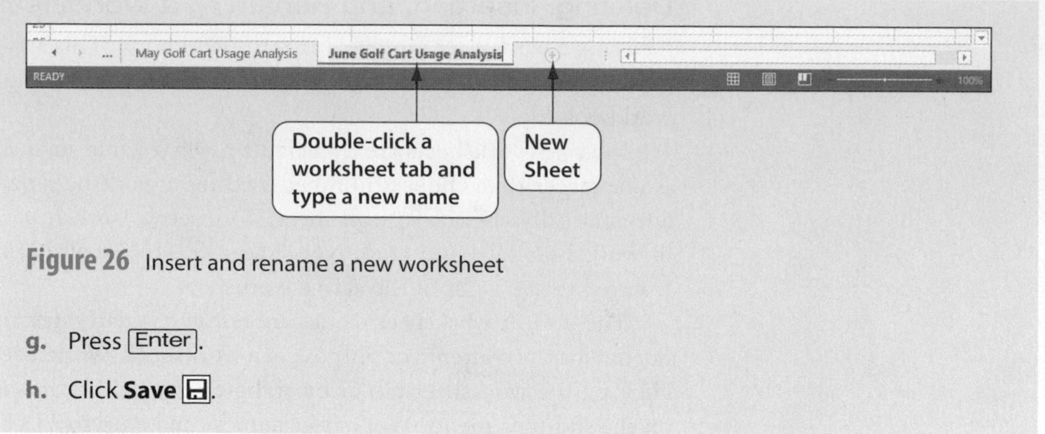

Figure 26 Insert and rename a new worksheet

g. Press Enter.

h. Click **Save**.

Using Series (AutoFill)

The **AutoFill** feature is a powerful way to minimize the effort required to enter certain types of data. AutoFill copies information from one cell, or a series in contiguous cells, into contiguous cells in the direction the fill handle is dragged. AutoFill is a smart copy that will try to guess how you want values or formulas changed as you copy. Sometimes, AutoFill will save significant time by changing the contents correctly. Other times, AutoFill changes the contents in a way you did not intend—when that happens, Auto Fill Options  makes options available that may be helpful.

The fill handle is a small green square in the bottom-right corner of the active cell border. To engage the AutoFill feature, drag the fill handle in the direction you wish to expand the active cell. When you point to and drag the fill handle, the mouse pointer is a thin black plus sign.

To make the June Golf Cart Usage Analysis worksheet ready for data entry, you need to copy and then clear some of the May data, and generate date information for June.

E01.21

To Quickly Generate Data Using AutoFill

a. In the e01ws01GolfCarts_LastFirst workbook, click the **May Golf Cart Usage Analysis** worksheet tab.

b. First you need to copy the contents of the May Golf Cart Usage Analysis worksheet to the June Golf Cart Usage Analysis worksheet. Press Ctrl + Home to make cell A1 the active cell, and then press Ctrl + A to select the entire worksheet.

c. On the HOME tab, in the Clipboard group, click **Copy**.

d. Click the **June Golf Cart Usage Analysis** worksheet tab, press Ctrl + Home to make A1 the active cell, and then click **Paste**.

e. Click cell **A11**. If necessary, scroll down until you can see cell A41. Press and hold Shift, and then click cell **A41**. Cell range A11:A41 should be selected. Press Delete.

f. Press Home. Cell A11 should be the active cell.

g. June contains one less day than May. You need to delete one row of the daily data. Right-click the header for row **12**, and then click **Delete** in the shortcut menu.

h. Click cell **A11**. Type 06/01/2015 and then press Ctrl + Enter.

i. Click and hold the **fill handle**, drag the fill handle down until the border around the cell range expands to include cells **A11:A40**, and then release the left mouse button.

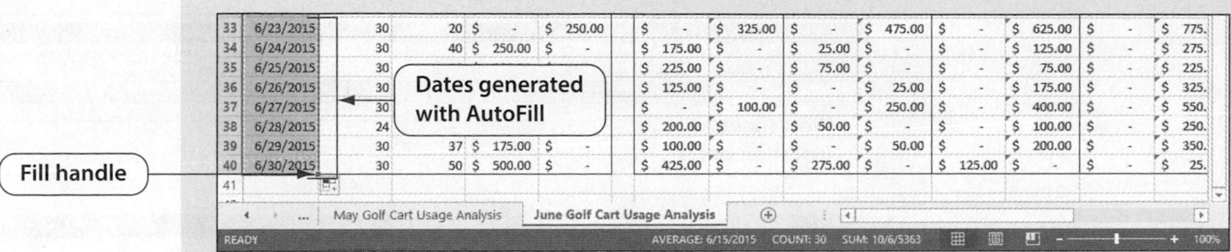

Figure 27 AutoFill dates for June Golf Cart Usage Analysis

Notice the date is incremented by one day in each cell from top to bottom.

j. Press Home to deselect the AutoFill range.

k. Click the **Documentation** worksheet tab, click cell **A22**, and then press Ctrl + ; to insert today's date. Press Tab, type June Golf Cart Usage Analysis and then press Tab. Type your last name, first name, press Tab, and then type G. Since you entered text, Excel examines other contiguous cells that contain content in the same column and using the AutoComplete feature, completes the entry other cell contents that begin with "G". Press Enter to accept the AutoComplete suggestion.

l. Click **Save**.

REAL WORLD ADVICE More on AutoFill, Anyone?

You just met Aidan Matthews, the chief technology officer at Painted Paradise Resort and Spa. You explained to him the work you have been completing for Barry. He urged you to explore AutoFill further as it is very flexible and can assist you in many ways. As he reminisced on his time conducting Excel training sessions earlier in his career, he remembered a file he gave trainees to practice AutoFill. If you would like to try some more AutoFill activities, open Aidan's file e01ws01AutoFill, and follow the instructions provided in cell comments. Knowing in-depth how AutoFill behaves can save you time!

Moving or Copying a Worksheet

The order of worksheets in a workbook can be changed by reordering the worksheet tabs. To move a worksheet, make the target worksheet the active worksheet by clicking on its tab. Click and hold on the worksheet tab, drag the worksheet tab to its new location, and drop it by releasing the mouse button. As a worksheet is dragged, a small black triangle will appear between worksheet tabs. This indicates the location where the worksheet will be inserted if the mouse button is released.

To copy a worksheet within a workbook, after clicking on the worksheet tab, press and hold Ctrl and drag a copy of the worksheet to a new location.

In the e01ws01GolfCarts_LastFirst workbook, the Documentation worksheet is the first—on the far left—worksheet. Painted Paradise Resort & Spa standards require the Documentation worksheet must be the far-right worksheet in a workbook. You must move the Documentation worksheet.

E01.22

To Move and Copy a Worksheet

a. In the e01ws01GolfCarts_LastFirst workbook, click and hold the **Documentation** worksheet tab. The mouse pointer will change to the move worksheet pointer. Move the mouse to the right until appears to the right of the June Golf Cart Usage Analysis worksheet tab.

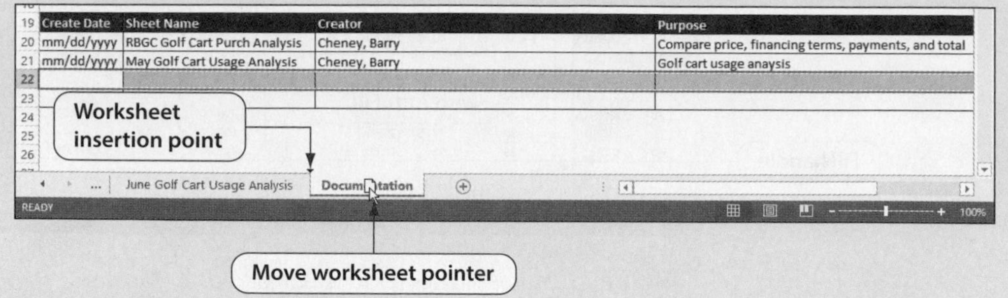

Figure 28 Move a worksheet

b. Release the mouse button to move the Documentation worksheet to the location of the ▼.

Barry has decided he wants the most recent golf cart usage analysis to be first (left) in the sequence of worksheets. You need to move the June Golf Cart Usage Analysis to the left of the May Golf Cart Usage Analysis.

c. Click and hold the **June Golf Cart Usage Analysis** worksheet tab. Move the ▼ pointer to the left until it is between the RBGC Golf Cart Purch Analysis and May Golf Cart Usage Analysis worksheets. Release the mouse button.

Barry also wants you to create a July Golf Cart Usage Analysis worksheet. He feels three months of usage data will help him better determine the number of carts to purchase. Rather than create a new worksheet and then copy a range of cells from another worksheet, this time copy the May Golf Cart Usage Analysis worksheet in its entirety to a new worksheet.

d. Click and hold the **May Golf Cart Usage Analysis** worksheet tab, and then press and hold Ctrl. The mouse pointer will change from to the Copy Worksheet pointer . Move the mouse to the left until ▼ appears to the left of the June Golf Cart Usage Analysis worksheet tab. Release the mouse button.

A copy of the May Golf Cart Usage Analysis worksheet has been created called "May Golf Cart Usage Analysi (2."

e. Double-click the **May Golf Cart Usage Analysi (2** worksheet tab, type July Golf Cart Usage Analysis and then press Enter.

f. Click cell **A11**. Type 07/01/2015 and then press Ctrl + Enter.

g. Click and hold the **fill handle**, drag the fill handle down until the border around the cell range expands to include cells **A11:A41**, and then release the mouse button.

h. Press Ctrl + Home to deselect the Auto Fill range.

i. Click the **Documentation** worksheet tab, click cell **A23**, and then press Ctrl + ; to insert today's date. Press Tab, type July Golf Cart Usage Analysis and then press Tab. Type your last name, first name; press Tab; and then type G and press Enter.

j. Click the **July Golf Cart Usage Analysis** worksheet tab.

k. Click **Save** .

Preview, Export, and Print Worksheets

Excel has a great deal of flexibility built into its printing functionality. To appropriately present your work in printed form, it is important that you understand how to take advantage of Excel's print features.

Barry Cheney is very pleased with the e01ws01Mowers_LastFirst workbook you created for him. He wants the workbook printed for the staff meeting. This will require that the analysis be printed on paper with appropriate headings and titles, and be exported to PDF for distribution via e-mail. In this section of the workshop, you will learn the different print features in Excel so your work can be most effectively presented on the printed page.

Exporting a Workbook to PDF

PDF is an acronym for Portable Document Format. It is a document representation standard developed by Adobe Systems and was made an open standard in 2008. One way to distribute a worksheet in a manner that allows it to be read—but not altered—by anyone with a free PDF reader application is to export it to a PDF.

Barry wants you to export the e01ws01GolfCarts_LastFirst workbook to PDF.

E01.23

To Export a Workbook to PDF

a. In the e01ws01GolfCarts_LastFirst workbook, click the **FILE** tab, and then click **Export**.

b. In the far-right pane, under Create a PDF/XPS Document, click **Create PDF/XPS**.

c. In the Publish as PDF or XPS dialog box, click **Options**. In the Options dialog box, under Publish what, click **Entire workbook**.

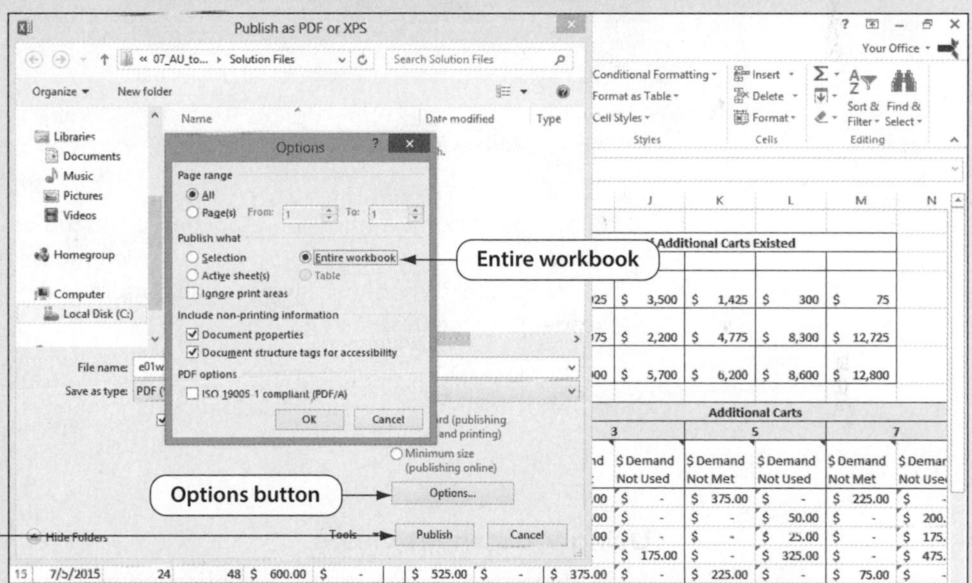

Figure 29 Export Options dialog box

d. Click **OK**. Be sure **Open file after publishing** is checked.

e. Navigate to where you are saving your Excel files, edit the filename listed in the File name box to display e01ws01GolfCartsP_LastFirst, and then click **Publish**.

Once the PDF file is created, it is opened in Modern Reader, the built-in Windows 8 PDF document viewer.

Troubleshooting

Your pdf file may not open in Modern Reader if a different pdf reader, such as Adobe Reader is installed as the default pdf file reader. If the pdf file dislpays in a different reader, close the reader and skip to Step h.

f. Right-click anywhere on the screen and a menu bar will appear at the bottom of the screen. Click **More**.

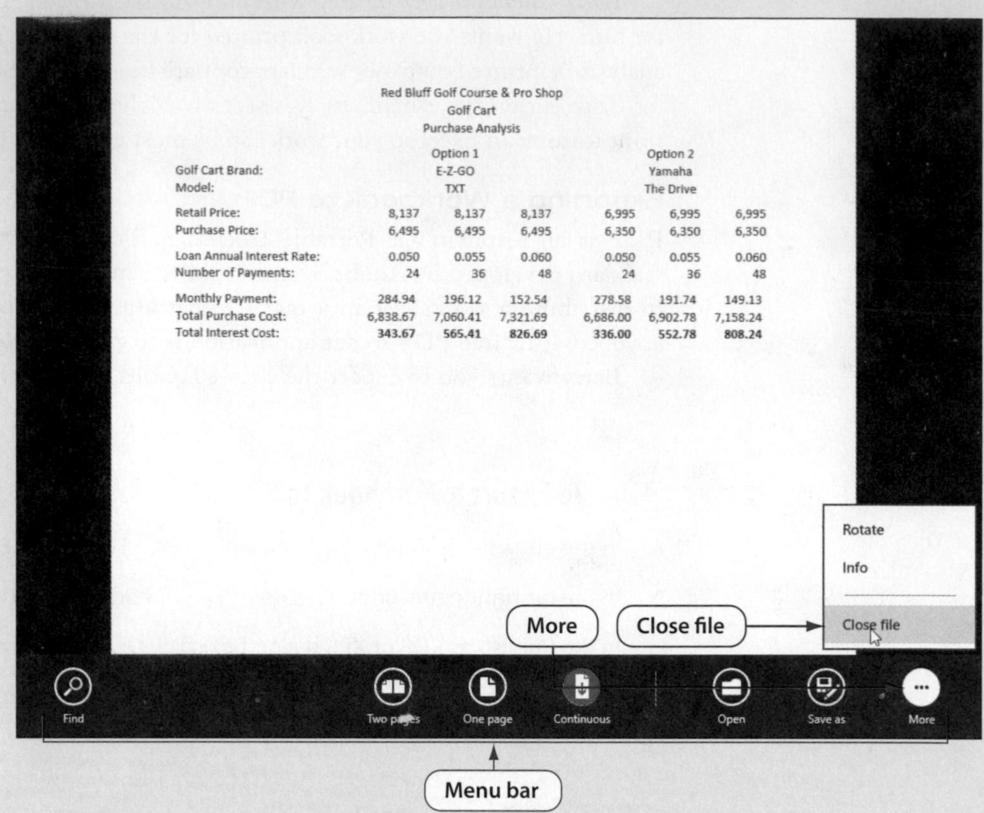

Figure 30 Modern Reader in Windows 8

g. Click **Close file**. Move the mouse pointer to the top edge of the screen. The pointer will change to a hand. Click and hold the left mouse button until the mouse pointer changes to, and then swipe to the bottom of the screen. This will close Modern Reader. Click the **Desktop** tile.

h. Click **Close** to close the e01ws01GolfCarts_LastFirst workbook. Submit the e01ws01GolfCartsP_LastFirst file as directed by your instructor.

Using Worksheet Views

In the bottom-right corner of the application window are three icons that control the worksheet view. Normal view is what you use most of the time when building and editing a worksheet. Only the cells in the worksheet are visible; print specific features such as margins, headers, footers, and page breaks are not displayed.

Page Layout view shows page margins, print headers and footers, and page breaks. It presents you with a reasonable preview of how a worksheet will print on paper.

Page Break Preview does not show page margins, headers or footers, but it allows you to manually adjust the location of page breaks. This is particularly helpful when you would like to force a page break after a set of summary values and/or between data categories and force part of a worksheet to print on a new page.

E01.24

To Switch Among Worksheet Views and Adjust Page Breaks

a. In the e01ws01Mowers_LastFirst workbook, click the **RBGC Mower Purchase Analysis** worksheet tab.

b. Click the **FILE** tab, and then click **Print**.

Notice that the worksheet does not print on a single page nor does information break across pages correctly.

c. Press Esc to leave Backstage view, and then click **Page Break Preview** on the status bar.

Only the part of the worksheet that will print is displayed. A dashed blue border indicates where printing will break from one page to another.

d. Use the **Zoom Slider** to adjust the zoom level to make the pages as large as possible without hiding any data off the visible application window.

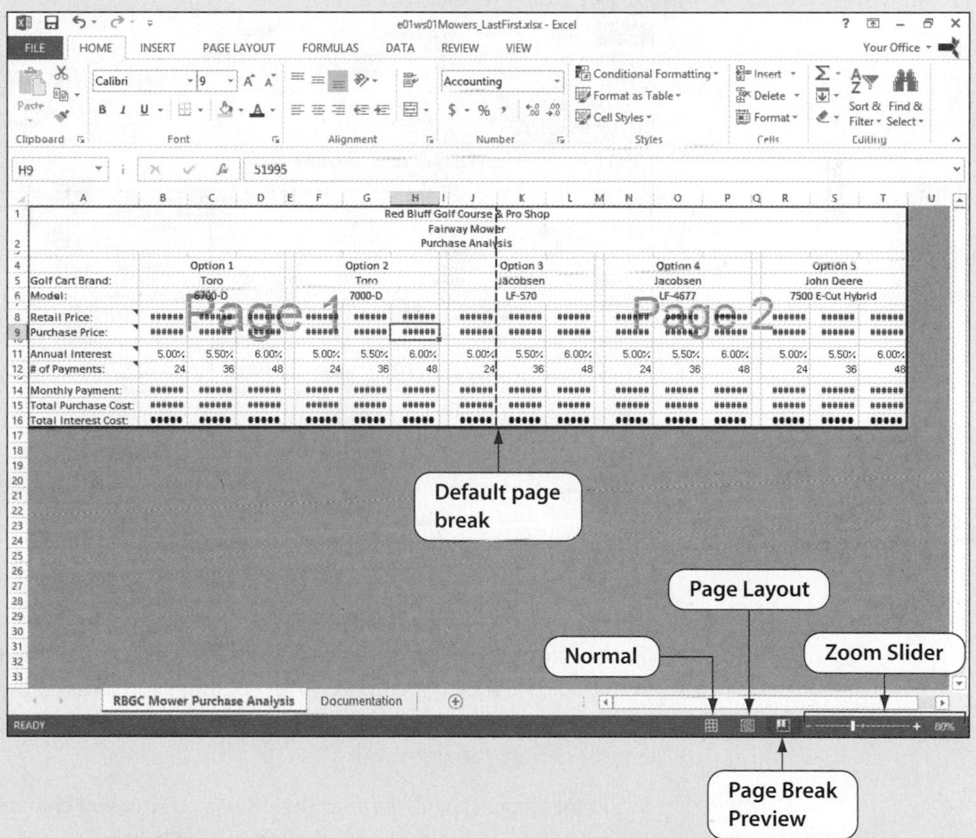

Figure 31 Page Break Preview

Now move the default page break since it divides Option 3 between two pages.

e. Move the pointer over the vertical dashed line between columns **J** and **K** to display the Vertical Page Break pointer ↔. Click and move the page break between columns **I** and **J**.

Notice the page break changes to a solid blue line. By moving the page break, you changed it from a default break to a hard page break. A **default page break** is placed by Excel wherever it is necessary to split content between pages. If the size of content changes, the location of a default break can change. A **hard page break** remains in its defined location until you move it. Changes in content size have no effect on the location of a hard page break.

Now you need to insert a new page break so that Option 5 will print on a separate page.

SIDE NOTE

Why Not Just Select R1?

You cannot select cell R1. Merge & Center is applied to cell range A1:T1.

f. Click the **PAGE LAYOUT** tab on the Ribbon—not Page Layout on the status bar.

Select cell **R2**. In the Page Setup group, click **Breaks**, and then click **Insert Page Break**.

Two page breaks are inserted, a horizontal page break above the active cell, and a vertical page break to the left of the active cell. You only want the vertical page break between columns Q and R.

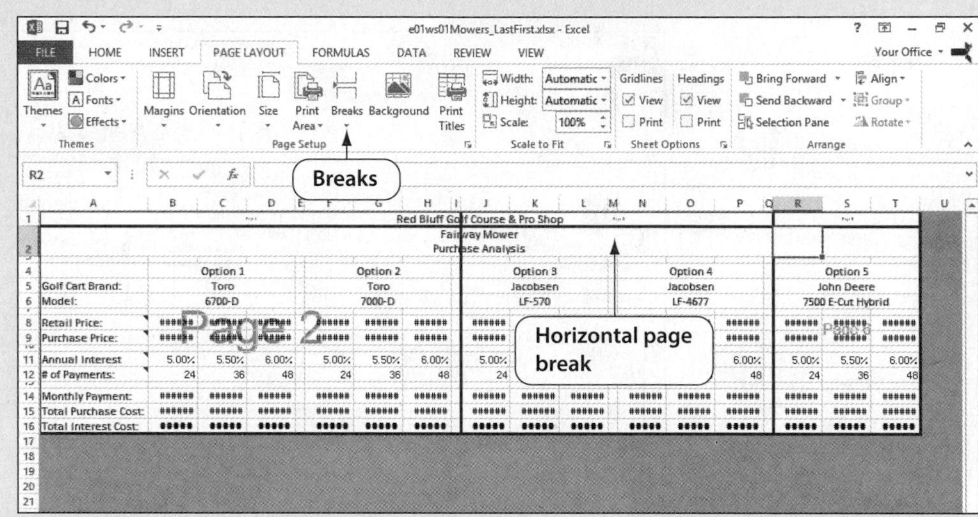

Figure 32 Insert horizontal and vertical page breaks in Page Break Preview

g. Point to the horizontal page break, and the mouse pointer will change to [↕]. Drag the **horizontal page break** off the bottom—or top—of the print area to remove it. There should now be page breaks after column I and after column Q.

Notice that the titles in rows 1:2 are split between two pages. You need to remove them from the print area.

h. Point to the top border, and the mouse pointer will change to the Horizontal Page Break pointer [↕]. Click and hold the left mouse button, and then move the top border down until it is between rows **2** and **3**.

i. Click **Page Layout** on the status bar, and then press Ctrl + Home. Page Layout view displays the worksheet with print margins. A thin border shows which part(s) of the worksheet will be printed on a page and also shows the location of the header.

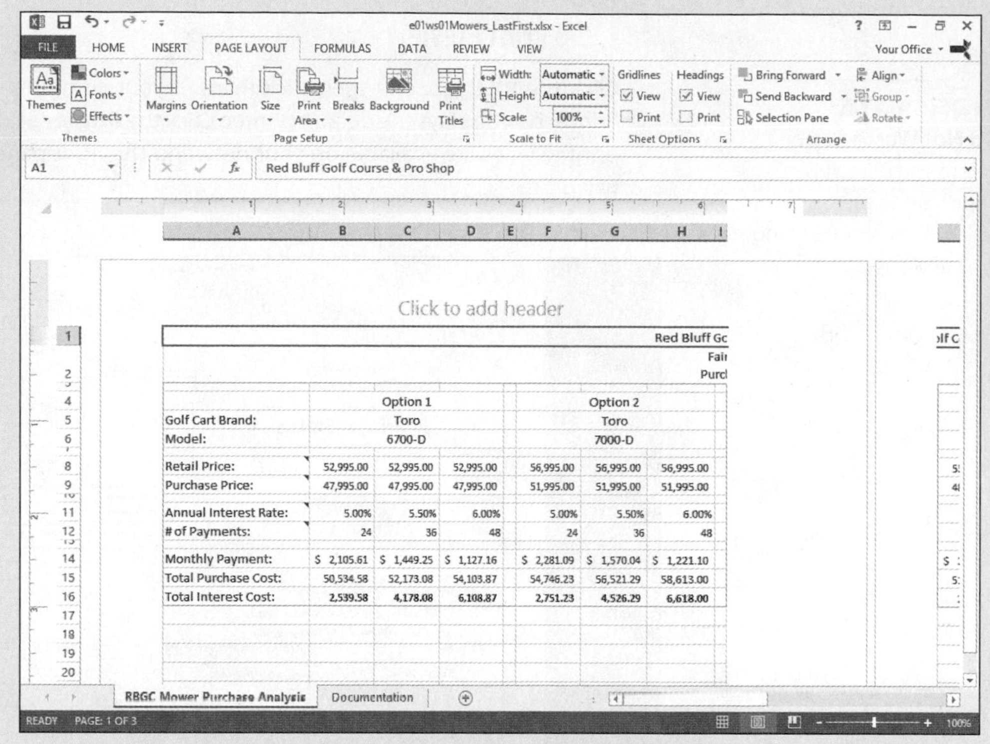

Figure 33 Page Layout view

j. Click **Normal** on the status bar. The thin lines between rows 2 and 3, rows 16 and 17, columns I and J, and columns Q and R show the print area and the locations of page breaks.

k. Click **Save**.

QUICK REFERENCE | **Switching Among Worksheet Views**

On the right side of the status bar do the following:

1. Click for Normal view.
2. Click for Page Layout view.
3. Click for Page Break Preview.

Using Print Preview and Printer Selection

Print Preview presents a view of your document as it will appear when printed. You can use the scroll bar on the right or the page navigation arrows on the bottom to view additional pages if your worksheet requires more than one page to print.

Often, a computer is connected to a local area network, or LAN. More than one print device can be made available to a computer via a LAN. You must be sure to select the printer/device you want to use. The default printer is selected automatically and is usually acceptable. When a different printer is required, click the Printer Status arrow to see a list of available devices.

Printing a worksheet is as simple as clicking the Print button on the Print tab in Backstage view. If more than one copy is desired, change the number in the Copies box to the right of the Print button. The copy count can be increased or decreased by clicking the arrows or by clicking in the Copies box and entering the number of copies from the keyboard.

E01.25

To Print Preview

SIDE NOTE

Do Not Waste Paper

Before you print, it is important to preview what will print to avoid wasting time and paper.

a. Click the **FILE** tab, and then click **Print**. If your computer has access to a printer, the Printer box displays the default printer. Click the **Printer Status** arrow to determine what print devices are available on your network. The right pane displays a preview of what will print.

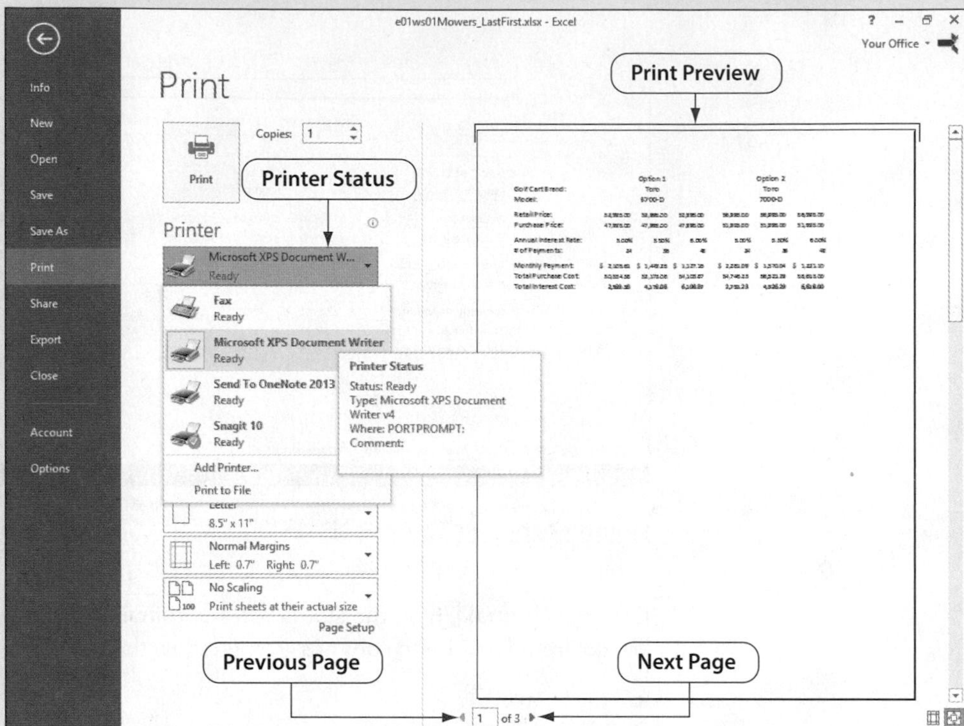

Figure 34 Print Preview and the Printer list

Troubleshooting

The list of devices displayed in the Printer list is determined by your installation, so the list of available printers will not match those shown in Figure 34.

b. Click **Next Page** to view page 2, and then click **Next Page** to view page 3.

Notice that pages 2 and 3 do not have any row headings. None of the pages have a page title. There is more to be done before this worksheet is ready for printing.

c. Press Esc to leave Backstage view.

Using Print Titles

When a worksheet is too large to print on a single page, it is often difficult to keep track of what information is being viewed from one page to another. Headers, such as those in column A of the golf cart analysis, are only printed on the first page.

Print titles can be included on each printed page so every column and/or row is labeled and easily identified from one page to another. Since you set page breaks between cart categories, you should print at least one column on each page that identifies cell contents in each row.

E01.26

To Specify Print Titles

a. Click the **PAGE LAYOUT** tab, and then in the Page Setup group, click **Print Titles**. The Page Setup dialog box will appear.

b. On the Sheet tab of the Page Setup dialog box, under Print titles, in the Columns to repeat at left box, type A:A.

The Print Titles feature requires the specification of a range, even when only a single column will be printed, thus the need to enter column A as A:A.

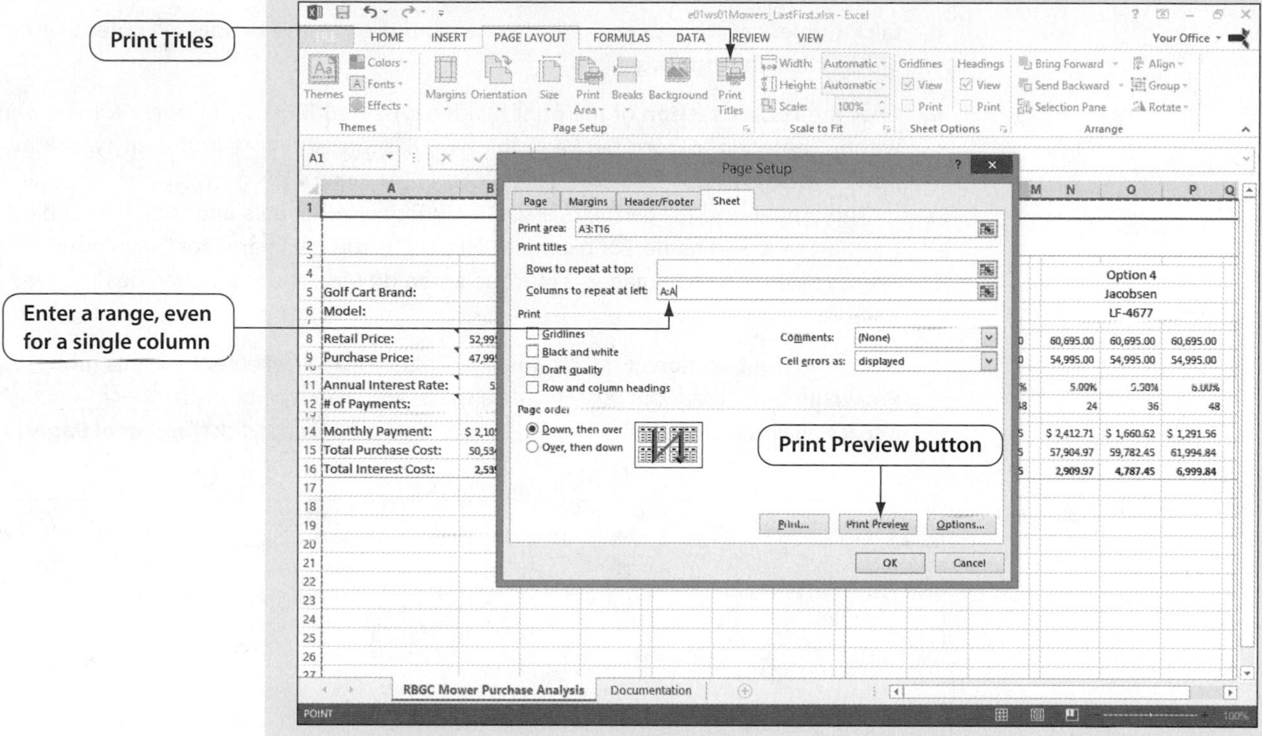

Figure 35 Sheet tab in the Page Setup dialog box for creating print titles

c. Click **Print Preview**. In the Print Preview pane, click **Next Page** to view page 2, and then click **Next Page** to view page 3.

Notice that pages 2 and 3 now have row headings.

d. Click **Save**.

Adding Headers and Footers

There are often items of information that should be included on a printed document that are not necessary in a worksheet. These items might include the following:

- Print date
- Print time
- Company name
- Page number
- Total number of pages
- Filename and location

Headers place information at the top of each printed page. Footers place information at the bottom of each printed page. The header and footer are divided into three sections: left, center, and right—information can be placed in any combination of the sections. You may include information in either or both the header and footer as deemed necessary.

E01.27

To Add a Header and Footer

a. Click the **RBGC Mower Purchase Analysis** worksheet tab, and then press Ctrl + Home to make A1 the active cell.

b. Click **Page Layout** on the status bar. If necessary, use the **Zoom Slider** to adjust zoom to 100%.

c. Select **Click to add header** in the top margin of Page Layout view. The DESIGN tab for HEADER & FOOTER TOOLS will appear on the Ribbon.

d. Click the **left section** of the print header, and then in the Header & Footer Elements group, click **Current Date**.

e. Click the **center section** of the print header, type Red Bluff Golf Course && Pro Shop without entering a space between the two "&"s, press Enter, and then type Mower Purchase Analysis.

The ampersand (&) performs a special function in headers and footers. It indicates the start of a field name. For example "&[Page]" is the field name for "page number." To display "&" in the print header, it must be entered twice, and it will then be displayed as a single character.

f. Select the **right section** of the print header. In the Header & Footer Elements group, click **Page Number**, press Spacebar to add a space, and then type of. Press Spacebar to add a space again, and then in the Header & Footer Elements group, click **Number of Pages**.

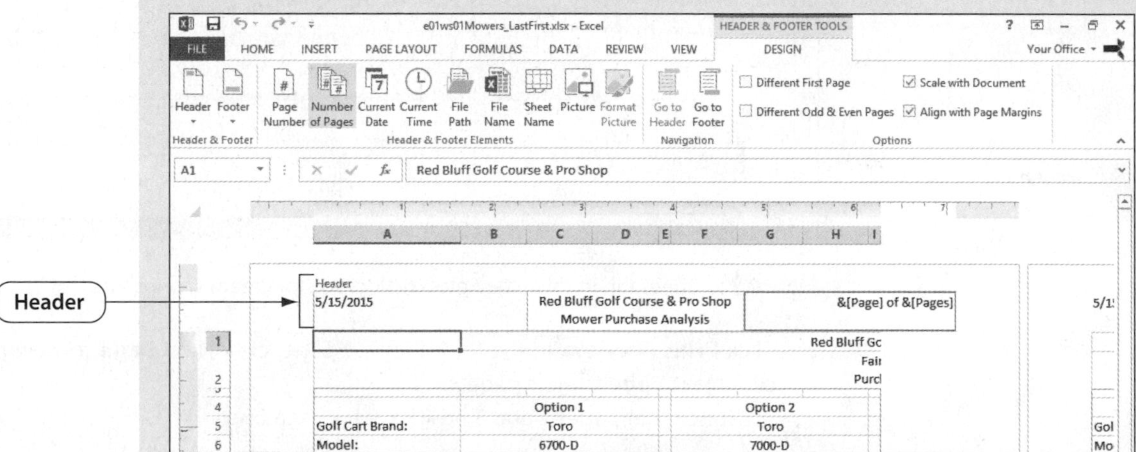

Figure 36 Page Layout view—Add information to the page header

g. In the Navigation group, click **Go to Footer**.

h. Click the **left section** of the print footer, and then in the Header & Footer Elements group, click **File Name**. Select any cell in the worksheet, press Ctrl + Home, and then on the status bar, click **Normal**.

i. Click the **FILE** tab, and then click **Print**. In the Print Preview pane, click **Next Page** to view page 2, and then click **Next Page** to view page 3.

Notice the header and footer are added to every page.

j. If your computer is attached to a printer, the Printer Status control displays the default printer. If you want to print to a different printer, click the **Printer Status** arrow next to the printer name, and then select the desired printer from the list. Click **Print** or submit your workbook file as directed by your instructor.

k. Click **Save**.

Changing Page Margins and Scaling

Page margins are the white space at the edges of the printed page. Normal margins for Excel are 0.7 inches on the left and right sides of the page, 0.75 inches on the top and bottom of the page, and 0.3 inches for the header and footer, if included.

Margins can be changed to suit conventions or standards for an organization, to better locate information on the page, or to avoid a page break at the last column or line of a worksheet.

It is not uncommon for worksheets to be too large to print on a single page, or to be so small that they appear lost in the top-left corner of the page. Scaling changes the size of the print font to allow more of a worksheet to be printed on a page or for a worksheet to be printed larger and use more page space. A printed worksheet that has been scaled to fit a sheet of paper generally looks more professional and is easier to read and understand than a worksheet that is printed on two pages that uses only a small part of the second page.

Barry Cheney looked at the printout you just produced and decided he wants to see the entire worksheet on a single page. Adjusting page margins and/or the print scaling can be used to print more of a worksheet on a single page.

E01.28

To Change Page Margins and Scaling

a. Click the **RBGC Mower Purchase Analysis** worksheet tab, click the **FILE** tab, and then click **Print**.

b. Under Settings, click the **Scaling** arrow—the last setting.

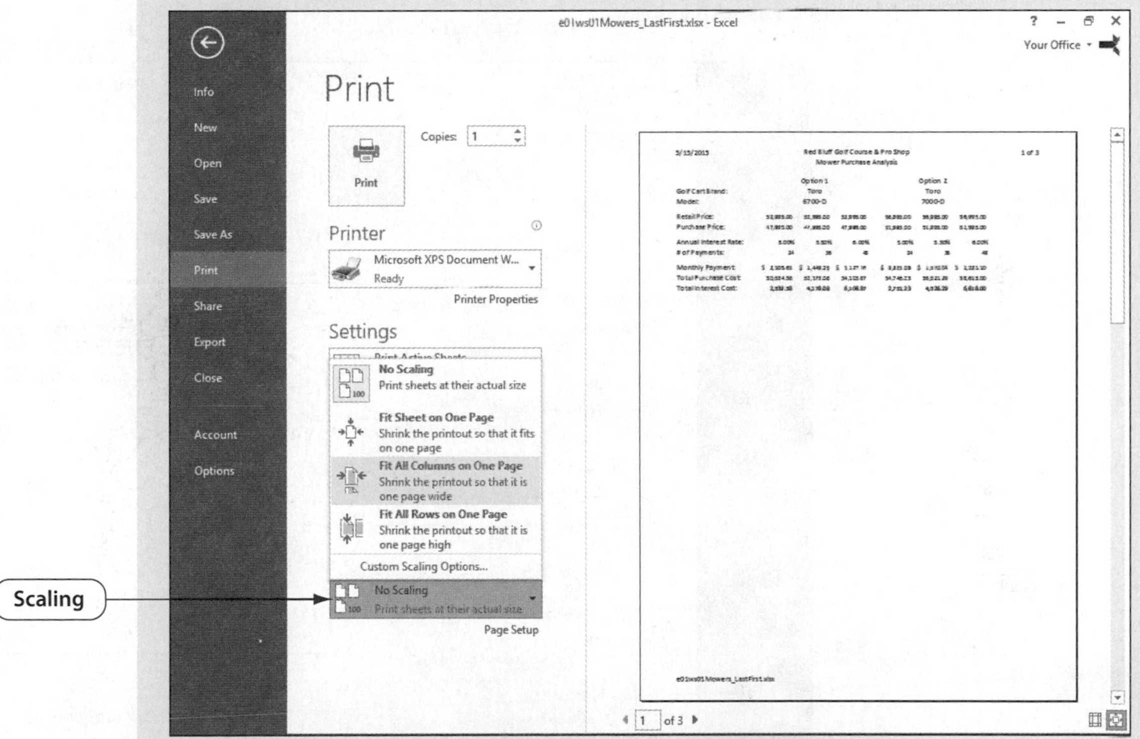

Figure 37 Print—Scaling control in Backstage view

c. Click **Fit All Columns on One Page**.

d. Click the **Margins** arrow, just above the Scaling setting, and then in the Margins list, select **Narrow**.

e. Click **Save**.

Changing Page Orientation and Print Range

Worksheets can be oriented to print on paper in one of two ways: **portrait**—the vertical dimension of the paper is longer, or **landscape**—the horizontal dimension of the paper is longer. Landscape orientation is generally used when a worksheet has too many columns to print well on a single page in portrait orientation. Scaling the worksheet to fit all columns on a single page can work in portrait orientation, but if scaling makes the data too small to be readable, landscape orientation is an option.

Print range defines what part of a workbook will be printed. The default is Print Active Sheets. This is often adequate, but you can also choose to print only a selected range of cells, or to print the entire workbook.

Barry Cheney does not like the last printout you produced either, the print is too small. He suggests changing the page orientation to landscape.

E01.29

To Change Page Orientation and Print Range

a. Click the **RBGC Mower Purchase Analysis** worksheet tab, click the **FILE** tab, and then click **Print**.

b. Click **Orientation**—fourth from the bottom under Settings—and then click **Landscape Orientation**. Narrow margins probably are not necessary at this point, so you should set them back to Normal.

c. Click the **Margins** control, and then select **Normal**.

d. Click the **Print Range** arrow—the first setting under Settings, and then click **Print Entire Workbook**.

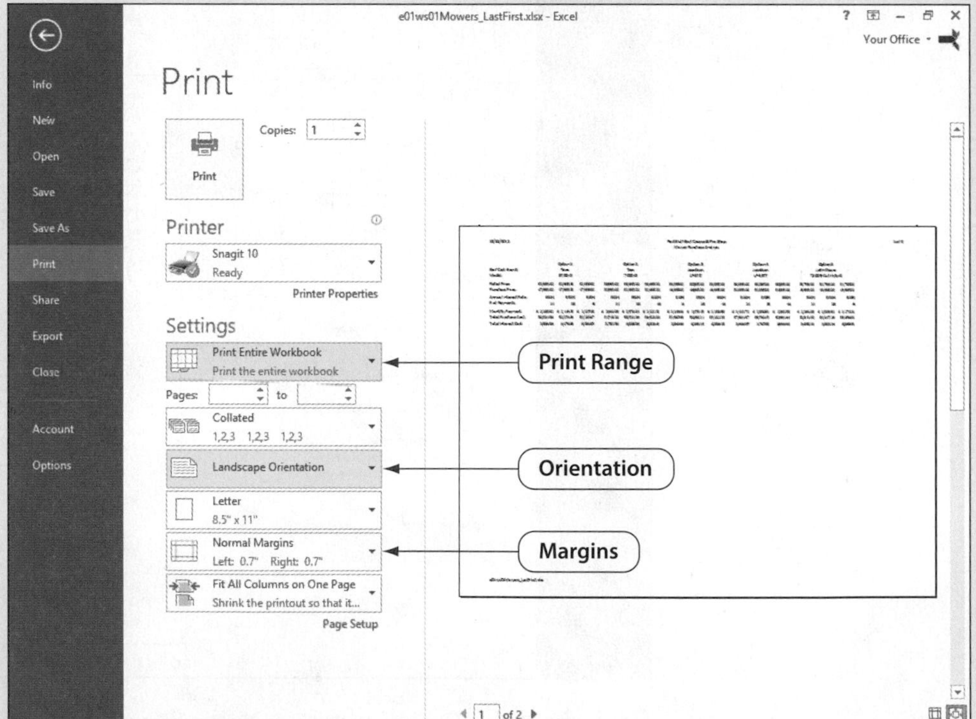

Figure 38 Page Orientation and Print Range

e. Click **Print** or submit your workbook file as directed by your instructor.

f. Click **Save** .

g. Click **Close** to close this workbook.

Concept Check

1. Explain the following terms for a reader who is not familiar with Excel:
   - Worksheet p. 380
   - Workbook p. 381
   - Cell p. 380
   - Row p. 380
   - Column p. 380
   - Spreadsheet p. 380
2. How do you quickly navigate to the last row in a worksheet that contains data? What happens when you press End in Excel? How do you move from one worksheet to another in Excel? What purpose does the Go To dialog box serve? How do you access the Go To dialog box? p. 383
3. Why is documentation important? Why do many people not properly document their workbooks? What are the possible costs associated with inadequate documentation? p. 386
4. What happens if you select a cell that contains important data, type "Jabberwocky" and then press Enter? How does the outcome change if you first double-click a cell that contains important data, type "Jabberwocky" and then press Enter? p. 389
5. How do you select noncontiguous cells? Is the ability to select noncontiguous cells important to the effective use of Excel? If yes, why? If no, why make use of noncontiguous cell selection? p. 392
6. Describe two ways in which columns and rows can be inserted and deleted. p. 400
7. How do you reorder worksheets in a workbook? p. 406
8. Explain the purpose of print titles, page headers, and page footers, and when you would use them. What are page orientation and scaling, and how can they be used in tandem to allow you to efficiently print a professional-looking worksheet? p. 412

Key Terms

Active cell 384
Active worksheet 383
AutoFill 410
Cell 380
Cell range 392
Cell reference 384
Column 380
Contiguous cell range 392
Date data 389
Destination cell 392
Field 380
Formula 380
Function 380
Keyboard shortcut 384
Landscape 422
Noncontiguous cell range 392
Numeric data 389
PDF 413
Portrait 422
Print Preview 417
Record 380
Row 380
Spreadsheet 380
Text data 389
Time data 389
Touch mode 386
What-if analysis 380
White space 396
Workbook 381
Worksheet 380
Worksheet navigation 384

Visual Summary

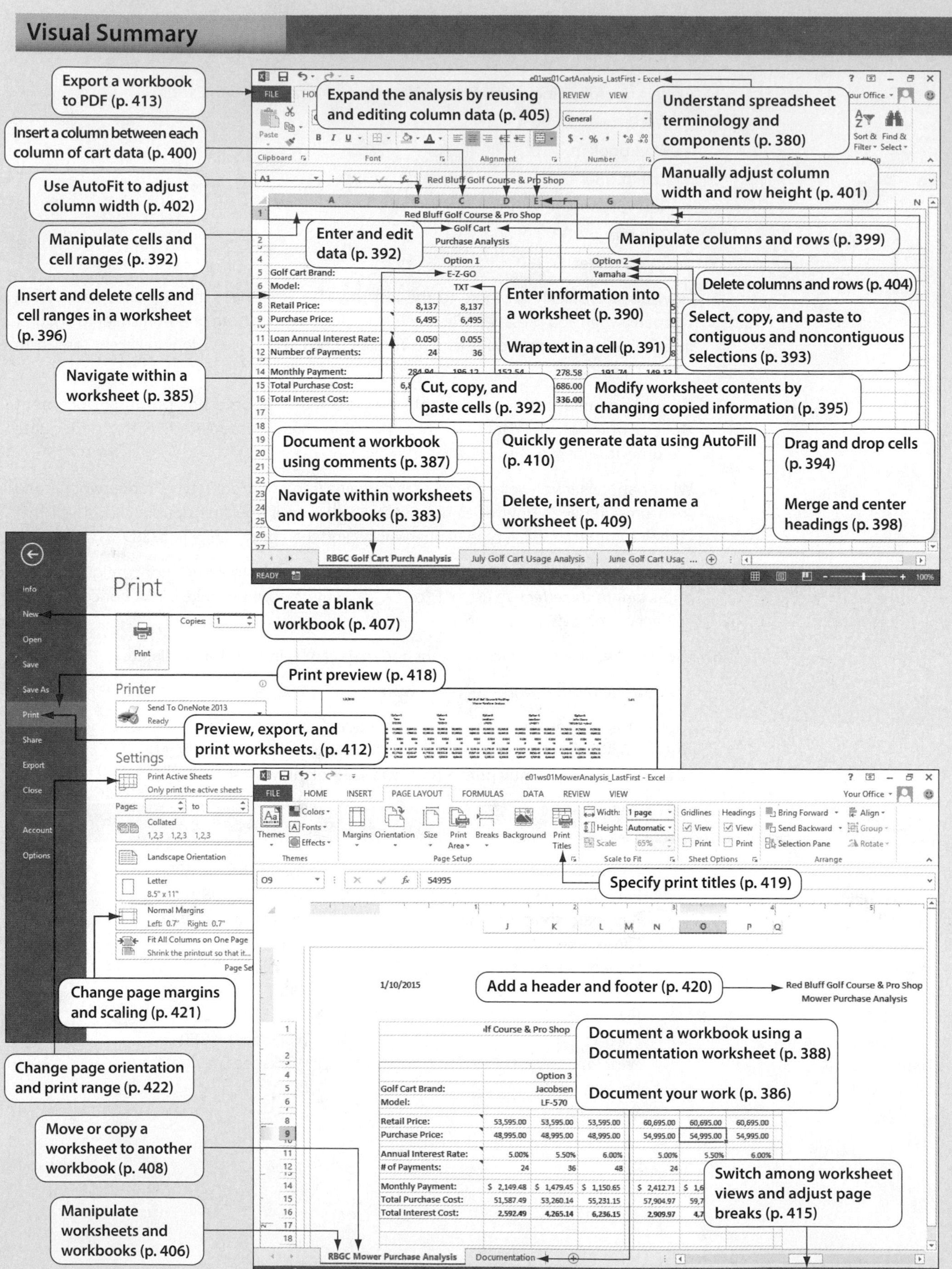

Figure 39 Red Bluff Golf Course and Pro Shop Golf Cart Purchase Analysis Final Document

Practice 1

Student data file needed:

 e01ws01WedPlan.xlsx

You will save your file as:

 e01ws01WedPlan_LastFirst.xlsx

e01ws01WedPlan_LastFirst.pdf

Red Bluff Resort Wedding Planning Worksheet

Sales & Marketing

Weddings are becoming an important part of the resort's business. Thus, Patti Rochelle started a worksheet to improve the wedding planning process for her staff. Last year, on average, the resort hosted three weddings per week and has done as many as six in a weekend. The worksheet Patti wants you to finish will allow for changes in pricing to be immediately reflected in the planning process.

You have been given a workbook that includes product/service categories, prices, and an initial worksheet structure in order to help standardize the process and pricing of weddings. You will build a worksheet that calculates the price of a wedding and doubles as a checklist to use as weddings are set up to ensure subcontractors, such as DJs, are reserved in a timely fashion and that all contracted services are delivered.

a. Start **Excel**, click **Open Other Workbooks**, and then double-click **Computer**. Click the disk drive in the left pane where your student data files are located, navigate through the folder structure, and then double-click **e01ws01WedPlan**. Click the **FILE** tab, click **Save As**, and then double-click **Computer**. In the Save As dialog box, navigate to the location where you are saving your files. In the File name box, type e01ws01WedPlan_LastFirst using your last and first name, and then click **Save**.

b. Double-click the **Sheet3** worksheet tab, type Wedding Planner and then press Enter. Double-click the **Sheet1** worksheet tab, and then type Documentation as the new name for the worksheet. Press Enter, click cell **B20**, and then type Wedding Planner. Press Ctrl + Home.

c. Right-click the **Sheet2** worksheet tab, and then select **Delete**.

d. Click the **Wedding Planner** worksheet tab.

e. Type the information into the indicated cells as follows.

Data Item	**Cell**	**Value**
Wedding Date	B2	6/18/2015
Start Time	D2	4:00 PM
End Time	D3	5:00 PM
Reception Start Time	G2	6:00 PM
Reception End Time	G3	12:00 AM
Total Hours	B5	8
Reception Hours	D5	6
Estimated Guests	B7	300
Piano Player (Hours)	C28	1
String Quartet (Hours)	C29	2
DJ (Hours)	C32	4
Discount	H33	-0.05

f. Click cell **E2**. Point to the border of the active cell, and when the mouse pointer changes, click and hold the left mouse button, drag cell **E2** to cell **G7**, and then release the mouse button.

g. Select cell range **F2:G3**, press Ctrl + X, click cell **H7**, and then press Ctrl + V. Select cell range **C2:D3**, press Ctrl + X, click cell **H4**, and then press Ctrl + V.

h. Select cell range **A2:B2**, press Ctrl + X, and then click cell **G3** to make it the active cell. Press Ctrl + V, and then select columns **G:H**. On the HOME tab, in the Cells group, click the **Format** arrow, and then click **AutoFit Column Width**.

i. Select columns **B:C**, and in the Cells group, click **Format**, and then click **Column Width**. Type 17 in the Column Width box, and then click **OK**. Click the header for column **E**, and then right-click and select **Delete** from the shortcut menu. In the Cells group, click the **Format** arrow, and then click **Column Width**. Type 2 in the Column Width box, and then click **OK**.

j. Press Ctrl + Home. Point to the border of the active cell, and when the mouse pointer changes to the move pointer, click and hold the left mouse button, and then drag cell **A1** to cell **F1**.

k. Select cell range **B9:C9**, press Ctrl and then select cell range **B34:C34**. In the Alignment group, click **Merge & Center**.

l. Click cell **A27**, and then in the Cells group, click the **Insert** arrow, and then click **Insert Sheet Rows**.

m. Click **Page Layout** on the status bar, scroll to the bottom of the worksheet, and then click **Click to add footer**. Click in the left section of the Footer. If necessary, under HEADER & FOOTER TOOLS, click the **DESIGN** tab. In the Header & Footer Elements group, click **File Name**, and then click a cell in the worksheet. Press Ctrl + Home, and then click **Normal** on the status bar.

n. Click the **Documentation** worksheet tab. Repeat Step m.

o. Click cell **A8**, and then type today's date in mm/dd/yyyy format. Click cell **B8**, and then type your last name, first name. Click cell **C8**, type Completed Ms. Rochelle's initial work - reorganized worksheet to function better as a checklist, and then press Ctrl + Home.

p. Click and hold the **Documentation** worksheet tab, and then move the **Documentation** worksheet to the right of the Wedding Planner worksheet.

q. Click the **Wedding Planner** worksheet tab, select cell range **F1:H35**, click the **FILE** tab, and then click **Print**. Under Settings, click the **Print Range** arrow, and then click **Print Selection**. If necessary, click the **Printer Status** arrow, select your printer, and then click **Print**. Press Ctrl + Home.

r. Click the **FILE** tab. Click **Print**. Click the **Scaling** arrow, and then select **Fit All Columns on One Page**. Press Esc. Click the **Documentation** worksheet tab. Click the **FILE** tab, and then click **Print**. Click the **Orientation** arrow, and then select **Landscape Orientation**. Click the **Scaling** arrow, and then select **Fit All Columns on One Page**.

s. Click **Export**, and then click **Create PDF/XPS**. Be sure **Open file after publishing** is not checked. Click **Options**. In the Options dialog box, under Publish what, click **Entire workbook**, and then click **OK**. Navigate to the folder where you are saving your files. In the File name box, type e01ws01WedPlan_LastFirst using your last and first name. Click **Publish**. Save and close the workbook.

t. Submit your file as directed by your instructor.

Problem Solve 1

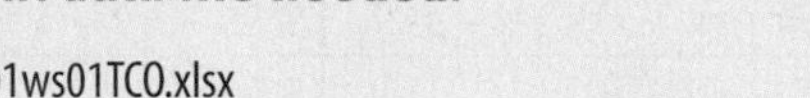

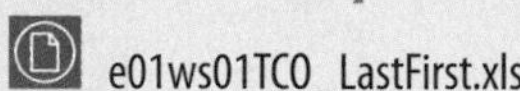

Finance & Accounting

Automobile Total Cost of Ownership

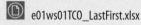

Most people own, or will at some time own, an automobile. Few actually take the time to calculate what owning an automobile actually costs—called "Total Cost of Ownership." This is an important calculation for both individuals and for businesses. In this Problem Solve, you will complete the development of an automobile total cost of ownership worksheet for your supervisor, Jan Bossy, CFO at your place of employment.

a. Start **Excel**, and then open **e01ws01TCO**. Save the workbook as e01ws01TCO_LastFirst using your last and first name.

b. Double-click the **Sheet1** worksheet tab, and then rename Sheet1 Documentation. Double-click the **Sheet2** worksheet tab, and then rename Sheet2 Auto TCO.

c. Type the Value information into the indicated cells as follows.

Data Item	Cell	Value
Model	B3	Scion TC
Purchase Price	B4	19547
Annual Interest Rate	B6	4.75%
Miles Driven / Year	E4	15000
Fuel Cost / Gallon	E5	3.90
MPG	E6	26

d. Merge and center the worksheet heading across cell range **A1:F1**.

e. Select cell range **C16:C22**, and then press Ctrl + C to copy the selected range to the Clipboard. Select cell range **D16:F16**, and press Ctrl + V to paste the Clipboard contents into the selected range.

f. Select cell range **B15:C15**. Use the AutoFill handle to expand the selected range to select **B15:F15**.

g. Select row **15** by clicking on the header, and then in the Cells group, click **Insert**.

h. Click cell **B15**, type 5-year Total Cost of Ownership Analysis and then select cell range **B15:F15**. In the Alignment group, apply **Center Across Selection**.

i. On the status bar, click **Page Layout**. Scroll to the bottom of the worksheet, and then click **Click to add footer**. In the Header & Footer Elements group, click **File Name**. Click a cell in the worksheet. Press Ctrl + Home. Click **Normal** on the status bar.

j. Click the **Documentation** worksheet tab, and then repeat Step i.

k. Click cell **A4**, and then enter today's date in mm/dd/yyyy format. Click cell **B4**, and then type your last name, first name. Click cell **C4**, and then type Completed Ms. Bossy's Automobile Total Cost of Ownership worksheet. Press Ctrl + Enter. Apply **Wrap Text** to cell C4. Click cell **B16**, type Auto TCO and then press Ctrl + Home.

l. Click the **Auto TCO** worksheet tab. Apply **AutoFit Column Width** to column **A**. Select columns **B:F**. On the HOME tab, in the Cells group, click the **Format** arrow, and then set **Column Width** to 12.

m. Right-click the **Sheet3** worksheet tab, and then select **Delete**.

n. Click and hold the **Auto TCO** worksheet tab. Move the Auto TCO worksheet to the left of the Documentation worksheet.

o. Click the **FILE** tab, and then click **Print**. Under Settings, click the **Orientation** arrow, select **Landscape Orientation**, and then press Esc. Click the **Documentation** worksheet tab. Click the **FILE** tab, and then click the **Print** tab. Click the **Orientation** arrow, and then select **Landscape Orientation**. Click the **Scaling** arrow, and then select **Fit All Columns to One Page**. Click the **Print Range** arrow, select **Print Entire Workbook**, and then click **Print**. Save and close the workbook.

p. Submit your file as directed by your instructor.

Perform 1: Perform in Your Career

Student data file needed:

e01ws01IncProp.xlsx

You will save your file as:

 e01ws01IncProp_LastFirst.xlsx

Finance & Accounting

Property Investment Analysis

You were recently hired by O'Miller Property Investment for an internship. A determining factor in Kelsie O'Miller's decision to give you this opportunity was your ability to work with Microsoft Excel. Ms. O'Miller just started a workbook that she wants to use to compare properties under consideration for acquisition.

She has asked you to finish the worksheet by doing a little formatting and expanding the worksheet to allow the side-by-side comparison of six properties.

a. Start **Excel**, and then open **e01ws01IncProp**. Save the workbook as e01ws01IncProp_ LastFirst.

b. Rename the Sheet3 worksheet Property Analysis and then rename the Sheet1 worksheet Documentation. Delete the **Sheet2** worksheet, and then click the **Property Analysis** worksheet tab.

c. Set the width of column A so that no portion of any row heading is hidden, and then delete column B.

d. Insert new rows into the worksheet above Loan APR, Income, Interest Paid Year 1, and Net Carrying Costs.

e. Copy all of the information for a loan and paste two more loan columns on the right. Use the AutoFit feature to adjust the column width of the new loan columns if necessary. Use the AutoFill handle to number the loans.

f. Type the following information into the indicated columns:

Data Item	**G**	**H**
Purchase Price	750000	499000
Down Payment	100000	100000
Loan APR	0.06	0.055
Income	97500	75000
Property Taxes	-6500	-5250
Repairs	-12000	-10000
Insurance	-5000	-4300
Advertising	-800	-550

g. Center the worksheet titles—the top two lines—across all columns that contain headings and data. Adjust row height where necessary so that titles are entirely visible.

h. Insert a column between the columns that contain loan information. For any column to the left of a column that contains loan data, set the column width to 3.

i. Move the values for Depreciation Years and Income Tax Rate one column to the right.

j. Add comments to the headings of Net Price, Interest Paid Year 1, Annual Depreciation, Net Carrying Costs, and Net Cash Flow that define each term.

k. In the Documentation worksheet, insert today's date into cell A4. Type your last name, first name into cell B4, and then type into cell C4 an appropriate description of your activities in this workbook. Change any other necessary information in the Documentation worksheet.

l. Add the File Name to the page footer in both worksheets.

m. Move a worksheet so that the worksheets are in the following order from left to right: Property Analysis, Documentation.

n. For printing the Property Analysis worksheet, set its orientation to Landscape. For the Documentation worksheet, set its orientation to Landscape, and then set scaling to Fit All Columns on One Page. Set Print Range to Print Entire Workbook.

o. Submit your file as directed by your instructor.

Additional Cases

Additional Workshop Cases are available on the companion website and in the instructor resources

WORKSHOP 2 | FORMAT, FUNCTIONS, AND FORMULAS

OBJECTIVES

Prepare Case

Red Bluff Golf Course & Pro Shop Sales Analysis

$

Finance & Accounting

The Red Bluff Golf Course & Pro Shop sells products ranging from golf clubs and accessories to clothing displaying the club logo. In addition, the Pro Shop collects fees for rounds of golf and services such as lessons from golf pro John Schilling.

Samot / Shutterstock

Manager Aleeta Herriott needs to track Pro Shop sales by category on a day-by-day basis. Sales, at least to some extent, are a reflection of traffic in the Pro Shop and can be used to help determine staffing requirements on different days of the week. In addition, summary sales data can be compared to inventory investments to determine if product mix is optimal, given the demands of clientele.

Each item or service at the time of sale is recorded in the Pro Shop point-of-sale (POS) system. At the end of each day, the POS system produces a cash register report with categorized sales for the day. This is the data source of each day's sales for the worksheet. Aleeta has created an initial layout for a sales analysis workbook, but she needs you to finish it.

REAL WORLD SUCCESS

"I worked in an insurance agency while I was in college. Part of my job was to administer marketing strategies. Every month we received data from our parent company that identified prospective clients. I used Excel to calculate a ranking so I could contact prospects with the highest potential value first. Agency performance was significantly improved as a result, and I received a regional award for efficiency improvement."

- Mike, alumnus and insurance agent

Student data files needed for this workshop:

 e01ws02WeekSales.xlsx

e01ws02red_bluff.jpg

You will save your file as:

 e01ws02WeekSales_LastFirst.xlsx

 e01ws02WSFormulas_LastFirst.pdf

Worksheet Formatting

To be of value, information must be effectively communicated. Effective communication of information generally requires that the information is formatted in a manner that aids in proper interpretation and understanding.

Some of the most revolutionary ideas in history have been initially recorded on a handy scrap of paper, a yellow legal pad, a tape recorder—even on a paper napkin. Communication of those ideas generally required they be presented in a different medium and that they be formatted in a manner that aided others' understanding. The content may not have changed, but the format of the presentation is important. People are more receptive to well-formatted information because it is easier to understand and to absorb. While accuracy of information is of utmost importance, what use is misunderstood accurate data? In this section, you will manipulate a worksheet by formatting numbers, aligning and rotating text, changing cell fill color and borders, using built-in cell and table styles, and applying workbook themes.

Format Cells, Cell Ranges, and Worksheets

There are several ways to present information. If different technologies, mediums, and audiences are considered, a list of more than 50 ways to present information would be easy to produce—the list could include such varied communication methods as books, speeches, websites, tweets, RSS feeds, and bumper stickers. An analysis of such a list however, would reveal a short list of generic communication methodologies:

- Oral
- Written narrative
- Tabular
- Graphical

Excel is an application specifically designed to present information in tabular and graphical formats. **Tabular format** is the presentation of text and numbers in tables—essentially organized in labeled columns and numbered rows. **Graphical format** is the presentation of information in charts, graphs, and pictures. Excel facilitates the graphical presentation of information via charts and graphs based on the tabular information in worksheets. This workshop is focused on formatting information for tabular presentation.

E02.00

To Get Started

a. Start **Excel**, and then open the student file **e01ws02WeekSales**.

b. Click the **FILE** tab, click **Save As**, double-click **Computer**, and then in the Save As dialog box, navigate to the location where you are saving your files. In the **File name** box type e01ws02WeekSales_LastFirst using your last and first name.

c. Click **Save** .

Number Formatting

Through number formatting, context can be given to numbers that can reduce the need for text labeling, such as for date and/or time values. Most of the world's currencies can be represented in Excel through number formatting. Financial numbers, scientific numbers, percentages, dates, times, and so on all have special formatting requirements and can be properly displayed in a worksheet. The ability to manipulate and properly display many different types of numeric information is a feature that makes Excel an incredibly powerful and ubiquitously popular application.

Numbers can be formatted in many ways in Excel, as shown in Table 1.

Format Name	Ribbon	Format List	Keyboard Shortcut	Example
Accounting	$ ▾			$ (1,234.00)
Comma[1]	,		Ctrl+Shift+!	(1,234.00)
Currency				-$1,234.00
			Ctrl+Shift+$	($1,234.00)
General		ABC 123	Ctrl+Shift+~	-1234
Number		General ▾		-1234.00
Percentage	%		Ctrl+Shift+%	7%
		%		-7.00%
Short Date				6/28/2015
			Ctrl+Shift+#	28-Jun-15
Time				6:00:00 PM
			Ctrl+Shift+@	6:00 PM

[1] Comma format is Accounting format without a currency symbol.

Table 1 Common number formats

MyITLab®
Workshop 2 Training

SIDE NOTE
More about the Comma Style
Comma Style is simply the Accounting Number Format without a monetary symbol.

E02.01

To Format Numbers

a. Click the **Weekly Sales** worksheet tab.

b. Select cell range **B6:H6**. Click the **HOME** tab, and then in the Number group, click **Accounting Number Format** $ ▾. The top row of numbers is often formatted with a currency symbol to indicate that subsequent values are currency as well.

> **Troubleshooting**
> If any of the cells you just formatted display number signs (#), select the cell(s), and in the Cells group, click Format, then on the Cell Size menu, click AutoFit Column Width.

c. Select cell range **B7:H8**, and then in the Number group, click **Comma Style** ,.

d. Select cell range **C29:C30**, press and hold Ctrl, click cell **C33**, and then select **C36:C38**. In the Number group, click **Percent Style** %, and then in the Number group, click **Increase Decimal** once.

e. Click cell **C31**, press Ctrl, and then click **C34**. In the Number group, click the **Number Format** General arrow, and then click **More Number Formats**. The Format Cells dialog box is displayed. Under Category, select **Currency**.

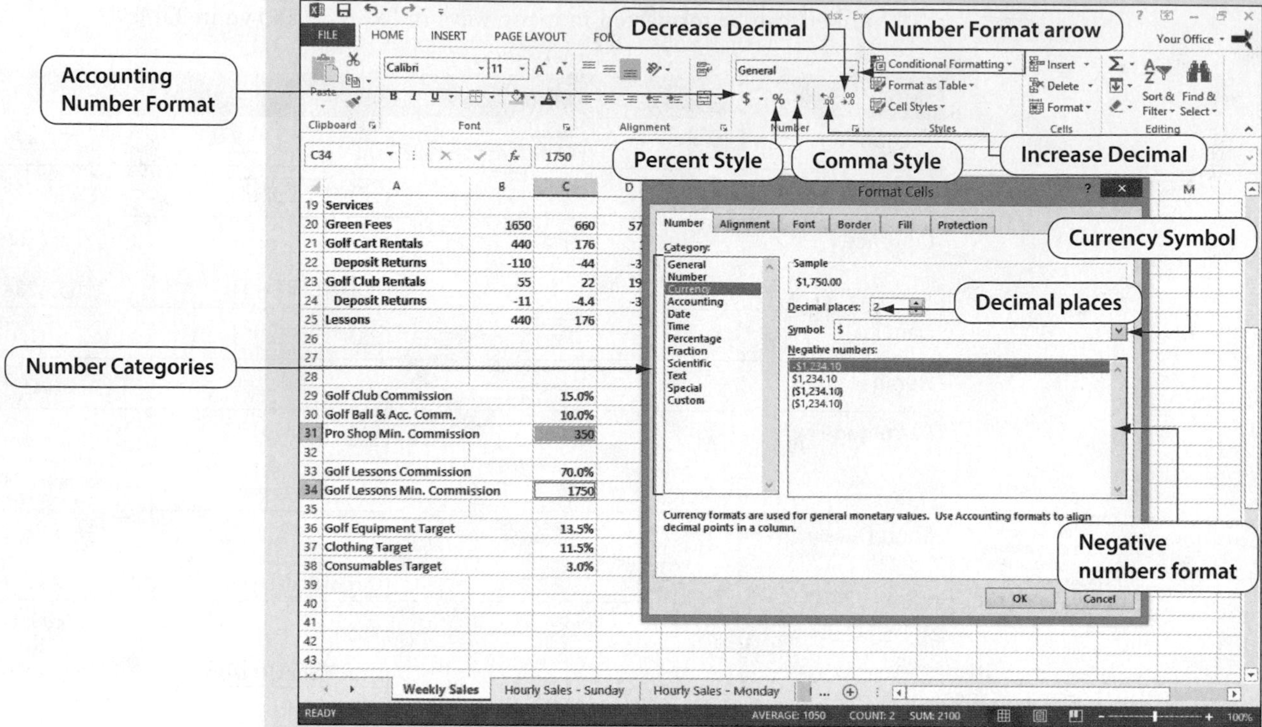

Figure 1 Number Format options

f. Double-click the **Decimal places** box, type 0 and then click **OK**.

g. Click **Save**.

REAL WORLD ADVICE **Accounting Number Format vs. Currency Number Format**

The Accounting and Currency number formats are both intended for monetary values. The Accounting format has the following characteristics:

- Negative numbers are surrounded in parentheses.
- The currency symbol is aligned to the left side of the cell.
- Zero values are displayed as a long dash (—) aligned at the decimal position.
- The decimal place is aligned.

The Currency format has the following characteristics:

- Negative numbers can be identified with a dash (-), parentheses, or displayed in red. The red color option can be combined with parentheses as well.
- The currency symbol is placed directly left of the value.
- Zero values are displayed as 0 with zeroes in each decimal place.

It is important to understand the differences so you can make intelligent formatting decisions.

Displaying Negative Values and Color

Negative numbers often require more than parentheses or a hyphen to call attention to the fact that a value is less than zero. The phrase "in the red" is often used to describe financial values that are less than zero, so, not surprisingly, Excel makes it very easy to display negative numbers in a red font color.

E02.02

To Display Negative Numbers in Red

a. Click the **Weekly Sales** worksheet tab.

b. Select cell range **B20:H22** (not B20:H25; you will format B23:H25 later). On the HOME tab, in the Number group, click the **Number Format** arrow [General], and then click **More Number Formats**.

c. Under Category, click **Number**. If necessary, enter 2 in the **Decimal places** box. Make sure **Use 1000 Separator (,)** is checked. Under Negative numbers, select the red negative number format **(1,234.10)**, and then click **OK**.

SIDE NOTE
Accounting Format in Red?
Conditional formatting, covered later in this workshop, can be used to display Accounting formatted numbers in red.

Troubleshooting
If the negative numbers in B22:H22 are not displayed in black, you didn't select the correct negative number format. Press Ctrl+Z and repeat Steps b–c.

d. Click **Save**.

CONSIDER THIS | **Accessibility and Color Blindness**

Approximately 8–12% of men of European descent are color blind. This does not mean they cannot see any color, but for about 99% of them, it means they have trouble distinguishing between reds and greens. How should this information affect the way you format your worksheets?

Formatting Date and Time

Excel stores a date and time as a number where the digits to the left of the decimal place are the number of complete days since January 1, 1900, inclusive. The right side of the decimal place is the decimal portion of the current day, which represents the current time. This date system allows Excel to use dates in calculations. For example, if you add 7 to today's date, the result is the date one week in the future.

While useful for computer systems and applications like Excel, people have not been taught to interpret time in this manner, so unformatted date and time values—those displayed in General format—mean little or nothing to us. Date and time formatting allows Excel date and time values to be displayed in a fashion that allows human interpretation. A heading that identifies a column as date values gives context to the information, but in the case of date information, without proper formatting, it is for the most part unusable by the reader.

E02.03

To Format a Cell or Cell Range as a Date or Time

a. Click the **Weekly Sales** worksheet tab.

b. Click cell **B4**; this is an unformatted date in Excel. On the HOME tab, in the Number group, click the **Number Format** arrow General, and then click **Short Date**. Click and hold down the left mouse button on the **fill handle**, and drag the **fill handle** right until the border around the active cell expands to include cells **B4:H4**, and then release the left mouse button. The date in cell B4 has been incremented by one day in each of the cells in C4:H4.

c. Notice the number signs in F4:H4. In the Cells group, click **Format**, and then click **AutoFit Column Width**.

d. Click the **Hourly Sales - Sunday** worksheet tab. Select cell range **A6:A7**. In the Number group, click the **Number Format** arrow General.

   Notice the Time format includes hours, minutes, and seconds. You have no need to display seconds, so you need to use the Format Cells dialog box to access additional time formats.

e. Click **More Number Formats**. Under Category, select **Time**. In the Type box, select **1:30 PM**.

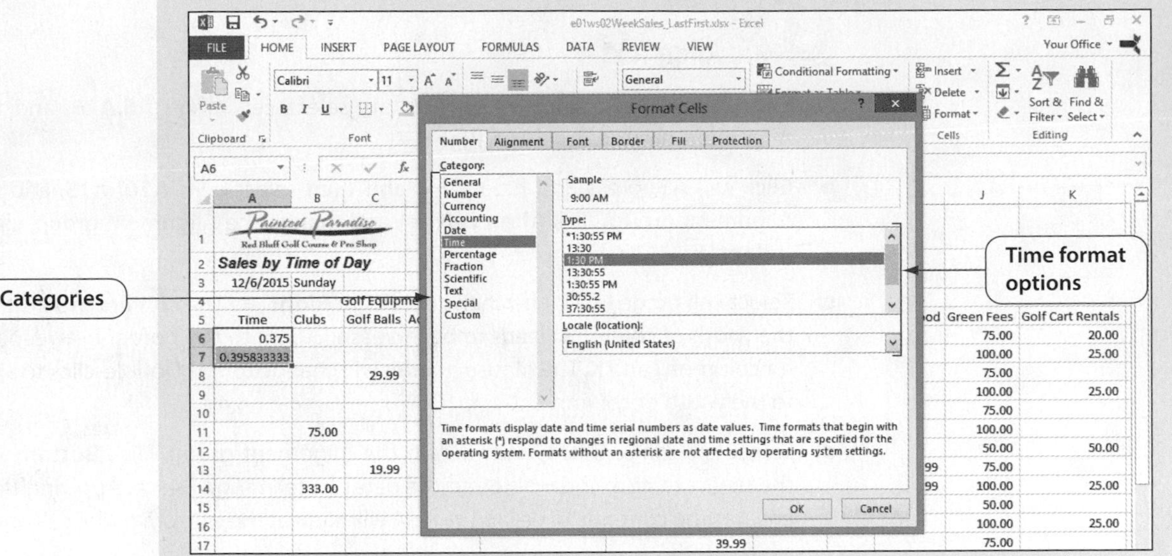

Figure 2 Time Formatting options

f. Click **OK**.

g. Click and hold the **fill handle**, and then drag the fill handle down to encompass cells **A6:A28**.

The series in cell range A6:A7 has been expanded through cell A28. Note that each cell is incremented by 30 minutes from the cell above. The 30-minute increment was determined by the time difference between cells A6 and A7. That is why you selected two cells before using Auto Fill in cell range A6:A28.

h. Click **Save**.

Excel stores time values as decimal portions of one day as follows:

- 1 = 1 day = 1,440 minutes
- .1 = 144 minutes = 2:24 AM
- .01 = 14.4 minutes = 12:14:24 AM

For this system to work in conjunction with date values, 0 and 1 are displayed as equivalent time values: 12:00:00 AM. However, in reality once a time value increases to 1, the date increments by 1 day and time reverts to 0. Would you be able to adapt if your digital watch or cell phone showed time the way Excel stores it? Would there be any advantages if time were actually displayed and handled in this format? What about date values?

Aligning Cell Content

Cell alignment allows cell content to be left-aligned, centered, and right-aligned horizontally, as well as top-aligned, middle-aligned, and bottom-aligned vertically. Certain cell formats align left or right by default. Number formats align right, including date and time formats. Text formatting aligns left by default, and for the most part, horizontal alignment changes will be made to alphabetic content such as titles, headings, and labels.

E02.04

To Align Text

a. Click the **Weekly Sales** worksheet tab, select cell range **A5:A25**, and then in the Alignment group, click **Align Right**.

b. Click cell **A5**, press and hold Ctrl, and then select cells **A10**, **A15**, and **A19**. In the Alignment group, click **Align Left**, and then in the Alignment group, click **Increase Indent**.

c. Select cell range **I4:J4**, and then click **Align Right**. The content in J4 is truncated, so the width of column J needs to be increased. Point to the border between the headers for columns **J** and **K**. The mouse pointer will change to ✚. Double-click to apply AutoFit to the width of column J.

d. Select cell range **B4:J4**, and then in the Alignment group, click **Bottom Align**. In the next exercise, you will rotate the dates in cell range B4:H4. Applying Bottom Align ensures the contents of cell range I4:J4 will align at the bottom of the cell once the dates are rotated.

e. Click **Save**.

Setting Content Orientation

Sometimes, it is helpful to display information at an angle or even vertically rather than the standard horizontal left to right. This is particularly true for tabular information. When formatting charts and graphs, rotating textual content can be very helpful in presenting information in a space-efficient, yet readable manner.

E02.05

To Rotate Text

a. Click the **Weekly Sales** worksheet tab.

b. Select cell range **B4:H4**.

c. In the Alignment group, click **Orientation**.

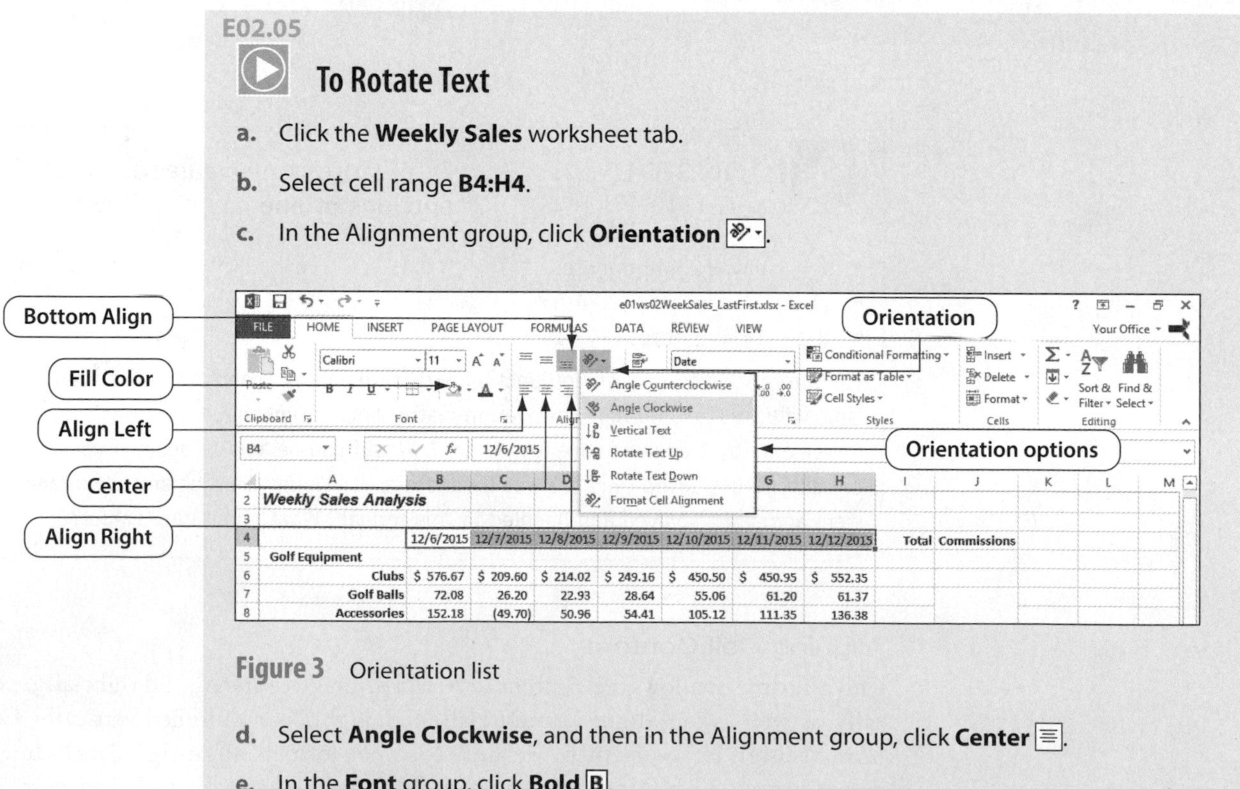

Figure 3 Orientation list

d. Select **Angle Clockwise**, and then in the Alignment group, click **Center**.

e. In the **Font** group, click **Bold**.

f. Click **Save**.

MODULE 1

Changing Fill Color

Fill color refers to the background color of a cell. It can be used to categorize information, to band rows or columns as a means of assisting the reader to follow information across or down a worksheet, or to highlight values.

It is generally a best practice to use muted or pastel fill colors. Bright colors are difficult to view for long periods of time and often make reading difficult. Bright background colors should only be used sparingly to highlight a value that requires attention, such as a value outside normal operating parameters.

E02.06

To Change Cell Background Color

a. Click the **Weekly Sales** worksheet tab.

b. Select the cell range **B4:H4**.

c. Press Ctrl, and then select cell range **A5:A25**. In the Font group, click the **Fill Color** arrow to display the color palette. Under Theme Colors, point to any color in the palette and a ScreenTip will appear identifying the color name. Select **Tan, Background 2, Darker 10%** (third column, second row).

d. Click cell **A4**, press Ctrl, and then select cell range **I4:J4**. Click the **Fill Color** arrow. Under Theme Colors, click **Tan, Background 2, Darker 25%.**

e. Click cell **A9**, press Ctrl, and then select cells **A14** and **A18**. In the Font group, click the **Fill Color** arrow, and then click **No Fill**. Click cell **A1**.

f. Click **Save**.

Adding Cell Borders

In the previous exercise, you changed the background color in a range of cells. When the background color is changed for a range of contiguous cells, cell borders are no longer visible. If it would be preferable to have visible cell borders, cell borders can be formatted to make them visible.

E02.07

To Format Cell Borders

a. Select cell range **B4:J4**, press Ctrl, and then select cell range **A5:A25**.

b. In the Font group, click the **Borders** arrow.

> **Troubleshooting**
>
> The Borders button may look different in your Excel application window than it does when referenced in this text; this is because the Borders button in the Font group of the Home tab displays the last border setting applied.

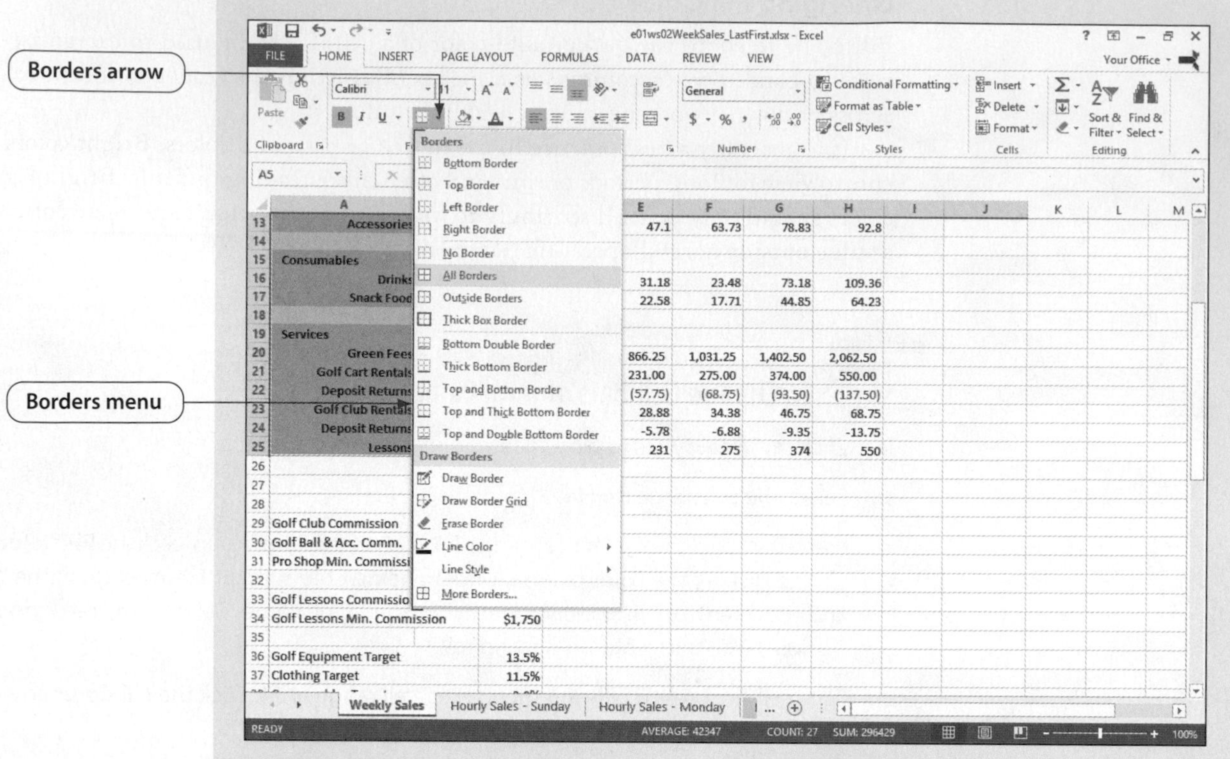

Figure 4 Borders list

c. In the Borders list, select **All Borders**.

d. Click cell **A5**, press Ctrl, and then select cells **A10**, **A15**, and **A19**. In the Font group, click the **Borders** arrow, and then in the Borders list, select **Thick Bottom Border**.

e. Click cell **J9**, click the **Borders** arrow, and then click **Top and Double Bottom Border**.

f. Select cell range **B9:I9**, press Ctrl, and then select cell ranges **B14:I14**, **B18:I18**, and **B26:I26**. Click the **Borders** arrow, and then click **Top and Bottom Border**.

g. Select cell range **B27:I27**, click the **Borders** arrow, and then click **Bottom Double Border**.

h. Click **Save**.

SIDE NOTE

Hide the Ribbon to See More of Your Worksheet

Double-click the Home tab to hide the Ribbon. Double-click the Home tab again to unhide it.

REAL WORLD ADVICE **Formatting—Less Is More**

Too much formatting results in a worksheet that is difficult to look at, that is difficult to read, and that conveys a sense that the designer lacked a plan. Here are some formatting guidelines:

- Format for a reason, not just for appearances.
- Use at most three fonts in a worksheet. Use each font for a purpose, such as to differentiate titles.
- Only use color to assist in readability, categorization, or identification purposes. For example, use organization colors for titles, bright colors to highlight small details, and background colors for categorization.
- Background colors should be pale, pastel colors. Bright background colors are tiring for the reader and can become painful to look at after a while.
- Special characters such as the ($) should be applied only as necessary. A $ sign in the first value of a column of numbers is often sufficient to identify its values as monetary. Then format subtotals and totals with a $ to differentiate them.

Copying Formats

Formatting a cell can consist of several steps involving fonts, colors, sizes, borders, alignment, and so on. You gain a significant efficiency advantage by reusing your work. Once a cell is formatted properly, you can apply the formatting properties to other cells. Copying formats from one cell to another saves a great deal of time.

Format Painter is a tool that facilitates rapid application of formats from one cell to other cells. To use the Format Painter, simply select the cell that is the source of the format you want to copy, click the Format Painter in the Clipboard group on the Home tab, and then select the cell or range of cells you want to "paint" with the source cell's formatting.

E02.08

To Use the Format Painter to Copy Formats

a. Click the **Weekly Sales** worksheet tab.

b. Click cell **B21**, and then in the Clipboard group, click **Format Painter**. The mouse pointer will change to . Select cell range **B23:H25**.

c. Click cell **B6**, double-click **Format Painter**, and then select cell range **B11:H11**. Select cell range **B16:H16**, select cell range **B20:H20**, and then click **Format Painter** to toggle it off. Cell B20 is not displayed properly after formatting. Point to the border between the headers for columns **B** and **C**. Double-click to apply AutoFit to the width of column B.

d. Click **Save**.

SIDE NOTE

How to Use the Format Painter Multiple Times

Double-click Format Painter, and it will remain active until you click it again, or press Esc.

Paste Options/Paste Special

When a cell is copied to the Clipboard, there is much more than a simple value ready to be pasted to another location. Formats, formulas, and values are all copied and can be selectively pasted to other locations in a workbook.

Different paste options are shown in Table 2. Although there are a large number of paste options, most worksheet activities require only a few of these options. Paste, , Paste Formatting , and Paste Values will accomplish most of what you will need to do. The various paste options are also additive, in that you can first paste a value to a copied cell and then paste the format from the copied cell, after which you could paste the formula from the copied cell.

Button	Function	Pastes
	Paste	All content from the Clipboard to a cell
	Formatting	Only the formatting from the Clipboard to a cell
	Values	Only the value from the Clipboard to a cell
	Formulas	Only the formula from the Clipboard to a cell
	Paste Link	A link (e.g., =A25) to the source cell from the Clipboard to a cell
	Transpose	A range of cells to a new range of cells with columns and rows switched

Table 2 Paste options

E02.09

To Use Paste Options to Copy Formats

a. Click the **Weekly Sales** worksheet tab.

b. Click cell **B7**. In the Clipboard group, click **Copy** to copy cell B7 to the Clipboard. Select cell range **B12:H13**, press Ctrl, and then select cell range **B17:H17**.

c. Right-click the **selected range**. The shortcut menu is displayed, which includes options that are determined by the context of the object that is the focus of the right-click.

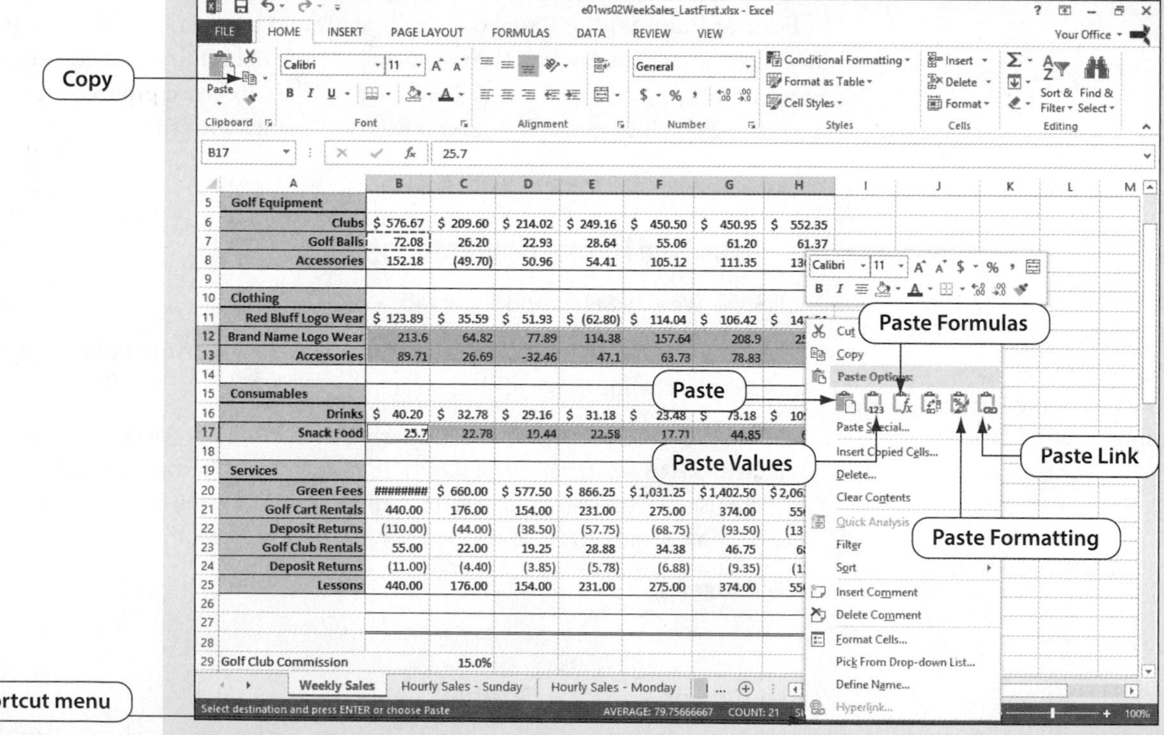

Figure 5 Paste Options menu

d. Point to each button on the Paste Options menu and notice what happens in the selected cell range.

e. On the Paste Options menu, click **Formatting**, and then press Esc to clear the Clipboard.

f. Click **Save**.

Using Built-In Cell Styles

Built-in cell styles are predefined and named combinations of cell- and content-formatting properties that can be applied to a cell or range of cells to define several formatting properties at once. A built-in cell style can set the font, font size and color, number format, background color, borders, and alignment with just a few clicks of the mouse. Built-in cell styles allow for rapid and accurate changes to the appearance of a workbook with very little effort.

E02.10

To Apply Built-In Cell Styles

a. Click the **Hourly Sales - Sunday** worksheet tab.

b. Click cell **B4**, press Ctrl, and then select cell **H4**. In the Styles group, click **Cell Styles**. The Cell Styles gallery appears.

Cell Styles gallery

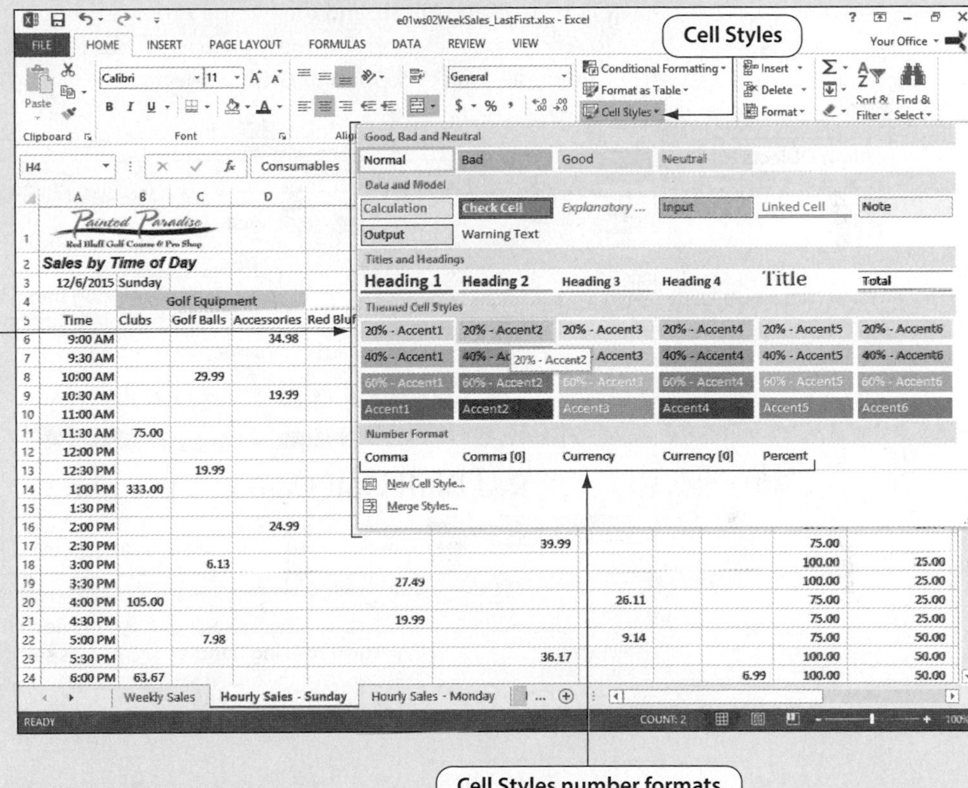

Figure 6 Cell Styles gallery

c. Under Themed Cell Styles, select **20% - Accent2**.

d. Click cell **E4**, press Ctrl, and then select cell **J4**. In the Styles group, click **Cell Styles**, and then select **40% - Accent2**.

e. Select cell range **A3:B3**, press Ctrl, and then select cell ranges **B4:P5** and **A5:A33**.

f. Click **Cell Styles**, and then under Titles and Headings, select **Heading 4**.
   Notice that in cell range B4:O4, the Accent2 cell background colors have not changed.

g. Select cell range **B29:P29**, and then in the Styles group, click **Cell Styles**, and then under Titles and Headings, select **Total**.

h. Click **Save**.

SIDE NOTE
Multiple Styles Can Be Applied to One Cell
How the cell is ultimately formatted is determined by the order in which styles are applied.

Inserting a Picture

Painted Paradise Resort & Spa has logos for each of its core businesses. All documents must include the appropriate logo whenever possible. Excel allows images, such as logos, to be inserted into a worksheet. Images are not contained in a cell, like data, but can be sized to fit cell borders using the Snap to Grid feature. In the next exercise, you will insert the Red Bluff Golf Course & Pro Shop image into the Weekly Sales worksheet.

E02.11

To Insert an Image into a Worksheet

a. Click the **Weekly Sales** worksheet tab.

b. Click cell **A1**. Click the **INSERT** tab, and then in the Illustrations group, click **Pictures**. In the Insert Picture dialog box, navigate to the location where your student data files are stored, click the **red_bluff** file, and then click **Insert**.

c. Click the **FORMAT** tab, and then in the Arrange group, click **Align Objects** . If Snap to Grid is not selected—it does not have a border around it as shown around View Gridlines—then click **Snap to Grid** to select.

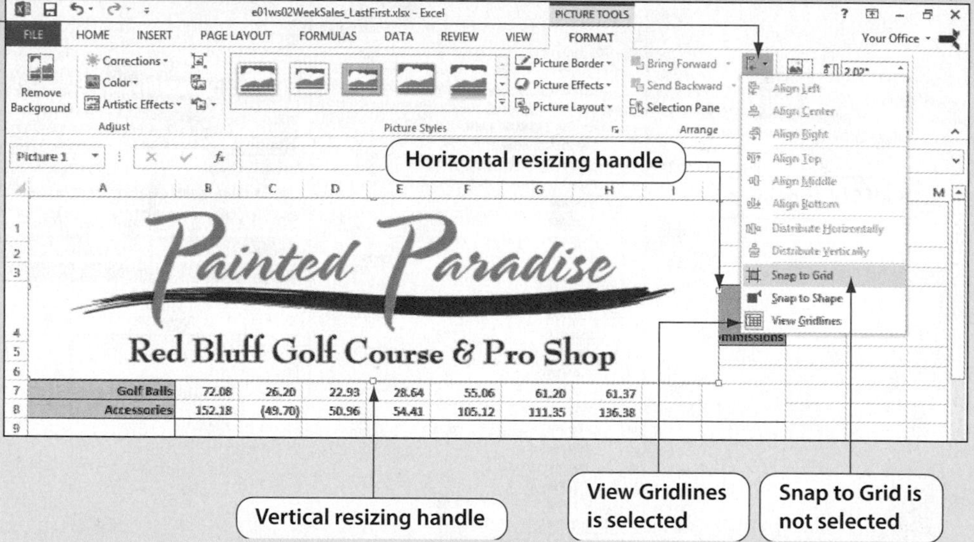

Figure 7 Insert a picture and toggle on Snap to Grid

d. Click and hold the right horizontal **resizing handle**, and then drag the edge of the **logo** to the left until it snaps to the border between columns **A** and **B**. Click and hold the bottom vertical **resizing handle**, and then drag the bottom edge of the **logo** up until it snaps to the border between rows **1** and **2**. Click cell **B6** to deselect the picture.

e. Click **Save** .

Applying Table Styles

A **table** is a powerful tabular data-formatting tool that facilitates data sorting, filtering, and calculations. Once a collection of data has been defined as a table by the application of a table style, it has special table properties not available to data simply entered into rows and columns of cells.

A **table style** is a predefined set of formatting properties that determine the appearance of a table. One of the useful features of a table style is the ability to "band" rows and columns. **Banding** is alternating the background color of rows and/or columns to assist in visually tracking information. Banding can be accomplished manually by changing the background color of a range of cells—a row for example—and then pasting the formatting into every other row. Manually banding a table is a tedious process at best. By applying a table style to a selected range of rows and columns, banding is accomplished in a couple of clicks. Most importantly, table banding is dynamic. If a row or column is inserted into—or deleted from—the worksheet, the banding is automatically updated. If banding is done manually, insertions and deletions require the banding to be manually updated as well.

Tables also allow for calculations in a total row such as summations, averages, or counts for each column in the table. These calculations are possible without table formatting; however, a table simplifies them.

E02.12

To Apply a Table Style to a Cell Range

a. Click the **Hourly Sales - Monday** worksheet tab.

b. Select the cell range **A5:P28**. Click the **HOME** tab, and then in the Styles group, click **Format as Table**. The Table Styles gallery appears.

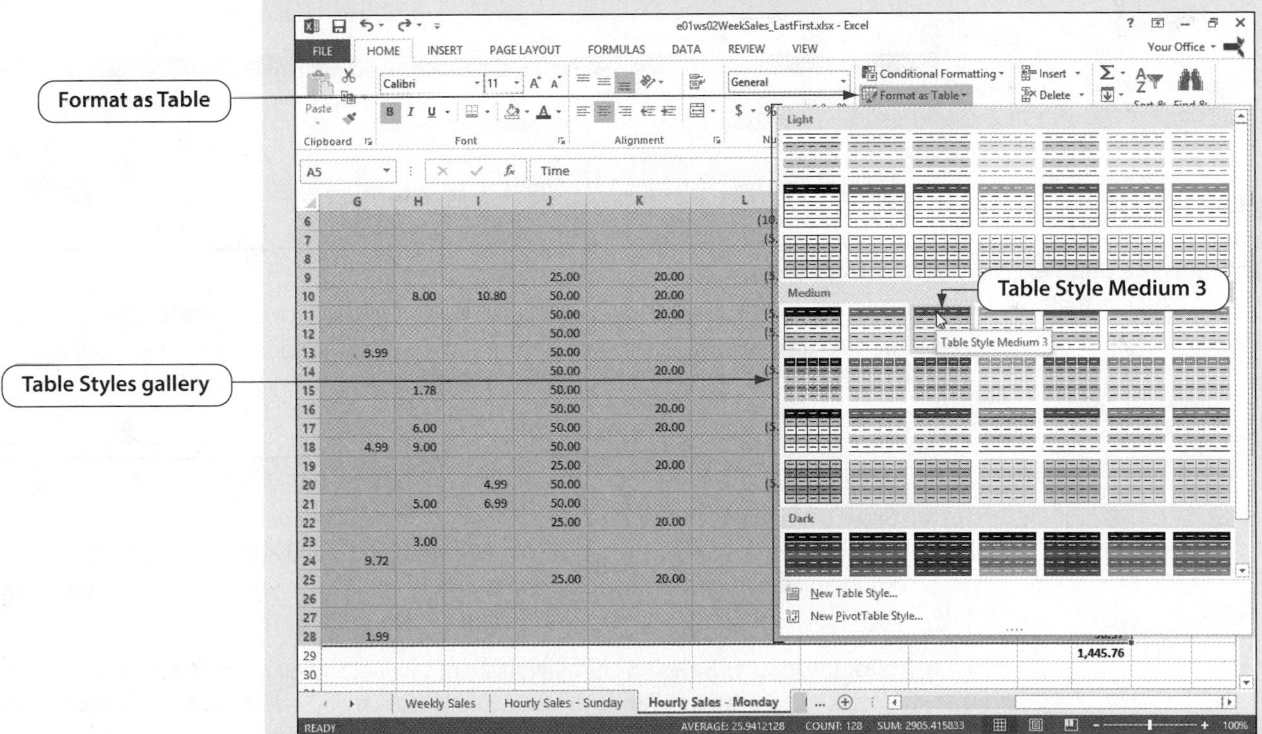

Figure 8 Table Style gallery

c. Under Medium table styles, select **Table Style Medium 3**. The Format As Table dialog box appears.

d. Since row 5 contains column headings, be sure **My table has headers** is checked, and then click **OK**. The TABLE TOOLS DESIGN tab is displayed.

Notice the rows of table data are in descending order by time. The arrow next to each column heading in the table in row 5 allows you to sort or filter the entire table by the information in each column.

e. Click cell **A6**, and then click the **Filter** arrow for the Time column (cell **A5**).

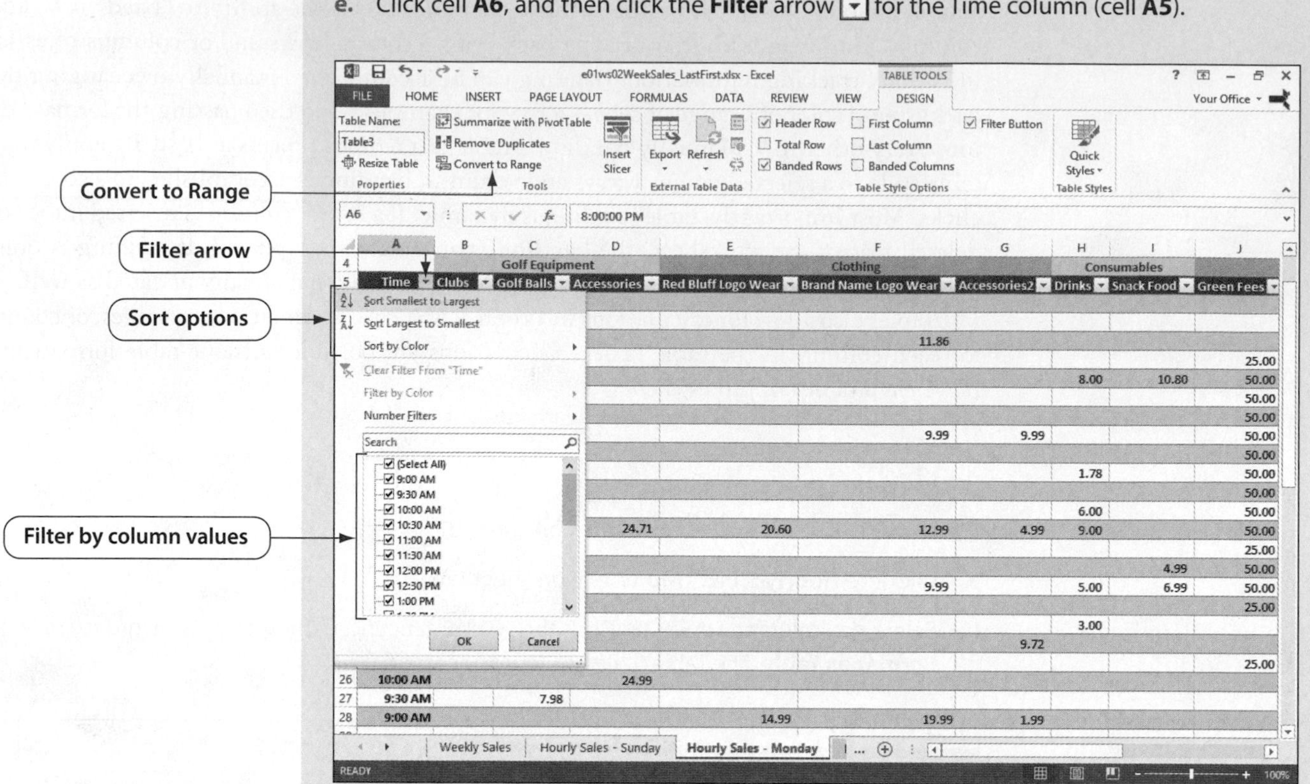

Figure 9 Table Tools Design tab and Table filter menu

f. On the displayed list, click **Sort Smallest to Largest**.

SIDE NOTE
Column Names in a Table Must Be Unique
Each table column must have a unique header. Excel appends a number to duplicates to make them unique.

> **Troubleshooting**
> Is the Table Tools Design tab not available when you want to select it? Check to make sure the active cell is somewhere in the table you formatted. A worksheet can contain many tables. Excel only makes the Table Tools Design tab available when the active cell is part of a formatted table.

g. Scroll down until row 5 disappears at the top of the window.

Notice what happens to the column headers. If the active cell is inside a table, when you scroll table column headings off the visible application window, table column headings replace worksheet column headings.

h. Click the **Hourly Sales - Sunday** worksheet tab. Select cell range **A5:P28**. In the Styles group, click **Format as Table**. Under Medium table styles, select **Table Style Medium 10**. The Format As Table dialog box appears. Be sure **My table has headers** is checked, and then click **OK**.

i. Click the **DESIGN** tab, and then in the Tools group, click **Convert to Range**. In the alert box that appears, click **Yes**.

Convert to Range removes all table functionality, but leaves in place the headers and cell formatting of the selected table design. This is a great way to quickly format a range with a theme and row banding, but if you do not want the data filtering and other table features, you can keep the visual formatting.

j. Click cell **B6**, and then click **Save**.

Changing Themes

A **theme** is a collection of fonts, styles, colors, and effects associated with a theme name. The **default** theme, the theme that is automatically applied unless you specify otherwise, is the Office theme. Changing the assigned theme is a way to very quickly change the appearance of the worksheets in your workbook. When a different workbook theme is applied, the built-in cell styles in the Styles group on the Home tab change to reflect the new workbook theme. Applying a workbook theme assures a consistent, well-designed look throughout your workbook.

E02.13

To Change the Theme

a. Click the **Hourly Sales - Sunday** worksheet tab.

b. Click the **PAGE LAYOUT** tab, and then in the Themes group, click **Themes**. The Themes gallery is displayed.

c. Click the **Parallax** built-in theme. Note that any cell that was assigned a cell style now reflects the corresponding cell style in the Parallax theme and that the default font has changed to Corbel.

d. Click the **Hourly Sales - Monday** worksheet tab. In the Themes group, click **Themes**, and then click the **Metropolitan** theme.

The table styles applied to these worksheets reveal the extent to which a change in theme can change the appearance of a worksheet. Note also that themes affect the entire workbook. A theme cannot be selectively applied to individual worksheets in a workbook.

e. Click the **Weekly Sales** worksheet tab. Click the **HOME** tab.

Notice that the background colors that were set using cell formatting are also affected by the new workbook theme. Also notice that for any cell where a font was not explicitly set, the font has changed to Calibri Light.

f. Click **Save**.

REAL WORLD ADVICE | **Formatting Does Not Change the Data Value, But Formatting Can Make Information More Valuable**

Formatting affects how information is displayed and understood. It does not change the value stored in a cell. Special formatting characters such as the dollar sign ($) and comma (,) are not stored with values, but they make financial values easier to read and to understand. Formatting helps turn data into information.

The next time you are adding formatting to a worksheet, ask "Does this formatting make my worksheet easier to understand?" or "Does this formatting add value in other ways?" such as confirming your organizational identity or its look and feel. If the answer to both questions is "No," maybe you should reconsider.

Remember, formatting does not change a data value, but it certainly can add information value. If formatting does not add value, it is likely unnecessary and may detract from the overall value of your worksheet. Consider your formatting decisions carefully.

Creating Information for Decision Making

In Excel, new information is most often produced through the use of functions or formulas to make calculations against data in the workbook.

Often, the objective is to improve decision making by providing additional information. In this section, you will manipulate data using functions and formulas and add information using conditional formatting to highlight or categorize information based on problem-specific parameters.

Create Information with Functions

Functions are one of Excel's most powerful features. A **function** is a program that performs operations on data. Function syntax takes the following form:

function name (argument 1,..., argument n)

where "function name" is the name of the function, and **arguments** inside the parentheses are the values the function requires. Different functions require different arguments. Arguments can be entered as letters, numbers, cell references, cell ranges, or other functions. Some functions do not require any arguments at all. There are more than 400 functions built into Excel that can be categorized as financial, statistical, mathematical, date and time, text, and several others—collectively these are referred to, not surprisingly, as **built-in functions**.

Part of what makes functions so useful is the use of cell references as arguments. Cell references enable you to use information from a particular cell or cell range in a function. Recall that a **cell reference** is the combination of a cell's column and row addresses. When a function that includes a cell reference as an argument is copied, the cell reference is changed to reflect the copied location relative to the original location. For example, say a function in cell B26 calculates the sum of cells B1:B25; if you copy the function from cell B26 to cell C26, the function in cell C26 will automatically be changed to summate C1:C25—the copied function will be relatively adjusted one column to the right.

Using the SUM, COUNT, AVERAGE, MIN, and MAX Functions

Of the more than 400 functions built into Excel, commonly used functions such as SUM, COUNT, AVERAGE, MIN, and MAX are readily available via the AutoSum Σ AutoSum button in the Function Library group on the Formulas tab, or in the Editing group on the Home tab. There are two ways to use AutoSum functions. You either select the **destination cell**, the cell that is to contain the function, or the "destination" of the AutoSum operation; you can also select the **source cell(s)**, the cell(s) that contain the data supplied to the function.

When you invoke AutoSum with the destination cell(s) selected, Excel inspects your worksheet and automatically includes a range adjacent to the active cell. Adjacent cells above the active cell are used by default. If there are no adjacent cells above, then adjacent cells to the left are used for the range. Excel does not inspect cell ranges to the right or below the active cell.

If a column of source cells is selected, if the cell at the bottom of the selected range does not contain data, the bottom cell is treated as the destination cell. If a row of source cells is selected, if the far-right cell in the selected range does not contain data, the far-right cell is treated as the destination cell. If the bottom or far-right cell contains data, the next open cell is used as the destination cell. Table 3 contains examples of the different ways in which data can be included in a function.

Type of Data	Function
Numbers	=SUM(1,3,5,7,11,13)
Cell range	=AVERAGE(B3:B25)
List of noncontiguous cells	=COUNT(B3,B9,C5,D14)
Column or columns	=SUM(J:J) or =AVERAGE(J:L)
Row or rows	=MIN(9:9) or =MAX(9:11)
Combination	=MIN(B3,B9:B15,C12/100,D:E)

Table 3 Function variations

Using the SUM Function by Selecting Destination Cells

The SUM function produces a sum of all numeric information in a specified range, list of numbers, list of cells, or any combination. In the next exercise you will generate new information in the Weekly Sales worksheet by selecting destination cells and inserting the SUM function.

E02.14

To Use the SUM Function by Selecting Destination Cells

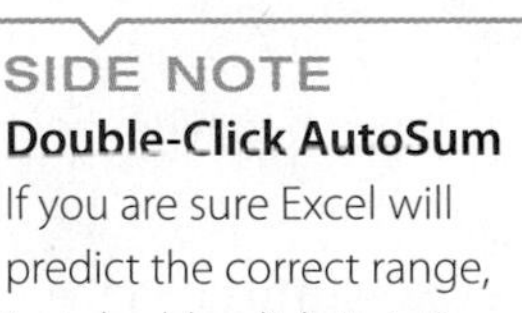

SIDE NOTE
Double-Click AutoSum
If you are sure Excel will predict the correct range, just double-click AutoSum.

a. Click the **Weekly Sales** worksheet tab.

b. Click cell **B9**. On the HOME tab, in the Editing group, click **AutoSum** [Σ AutoSum]. Excel inspects the cells above B9 and suggests that you want to sum range B6:B8 by surrounding it with a dashed, moving border. Since the suggested range is correct, press [Enter].

c. Select cell range **C9:H9**, press and hold [Ctrl], and then select cell ranges **B14:H14, B18:H18, B26: H26, I6:I9, I11:I14, I16:I18**, and **I20:I26**. Click **AutoSum** [Σ AutoSum].

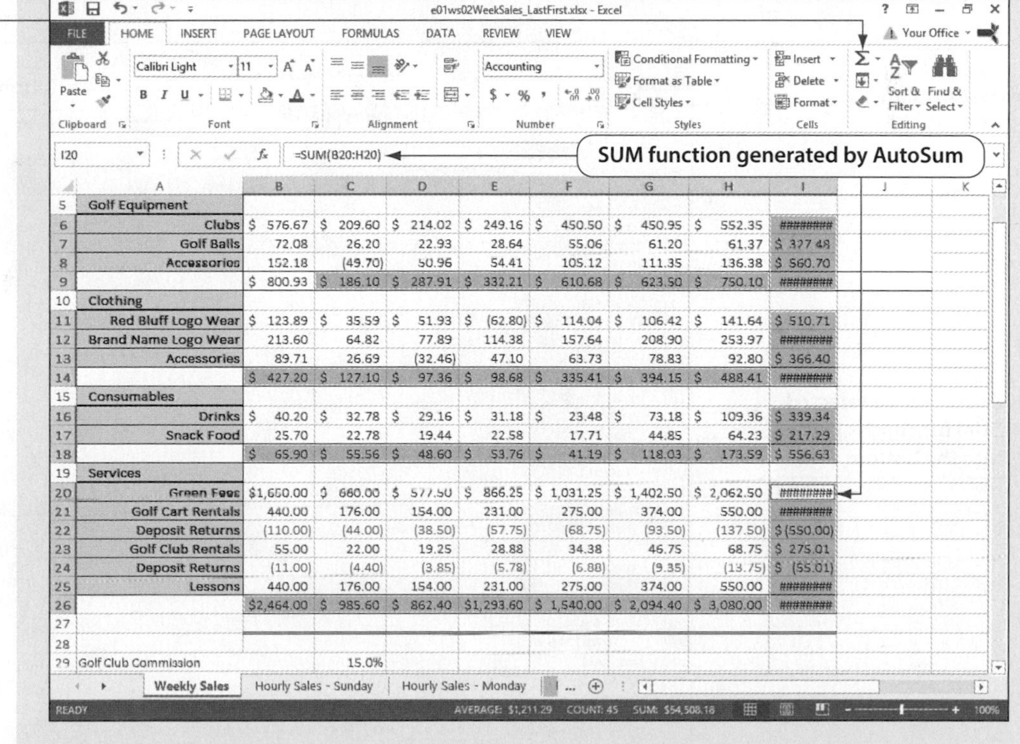

Figure 10 SUM function

d. In the Cells group, click **Format**, and then click **AutoFit Column Width**.

AutoSum will operate on noncontiguous cell ranges as well, but it must be handled a little differently. To calculate the total sales for each day, you must sum the category totals.

e. Click cell **B27**, and then click **AutoSum** [Σ AutoSum ▾]. AutoSum recognizes that cell B26 contains a SUM function and only selects B26 as the predicted range. Press and hold Ctrl, select cells **B18**, **B14**, and **B9**, and then click **AutoSum** [Σ AutoSum ▾] again.

f. Drag the **fill handle** and expand the active cell to encompass cell range **B27:I27**. If any of the cells display number signs, in the Cells group, click **Format**, and then click **AutoFit Column Width**.

g. Click **Save** [💾].

SIDE NOTE
SUM Shortcut
SUM can be quickly invoked by pressing Alt+=.

Using the SUM Function by Selecting Source Cells

Inserting a function using AutoSum after selecting source cells works particularly well when the source range does not contain contiguous data, as in the Hourly Sales - Sunday worksheet. In the next exercise, you will generate new information in the Hourly Sales - Sunday worksheet by selecting source cells and inserting a SUM function using the AutoSum button.

E02.15

To Use the SUM Function by Selecting Source Cells

a. Click the **Hourly Sales - Sunday** worksheet tab. Double-click the **HOME** tab to hide the Ribbon and make more of the worksheet visible.

b. Select cell range **B29:B6**. If you start your selection with the cell where you wish to insert the SUM(), then when the function is inserted you will see it in the formula bar. Press Alt+= to insert a SUM function.

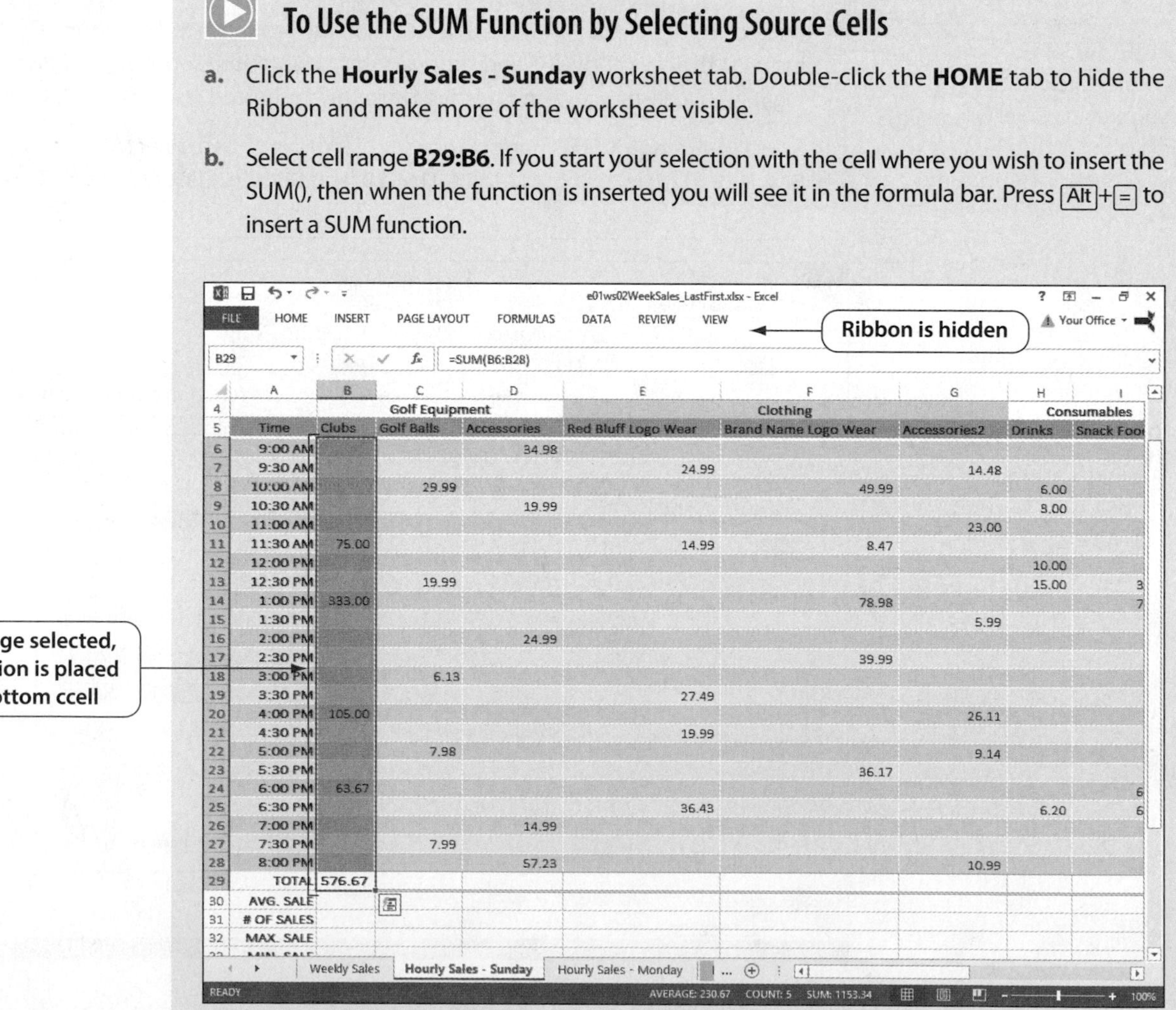

Figure 11 Inserting a SUM function with source cells selected

Since the bottom cell in the selected range did not contain data, the SUM function is placed into cell B29.

c. Select cell range **B6:O6**, and then press Alt+=.
Since the far-right cell in the selected range contained data, the SUM function is placed into cell P6, the next open cell to the right. Now you could use Auto Fill to complete the summations for columns C:P and rows 7:28, but there is a way to use AutoSum to insert all of the formulas at once.

d. Select cell range **B6:P29**. You have included a row of empty cells below your destination range and a column of empty cells to the right of your destination range. In this case, you are actually selecting both the source and destination cells. Press Alt+=. You may have to scroll to the right to see column P.

e. Double-click the **HOME** tab to unhide the Ribbon, press Ctrl+Home to deselect the selected range and select cell **A1**. Click **Save**.

Using COUNT and AVERAGE

The **COUNT function** returns the number of cells in a cell range that contain numbers. It can be used to generate information such as the number of sales in a period by counting invoice numbers, the number of people in a group by counting Social Security numbers, and so on.

The **AVERAGE function** returns a weighted average from a specified range of cells. The sum of all numeric values in the range is calculated and then divided by the count of numbers in the range. Essentially the AVERAGE function is SUM/COUNT.

COUNT and AVERAGE can be inserted in any manner by which the SUM function can be inserted. In the next exercise, you will calculate averages and counts for the Hourly Sales - Sunday worksheet and take advantage of AutoSum's feature that places results in the first open cell following a selected destination range.

E02.16

To Use the COUNT and AVERAGE Functions

a. Click the **Hourly Sales - Sunday** worksheet.

b. Select cell range **B6:P28**. In the Editing group, click the **AutoSum** arrow Σ AutoSum ▾.

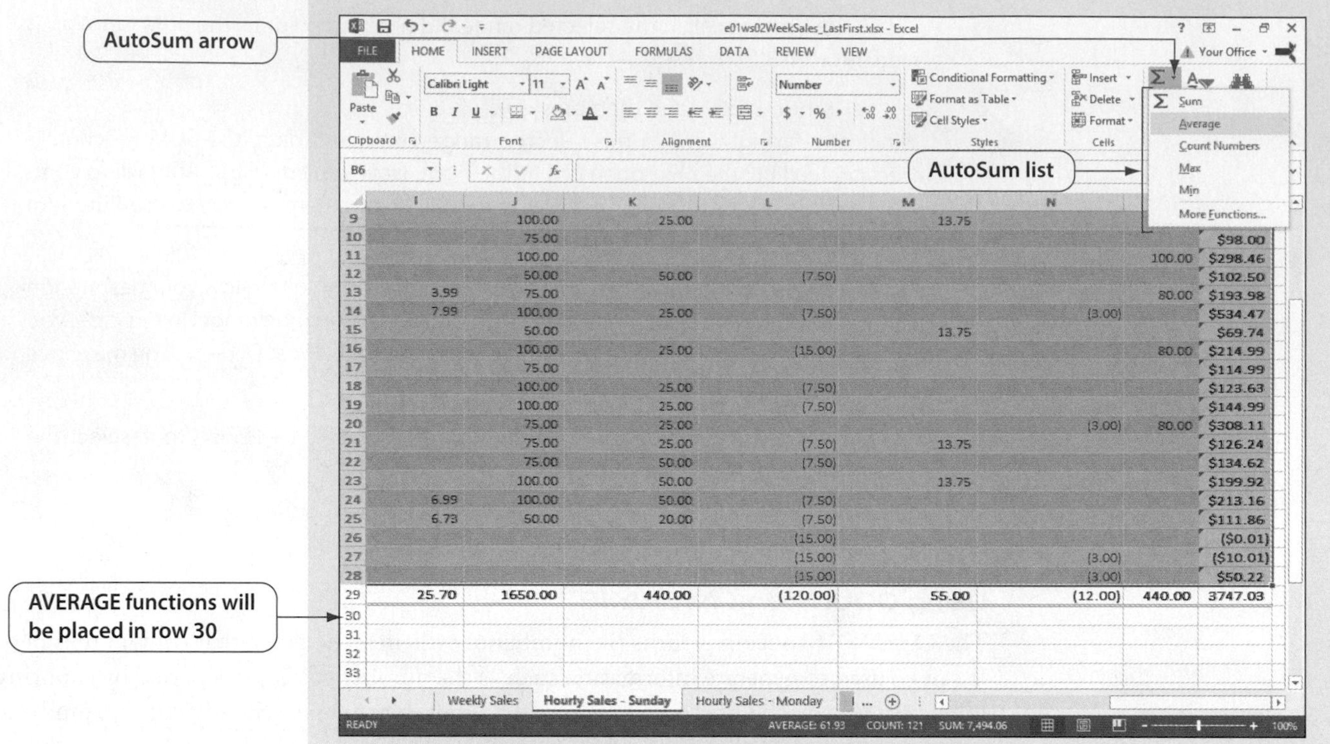

Figure 12 AutoSum AVERAGE function

Select **Average**. Click cell **P30**.

Notice that Excel expanded the selected range to include row 29, but inserted the AVERAGE functions into row 30, the first available empty cells below the selected destination range. Also notice that the AVERAGE function in cell P30 does not include row 29; it includes the rows specified in the originally selected range.

c. Select cell range **B6:O28**, click the **AutoSum** arrow [Σ AutoSum ▾], and then select **Count Numbers**. You do not select column P for this calculation because a count of the number of half-hour periods in the sales day, which is what a count of the numbers in column P would represent, would not be of any value.

Once again, AutoSum expanded the selected range to include row 29, but this time inserted the COUNT functions into row 31, the first available empty cells below the selected destination range.

d. Click **Save** [save icon].

SIDE NOTE

Shift+↑

Use this key combination to decrease the selected range by 1 row rather than reselect the entire range.

Using MIN and MAX

An average gives you an incomplete picture. If your instructor stated that the average on the exam is 75%, you do not have any information about the actual score distribution. Everyone in the class may have gotten a C with the low of 71% and high of 79%. Conversely, no one may have gotten a C with half the class getting an A and half getting an F. Both situations could have a 75% average but are very different distributions. The average should never be relied on without looking at additional statistics that help complete the picture. While many statistics exist to do this, the minimum and the maximum value provide at least a little more insight into the distribution of data by defining the extremes. The **MIN function** and **MAX function** examine all numeric values in a specified range and return the minimum value and the maximum value, respectively.

E02.17

To Use the MIN and MAX Functions

a. Click the **Hourly Sales - Sunday** worksheet tab.

b. Select cell range **B6:P28**, click the **AutoSum** arrow [Σ AutoSum ▾], and then select **Max**.
The MAX functions were inserted into row 32, the first available empty row below the selected destination range.

c. Rather than select cell range **B6:P28** over again, press [Shift]+[↑] to remove row 29 from the selected range. Cell range B6:P28 should now be selected. Click the **AutoSum** arrow [Σ AutoSum ▾], and then select **Min**.
The MIN functions were inserted into row 33, the first available empty row below the selected destination range. The functions inserted into the Hourly Sales - Sunday worksheet can be used to calculate the same values in the Hourly Sales - Monday worksheet. They simply need to be copied between worksheets.

d. Click the header for row **29**, press and hold [Shift], and then click the header for row **33**. In the Clipboard group, click **Copy**.

e. Click the **Hourly Sales - Monday** worksheet tab, click cell **A29**, and then in the Clipboard group, click **Paste**.

29	TOTAL	209.60	26.20	49.70	35.59	64.82	26.69	32.78	22
30	AVG. SALE	69.87	8.73	24.85	17.80	12.96	6.67	5.46	7
31	# OF SALES	3	3	2	2	5	4	6	
32	MAX. SALE	75.00	9.90	24.99	20.60	19.99	9.99	9.00	10
33	MIN. SALE	63.67	7.98	24.71	14.99	9.99	1.99	1.78	4

Weekly Sales | Hourly Sales - Sunday | Hourly Sales - Monday

READY AVERAGE: 55.60156257 COUNT: 79 SUM: 4114.51563 100%

Figure 13 AVERAGE, COUNT, MAX, and MIN functions

The functions in rows 29:33 in the Hourly Sales - Sunday worksheet have been copied to the same locations in the Hourly Sales - Monday worksheet.

f. Click **Save**.

Calculate Totals in a Table

When a range is formatted as a table, the range is structured such that every column is assigned a name, either by the user or automatically by Excel. Data in a table can be easily sorted and/or filtered by the values in each column. When you filter data, you choose which data are visible and which data are not. Visible data are included in table calculations and hidden data are not.

Using Tables and the Total Row

An Excel table can include a total row that allows you to calculate a number of different statistics for each column in the table. The Hourly Sales - Monday worksheet has been formatted as a table. In the next exercise, you will add a total row and use the total row to sum each column in the table.

To generate a statistic such as the sum, average, or standard deviation in a total row, you click the filter arrow and select from the menu. A table total row uses the SUBTOTAL function to generate values. The **SUBTOTAL function** calculates results based on only data that is visible in a table, so you can filter table data and the SUBTOTAL values will automatically recalculate.

Further, when calculating values from a table, you can reference data in the table using structured references. An extensive discussion of structured references is outside the scope of this workshop, but since a table is a data structure defined by its column titles, you can perform calculations by referencing the column titles—the structure identifiers—in the table.

E02.18

To Use Sum in a Table Total Row and Filter the Results

a. Click the **Hourly Sales - Monday** worksheet tab.

b. Click cell **B28** to place the active cell inside the table range. The TABLE TOOLS DESIGN tab is displayed. Click the **DESIGN** tab, and then in the Table Style Options group, click the **Total Row** check box.

This adds a special total row that works with the table format to total each column as you specify. Notice that the formulas you copied into this worksheet in the previous exercise have been moved down one row.

c. Click cell **B29**, and then click the **function list** arrow next to cell B29.

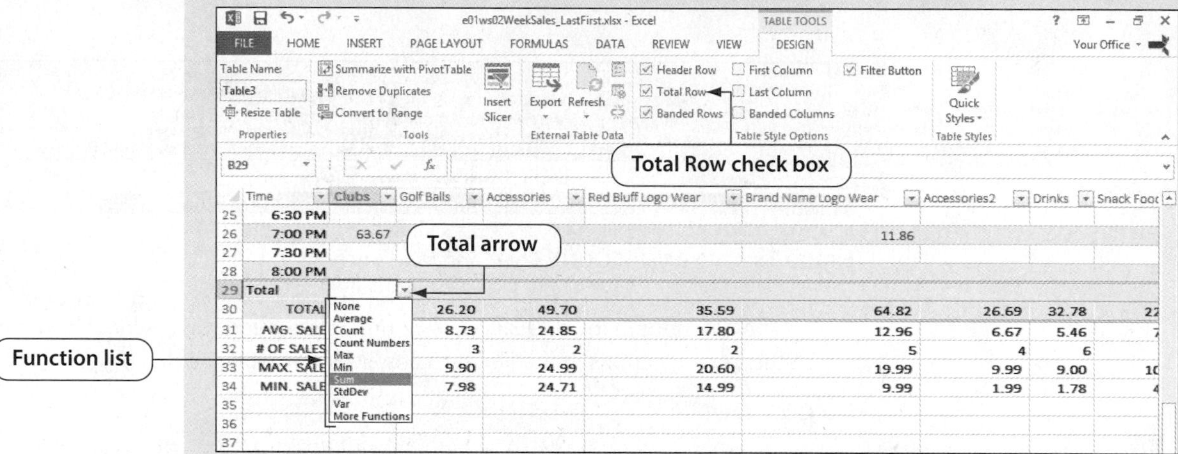

Figure 14 Calculating the sum in a table total row

d. Select **Sum**.

Excel does not need to predict the summed range for a table. It automatically sums all the visible rows in the table column. Notice the formula bar. Even though you selected Sum from the Table Totals menu, Excel uses a SUBTOTAL function in a table total row. The **SUBTOTAL function** can return any of 11 different values including all of the AutoSum functions, the product, standard deviation, and variance.

SIDE NOTE

What Is the SUBTOTAL Function?

To learn more about the SUBTOTAL function, press F1, type SUBTOTAL into Search Help, and then press Enter.

e. Drag the **fill handle** to copy cell B29 to cell range **C29:P29**. If the table range is scrolled off the top of the window, expand the cell range to include the column titled **Total.** If any cells in the total row contain # signs, select those cells. Click the **HOME** tab, and then in the Cells group, click **Format**, and then select **AutoFit Column Width**.

f. Press Ctrl+Home, and then click the **filter** arrow in cell **A5**. Since this is the Time column, you can filter the table data by selecting—or deselecting—values in the time column. Click **(Select All)** to deselect all time values in the table. Then click **9:00, 9:30, 10:00, 10:30, 11:00** and **11:30.** This will filter the table to display only sales in the morning hours.

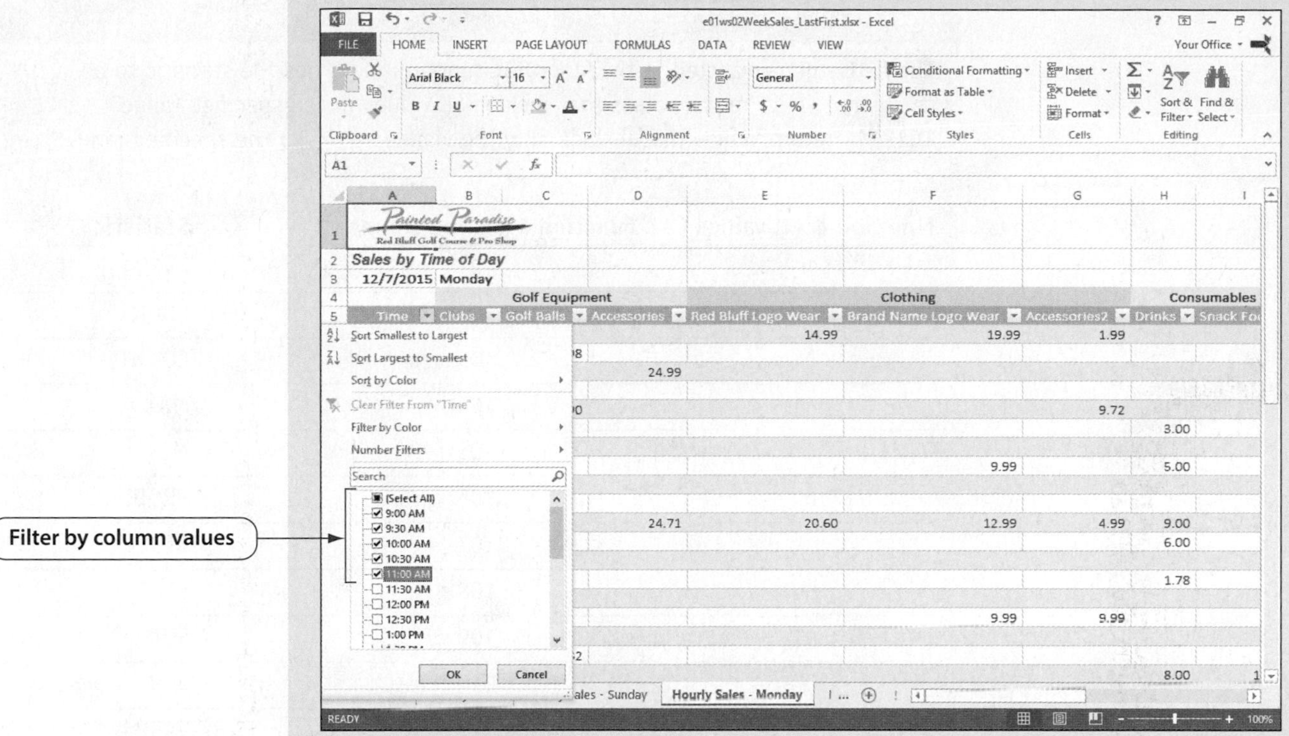

Figure 15 Table filter menu

g. Click **OK**, and then click cell **B29**.

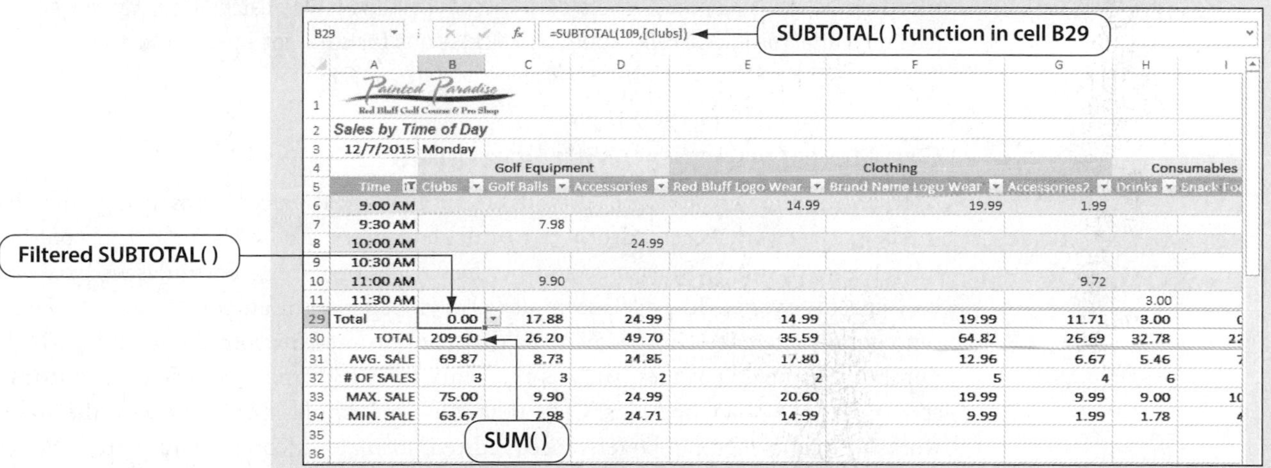

Figure 16 Filtered table total row

Notice in Figure 16 that the Total values in row 29 no longer equal the TOTAL values in row 30. The SUBTOTAL function used to calculate the sums in row 29 only include the visible data. You filtered the table to exclude all hours 12:00 PM or later, notice that rows 12:28 are hidden—rows 12:28 are not included in the SUBTOTAL calculations in row 29.

In Figure 16, notice the formula bar displays the function in cell B29: =SUBTOTAL(109,[Clubs]). This formula uses a structured reference that is unique to tables in Excel. It is the equivalent of =SUBTOTAL(109,B6:B28), but it uses the column name in the table to identify the range against which the function is to act. The number "109" indicates that the SUBTOTAL function is to calculate a sum. The following Quick Reference lists the values for different SUBTOTAL statistics.

h. Click **Save**.

QUICK REFERENCE | **The SUBTOTAL Function**

The first argument listed in the SUBTOTAL function identifies the statistic to be calculated. 1–11 return values that include all values in the specified range. 101–111 return values that include only the visible values in the specified range.

Function # All values	Function # Visible values	Statistic
1	101	AVERAGE
2	102	COUNT
3	103	COUNTA
4	104	MAX
5	105	MIN
6	106	PRODUCT
7	107	STDEV
8	108	STDEVP
9	109	SUM
10	110	VAR
11	111	VARP

One quirk associated with the SUBTOTAL function is that when it is used to calculate statistics against a table, the function number visibility is irrelevant. For example, if you specify function number 9, and then filter the table data such that only part of the table data is visible, only visible data will be included in the calculation. Value visibility is only a factor in SUBTOTAL function calculations for data not included in a table.

Create Information with Formulas

A **formula** allows you to perform basic mathematical calculations using information in the active worksheet and others to calculate new values; formulas can contain cell references, constants, functions, and mathematical operators. Formulas in Excel have a very specific syntax. In Excel, formulas always begin with an equal sign (=). Formulas can contain references to specific cells that contain information; a **constant**, which is a number that never changes, such as the value for π (pi); **mathematical operators** such as +, – , *, /, ^; and functions. Cells that contain formulas can be treated like any other worksheet cell. They can be referenced, edited, formatted, copied, and pasted.

If a formula contains a cell reference, when copied and then pasted into a new location, the cell reference in the formula changes. The new cell reference reflects a new location relative to the old location. This is called a **relative cell reference**. For example, as shown in Figure 17, when the formula in the left column is copied one column to the right and two rows down, the cell references in the formula change to reflect the destination cell relative to the original cell. Consequently, columns A and J are changed to B and K respectively—one column right, and rows 3 and 12 are changed to 5 and 14, two rows down. Note that the column and row numbers of the cells that contain the formulas are not shown in Figure 17. The active cell address does not matter in relative addressing. All that matters is the relative shift in columns and rows from source to destination, and the cell references in the formula.

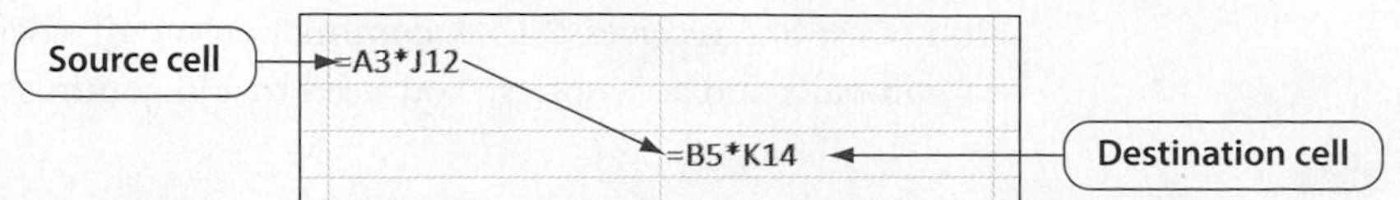

Figure 17 Relative referencing when copying from a source cell to a destination cell

Relative cell references allow you to reuse formulas in a well-designed worksheet. You can enter a formula once and use it many times without having to reenter it in each location and change the cell references. Simply copy and paste it to a new location.

Further, relative references adjust formulas to ensure correctness when the structure of the worksheet changes. If a column is inserted to the left of a cell referenced in a formula, or a row is inserted above a cell referenced in a formula, the cells referenced by the formula will be adjusted to ensure the formula still references the same relative locations.

Using Operators

Excel formulas are constructed using basic mathematical operators very similar to those used in a mathematics and exactly the same as used in most programming languages. Table 4 contains the mathematical operators recognized in Excel.

Operation	Operator	Example	Formula Entered in Current Cell
Addition	+	=B4+B5	Assign the sum of B4 and B5 to the current cell.
Subtraction	-	=B5-B4	Assign the difference of B4 and B5 to the current cell.
Multiplication	*	=B5*3.14	Assign B5 multiplied by 3.14 to the current cell.
Division	/	=B5/B4	Assign the result of dividing B5 by B4 to the current cell.
Exponentiation	^	=B4^2	Assign the square of B4 to the current cell.

Table 4 Mathematical operators in Excel

SIDE NOTE
Copy a Formula and Not Change Relative References
Select the formula in the formula bar, click [copy icon], press Esc, and then Paste.

SIDE NOTE
How to Remember Order of Operations
P arentheses
E xponentiation
D ivision and/or
M ultiplication
A ddition and/or
S ubtraction.

Applying Order of Operations

Order of operations is the order in which Excel processes calculations in a formula that contains more than one operator. Mathematical operations execute in a specific order:

1. Parentheses
2. Exponentiation
3. Multiplication and division
4. Addition and subtraction

Excel scans a formula from left to right while performing calculations using the above order of operation rules. Thus you can control which part of a calculation is performed first by enclosing parts of a formula in parentheses. Portions of a formula enclosed in parentheses are evaluated first, following the previously listed order. Table 5 contains some examples of the effect of order of operations on formula results.

Formula	Result	Formula	Result
=4-2*5^2	-46	=(5+5)*4/2-3*6	2
=(4-2)*5^2	50	=(5+5)*4/(2-3)*6	-240
=5+5*4/2-3*6	-3	=(5+5)*4/(2-3*6)	-2.5

Table 5 Order of operations

Golf pro John Schilling is paid a commission of sales. He receives 70% of all lesson fees received by the Pro Shop. Pro Shop manager Aleeta Herriott is in charge of all golf club sales. She receives a 15% commission on all sales of clubs and a 10% commission on golf balls and accessories. You need to add commission calculations to the worksheet.

E02.19

To Calculate Commissions Using Formulas

a. Click the **Weekly Sales** worksheet tab.

b. Select cell **J25**. In this cell, you will calculate the commissions John Schilling earned on golf lessons. The total revenue from golf lessons for the week is in cell I25, and the commission paid for golf lessons is in cell C33. Type =I25*C33.

SIDE NOTE
Enter Formulas with the Mouse
To enter the formula in J25 without typing cell references, type =, click cell I25, type *, click cell C33, and press Enter

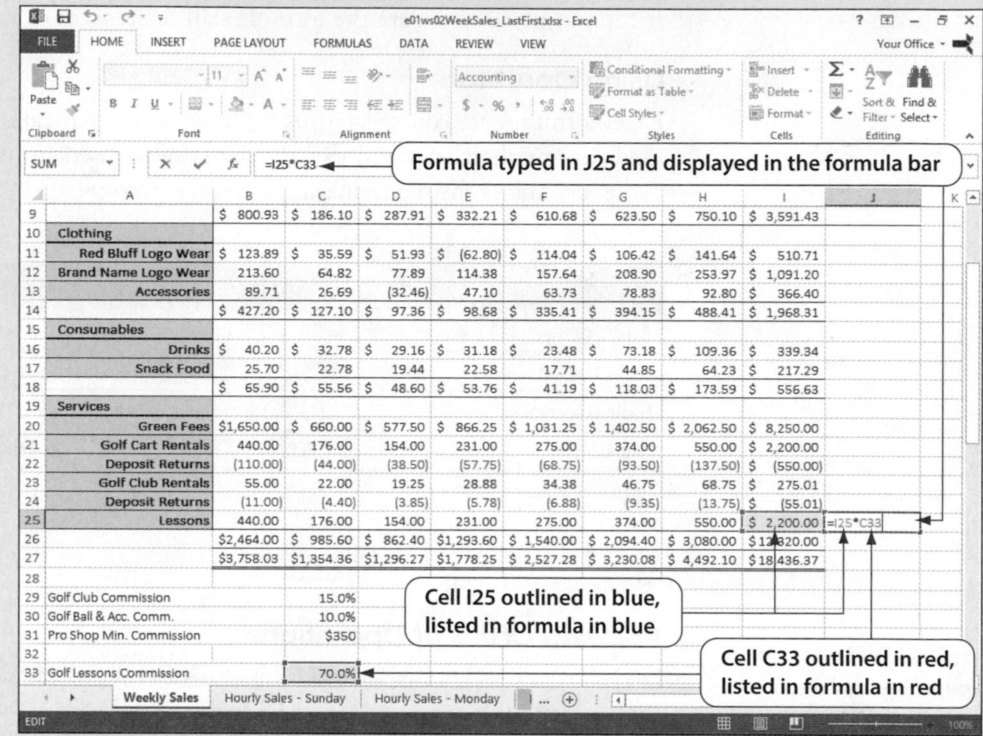

Figure 18 Entering a formula into a cell

c. Press Enter.

d. Click cell **J6**. In this cell, you need to calculate the commissions that Aleeta Herriott earned selling golf clubs in the Pro Shop. To multiply the total golf club sales for the week by the commission percentage on golf club sales, type =I6*C29 and then press Enter.

e. In cell **J7**, calculate the commission earned on Pro Shop accessories. To multiply the sum of golf ball and accessory sales for the week by the appropriate commission, type =(I7+I8)*C30 and then press Enter.

f. In cell **J9**, sum Aleeta Herriott's commissions. Type =SUM(J6:J7), and then press Enter.

g. Click **Save**.

SIDE NOTE
A Faster Way to Sum Commissions
In cell J9, double-click AutoSum Σ and you will generate the same result without typing the formula.

Troubleshooting

Excel allows you to copy formulas from one location to another and adjusts cell references to ensure calculation accuracy. This is not necessarily true when a formula is moved from one location to another, however. If you move a formula by dragging it from one location to another, cell references do not change. Be sure you double-check a formula after you move it to ensure it is still producing a correct result.

REAL WORLD ADVICE An Alternative to Typing Cell References

An alternative, and more accurate, method to typing cell references into a formula is to type only the operators and then select the cells from the worksheet. The steps to enter the daily sales total in the Weekly Sales worksheet would be as follows:

1. Select cell B27.
2. Type =.
3. Click cell B9, and then type +.
4. Click cell B14, and then type +.
5. Click cell B18, and then type +.
6. Click cell B26, and then press Enter.

This method of building formulas is much less error prone than typing cell references. Learning this methodology would be worth your effort.

Use Conditional Formatting to Assist Decision Making

As discussed previously, one of the primary purposes of information analysis in Excel worksheets is to assist in decision making. People are often influenced by the format by which information is presented. Worksheets can be huge—thousands of rows and dozens of columns of information. The number of calculated items can be daunting to analyze, digest, and interpret. To the extent Excel can be used to assist the decision maker in understanding information, decision making speed and quality should improve.

Conditional formatting is one way Excel can aid the decision maker by changing the way information is displayed based on rules specific to the problem the worksheet is designed to address.

Highlighting Values in a Range with Conditional Formatting

Conditional formatting allows the specification of rules that apply formatting to a cell as determined by the rule outcome. It is a way to dynamically change the visual presentation of information in a manner that adds information to the worksheet.

Conditional formatting can be used to highlight information by changing cell fill color, font color, font style, font size, border, number format, and by adding visual cues like scales and icons. In the next exercise, you will apply conditional formatting to highlight the sales figures in each category that are above average for each day's sales.

E02.20

To Highlight High and Low Category Sales and to Display Negative Accounting Number Formatted Cells in Red

a. Click the **Weekly Sales** worksheet tab.

b. Select cell range **B9:H9**. Click the **HOME** tab, and then in the Styles group, click **Conditional Formatting**. Point to **Top/Bottom Rules**, and then select **Top 10 Items**. In the Top 10 Items dialog box, in the Format cells that rank in the TOP box, double-click **10**, and then type 1. Click the **with** arrow.

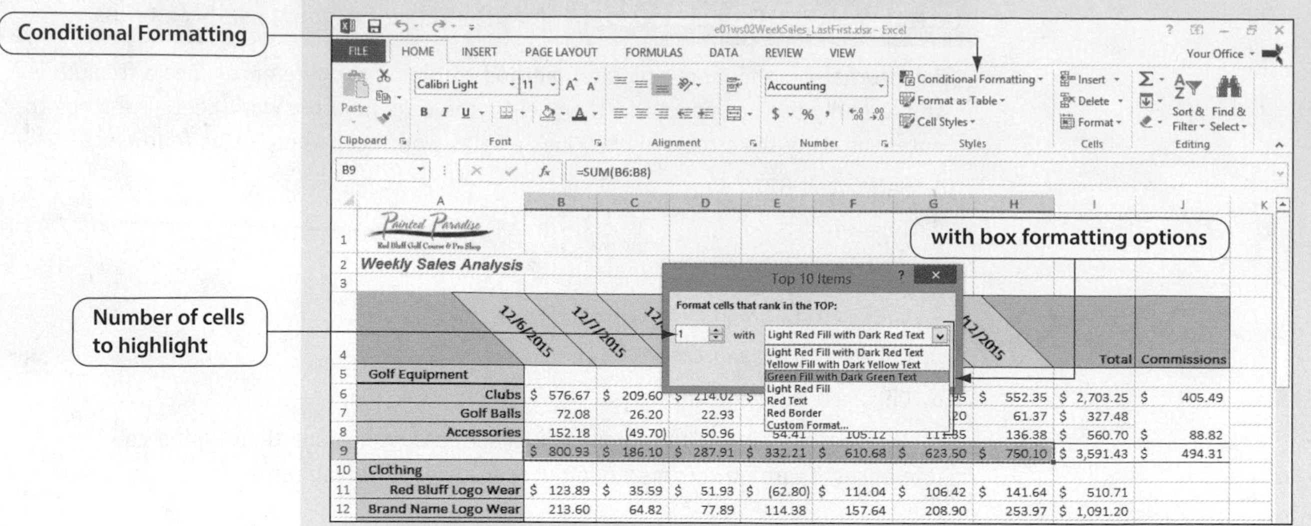

Figure 19 Top 10 Items dialog box

c. Select **Green Fill with Dark Green Text**, and then click **OK**.

d. In the Styles group, click **Conditional Formatting**, point to **Top/Bottom Rules**, and then select **Bottom 10 Items**. In the Bottom 10 Items dialog box, in the Format cells that rank in the BOTTOM box, double-click **10**, and then type 1. Click **OK**.

Now you can copy the formatting you just added to B9:H9 to the other category totals and to the overall totals in the Weekly Sales worksheet.

e. With cell range **B9:H9** still selected, in the Clipboard group, double-click **Format Painter**. Select cell ranges **B14:H14**. Select cell range **B18:H18**. Select cell range **B26:H26**. Select cell range **B27:H27**. Click **Format Painter** to turn off the Format Painter.

Recall that Accounting Number Format does not include the option to display negative numbers in red—notice cell C8. This can be accomplished with conditional formatting.

f. Select cell range **B6:I27**. In the Styles group, click **Conditional Formatting**, point to **Highlight Cells Rules**, and then click **Less Than**. In the Format cells that are LESS THAN box, type 0. Click the **with** box arrow, and then select **Red Text**. Click **OK**.

g. Click **Save**.

SIDE NOTE
(Numbers) in Blue?
In the with box, click Custom Format, click Color, and choose a different color for negative numbers.

Troubleshooting

Be sure to double-check the results of any copy-and-paste activity when conditional formatting is involved. A row of cells that contain conditional formatting was copied to the Clipboard. The row must be pasted from the Clipboard, using Paste Formatting one row at a time, or the conditional formatting rules will be broken.

Applying Conditional Formatting to Assess Benchmarks Using Icon Sets

Conditional formatting can also be used to highlight whether or not a value satisfies a particular criteria such as a benchmark. The staff in the Pro Shop is guaranteed a minimum commission amount—stored in cells C31 and C34. It is much preferable that a staff member's commissions exceed the minimum. You can use conditional formatting to clearly identify whether or not Aleeta Herriott's commissions in the Pro Shop and John Schilling's commissions for lessons exceed the contractual minimum.

E02.21

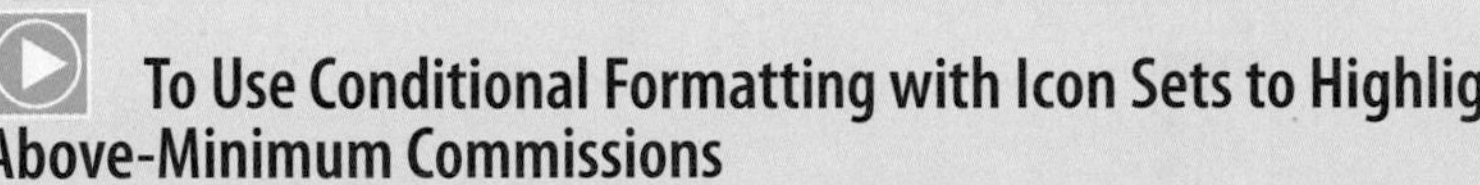

To Use Conditional Formatting with Icon Sets to Highlight Above-Minimum Commissions

a. Click cell **J9**. In the Styles group, click **Conditional Formatting**, point to **Icon Sets**, and then click **More Rules**. In the New Formatting Rule dialog box, under Select a Rule Type, make sure **Format all cells based on their values** is selected.

b. Under Edit the Rule Description, click the **Icon Style** arrow, and then click the first item in the list, **3 Arrows (Colored)**—you will have to scroll up.

c. Under **Icon**, click the **arrow** next to the yellow arrow, and then select the **red down arrow** for the middle Icon box—the Icon Style box will change to Custom. In the bottom Icon box, select **No Cell Icon**, and then select **Number** in both Type boxes.

d. Double-click in the top **Value** box and then press Delete. Click **Collapse dialog box** in the top Value box, select cell **C31**—the minimum commission for the Pro Shop manager, and then click the **Expand dialog box** icon.

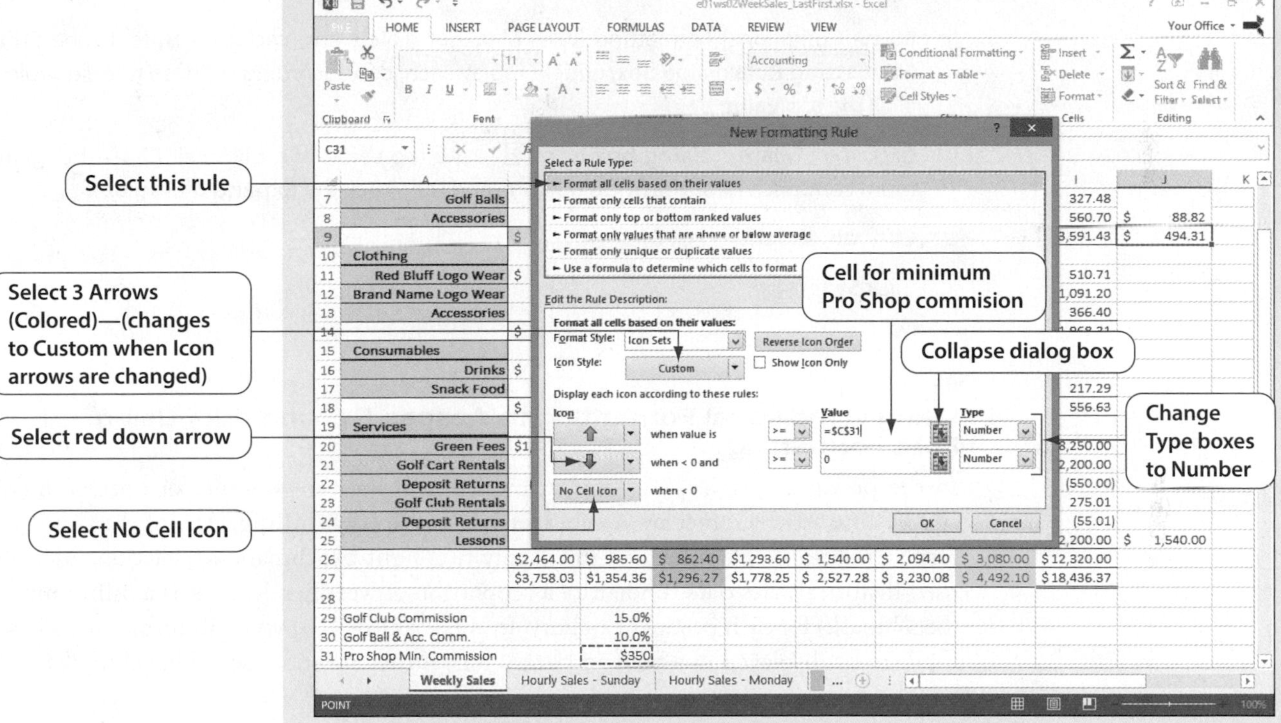

Figure 20 Conditional formatting using icon sets

e. Click **OK**. Now you can use the conditional format you just created for the golf lessons commission in cell J25.

f. With cell **J9** selected, click **Format Painter**, and then click cell **J25** to paste formatting, including conditional formatting.

g. In the Styles group, click **Conditional Formatting**, and then select **Manage Rules**. The Conditional Formatting Rules Manager dialog box is displayed.

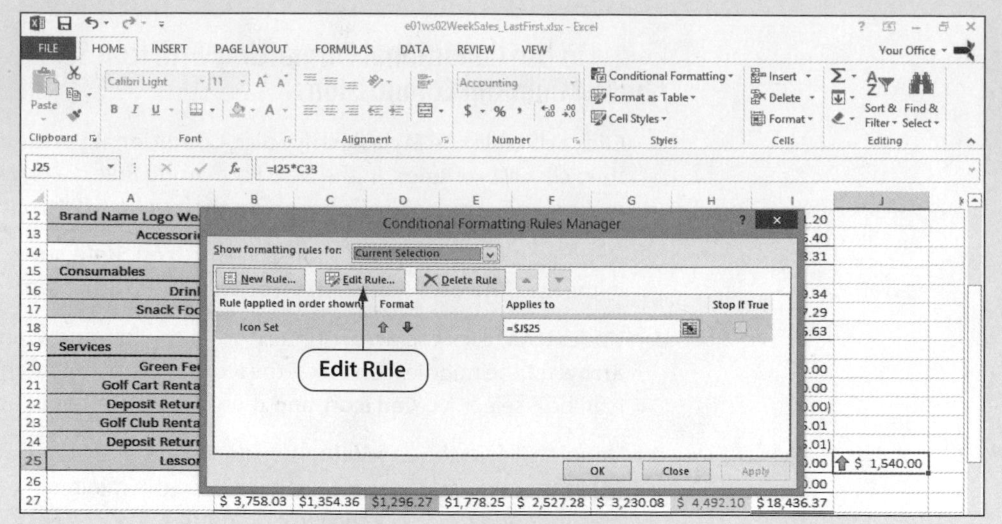

Figure 21 Conditional Formatting Rules Manager dialog box

h. In the Conditional Formatting Rules Manager dialog box, click **Edit Rule**. In the **Edit Formatting Rule** dialog box, under Display each icon according to these rules, double-click the top **Value** box.

i. Click the **Collapse dialog box** icon in the top Value box. Click cell **C34**—the minimum commission for the RBGC golf pro, and then click the **Expand dialog box**.

j. Click **OK**, and then click **OK**.

k. Click **Save**.

Using Conditional Formatting to Assess Benchmarks Using Font Formatting

In the previous exercise, you used arrow icons to indicate whether or not commission minimums had been met by Aleeta Herriott and John Schilling. Any of the conditional formatting features can be used to visually highlight benchmark satisfaction. Aleeta has used historical sales data to identify a proportion of weekly sales that is a minimum goal (benchmark) for each product category. In the next exercise, you will format weekly sales totals to be displayed in a bold and green font if they meet or exceed benchmarks.

E02.22

To Highlight Sales that Meet or Exceed Benchmarks

a. Click cell **I9**. In the Styles group, click **Conditional Formatting**. Point to **Highlight Cells Rules**, and then select **More Rules**. In the New Formatting Rule dialog box, under Select a Rule Type, click **Use a formula to determine which cells to format**.

b. In the **Format values where this formula is true** box, type =I9/I27>=C36 (golf equipment percentage of total sales compared to the golf equipment benchmark percentage of sales). Click **Format**. On the Font tab, in the Font style box, click **Bold**. Click the **Color** arrow.

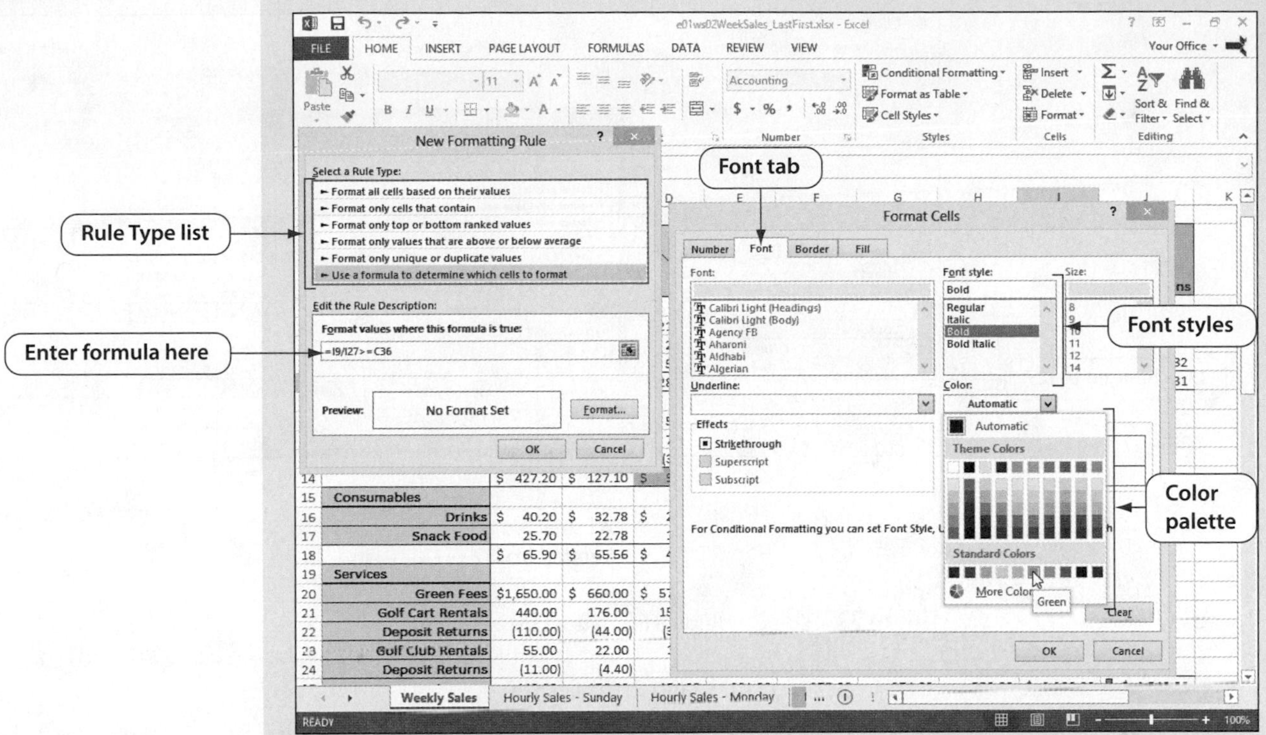

Figure 22 Conditional formatting using a formula

c. Under Standard Colors, click **Green**. Click **OK** two times. In the Cells group, click **Format**, and then select **AutoFit Column Width**. Now copy formatting from cell **I9** to the cells that contain the week's total sales for **Clothing** and **Consumables**.

d. With **I9** selected, double-click **Format Painter**. Click cell **I14**, and then click cell **I18**. Click **Format Painter** to turn it off. Copying formatting will have made some incorrect relative changes to the cell references in the formula you entered in Step b so you need to edit the copied rules.

e. Click cell **I14**, and then in the Styles group, click **Conditional Formatting**, and then select **Manage Rules**. Click the **Formula: = I14/I32>=C41** rule, and then click **Edit Rule**.

The source formula: =I9/I27>=C36 was adjusted relatively to =I14/I32>=C41. I32 is not the correct cell reference for the total sales weekly total, and C41 is not the correct cell reference for the benchmark percentage for Clothing.

f. In the **Format values where this formula is true** box, double-click **I32**, type I27, and then double-click **C41**.

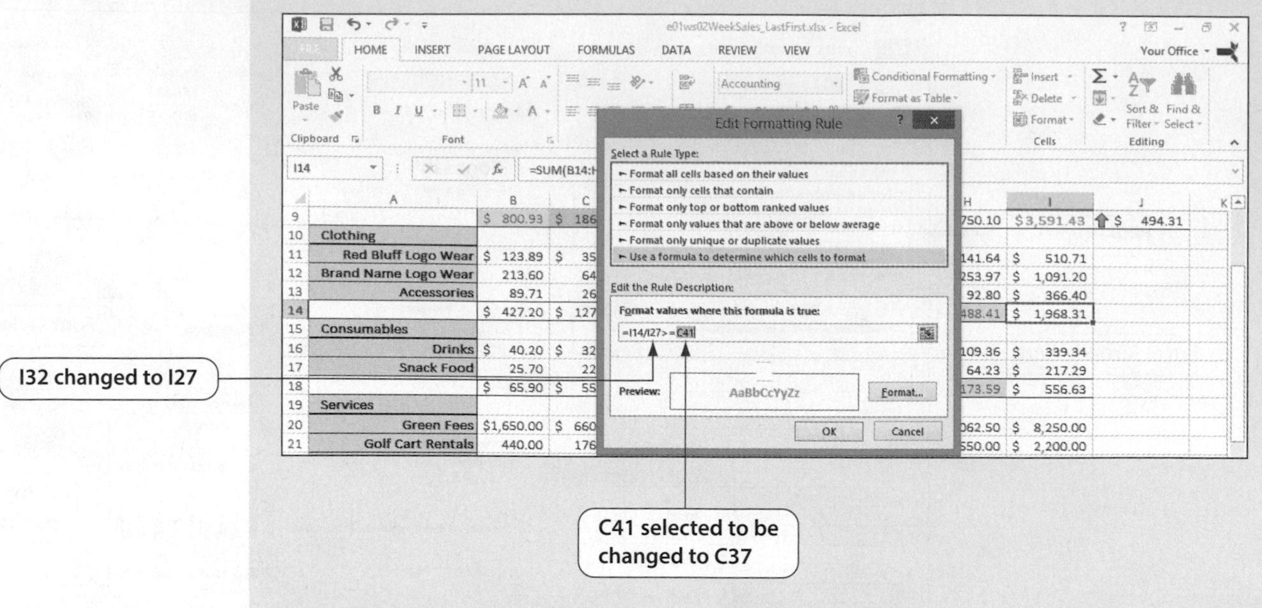

Figure 23 Edit conditional formatting using the Rules Manager

g. Type C37, click **OK**, and then click **OK**.

h. Click cell **I18**, and then in the Styles group, click **Conditional Formatting**, and then select **Manage Rules**. Click the **Formula: = I18/I36>=C45** rule, and then click **Edit Rule**.

i. In the **Format values where this formula is true** box, double-click **I36**, and then type I27. Double-click **C45**, type C38, click **OK**, and then click **OK**.

j. Click **Save**.

Removing Conditional Formatting

Once conditional formatting has been applied to a cell or range of cells, it may be necessary to remove the conditional formatting without affecting other cell formatting or cell contents. Conditional formatting can be removed from a selected cell or cell range, and it can be removed from the entire sheet, depending upon which option is chosen.

When you applied the conditional formatting to cell range B6:I27 that displayed negative numbers in red regardless of the number format, several cells that did not contain data were also conditionally formatted. Although applying conditional formatting to a large range of cells all at once is efficient, applying it to cells that do not contain data in the current design may cause unforeseen problems as the worksheet is modified in the future. You need to remove the conditional formatting in the empty cells.

CONSIDER THIS
How Might You Use Conditional Formatting?

Can you think of ways you could use conditional formatting in worksheets to aid personal decisions? Could you use conditional formatting as an aid in tracking your stock portfolio? Monthly budget and expenses? Checking account?

SIDE NOTE

View More of the Worksheet

Click the View tab, and in the Show group, uncheck Formula Bar. Double-click any Ribbon tab to hide the Ribbon.

E02.23

To Remove Conditional Formatting from a Range of Cells

a. Select cell range **B10:I10**, press Ctrl, and then select cell ranges **B15:I15** and **B19:I19**.

b. In the Styles group, click **Conditional Formatting**, and then click **Manage Rules**. Click the **Show formatting rules for** arrow, and then select **Current Selection**. The Conditional Formatting Rules Manger will display the rules applied in the currently selected cells. Click the **Cell Value < 0** rule.

Notice the Cell Value < 0 rule that was applied to the selected ranges even though the ranges do not contain any data.

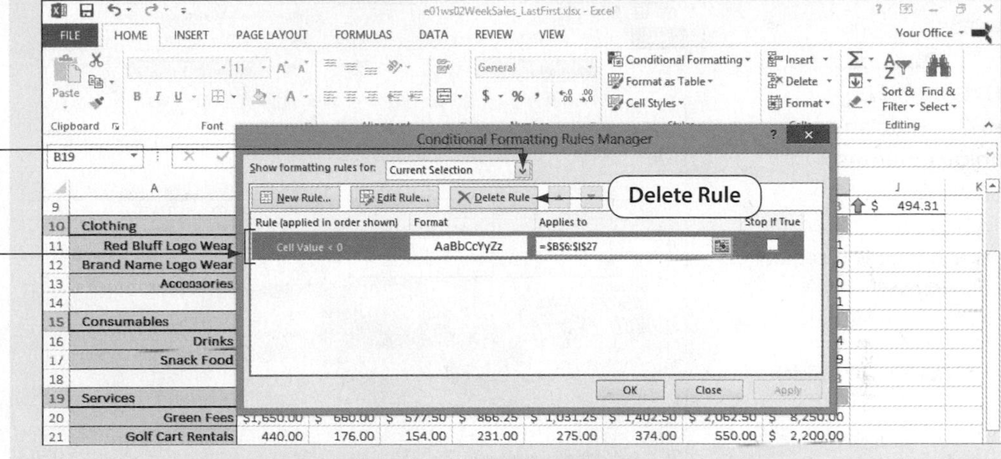

Figure 24 How to remove conditional formatting

c. Click **Delete Rule**, and then click **OK**.

d. Click **Save**.

SIDE NOTE

Another Way to Remove Conditional Formatting

Click Conditional Formatting, point to Clear Rules, and then select Clear Rules from Selected Cells.

Hide Information in a Worksheet

A worksheet can contain information that may not be necessary, or even desirable, to display. This is often true of a list of parameters. A **parameter** is a term generally used to describe a value included for calculation or comparison purposes that is stored in a single location such as a worksheet cell so that it can be used many times but be edited in a single location. Another example of hidden information would be hiding detailed information used to calculate totals until such time that the person using the worksheet would like to see it.

Hiding information in a worksheet is relatively simple. Entire worksheet rows and columns can be hidden. Simply select the rows and/or columns to be hidden by clicking on the row or column heading. Right-click with the mouse pointer over the heading or in the selected row(s) or column(s), and click Hide on the shortcut menu that appears.

Gridlines are very helpful in visualizing and navigating a workbook during development, but some feel they clutter a worksheet. Gridlines can be "hidden" simply by unchecking the Gridlines box in the Show group of the View tab.

Hiding Worksheet Rows

In the Weekly Sales worksheet, rows 29:38 contain parameters that are used to calculate commissions, to identify minimum commission levels, and to specify sales percentage benchmarks for golf equipment, clothing, and consumables. Once the Weekly Sales worksheet has been fully developed, there is little need to have this data visible. In fact, having this kind of data visible can be problematic in that a user could inadvertently, or intentionally, change the data and cause the worksheet to display incorrect information. In the next exercise you will hide rows 29:38 from view in the Weekly Sales worksheet.

E02.24

To Hide Rows in a Worksheet

SIDE NOTE
Unhide Hidden Rows
Select the rows above and below the hidden rows, right-click the selection, and then click Unhide in the shortcut menu.

SIDE NOTE
You Can Hide and Unhide Columns as Well
Select columns instead of rows, and use the shortcut menu just as when you hide or unhide rows.

a. Click the heading for row **29** in the **Weekly Sales** worksheet, press and hold Shift, and then click the **heading** for row **38**.

b. Right-click anywhere in the selected rows.

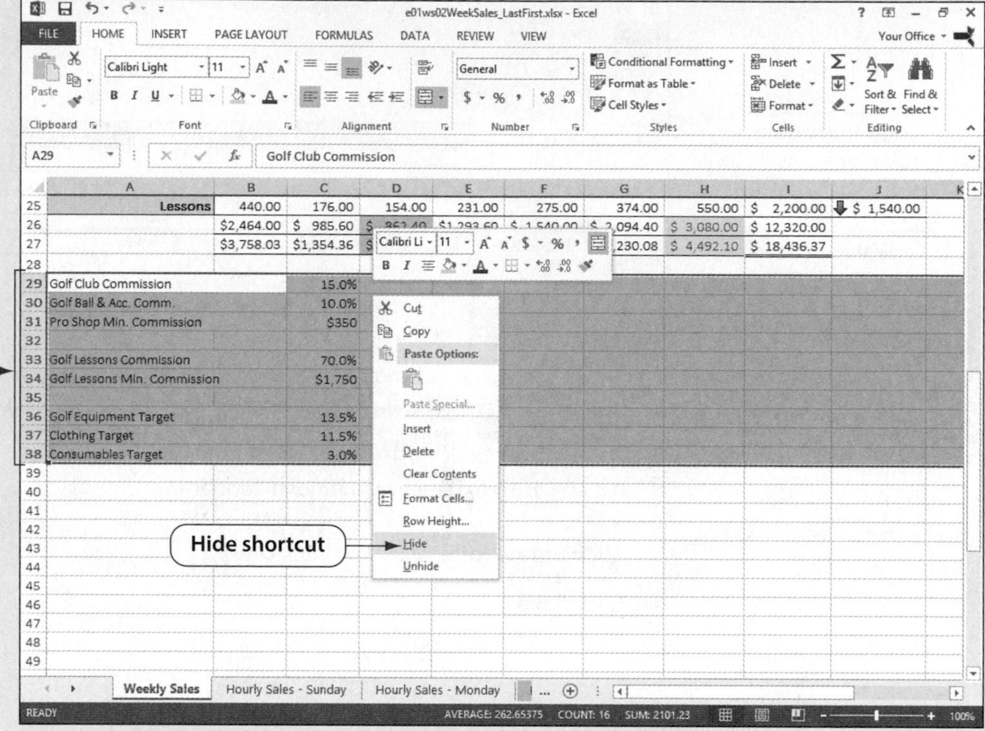

Figure 25 Hide rows using the shortcut menu

c. Select **Hide** on the shortcut menu.

d. Press Ctrl+Home, then click **Save**.

Hiding Worksheet Gridlines

Gridlines assist in identifying cells when manipulating a worksheet. Once a worksheet is complete, some people feel gridlines detract from a worksheet's professional appearance. In the next exercise, you will turn off, or hide, gridlines in the Weekly Sales worksheet.

E02.25

To Hide Gridlines in a Worksheet

a. Click the **VIEW** tab, and then in the Show group, click **Gridlines** to toggle gridlines off.
Notice that the worksheet now has a white background. To many users, this is much more visually appealing than a worksheet where gridlines are visible.

b. Click **Save**.

Document Functions and Formulas

An important part of building a good worksheet is documentation. Ms. Herriott included the standard documentation worksheet in the e01ws01WeeklySales workbook and updated it to reflect what she had accomplished prior to assigning completion of the workbook to you.

Showing Functions and Formulas

What is displayed in a cell that contains a function or a formula is the calculated result. The function or formula that generated the displayed value is only visible one cell at a time by selecting a cell and then looking at the formula bar. When Show Formulas is on, the calculated results are hidden, and functions and formulas are shown in the cells instead, whenever applicable.

Show Formulas is very helpful in understanding how a worksheet is structured. It is an essential aid when correcting errors or updating the function of a worksheet. A worksheet that has Show Formulas turned on can be printed and/or exported for documentation purposes.

E02.26

To View Worksheet Formulas and Export to PDF

a. Click the **Weekly Sales** worksheet tab.

b. Click the **FORMULAS** tab, and then in the Formula Auditing group, click **Show Formulas** .

Cells now display formulas rather than values. Notice that Show Formulas also displays cell data without formatting.

c. Use the **Zoom Slider** on the status bar to move the zoom level so you can view the entire worksheet on the monitor.

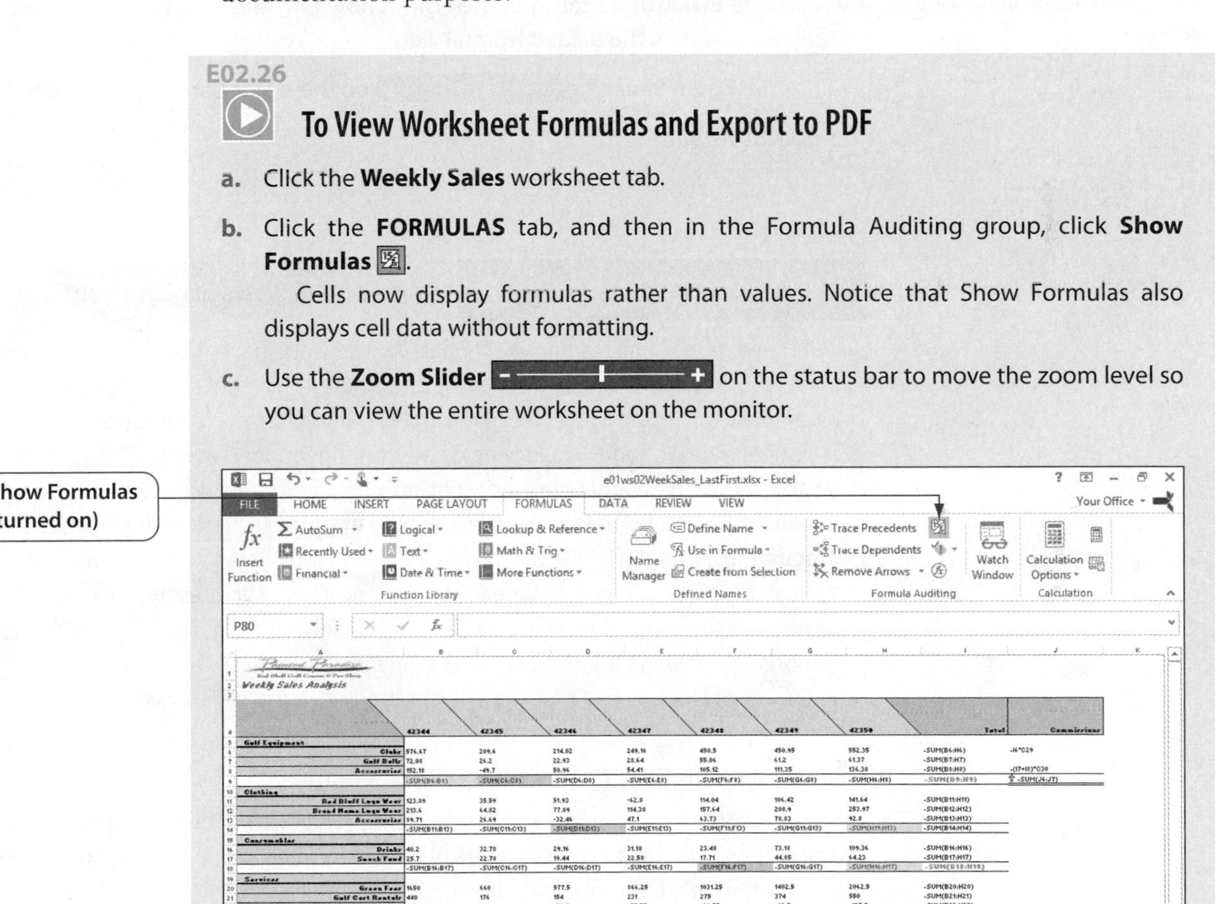

Figure 26 Show Formulas

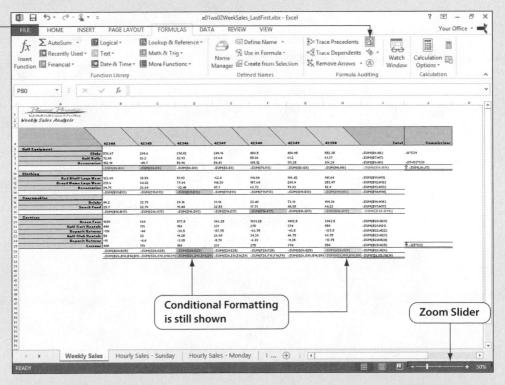

d. Click the **PAGE LAYOUT** tab, and then in the Scale to Fit group, click the **Width** arrow, and then click **1 page**. This will scale your worksheet to print in the width of a single page.

e. In the Scale to Fit group, click the **Height** arrow, and then click **1 page**. This will scale your document to print in the height of a single page.

f. In the Page Setup group, click **Orientation** and then select **Landscape**.

g. Click the **FILE** tab to enter Backstage view, and then click **Export**. Under Create a PDF/XPS Document, click **Create PDF/XPS**. In the Publish as PDF or XPS dialog box, double-click the **File name** box, and then type e01ws02WSFormulas_LastFirst, using your last and first name. Make sure **Open file after publishing** is checked. Click **Publish**.

SIDE NOTE

Shortcut to Toggle Show Formulas

Press Ctrl+~ to toggle Show Formulas on and off.

h. The Weekly Sales worksheet with Show Formulas turned on is displayed as a PDF document in Modern Reader. Move the pointer to the top of the screen. Click and hold the left mouse button and swipe to the bottom of the screen to close Modern Reader. Click the **Desktop** tile to return to Excel.

i. Click the **FORMULAS** tab, and then click **Show Formulas** to toggle Show Formulas off and return to the default Normal view.

j. Use the **Zoom Slider** on the status bar to set the zoom to **100%**.

k. Click **Save**.

REAL WORLD ADVICE | **Print Formula View for Documentation**

You need to document your workbooks. As the worksheets you develop become more complex—use more functions and formulas—the need for documentation increases. Once your worksheet is complete, one vital documentation step is to print a Formula view of your worksheet. If anything ever goes wrong with your worksheet in the future, a Formula view printout may be the fastest way to fix it. Remember, an environmentally friendly documentation option can be to print to PDF. **Portable Document Format (PDF)** was developed by Adobe Systems in 1993 and is a file format that has become a standard for storing files. PDF preserves exactly the original "look and feel" of a document but allows its viewing in many different applications. Exporting to PDF is a great way to document your worksheets.

Updating Existing Documentation

You have made some significant and very important improvements to the e01ws02WeekSales_LastFirst workbook. You must document those updates that require identification or explanation.

E02.27

To Update Existing Documentation

a. Click the **Documentation** worksheet tab.

b. Complete the following:
   - Click cell **A8**, type today's date in mm/dd/yyyy format, and then press Enter.
   - Click cell **B8**, type your name in Lastname, Firstname format, and then press Enter.
   - Click cell **C8**, type Green background - high sales for the week, and then press Enter.
   - In cell **C9**, type Red background - low sales for the week, and then press Enter.
   - In cell **C10**, type Bold and green week total - sales proportion benchmark met, and then press Enter.
   - In cell **C11**, type Commission - green arrow - minimum met, and then press Enter.
   - In cell **C12**, type Commission - red arrow - minimum not met, and then press Enter.

c. Click the **Weekly Sales** worksheet tab.

d. Click the **FILE** tab, and then click **Print**. Under Settings, click the **Print Active Sheets** arrow, and then click **Print Entire Workbook**. Submit your work as directed by your instructor.

e. Click **Save**.

f. Close **Excel**.

REAL WORLD ADVICE **The Power and Risk of "Machine Decision Making"**

Never forget that tools like Excel are decision-making aids, not decision makers. Certainly there are highly structured decisions that can be programmed into a worksheet in Excel such that the result is the decision, such as a product mix problem. Excel is often used for the analysis of information in less highly structured problems. In addition, generally not all factors in a decision can be quantified and programmed into a worksheet.

Computers make calculations; people make decisions.

Concept Check

1. Why should you format data in Excel? How might you format data for a person who is color blind? p. 430–434
2. What are the different functions made available via the AutoSum button? What does each function calculate? p. 446
3. What are the advantages of calculating totals in a table total row? p. 451–452
4. What operator begins all formulas and functions in Excel? What purpose do parentheses serve in Excel formulas? p. 454–455
5. What is conditional formatting? How can conditional formatting assist in decision making? p. 457
6. List two reasons why it may be necessary to hide rows or columns of information in a worksheet. p. 463
7. Why is the PDF file format good for saving documentation? p. 466

Key Terms

Argument 446
AVERAGE function 449
Banding 443
Built-in cell style 441
Built-in function 446
Cell alignment 435
Cell reference 446
Conditional formatting 457
Constant 454
COUNT function 449
Default 445
Destination cell 446
Fill color 437
Format Painter 439
Formula 454
Function 446
Graphical format 430
Mathematical operator 454
MAX function 450
MIN function 450
Order of operations 455
Parameter 463
Portable Document Format (PDF) 466
Relative cell reference 454
Source cells 446
SUBTOTAL function 451
Table 442
Table style 443
Tabular format 430
Theme 445

Visual Summary

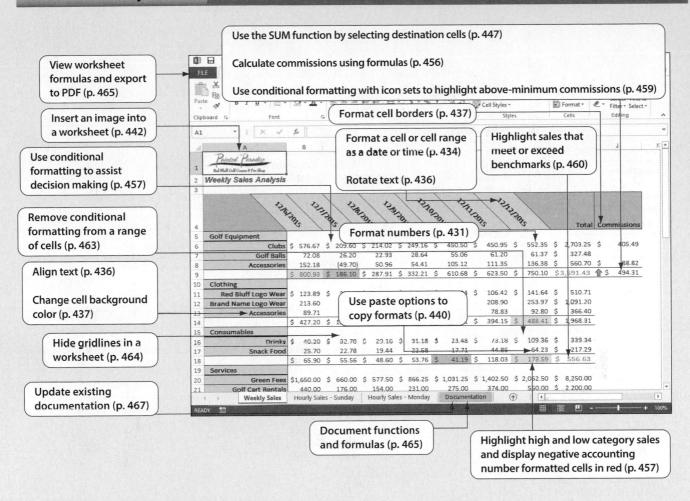

Use the SUM function by selecting destination cells (p. 447)

Calculate commissions using formulas (p. 456)

Use conditional formatting with icon sets to highlight above-minimum commissions (p. 459)

View worksheet formulas and export to PDF (p. 465)

Insert an image into a worksheet (p. 442)

Format cell borders (p. 437)

Format a cell or cell range as a date or time (p. 434)

Rotate text (p. 436)

Highlight sales that meet or exceed benchmarks (p. 460)

Use conditional formatting to assist decision making (p. 457)

Remove conditional formatting from a range of cells (p. 463)

Format numbers (p. 431)

Align text (p. 436)

Change cell background color (p. 437)

Use paste options to copy formats (p. 440)

Hide gridlines in a worksheet (p. 464)

Update existing documentation (p. 467)

Document functions and formulas (p. 465)

Highlight high and low category sales and display negative accounting number formatted cells in red (p. 457)

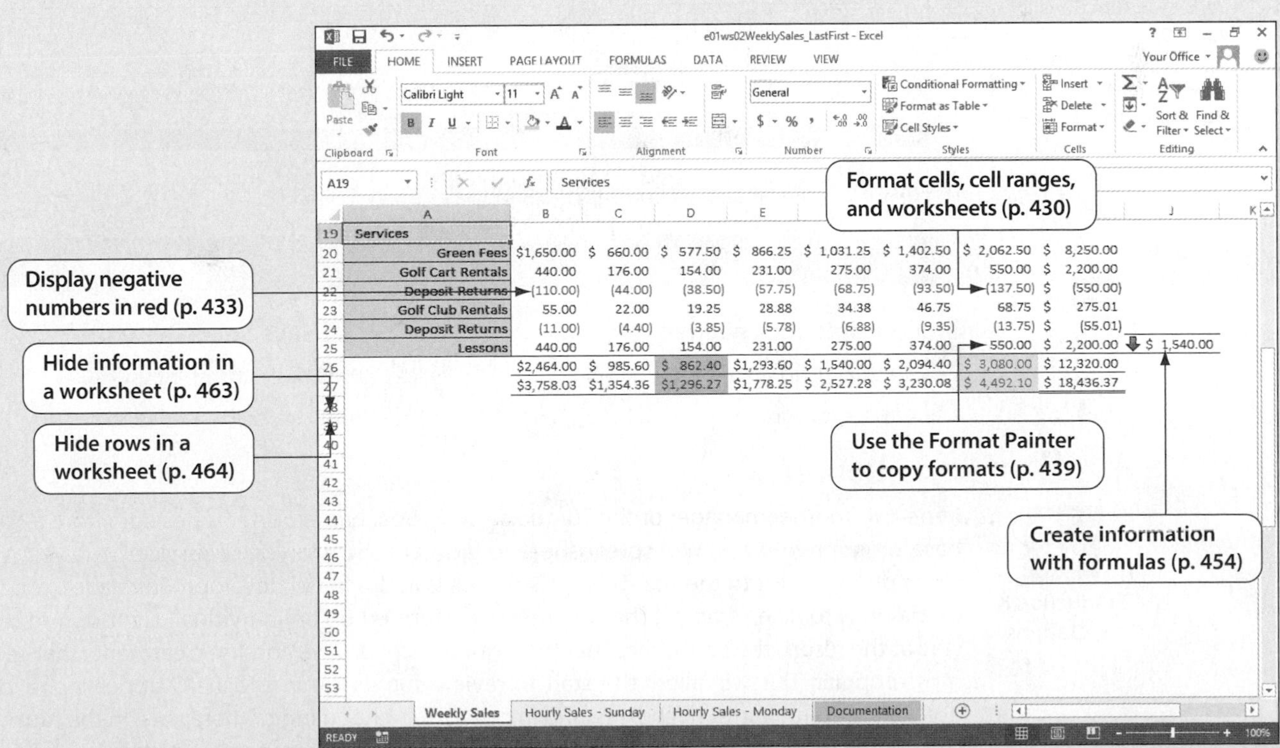

Apply a table style to a cell range (p. 443)

Change the theme (p. 445)

Use SUM in a table total row and filter the results (p. 452)

Calculate totals in a table (p. 451)

Apply built-in cell styles (p. 441)

Use the SUM function by selecting source cells (p. 448)

Create information with functions (p. 446)

Use the COUNT and AVERAGE functions (p. 449)

Use the MIN and MAX functions (p. 451)

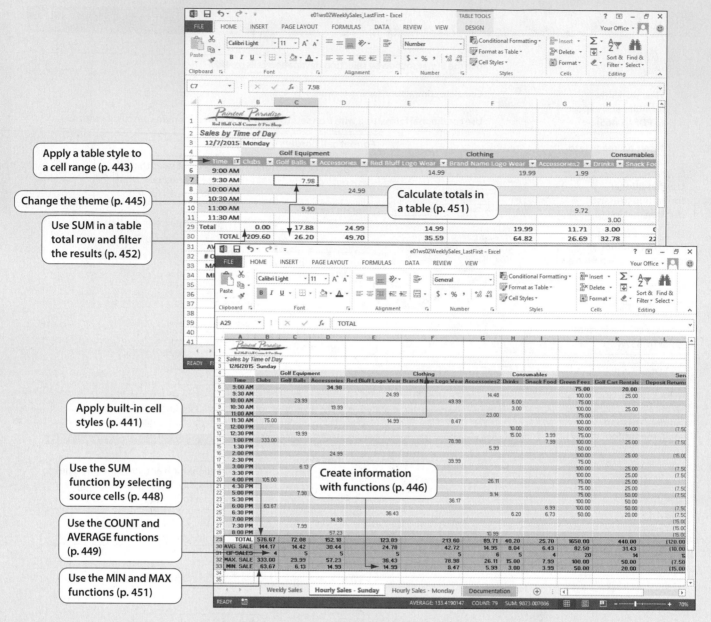

Figure 27 Red Bluff Golf Course & Pro Shop Sales Analysis Final

Practice 1

Student data files needed:

e01ws02SpaSchd.xlsx

turquoise_oasis.jpg

You will save your files as:

e01ws02SpaSchd_LastFirst.xlsx

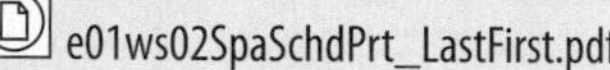

e01ws02SpaSchdPrt_LastFirst.pdf

Spa Schedule

Production & Operations

Irene Kai, another manager of the Turquoise Oasis Spa, has exported sales data from a database program into an Excel spreadsheet to facilitate the analysis of services received by a client during a visit to the spa. This spreadsheet is in the initial development stages, but the intention is to keep track of the treatments performed on an individual client during their stay at the resort, the consultant that performed each service, and the treatments that seem most popular. This will allow the staff to review spa usage in a visually appealing layout, notice trends in treatment choices, and improve the scheduling of therapists. In the future, it might lead to the mailing of special promotions to regular or repeat customers, a reevaluation of pricing, or the addition or deletion of treatments based on popularity.

Irene has imported the data and created a workbook that will consist of three worksheets. One worksheet contains the clients' names, a list of the dates of service, type of treatment administered, the cost of the treatment, and the consultant that performed that service. A second worksheet has a list of spa therapists and the days of the week and times that each is available.

a. Start **Excel**, click **Open Other Workbooks**, double-click **Computer**, navigate to where your student data files are located, and then open **e01ws02SpaSchd**. Click the **FILE** tab, click **Save As**, and then double-click **Computer**. In the Save As dialog box, navigate to the location where you are saving your files. In the **File name** box, type e01ws02SpaSchd_LastFirst using your last and first name, and then click **Save**.

b. Click the **Documentation** worksheet tab, click cell **A8**, and then press Ctrl+; to enter the current date. Press Tab. In cell **B8**, type your name in Lastname, Firstname format.

c. Click the **Schedule by Date** worksheet tab. Click the **PAGE LAYOUT** tab, and then in the Themes group, click **Themes**, and then select **Organic** from the gallery.

d. Click cell **A1**. Click the **HOME** tab, and then in the Cells group, click **Format**, and then click **Row Height**. Type 50 in the **Row height** box, and then click **OK**.

e. Click cell **D1**. Click the **INSERT** tab, and then in the Illustrations group, click **Pictures**. Navigate to the location where your student data files are stored, click **turquoise_oasis**, and then click **Insert**. Click the **FORMAT** tab, and then in the Arrange group, click **Align**, and then if Snap to Grid is not selected, click **Snap to Grid**. Click the right horizontal **resizing handle** and snap the right **edge** of the logo to the border between columns **F** and **G**. Click the bottom vertical **resizing handle**, and snap the bottom edge of the logo to the border between rows **1** and **2**.

f. Select the cell range **A2:J2**. Click the **HOME** tab, and then in the Alignment group, click **Merge & Center**. In the Style group, click **Cell Styles**, and then select **Heading 4** in the gallery.

g. Select cell range **A4:J4**, click **Cell Styles**, and then select **Heading 3** in the gallery.

h. Click cell **A2**, and then in the Clipboard group, click **Copy**. Select cell range **A26:A30**, right-click cell **A26**, and then in the Paste Options shortcut menu, select **Formatting**. In the Alignment group, click **Align Left**.

i. Click cell **A6**. In the Clipboard group, click **Format Painter**, and then select cell range **A7:A23**.

j. Select cell range **I6:I23**. In the Number group, click the **Number Format** arrow, and then select **Currency**. In the Number group, click **Decrease Decimal** two times.

k. Select cell range **C6:C23**. Click the **Number Format** arrow, and then click **More Number Formats**. In the **Type** box, select **1:30 PM**, and then click **OK**.

l. Select cell **J10**, press Alt+=, select the cell range **I6:I9**, and then press Enter. Select cell **J13**, press Alt+=, select cell range **I11:I12**, and then press Enter. Select cell **J18**, press Alt+=, select cell range **I14:I17**, and then press Enter. Select cell **J21**, press Alt+=, select cell range **I19:I20**, and then press Enter. Select cell **J24**, press Alt+=, select cell range **I22:I23**, and then press Enter.

m. Select cell **C28**, and then type =MAX(J6:J24). Press Ctrl+Enter, click cell **J24**, click the **Format Painter**, and then click cell **C28**.

n. Right-click the **column H** header, and then select **Hide** from the shortcut menu.

o. Select cell range **A4:J24**. In the Styles group, click **Format as Table**, and then select **Table Style Medium 2** from the gallery menu. In the Format as Table dialog box, check **My table has headers**, and then click **OK**. In the Table Style Options group, click **Total Row**. Click the **HOME** tab, click cell **J10**, click the **Format Painter**, and then click cell **J25**.

p. In the Editing group, click **Sort & Filter**, and then click **Filter** to turn off column filters.

q. Select cell **J10**, press and hold Ctrl, and then select cells **J13**, **J18**, **J21**, and **J24**. In the Styles group, click **Conditional Formatting**, point to **Highlight Cells Rules**, and then select **Greater Than**. Type =C$31 in the **Format cells that are GREATER THAN** box. Click the **with** arrow, and then select **Custom Format**. In the Format Cells dialog box, on the Font tab, in the Font style box, click **Bold**. Click the **Color** arrow, and select **Green, Accent1** from the palette. Click **OK**, and then click **OK** again.

r. Click the **Therapist Schedule** worksheet tab. Select cell **C8**, type Monday, and then press Ctrl+Enter. Click and hold the **fill handle**, and then expand the active cell to encompass cell range **C8:C14**. Press Ctrl+C. Click cell **C16**, press and hold Ctrl, and then click cell **C24**. Press Ctrl+V.

s. Select cell range **A6:D6**. In the Styles group, click **Cell Styles**, and then select **40% - Accent5** from the gallery menu. In the Font group, click **Bold**.

t. Select cell range **A8:A14**. Press Ctrl, and then select cell ranges **B8:B14**, **A16:A22**, **B16:B22**, **A24:A30**, and **B24:B30**. In the Alignment group, click **Merge & Center**. In the Alignment group, click **Orientation**, and then select **Vertical Text**. In the Alignment group, click **Middle Align**. In the Font group, click **Bold**. Select columns **A:B**. In the Cells group, click **Format**, and select **AutoFit Column Width**.

u. Right-click the **header** for row **5**, and then click **Delete**.

v. Click the **Documentation** worksheet tab. Click cell **C8**, and then type Calculated daily totals. Press Enter. Type Determined maximum day's sales. Press Enter. Type Formatted daily sales totals that met target as green and bold. Press Enter. Type Finished and formatted the Therapist Schedule worksheet. Press Ctrl+Home.

w. Click the **Schedule by Date** worksheet tab. Click the **PAGE LAYOUT** tab, and then in the Page Setup group, click **Orientation**, and then select **Landscape**. In the Scale to Fit group, click the **Width** arrow, and then click **1 page**.

x. Click the **FORMULAS** tab, and then in the Formula Auditing group, click **Show Formulas**. Click the **FILE** tab, click **Export**, and then under Create a PDF/XPS Document, click **Create PDF/XPS.** Be sure **Open file after publishing** is not checked. Click **Options**. In the Options dialog box, under Publish what, click **Entire workbook**, and then click **OK**. Navigate to the folder where you are saving your files. In the File name box, type e01ws02SpaSchdPrt_LastFirst using your last and first name, and then click **Save**.

y. Submit your files as directed by your instructor.

Problem Solve 1

Student data file needed:

You will save your file as:

e01ws02Portfolio_LastFirst.xlsx

Stock Portfolio Monthly Dividend Income

Finance & Accounting

One method that is used by retirees to provide income during their retirement years is investing in dividend-paying stocks. The dividends allow the investor to make withdrawals from their retirement account without having to reduce their invested principal. Michael Money, president and chief investment officer of your new employer, Excellent Wealth Management, has developed a worksheet to show how a portfolio of stocks can create an additional income stream for his clients. You are asked to determine how much income the current portfolio is generating in order to assist with future investment decisions, in the form of adding to current investments, or diversifying and adding other dividend-paying investments.

a. Start **Excel**, and then open **e01ws02Portfolio**. Save the workbook as e01ws02Portfolio_LastFirst replacing Last and First with your name.

b. Center and bold cell range **B2:F3**.

c. Merge and center cell range **A1:N1**. Apply the **Title** cell style, and then **Bold** the range.

d. Select cell range **N12:N16**, and then calculate row totals using the AutoSum SUM function.

e. Calculate the average of Total Dividends Received in cell **G8**.

f. Apply cell style **Heading 3** to cells **G7**, **B10**, and **B18**.

g. Apply the **Currency** format to cell ranges **B4:F4**, **B6:G4**, **B8:G8**, **B12:N16**, and **B20:N25**.

h. In cell **B7**, calculate the yield of Prime Steel—the annual dividends per share divided by the price per share. Copy the formula to cell range **C7:F7**. Format the yield figures as **Percent Style** with 2 decimal places.

i. Hide rows **10:17**.

j. Format cell range **A19:N24** as a table with headers and a total row. Apply **Table Style Light 11**. Sort by STOCK from A-Z, and then turn off Filters.

k. Select cell range **B20:N25**. Use the AutoSum SUM function to calculate row and column totals.

l. Apply a top border to cell range **A25:N25** and a left border to cell range **N19:N25**.

m. Apply cell style **20% - Accent3** to cell ranges **A20:A25**, **B25:N25**, and **N20:N24**.

n. Apply **Conditional Formatting** to cell range **B20:M24**. Display the **Top 10 Items** as **Green Fill with Dark Green Text**.

o. Apply **Conditional Formatting** to cell range **B25:M25**. Display the **Above Average** values with a **Double** underline.

p. Apply **Conditional Formatting** to cell range **N20:N24**. Display the **Above Average** values with a **Double** underline.

q. Turn off gridlines in the **Dividend Portfolio** worksheet.

r. In the **Documentation** worksheet, enter today's date in mm/dd/yyyy format into cells **A4** and **A16**. Type your name in Lastname, Firstname format into cell **B4**. In cell **C4**, type Completed Mr. Money's Monthly Dividend Income worksheet. In cell **B16**, type Dividend Portfolio. Make cell **A1** the active cell.

s. For the **Dividend Portfolio** worksheet, set Orientation to **Landscape**, and then set Scaling to **Fit All Columns on One Page**. Change print settings to **Print Entire Workbook**. Print and/or submit your workbook file as directed by your instructor.

t. Save and close the workbook.

Perform 1: Perform in Your Life

Student data file needed:

e01ws02PriceChngs.xlsx

You will save your file as:

e01ws02PriceChngs_LastFirst.xlsx

Tracking Stock Price Movements

Finance & Accounting

Excel can be used to track changes in stock prices over time. Not only can you record the actual prices, but by using formulas and some formatting you can easily calculate the percentage changes in price and pick out the winners and losers in your portfolio.

After demonstrating your Excel skills for Mr. Money, he would like you to work with some real data for a client (your instructor). The client may decide to modify the specifications given below. Because customer service is of the utmost importance to Excellent Wealth Management, be sure to follow any client requests very carefully.

a. Start **Excel**, and then open **e01ws02PriceChngs**. Save the workbook as e01ws02PriceChngs_LastFirst replacing Last and First with your name.

Use a website that provides access to historic stock price data for Steps b–d. Options include, but are not limited to, finance.yahoo.com or google.com/finance.

b. Select five (5) companies that are publicly traded. Enter the company name in each cell, starting with B3:F3. In the cell immediately below each company name, enter the ticker symbol—the abbreviation that the company's stock uses.

c. Enter the eight (8) most recent dates that denote the first trading day of a quarter starting in cell A5:A12. For example, the first trading day of 1Q2011 was 1/3/2011. The first trading day of 2Q was 4/2/2011. Format the dates entered as Long Date. Adjust the widths of columns A:F to fit the data you entered.

d. Look up the historic closing prices for each stock for the dates entered in Step d, and then enter these values into the corresponding cells.

e. Under the first company's historic closing price data, calculate the minimum price that was observed. Copy the formula to the cells under each of the other companies' historic price data.

f. Under the minimum price that was calculated, determine the maximum closing price that was observed. Copy the formula to the appropriate cell for each of the other companies.

g. For each company, calculate the Current Gross Margin as the closing price at the end of the most recent quarter—the closing price at the end of the first quarter.

h. Format the historic price data, the minimum and maximum closing prices, and the current gross margin with an appropriate format.

i. Select the range that contains the historic closing prices for the first company. Apply conditional formatting to the range using the Gradient Fill Green Data Bar.

j. Apply the same conditional formatting to each of the other companies using the Format Painter.

k. Use conditional formatting to highlight the largest Maximum, smallest Minimum, largest Current Gross Margin, and smallest Current Gross Margin calculated in Steps e–g.

l. Right align the text of the headings in cells A3:A15. Center the company names and tickers for each range. Merge and center **Price Performance** across the respective data ranges. Merge and center **Excellent Wealth Management** across all of the columns used in the worksheet, and then apply the Heading1 cell style. Make sure all of the data is visible in each of the cells.

m. Apply the Heading4 cell style to all row and column headings, and then apply the Output cell style to the ticker symbols.

n. Apply an appropriate workbook theme, and then adjust the widths of columns A:F if necessary.

o. Copy the worksheet to a new worksheet named Auditing. Show the formulas in this worksheet, and then adjust the column widths of columns A:F to fit the displayed content.

p. Update the Documentation worksheet to reflect the changes that have been made to the workbook.

q. Click the **Stocks** worksheet tab, and then adjust print settings to ensure a usable printed worksheet and to print all worksheets in the workbook. Submit your file as directed by your instructor.

Additional Cases

Additional Workshop Cases are available on the companion website and in the instructor resources.

MODULE CAPSTONE

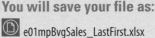

More Practice 1

Student data files needed:

 e01mpBvgSales.xlsx

e01mpIndigo5.jpg

You will save your file as:

e01mpBvgSales_LastFirst.xlsx

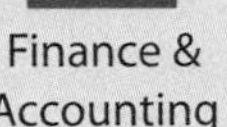

Finance & Accounting

Production & Operations

Beverage Sales and Inventory Analysis

The Painted Paradise Resort and Spa offers a wide assortment of beverages through the Indigo5 restaurant and bar. The resort must track the inventory levels of these beverages as well as the sales and costs associated with each item. Analyze the inventory and sales data found in the worksheet. There are four categories of beverages: Beer, Wine, Soda, and Water. You also have three inventory figures: Starting, Delivered, and Ending. Resort management wants you to generate an analysis of beverage sales in which you identify units sold of each beverage, cost of goods sold, revenue, profit, profit margin, and appropriate totals and averages.

a. Start **Excel**, and then open **e01mpBvgSales**. Save the file with the name e01mpBvgSales_LastFirst, using your first and last name.

b. Click the **Documentation** worksheet tab, click cell **A6**, press Ctrl, and then select cells **A8** and **A20**. Press Ctrl+; and then press Ctrl+Enter to enter today's date. Click cell **B6**, press Ctrl, and then select cells **B8** and **C20**. Type your Last name, First name, and then press Ctrl+Enter. Click cell **C6**, type Formatting Beverage Sales worksheet and then press Enter. In cell **B20**, type Beverage Sales. In cell **D20**, type Weekly beverage sales analysis.

c. Click the **Beverage Sales** worksheet tab, select cell range **D2:J2**, and then click **Merge & Center** for the selected range. Apply the **Title** cell style to the selected range.

d. Select cell range **D3:J3**, and then click **Merge & Center** for the selected range. Apply the **Heading 4** cell style to the selected range.

e. Insert a **hard return** at the specified locations in the following cells—be sure to remove any spaces between the words, and then press Alt+Enter to insert the hard return.
   - Between **Starting** and **Inventory** in **C6**
   - Between **Inventory** and **Delivered** in **D6**
   - Between **Ending** and **Inventory** in **E6**

f. Make the following formatting changes.
   - Format the height of row 6 to 30.
   - Select cell range **A6:K29**, and then apply **AutoFit Column Width**.
   - Select cell range **C6:K6** along with cells **B13**, **B19**, **B26**, **B30**, and **B31**. Apply **Align Right**.
   - Select cell ranges **C13:K13**, **C19:K19**, **C26:K26**, and **C30:K30**. Add a **Top and Bottom Border** to the selected cell ranges. Select cell range **C31:K31**, and then add a **Bottom Double Border** to the selected range.

g. Select cell range **C7:F31**. Format the selected range as **Number** with a comma separator and zero decimal places. Select cell range **G7:J31**, and then format the selected range as **Number** with a comma separator and two decimal places.

h. Make the following calculations.
   - Click cell **F7**. Calculate Units Sold by adding Starting Inventory to Inventory Delivered and then subtracting Ending Inventory. Type =C7+D7-E7, and then copy cell **F7** to cell ranges **F8:F12**, **F15:F18**, **F21:F25**, and **F28:F29**. If any cells contain pound signs (#), select the column, and then apply **AutoFit Column Width**.
   - Click cell **H7**. Calculate Cost of Goods Sold as Units Sold multiplied by Cost Per Unit. Type =F7*G7, and then copy cell **H7** to cell ranges **H8:H12**, **H15:H18**, **H21:H25**, and **H28:H29**. If any cells contain a string of pound signs (#), select the column, and then apply **AutoFit Column Width**.
   - Click cell **J7**. Calculate Revenue as Units Sold multiplied by Sale Price Per Unit. Type =F7*I7, and then copy cell **J7** to cell ranges **J8:J12**, **J15:J18**, **J21:J25**, and **J28:J29**. If any cells contain a string of pound signs (#), select the column, and then apply **AutoFit Column Width**.
   - Click cell **K7**. Calculate Profit Margin as (Revenue - Cost of Goods Sold)/Revenue. Type =(J7-H7)/J7. Copy cell **K7** to cell ranges **K8:K12**, **K15:K18**, **K21:K25**, and **K28:K29**.

i. Select cell ranges **C13:F13**, **C19:F19**, **C26:F26**, **C30:F30** and cells **H13**, **J13**, **H19**, **J19**, **H26**, **J26**, **H30** and **J30**. Click **AutoSum**. If any cells contain a string of number signs (#), select the cells, and then apply **AutoFit Column Width**.

j. Click cell **C31**. Calculate the total number of items in Starting Inventory for all categories combined by using the SUM() function. Type =SUM(C13,C19,C26,C30) and then copy cell **C31** to cell range **D31:F31** as well as cells **H31** and **J31**. If any cells contain a string of number signs (#), select the cells, and then apply **AutoFit Column Width**.

k. Copy cell **K12**, and then from **Paste Options**, paste **Formulas** into cells **K13**, **K19**, **K26**, **K30**, and **K31**. Select cell range **K7:K31**. Format the selected range as **Percentage** with one decimal place. If any cells contain a string of pound signs (#), select the cells, and then apply **AutoFit Column Width**.

l. Select cells **H13**, **J13**, **H19**, **J19**, **H26**, **J26**, **H30**, **J30**, **H31**, and **J31**. Format the selected cells as **Currency**. If any cells contain a string of pound signs (#), select the cells, and then apply **AutoFit Column Width**.

m. Select cell range **F7:F12**. Use conditional formatting to highlight the beer with the highest number of units sold for the week as **Green Fill with Dark Green Text**. Use **Top 10 Items** in Top/Bottom Rules, and then change the number of ranked items to **1**.

n. Copy cell **F12**. Select cell range **J7:J12**. Right-click the selected cell range, and then under Paste Options, click **Paste Formatting**. Continue pasting conditional formatting as follows.
   - Select cell range **F15:F18**, and then click **Paste Formatting**.
   - Select cell range **J15:J18**, and then click **Paste Formatting**.
   - Select cell range **F21:F25**, and then click **Paste Formatting**.
   - Select cell range **J21:J25**, and then click **Paste Formatting**.
   - Select cell range **F28:F29**, and then click **Paste Formatting**.
   - Select cell range **J28:J29**, and then click **Paste Formatting**.

o. Select cell range **J7:J12**, press Ctrl, and then select cell ranges **J15:J18**, **J21:J25**, and **J28:J29**. Click **Increase Decimal** two times.

p. Select cell range **A6:K6**, press Ctrl, and then click cells **A14**, **A20**, and **A27**. In the Themed Cell Styles group, apply **Accent6** to the selected cells. With the cells still selected, press Ctrl, and then select cell ranges **B13:K13**, **B19:K19**, **B26:K26** and **B30:K31**. Click **Bold**.

q. Delete row 4.

r. Press Ctrl+Home. Click the **INSERT** tab, and then in the Illustrations group, click **Pictures**. Navigate to the location of your student data files, and then click

e01mpIndigo5. Click **Insert**. Under PICTURE TOOLS, on the FORMAT tab, in the Arrange group, click **Align**, and then click **Snap to Grid**. Drag the square resizing handle on the right side of the logo left until the right border is between columns **B** and **C**. Drag the square resizing handle on the bottom of the logo and up until the bottom border is between rows **4** and **5**.

s. Click the **PAGE LAYOUT** tab, and then in the Themes group, click Themes, and then click **Wood Type** to change the workbook theme. Apply **AutoFit Column Width** to columns **A:K**. Set Page Orientation to **Landscape**, set the Width to **1 page**, and then press Ctrl+Home.

t. Click the **Documentation** worksheet tab. Click cell **C8**, and then enter a descriptive sentence or two that accurately reflects the activities in this exercise. Press Ctrl+Home. Click the **Beverage Sales** worksheet tab.

u. Click **Save**. Close Excel. Submit your file as directed by your instructor.

Problem Solve 1

MyITLab® Grader
Homework 1

Student data files needed:

e01ps1HotelDisc.xlsx

e01ps1PaintedPar.jpg

You will save your file as:

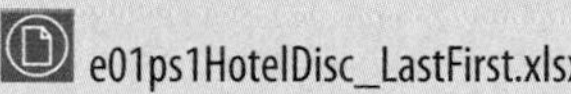

e01ps1HotelDisc_LastFirst.xlsx

Finance & Accounting

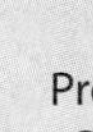

Production & Operations

Analysis of Hotel Sales Discounts

The Painted Paradise Resort and Spa has 700 rooms. The Painted Paradise Resort and Spa gives discounts to guests who meet certain conditions. First, the Paradise Club discount, a 9% discount applicable to all products and services at the resort, is offered to guests who opt into the resort's rewards program. Another 10% discount, good on hotel rooms and services, is offered to groups who book a large block of rooms. Finally, at the discretion of the resort management, rooms may be charged at a complimentary rate. The resort's management would like to get an idea of how much revenue is lost to discounts on Friday and Saturday nights, the busiest nights of the week.

a. Start **Excel**, and then open **e01ps1HotelDisc**. Save the file with the name e01ps1HotelDisc_LastFirst, using your first and last name.

b. Click the **Documentation** worksheet tab, click cell **A6**, press Ctrl, and then select cells **A8** and **A20**. Press Ctrl+; and then press Ctrl+Enter to enter today's date. Click cell **B6**, press Ctrl, and then select cells **B8** and **C20**. Type your Last name, First name and then press Ctrl+Enter. Click cell **C6**, type Formatting Hotel Discounts worksheet and then press Enter. Click cell **B20**, and then type Hotel Discounts. Click cell **D20**, and then type Analysis of weekend hotel room discounts by room type.

c. Click the **Hotel Discounts** worksheet tab. Set the height of row **1** to 40. Click cell **C1**. Click the **INSERT** tab, and then in the Illustrations group, click **Pictures**. Navigate to the location of your student data files, and then click the **e01ps1PaintedPar** file. Click **Insert**. Click the **FORMAT** tab, and then in the Arrange group, click **Align**. Make sure **Snap to Grid** is selected. Drag the resizing handle on the right side of the logo to the left until the right border is between columns **F** and **G**. Drag the resizing handle on the bottom of the logo up until the bottom border is between rows **1** and **2**.

d. Apply the **Heading 4** cell style to cells **A2**, **A12**, **A24**, and **A41**.

e. Apply the **Heading 3** cell style to cells **A3:G3** and **A7:G7**.

f. Change the font color in cells **A4:A5** and **A8:A10** to **Dark Blue, Text 2**, and then apply **Bold**.

g. Format the range **B8:G10** as **Percent Style** with one decimal place.

h. Apply Table Styles as follows.
   - Format cells **A13:G17** as **Table Style Light 9** with the option **My table has headers** checked. Under TABLE TOOLS, on the DESIGN tab, in the Table Style Options group, check **First Column**, in the Tools group, click **Convert to Range**, and then click **Yes**.
   - Format cells **A18:G22** as **Table Style Light 9** with **My table has headers** checked. Check **First Column**, click **Convert to Range**, and then click **Yes**.
   - Format cells **A25:H31** as **Table Style Medium 2** with **My table has headers** checked. Check **First Column** and **Last Column**, click **Convert to Range**, and then click **Yes**.
   - Format cells **A33:H39** as **Table Style Medium 2** with **My table has headers** checked. Check **First Column** and **Last Column**, click **Convert to Range**, and then click **Yes**.
   - Format cells **A42:H46** as **Table Style Medium 2** with **My table has headers** checked. Check **First Column** and **Last Column**, click **Convert to Range**, and then click **Yes**.

i. Apply number formatting as follows:
   - Format cells **B26:G29**, **B34:G37**, and **B43:G45** as **Number**. Negative numbers should not be displayed in red. Make sure to display **2 decimal places** and that **Use 1000 Separator (,)** is checked.
   - Format cells **B30:H31**, **H26:H29**, **B38:H39**, **H34:H37**, **B46:H46**, and **H43:H45** as **Accounting**.

j. Calculate the following:
   - In cell **B26**, enter a formula to multiply the total number of One Double rooms rented on Friday by the Standard Rate for a One Double room. Click **AutoSum**, and then select the cell range **B14:B17**. Edit the formula to multiply the SUM() function by the Standard Rate for a One Double room in cell **B5**.
   - In cell **B27**, calculate the discount total for the Paradise Club for One Double rooms for Friday night. Enter a formula to multiply the number of Paradise Club One Double rooms rented on Friday by the Standard Rate for a One Double room by the Paradise Club discount. The result of the formula will be a negative number to reflect the discount total.
   - In cell **B28**, calculate the Group discount total. Multiply the Standard Rate for a One Double room by the number of Group Discount rooms sold for Friday night by the Group Discount.
   - In cell **B29**, calculate the Comp discount total. Multiply the Standard Rate for a One Double room by the number of Comp Discount rooms sold for Friday night by the Comp Discount.

k. Select cell range **B26:B29**. Click and hold the **fill** handle, and then expand the selection to include **B26:G29**.

l. Calculate the following:
   - In cell **B34**, Gross Sales for One Double rooms for Saturday night. Multiply the Standard Rate for each room type by the number of rooms rented of that type for Saturday night (sum all four types of sales).
   - In cell **B35**, Paradise Club discount total for One Double rooms for Saturday night. Multiply the number of Paradise Club rooms sold Saturday night by the Standard Rate by the Paradise Club Discount.
   - In cell **B36**, Group discount total for One Double rooms for Saturday night. Multiply the Standard Rate by the number of Group One Double rooms sold Saturday night by the Group Discount.
   - In cell **B37**, comp discount total for One Double rooms for Saturday night. Multiply the Standard Rate by the number of Comp One Double rooms sold Saturday night by the Comp Discount.

m. Select cell range **B34:B37**. Click and hold the **fill** handle, and then expand the selection to include **B34:G37**.

- In cell **B43**, calculate the Paradise Club discounts for Friday and Saturday night for One Double rooms. Add the Friday Paradise Club discounts to the Saturday Paradise Club discounts.
- Use the **fill** handle to copy cell **B43** to cell range **B44:B45**. In the Auto Fill Options menu, select **Fill Without Formatting**.

n. Copy cell range **B43:B45** to cell range **C43:G45**.

o. Calculate the Net Sales for each room type on each night, the total sales and discounts for all room types on each night, the Total Discounts for each room type for both nights, and the Total of each discount type for the weekend.
- Select cell ranges **B30:G30**, **H26:H30**, **B38:G38**, **H34:H38**, **B46:G46** and **H43:H46**. Click **AutoSum**.

p. In cell **B31**, calculate Total Discounts for Friday for One Double rooms by subtracting Gross Sales from Net Sales. Copy the formula to cell range **C31:H31**.

q. Copy the formulas in cell range **B31:H31** to cell range **B39:H39**.

r. Apply **Bold** to cell ranges **B31:H31**, **B39:H39**, and **B46:G46**. Apply **AutoFit Column Width** for columns **A:H**. Use the resizing handles to reposition the right side of the logo in row 1 between columns **F** and **G**, and then click cell **A1**.

s. On the PAGE LAYOUT tab, set Orientation to **Landscape**, and then set Width to **1 page**.

t. In the **Documentation** worksheet, in cell **C8**, enter a descriptive sentence or two that accurately reflects the activities in this exercise. Press Ctrl+Home. Click the **Hotel Discounts** worksheet tab.

u. Click **Save**, and then close Excel, submit your file as directed by your instructor.

Problem Solve 2

Student data file needed:

You will save your file as:

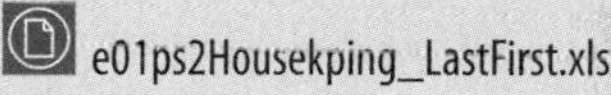

Production & Operations

Human Resources

Housekeeping Staff Performance

The Painted Paradise Resort and Spa takes great pride in the efficiency of its housekeeping staff. The housekeeping staff at the Painted Paradise Resort and Spa is expected to properly clean a hotel room in an average of 25 minutes and never more than 30 minutes. Management is interested in how long it takes to actually begin cleaning rooms after guests check out. This is referred to as lag time—time when a room cannot be rented. The Painted Paradise Resort and Spa wants guests to be able to check in early at no charge as long as there is a room available. By keeping lag time to a minimum, room availability is maximized.

a. Start **Excel**, and then open **e01ps2Housekping**. Save the file as e01ps2Housekping_LastFirst, using your first and last name.

b. Click the **Documentation** worksheet tab, and then select cells **A6**, **A8**, and **A20**. Press Ctrl+; and then press Ctrl+Enter to enter today's date. Select cells **B6**, **B8**, and **C20**. Type your Last name, First name and then press Ctrl+Enter. Click cell **C6**, and then type Completed the Housekeeping Analysis worksheet. In cell **B20**, type Housekeeping Analysis. In cell **D20**, type Analyze housekeeping efficiency.

c. Click the **Housekeeping Analysis** worksheet tab. In cell range **C8:F8**, replace hyphens and any surrounding spaces with a **hard return**. In cell **B8**, replace the space between **Checkout** and **Time** with a **hard return**.

d. Apply formatting as follows.
   - **Merge** cell ranges **A24:B24**, **A25:B25**, **A26:B26**, **A27:B27**, and **A29:B29**.
   - Apply **Merge & Center** to cell ranges **B7:D7**, **C22:D22**, and **E22:F22**.
   - Apply **AutoFit Column Width** in columns **A:H**.
   - Apply **Align Right** to cell ranges **A3:A5**, **E3:E4**, **A24:A29**, **C23:F23**, and cells **A8**, **C3**, and **H8**.
   - **Center** align the cell range **B8:F8**.
   - Apply the **40% - Accent2** cell style to cells **A2**, **B7**, and **C22**. Apply the **60% - Accent2** cell style to cell **E22**.
   - Apply the **Heading 2** cell style to cell **A2**.
   - Apply the **Heading 3** cell style to cell range **A8:H8** and cells **B7**, **C22**, and **E22**.
   - Apply the **Heading 4** cell style to cell ranges **A3:A5**, **E3:E4**, **A24:A29**, **C23:F23**, and cell **C3**.

e. Adjust the column width for the following columns.
   - Column **A** to **18**
   - Columns **B:F** to **12**
   - Column **H** to **10**

f. Calculate the following.
   - Room Clean Lag Time in cell **E9** by subtracting the Checkout Time from the Room Clean Start Time. Copy the formula you just created to cell range **E10:E20**.

     Notice the cells that contain formulas that subtract one time value from another time value are automatically formatted as time values.
   - Room Clean Duration in cell **F9** by subtracting the Room Clean Start Time from the Room Clean End Time. Copy the **formula** you just created to cell range **F10:F20**.
   - Total Room Cleaning Time—Lag in cell **D24** by summing all individual Room Clean Lag Time.
   - Total Room Cleaning Time—Duration in cell **F24** by summing all individual Room Clean Duration.
   - Average Room Cleaning Time—Lag and Duration in cells **D25** and **F25**, respectively.
   - Minimum Room Cleaning Time—Lag and Duration in cells **D26** and **F26**, respectively.
   - Maximum Room Cleaning Time—Lag and Duration in cells **D27** and **F27**, respectively.
   - Calculate the number of Maintenance Issues Reported in cell **C29**. Format cell **C29** as **Number** with zero decimal places.
   - Apply **Conditional Formatting** to the cell range **E9:E20** so Room Clean Lag Times that are greater than the Allowed Average Room Cleaning Time Lag display cell values in **Red Text**.

     Apply **Conditional Formatting** to the cell range **F9:F20** so Room Clean Durations that are greater than the Allowed Average Room Cleaning Time Duration displays cell values in **Red Text**.

     Apply **Conditional Formatting** to cell **D24** to change the font color to **Red Text** if the value in D24 is greater than the value in cell C24: under Format cells that are GREATER THAN:, in the far-left box, type =C24. Copy formatting from cell D24 to cell ranges **D25:D27** and **F24:F27**.

g. Format the cell ranges **E9:F20**, **D24:D27** and **F24:F27** with the standard color Green font color.

h. Apply the **Retrospect** workbook theme.

i. Turn off the worksheet gridlines.

j. On the PAGE LAYOUT tab, set Width to **1 page**.

k. In the **Documentation** worksheet, in cell **C8**, enter a descriptive sentence or two that accurately reflects the activities in this exercise. Press Ctrl+Home.

l. Click the **Housekeeping Analysis** worksheet tab, and then press Ctrl+Home.

m. Click **Save**, and then close Excel. Submit your file as directed by your instructor.

Perform 1: Perform in Your Life

Student data file needed:	You will save your file as:
Blank Excel workbook	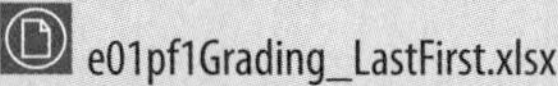 e01pf1Grading_LastFirst.xlsx

Grade Analysis

Information Technology

Most students are concerned about grades and want to have some means of easily tracking grades, analyzing performance, and calculating the current grade (as much as is possible) in every class.

a. Start **Excel**, and then open a blank workbook. Save the file as e01pf1Grading_LastFirst using your first and last name. Rename Sheet1 with a name appropriate for this exercise.

b. Enter the standard 90-80-70-60 grading scale into your worksheet. Build the scale in descending order with letter grades in the cell to the right of the point score.

c. Look in your syllabus for a list of assignments, exams, and other point-earning activities. Enter the assignments into Excel. For completed assignments, enter the points possible and your score. Be sure to label all data items.

d. Include the following calculations:
   - Calculate the percentage score for each point-earning activity, and then use conditional formatting to indicate whether you received an "A," "B," "C," or below a "C" on each assignment.
   - Calculate the possible points earned to date and total points earned to date in the class.
   - Calculate the current overall percentage earned in the class.
   - Calculate the percentage you need to earn on the final examination to achieve an "A," "B," and "C" given the points possible to date and points earned to date.

e. Conditionally format the percentage required to achieve an "A" in the course to visually indicate how hard you may have to study for the final examination.

   For example, if you will have to score at least an 80% on the final examination to achieve an "A" in this course, color the cell that contains the points required to achieve an "A" red to show that you have to study pretty hard for the final examination. Use other colors to indicate whether or not you must score less than 80% or less than 70% on the final examination to achieve an "A" in the course. Use parameters to identify the cutoff values for "A," "B," and "C."

f. Repeat Step h for the percentage required to achieve a "B" in the course.

g. Repeat Step h for the percentage required to achieve a "C" in the course.

h. Apply the following conditional formatting:
   - Add conditional formatting to visually indicate if an "A" is not possible because the percentage required on the final examination to achieve an "A" exceeds 100%.
   - Add conditional formatting to visually indicate if an "B" is not possible because the percentage required on the final examination to achieve an "B" exceeds 100%.
   - Add conditional formatting to visually indicate if an "C" is not possible because the percentage required on the final examination to achieve an "C" exceeds 100%.

i. Ask your instructor whether to include any other courses you are currently taking.

j. Include a completed and well-structured Documentation worksheet.

k. Insert the File Name in the left footer of all worksheets.

l. Modify any page settings to ensure your worksheets each will print on a single page. Specify portrait or landscape orientation as is appropriate to maximize readability.

m. Save your file, and then close Excel. Submit your file as directed by your instructor.

Perform 2: Perform in Your Career

Student data file needed:

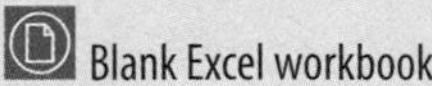
Blank Excel workbook

You will save your file as:

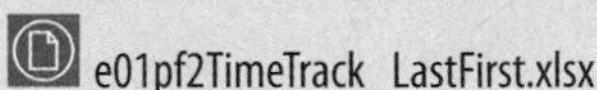
e01pf2TimeTrack_LastFirst.xlsx

Personal Time Tracking

Finance & Accounting

Human Resources

You have started working as a computer programmer with BetaWerks Software Corporation. The company requires you to track the time that you spend doing different things during the day each week. This helps the company determine how many of your hours are billable to customers. You have several different projects to work on as well as a few training sessions throughout the week. The company pays for one 15-minute coffee break and a one-hour lunch each day. Any additional time is considered personal time.

a. Start **Excel**, and then open a blank workbook. Save the file as e01pf2TimeTrack_LastFirst using your first and last name. Rename Sheet1 with a name appropriate to this exercise.

b. Create a worksheet to track your time for the company this week. The following requirements must be met:
   - The worksheet should identify the first day of the workweek with a title such as: Week of mm/dd/yyyy.
   - Your time must be broken down by project/client and weekdays.
   - Time not billable to a project should be classified as Unbillable.
   - Unbillable time should be broken into at least two categories: Breaks and Work.

c. Set up your worksheet so you can easily calculate the amount of time you spent working on each account, in meetings, in training, and on breaks according to the information below:
   - Monday, you spent two hours in a meeting with your development team. This is billable to the BetaWerks Software company as unbillable hours. Following the meeting, you took a 20-minute coffee break. After your break, you spent two hours and 15 minutes working on your project for the Garske Advising. After a one-hour lunch, you attended a two-hour training and development meeting. Before heading home for the day, you spent two hours working on the ISBC Distributing project.
   - Tuesday morning you spent four hours on the Klemisch Kompany project. To help break up the morning, you took a 20-minute coffee break at 10:00. You only had time for a 30-minute lunch because you had to get back to the office for a team-building activity. The activity lasted 40 minutes. To finish the day, you spent four hours working on the Garske Advising assignment.
   - Wednesday morning, you spent two hours each on the Garske Advising and Klemisch Kompany projects. Lunch was a quick 30 minutes because you had a conference call with Mr. Atkinson from ISBC at 1 p.m. The conference call took one hour, and then you spent an additional three hours working on the project.
   - Thursday, the day started with a 30-minute update with your supervisor. Following the meeting, you were able to spend two hours on the ISBC project. After a 15-minute coffee break, you started on a new project for K&M Worldwide for 90 minutes.

You took a 45-minute lunch break, and then spent two and a half hours on the Klemisch Kompany project and two hours on your work for L&H United.

- Friday started with a two-hour training and development session about a new software package that BetaWerks is starting to implement, followed by a 15-minute coffee break. After your coffee break, you were able to squeeze in two more hours for L&H United before taking a one-hour lunch. After lunch, you put in four hours on the Klemisch Kompany project before finally going home for the week.

d. BetaWerks bills your time spent on each account according to the following rates:

Klemisch Kompany	$275
Garske Advising	$250
ISBC Distributing	$225
K&M Worldwide	$175
L&H United	$200

e. Your salary is $100,000/year with benefits. Given two weeks of vacation, you cost BetaWerks $2,000 in salary and benefits per week.

f. Include in your worksheet a calculation of your profit/loss to BetaWerks for the week.

g. Be sure to document your worksheet using a separate Documentation worksheet, comments, and instructions.

h. Modify any page settings to ensure your worksheets each will print on a single page. Specify portrait or landscape orientation as is appropriate to maximize readability.

i. Insert the **File Name** in the left footer of all worksheets.

j. Save your file, and then close Excel. Submit your file as directed by your instructor.

Perform 3: Perform in Your Team

Student data file needed:

Blank Excel workbook

You will save your file as:

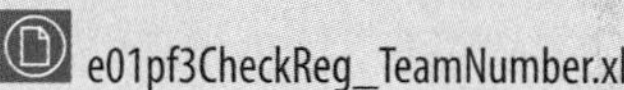

e01pf3CheckReg_TeamNumber.xlsx

Check Register

Finance & Accounting

You volunteer your time with a local nonprofit, the Mayville Community Theatre. Because of your business background, the board of directors has asked you to serve as the new treasurer and to track all of the monetary transactions for the group.

a. Select one team member to set up the document by completing Steps b through e. Then continue with Step d.

b. Open your browser, and then navigate to either **https://www.skydrive.live.com**, **https://www.drive.google.com**, or any other instructor assigned location. Be sure all members of the team have an account on the chosen system—a Microsoft or Google account.

c. Create a new workbook, and then name it e01pf3CheckReg_TeamNumber. Replace Number with the number assigned to your team by your instructor.

d. Rename Sheet1 as Check Register - Team #. Replace # with the number of your team.

e. Share the worksheet with the other members of your team. Make sure that each team member has the appropriate permission to edit the document.

f. Hold a team meeting, and make a plan. Layout the worksheet you are going to build on paper, discuss the requirements of each of the remaining steps, and then divide the remaining steps (g–n) among team members. Note that the steps should be completed in order, so as each team member completes his or her steps, he or she should notify the entire team, not just the team member responsible for the next step.

g. Create the Check Register worksheet to track receipts and expenditures that should be assigned to one of the following categories: **Costumes**, **Marketing**, **Operating and Maintenance**, **Scripts and Royalties**, and **Set Construction**. Also track the following for each receipt or expenditure: the date, amount of payment, check/reference number, recipient, and item description.

h. Enter the following receipts and expenditures under the appropriate category.

Date	Item	Paid To	Check or Ref. #	Amount
11/1/2015	Starting Balance	N/A		$1793.08
11/2/2015	Royalties for "The Cubicle"	Office Publishing Company	9520	–$300.00
11/2/2015	Scripts for "The Cubicle"	Office Publishing Company	9521	–$200.00
11/5/2015	Building Maintenance—Ticket Office	Fix It Palace	9522	–$187.92
11/8/2015	Patron Donation	N/A	53339	$1,000.00
11/12/2015	Costumes for "The Cubicle"	Jane' s Fabrics	9523	–$300.00
11/22/2015	Building Materials for set construction of "The Cubicle"	Fix It Palace	9524	–$430.00
11/30/2015	TV and Radio ads for "The Cubicle"	AdSpace	9525	–$229.18
11/30/2015	General Theater Operating Expenses—November	The Electric Co-op, City Water Works	9526	–$149.98
12/15/2015	Ticket Revenue from "The Cubicle"	N/A	59431	$1,115.50
12/30/2015	General Theater Operating Expenses—December	The Electric Co-op, City Water Works	9527	–$195.13

i. Periodically, money is deposited into the checking account. Include a way to track deposits.

j. Finally, include a running balance. This should be updated any time money is deposited or withdrawn from the account.

k. If the running account balance drops below $1,000, there should be a conditional formatting alert for any balance figure below the threshold.

l. Document the check register using a separate Documentation worksheet, explicit instructions, and comments where helpful.

m. Modify any page settings to ensure your worksheets each will print on a single page. Specify portrait or landscape orientation as is appropriate to maximize readability.

n. Insert the File Name in the left footer on all worksheets in the workbook. Include a list of the names of the students in your team in the right section of the footer.

o. Press Ctrl+Home, save your file, and then close Excel. Submit your file as directed by your instructor.

Perform 4: How Others Perform

Student data file needed:

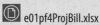

You will save your file as:

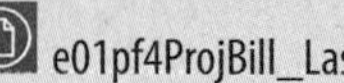

Project Management Billing

Finance & Accounting

John Smith works with you at the Excellent Consulting Company. Each week, consultants are required to track how much time they spend on each project. A worksheet is used to track the date, start time, end time, project code, a description of work performed, and the number of billable hours completed. At the bottom of the worksheet, the hours spent on each project are summarized so clients can be billed. In your role as an internal auditor, you have been asked to double-check a tracking sheet each week. By random selection, Mr. Smith's tracking worksheet needs to be checked this week. Make sure his numbers are accurate, and ensure that his worksheet is set up to minimize errors. His worksheet is also badly in need of some formatting for appearance and clarity.

a. Start **Excel**, and then open **e01pf4ProjBill**. Save the file as e01pf4ProjBill_LastFirst replacing LastFirst with your own name.

b. Make sure all calculated figures are correct. If you subtract Start Time from End Time and multiply the difference by 24, the result is the number of hours between the two times.

c. Examine client totals, and then correct any problems with formulas.

d. Apply formatting such as cell styles, bold, a theme, and so on to improve the appearance of the worksheet.

e. Apply any data formatting that will make the data easier to interpret.

f. Add documentation.

g. Insert the File Name in the left footer on all worksheets in the workbook.

h. Modify any page settings to ensure the worksheets each will print on a single page. Specify portrait or landscape orientation as is appropriate to maximize readability.

i. Save your file, and then close Excel. Submit your file as directed by your instructor.

WORKSHOP 3 | CELL REFERENCES, NAMED RANGES, AND FUNCTIONS

OBJECTIVES

Prepare Case

Painted Paradise Resort and Spa Wedding Planning

Sales & Marketing

Finance & Accounting

Clint Keller and Addison Ryan just booked a wedding at Painted Paradise Resort and Spa. When requested by a happy couple, the Turquoise Oasis Spa coordinates a variety of events including spa visits, golf massages, and gift baskets made up of various spa products. Given the frequency of wedding events at the Turquoise Oasis Spa, Meda Rodate has asked for your assistance in designing an Excel workbook that can be used and reused to plan these events in the future.

Vladimir Voronin / Fotolia

REAL WORLD SUCCESS

"The skills I have learned through Excel have become incredibly valuable in my everyday life. I recently worked at a private golf course, and was asked to create an inventory workbook to track Beverage Cart sales. This would allow the golf course to forecast demand and predict the amount of starting inventory we needed to maintain. In addition, we needed to use functions that would be user-friendly for the beverage cart employees. At the end of the day, the beverage cart employees would count to see how many items from the set amount of inventory were missing, input the numbers into the Excel workbook, and Excel would compute the amount of sales the beverage cart employee would need to turn in. The remaining amount would equal the tips the employee had earned. The use of Excel functions not only helped the Golf Course track its inventory, but also its profits."

- Kristen, alumnus

Student data file needed for this workshop:

e02ws03Wedding.xlsx

You will save your file as:

e02ws03Wedding_LastFirst.xlsx

Referencing Cells and Named Ranges

The value of Excel expands as you move from using the spreadsheet for displaying data to analyzing data in order to make informed decisions. As the complexity of a spreadsheet increases, techniques that promote effective and efficient development of the spreadsheet become of utmost importance. Integrating cell references within formulas and working with functions are common methods used in developing effective spreadsheets. These skills will become the foundation for more advanced skills.

A **cell reference** is used in a formula or function to address a cell or range of cells. A cell reference contains two parts, a column reference—the alphabetic portion that comes first, and a row reference—the numeric portion that comes last. For example, cell reference B4 refers to the intersection of column B and row 4. When a formula is created, you can simply use values, like =5*5. However, writing a formula without cell references is limiting. Formulas with cell references are substantially more powerful. For example, the formula =B4*C4, where cells B4 and C4 contain values to be used in the calculation, allows the formula to reference a cell (or cell range) rather than a value (or values). This means that when data changes in an individual cell, any formulas that reference the cell are automatically recalculated. In this section you will use cell referencing and named ranges to build a worksheet model for planning events at the Turquoise Oasis Spa.

Understand the Types of Cell References

There are three different types of cell referencing: relative, absolute, and mixed. A **relative cell reference** changes when the formula or function is copied to another location. The change in the cell reference will reflect the number of rows and/or columns that the cell was copied from, relative to its original location. An **absolute cell reference** does not change if a formula or function is copied to another location. An absolute reference is specified by placing a dollar sign ($) sign in front of both the column letter(s) and row number. For example, to make B4 an absolute reference you would specify $B$4. A **mixed cell reference** is essentially a combination of relative and absolute cell references. In a mixed cell reference, the column or row portion of the reference is absolute and the corresponding row or column is relative. For example, $B4 is a mixed reference where the column is absolute and the row is relative. B$4 is a mixed reference where the column is relative and the row is absolute. In essence, the dollar sign ($) sign locks down the letter or number it precedes so it will not change when copied.

QUICK REFERENCE | **Types of Cell Referencing**

Below are examples of the three types of cell referencing for cell A4:

1. Relative cell referencing: =A5+B5
2. Absolute cell referencing: =$A$5+B5
3. Mixed cell referencing: =$A5+B5

Cell referencing is a useful feature when formulas need to be copied across ranges in a spreadsheet. When creating a spreadsheet and developing a formula that will not be copied elsewhere, relative and absolute cell referencing is not necessary. However, data arranged in a table may require a formula to perform calculations on each row, or record. Excel allows this process to be completed quickly and easily by using cell referencing. The formula can be constructed once and then quickly copied across a range of cells.

MODULE 2

REAL WORLD ADVICE Creating Dynamic Workbooks

The use of cell references in formulas helps make spreadsheets in Excel extremely powerful. By using a cell reference to refer to a value in a formula you can make your spreadsheet flexible. In other words, using cell references makes your spreadsheet easier to use and more efficient. If something about your business changes and requires an update to a value in your spreadsheet, you need only make the update in one place.

Open the Starting File

Meda Rodate would like for the Turquoise Oasis Spa to become more efficient in planning for wedding events. She has asked for your help in designing an Excel workbook to accomplish this goal. You will begin by opening the wedding planning workbook and organizing the number and pricing of spa gift baskets by constructing common Excel functions using various types of cell referencing.

E03.00

To Open the Excel Workbook

a. Start **Excel**, click **Open Other Workbooks**, double-click **Computer**, and then browse to your student data files. Locate and select **e02ws03Wedding**, and then click **Open**.

b. Click the **FILE** tab, click **Save As**, and then Browse to your student files. In the File name box, type e02ws03Wedding_LastFirst using your last and first name, and then click **Save**.

c. Click the **INSERT** tab, and then in the Text group, click **Header & Footer**.

d. On the HEADER & FOOTER TOOLS DESIGN tab, in the Navigation group, click **Go to Footer**. If necessary, click the left section of the footer, and then click File Name in the Header & Footer Elements group.

e. Click any cell on the spreadsheet to move out of the footer, press Ctrl+Home, click the **VIEW** tab, and then in the Workbook Views group, click **Normal**, and then click the **HOME** tab.

Using Relative Cell Referencing

Relative cell referencing (as shown in Figure 1) is the default reference type when constructing formulas in Excel. Remember that relative cell referencing changes the cells in a formula if it is copied or otherwise moved to another location. This includes the use of copy and paste or the AutoFill feature to copy a formula to another location. If a formula is copied to the right or left, the column references will change in the formula. If a formula is copied up or down, the row references will change in the formula.

Relative cell referencing is useful in situations where the same calculation is needed in multiple cells but the location of the data needed for the calculation changes relative to the position of the calculation cell. The GiftBaskets worksheet contains a list of individual items that are included in the different types of gift baskets offered at the Turquoise Oasis Spa. The worksheet contains the prices for individual items in the baskets, the number of each item in the basket, and the prices of each basket.

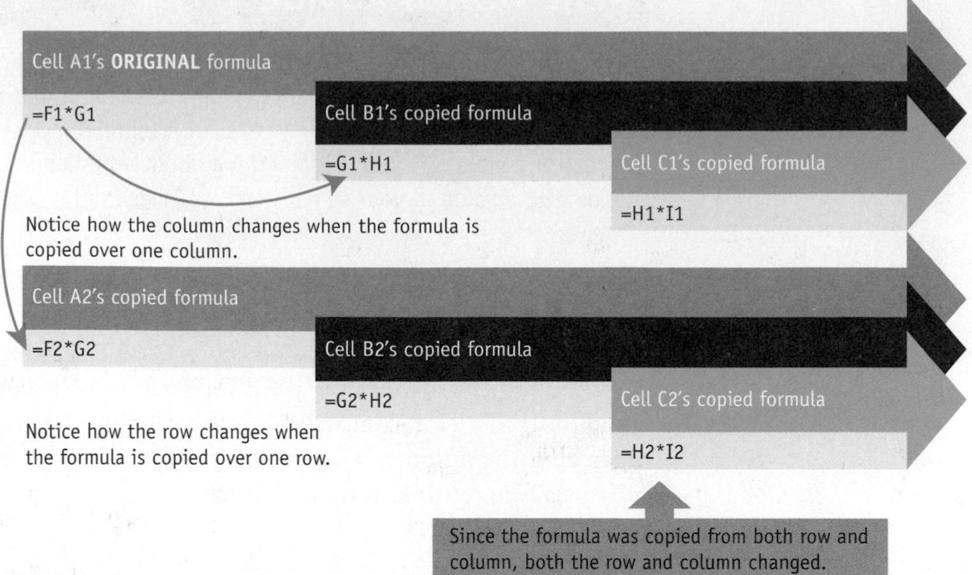

Figure 1 Understanding relative cell referencing

The Turquoise Oasis Spa allows wedding parties to specify up to three different kinds of custom gift baskets. Each gift basket can contains up to four different items in each basket. The workbook has been set up such that cells with a blue fill need to be changed from one event to another. In this exercise you will use relative cell referencing to display the total number of items in each type of gift basket.

MyITLab®
Workshop 3 Training

SIDE NOTE
Alternate Method
You can also use AutoFill with a formula in a horizontal range by selecting the range and pressing Ctrl and typing R.

E03.01

To Use Relative Cell Referencing

a. Click the **GiftBaskets** worksheet, and then click cell **F9**.

b. Type =SUM(B9:E9) and then press Ctrl+Enter.

c. Click the **AutoFill handle** + on the bottom-right corner of cell **F9**, and then drag down to copy the formula to cell **F11**.

Notice that the formula in cell F11 refers to cells B11:E11. Since the formula copied down, the row reference changed from 9 to 10 and finally to 11.

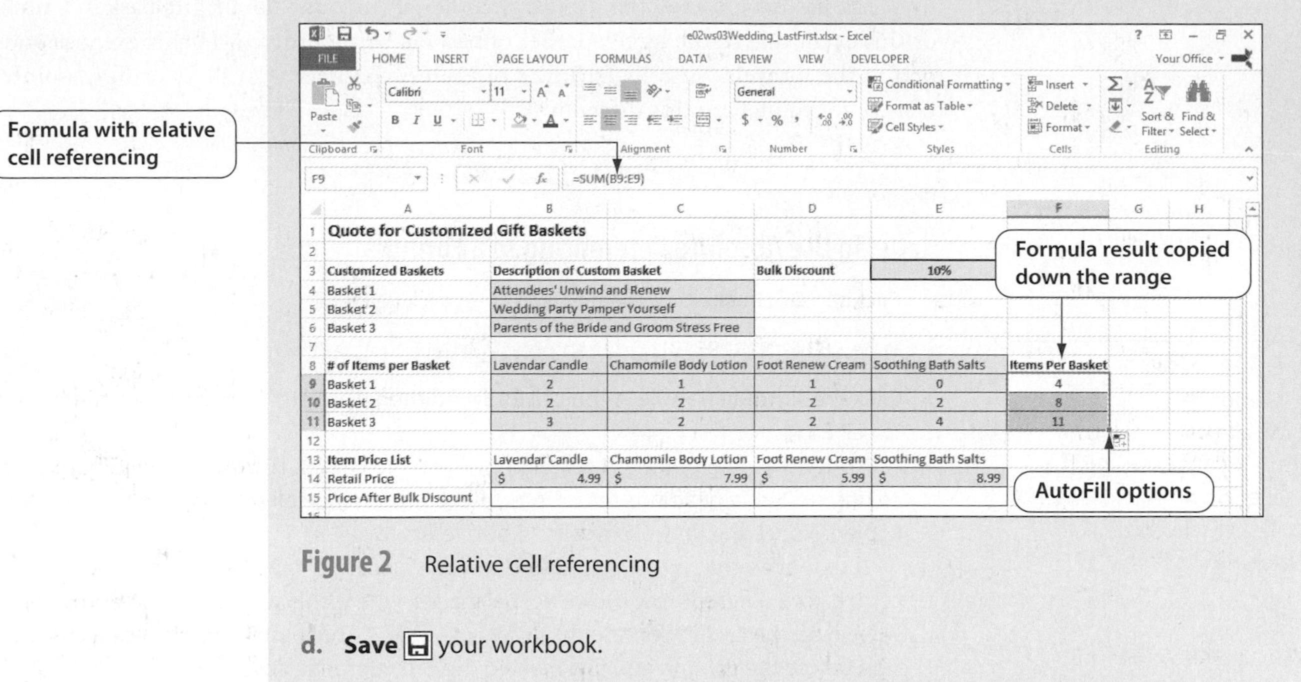

Figure 2 Relative cell referencing

d. **Save** your workbook.

Using Absolute Cell Referencing

Absolute cell referencing (as shown in Figure 3) is useful when a formula needs to be copied and the reference to one or more cells within the formula must not change as the formula is copied. Thus, the column and row address of a referenced cell remains constant regardless of the position of the cell when the formula is copied to other cells.

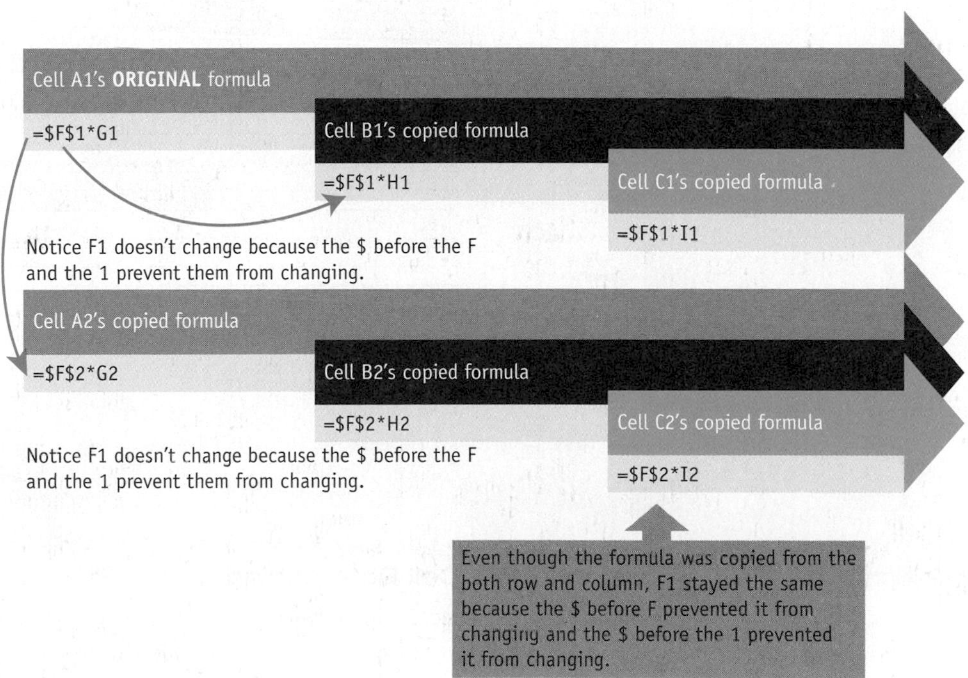

Figure 3 Understanding absolute cell referencing

Meda has decided to offer a bulk percentage discount on all gift baskets purchased for this event due to the large number of baskets being ordered. In this exercise you will modify the formulas in cells B15:E22 of the GiftBaskets worksheet using absolute cell referencing to include this discount.

E03.02

To Use Absolute Referencing to a Formula

a. Click the **GiftBaskets** worksheet, and then click cell **B15**.

b. Type =B14-(B14*$E$3) and then press Ctrl+Enter.

c. Click the **AutoFill handle** on cell **B15**, and then drag to the right to copy the formula to cell **E15**.

Notice that the formula in cell E15 now refers to cell E3. The dollar sign in front of the column and row headings force Excel to keep the same cell reference as the formula is copied. Notice the formula in cell E15 also refers to cell E3.

Also, notice that the $ sign before row 3 is not required since the formula was not copied to a different row. However, no matter where this formula is copied to on the worksheet the calculation should always use cell E3. Thus, common practice is to put a $ sign before the column and row making the cell reference absolute.

SIDE NOTE

Using F4

An alternative to typing the $ signs is to press F4 after typing or selecting the cell reference.

Formula with absolute reference for cell E3

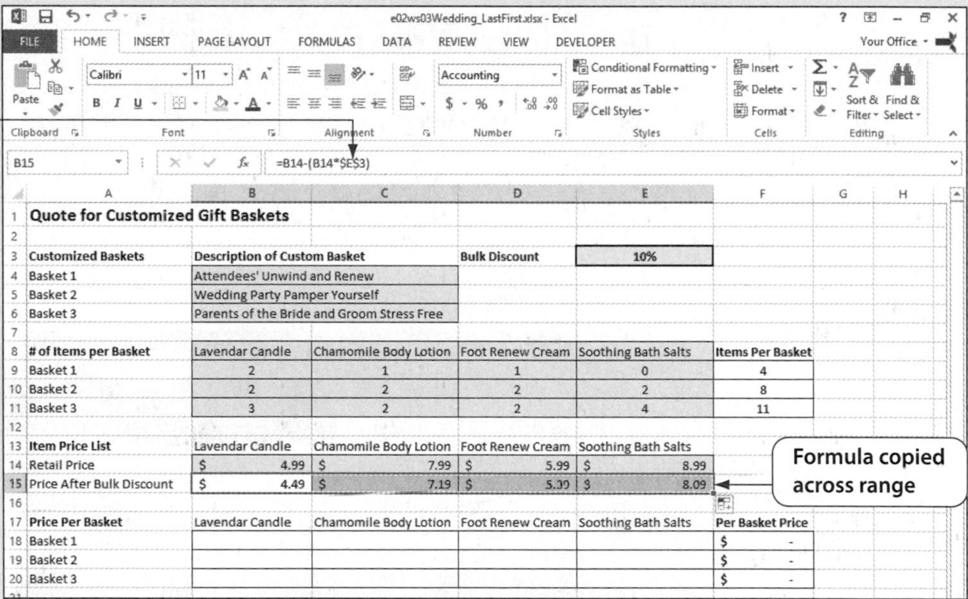

Figure 4 Absolute cell referencing

d. **Save** your workbook.

Using Mixed Cell Referencing

Mixed cell references can be very useful in the development of spreadsheets. Mixed cell references refer to referencing a cell within the formula where part of the cell address is preceded by a dollar sign to lock—either the column letter or the row value—as absolute reference. This will leave the other part of the cell as relatively referenced when the formula is copied to new cells. Figure 5 shows a representation of how mixed cell referencing works.

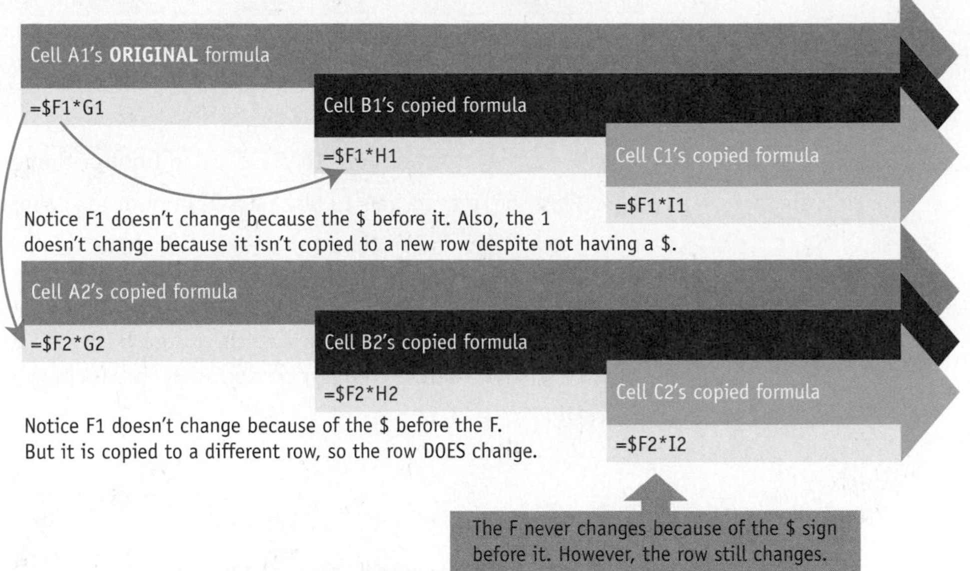
Cell A1's ORIGINAL formula
=$F1*G1
Cell B1's copied formula
=$F1*H1
Cell C1's copied formula
=$F1*I1
Notice F1 doesn't change because the $ before it. Also, the 1 doesn't change because it isn't copied to a new row despite not having a $.
Cell A2's copied formula
=$F2*G2
Cell B2's copied formula
=$F2*H2
Cell C2's copied formula
=$F2*I2
Notice F1 doesn't change because of the $ before the F. But it is copied to a different row, so the row DOES change.
The F never changes because of the $ sign before it. However, the row still changes.

Figure 5 Understanding mixed cell referencing

REAL WORLD ADVICE **Layout of a Spreadsheet Model**

Think of a spreadsheet model as an interactive report. Some of the data is static and may not change often, if ever. Some of the data, as in the Wedding Planning workbook, will need to change with each use of the spreadsheet. It can be helpful to color-code cells so anyone using the spreadsheet can easily see which cells require a change and which should be left alone. For example, in the Wedding Planning workbook cells with a blue fill are cells that need to be updated from one event to another.

If you need to verify that the formula has the correct relative and absolute referencing after it has been copied or moved into other cells within the spreadsheet, a quick and easy verification is to examine one of the cells in edit mode. Best practice dictates following these steps:

1. Double-click a cell containing the formula to enter edit mode.
2. In edit mode, notice the color-coded borders around cells match the cell address references in the formula. Using the color-coding as a guide, verify that the cell(s) are referenced correctly.
3. If the referencing is incorrect, notice which cells are not referenced correctly.
4. Exit out of edit mode by pressing Esc and returning to the original formula.
5. Edit the cell references, and then copy the corrected formula again.
6. Always recheck the formula again to see if your correction worked when copied into other cells or cell ranges.

Repeat this process as needed. Instead of typing the dollar signs within your cell references, F4 can be used to change the type of cell referencing. If the insertion point is placed within a cell reference in your formula, press F4 one time and Excel will insert dollar signs in front of both the row reference and column reference. If you press F4 again, Excel places a dollar sign in front of the row number only. If you press F4 a third time, Excel places a dollar sign in front of the column reference and removes the dollar sign from the row reference. Pressing F4 a fourth time returns the cell to a relative reference.

QUICK REFERENCE | Using F4

F4 can be used to change the type of cell referencing.

1. Press F4 one time to place a $ in front of both the column and row value (absolute reference).
2. Press F4 a second time to place a $ in front of the row value only (mixed reference).
3. Press F4 a third time to place a $ in front of the column value only (mixed reference).
4. Press F4 a fourth time to remove all $ characters (relative reference).

In this exercise you will update the range B18:E20 to include formulas that calculate the price of individual items included in each basket type using mixed cell referencing.

E03.03

To Use Mixed Cell Referencing

a. Click the **GiftBaskets** worksheet, and then click cell **B18**.

b. Type =B9*B$15 and then press Ctrl+Enter.

c. Click the **AutoFill handle** on cell **B18**, and then drag down to copy the formula to cell **B20**.

Notice that the formula in cell B20 still refers to cell B15. The dollar sign in front of the row heading forces Excel to use row 15 as the referenced row no matter where the formula is copied to. However, the column will change as the formula is copied to the left or right in the worksheet.

d. With range **B18:B20** still selected, click the **AutoFill handle** on cell B20, and then drag to the right to copy the formulas to the range **E18:E20**. Notice that as the formulas are copied column B changes while the row reference to row 15 remains unchanged as the formula is copied to the range.

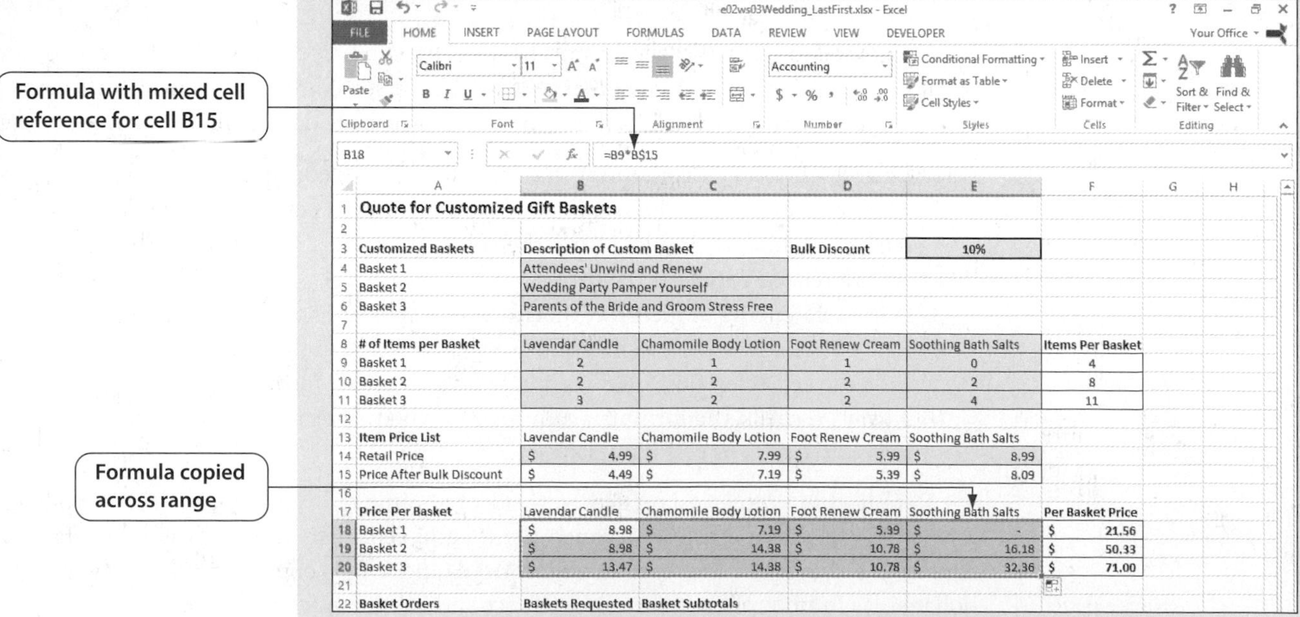

Figure 6 Mixed cell referencing

e. Click cell **E14**, type 11.99 and then press Enter.

Notice that the values in cells E19:E20 have been updated. For reference, E20 previously displayed $32.36; now it displays $43.16.

f. **Save** your workbook.

MODULE 2

CONSIDER THIS | **Cell Referencing**

In cell B18 of the GiftBaskets worksheet the formula uses mixed cell referencing by referring to cell B$15. Would there have been a different result if absolute referencing would have been used? Would there have been a different result if relative referencing had been used? Why would these options be incorrect?

REAL WORLD ADVICE | **Building for Scalability**

When you develop a spreadsheet you should consider the potential for the model to expand. A good spreadsheet model allows the user to add more data as needed. Instead of assuming current conditions will never change, your spreadsheet should be built to accommodate growth. While developing the model, you may consider using hypothetical data so you can see how the model will look when it has real data.

QUICK REFERENCE | **Understanding Referencing Based on Copy Destination**

Cell references in a formula can change when copied. To understand where to put a $ sign, you must understand how the cell references will change when copied. Excel determines what to change by the original location and the copy destination. Remember, the $ locks down the letter or number it precedes so it will not change.

Original Location	Copy Destination	Column Becomes	Row Becomes	Considerations
A1	Formula will not be copied.	N/A	N/A	Cell referencing is irrelevant.
A1	A5	The column references will not change.	The row references will change by 4 rows.	Adding a $ sign before the column is irrelevant. Add a $ before the row if the row should not change.
A1	C1	The column references will change by 2 columns.	The row references will not change.	Add a $ before the column if the column should not change. Adding a $ before the row is irrelevant.

(Continued)

QUICK REFERENCE	Understanding Referencing Based on Copy Destination *(Continued)*

Original Location	Copy Destination	Column Becomes	Row Becomes	Considerations
A1	C5	The column references will change by 2.	The row references will change by 4.	Since both the column and row references will change, add a $ before any references that should not change.

Create Named Ranges

Once you are comfortable working with formulas and cells there is a natural progression to using named ranges and functions. A **named range** is a group of cells that have been given a name that can then be used within a formula or function. Named ranges are an extension of cell references and provide a quick alternative for commonly used cell references or ranges.

Spreadsheet formulas that use cell references such as =C5*C6 may be easy to interpret when simple. However, as the size and complexity of the workbook increases, so does the difficulty and time needed to incorporate cell references in formulas. This is especially the case with workbooks that use multiple worksheets. The use of named ranges enables a developer to quickly develop formulas that make sense. It also increases the legibility of formulas to other individuals using the same workbook. For example, the formula =SUM(BasketSubtotals) is much easier to interpret than =SUM(C23:C25). You can quickly understand the formula if it is written with assigned names you designate.

Creating Named Ranges Using the Name Box

Named ranges are easy to create as you develop a spreadsheet. A named range can be either a single cell or a group of cells. Most named ranges are groups of cells used within multiple formulas. A simple way to name a range is to select the range and use the Name Box to create the name. This allows for a custom name to be given to the range. When naming ranges, a descriptive name should be used for the range being named. Named ranges do have some restrictions for the types of characters that can be used. Named ranges cannot start with a number, cannot contain spaces, and the name cannot resemble a cell reference.

QUICK REFERENCE	Conventions for Naming Ranges

Below is a list of conditions that must be meet when creating named ranges.

1. Names for ranges must start with a letter, an underscore (_), or a backslash (\ ).
2. Create names that provide specific meaning to the range being named.
3. Spaces cannot be used while created a named range. Instead use an underscore, a hyphen character, or capitalize the first letter of each word. For example, HairStyles.
4. Do not use combinations of letters and numbers that resemble cell references.

In this exercise you will create a named range using the Name box. This named range can then be used in future calculations as an absolute cell reference.

E03.04

To Create a Named Range Using the Name Box

a. Click the **GiftBaskets** worksheet, and then select the range **C23:C25**.

b. Click in the **Name** box to select the existing text. Type **BasketSubtotals** and then press Enter to create a new named range. Notice that when the range C23:C25 is selected the text BasketSubtotals will be displayed in the Name box.

SIDE NOTE

Selecting a Range

The name box will display a list of all named ranges in a workbook. Click any named range in the name box to select that range in a sheet.

Named range displayed in Name box

Named range selected

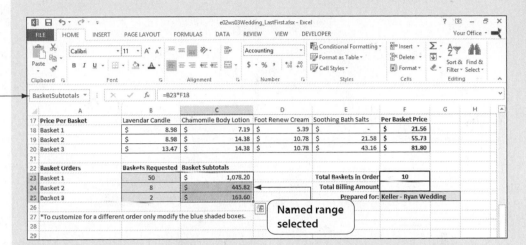

Figure 7 Name range applied to C23:C25

Troubleshooting

If you click outside of the Name Box before pressing Enter, the named range will not be created.

c. **Save** your workbook.

Modifying Named Ranges

If a named range has been created incorrectly it can be redefined by selecting the correct data and naming the range again. Alternatively, the Name Manager can be used to modify an existing range or to view a list of already defined ranges. The **Name Manager** can be used to create, edit, delete, or troubleshoot named ranges in a workbook.

Currently the range BasketsRequested only includes gift basket option 2 and 3. In this exercise you will modify a named range that was previously created in the workbook.

E03.05

To Modify a Named Range

a. Click the **GiftBaskets** worksheet, click the **Name** box arrow, and then click **BasketsRequested**.

   Notice that the range selected is B24:B26. This is the incorrect range. The correct range is B23:B25.

b. Click the **FORMULAS** tab, and then in the Defined Names group, click **Name Manager**.

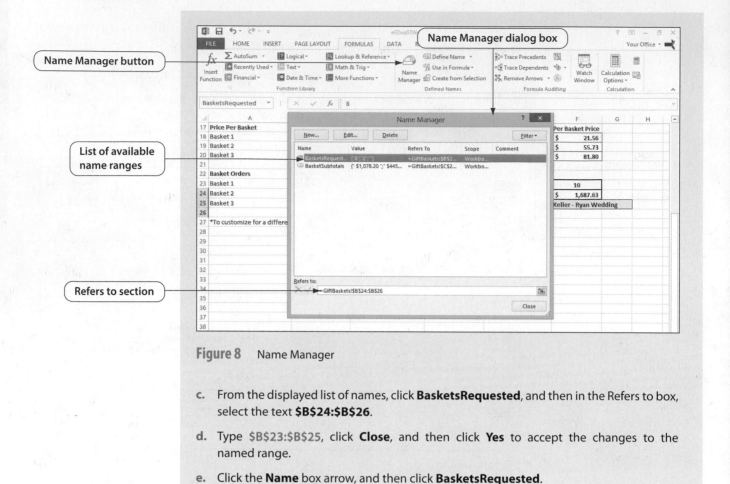

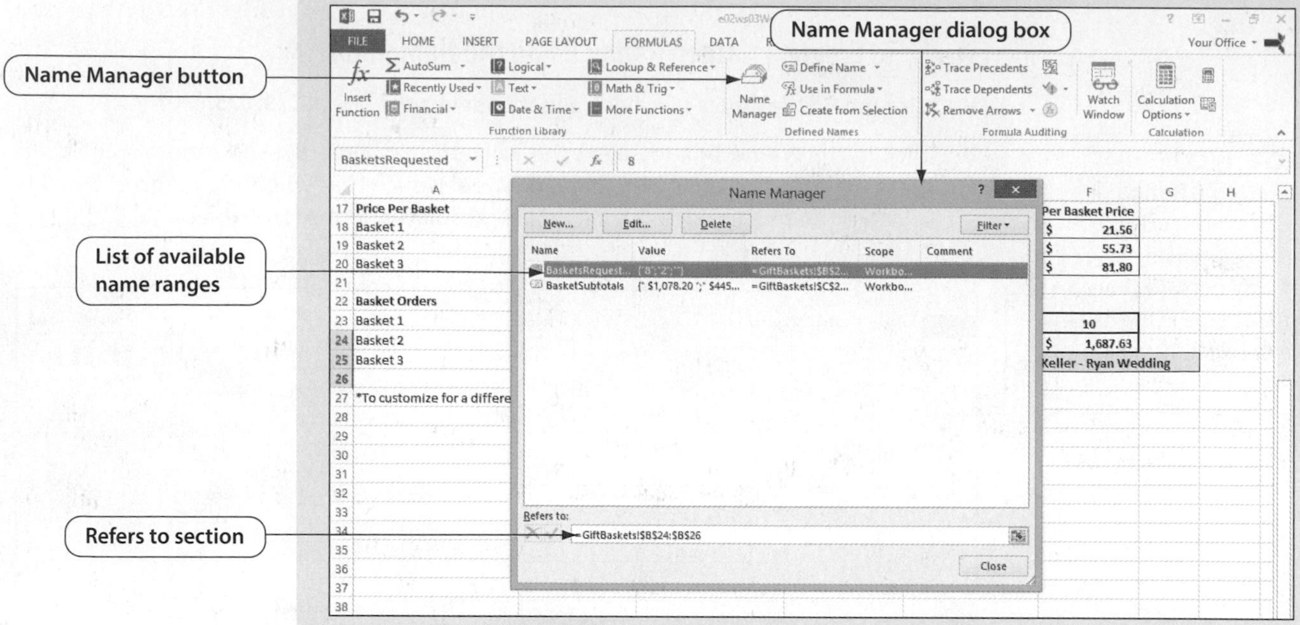

Figure 8 Name Manager

c. From the displayed list of names, click **BasketsRequested**, and then in the Refers to box, select the text **$B$24:$B$26**.

d. Type $B$23:$B$25, click **Close**, and then click **Yes** to accept the changes to the named range.

e. Click the **Name** box arrow, and then click **BasketsRequested**.
Notice that the correct range, B23:B25, is now selected.

f. **Save** your workbook.

Using Named Ranges

Using named ranges in place of cell references is a simple process. Instead of typing the cells that you want to use in a formula, you can type the range name you have created. Excel will begin to recognize the name you are typing and offer to automatically complete the name for you. Another method of using named ranges is to use the Paste Name feature in Excel. While typing a formula you can press F3 to view a list of named ranges in the workbook and then insert it into the formula you are constructing.

Meda has requested that the worksheet display the total amount that the wedding party is to be billed for the gift baskets being made. In this exercise you will use a named range to create a calculation to display the total price of the requested gift baskets in the worksheet.

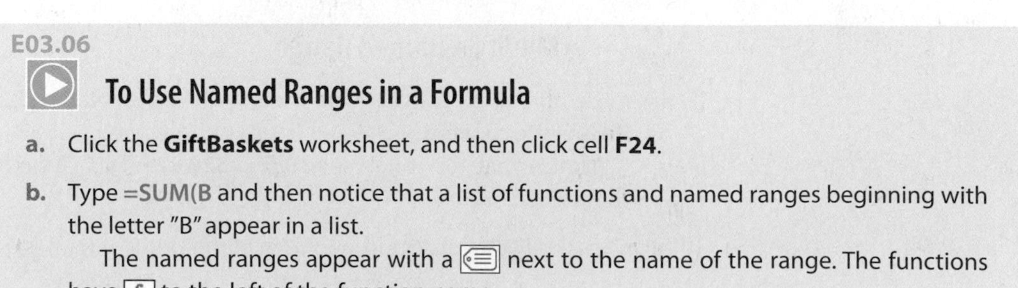

E03.06

To Use Named Ranges in a Formula

a. Click the **GiftBaskets** worksheet, and then click cell **F24**.

b. Type =SUM(B and then notice that a list of functions and named ranges beginning with the letter "B" appear in a list.
The named ranges appear with a next to the name of the range. The functions have to the left of the function name.

c. Type ask, press [↓], and then press [Tab] to select the **BasketSubtotals** named range. Press [Ctrl]+[Enter] to complete the formula.

d. **Save** your workbook.

Creating Named Ranges from Selections

At times your worksheet's data will be organized in such a way that the names for your ranges exist in a cell in the form of a heading, either for each row or each column in the data set. Rather than selecting each row or column separately in a time-consuming process, you can use the Create from Selection method.

The Create from Selection method is a process that produces multiple named ranges from the headings in rows, columns, or both, from the data set. The key element is to realize that the names for the ranges need to exist in a cell adjacent to the data range. Most commonly, these names are column headers that make for very convenient names for each column of data.

In this exercise you will create named ranges for the item subtotals for each type of gift basket. You will then apply the named ranges to the formulas in cells F18:F20.

E03.07

To Created Named Ranges and Apply the Names to Formulas

a. Click the **GiftBaskets** worksheet, and then select the range **A18:E20**.

b. On the FORMULAS tab, in the Defined Names group, click **Create from Selection**.

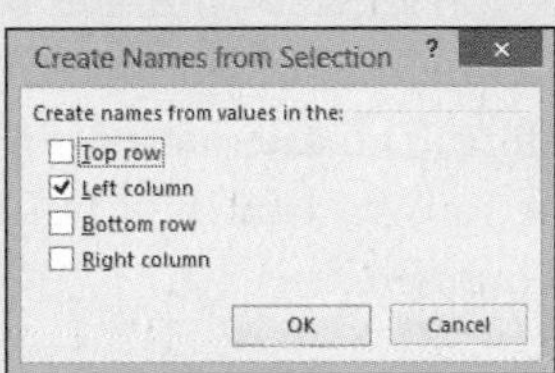

Figure 9 Create from Selection dialog box

SIDE NOTE
Create from Selection
After selecting the range of data you wish to name, the keyboard shortcut [Ctrl]+[Shift]+[F3] will create a single or multiple named ranges from the selection.

c. Confirm that the **Left column** check box is selected, and then click **OK**.

d. Select the range **B18:E18**.

Notice that the Name box displays the name **Basket_1**. In creating the named range Excel substituted all space characters in the name with underscore characters. Ranges B19:E19 and B20:E20 will appear similarly.

e. Select the range **F18:F20**, and then in the Defined Names group, click the **Define Name** arrow, and then click **Apply Names**. Notice that Excel has detected three potential named ranges that can be substituted into the formulas in the selected range.

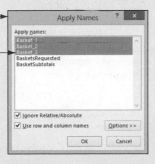

Figure 10 Apply Names dialog box

f. Click **OK**. Notice that the formula in cell F18 now reads =SUM(Basket_1).

g. **Save** your workbook.

REAL WORLD ADVICE | **When to Use Named Ranges**

Like any useful feature, Named ranges can be overused. Named ranges make it easy to understand formulas and can be used to select a range of cells quickly. However, you must invest time and effort to create and use the named ranges. Named ranges have the most value when sets of data are used in multiple formulas or when other users need to understand the construction of the spreadsheet. Not every cell or range in your workbook needs to be a named range. If you need a formula to copy across a range of cells with the references remaining relative, named ranges are not the best option. You should do a mental cost-benefit analysis to ensure it is worth the time and effort. Your decision on when to use named ranges will become easier with practice and experience.

Understanding Functions

A **function** is a named calculation where Excel calculates the output based on the input provided. These can be fairly simple such as using the SUM function that adds any cell address range as input. Conversely, functions can be more complex. For example, calculating a monthly loan payment is accomplished by indicating various arguments—the loan amount, number of payments, and interest rate. **Arguments** are any inputs used by a function to compute the solution. As long as you have the correct inputs, Excel will perform the calculation for the function. In this section, you will use common business functions to continue building the worksheet module used for planning events at the Turquoise Oasis Spa.

Create and Structure Functions

Functions are composed of several elements and need to be structured in a particular order. When discussing functions, you need to be aware of the syntax of an Excel function. The **syntax** is the structure and order of the function and the arguments needed for Excel to perform the calculation. If you understand the syntax of a function, you can easily learn how to use new functions quickly. The syntax for a function is represented in Figure 11.

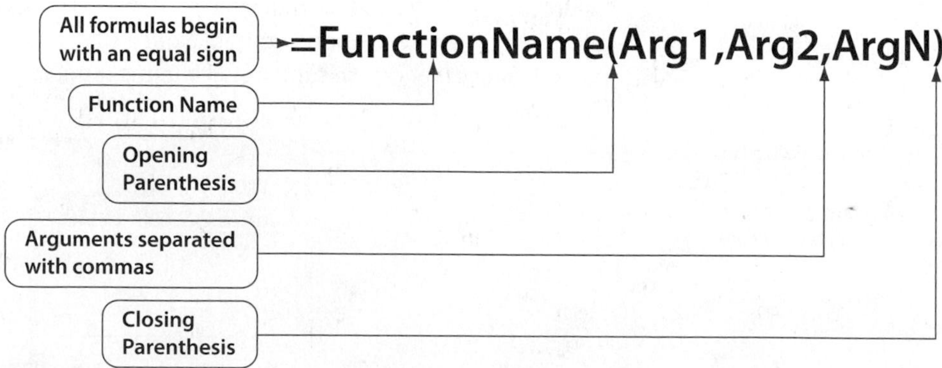

Figure 11 Syntax of a function

The FunctionName is any function that is in the Excel library. Examples are SUM, COUNT, and TODAY. With all functions, a pair of parentheses () are required after the FunctionName that may contain arguments associated with the function. Functions such as SUM() have one or more arguments that are required. If the required argument(s) are not supplied an error will occur. Some functions, like TODAY() do not have any arguments. These functions do not need any inputs to be able to generate output. The TODAY() function simply uses the clock on the computer to return the current date. Even though there are no arguments needed, the () parentheses are always included, which helps Excel understand that a function is being used.

Arguments can either be required or optional. The required arguments always come before any optional arguments. All arguments are separated with commas. Optional arguments are identified with square brackets [] around the argument name. You never type the square brackets into the actual construction of the function. They are only used to inform you that the argument is optional.

For example, the syntax for the SUM function is:

=SUM(number1, [number2], ...)

The first argument is required; the SUM function must have a number, cell, or range to begin the calculation. The second argument—a second cell or range—is optional. Notice that the second argument uses square brackets to identify that it is optional. The periods following the second argument indicate that one or more arguments can be added as needed. The SUM function can hold up to 255 arguments.

Arguments, like variables in a math equation, need to be appropriate values that are suitable for the function. With Excel, the acceptable values can take six common forms, including other functions, as shown in Table 1.

Form of Input	Example	Explanation
Numeric value	5	Type the value
Cell reference	C5	Type the cell or range of cells
Named range	SALES	Type the name of the range
Text string	"Bonus"	Type the text with quotes " " so Excel will recognize it as a text string rather than a named range
Function	SUM(C5:C19)	Type a function following the correct syntax of the function name, pair of parentheses, and any arguments
Formula	(C5+D5)/100	Type the formula following correct mathematical formula structure

Table 1 Function argument formats

Functions are typically categorized for easy access. The primary categories are shown in Table 2. Functions can be found in the Formulas tab under these categorical names. They can also be searched to find the usage and syntax of functions that are unfamiliar.

Category	Description
Compatibility	A set of functions that are compatible with older versions of Excel
Cube	Working with data and filtering, similar to pivot tables
Database	Performing calculations in Excel on data that meets specific criteria
Date & Time	Working with serial date and time values
Engineering	Working with engineering formulas and calculations
Financial	Working with common financial formulas
Information	Providing data about cell content within a worksheet
Logical	Evaluating expressions or conditions as being either true or false
Lookup & Reference	Working with indexing and retrieving information from data sets
Math & Trig	Working with mathematics
Text	Working with text strings
Statistical	Working with common statistical calculations
User Defined	Working with functions created by the user or by third-party add-ins
Web	Working with URL, XML, and web services connections

Table 2 Function categories

Use and Understand Math and Statistical Functions

At the most fundamental level, spreadsheets are used to perform calculations. These calculations may result in loan payments, GPA calculations, profit margins, or even age calculations. Excel has a large array of functions available for simple and complex mathematical functions. There are functions available to sum, count, perform algebra or trigonometry, and create a wide range of statistical calculations.

Using Math and Trig Functions

The math and trigonometry functions are useful for various numerical manipulations. For example, there are several functions that round data in a cell or calculation. The **ABS function**, for example, returns the absolute value of the number analyzed by the function. A cell or calculation resulting in the number –4 would be returned as 4 by the ABS function. The **INT function** rounds down any decimal values associated with a number to the nearest whole number. The **ROUND function** is important when you want to round a number to a specific number of digits. The ROUND function can round values to the left or right of the decimal in a number. For example, using the ROUND function you could change the number 115.89 to 116 by rounding to the ones place. You could also display 120 by rounding to the integer value to the tens place. While ROUND will round to the nearest digit, ROUNDDOWN and ROUNDUP can be used to force the rounding in a particular direction. Commonly used math functions are shown in Table 3.

When a function is used to round data, the result of that function is used in future calculations. This is different from formatting a cell to a specific number of decimal places as formatting does not change the underlying data.

Function	Usage
ABS(Number)	Returns the absolute value of a number
INT(Number)	Rounds a number down to the nearest integer
RAND( )	Returns a random number from 0 to less than 1
RANDBETWEEN(Bottom,Top)	Returns a random integer between the numbers you specify
ROUND(Number,Num_digits)	Rounds a number to a specified number of digits
ROUNDDOWN(Number,Num_digits)	Rounds a number down to a specified number of digits
ROUNDUP(Number,Num_digits")	Rounds a number up to a specified number of digits

Table 3 Commonly used math functions

There are two common methods for creating functions: by using the Function Arguments dialog box and by typing the function in the cell. The **Function Arguments** dialog box provides additional information and previews results of the formula being constructed. When first developing the skills for using functions in Excel, the Function Arguments dialog box can be very valuable. As more experience with functions are gained, the Function Arguments dialog box may become less useful, particularly when nesting multiple functions together.

Meda has received some historical data on wedding events that she would like to have summarized. When planning new events, this historical data will be helpful to refer to. The data contains four items of interest:

1. The number of days spent by wedding parties at the Painted Paradise Resort and Spa—the value was previously calculated used decimals based on check-in and checkout times. Meda would like this data to be in integers or whole number of days. Since wedding parties receive a late checkout time, these values would need to be rounded down to the nearest whole number.
2. The price of merchandise that was returned after the wedding took place—the price in the column represents the money refunded to customers for the merchandise. The system used at the spa erroneously allowed employees to enter some of this data as a negative value or as a positive value. This data must be displayed as positive values.
3. Data displaying the amount spent in total by each wedding party at the Turquoise Oasis Spa—the average of this column has been calculated in the WeddingSummary worksheet cell C2. Currently, the average is formatted to display too many decimal places. However, the actual value of the cell has many more than two decimals. Meda plans to use this average in subsequent calculations. Formatting the cell to two decimals will not change the value of the cell. Thus, the value needs rounded to two decimals.
4. Data indicating whether the bridal party from the wedding is a member of the spa—the system used by the spa indicates a 1 for spa members and a null value for nonmembers. When this data was imported into Excel the result for nonmembers was the text "Null".

E03.08

To Use the INT and ABS Functions

> **SIDE NOTE**
> **Alternate Method**
> Instead of typing B9 in the Function Arguments dialog box, you can click cell B9. The cell reference will be supplied automatically.

a. Click the **WeddingSummary** worksheet, and then click cell **C9**.

b. To the left of the formula bar, click **Insert Function** [fx]. Click the **Or select a category** arrow, and then select **Math & Trig**.

c. In the **Select a function** box, scroll down, click **INT**, and then click **OK**.

d. Type B9 and notice that to the right of the dialog box, you see the value currently in cell B9. Under the current value you will see a preview of the result of the INT function.

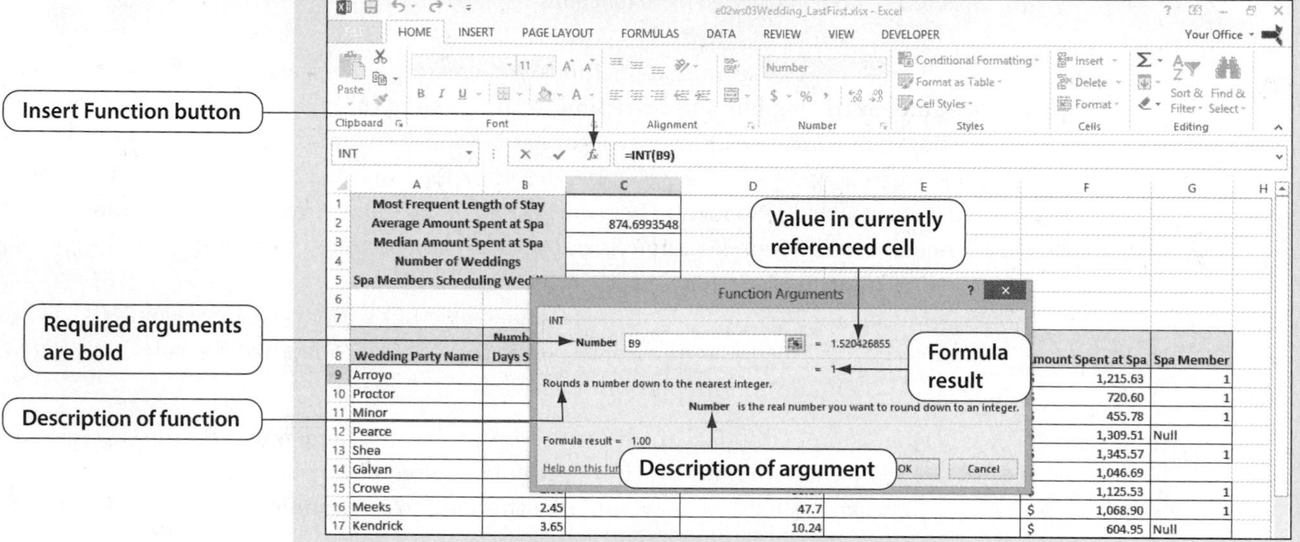

Figure 12 Function Arguments dialog box

e. Click **OK**, and then double-click the **AutoFill handle** [+] to copy cell **C9** down to **C39**.
Notice the values in column B have now been rounded down to the nearest whole number. Illustratively, the value of cell C24 is 4.00 even though the value in cell B24 is 4.50. Since all of the values are now whole days without a decimal value, the format for C9:C39 needs to have decimals decreased to zero decimals.

f. With the range **C9:C39** selected, click the **HOME** tab, and then in the Number group, click **Decrease Decimal** [.00→.0] twice.

> **SIDE NOTE**
> **Function Help**
> Click the Help on this function link in the lower left of the Function Arguments dialog box to open Excel Help for the function being used.

g. Click cell **E9**, and then click **Insert Function** [fx]. If necessary, click the **Or select a category** arrow, and then select **Math & Trig**.

h. In the Select a function box, click **ABS**, and then click **OK**.

i. In the Function Arguments dialog box, in the Number box, type D9 and then click **OK**. Double-click the **AutoFill handle** [+] to copy cell **E9** down to **E39**. All values in column D now appear as positive numbers.

j. **Save** [save icon] your workbook.

MODULE 2

CONSIDER THIS | **Exploring Functions**

Use the Insert Function button in the formula bar to find a function with which you are not familiar. Read the description for the function in the Insert Function dialog box. Use Microsoft Help or the Internet to learn more about the function, and share it with another person. Did you have any trouble understanding the function? Is the Insert Function button a useful tool for exploring new functions?

Inserting a Function Using Formula AutoComplete

Functions can also be constructed without using the Function Arguments dialog box. This is accomplished by typing the equal sign and typing the function name directly into the cell. Excel will still provide guidance using this method. Additionally, as needed, you can always enter the Function Arguments dialog box to get more assistance.

When you initially type in the beginning of a function name, the Formula AutoComplete listing of functions will be shown from which you can select the appropriate function. Formula AutoComplete will provide a list of functions and named ranges that match the text following the equal sign. The list will automatically reflect changes as you type in more letters. Excel will even display a short description of the function when the function name is highlighted. As the function names appear you can use ↓, ↑, →, ←, or your mouse to move through the listing. To select a function, press Tab or double-click the selected function.

Once the function is selected, the arguments will be listed in a movable tag, called a ScreenTip, to provide guidance in completing the function. The argument you are currently editing will be displayed in bold. If you have entered some of the arguments, you can click the argument in the ScreenTip, and Excel will relocate the insertion point to that argument. In this exercise you will insert the ROUND function using Formula AutoComplete.

E03.09

To Insert a Function Using Formula AutoComplete

a. Click the **WeddingSummary** worksheet, and then double-click cell **C2** to begin editing the function.

b. Click after the **equal sign** to place the insertion point before the AVERAGE function. Type ROUND(to begin the new function.

Notice how the Formula AutoComplete suggested possible functions while you typed "round". Also, notice that the number argument is shown in bold font to indicate that this is the argument being edited.

c. Point to the **left edge** of the ScreenTip box, and then drag the ScreenTip to the right of cell **C2**.

SIDE NOTE
Formula AutoComplete
To reduce typing and possible errors, you can use the arrow keys or the mouse to select functions from the Formula AutoComplete list.

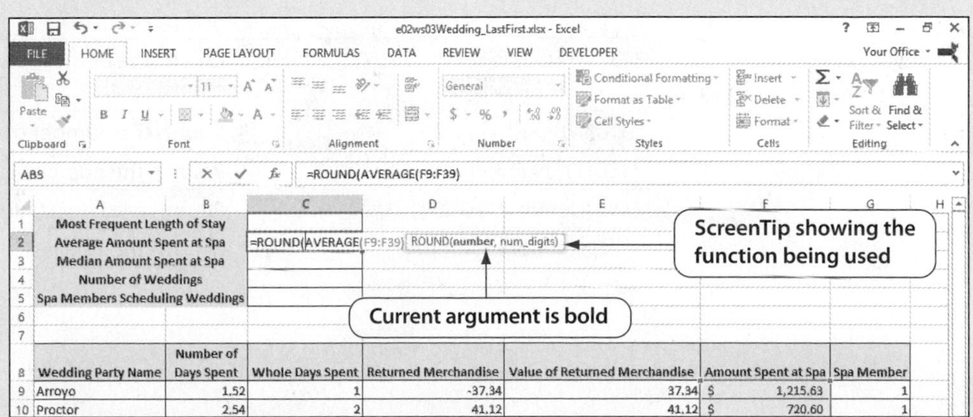

Figure 13 ScreenTip showing the ROUND function

d. Click after the **ending parenthesis** for the AVERAGE function, type , and then notice the num_digits argument of the ROUND function is in bold.

e. Type 2) to complete the num_digits argument. This will round the result of the AVERAGE function to two decimal places.

f. Press Ctrl+Enter.

Notice that the value in cell C2 is now $874.70, or rounded to two decimal places. Importantly, if you had formatted cell C2 to display only two decimal places, the cell would also show $874.70 on the screen. However, formatting does not change the value. So, even though the cell would show $874.70, the cell value used in subsequent mathematical calculations would still be $874.699355. If you increase the number of decimals for cell C2 after using the ROUND function, you will see the cell value is changed to $874.700000.

g. **Save** your workbook.

REAL WORLD ADVICE | **Rounding vs. Formatting**

Formatting text as currency will only give the appearance of true rounding. Any calculations using a cell formatted as currency but containing extra decimal places will include all decimal places in the calculation. Using the ROUND function will eliminate extra decimal places. Thus, future calculations will use the value displayed as a result of the ROUND function.

Using Statistical Functions

Similar to mathematical functions, statistical functions, as shown in Table 4, handle common statistical calculations such as averages, minimums, and maximums. Statistical functions are extremely useful for business analysis as they aggregate and compare data. Common descriptive statistics are used to describe the data. The average, median, and mode are common descriptive statistics that help describe the nature of a data set. They help understand and predict future data.

Statistical Functions	Usage
AVERAGE(Number1,[Number2],...)	Returns the mean from a set of numbers
COUNT(Value1,[Value2],...)	Counts the number of cells in a range that contain numbers
COUNTA(Value1,[Value2],...)	Counts the number of cells in a range that are not empty
COUNTBLANK(Range)	Counts the number of empty cells in a range
MEDIAN(Number1,[Number2],...)	Returns the number in the middle of a set of numbers
MAX(Number1,[Number2],...)	Returns the largest number from a set of numbers
MIN(Number1,[Number2],...)	Returns the smallest number from a set of numbers
MODE.SNGL(Number1,[Number2],...)	Returns the value that occurs most often within a set

Table 4 Commonly used statistical functions

MODULE 2

The **MEDIAN function** is used to measure the central tendency or the location of the middle of a set of data. For example, in a range from 1 to 3, 2 would be the middle of the data or the median. Another measure commonly used to locate data in a range is mode. There are three methods for calculating the mode of a range of data in Excel 2013. The **MODE.SNGL function** returns the most frequently occurring value in a range of data. If more than one number occurs multiple times in a range of data, the **MODE.MULT function** can be used to return a vertical array, or list, of the most frequently occurring values in a range of data.

The **MODE function**, like MODE.SNGL, returns the most frequently occurring value in a range of data. It is important to note that in Excel 2010 this function was replaced by MODE.SNGL and MODE.MULT. The MODE function is still available in Excel 2010 and 2013 to provide backwards compatibility with earlier versions of Excel. Because of this, the function will appear in the Formula AutoComplete menu with a warning icon  next to it.

The **COUNTA function** is useful for counting the number of cells within a range that contain any type of data. This is distinct from the **COUNT function** that only counts cells in a given range that contain numeric data. Using COUNTA is a great method to count the number of records in a data set. On the WeddingSummary worksheet column G contains a list of whether or not the bridal party was a member of the spa. When the data was imported into Excel the system used by the spa marked members with the number one. Nonmembers were marked with the text "Null".

E03.10

To Use Statistical Functions

a. Click the **WeddingSummary** worksheet, and then click cell **C1**.

b. Type =MODE.SNGL(C9:C39) and then press Ctrl+Enter.
Cell C1 now displays the most frequently occurring number of days stayed by a wedding party, 4.

c. Click cell **C3**, type =MEDIAN(F9:F39) and then press Enter.
Cell C3 now displays the median amount spent by wedding parties at the spa, $899.77, representing the middle value as compared to the data for the average amount spent at the spa.

d. Click cell **C4**, type =COUNTA(A9:A39) and then press Enter.
The COUNTA function counts all of the cells in the range A9:A39 to display the 31 wedding parties represented in the data.

e. Click cell **C5**, type =COUNT(G9:G39) and then press Ctrl+Enter.
The COUNT function counts the numbers occurring in column G. Notice that since the only values in column G are numbers, COUNTA would also work in this instance.

f. **Save** your workbook.

Use and Understand Date and Time Functions

Date and time functions are useful for entering the current day and time into a worksheet as well as calculating the intervals between dates. This category of functions is based on a serial date system where each day is represented sequentially from a starting point. In Microsoft applications, that standard is 1/1/1900, which has a serial number of 1. Thus, dates prior to that will not be recognized by the system. Interestingly, when Apple initially made its starting point, it began in 1904. Excel settings can be changed to use the Apple starting point, but it is generally accepted practice to keep the default setting of 1/1/1900 as the starting point. Using two different starting points for dates in Excel spreadsheets can cause significant problems. Common date and time functions are shown in Table 5.

Function	Usage
DATE(Year,Month,Day)	Returns the number that represents the date in Microsoft Excel date-time code
DATEDIF(Date1,Date2,Interval)	Returns the time unit specified between two dates, including the two dates (inclusive)
DAY(Serial_number)	Returns the day of the month, a number from 1 to 31
MONTH(Serial_number)	Returns the month, a number from 1 to 12
NETWORKDAYS(Start_date,End_date,[Holidays])	Returns the number of whole workdays between two dates, inclusive; does not count weekends and can skip holidays that are listed
TODAY( )	Returns the computer system date
WEEKDAY(Serial_number,[return_number],[Return_type])	Returns a number from 1 to 7 representing the day of the week. Can be set to return 0–6 or 1–7
WEEKNUM(Serial_number, [Return_type])	Returns the week number in the year, which week of the year the date occurs
YEAR(Serial_number)	Returns the year of a date, an integer in the range 1900–9999

Table 5 Common date functions

CONSIDER THIS | **Dates in Microsoft Applications**

Do you suppose the same Microsoft employees developed Access, Excel, Word, and PowerPoint? Is it possible that even within a company, there may have been differences in the starting date? Does Access use the same 1/1/1900 for its date starting point? See if you can find out.

Using Date and Time Functions

Excel tracks time by the number of days that have occurred since 1/1/1900. Time is represented by the decimal portion of this number. The decimal is based on the number of minutes in a day (24*60=1440). Thus, a 0.1 decimal is equal to 144 minutes. A full date and time value—such as 5/14/2015 8:35 AM—would appear as 42138.35804. There are 42138 days between 1/1/1900 and 5/14/2015. The time of 8:35 AM is represented by the .35804 portion of the number.

The TODAY and NOW functions are two common functions for inserting the current date into a spreadsheet. There is a slight—but significant—difference between the TODAY and NOW functions. The key difference is that the **TODAY function** simply puts in the current date while the **NOW function** puts in the current date and time. If you think about it, the TODAY function only works with integer representation of days while the NOW function uses decimals to include the time in addition to the day. Both functions can be formatted to show just the date, and you can work with time calculations that mix the two functions. Common time functions are listed in Table 6.

Function	Usage
HOUR(Serial_number)	Returns the hour in a time value, from 0 to 23
MINUTE(Serial_number)	Returns the minute in a time value, from 0 to 59
MONTH(Serial_number)	Returns the month, a number from 1 to 12
SECOND(Serial_Number)	Returns the number of seconds in a time value, from 0 to 59
NOW( )	Returns the computer system date and time

Table 6 Common time functions

REAL WORLD ADVICE **NOW vs. TODAY**

Be careful using NOW versus TODAY, especially when doing date calculations. Both functions use a serial number, counting from 1/1/1900. But, the NOW function also includes decimals for the time of day while TODAY works with integer serial numbers. At noon, on 5/1/2015 the NOW function has the value of 42125.5 while the TODAY function has a value of 42125.0. If you are using these date functions inside another function this could change the result if you are comparing a date the user provided. It is suggested to use the TODAY function if a user will be inserting the date into Excel by hand so the hand-typed value will be compared or used in a calculation with the function, eliminating the decimal issue.

DATEDIF is a useful date function because it enables you to calculate the time between two dates. The function can return the time unit as days, months, or years. However, while all the other functions are listed and can be found in Excel, Help and the Function Library do not offer any information about the DATEDIF function. You will not find any information on the DATEDIF function unless you search the Microsoft site. Since no information exists on it within Excel, this is one function that you must hand type and do the research to understand the syntax. Nonetheless, DATEDIF is one of the more useful date functions.

The syntax of the function is as follows:

=DATEDIF(Date1, Date2, Interval)

The first argument is the starting date in time—the older date—while the second argument is the ending date in time—the newer, more recent date. It may be helpful to remember that time lines are usually depicted as moving left to right, just as they would be listed in the DATEDIF function. The third argument is the interval that should be used, like the number of months or days between the two dates. The unit is expressed as a text value and therefore must be surrounded by quotes for correct syntax. The viable unit value options are shown in Table 7.

Unit Value	Description
"D"	Returns the number of complete days between the dates
"M"	Returns the number of complete months between the dates
"Y"	Returns the number of complete years between the dates
"MD"	Returns the difference between days in two dates, ignoring months and years
"YM"	Returns the difference between months in two dates, ignoring days and years
"YD"	Returns the difference between days in two dates, ignoring years

Table 7 Unit value options for DATEDIF

The options "D", "M", and "Y" are commonly used to calculate differences between dates. For example, using "Y" for the Interval argument is common practice for calculating an age. The options "YM", "YD", and "MD" are not as commonly used because they ignore certain aspects of the date structure. For example, using "YM" for the Interval argument with the dates 7/1/2014 and 9/12/2015 will result in a value of 2. This is because the "YM" unit value ignores the years in the two dates and only calculates the number of whole months between July (7) and September (9). Using "M" in the Interval argument will result in the value 14, the more commonly expected result.

Meda has asked for your help in completing an analysis of customers in the Keller-Ryan wedding party that have requested spa services. As part of the spreadsheet model she would like the current date to appear in cell B1 and the current age of customers to appear in column C. In this exercise you will use common date functions to complete the analysis.

E03.11

To Use Date and Time Functions

a. Click the **SpaServices** worksheet tab, and then click cell **B1**.

b. Type =TODAY() and then press Ctrl+Enter.

Notice that cell B1 now displays the current date. Each time the worksheet is opened, or when a cell is edited, the current date will be updated and displayed in cell B1. Since the time of day is not relevant here, the TODAY function is preferred over the NOW function.

c. Click cell **C5**, type =DATEDIF(B5,TODAY(),"Y") and then press Ctrl+Enter.

The TODAY function is nested inside of the DATEDIF function. Since the interval is set to year, using "Y", the result is that the age of the guest is always current in this calculation.

Troubleshooting

No ScreenTip help will appear when typing the DATEDIF function. If the DATEDIF function returns a #NUM! error the most likely problem is mixing up the order of the two dates within the function. The first date should be the earliest date and the second date the most recent one. The other common error is actually typing in a date as the argument. Typing 12/3/2015 will be interpreted as division instead of a date. The value must either be in serial date format or typed inside of quotation marks.

d. Double-click the **AutoFill handle** + to copy cell **C5** down to **C22**. The current ages of all guests are now displayed in column C.

e. **Save** your workbook.

CONSIDER THIS | Calculating Days

Since Excel uses the 1900 date system, do you really need to use the DATEDIF function to calculate the difference between days—the "D" unit? What other way could you calculate the difference? What would that formula look like?

Use and Understand Text Functions

Excel is frequently used to bring data together from multiple different locations and/ or systems, including text data. Many times, the data is inconsistent from one source to another. For example, one workbook could list First Name Last Name—Olivia Stone— and the next may list names Last Name, First Name—Stone, Olivia. In situations like this, knowing how to alter text data is extremely valuable and time saving.

There are a multitude of reasons why text data in a cell may need to be altered. Names in a cell may need to be separated or combined. Several pieces of data may be stored in a single cell but need to be separated into many columns of data for easier analysis. Excel contains a wide array of functions and features that allow for the manipulation of text data. Some newer features in Excel are optimized for touch-screen devices. This makes it easier to manipulate data when using Excel on a mobile device such as a tablet computer.

Text functions can be used to change the appearance of data, such as displaying text in all lowercase letters. Text functions can also be used to cleanse text. Cleansing text involves removing unwanted characters, rearranging data in a cell, or correcting erroneous data.

Using Text Functions

Text functions help manage, manipulate, and format text data. Data stored as text is commonly referred to as a string. Text functions can change the way data is viewed, cut a string of text into multiple pieces, or combine multiple pieces of text together into one string of text. While most text functions can be used individually, they become increasingly powerful when nested together to transform text. A list of common text functions are listed in Table 8.

The **LEFT function** returns a set number of characters from the left side of a cell. The number of characters the LEFT function will return is defined in the num_chars argument. This number can be simply typed in, or it can be more dynamically calculated using other functions. The **FIND function** searches for a specified string of text in a larger string of text and returns the position number where the specified text begins. By using the FIND function in the num_chars argument of the LEFT function, a dynamic formula can be constructed to separate a portion of text from one cell into another.

Function	Usage
CONCATENATE(text1,text2,...)	Joins text1, text2,...,textn together in order into a single string value
FIND(find_text,within_text,[start_num])	Finds find_text in within_text. The search begins at start_num (start_num defaults to 1) and is case sensitive. The starting position of find_text is returned. If the find_text is not present an error will be returned.
LEFT(text,[num_chars])	Returns a string num_chars long from the left side of text
LEN(text)	Returns a number that represents the number of characters
MID(text,start_num,num_chars)	Returns a string extracted from text beginning in position start_num that is num_chars long
RIGHT(text,[num_chars])	Returns a string num_chars long from the right side of text
TRIM(text)	Returns text with any leading, trailing, or extra spaces between words removed
UPPER(text)	Returns text with all characters in uppercase
PROPER(text)	Returns text with only the first letter in uppercase, all other letters will return in lowercase
SEARCH(find_text,within_text,[start_num])	Finds find_text in within_text. The search begins at start_num (start_num defaults to 1) and is case insensitive. The starting position of find_text is returned. If the find_text is not present an error will be returned.
TEXT(value,format_text)	Returns a number value as a string with the format specified in format_text

Table 8 Common text functions

Meda has asked that you rearrange some of the data on the SpaServices worksheet. Column A contains a list of guests first and last names. To provide better customer service Meda would like the first names of the guests in a separate column that can be used later. The names in column A are arranged in a consistent format. The text in the cell begins with the guest's first name followed by a single space character. After the space character is the guest's last name. Given this format, the space character can be used by text functions to separate the first name from the last name. You will use the FIND and LEFT functions to display only the first name of the guest in column D.

E03.12

To Nest the FIND and LEFT Functions

a. Click the **SpaServices** worksheet, and then click cell **D5**.

b. Type =LEFT(A5, to begin the text function. The LEFT function will begin at the left side of cell A5 and return all characters from position 1 until the number specified by the num_chars argument.

c. Type FIND(" ",A5)) and then press Ctrl+Enter to complete the function.

Notice the name Olivia appears in cell D5. To separate the first name, you take advantage of the text pattern of the space. To separate text, you must identify the text pattern. The pattern must be consistent in some way to use text functions. Here the FIND function looks for the space character that separates the first and last names. For cell A5, the FIND function returns a 7 because the name Olivia contains six characters and the space after the name is the seventh character. Since you will not want to include the space character, the TRIM function can be used to remove it.

SIDE NOTE
Alternate Method
Subtracting a 1 from the Find function returns a 6 instead of a 7. The result is the same as using TRIM.

d. Double-click cell **D5** to begin editing the function. Click after the **equal sign** to place the insertion point before the LEFT function. Type Trim(to begin the TRIM function.

e. Click after the last closing parenthesis. Type) and then press Ctrl+Enter to complete the TRIM function. The number of characters in cell D5 is now 6 as the trailing space character has been removed.

f. Double-click the **AutoFill handle** ➕ to copy cell **D5** down to **D22**. The first names of all guests are now displayed in column D.

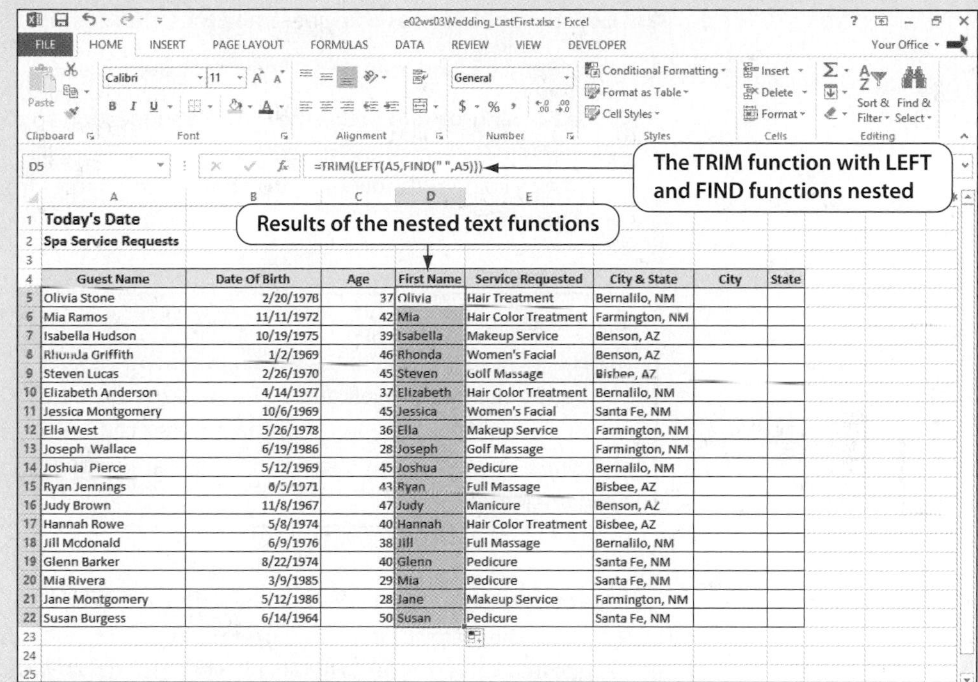

Guest Name	Date Of Birth	Age	First Name	Service Requested	City & State	City	State
Olivia Stone	2/20/1978	37	Olivia	Hair Treatment	Bernalilo, NM		
Mia Ramos	11/11/1972	42	Mia	Hair Color Treatment	Farmington, NM		
Isabella Hudson	10/19/1975	39	Isabella	Makeup Service	Benson, AZ		
Rhonda Griffith	1/2/1969	46	Rhonda	Women's Facial	Benson, AZ		
Steven Lucas	2/26/1970	45	Steven	Golf Massage	Bisbee, AZ		
Elizabeth Anderson	4/14/1977	37	Elizabeth	Hair Color Treatment	Bernalilo, NM		
Jessica Montgomery	10/6/1969	45	Jessica	Women's Facial	Santa Fe, NM		
Ella West	5/26/1978	36	Ella	Makeup Service	Farmington, NM		
Joseph Wallace	6/19/1986	28	Joseph	Golf Massage	Farmington, NM		
Joshua Pierce	5/12/1969	45	Joshua	Pedicure	Bernalilo, NM		
Ryan Jennings	6/5/1971	43	Ryan	Full Massage	Bisbee, AZ		
Judy Brown	11/8/1967	47	Judy	Manicure	Benson, AZ		
Hannah Rowe	5/8/1974	40	Hannah	Hair Color Treatment	Bisbee, AZ		
Jill Mcdonald	6/9/1976	38	Jill	Full Massage	Bernalilo, NM		
Glenn Barker	8/22/1974	40	Glenn	Pedicure	Santa Fe, NM		
Mia Rivera	3/9/1985	29	Mia	Pedicure	Santa Fe, NM		
Jane Montgomery	5/12/1986	28	Jane	Makeup Service	Farmington, NM		
Susan Burgess	6/14/1964	50	Susan	Pedicure	Santa Fe, NM		

Figure 14 Result of nesting the FIND function

g. **Save** your workbook.

Using the Flash Fill

The Flash Fill feature in Excel 2013 makes data cleansing easier and faster than using traditional text functions. **Flash Fill** recognizes patterns in data as you type and automatically fills in values for text and numeric data. Flash Fill involves less typing than text functions, which makes it easier to use on mobile or touch-screen devices.

To work correctly Flash Fill must be completed in a column adjacent to the data being manipulated. There are two ways to use the Flash Fill. Providing two suggested values will initiate the automatic Flash Fill to a suggestion for cleansing your data. This suggestion will preview along the column adjacent to the data. Pressing Enter will accept the suggestion and populate the column of cells. Flash Fill can also be initiated on the Data tab. This is useful for cleansing data in cells that are not directly adjacent to the data or for numeric data. Flash Fill will not automatically suggest values for numeric data.

The SpaServices worksheet includes a list of the city and state of origin for each guest attending the wedding. Separating these values into individual columns will be helpful for future tasks such as counting the number of guests from each state. In this exercise you will use the Flash Fill feature to separate the guest's city and state of origin into individual columns.

E03.13

To Use Flash Fill

a. Click the **SpaServices** worksheet, and then click cell **G5**.

b. Type Bernalilo and then press Enter to move to cell G6.

c. Type Farmington and notice the Flash Fill suggestion appears down the column of data. Press Enter to accept the suggestion.

Notice column G now contains only the city names from the list of cities and states in column F.

> **Troubleshooting**
> The Flash Fill feature requires two suggested values before it will offer a suggestion for the column of data you are in. These two suggested values must be typed in consecutive actions. If you clicked in another cell or pressed another key on the keyboard between typing "Bernalilo" and "Farmington"—Flash Fill will not offer a suggestion.

d. Select cell **H5**, type NM and then press Ctrl+Enter.

Since the State column is not next to the column with the city and state text, typing a suggested value for Flash Fill will not work. Using the Flash Fill button from the DATA tab will accomplish the task of isolating the state from column F.

e. Click the **DATA** tab, and then in the Data Tools group, click **Flash Fill**.

Notice column H now contains only the state abbreviations from the list of cities and states in column F. Importantly, notice that Flash Fill inserts static data. Thus, if the values in column F change, columns G and H will not be automatically updated. If you needed them to be automatically updated, you would need to use text functions.

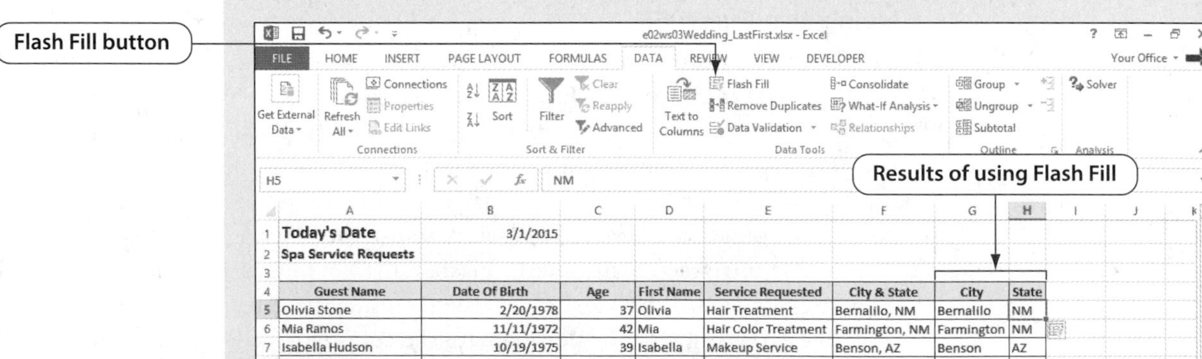

Figure 15 City names and state abbreviations separated with Flash Fill

f. **Save** your workbook.

REAL WORLD ADVICE **Flash Fill vs. Text Functions**

The Flash Fill feature of Excel 2013 is a quick, powerful, and touch-screen friendly way to work with text and numeric data. It is easy to use, but the data you insert using Flash Fill is not automatically updated if the underlying data changes. Flash Fill will not update prior values if new data is added or if the existing data changes. Text functions will update their results if underlying data changes, and they can be easily copied to accommodate new data. If data will be added or changed in your workbooks on a regular basis, use text functions!

Use Financial and Lookup Functions

Excel has many functions available to help businesses make decisions. These decisions may include calculating payments on a loan or returning data from a table based upon a specific value in a worksheet. The ability to combine these processes in more complex tasks is even more powerful. For example, a lookup function can retrieve an interest rate from a table of data to be used in a subsequent loan calculation. As with other functions, lookup and reference functions when combined with financial functions can be an effective combination.

Using Lookup and Reference Functions

Lookup and reference functions look up matching values in a table of data. Lookup and reference functions can be used for simple matches or complex retrieval tasks. This can be as simple as retrieving a value from a vertical or horizontal list, or as complex as finding the value of a cell within a table of data at a given row and column intersection. Common lookup and reference functions can be found in Table 9.

Function	Usage
HLOOKUP(lookup_value,table_array, row_index_num,[range_lookup])	Finds lookup_value in the top row of table_array and returns a value from row_index
INDEX (array,row_num,[column_num])	Returns a value from array by indexes specified as row_num and column_num
MATCH(lookup_value,lookup_array, [match_type])	Finds lookup_value in lookup_array
VLOOKUP(lookup_value,table_array, col_index_num,[range_lookup])	Finds lookup_value in the first column of table_array and returns a value from column_index

Table 9 Common lookup and reference functions

The **VLOOKUP function** matches a provided value in a table of data and returns a value from a subsequent column similar to looking up a phone number in a phone book. The "V" signifies that the function matches the provided value vertically, in the first column of the table of data. The syntax of a VLOOKUP is as follows:

=VLOOKUP(lookup_value, table_array, col_index_number, [range_lookup])

The lookup_value argument can be any text, number, or a reference to a cell that contains data. The table_array argument is a range in a spreadsheet. The range can be a single column of cells or multiple columns of cells. The VLOOKUP function will match the lookup_value on the first column of the supplied table_array. The col_index_number is the column number of the corresponding value that will be returned. The optional range_lookup argument allows the VLOOKUP to perform an approximate or exact match.

The range_lookup argument is TRUE for an approximate match. An approximate match allows the VLOOKUP to return the first value less than the range_lookup on the first column of the table_array. For example, looking up the value 50 on a range containing 45 and 55 would return 45. The range_lookup argument is FALSE for an exact match. An exact match will force the VLOOKUP to find the same value supplied in the lookup_value in the first column of the table_array. If the value cannot be found, the function will return an error.

The Turquoise Oasis Spa has recently partnered with a local bank to offer financing to customers that are booking large, costly events. Booking spa services usually is one of the last things guests will book. Thus, some guests will book less than they desire due to budget concerns. The spa is hoping that offering a financing package and discounts for large events will increase spa revenue.

As part of the workbook you are building for the spa, Meda has asked that you finish the WeddingFinancing worksheet that she started. This worksheet contains cells for guests to enter information about the wedding being planned. The worksheet already has cells prepared for entering the cost of the event, the down payment supplied by the guest, the annual interest rate, and the term of the loan in years. You have been asked to complete this worksheet so that when a wedding is scheduled, the guest will have an understanding of the basic elements of the financing plan. In this exercise you will use a lookup function to return the discount that the spa will provide based on the total cost of the wedding event being planned.

E03.14

To Use the VLOOKUP function

a. Click the **WeddingFinancing** worksheet tab, and then click cell **B7**.

b. Type =VLOOKUP(B3, to begin the VLOOKUP function.

This will use the value in B3 as the lookup value to match on the list of discounts.

c. Type E4:F8,2,TRUE) and then press Enter to complete the VLOOKUP function.

The VLOOKUP matches the value in B3 on the range E4:E8. When a match is found, the corresponding row value from column F will be returned. By placing TRUE as the range_lookup argument the VLOOKUP will perform an approximate match. This means an event costing $37,000 will returns a 5.0% discount.

Troubleshooting

If the VLOOKUP function returns a #N/A error, check to make sure the range_lookup argument is TRUE. Using FALSE for the argument will force the VLOOKUP into an exact match. Since $37,000 is not listed in E4:E8, an error will be returned.

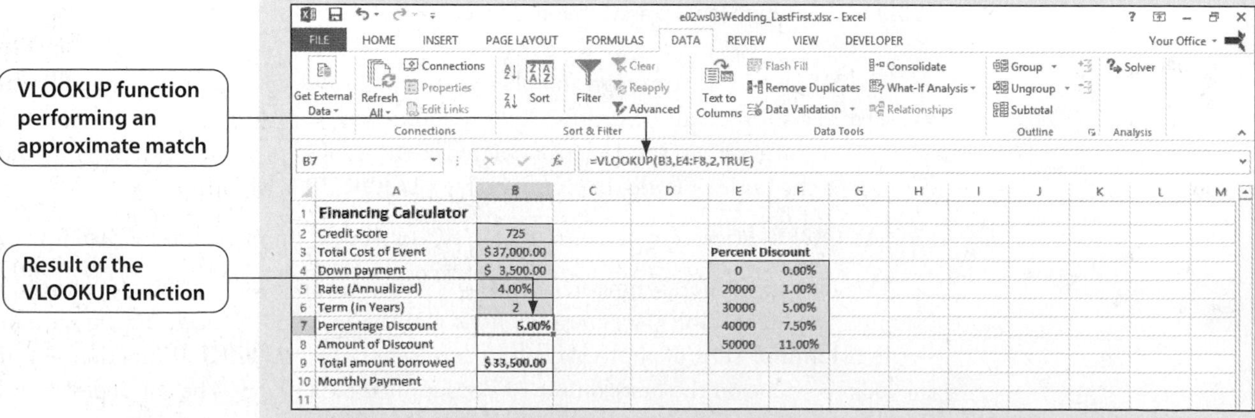

Figure 16 WeddingFinancing worksheet using the VLOOKUP function

d. Click cell **B8**, type =B3*B7 and then press Ctrl+Enter.

This will apply the 5.0% discount to the $37,000 event cost resulting in a discount of $1,850.

e. **Save** your workbook.

REAL WORLD ADVICE **Approximate and Exact Matches**

If the range_lookup argument is left blank it will default to TRUE for an approximate match. If the range_lookup should be FALSE, but is mistakenly left blank an incorrect result will be returned. Best practice dictates that you should always specify the range_lookup even though it is optional.

Using Financial Functions

A foundation for a successful business is generating revenue—any income brought into the business, prior to paying any expenses out—and hopefully yielding net profits. This also applies to personal finances where individuals generate income with the main goal of covering their expenses as they go through life with a net profit to spare. Having a foundational knowledge of financial terms is thus an important element of succeeding in both your personal and professional life. Some common financial terms that you will see and hear or possibly make use of in an Excel spreadsheet are shown in Table 10.

Financial Term	Definition
APR	The annual percentage rate; an interest rate expressed in an annual equivalent
Compounding interest	A process of charging interest on both the principal and the interest that accumulates on a loan
Interest payment	The amount of a payment that goes toward paying the interest accrued
NPV	The net present value of future investments
Period	The time period of payments, such as making payments monthly
Principal payment	The amount of a payment that goes toward reducing the principal amount
Principal value	The original amount borrowed or loaned
PV	Present value—the total amount that a series of future payments is worth now
Rate (and APR)	The interest rate per period of a loan or an investment
Simple interest	The interest charged on the principal amount of a loan only
Term	The total time of a loan, typically expressed in years or months
Time value of money	Recognizing that earning one dollar today is worth more than earning one dollar in the future

Table 10 Financial terminology

Financial functions are a set of predefined functions that can be used for calculating interest rates, payments, and analyzing loans. Some common financial functions are listed in Table 11.

Financial Functions	Usage
PMT(rate,nper,pv,[fv],[type])	Calculates periodic payment for a loan based on a constant interest rate and constant payment amounts
IPMT	Calculates periodic interest payment for a loan based on a constant interest rate and constant payment amounts
PPMT	Calculates periodic principal payment for a loan based on a constant interest rate and constant payment amounts
NPV	Calculates the net present value based on a discount interest rate, a series of future payments, and future income

Table 11 Common financial functions

A common and useful financial function in Excel is the PMT function. The **PMT function** determines the periodic payment for a loan based upon constant payments and interest rate. The PMT function by default returns a negative value. The function is really calculating an outflow of cash, a payment to be made. Within the financial and accounting industry, an outflow of cash is considered a negative value. In other words, this function assumes you are actually making a payment—taking money out of your pocket to give to someone else, or a negative value. Since some people may be confused seeing the value as negative, the value can be made positive by simply inserting a negative sign prior to the function or placing the absolute value function—ABS() —around the PMT function.

The syntax of the PMT function is as follows:

=PMT(rate,nper,pv,[fv],[type])

The first argument is the rate, which is the periodic interest rate. Importantly, the interest rate must be for each period. Most loans are discussed in terms of annual percentage rate (APR), while the period would be a shorter time period such as quarterly or monthly. The APR would need to be divided by 12 to get an equivalent monthly interest rate.

The second argument is nper, which is the number of periods or total number of payments that will be made for the loan. Again, many loans are discussed in years while the payments would be monthly. Thus, you will often need to determine the total number of periodic payments with a calculation.

The third required argument is PV, which is the present value of an investment or loan—the amount borrowed that needs to be paid back. The last two arguments are optional. The FV argument is the future value attained after the last payment is made. If this argument is left blank, the PMT function assumes FV to be zero. The Type argument indicates when a payment is due. If left blank, the PMT function assumes payments are due at the end of a period, if a one is supplied then payments are assumed due at the beginning of a period.

In this exercise, you will calculate the monthly payment for the customer for the event being planned using the PMT function.

E03.15

To Use the PMT Function

a. Click the **WeddingFinancing** worksheet, and then click cell **B10**.

b. Type =-PMT(to begin the PMT function.

As previously mentioned the PMT function is calculated by default as a negative value. The negative sign before the PMT function will display the final result as a positive number.

c. Type B5/12, to complete the rate argument. Because the interest rate in cell B5 is annual, you need to divide by 12 to get the interest rate per payment—in this case monthly.

d. Type B6*12, to complete the number of periods argument. Because the term of the loan is in years, you will need to multiply the term by 12 to get the total number of payments—in this case months—in the loan.

SIDE NOTE
Unit Conversions
Be careful when converting the arguments of the PMT function. Monthly payments are converted using 12, quarterly are converted using 4.

e. Type B9) and then press Ctrl+Enter to supply the present value of the loan and complete the PMT function.

The original loan amount was $37,000. Cell B9 takes the original amount in B3, subtracts the down payment supplied in cell B4, and subtracts the amount of the discount in cell B8.

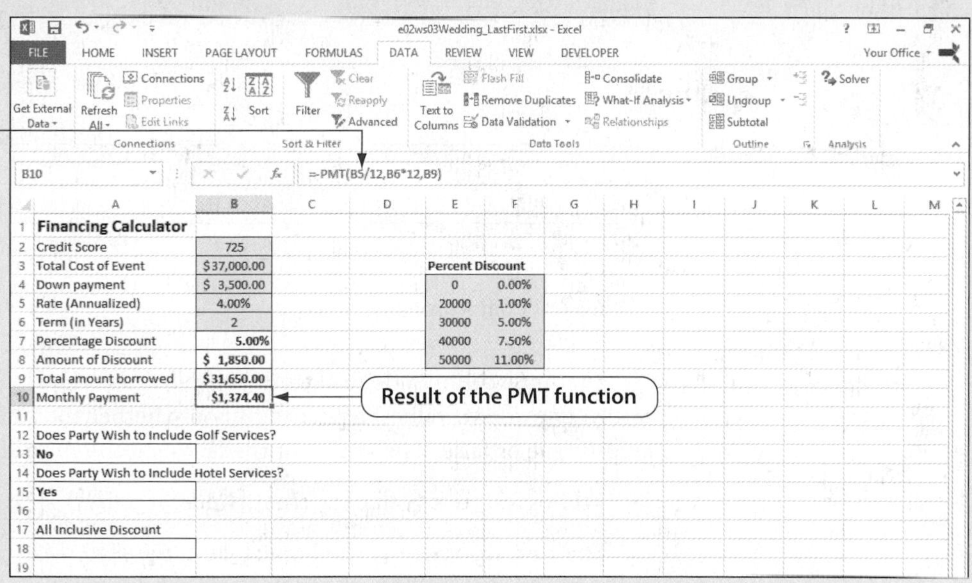

Figure 17 PMT function used to calculate a monthly payment

f. **Save** your workbook.

Use Logical Functions and Troubleshoot Functions

When constructing a spreadsheet the need will often arise to evaluate criteria in a range of cells and make a decision based on those criteria. Excel contains functions that can evaluate a wide range of criteria and return customized results. For example, a comparison of two cells to see if their values are the same may result in a cell displaying TRUE, a customized text response, or even performing another calculation. As the formulas in a spreadsheet become more complicated errors may occur in the spreadsheet. Understanding some basic spreadsheet troubleshooting techniques can easily correct these errors.

Using Logical Functions

Logical functions evaluate statements, or declarations, as being either true or false. For example, the statement "the sky is blue" is a declaration that can be evaluated as true. If the statement was "Is the sky blue?" the response would be a yes/no instead of true/false. So, all logical functions are structured around the concept of declaring a position or statement that Excel will evaluate and return as True or False.

The best way to think of a declaration is to think of using comparison symbols like the =, >, <, or >= symbols as shown in Table 12. When you set up a statement of X>Y, Excel can evaluate that comparison as true or false.

Comparison Operator Symbol	Example	Declarative Clause
<	A < B	A is less than B
>	A > B	A is greater than B
=	A = B	A is equal to B
<=	A <= B	A is less than or equal to B
>=	A >= B	A is greater than or equal to B
<>	A <> B	A does not equal B

Table 12 Comparison operators

The most common logical function to learn is the IF function. The **IF function** will return one of two values depending upon whether the supplied logical test being evaluated is true or false. The syntax of the IF function is as follows:

=IF(logical_test,[value_if_true],[value_if_false])

The first argument is the logical_test, the statement you want to evaluate as TRUE or FALSE. Excel will then evaluate it as either true or false. The second argument is the result you want returned in the cell if the expression is evaluated as true. The third argument is the result you want in the cell if the expression is evaluated as false.

Notice that only the logical_test argument is required. The last two arguments are optional. If you leave them out, Excel will automatically return TRUE or FALSE as the result of the function. However, it is much more common and expected that you will supply something for all three arguments. If you consider the context, logical statement, and results of the IF function, the structure begins to fall into place.

It is possible to create intricate logical statements using the AND and the OR functions. These functions allow you to evaluate multiple logical statements within a single IF function. The **AND function** returns TRUE if all logical tests supplied are true; otherwise, it returns FALSE. The **OR function** returns TRUE if any one logical test supplied is true; otherwise, it returns FALSE. The components can incorporate values, cells, named ranges, and even other functions. Common logical functions and their usage are listed in Table 13.

Logical Functions	Usage
IF(logical_test,[value_if_true],[value_if_false])	Returns one of two values, depending upon whether the logical statement is evaluated as being true or false
IFERROR(value,value_if_error)	Returns a specified value if a function or formula returns an error; otherwise, it returns the value of the function or formula
AND(logical1,logical2,...)	Returns true if logical1, logical2,...logicaln all return true
OR(logical1,logical2,...)	Returns true if any one of logical1, logical2,...logicaln return true

Table 13 Common logical functions

CONSIDER THIS | **Variations in Constructing Formulas**

In Excel, there can be many ways that a formula can be written. Some are more efficient than others. At a minimum, every IF statement can be written two ways. Why? Provide an example with both ways.

To encourage couples getting married to use the resort for all of their wedding services, the Painted Paradise Resort and Spa is offering an all-inclusive discount of $500.00. The availability of the discount to the guests must be evaluated in two steps. First, the discount can only be offered if the guest's credit score is at least 650. Secondly, the wedding party must use both the golf course and hotel as part of their event. Common logical functions can be used to evaluate if a wedding party is eligible for the all-inclusive discount. If the wedding party is eligible, they will receive a $500 discount. If they are not eligible, the cell should display a zero.

E03.16

To Use the IF and the AND functions

a. Click the **WeddingFinancing** worksheet, and then click cell **C10**.

b. Type =IF(to begin the IF function and enter the logical_test argument.

   The credit score of the guest is located in cell B2. The IF function will need to test for a value in this cell of greater than or equal to 650.

c. Type B2>=650, to complete the logical_test argument and enter the value_if_true argument.

   The IF function should return the text "Sufficient Credit Score" if the value in B2 is 650 or greater. If the value is less than 650 the text "Insufficient Credit Score" should be returned.

d. Type "Sufficient Credit Score", "Insufficient Credit Score") and then press Ctrl+Enter to complete the IF function. If necessary, use the AutoFit feature on column C.

   Notice that since the value in B2 is 725, the text "Sufficient Credit Score" is returned by the IF function.

e. Click cell **A18**, and then type =IF(to begin the IF function and enter the logical_test argument. Since the discount requires both golf services and hotel services to be used by the wedding party, the AND function will be used in the logical test of the IF function to evaluate this criteria.

SIDE NOTE
Using Quotes
Quotation marks must be used in an IF function to return text values. To return numeric data do not use quotation marks.

f. Type AND(A13="Yes",A15="Yes"), to insert the AND function into the IF function and complete the logical_test argument.

The AND function will now return TRUE if cells A13 and A15 both contain the text "Yes". Otherwise it will return FALSE to the IF function.

g. Type 500, to complete the value_if_true argument.

If the AND function returns TRUE, the number 500 will be displayed in cell A18. This will give a $500 discount to the wedding party.

h. Type 0) to complete the value_if_false argument and complete the IF function.

If the AND function returns FALSE, the number 0 will be displayed in cell A18 and no discount will be given. Notice that no discount is currently given as cell A13 displays No.

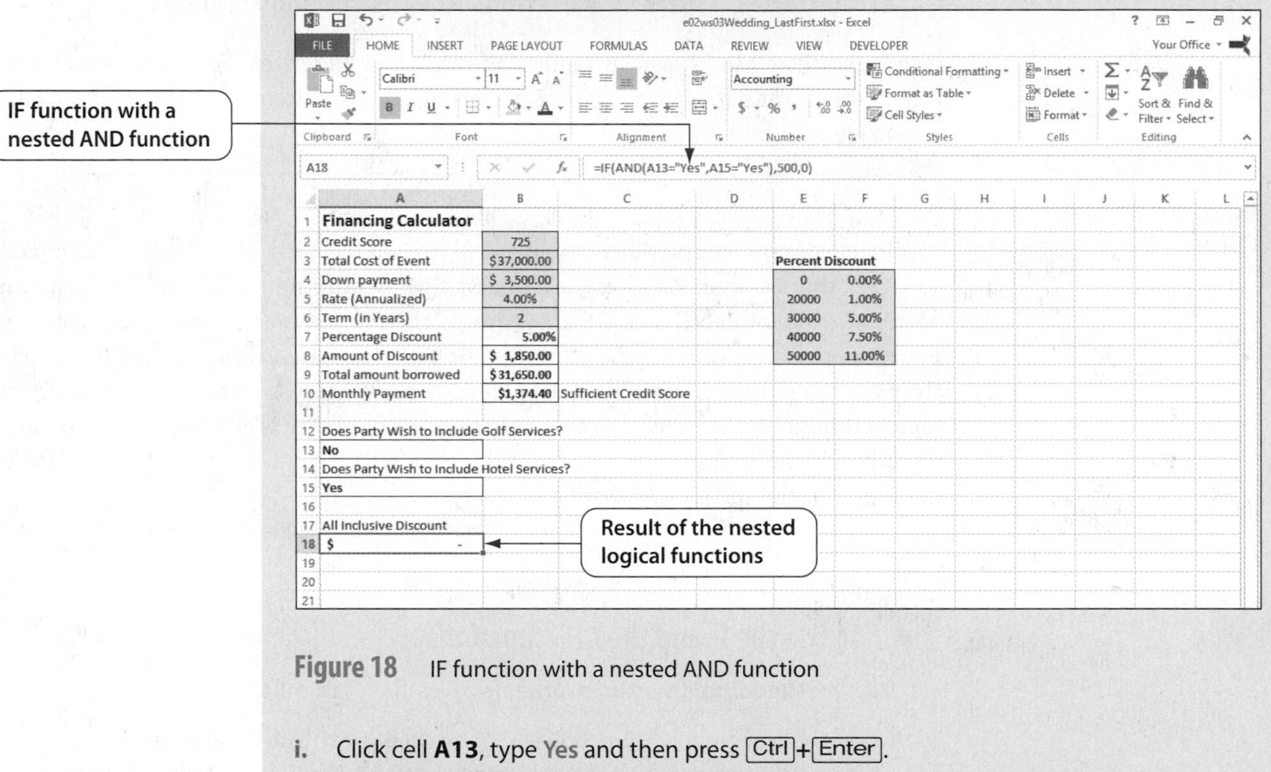

Figure 18 IF function with a nested AND function

i. Click cell **A13**, type Yes and then press Ctrl+Enter.

Cell A18 now displays a discount as both cells A13 and A15 display Yes.

j. **Save** your workbook.

IF functions can range from simple tests of a statement to complex, nested formulas. Table 14 shows four examples of IF functions with varying levels of complexity.

Context: Display the word "Good" if the exam score in J10 is better than or equal to the target goal of 80, which is in cell B2. If it is worse than 80, display the word "Bad".

Example: =IF(J10>=$B$2,"Good", "Bad")

Interpretation: If the value of cell J10 is greater than or equal to the value in B2, the text "Good" is displayed. Otherwise, the text "Bad" is displayed.

Context: Display the status of an employee meeting his or her goal of getting a number of transactions, where transactions are listed in the range of A2:A30 and the target number of transactions are in cell C3.

Example: =IF(COUNT(A2:A30)>=C3,"Met Goal", "")

Interpretation: If the count of transactions that are listed in range A2:A30 is greater than or equal to the value in C3 (the target goal for the employee), then the employee met his or her goal and the text "Met Goal" should be displayed. Otherwise, the goal was not met and no value should be displayed. This can be accomplished by supplying two quotation marks with no characters typed between them.

Context: For tracking any projects that have not been completed, check the text in H20, and if it does not say "Complete", assume the project is not complete and calculate how many months are left when A3 has today's date and A4 has the targeted completion date.

Example: =IF(H20<>"Complete", DATEDIF(A3,A4,"M"),0)

Interpretation: If H20 does not say "Complete" to represent a completed project, calculate the number of months left, based on dates in cells A3 and A4. Otherwise, show a zero.

Context: Determine salary by checking if the employee generated less revenue than their goal, listed in B2. If so, they simply get their base pay. If they do meet their goal or generate more revenue than their goal, they get a bonus, which is a percent of sales added to their base pay. Since this may result in a value that has more than two decimals, the result needs to be rounded to two decimals.

Example: =ROUND(IF(SUM(Sales<B2,Base,Base+BonusPercent*(Sum(Sales))),2)

Interpretation: The ROUND( ) function will round the result to two decimals. Inside the ROUND function, the SUM(Sales) functions will sum the range named Sales to give the total sales. The IF statement then indicates that IF the total Sales is less than the value in B2 (the sales goal), provide the value that is in the range called Base (Base pay). Otherwise, the total Sales must be greater than B2 and the pay would be calculated as the Base (Base pay) plus the value in the named range, BonusPercent times the total Sales.

Table 14 Examples of IF functions

> **CONSIDER THIS | What IF There Are Three Options?**
>
> An IF statement can handle just two results: true and false. Are most real-world situations that simple? How could you use an IF statement if there are more than two results? It is possible!

Troubleshooting Functions

Logical functions dramatically increase the value of a spreadsheet. However, on the path to learning how to use functions, and even as an experienced spreadsheet user, you will still make typing errors during the development of functions. Excel does an excellent job of incorporating cues to help you determine where you have gone astray with a function.

When you make a mistake with a function that prevents Excel from returning a viable result, Excel will provide an error message. While these may seem cryptic initially, they actually can be interpreted. Typically an error message will be prefaced with a number symbol (#). Examples would be #VALUE!, #N/A, #NAME?, or #REF!. Over time you will learn to recognize common issues that would cause these error messages.

QUICK REFERENCE | **Common Error Messages**

1. #NAME?—This error indicates that text in a formula is not recognized. Excel treats unrecognized text as a named range that does not exist. This is often due to missing quotes around a text string or mistyping the function or range name.
2. #REF!—This error indicates a reference that Excel cannot find. This is often due to changes like a deleted worksheet, column, row, or cell.
3. #N/A—This error indicates that a value is not available in one or more cells specified. Common causes occur in functions that try to find a value in a list but the value does not exist. Rather than returning an empty set—no value—Excel returns this error instead.
4. #VALUE!—This error occurs when the wrong type of argument or operand is being used, such as entering a text value when the formula requires a number. Common causes can be the wrong cell reference that contains a text value rather than a numeric value.
5. #DIV/0!—This is a division by 0 error and occurs when a number is divided by zero or by a cell that contains no value. While it can occur due to an actual error in the design of a formula, it also may occur simply due to the current conditions within the spreadsheet data. In other words, this is common when a spreadsheet model is still in the creation process and data has not yet been entered into the necessary cells. Once proper numeric data does exist, the error disappears.

There are numerous ways to troubleshoot erroneous functions in Excel. When you encounter an error, you can quickly check the cell references and arguments of the function by double-clicking the cell to edit the function. This is beneficial since, while a function is being edited, Excel will outline any cells or ranges included in the function and display the ScreenTip for the function.

On the Commission worksheet, Meda has set up a quick analysis that rewards the employee scheduling the event with a commission of the total cost of the event. The commission earned is then added to the base event pay for the employee. The base event pay is contingent upon the employee level. After setting up the worksheet, she noticed an error in one of the cells. Additionally, the table located in the Commission worksheet states that managers have a base event pay of $1,250. However, the value shown for the manager in the worksheet is only $750.

E03.17

To Troubleshoot a Function

a. Click the **Commission** worksheet tab, and then click cell **B4**.

   Notice the #N/A error being returned by the VLOOKUP function in the cell. Recall that this error commonly occurs because a value cannot be found on a list.

b. Click the **Error Message** button next to cell B4. Notice that the error message states a value is not available.

c. Double-click cell **B4** to edit the formula.

Notice the outlines around the cells that are part of the VLOOKUP function. From this view you can verify that cell B3 is correctly referenced as the lookup value. Cells E4:F8 are correctly referenced as the table array. The column index number will return a value from column F if a value is found in column E.

Notice the range_lookup argument is set to FALSE. This means the lookup is performing an exact match. Since $17,000 does not occur in the range E3:E7, the VLOOKUP will return a #N/A error.

d. Place the insertion point at the end of the **range_lookup** argument, and then delete the text **FALSE**. Type TRUE and then press Ctrl+Enter to fix the formula. Notice that the value 5% now appears in cell B4.

e. Double-click cell **B8** to edit the formula.

Notice the range_lookup argument is set to TRUE. This means the lookup is performing an approximate match and is returning the incorrect base event pay rate.

f. Place the insertion point at the end of the **range_lookup** argument, and then delete the text **TRUE**. Type FALSE and then press Ctrl+Enter to fix the formula. Notice that the value $1,250 now appears in cell B8.

g. Complete the Documentation worksheet, **save** your workbook, and then **close** Excel. Submit your work as directed by your instructor.

REAL WORLD ADVICE Function Construction Guidelines

As you develop a spreadsheet, follow these guidelines for creating formulas and functions:

1. Use parentheses for grouping operations in calculations in order to get the correct order. However, do not overuse parentheses as it quickly adds to the complexity of the formula. For example, use =SUM(Sales) instead of =(SUM(Sales)).
2. When inserting numbers into a function, use formatting such as 10000. Do not enter 10,000 using a comma. The comma is a formatting element, and in Excel it is used to separate arguments. Best practice for functions and formulas dictates entering the 10,000 value in a cell and then using the cell address in the formula.
3. Insert currency as 4.34 instead of $4.34 as this will get confusing with relative and absolute cell referencing. Then, format the cell that will contain the result as Accounting or Currency. Best practice for functions and formulas dictates entering the 4.34 value in a cell and then using the cell address in the formula.
4. Enter percentages as decimals, such as .04. Then, format the number as a percentage.
5. Logical conditions have three parts—two components to compare and the comparison sign. Do not type ">5" when there is no value to evaluate as being greater than 5.
6. Use the negative sign, such as -333 to indicate negative numbers in formulas as opposed to (333).
7. Always put quotes around text unless it is a named range. Numeric values do not require quotes unless the number will be used in a textual context and not for a mathematical equation, such as displaying a zip code or telephone number.
8. Avoid unneeded spaces in formulas. Excel will allow a function such as = SUM(A2:A10). Best practice dictates typing the function as =SUM(A2:A10) with no extra spaces.

Concept Check

1. Explain the three different types of cell referencing. p. 488
2. Why are named ranges useful? What limitations are there in creating the names for ranges? p. 496
3. Why is the syntax of an Excel function important? How can you distinguish between required and optional portions of a function? p. 501–502
4. In the math and statistical functions, what are the differences between the ROUND function and the INT function? Give a business example of when you would use each. p. 502-503
5. What is the difference between the TODAY() and NOW() functions? Why is this difference important? p. 509
6. What are common uses for text functions? Why is the Flash Fill feature useful on mobile devices? p. 511, 513
7. Explain the difference between the TRUE and FALSE parameters for the range_lookup argument of a VLOOKUP function. Give a business example of how you would use a VLOOKUP with a PMT function. p. 516
8. Give a business example where an IF function would be useful. How would using the AND or OR functions in the logical_test argument change the way the IF function works? p. 521

Key Terms

ABS function 502
Absolute cell reference 488
AND function 520
Argument 500
Cell reference 488
COUNT function 507
COUNTA function 507
Date and time functions 508
DATEDIF function 509
Financial functions 518
FIND function 511
Flash Fill 513
Function 500
Function arguments 503
IF function 520
INT function 502
LEFT function 511
Logical functions 520
Lookup and reference functions 515
MEDIAN function 507
Mixed cell reference 488
MODE function 507
MODE.MULT function 507
MODE.SNGL function 507
Name Manager 497
Named range 496
NOW function 509
OR function 520
PMT function 518
Relative cell reference 488
ROUND function 502
Syntax 500
Text functions 511
TODAY function 509
VLOOKUP function 515

Visual Summary

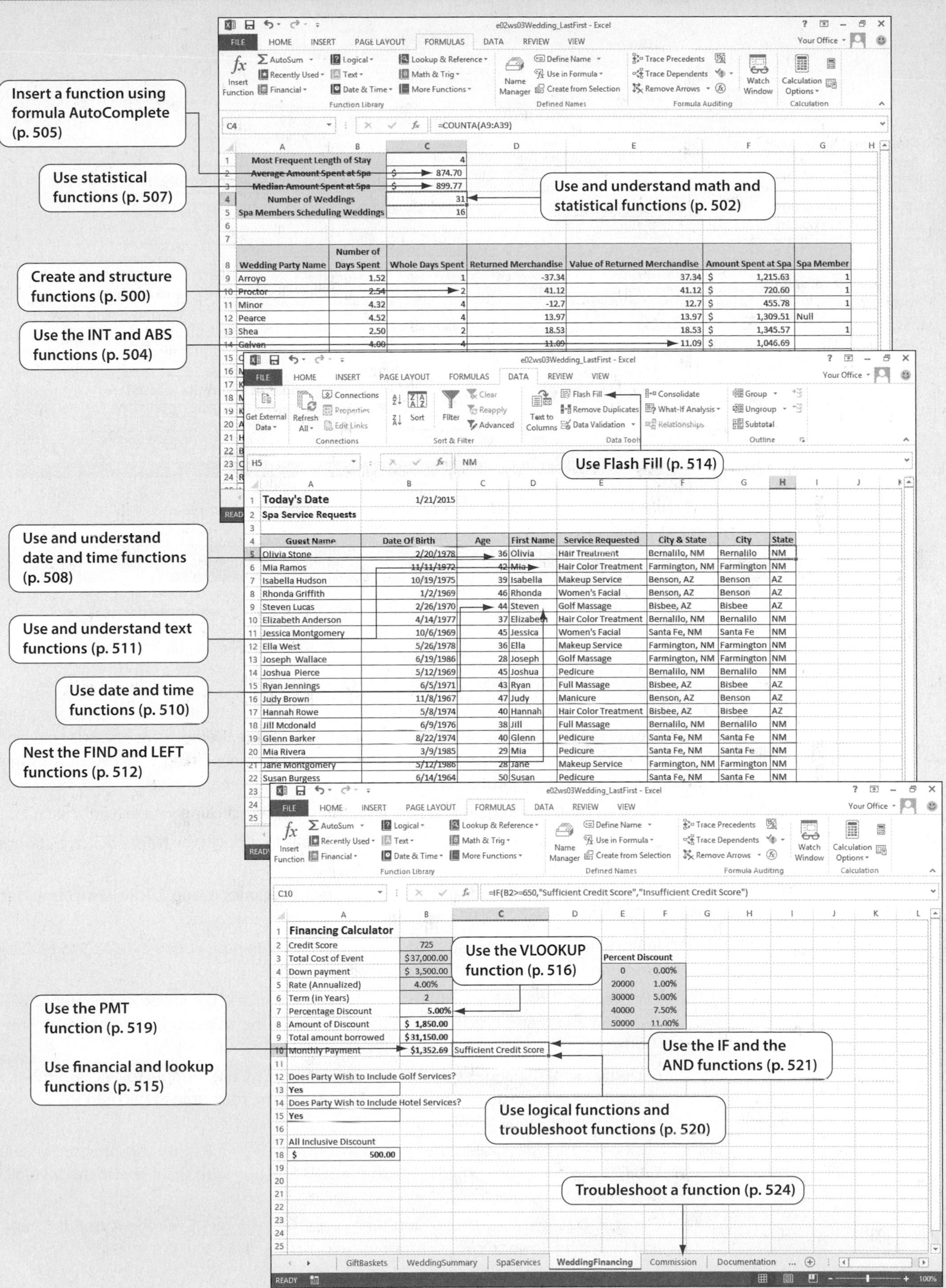
Insert a function using formula AutoComplete (p. 505)
Use statistical functions (p. 507)
Use and understand math and statistical functions (p. 502)
Create and structure functions (p. 500)
Use the INT and ABS functions (p. 504)
Use Flash Fill (p. 514)
Use and understand date and time functions (p. 508)
Use and understand text functions (p. 511)
Use date and time functions (p. 510)
Nest the FIND and LEFT functions (p. 512)
Use the VLOOKUP function (p. 516)
Use the PMT function (p. 519)
Use financial and lookup functions (p. 515)
Use the IF and the AND functions (p. 521)
Use logical functions and troubleshoot functions (p. 520)
Troubleshoot a function (p. 524)
=COUNTA(A9:A39)
=IF(B2>=650,"Sufficient Credit Score","Insufficient Credit Score")

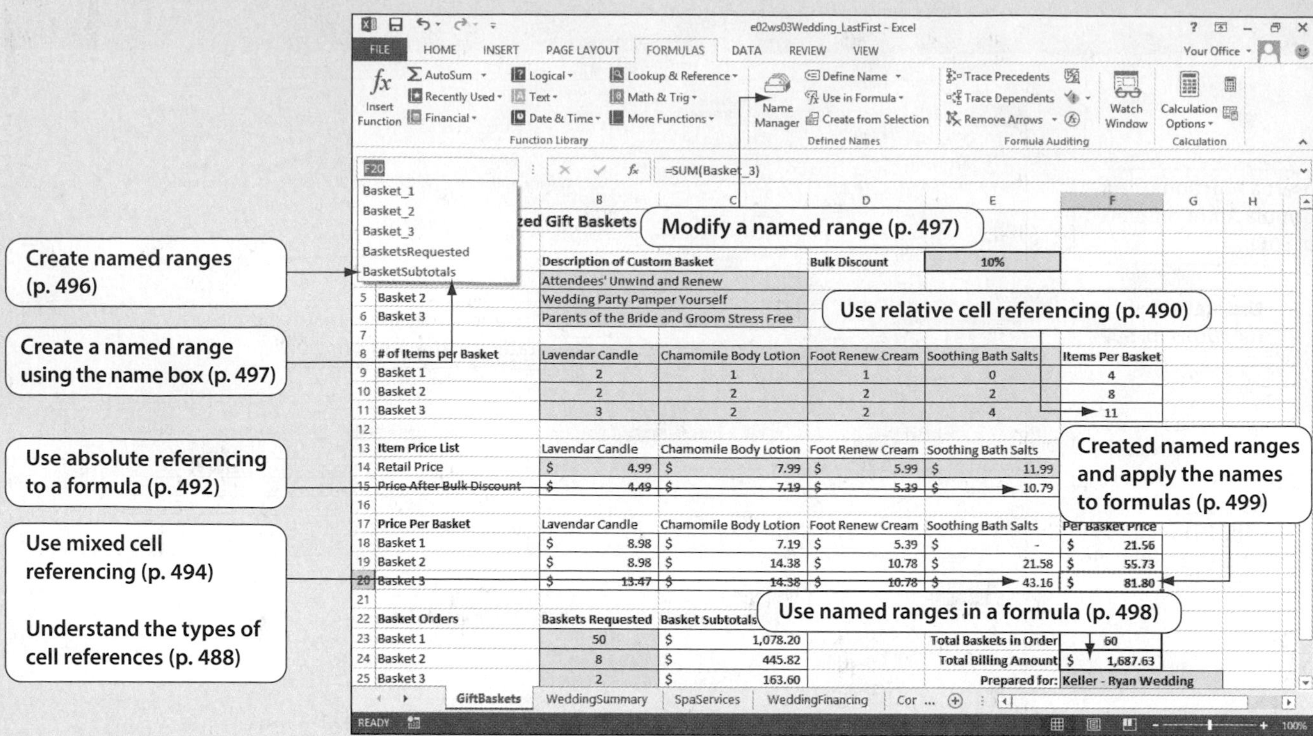

Figure 19 Painted Paradise Resort and Spa Wedding Planning Complete

Practice 1

Student data file needed:

e02ws03Bonus.xlsx

You will save your file as:

e02ws03Bonus_LastFirst.xlsx

Massage Therapist Bonus Workbook

Human Resources

Meda Rodate has been constructing a workbook that would enable her to analyze the goals for massage therapists and calculate their pay. The massage therapists have a base pay and earn commission on massages along with a bonus. Meda has asked that you make some modifications to the workbook that she began to facilitate her analysis.

a. Open **e02ws03Bonus**. Save it as e02ws03Bonus_LastFirst using your last and first name.

b. Click the **Bonus** worksheet tab, and then click cell **J17**. Click in the **Name** box, type Bonus and then press Enter.

c. Click the **FORMULAS** tab, and then in the Defined Names group, click **Name Manager**. Click **Christy** in the list of named ranges in the workbook.

d. In the Refers to box, delete the existing range, and then type =Bonus!$B$12:$K$12. Click **Close**, and then click **Yes** to save changes.

e. Click cell **B4**. Type =B3, and then press F4 twice to create the mixed cell reference B$3. Type *A4 and then press F4 three times to create the mixed cell reference $A4. Press Ctrl+Enter.

f. Click the **AutoFill** handle, and then drag down to copy the formula to cell **B8**. With the range B4:B8 still selected, click the **AutoFill** handle, and then drag to the right to copy the formulas to the range **B4:K8**.

g. Click cell **F19**, type =SUM(Christy), and then press Enter. Repeat this process for cells F20:F22, replacing the named range in the SUM function with the name of the therapist in cells A20:A22 respectively.

h. Click cell **D25**, type =C19*C25, and then press Ctrl+Enter. Click the **AutoFill** handle, and then drag down to copy the formula to cell **D28**.

A bonus is earned if the therapist attains two goals. First, if the generated actual revenue for a therapist is greater than the goal for that therapist. Second, if the actual number of massages completed for a therapist was greater than or equal to the goal of that therapists. If the goal is met, cells D19:D22 and G19:G22 should display a 1; otherwise, they should display a 0.

i. Click cell **D19**, type =IF(C19>B19,1,0) and then press Ctrl+Enter. Click the **AutoFill** handle, and then drag down to copy the formula to cell **D22**.

j. Click cell **G19**, type =IF(F19>=E19,1,0) and then press Ctrl+Enter. Click the **AutoFill** handle, and then drag down to copy the formula to cell **G22**. If both goals are met, cells E25:E28 should display the bonus amount in cell J17; otherwise, they should display 0.

k. Click cell **E25**, type =IF(AND(D19=1,G19=1),Bonus,0) and then press Ctrl+Enter. Click the **AutoFill** handle, and then drag down to copy the formula to cell **E28**.

l. Click cell **F25**, type =B25+D25+E25, and then press Ctrl+Enter. Click the **AutoFill** handle, and then drag down to copy the formula to cell **F28**.

m. On the **INSERT** tab, in the Text group, click **Header & Footer**. On the HEADER & FOOTER TOOLS DESIGN tab, in the Navigation group, click **Go to Footer**. Click in the **left footer** section, and then in the Header & Footer Elements group, click **File Name**.

n. Click any **cell** on the spreadsheet to move out of the footer, and then press Ctrl+Home. On the **VIEW** tab, in the Workbook Views group, click **Normal**.

o. Click the Documentation worksheet. Click cell **A6**, and then type in today's date. Click cell **B6**, and then type in your first and last name. Complete the remainder of the Documentation worksheet according to your instructor's direction.

p. Click **Save**, close Excel, and then submit your files as directed by your instructor.

Problem Solve 1

Production & Operations

Student data file needed:

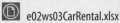

e02ws03CarRental.xlsx

You will save your file as:

e02ws03CarRental_LastFirst.xlsx

Express Car Rental

Jason Easton is a member of the support/decision team for the San Diego branch of Express Car Rental. He created a worksheet to keep track of weekly rentals in an attempt to identify trends in choices of rental vehicles, length of rental, and payment method. This spreadsheet is designed only for Jason and his supervisor to try and find weekly trends and possibly use this information when marketing and forecasting the type of cars needed on site. The data for the dates of rental, daily rates, payment method, and gas option have already been entered.

a. Open **e02ws03CarRental**, and then save the file as e02ws03CarRental_LastFirst using your last and first name.

b. On the RentalData worksheet, in cell **E6**, enter a date formula to determine the length of rental in days. Copy this formula to the range **E7:E32**.

c. Name the range **A37:B40** RentalRates.

d. In cell **G6**, use the appropriate lookup and reference function to retrieve the rental rate from the named range **RentalRates**. The function should look for an exact matching value from column A in the data. Copy the function down the column to cell **G32**.

e. Name the range **B42** Discount and then name the range **B44** GasCost.

f. In cell **H6**, enter a formula to determine any discount that should be applied. If the payment method was Express Miles or Rewards, the customer should receive the discount shown in B42. If no discount should be applied, the formula should return a zero. Use the named range for cell **B42**, not the cell address, in this formula. Copy the function down the column to cell **H32**.

g. In cell **J6**, enter the correct formula to determine the cost of gas if the customer chose that option as indicated in column I. Use the named range for cell **B44** in this formula. Copy the function down the column to cell **J32**.

h. In cell **K6**, enter the correct formula to determine the total cost of the rental by based on the daily rate, the number of days rented, the cost of gas, and any discount given to the customer. Copy the function down the column to cell **K32**.

i. In cell **B46**, use the appropriate function to calculate the Median length of rental in days.

j. In cell **B47**, use the appropriate function to count the number of rentals in the data.

k. Complete the Documentation worksheet according to your instructor's direction. Insert the **filename** in the left custom footer section of the Header/Footer tab in the Page Setup dialog box on all worksheets in the workbook.

j. Click Save, close Excel, and then submit your files as directed by your instructor.

Perform 1: Perform in Your Life

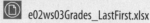

Student data file needed:

e02ws03Grades.xlsx

You will save your file as:

e02ws03Grades_LastFirst.xlsx

Calculate Your Grade

Information Technology

Using the e02ws03Grades workbook construct an evaluation of your grades in a class you are currently taking. The workbook provided has an example grading scale, though this can be modified to meet the requirements of the course you are taking.

a. Open **e02ws03Grades**, and then save the file as e02ws03Grades_LastFirst.

b. Create a basic structure for entering the names of assignments, the points possible on an assignment, and the current percentage grade of an assignment. Enter your assignments and respective grades in the worksheet.

c. Create named ranges for the points possible, points earned, and the grading scale ranges. Use these named ranges in calculations as appropriate.

d. In an adjacent column calculate your percentage grade on each assignment. Use the appropriate function to round the resulting percentage to two decimal places.

e. In an adjacent column use the appropriate function to look up the letter grade on the assignment using the grading scale provided.

f. Summarize the total points possible and your total points earned. Calculate your course grade as a percentage of the total points possible. Use the appropriate function to round the resulting percentage to two decimal places.

g. Calculate your letter grade for the course using the appropriate function.

h. Some courses provide extra credit. Create a cell that displays Yes if your course offers extra credit or No if it does not. Create another cell that displays the number of credits you have earned.

i. Construct an IF function that adds the extra credit points earned into your course grade if extra credit for the course is available and the extra credit points earned is greater than zero.

j. Complete the Documentation worksheet according to your instructor's direction. Insert the **filename** in the left custom footer section of the Header/Footer tab in the Page Setup dialog box on all worksheets in the workbook.

k. Click Save, close Excel, and then submit your files as directed by your instructor.

Additional Cases

Additional Workshop Cases are available on the companion website and in the instructor resources

WORKSHOP 4 | EFFECTIVE CHARTS

OBJECTIVES

1. Explore chart types, layouts, and styles p. 532
2. Explore the positioning of charts p. 536
3. Understand different chart types p. 539
4. Change chart data and styles for presentations p. 548
5. Edit and format charts to add emphasis p. 557
6. Use sparklines and data bars to emphasize data p. 561
7. Recognize and correct confusing charts p. 564

Prepare Case

Turquoise Oasis Spa Sales Reports

Sales & Marketing

The Turquoise Oasis Spa managers, Irene Kai and Meda Rodate, are pleased with your work and would like to see you continue to improve the spa spreadsheets. They want to use charts to learn more about the spa. To do this, Meda has given you a spreadsheet with some data, and she would like you to develop some charts. Visualizing the data with charts will provide knowledge about the spa for decision-making purposes.

PhotoSG / Fotolia

REAL WORLD SUCCESS

"In my internship, I used a combo chart to analyze inventory trends over time, presenting inventory buildup or shrinkage on one axis and production levels on another. I was able to use this visual representation to better understand supply chain coordination throughout a quarter, providing my superiors with data to improve our operating efficiency. By combining these charts with charts presenting demand variance, our company was able to pinpoint sources of inventory buildup and higher operating costs."

- Steven, alumnus

Student data files needed for this workshop:

 e02ws04SpaSales.xlsx

 e02ws04TurquoiseOasis.jpg

You will save your file as:

 e02ws04SpaSales_LastFirst.xlsx

Designing a Chart

With Excel you can organize data so it has context and meaning, converting data into meaningful information. **Data visualization** is the graphical presentation of data with a focus upon qualitative understanding. It is central to finding trends and supporting business decisions. Modern data visualization can include beautiful and elegant charts that include movement and convey information in real time. Even basic charts are at the heart of data visualization. Charts enlighten you as you compare, contrast, and examine how data changes over time. Learning how to work with charts means not only knowing how to create them but also realizing that different knowledge can be discovered or emphasized by each type of chart.

While it may seem simple to create a pie chart or bar chart, there are many considerations in creating your charts. Charts, as with pictures, are worth a thousand words. However, people interpret charts differently if the chart is not well developed. A well-developed chart should provide context for the information, without overshadowing key points. Finally, it is easy to confuse people with the choice and layout of a chart. You should create charts that use accurate, complete data, and your objective should be to provide a focused, clear message. In today's data-rich world, many interpretations or messages can be extracted from the data. There are three primary objectives businesses have in charting: data exploration, hypothesis testing, and argumentation.

Using the **data exploration objective**, you simply manipulate the data, and try to evaluate and prioritize all the interpretations or messages. There may be a need to create multiple charts, using a variety of data sources, layouts, and designs as you interpret the data. In this case, examine the data and let the charts tell a story.

Using the **hypothesis testing objective**, you may have some ideas or hypotheses about the data. Maybe you believe that a certain salesperson performs better than the others. Or maybe you believe that certain types of massages are more popular with particular types of customers. Charts can visually support or refute a hypothesis.

Using the **argumentation objective**, you have a position you want the data to visually support. You will need to select a specific and appropriate chart layout, use the necessary data, and design a chart that conveys your message clearly and unambiguously. Further, you have an ethical obligation to accurately represent the data. Misrepresenting data can result in lawsuits, loss of your job, or even cost lives.

Regardless of the objective, just a small set of data allows you to create a variety of charts, each offering a different understanding of the data. In this workshop, you will start with understanding the concepts for creating a chart in Excel, and understand which type of chart will depict the information in the best and most efficient manner.

Explore Chart Types, Layouts, and Styles

When you decide to represent data visually, you need to make some initial decisions about the basic design of the chart. These initial decisions include the location of the chart, the type of chart, the general layout and style, and what data you will be using. These elements can be set initially and modified later. Best practice dictates that you first consider and develop the basic design of the chart.

Regardless of the location or type of chart, the process of creating a chart starts with the organization of the data on the spreadsheet. The typical structure is to have labels across the top of the data, along the left side of the data, or both. While the labels do not have to be directly next to the data, it helps when selecting data and making your chart. The data may have been brought in from an external data source, like Access. The data may need to be filtered, calculated, or reorganized prior to creating a chart.

When you are ready to create a chart, select the cells that contain both the label headings and the data. People rarely create a perfect chart the first time. Initially, you may start a chart, work with it for a while, and then realize a different chart type would better convey the information. Fortunately, Excel provides ample flexibility when designing charts. Thus, if you change your mind, you can modify the chart or simply start over.

MODULE 2

Opening the Starting File

A chart in Excel is an object that sits above the worksheet. Clicking on the chart will allow you to modify aspects of the chart or even change the type of chart. You have been asked to review a pie chart that displays the use of portable massage tables by different therapists.

E04.00

To Open the SpaSales Worksheet

a. Start **Excel**, click **Open Other Workbooks**, and browse to your student data files. Locate and select **e02ws04SpaSales**, and then click **Open**.

b. Click the **FILE** tab, and then click **Save As**. Browse to the location where you are saving your files. In the File name box, type e02ws04SpaSales_LastFirst, using your last and first name, and then click **Save**.

c. On the **INSERT** tab, in the **Text** group, click **Header & Footer**.

d. On the **HEADER & FOOTER TOOLS DESIGN** tab, in the Navigation group, click **Go to Footer**. If necessary, click the **left section** of the footer, and then in the Header & Footer Elements group, click **File Name**.

e. Click any **cell** on the worksheet to move out of the footer, press Ctrl + Home, and then on the status bar, click **Normal**.

Modifying an Existing Chart

When you click an existing chart, you are activating the chart area. It will be highlighted on the border while the middle of the sides and the corners will have selection handles used to resize the chart. The chart border can also be used to move the entire chart to a new location within the spreadsheet. The Chart Tools contextual tab will appear on the Ribbon, and to the right of the chart three buttons will appear that provide quick access to common functions such as modifying chart elements, changing the chart layout, or filtering the chart data.

When a chart is selected, the data used in creating the chart will be highlighted in the worksheet, offering a visual clue of the associated data. In the TableUse worksheet you will see a pie chart describing the use of massage tables by individual therapists at the spa. A purple border surrounds the data that represents the legend labels. The range with a blue border is the data that represents the data series for the pie slices. A **data series** is a group of related data values to be charted. A **data point** is an individual data value in a data series. A chart may contain multiple data series or a single data series.

Subcomponents of the chart can also be selected, such as the background, various text elements, and even the individual chart elements themselves. Click components to make them active, and adjust specific items through either the Ribbon options or by right-clicking to display the shortcut menu to see available options. In this exercise, you will modify an existing pie chart on the TableUse worksheet.

REAL WORLD ADVICE First Impressions

First impressions are important with charts. You want the audience to receive the correct message during the initial moments. If the audience is distracted by the look and feel of the chart, they may stop looking for the message in the chart or extend the chaotic personality of the chart to the presenter. Thus, the chart can become a reflection upon you and your company.

MyITLab® Workshop 4 Training

SIDE NOTE
Alternate Method
Any action completed in the Chart Formatting Control can be completed through the Chart Tools contextual tab on the Ribbon.

E04.01

To Modify an Existing Chart

a. Click the **TableUse** worksheet tab. Notice the pie chart located below the data on this worksheet.

b. Click the **chart border** of the chart to select the chart and display the CHART TOOLS contextual tabs.

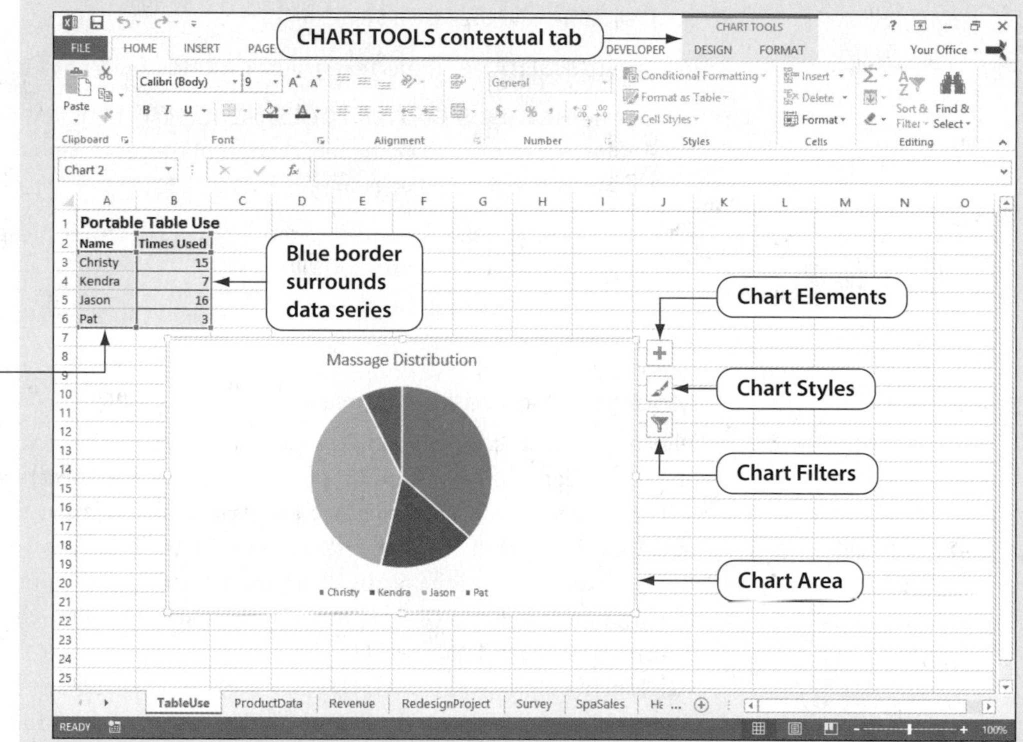

Figure 1 Selected pie chart

c. To the right of the chart, click **Chart Elements** [+], and then click **Data Labels**. This will display the number of times each therapist used a portable massage table in the corresponding slice of the pie chart.

d. Click the **Data Labels** arrow, and then select **More Options**. This will open the Format Data Labels task pane.

e. Under the **LABEL OPTIONS** group, click to deselect **Value**, and then click **Percentage**.

SIDE NOTE

Hover to See Icon Information

When presented with a set of icons, hover the mouse over an icon, and a ScreenTip will appear offering descriptive information.

f. Click the **chart border** of the chart, click **Chart Styles** , and then scroll down and point to **Style 7**. Notice the chart changes to display a live preview of the style. Click **Style 7**, and then click **Chart Styles** to close the control. This chart now displays the percent of portable table usage for each massage therapist at the spa.

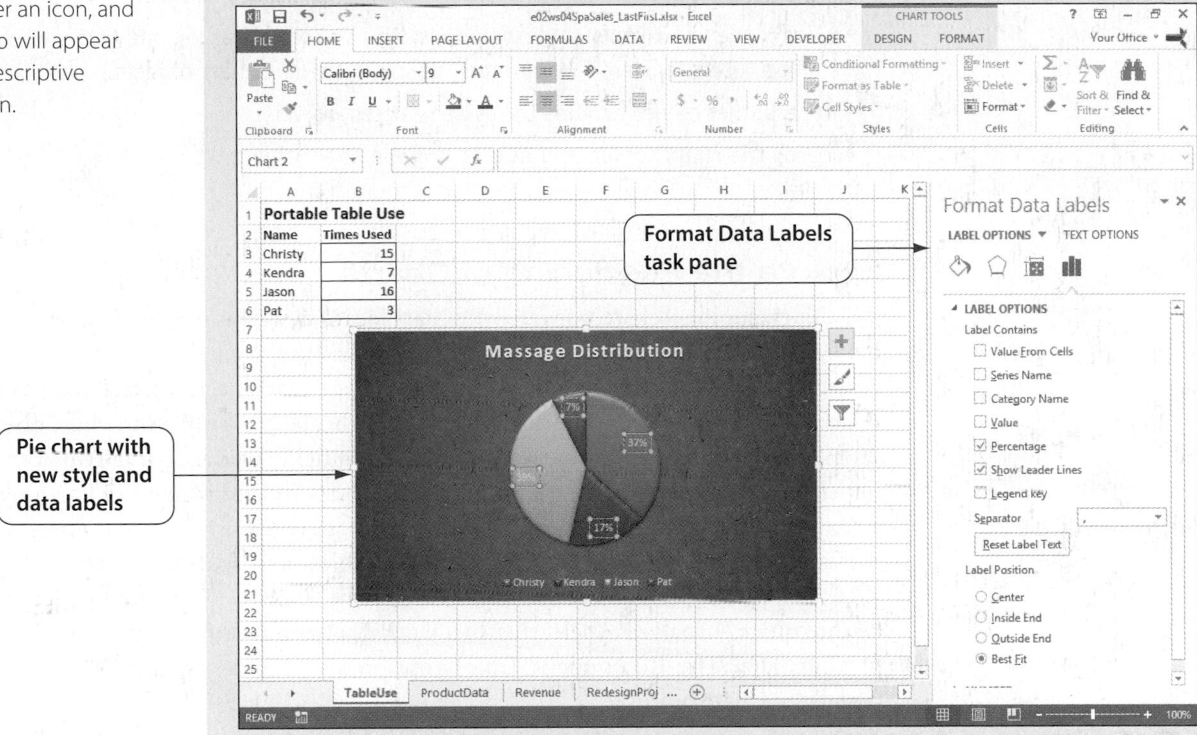

Figure 2 Modified chart

g. Close the Format Data Labels task pane, and then click **Save** .

CONSIDER THIS | **Misleading Charts**

Charts are supposed to frame information. But, have you ever seen a chart in a newspaper, online article, or magazine that would lead the viewer to an incorrect assumption or conclusion? Look for a chart that is misleading, discuss the context and possible incorrect conclusions that could be made, and consider the ethical aspect for the creator of the chart.

QUICK REFERENCE | **Working with Chart Objects**

It is possible to navigate through a chart using some of these guidelines:

- Click the chart border to activate the Chart Tools contextual tabs.
- Click chart objects to select individual chart components.
- Click outside a chart object or press Esc to deselect an object.
- Under the Chart Tools contextual tabs, on the Format tab, in the Current Selection group, use the Chart Elements box to select specific chart objects.
- Use border corner handles to resize selected objects.
- Click the chart border, and drag to move a chart object.

Explore the Positioning of Charts

When developing a chart, consider the chart location, as this might affect the flexibility of moving and resizing your chart components. There are two general locations for a chart—either within an existing worksheet or on a separate worksheet, referred to as a chart sheet. A **chart sheet** is a special worksheet that is dedicated to displaying chart objects. Excel 2013 has several new features that allow you to quickly analyze data. Two of these are the Quick Analysis tool and the Recommended Charts feature. The **Quick Analysis** tool is a contextual tool that appears when you select data in a worksheet and offers single-click access to formatting, charts, formulas, PivotTables, and sparklines. The Recommended Charts feature is located on the Insert tab on the Ribbon. The **Recommended Charts** feature quickly analyzes a selection in a worksheet and recommends chart types that best fit your data. The Recommend Charts option also appears in the Quick Analysis tool under the Chart heading.

Creating Charts in an Existing Worksheet

Placing a chart within a worksheet can be very helpful, allowing you to display the chart beside the associated data source. When comparing charts side by side, placing the charts on the same worksheet can also be handy. Additionally, placing a chart within the worksheet may offer easy access to chart components when copying and pasting components into other applications.

Your manager, Irene, would like you to work with some data. Irene would like the data organized and presented in an effective graphical manner to aid in the analysis of the data so it is more informative. Specifically she would like to compare the total number of massages given over an eight-week period of time.

E04.02

To Create a Chart in an Existing Worksheet

a. Click the **ProductData** worksheet tab, and then select the range **A2:B12** as the data to use for creating a chart. Notice that once the data is selected, the Quick Analysis tool is displayed below and to the right of cell B12.

b. Click **Quick Analysis** , and then click **CHARTS**.

c. Point to the **Clustered Column** chart suggestion. Notice that a live preview of the chart is displayed.

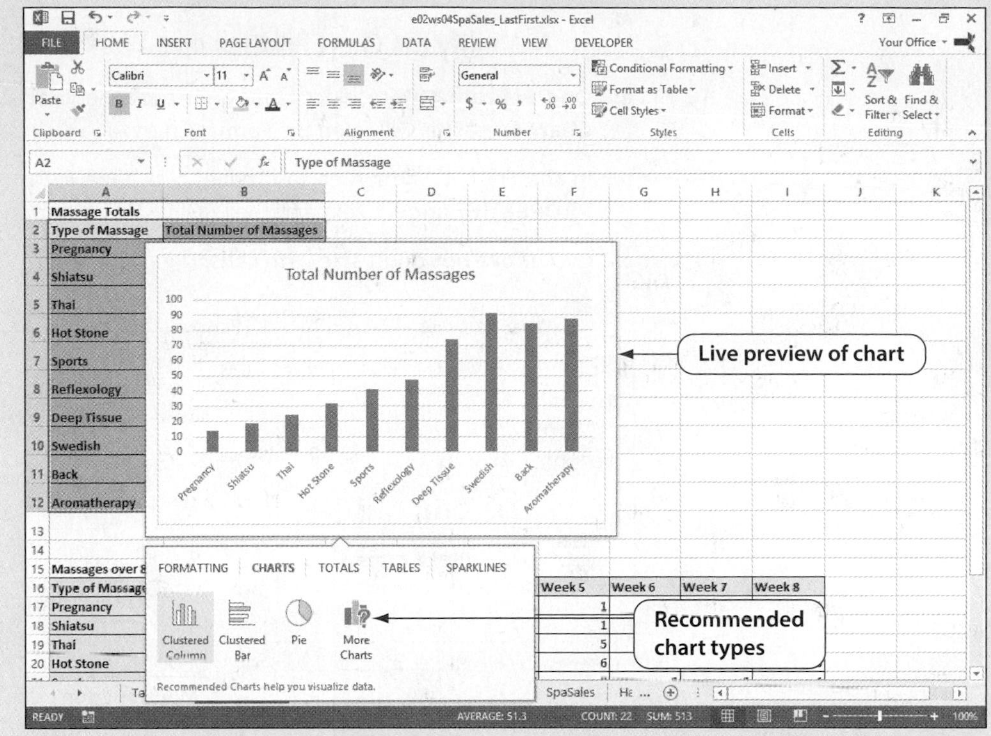

Figure 3 Quick Analysis tool with a suggested chart

d. Click **Clustered Column** to insert the chart into the worksheet.

Notice the chart appears on the currently active worksheet and shows colored borders surrounding the associated data linked to the chart. This chart displays the total number of each type of massage offered by the Spa.

e. Click the **chart border** when the pointer appears as a four-way arrow. Be careful not to click the corners or middle areas of the border that are designated by small handles and used for resizing the chart. Drag the **border** to move the chart to the right of the data so the top-left chart corner is approximately in cell **D2**.

f. Click **Save**.

Modifying a Chart's Position Properties

Charts created within the worksheet will appear as objects that "float" on top of the worksheet. The default property settings resize the chart shape if any of the underlying rows or columns are changed or adjusted. Therefore if the width of a column that lies behind the chart is increased, the chart width will increase accordingly. It is possible to change this setting, locking the size and position of the chart so it does not resize or move when columns or rows are resized, inserted, or deleted.

For example, additional data may be added to the ProductData worksheet. This data may require underlying columns to be widened or new columns inserted. Without adjusting the default settings on the chart, it could become distorted when changes are made to the worksheet.

E04.03

To Modify the Chart Position on a Worksheet

a. On the **ProductData** worksheet, right-click the **chart border**, and then click **Format Chart Area**. This will open the Format Chart Area task pane.

b. In the Format Chart Area task pane, click **Size & Properties**, and then click the **PROPERTIES** arrow to expand the PROPERTIES group.

c. Click **Move but don't size with cells.**

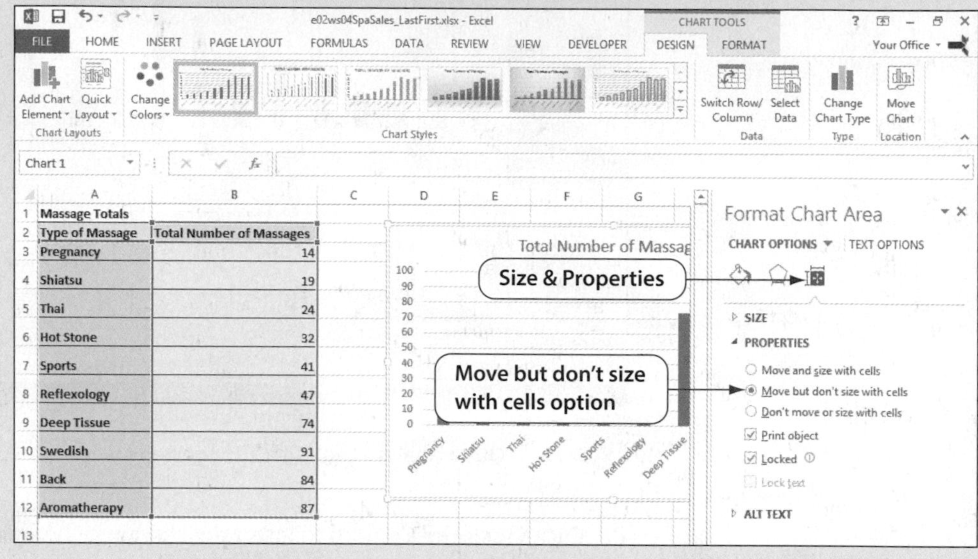

Figure 4 Format Chart Area task pane

d. Close the Format Chart Area task pane, and then click **Save**.

The chart size will not be resized if the width or height of the columns or rows underneath are changed or adjusted, but the chart will move along with the cells that it is sitting over. From here, you can easily move the chart by dragging the border, or you can resize the chart by clicking and dragging the corners.

Placing Charts on a Chart Sheet

As previously defined, a chart sheet is a worksheet that only contains chart objects. The familiar cell grid is replaced with the actual chart. Having the chart on a separate chart sheet can make it easier to isolate and print on a page. Chart sheets are also useful when you want to create a set of charts and easily navigate between them by worksheet names rather than looking for them on various worksheets. Due to the nature of chart sheets, the data associated with the chart will be on a different worksheet.

Irene has mentioned that she would like to use this chart in future presentations and would like to be able to easily isolate and print the chart. To facilitate this you will move the chart to a chart sheet.

MODULE 2

E04.04

To Move a Chart to a Chart Sheet

SIDE NOTE

Moving a Chart

The Move Chart button is a simple method for moving a chart from a worksheet to a chart sheet.

a. On the **ProductData** worksheet, select the **clustered column chart**.

b. On the **CHART TOOLS DESIGN** tab, in the **Location** group, click **Move Chart**. The Move Chart dialog box is displayed.

c. In the Move Chart dialog box, click the **New sheet** option. In the New sheet box, clear the **existing name**, and then type TotalNumberOfMassages. Click **OK**. Notice that you now have a new chart sheet tab in your workbook file. This chart sheet is exclusively for the chart and will not have the normal worksheet appearance.

d. Applying a color to the worksheet tab will allow the chart sheet to be easily distinguished from the rest of the worksheets in the workbook. Right-click the **TotalNumberOfMassages** worksheet tab. Point to **Tab Color**, and then click **Blue, Accent 1** in the first row, fifth column as the tab color.

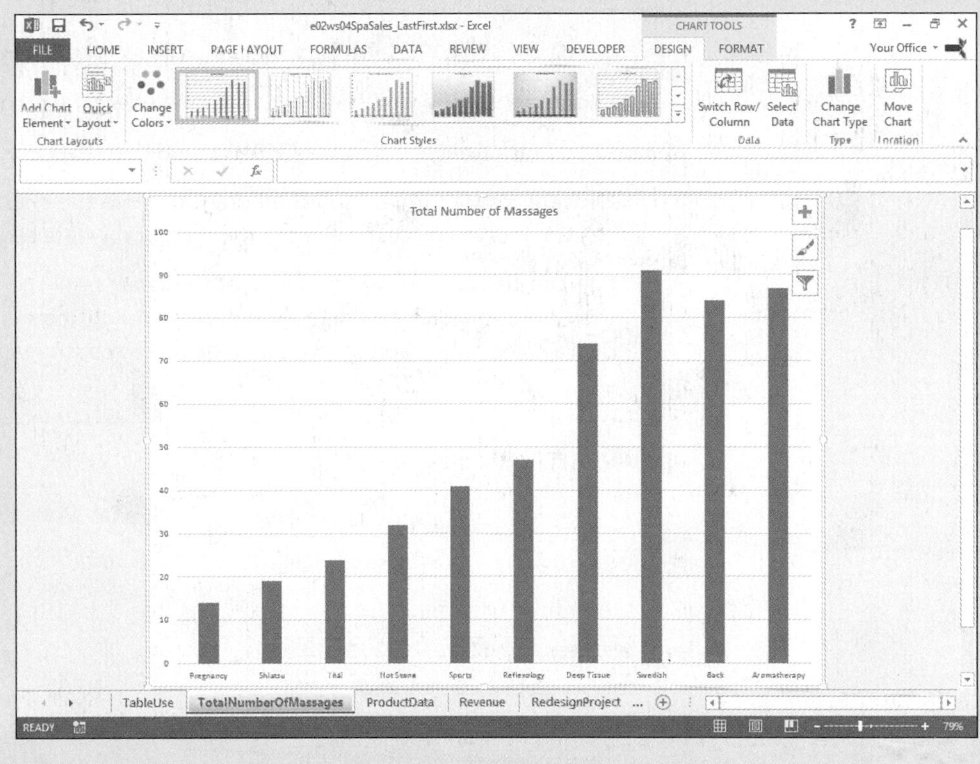

Figure 5 TotalNumberOfMassages chart sheet

e. Click **Save** .

Understand Different Chart Types

When creating a chart it is important to choose the correct type of chart to use. Each chart type conveys information differently. The chart type sets the tone for the basic format of the data and what kind of data is included. Thus, it helps to become familiar with the types of charts that are commonly used for business decision making and for presentations. Always consider which type is appropriate for the message you are trying to convey.

Creating Pie Charts

Pie charts are commonly used for depicting the relationships of the parts to the whole such as comparing staff performance within a department or comparing the number of transactions of each product category within a time period.

For a pie chart you need two data series—the labels and a set of corresponding values. This is similar to the data selection made in the TableUse sheet to indicate the percentage of times each person used the portable massage table. Note that the data can be described as a percentage of the whole as in the chart.

The questions you have will influence what textual data you will include in any chart. If you are exploring a use fee, then having the percentage would indicate which therapist would be contributing the most fees, and the actual numbers may not be a crucial element. When you create a chart, examine it to see if it answers your questions.

In this exercise, you will create a simple pie chart that shows the proportion of revenue each of four different massage types earned for the spa in the month of June.

E04.05

To Create a Pie Chart

a. Click the **Revenue** worksheet tab, and then select the range **A1:E2**.

b. Click **Quick Analysis** , click **CHARTS**, and then click **Pie**.

c. Click the **chart border**, and then drag to move the chart to the upper left corner of cell **G4**. This will place the chart to the right of the data set.

d. Point to the **bottom-right corner** of the chart until the pointer changes to , and then drag to resize the chart so the bottom-right corner is over cell **M17**. This chart displays the proportion of revenue generated by each massage type.

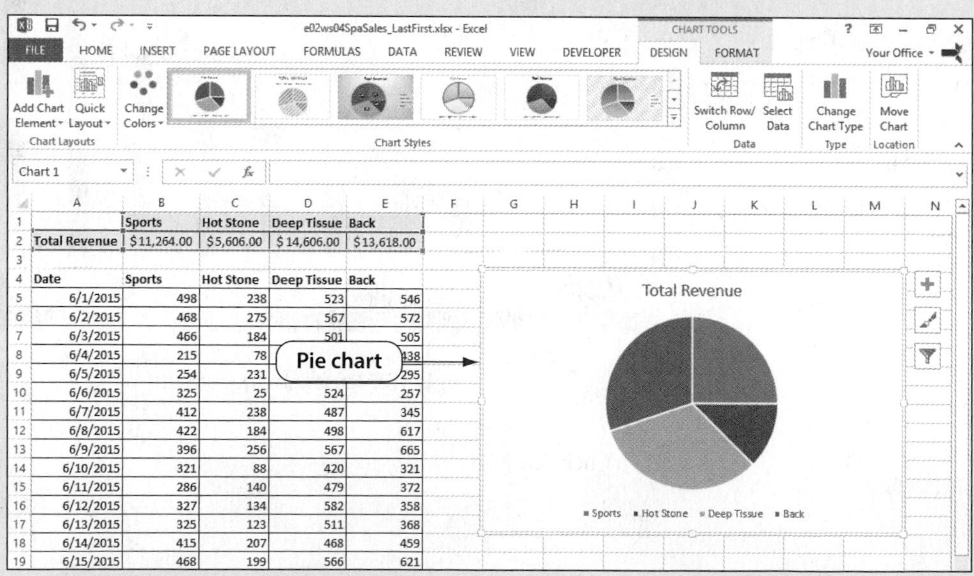

Figure 6 Total Revenue pie chart

e. Click **Save** .

Even though all the data is used to show every massage type, you do not have to use all the data. If the goal is to examine the data and extract a portion of the information, like the fact that several massage types have low or high average ratings, it may be better to only show a few massage types rather than include too much information. Showing a subset of massage types may help to emphasize particular ratings.

In determining how to proceed once the data has been initially examined, start developing hypotheses and questions. For example, it may be that hot stone massages are very new and need to be marketed more as they currently represent a small portion of revenues. Develop questions, and then use the data to determine the validity of the questions and make strategic decisions.

Creating Line Charts

Line charts help convey change over a period of time. They are great for exploring how data in a business, such as sales or production, changes over time. Line charts help people to interpret why the data is changing and to make decisions about how to proceed. For example, when a doctor examines a heart rate on an electrocardiogram, he or she is looking at data over time to see what has been happening. The doctor wants to determine if there are issues, and then make decisions whether the patient should go home, be given medications, or have surgery.

To create a line chart you need to have at least one set of labels and at least one set of corresponding data. It is possible to have multiple data series, each series representing a line on the chart. You have been provided with data listing revenue generated by four different types of massages. The data is organized by day throughout the month of June. In this exercise, you will create a line chart displaying daily revenue by massage type in June. Each day will appear as a point on the line that is created. Each massage type would be a separate line on the chart.

E04.06

To Create a Line Chart

a. On the **Revenue** worksheet, select cell **A4**, press Ctrl, and then press A to select the entire data set, including the labels.

b. Click **Quick Analysis**, click **CHARTS**, and then click **Line**.

c. On the **CHART TOOLS FORMAT** tab, in the Current Selection group, click the **Chart Elements** arrow, and then click **Chart Title**. Type Revenue by Massage Type for June and then press Enter.

d. Click the **chart border**, and then drag to move the chart to place the top-left corner in cell **G20**. This will place the chart to the right of the data set.

e. Point to the **bottom-right corner** of the chart until the pointer changes to , and then drag to resize the chart so the bottom-right corner is over cell **M33**. This chart displays the revenue generated by each type of massage through the month of June.

SIDE NOTE

Inserting a Chart

Charts can also be inserted by clicking the Insert tab, and then in the Charts group, clicking Recommended Charts.

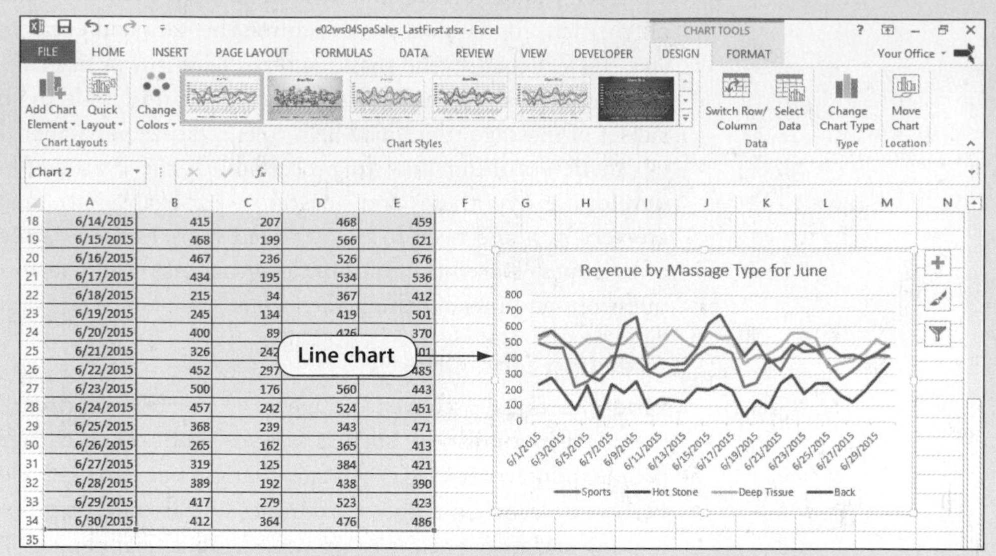

Figure 7 Revenue by Massage Type for June line chart

> **Troubleshooting**
>
> If you end up with a chart that looks dramatically different than what you would expect, check the colored borders around the linked data set. It is very common to select all the data in a table when the intention was to select just part of the data. If too much data was selected, you can delete the selected chart by pressing Delete. Alternatively, you could select the corner of a colored link data border and drag the border to adjust the set of data. The blue-border data is displayed in the chart. When that border is adjusted, the associated label data is automatically adjusted accordingly. The chart is also automatically adjusted so changes can be immediately seen.

f. Click **Save**.

Creating Column Charts

Column charts are useful for comparing data sets that are categorized, like departments, product categories, or survey results. Column charts are also useful for showing categories over time where each column represents a unit of time. Column charts are good for comparisons both individually, in groups, or stacked. Column chart data can easily allow for grouping of data so comparisons of the groups can occur.

In the TotalNumberOfMassages chart it is easy to interpret that pregnancy massages represent a small portion of the total massages provided. On the other hand, Swedish, aromatherapy, back, and deep tissue massages represent a large portion of the data.

Creating Bar Charts

Bar charts are useful for working with categorical data. Bar charts are similar to column charts except the bars are horizontal representations of the data rather than vertical. Like column charts, bar charts can depict a single piece of data, can be grouped data series, and can be stacked.

Because bar charts typically use groups and sum data, stacked bar charts can be useful when you want to see how the individual parts add up to create the entire length of each bar. For example, with the data on the ProductData worksheet, you may want to compare each type of massage, summing revenue or counting sales for each type of massage.

The x-axis would be number of massages or revenue. While it is the same data as used for the line chart, it conveys information about an output without the emphasis on time that is inherent with the line chart.

While bar charts are often viewed as simply being column charts turned on their sides, there is a particular bar chart that does use time values on the x-axis. It is a **Gantt chart**, which shows a project schedule where each bar represents a component or task within the project. The breakdown of tasks is useful for scheduling. Gantt charts are commonly used with project management. Gantt charts can be complex showing start times, end times, sequence of tasks, and people assigned to each task. A basic Gantt chart can be created that is informative and helps a team successfully complete a project. You have been asked to create a Gantt chart that will assist Irene and Meda visualize the timeline of a project to redesign the massage therapy rooms.

E04.07

To Create a Bar Chart

a. Click the **RedesignProject** worksheet tab, and then select the range **A3:D8**.

b. Click **Quick Analysis**, click **CHARTS**, and then click **More Charts**.

c. In the Insert Chart dialog box, click the **All Charts** tab, and then click **Bar** from the list of chart types. Click **Stacked Bar**, and then click **OK**.

d. Click the **Chart Title**, type Project Schedule and then press Enter.

e. Click the **blue data bar** within the chart corresponding with the Series "Start Date" to select the data series. **Right-click** a blue data bar, and then select **Format Data Series**. In the Format Data Series task pane, click **Fill & Line**.

f. Click the **FILL** arrow to expand the FILL group, and then click **No Fill**.

g. Click the **BORDER** arrow to expand the BORDER group, and then click **No Line**.

h. Click the **Vertical (category) Axis** corresponding to the project tasks. In the Format Axis task pane, click **Axis Options**, and then select **Categories in reverse order**.

i. Click the **Horizontal (value) Axis** corresponding to the start dates above the plot area. In the Format Axis task pane, click **TEXT OPTIONS**, and then click **Textbox**. Click in the box for **Custom angle**, if necessary delete the existing value, and then type 45. Press Enter.

j. Click the **chart border**, and then drag so the top-left corner is over cell **A11**. This chart visually displays both the number of days completed and the number of days remaining for each project listed in the worksheet.

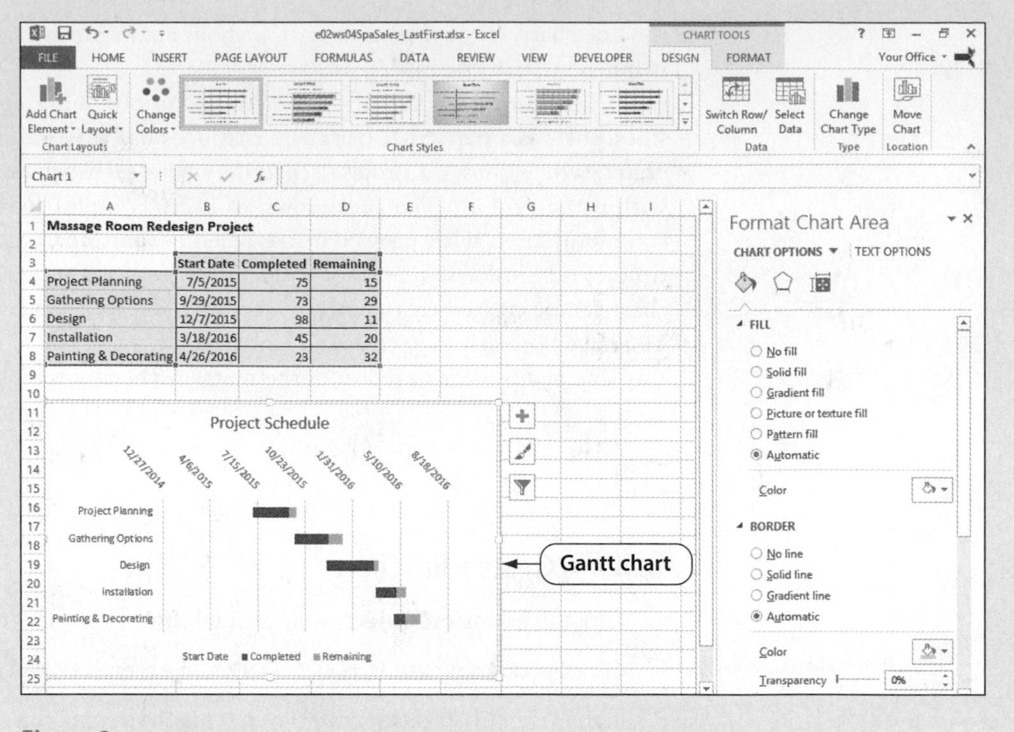

Figure 8 Completed Gantt chart

k. Close [X] the Format Chart Area task pane, and then click **Save** [Save].

The resulting Gantt chart depicts the time for each task in the project. For each bar, the task is set up with the amount completed and the amount that is remaining. The tasks are staggered to show the relation of each task to the other.

Creating Scatter Charts

Scatter charts, also called scatter plots, are a particular type of chart that conveys the relationship between two numeric variables. This type of chart is very common as a statistical tool depicting the correlation between the two variables. The standard format is to have the x-axis data on the far-left column and the y-axis data in a column on the right side.

Irene and Meda have data from a survey showing the requested temperature of the room used for massages and the age of the customer. This data may reveal important information as to what temperature is typically requested by different age groups. They have asked you to create a scatter chart of the requested temperatures of rooms and ages of customers.

E04.08

To Create a Scatter Chart

a. Click the **Survey** worksheet tab, and then select the range **A2:B53**. This will include the data and labels for Age and Temp.

b. Click **Quick Analysis** , click **CHARTS**, and then select **Scatter**.

c. Click the **chart border**, and then drag to move it to the right of the data so the top-left corner is over cell **E2**.

   The default scale of the chart does not bring out any trends to the data. Adjusting the scaling of the y-axis will help display any trends in the data.

d. Double-click the **Vertical (Value) Axis** corresponding to the temperature requested. In the Format Axis task pane, click **Axis Options** , click the **AXIS OPTIONS** arrow to expand the AXIS OPTIONS group, and then click in the box for **Minimum**.

e. Select the existing number, type 65 and then press Enter.

   Notice the resulting scatter plot has a slight upward trend as the age of the customer increases. This knowledge may lead to decisions that help provide better customer service.

f. Click the **Chart Title**, type Relationship Between Age and Temperature, and then press Enter. This chart shows the relationship between increasing age and temperatures requested for massages.

g. Close the Format Chart Title task pane, and then click **Save** .

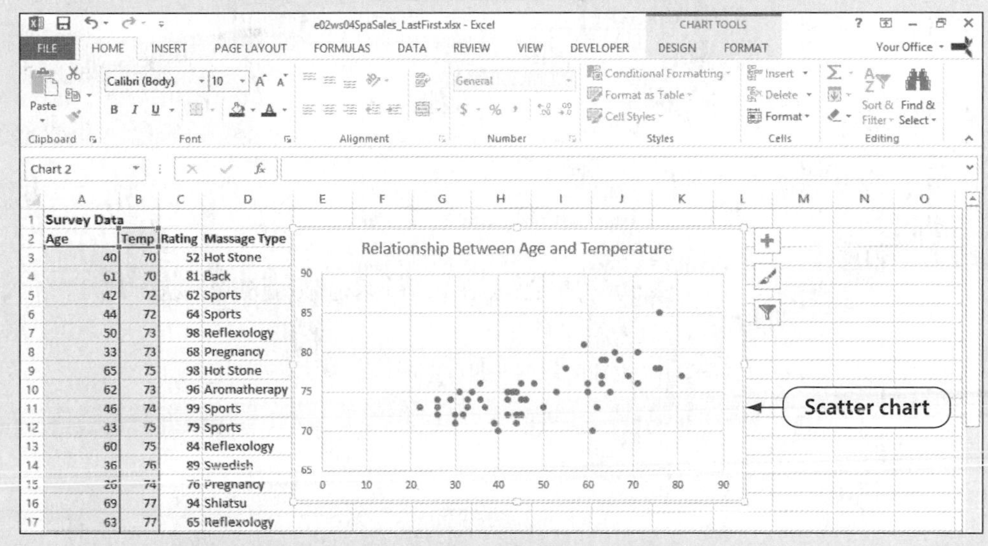

	A	B	C	D
1	Survey Data			
2	Age	Temp	Rating	Massage Type
3	40	70	52	Hot Stone
4	61	70	81	Back
5	42	72	62	Sports
6	44	72	64	Sports
7	50	73	98	Reflexology
8	33	73	68	Pregnancy
9	65	75	98	Hot Stone
10	62	73	96	Aromatherapy
11	46	74	99	Sports
12	43	75	79	Sports
13	60	75	84	Reflexology
14	36	76	89	Swedish
15	26	74	76	Pregnancy
16	69	77	94	Shiatsu
17	63	77	65	Reflexology

Figure 9 Scatter chart of temperature requested and age

Creating Area Charts

An **area chart** is a variation of a stacked line chart that emphasizes the magnitude of change over time and visually depicts a trend. The area chart stacks a set of data series and colors each area that is created. This type of chart has a nice visual characteristic because each colored layer changes, growing or shrinking, as it moves across time periods. Thus, with an area chart, the x-axis is typically a time sequence. The area chart could also use categories instead of time on the x-axis where each layer again is showing the individual contribution to the area; thus, it is a quantitative chart that shows growth or change in totals.

Irene has asked you to create a chart to further understand the differences in the types of massages given over the past eight weeks at the spa. You will create an area chart for this purpose.

E04.09

To Create an Area Chart

a. Click the **ProductData** worksheet tab, and then select the range **A16:I26**.

b. Click **Quick Analysis** [icon], click **CHARTS**, and then select **Stacked Area**.

c. Click the **Chart Title**, type Massage Types Over Past 8 Weeks and then press Enter.

d. Click the **chart border**, and then drag to move the chart so the top-left corner is over cell **D3**. This chart shows the total number of massages offered for each of the past eight weeks with emphasis placed on the different massage types.

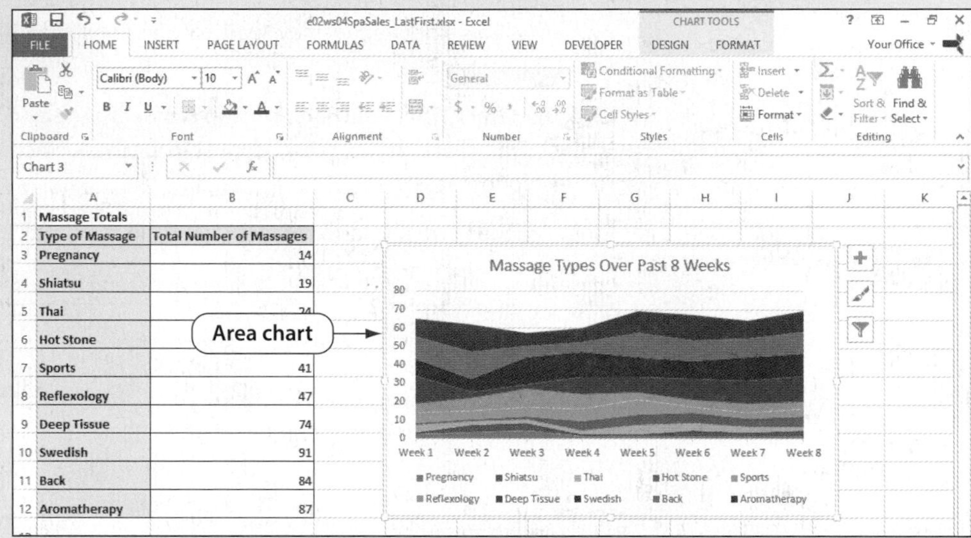

Figure 10 Area chart of massage types over past 8 weeks

e. Click **Save** [icon].

QUICK REFERENCE — Chart Selection Guidelines

The common types of charts and their usage are listed below:

- Pie—Used for comparing the relationship of parts to a whole
- Line—Shows changes within a data series; often used with time on the x-axis
- Column—Compares data vertically; can incorporate a time element and groups
- Bar—Compares data horizontally; stacked bar can show progress, growth
- Scatter—Used for correlations, exploring the relationship between two variables
- Area—Used to highlight areas showing growth over time or for categories; a variation of a line chart list

Creating Combination Charts

A **combination chart** displays two different types of data by using multiple chart types in a single chart object. Combination charts can enhance the understanding of data when the scale of data needing to be charted varies greatly. For example, consider monitoring the number of items sold in the spa to customers over a 12-month span of time. To fully comprehend the data it would be helpful to explore both the number of items sold and the profit from items sold. However, a single item may cost hundreds of dollars. This makes creating a chart to compare these two pieces of data difficult. In prior versions of Excel, creating a combination chart was a difficult and time-consuming process. In Excel 2013, combination charts are a standard chart type.

Meda has asked that you analyze the quantities of spa products sold from the prior year's sales and compare that to the profits over the same time span. Currently, only data from January to November is available. Meda has asked that you proceed with creating a chart and add the December data when it becomes available.

E04.10

To Create a Combination Chart

a. Click the **SpaSales** worksheet tab, and then select the range **A1:C12**.

b. Click **Quick Analysis** [icon], click **CHARTS**, and then select **More Charts**.

c. In the Insert Chart dialog box, click the **All Charts** tab. From the list of charts, click **Combo**.

   Before you insert the chart, you will have an opportunity to customize how the data will look. The default chart shows the month on the x-axis while using a line chart for profit—in red, and a clustered column chart for quantity sold—in blue.

d. Next to **Profit**, click to select the **Secondary Axis** check box. This scales the line chart for profit on a separate axis from quantity, allowing the trend over time between the two to be compared. Click **OK**.

e. Click the **Chart Title**, type Quantity Sold and Profit and then press Enter.

f. Click the **chart border**, and then drag to move the chart so the top-left corner is over cell **E2**.

   This chart compares the number of spa products sold and the profit from products sold in the same chart. Notice that in January the profit for items sold is lower than might be expected by the quantity sold.

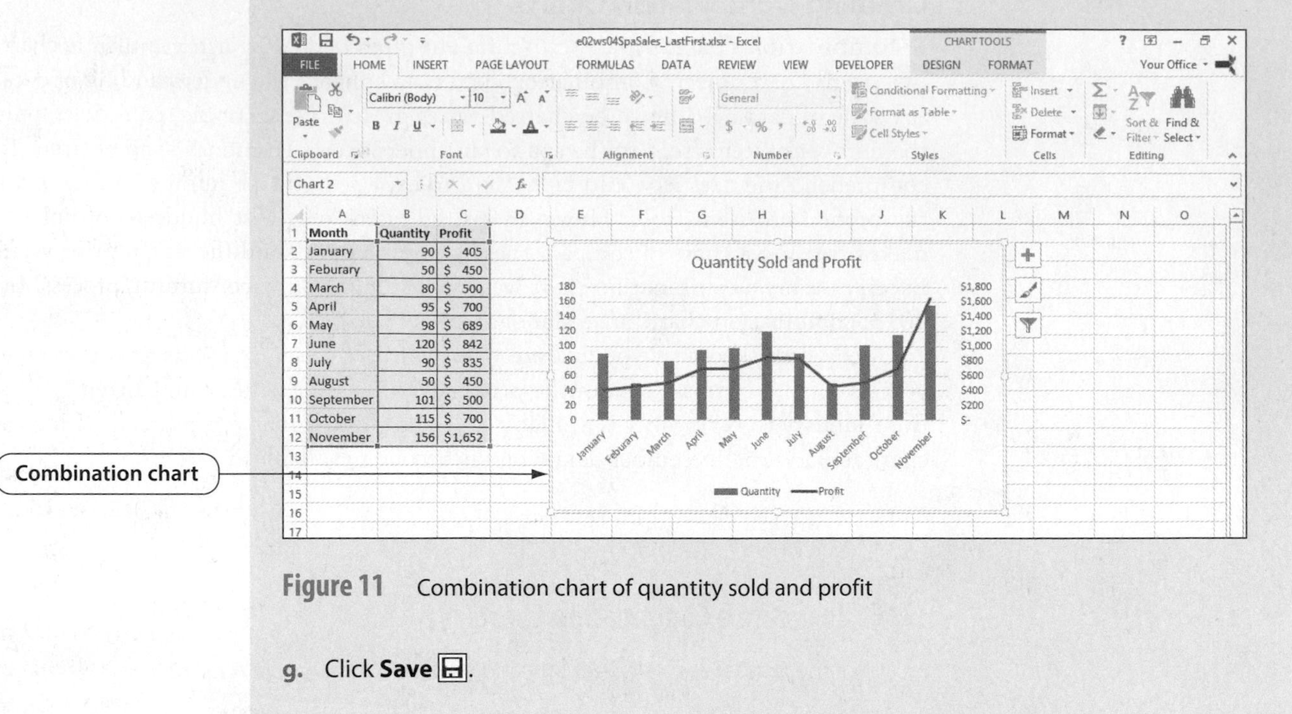

Figure 11 Combination chart of quantity sold and profit

g. Click **Save**.

Exploring Chart Layouts

As you have seen, a chart can help answer questions and may even generate more questions. This helps move toward the understanding of information, which can also lead to better decision making. Creating these initial charts to explore data is quick and efficient and informs the user.

When presenting a chart to others, the context of the chart is of utmost importance. Without context, your audience will try to guess the context. You need to provide meaning.

Providing context means providing textual guidance to the audience. The audience will see the pie chart, but you need to inform them more about the data. Thus, labels are another crucial element needed to provide context in charts. The labels include the chart title and axes titles, the legend, and the labels for the data. All these elements should work cohesively to convey a complete picture of what the chart is trying to convey to the audience. In this section, you will change the appearance of charts by altering their layout and color patterns. You will also add chart titles and modify the titles of the chart axis.

Change Chart Data and Styles for Presentations

While the default chart settings are pleasant visually, you can still improve the look and feel of the chart. The chart layouts are available under the Chart Tools contextual tabs, on the Design tab, in the Chart Layouts group. Excel provides many options for arranging the components on a chart. This includes placement of the titles and legend as well as the display of information such as the data point values.

Chart styles are a variation of chart layouts. Where chart layouts focus on location of components, styles focus more on the color coordination and effects of the components. Chart styles are located on the Chart Tools Design tab, in the Chart Styles group. For easier access, Excel 2013 displays the Chart Styles icon to the right side of any chart when it is selected. The choices mix color options with shadows and 3-D effects to create a variety of templates. You can also start with a template, and then adapt it to suit your tastes.

Chart data is the underlying data for the chart and labels. There can be many reasons for modifying data, and it can be accomplished through various methods. For example, if the data needs to be swapped between the data points and the axis data, you can use the Data group to switch rows and columns or select new data for a chart.

Changing the Appearance of a Chart

Because charts in Excel are connected to data on the worksheet, changes to the data are automatically reflected in the chart. This is extremely useful if you have a model that is using some calculations that are then used in a chart. You can do what-if analysis by changing data in a worksheet; the corresponding changes will appear on the chart.

Charts may need to be modified when the amount of data being charted needs to be changed. For example, a chart might have too much information included, making it difficult to get a clear picture. Conversely, a chart may need to be modified as new data becomes available. If the new data is adjacent to the existing data, it is a simple process to expand the existing data series. This is achieved by resizing the borders around the data series after activating the chart. Irene has just provided you with the December data for quantity and profit for the spa. You need to add this data to the SpaSales worksheet and adjust the combination chart accordingly. Additionally you will modify the appearance of the chart.

E04.11

To Modify the Layout and Data in an Existing Chart

a. On the **SpaSales** worksheet, click cell **A13** to select it.

b. Type December and then press Tab. Type 165 and then press Tab. Type 1701 and then press Ctrl + Enter.

c. Click the **chart area** portion of the chart. Click the **sizing handle** on the lower edge between cells **A12** and **B12**, and then drag the sizing handle down one row so that the range **A2:C13** is now being charted. The chart will now display the quantity sold and profits for the month of December.

d. On the **CHART TOOLS DESIGN** tab, in the Type group, click **Change Chart Type**.

e. Near the bottom of the Change Chart Type dialog box, next to the Profit series, click the **Chart Type** arrow. Select **Area**, and then click **OK**.

f. To the right of the chart, click **Chart Styles**, scroll down, and then click **Style 6**. Click **Chart Styles** to close the style gallery.

g. On the **CHART TOOLS DESIGN** tab, in the Chart Layouts group, click **Quick Layout**. In the displayed gallery, click **Layout 9**. Notice that the new layout added labels for the x- and y-axis on the chart. These axis titles will be revised at a later point.

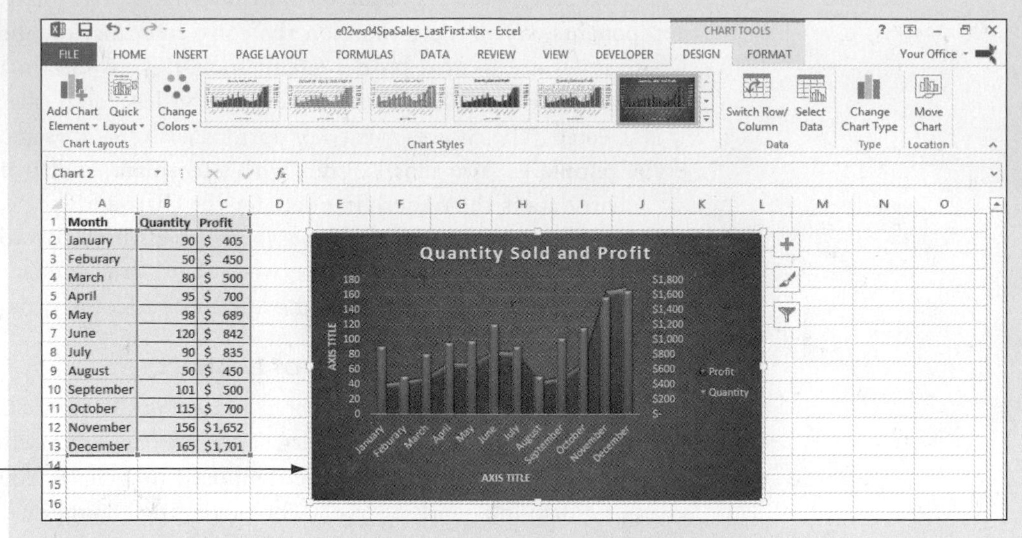

Combination chart with modified style and labels

Figure 12 Modified combination chart

h. Click **Save** .

Inserting Objects

If you work for a company, it would be useful to insert the company logo into any chart that is used outside the company. After all, marketing occurs everywhere. It may also be useful to use images to help convey the tone of the presentation. This can be accomplished with an image inserted into the chart. Irene mentioned she would be using the chart sheet in the workbook in a variety of presentations. Given this, you will modify the appearance of the chart by inserting the Turquoise Oasis Spa logo and a shape object containing the title of the chart.

E04.12

To Insert Objects into a Chart

a. Click the **TotalNumberOfMassages** chart worksheet tab, and then select the **chart**, if necessary.

b. Click the **INSERT** tab, and then in the Illustrations group, click **Pictures**. In the left pane of the Insert Picture dialog box, navigate to the location where you store your student data files, and then click **e02ws04TurquoiseOasis**. Click **Insert**.

c. On the **PICTURE TOOLS FORMAT** tab, in the Size group, click the **Shape Height** box. Clear any existing text, type 0.9 and then press Enter.

d. Click in the **Chart Area**. On the **CHART TOOLS DESIGN** tab, in the **Chart Layouts** group, click **Quick Layout**. In the gallery that appears, click **Layout 4**. Notice that the new layout added labels for the x-axis on the chart.

e. Click any of the **columns** in the chart. On the **CHART TOOLS FORMAT** tab, in the **Shape Styles** group, click the **More** arrow, and then click **Subtle Effect - Orange, Accent 6** in the fourth row, seventh column.

f. Click the **INSERT** tab, and then in the Illustrations group, click **Shapes**. In the displayed gallery, in the Rectangles group, click **Rounded Rectangle**—the second option. Click to place the **rectangle** below the Turquoise Oasis Spa logo.

g. Type Number of Massage Services by Type. On the **DRAWING TOOLS FORMAT** tab, in the Size group, click the **Shape Height** box, type 0.8 and then press Enter. In the **Shape Width** box, type 2.2 and then press Enter.

h. In the Shape Styles group, click the **More** arrow, and then select **Subtle Effect - Orange, Accent 6** in the fourth row, seventh column.

i. Click the **HOME** tab, and then in the Font group, click the **Font Size** arrow, and then select **16**.

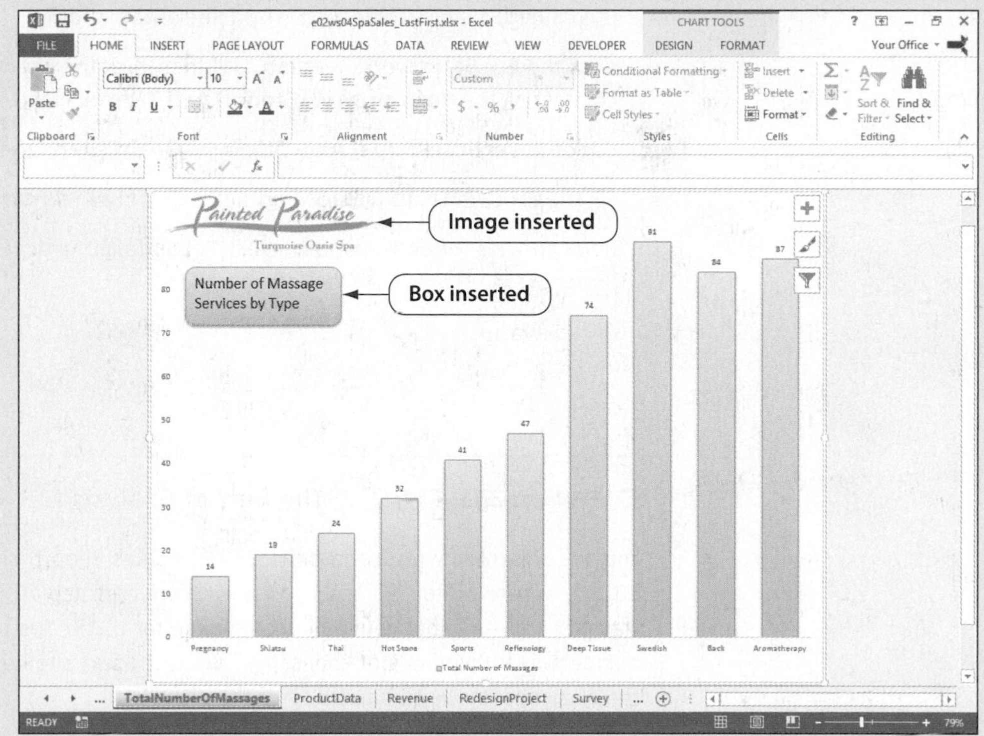

Figure 13 Picture and shape inserted into a chart

j. Click **Save**.

Exploring Titles for the Chart and Axes

Chart and axes titles are added easily under the Chart Tools Format tab or with the Chart Elements button that appears on the right side of charts in Excel 2013. Chart titles can be added within the chart or they can reference cells on the spreadsheet for easy updating. You have been asked by Meda to alter the title of the Gantt chart on the RedesignProject worksheet to match the text in cell A1. She has also asked you to clarify the horizontal and vertical axis labels on the combination chart in the SpaSales worksheet.

E04.13

To Modify Chart Titles and Axis Labels

a. Click the **RedesignProject** worksheet tab, and then click the **chart border** of the Gantt chart.

b. Click the **chart title** at the top of the chart, and then click the **formula bar**. Type = and then click cell **A1**.

c. Press Enter.

Notice the title of the chart now matches the contents of cell A1. If the text in cell A1 is changed, the chart title will be updated automatically.

d. Click the **SpaSales** worksheet tab, and then click the **chart border** of the combination chart. Click the **Horizontal (Category) Axis Title** box, and then press Delete.

e. Click the **Vertical (Value) Axis Title**, type Quantity and then press Enter.

f. On the **CHART TOOLS DESIGN** tab, in the Chart Layouts group, click **Add Chart Element**.

g. Point to **Axis Titles**, and then select **Secondary Vertical**. Type Profit and then press Enter.

h. Click **Save**.

CONSIDER THIS | **The Unit of Analysis**

You are presented with a chart titled "2013 Sales Report" and the x-axis is showing 20, 30, 40, and so on for the scale. What is this report depicting? Is it the number of sales transactions—number sold—or the revenue for 2013? Are the 20, 30, and 40 the actual numbers or in hundreds or thousands? What context should there be to make certain the audience knows the meaning of the chart?

Working with the Legend and Labeling the Data

The legend is an index within a chart that provides information about the data. With some charts the legend is added automatically. With other charts, such as pie charts, it is possible to incorporate the same information beside each pie slice as labels.

When the parts are labeled on the chart, the legend is not needed and can be removed. Labels can also be added alongside the data on the chart. This is quite informative as it moves the information from a legend to the data. This can be a visually useful addition.

The data labels can be added, moved, or removed through the Chart Elements button that appears to the right of a selected chart or through the Chart Tools Design tab.

E04.14

To Work with Legends and Data Labels

a. Click the **Revenue** worksheet tab, and then click the **chart border** of the line chart.

b. To the right of the chart, click **Chart Elements** [+], move the pointer over Legend and click the **Legend** arrow, and then click **Right**.

c. Click the **chart border** of the pie chart. To the right of the chart, click **Chart Elements** [+], and then click to select the **Data Labels** check box. Click the arrow next to **Data Labels**, and then select **Data Callout**.

d. Click **Legend** to clear the check box. This will remove the legend from the pie chart.

e. Click **Chart Elements** [+] again to close it, and then click **Save** [Save].

Troubleshooting

Adding and removing chart elements may alter the position of other elements of your chart. You may need to reposition existing or new elements in the chart to clarify the meaning of the chart.

SIDE NOTE

Deleting Chart Elements

Chart elements can be easily removed by selecting them in the chart and pressing [Delete].

Modifying Axes

The x-axis and y-axis scales are automatically created through a mathematical algorithm within Excel. However, sometimes the scale needs to be modified as you have already seen. For example, when the scale of numbers is large, a significant gap can exist from 0 to the first data point. In this case, you can modify the scale to start at a more appropriate number instead of 0—the standard minimum value for Excel. When you need to compare two or more charts, the scales must be consistent. Any time you put charts side by side, you need to also make sure your x-axis and y-axis scales are the same. Your audience may not realize otherwise and make incorrect assumptions or decisions. The axis data may also be too crowded, making it difficult to read. In this situation, you would be able to modify the layout of the scale by adjusting the alignment of the data. The data on the axis can be vertical, horizontal, or even placed at an angle.

The Format Axis task pane is used to manually set the axis options for consistency between a set of charts. Under the Axis Options, the default Excel scale minimum and maximums are set automatically based on data. This setting can be changed to allow for customized minimum and maximum values to be applied to the chart. If the source data for the chart is changed, the scale will remain fixed and will not automatically be updated; therefore, any fixed values may also need to be reevaluated as source data changes.

E04.15

To Modify a Chart Axis

a. Click the **RedesignProject** worksheet tab, and then click the **chart border** of the Gantt Chart.

b. Double-click **Horizontal (Value) Axis** at the top of the chart. This will open the Format Axis task pane to the Axis Options group. Click the **Minimum** box. The value displayed is the Excel serial number for the date 12/27/2014.

c. Delete the existing value, type 7/1/2015 and then press Enter. Excel will recognize that you have typed a date into the field and translate this into the serial number 42186.

d. Close the Format Axis task pane.

> **SIDE NOTE**
> **Format Task Pane**
> If the Formatting task pane is open, click an element within the chart to activate the corresponding options within the pane.

Troubleshooting

If the value you type in any of the Axis Options boxes does not work for your chart, click the Reset button to the right of the box to change the value back to the chart default.

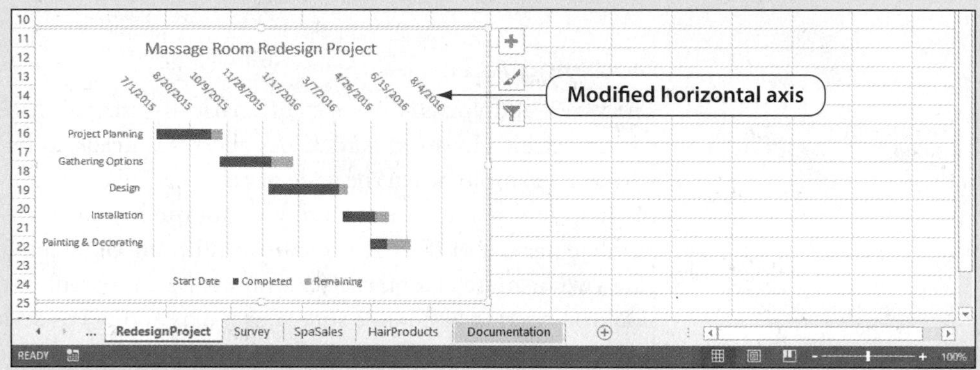

Figure 14 Gantt chart with a modified axis

e. Click **Save**.

Changing Gridlines

Gridlines are the lines that go across charts to help gauge the size of the bars, columns, or data lines. In Excel, the default is to display the major gridlines—the gridlines at the designated label values, and not to display the minor gridlines—the gridlines between the label values. If the chart is a line or column chart it puts in the horizontal major gridlines while the bar chart puts in vertical major gridlines. The default is a good starting point, but personal preferences can dictate which lines to display. The Format Major Gridlines task pane allows for the customization of gridlines in a chart.

E04.16

To Modify Gridlines on a Chart

a. Click the **Revenue** worksheet tab, and then click the **chart border** of the line chart.

b. To the right of the chart, click **Chart Elements** [+], move the pointer over Gridlines and click the **Gridlines** arrow, and then select **Primary Major Vertical**.

c. Click **Chart Elements** [+] again to close it.

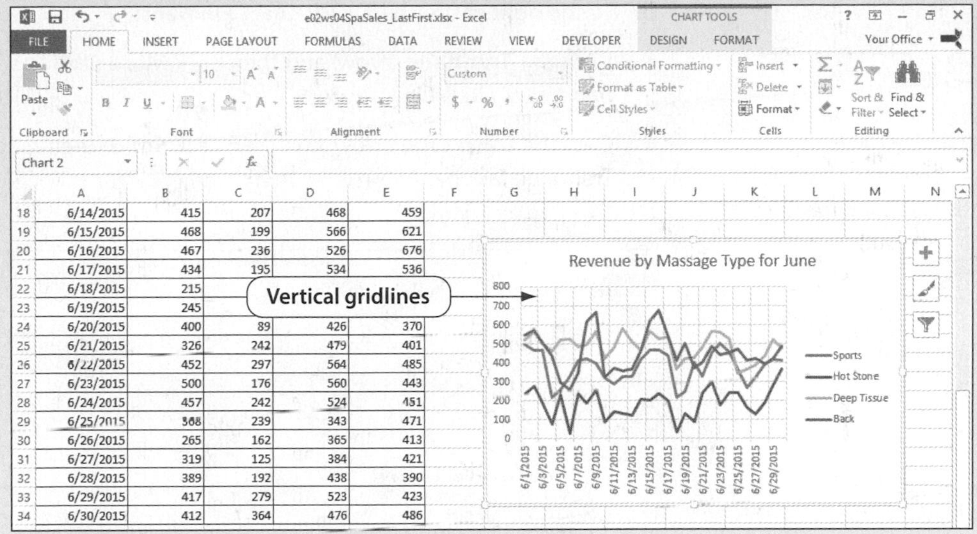

Figure 15 Vertical gridlines added to a line chart

d. Click **Save** [💾].

Analyzing with Trendlines

A common analysis tool to use within a chart is the trendline. A **trendline** is a line that uses current data to show a trend or general direction of the data. Data, however, can have a variety of patterns. For scatter plots that explore how two variables interact, a linear trend may be seen. If data fluctuates or varies a great deal, it may be more desirable to use a moving average trendline. Instead of creating a straight line based on all the current data, the moving average trendline uses the average of small subsets of data to set short trend segments over time. The moving average trendline will curve and adjust as the data moves up or down.

The trend or pattern of the data may suggest or predict what will happen in the future. For linear trends, the predicted data can be charted using a linear trendline added to a scatter chart and the current trend of the data.

Adding a trendline for the scatter chart on the Survey worksheet data may help confirm the hypothesis that older customers desire a warmer room than younger customers. This may lead the staff to adjust the room temperature prior to a customer arriving. The staff could predict the desired temperature based on the age of the customer. This could help improve customer satisfaction. Again, you may want to consider other demographics—characteristics—of the customers that allow for providing a customized and personalized service that will build customer loyalty and repeat business. It is easier to retain existing customers than find new customers.

For example, the scatter chart on the Survey worksheet shows that as the age of the customer increases so does the temperature of the room they request. Adding a trendline to this chart will further illustrate this relationship.

E04.17

To Insert a Trendline

a. Click the **Survey** worksheet tab, and then click the **chart border** of the scatter chart.

b. To the right of the chart, click **Chart Elements** [+], and then click **Trendline**.

c. Click the **Trendline** arrow, and then click **More Options**. In the Format Trendline task pane, click **Fill & Line**.

d. Click the **Dash type** arrow, and then click **Solid** (the first option). Close [X] the Format Trendline task pane.

SIDE NOTE
Types of Trendlines
Different types of trendlines can be added to a chart using the Chart Elements button.

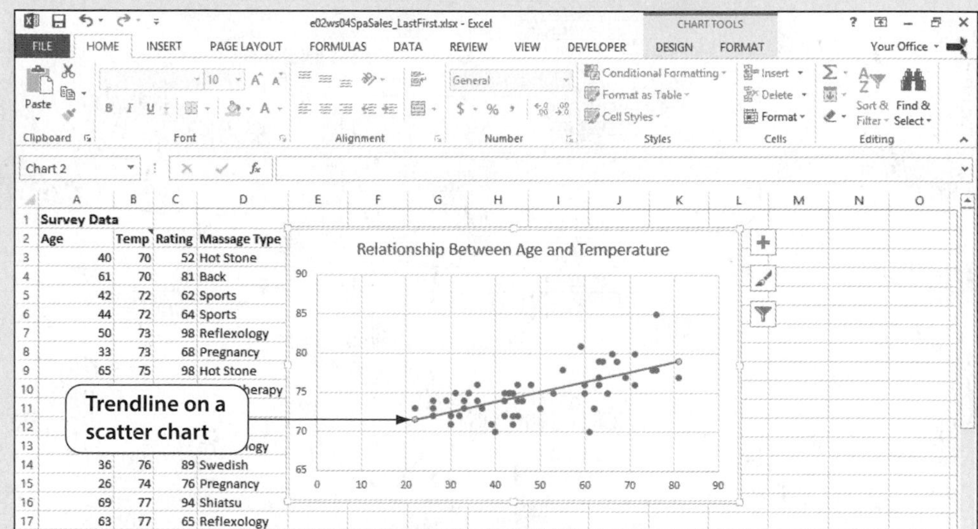

Figure 16 Scatter chart of age and temperature

e. Click **Save**.

QUICK REFERENCE | **Chart Trendlines**

The following is a listing of the types of trendlines available within Excel:

- Linear trendline—Adds/sets a linear trendline for the selected chart series
- Exponential trendline—Adds/sets an exponential trendline for the selected chart series
- Linear Forecast trendline—Adds/sets a linear trendline with a two-period forecast for the selected chart series
- Two-Period Moving Average trendline—Adds/sets a two-period moving average trendline for the selected chart series

MODULE 2

REAL WORLD ADVICE **The Timing of Trends**

Trends show patterns over time. When looking at hourly sales at a restaurant, it becomes important to look at more than one day's worth of hourly sales to obtain a better understanding of the trend. Charting multiple days reveals any trends and consistent patterns. For example, maybe it is discovered that on Friday and Saturday, hourly sales are consistently higher than other days of the week. This would suggest a need for scheduling more people to work on those days. If only one day had been charted, or even just one week, the overall weekly trends may have been missed or interpreted incorrectly.

Edit and Format Charts to Add Emphasis

When formatting a chart, it is important to have a plan in mind as to the overall layout and look and feel. With a well-thought-out plan, it will be easy to apply the desired adjustments to the components with regard to position, color, and emphasis. Typically, you can either create a unique layout or modify one of Excel's many layouts. Either way, being able to make formatting changes is easy and a very useful and powerful way to convey information. In this section, you will explore various ways to format a chart.

Adding Color to Chart Objects

Working some color into charts can be helpful from a marketing perspective. Excel offers options that allow changing the interior color as well as the border color. Chart colors can be added to match a company's color scheme or to highlight certain important aspects of the data. Remember, while it is possible to add value to charts with color, it is also possible to overdo it. Irene has mentioned to you that she will be using the pie chart on the Revenue worksheet in a presentation. She would like for you to enhance the visual appeal of the chart before her presentation.

To Change the Coloring of a Chart

a. Click the **Revenue** worksheet tab, and then click the **chart border** of the pie chart.

b. On the **CHART TOOLS DESIGN** tab, in the Chart Styles group, click **Change Colors**, and then in the gallery that appears, select **Color 4** (the fourth option).

c. On the **CHART TOOLS FORMAT** tab, in the Shape Styles group, click **Shape Fill**, and then select **Orange, Accent 6, Lighter 40%**.

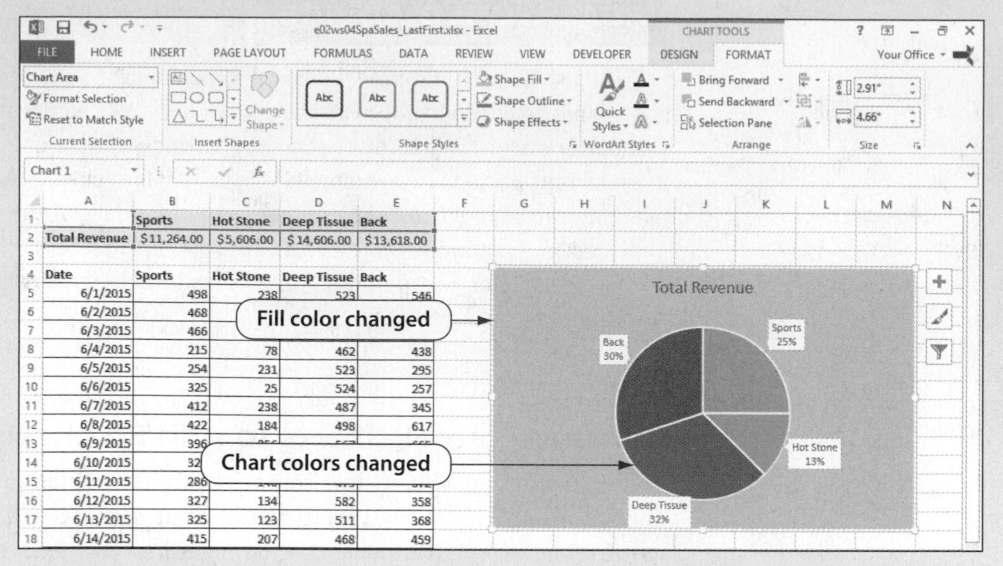

Figure 17 Pie chart with added color

d. Click **Save** .

Working with Text

Whether the text is in a box, title, legend, or axis scale, you can change the formatting of text and the backgrounds of the text objects in charts. The text can be formatted as WordArt, and shapes can be modified to common Shape Styles. The pie chart that was modified with a new color scheme now has a title that is difficult to read. Increasing the font size and bolding the font in the chart title box will address this problem.

E04.19

To Format Text Within a Chart

a. On the **Revenue** worksheet, if necessary click the **chart border** of the pie chart.

b. Click the **Chart Title**, and then on the **HOME** tab, in the Font group, click **Bold** B. In the Font group, click the **Font Size** 11 arrow, and then select **16**.

c. Click **Save** .

Exploding Pie Charts

The traditional pie chart is a pie with all the slices together. Preset options offer a pie chart with a slice pulled slightly away from the main pie, or you can manually move a slice outward creating an exploded pie chart. This technique allows for highlighting a particular piece of the pie. As part of her presentation, Irene wants to emphasize the hot stone massage type as it represents the least amount of revenue in the data series. Visual emphasis on this point can be easily created by exploding the slice of the pie chart representing the revenue percentage of hot stone massages.

E04.20

To Create an Exploding Pie Chart

a. On the **Revenue** worksheet, if necessary click the **chart border** of the pie chart.

b. Click the **plot area.** Notice that the entire pie is selected.

c. Click the **Hot Stone** slice of the pie, and then drag the **slice** slightly to the right.

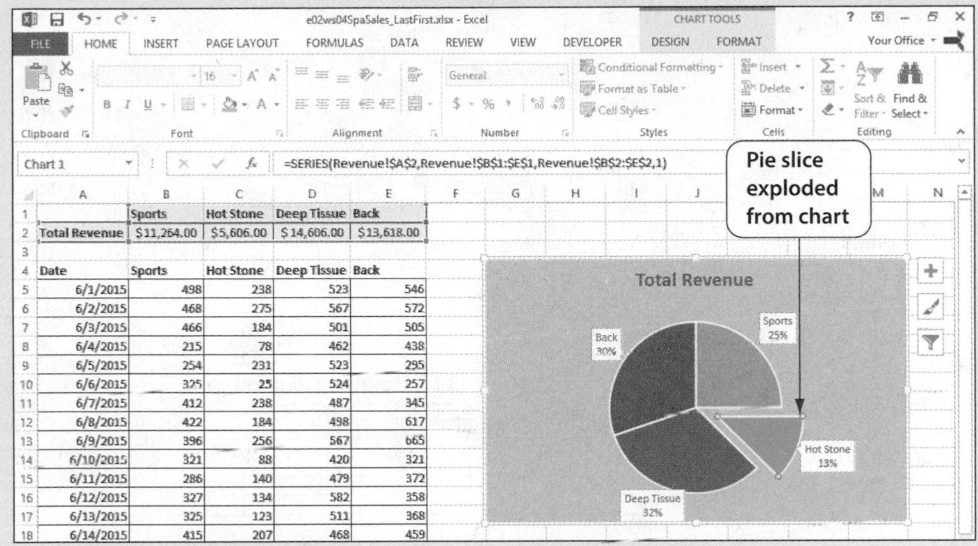

Figure 18 Exploded pie chart

d. Click **Save** .

Changing 3-D Charts and Rotation of Charts

The 3-D effect and rotation of charts is something that should be used conservatively. The effect can be done well, or it can be overused, resulting in a chart that goes overboard and distracts from the intended message. You can choose the 3-D effect when starting to develop a chart. Additionally, options are available to rotate the 3-D effect, giving the chart a crisp distinctive look. The 3-D format can be applied to a variety of objects. The 3-D Rotation setting is intended for the chart area only. The pie chart showing the total revenue by massage type can be enhanced with 3-D effects and rotation.

E04.21

To Change the Chart Type to 3-D

a. On the **Revenue** worksheet, if necessary click the **chart border** of the pie chart.

b. On the **CHART TOOLS DESIGN** tab, in the Type group, click **Change Chart Type**.

c. In the Change Chart Type dialog box, click the **All Charts** tab, click **3-D Pie**, and then click **OK**.

d. Double-click the **chart area** to open the Format Chart Area task pane. Click **Effects** , and then click the **3-D ROTATION** arrow to expand the 3-D ROTATION group.

e. Click in the box for **Y Rotation**, delete the existing value, and then type 50. Click in the box for **Perspective**, delete the existing value, and then type 30.

f. Click the **3-D FORMAT** arrow to expand the 3-D FORMAT group. Click the **Top Bevel** arrow, and then select **Cool Slant** in the first row, fourth column. Close [X] the Format Chart Area task pane.

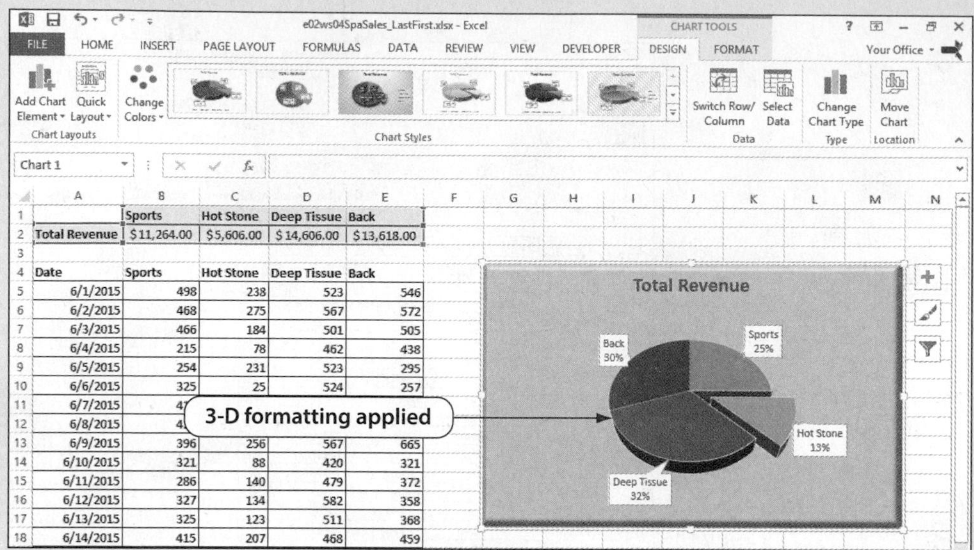

Figure 19 Pie chart with 3-D formatting applied

g. Click **Save** [Save].

QUICK REFERENCE — Formatting Options for Chart Objects

Below are format options for charts and their descriptions:

- Number—Format data as currency, date, time, and so on.
- Fill—Fill the background of a component with a color, picture, or pattern.
- Border Color—Set the color of the border for a component.
- Border Styles—Set the thickness and type of border for a component.
- Shadow—Add shadowing effect to a component.
- Glow and Soft Edges—Add glow and edge effects to a component.
- 3-D Format—Add 3-D effects to component.
- Alignment—Align text direction for a component, such as left, top, vertical, or horizontal.

Effectively Using Charts

The effectiveness of a chart is dependent on the chart type, the layout, and the formatting of the data. Charts should provide clarity and expand the understanding of the data. Charts used in a presentation should support the ideas you want to convey. The charts should highlight key components about an issue or topic being addressed in the presentation. Providing too much information on a chart can confuse or hide the issue being discussed. It can be difficult to get a point across if the chart is confusing, cluttered, or packed with too much information. In this section, you will use sparklines and data bars to emphasize data. You will also recognize and correct confusing charts.

Use Sparklines and Data Bars to Emphasize Data

The same data can be viewed through various perspectives, emphasizing different parts of information. Charts typically do three things:

- Support or refute assertions
- Clarify information
- Help the audience understand trends

Sparklines and data bars are tools in Excel that can accomplish these three goals.

Emphasizing Data

As with any set of data, you can reasonably expect to find multiple ideas that could be emphasized in a chart. Typically within a business, one to three key issues might be chosen for discussion. The idea is to eliminate any extraneous data from the chart that does not pertain to the issues being emphasized. Common methods can be employed to emphasize the idea in the chart. When using a single chart, highlight a particular data set within the chart to help focus attention to a key point. Depending on the chart type, the emphasis may be depicted differently as shown in Table 1.

Single Chart Types	Common Emphasis Methods
Pie chart	Explode a pie slice
Bar/Column	Use an emphasizing color on the bar/column
Line	Line color, weight, and marker size
Scatter	Adding a trendline

Table 1 Emphasis methods for single chart types

Exploring Sparklines

Sparklines are small charts that are embedded into the cells in a worksheet, usually beside the data, to facilitate quick analysis of trends. A sparkline can be used within a worksheet to give an immediate visual trend analysis, and it adjusts as the source data changes. The sparkline can graphically depict the data over time through either a line chart or a bar chart that accumulates the data. Sparklines can also depict data points in the series as a win/loss chart. The default setting is for values above 0 to be a win, while values below 0 are a loss. This value can be modified under the Format tab using the Sparkline Axis button.

Irene and Meda would like to better examine sales of hair products at the spa. They have collected some data for you to analyze from the last eight weeks. Adding sparklines adjacent to the data will emphasize the trend in products over time.

E04.22

To Insert Sparklines

a. Click the **HairProducts** worksheet tab, and then select the range **A3:A7**.

b. Click the **INSERT** tab, in the Sparklines group, click **Line**. In the Create Sparklines dialog box, in the **Data Range** box, type C3:N7 and then click **OK**.

c. On the **SPARKLINE TOOLS DESIGN** tab, in the Style group, click the **More** arrow, and then select **Sparkline Style Accent 2, Darker 50%** (first row, second column). The sparklines show the changes in hair products sold over the 12 months represented by the data.

d. Click cell **A1** to deselect the sparklines.

SIDE NOTE
Alternate Method
Sparklines can also be inserted to the right of any data using the Quick Analysis tool.

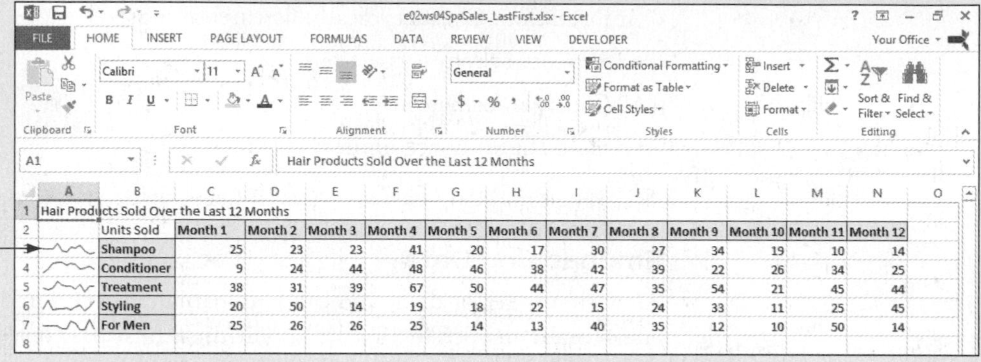
Hair Products Sold Over the Last 12 Months

Units Sold	Month 1	Month 2	Month 3	Month 4	Month 5	Month 6	Month 7	Month 8	Month 9	Month 10	Month 11	Month 12
Shampoo	25	23	23	41	20	17	30	27	34	19	10	14
Conditioner	9	24	44	48	46	38	42	39	22	26	34	25
Treatment	38	31	39	67	50	44	47	35	54	21	45	44
Styling	20	50	14	19	18	22	15	24	33	11	25	45
For Men	25	26	26	25	14	13	40	35	12	10	50	14

Figure 20 Sparklines applied to hair products data

e. Click **Save**.

The sparklines show the trend in units of hair products sold over a 12-month time frame by type of product. For example, notice that the sales of the For Men products were steady until Month 7 when they spiked, came back down in month 9, and then spiked again in Month 11. This is very easy to visualize with sparklines next to the data.

QUICK REFERENCE | **Working with Sparklines**

Using the following process will help in the development of sparklines:

- Select any cell within the added sparklines to display the Sparkline Tools contextual tabs.
- Ungroup sparklines using the Ungroup button on the Sparkline Tools Design tab.
- Group sparklines again using the Group button on the Design tab.
- Change colors and styles using the options available in the Style group.
- Choose to show high or low points using the options in the Show group.

Inserting Data Bars

Data bars are graphic components that are overlaid onto data in worksheet cells. The graphic component is added to a cell and interprets a set of data in a range adjusting the bar and, if necessary, the bar color to help a spreadsheet user gain a quick understanding of the data. Data bars can be applied as a one-color solid fill or a gradient fill from left to right as the numerical value gets bigger.

Data bars are components of the Conditional Formatting feature. This technique can be employed with scores, ratings, or other data where the user would want to do a visual inspection to see a relative scale on the data. Irene and Meda have requested one more enhancement to the hair products analysis you have already begun. They would like a small visual cue added to a list of profits by hair product type. Adding data bars to the profits of all hair products sold at the spa over the past 12 months will provide emphasis on which products were and were not profitable.

E04.23

To Insert Data Bars

a. On the **HairProducts** worksheet, select the range **C10:C14**.

b. Click the **HOME** tab, and then in the Styles group, click **Conditional Formatting**, and then point to **Data Bars**.

c. Under Gradient Fill, select **Green Data Bar** (row one, second option). The inserted data bars clearly show that Conditioner is the highest grossing product while For Men is the lowest grossing product.

d. Click cell **A1** to deselect the data bars.

> **SIDE NOTE**
> **Alternate Method**
> Data bars can also be inserted from the Quick Analysis tool. The default color is blue if this method is used.

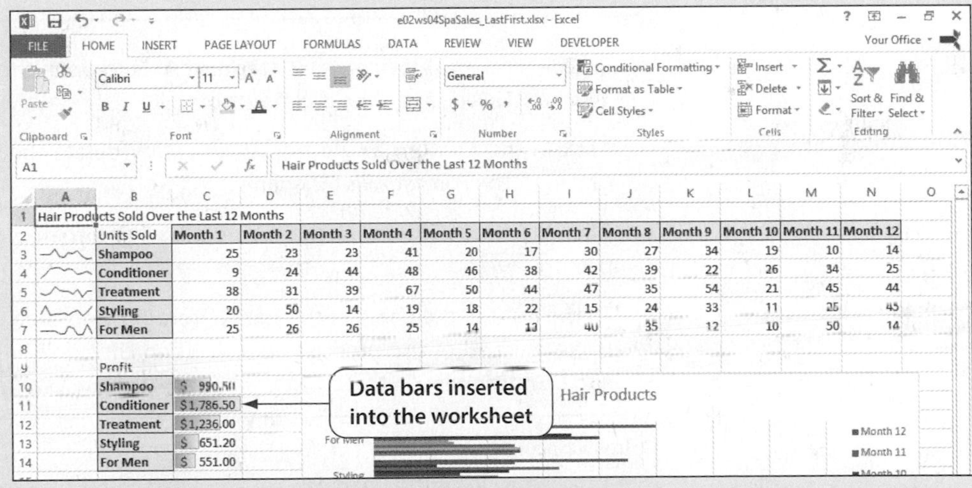

Figure 21 Data bars inserted

e. Click **Save**.

Recognize and Correct Confusing Charts

The process of working with and creating visually appealing charts with clear messages involves recognizing when you have a confusing chart. It is possible to have too much information or ambiguous information. This could include missing labels or legends, or textual information on a chart that is not clear. Additionally, a commonly made error is to use the incorrect chart type when analyzing data.

Correcting a Confusing Chart

Irene has pointed out that on the HairProducts sheet, a clustered bar chart was created that is difficult to interpret. The chart is based on the same data from which you created sparklines. Irene would like to be able to use the chart to compare different lines of product. The chart that was created shows the number of units sold as the bars, with each product having a different bar for each month in the data.

E04.24

To Correct a Confusing Chart

a. On the **HairProducts** worksheet, click the **chart border** of the clustered column chart.

b. On the **CHART TOOLS DESIGN** tab, in the Type group, click **Change Chart Type**. In the Change Chart Type dialog box, on the **All Charts** tab, click **Line**, and then click **OK**.

c. In the **Data** group, click **Switch Row/Column**. Since the data being charted is time sensitive, the time element should be shown on the x-axis.

Troubleshooting

Depending on your data, Excel may suggest a chart with the x- and y-axis already switched, saving you a step.

d. Double-click the **Horizontal (Category) Axis** to open the Format Axis task pane. Click **TEXT OPTIONS**, and then click **Textbox**.

e. Click in the **Custom angle** box, if necessary delete the existing value, and type 45. Close the Format Axis task pane.

f. Click the **Chart Title**, click the **formula bar**, and then type =. Click cell **A1**, and then press Enter.

g. To the right of the chart, click **Chart Filters**, and then under SERIES, click **Select All** to deselect all of the product options. Then click only the check boxes for **Shampoo** and **Conditioner**.

Troubleshooting

If the Chart Elements, Chart Styles, and Chart Filter buttons do not automatically appear to the right of the selected chart, use the horizontal scroll bar to create more space to the right of the selected chart. The buttons will only appear if there is enough space beside the chart.

h. Click **Apply**, and then click **Chart Filters** again to close it. Notice that the lines for these two products do not show similar trends as might be expected.

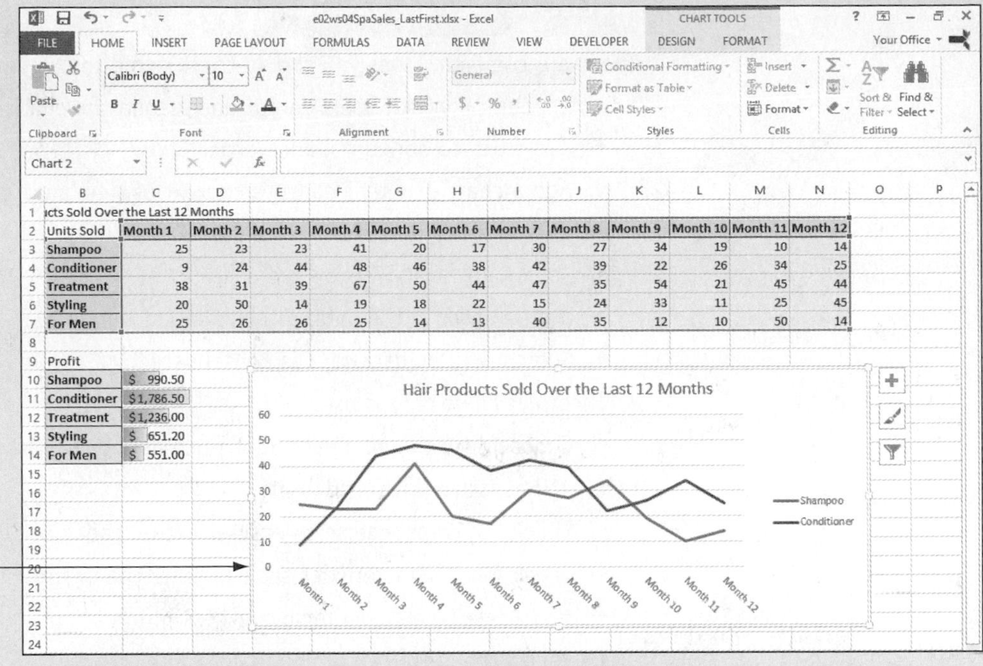

	Units Sold	Month 1	Month 2	Month 3	Month 4	Month 5	Month 6	Month 7	Month 8	Month 9	Month 10	Month 11	Month 12
3	Shampoo	25	23	23	41	20	17	30	27	34	19	10	14
4	Conditioner	9	24	44	48	46	38	42	39	22	26	34	25
5	Treatment	38	31	39	67	50	44	47	35	54	21	45	44
6	Styling	20	50	14	19	18	22	15	24	33	11	25	45
7	For Men	25	26	26	25	14	13	40	35	12	10	50	14

	Profit	
10	Shampoo	$ 990.50
11	Conditioner	$1,786.50
12	Treatment	$1,236.00
13	Styling	$ 651.20
14	For Men	$ 551.00

Hair products chart after changes

Figure 22 Corrected line chart

> **Troubleshooting**
> If you click the chart to see the source data associated with the chart and only see some of the data selected with a blue border, a chart component might have been clicked by mistake instead of the full chart area. To get the data set associated with the entire chart, under Chart Tools, click the Format tab. In the Current Selection group, change the Chart Element to Chart Area. Data associated with the selected component will be highlighted with a colored border.

i. Click **Save**.

Preparing to Print a Chart

Printing charts uses essentially the same process as printing a worksheet. When printing a chart sheet, select the chart sheet, go through the normal printing process, and adjust print options as you would for a worksheet. The chart will be a full-page display. If the chart is on a regular worksheet, it will be printed if you choose to print everything on the worksheet. In this case, the chart will be the size you developed on the worksheet. This is convenient when you want to print some tables or other data along with the chart. Finally, if you want to print just the chart on the worksheet, select the chart first, then choose the Print Selected Chart print option to print only the current chart.

Another useful technique when exploring data through charts is the ability to create static copies of the chart that can be used to compare with later versions. You can, in essence, take a picture of a chart that will not retain the underlying data. In this manner, subsequent versions of the chart can be made into images for comparisons. The process of creating a picture of the chart is to select the chart, copy it, then use the Paste Special option and paste it as a picture. When pasting as a picture, there are multiple picture format options such as a PNG, JPEG, or GIF files.

QUICK REFERENCE | **Common Charting Issues**

These are common issues you should try to avoid in the development of charts.

- Not enough context; users do not understand the chart.
  - Add titles to horizontal and vertical axis.
  - Add a chart title that conveys context of time and scope.
  - Add data labels to show percentages or values of chart elements.
- Too much information is on the chart.
  - Use a subset of the data, rather than all the data.
  - Summarize the data so it is consolidated.
- Incorrect chart type is used.
  - Choose a type more appropriate, such as a line chart for trends.
- Chart has issues with readability.
  - Check the color scheme to ensure text is readable.
  - Check font characteristics such as font type or font size.
  - Move data labels, and remove excess information.
  - Resize the overall chart to provide more area to work.
  - Check the color scheme and formatting so it is professional and does not hide chart information or text.
- Information or labeling is misleading.
  - Check the scaling to ensure it is appropriate and labeled for the correct units.
  - Consider the following wording: Does "Sales" mean the number of transactions or the total revenue?

E04.25

To Print a Chart

a. On the **HairProducts** worksheet, click the **chart border** of the line chart.

b. On the **FILE** tab, click **Print**. Notice that under Settings, the option for Print Selected Chart is selected by default.

c. Verify that the selected chart fits within the orientation of the page. If necessary, change the orientation of the page to **Landscape Orientation**.

d. Verify that the correct printer—as directed by your instructor—appears on the Printer button. Choices may vary depending on the computer you are using. If the correct printer is not displayed, click the **Printer** button arrow, and then click to choose the correct or preferred printer from the list of available printers. If your instructor asks you to print the document, click the **Print** button.

e. Complete the Documentation worksheet and submit your workbook as directed by your instructor. Click **Save**, and then close Excel.

Concept Check

1. What are some important items to consider when choosing the design and layout of a chart? p. 532
2. What are the two possible locations for a chart in Excel? Why would you choose one over the other? p. 536
3. Compare the purpose of a column chart and a pie chart. Give an example scenario for using the two different types of charts. p. 539–542
4. Why is it important to add elements and styles to charts such as titles, legends, and labels? p. 548
5. List two possible ways to add emphasis to an existing chart. p. 557
6. How are sparklines and data bars different from other chart objects in Excel? What are they commonly used for? p. 561–563
7. What are common mistakes that can be made when designing charts? Why is it important to correct these mistakes in existing charts? p. 564

Key Terms

Area chart 545
Argumentation objective 532
Bar chart 542
Chart sheet 536
Column chart 542
Combination chart 547
Data bars 563
Data exploration objective 532
Data point 533
Data series 533
Data visualization 532
Gantt chart 543
Hypothesis testing objective 532
Line chart 541
Pie chart 540
Quick Analysis 536
Recommended Charts 536
Scatter chart 544
Sparkline 561
Trendline 555

Visual Summary

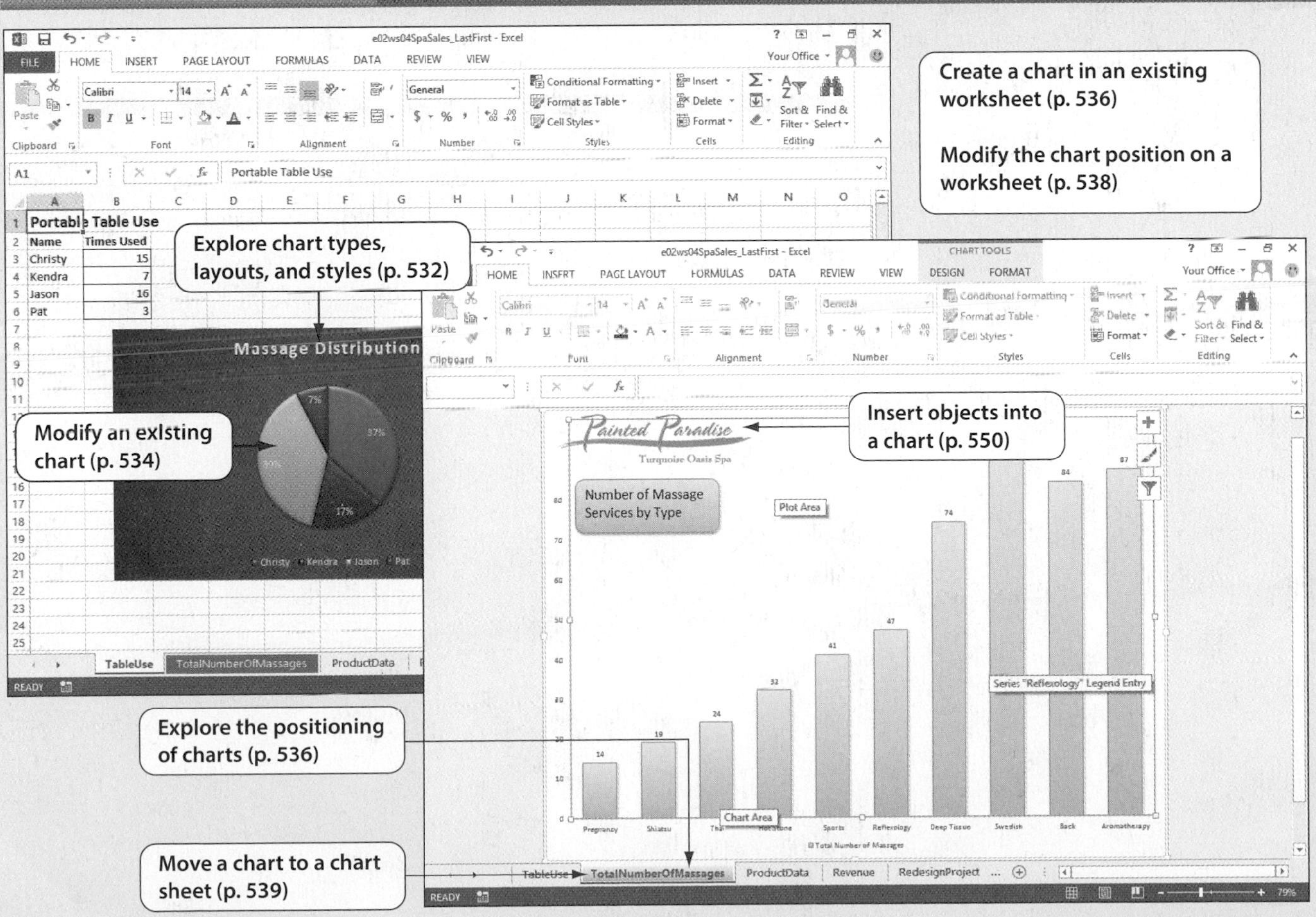

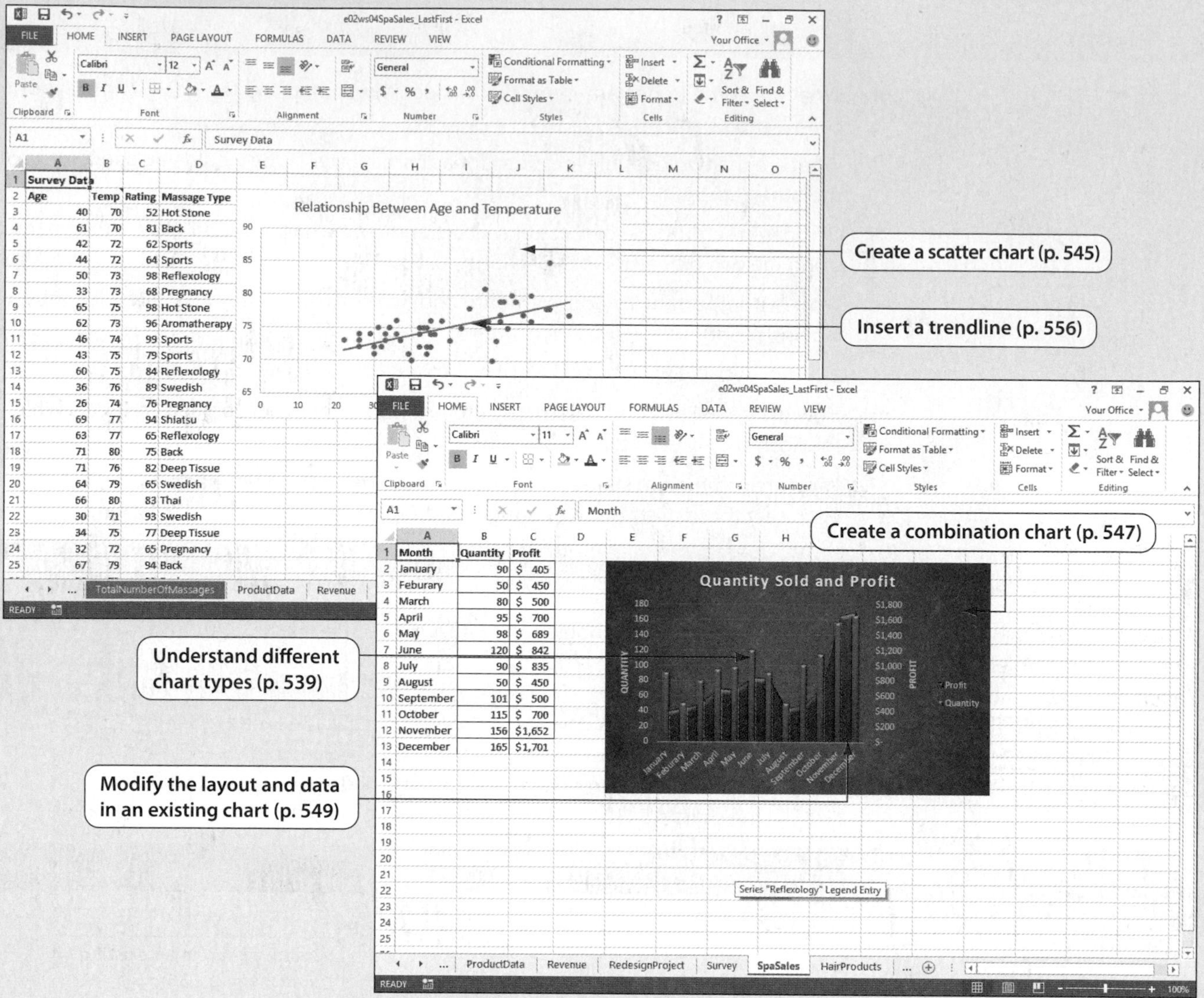

Relationship Between Age and Temperature
Create a scatter chart (p. 545)
Insert a trendline (p. 556)
Create a combination chart (p. 547)
Quantity Sold and Profit
Understand different chart types (p. 539)
Modify the layout and data in an existing chart (p. 549)

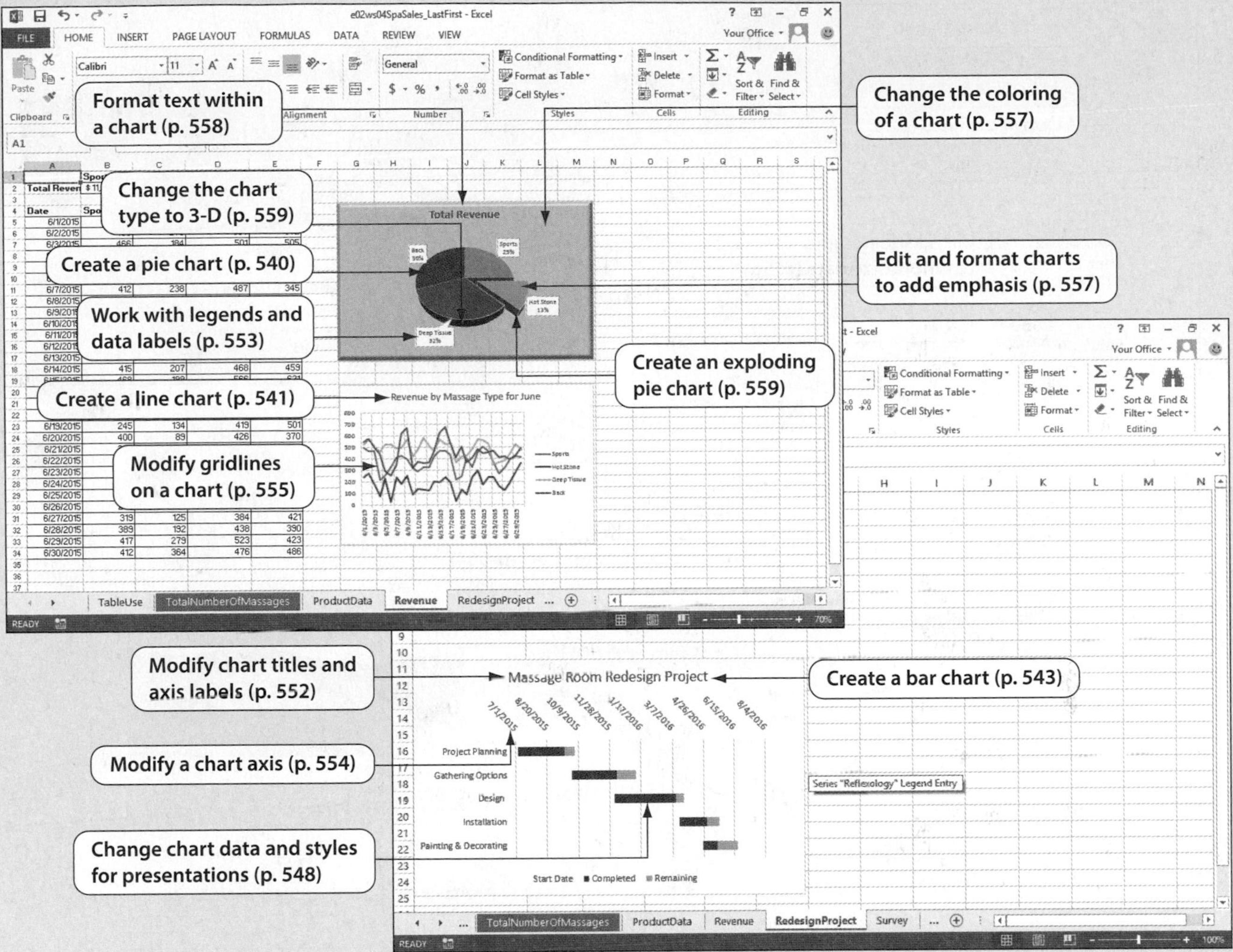
Format text within a chart (p. 558)
Change the coloring of a chart (p. 557)
Change the chart type to 3-D (p. 559)
Create a pie chart (p. 540)
Edit and format charts to add emphasis (p. 557)
Work with legends and data labels (p. 553)
Create an exploding pie chart (p. 559)
Create a line chart (p. 541)
Modify gridlines on a chart (p. 555)
Modify chart titles and axis labels (p. 552)
Create a bar chart (p. 543)
Modify a chart axis (p. 554)
Change chart data and styles for presentations (p. 548)
Total Revenue
Revenue by Massage Type for June
Massage Room Redesign Project
Project Planning
Gathering Options
Design
Installation
Painting & Decorating
Start Date
Completed
Remaining

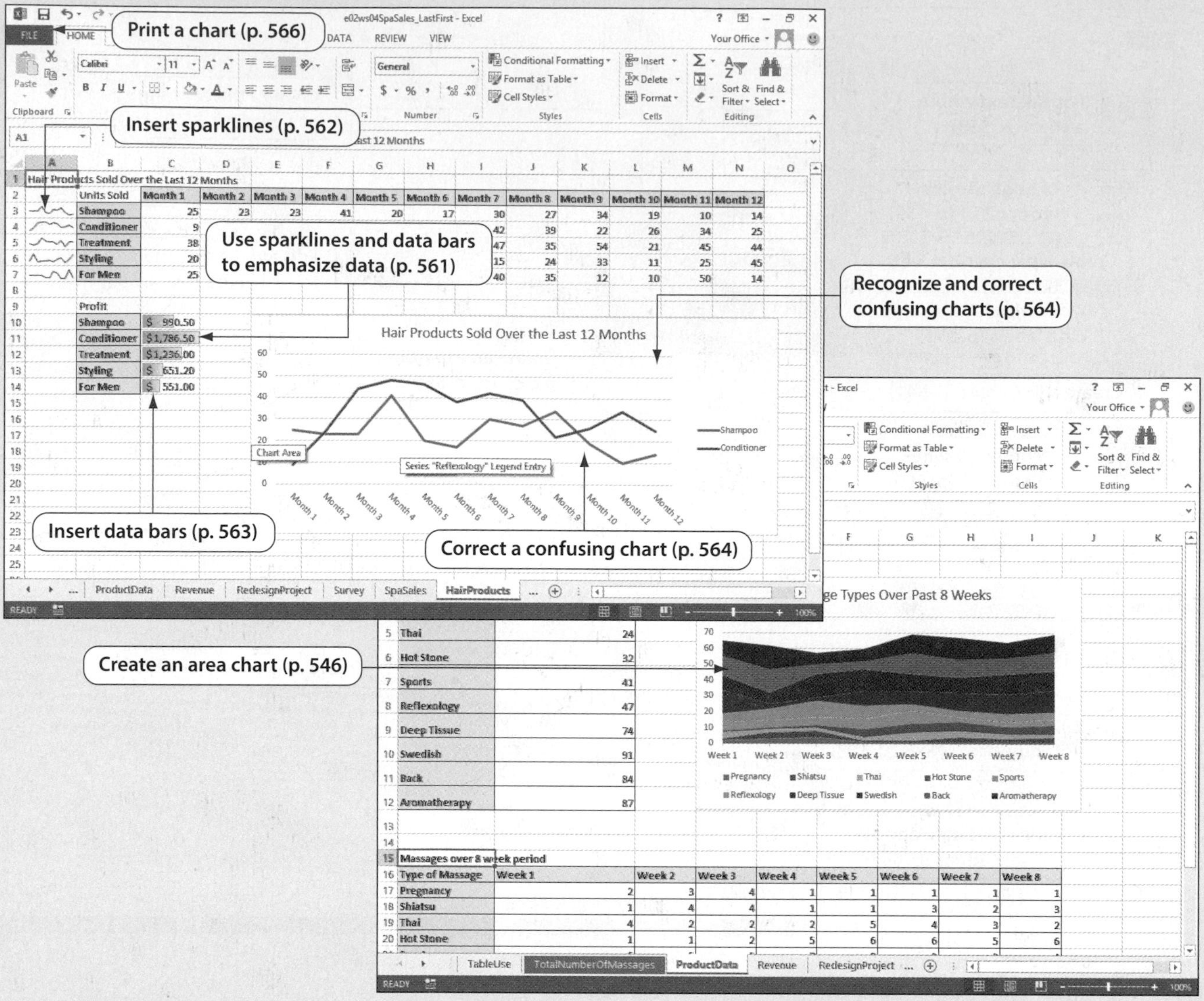

Figure 23 Turquoise Oasis Spa Sales Reports Final Document

Practice 1

Student data file needed:

 e02ws04Summary.xlsx

You will save your file as:

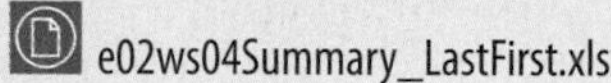

e02ws04Summary_LastFirst.xlsx

Product Sales Report

Sales & Marketing

Irene Kai and Meda Rodate have pulled together data pertaining to sales by the spa's massage therapists. In addition to massages, the therapists should also promote skin care, health care, and other products. With the monthly data, the managers want a few charts developed that will enable them to look at trends, compare sales, and provide feedback to the therapists. You are to help them create the charts.

a. Open the **e02ws04Summary** workbook. Save its as e02ws04Summary_LastFirst using your last and first.

b. Click the **Projections** worksheet tab, and then select the range **A4:B12**. Click **Quick Analysis**, click **CHARTS**, and then click **Clustered Column**. Click the **chart border**, and position the chart so that the top-left corner is over cell **D4**.

c. Click the **Chart Title**, and then click in the **formula bar**. Type = Projections!$A$1 and then press Enter.

d. To the right of the chart, click **Chart Styles**, and then select **Style 6** from the list. Click Chart Styles again to close the gallery.

e. Double-click the **Vertical (Value) Axis** to open the Format Axis task pane. Click in the **Minimum** box, clear the existing text, and then type 100. Close the Format Axis task pane.

f. Click the **Transactions** worksheet tab. Select the range **B5:J5**, press and hold Ctrl, and then select the range **B10:J10**. On the **INSERT** tab, in the **Charts** group, click the **Insert Pie or Doughnut Chart** arrow. Click **Pie**, the first option under 2-D Pie. Click the **chart border** of the chart, and position the chart so that the top-left corner is over cell **C12**.

g. Click the **Chart Title**, type Total Transactions by Therapist, and then press Enter.

h. To the right of the chart, click **Chart Elements**. Click the **Data Labels** arrow, and then click **More Options**. In the Format Data Labels task pane, under LABEL OPTIONS, under Label Contains, select **Percentage**. Under Label Position, select **Outside End**. Close the Format Data Labels task pane.

i. To the right of the chart, click **Chart Elements**. Click the **Legend** arrow, and then click **Right**.

j. Click the **Pie**—be careful not to click the label text. Click once again on the **red pie slice** for Meda that has the associated label 15, 6%. Drag the slice slightly **to the right** so it is exploded from the rest of the pie.

k. Click the **Revenue** worksheet tab, and then select the range **B10:J10**. Click the **INSERT** tab, and then in the Sparklines group, click **Line** to add sparklines to the worksheet. In the **Data Range** box, type B6:J9 and then click **OK**. Click any **cell** outside of the sparklines to deselect the sparklines.

l. On the INSERT tab, in the Text group, click **Header & Footer**. Under **HEADER & FOOTER TOOLS**, on the **DESIGN** tab, in the **Navigation** group, click **Go to Footer**. Click in the **left footer section**, and then in the **Header & Footer Elements** group, click **File Name**.

m. Click any **cell** on the worksheet to move out of the footer, and then press Ctrl + Home. On the status bar, click **Normal**.

n. Click the **Documentation** worksheet. Click cell **A6**, and then type in today's date. Click cell **B6**, and then type in your first and last name. Complete the remainder of the **Documentation** worksheet according to your instructor's direction.

o. Click **Save**, close Excel, and then submit your file as directed by your instructor.

Problem Solve 1

Student data file needed:

e02ws04Express.xlsx

You will save your file as:

e02ws04Express_LastFirst.xlsx

Express Car Rental

Research & Development

Thomas Reynolds is the corporate buyer for vehicles put into service by Express Car Rental. Tom has the option to buy several lots of vehicles from another rental agency that is downsizing. He wants to get a better idea of the number of rentals nationwide by vehicle type. The corporate accountant has forwarded Tom a worksheet containing rental data for last year. Tom wants to use this summarized data but feels that embedding charts will provide a quicker analysis in a more visual manner for the chief financial officer at their meeting next week.

a. Open **e02ws04Express**, and then save the file as e02ws04Express_LastFirst. Replace LastFirst with your actual name.

b. Use the data on the **AnnualData** worksheet, and create a **3-D Pie** chart of the number of annual rentals for the six car types. Reposition the chart below the monthly data.

c. On the 3-D pie chart, change the title to Annual Rentals. Change the font of the title to **Arial Black**, **16** pt, and **bold**. Adjust the data labels on the pie chart to include the **category name** and **percentage** only. Position the label information outside of the chart. Change the font size of the labels to **8** and apply **bold**. Delete the legend.

d. On the pie chart, explode the slice of the chart that represents the auto type with the **lowest percentage of annual rentals**.

e. Increase the data used in the column chart to include the months of **July**, **August**, and **September**.

f. Select the **clustered column** chart located below the monthly data. Change the chart type to **Line with Markers**. Switch the row and column data so that the months **July to December** are represented on the x-axis.

g. Change the chart style to **Style 6**. On the line chart, add **primary major vertical grid lines**. Change the chart title to Rentals by Auto Type for July to December.

h. Create a **3-D clustered column** chart using the data for the **Semi-Annual Totals** for all auto types on the AnnualData worksheet. The primary horizontal axis should be the auto types.

i. Move the 3-D column chart from the AnnualData worksheet to a chart sheet, and then name that sheet SemiAnnualReport. If necessary, add the chart title Semi-Annual Total to the chart. Adjust the 3-D Rotation of the chart to the following.
   - X Rotation of **20**
   - Y Rotation of **15**
   - Perspective of **15**

j. Reposition the **SemiAnnualReport** worksheet after the AnnualData worksheet.

k. Complete the **Documentation** worksheet according to your instructor's direction. Insert the **filename** in the left custom footer section of the Header/Footer tab in the Page Setup dialog box on all worksheets in the workbook.

l. Click Save, close Excel, and then submit the file as directed by your instructor.

Perform 1: Perform in Your Career

Student data file needed:

 e02ws04Costume.xlsx

You will save your file as:

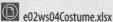

e02ws04Costume_LastFirst.xlsx

Costume Sales

Sales & Marketing

You work for a costume store. The store has recently compiled a summary of units sold and profit over the past year. Adding some charts to the worksheet would help them to better understand their customer demands and sales trends. The store would like you to visually represent the monthly units sold and the profit so the managers can visually identify any instances where units sold and profit do not correspond.

a. Open **e02ws04Costume**, and then save the file as e02ws04Costume_LastFirst. Replace LastFirst with your actual name.

b. Create a combination chart to the right of the monthly sales data. Represent the number of costumes sold as a column chart and profit as a line chart. Plot the profit data on a secondary axis.

c. Apply a **style** to the chart, and then add an appropriate chart title. Include a legend to describe the data being charted.

d. Adjust the primary vertical axis to have a minimum of 170 and the secondary vertical axis to have a minimum of 3000.

e. Create an appropriate chart under the combination chart that visually depicts the percentage of the number of costumes sold by each costume type. Apply **3-D** formatting to the chart and label appropriately.

f. Superhero costumes should be the largest percentage of sales in the data. Emphasize this in the chart by changing the presentation of the chart item that represents Superhero costumes sold.

g. Apply data bars to the Profit data for Costume Type to visualize the profit by costume type. Choose any gradient fill color.

h. Complete the **Documentation** worksheet according to your instructor's direction. Insert the **filename** in the left custom footer section of the Header/Footer tab in the Page Setup dialog box on all worksheets in the workbook.

i. Click Save, close Excel, and then submit the file as directed by your instructor.

Additional Cases

Additional Workshop Cases are available on the companion website and in the instructor resources.

MODULE CAPSTONE

More Practice 1

Student data file needed: e02mpSales.xlsx

You will save your file as: 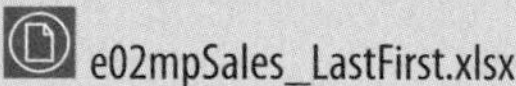

Restaurant Marketing Analysis

Sales & Marketing

The accounting system at the Indigo5 Restaurant tracks data on a daily basis that can be used for analysis to gauge its performance and determine needed changes. The restaurant is considering entering into a long-term agreement with a poultry company and getting a new refrigeration unit to store the chicken. If Indigo5 enters the agreement, the poultry company agrees to give Indigo5 a substantial discount for a specified period of time. Management would like to stimulate sales for the lowest revenue producing chicken item and any chicken items not meeting a sale performance threshold. Thus, some of this savings will be passed to the guests by placing these chicken items on sale.

a. Start **Excel**, and then open **e02mpSales**.

b. Save the file as e02mpSales_LastFirst, using your last and first name.

c. Click the **Indigo5ChickenSales** worksheet, and then click cell **D2**. Type =TODAY() and then press Enter.

Notice the data on the worksheet. The range A13:E18 contains four months of actual sales quantities for each menu item. Whereas, the range A22:E27 contains the sales projections that Indigo5 made for the same four months prior to the start of each month.

d. Click cell **B4**, type =SUM(B22:E22) and then press Ctrl+Enter. In cell **B4**, double-click the **AutoFill** handle to automatically fill cell range **B4:B9**. The range now returns the total quantity projection over the four months for each item.

e. Click cell **C4**, type =SUM(B13:E13) and then press Ctrl+Enter. In cell **C4**, double-click the **AutoFill** handle to automatically fill cell range **C4:C9**. The range now returns the total quantity of actual sales over the four months for each item.

f. Click cell **D4**, type =AVERAGE(B13:E13) and then press Ctrl+Enter. In cell **D4**, double-click the **AutoFill** handle to automatically fill cell range **D4:D9**. The range now returns the average monthly quantity for actual sales over the four months for each item.

g. Now you need to determine the price for each item to use in revenue calculations. Notice a list of menu prices is in cells A30:B44. Select the range **A30:B44**. Click the **Name** box, type Prices and then press Enter. The price listing is now named Prices to use in later calculations.

h. Click cell **E4**, type =VLOOKUP(A4,Prices,2,FALSE) and then press Ctrl+Enter. In cell **E4**, double-click the **AutoFill** handle to automatically fill the cell range **E4:E9**. The range now returns the price of each item by looking up the item and exactly matching the item name in the Prices list.

i. Click cell **F4**, type =E4*C4 and then press Ctrl+Enter. In cell **F4**, double-click the **AutoFill** handle to automatically fill cell range **F4:F9**. The range now returns the total revenue for each item.

j. Now you need to determine whether the item fell short or exceeded the sales projection.

Click cell **G4**, type =ROUND(C4/B4,2) and then press Ctrl+Enter. In cell **G4**, double-click the **AutoFill** handle to automatically fill cell range **G4:G9**. The range now returns a projection percentage. An item that fell short of the sales projection will be under 100%. An item that exceeded the sales projection will be over 100%.

k. Now you need to determine what item has the highest revenue. Click cell **H4**, type =IF(F4=MAX($F$4:$F$9),"Best Item","") and then press Ctrl+Enter. In cell **H4**, double-click the **AutoFill** handle to automatically fill cell range **H4:H9**. The range now returns a blank for all items except the one with the highest sales revenue—which returns Best Item.

l. Now you need to determine which items to put on sale to stimulate sales. An item should be put on sale if its % of Projection is less than the Sale Threshold in cell L4. An item should also be put on sale if its sales revenue is the lowest. Click cell **I4**, type =IF(OR (G4<$L$4,G4=MIN($F$4:$F$9)),"Put on Sale","") and then press Ctrl+Enter. In cell **I4**, double-click the **AutoFill** handle to automatically fill cell range **I4:I9**.

The range now returns Put on Sale for two items—the item with the lowest sales revenue and two items with a % of Projection less than 95%. All other items return a blank.

m. Now you need to how many days the sale will last based on dates given by the poultry company. Click cell **L7**, type =DATEDIF(L5,L6,"d") and then press Ctrl+Enter.

n. Select the range **B13:E18**. Click the **INSERT** tab, and then in the Sparklines group, click **Line**. Select the location range **F13:F18**, and then click **OK**. Click the **DESIGN** tab, and then in the Show group, click the **Markers** check box.

o. Now you need to create a chart comparing the percentage of all sales each item represents.
Select the range **A3:A9**. Press and hold Ctrl, and then select the range **F3:F9**.

- Click the **INSERT** tab, and then in the Charts group, click the **arrow** next to the Insert Pie or Doughnut Chart button. Select the first option for a **Pie Chart**.
- Click the **chart border**, and then drag to move the chart so the top-left corner is over the top-left corner of cell **G10**. Click on the **right resizing handle**, and then drag the right chart border to the border between columns **L** and **M**. Click the **bottom resizing handle**, and then move the bottom of the chart to the border between rows **22** and **23**.
- On the DESIGN tab, in the Chart Styles group, select **Style 3**.
- Click the chart title, **Total Revenue**. Click a second time on **Total Revenue** to place your cursor into the title. Erase "Total Revenue", and then type Chicken Sales Revenue by Menu Item.

p. Now you need to look at loan options for the new refrigeration unit. Click the **Poultry Loan** worksheet tab.

q. You need to look at a quarterly payment as it varies for different numbers of payments—or terms in years—and the annual interest rate. Indigo5 would like to make quarterly payments—four payments per year. Click cell **C12**, and type =-PMT($B12/4,C$11*4,$C$6) and then press Ctrl+Enter. In cell **C12**, double-click the **AutoFill** handle to automatically fill cell range **C12:C14**. With C12:C14 selected, drag the **AutoFill** handle to column **E** to fill the range **C12:E14**.

Notice that the mixed cell addressing of the $ before the B will make the B stay the same and not change when copied—same for the $ before the 11. Notice that when copied, the formula will always contain $C$6 since it has an absolute reference of a $ before both the column and the row.

r. Indigo5 would like to use the option that keeps the payment under $2,000, has the shortest term, and the lowest interest rate. Click cell **D12**, and then click the **Bold** button to indicate that option as the best.

s. Click the **Indigo5ChickenSales** worksheet tab. Click the **PAGE LAYOUT** tab, and then in the Page Setup group, click the **Page Setup Dialog Box Launcher**. Click the **Header/Footer** tab. Click **Custom** Footer, then click the **Insert File Name** button to place the file name in the left section of the footer. Click **OK** twice. Repeat this step for the **PoultryLoan** worksheet.

t. Click the **Documentation** worksheet. Click cell **A6**, and then type in today's date. Click cell **B6**, and then type in your first and last name. Complete the remainder of the **Documentation** worksheet according to your instructor's direction.

u. Click **Save**, close Excel, and then submit your file as directed by your instructor.

Problem Solve 1

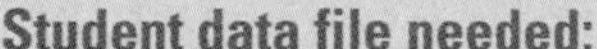

Student data file needed:

e02ps1Raises.xlsx

You will save your file as:

e02ps1Raises_LastFirst.xlsx

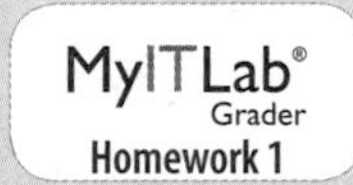

MyITLab® Grader Homework 1

Human Resources

Employee Raise Evaluation

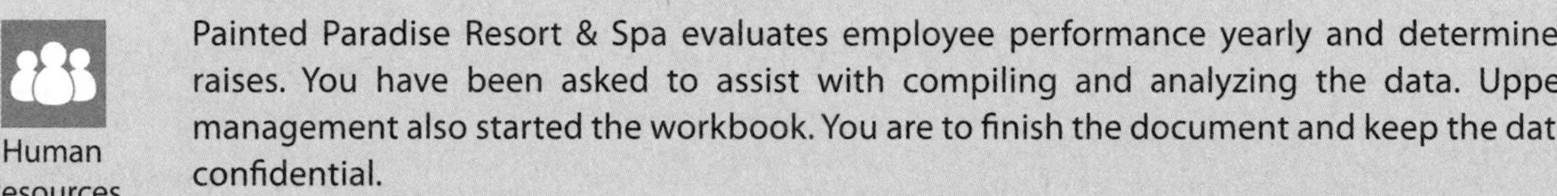

Painted Paradise Resort & Spa evaluates employee performance yearly and determines raises. You have been asked to assist with compiling and analyzing the data. Upper management also started the workbook. You are to finish the document and keep the data confidential.

a. Start **Excel**, and then open **e02ps1Raises**. Save the file as e02ps1Raises_LastFirst.

b. The **Addresses** worksheet includes data from the payroll database. You need to cleanse the data so this worksheet can be used in a mail merge to create salary notice letters. Add the following.

- In column **E**, extra spaces and a dash were left in the data by the database in case the zip code had an extension. In cells **F7:F14**, enter a LEFT function to return the ZipCode without the unnecessary "–".
- In column **G**, the database did not export the formatting for the phone numbers. In cells **H7:H14**, use Flash Fill to add formatting back to the phone number. If done correctly, cell H7 will return **(505) 555-1812**. Hint: There is only one space between the ")" and the 5.

c. The **Evaluations** worksheet includes evaluation data collated from various managers. Managers rated employees both quantitatively—numerically—and qualitatively—written notes. The number scores and notes support the raise recommendation made by the manager. Add the following.

- In cells **I3:I10**, calculate the average numerical ratings for each employee. Only managers get evaluated by the Leadership rank in column **H**. Column **C** indicates whether the employee is a manager. Thus, the average calculation should only include the values in column **H** if the employee is a manager. Even if a rating is given to a non-manager employee in column **H**, that number should not be included in the average in column **I**. Hint: This calculation requires the use of an IF statement.
- In cells **B13:B20**, exported data from the rating system combines the manager's raise recommendation of High, Standard, or Low followed by the manager's notes. In cells **J3:J10**, use a combination of text functions to return just the manager's raise recommendation—High, Standard, or Low. The values returned should not have extra spaces before or after the word. Hint: The names in A3:A10 are in the same order as A13:A20. Also, notice the text pattern is always the recommendation followed by a space.

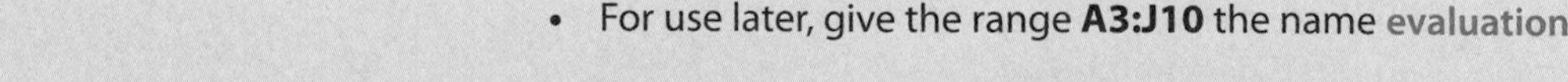

- For use later, give the range **A3:J10** the name evaluations.

d. On the **Payroll** worksheet, there is an analysis for raises you need to finish. First, you need to get all the applicable data to making the raise determination on this worksheet. Add the following.
   - In cell **F1**, enter a formula to always return the current date.
   - In cells **E6:E13**, add a DATEDIF function that will calculate the years employed based on today's date in cell F1 and the HireDate in column **B**.
   - In cells **F6:F13**, add a VLOOKUP function that returns the raise recommendation—High, Standard, or Low—for each employee by exactly matching the Name in column **A** in the range you named **evaluations**.
   - In cells **G6:G13**, add a VLOOKUP function that returns the starting raise percentage based on the ranges in the Standard Raise table in cells **A16:B19** and the number of years employed in column **E**.

e. On the **Payroll** worksheet, you now need to begin determining the employee's final raise. Add the following.
   - In cells **H6:H13**, add an IF function that will award anyone with a Raise Recommend of High an extra bonus listed in cell **F2**. All other employees get zero bonus.
   - In cells **I6:I13**, add an IF function that will give anyone with a Raise Recommend of Low a deduction listed in cell **F3**. All other employees get zero deduction.
   - In cells **J6:J13**, add a calculation that returns the final raise amount with the value—not just formatted—rounded to the hundreds position. For example, a final raise of $1,625 rounded to the hundreds returns a value of $1,600. The final raise amount is the salary multiplied by the Standard Raise % and then adding any bonus and subtracting any deduction. Hint: The num_digits argument will need to be negative.
   - In cells **K6:K13**, add a calculation that returns the Final % Increase. The final increase is determined by dividing the Raise Amt by the Salary.
   - In cells **L6:L13**, add a calculation that returns the New Salary by adding the Salary and Raise Amt.

f. On the **Payroll** worksheet, you now need to add a few summary measures for upper management. Add the following.
   - In cell **J1**, add a function that calculates the Net Payroll Increase based on the Raise Amt in cells **J6:J13**.
   - In cell **J2**, add a function that calculates the Average Raise % based on the Final % Increase in cells **K6:K13**.
   - Based on the data in cells **A5:A13** and **K5:K13**, add a **3-D Clustered Column**. Hint: Use Ctrl to select noncontiguous ranges for the chart.
   - Under chart styles, set the chart to **Style 3**. Change the vertical axis to start at a lower bound of **0.01**—for 1%. Then, change the title to read **Final % Increase Comparison**.
   - Move and resize the chart so the upper-left corner is in cell **F14** and the lower-right corner is in cell **L22**. Set the chart title to **11** pt font. Set the vertical and horizontal axis labels to **9** pt font.

g. Complete the **Documentation** worksheet according to your instructor's direction. Insert the filename in the left custom footer section of the Header/Footer tab in the Page Setup dialog box on all worksheets in the workbook.

h. Click Save, close Excel, and then submit the file as directed by your instructor.

Problem Solve 2

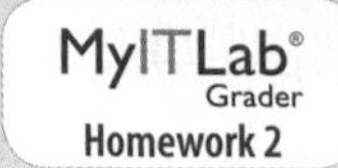

Sales & Marketing

Student data file needed:

e02ps2Advertising.xlsx

You will save your file as:

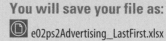

e02ps2Advertising_LastFirst.xlsx

Advertising Review

The Painted Paradise Resort & Spa has been investing in advertising using different advertising media. When guests check in, the employee asks the guest how they heard about Painted Paradise Resort & Spa. Based on the customer's response, the employee then notes in the system either magazine, radio, television, Internet, word of mouth, or other. Since almost every guest is asked, the number surveyed represents a significant portion of the actual guests. The past year's data is located on the GuestData worksheet. Every time a guest answers an advertising source—such as a magazine—as how he or she heard about the resort, it is considered a guest result. Ideally, the resort wants to purchase advertising at a low cost but then see as many guest results as possible.

Every year, upper management sets the advertising budget before the beginning of the fiscal year—July 1 start. For this next year, upper management gave you more television budget because of a new video marketing campaign. Also, the advertising contracts get negotiated every year, as the media vendors require a one-year commitment. The contracts are negotiated after the budget is set. You will develop charts for an upcoming presentation that will discuss a marketing strategy, potential changes to the budget given the new media prices, anticipated monthly guest results, and prospects of hiring a marketing consulting company with a high retainer that would require a loan.

a. Start Excel, and then open **e02ps2Advertise**. Save the file as e02ps2Advertise_LastFirst.

b. On the **GuestData** worksheet in the cells **A6:J17**, the data indicates the number of guests responding that he or she heard of the resort from the listed method—Guest Results. Add the following.

- In cell **H2**, add a COUNTA function to determine the number of months listed in cells A6:A17.
- In cell **J2**, add a DATEDIF to calculate the survey duration in years using the 2014 Fiscal Start date and 2015 Fiscal Start date.
- In cells **B6:B17**, use Flash Fill to return the three character code for the month—JUL for July.
- Select cells **L6:M17**, and then name the range season.
- In cells **C6:C17**, add a VLOOKUP that will exactly match the month in column **B** to return the correct season—Low, Mid, or High—based off the named range **season**.
- In cells **D19:J19**, calculate the averages for each column with a rounded value—not just formatted—to zero decimal places.
- For later use, create the following named ranges.

Cell	Name
D19	AvgMagazine
E19	AvgRadio
F19	AvgTelevision
G19	AvgInternet

c. On the **AdvertisingPlan** worksheet, an analysis of past Guest Results and the new budget has been started. First, you need to finish out the past year analysis. Add the following.

- In cell **F2**, enter a function that will return the current date.
- Set the following cells to these formulas.

Cell	Name
D6	=AvgMagazine
D7	=AvgRadio
D8	=AvgTelevision
D9	=AvgInternet
* Note that these are monthly averages. Thus all calculations on this worksheet are estimates based on the monthly average.	

- In cells **E6:E9**, calculate the Amount Spent—this is a monthly figure—by multiplying the Cost Per Ad and the Ads Placed.
- In cells **F6:F9**, calculate the Cost per Guest Result by dividing the Amount Spent by the Past Guest Results.
- In cells **C10:F10**, calculate the appropriate totals for each column.

d. On the **AdvertisingPlan** worksheet, you need to finish out the new budget year analysis. Add the following.

- In cells **I6:I9**, calculate the Number of Ads that can be purchased based off the New Budget and the New Cost Per Ad in columns **G** and **H**. Hint: A partial ad cannot be purchased. Further, $324 would not be enough to purchase one radio ad since the cost per ad is $325.
- In cells **J6:J9**, calculate the Amount to Spend—this is a monthly figure—by multiplying the New Cost Per Ad and the Ads to Place.
- In cells **G10** and **I10:J10**, calculate the appropriate totals for each column. If necessary, change the format for cell I10 to general.
- In cell **H11**, calculate the amount of the budget remaining by subtracting the Amount to Spend total from the New Budget total. Note, the totals are in row 10. A negative number indicates the new plan is over budget. A positive number indicates the new plan is under budget and has excess spendable funds.
- In cells **K6:K9**, add a formula that will return Increase? if the Ads to Place is equal to zero or if the New Cost Per Ad is less than or equal to the Budget +/- in cell H11. Any others should return Decrease?. This column now indicates the media types for which the resort may want to consider an increase or decrease to the Ads to Place—along with any necessary budget adjustment.
- In cells **L6:L9**, calculate the Anticipated Guest Results by dividing the Amount to Spend by the Cost per Guest Result—column F. The resulting value—not the just the format—should be rounded to zero decimals.
- In cell **L10** calculate the appropriate total for Anticipated Guest Results.
- In cell **L11**, calculate the amount of anticipated guest results compared to the past by subtracting the Past Guest Results total from the Anticipated Guest Results total. Note, the totals are in row 10. A negative number indicates an anticipated decrease in Guest Results. A positive number indicates an anticipated increase in Guest Results.
- Evaluate the statements in cells **H15:L18**. Bold any false statements.

e. Starting on the **AdvertisingPlan** worksheet, you need to make two charts for your presentation. Create the following two charts.

- Based on the data in cells **A5:A9**, **D5:D9**, and **L5:L9**, add a **3-D Clustered Column** chart. Hint: Use Ctrl to select noncontiguous ranges for the chart.
- Under chart styles, set the chart to **Style 6**. Then, change the title to read PAST V. ANTICIPATED MONTHLY GUEST RESULTS.
- Move and resize the chart so the upper-left corner is in cell **A11** and the lower-right corner is in cell **F22**. Set the chart title to **12** pt font.

- Based on the data in cells **A5:A9**, **D5:D9**, and **E5:E9**, add a **Clustered Column - Line on Secondary Axis Combo Chart**. Hint: Use Ctrl to select noncontiguous ranges for the chart. Make this chart appear on its own worksheet—chart sheet—named GuestResultsBySpending.
- Under chart styles, set the chart to **Style 6**. Then, change the title to read Past Advertising Amount Spent compared to # of Guest Results Experienced, monthly.
- Set the chart title to **16** pt font, set all axis data labels to **18** pt font, and then set all legend text to **12** pt font.

f. On the **MarketingConsultants** worksheet, a monthly loan payment analysis has been started. The resort is considering hiring marketing consultants. However, they require a large up-front retainer fee. The resort would need to take out a loan to cover the cost. The resort needs an analysis of the loan payment by varying interest rate and down payment amount. Add the following.
    - In cells **D10:H13**, add a **PMT** function to calculate the monthly payment. Enter one formula that can be entered in cell **D10** and filled to the remaining cells. Hint: Think carefully about where $ signs are needed for mixed and absolute cell addressing. Also, the down payment can be subtracted from the Retainer—or Principal—Amount in the third argument of the PMT function.

g. Complete the **Documentation** worksheet according to your instructor's direction. Insert the **filename** in the left custom footer section of the Header/Footer tab in the Page Setup dialog box on all worksheets in the workbook.

h. Click Save, close Excel, and then submit the file as directed by your instructor.

Perform 1: Perform in Your Life

Student data file needed:

Blank Excel workbook

You will save your file as:

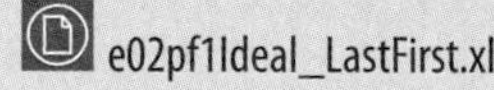
e02pf1Ideal_LastFirst.xlsx

Your Ideal Career Start

Human Resources

Even if this is your first semester, you have probably already begun to think about the type of job or career you want. Further, when you are studying long hours, it can be fun to imagine the new car you might buy at your ideal career start after graduation. For this project, pretend—if you need to—that you are graduating this semester. In this project, you need to find currently available jobs and establish criteria to help you pick your most desired position. Then, you will find the ideal new car to purchase, but your new position's salary must be able to afford the monthly payment.

a. Open a blank Excel workbook. Save the workbook as e02pf1Ideal_LastFirst. Apply a **Theme**, and then use cell styles where appropriate. Keep the workbook professional, but feel free to optionally add elements such as a picture of your ideal career start or new car.

b. Create a worksheet named JobData. Go to the Internet, and then find five or more jobs that interest you. You can grab positions from multiple websites or just one website—from the same website will be easiest. Copy and paste that data into the **JobData**. On the JobData worksheet, accomplish the following.
    - The goal is to get separate columns of data listed below by copying from the Internet and separating—or cleaning—the data using Excel's Flash Fill feature and/or text functions. Depending on how you copy and paste from the web, this will be harder or easier. You can gather more data than listed below if it is relevant for you to picking the ideal job. At a minimum, you must have the following.

Data (no extra characters in or around the data)	Description
Company Name	Full name as you would address a letter to the company
Job Title	Full job title and needs to be descriptive of the position. For example, "Entry Level" is not a sufficient title. "Application Support Analyst— Entry Level" is a sufficient title.
State	State position is located in. State should be in a column by itself, not in combination with the city or address.
Pay or Pay Range	Salary or hourly rate. If a pay range is provided, separate out the low and high end of the range separately. Hint: Try not to mix pay types. For example, if you are looking for a salary position, choose all salary positions.

Table 1 Required minimum job position data

- Add headers, comments, and/or notes to make clear to your instructor what Excel steps you took to get to the final job data. Leave all formulas you create in the worksheet—show your work, and don't delete it. Indicate where Flash Fill was used. Keep your work organized.
- Indicate on the worksheet the website you used to find the job posting, for example Monster.com or CareerBuilder.com. Also, indicate the date and your full name on the worksheet somewhere.

c. Create another worksheet called **JobAnalysis**. In an organized fashion, copy onto the worksheet only the clean copies of data that you intend to use. Add the following elements to this worksheet.
- Use an IF statement in combination with any other Excel formulas/functions to indicate whether a job is in a state you find desirable. You should indicate a minimum of two states as desirable.
- Create a table that establishes pay range categories for Below Expected, Expected, and Above Expected based on your personal job expectations. Use this table in a VLOOKUP to determine which category for each of the positions you are evaluating.
- Add any other additional formulas and functions to help you determine the most desirable position.
- The worksheet must ultimately indicate one final **Most Desired** job position.

d. Create another worksheet called **MyNewCar**. Add the following elements to this worksheet.
- Cells that indicate the following information about the car you would like: Manufacturer, Model, Year, Price, and URL to a webpage that provides this information. You may pick a preowned car if you indicate that on the worksheet.
- A loan analysis for a monthly payment. Your monthly payment will vary by the price of the car, down payment, term or number of payments, and annual interest rate. Research realistic current interest rates for the type of car you wish to purchase. Your analysis should evaluate various options for two of the following: interest rate, term, or down payment.
- Somewhere on the worksheet, calculate or input the monthly income from your Most Desired job on the JobAnalysis worksheet.
- You need to be able to afford the car you pick. The amount you will be able to afford will vary greatly on individual circumstances—such as marital status, credit card debt, and homeowner status. For the purposes of this project, the car you pick cannot have a monthly payment greater than 10% of your gross—pretaxes or deductions—salary for your Most Desired job. Create an analysis of the percentage your loan payment represents of your monthly salary. Bold or otherwise indicate feasible loan options. If none of the loan options are under 10%, you will have to do one or a combination of the following: pick a new car, increase your down payment, extend your term, or find a lower interest rate.

e. Build at least one meaningful chart on either the JobAnalysis or MyNewCar worksheet. Include at least a one-sentence explanation near the chart explaining the chart's significance.

f. Complete the **Documentation** worksheet according to your instructor's direction. Insert the **filename** in the left custom footer section of the Header/Footer tab in the Page Setup dialog box on all worksheets in the workbook.

g. Save your work, and then close Excel. Submit the file as directed by your instructor.

Perform 2: Perform in Your Career

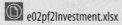

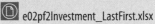

Student data file needed: e02pf2Investment.xlsx

You will save your file as:  e02pf2Investment_LastFirst.xlsx

Investment Portfolios

Finance & Accounting

You have started working as an investment intern for a financial company that helps clients invest in the stock market. Your manager gives you a spreadsheet detailing some periodic investments in Nobel Energy, Inc. (NBL) made by one of the clients. The client would like a report and charts on the NBL investment and the stock's performance. Your manager has asked you to finish this report.

a. Open workbook **e02pf2Investment.** Save the workbook as e02pf2Investment_LastFirst. Apply a **theme**, and then use cell styles where appropriate for a professional looking spreadsheet.

b. On the NBLInvestment worksheet, add the following calculations.
   - In column **F**, a formula to calculate total value was already entered by your manager. Update the formula to return a value of only two decimals. Hint: The cell value needs to change, which is different than merely formatting to two decimals.
   - In column G, starting in the second row—cell **G22**—enter a formula to sum up the quarterly investments as of the date in column A to provide a cumulative total. For example, cell G22 should return the sum of the Quarterly investments on 1/2/2013 and 4/1/2013. Next, cell G23 should return the sum of the Quarterly investments on 1/2/2013, 4/1/2013, and 7/1/2013. Thus, column G returns a running total of investments so that the last cell—G33—reflects the total of all investments from 1/2/2013 thru 1/3/2016.
   - In column **H**, calculate the total growth. If total value is more than 0, then total growth is total value – total investment. Otherwise, the total growth is either 0 or a negative value. A negative value means that the investment shrunk instead of grew.
   - In column **I**, calculate the total growth %: if total value is more than 0, then total growth % is total growth / total investment; otherwise, the total growth % is 0.
   - In column **J**, calculate the quarterly growth: if total value is more than 0, then quarterly growth is total growth—total growth from the previous quarter; otherwise, quarterly growth is 0.
   - In column **K**, calculate quarterly growth %: if total value is more than 0, then quarterly growth % is quarterly growth / total investment; otherwise, quarterly growth % is 0.

c. Create a **combo chart** for Total Portfolio Performance that displays the Total Value, Total Investment and Total Growth % over time. Hint: You will need to show a secondary axis for Total Growth %.

d. Create a **combo chart** for Quarterly Performance that displays the Quarterly Growth and the Quarterly Growth % over time. Hint: You will need to show a secondary axis for Quarterly Total Growth %.

e. Complete the **Documentation** worksheet according to your instructor's direction. Insert the **filename** in the left custom footer section of the Header/Footer tab in the Page Setup dialog box on all worksheets in the workbook.

f. Save your work, and then close Excel. Submit the file as directed by your instructor.

Perform 3: Perform in Your Team

Student data file needed:

 e02pf3WhirlyWind.xlsx

You will save your file as:

 e02pf3WhirlyWind_TeamName.xlsx

Theme Park Expansion

Production & Operations

You work for Whirly Wind Theme Park—a preeminent amusement park next to a large lake. Whirly Wind is primarily a thrill and roller-coaster park. While Whirly Wind has a water section in the park, it is small and outdated. Your manager assigned you to a team to help with the analysis for an expansion of the park's water area and overall capacity. Your manager needs help looking at past sales, sales trends, loan options, and project management. Your manager has provided you with a starting workbook that needs work and elaboration.

a. Select one team member to set up the document by completing Steps b–d.

b. Open your browser and navigate to either **https://www.skydrive.live.com**, **https://www.drive.google.com**, or any other instructor assigned location. Be sure all members of the team have an account on the chosen system—such as a Microsoft or Google account.

c. Open **e02pf3WhirlyWind**, and then save the file as e02pf3WhirlyWind_TeamName replacing TeamName with the name assigned to your team by your instructor.

d. Share the spreadsheet with the other members of your team. Make sure that each team member has the appropriate permission to edit the document.

e. Hold a team meeting and discuss the requirements of the remaining steps. Make an action and communication plan. Consider which steps can be done independently and which steps require completion of prior steps before starting.

f. On the **RevenueHistory** worksheet, you will find data about past revenue—earned income before any costs. Whirly Wind is only open from the first of April until the end of October every year. Whirly Wind is located in the Midwest of the United States with typical Midwest weather. Whirly Wind offers discounted season passes during the month of April and October every year. Below is a description of the provided data.

Data	Description
Month	The first day of the month for the data in that row.
Monthly Revenue	All revenue from all sources for that month—April through October.
Attendance	The number of guests that entered the park that month. The guests may have been paid guests or season pass/comp guests who did not have to pay. Attendance is not reflective of time spent in the park. If a guest leaves and comes back into the park, the guest is still only counted once. The Max Monthly Capacity is also listed in cell J4.
Ticket Sales (Any Kind)	All ticket sales that month. This includes single day, multiple day, and all variations of a season pass. If a guest buys a season pass in April, the revenue is accounted for in April. However, the guest can still enter the park from May to October of that year without adding any money to the monthly ticket sales.
Food & Merch Sales	All other revenue besides ticket sales. This is primarily food and merchandise. However, it also includes a few other things such as parking.
Avg Temp (Degrees)	The average temperature for the park that particular month.

Table 2 Whirly Wind revenue data

g. The data on the **RevenueHistory** worksheet could be analyzed in several ways. At a minimum, add the following to the worksheet.
    - Calculations for appropriate averages, mode for attendance, and average ticket cost per guest in attendance that month.
    - Each team member should independently create 1–2 charts about the data on this worksheet.
    - The team should meet and decide which charts to include in the final file. The final file should have a minimum of four charts and a maximum of six charts. The team should pick the charts that provide insight into the sales trends of the park.

h. On the **Loan** worksheet, you will find the basic information about three loan options to finance Whirly Wind's expansion. Make the following updates to the loan worksheet.
    - In column **F**, calculate the loan—or funding—needed to do the expansion.
    - In column **G**, calculate the cost per extra capacity—or amount per extra guest attendance based off the total cost in column **D**.
    - In column **H**, research and provide current interest rates applicable to these three loan options.
    - Below row **7**, add a loan analysis to provide the monthly payment amount for the three loan options. Whirly Wind is considering a term of 2, 3, or 5 years only.
    - Below row **7**, add an analysis indicating which loan options are Ideal or Not Preferred. If the loan meets Whirly Wind's Preferences in columns J:L, the loan is Ideal. Any loan not meeting all of those preferences is Not Preferred.
    - Add any other calculations your team feels is relevant to determining the best loan for Whirly Wind.

i. On the TimeLine worksheet, you will see the applicable dates and project days needed to complete each state of the expansion project. On this worksheet, add the following.
    - In column **E**, add a calculation to determine the number of Total Needed days based on the Start Date and Projected End Date.
    - In column **D**, add a calculation to determine the number of days remaining based on the Total Needed and Completed.
    - On the worksheet somewhere, calculate the total project duration in months.
    - On the worksheet somewhere, calculate the current project date with the TODAY function.
    - Add a Gantt chart for the project timeline.

j. Apply a **Theme**, and then use **cell styles** where appropriate and to make professional.

k. As a team, answer the questions on the TeamComments worksheet.

l. Complete the **Documentation** worksheet according to your instructor's direction. Minimally, include enough detail to identify which parts of the worksheets/workbook each team member completed.

m. Insert the **filename** in the left custom footer section of the Header/Footer tab in the Page Setup dialog box on all worksheets in the workbook. In a custom header section, include the **names** of the students in your team—spread the names evenly across each of the three header sections: left section, center section, and right section.

n. Save your work, and then close Excel. Submit the file as directed by your instructor.

Perform 4: How Others Perform

Student data file needed:

 e02pf4Fit.xlsx

You will save your file as:

e02pf4Fit_LastFirst.xlsx

BMI Health Analysis

Research & Development

A state health agency wants to examine health data on college students starting with the body mass index (BMI). You recently started as an intern to the school's grant-funded initiative, Fit School. Fit School works with the state health agency and counsels student clients on improving health. The agency gave your manager this file with historical data from 1952 through 2011, current data from your school, and a health counselor's tool to help analyze a client's health condition. Your manager thought the file was confusing and had errors. Your manager asked you to look at the data, correct the errors, and create some new components on the spreadsheet.

You calculate BMI using a person's height (in inches) and weight (in pounds). The formula for BMI is as follows:

Weight/Height^2 * 703 (the notation in Excel to square height is Height^2)

For example, if a client weighs 120 pounds and is 5 feet 6 inches tall, their BMI is as follows: 120/66^2 * 703=19.37

The BMI has categories as follows.

- Underweight: less than 18.5
- Normal: 18.5 or greater and less than 25
- Overweight: 25 or greater and less than 30
- Obese: 30 or greater

a. Start Excel, and then open **e02pf4Fit**. Save the file as e02pf4Fit_LastFirst.

b. Throughout the workbook, **cell styles** should be applied to appropriate headings and titles using an appropriate **theme**. Also, BMI calculations do not have many decimals. Change BMI values—not just the format—to be rounded to two decimals except those on the Historical worksheet.

c. The **Historical** worksheet shows average BMI numbers for males and females from 1952 to 2011. The agency wants to see the trend of average BMI index numbers for males and females over the entire time period. The current chart is confusing. Update the chart as follows.
   - The chart should be a more appropriate chart type.
   - The chart should have a more descriptive title and clean, understandable x-axis and y-axis labels.
   - The chart should have a professional, business look so it can be used by the state agency in a presentation.
   - Adjust the scales and create gridlines that help convey the context as appropriate.

d. The **CurrentData** worksheet has data for students at your school. This worksheet has errors and needs some additions. Update this worksheet as follows.
   - The Weight Category in column F looks up the BMI Category from a table located on the BMICategories worksheet with the range named BMICategory. This calculation is not working correctly and produces erroneous #N/A errors. Fix errors in this workbook that cause this formula to not work correctly. Hint: Look carefully at the construction of the BMICategory look up table values and name range definition.

- The Female and Male BMIs are being separated in columns G and F. This separation will allow separate averages for male and female to be calculated. The formulas are returning male results for females and female results for males. Update the formulas so the correct values are showing.
- Add averages appropriately to the bottom of the data set.

e. The **HealthAnalysis** worksheet is a tool for counselors to help clients assess their current health and set goals. This worksheet has errors and needs additions. Update this worksheet as follows.
   - The BMI Calculation in cell B6 will return an error if height—B4—and weight—B5—are blank. Modify cell **B6** to return a blank value if either height or weight is blank.
   - In the prior step, you fixed the BMI category lookup on the CurrentData worksheet to work correctly. Cell B7 uses the same name range for the table—BMICategory. Cell B7 contains a different error causing it to work incorrectly. Find and fix the error. Then, modify cell B7 to return a blank value if cell B6 is blank.
   - Cell C7 contains a formula that should return the words "At Risk BMI" for Overweight and Obese clients. For all other clients, cell C7 should return a blank. Even after fixing cell B7, this formula returns incorrect results. Find and fix the error.
   - Cell B11 should calculate the client's age. This formula is returning an error. Find and fix the error. Then, modify cell **B11** to return a blank value if cell B10 is blank.
   - The worksheet coloring should be professional and help indicate to the counselor which cells should be modified or changed when meeting with a client.

f. The **BMIEstimateTable** is for counselors to print out and give to clients for future estimation of BMI as the client's weight changes. This worksheet is not working properly. Update this worksheet as follows.
   - The formulas in cells **C4:Q21** are not returning the correct results. Fix the formulas.
   - The worksheet does not print well. Update the **settings** and **coloring** to look professional when printed in black and white ink.

g. Insert the **filename** in the left custom footer section of the Header/Footer tab in the Page Setup dialog box on all worksheets in the workbook. Complete the **Documentation** worksheet according to your instructor's direction.

h. Save your work, and then close Excel. Submit the file as directed by your instructor.

Microsoft Office Access 2013

Module 1

Understanding and Using a Relational Database

WORKSHOP 1 | THE FOUR MAIN DATABASE OBJECTS

OBJECTIVES

1. Understand what Access is p. 588
2. Maneuver in the Navigation Pane p. 592
3. Understand what a table is p. 595
4. Manually navigate a database p. 601
5. Understand what a query is p. 604
6. Understand what a form is p. 611
7. Understand what a report is p. 613
8. Back up a database p. 617
9. Compact a database p. 618

Prepare Case

Red Bluff Golf Club Putts for Paws Charity Tournament

Production & Operations

The Red Bluff Golf Club is sponsoring a charity tournament, Putts for Paws, to raise money for the Santa Fe Animal Center. An intern created a database to help run the tournament but did not finish it before leaving. You have been asked to finish the database to track the participants who enter the tournament, the orders they have placed, and the items they have purchased.

Kati Molin / Shutterstock

REAL WORLD SUCCESS

"I used Access to create *ad hoc* reports for managers. My ability to quickly provide data has made me their 'go to' person."

- Art, alumnus, materials analyst

Student data files needed for this workshop:

 a01ws01Putts.accdb

 a01ws01Participant.accdb

You will save your file as:

 a01ws01Putts_LastFirst.accdb

Understanding Database Basics and Tables

Businesses keep records about everything they do. If a business sells products, it keeps records about its products. It keeps records of its customers, the products it sells to each customer, and each sale. It keeps records about its employees, the hours they work, and their benefits. These records are collected and used for decision making, for sales and marketing, and for reporting purposes. A **database** is a collection of these records. The purpose of a database is to store, manage, and provide access to these business records.

In the past, many databases were paper based. Paper records were stored in files in file cabinets. Each file would be labeled and put in a drawer in a file cabinet. Elaborate filing schemes were developed so that one record could be located quickly. This was highly labor intensive and error-prone. Today, while most businesses use automated databases to store their records, you still see the occasional paper-based system. For example, your doctor's office may still use paper files for patient records.

Data are facts about people, events, things, or ideas, and they are an important asset to any organization as data allows companies to make better business decisions after converting it into useful information. **Information** is data that has been manipulated and processed to make it meaningful. For example, if you saw the number 2,000 out of context, the number has no meaning. If you are told that 2,000 represents the amount of an order in dollars, that piece of data becomes meaningful information. Businesses can leverage meaningful information to gain a competitive advantage, such as by providing discounts to those who order more expensive items. An automated database management system, such as Microsoft Access 2013, makes that possible.

Databases are used for two major purposes: for operational processing and for analytical purposes. In operational or transaction-based databases, each sale or transaction that a business makes is tracked. The information is used to keep the business running. Analytical databases are used for extracting data for decision making. The data in these databases are summarized and classified to make information available to the decision makers in the firms.

Automated databases provide many advantages over paper databases. The information in the databases is much easier to find in automated form. The information can be manipulated and processed more rapidly. Automated databases can be used to enforce accuracy and other quality standards. In today's fast-paced world, a business needs to manipulate information quickly and accurately to make decisions. Without today's automated databases, a business cannot compete. In this section, you will learn what Access is and learn about the four main object types in an Access database.

Understand What Access Is

Access is a relational **database management system (DBMS)** program created by Microsoft. It provides a tool for you to organize, store, and manipulate data, as well as to select and report on data.

Access stores data in tables. Similar data are stored in the same table. For example, if you are storing data about participants in an event, you would include all the participants' names, addresses, and telephone numbers in one table.

The power of a database system comes with the ability to link tables together. A separate table of purchases for the tournament can be linked with the participant table. This allows users to easily combine the two tables; for example, the tournament manager would be able to print out the participants with a record of their tournament purchases.

REAL WORLD ADVICE What Advantage Does Using Access Give You?

There are many database management system (DBMS) software packages available. Why should you use Access?

- Access is an easily available DBMS. It is included with many Microsoft Office suites, which makes Access very attractive to businesses.
- Access is a relational DBMS. What you learn about Access is transferable to other relational DBMSs.
- Access allows for easy interaction with other products in the Office suite. You can export data and reports into Word, PowerPoint, or Excel. You can also import from Excel and Word into Access.
- Access is often used as a stand-alone DBMS, meaning a DBMS used by a single user. Even if a company uses another DBMS for many users, you can easily link to that database with Access. You can use Access queries to output the data you need to interact with other Office applications to perform tasks such as mail merges.
- Access allows you to create an app database and either give it to others or put it on the Windows App Store.

Understanding the Four Main Objects in a Database

Access has four main database **objects**: tables, queries, forms, and reports. A **table** is the database object that stores data organized in an arrangement of columns and rows. A **query** object retrieves specific data from other database objects and then displays only the data that you specify. Queries allow you to ask questions about the data in your tables. You can use a **form** object to enter new records into a table, edit or delete existing records in a table, or display existing records. The **report** object summarizes the fields and records from a table or query in an easy-to-read format suitable for printing.

QUICK REFERENCE Access Object Types

There are four main database object types:

1. Table objects store data. Each row is a person, place, or thing. Each column is a field.
2. Query objects allow you to ask questions about your data. You can select, summarize, and sort data in a query.
3. Form objects give you a formatted way to add, modify, or delete data in your tables. They can also be used to display data.
4. Report objects provide an easy-to-read view of your data that is suitable for business purposes. Data in reports can be grouped, sorted, and totaled.

Access objects have several views. Each **view** gives you a different perspective on the objects and different capabilities. For example, the **Datasheet view** of a table shows the data contents within a table. Figure 1 shows Datasheet view of a participant table. **Design view** shows how fields are defined. Depending on the object, other views may exist. Figure 1 shows a toggle button you can use to switch between Datasheet view and Design view. Figure 2 shows how a participant table would appear in Design view.

In Datasheet view, you see the actual participants and their related information. In Design view, you see how the information is defined and structured. Figure 1 shows the charity event participant table. Each row contains corresponding pieces of data about the participant listed in that row. Each row in Access is called a **record**. A record is all of the data pertaining to one person, place, thing, or event. There are 17 participant records in the table. The second participant is John Trujillo.

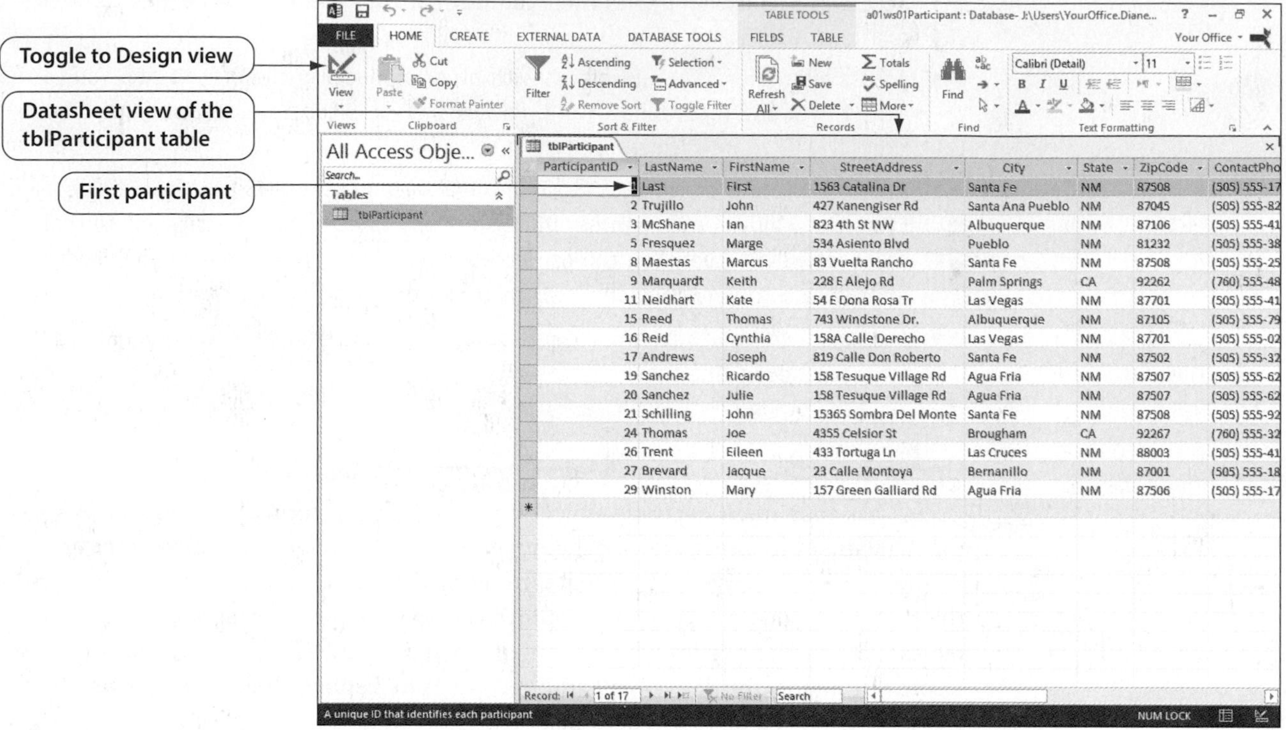

Figure 1 Datasheet view of the tblParticipant table

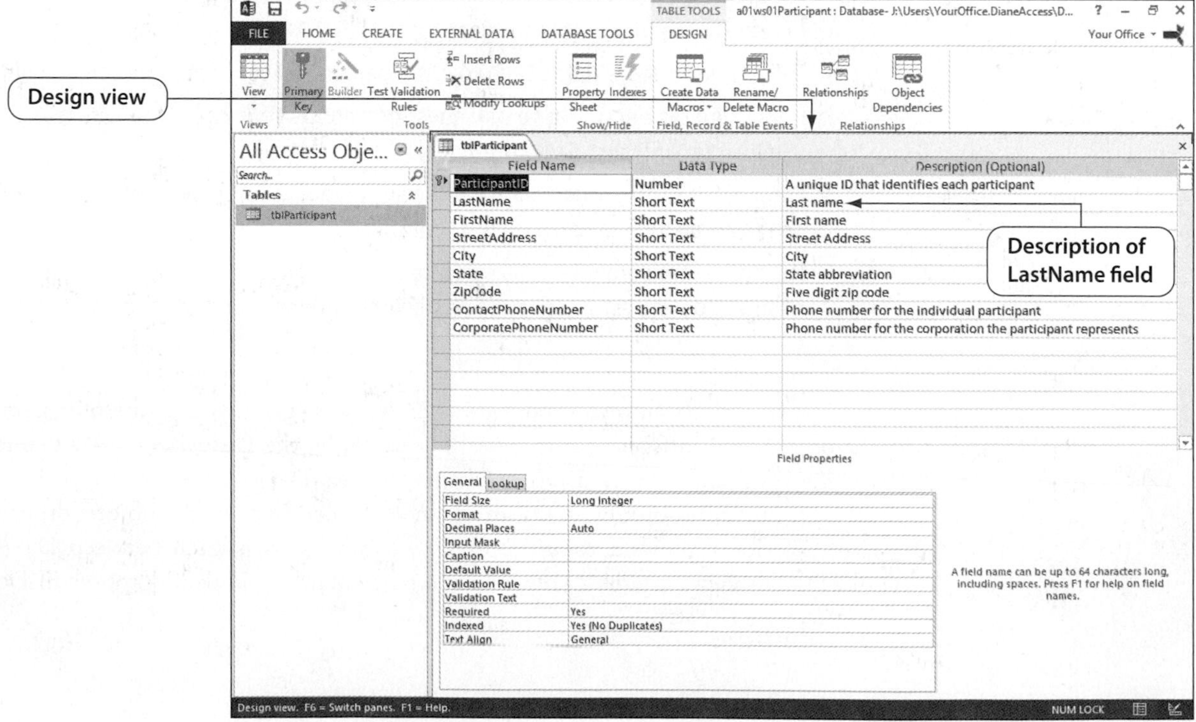

Figure 2 Design view of the tblParticipant table

Each column in Access is called a **field**. A field is a specific piece of information that is stored in every record. LastName is a field that shows the participant's last name. As you go across the table rows, you will see fields that represent the participant's first name and address.

Creating a New Database and Templates

When you create a new database, you can design it yourself starting with an empty database. If you take this approach, you develop the tables, fields, and the relationships—or links—between the tables. This requires you to decide what information you want to keep in your database, how this information should be grouped into tables, what relationships you need, and what queries and reports you need.

The other option in creating a new database is to start with a prebuilt template. A **template** is a structure of a database with tables, fields, forms, queries, and reports. Templates are professionally designed databases that you can either use as is or adapt to suit your needs. You can download a wide variety of templates from Microsoft's website Office.com. Microsoft provides sample database templates used for managing assets, contacts, issues, projects, and tasks.

Templates are created by Microsoft employees or other users. Microsoft then allows users to rate the template so you can see what others have found useful. You can also download sample databases to experiment with. The difference between a template and a sample database is that a sample database has presupplied data, whereas a template is empty except for the structure and definitions. One of the popular sample databases among Access users is Microsoft's Northwind database, which has sales, customer, and employee data for a fictitious company named Northwind Traders.

For the tournament, the intern created a new database and defined tables specifically for Putts for Paws. You will work with the database that has already been created. You need to start Access and open the database to get started.

SIDE NOTE

Do Not Confuse a DBMS with a Database

Access is DBMS software while a database is a collection of data. You could use paper files to manage your database, but you choose to use Access DBMS software instead.

A01.00

To Start Access and Open a Database

a. From the Windows Start screen or desktop, point to the **bottom-right corner** of the screen. The Charms will be displayed on the right side of the screen.

b. Note the labels underneath each of the charms. Click the **Search** charm.

c. Click inside the **search** box at the top of the page. Type Access.

d. Click **Microsoft Access 2013** in the search results.

e. Click **Open Other Files** on the Access Start Screen, and then click **Computer**. Navigate to your student data files, click **a01ws01Putts**, and then click the **Open** button.

f. Click the **FILE** tab, and then click **Save As**. Under **File Types**, make sure **Save Database As** is selected. Under **Save Database As**, make sure **Access Database** is selected. Click **Save As**, and then navigate to the location where you are saving your files. In the **File name** box, type a01ws01Putts_LastFirst, using your last and first name. Click **Save**.

g. If the Security Warning message appears, click the **Enable Content** button.

REAL WORLD ADVICE	Why Does Access Give You a Security Warning About Your Database?

Access databases can contain dangerous code that can infect your computer with a virus. Therefore, Access displays a security warning asking you whether you trust the content of the database. Until you tell Access that you trust this content, Access disables features that might allow the virus to infect your computer.

- Make sure you run a virus scan on any file before you say it should be trusted. You do not want to trust content that you are unsure about.
- You can trust the content for a single use. Click Enable Content to say that you trust the file.
- To trust a database permanently, you can store it in a trusted location. Depending on your computer and operating system, certain locations are predefined as trusted. Click the File tab, click Options, and then select Trust Center for the Access Trust Center, where you can add other locations to the trusted locations.

Maneuver in the Navigation Pane

When you open a database, Access displays the **Navigation Pane** on the left side as shown in Figure 3. This pane allows you to view the objects in the database. The standard view in the Navigation Pane shows all objects in the database organized by object type. You can see that the database has three tables: tblItem, tblOrder, and tblOrderLine. There is one query, one form, and one report.

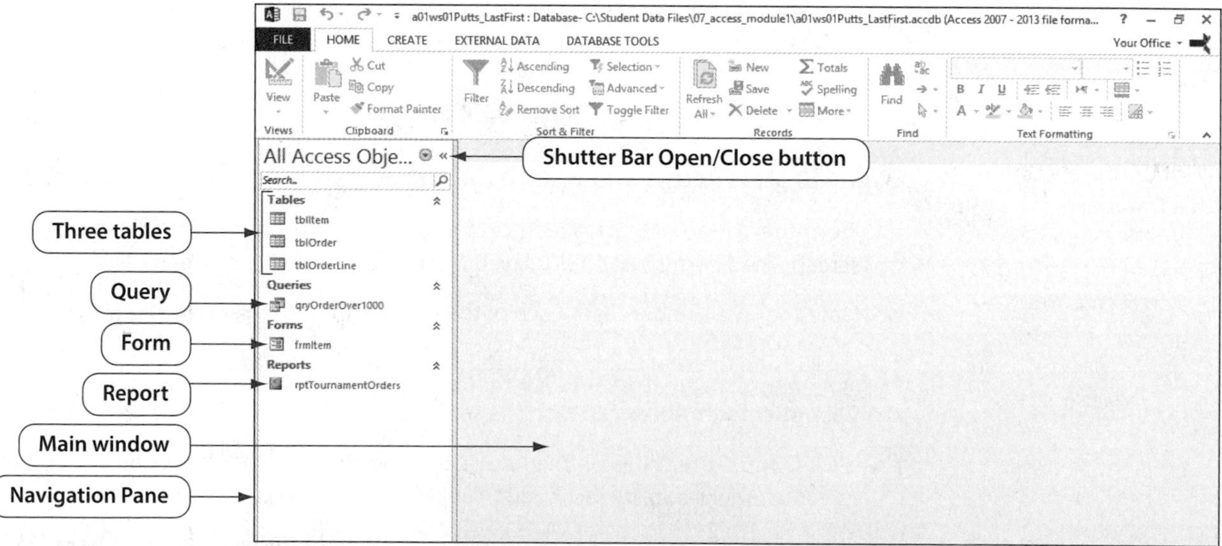

Figure 3 Opening screen for a01ws01Putts_LastFirst

Opening and Closing the Shutter Bar

You can work in Access with the Navigation Pane open or closed. The Shutter Bar Open/Close button at the top of the pane opens and closes the pane.

MyITLab®
Workshop 1 Training

A01.01

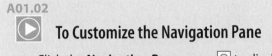

To Open and Close the Navigation Pane

a. Click the **Shutter Bar Close** button « to close the Navigation Pane. Access closes the pane, allowing for a larger workspace in the database, but it leaves the Navigation Pane on the side of the window for when you need it.

b. Click the **Shutter Bar Open** button » to open the pane again.

MODULE 1

Customizing the Navigation Pane

While the default view of the Navigation Pane shows all objects such as tables, queries, forms, and reports, organized by object type, you have several choices of views.

A01.02

To Customize the Navigation Pane

a. Click the **Navigation Pane** arrow to display the Navigation Pane view options. The default view is displayed, which is Object Type and All Access Objects.

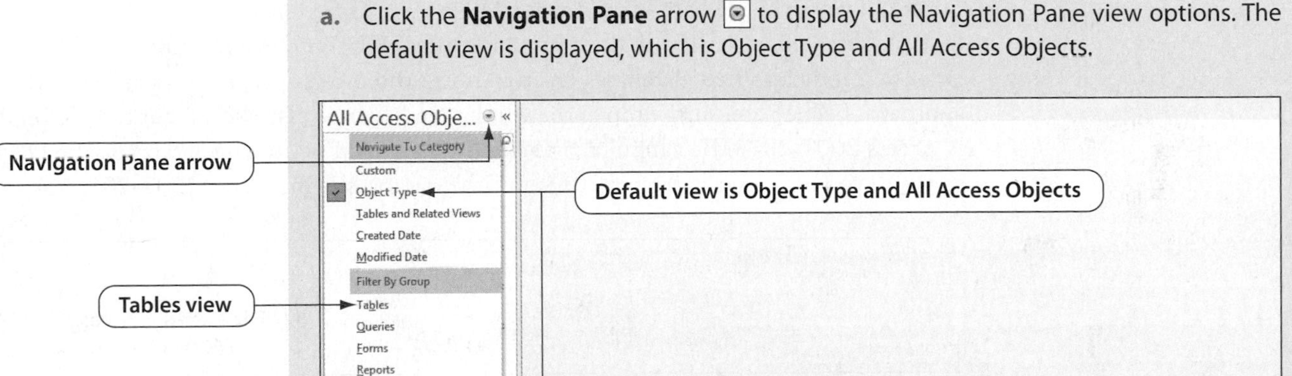

Figure 4 Navigation Pane options—default view

b. Click **Tables**.

Only the three tables are displayed in the Navigation Pane. When you have many objects in a database, it helps to restrict objects that are shown in the Navigation Pane.

c. Click the **Navigation Pane** arrow again, and then click **Tables and Related Views**.

The objects are organized by tables. Any query, report, or form related to a table is listed with that table.

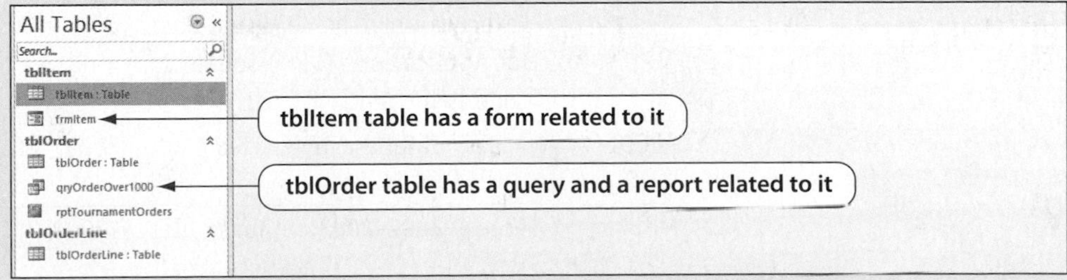

Figure 5 Tables and related views in Navigation Pane

Using the Search Box

Currently, there are only a few objects in your database. However, as you work with a database, more objects may be added as you develop reports and queries. As a result, to help you find objects, Access provides a Search box.

A01.03

To Search for an Object

a. In the **Search** box at the top of the **Navigation Pane**, type Order. Access searches for and displays all objects with the word **Order** in their name.

b. Click the **Clear Search String** button to see all objects again.

c. Click the **Navigation Pane** arrow, click **Object Type**, click the **Navigation Pane** arrow again, and then select **All Access Objects**. This returns you to the default view, which is what will be used throughout this text.

Understanding File Extensions in Access

A **file extension** is the suffix on all file names that helps Windows understand what information is in a file and what program should open the file. However, Windows automatically hides these extensions so you often do not notice them. The file name in Figure 6 shows the file name and location followed by its extension ".accdb". Access 2013 uses the same file extension that was used in Access 2010 and Access 2007. This ".accdb" extension indicates that databases created in the three versions are compatible with one another. The file name at the top of the window in Figure 6 also shows that the file version is Access 2007-2013. Be careful not to confuse the DBMS with the database. The DBMS software you are using is Access 2013, but the database is in Access 2007-2013 format.

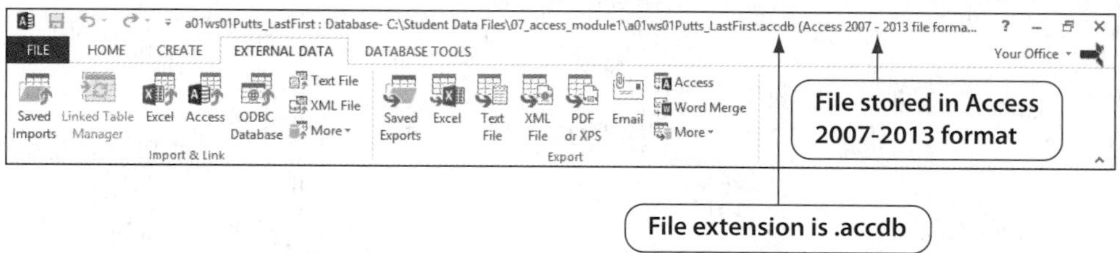

Figure 6 Title bar showing file extension

QUICK REFERENCE | **Access File Extensions**

Extension	Description	Version of Access	Compatibility
ACCDB	Access database files	2007-2013	Cannot be opened in Access 2002-2003
ACCDE	Access database files that are in "execute only" mode Visual Basic for Applications (VBA) source code is hidden.	2007-2013	Cannot be opened in Access 2002-2003
ACCDT	Access database templates	2007-2013	Cannot be opened in Access 2002-2003
MDB	Access 2002-2003 database files	2002-2003	Can be opened in Access 2007-2013 Access 2007-2013 can save files in this format.
MDE	Access database files that are in "execute only" mode Visual Basic for Applications (VBA) source code is hidden.	2002-2003	Can be opened in Access 2007-2013 Access 2007-2013 can save files in this format.

Understand What a Table Is

Tables store data organized in an arrangement of columns and rows. For illustration, think about the charity event, Putts for Paws. There are many ways participants and companies can participate in the event and help the charity. For example, a participant can play in the event, a company can pay for a foursome to play in the event, or the company can sponsor various items such as a cart, hole, or flag. As a result, Painted Paradise needs to keep a record of the available options and what corporations or participants have purchased, as shown in Table 1.

Item ID	Item Description	Quantity Available	Amount To Be Charged	Notes
G1	Golfer—one	100	$200.00	
TEAM	Golfers—team of four	10	$550.00	
CTEAM	Golfers—corporate team of four	10	$850.00	Includes hole sponsorship
CART	Cart sponsor	40	$2,000.00	Logo or brand displayed on cart
HOLE	Hole sponsor	18	$500.00	Logo or brand displayed on hole
FLAG	Flag sponsor	18	$500.00	Logo or brand displayed on flagstick

Table 1 Data in the tblItem table

As mentioned previously, the power of a **relational database** comes when you link tables. A relational database is a database where data is stored in tables with relationships between the tables. The tblItem table shown in Table 1 contains information about items that a participant or corporation can buy to support the charity, including the items available, a description, the quantity available to be sold, the amount that will be charged for the item, and notes about the item. However, you cannot see who has ordered these items. That additional information becomes available when you use relationships to look at other tables.

Importing a Table

Recently, a colleague compiled a list of participants in the charity event in an Access table in another database. You will begin your work for Putts for Paws by importing this participant table from the Participant database into your database. **Importing** is the process of copying data from another file, such as a Word file or Excel workbook, into a separate file, such as an Access database.

A01.04

To Import an Access Object

a. Click the **EXTERNAL DATA** tab, and then in the Import & Link group, click **Access**. The Get External Data - Access Database dialog box is displayed.

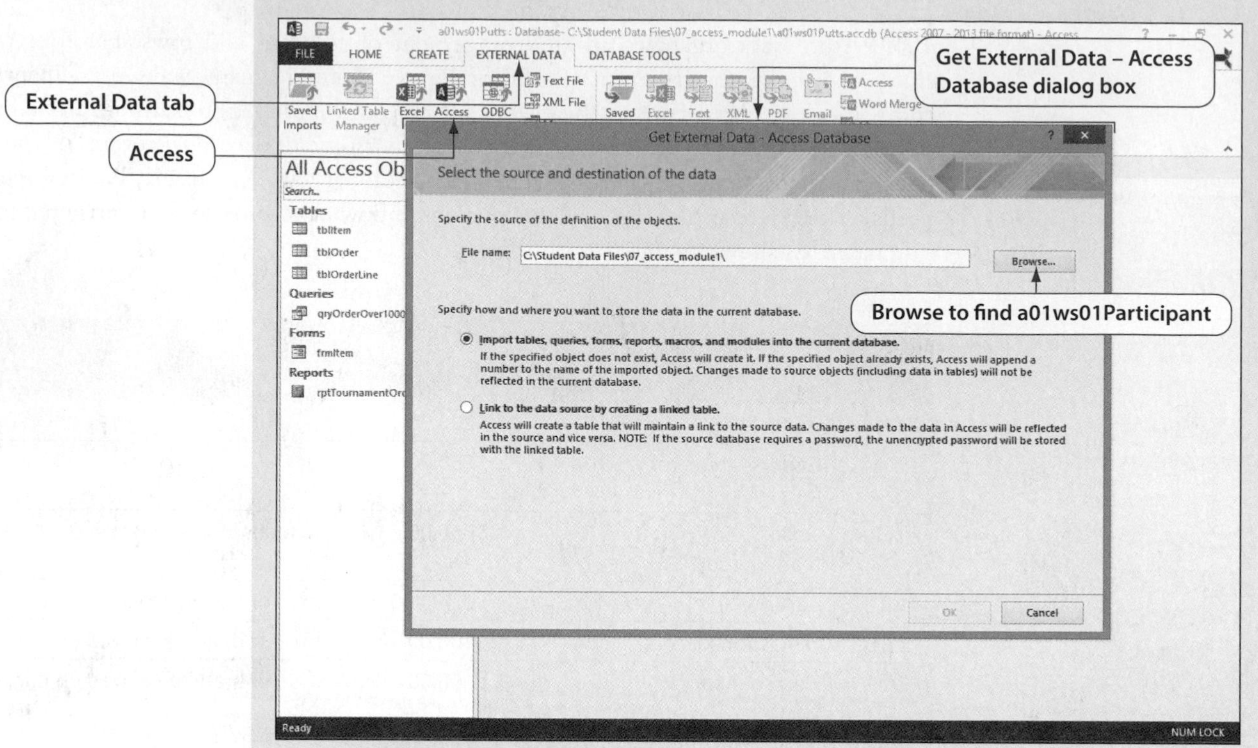

Figure 7 Get External Data – Access Database dialog box

b. Click **Browse**, navigate to your student data folder, and then select the **a01ws01Participant** database. Click **Open**, and then click **OK**. Access opens the Import Objects dialog box.

> **Troubleshooting**
> If you do not see the Import Objects dialog box, you may have chosen Access from the Export group on the Ribbon rather than from the Import & Link group.

c. If necessary, click the **Tables** tab. Click **tblParticipant**, and then click **OK**. Access displays the message: All objects were imported successfully.

d. Click **Close** at the bottom of the dialog box.

e. Double-click **tblParticipant** in the Navigation Pane.

Access opens the table. You may not see exactly the same number of columns and rows in your table because how much of the table is visible is dependent on how large your Access window is. You can change the size of the Access window by using your mouse to resize it or by clicking the Maximize button [□] to maximize the Access window.

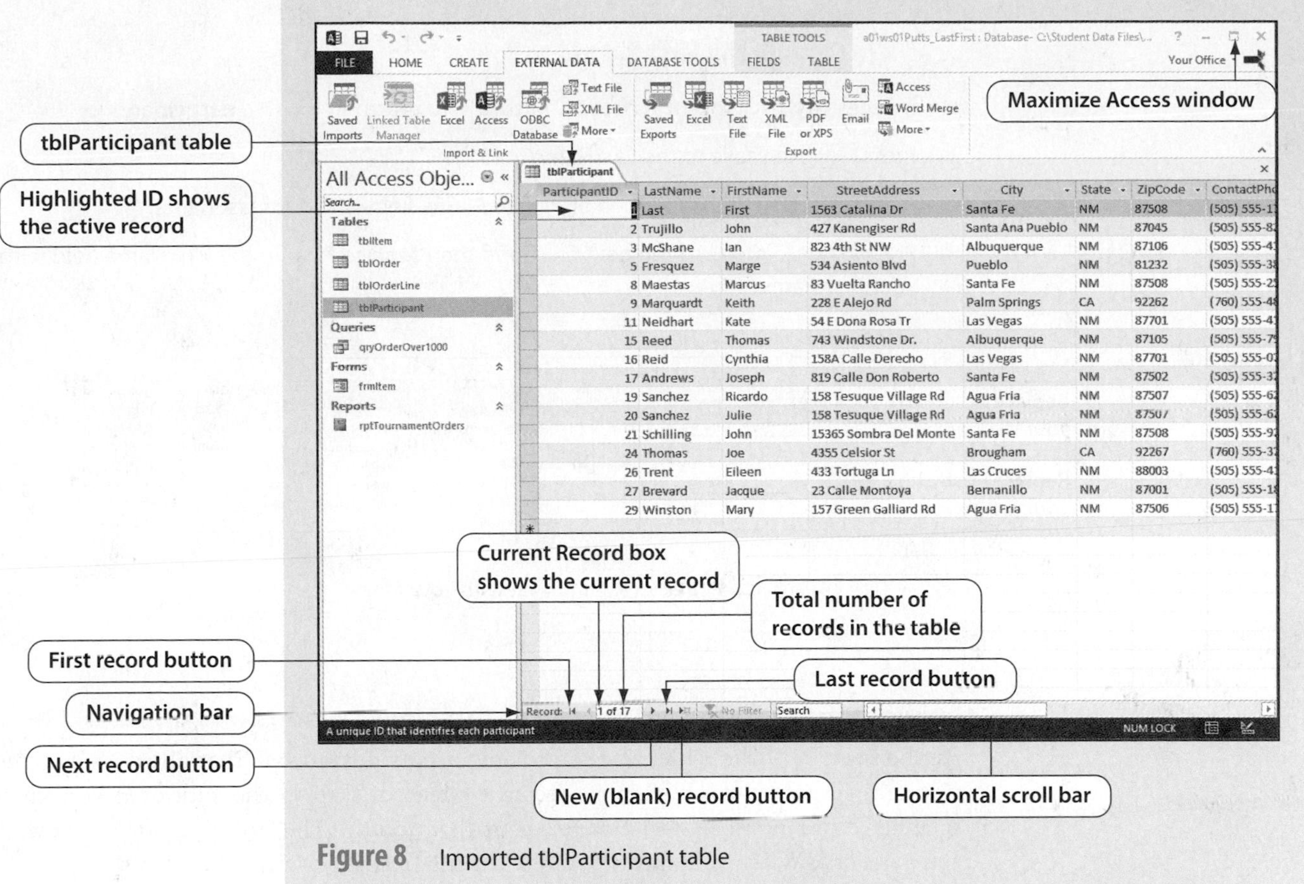

Figure 8 Imported tblParticipant table

REAL WORLD ADVICE What Should You Name Your Tables?

If other people use the database and cannot find the right table, how useful is your database? Thus, you want to use names that are easy to understand. While Access allows you to give any name you want to a table, the name "tblParticipant" follows a standard naming convention:

- Use a name that starts with "tbl". That allows you to distinguish tables from queries at a glance.
- Follow with a name that is descriptive. You want it to be easy to remember what is in the table.
- Make the name short enough that it is easy to see in the Navigation Pane.
- You can use spaces in table names (e.g., tbl Participant), but avid Access users avoid them because it makes advanced tasks more difficult.
- You can use special characters in names. Some people use underscores where a space would otherwise be, such as tbl_Participant.

Navigating Through a Table

Carefully examine the tblParticipant table. Each row of data contains information about the participant listed in the LastName field. There are 17 participant records in the table, with the second record being John Trujillo. You will change the name in the record for the first participant to your name.

A01.05

To Change the First Record to Your Name

a. If necessary, click the **First record** button to return to the first participant.

b. Press Tab to move to the LastName field.

c. Replace **Last** in the first record of the LastName field with your last name.

d. Press Tab to move to the next field, and then replace **First** in the FirstName field with your first name.

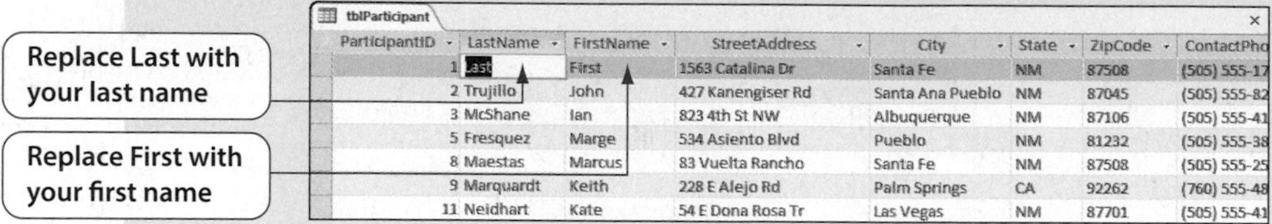

ParticipantID	LastName	FirstName	StreetAddress	City	State	ZipCode	ContactPho
1	Last	First	1563 Catalina Dr	Santa Fe	NM	87508	(505) 555-17
2	Trujillo	John	427 Kanengiser Rd	Santa Ana Pueblo	NM	87045	(505) 555-82
3	McShane	Ian	823 4th St NW	Albuquerque	NM	87106	(505) 555-41
5	Fresquez	Marge	534 Asiento Blvd	Pueblo	NM	81232	(505) 555-38
8	Maestas	Marcus	83 Vuelta Rancho	Santa Fe	NM	87508	(505) 555-25
9	Marquardt	Keith	228 E Alejo Rd	Palm Springs	CA	92262	(760) 555-48
11	Neidhart	Kate	54 E Dona Rosa Tr	Las Vegas	NM	87701	(505) 555-41

Figure 9 Replace Last and First with your name

Navigating Through a Table with the Navigation Bar

At the bottom of the table, Access provides a **Navigation bar** that allows you to move through the table. You can move record by record, skip to the end, or if you know a specific record number, you can jump to that record. The highlighted ID shows the active record. When you open the table, the first record is active.

Examine the various parts of the Navigation bar as shown in Figure 8. The Current Record box shows which record is active and how many records are in the table. There are four arrow buttons in the Navigation bar that you can use to move between records.

A01.06

To Navigate Through the Table Using the Navigation Bar

a. Click the **Next record** button to move to the second record. The **Current Record** box changes to show **2 of 17**. Access highlights the first name of participant John Trujillo.

b. Click the **Next record** button again to move to the third participant. The **Current Record** box changes to show **3 of 17**.

c. Click the **First record** button to return to the first participant.

d. Click the **New (blank) record button** to go to the first blank row. Alternatively, you could click in the ParticipantID field of the first blank row.

The first blank row at the end of the table is the **append row**. This row allows you to enter new records to the table. Notice that Access displays an asterisk in the **record selector** box—it is the small box at the left of the record—to indicate that it is the append row. When you type information here, you create a new participant record. Whenever you add a participant, you want to make sure you are in the append row so you are not changing the information for an existing participant. You will add a participant to this empty row.

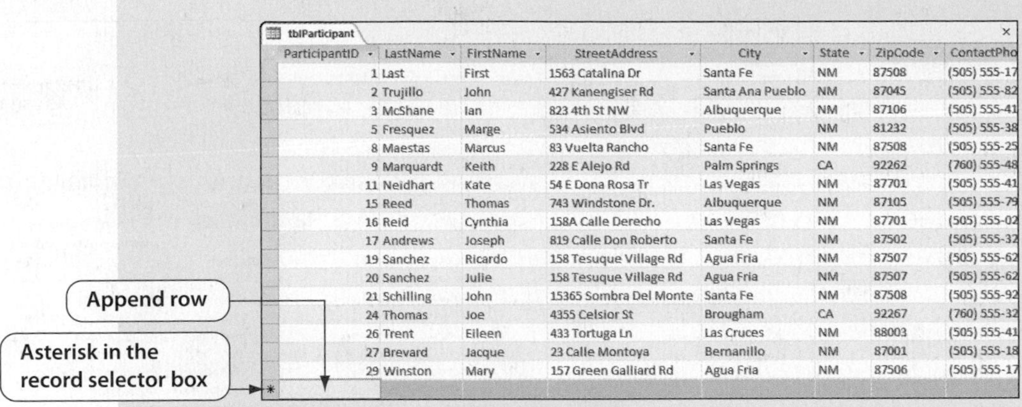

Figure 10 Append a new record

e. Make sure that the append row (blank row) is selected and that the record selector box contains an asterisk. In the ParticipantID field, type 30. Press Tab to move to the next field, and then in the **LastName** column, type Fox.

Alternatively, you can press Enter after typing text in a field to move to the next field. Also, notice that when you start typing, the record indicator changed from an asterisk to a pencil. The pencil means that you are in edit mode. The record after Fox now becomes the new append row. Press Enter, and then in the FirstName column, type Jeff.

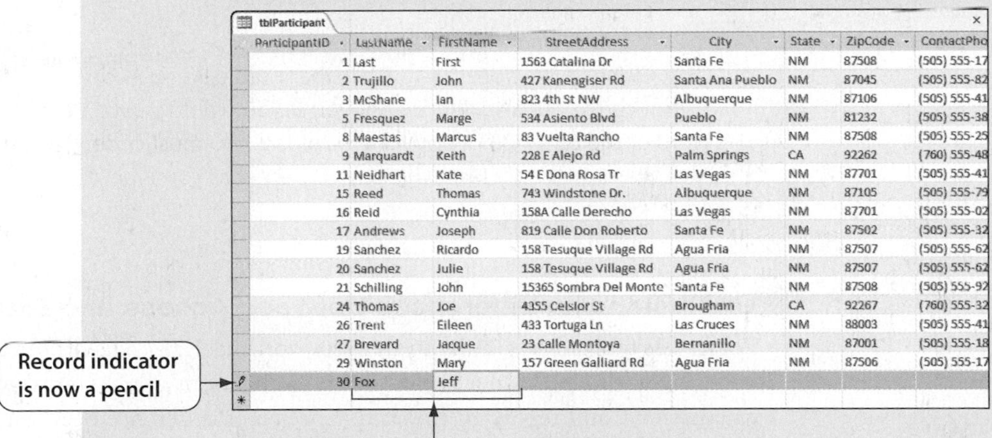

Figure 11 Enter participant Jeff Fox into the append row

f. Continue entering the data for Jeff Fox using the following information:

StreetAddress	1509 Las Cruces Drive
City	Las Cruces
State	NM
ZipCode	88003
ContactPhoneNumber	(505) 555-8786
CorporatePhoneNumber	(leave blank)

MODULE 1

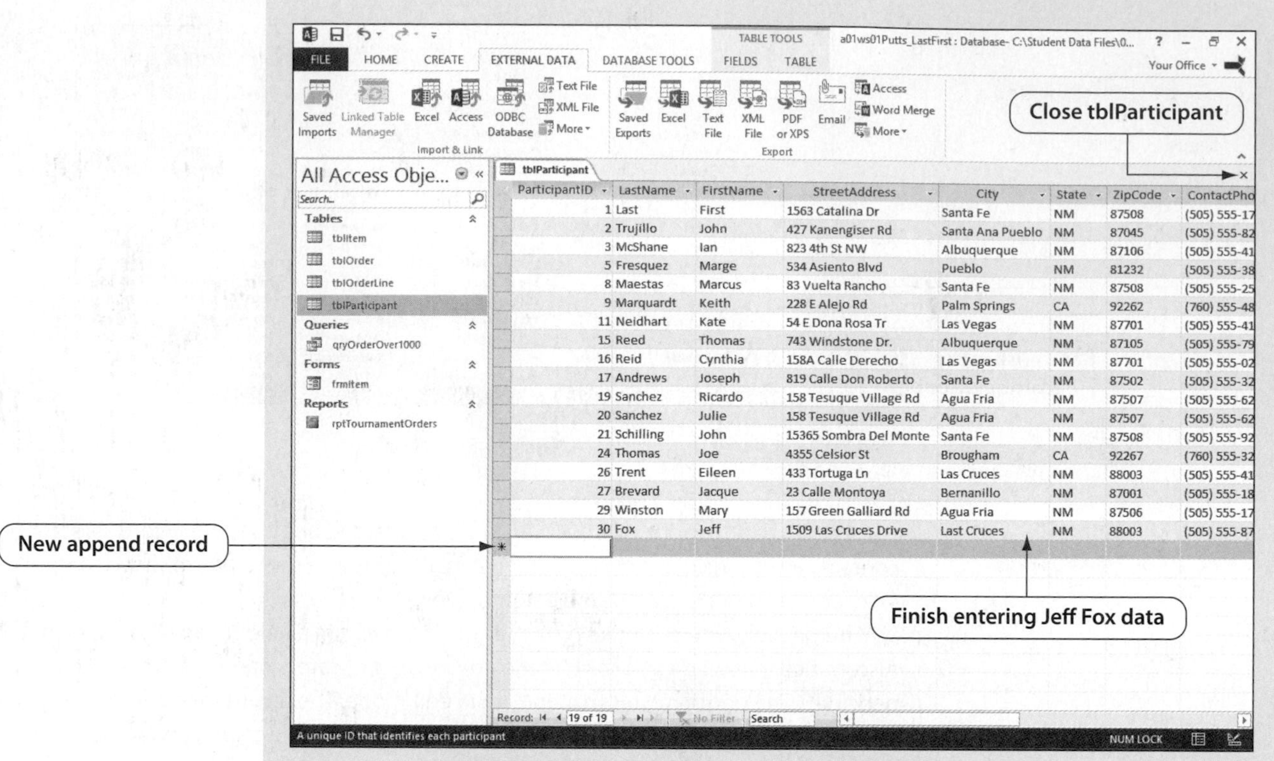

Figure 12 Finish entering the record for Jeff Fox

g. Click **Close** [X] to close the tblParticipant table. Keep Access and the database open.

Notice that Access did not ask you if you want to save the table. Access is not like Word or the other Office applications where you must choose an option to save the file. Access automatically saves the data you enter as you type it.

Understanding Differences Between Access and Excel

An Access table looks similar to an Excel worksheet. Both have numbered rows of data and columns with labels. In addition, both applications allow you to manage data, perform calculations, and report on the data. The major difference between the two applications is that Access allows multiple tables with relationships between the tables, thus the term "relational database". For example, if you are keeping track of participants and the items that they order, you create a table of participants and another table of orders. Excel 2013 has some of these features so it now blurs the distinction between spreadsheets and relational databases.

When you look at Access, you notice that several tables are used for an order. Why use multiple tables for a single order? Figure 13 shows how an order would look in Access and in Excel. The Excel version has to repeat the participant's information on multiple lines. This leads to problems:

- Data redundancy—With repetition, you create redundant information. John Trujillo bought a cart and a team, so in Excel you have two rows. You would have to repeat the address information on both records. It is not efficient to enter the address information twice.
- Errors—Redundant information leads to errors. If the address needs to be changed, you have to look for all records with that information to make sure it is fixed everywhere.
- Loss of data—Suppose that John Trujillo orders just one item. If you deleted the ordered item, it would mean deleting all the information about him as well as the order.

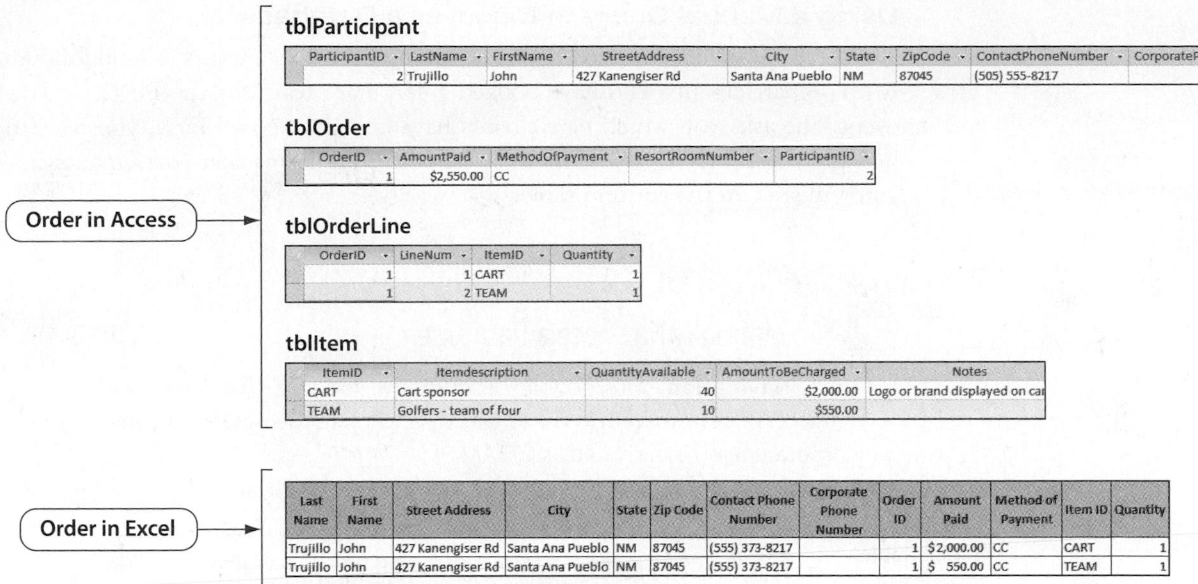

tblParticipant

ParticipantID	LastName	FirstName	StreetAddress	City	State	ZipCode	ContactPhoneNumber	CorporatePho
2	Trujillo	John	427 Kanengiser Rd	Santa Ana Pueblo	NM	87045	(505) 555-8217	

tblOrder

OrderID	AmountPaid	MethodOfPayment	ResortRoomNumber	ParticipantID
1	$2,550.00	CC		2

tblOrderLine

OrderID	LineNum	ItemID	Quantity
1	1	CART	1
1	2	TEAM	1

tblItem

ItemID	Itemdescription	QuantityAvailable	AmountToBeCharged	Notes
CART	Cart sponsor	40	$2,000.00	Logo or brand displayed on ca
TEAM	Golfers - team of four	10	$550.00	

Last Name	First Name	Street Address	City	State	Zip Code	Contact Phone Number	Corporate Phone Number	Order ID	Amount Paid	Method of Payment	Item ID	Quantity
Trujillo	John	427 Kanengiser Rd	Santa Ana Pueblo	NM	87045	(555) 373-8217		1	$2,000.00	CC	CART	1
Trujillo	John	427 Kanengiser Rd	Santa Ana Pueblo	NM	87045	(555) 373-8217		1	$ 550.00	CC	TEAM	1

Figure 13 John Trujillo's order in Access and in Excel

Because Access and Excel have so many common functionalities, many people use the tool that they are more confident using. If you prefer to use both, however, you can easily switch by exporting your data from Access to Excel or from Excel into Access. You can also use one tool for most uses and import your data into the other when you need to.

REAL WORLD ADVICE **When Do You Use Access Instead of Excel?**

Generally, Access is designed to store data, and Excel is designed to analyze data and model situations. Fortunately, you can easily store data in Access and export a query to Excel for analysis.

Use Access for the following:

- You need to store data in multiple tables.
- You have a very large amount of data, as in thousands of records.
- You have large amounts of nonnumeric data.
- You want to run many different queries and reports from your data.
- You have multiple users accessing your data.

Use Excel for the following:

- Your data fits well into one table.
- You want to primarily do calculations, summaries, or comparisons of your data.
- You are using a report that you create just one time or in just one format.

Manually Navigate a Database

Before you explore the database using Access queries, you will explore the database manually. This will give you an understanding of what Access can do. Additionally, before you write queries and reports, you should examine your tables and fields so that you understand the database.

Using a Manual Query to Discover a Database

Patti Rochelle, the events coordinator at Painted Paradise, wants to send follow-up letters to those participants who have booked a corporate team for the Putts for Paws charity event. She asks you which participants have booked a team. First, you have to discover how a team is indicated in the database. Teams are items that participants can order, so you will start in the tblItem table.

A01.07

To Manually Navigate a Database

a. In the **Navigation Pane**, double-click **tblItem**.

Access opens tblItem in Datasheet view. Explore the data, and you will notice that a corporate team is indicated as CTEAM.

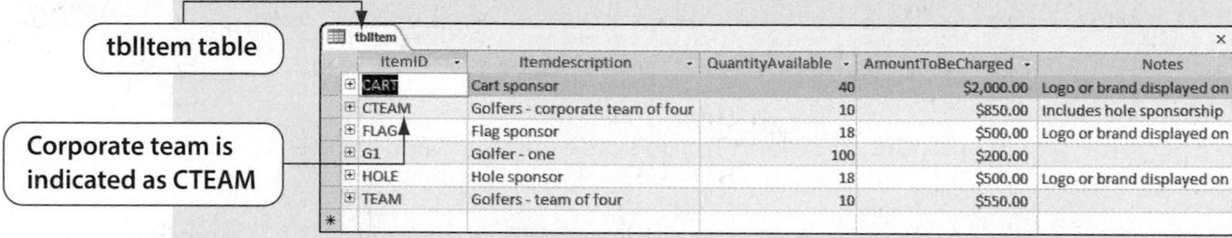

ItemID	Itemdescription	QuantityAvailable	AmountToBeCharged	Notes
CART	Cart sponsor	40	$2,000.00	Logo or brand displayed on
CTEAM	Golfers - corporate team of four	10	$850.00	Includes hole sponsorship
FLAG	Flag sponsor	18	$500.00	Logo or brand displayed on
G1	Golfer - one	100	$200.00	
HOLE	Hole sponsor	18	$500.00	Logo or brand displayed on
TEAM	Golfers - team of four	10	$550.00	

Figure 14 tblItem table

b. **Close** ☒ the tblItem table.

Next you need to determine which orders include CTEAM. Orders are composed of data from tblOrderLine and tblOrder.

c. Double-click **tblOrderLine** to open the table.

Scan for orders that include CTEAM. There are two, OrderID 4 and OrderID 11.

d. **Close** ☒ the tblOrderLine table.

e. Double-click **tblOrder** to open the table, and then find OrderID **4** and **11**.

You need to find which participants placed these orders. Access uses common fields to relate tables. tblParticipant and tblOrder have ParticipantID in common. You find that the ParticipantID for OrderID 4 is 5, and for OrderID 11 the ParticipantID is 19.

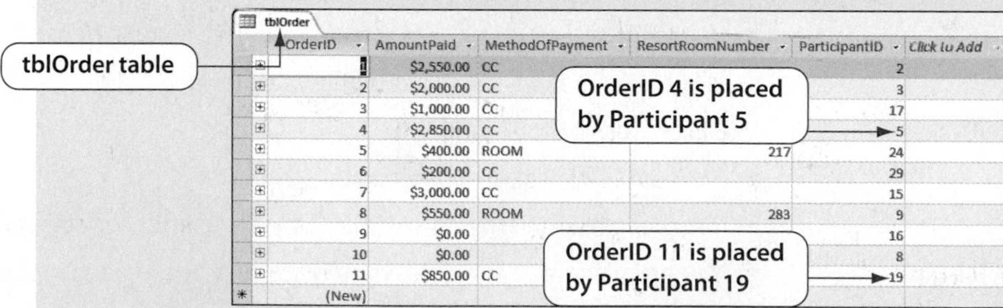

OrderID	AmountPaid	MethodOfPayment	ResortRoomNumber	ParticipantID	Click to Add
1	$2,550.00	CC		2	
2	$2,000.00	CC		3	
3	$1,000.00	CC		17	
4	$2,850.00	CC		5	
5	$400.00	ROOM	217	24	
6	$200.00	CC		29	
7	$3,000.00	CC		15	
8	$550.00	ROOM	283	9	
9	$0.00			16	
10	$0.00			8	
11	$850.00	CC		19	
(New)					

Figure 15 tblOrder table

f. **Close** ☒ the tblOrder table.

g. Double-click **tblParticipant** to open the table.

Scan for the participants that match the two ParticipantIDs you identified earlier, 5 and 19. You find that OrderID 4 was placed by ParticipantID 5, Marge Fresquez. In addition, OrderID 11 was placed by ParticipantID 19, Ricardo Sanchez.

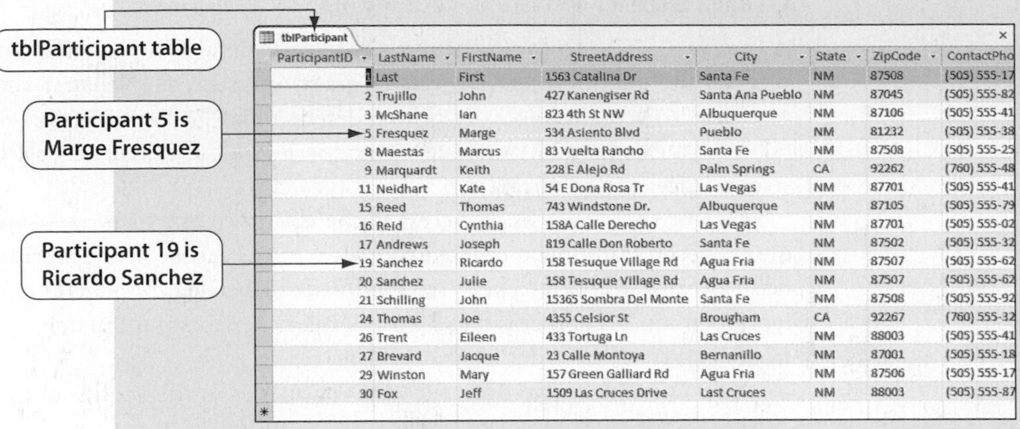

ParticipantID	LastName	FirstName	StreetAddress	City	State	ZipCode	ContactPho
1	Last	First	1563 Catalina Dr	Santa Fe	NM	87508	(505) 555-17
2	Trujillo	John	427 Kanengiser Rd	Santa Ana Pueblo	NM	87045	(505) 555-82
3	McShane	Ian	823 4th St NW	Albuquerque	NM	87106	(505) 555-41
5	Fresquez	Marge	534 Asiento Blvd	Pueblo	NM	81232	(505) 555-38
8	Maestas	Marcus	83 Vuelta Rancho	Santa Fe	NM	87508	(505) 555-25
9	Marquardt	Keith	228 E Alejo Rd	Palm Springs	CA	92262	(760) 555-48
11	Neidhart	Kate	54 E Dona Rosa Tr	Las Vegas	NM	87701	(505) 555-41
15	Reed	Thomas	743 Windstone Dr.	Albuquerque	NM	87105	(505) 555-79
16	Reid	Cynthia	158A Calle Derecho	Las Vegas	NM	87701	(505) 555-02
17	Andrews	Joseph	819 Calle Don Roberto	Santa Fe	NM	87502	(505) 555-32
19	Sanchez	Ricardo	158 Tesuque Village Rd	Agua Fria	NM	87507	(505) 555-62
20	Sanchez	Julie	158 Tesuque Village Rd	Agua Fria	NM	87507	(505) 555-62
21	Schilling	John	15365 Sombra Del Monte	Santa Fe	NM	87508	(505) 555-92
24	Thomas	Joe	4355 Celsior St	Brougham	CA	92267	(760) 555-32
26	Trent	Eileen	433 Tortuga Ln	Las Cruces	NM	88003	(505) 555-41
27	Brevard	Jacque	23 Calle Montoya	Bernanillo	NM	87001	(505) 555-18
29	Winston	Mary	157 Green Galliard Rd	Agua Fria	NM	87506	(505) 555-17
30	Fox	Jeff	1509 Las Cruces Drive	Last Cruces	NM	88003	(505) 555-87

Figure 16 tblParticipant table

h. **Close** [X] the tblParticipant table.

You now can tell Ms. Rochelle which participants have booked corporate teams and the address that the follow-up should be sent to. However, it may seem like a lot of work to find out who booked the corporate teams. Access queries make this task easier. It is important to know what data is in your database. While Access will do the hard part of matching tables on common fields and finding the results, you still need to tell it what fields you want and where the fields are located.

REAL WORLD ADVICE — Closing Tables

While Access allows you to leave several tables open at the same time, it is a good idea to get into the habit of closing a table when you are done with it.

- First, there are many Access functions that use a table that cannot be completed while the table is open. If you close the table, you no longer risk running into this problem.
- Second, closing tables makes it less likely that you will accidently change the wrong table.
- Third, each open table requires more memory for Access. With larger tables, Access could be slowed down by having multiple tables open.

Understanding Queries, Forms, and Reports

You have explored tables, the first of the four main object types in Access. As mentioned previously, the other three object types are queries, forms, and reports. Each object provides a different way to work with data stored in tables. A query is used to ask questions about your data. A form is primarily used to enter data into your database or display data in your database. Reports are used to provide professional looking displays of your tables that are suitable for printing. In this section, you will work with queries, forms, and reports within your database.

Understand What a Query Is

A query is a way to ask questions about your data. For your charity golf tournament, you can use queries to get answers to questions, such as "What is Ian McShane's phone number?", "What has John Trujillo ordered?", and "What orders are over $1,000?"

You can also conduct more complex queries such as calculating a score given a player's strokes and their handicap.

One of the strengths of Access is the ability to ask such questions and get answers quickly. You traced who ordered corporate teams earlier in the workshop. That was difficult because you had to keep track of fields such as ParticipantID in one table and then look them up in another table. By using queries, Access will match common fields in the tables and trace the order for you.

You will look at two different views of queries in this workshop:

- Datasheet view shows the results of your query.
- Design view shows how the query is constructed. It shows the tables, fields, and selection criterion for the query.

Creating a Query Using a Wizard

Access provides wizards to help you with tasks. A **wizard** is a step-by-step guide that walks you through tasks by asking you questions to help you decide what you want to do. Once you have some experience, you can also do the task yourself without a guide. You would like to know which participants are from Santa Fe, New Mexico. You will use the Query Wizard to create the query getting all participants, and then you will modify the query design to select those from Santa Fe.

REAL WORLD ADVICE | **Using Wizards in Access**

Wizards can sometimes save you time! Access wizards are shortcuts to building objects such as queries, reports, and forms. They select fields, format the data, and perform calculations. After the wizard does the initial formatting, you can always modify the resulting query, report, or form to get exactly what you want.

However, anything that can be done with a wizard could also be done without a wizard. A wizard may limit your choices. On the other hand, starting in design view requires you to make choices without guidance. Whether you start with a wizard or with design view is usually personal choice. As you become more comfortable with Access, pick the method that you prefer. The results will be the same.

A01.08

To Create a Query with a Wizard

a. Click the **CREATE** tab, and then in the Queries group, click **Query Wizard**.

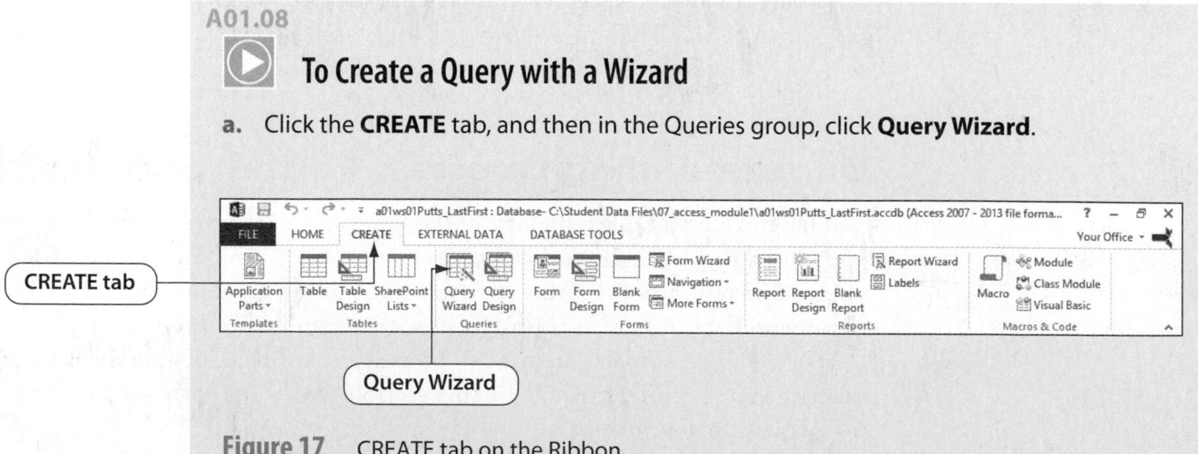

Figure 17 CREATE tab on the Ribbon

Access displays the New Query dialog box and asks you what kind of query you want.

Troubleshooting
If this is the first time that you have used an Access wizard, Access will need to set up the wizards. You will get a message "Setting up wizard" and will need to wait while the wizards are installed.

b. If necessary, click **Simple Query Wizard**, and then click **OK**.
   Access asks you which fields you want to include in the query. You have choices of tables or queries as the source for your fields. Your database has four tables to select as a source. You will choose only one table. You could choose fields from multiple tables, but that is not necessary in this query.

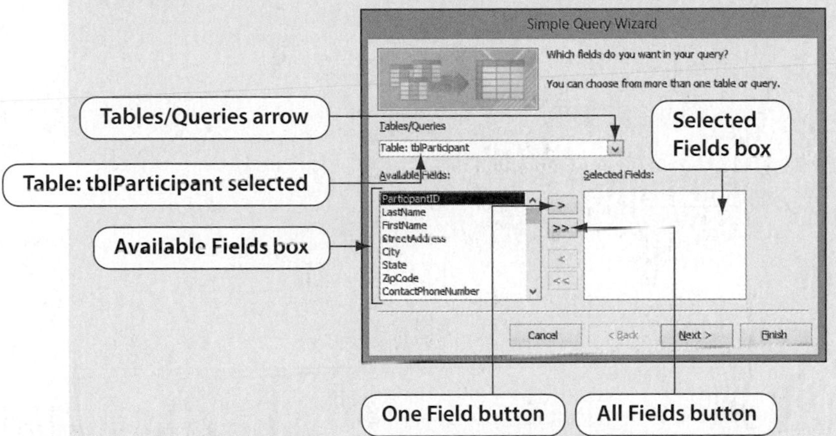

Figure 18 Select tblParticipant

c. Click the **Tables/Queries** arrow to see available field sources, and then select **Table: tblParticipant** as the source of your fields.
   The dialog box has two lists. The box on the left shows you all available fields from the selected table or query. The box on the right shows you all the fields that you have selected for this query. You use the buttons between the two lists to move fields from one box to the other. Selecting a field and clicking the One Field button [>] moves that field from the Available Fields box to the Selected Fields box. Clicking the All Fields button [>>] moves all fields.

d. Under Available Fields, click **LastName**, and then click the **One Field** button [>]. Access moves the LastName field to the Selected Fields box.

e. Click **FirstName**, and then click the **One Field** button [>].

f. Click **City**, and then click the **One Field** button [>].
   Your field list in the right box should display fields in the following order: LastName, FirstName, and City.

Troubleshooting
If you accidently add the wrong field to the Selected Fields box, select the field and use the One Field Back button [<] to place it back in the Available Fields box.
   If you select the fields in the wrong order, Access does not have a way to reorder the fields. It is best to place them all back in the Available Fields box using the All Fields Back button [<<] and then select them again in the right order.

g. Click **Next** to continue to the next page of the wizard. In the **What title do you want for your query?** box type **qryParticipantSantaFe_initialLastname** using your first initial and last name.

h. Click **Open the query to view information**, and then click **Finish**.
Access shows you the results of your query. Once you have created this query, the query name is displayed under All Access objects in the Navigation Pane.

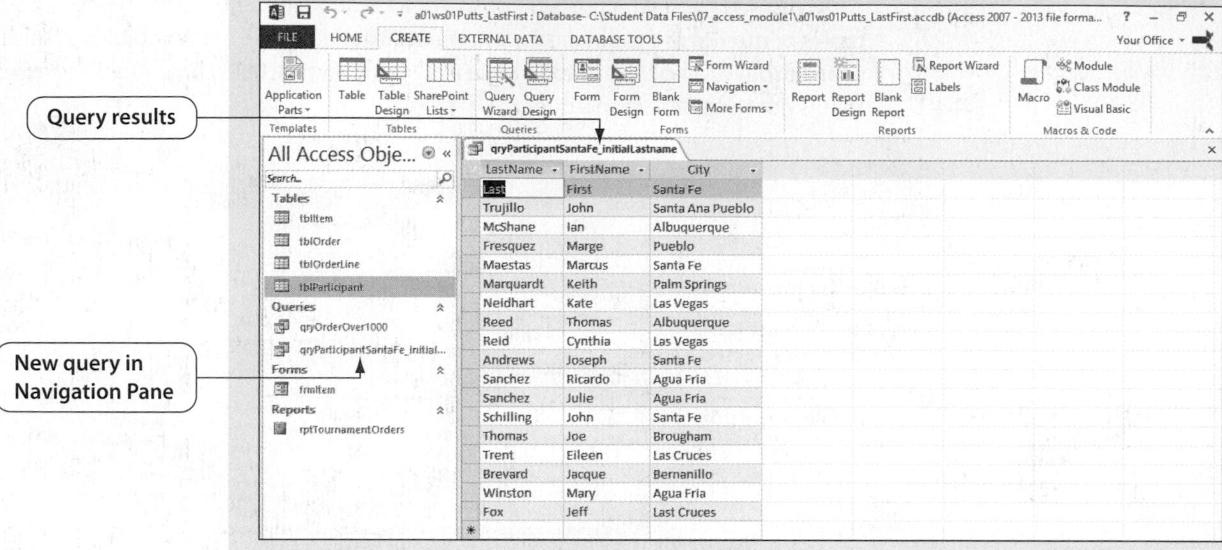

Figure 19 Results of your query

i. Click **Save** to save the query, and then **close** the query.

SIDE NOTE
Saving Design Changes
While Access automatically saves data changes, you need to tell it to save design changes. A new query is a design change.

Query results are a recordset that provide an answer to a question posed in a query. The query results show records and fields created at **run time**, which means that the results are created each time you run the query. This run time table is referred to as a **recordset**. The method to create the query is saved but not the actual results. That means that if you add a participant who meets the query criteria to the participant table, the next time you run this query, that participant will appear in the results of this query.

REAL WORLD ADVICE Naming Your Queries

Similar to tables, Access will allow you to give your query any name you want. There are two important considerations:

- You want to remember what a query does, so make the name as descriptive as possible. A query named "tblParticipant Query" will probably have no meaning for you in a few days. It will be easier to remember that "qryParticipantSantaFe" shows participants from Santa Fe.
- When you are looking at field sources, you often have a choice between tables and queries. Starting all your tables with "tbl" and all your queries with "qry" makes it easy to distinguish what you are choosing.

MODULE 1

Selecting a Value Using Design View

The Query Wizard uses a question-and-answer dialog box to create a query. The other method of creating a query is to use Design view. Design view goes behind the scenes of the data and shows you the detailed structure of an Access object. You can also use Design view to modify an existing query.

A01.09

To Switch to Design View of a Query

a. Right-click **qryParticipantSantaFe_initialLastname** in the Navigation Pane.

b. Select **Design View** from the shortcut menu.
   Access opens the Design view of your query. The DESIGN tab is open on the Ribbon. The left side of the screen shows the Navigation Pane. The top half of the screen shows the **query workspace**, which is the source for data in the query. In this case, the source is the table tblParticipant. The bottom half is called the **query design grid**. It shows which fields are selected in this query: LastName, FirstName, and City.

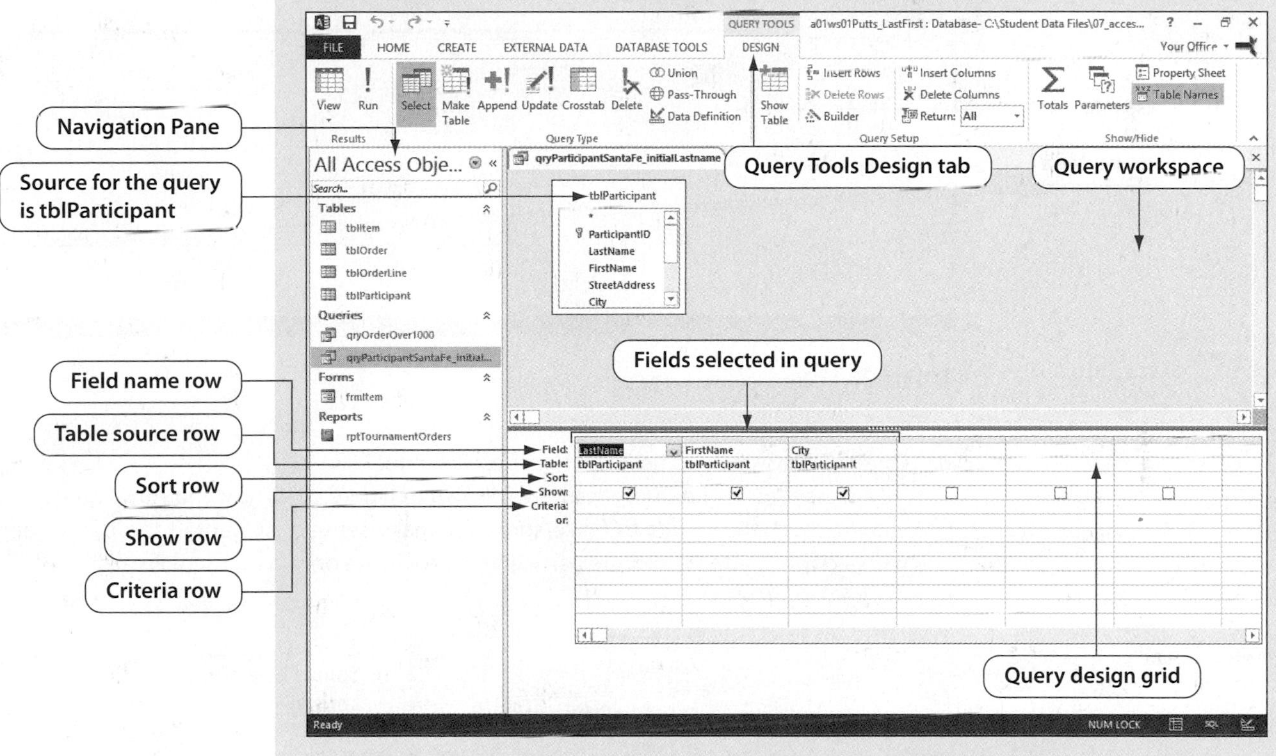

Figure 20 Design view for qryParticipantSantaFe_initialLastname

Selecting Values in a Query

Each row in the design grid shows information about the field. The top row is Field name. The next row shows the table or source for this field. The Sort row allows you to specify the order of records shown in your query results by setting one or more sort fields. The Show row is a check box that specifies whether the field is shown in the table of query results. The Criteria rows allow you to select certain records by setting conditions for the field contents. You are going to change this query to see which participants are from Santa Fe. You will do that by adding selection criteria.

A01.10

To Select a Value in a Query

a. Click the **Criteria** cell in the City column.

b. Type Santa Fe.

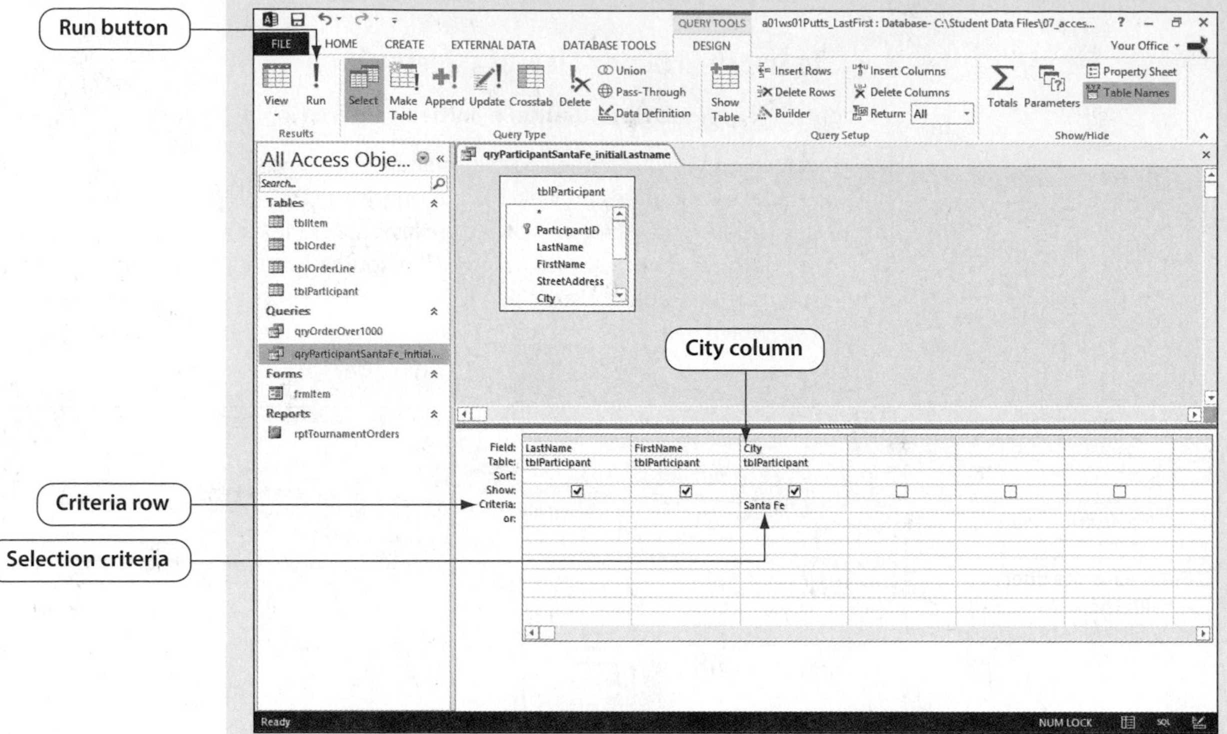

Figure 21 Enter criteria in a query selection

SIDE NOTE

Query Criteria

Because "City" is a text field, the criteria is treated as text, and Access adds quotation marks. You can also type the quotation marks.

c. On the DESIGN tab, in the Results group, click **Run**.

Access returns the query results as shown in Figure 22. When you run a query, you should check the results to make sure they make sense. You wanted the participants with a city of Santa Fe, and the participants shown are only from Santa Fe.

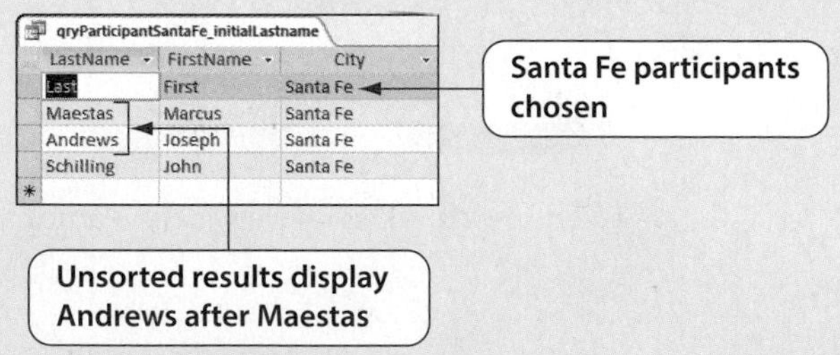

Figure 22 Unsorted query results showing participants from Santa Fe

Troubleshooting

If your query results are not what you expect (compare to Figure 22), you made an error in entering your selection criteria. Click the View button on the Home tab to switch back to Design view. Compare your criteria with Figure 21. Make sure that you spelled "Santa Fe" correctly and that it is in the City column.

QUICK REFERENCE | **Selecting in a Query**

When you typed Santa Fe in the criteria, you asked Access to select those participants who had a city equal to "Santa Fe". The equals sign is implied, though you can enter it if you wish. Other operators that can be entered in the selection criteria follow:

Operator	Meaning	Description
=	Equal to	Selects the records where the field value is equal to the value provided. If no operator is used, equal to is assumed.
<	Less than	Selects the records where the field value is less than the value provided.
>	Greater than	Selects the records where the field value is greater than the value provided.
< =	Less than or equal to	Selects the records where the field value is less than or equal to the value provided.
> =	Greater than or equal to	Selects the records where the field value is greater than or equal to the value provided.
< >	Not equal	Selects the records where the field value is not equal to the value provided.
Between	Between	Selects the records where the field values listed are within the two values. For example, between 1 and 7 is true for any value between 1 and 7—this includes the value of 1 and the value of 7.

Sorting Query Results

When Access runs a query, it puts the results in a default order based on how the table is defined. As shown in Figure 22, the order of the participants does not make much sense with Joseph Andrews after Marcus Maestas. In addition, if the query result shows many records, it will be difficult to find a specific record. Usually you will want to change the sort order so that the order of the results makes sense. In this query, you will choose to put the participants in alphabetical order.

A01.11

To Sort Query Results

a. In the Views group, click the **View** arrow, and then select **Design View**.

b. Click the **Sort cell** in the LastName column, click the **Selection** arrow, and then select **Ascending**.

c. Click the **Sort cell** in the FirstName column, click the **Selection** arrow, and then select **Ascending**.

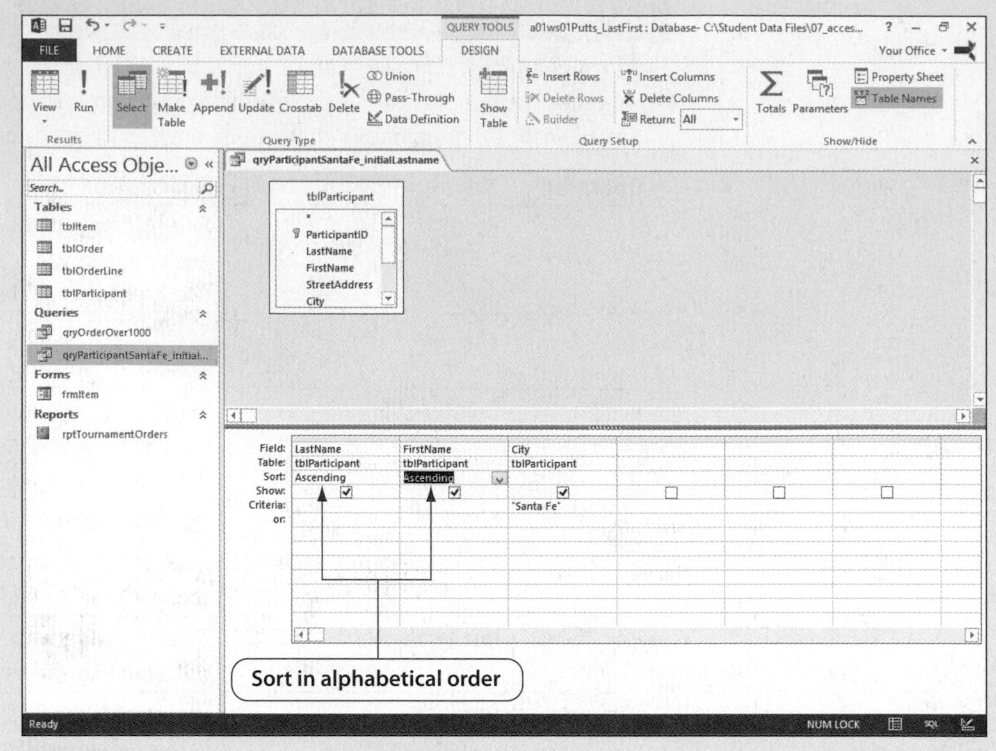

Figure 23 Sorting results of a query

d. On the DESIGN tab, in the Results group, click **Run**.

Access puts the participants in alphabetical order by Last name. If there were two participants with the same Last name, they would be sorted alphabetically by First name.

Printing Query Results

If you want to print your query results, you can do this on the File tab. Printing tables is done the same way.

A01.12

To Print a Query

a. Click the **FILE** tab to display Backstage view.

b. Click **Print**, and then click **Print Preview** to see what the results would look like if printed.

c. If your instructor asks you to print your results, on the PRINT PREVIEW tab, click **Print**. In the Print dialog box, select the correct printer, and then click **OK**.

d. On the PRINT PREVIEW tab, click **Close Print Preview**.

e. Click **Save** [Save icon].

f. **Close** [X] the qryParticipantSantaFe_initialLastname query.

> **Troubleshooting**
>
> If you accidently closed Access instead of just the query, open Access the same way you did at the beginning of the workshop. In the Recent databases, click the name a01ws01Putts_LastFirst to open the database again.

REAL WORLD ADVICE | **Do You Need to Print?**

Before you decide to print the results of a query, you may want to consider whether you really need a printed version. If you want to share the results with someone else, often you can share them via e-mail. Access provides an export-to-PDF feature for a query or table that allows you to save the results in PDF format. Right-click the object in the Navigation Pane, point to Export, and then select PDF or XPS. You can then publish your object as a PDF file, which you can e-mail to someone. Alternatively, you can use the External Data tab to export to a PDF format.

Understand What a Form Is

A form provides another interface to a table or query beyond the table in Datasheet view. In corporate databases, end users of a database computer system often use forms to enter and change data. You can also use forms to limit the amount of data you see from a table. In a personal database, you can create forms for entering data if you wish.

Forms have three views:

- **Form view** shows the data in the form. This is the view you use to enter or change data. You cannot change the form design in this view.
- **Layout view** shows the form and the data. Some of the form design such as field lengths and fonts can be changed in this view. The data cannot be changed.
- Design view shows the form design but not the data. Any aspect of the form design can be changed. The data cannot be changed.

REAL WORLD ADVICE | **Layout View vs. Design View**

Both Layout view and Design view allow you to change the design of forms. Which view is best for changing design? Part of this is personal preference, but some features are only able to be changed in Design view. Some considerations:

- Layout view shows both the form and the data. When changing column widths or field lengths, it is often easier if you see both. You can adjust the sizes while seeing the data and make sure you pick a size that is appropriate.
- Many features can only be changed in Design view. How do you remember which ones? If you prefer Layout view, try it in that view first, and switch to Design view whenever you have trouble changing something.

Creating a Form

You want to create a form to make it easier to enter participants. There are different types of forms that can be created. The default form shows one participant at a time and has each field clearly labeled.

A01.13

To Create a Form

a. Click **tblParticipant** in the Navigation Pane. Click the **CREATE** tab, and then in the Forms group, click **Form**.

b. Click **Save** to save the form. In the Save As dialog box, type **frmParticipant_initialLastname** using your first initial and last name, and then click **OK**.

Access creates a form. Notice that the form displays the same Navigation bar that you had in the table. That is because a form is a data entry or display tool for the table. You can use it to navigate through your table. The form is created in Layout view, which allows you make minor changes to the design.

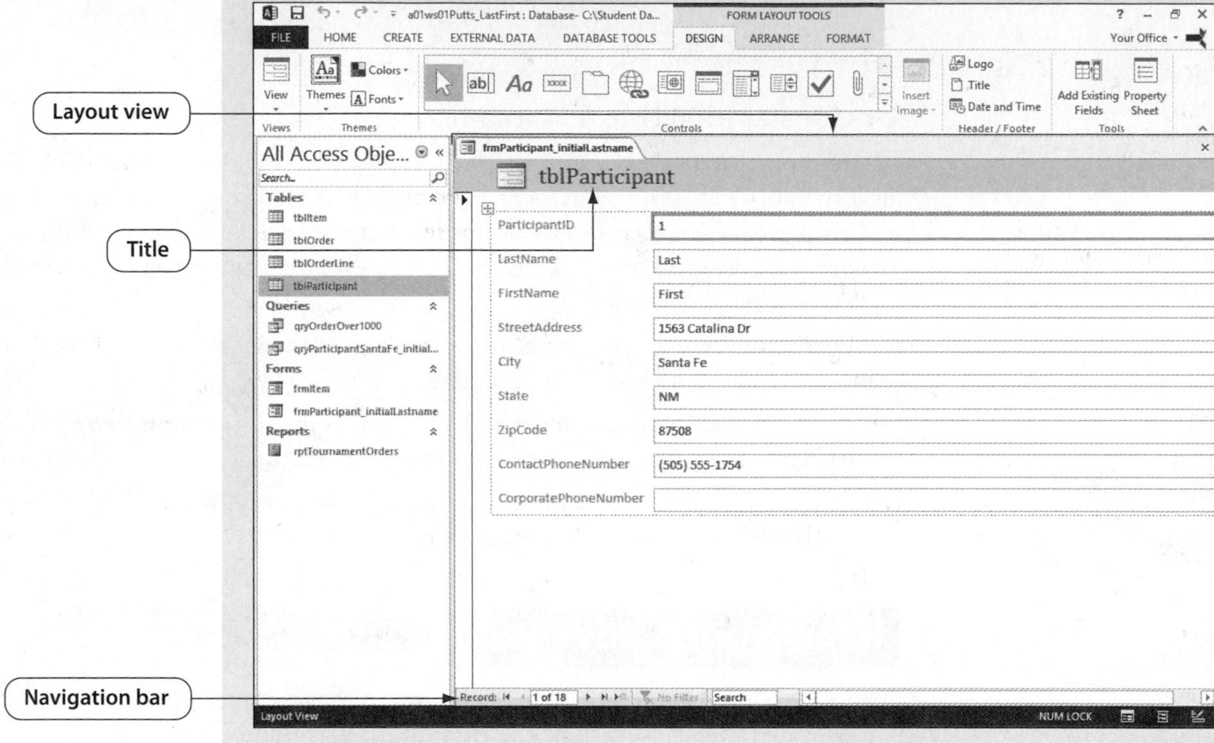

Figure 24 Form in Layout view

c. Click the **title** of the form, and then click again to select the **title**. Replace the current title with **Participant form by initial Lastname** using your first initial and last name.

d. Press Enter, and then click **Save** to save your form.

Entering Data via a Form

Jackie Silva has asked to register for the tournament. You will use your newly created form to add her to the participant table. It is very important that you navigate to the append row so you enter her information into a blank form. If you see data about a participant in the form, you will be replacing that participant with Jackie Silva instead of adding a new participant.

A01.14

To Enter Data Using a Form

a. Click the **DESIGN** tab, in the Views group, click the **View** arrow, and then click **Form View**. This view allows you to use the form to enter data into the table.

b. Click the **New (blank) record button** on the Navigation bar. If you see a participant's name in the form, try again. This will be record 19 of 19 in the Navigation bar.

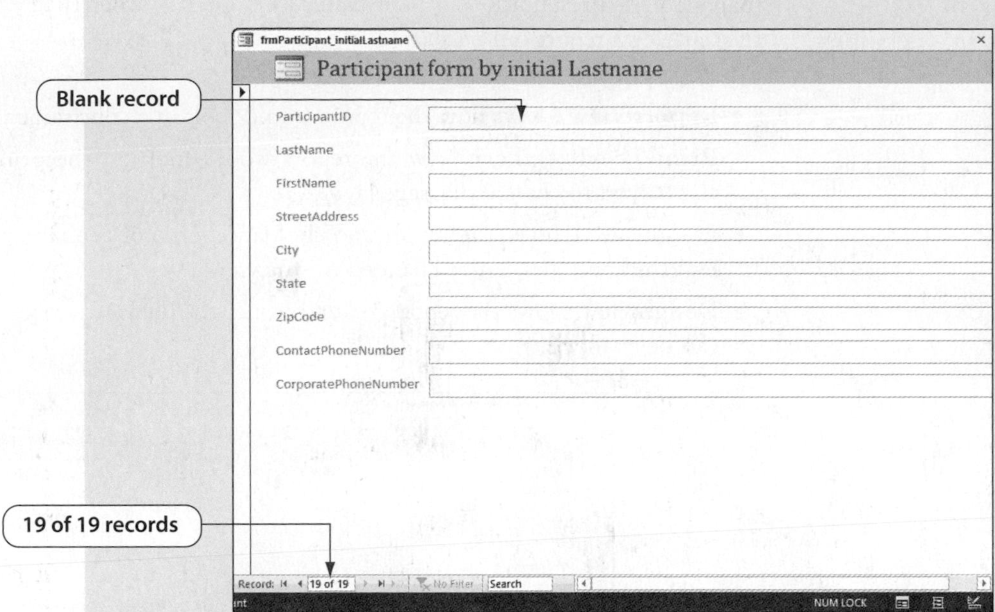

Figure 25 Blank append record

SIDE NOTE
Saving in Access
Unlike Word, Access saves your data as it is entered. Typing over the data in another record means that you lose the data that was there.

c. Type the following information into the form. Press Enter or Tab to move to each field.

ParticipantID	31
LastName	Silva
FirstName	Jackie
StreetAddress	1509 Main Street
City	Santa Ana Pueblo
State	NM
ZipCode	87044
ContactPhoneNumber	(505) 555-3355
CorporatePhoneNumber	(leave blank)

d. **Close** the form. The participant data you entered in the form is saved to the table.

e. On the Navigation Pane, under Tables, double-click **tblParticipant**.

f. Click the **Last Record button** on the Navigation bar. Verify that Jackie Silva has been added to your table.

g. **Close** the table.

CONSIDER THIS | **Adding Data Directly into a Table vs. Adding Data via a Form**

You have added two participants to your table. Earlier, you added a row to the table and added Jeff Fox. Now, you have added Jackie Silva via a form. Which was easier for you? Why would most companies use forms to enter data?

Understand What a Report Is

A report provides an easy-to-read format suitable for printing. A sample report is shown in Figure 26. As you can see, the report has page headers—the column headings—and a footer. You can easily provide column totals as needed. When printing data for management presentations, you usually use a report rather than a query. The source of the data for a report can be a table or query.

Reports have four views:

- **Report view** shows how the report would look in a continuous page layout.
- **Print Preview** shows how the report would look on the printed page. This view allows you to change the page layout.
- Layout view shows the report and the data. Some of the report design such as field lengths and fonts can be changed in this view.
- Design view shows the report design but not the data. Any aspect of the report design can be changed.

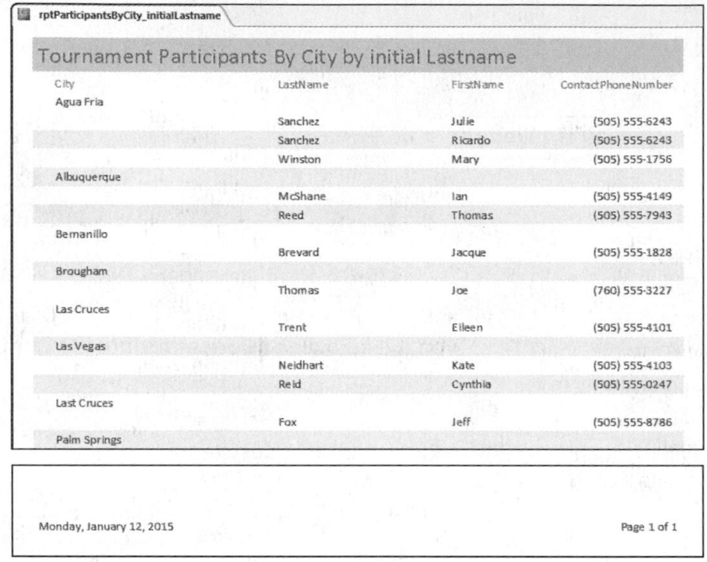

rptParticipantsByCity_initialLastname

Tournament Participants By City by initial Lastname

City	LastName	FirstName	ContactPhoneNumber
Agua Fria			
	Sanchez	Julie	(505) 555-6243
	Sanchez	Ricardo	(505) 555-6243
	Winston	Mary	(505) 555-1756
Albuquerque			
	McShane	Ian	(505) 555-4149
	Reed	Thomas	(505) 555-7943
Bernanillo			
	Brevard	Jacque	(505) 555-1828
Brougham			
	Thomas	Joe	(760) 555-3227
Las Cruces			
	Trent	Eileen	(505) 555-4101
Las Vegas			
	Neidhart	Kate	(505) 555-4103
	Reid	Cynthia	(505) 555-0247
Last Cruces			
	Fox	Jeff	(505) 555-8786
Palm Springs			

Monday, January 12, 2015 Page 1 of 1

Figure 26 An Access report

Creating a Report Using a Wizard

The report feature in Access allows you to easily design reports that can serve management purposes and look professional. You will create a report listing the participants in the database. You will use the Report Wizard to create the report.

The Report Wizard starts similarly to the Query Wizard in selecting fields for the report. After that the wizard asks questions about report formatting that were not part of the Query Wizard.

You want to create a list of participants entered in the tournament with their contact phone numbers. You will group all the participants in a single city into a single group. You will print the participants in alphabetic order within each group.

A01.15

To Create a Report Using a Wizard

a. Click the **CREATE** tab, and then in the Reports group, click **Report Wizard**. Click the **Tables/Queries** arrow, and then click **Table: tblParticipant**.

b. Using the One Field button >, move these fields to the Selected Fields box: **LastName**, **FirstName**, **City**, and **ContactPhoneNumber**.

c. Click **Next**. The wizard asks if you want to add grouping levels.

d. Click to select **City**, and then click the **One Field** button > to group by City. When you make this selection, the box on the right of the dialog box shows a preview of what the report grouping will look like.

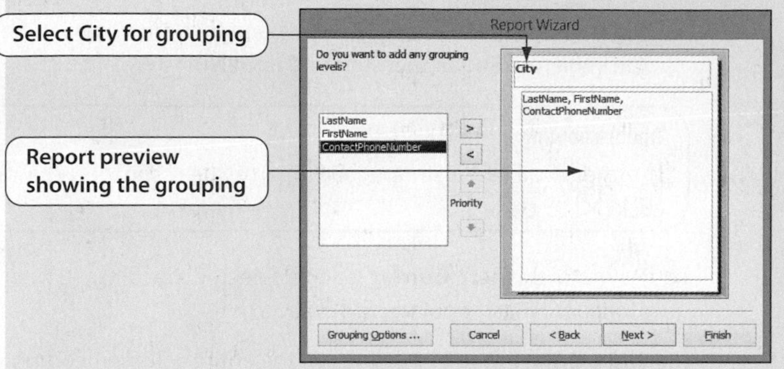

Figure 27 Add grouping levels

e. Click **Next**.

The wizard asks what sort order you want. You always want to put your report in some order that makes it easy to read and understand. Otherwise, a report with a lot of information is difficult to understand. In this report, you will list participants alphabetically.

f. In the **1** box, click the **arrow**, and then select **LastName**. If necessary, make sure that the sort order is **Ascending**, meaning in alphabetical order from A to Z.

g. In the **2** box, click the **arrow**, and then select **FirstName**.

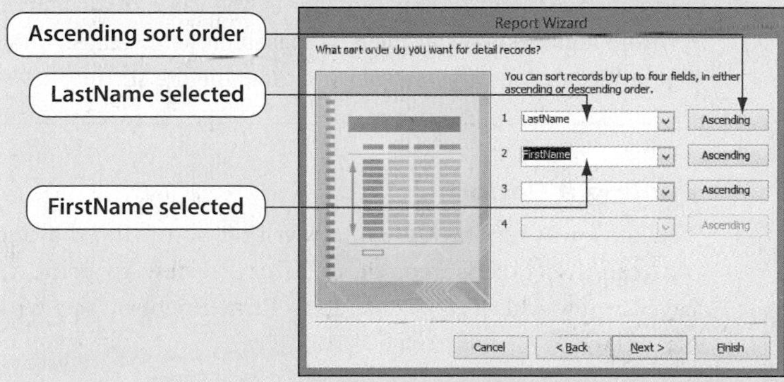

Figure 28 Add sorting

h. Click **Next**. If necessary, change the layout to **Stepped** and the orientation to **Portrait**.

i. Click **Next**. In the **What title do you want for your report?** box, type **rptParticipantsByCity_initialLastname** using your first initial and last name.

j. Click **Finish**.

Access displays the report in Print Preview. You notice that the ContactPhoneNumber heading is not fully shown. You can fix that easily in Layout view.

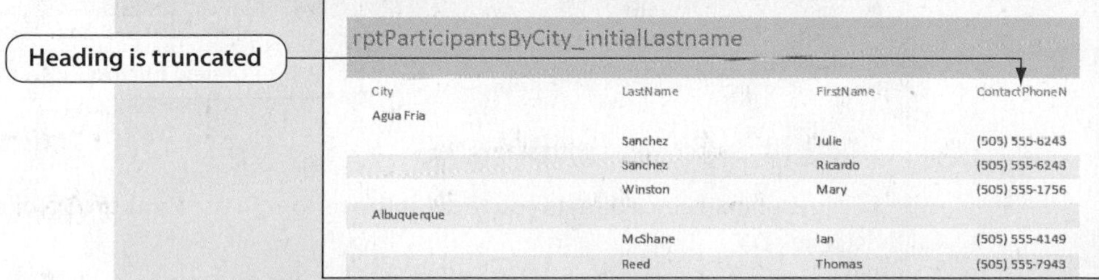

Figure 29 Report in Print Preview

k. Right-click anywhere on the report, and then click **Layout View** from the shortcut menu. Click the heading of the **ContactPhoneNumber** column.

> **Troubleshooting**
> If either the Field List Pane or Property Sheet show on the right side of the field, click [X] to close it.

l. Point to the **left border** of the selected heading (ContactPhoneNumber) until the Horizontal Resize pointer is displayed [↔].

m. Drag to the left until you can see the entire column heading.

n. Double-click the **title** of the report, and then change the report title to Tournament Participants By City by initial Lastname using your first initial and last name. Your report should look like Figure 26.

o. Click **Save** [💾] to save the report.
Notice that the City data is a line above the data in the other columns. That is because the participants are grouped by city. Within a city, participants are sorted alphabetically.

> **CONSIDER THIS | Grouping vs. Sorting**
> Grouping arranges records together by the value of a single field. Sorting puts the records within a group in a specific order based on field values. When would you choose to sort your records, and when would you group before sorting?

Printing a Report

You can print reports the same way that you printed a query earlier using the File tab. You can also take advantage of Print Preview to print a report. You are currently in Layout view and need to change to Print Preview. You will use the button on the status bar to switch views.

A01.16

To Print a Report

a. Click **Print Preview** [icon] to change to Print Preview. Alternatively, you could change to Print Preview using the button on the Ribbon as you have done before.

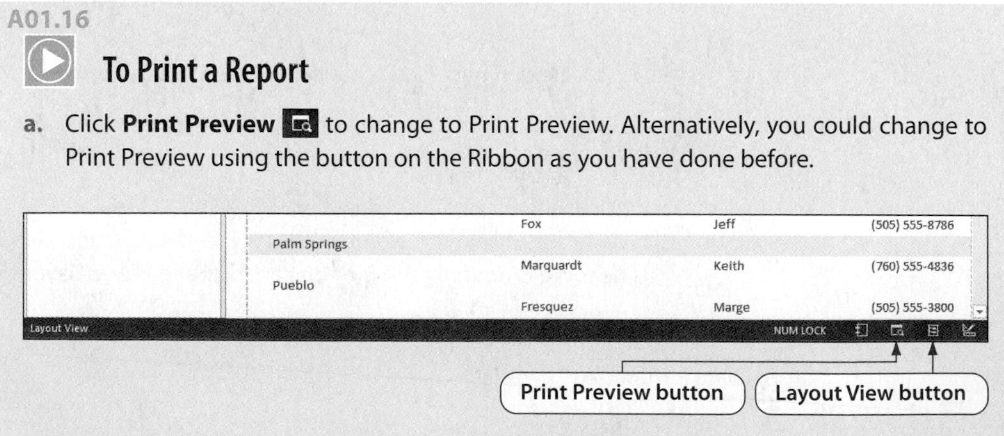

Figure 30 Switch views with status bar

b. If your instructor directs you to print the report, in the Print group, click **Print**, and then click **OK**.

c. In the Close Preview group, click **Close Print Preview**, and then **close** [X] the report.

REAL WORLD ADVICE **When Do You Use a Report vs. a Query?**

Both reports and queries can be used to report on your data. A report provides a more formal presentation of your data and is designed for printing. A query has more selection capabilities, but the formatting is not as attractive. You can combine the two capabilities by first creating the query object and then creating a report using the query as your source.

Back Up a Database

A **backup database** is an extra copy of your database that you can use to protect yourself from the accidental loss of your database. Backups can help in cases of accidental deletion of data. You can return to the backup copy if you accidently delete the real database. The backup copy may not be as current as your real database, but it may save you from having to recreate the whole database. If you store the backup on another storage medium, it can also help in cases of hardware failure such as a hard drive crash.

Creating a Backup

In Access, you make backups by using the Back Up Database command, which is available on **Backstage view** under Save As. If you make multiple backup copies, you will want to give them different names. The backup feature appends the current date to the suggested file name. That allows you to easily distinguish between various versions of the backups. You can be sure that you are getting the most recent one.

If you ever need a backup, simply return to the most recent copy that you have and start working with that file. You can save it as the name of the file you want to work with.

A01.17

To Back Up a Database

a. Click the **FILE** tab, and then click **Save As**. Make sure that **Save Database As** is selected under File Types. Access displays Save Database As options in the right pane.

b. Under **Advanced**, click **Back Up Database**, and then click the **Save As** button. The Save As dialog box appears with a suggested file name that has the date appended.

c. Navigate to the drive and folder where you want to store your backup. Change the file name if necessary, and then click **Save**.

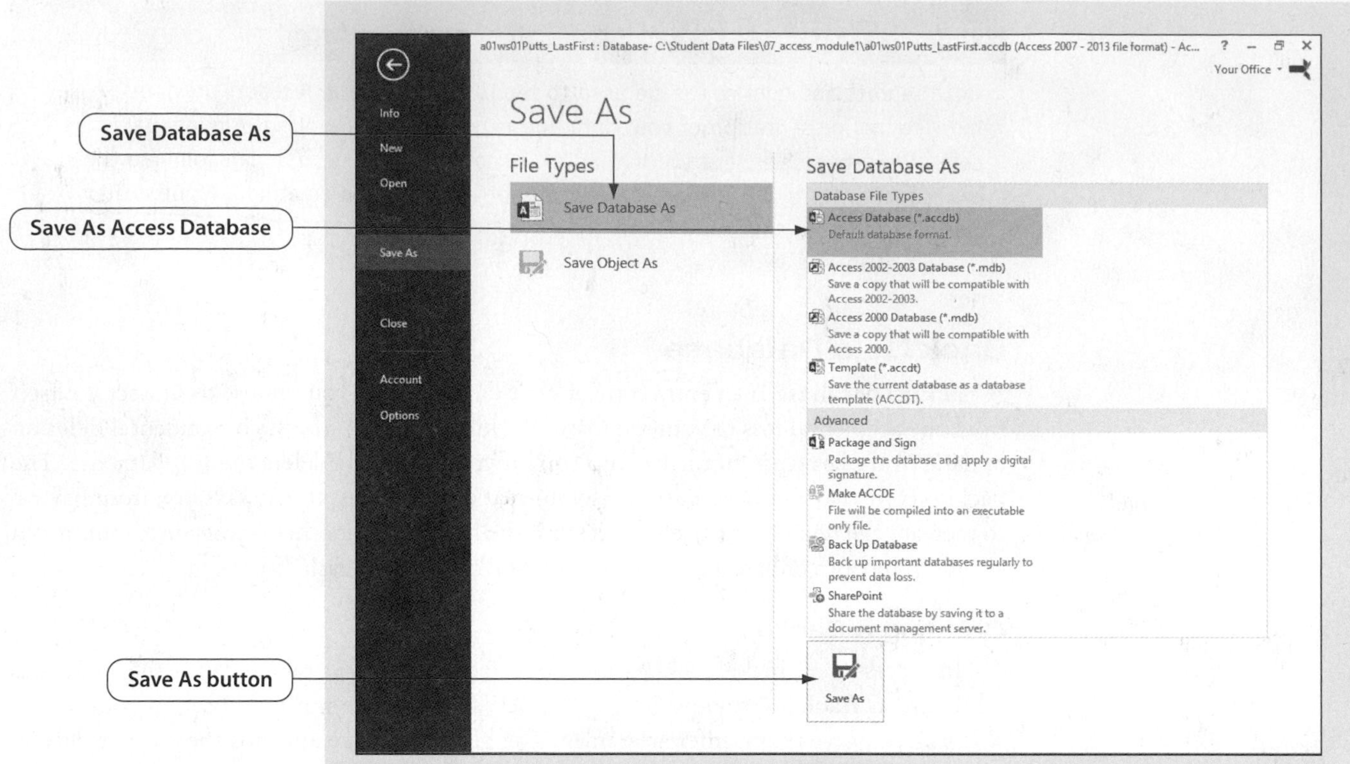

Figure 31 Make a backup copy of your database

> **CONSIDER THIS | Backups**
>
> What would you lose if your PC's hard drive crashed? Do you have copies of school work, photographs, or music? You may never need to retrieve the backup, but which would be worse: making unnecessary backups or losing all your files?

Compact a Database

While you work on an Access database, the size of the database file increases. When you delete a record or object, or if you make changes to an object, Access does not reuse the original space. Access provides a compacting feature that makes more efficient use of disk space. **Compacting** rearranges objects to use disk space more efficiently, thus releasing the now unused space to be used again. If you do not compact your database, its size can get very large quickly. The compact option also looks for damaged data and tries to repair it.

Compacting Your Database

You have two options for compacting: (1) You can perform a single Compact and Repair Database action at any time, or (2) You can select Compact on Close. If you select Compact on Close, Access automatically compacts your database anytime you close it. Both options are available on Backstage view.

MODULE 1

A01.18

To Compact a Database

a. Click the **FILE** tab.

b. Click **Compact & Repair Database**.

Access compacts your database, fixes it if necessary, and returns you to the HOME tab. On a small database such as Putts for Paws, this action is very fast. On a larger database with many changes made, there may be a noticeable delay.

c. Click the **FILE** tab, and then click **Options**.

d. Click **Current Database** in the left pane, and then under Application Options, click the **Compact on Close** check box.

By default, Compact on Close is turned off. Many professionals like to turn on Compact on Close so they do not need to remember to compact the database themselves.

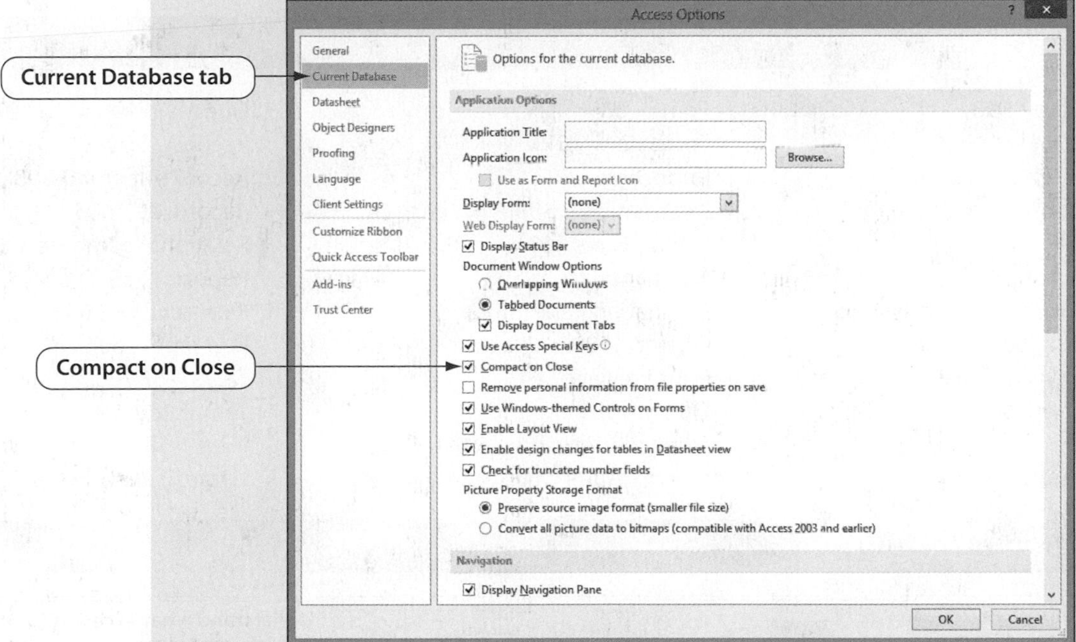

Figure 32 Select Compact on Close

e. Click **OK** to turn this option on. Access warns you that the option will not take effect until you close and reopen the database.

f. Click **OK**, and then **close** ✕ Access.

Concept Check

1. What is Access? When would you use Access instead of Excel? p. 588, 598
2. What is the Navigation Pane? Where do you find it? p. 592
3. What is a record? What is a field? How are they represented in Access? p. 597–600
4. How do you manually navigate a database? p. 601–603
5. How is a query used? What is the difference between Datasheet view and Design view of a query? p. 603–604
6. How is a form used? p. 611
7. How is a report used? What is Report Layout view? p. 613–614
8. What is a database backup, and how is it used? p. 617
9. What does it mean to compact and repair your database? What is the difference between a single compact and a compact on close? p. 618

Key Terms

Append row 598
Backstage view 617
Backup database 617
Compacting 618
Data 588
Database 588
Database management system (DBMS) 588
Datasheet view 589
Design view 589
Field 591
File extension 594
Form 589
Form view 611
Importing 595
Information 588
Layout view 611
Navigation bar 598
Navigation Pane 592
Object 589
Print Preview 614
Query 589
Query design grid 607
Query results 606
Query workspace 607
Record 590
Record selector 598
Recordset 606
Relational database 595
Report 589
Report view 614
Run time 606
Table 589
Template 591
View 589
Wizard 604

Visual Summary

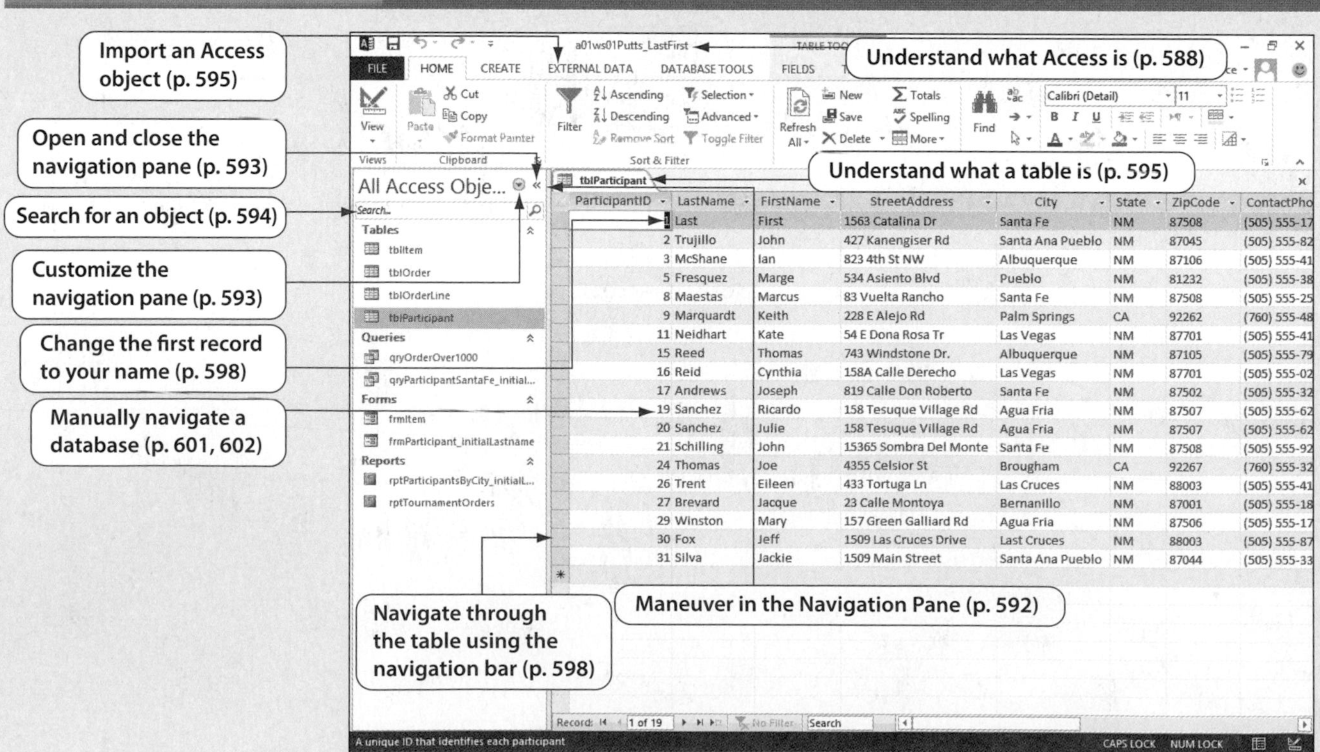

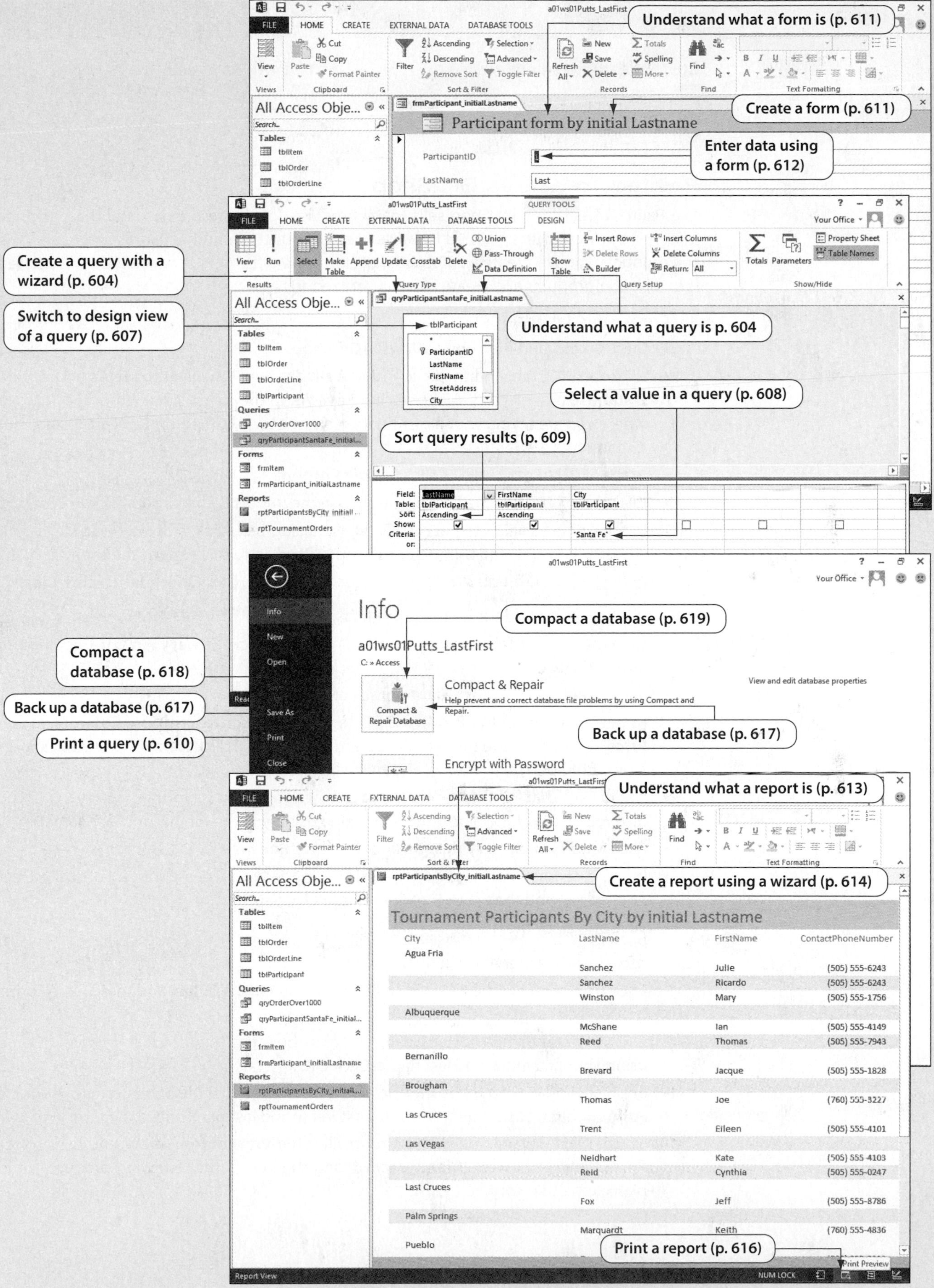

Figure 33 Putts for Paws Charity Tournament Participants Final Database

Practice 1

Student data files needed:

a01ws01Giftshop.accdb

a01ws01Products.accdb

You will save your file as:

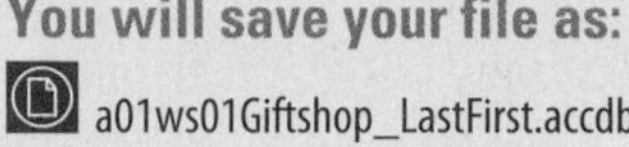

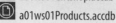

a01ws01Giftshop_LastFirst.accdb

Painted Treasures Gift Shop

Sales & Marketing

The Painted Treasures Gift Shop sells many products for the resort patrons. These include jewelry from local artists, Painted Paradise linens, products from the resort's restaurant, and spa products. You will create a database that stores the gift shop's products. You will create a form to enter products and create an inventory report.

a. Create your database.
   - Start **Access**, and then open **a01ws01Giftshop**.
   - Click the **FILE** tab, and then click **Save As**. Make sure **Save Database As** and **Access Database** are selected, and then click **Save As**. In the Save As dialog box, navigate to where you are saving your files, and then type a01ws01Giftshop_LastFirst, using your last and first name. Click **Save**.
   - In the SECURITY WARNING, click **Enable Content**.
   - Click the **EXTERNAL DATA** tab, and then in the Import & Link group, click **Access**.
   - In the Get External Data - Access Database dialog box, click **Browse**, navigate to your student data files, and then select **a01ws01Products**. Click **Open**, and then click **OK**.
   - In the **Import Objects** dialog box, select **tblProduct**, click **OK**, and then click **Close**.

b. Create a query to find the clothing products.
   - Click the **CREATE** tab, and then in the Queries group, click **Query Wizard**. Click **Simple Query Wizard**, and then click **OK**.
   - Select **Table: tblProduct** as the source of your fields.
   - In this order, select the **ProductID**, **Category**, **ProductDescription**, **Color**, **Size**, and **Price** fields and move them to the Selected Fields box. Click **Next**, click **Detail (shows every field of every record)**, and then click **Next**.
   - Under **What title do you want for your query?**, type qryProductsClothingType_initialLastname using your first initial and last name.
   - Click **Modify the query design**, and then click **Finish**.
   - In the Category Criteria cell, type Clothing, in the ProductDescription Sort cell, select **Ascending**, and then click **Run** in the Results group.
   - Save and close the query.

c. Create a form to enter new products.
   - Click **tblProduct** in the Navigation Pane. Click the **CREATE** tab, and then in the Forms group, click **Form**.
   - Click **Save**, and then in the Save As dialog box, type frmProduct_initialLastname using your first initial and last name. Click **OK**.
   - In Layout view, select the **form title**, and then change the title of the form to Products Form by initial Lastname using your first initial and last name. Save the form.
   - On the DESIGN tab, in the Views group, click the **View** button arrow, and then select **Form View**. Click **New (blank) record**, and then enter the following product in the blank append record.

ProductID	42
ProductDescription	Polo Shirt
Category	Clothing
QuantityInStock	35
Price	30.00
Size	L
Color	Blue

- Close the form.

d. Create an inventory report.
- Click the **CREATE** tab, and then in the Reports group, click **Report Wizard**.
- Click the **Tables/Queries** arrow, and then click **Table: tblProduct**.
- Select the fields in the following order: **Category**, **ProductDescription**, **Color**, **Size**, and **QuantityInStock**, and then click **Next**.
- Under **Do you want to add any grouping levels?**, double-click **Category** and **ProductDescription**, and then click **Next**.
- In the **1** box, click the **arrow**, and then select **Color**. In the **2** box, click the **arrow**, select **Size**, and then Click **Next**.
- Change the Layout to **Stepped**, the Orientation to **Landscape**, and then click **Next**.
- Type rptInventory_initialLastname, using your first initial and last name, as the title for your report, and then click **Finish**.
- Switch to **Layout** view, and then change the report title to Inventory Report by initial Lastname using your first initial and last name.
- Save and close the report, and then close the database. Submit your file as directed by your instructor.

Problem Solve 1

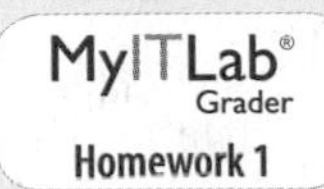

Student data files needed:

 a01ws01Arena.accdb

 a01ws01Employee.accdb

You will save your file as:

 a01ws01Arena_LastFirst.accdb

Sunshine Event Arena

Production & Operations

The Sunshine Event Arena (SEA) is an arena that hosts such local events as banquets, concerts, and sporting events. The database contains tables that track events, ticket sales, and patrons of the arena.

You will expand the database by importing an employee table and creating a form, a report, and a query.

a. Start **Access**, and then open **a01ws01Arena**.

b. Click the **FILE** tab, and then click **Save As**. Make sure **Save Database As** and **Access Database** are selected, and then click **Save As**. Browse to where you are storing your files, name your database a01ws01Arena_LastFirst, using your last and first name, and then click **Save**. Click **Enable Content** in the SECURITY WARNING.

c. Import tables from the Access database **a01ws01Employee**, selecting the **tblEmployee** table. Do not save the import steps.

d. Create a form for **tblEmployee**, and then save the form as frmEmployee_initialLastname.

e. Change the title of the form to Employee Form by initial Lastname using your first initial and last name.

f. Switch to Form view. Use the navigation bar at the bottom of the screen to navigate to the **New (blank) record** for tblEmployee. Make sure the employee fields are blank, and enter the following information for a new employee:

Employee ID	**(Access will fill)**
First Name	Your actual first name
Last Name	Your actual last name
Address	1020 Range Drive
City	Pueblo
State	NM
Phone	(505) 555–1222

g. A patron named Elaine called, and you want to call her back but need her number. Use the Query Wizard to create a query listing **FirstName**, **LastName**, and **Phone** from tblPatrons. Save your query as qryPatronNamedElaine_initialLastname.

h. In **Design** view for **qryPatronNamedElaine_initialLastname**, select the patrons with a FirstName of Elaine. Sort the results by **LastName**, and then run the query.

i. Create a report on events showing **EventDate**, **EventName**, **EventType**, **TicketsAvailable**, and **TicketPrice** from tblEvents. Group by **EventType**, sort by **EventDate**, and then change to **Landscape** orientation. Name your report rptEvents_initialLastname. In Layout view, change the report title to read Event Report by initial Lastname.

j. Close the database. Submit your file as directed by your instructor.

Perform 1: Perform in Your Career

Student data file needed:

 a01ws01Roadhouse.accdb

You will save your file as:

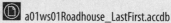

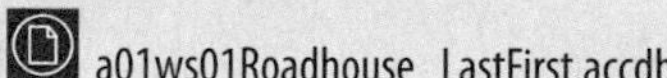
a01ws01Roadhouse_LastFirst.accdb

Beverage Database at The Roadhouse Bar and Grill

Production & Operations

You are the bar manager at The Roadhouse Bar and Grill, a local restaurant that specializes in home-cooked meals for breakfast, lunch, and dinner. You have a database that you use for managing the inventory of beverage items.

You will expand the database by creating a form, reports, and queries.

a. Start **Access**, open the student data file **a01ws01Roadhouse**, and then save it as a01ws01Roadhouse_LastFirst, using your first and last name. Manually navigate the tables in the database to explore the types of data in the database.

b. Create a form for **tblSuppliers** and name it frmSuppliers_initialLastname. Use your form to change the name of the first supplier to your full name.

c. Create a report showing suppliers and name it rptSuppliers_initialLastname.

d. Create a query that shows what types of beverages you have that are in a can and name it qryCannedBeverage_initialLastname.

e. Create another report that you would find useful in your job.

f. Create another query that you would find useful in your job.

g. If your instructor asks you to print your results, print all reports and queries.

h. Close your database. Submit your file as directed by your instructor.

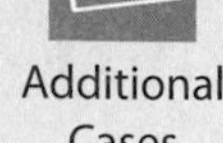

Additional Cases

Additional Workshop Cases are available on the companion website and in the instructor resources.

Microsoft Office Access 2013

Module 1

Understanding and Using a Relational Database

WORKSHOP 2 | TABLES, KEYS, AND RELATIONSHIPS

OBJECTIVES

1. Understand database design p. 626
2. Import data from other sources p. 629
3. Enter data manually p. 637
4. Create a table in Design view p. 640
5. Understand masks and formatting p. 644
6. Understand and designate keys p. 647
7. Understand basic principles of normalization p. 652
8. Understand relationships between tables p. 653
9. Create a one-to-many relationship p. 655
10. Create a many-to-many relationship p. 659
11. Understand referential integrity p. 664

Prepare Case

Red Bluff Golf Club Putts for Paws Charity Tournament Database

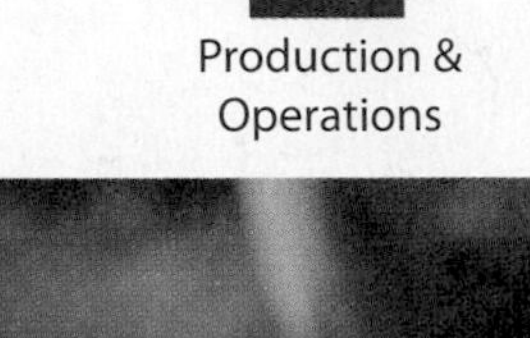

Production & Operations

Nico Traut / Shutterstock

The Red Bluff Golf Club is sponsoring a charity tournament, Putts for Paws, to raise money for the local pet shelter. You are modifying a database for the tournament that tracks money being raised from the event. The scope of this database is limited to tracking monies. Thus, in this instance, you are not tracking whether a participant is a golfer, volunteer, or other role. Anyone can donate money in the form of hole sponsorship or other donation item. You will want to track monies derived from corporate sponsorship. You will bring in data for the event from various sources including Excel worksheets and text files.

REAL WORLD SUCCESS

"Reports on open issues were very important to my project manager. I set up a database with a main table of open issues. I used foreign keys to link it to employee tables and to a table of priorities. That way I could give a report on the issue and who reported it with how important it was."

\- Joseph P., IT intern

Student data files needed for this workshop:

 a01ws02Putts.accdb

a01ws02PuttsVol.xlsx

 a01ws02PuttsGolf.xlsx

a01ws02PuttsDon.txt

 a01ws02PuttsCont.xlsx

You will save your files as:

 a01ws02Putts_LastFirst.accdb

 a01ws02PuttsDon_LastFirst.txt

Inserting Data into a Database

In designing a database, you will develop the tables, fields, and relationships of the tables. To manage the golf tournament, you will need to keep track of participants, the corporations that participate, the tee times, and the items each of the participants purchase. Each of these will be a table in your database. In this section, you will load tables from already existing databases and from Excel worksheets, in addition to creating two new tables.

Understand Database Design

Database design can be thought of as a three-step process:

1. Identify your entities—they become the tables.
2. Identify the attributes—they become the fields.
3. Specify the relationships between the tables.

An **entity** is a person, place, item, or event that you want to keep data about. You decide that you need to keep track of participants including golfers, donors, and corporate representatives. You need a participant table to track these people. A single participant is an instance of the participant entity and will become a record in the participant table.

An **attribute** is information about the entity. For example, for each participant you will want to keep information, such as name and address. These attributes will become the fields in your table.

A **relationship** is an association between tables based on common fields. You can see the power of Access when you relate tables together. For example, you can relate participants to orders that the participants place.

Later in the workshop, you will look more closely at designing a database. While you explore the database tables and data, think about these general principles or steps to follow.

1. Brainstorm a list of all the types of data you will need.
2. Rearrange data items into groups that represent a single entity. These groups will become your tables.
3. If one item can have several attributes, such as a credit card number, expiration date, name on a card, and security code, then put it into one group that will later become a table of its own. In this example, it would be a group named "credit card".
4. Break each attribute into the smallest attributes; they will become the fields. Give each attribute a descriptive name. For example, split addresses into street, city, state, and zip code.
5. Do not include totals, but do include all of the data needed so the calculation can be done in a query. For example, include the price of an item and the quantity ordered so the total cost can be calculated.
6. Remove any redundant data that exists in multiple groupings. For example, do not repeat customer names in both the customer grouping and the sales grouping.
7. Ensure common fields connect the groupings. For example, make sure that there is a common field between the customer grouping and the sales grouping so they can be connected. Later in this workshop, you will learn more about common fields.

You start with the participant entity, which is the tblParticipant table. You notice that it contains the fields shown in Table 1 to track the participants in the tournament.

Field Name	Data Type	Description	Field Size
ParticipantID	Number—Long Integer	A unique ID that identifies each participant	
LastName	Short Text	Last name	25
FirstName	Short Text	First name	20
StreetAddress	Short Text	Street address	35
City	Short Text	City	25
State	Short Text	State abbreviation	2
ZipCode	Short Text	Five digit zip code	5
ContactPhoneNumber	Short Text	Phone number for the individual participant	14
CorporatePhoneNumber	Short Text	Phone number for the corporation the participant represents	14

Table 1 Fields for tblParticipant

REAL WORLD ADVICE **Break Compound Fields into Their Parts**

You might wonder why the name field and address fields are divided into multiple fields. Would it not be easier to have a single field for Name and a single field for Address? It might be easier for data entry, but it is much more difficult for reporting.

- Break names into first name and last name fields. That means you can sort on people alphabetically by last name, and if two people have the same last name, by first name.
- Break addresses into fields such as StreetAddress, City, State, and ZipCode. This allows reporting by state, city, or other fields.
- For other fields, consider whether you might want to report on smaller parts of the field. For example, for PhoneNumber in some applications, you might want to report on AreaCode. However, that would be rare, and so you usually use just one field.

Illustrating some of the basic principles of database design, notice that the participant's name is split into two fields and the address is split into four fields. Why should you do this? When you have fields such as name or address that are composed of several smaller fields, you should split them into their component parts. This allows for more flexibility for reporting. For example, often a report is needed in alphabetic order by last or first name. You could not do this if you had stored the first and last name combined in the same field. Further, a field named "Name" is confusing, leading to inconsistent data such as nicknames and incomplete names. This also allows you to report or query on just part of the field such as which participants are from a particular state.

CONSIDER THIS | **Street Address Components**

Street addresses contain two parts, the number and street name. While some databases split these apart, this is not necessary for most business uses. What are some businesses that would benefit from separating these?

REAL WORLD ADVICE First and Last Names

Painted Paradise is a U.S. company with guests who primarily use a first name followed by a last name. However, not all cultures around the world break names into first and last. For example, Korean names are designated as family name followed by given name. Designing database fields to accommodate all of the different cultures in the world is challenging. Always keep in mind the typical name for the database, but try to design it in such a way that other naming practices can fit into the database. Because businesses today are global, designing a database sensitive to all global cultures is difficult but important.

Opening the Starting File

For the golf tournament, you will need to keep track of participants, the corporations that participate, and the items each of the participants purchase. There are several files that tournament organizers have been keeping about the tournament. You will import all the files into your Access database.

A02.00

To Open the a01ws02Putts Database

a. Start **Access**, and then open the student data file named **a01ws02Putts** in the folder location designated by your instructor.

b. Click the **FILE** tab, click **Save As,** click **Save Database As**, click **Save As** and then locate the folder or location designated by your instructor. Save the file as an Access Database in the location where you save your files with the name a01ws02Putts_LastFirst using your last and first name. If necessary, enable the content.

Understanding Data and Design Views of Tables

Tables have two views: Datasheet view and Design view. Datasheet view shows the values of the data within the table. The Design view shows the structure of the table with the fields and their definitions.

A02.01

MyITLab®
Workshop 2 Training

To View Table Design View

a. Double-click the **tblParticipant** table to open it.
   When you open the tblParticipant table, it opens in Datasheet view. In Datasheet view, you can see the information about the participants.

b. If necessary, click the **First record** button [I◄] in the Navigation bar to return to the first participant.

c. Press [Tab] to move to the **LastName** column.

d. Replace **Last** in the first record of the LastName column with your last name, press [Tab] to move to the next column, and then replace **First** in the FirstName column with your first name.

Replace Last and First with your last and first name

tblParticipant

ParticipantID	LastName	FirstName	StreetAddress	City	State	ZipCode	ContactPho
1	Last	First	1563 Catalina Dr	Santa Fe	NM	87508	(505) 555-17
2	Trujillo	John	427 Kanengiser Rd	Santa Ana Pueblo	NM	87045	(505) 555-82
3	McShane	Ian	823 4th St NW	Albuquerque	NM	87106	(505) 555-41
5	Fresquez	Marge	534 Asiento Blvd	Pueblo	NM	81232	(505) 555-38
8	Maestas	Marcus	83 Vuelta Rancho	Santa Fe	NM	87508	(505) 555-25

Figure 1 Datasheet view of tblParticipant

e. Click the **HOME** tab, and then in the Views group, click the **View** arrow, and then select **Design View**. When you switch to Design view, you see the structure of the fields and the field properties.

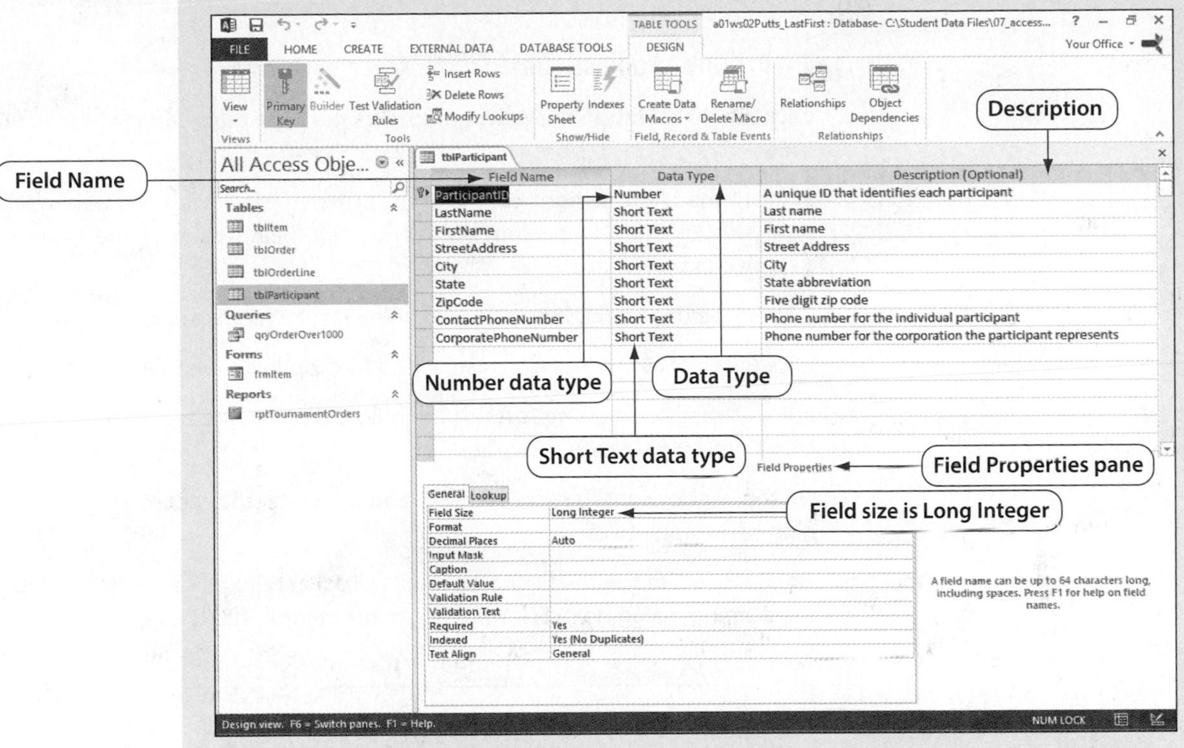

Figure 2 Design view of tblParticipant

The upper pane of Design view has three columns: Field Name, Data Type, and Description. The Field Name is the column label in Datasheet view. **Data types** define the kind of data that can be entered into a field, such as numbers, text, or dates. The data type tells Access how to store and display the field. Number and Short Text are the two most common data types. In this table, you can see that one field is stored as a **Number data type**. That means that the data can only contain numeric characters. The **Short Text data type** allows any text and numeric characters to be stored. Street Address is the Short Text data type, so a street address in this database can contain numbers, letters, and special characters. The third column, Description, helps the user discern the meaning of the field.

The Field Properties pane in Design view gives more information on how the data is stored, entered, and processed. If the ParticipantID field is selected, you can see that its Field Size is Long Integer.

Import Data from Other Sources

Painted Paradise has had different employees collecting data in different ways. Luckily, the applications within the Microsoft Office suite work together. This allows you to import—move data— easily between Excel and Access. You will import the files from Excel, Access, and Notepad. After importing the data, you will be able to further analyze and refine the table structure for the database. Even though other employees have kept track of the roles that each participant plays, remember that the scope of this database does not include tracking the participants' roles in the event. You are only tracking corporate involvement.

Copying and Pasting

Only a few golfer participants were entered into the tblParticipant table. Some others were put in an Excel worksheet. You will copy and paste them from Excel into your Access table.

A02.02

To Copy and Paste Data from Excel

a. Click the **HOME** tab, in the Views group, click the **View** arrow, and then select **Datasheet View**.

b. Point to the **bottom-right corner** of the screen. The Charms will be displayed on the right side of the screen. Note the labels underneath each of the charms. Click the **Search** charm.

c. Click inside the **search box** at the top of the page. Type Excel.

d. Click **Excel 2013** in the search results, and then open **a01ws02PuttsGolf**.

e. In Excel, drag to select **cells A1** through **I9**. On the HOME tab, in the Clipboard group, click **Copy** to copy these cells.

f. On the Windows taskbar, click **Access**, and then click the **record selector** at the beginning of the append row.

g. On the HOME tab, in the Clipboard group, click **Paste** to paste the golfers into Access. In the warning dialog box, click **Yes** to paste the records into the table.

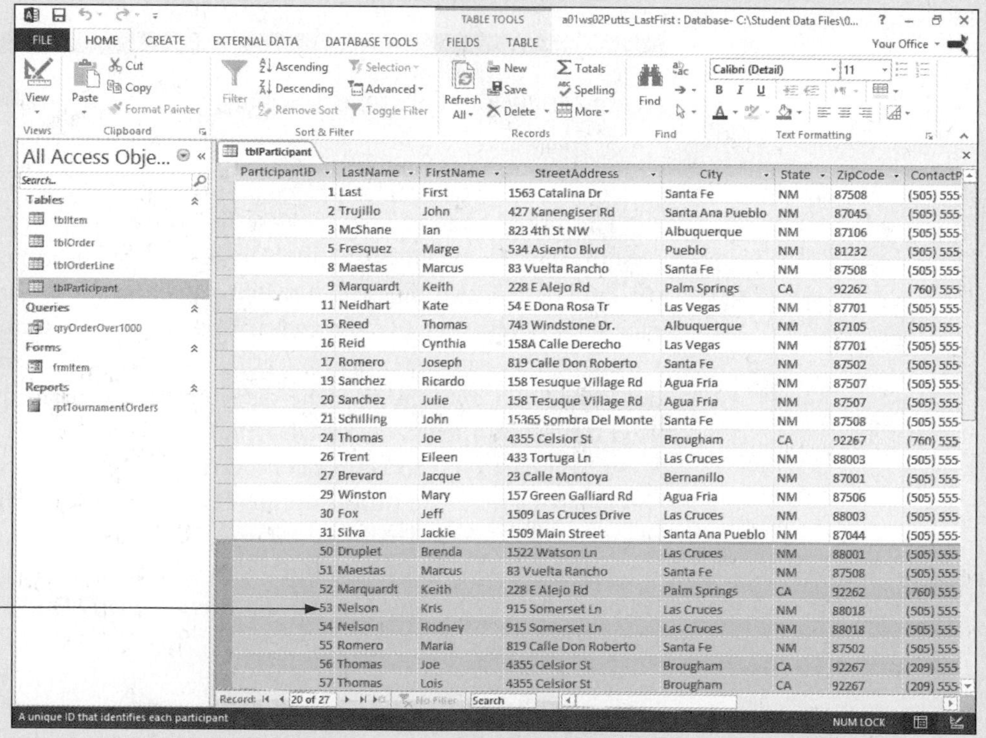

Figure 3 New golfers at the end of the tblParticipant table

MODULE 1

Troubleshooting

If you accidently click in a single cell of the append row and try to paste there, you get the error message "The text is too long to be edited." It appears that you are trying to paste all the data into one cell, and Access will not let you continue. If this happens, click OK, indicating that you do not want to put all the text into the one cell.

After that it may be difficult to exit that row and click in the record selector column. It appears you are trying to paste an invalid row, and Access will not let you continue. You will get an error message saying "Index or primary key cannot contain a Null value." When you click OK and try to recover, the message will reappear. If this happens, press Esc indicating that you do not want to keep that record.

h. **Close** ☒ the tblParticipant table.

REAL WORLD ADVICE **Copying and Pasting from Excel into Access**

Copying and pasting requires that the columns be exactly the same in Excel and Access. There cannot be missing columns or columns in different orders. You cannot paste fields that are nonnumeric into numeric fields. If you have any doubt about the data being compatible, use the Import feature to append the data to the table.

Use Copy and Paste when:

- You started in Access and exported the data to Excel, made additions, and now want to import it into Access. That way you know that the columns are the same.
- You are copying and pasting the contents of a single field from Excel into Access, such as a street address.

Importing a Worksheet

Access allows you to import an entire worksheet or a smaller portion of a worksheet into a table. This is quite useful as Excel is so frequently used in organizations. Excel column headings are frequently imported as field names.

The golf club has been keeping corporate contacts for the event in an Excel worksheet. You will import this Excel worksheet into your tblParticipant table.

A02.03

To Import an Excel Spreadsheet

a. On the Windows taskbar, click **Excel**, click the **FILE** tab, and then click **Close**.

b. Click the **FILE** tab, and then click **Open**. Navigate to your student data files, click **a01ws02PuttsCont**, and then click **Open**.

Notice that the contacts data looks like the tblParticipant table in many ways. However, the corporate phone number immediately follows the participant's name rather than being at the end of the record as it is in the Access table. An import from Excel into an existing Access table is ideal for this type of import because as long as the columns have the same name, Access will match up the columns, skipping any missing column. You cannot copy and paste the way you did earlier because the columns are not arranged in the same order.

CorporatePhoneNumber immediately follows FirstName

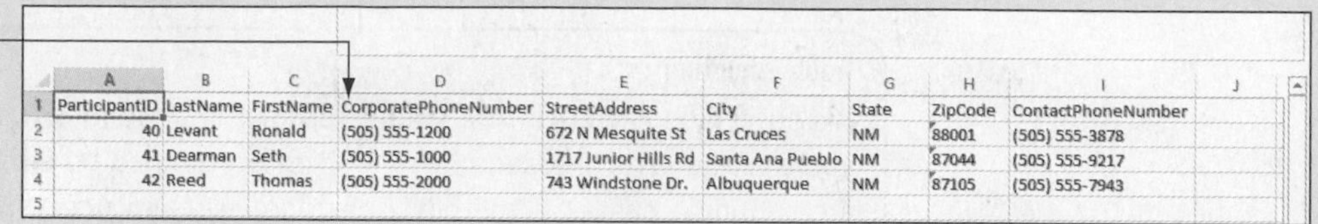

	A	B	C	D	E	F	G	H	I	J
1	ParticipantID	LastName	FirstName	CorporatePhoneNumber	StreetAddress	City	State	ZipCode	ContactPhoneNumber	
2	40	Levant	Ronald	(505) 555-1200	672 N Mesquite St	Las Cruces	NM	88001	(505) 555-3878	
3	41	Dearman	Seth	(505) 555-1000	1717 Junior Hills Rd	Santa Ana Pueblo	NM	87044	(505) 555-9217	
4	42	Reed	Thomas	(505) 555-2000	743 Windstone Dr.	Albuquerque	NM	87105	(505) 555-7943	
5										

Figure 4 Contact data in Excel

c. **Close** [X] Excel.

d. In Access, click the **EXTERNAL DATA** tab, and then in the Import & Link group, click **Excel**. The Get External Data - Excel Spreadsheet dialog box appears.

e. Click **Browse**, navigate to your student data files, click **a01ws02PuttsCont**, and then click **Open**. Select **Append a copy of the records to the table**, click the **arrow**, select **tblParticipant**, and then click **OK**.

The Import Spreadsheet Wizard opens, which displays worksheets and named ranges in the Excel workbook.

f. Make sure **Show Worksheets** is selected and the **Corporate contacts** worksheet is highlighted, and then click **Next**.

Access displays the next page of the wizard. This shows that Access found the column headings in Excel and matched them to the field names in Access.

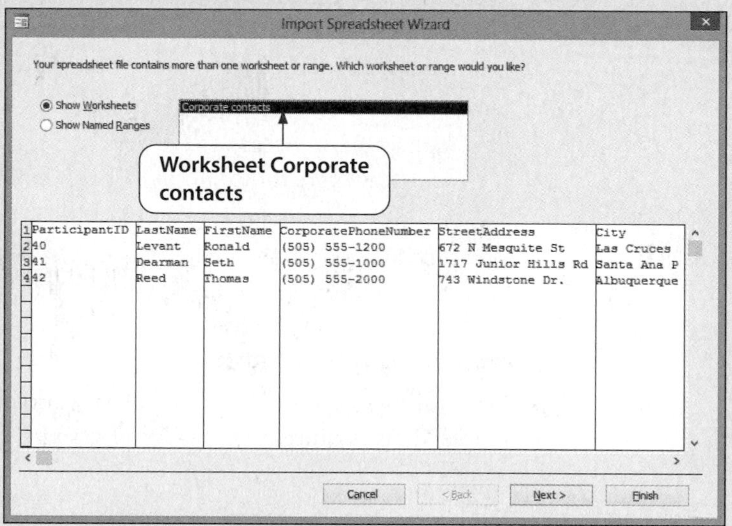

Figure 5 Worksheet to be imported

g. Click **Next**, click **Finish**, and then click **Close**.

h. In the Navigation Pane, double-click the **tblParticipant table** to open the table.

Your table has the three corporate contacts added. The contacts were imported and because the field names in Access matched the Excel column headings, the fields were rearranged to match the Access table order.

SIDE NOTE

Tables Are Ordered by Primary Key

When you added the contacts, they were added in the middle of the table because Access orders tables by primary key.

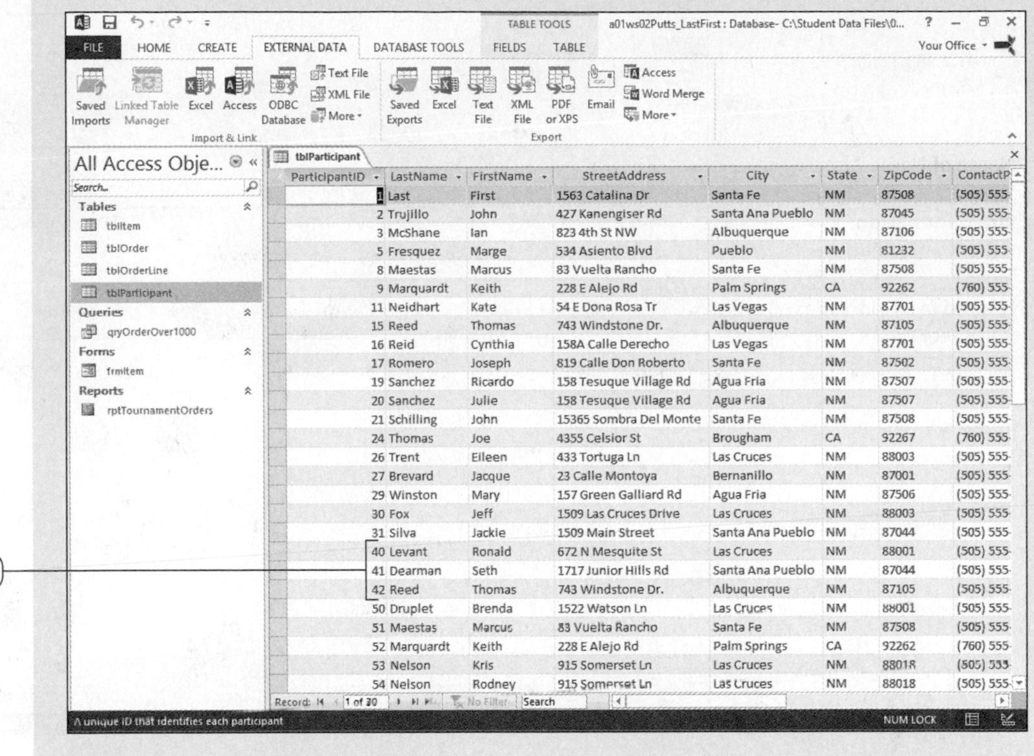

Figure 6 Corporate contacts imported into tblParticipant table

i. **Close** [X] the tblParticipant table.

Importing from a Named Range

Access allows you to import a smaller portion of a worksheet, known as a named range, into a table. A named range is a group of cells that have been given a name that can then be used within a formula or function. This part of the worksheet can then be referenced in formulas or charts by name rather than by cell address or range address.

The golf club has been keeping information about the volunteers for the event in an Excel worksheet. This worksheet contains other information about volunteering that you will not need. The range containing the contact information for the volunteers has been named VolunteerNamesAddress.

A02.04

To Import a Named Range

a. Start **Excel 2013**, and then open **a01ws02PuttsVol**.

Notice the Volunteers worksheet contains the volunteer information as well as other data.

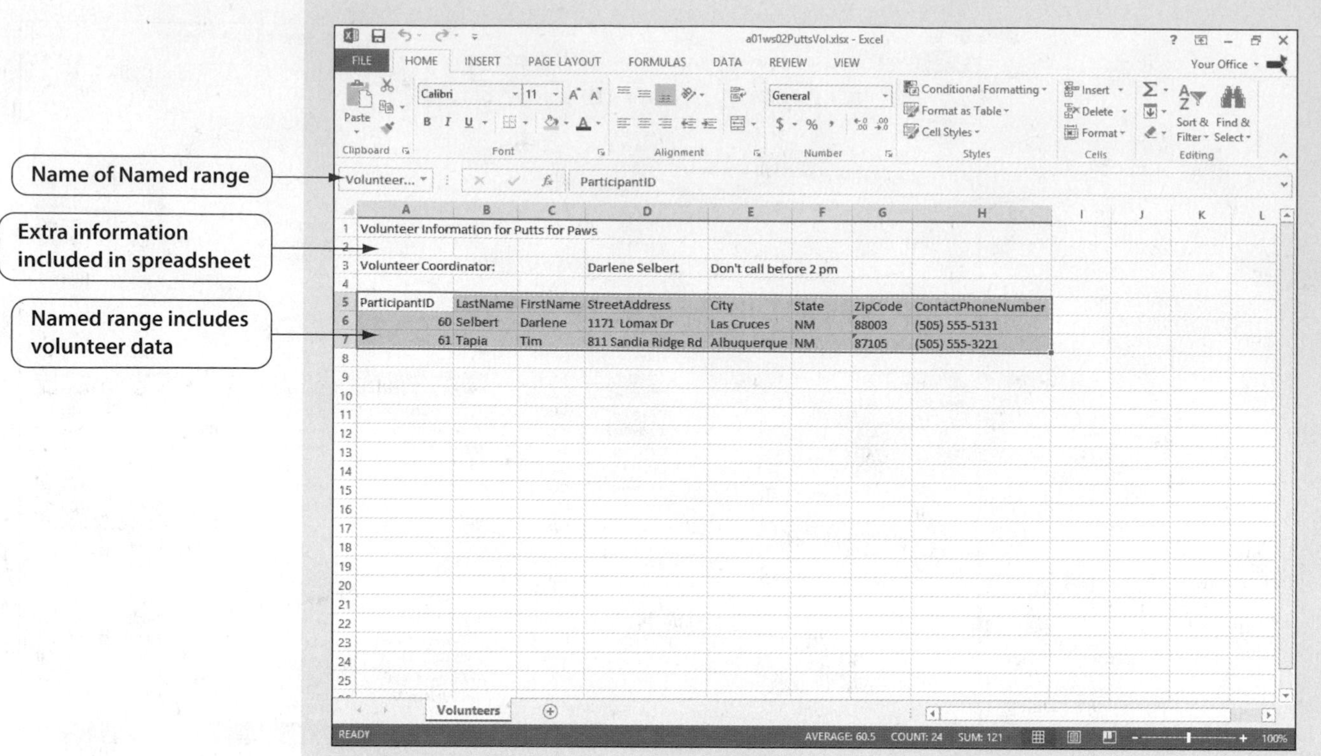

Figure 7 Volunteers worksheet with extra information

b. **Close** ☒ Excel.

c. In Access, click the **EXTERNAL DATA** tab, and then in the Import & Link group, click **Excel**. The Get External Data - Excel Spreadsheet dialog box appears.

d. Click **Browse**, navigate to your student data files, click **a01ws02PuttsVol**, and then click **Open**.

e. Select **Append a copy of the records to the table**, click the **arrow**, and then select **tblParticipant**.

f. Click **OK**, and then click **Show Named Ranges**.
   One named range, VolunteerNamesAddress, is displayed and highlighted in the list box.

g. Click **Next**. Access tells you that it found your column headings in Excel and matched them to the field names in Access. Click **Next**.

h. Click **Finish**, and then click **Close**.

i. In the Navigation Pane, double-click the **tblParticipant table** to open the table. Your table has the two volunteers added.

j. **Close** ☒ the tblParticipant table.

Importing from a Text File

Access enables you to import data from text and Word files. Typically these files would have data organized in tables. In Word, these tables will have actual rows and columns. In text files, the tables are implied by the separation of the columns. This separation is done by delimiter characters. A **delimiter** is a character such as a tab or comma that separates the fields. The rows in the text tables will be imported as records into your Access table.

The golf course has been keeping information about the donors for the event in a text file. You want to import that data into your Access database.

A02.05

To Import from a Text File

a. Point to the **bottom-right corner** of the screen. The Charms will be displayed on the right side of the screen. Click the **Search** charm.

b. Click inside the **search box** at the top of the page, type Notepad and then click **Notepad** in the search results.

c. Click **File**, click **Open**, and in the Open dialog box in the left pane, navigate to your student data files, click **a01ws02PuttsDon**, and then click **Open**.

   Notice that there are three donors in this file. The fields are separated by unseen tabs.

d. **Close** Notepad.

> **Troubleshooting**
>
> Your columns may not line up the way that Figure 8 shows them lining up. This happens because Notepad does not save font formatting. Notepad does save tabs so you do not need to worry about any display differences.

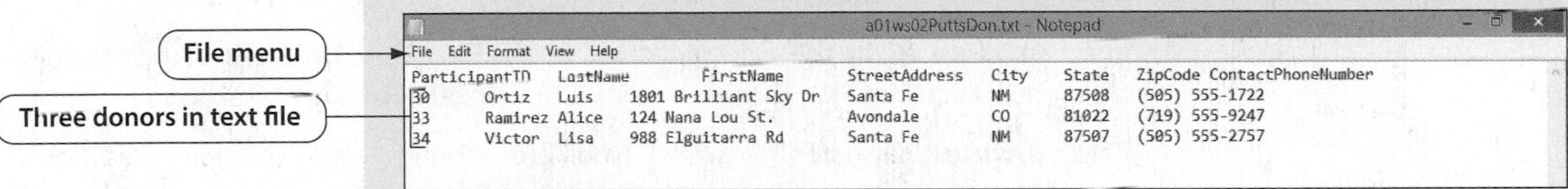

Figure 8 Donor text file in Notepad

e. In Access, click the **EXTERNAL DATA** tab, and then in the Import & Link group, click **Text File**. The Get External Data - Text File dialog box appears.

f. Click **Browse**, navigate to your student data files, click **a01ws02PuttsDon**, and then click **Open**.

g. Click **Append a copy of the records to the table**, click the **arrow** to select **tblParticipant**, and then click **OK**. Access recognizes that this data has columns that are delimited—separated by tabs or commas.

h. Click **Next**, select the **Tab** delimiter, and then click to select the **First Row Contains Field Names** check box.

i. Click **Next**, and then click **Finish**.

   An error message appears saying that Access is unable to append all the data to the table and that one record was lost because of key violations. The first field in your table is a primary key that must be unique. Apparently one of the donors has a ParticipantID that was already used in the Access table.

j. Click **No**, click **OK**, click **OK**, and then click **Cancel**.

k. Double-click **tblParticipant** to open the table in Datasheet view.

l. Open **Notepad**, click **File,** select **Open...**, navigate to your student data files, click **a01ws02PuttsDon**, and then click **Open**. There are three donors in the file that have ParticipantIDs of 30, 33, and 34 as shown in Figure 8.

m. Compare the donor data in the text file to the records in the tblParticipant table. Notice ParticipantID 30 has been used twice, once for Jeff Fox in the Access table and once for Luis Ortiz in the Notepad file. You talk to the person keeping records of donors and discover she meant to type "32" for Luis Ortiz.

n. In Notepad, click **File**, and then click **Save As**. In the Save As dialog box, navigate to the location where you are saving your files. In the **File** name box, type a01ws02PuttsDon_LastFirst using your last and first name. Click **Save**.

> **Troubleshooting**
> If your Save As dialog box does not show folders, click Browse Folders at the bottom of the dialog box.

o. In Notepad, select the text **30**, and then type 32.

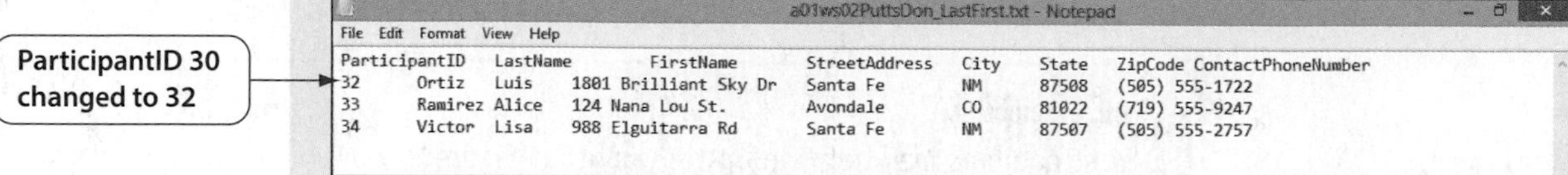

Figure 9 Change ParticipantID from 30 to 32

p. **Close** Notepad, and then save the file.

q. In Access, **close** the tblParticipant table. On the EXTERNAL DATA tab, in the Import & Link group, click **Text File**. The Get External Data - Text File dialog box appears.

r. Click **Browse**, navigate to where you are storing your solution files, click **a01ws02PuttsDon_LastFirst**, and then click **Open**.

s. Repeat the import Steps g–i. This time Access successfully imports the donors.

t. Click **Close**. Double-click **tblParticipant** to open the table and verify that the records for Luis Ortiz, Alice Ramirez, and Lisa Victor were imported.

u. **Close** the tblParticipant table.

REAL WORLD ADVICE | Importing an Excel Worksheet into a New Table

In all the previous examples of importing, you imported into an already existing table. You can also import into a new table. Access creates a table using the column headings for field names. Access defines fields with default definitions. After performing the import, open the table in Design view and adjust fields and properties as necessary. Some things that you should consider in these adjustments are the following:

- What field did Access assign as the primary key for the table? Access defaults to creating a new field called ID for the primary key. Later in the workshop, you will learn what field might work better as a primary key.
- The default length for all short text fields is 255 characters. Adjust the field size properties to sizes that are appropriate for your fields. Check all field definitions for errors.
- Are the field names descriptive? The column headings from Excel might not be appropriate as field names in Access.

Enter Data Manually

If the data does not already exist in another form, you can type the data directly into Access. There are two methods: entering data directly into the table or entering the data in a form.

Entering Data Using Datasheet View

When you open a table in Datasheet view, you can type data directly into the table. You want to enter a new order. You will need to enter data into tblOrder and the details of the order in tblOrderLine. The order to enter is your own; you are entering the tournament as a golfer.

A02.06

To Enter Data in Datasheet View

a. In the Navigation Pane, double-click **tblOrder**, click in the **AmountPaid** column of the append row, and then type 200.

As you type the "200", a pencil icon appears in the record selector on the left. The pencil icon means that this record is actively being modified. Additionally, the OrderID was filled in with "12". This happens because the field has a data type of AutoNumber, which means that Access assigns the next highest number.

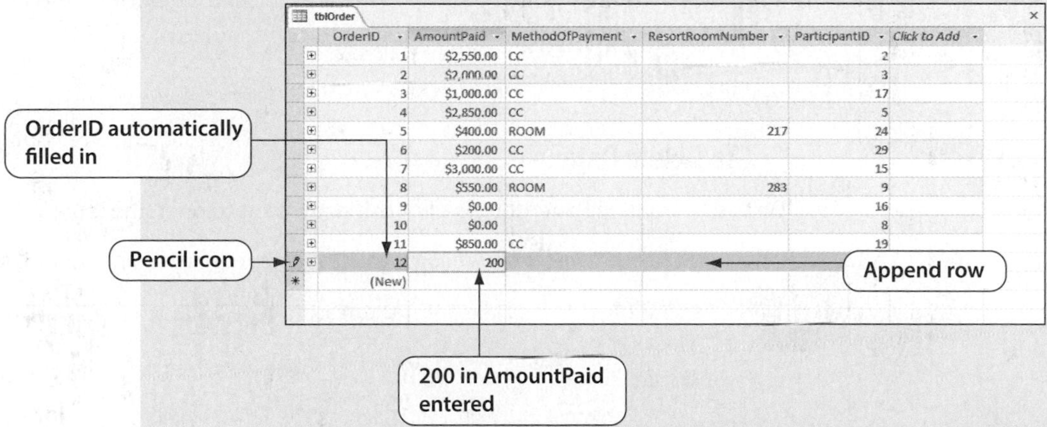

Figure 10 Type 200 in AmountPaid

b. Press Tab to continue filling in the record with a MethodOfPayment of CC, leave the ResortRoomNumber empty, and then type 1 in ParticipantID.

c. Press Tab to go to the next record. The pencil icon disappears. Unlike Word and Excel, Access immediately saves the data change.

d. **Close** X the tblOrder table.

e. In the Navigation Pane, double-click **tblOrderLine**, click in **OrderID** of the append row, and then type 12.

f. Press Tab to continue filling in the record with LineNum 1, ItemID G1, and Quantity 1.

g. **Close** X the tblOrderLine table.

REAL WORLD ADVICE | Undoing in Access

Access immediately saves the changes you make to data. There is very limited undo/redo functionality in Access. If the Undo button is dimmed, you cannot undo the change you made.

- Typically you can undo a single typing change even if you have gone on to the next record. However, if you made several changes to different records, you cannot undo more than the changes to the last record.
- If you have made changes to several fields in a single record, you can click Undo to undo each of them.
- You can also press Esc to stop editing a record and revert to the record data as it appeared before you started changing the record.
- If you make an error, you can press Esc to get out of the error.

Because of the limited undo features in Access, do not count on undoing your changes. You will often find that you cannot undo. For example, when you delete a record or records, you cannot undo the deletion.

Design changes are not saved until you save the object you changed. Thus, you can undo design changes until you save.

Removing Data

You can delete records from a table. These are permanent deletions and cannot be undone. Golfer Kate Neidhart needs to withdraw from the tournament.

A02.07

To Delete Data in Datasheet View

a. In the Navigation Pane, double-click **tblParticipant** to open the table in Datasheet view.

b. Click the **record selector** for record 7, Kate Neidhart, ParticipantID 11, to select the row.

Figure 11 Delete Kate Neidhart record

c. Right-click the **row**, and then select **Delete Record**. Because you cannot undo a delete, Access asks if you are sure you want to delete this record.

d. Click **Yes**. The record is deleted.

> **Troubleshooting**
> If you do not get the Access confirmation message asking if you are sure you want the deletion to occur, the confirmation message setting may be turned off. If you would like to turn it back on, on the File tab, click Options, and then click Client Settings. Scroll down to find the Confirm section under Editing, click the Document deletions check box, and click OK.

You can also delete individual fields from a table. These are also permanent deletions and cannot be undone. You decide that you will create a table for corporations involved with the tournament, tblCorporate, and that the CorporatePhoneNumber will be a part of that table. Thus, you will not need CorporatePhoneNumber for each tblParticipant record, and you will delete that field. You can delete a field in either Design view or Datasheet view. In Datasheet view, you can see the contents of the field that you are deleting, which gives you an extra check on whether you really want to delete the field.

A02.08

To Delete a Field in Datasheet View

a. Scroll to the right to find the **CorporatePhoneNumber** column. Point to the **column heading** until it changes to a black down arrow, and then click so the entire column is highlighted. Make sure that you selected **CorporatePhoneNumber** and not **ContactPhoneNumber**.

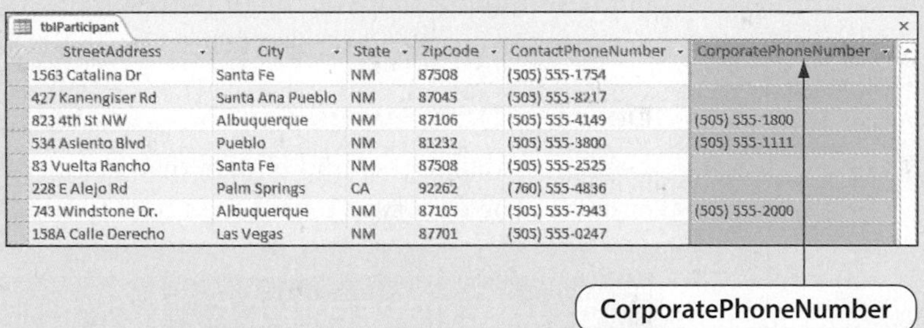
tblParticipant

StreetAddress	City	State	ZipCode	ContactPhoneNumber	CorporatePhoneNumber
1563 Catalina Dr	Santa Fe	NM	87508	(505) 555-1754	
427 Kanengiser Rd	Santa Ana Pueblo	NM	87045	(505) 555-8217	
823 4th St NW	Albuquerque	NM	87106	(505) 555-4149	(505) 555-1800
534 Asiento Blvd	Pueblo	NM	81232	(505) 555-3800	(505) 555-1111
83 Vuelta Rancho	Santa Fe	NM	87508	(505) 555-2525	
228 E Alejo Rd	Palm Springs	CA	92262	(760) 555-4836	
743 Windstone Dr.	Albuquerque	NM	87105	(505) 555-7943	(505) 555-2000
158A Calle Derecho	Las Vegas	NM	87701	(505) 555-0247	

Figure 12 Select the CorporatePhoneNumber column

b. Click the **HOME** tab, and then in the Records group, click **Delete**.
Because you cannot undo a delete, Access asks, "Do you want to permanently delete the selected field(s) and all the data in the field(s)? To permanently delete the field(s), click Yes." Because you are in Datasheet view, you can glance at it and make sure this is the data you want to delete.

c. Click **Yes**. The column is deleted.

d. **Close** [X] the tblParticipant table.

> **Troubleshooting**
> If when you clicked in the column heading you accidently double-clicked and then clicked Delete, Access blanked out the field name rather than deleting the column. This put you in edit mode, ready to rename the field. Press [Esc] to cancel edit mode and try again.

Understanding Tables and Keys

Now that you have imported data into the tblParticipant table, you need to further examine and evaluate how the tables have been set up. Tables represent entities—or people, places, things, or events that you want to track. Each row represents a single person, place, and so on. To identify that entity, you use a primary key field. A **primary key** field is a field that uniquely identifies the record; it can be any data type, but it should be a field that will not change. For example, a person's name is not a good primary key for two reasons. First of all, it is not unique—several people may have the same name, and second, a person's name could change. If you define a primary key for a table, the field cannot be blank.

In this section, you will create a table from scratch, minimize file size, facilitate quick data entry, minimize errors, and encourage data consistency as shown in Table 2.

Goal	Example
Minimize file size	If a field is an integer that is always less than 32,767, use Integer rather than Long Integer to define the field.
Facilitate quick data entry, including removing redundant data	Store a state abbreviation rather than the state name spelled out.
Minimize errors	Use the Date/Time data type for dates and not a Text data type. Access will then only accept valid dates, and not 2/31/2013, which is invalid.
Encourage data consistency	Use a Yes/No check box rather than having the word Yes or No typed into a text field where misspellings could occur.

Table 2 Table design goals

Create a Table in Design View

You want to keep track of corporations who are involved with the tournament. You do not have a source that you can import, so you will need to design and create the table. You will use Design view to enter fields, data types, and descriptions.

Defining Data Types

Data types define the kind of data that can be entered into a field, such as numbers, text, or dates. The data type tells Access how to store and display the field.

QUICK REFERENCE | **Data Types**

Data Type	Description	Examples
Short Text	Used to store textual or character information. Any character or number can be entered into this type of field. You should store any data that will never be used in calculations, such as a Social Security number, as text, not a number. There is an upper limit of 255 characters that can be stored in a Short Text field.	Names, addresses
Long Text	Used to capture large amounts of text. Can store up to 1 gigabyte of characters, of which you can display 65,535 characters in a control on a form or report. This is a good data type to use if you need more than 255 characters in one field.	Comments
Number	Used for numeric data.	Quantity

Data Type	Description	Examples
Date/Time	Used to store a date and/or time.	Start time
Currency	A numeric value that is used for units of currency. It follows the regional settings preset in Windows to determine what the default currency should be. In the United States, the data is displayed with a dollar sign and two decimal places.	Salary
AutoNumber	Used for keys. Access generates the value by automatically incrementing the value for each new record to produce unique keys. For example, it would set the value as 1 for the first record, 2 for the next, and 3 for the third.	ProductID
Yes/No	A checked box where an empty box is no, and a checked box is yes.	EntryPaid
OLE Object	Use to attach an OLE object, such as a Microsoft Office Excel worksheet, to a record. An OLE object means that when you open the object, you open it in its original application such as Excel. It allows cross-application editing.	SalarySpreadsheet
Hyperlink	Text or combinations of text and numbers stored as text and used as a hyperlink address.	CompanyWebsite
Attachment	Images, worksheet files, documents, charts, and other types of supported files that are attached to the records in your database, similar to attaching files to e-mail messages.	EmployeePhoto
Calculated	A field calculated from other fields in the table. A calculated field may not be edited as it performs a calculation on other data that is entered.	GrossPay, which is calculated based upon HoursWorked and HourlySalary
Lookup Wizard	Lists either values retrieved from a table or query, or a set of values that you specified when you created the field.	ProductType, which gives a list of valid types

REAL WORLD ADVICE **Number or Text?**

Any character can be used in a text field. However, if you expect a field to contain only numbers, you should only store the data in a text field if the numbers will never be used in a calculation. If you store numbers as text, you cannot use them in calculations. Conversely, if you improperly store numeric text as a number, Access will remove any leading zeros. For example, you would not use zip codes in calculations, so a zip code should be stored as text. A person living in Boston might have a zip code of 02108. If you stored the zip code as a number, Access would convert this to 2108.

Determining Field Size

Field size indicates the maximum length of a data field. Whenever you use a Text data type, you should determine the maximum number of text characters that can exist in the data to be stored. That number would then be the field size. For example, a state abbreviation can only be two characters long, so the size for this field should be 2. If you allow more than two characters, you are likely to get a mix of abbreviations and spelled-out state names. Limiting the size will limit errors in the data. There is an upper limit of 255 characters for a Short Text field. If you need more than 255 characters, use a Long Text data type.

For numeric fields, the type defines the maximum length or range of values. You should use the number size that best suits your needs. For example, if a value in a field is always going to be a whole number and is never going to be above 32,768 then Integer is the best field size. If the number is currency, you should use the Currency data type instead of Number.

QUICK REFERENCE | **Number Field Sizes**

Field Size	Description
Byte	For integers that range from 0 to 255. These numbers can be stored in a single byte.
Integer	For integers that range from –32,768 to +32,767. Must be whole numbers. Integers cannot have decimal places.
Long Integer	For integers that range from –2,147,483,648 to +2,147,483,647. Long Integers cannot have decimal places. (AutoNumber is a long integer.)
Single	For large numbers with up to seven significant digits. Can contain decimal places. Numbers can be negative or positive. For numeric floating point values that range from -3.4×10^{38} to $+3.4 \times 10^{38}$.
Double	For very large numbers with up to 15 significant digits. Can contain decimal places. Numbers can be negative or positive. For numeric floating point values that range from -1.797×10^{308} to $+1.797 \times 10^{308}$.
Decimal	For numeric values that contain decimal places. Numbers can be negative or positive. For numeric values that range from $-9.999... \times 10^{27}$ to $+9.999... \times 10^{27}$.

You determine that your corporation table, tblCorporate, should contain the company name, address, and phone number.

A02.09

To Create a Table in Design View

a. Click the **CREATE** tab, and then in the Tables group, click **Table Design**.
   Access opens a blank table in Design view. You will enter each field in the appropriate row.

b. Type **CompanyName** for the Field Name, and then press Tab to move to the Data Type column.
   Notice that Short Text is the default data type, so you do not need to make a selection to keep Short Text for this field. For other data types, click the arrow and select the data type.

c. Press Tab to move to the Description column, and then type **Company name**.

d. In the Field Properties pane, type **50** in the Field Size box.

SIDE NOTE
Select Data Type
Alternatively, you can type the first letter of the data type, and it will appear, such as "N" for Number.

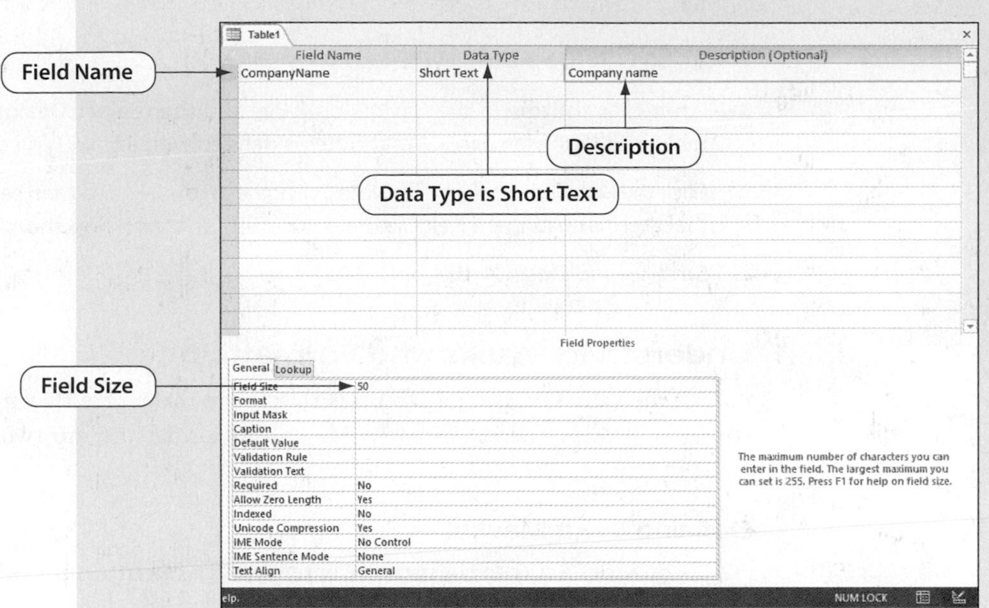

Figure 13 First field in the tblCorporate table

e. Continue defining the table with the following information, being sure to enter maximum length in the Field Size box.

Field Name	Data Type	Description	Field Size
StreetAddress	Short Text	Company's street address	40
City	Short Text	Company's city	40
State	Short Text	State abbreviation	2
ZipCode	Short Text	Zip code either 5- or 9-character format	10
PhoneNumber	Short Text	Phone number with area code	14

f. **Save** the table, and name it tblCorporate and then click **OK**. In the warning message that asks if you want to create a primary key, click **No**. You will define a key later.

g. **Close** the tblCorporate table.

Changing Data Type

In Design view, you can change the size of a field. If you decide that a field length needs to be longer, you can change the field without concern. If you make a field length shorter and there were data that needed the longer length, you may truncate those values. For that reason, Access will always warn you that data may be lost if you change the length to a smaller size.

The tblItem table has a Notes field that has a data type of Short Text. The tournament director asks you to change that to have a data type of Long Text so that full comments can be added for items.

A02.10

To Change a Data Type

a. Right-click **tblItem** in the Navigation Pane, and then select **Design View** to open the table in Design view. Notice that Notes is defined with a Data Type of Short Text.

b. Click the **Data Type** column for Notes, click the **arrow** [▾], and then select **Long Text**. Note that there is no longer a Field Size field. Long Text does not show the maximum field length.

c. **Save** [💾] and **close** [X] the table.

Understand Masks and Formatting

One of the values of using a DBMS is that it can make sure that information is entered, stored, and displayed consistently. Masks and formatting are two of the methods that assist in that process.

Defining Input Masks

Access provides a way to consistently enter data, called **input masks**. For example, phone numbers can be typed (555) 555-5555, 555-5555, or 555-555-5555. An input mask defines a consistent template and provides the punctuation, so you do not have to type it. Access also has a wizard that creates automatic masks for Social Security numbers, zip codes, passwords, extensions, dates, and times. You can also create your own custom masks. Input masks can affect how data is stored.

A02.11

To Create an Input Mask

a. Right-click **tblCorporate** in the Navigation Pane, and then select **Design View** to open the table in Design view.

b. Click the **PhoneNumber** Field Name to select the PhoneNumber field. In the Field Properties pane, click in the **Input Mask** box.

c. Click the **Build** button [...] to start the Input Mask Wizard. If necessary, select **Phone Number**.

d. Click **Next** to start the phone number Input Mask Wizard.

   Access suggests the format !(999) 000-0000. This means that the area code is optional and will be enclosed in parentheses. The rest of the phone number is required and will have a dash between the two parts. The exclamation mark specifies that characters should be typed from left to right.

e. Click **Next** to accept the format.

f. Access asks if you want to store the symbols with the data. Select **With the symbols in the mask, like this**.

g. Click **Next**, and then click **Finish**.

SIDE NOTE

Semicolons in Mask

The semicolons indicate that there are three sections of the mask. The dash in the last section shows the placeholder.

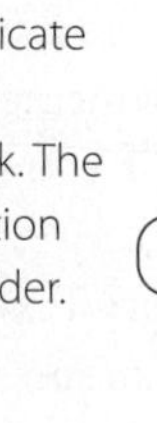

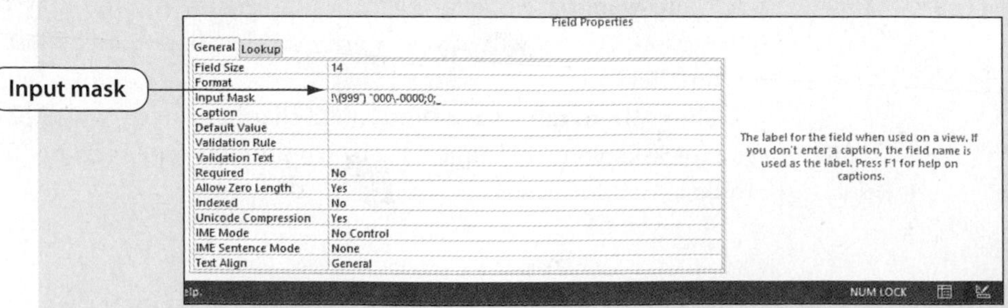

Figure 14 Finished input mask

h. **Save** [save icon] the table design. On the DESIGN tab, in the Views group, click the **View** arrow, and then select **Datasheet View**.

i. Notice that the columns are not wide enough for the entire heading text to show. Move your mouse pointer to the border between **CompanyName** and **StreetAddress** until it becomes the Horizontal resize pointer [+], and then double-click the **border** to widen the column.

j. Double-click the **border** after the **StreetAddress** and **PhoneNumber** headings to widen the columns.

k. Click in the **append row** for **CompanyName**, and then type Tesuque Mirage Market. Press Tab to move to **StreetAddress**.

l. Continue entering the records as follows.

CompanyName	StreetAddress	City	State	ZipCode	PhoneNumber
Tesuque Mirage Market	8 Tesuque Mirage Rd	Santa Fe	NM	87506	(505) 555-1111
Hotel Playa Real	125 Madison Avenue	Santa Fe	NM	87508	(505) 555-1800
Bouzouki Museum	716 Camino Cercano	Santa Fe	NM	87505	(505) 555-1200
McDoakes Restaurant	2017 High St	Santa Fe	NM	87501	(505) 555-1000
Benson & Diaz	1953 A Piazza Pl, Suite 101	Santo Domingo	NM	87052	(505) 555-2000

m. **Close** [X] the tblCorporate table, and then in the Microsoft Access dialog box click **Yes** to save the layout.

SIDE NOTE

Masks Save Keystrokes

Notice that the phone number mask that you entered means that you do not need to type the parentheses and dashes in the phone number.

Formatting

In a table design, you can define a Format field property that customizes how data is displayed and printed in tables, queries, reports, and forms. The **Format** property tells Access how data is to be displayed. It does not affect the way the data is stored. For example, you can specify that currency fields are displayed in dollars, such as $1,234.56 in American databases, or in euros, such as €1.234,56 in European databases. Formats are available for Date/Time, Number, Currency, and Yes/No data types. You can also define your own custom formats for Short Text and Long Text fields.

QUICK REFERENCE | Format Field Property

Data Type	Format	Example
Date/Time	General Date	11/9/2015 10:10:10 PM
	Long Date	Wednesday, November 9, 2015
	Medium Date	9-Nov-15
	Short Date	11/9/2015
	Long Time	10:10:10 PM
	Medium Time	10:10 PM
	Short Time	22:10
Number and Currency	General Number	Display the number as entered
	Currency	Follows the regional settings preset in Windows. In the United States: $1,234.56. In much of Europe, €1.234,56.
	Euro	Uses the euro symbol regardless of the Windows setting.
	Fixed	Displays at least one digit after the decimal point. In the Decimal Places property, you choose how many fixed digits to show after the decimal point.
	Standard	Use the regional settings preset in Windows for the thousands divider. 1,234 in the United States; 1.234 in much of Europe.
	Percent	Multiply the value by 100 and follow with %.
	Scientific	Use standard scientific notation, for example, 4.5E + 13.
Yes/No	Yes/No	Yes or No display options.
	True/False	True or False display options.
	On/Off	On or Off display options.

A02.12

To Define a Date Field

a. In the Navigation Pane, right-click **tblOrder**, and then select **Design View**.

b. In the first **blank row**, in the Field Name column, type OrderDate. Select a Data Type of **Date/Time**, and then enter a Description of Date order was placed.

c. Click in the **Format** box in the Field Properties pane.

d. Click the **Format** arrow, and then select **Short Date**.
Notice that the Property Update Options button appears. Clicking it would display an option to change the format of OrderDate wherever else it appears. Because it does not appear anywhere else yet, you do not need to click the button.

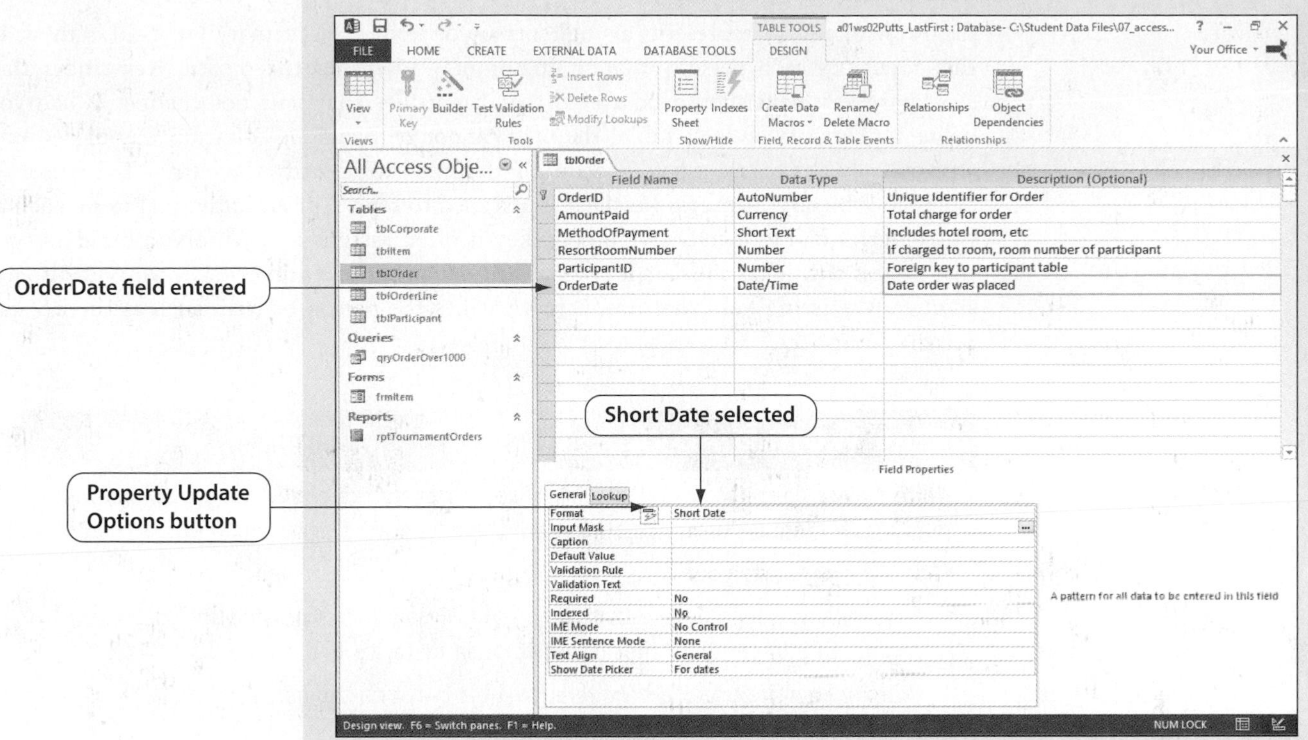

Figure 15 Adding a Short Date field

e. **Save** the table design, and then in the Views group, click the **View** button to switch to Datasheet view.

   The orders were placed on May 4, 2015, but no date was entered.

f. For the first order, in the OrderDate field type May 4, 2015. Press [↓] to move to the next record. Notice the display changes to **5/4/2015**, the short date format.

g. For the second order, type 05/04/2015 and then press [↓] to move to the next record. Again, the display changes to the new format.

h. For the next order, type May 4 15 and then press [↓] to move to the next record. Once again, the display changes to 5/4/2015.

i. Continue typing May 4 15 for all the orders.

j. **Close** the table.

CONSIDER THIS | Database Design Principles

Some principles for database design are shown in Table 2. How do field sizes, formatting, and input masks facilitate these principles? When would you use a format? When would you use an input mask?

Understand and Designate Keys

Each table should have a field that uniquely identifies each of the records in the table. This field is called the primary key. If you know the primary key, you know exactly what record you want. Another type of key is a **foreign key**. A foreign key is a value in a table that is the primary key of another table. The primary and foreign keys form the common field between tables that allow you to form a relationship between the two tables.

Understanding Primary Keys

Each row of a table represents a single person or item. The primary key field is the field that identifies each person or item. It uniquely identifies the record. Remember that a primary key field should be a field that has values that will not change. When you define a primary key for a table, the field cannot be blank. A common way of defining a primary key is to use a field specifically designed to identify the entity. This is sometimes an arbitrary **numeric key** that is assigned to represent an individual item, such as CustomerID or ProductID. A numeric key is often assigned an AutoNumber data type that Access will fill as the data is entered. Instead of using a numeric key, you can also use an already existing field that uniquely identifies the person or item such as their Social Security number.

REAL WORLD ADVICE | **Do You Need a Primary Key?**

While Access does not require a primary key for every table, you almost always want to give the table a primary key. What are the advantages of having a primary key?

- It helps organize your data. Each record is uniquely identified.
- Primary keys speed up access to your data. Primary keys provide an index to a record. In a large table, that makes it much faster to find a record.
- Primary keys are used to form relationships between tables.

Understanding Foreign Keys

A foreign key is a field in a table that stores a value that is the primary key in another table. It is called foreign because it does not identify a record in this table; it identifies a record in another—foreign—table. For example, you have two tables, tblParticipant and tblOrder, in your database. You want to know which participants have placed certain orders. The primary key for your Participant table is ParticipantID. You can add a field called ParticipantID to the Order table that indicates which participant placed the order. ParticipantID is the foreign key in the tblOrder table; it identifies the participant in the tblParticipant table. Figure 16 illustrates this relationship. Foreign keys do not need to be unique in the table. Participants can place several orders.

You will use the ParticipantID to form a relationship between the two tables later in this workshop.

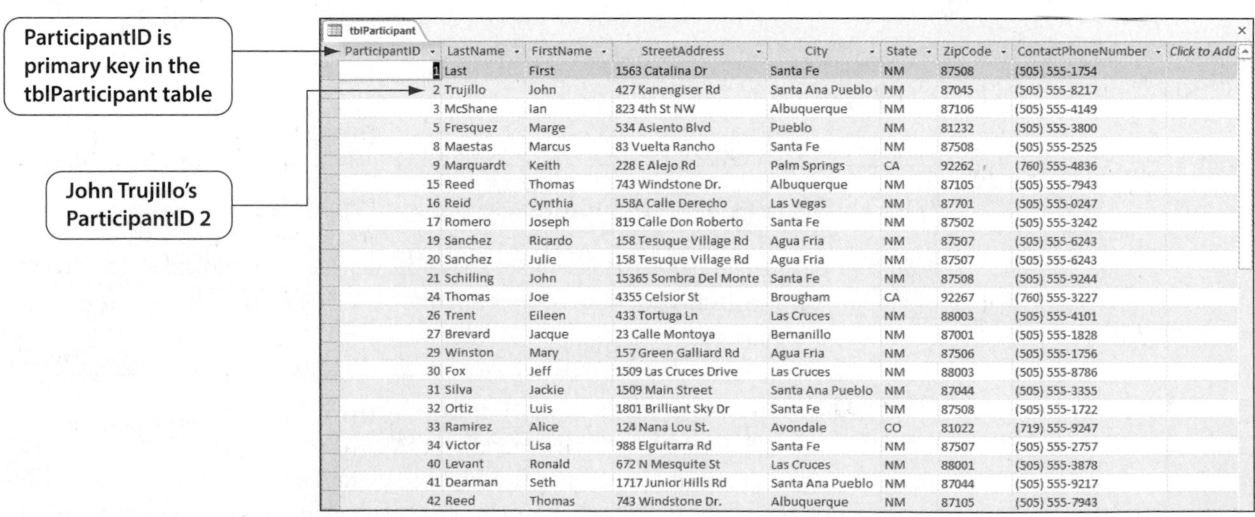

ParticipantID	LastName	FirstName	StreetAddress	City	State	ZipCode	ContactPhoneNumber	Click to Add
1	Last	First	1563 Catalina Dr	Santa Fe	NM	87508	(505) 555-1754	
2	Trujillo	John	427 Kanengiser Rd	Santa Ana Pueblo	NM	87045	(505) 555-8217	
3	McShane	Ian	823 4th St NW	Albuquerque	NM	87106	(505) 555-4149	
5	Fresquez	Marge	534 Asiento Blvd	Pueblo	NM	81232	(505) 555-3800	
8	Maestas	Marcus	83 Vuelta Rancho	Santa Fe	NM	87508	(505) 555-2525	
9	Marquardt	Keith	228 E Alejo Rd	Palm Springs	CA	92262	(760) 555-4836	
15	Reed	Thomas	743 Windstone Dr.	Albuquerque	NM	87105	(505) 555-7943	
16	Reid	Cynthia	158A Calle Derecho	Las Vegas	NM	87701	(505) 555-0247	
17	Romero	Joseph	819 Calle Don Roberto	Santa Fe	NM	87502	(505) 555-3242	
19	Sanchez	Ricardo	158 Tesuque Village Rd	Agua Fria	NM	87507	(505) 555-6243	
20	Sanchez	Julie	158 Tesuque Village Rd	Agua Fria	NM	87507	(505) 555-6243	
21	Schilling	John	15365 Sombra Del Monte	Santa Fe	NM	87508	(505) 555-9244	
24	Thomas	Joe	4355 Celsior St	Brougham	CA	92267	(760) 555-3227	
26	Trent	Eileen	433 Tortuga Ln	Las Cruces	NM	88003	(505) 555-4101	
27	Brevard	Jacque	23 Calle Montoya	Bernanillo	NM	87001	(505) 555-1828	
29	Winston	Mary	157 Green Galliard Rd	Agua Fria	NM	87506	(505) 555-1756	
30	Fox	Jeff	1509 Las Cruces Drive	Las Cruces	NM	88003	(505) 555-8786	
31	Silva	Jackie	1509 Main Street	Santa Ana Pueblo	NM	87044	(505) 555-3355	
32	Ortiz	Luis	1801 Brilliant Sky Dr	Santa Fe	NM	87508	(505) 555-1722	
33	Ramirez	Alice	124 Nana Lou St.	Avondale	CO	81022	(719) 555-9247	
34	Victor	Lisa	988 Elguitarra Rd	Santa Fe	NM	87507	(505) 555-2757	
40	Levant	Ronald	672 N Mesquite St	Las Cruces	NM	88001	(505) 555-3878	
41	Dearman	Seth	1717 Junior Hills Rd	Santa Ana Pueblo	NM	87044	(505) 555-9217	
42	Reed	Thomas	743 Windstone Dr.	Albuquerque	NM	87105	(505) 555-7943	

Figure 16 Relationship between tblParticipant and tblOrder tables

Continued

Continued

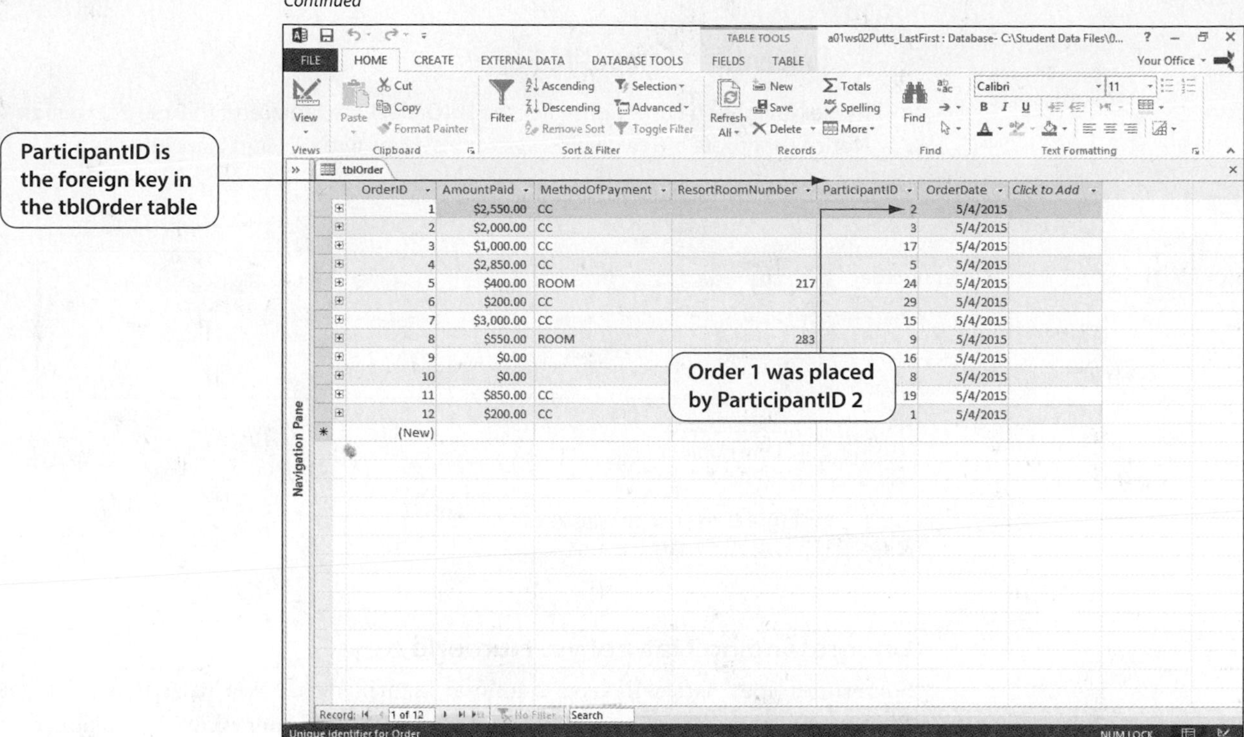

Figure 16 Relationship between tblParticipant and tblOrder tables

Composite Keys

Sometimes, two fields are needed to uniquely identify a record. In that case, both fields are used to create the key and are called a **composite key**. For example, a university might identify a class by subject area and course number. The university could have classes Math 101, Math 102, and MIS 101. It takes both subject and course number to identify a single course. The combination of the two fields is called a composite key.

A typical use of a composite key is on an order form. Figure 17 shows a paper form that the golf tournament organizers used before they used Access. To uniquely identify the items that have been ordered, a composite key can be made combining the order number with the line number of the order form. You notice that this composite key is used for orders in the golf tournament database.

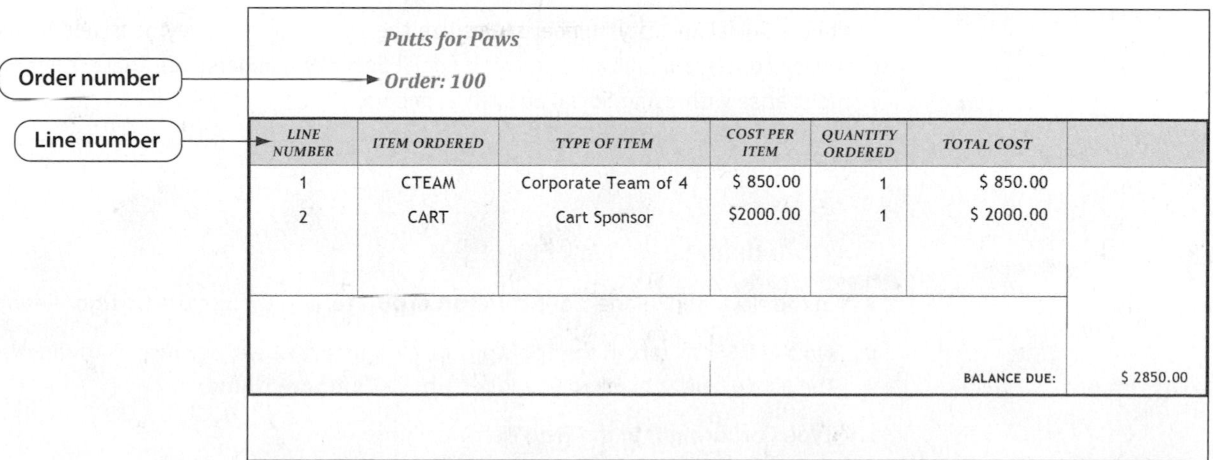

Putts for Paws

Order: 100

LINE NUMBER	ITEM ORDERED	TYPE OF ITEM	COST PER ITEM	QUANTITY ORDERED	TOTAL COST
1	CTEAM	Corporate Team of 4	$ 850.00	1	$ 850.00
2	CART	Cart Sponsor	$2000.00	1	$ 2000.00
					BALANCE DUE: $ 2850.00

Figure 17 Composite key on a paper order form

A02.13

To Identify a Composite Key

a. In the Navigation Pane, right-click the **tblOrderLine** table, and then select **Design View**. Notice that there are two fields marked as a key: OrderID and LineNum.

b. **Close** [X] the tblOrderLine table.

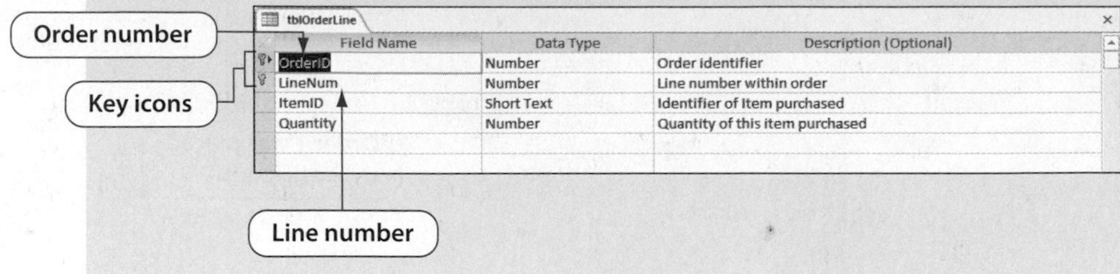

Figure 18 Composite key in the tblOrderLine table

Understanding Natural vs. Numeric Keys

Sometimes your data will have a unique identifier that is a natural part of your data. When that is true, you can use the field as a **natural primary key**. If you already identify orders by order number, that would make a good primary key.

The important point is that the natural primary key is a value that will not change. You might start by thinking that telephone number is a natural way to identify a customer. But people change their telephone numbers. When the natural key might change, it is better to use an arbitrary unique number to identify the customer. When natural keys do exist, they are favored over numeric keys.

You can use the data type AutoNumber for the primary key. In that case, Access will automatically assign a unique value for every record. You can also define a key as numeric, and fill the key values yourself.

You decide that you need to create a numeric primary key for your tblCorporate table named CorporateID. You will let Access automatically create the key by using an AutoNumber data type.

CONSIDER THIS | Social Security Number as a Primary Key

While a Social Security number seems like the perfect primary key, it is seldom used. What privacy concerns might arise in using Social Security numbers? Are there other issues that might arise with using Social Security numbers?

A02.14

To Define a Primary Key

a. In the Navigation Pane, right-click **tblCorporate**, and then select **Design View**.

b. On the DESIGN tab, in the Tools group, click **Insert Rows**. Because CompanyName was the active field, a blank row is added above **CompanyName**.

c. Type CorporateID in the Field Name column.

d. Select **AutoNumber** as the Data Type. The field size is set to Long Integer.

e. Type Unique corporate identifier in the Description column.

f. With the CorporateID row still selected, on the DESIGN tab, in the Tools group, click **Primary Key** to make "CorporateID" the primary key. A key icon is displayed in the record selector bar.

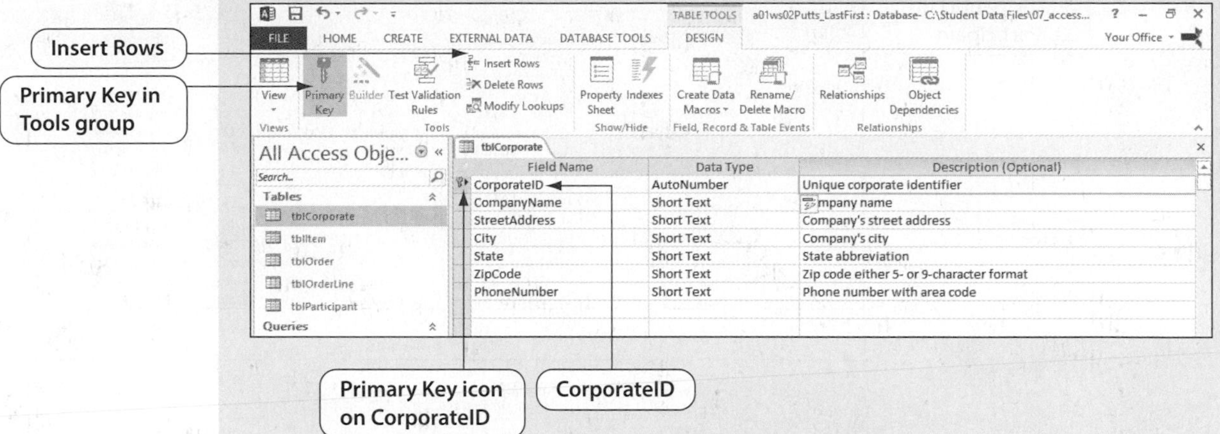

Figure 19 Defining a primary key

g. **Save** your table design. Click the **HOME** tab, and then in the Views group, click **View**. Notice that Access has populated the CorporateID field with automatic numbers starting at 1 and going through 5.

h. **Close** the tblCorporate table.

REAL WORLD ADVICE **Read Your Error Messages**

The error message "Index or primary key cannot contain a Null value" is one example of an error message that Access displays when you make changes to an Access database that would break the rules you set up in your table design. You should read the error message carefully to understand what it is telling you.

If you get the error message "Index or primary key cannot contain a Null value," that means that one of your records has no entry in the primary key field. Enter the primary key. Often the issue is that you accidently entered data in the append record. If you do not want that record to be created, press Esc to cancel the addition of the record.

Understanding Relational Databases

One of the benefits of using Access is the ability to add relationships to the tables. This allows you to work with two or more tables in the same query, report, or form. For the tournament database, when you relate tables together, you can ask such questions as "What golfers are playing for the Tesuque Mirage Market?", "Did the market agree to purchase any other items?", and "Have they paid for those items yet?"

Relationships in a relational database are created by joining the tables together. A **join** is created by creating a relationship between two tables based upon a common field in the two tables, as shown in Figure 20. The tblParticipant table has a field—column—named ParticipantID. tblOrder also has a field named ParticipantID. When you create the relationship, Access will match the ParticipantIDs between the two tables to find those participants that placed an order. Looking at the table, you can mentally join the two tables to see that John Trujillo has placed an order for $2,550. When Access runs a query, it uses an existing join to find the results. In this section, you will form relationships between tables, create a report, and check to make sure the relationships you are creating between tables make sense.

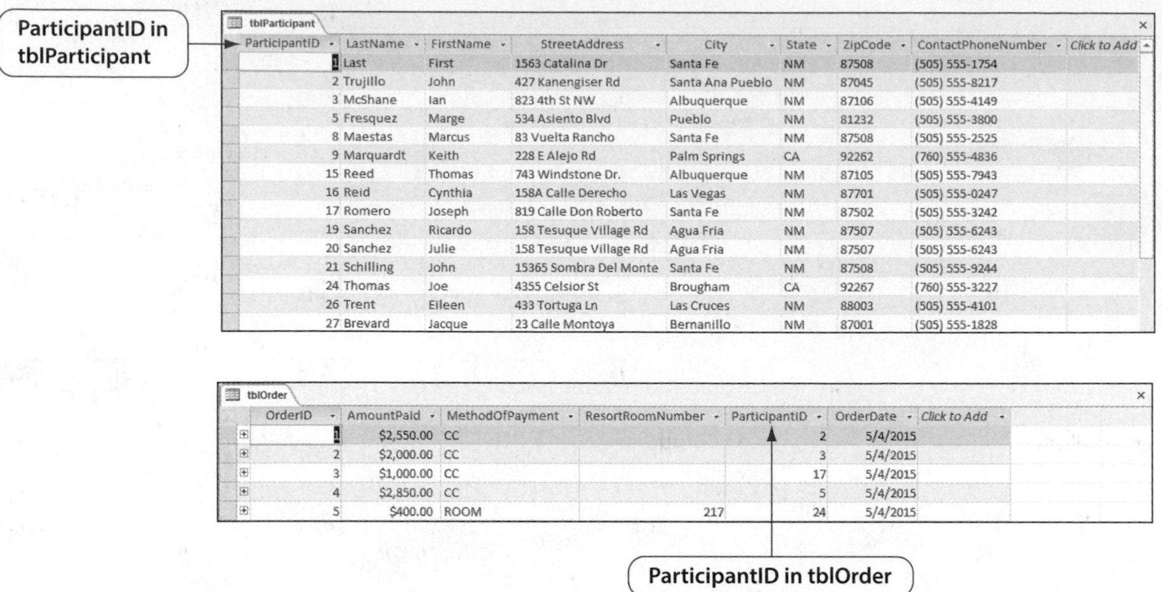

ParticipantID	LastName	FirstName	StreetAddress	City	State	ZipCode	ContactPhoneNumber	Click to Add
1	Last	First	1563 Catalina Dr	Santa Fe	NM	87508	(505) 555-1754	
2	Trujillo	John	427 Kanengiser Rd	Santa Ana Pueblo	NM	87045	(505) 555-8217	
3	McShane	Ian	823 4th St NW	Albuquerque	NM	87106	(505) 555-4149	
5	Fresquez	Marge	534 Asiento Blvd	Pueblo	NM	81232	(505) 555-3800	
8	Maestas	Marcus	83 Vuelta Rancho	Santa Fe	NM	87508	(505) 555-2525	
9	Marquardt	Keith	228 E Alejo Rd	Palm Springs	CA	92262	(760) 555-4836	
15	Reed	Thomas	743 Windstone Dr.	Albuquerque	NM	87105	(505) 555-7943	
16	Reid	Cynthia	158A Calle Derecho	Las Vegas	NM	87701	(505) 555-0247	
17	Romero	Joseph	819 Calle Don Roberto	Santa Fe	NM	87502	(505) 555-3242	
19	Sanchez	Ricardo	158 Tesuque Village Rd	Agua Fria	NM	87507	(505) 555-6243	
20	Sanchez	Julie	158 Tesuque Village Rd	Agua Fria	NM	87507	(505) 555-6243	
21	Schilling	John	15365 Sombra Del Monte	Santa Fe	NM	87508	(505) 555-9244	
24	Thomas	Joe	4355 Celsior St	Brougham	CA	92267	(760) 555-3227	
26	Trent	Eileen	433 Tortuga Ln	Las Cruces	NM	88003	(505) 555-4101	
27	Brevard	Jacque	23 Calle Montoya	Bernanillo	NM	87001	(505) 555-1828	

OrderID	AmountPaid	MethodOfPayment	ResortRoomNumber	ParticipantID	OrderDate	Click to Add
1	$2,550.00	CC		2	5/4/2015	
2	$2,000.00	CC		3	5/4/2015	
3	$1,000.00	CC		17	5/4/2015	
4	$2,850.00	CC		5	5/4/2015	
5	$400.00	ROOM	217	24	5/4/2015	

Figure 20 Tables joined between primary and foreign keys

Understand Basic Principles of Normalization

When you work with tables in Access, you want each table to represent a single entity and have data only about that entity. For example, you want a tblParticipant table to have data about participants and nothing else. You do not want to have data about the corporation they represent or the order they placed. You want the data about the participant to be in the participant table and no data about any other entity in the tblParticipant table as shown in Figure 20. There is no data that is about any other entity in the tblParticipant table. This is why you deleted the CorporatePhoneNumber field earlier in the exercise.

Representing Entities and Attributes

Recall that an entity is a person, place, or item that you want to keep data about. The data you keep about an entity are called attributes. An entity is generally stored in a single table in a relational database. The attributes form the fields or columns of the table. **Normalization** is the process of minimizing the duplication of information in a relational database through effective database design. If you know the primary key of an entity in a normalized database, each of the attributes will have just one value. When you normalize a database, you will have multiple smaller tables, each representing a different thing. There will be no redundant data in the tables. A complete discussion of normalization is beyond the scope of this workshop, but the following sections will give you an idea of why you normalize your tables.

Table 3 shows a nonnormalized view of tblParticipant. Suppose John Trujillo places two orders, Order 1 for $2,550 and Order 2 for $500. You can easily fill in his name and address. However, when you get to the order fields, you cannot fill in the attributes with just one value. You want to enter Order 1 for Order ID and Order 2 for Order ID. You want to enter $2,550 for AmountPaid and $500 for AmountPaid. But you only have one field for each.

Participant ID	Last Name	First Name	Street Address	Other Address Fields	Order ID	Amount Paid
2	Trujillo	John	427 Kanengiser Rd		??????	????

Table 3 Nonnormalized tblParticipant table

For each record's ParticipantID, you do not have a single value for OrderID and AmountPaid because each participant may make several orders. You could have a column for OrderID1 and OrderID2. But, how many columns would you make? What if this was for a grocery store where one transaction might contain hundreds of items? Any time you do not know how many columns to repeat, the table is not normalized and you need another table. Thus, this table does not fit the principles of normalization. It has two entities in the table: participants and orders.

CONSIDER THIS | Why Is a Nonnormalized Table Undesirable?

If you have a table as shown in Table 3, you could simply enter a record for each item. So, if you had five items, you would enter five records in the table. What kind of redundancy does that create? If you used this method, is there a primary key?

Minimizing Redundancy

Table 4 shows a nonnormalized view of the tblOrder table. In this case, when you know the OrderID, you do know the value of each field.

OrderID	Amount Paid	Method of Payment	Last Name	First Name	Address	Other Address Fields
1	$2,550.00	CC	Trujillo	John	427 Kanengiser Rd	
12	$500.00	CC	Trujillo	John	427 Kanengiser Rd	

Table 4 Nonnormalized tblOrder table

However, the table has redundant data. **Redundancy** occurs when data is repeated several times in a database. All of the data about John Trujillo is repeated for each order he makes. That means that the data will need to be entered multiple times. Beyond that, if the data changes, it has to be changed in multiple places. If his address or phone number changes, it will need to be changed on all his order records. Forgetting to change it in one place will lead to inconsistent data and confusion. Again, this table is not normalized because it contains data about two different entities: participant and orders.

In a normalized database, redundancy is minimized. The foreign keys are redundant, but no other data about the entity is repeated.

Understand Relationships Between Tables

To normalize the database, you need to have two tables: one for participants and one for orders. How then do you form a relationship between them? A table represents an entity—or the nouns—in the database. The relationship represents the verb that connects the two nouns. In the example, the two nouns are "participant" and "order." Is there a relationship between these two nouns? Yes. You can say that a participant places an order.

Once you determine that there is a relationship between the entities, you need to describe the relationship. You do that by asking yourself two questions starting with each entity in the relationship:

- Question 1, starting with the Participant entity: If you have one participant, what is the maximum number of orders that one participant can place? The only two answers to consider are one or many. In this case, the participant can place many orders.
- Question 2, starting with the Order entity: If you have one order, what is the maximum number of participants that can place that order? Again, the only answers to consider are one or many. An order is placed by just one participant.

The type of relationship where one question is answered "one" and the other is answered "many" is called a one-to-many relationship. A **one-to-many relationship** is a relationship between two tables where one record in the first table corresponds to many records in the second table. One-to-many is called the cardinality of the relationship. **Cardinality** indicates the number of instances of one entity that relates to one instance of another entity.

Using the Relationships Window

Access stores relationship information in the Relationships window as shown in Figure 21.

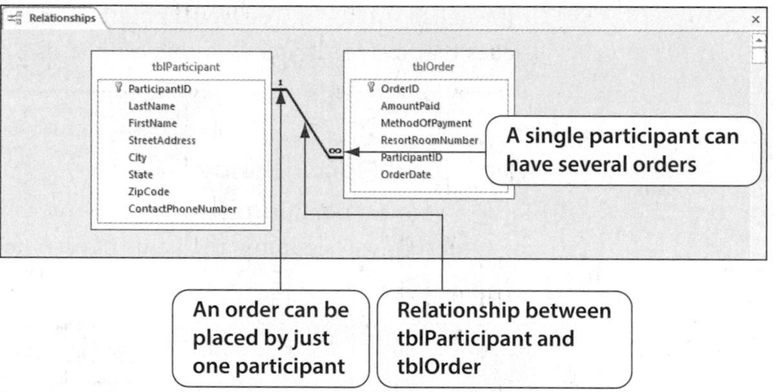

Figure 21 Relationships window

The Relationships window shows tables and the relationships between those tables. Notice the join line between tblParticipant and tblOrder. There is an infinity symbol on the line next to tblOrder. The infinity symbol indicates that a single participant can have several orders. There is a "1" on the line next to tblParticipant. The "1" indicates that an order can be placed by just one participant. Access indicates a one-to-many relationship in this way, putting a "1" on the one side of the join line and an infinity symbol on the many side.

REAL WORLD ADVICE | **Other Uses for the Relationships Window**

The Relationships window gives you an overview of all your tables and the relationships between them. It also shows all the fields in all the tables. It is often helpful to return to the Relationships window when developing queries and reports.

A02.15

To Open the Relationships Window

a. Click the **DATABASE TOOLS** tab, and then in the Relationships group, click **Relationships**.
   The Relationships window opens. The window shows tables and the relationships between those tables.

Determining Relationship Types

The relationship between tblParticipant and tblOrder is a one-to-many relationship. There are other types of relationships. Consider the relationship between tblOrder and tblItem. There is a relationship: an item can be on an order. What is the cardinality? You need to ask yourself the two questions to determine the cardinality:

- Question 1, starting with the Order entity: If you have one order, what is the maximum number of items that can be part of that order? You care only about two answers: one or many. In this case, the order can contain many items. For example, a golfer could buy an entry into the tournament and a T-shirt.
- Question 2, starting with the Item entity: If you have one item, what is the maximum number of orders that that item can be part of? Again, the only answers to consider are one or many. Obviously you want more than one person to be able to order an entry to the tournament. Therefore, you say that an item can be on many orders.

With both answers being many, this is a many-to-many relationship. A **many-to-many relationship** is a relationship between tables in which one record in one table has many matching records in a second table, and one record in the related table has many matching records in the first table. Because these two tables in the charity database do not have a common field, in Access this kind of many-to-many relationship must have an additional table in between these two. This intermediate table is referred to by several synonymous terms: "intersection," "junction," or "link table." You will look at this later in the workshop.

A one-to-one relationship occurs when each question is answered with a maximum of one. A **one-to-one relationship** is a relationship between tables where a record in one table has only one matching record in the second table. In a small business, a department might be managed by no more than one manager, and each manager manages no more than one department. That relationship in that business is a one-to-one relationship.

There are three types of relationships: one-to-many, many-to-many, and one-to-one. The relationship type is based upon the rules of the business. In the charity golf tournament, the relationship between the order and the item is many-to-many, but in another business it might not be. For example, consider a business that sells custom-made jewelry where each item is one of a kind. In this case, an item can appear on just one order. Thus, the relationship between order and item in that business would be one-to-many.

REAL WORLD ADVICE | **Use of One-to-One Relationships**

When you have a one-to-one relationship, you could combine the two tables into a single table. A single table is simpler than two tables with a one-to-one relationship between them.

- You could keep the two tables separate when the two tables are obviously two different things like manager and department. You might want to keep private information about the manager in the manager table. Additionally, this would be easier to change if business rules change and multiple managers might manage the same department.
- You should combine the two tables when there are just a few attributes on one of the tables. For example, suppose you only wanted to keep the manager's name in the manager table with no other information about the manager. Then you might consider the manager's name to be an attribute of the department.

Create a One-to-Many Relationship

Consider the relationship between tblParticipant and tblOrder. This is a one-to-many relationship. To form a relationship between two tables, you need the tables to have a field in common. The easiest way to accomplish this is to put the primary key from the table on the one side in the table on the many side. In this case, this means that you use the ParticipantID from the one side table and add it as a field to the tblOrder table. The field that you add to the many side is called a foreign key because it is a key to another, or foreign, table. ParticipantID is already a field on the many side table, so you can use it to form the relationship.

QUICK REFERENCE	Creating a One-to-Many Relationship in Access

Creating a one-to-many relationship in Access takes three steps:

1. Make sure the two tables have a field in common. Use the primary key from the one side, and add it as a foreign key in the many side table.
2. Form the relationship in the Relationships window. This is done by connecting the primary key of the one side table to the foreign key in the many side table.
3. Populate the foreign key by adding data to the foreign key in the many side table.

Forming the Relationship

Because the tblParticipant and tblOrder tables already have a field in common, you can form the relationship. You will connect the primary key of the one side table to the foreign key on the many side table.

A02.16

To Form a Relationship

a. On the DATABASE TOOLS tab, in the Relationships group, click **Show Table**, click **tblParticipant**, and then click **Add**.

b. Click **Close** to close the Show Table dialog box, and then drag the **tblParticipant** table to appear below tblOrder in the Relationships window.

c. Use your pointer to resize **tblParticipant** by dragging the corner of the field list so all fields show. Drag **tblOrder** to the right.

SIDE NOTE
Adding Tables to the Relationships Window
You can also add tables to the Relationships window by clicking on a table in the Navigation Pane and dragging it to the window.

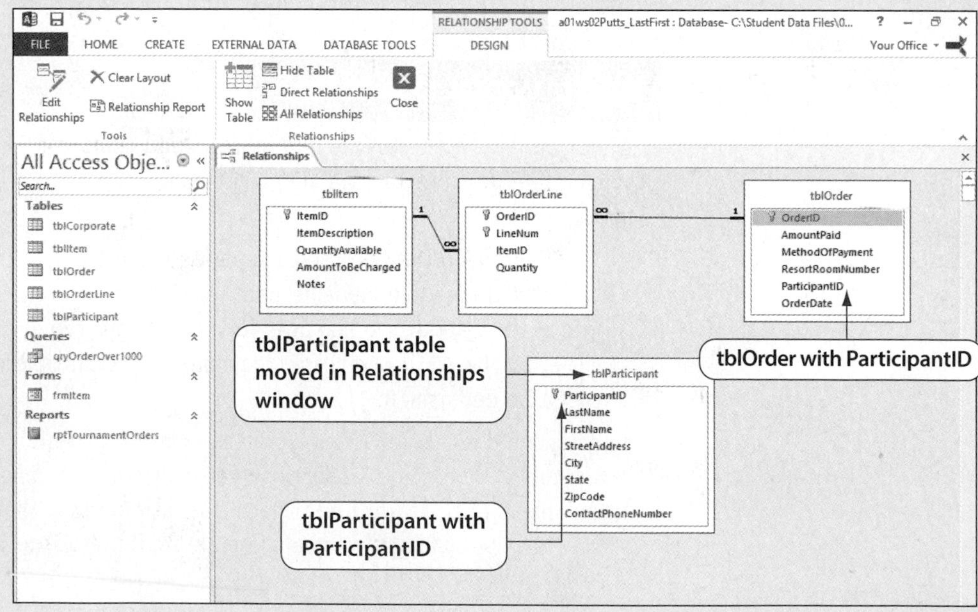

Figure 22 Move the table in the Relationships window

SIDE NOTE
Tables in the Relationships Window
Do not add a table twice to Relationships. If you do, close the window without saving and start over. A hidden table is still there.

d. Drag the primary key, **ParticipantID**, from tblParticipant to **ParticipantID** in tblOrder. Alternatively, you could drag from ParticipantID in tblOrder to ParticipantID in tblParticipant.

The Edit Relationships dialog box is displayed. Check that the fields shown in the box are both ParticipantID.

> **Troubleshooting**
> If you do not see two fields named ParticipantID in the Edit Relationships dialog box, click Cancel and retry Step d.

Notice that Access calls the relationship a one-to-many relationship. This is because the relationship is between a primary key and a foreign key.

e. Click **Enforce Referential Integrity** to select it, and then click **Create**. Later in the workshop you will look further at what referential integrity accomplishes.

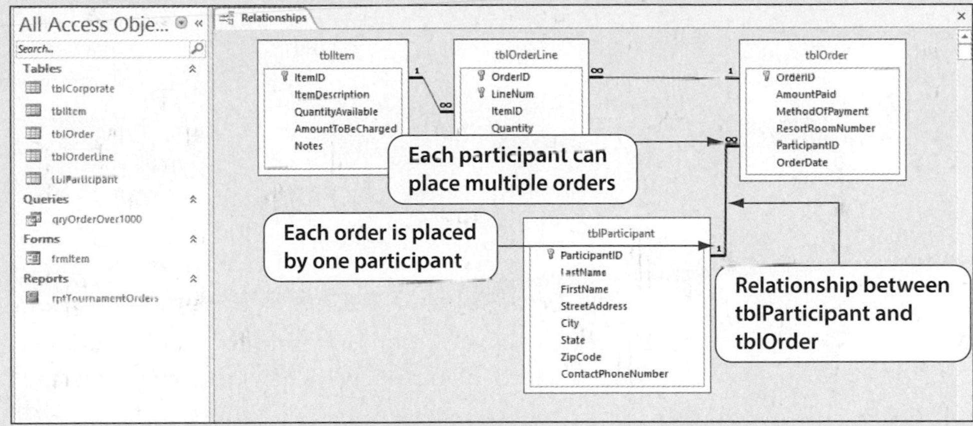

Figure 23 tblParticipant and tblOrder relationship

f. **Save** your relationships, and then **close** the Relationships window.

> **Troubleshooting**
> If you get the error message "The database engine could not lock table 'tblParticipant' because it is already in use by another person or process," this means that the tblParticipant table is still open. Close the table, and try again to form the relationship. You should get in the habit of closing tables when you are done with them.
>
> If you get the error message "Relationship must be on the same number of fields with the same data type," this means that the data types for the primary key and the foreign key are different. For example, they must be both Numeric and Long Integer or both Text. Make sure that you are creating the relationship between the correct fields. If you are, check the table designs, and fix the field with the wrong data type.
>
> If you add a relationship that you do not want, right-click the join line and click Delete. If you want to edit a relationship, right-click the join line and click Edit Relationship.

QUICK REFERENCE	Three Types of Relationships	
Type of Relationship	**Alternate Notations**	**Meaning**
One-to-many	1:N or 1:M 1-to-N	A relationship between two tables where one record in the first table corresponds to many records in the second table; however, each record in the second table corresponds to just one record in the first table.
Many-to-many	M:N M-to-N	A relationship between two tables where one record in the first table corresponds to many records in the second table; and, each record in the second table corresponds to many records in the first table.
One-to-one	1:1 1-to-1	A relationship between two tables where a record in one table has only one matching record in the second table; and, each record in the second table corresponds to just one record in the first table.

Using Two Related Tables in a Report

The reason you create a relationship is to join two tables for queries, reports, and forms. You will create a simple report showing participants and their orders.

A02.17

To Create a Report from Two Tables

a. Click the **CREATE** tab, and then in the Reports group, click **Report Wizard**.

b. In the Report Wizard dialog box, click the **Tables/Queries** arrow, and then select **Table: tblParticipant**. Select the **LastName** field, and then click **One Field** [>]. Select the **FirstName** field, and then click **One Field** [>].

c. Click the **Tables/Queries** arrow, and then select **Table: tblOrder**. Select the **OrderID** field, and then click **One Field** [>]. Select the **AmountPaid** field, and then click **One Field** [>].

> **Troubleshooting**
> If you clicked Next instead of selecting the tblOrder fields, you can go back a step in the wizard by clicking Back.

d. Click **Next**.

You can see a preview of how your report will look if you group the participants by tblParticipant. Access uses the "one" side of a one-to-many relationship as the default for the grouping. This is the grouping you want.

e. Click **Next**. The wizard asks if you want more grouping levels; however, you do not want any other grouping levels.

f. Click **Next**.

g. Use the arrow to select **OrderID**. Ascending sort order is already selected. Click **Next**.

The wizard asks you to choose a layout and orientation for your report. You will accept the default layout and orientation.

h. Click **Next**.

i. Title your report rptParticipantOrders_initialLastname using your first initial and last name. Click **Finish**.

Access connects the participants and orders in a report.

j. Right-click anywhere on the report, and then select **Layout View** from the shortcut menu.

> **Troubleshooting**
>
> If the Field List shows on the right side of the Access window, close it so you can see the entire report layout.

k. Double-click the **title** of the report. Change the report title to Participant and Orders by initial Lastname using your first initial and last name and press Enter. **Save** your report.

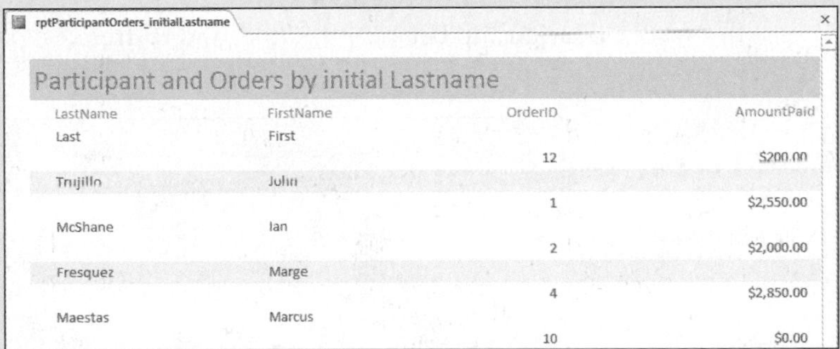

Figure 24 Complete report

l. If your instructor directs you to print the report, right-click anywhere on the report, switch to **Print Preview**, click **Print** in the Print group, and then click **OK**.

m. **Close** your report.

Create a Many-to-Many Relationship

Unless you are connecting a common field such as a foreign key to the same foreign key in a different table, Access cannot form a many-to-many relationship with a single relationship. Instead you need to make two one-to-many relationships to represent the many-to-many relationship. As stated before, tblOrder and tblItem have a many-to-many relationship. An order can have many items on it. Each item can be on many orders. To form this relationship, a new table, tblOrderLine needs to be added. Both tblOrder and tblItem are related to the new table. The third table is called a junction table. A **junction table** breaks down the many-to-many relationship into two one-to-many relationships.

Look at the relationship between tblOrder and tblOrderLine in Figure 25. It is a one-to-many relationship with orders having many order lines but each order line on just one order. There is also a relationship between tblOrderLine and tblItem. It also is a one-to-many relationship with each order line having just one item but an item able to be on many order lines as shown in Figure 25.

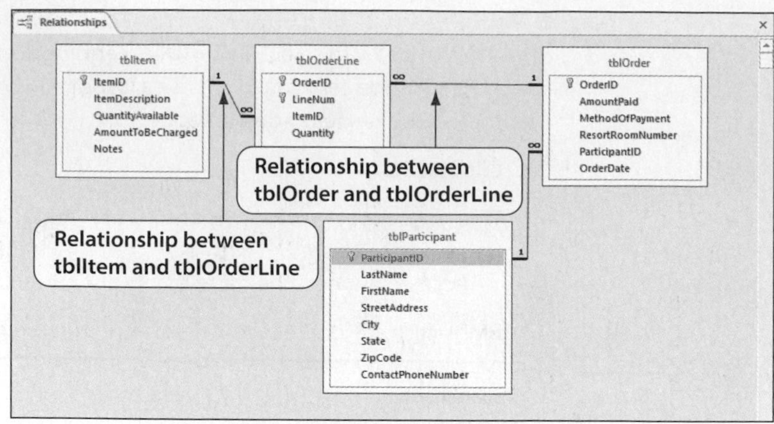

Figure 25 Relationship between tblOrder and tblItem with tblOrderLine

As shown in Figure 26, OrderID 4 has two order lines: one with an item of a corporate team and one with a cart. By traveling left to right across the three tables, you see that OrderID 4 has many items on it. OrderID 6 has one line: an entry to the tournament. By traveling from right to left across the three tables, you see that an entry to the tournament can be on many orders. Hence the junction table tblOrderLine forms a many-to-many relationship between tblOrder and tblItem.

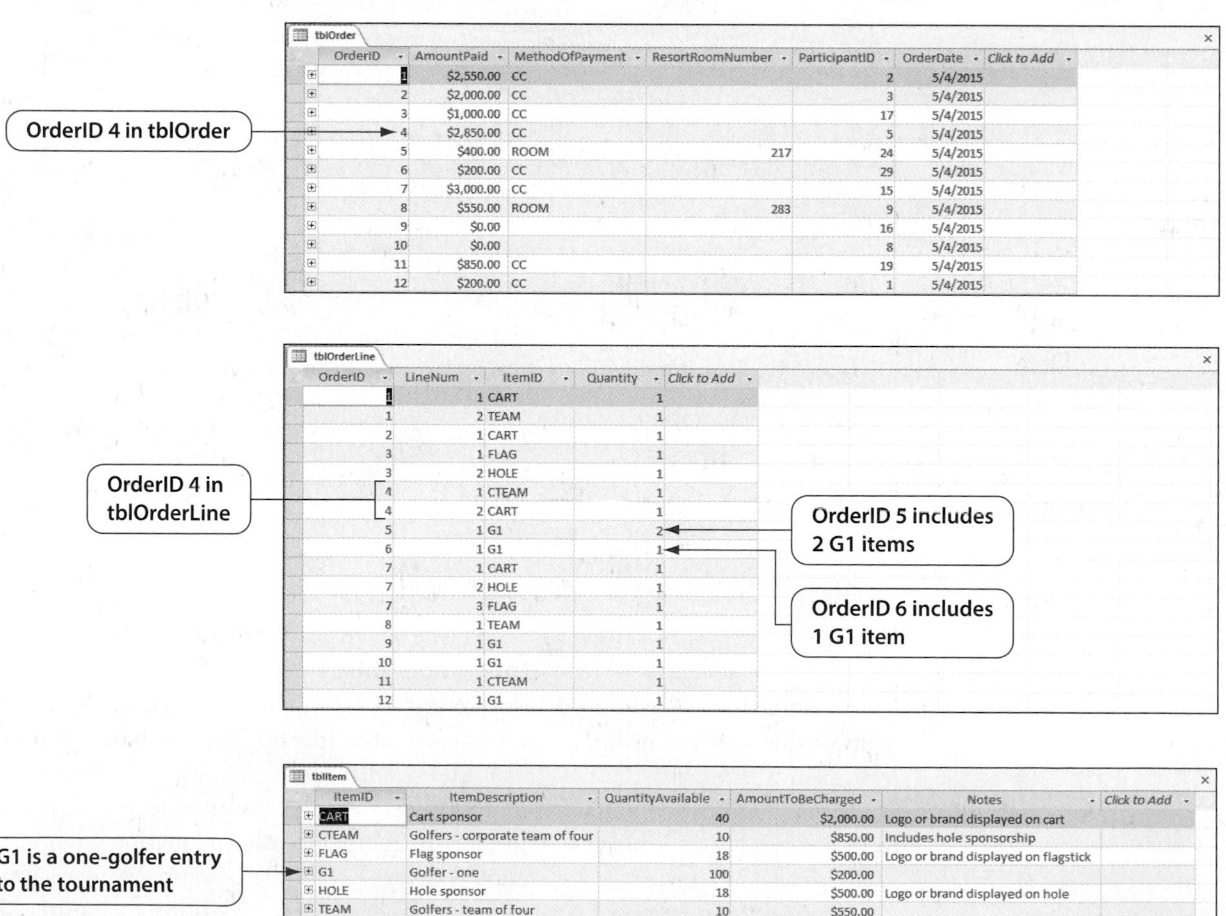

tblOrder

OrderID	AmountPaid	MethodOfPayment	ResortRoomNumber	ParticipantID	OrderDate	Click to Add
1	$2,550.00	CC		2	5/4/2015	
2	$2,000.00	CC		3	5/4/2015	
3	$1,000.00	CC		17	5/4/2015	
4	$2,850.00	CC		5	5/4/2015	
5	$400.00	ROOM	217	24	5/4/2015	
6	$200.00	CC		29	5/4/2015	
7	$3,000.00	CC		15	5/4/2015	
8	$550.00	ROOM	283	9	5/4/2015	
9	$0.00			16	5/4/2015	
10	$0.00			8	5/4/2015	
11	$850.00	CC		19	5/4/2015	
12	$200.00	CC		1	5/4/2015	

tblOrderLine

OrderID	LineNum	ItemID	Quantity	Click to Add
1	1	CART	1	
1	2	TEAM	1	
2	1	CART	1	
3	1	FLAG	1	
3	2	HOLE	1	
4	1	CTEAM	1	
4	2	CART	1	
5	1	G1	2	
6	1	G1	1	
7	1	CART	1	
7	2	HOLE	1	
7	3	FLAG	1	
8	1	TEAM	1	
9	1	G1	1	
10	1	G1	1	
11	1	CTEAM	1	
12	1	G1	1	

tblItem

ItemID	ItemDescription	QuantityAvailable	AmountToBeCharged	Notes	Click to Add
CART	Cart sponsor	40	$2,000.00	Logo or brand displayed on cart	
CTEAM	Golfers - corporate team of four	10	$850.00	Includes hole sponsorship	
FLAG	Flag sponsor	18	$500.00	Logo or brand displayed on flagstick	
G1	Golfer - one	100	$200.00		
HOLE	Hole sponsor	18	$500.00	Logo or brand displayed on hole	
TEAM	Golfers - team of four	10	$550.00		

Figure 26 Data in tblOrder, tblOrderLine, and tblItem

tblOrderLine has foreign keys to tblOrder and tblItem. This allows the relationships to be formed. Notice that the relationship between tblOrder and tblOrderLine is formed with OrderID in tblOrder joined to OrderID in tblOrderLine. Similarly the relationship between tblItem and tblOrderLine is formed from ItemID in tblItem to ItemID in tblOrderLine.

The junction table, tblOrderLine, has one field beyond the key fields: Quantity. This indicates the quantity of each item on the order. As shown in Figure 26, OrderID 5 included two entries to the tournament.

Forming a New Many-to-Many Relationship

Consider the relationship between your new table, tblCorporate, and tblParticipant. There is a relationship: a participant can represent a corporation. A participant can be a golfer for a corporation, the corporate representative, or a donor. What is the cardinality? You need to ask yourself the two questions to determine the cardinality:

- Question 1, starting with the Corporate entity: If you have one corporation, what is the maximum number of participants that can represent that corporation? You care only about two answers: one or many. In this case, the corporation could be represented by many participants. A corporate team might have four golfer participants.
- Question 2, starting with the Participant entity: If you have one Participant, what is the maximum number of roles that Participant can represent for the corporation? Again, the only answers to consider are one or many. A Participant could be a golfer representing the corporation and also be a corporate representative.

QUICK REFERENCE | **Creating a Many-to-Many Relationship in Access**

Creating a many-to-many relationship in Access takes four steps:

1. Create a junction table. Create a primary key that will be a unique field for the junction table, and add two foreign keys, one to each of the many-to-many tables. Alternatively you can create a composite key made up of the two foreign keys.
2. Determine if there are any fields that you want to add to the junction table beyond the keys.
3. Form two relationships in the Relationships window. This is done by connecting the primary key of one of the original tables to the appropriate foreign key of the junction table. Repeat for the second of the original tables. The junction table is on the many side of both relationships.
4. Populate the junction table.

Creating a Junction Table

Because the relationship between tblCorporate and tblParticipant is many-to-many, you need a junction table. Recall that the junction table breaks down the many-to-many relationship into two one-to-many relationships. In this case, the junction table will indicate the role that the participant has for the corporation. The primary key for the junction table will be ParticipantRoleID, an AutoNumber field. You will have two foreign keys, the CorporateID field and the ParticipantID field. You will also add a field named Role that describes the role of the participant. Because the table represents roles, you will call the table tblParticipantRole.

A02.18

To Create a Junction Table in Table Design View

a. Click the **CREATE** tab, and then in the Tables group, click **Table Design**.
   Access opens a blank table in Design view. You will enter each field in the appropriate row.

b. In the Field Name column, type ParticipantRoleID. Press Tab to move to the Data Type column, click the **arrow**, and then select the **AutoNumber** data type.
   Alternatively, you can type the "A," and "AutoNumber" will appear.

c. Notice that Field Size in the Field Properties pane defaults to Long Integer. Press Tab to move to the Description column, and then type Primary key for tblParticipantRole.

d. On the DESIGN tab, in the Tools group, click **Primary Key** to make the ParticipantRoleID field the primary key.

e. Press Tab to move to the next field. Continue filling in the table with the following information, being sure to enter the field size in the Field Properties pane.

Field Name	Data Type	Description	Field Size
CorporateID	Number	Foreign key to tblCorporate	Long Integer
ParticipantID	Number	Foreign key to tblParticipant	Long Integer
Role	Short Text	Role that this participant fills for the corporation	40

f. **Close** X the table, and then in the Microsoft Access dialog box click **Yes**. Name the table tblParticipantRole and then click **OK**.

Creating Two One-to-Many Relationships

The many-to-many relationship will turn into two one-to-many relationships between each of the original tables and the junction table. The rule is that the junction table is on the many side of the two relationships. But you can ask yourself the two questions to determine the cardinality:

- Question 1, starting with the Corporate entity: If you have one corporation, what is the maximum number of participant roles that can represent that corporation? You care only about two answers: one or many. In this case, the corporation could be represented by many participant roles. A corporation could have golfers and corporate contacts.
- Question 2, starting with the ParticipantRole entity: If you have one ParticipantRole, what is the maximum number of corporations that the participant can represent? Again, the only answers to consider are one or many. A ParticipantRole is for a single participant.

Thus tblCorporate to tblParticipantRole is a one-to-many relationship with Corporate on the "one" side.

You can ask the same questions between tblParticipant and tblParticipantRole.

A02.19

To Form Two Relationships to the Junction Table

a. Click the **DATABASE TOOLS** tab, and then in the Relationships group, click **Relationships**.

b. On the DESIGN tab, in the Relationships group, click **Show Table**. Select **tblCorporate**, click **Add**, select **tblParticipantRole**, and then click **Add**.

c. **Close** the Show Table dialog box, and then drag the **tables** in the Relationships window, so there is some space between the tables to form the relationships.

d. Drag the primary key **ParticipantID** from tblParticipant to **ParticipantID** in tblParticipantRole. Alternatively, you could drag from ParticipantID in tblParticipantRole to ParticipantID in tblParticipant.

e. Access displays the Edit Relationships dialog box. Click **Enforce Referential Integrity** to select it, and then click **Create**.

f. Drag the primary key **CorporateID** from tblCorporate to **CorporateID** in tblParticipantRole.

g. Access displays the Edit Relationships dialog box. Click **Enforce Referential Integrity** to select it, and then click **Create**.

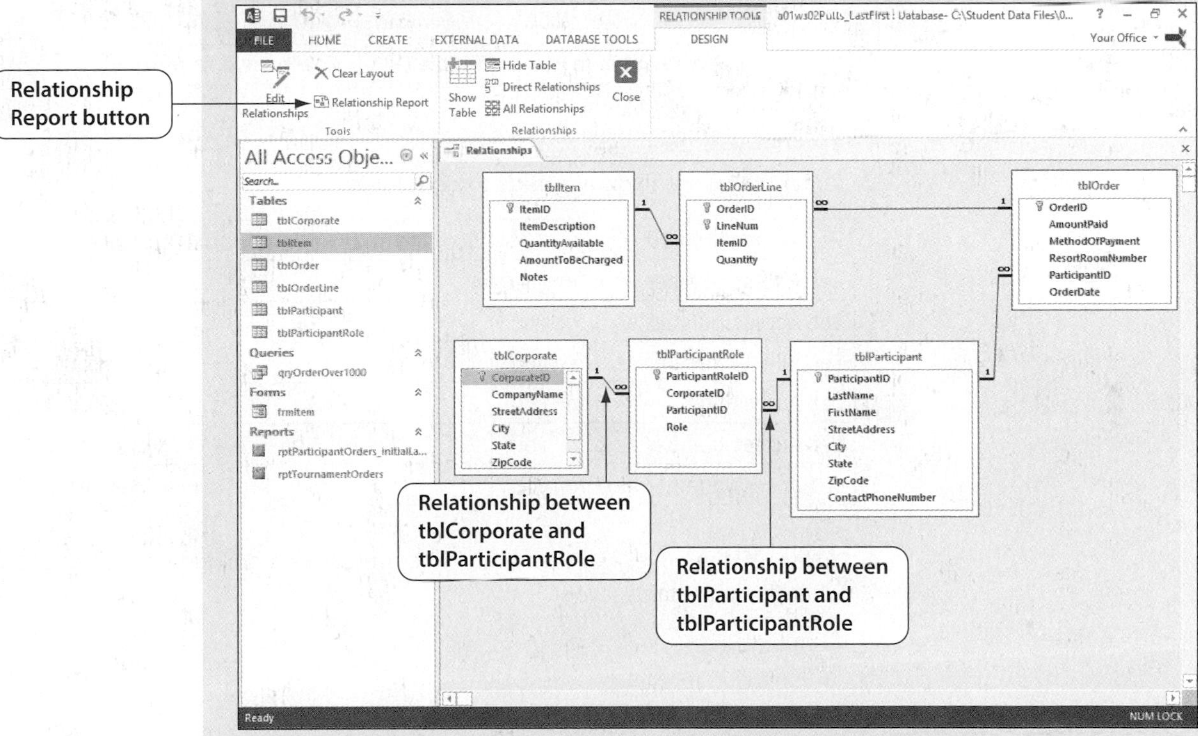

Figure 27 Completed Relationships window

h. On the DESIGN tab, in the Tools group, click **Relationship Report** to create a report for your relationships. **Save** the report, accepting the report name **Relationships for a01ws02Putts_LastFirst**, and then click **OK**.

i. If your instructor asks you to print your report, on the PRINT PREVIEW tab, in the Print group, click **Print** to print the report. **Close** the Relationships report.

j. **Close** the Relationships window.

Populating the Junction Table

To complete the many-to-many relationship, you need to populate the junction table.

A02.20

To Populate the Junction Table

a. Double-click **tblParticipantRole** to open the table in Datasheet view.

b. Click in the **CorporateID append row**. Enter a CorporateID of 1, a ParticipantID of 5 and a Role of Corporate Contact. Access automatically numbers ParticipantRoleID as "1".

c. Because the last field is not totally visible, place your pointer in the **border** on the right of the **Role** column heading. When your pointer is a double-headed arrow [+], double-click the **border** to resize the column. This resizing is called AutoFitting. Repeat for each field.

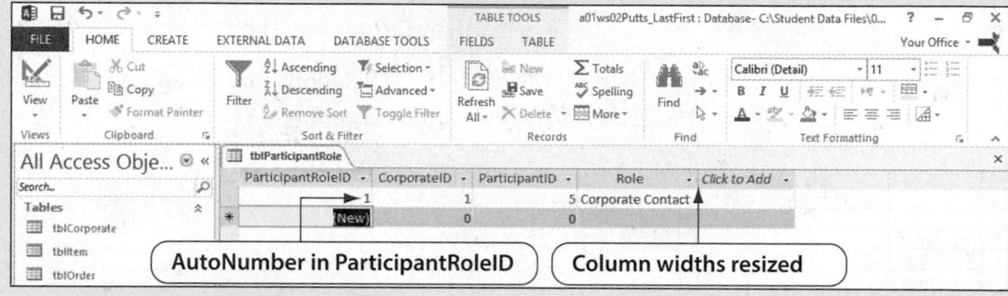

Figure 28 tblParticipantRole columns resized

d. Enter the following data in the records as follows.

ParticipantRoleID	CorporateID	ParticipantID	Role
Let Access number as 2 for you	1	5	Golfer
Let Access number as 3 for you	1	26	Golfer
Let Access number as 4 for you	2	1	Golfer
Let Access number as 5 for you	2	3	Golfer
Let Access number as 6 for you	2	54	Corporate Contact
Let Access number as 7 for you	2	54	Golfer

e. **Close** [X] the table, and then in the Microsoft Access dialog box click **Yes** to save the changes to the table layout.

Defining One-to-One Relationships

One-to-one relationships in Access are formed very similarly to one-to-many relationships. You can put a foreign key in either table and establish the relationship by dragging with the primary key in one table joined to the foreign key. You can also make both tables have the same primary key.

Understand Referential Integrity

Referential integrity is a database concept that ensures that relationships between tables remain consistent. When one table has a foreign key to another table, the concept of referential integrity states that you may not add a record to the table that contains the foreign key unless there is a corresponding record in the linked table. Recall that when you created the relationship between tblParticipant and tblOrder, you told Access to enforce referential integrity.

Enforcing Referential Integrity

Enforcing referential integrity ensures that the following rules will be applied when you define the fields in Design view:

- The values in the field on the one side of the relationship is unique in the table. You must either use the primary key of the one side in the relationship or a field that you have set as unique in the table.
- You cannot add a foreign key value in the many side that does not have a matching primary key value on the one side.
- The matching fields on both sides of the relationship are defined with the same data types. For example, if the primary key is numeric and Long Integer, the foreign key must be numeric and Long Integer too. (For purposes of relationships, an AutoNumber primary key is considered Long Integer.)

If these rules are violated, when you try to form the relationship, you will get the following error message: "Relationship must be on the same number of fields with the same data type."

Double-check how you defined the relationship between tblParticipant and tblOrder.

To Check and Test Referential Integrity

a. Click the **DATABASE TOOLS** tab, and then in the Relationships group, click **Relationships**.
   The Relationships window is displayed. Notice the relationship that was formed between ParticipantID in tblParticipant and ParticipantID in tblOrder.

b. **Close** [X] the Relationships window.

c. Right-click **tblParticipant**, and then select **Design View**. Notice that ParticipantID is defined as Number and Long Integer. **Close** [X] tblParticipant, right-click **tblOrder**, select **Design View**, and then click the **ParticipantID** field. Notice that ParticipantID is also defined as Number and Long Integer in the tblOrder table.
   Referential integrity means that Access will also enforce rules when you work with the data in the tables. You cannot enter a value in the foreign key field on the "many" side table that is not a primary key value on the "one" side table. For example, you cannot add a participant that does not exist in tblParticipant to a team. However, you can leave the foreign key unfilled, indicating that this participant is not part of a team.

d. Click the **HOME** tab, and then in the Views group, click the **View** button to switch to Datasheet View for tblOrder.

e. In the ParticipantID for the last record in the table, type 70 and then press Enter twice.
   Access responds with the error message "You cannot add or change a record because a related record is required in table tblParticipant." That is, you cannot add an order to participant 70 because there is no participant 70.

f. Click **OK**, and then change the ParticipantID for the last order back to 1. Press Enter twice. ParticipantID 1 is a valid participant so you can make that change.

g. **Close** [X] the tblOrder table.

CONSIDER THIS | **Why Enforce Referential Integrity?**

You can decline to enforce referential integrity on a relationship. What are the pros and cons of enforcing referential integrity? What are the pros and cons of not enforcing referential integrity?

If you enforce referential integrity, you cannot delete a record from the "one" side table if matching records exist in the "many" side table. If you want to delete the record, you must delete the matching records or use Cascade Delete as explained later.

A02.22

To Understand Relationships Between the One and Many Side Tables

a. In the Navigation Pane, double-click **tblParticipant** to open it in Datasheet view.

b. Click the **record selector** of the second row, John Trujillo.

c. Click the **HOME** tab, and then in the Records group, click **Delete**.
Access responds that "The record cannot be deleted or changed because table 'tblOrder' includes related records." That means John Trujillo has placed an order.

d. Click **OK**.

e. **Close** [X] the tblParticipant table.

f. **Close** [X] the database and Access.

You also cannot change the primary key value in the "one" side table if that record has related records.

QUICK REFERENCE | **Referential Integrity**

Access enforces the following rules on defining a relationship with referential integrity:

1. The primary key field values on the one side of the relationship must be unique in the table.
2. The foreign key values on the many side of the relationship must exist as the primary key field for a record on the one side of the relationship.
3. The matching fields on both sides of the relationship are defined with the same data types.

The following rules are applied to data changes when referential integrity is enforced:

1. You cannot enter a value in the foreign key field on the "many" side table that is not a primary key on the "one" side table. However, you can leave the foreign key unfilled, indicating that this record is not in the relationship. It is not good practice to do this however.
2. You cannot delete a record from the "one" side table if matching records exist in a "many" side table, unless Cascade Delete has been selected for the relationship, in which case all the matching records on the many side are deleted.
3. You cannot change a primary key value in the "one" side table if that record has related records in the "many" side, unless Cascade Update has been selected for the relationship, in which case all the matching records on the many side have their foreign key updated.

Selecting Cascade Update

When you ask Access to enforce referential integrity, you can also select whether you want Access to automatically cascade update related fields or cascade delete related records. These options allow some deletions and updates that would usually be prevented by referential integrity. However, Access makes these changes and replicates or cascades the changes through all related tables so referential integrity is preserved.

If you select Cascade Update Related Fields when you define a relationship, then when the primary key of a record in the one side table changes, Access automatically changes the foreign keys in all related records. For example, if you change the ItemID in the tblItem table, Access automatically changes the ItemID on all order lines that include that item. Access makes these changes without displaying an error message.

If the primary key in the "one" side table was defined as AutoNumber, selecting Cascade Update Related Fields has no effect, because you cannot change the value in an AutoNumber field.

Selecting Cascade Delete

If you select Cascade Delete Related Records when you define a relationship, any time that you delete records from the one side table, the related records in the many side table are also deleted. For example, if you deleted a tblParticipant record, all the orders made by that participant are automatically deleted from the tblOrder table. Before you make the deletion, Access warns you that related records may also be deleted.

CONSIDER THIS | Should You Cascade Delete Related Records?

Should you cascade delete related records? Consider a customer who has made many orders. If the customer asks to be removed from your database, do you want to remove his or her past orders? How do you think the accountants would feel?

Concept Check

1. What is an entity? What is an attribute? What is a relationship? p. 626
2. If you have data in an Excel worksheet, what methods could you use to move the data in Excel to Access? How would you decide between the methods? p. 629–636
3. Why is it important to type a new record in the blank (append) row rather than on top of another record? p. 638
4. What data types would you use for the following fields: price, phone number, street address, ZIP code, and notes about product usage? p. 640–641
5. What is a mask used for? What is a format used for? Which can affect the way that data is stored? p. 644–647
6. What is the purpose of a primary key? p. 647–648
7. Why is redundancy of data undesirable? p. 652–653
8. What does it mean to say that there is a relationship between two tables? p. 653–655
9. How do you create a one-to-many relationship in Access? p. 655–657
10. How do you create a many-to-many relationship in Access? p. 659–661
11. What does it mean for a relationship to have referential integrity enforced? p. 664–666

Key Terms

Attribute 626
Cardinality 654
Composite key 649
Data type 629
Delimiter 634
Entity 626
Field size 641
Foreign key 647
Format 645
Input mask 644
Join 651
Junction table 659
Many-to-many relationship 655
Natural primary key 650
Normalization 652
Number data type 629
Numeric key 648
One-to-many relationship 654
One-to-one relationship 655
Primary key 640
Redundancy 653
Relationship 626
Text data type 629

Visual Summary

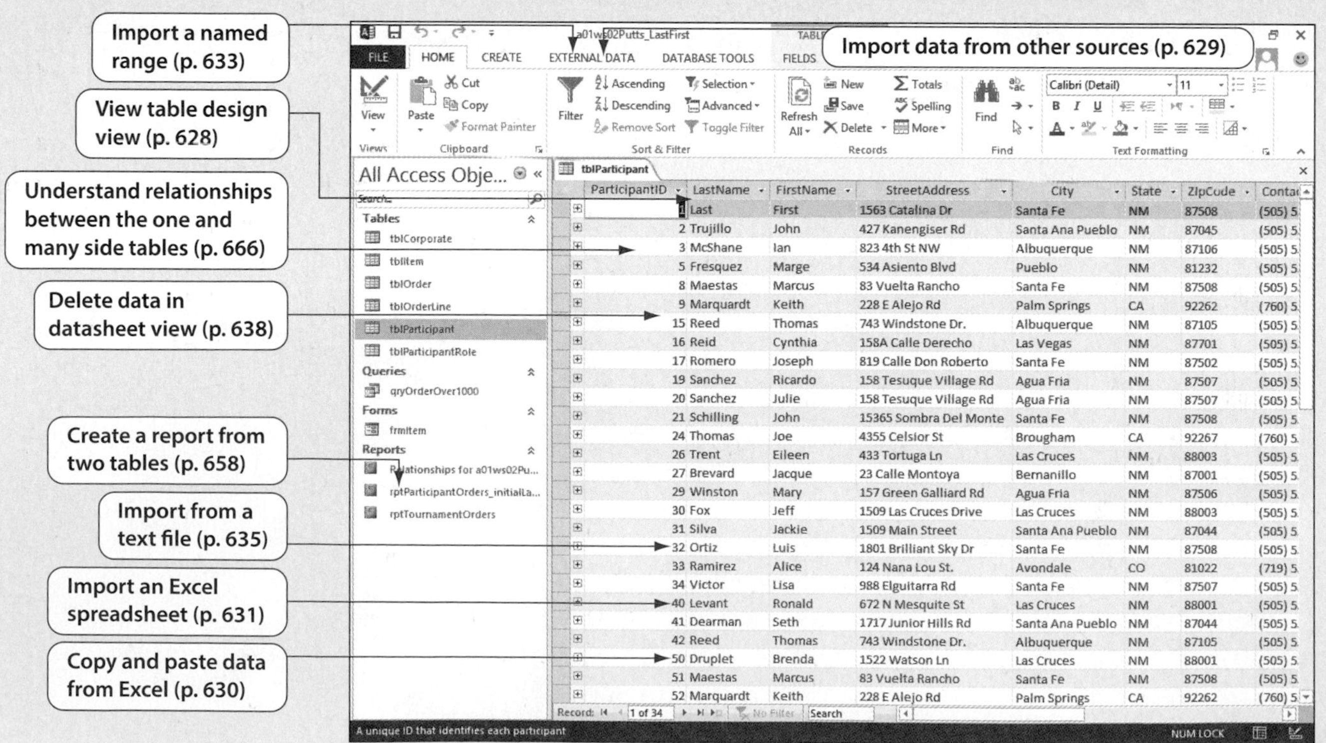

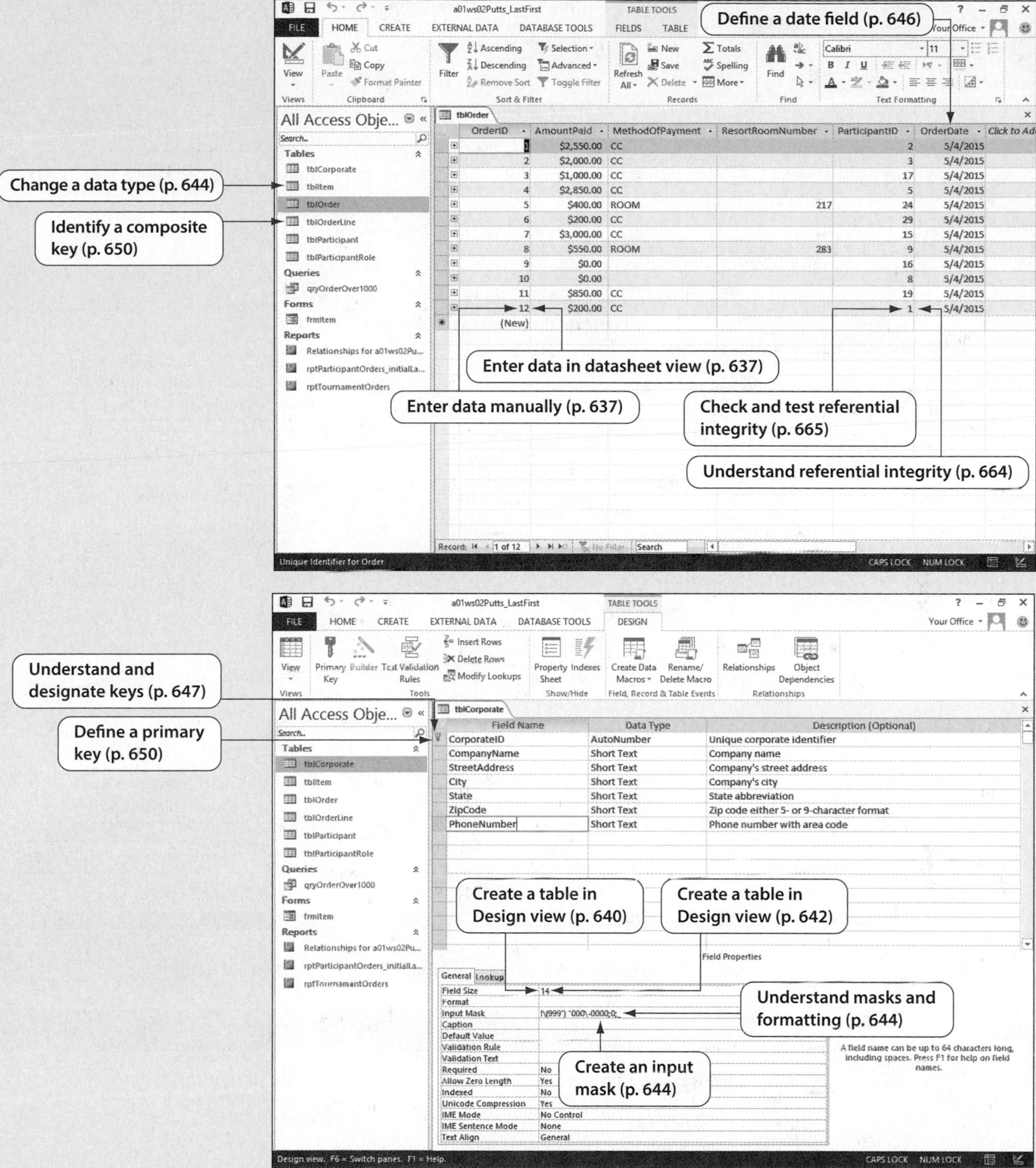

Define a date field (p. 646)
Change a data type (p. 644)
Identify a composite key (p. 650)
Enter data in datasheet view (p. 637)
Enter data manually (p. 637)
Check and test referential integrity (p. 665)
Understand referential integrity (p. 664)
Understand and designate keys (p. 647)
Define a primary key (p. 650)
Create a table in Design view (p. 640)
Create a table in Design view (p. 642)
Understand masks and formatting (p. 644)
Create an input mask (p. 644)

Create a junction table in table Design view (p. 662)

Populate the junction table (p. 664)

Understand relationships between tables (p. 653)

Open the relationships window (p. 654)

Form two relationships to the junction table (p. 663)

Create a many-to-many relationship (p. 659)

Create a one-to-many relationship (p. 655)

Form a relationship (p. 656)

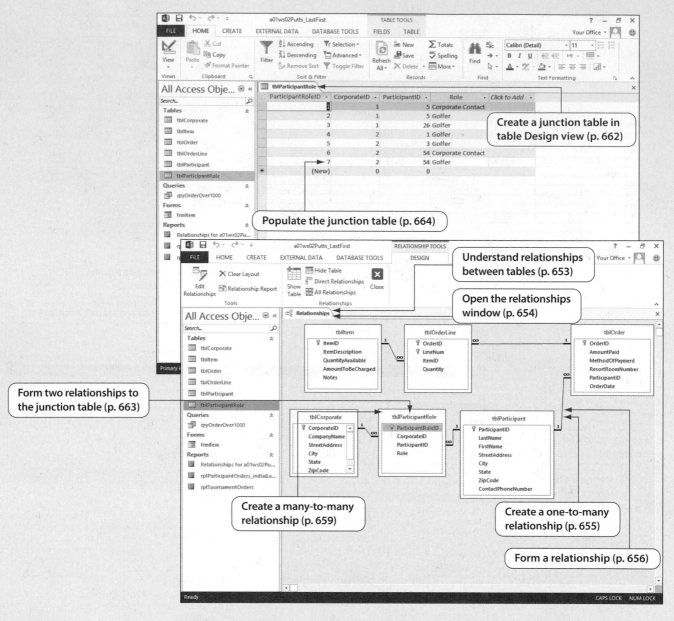

Figure 29 Putts for Paws Charity Tournament Imported Data Final Database

Practice 1

Student data files needed:

a01ws02Giftshop.accdb

a01ws02Products.xlsx

a01ws02Customers.xlsx

You will save your file as:

a01ws02Giftshop_LastFirst.accdb

Painted Treasures Gift Shop

The Painted Treasures Gift Shop sells many products for the resort patrons including jewelry, clothing, and spa products. You will create a database of customers and their purchases. The three tables that you need are customers, purchases, and products. What are the relationships between these three tables? You will need to add a junction table between the two tables with a many-to-many relationship.

a. You will import the tblProduct table from Excel. When you import a new table from Excel, you need to change the field definitions in Access.

- Start **Access**, and then open **a01ws02Giftshop**.

- Click the **FILE** tab, and save the file as an Access database in the location where you are saving your files with the name a01ws02Giftshop_LastFirst using your last and first name. If necessary, enable the content.
- Click the **EXTERNAL DATA** tab, and then in the Import & Link group, click **Excel**.
- Click **Browse.** Navigate to your student data files, select **a01ws02Products**, and then click **Open**. Make sure **Import the source data into a new table in the current database** is selected, and then click **OK**.
- In the Import Spreadsheet Wizard, note that **tblProduct** is selected, and then click **Next**.
- Be sure that the **First Row Contains Column Headings** check box is selected, click **Next**, and then click **Next** again.
- Select **Choose my own primary key**, click the **Primary Key** arrow, select **ProductID**, and then click **Next**.
- In the **Import to Table** box, keep the entry **tblProduct**, click **Finish**, and then click **Close**.
- Right-click **tblProduct**, and then select **Design View**.
- Change the data types as shown in the following table. Enter descriptions and change field sizes as noted.

Field Name	Data Type	Description	Field Size/Format
ProductID	Number	Unique identifier for product	Change Field Size to Long Integer
ProductDescription	Short Text	Description of product	Change Field Size to 40
Category	Short Text	Product category	Change Field Size to 15
QuantityInStock	Number	Quantity of product in stock	Change Field Size to Integer
Price	Change to Currency	Price to charge customer	Change format to Currency
Size	Short Text	Size of product	Change Field Size to 10
Color	Short Text	Color of product	Change Field Size to 15

- Save the table. Access tells you that some data might be lost because you are making fields shorter in length. Accept this by clicking **Yes**, and then close the table.

b. You will create a table named tblCustomer in Design view and import data to populate it.

- Click the **CREATE** tab, and then click **Table Design**. Access opens a blank table in Design view.
- Fill in the fields and change field sizes as noted.

Field Name	Data Type	Description	Field Size
CustomerID	AutoNumber	A unique ID that identifies each customer	**Long Integer**
LastName	Short Text	The customer's last name	25
FirstName	Short Text	The customer's first name	20
StreetAddress	Short Text	Street address	40
City	Short Text	City address	25
State	Short Text	State abbreviation	2
ZipCode	Short Text	Five-digit zip code	5
ResortHotelRoom	Short Text	Leave blank if not guest	6

- Highlight the **CustomerID** row by clicking the record selector to the left of the field, and then in the Tools group, click **Primary Key** to make CustomerID the primary key.
- Save your table design, naming it tblCustomer, click **OK**, and then close your table.
- Click the **EXTERNAL DATA** tab, and then in the Import & Link group, click **Excel**.
- Click **Browse**. Navigate to your student data files, click **a01ws02Customers**, and then click **Open**.
- Click **Append a copy of the records to the table** if necessary, click the arrow to select **tblCustomer**, and then click **OK**.
- Click **Next** twice, and then in the Import Spreadsheet Wizard dialog box, under Import to Table, in the Import to Table box accept the name **tblCustomer**. Click **Finish**, and then click **Close**. Double-click **tblCustomer** to open it in Datasheet view.
- In the first record in the table, change the **LastName** and **FirstName** fields to your last name and first name. Close the table.

c. Create relationships between your tables.

- Click the **DATABASE TOOLS** tab, and then in the Relationships group, click **Relationships**, and then click **Show Table**, if necessary.
- Add all four tables in the order **tblCustomer**, **tblPurchase**, **tblPurchaseLine**, and **tblProduct** to the Relationships window, and then close the Show Table dialog box.
- Drag the primary key **CustomerID** from tblCustomer to **CustomerID** in tblPurchase.
- Click **Enforce Referential Integrity**, and then click **Create**.
- Drag the primary key **PurchaseID** from tblPurchase to **PurchaseID** in tblPurchaseLine. Click **Enforce Referential Integrity**, and then click **Create**.
- Drag the primary key **ProductID** from tblProduct to **ProductID** in tblPurchaseLine. Click **Enforce Referential Integrity**, and then click **Create**.
- Click **Relationship Report**, and then save the report, accepting the name **Relationships for a01ws02Giftshop_LastFirst**. If your instructor directs you to print your results, print the report.
- Close the report, and then close the Relationships window.

d. Create a report of the customers, purchases, and products.

- Click the **CREATE** tab, and then in the Reports group, click **Report Wizard**.
- In the Report Wizard dialog box, click the **Tables/Querles** arrow, and then select **Table: tblCustomer**. Select the **LastName** and **FirstName** fields.
- Click the **Tables/Queries** arrow, click **Table: tblPurchase**, and then select **PurchaseDate**.
- Click the **Tables/Queries** arrow, click **Table: tblPurchaseLine**, and then select **Quantity**.
- Click the **Tables/Queries** arrow, click **Table: tblProduct**, select **ProductDescription**, and then click **Next**.
- Accept grouping by **tblCustomer** and then by **PurchaseDate** by clicking **Next**.
- You do not want any other grouping levels, click **Next**.
- Click the **arrow** to sort your report by ascending **ProductDescription**, and then click **Next**.
- Change the Orientation to **Landscape**, and then click **Next**.
- Title your report rptCustomerPurchases_initialLastname using your first initial and last name, and then click **Finish**.

- Switch to Layout view.
- Change the title of your report to Customer and Purchases by initial Lastname using your first initial and last name.
- Click the **column heading** for Quantity, press Shift, and then click the **first value** for Quantity so both the column heading and values are selected. With your pointer, move the right border to the left of the dotted blue line. Save your report.
- If your instructor directs you to print your results, print the report.
- Close the report, and then exit Access. Submit your file as directed by your instructor.

Problem Solve 1

Student data files needed:

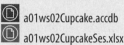

 a01ws02Cupcake.accdb

a01ws02CupcakeSes.xlsx

You will save your file as:

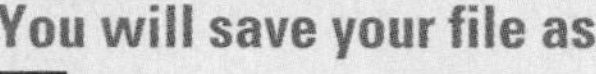

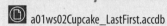

a01ws02Cupcake_LastFirst.accdb

Managing Employees at Jellybean's Cupcakes

Production & Operations

You are the manager of the Human Resources Department of Jellybean's Cupcakes, a bakery franchise specializing in traditional and trendy cupcakes. You need to create a database that will help you track current employees along with training efforts for all of the bakeries' employees. You have a database with employee data. You will add the training sessions from an Excel spreadsheet. You will have to create a relationship between employees and training sessions. Each employee can take many training sessions, and each training session can be attended by many employees, so you will need to create a junction table.

a. Start **Access**, and then open **a01ws02Cupcake**. Click the **FILE** tab, and then save the file as a01ws02Cupcake_LastFirst using your last and first name. If necessary, enable the content.

b. Open the **tblEmployee** table, and then change the name in record 25 to your name.

c. Switch to Design view, and then add two new fields to tblEmployee.

Field Name	Data Type	Description	Field Size/Format
MobilePhone	Short Text	The employee's cell phone number	14
DOB	Date/Time	The employee's date of birth	**Short Date**

d. Add an input mask for MobilePhone. Use a mask that will show phone numbers as **(555) 555-5555** with a place holder "-" and then save with the symbols in the mask.

e. Import a new table, **tblSessions**, from the Excel workbook **a01ws02CupcakeSes**. Do not set a primary key during the import. Make the following changes to the table in Design view.

- Add a new field SessionID and then assign a data type of **AutoNumber**. Make this field a primary key.
- Make the changes shown to Data Type, Description, and Field Size/Format.

Field Name	Data Type	Description	Field Size/Format
SessionID		The key that identifies each training session	
SessionName		The name of the training session	50
Description	Long Text	The description of the training session	
SessionDate		The date this session was held	Short Date

f. Create a new table in Design view. This table will serve as the junction table. Add the following fields, data types, and descriptions.

Field Name	Data Type	Description	Field Size
EmpTrnID	AutoNumber	The key that identifies each training session and employee	
SessionID	Number	The foreign key to tblSessions	Long Integer
EmployeeID	Number	The foreign key to tblEmployee	Long Integer

Assign **EmpTrnID** as the primary key, and then save the table as tblEmployeeTraining.

g. Open the **Relationships** window, and then create a one-to-many relationship between **EmployeeID** in tblEmployee and **EmployeeID** in tblEmployeeTraining. Enforce referential integrity.

h. Create a one-to-many relationship between **SessionID** in tblSessions and **SessionID** in tblEmployeeTraining, and then enforce referential integrity. Do not cascade update or cascade delete.

i. Create a relationship report, accepting the default report name.

j. Enter the following data into **tblEmployeeTraining**.

EmpTrnID	SessionID	EmployeeID
Let Access autonumber as 1	1	13
Let Access autonumber as 2	1	21
Let Access autonumber as 3	1	18
Let Access autonumber as 4	2	5
Let Access autonumber as 5	2	25
Let Access autonumber as 6	10	3
Let Access autonumber as 7	10	5
Let Access autonumber as 8	10	25
Let Access autonumber as 9	10	21
Let Access autonumber as 10	10	4

k. Create a query named qryChocolate101_initialLastname that selects **LastName**, **FirstName**, **HomePhone**, and **SessionName**. Select those employees that signed up for **Chocolate 101**, and then sort by **LastName** and **FirstName**.

l. Close your database. Submit your file as directed by your instructor.

Perform 1: Perform in Your Career

Student data files needed:

a01ws02Interns.accdb

a01ws02InternsCo.xlsx

You will save your file as:

a01ws02Interns_LastFirst.accdb

Internship Coordinator

Production & Operations

You take a job with an organization that matches students from Indiana schools to internship opportunities. You have a database with a table of information about interns and an Excel spreadsheet with companies that offer internships. You want to create a record of each intern's interviews. An intern can have many interviews, but an interview is with just one intern. A company can schedule many interviews, but an interview is with just one company.

a. Start **Access** and then open **a01ws02Interns**. Click the **FILE** tab, and save the file as an Access Database in the location where you save your files with the name a01ws02Interns_LastFirst.

b. Open **tblIntern**, familiarize yourself with the fields, add yourself as a new intern, and then close the table.

c. Start **Excel**, and then open **a01ws02InternsCo**. Familiarize yourself with the fields, and then close the workbook.

d. Import the companies from Excel into Access, creating a new table for companies called tblCompany. Fix data types and field sizes as appropriate. Add descriptions, and then set the **CompanyID** field as primary key.

e. Add a contact phone number field to the table formatted appropriately. Populate the phone number with the following information:

Company Name	Contact Phone Number
FreeMarkets	(408) 555-2049
BNY Mellon	(202) 555-8000
Adobe Systems, Incorporated	(408) 555-6799
Kraft Foods, Incorporated	(847) 555-9100
Oracle Corporation	(650) 555-3200

f. Design a table for interviews that will have the date of the interview and whatever primary keys and foreign keys you need. Create this table naming it tblInterview.

g. Form the relationships you need, and then create a relationship report accepting the default name.

h. Populate the interview table with the following information:

- Gloria Perry has an interview with BNY Mellon on 2/16/2015.
- You have an interview with Oracle Corporation on 2/13/2015.
- Thomas Jackson has an interview with Oracle Corporation on 2/13/2015.
- You have an interview with Adobe Systems, Incorporated, on 2/20/2015.
- Gloria Perry has an interview with FreeMarkets on 3/2/2015.

i. Create a report showing all companies and the interviews that are scheduled. Save the report as rptCompanyInterviews_initialLastname. Fix the columns as necessary to show them all.

j. Submit your file as directed by your instructor.

Additional Cases

Additional Workshop Cases are available on the companion website and in the instructor resources.

MODULE CAPSTONE

More Practice 1

Student data files needed:

a01mpRecipe.accdb
a01mpRecipePrep.xlsx
a01mpRecipeIng.xlsx
a01mpRecipeJunc.csv

You will save your file as:

a01mpRecipe_LastFirst.accdb

Indigo5 Restaurant

Production & Operations

Robin Sanchez, the chef of the resort's restaurant, Indigo5, wants to keep track of recipes and the ingredients that they include in an Access database. This will allow her to plan menus and get reports and queries on the ingredients that are needed. Ingredients have already been stored in Excel worksheets and can be imported from Excel into Access. The dish preparation instructions can be copied from Excel and pasted into Access. Other data will need to be entered. Complete the following tasks:

a. Start **Access**, and then open the student data file **a01mpRecipe**. Click the **FILE** tab, and then save the file as an Access database in the location designated by your instructor with the name a01mpRecipe_LastFirst using your last and first name. If necessary, enable the content.

b. Create a new table in **Design** view. This table will store specific recipe items.

- Add the following fields, data types, and descriptions. Change field sizes as noted.

Field Name	Data Type	Description	Field Size
RecipeID	**Short Text**	The recipe ID assigned to each menu item (primary key)	6
RecipeName	**Short Text**	The recipe name	30
FoodCategory	**Short Text**	The food category	15
TimeToPrepare	**Number**	Preparation time in minutes	**Integer**
Servings	**Number**	The number of servings this recipe makes	**Integer**
Instructions	**Long Text**	Cooking instructions	

- Designate **RecipeID** as the primary key. Save the new table as tblRecipes and then close the table.

c. Create a form to enter recipes. Select **tblRecipes**, click the **CREATE** tab, and then in the Forms group, click **Form**. Save the form as frmRecipes_initialLastname using your first initial and last name.

- Enter the following data into frmRecipes_initialLastname in Form view.

RecipeID	RecipeName	FoodCategory	TimeToPrepare	Servings
REC001	Chicken Soup	Soup	45	8
REC002	Black Beans	Beans	90	6

d. Start Excel, and then open **a01mpRecipePrep**. For each recipe, copy the **Cooking Instructions** from the Excel worksheet and paste the recipe instructions into the Access field **Instructions**. Close the form, and then close Excel.

e. Import Excel file **a01mpRecipeIng**, appending it to **tblIngredients**. Use the **Ingredients** worksheet. There are headers in the first row of this worksheet. Do not save the import steps.

f. Create a new table in **Design** view. This table will serve as the junction table between the tblIngredients and tblRecipes tables.
   - Add the following fields, data types, and descriptions, in this order. Change field sizes as noted.

Field Name	Data Type	Description	Field Size
RecipeIngredientID	**AutoNumber**	The recipe ingredient ID automatically assigned to each recipe ingredient (primary key)	
RecipeID	**Short Text**	The recipe ID from tblRecipes (foreign key)	6
IngredientID	**Number**	The ingredient ID from tblIngredients (foreign key)	**Long Integer**
Quantity	**Number**	The quantity of the ingredient required in the recipe	**Double**

   - Assign **RecipeIngredientID** as the primary key.
   - Save the new table as tblRecipeIngredients.
   - Close the table.

g. Open the **Relationships** window and add all three tables to the window.
   - Create a one-to-many relationship between **RecipeID** in tblRecipes and **RecipeID** in tblRecipeIngredients. Enforce referential integrity. Do not cascade update or cascade delete.
   - Create a one-to-many relationship between **IngredientID** in tblIngredients and **IngredientID** in tblRecipeIngredients. Enforce referential integrity. Do not cascade update or cascade delete.
   - Create a relationships report accepting the default name.
   - Save the relationships, and then close the Relationships window.

h. The Recipe Ingredients junction data were stored in a comma-separated values file or csv file. This is a comma-delimited format that can be read by Excel. Access treats a csv file as a text file. Import **a01mpRecipeJunc** as **Text** appending it to **tblRecipeIngredients**. Select **Delimited**, **Comma**, and **First Row Contains Field Names**. Do not save the import steps.

i. Use the Simple Query Wizard and the data in tblRecipes, tblRecipeIngredients, and tblIngredients to create a query that displays the ingredients for each dish. The query results should list **RecipeName**, **Quantity**, **Ingredient**, and **Units**. This will be a **Detail** query. Run your query. Adjust the width of the query columns as necessary. Save your query as qryRecipeIngredients_initialLastname.

j. Create a report with the source **qryRecipeIngredients_initialLastname** using the Report Wizard. Select all fields, group by **RecipeName**, and then sort by **ingredient**. Accept all other defaults. Name your report rptRecipeIngredients_initialLastname and then modify the report title to be your Recipe Ingredients Report by initial Lastname. Adjust the report columns as necessary.

k. Close the database. Submit the file as directed by your instructor.

Problem Solve 1

Student data files needed:

a01ps1Hotel.accdb

a01ps1HotelGuest.accdb

a01ps1HotelRes.xlsx

a01ps1HotelRooms.csv

You will save your file as:

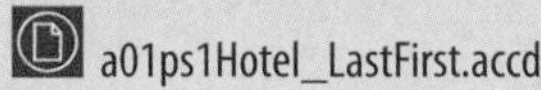

a01ps1Hotel_LastFirst.accdb

Hotel Reservations

Production & Operations

The main portion of the resort is the hotel. The hotel wants to store information about hotel guests, reservations, and rooms. You will design tables, import data from Access and Excel, and create relationships. Then you will be able to create queries and reports from the data. Complete the following tasks:

a. Start **Access**, and then open **a01ps1Hotel**. Click the **FILE** tab, and save the file as an Access database with the name a01ps1Hotel_LastFirst using your last and first name. If necessary, enable the content.

b. Import a table from the Access database **a01ps1HotelGuest**, selecting the **tblGuests** table. Do not save the import steps.

c. Open **tblGuests**, and then change the guest name in record **25** to your first and last name. Close the table.

d. Create a new table in **Design** view. This table will store reservations.

- Add the following fields, data types, and descriptions, in this order. Change field sizes as noted.

Field Name	Data Type	Description	Field Size/ Format
ReservationID	**AutoNumber**	A unique identifier for the reservation (primary key)	**Long Integer**
GuestID	**Number**	The guest ID from tblGuests (foreign key)	**Long Integer**
RoomNumber	**Short Text**	The room number from tblRooms (foreign key)	30
CheckInDate	**Date/Time**	The date the guest will check in	**Short Date**
NightsStay	**Number**	How many nights the guest will stay	**Integer**
NumberOfGuests	**Number**	The number of guests on this reservation	**Integer**

- Assign **ReservationID** as the primary key.
- Save the new table as tblReservations.

e. Import **a01ps1HotelRes** from Excel, appending it to **tblReservations**. The Excel column headers match the Access field names.

f. Select **tblReservations**, click the **CREATE** tab, and then in the Forms group, click **Form** to create a form to enter reservations. Save it as frmReservations_initialLastname, using your first initial and last name.

- Enter the following data in the new (blank) record in frmReservations_initialLastname.

ReservationID	GuestID	RoomNumber	CheckInDate	NightsStay	NumberOfGuests
AutoNumber	25	105	4/20/2015	8	1

g. Create a new table in **Design** view. This table will store information about the hotel rooms.
   - Add the following fields, data types, and descriptions, in this order. Change field sizes as noted.

Field Name	Data Type	Description	Field Size
RoomNumber	**Short Text**	The resort's room number or name (primary key)	30
RoomType	**Short Text**	The type of room this is	20

   - Assign **RoomNumber** as the primary key.
   - Save the new table as tblRooms.

h. The Hotel Rooms data was stored in a comma-separated values file or csv file. This is a comma-delimited format that can be read by Excel. Access treats a csv file as a text file. Import **a01ps1HotelRooms** as text, appending it to **tblRooms**. Select **Delimited**, **Comma**, and **First Row Contains Field Names**. Do not save the import steps.

i. Open the **Relationships** window, add **tblGuests**, **tblReservations**, and **tblRooms**. Create a one-to-many relationship between **GuestID** in tblGuests and **GuestID** in tblReservations. Enforce referential integrity. Do not cascade update or cascade delete.

j. Create a one-to-many relationship between **RoomNumber** in tblRooms and **RoomNumber** in tblReservations. Enforce referential integrity. Do not cascade update or cascade delete. Create a relationships report accepting the default name.

k. Use the Simple Query Wizard to create a query. The query results should list **GuestID**, **GuestFirstName**, **GuestMiddleInitial**, **GuestLastName**, **CheckInDate**, **NightsStay**, and **RoomType**. This query should show every field of every record.

l. Save your query as qryMyReservations_initialLastname. Run the query.

m. In Design view for **qryMyReservations_initialLastname**, select the guest with **GuestID** = 25. Sort by **CheckInDate**. Run the query.

n. Use the Report Wizard to create a report showing **ReservationID**, **CheckInDate**, **NightsStay**, and **RoomType**. View by **tblRooms** and sort by **CheckInDate** and **ReservationID**. Name your report rptReservations_initialLastname. Change the title to Reservations Report by initial Lastname. Adjust the report columns as necessary.

o. Close the database. Submit the file as directed by your instructor.

Problem Solve 2

MyITLab® Grader
Homework 2

Student data files needed:

a01ps2HotelStaff.accdb
a01ps2HotelEmp.xlsx
a01ps2HotelAreas.accdb

You will save your file as:

a01ps2HotelStaff_LastFirst.accdb

Human Resources

Hotel Reservations

The Hotel general manager needs a human resource database to store information on employees, the areas they work in, and the hours they are scheduled to work. The database will have three new tables: tblHotelAreas, tblEmployee, and tblSchedule.

Complete the following tasks:

a. Start **Access**, and then open the student data file **a01ps2HotelStaff**. Click the **FILE** tab, and save the file as an Access Database in the location designated by your instructor with the name a01ps2HotelStaff_LastFirst using your first and last name. If necessary, enable the content.

b. Create a new table in **Design** view. This table will store employees.

   - Add the following fields, in this order. Where necessary, you decide upon data types and field sizes.

Field Name	Data Type	Description	Field Size
EmployeeID	**AutoNumber**	A unique identifier for the employee (primary key)	
AreaID	**Number**	The area ID from tblHotelAreas (foreign key)	**Long Integer**
FirstName	**Pick appropriate type**	The employee's first name	30
LastName	**Pick appropriate type**	The employee's last name	30
StreetAddress	**Pick appropriate type**	Home street address	40
City	**Pick appropriate type**	City	30
State	**Pick appropriate type**	State abbreviation	Pick appropriate size
ZipCode	**Pick appropriate type**	Zip code (5 digit)	Pick appropriate size
Phone	**Pick appropriate type**	Home phone number	14
HireDate	**Pick appropriate type**	Date employee was hired	**Short Date**
JobTitle	**Pick appropriate type**	Employee job title	30

   - Make sure you have assigned the most appropriate field to be the primary key.
   - Save the new table as tblEmployee.
   - Define an input mask for the phone number. Use a mask that will show phone numbers as **(555) 555-5555** with a place holder of "-" and save with the symbols in the mask.

c. Import **a01ps2HotelEmp** from Excel, using the **Employee** worksheet and appending it to **tblEmployee**. Change the name and street address of the last employee to your name and address.

d. Import the **tblHotelAreas** table from the **a01ps2HotelAreas** Access database and create a new table.

e. Import **a01ps2HotelEmp** from Excel, using the **Area** worksheet and appending it to **tblHotelAreas**.

f. Create a new table in **Design** view. This table will store information about an employee's schedule.

- Add the following fields, data types, and descriptions, in this order.

Field Name	Data Type	Description	Field Size
ScheduleID	**AutoNumber**	A unique identifier for the schedule (primary key)	**Long Integer**
ScheduleDay	**Date/Time**	The day the schedule applies to	**ShortDate**
StartTime	**Date/Time**	Starting time for the shift	**MediumTime**
HoursScheduled	**Number**	Number of hours on shift	**Integer**
EmployeeID	**Number**	The person being scheduled	**Long Integer**

- Make sure you have assigned the most appropriate primary key.
- Save the new table as tblSchedule.

g. Import **a01ps2HotelEmployees** from Excel, using the **Schedule** worksheet, and appending it to **tblSchedule**.

h. Open the **Relationships** window, add the tables **tblSchedule**, **tblEmployee**, and **tblHotelAreas**. Create a one-to-many relationship between **EmployeeID** in tblEmployee and **EmployeeID** in tblSchedule. Enforce referential integrity. Do not cascade update or cascade delete.

i. Create a one-to-many relationship between **AreaID** in tblHotelAreas and **AreaID** in tblEmployee. Enforce referential integrity. Do not cascade update or cascade delete. Create a relationships report accepting the default name.

j. Create a form for **tblEmployee**. Notice that Access automatically includes the related records from tblSchedule at the bottom of the form. Save the form as frmEmployeeSchedule_initialLastname.

k. Using **frmEmployeeSchedule_initialLastname**, add a new schedule for yourself to work on January 3, 2015, starting at 8 am and working for 8 hours.

l. Use data in **tblHotelAreas**, **tblEmployee**, and **tblSchedule** to create a schedule query. The query results should list **AreaID**, **AreaName**, **FirstName**, **LastName**, **ScheduleDay**, **StartTime**, and **HoursScheduled**. Save your query as qryCoffeeShopSchedule_initialLastname.

m. In Design view for **qryCoffeeShopSchedule_initialLastname**, select only the data from **AreaID 4**. Run the query.

n. Create a report from **qryCoffeeShopSchedule_initialLastname**. Select these fields: **FirstName**, **LastName**, **ScheduleDay**, **StartTime**, and **HoursScheduled**. View by **tblSchedule**. Sort by **ScheduleDay**, **StartTime** and **LastName**, and then change to **Landscape** orientation. Name your report rptCoffeeShopSchedule_initialLastname. Modify the report title to be Coffee Shop Schedule by initial Lastname.

o. Close the database. Submit the file as directed by your instructor.

Perform 1: Perform in Your Life

Student data file needed:

 Blank Access database

You will save your file as:

 a01pf1Club_LastFirst.accdb

Track Events for Your Organization

Research & Development

Pick an organization that you belong to. You want to track the members of the organization, events, and member attendance at the events. Because a member can attend many events and an event can be attended by many members, you will need a junction table. You will start by creating three tables, the relationships between the tables, and reports on attendance. Next, you will decide on one other table that makes sense for your organization, define that table, and relate it to one of the already existing tables.

a. Start **Access**, and then click **Blank desktop database**. Browse to where you are storing your data files, and name your database a01pf1Club_LastFirst.

b. Design a table to store members. Choose appropriate fields that would describe the members of your organization.
   - Assign a field to be primary key, and then make it **AutoNumber**. For all fields, enter appropriate data types, descriptions, field sizes, and masks. Save your table as tblMember.

c. Enter yourself and a friend into the table. Enter as many other members as you wish.

d. Design a table to store events. Use the following fields: EventID, EventName, EventDate, and PlaceName. You may add other fields as appropriate.
   - Assign EventID to be primary key, and then make it an AutoNumber. Enter appropriate data types, descriptions, and field sizes. Save your table as tblEvent.

e. Enter two events that you attended into the table. Enter as many other events as you wish.

f. Design a junction table to relate members and attendance at events. Use the following fields: EventID and the primary key of your member table.
   - EventID is a foreign key and should be Number, Long Integer. Enter an appropriate description.
   - Use the primary key of your member table as a foreign key in this table. Enter an appropriate type and description.
   - Create a composite primary key using both EventID and the primary key from your member table.
   - Save your table as tblAttendance.

g. Create relationships as appropriate for the tblMember, tblAttendance, and tblEvent tables.

h. Enter the following data into tblAttendance.

EventID	MemberID
Use the EventID for the first event	Your primary key in the member table
Use the EventID for the first event	Your friend's primary key in the member table
Use the EventID for the second event	Your primary key in the member table

i. Create a report on Events using **EventName**, **EventDate**, and **PlaceName**. Sort by EventDate. Name your report rptEventReport_initialLastname and then modify the report title to be Event Report by initial Lastname.

j. Create a query on Events including **EventName**, **EventDate**, and **PlaceName**. Save the query as qryEventName_initialLastname and then modify the query design to select the EventName for the first event. Run the query.

k. Create a report on event attendance. Use **EventName** and **EventDate** from tblEvent and the member's name. Group the report by **Event**. Sort the report by **LastName** and **FirstName**. Name your report rptEventAttendance_initialLastname and then modify the report title to be Event Attendance by initial Lastname.

l. Determine one additional table that would make sense for your organization to keep data in.

m. Design this table and the appropriate fields. Make sure to assign a primary key.

n. Enter data into the new table. Create relationships between this new table and your existing tables as appropriate. Ask yourself the two questions to determine the relationships. Create a relationships report accepting the default name.

o. Create a report showing data from your new table and data from another table that it is related to.

p. Submit the file as directed by your instructor.

Perform 2: Perform in Your Career

Student data file needed:	You will save your file as:
Blank Access database	 a01pf2PetStore_LastFirst.accdb

Pet Store

Sales & Marketing

A pet store owner wants to create a database for the store. The database needs to include information about animals and the breeds of the animals. An animal is of one breed. The pet store can have many animals of each breed. The pet owner will want to keep records of the purchases and the customers that bought each animal. You will need to decide what tables you need to record purchases and customers. You will also need to decide what relationships you want to create.

a. Start **Access**, and then click **Blank desktop database**. Browse to where you are storing your data files, and name your database a01pf2PetStore_LastFirst.

b. Design a table to store breeds. Use the following fields: BreedID, AnimalType, BreedName, MaximumSize (in pounds), LengthOfLife (in years).

- Assign **BreedID** to be primary key with the AutoNumber data type.
- For all fields, enter appropriate data types, descriptions, and field sizes. Save your table as tblBreed.

c. Enter the following data into the table, in this order.

BreedID	AnimalType	BreedName	MaximumSize	LengthOfLife
1	Dog	Akita	110	12
2	Dog	Papillon	9	15
3	Cat	Devon	7	18
4	Cat	Birman	10	19
5	Chinchilla	Silver Mosaic	1	15

d. After entering those five breeds, pick another breed and add it to the table.

e. Design a table to store animals. Use the following fields: AnimalID, DateOfBirth, Price, Weight, Color, Sex, and BreedID.

- Assign **AnimalID** to be primary key with the AutoNumber data type.
- BreedID is the foreign key to tblBreed.
- For all fields, enter appropriate data types, descriptions, and field sizes.
- Save your table as tblAnimal.

f. Enter the following data into tblAnimal, in this order.

AnimalID	DateOfBirth	Price	Weight	Color	Sex	BreedID
1	6/17/2014	$125.00	28	White	M	1
2	6/17/2014	$125.00	30	White	M	1
3	7/25/2014	$610.00	4	Tan	F	2
4	8/7/2014	$610.00	3	White	F	2
5	8/7/2014	$550.00	3	White	M	2
6	5/10/2014	$225.00	2	Blue	F	3
7	5/10/2014	$225.00	2	Gray	M	3
8	6/26/2014	$150.00	2	White	F	4
9	7/17/2014	$125.00	2	Gray	M	4
10	8/18/2014	$ 30.00	1	Silver	F	5

g. After adding the 10 animals, add another animal which is of the breed you entered for the prior table.

h. Open the Relationships window. Create a one-to-many relationship between BreedID in tblBreed and BreedID in tblAnimal. Enforce referential integrity. Do not cascade update or cascade delete.

i. Determine the tables that the store owner would need to keep store customers and their purchases.

- Design these tables and the appropriate fields. Make sure to assign primary keys.
- Create relationships between these new tables and your existing tables as appropriate. Ask yourself the two questions to determine the relationships. Add foreign keys as appropriate. Create a relationships report accepting the default name.

j. Enter the appropriate customer and purchase data to capture the following events.

- You bought the chinchilla with AnimalID = 10 yesterday.
- A friend bought the Birman cat with AnimalID = 9 and the Akita with Animal ID = 1 today.

k. Create a report showing animals by breed. Show **AnimalType**, **BreedName**, **AnimalID**, **DateOfBirth**, and **Price**. Select correct groupings and sort orders.

l. Create a query to find out who purchased AnimalID = 10. Show **Customer name** (FirstName and LastName), **AnimalID**, **AnimalType**, and **BreedName**.

m. Create a report showing the animals purchased on all dates. Group and sort appropriately.

n. Submit the file as directed by your instructor.

Perform 3: Perform in Your Team

Student data files needed:

Blank Access database

Blank Word document

You will save your files as:

a01pf3Music_TeamName.accdb

a01pf3MusicPlan_TeamName.docx

Independent Music Label

Production & Operations

The owner of an independent music label needs to keep track of the groups, musicians, and their music. You have been asked to create a database for the label.

The label owner would like to be able to get a list of groups with all musicians, get a list of groups with albums, select an album and see all songs in the album, and select a group and see their albums with all songs in the album. You will need to design tables, fields, relationships, queries, and reports for the label.

Because databases can only be opened and edited by one person at a time, it is a good idea to plan ahead by designing your tables in advance. You will use a Word document to plan your database and to plan which team member will do what. You will use SkyDrive to store your Word document and Access database.

a. Select one team member to set up the Word document and Access database by completing Steps b–e.

b. Open your browser and navigate to **https://www.skydrive.live.com**, create a new folder, and name it a01pf3MusicFolder_TeamName. Replace TeamName with the name assigned to your team by your instructor.

c. Start **Access**, and then click **Blank desktop database**. Create a blank database, and then name it a01pf3Music_TeamName. Replace TeamName with the name assigned to your team by your instructor. Click the **Create** button to create the database.

d. Upload the **a01pf3Music_TeamName** database to the **a01pf3MusicFolder_TeamName** folder, and then share the folder with the other members of your team. Verify that the other team members have permission to edit the contents of the shared folder and that they are required to log in to SkyDrive to access it.

e. Create a new Word document in the assignment folder in SkyDrive, and then name it a01pf3MusicPlan_TeamName. Replace TeamName with the name assigned to your team by your instructor.

f. In the Word document, each team member must list his or her first and last name as well as a summary of their planned contributions. As work is completed on the database, this document should be updated with the specifics of each team member's contributions.

g. Use the Word document to list the fields you need in each table, the primary keys for each table, and the foreign keys.

h. In Access, your team members will need to complete the following steps.
   - Design your tables.
   - Enter data for three music groups into your tables.

Groups	Group Members	Albums	Songs
Clean Green, an Enviro-Punk band	Jon Smith (vocalist and guitar) Lee Smith percussion and keyboard)	Clean Green	Esperando Verde Precious Drops Recycle Mania Don't Tread on Me
		Be Kind to Animals	It's Our Planet Too Animal Rag Where Will We Live?
Spanish Moss, a Spanish Jazz band	Hector Caurendo (guitar) Pasquale Rodriguez (percussion) Perry Trent (vocalist) Meredith Selmer (bass)	Latin Latitude	Attitude Latitude Flying South Latin Guitarra Cancion Cancion
Your band	Your team members	You decide	You decide

   - Create your relationships. Create a relationships report.
   - Create a report showing all groups with all musicians.
   - Create a report showing all groups, the group type, and their albums.
   - Create a query to select an album from your band and see all songs in the album.
   - Create a query to select your band and see all your albums with all songs in the albums.

i. Once the assignment is complete, share the **a01pf3MusicFolder_TeamName** folder with your instructor. Make sure that your instructor has permission to edit the contents of the folder.

Perform 4: How Others Perform

Student data file needed:

a01pf4Textbook.accdb

You will save your files as:

a01pf4Textbook_LastFirst.accdb

a01pf4Textbook_LastFirst.docx

College Bookstore

Production & Operations

A colleague has created a database for your college bookstore. He is having problems creating the relationships in the database and has come to you for your help. What problems do you see in his database design? He has three tables in his database: one for sections of courses, one for instructors, and one for textbooks, as shown in Figures 1, 2, and 3.

a. Start **Access**, and then open the student data file **a01pf4Textbook**. Save the file as a01pf4Textbook_LastFirst. You do not need to make changes to this database, but you will want to look at the database in more detail than is shown in the figures.

b. Create a Word document named a01pf4Textbook_LastFirst where you will answer the remaining questions.

c. Are there any errors in the way that fields are defined or named in the tables? In your a01pf4TextbookAnswers_LastFirst Word document, list your errors by table.

d. Are there any errors in the way that tables are named or defined? In your a01pf4TextbookAnswers_LastFirst Word document, list your errors by table.

e. He wants to define these relationships. How would you want to define the relationships?
   - An instructor can teach many sections; a section is taught by just one instructor.
   - A section can have many textbooks; a textbook can be used in many sections.

f. In your a01pf4TextbookAnswers_LastFirst Word document, describe how you would define the relationships.

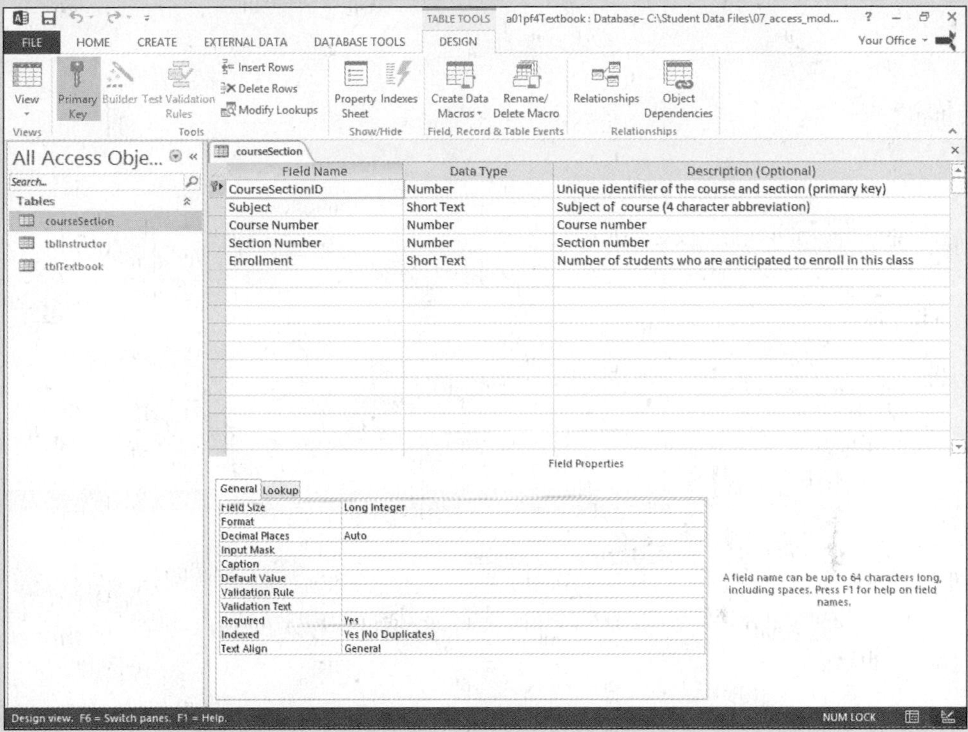

Figure 1 Table design for courseSection

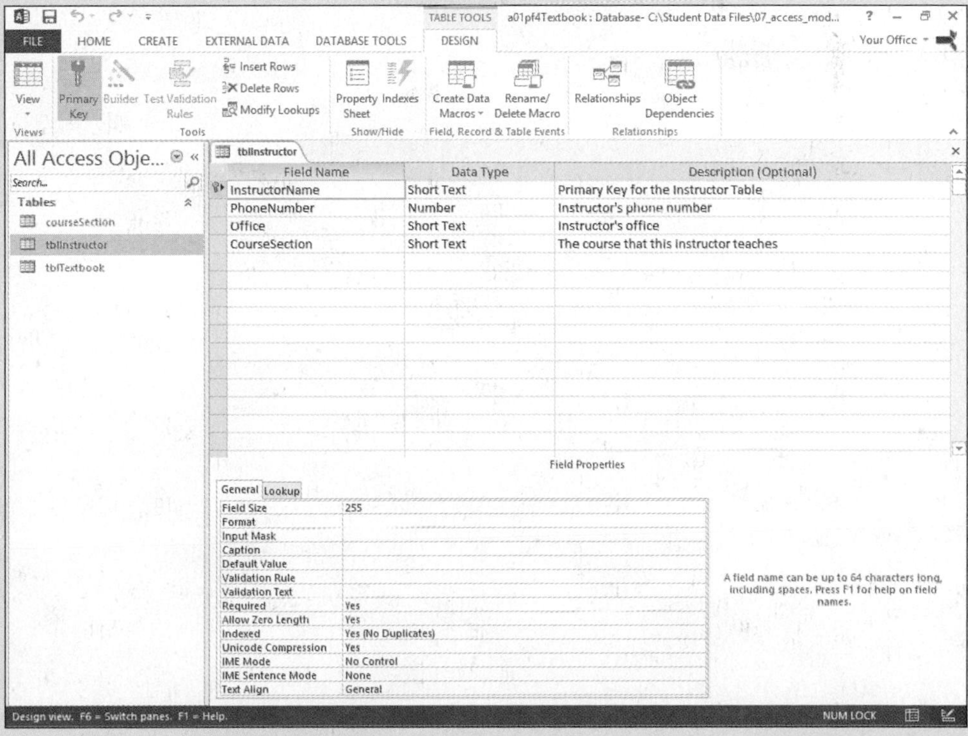

Figure 2 Table design for tblInstructor

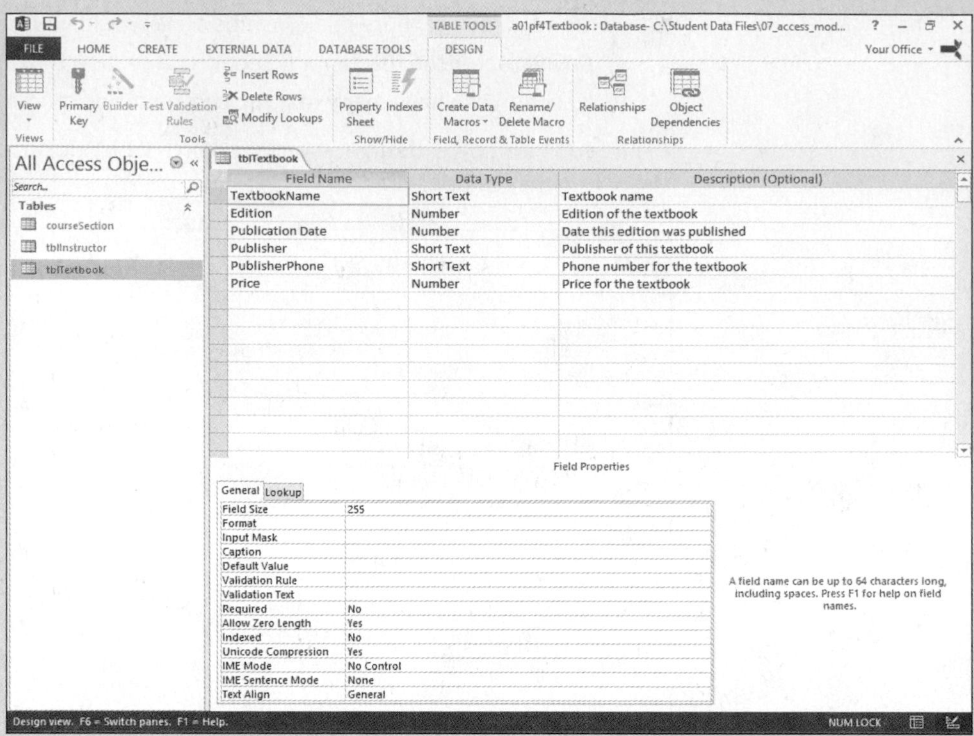

Figure 3 Table design for tblTextbook

g. Submit the files as directed by your instructor.

WORKSHOP 3 | QUERIES AND DATA ACCESS

OBJECTIVES

1. Find and replace records in the datasheet p. 690
2. Modify datasheet appearance p. 695
3. Run query wizards p. 697
4. Create queries in Design view p. 699
5. Sort query results p. 706
6. Define selection criteria for queries p. 708
7. Create aggregate functions p. 723
8. Create calculated fields p. 729

Prepare Case

Turquoise Oasis Spa Data Management

Production & Operations

The Turquoise Oasis Spa has been popular with resort clients. The owners have spent several months putting spa data into an Access database so they can better manage the data. You have been asked to help show the staff how best to use the database to find information about products, services, and customers. For training purposes, not all the spa records have been added yet. Once the staff is trained, the remaining records will be entered into the database.

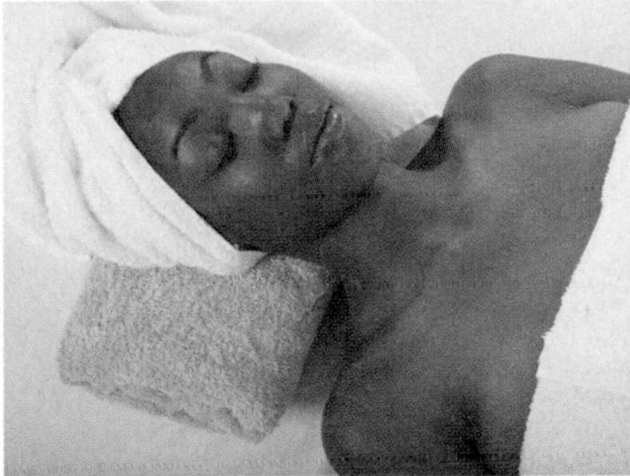

Dewayne Flowers / Shutterstock.com

REAL WORLD SUCCESS

"My company sells luxury appliances. Sometimes, we run out of products and don't have time to wait for the supplier. In the past, I'd have to get on the phone and call all our other locations in the region to see if they had extra that they could spare. Now, I run a query and in less than a minute I know who has it and when they need it. The queries are so popular that I've shared them with all of the managers."

- David, alumnus and procurement specialist

Student data file needed for this workshop:

 a02ws03Spa.accdb

You will save your file as:

 a02ws03Spa_LastFirst.accdb

Working with Datasheets

Datasheets are used to view all records in a table at one time. Each record is viewed as a row in the table. Records can be entered, edited, and deleted directly in a datasheet. When a table becomes so large that all the records and fields are no longer visible in the datasheet window without scrolling, the Find command can be used to quickly find specific values in a record. In this section, you will find records in a datasheet as well as modify the appearance of a datasheet.

Find and Replace Records in the Datasheet

The Navigation bar allows you to move to the top and bottom of a table or scroll to a specific record; however, this can be inefficient if your table is large. To manage larger tables, Access provides ways for you to quickly locate information within the datasheet. Once that information is found, it can then be easily replaced with another value using the **Replace command**.

If you do not know the exact value you are looking for because you do not know how it is spelled or how someone entered it, you can use a wildcard character. A **wildcard character** is used as a placeholder for an unknown part of a value or to match a certain pattern in a value. For example, if you know the value you are looking for contains the word "market" you can use a wildcard character at the beginning and end such as *market*.

Opening the Starting File

The owners of the spa have spent several months entering spa data into an Access database so they can better manage the data. You have been asked to help show the staff how best to use the database to find information about products, services, and customers. For training purposes, not all the spa records have been added yet.

A03.00

To Open the a02ws03Spa Database

a. Start **Access**, and then open the student data file **a02ws03Spa**.

b. On the **FILE** tab, save the file as an **Access Database** in the location designated by your instructor with the name a02ws03Spa_LastFirst using your first and last name. If necessary, enable the content.

Finding Records in a Table

In Datasheet view, you can use the **Find command** to quickly locate specific records using all or part of a field value. For this project, a staff member found a book left by one of the guests. A first name was printed on the inside of the book cover. The staff member remembers helping a gentleman named Guy who said he was from North Carolina, but is not certain of his last name. You will show the staff how to use the Find command to quickly navigate through the table to search for this guest.

MyITLab®
Workshop 3 Training

A03.01

To Find Records in the Datasheet

a. In the Navigation Pane, double-click **tblCustomer** to open the table.

b. Add a record at the end of the table with your first name, last name, address, city, state, phone and e-mail address. Press Tab until the record selector is on the next row and your record has been added to the table.

SIDE NOTE
Find Shortcut
Ctrl+F is the keyboard shortcut for Find.

SIDE NOTE
Spelling Counts
Spelling counts in Access, so if you enter a search item and Access cannot find it, your search value may be spelled wrong.

MODULE 2

c. On the Navigation bar, click **First Record** to go to the first record in the table. On the HOME tab, in the Find group, click **Find** to open the Find and Replace dialog box.

d. Replace the text in the Find What box with Guy. Click the **Look In** arrow, and then select **Current document**.

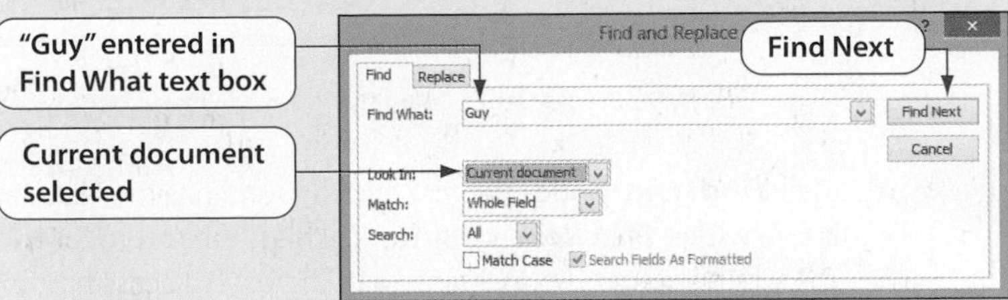

Figure 1 Find and Replace dialog box to find all records for "Guy"

e. Click **Find Next**. Access highlights the first record found for Guy Bowers from Derby, North Carolina (NC). This is a possibility, but there might be a second Guy.

f. Click **Find Next** again to check for more records with Guy. Guy Blake from Suffolk, Wisconsin, is found.

g. Click **Find Next** again to check for more records with Guy. When Access is done searching and cannot find any more matches, you will see the message "Microsoft Access finished searching the records. The search item was not found."

h. Click **OK**, and then click **Cancel** to close the Find and Replace dialog box.

Troubleshooting
If you did not get the results shown above, go back and carefully check the settings in the Find and Replace dialog box. Make sure Match Case is not checked. When Match Case is checked, the search will be case sensitive. Also check to make sure the Look In box shows Current document. If the Look In box shows Current field, Access will only look in the field selected.

Finding and Replacing Data in a Datasheet

Not only can you find records using the Find command, but you can also replace records once you find them with the Replace command. In a large table, it is helpful to locate a record using the Find command, and then replace the data using the Replace command.

For this project, the receptionist receives a notice from Erica Rocha about her upcoming marriage. The receptionist wants to go through the database and find any records related to Erica and change her last name to her married name, Muer. You will show the receptionist how to find Erica in the database and replace her last name of Rocha with Muer.

A03.02

To Find and Replace Records

a. On the HOME tab, in the Find group, click **Find** to open the Find and Replace dialog box.

b. In the Find and Replace dialog box, click the **Replace** tab. In the Find What box, type Rocha and then in the Replace With box, type Muer.

c. Verify that Look in: Current document is selected. Leave all other options as they are.

SIDE NOTE

Data Is Automatically Saved

Access automatically saves data changes when you close the table without prompting you to save it.

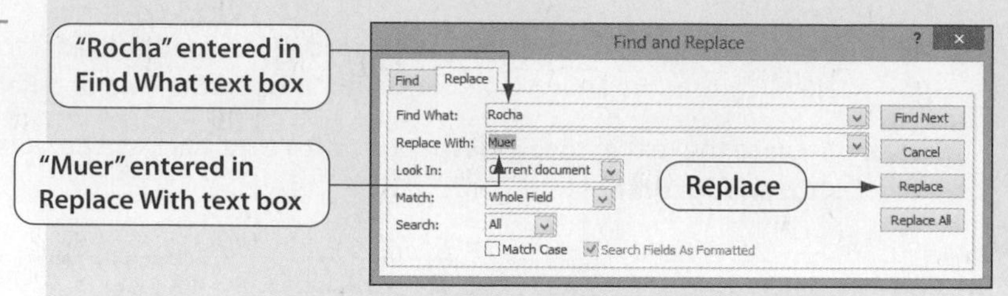

Figure 2 Find and Replace box options

d. Click **Find Next**. Notice the first record found has the last name Rocha, but the first name is Emily. Click **Find Next** again. Notice this is the record for Erica Rocha. Click **Replace**. Click **OK** when you get the message that Microsoft Access has finished searching the records. The Last Name should now be Muer instead of Rocha. Click **Cancel** to close the Find and Replace dialog box.

e. **Close** [X] the table.

Using a Wildcard Character

A wildcard character, as shown in Table 1, is used as a placeholder for an unknown part of a value or to match a certain pattern in a value. A wildcard character can replace a single character or multiple characters and both text and numbers.

Wildcard Character	Example
*	To match any number of characters; to search for a word that starts with "ar" you would enter ar*.
#	To match any single numeric character; to search for a three-digit number that starts with "75" you would enter 75#.
?	To match any single character; to search for a three-letter word that starts with "t" and ends with "p" you would enter t?p.
[ ]	To match any single character within the brackets; to search for a word that starts with "e," contains any of the letters "a" or "r," and ends with "r," you would enter e[ar]r and get "ear" or "err" as a result.
!	To match any single character NOT within the brackets; to search for a word that starts with "e," contains any letter other than "a" or "r," and ends with "r," you would enter e[!ar]r to get anything except "err" or "ear".
-	To match any range of characters in ascending order—"a" to "z"; to search for a word beginning with "a" and ending in "e" with any letter between "b" and "t" in between, you would enter a[b-t]e.

Table 1 Wildcard characters

For this project, the staff is looking for products with the word "butter" in the name so they can put together a weekly promotion for all these products. You will show them how to use a wildcard character to find the products.

A03.03

To Use a Wildcard Character to Find a Record

a. Double-click **tblProduct** to open the table.

b. In the first record, click the **ProductDescription** field. In the Find group, click **Find** to open the Find and Replace dialog box. Replace the text in the Find What box with *butter*. Click the **Look In** arrow, and then click **Current field**.

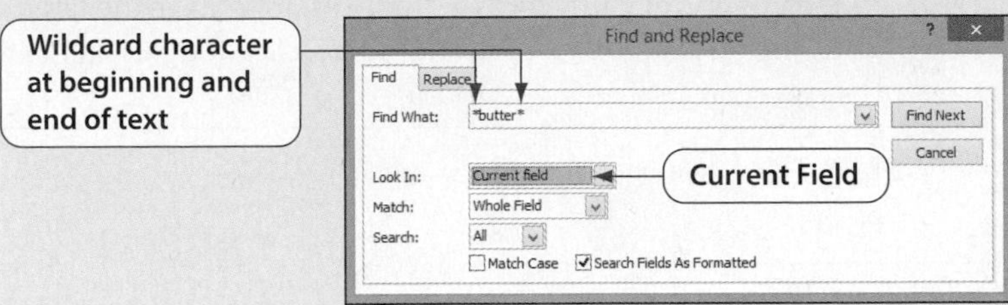

Figure 3 Find records with "butter" in the ProductDescription field

c. Click **Find Next**. The first record found is for ProductID P018 Cocoa Body Butter. Click **Find Next** again to find the record for ProductID P021 Lemon Body Butter.

d. Click **Find Next** again until Access has finished searching the records. When Access is done searching and cannot find any more matches, you will see the message "Microsoft Access finished searching the records. The search item was not found." Click **OK**, and then click **Cancel** to close the Find and Replace dialog box.

> **Troubleshooting**
> If Access highlights a record in the table and you cannot see it, drag the Find and Replace dialog box to another area of the screen.

e. **Close** [X] the table.

Applying a Filter to a Datasheet

A **filter** is a condition you apply temporarily to a table or query. All records that do not match the filter criteria are hidden until the filter is removed or the table is closed and reopened. A filter is a simple technique to quickly reduce a large amount of data to a much smaller subset of data. You can choose to save a table with the filter applied so when you open the table later the filter is still available.

You can filter a datasheet by selecting a value in a record and telling Access to filter records that contain some variation of the record you choose, or you can create a custom filter to select all or part of a field value.

Filtering by Selection

When you **filter by selection**, you select a value in a record and Access filters the records that contain only the values that match what you have selected. For this exercise, a customer came into the spa and stated that she was from Minnesota and had previously been a spa customer but was just browsing today. She left her glasses on the counter, and the staff wants to return them to her. You will help the staff members find all customers from Minnesota to see if they recognize the customer's name.

A03.04

To Select Specific Records Using a Selection Filter

SIDE NOTE
How to Clear Filters
To delete filters from the table, click Advanced in the Sort & Filter group, and select Clear All Filters.

a. Double-click **tblCustomer** to open the table, locate the first record with an address in the state of Minnesota (MN), and then click the **State** field. In the Sort & Filter group, click **Selection**, and then click the **Equals "MN"** option.

Access displays three records where all states are MN for Minnesota. The Toggle Filter in the Sort & Filter group allows you to go back and forth between viewing the filtered records and all the records in the table. To remove the filter, click Toggle Filter in the Sort & Filter group. To show the filter again, click Toggle Filter in the Sort & Filter group.

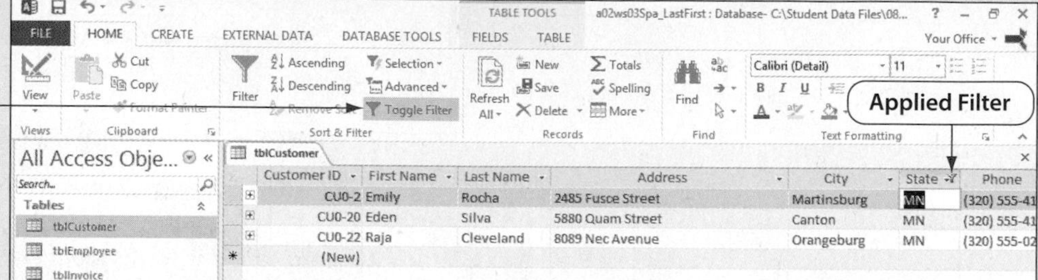

Figure 4 Filtered table for all records containing a state of MN

b. The filter is temporary unless you choose to save it with the table or query. If you do save it, the next time you open the table or query, you only have to click Toggle Filter to see the records from the state of Minnesota. Click **Save** on the Quick Access Toolbar. This saves the table with the filter. Close the table.

c. Double-click **tblCustomer** to open the table. On the HOME tab, in the Sort & Filter group, click **Toggle Filter** to see the filtered records. **Close** the table.

CONSIDER THIS | **Finding Records**

You have now found records using Find and Replace and using a selection filter. What are the advantages of each method? When would you use each?

Using a Text Filter

Text filters allow you to create a custom filter to match all or part of the text in a field that you specify. For this exercise, the staff wants to create a mailing of sample products but cannot send the products to customers with a post office box. You will help the staff find all customers who have "P.O. Box" as part of their address.

A03.05

To Select Specific Records Using a Text Filter

a. Double-click **tblCustomer** to open the table. Select the entire **Address** column by clicking the column name. In the column heading, click the **filter** arrow in the column heading, point to **Text Filters**, and then click **Begins With**.

b. In the Custom Filter dialog box, type P and then click **OK**.

Access retrieves the nine records where the addresses contain a P.O. box number. Notice that Toggle Filter in the Sort & Filter group is selected and the Filtered indicator in the Navigation bar is highlighted. You can toggle between the filtered table and the whole table by clicking on either Toggle Filter or the Filtered indicator. The filter indicator in the column heading indicates whether a filter is currently applied.

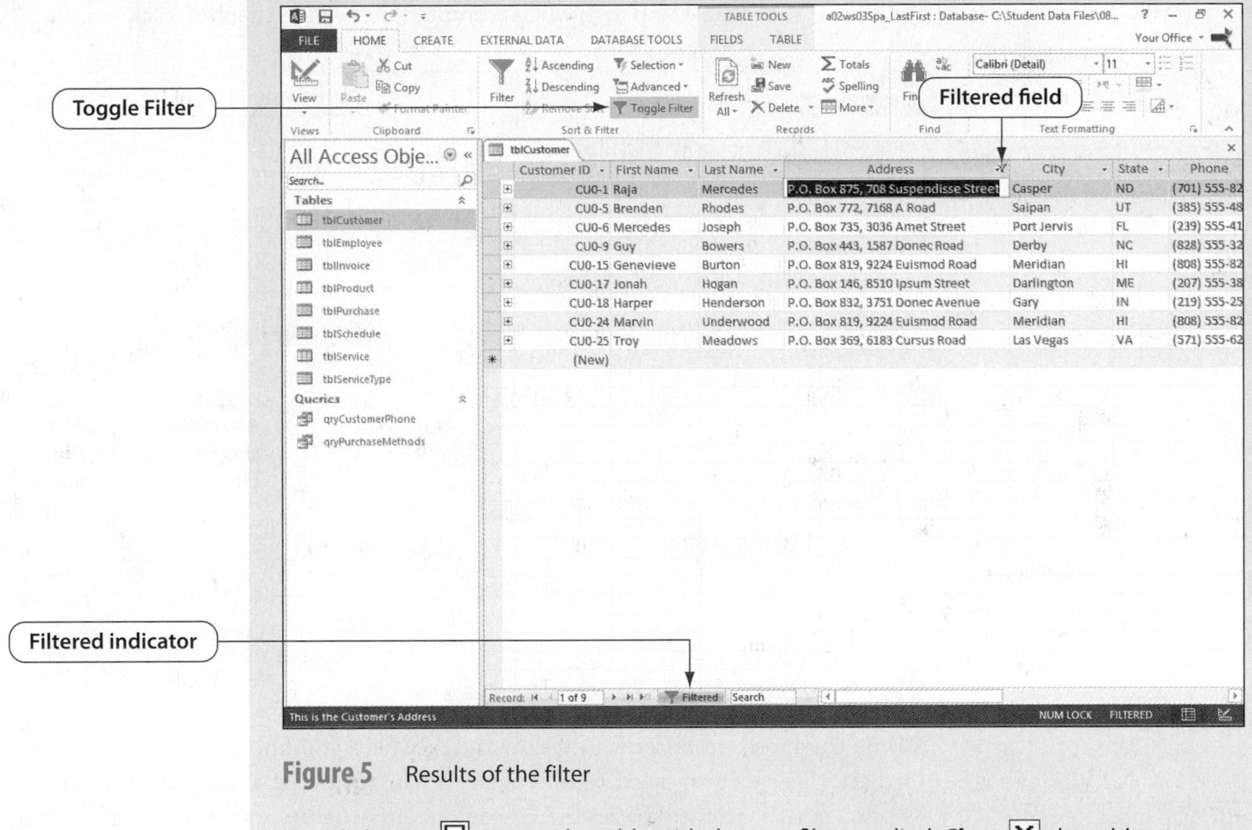

Figure 5 Results of the filter

c. Click **Save** to save the table with the new filter applied. **Close** the table.

Modify Datasheet Appearance

You can change the appearance of your datasheet by changing the font type, font size, column widths, and background colors to make it more readable. **AutoFit** is a feature that can change the column width of the data to match the widest data entered in that field. That allows you to see all the data in a particular field.

Changing the Look of a Datasheet

For this exercise, the manager is upset because the font is too small and she cannot see all the field headings in the invoice table. You will show her how to make the text larger and the columns wider.

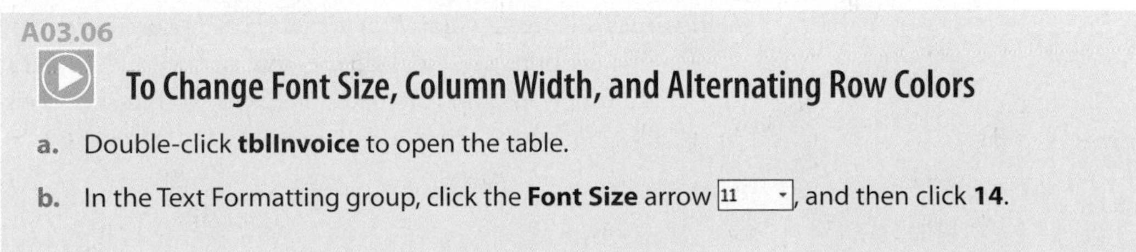

A03.06

To Change Font Size, Column Width, and Alternating Row Colors

a. Double-click **tblInvoice** to open the table.

b. In the Text Formatting group, click the **Font Size** arrow 11, and then click **14**.

SIDE NOTE

Alternate Method for Changing Column Width

You can also drag a column border to make the column wider.

c. Point to the **right border** of the first field name and double-click. The AutoFit feature resizes the column to best fit the data. Repeat this action for all the columns.

d. In the Text Formatting group, click the **Alternate Row Color** arrow, and then under Theme Colors select **Olive Green, Accent 3, Lighter 40%**. This is the seventh column and the fourth row under Theme Colors. The rows will still be alternating colors, but they will be changed to olive green.

e. **Close** the table, and then when prompted to save the changes, click **Yes**.

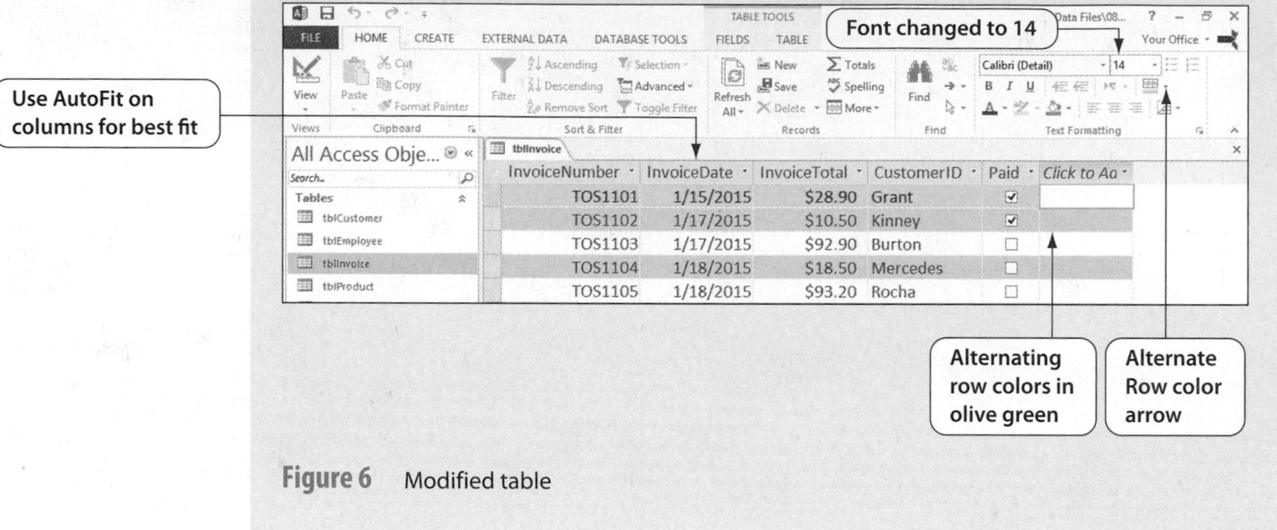

Figure 6 Modified table

Querying the Database

While the Find and Filter features can quickly help you find data, a query can be created for data that you may need to find again in the future. If you recall, the Simple Query Wizard is used to display fields from one or more tables or queries with the option to choose a detailed or summary query if working with more than one table. The Simple Query Wizard does not provide the opportunity to select data criteria.

In addition to the Simple Query Wizard, there are three additional query wizards available to make quick, step-by-step queries.

1. **Crosstab**: Used when you want to describe one field in terms of two or more fields in the table. Example: summarizing information or calculating statistics on the fields in the table.
2. **Find Duplicates**: Used when you want to find records with the same specific value. Example: duplicate e-mail addresses in a customer database.
3. **Find Unmatched**: Used when you want to find the rows in one table that do not have a match in the other table. Example: identifying customers who currently have no open orders.

Queries can also be created in Query Design view, which not only allows you to choose the tables and fields to include in the query, but also allows you to select criteria for the field values, create calculated fields, and select sorting options.

In this section, you will create and define selection criteria for queries and create aggregate functions and calculated fields as well as sort query results.

Run Query Wizards

Two other query wizards, the Find Duplicates Query Wizard and the Find Unmatched Query Wizard, allow you to find duplicate records or identify orphans by selecting criteria as part of the wizard steps. An **orphan** is a foreign key in one table that does not have a matching value in the primary key field of a related table.

Creating a Find Duplicates Query

The **Find Duplicates Query Wizard** finds duplicate records in a table or a query. You select the fields that you think may include duplicate information, and the wizard creates the query to find records matching your criteria.

For this exercise, the spa receptionist sends out mailings and reminders to spa customers throughout the year. She wants to be able to prevent multiple mailings to the same address to help reduce costs. You will show her how she can use a Find Duplicates query to check for duplicate addresses.

A03.07

To Find Duplicate Customer Information

a. Click the **CREATE** tab, and then in the Queries group, click **Query Wizard**. Access displays the New Query dialog box and lists the different queries you can select.

b. Select **Find Duplicates Query Wizard**, and then click **OK**.

c. Select **Table: tblCustomer** as the table to search for duplicate field values, and then click **Next**.

> **Troubleshooting**
> If you get a Security Notice, click Open.

d. Under Available fields, click **CustAddress**, and then click the **One Field** button [>]. Access moves the CustAddress field to the Duplicate-value fields list. This is the field you think may have duplicate data.

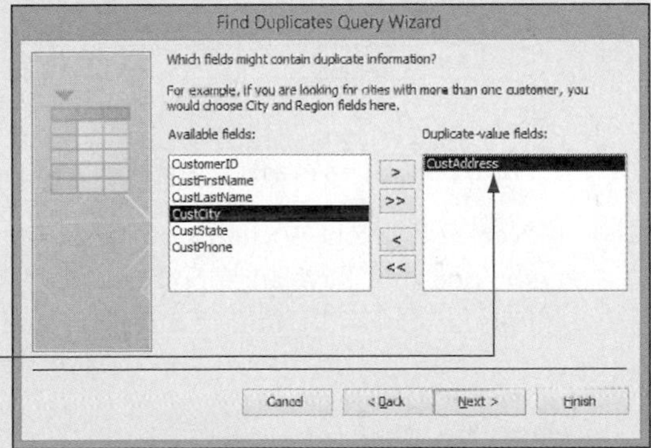

Figure 7 Select the field that may have duplicate data

e. Click **Next**. Click the **All Fields** button [>>] to move all available fields to the Additional query fields list to display all the fields in the query results. Click **Next**.

f. Under "What do you want to name your query?", type **qryDuplicateCustomers_initialLastname**, using your first initial and last name, and then click **Finish**. The result of the query should have two records with the same address.

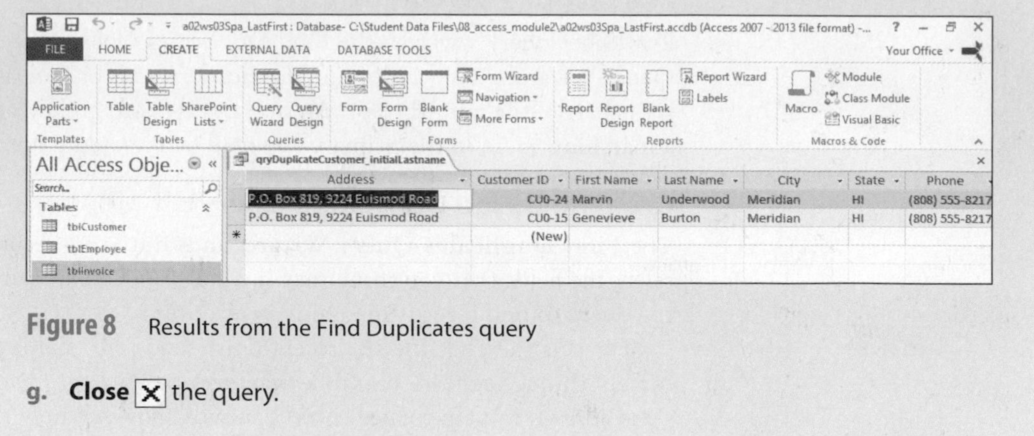

Figure 8 Results from the Find Duplicates query

g. **Close** [X] the query.

Creating a Find Unmatched Query

The **Find Unmatched Query Wizard** is designed to find records in a table or query that have no related records in a second table or query. This can be very helpful if you wantto contact inactive customers or mail a notice to past clients who are still listed in the database. The wizard uses the primary key from the first table and matches it with the foreign key in the second table in order to determine if there are unmatched records. If a one-to-many relationship exists between the two tables, then the wizard will join the two correct fields automatically.

The wizard will try to match the primary key field and the foreign key field if there is a one-to-many relationship between the two tables. If there is not a one-to-many relationship, you can select the fields to be matched manually.

For this project, spa management would like to identify customers who have used the spa's services in the past but do not have a current appointment. This means a record for the customer would be listed in the customer table but not in the schedule table as shown in Figure 9.

Customer Table

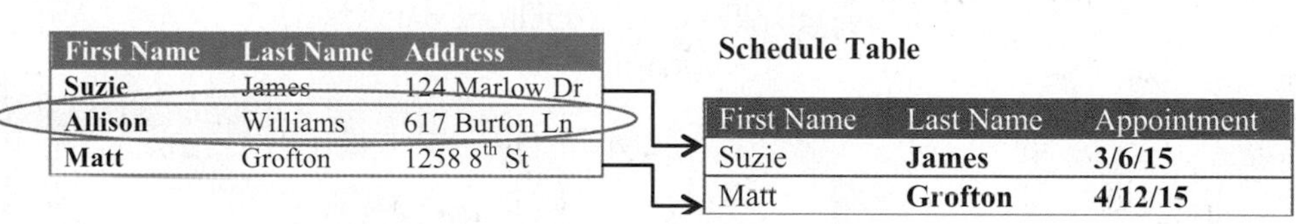

First Name	Last Name	Address
Suzie	James	124 Marlow Dr
Allison	Williams	617 Burton Ln
Matt	Grofton	1258 8th St

Schedule Table

First Name	Last Name	Appointment
Suzie	James	3/6/15
Matt	Grofton	4/12/15

Figure 9 Tables in a Find Unmatched query

Notice Allison Williams is a past customer so she is listed in the customer table, but she does not have an appointment scheduled in the schedule table. Her record would be found in a Find Unmatched query comparing the customer and schedule tables.

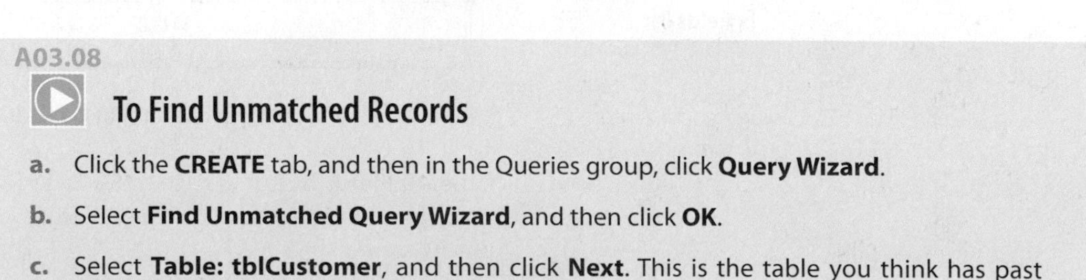

A03.08

To Find Unmatched Records

a. Click the **CREATE** tab, and then in the Queries group, click **Query Wizard**.

b. Select **Find Unmatched Query Wizard**, and then click **OK**.

c. Select **Table: tblCustomer**, and then click **Next**. This is the table you think has past customers with no upcoming appointments.

d. Select **Table: tblSchedule**, and then click **Next**. This is the table that has customers with upcoming appointments you want to compare to the main tblCustomer table.

e. Under Fields in 'tblCustomer', verify **CustomerID** is selected, and then under Fields in 'tblSchedule', verify **Customer** is selected. This is the common field that the wizard will use to compare the tables.

SIDE NOTE
Manually Select Fields to Match
If your tables are not in a one-to-many relationship, select the fields manually and use the button to move them to the Matching fields box.

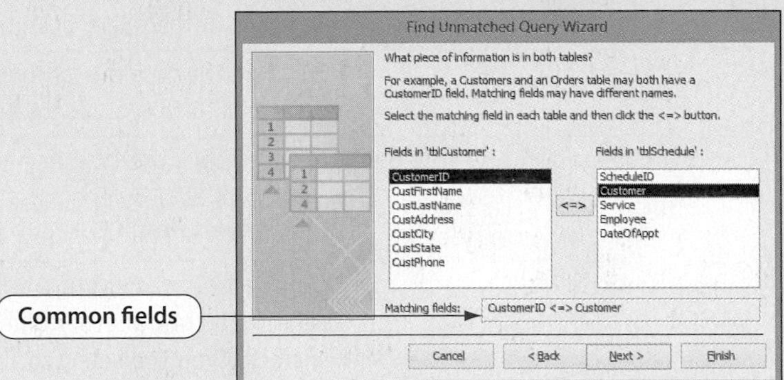

Figure 10 Compare the two tables using their common field

f. Click **Next**, click the **All Fields** button [>>] to add all the fields to the Selected fields list, and then click **Next**.

g. Under "What would you like to name your query?", type qryCustomersWithout Appointments_initialLastname, using your first initial and last name, and then click **Finish**. You should see the names and e-mails of three customers who do not currently have appointments at the spa including yourself. **Close** [X] the query.

Create Queries in Design View

The query wizards work by prompting you to answer a series of questions about the tables and fields to display and then creating the query based upon your responses. Alternatively, you can use Design view to manually create queries. The query window in Design view allows you to specify the data you want to see by building a **query by example**. A query by example provides a sample of the data you want to see in the results. Access takes that sample of data and finds records in the tables you specify that match the example. In the query window, you can include specific fields, define criteria, sort records, and perform calculations. When you use the query window, you have more control and more options available to manage the details of the query design than with the Simple Query Wizard.

When you open Design view, by default, the Show Table dialog box opens with a list of available tables and queries to add. You can either select a table name and click Add, or you can double-click the table name. Either way the table will be added to the query window. If the Show Table dialog box is closed, you can drag a table or query from the Navigation Pane to the query window to add it to the query.

The next step in building your query is to add the fields you want to include from the various tables selected to the query design grid. There are a number of ways to add fields to the query design grid.

QUICK REFERENCE	Methods to Add Fields to a Query Design Grid
Action	**Description**
Drag	Once you click the field name, drag it to any empty column in the query design grid.
Double-click field name	Double-click the field name to add it to the first empty column in the query design grid.
Select from list	Click in the first row of any empty column, click the selection arrow, and select the field name from the list.
Double-click the title bar	Double-click the title bar for the table with the fields you want to add, and all the fields will be selected. Drag the fields to the first empty column.
Click, Shift, Click	Click a field name, press and hold down the Shift key, and then click another name to select a range of field names. Drag the selected fields to the query design grid.

If you add a field to the wrong column in the query design grid, you can delete the column and add it again, or you can drag it to another position in the grid.

All fields that have values you want included in a query—either for the criteria or to show in the results—must be added to the query design grid. For example, you may want to find all customers from New Mexico, but not necessarily show the state field in the query results. You can use the Show check box to indicate which fields to show in the results and which fields not to show.

REAL WORLD ADVICE **Increasing Privacy Concerns**

There are many instances where the person running the query does not have the right to see confidential information in the database. An example of this is Social Security numbers. Although companies are doing away with this practice, many existing databases still use Social Security numbers as a unique identifier. You can include a Social Security number in query criteria, but uncheck the Show box so the actual value does not show in the query results.

Creating a Single-Table Query

A single-table query is a query that is based on only one table in your database.

For this exercise, the manager of the spa needs your help to print out a price list for all the products. She wants to see the product description, size, and price for each product, and she wants to see all the records. You will show her how to add only the fields she wants to the query.

A03.09

To Create a Single-Table Query

a. Click the **CREATE** tab, and then in the Queries group, click **Query Design** to open the query window with the Show Table dialog box.

b. In the Show Table dialog box, select **tblProduct**, and then click **Add**. Click **Close** to close the Show Table dialog box.

> **Troubleshooting**
> If you cannot see the query design grid at the bottom of the query design window, use the pointer [pointer icon] to drag the top border of the grid up.

SIDE NOTE
Seeing All Fields in a Table
Alternatively, you can scroll down to see all the fields.

c. Use your pointer to drag the lower border of **tblProduct** down to see all the fields.

d. Double-click **ProductDescription** to add it to the first column of the query design grid. Repeat for **Price** and **Size**.

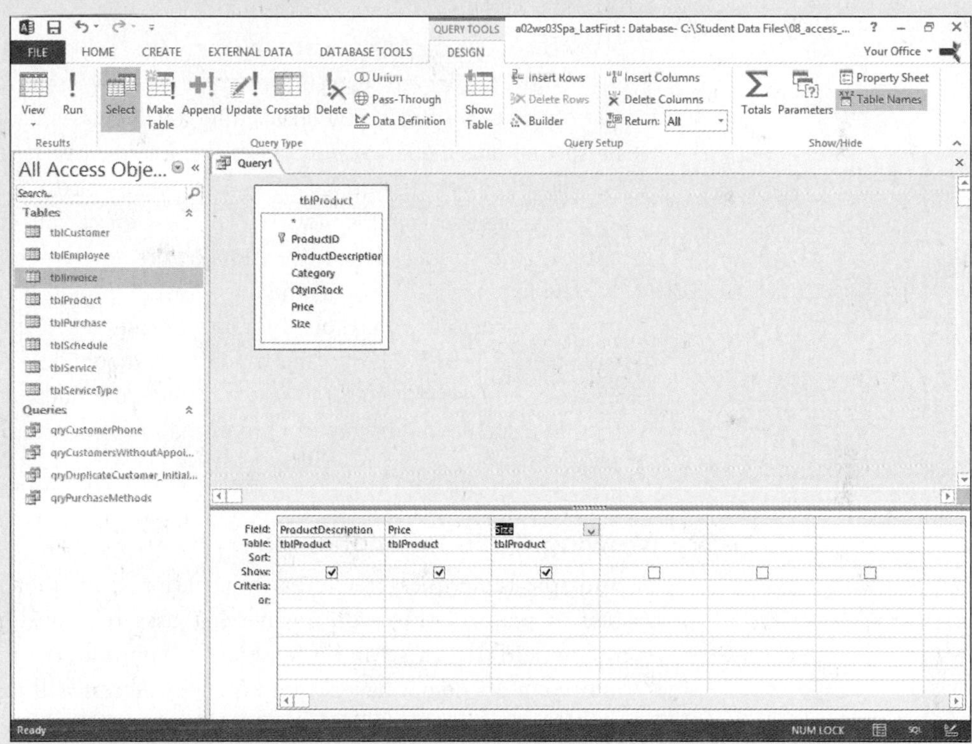

Figure 11 Fields from tblProduct added to the query design grid

e. In the Results group, click **Run** to run the query. You should have 25 records showing the ProductDescription, Price, and Size (ounces) fields.

f. In the Views group, click the **View** arrow, and then click **Design View**. To move the Size field to the left of the ProductDescription field, click the **top border** of the **Size** field to select the column. Again pointing to the top border of the field, drag the **Size field** to the left of the **ProductDescription** field. In the Results group, click **Run** to run the query again. The query will still have 25 records, but the field order will be Size, ProductDescription, and Price.

g. Click **Save** [Save icon] on the Quick Access Toolbar. In the Save As dialog box, type qryProductPriceList_initialLastname, using your first initial and last name, and then click **OK**. **Close** [X] the query.

QUICK REFERENCE | **Opening or Switching Views**

Access gives you several methods to open objects in different views or to switch views.

1. To open an object in default view, double-click it in the Navigation Pane.
2. To open an object in design view, right-click it in the Navigation Pane, and select Design View.
3. To switch views for an already open object, on the Home tab, in the Views group, click the View arrow, and then select your preferred view.
4. To switch views for an already open object, right-click the object tab, and then select the preferred view.
5. To switch views for an already open object, the right side of the status bar has small icons for each available view. Hover over the icon to see the ScreenTip. Click the icon to switch to the preferred view.

REAL WORLD ADVICE | **The Importance of Knowing Your Data**

Many times databases are shared by many users. Different people may enter data differently causing errors or inconsistency. Inconsistent data entry can affect the validity of query results. By misspelling a value or abbreviating a value that should be spelled out, a query may not find the record when it searches using criteria. You must know what your data looks like when you create queries. A quick scan of the records, or using Find with a wildcard for certain values, may help you find misspellings or other data entry errors before you run your query.

Having some idea of what the query results should look like will also help make sure your query has found the right record set. For example, if you query all customers from New Mexico and think there should be a dozen, but your query shows 75, you should check your table records and your query criteria to see why there might be such a big discrepancy from what you expected.

Viewing Table Relationships

A multiple-table query retrieves information from more than one table or query. For Access to perform this type of query, it uses relationships between the tables, or the common field that exists in both tables to "connect" the tables.

If two tables do not have a common field, Access will join the two tables by combining the records, regardless of whether they have a matching field. This is called the **multiplier effect**. For example, if one table has 10,000 records and another table also has 10,000 records, and if these two tables do not have a common field, all records in the first table will be matched with all records in the second table for a total of 100,000,000 records! Depending on the processing power and memory on the computer, Access could take a long time to run the query or even become nonresponsive.

You can view how your tables are related in the Relationships window. **Join lines** are the lines connecting the tables that represent relationships. The field that the line is pointing to in each table represents the common field between the tables. It is helpful to understand how tables are related before you try and create a multiple table query.

A03.10

To View Table Relationships

a. On the **DATABASE TOOLS** tab, in the Relationships group, click **Relationships**. Click the **Shutter Bar Open/Close button** « to hide the Navigation Pane and display the whole Relationships window. Take a moment to study the table relationships.

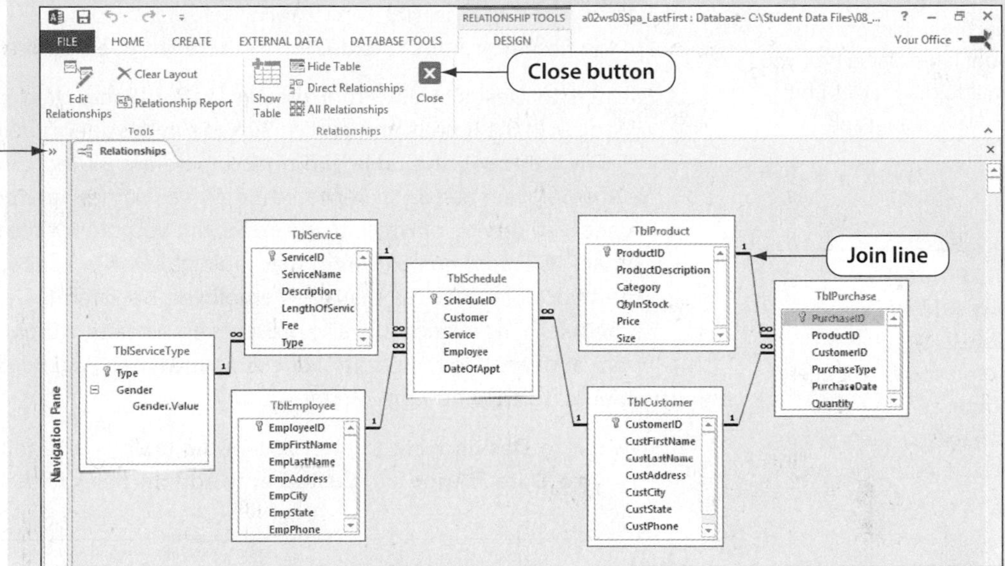

Figure 12 Spa Database table relationships

b. Click the **DATABASE TOOLS** tab, and then in the Relationships group, click **Close** to close the Relationships window. Click the **Shutter Bar Open/Close button** » to show the Navigation Pane again.

REAL WORLD ADVICE — Which Tables to Choose?

You should only select the tables you need when creating a query in the query window. Access treats all the tables selected as part of the query when it executes the query, which means unnecessary tables added to the query may cause performance problems or incorrect results. Best practice is to do the following:

- Understand the table structure and relationships before you construct your query—refer to the Relationships window often.
- Choose only those tables from which you need data.
- If no data from a table is needed, do not add the table. The exception to this rule is if a table is required to link the many-to-many relationship together. In other words, no table will be left unconnected and tables can be added to create that connection.

Creating a Query from Multiple Tables

All tables added to a query should be connected by relationships and have a common field. For this project, the staff would like to see one recordset that includes the services scheduled for each employee. tblEmployee includes the employee names, and tblSchedule lists the services scheduled for each employee. You will create a query that combines the two tables into one query.

A03.11

To Create a Query from Multiple Tables

SIDE NOTE

Adding Tables from the Navigation Pane

Remember, in addition to selecting tables from the Show Table dialog box, you can also drag tables from the Navigation Pane.

SIDE NOTE

Only Add Necessary Tables

Adding a table to a query without adding fields changes the query results, and the results may not make sense.

a. Click the **CREATE** tab, and then in the Queries group, click **Query Design**, click **tblEmployee**, and then click **Add**. Close the Show Table dialog box.

b. Double-click **EmpFirstName** and **EmpLastName** in that order to add the fields to the query design grid.

c. In the Results group, click **Run**. Notice there are 14 employee records.

d. Switch to **Design** view. From the Navigation Pane, drag **tblSchedule** to the query window. In the Results group, click **Run** to run the query again.

Scroll through the table and notice there are 53 records in the query results now and employees names are repeated. Employee names have been matched up with each scheduled service, of which there are 53, but you cannot see any information about the services because no fields from that table have been added. The relationship between the two tables dictates that each employee be listed for each service he or she has scheduled. The relationship also prevents employees without a scheduled appointment from appearing in the results. For example, Mariah Paul does not appear here because she has no appointments scheduled.

e. Switch to **Design** view. In the tblSchedule table, in the following order, double-click **Service**, **DateOfAppt**, and **Customer** to add the fields to the query design grid.

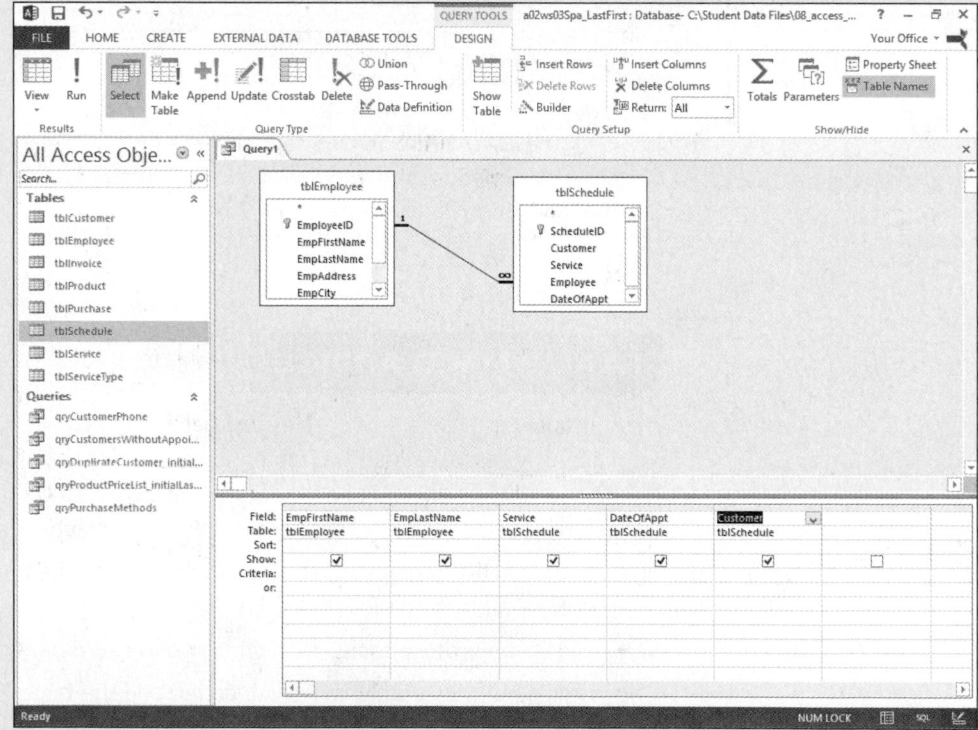

Figure 13 Query window for multiple-table query

f. In the Results group, click **Run** to run the query.

Notice there are 53 records again for each service scheduled, but now the detail for those services are included in the query because you added the fields to the query design grid.

g. Click **Save** on the Quick Access Toolbar, under Query Name type **qryEmployeeSchedule_initialLastname** using your first initial and last name, and then click **OK**. **Close** the query.

Removing a Table from a Query to Fix an Undesirable Multiplier Effect

When two tables without a common field are used in a query, you will see the multiplier effect. Recall that the multiplier effect occurs when each record in the first table is matched to each record in the second table.

For this exercise, someone in the spa wanted to find the phone number for each customer, but they created a multiple table query using two tables without a common field. One table has 25 records and the other has 26, so the multiplier effect caused the query result to have 650 records! You will run their query, and then fix it by removing the second table from the query.

A03.12

To Remove a Table from a Query

a. Double-click **qryCustomerPhone** to run the query.

Notice there are 650 records because every customer name is matched with every product. Since there are 25 products, each of the 26 customers is matched with every product for 25 times 26 = 650 records.

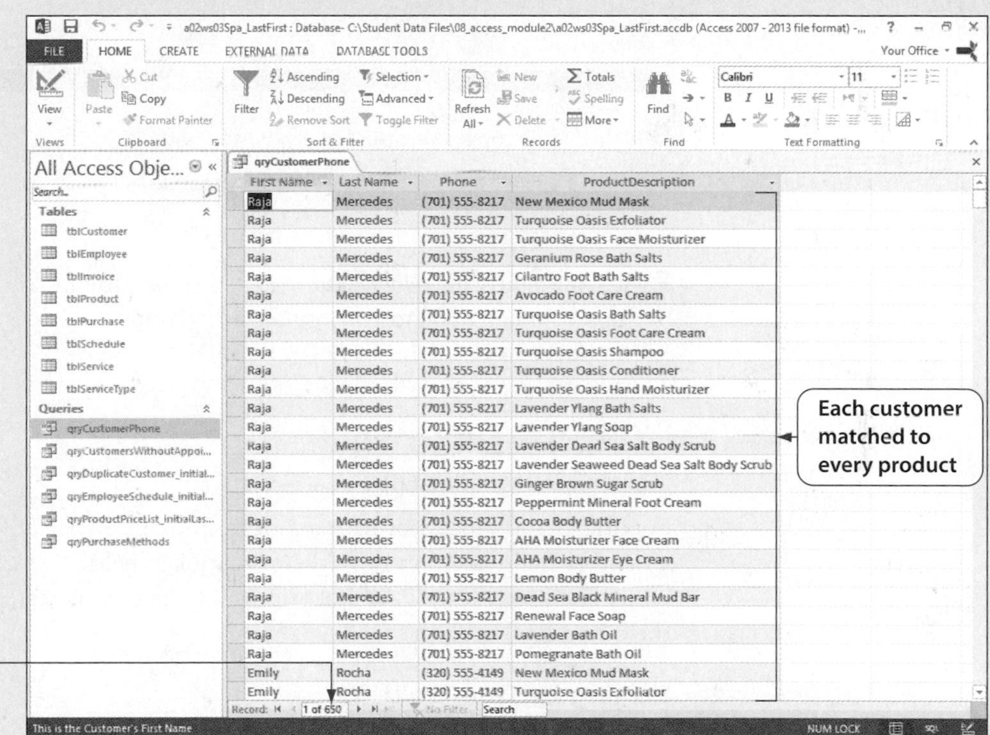

Figure 14 Query with multiplier effect

b. Switch to **Design** view. Notice there is no relationship between tblProduct and tblCustomer, which caused the multiplier effect. You will remove tblProduct from the query.

c. Right-click **tblProduct** in the query window, and then select **Remove Table**. The table is removed from the query window, and the ProductDescription is removed from the fields.

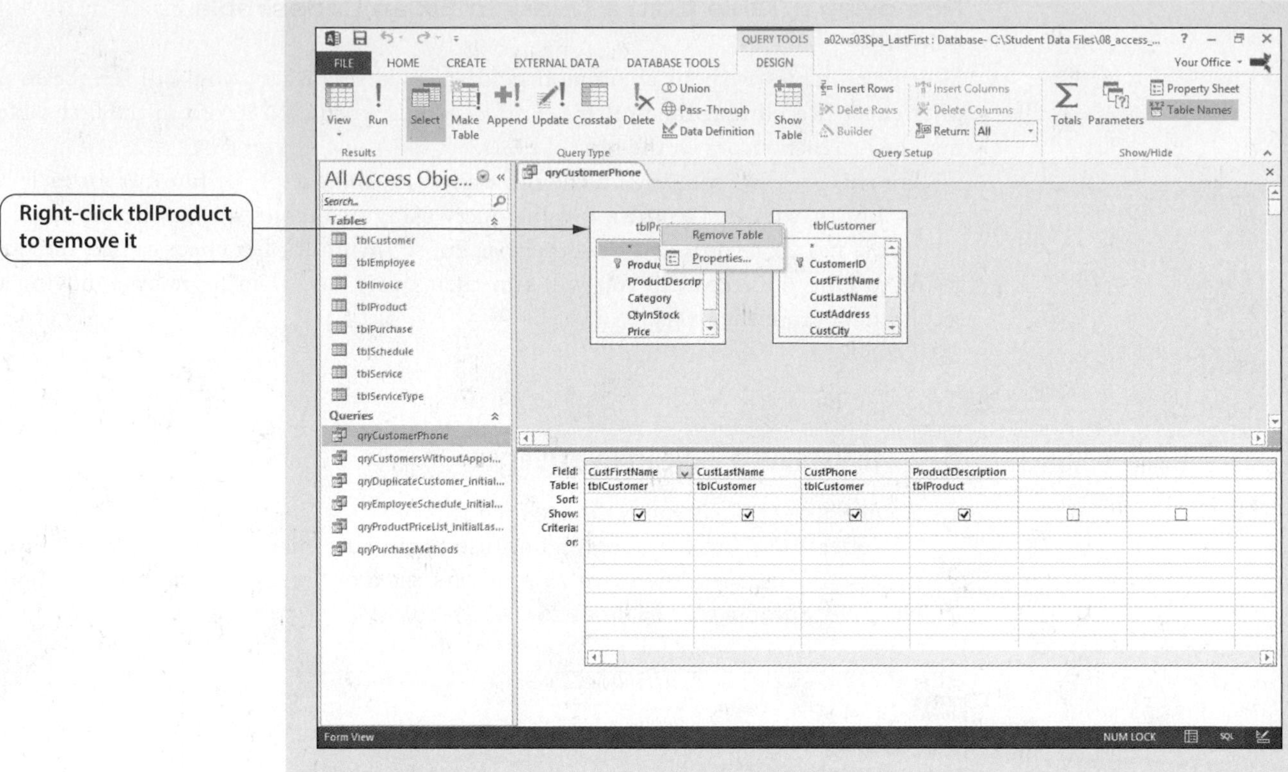

Figure 15 Remove table from query

d. Click **Run** to run the query.
   Notice there are now only 26 records.

e. On the **FILE** tab, select **Save As**, click **Save Object As**, click **Save As**, under Save 'qryCustomerPhone' to, type qryCustomerPhone_initialLastname using your first initial and last name, and then click **OK**. Close the query.

Sort Query Results

Sorting is the process of rearranging records in a specific order. By default, records in a table or query are sorted by the primary key field. You can change the sort order of a table in a query, which will not affect how the data is stored, only how it will appear in the query results.

Sorting by One Field

To sort records, you have to select a **sort field**, or a field used to determine the order of the records. The sort field can be a Short Text, Long Text, Number, Date/Time, Currency, AutoNumber, Yes/No, or Lookup Wizard field as shown in Table 2. A field may be sorted either in ascending order or descending order.

Type of Data	Sorting Options
Short and Long Text	Ascending (A to Z); Descending (Z to A)
Numbers (including Currency & AutoNumber)	Ascending (lowest to highest); Descending (highest to lowest)
Date/Time	Ascending (oldest to newest); Descending (newest to oldest)
Yes/No	Ascending (yes, then no values); Descending (no, then yes values)

Table 2 Methods for sorting data

MODULE 2

If you have numbers that are stored as text—phone numbers, Social Security numbers, zip codes—then the characters 1 to 9 come before A to Z in the appropriate order sorted as alphanumeric text.

A table may be sorted by a single field in Datasheet view. When a table is sorted using a single field, a sort arrow will appear in the field name so you can see that it is sorted. For this project, you will show the spa manager how to sort the tblProduct table by category.

SIDE NOTE
Alternative Method to Sorting Fields
Alternatively, you can select the field to be sorted and click Ascending or Descending on the Home tab in the Sort & Filter group.

A03.13

To Sort a Table by a Single Field

a. Double-click **tblProduct** to open the table.

b. Click the Category column heading arrow, and then click **Sort A to Z**. This will sort the records by the Category field in ascending order.

c. **Close** [X] the table, and then click **Yes** when prompted to save the changes.

Sorting by More than One Field

You can also sort by multiple fields in Access. The first field you choose to sort by is called the **primary sort field**. The second and subsequent fields are called **secondary sort fields**.

In datasheet view, you can sort multiple fields by selecting all the fields at one time and using the Sort & Filter group sorts, but there are some restrictions. First, the fields in datasheet view must be next to each other and the sort is executed left to right; that is, the far-left field is the primary sort field, the next field is a secondary sort field, and so on. Secondly, you can only sort in ascending or descending order for all fields, you cannot have one field sorted in ascending order and another in descending order. These two restrictions do not exist if sorting is set in Design view. Thus, it is more efficient to create a query and sort by multiple fields using Design view.

Using Design view to sort records allows you to sequence the fields from left to right in an order that makes sense for your desired sort results and allows you to combine ascending and descending sorts. You can also sort in an order different than left to right by adding a field multiple times and clearing the Show check box. For this exercise, you will show the staff how to sort the tblSchedule table by Employee, then Date, and then Service by creating a query from the table and setting up the sort options.

A03.14

To Sort a Query by More than One Field

a. Click the **CREATE** tab, and then in the Queries group, click **Query Design**. Double-click **tblEmployee** and **tblSchedule** to add the tables to the query. Click **Close** to close the Show Table dialog box.

b. Double-click **EmpLastName**, **EmpFirstName**, and **EmpPhone** from tblEmployee to add those fields to the query design grid. Double-click **DateOfAppt**, **Service**, and **Customer** from tblSchedule to add those fields to the query design grid.

c. Click the **Sort** row for **EmpLastName**, click the **selection** arrow, and then click **Ascending**. Click **Ascending** for the **EmpFirstName**, **DateOfAppt**, and **Service** fields.

Notice that unlike sorting in Datasheet view, your sorting fields do not need to be next to each other to be sorted in a query.

SIDE NOTE
How Many Fields Is Too Many?
You may choose up to 10 fields to sort by in Design view.

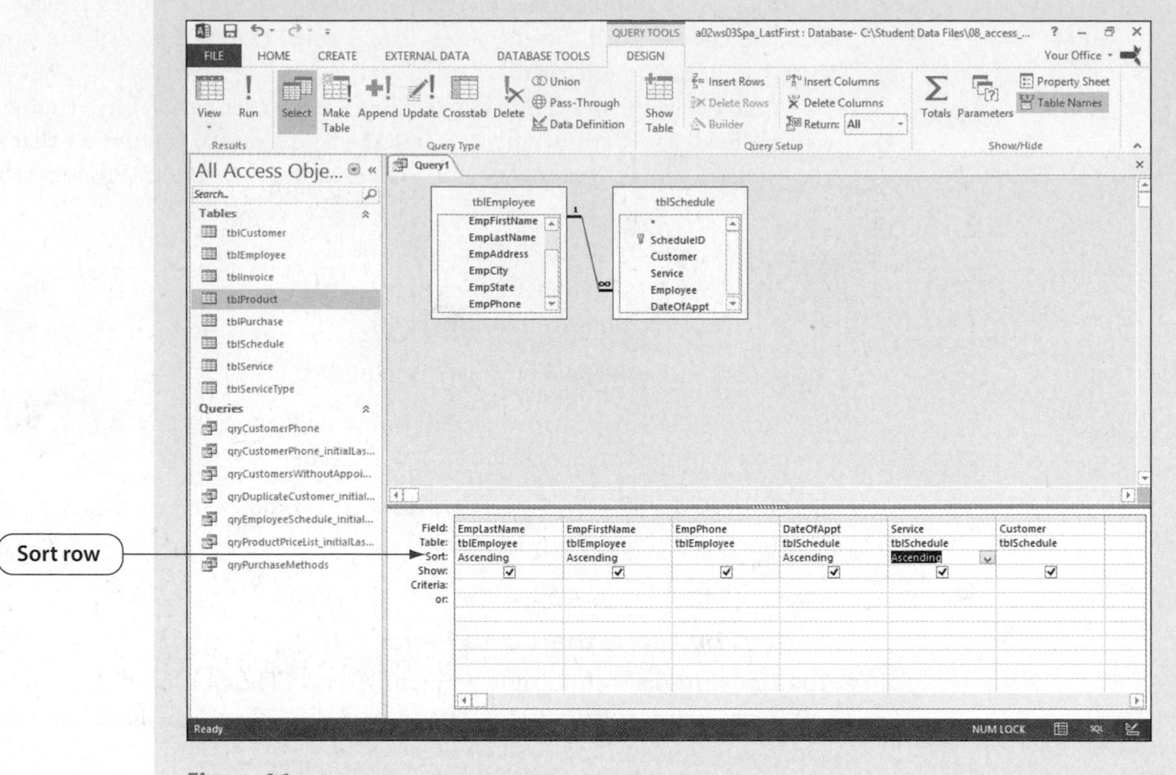

Figure 16 Sort options selected

d. Click **Run** to run the query. The table should be sorted by Employee, then Date, then Service.

e. Click **Save** on the Quick Access Toolbar, name the query qryEmployeeAppointments_initialLastname using your first initial and last name, and then click **OK**. **Close** the query.

Define Selection Criteria for Queries

Databases, including Access, provide a robust set of selection criteria that you can use to make your queries well focused. You can use the different kinds of operators described below to choose criteria for one or more fields in one or more tables.

Using a Comparison Operator

Comparison operators compare the values in a table or another query to the criteria value you set up in a query. The different comparison operators, descriptions, and examples are shown in Table 3. Comparison operators are generally used with numbers and dates to find a range or a specific value. Equal to and not equal to can also be used with text to find an exact match to criteria. For example, to find all states that are not NY you could enter < >"NY" for the state criteria.

In query criteria, text is identified by quotation marks around it and dates with # in front of and at the end of the date. For example, 1/1/16 would appear as #1/1/16#. Access adds the necessary quotation marks and pound signs, but it is a good idea to double-check.

Operator	Description
=	Equal to
<=	Less than or equal to
<	Less than
>	Greater than
>=	Greater than or equal to
< >	Not equal to

Table 3 Comparison operators

For this project, the manager of the spa wants to see all products $10 and under so she can plan an upcoming special on the spa's lower-priced products. You will show her how to use a comparison operator in a query to find those products.

A03.15

To Use a Comparison Operator in a Query

a. Click the **CREATE** tab, and then in the Queries group, click **Query Design**, click **tblProduct**, and then click **Add**. Click **Close** to close the Show Table dialog box.

b. In the following order, double-click **ProductID**, **ProductDescription**, **Size**, **Category**, **QtyInStock**, and **Price** to add the fields to the query design grid.

c. Click in the **Criteria** row for the **Price** field, and then type <=10.

d. Click **Run** to run the query. The results should show six records all with prices $10 or less.

e. Click **Save** on the Quick Access Toolbar, under Query Name type qryLowPriceProducts_initialLastname using your first initial and last name, and then click **OK**. **Close** the query.

Hiding Fields That Are Used in a Query

For a field to be used in a query, it must be added to the query grid. If you just want to use the field to define criteria but do not want to see the results of that field in the query, it cannot be removed from the query grid, but it can be hidden from the results.

For this project, the manager is happy with the results of the low-price products query you created above, but she would like to post a list of the products without the prices so she can advertise the list as all under $10. You tell her that is possible by using the Show check box in the query design grid.

A03.16

To Use a Field Value in a Query but Not Show the Field in the Results

a. Open **qryLowPriceProduct_initialLastname** in Design view.

b. In the Price field, click the **Show** check box to clear the check mark.

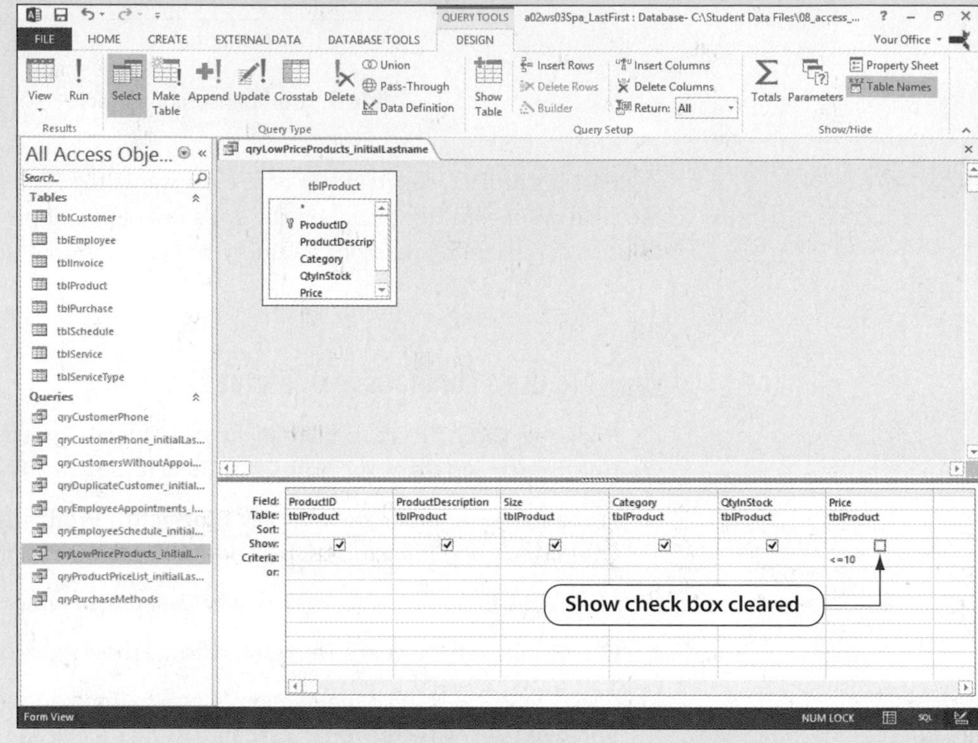

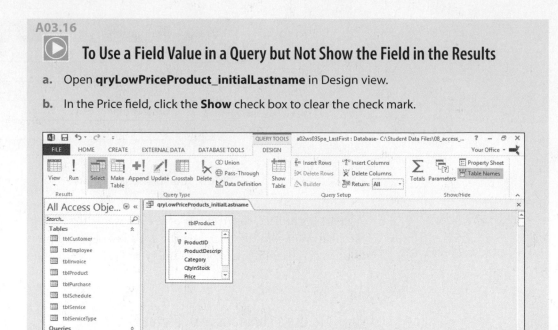

Figure 17 Clearing the Show check box

c. In the Results group, click **Run** to run the query. The results should show the same six records you found in the previous query, but without the price field showing.

d. On the **FILE** tab, select **Save As**, select **Save Object As**, and then click **Save As**. In Save 'qryLowPriceProducts_initialLa…' to: type qryTenAndUnder_initialLastname using your first initial and last name, and then click **OK**. **Close** [X] the query.

Sorting on a Field That You Do Not Show

The manager liked the employee schedule query you created, but she would like it to show employee first name first in the query results. If you put first name first in the grid and then last name, Access will sort by first name first. You will show her how to add a field multiple times to the query design grid to sort fields one way but display them another way.

A03.17

To Sort a Query by Multiple Fields in a Different Sort Order

a. Click the **CREATE** tab, and then in the Queries group, click **Query Design**. Double-click **tblEmployee** and **tblSchedule** to add the tables to the query. Click **Close** to close the Show Table dialog box.

b. Double-click **EmpFirstName** and **EmpLastName** from tblEmployee to add those fields to the query design grid. Double-click **DateOfAppt**, **Service**, and **Customer** from tblSchedule to add those fields to the query design grid.

c. Click the **Sort** row for **EmpFirstName**, click the **selection** arrow, and then click **Ascending**. Click **Ascending** for the **EmpLastName**, **DateOfAppt**, and **Service** fields.

d. In the Results group, click **Run** to run the query.

Notice that the results are sorted by first name and not last name, for example, Alex Weaver is shown before Amanda Johnson. You will need to add another first name field to fix the sort order.

e. Switch to **Design** view. Double-click **EmpFirstName** in tblEmployee to add it to the query design grid. Click at the top of the second **EmpFirstName** field to select it, and then drag it to the right of EmpLastName.

f. Click the **Sort** row for the first **EmpFirstName**, and then change it to **(not sorted)**. Click the **Sort** row for the second **EmpFirstName**, and then change it to **Ascending**. Click the **Show** check box under the second EmpFirstName field in the third column to clear it.

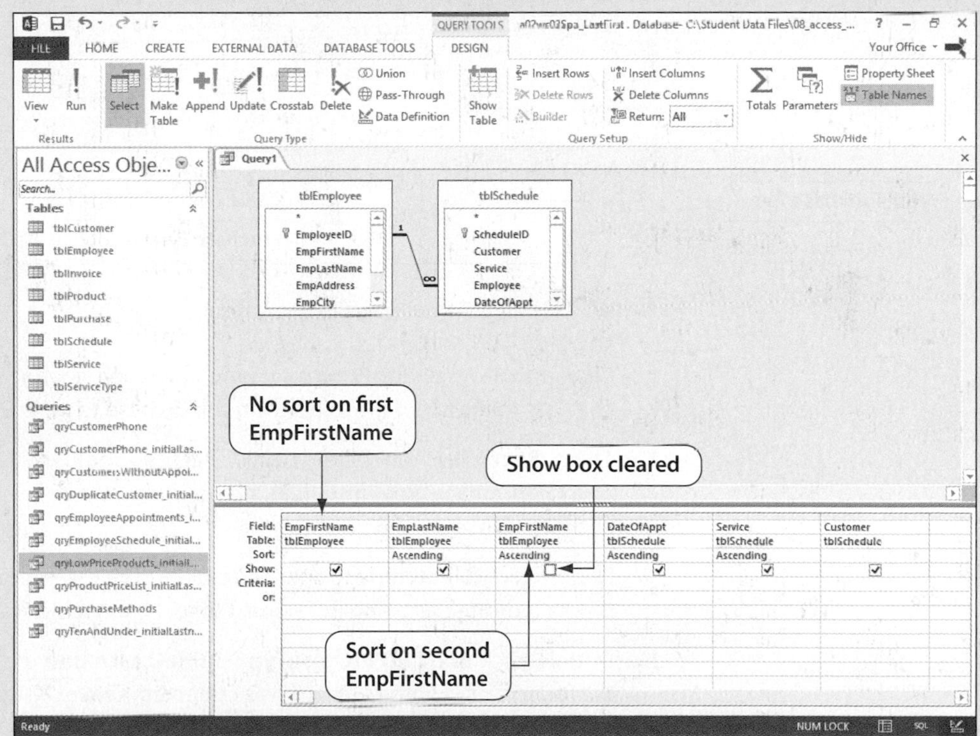

Figure 18 Sort options selected and EmpFirstName Show check box cleared

g. Click **Run** to run the query. The results should show 53 records sorted by employee last name, first name, date, and service. Notice that the main sort is by last name but Alex Weaver comes before Joseph Weaver.

h. Click **Save** on the Quick Access Toolbar, name the query **qryEmployeeSort_initialLastname** using your first initial and last name, and then click **OK**. **Close** the query.

Using Is Null Criteria

You practiced entering a criteria value to get all records that meet the criteria. You can also select any records that have no value in a field using the Is Null criteria. Null is the absence of any value and is different from blank or zero.

For this exercise, one of the spa workers has created a purchase record without specifying that the order was placed in person. You will show the manager how to locate a record that is missing a value. You will also show her how to change the value in the query and have it changed in the table.

A03.18

To Use Is Null Criteria

a. Click the **CREATE** tab, and then in the Queries group, click **Query Design**. Double-click **tblPurchase**, and **tblCustomer** to add the tables to the query window. Click **Close** to close the Show Table dialog box.

b. In the following order, double-click **PurchaseType** and **PurchaseDate** from tblPurchase, and **CustFirstName** and **CustLastName** from tblCustomer to add them to the query design grid.

c. Click in the **Criteria** row for the PurchaseType field, and then type Is Null.

d. Click **Run** to run the query. The results show one record that was the purchase by Omar Hinton on 1/18/2015. That is the one that the employee forgot to enter.

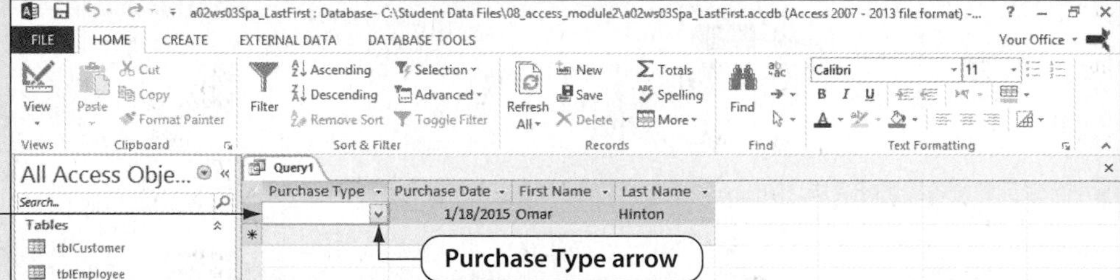

Figure 19 Change null value in query results

e. Click the arrow under **Purchase Type**, and then change the value to **In Person**. This changes the result in the underlying tblPurchase to be In Person.

f. Click **Save** on the Quick Access Toolbar, under **Query Name** type qryNullPurchaseType_initialLastname using your first initial and last name, and then click **OK**. **Close** the query.

g. Double-click **tblPurchase** to open the table. Notice that Hinton's purchase (PurchaseID = 25) is now indicated as being In Person. **Close** the table.

h. Double-click **qryNullPurchaseType_initialLastname** to run it. Notice that no records are found since Hinton's record was corrected. **Close** the query.

Using the AND Logical Operator

When you create a query, you can select criteria for one field or for multiple fields. If you use multiple criteria, then you must also use **logical operators** to combine these criteria. Logical operators are operators that allow you to combine two or more criteria, as shown in Table 4. For example, if you want a record selected when both criteria are met, then you would use the AND logical operator, but if you want a record selected if only one of the criteria is met, then you would use the OR logical operator. For an even more advanced query, you can combine the AND and the OR logical operators.

Operator	Description
AND	Returns records that meet both criteria
OR	Returns records that meet one or more criteria
NOT	Returns records that do not meet the criteria

Table 4 Logical operators

When you want to specify multiple criteria, and all criteria must be true for a record to be included in the results, then the AND logical operator is used, and the criteria must be in the same Criteria row in the query design grid. Access will look at the first field in the query design grid for criteria and continue moving from left to right looking for criteria. When criteria are in the same row, all criteria must match for the record to be included in the query results. For this project, you want to help the manager narrow down a sales strategy. She is trying to determine which customers place phone orders for products over $10.

A03.19

To Use the AND Logical Operator

a. Click the **CREATE** tab, and then in the Queries group, click **Query Design**. Double-click **tblProduct**, **tblPurchase**, and **tblCustomer** to add the tables to the query window. Click **Close** to close the Show Table dialog box.

b. In the following order, double-click **PurchaseType** from tblPurchase, **ProductDescription** and **Price** from tblProduct, and **CustFirstName** and **CustLastName** from tblCustomer to add them to the query design grid.

c. Click in the **Criteria** row for the PurchaseType field, type Phone, and then for the Price field type >10.

d. Click in the **Sort** row for the **ProductDescription** field, and then select **Ascending**.

SIDE NOTE

Looks Do Not Matter

How the tables are laid out in the query window does not affect the results. You can move the tables by dragging them to a new location.

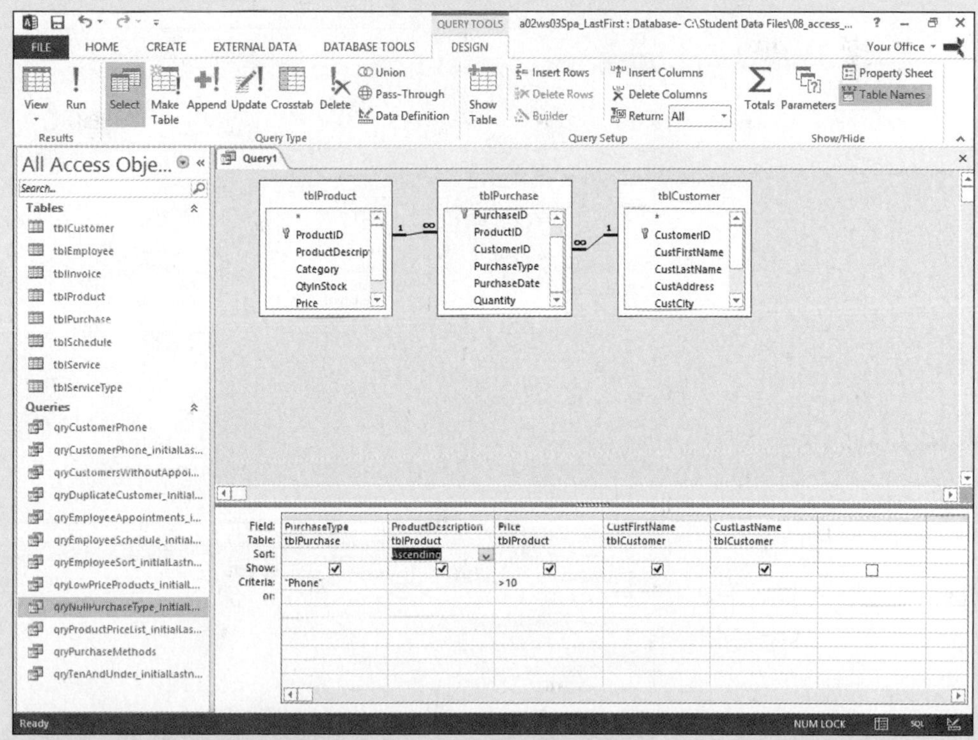

Figure 20 Criteria added for PurchaseType and Price fields

e. Click **Run** to run the query. The results show five records, with Phone as the purchase type and a price greater than $10. The results are sorted by ProductDescription.

f. Click **Save** on the Quick Access Toolbar, under Query Name type qryPhoneAndTen_initialLastname using your first initial and last name, and then click **OK**. **Close** the query.

Using the OR Logical Operator

When you want to specify criteria in multiple fields, and at least one of the criteria must be true for a record to be included in the results, then the OR logical operator is used, and the criteria must be in different Criteria rows in the query design grid. Access will look at the first field in the first Criteria row for criteria and continue moving from left to right. Then it will start at the left again on the next criteria row that is labeled "or". For this exercise, you want to help the manager find all customers who make purchases either by phone or online.

A03.20

To Use the OR Logical Operator

a. Click the **CREATE** tab, and then in the Queries group, click **Query Design**. Double-click **tblProduct**, **tblPurchase**, and **tblCustomer** to add the tables to the query. Click **Close** to close the Show Table dialog box.

b. Double-click **PurchaseType** from tblPurchase, double-click **ProductDescription** from tblProduct, and then double-click **CustFirstName** and **CustLastName** from tblCustomer in that order to add them to the query design grid.

c. Click in the **Criteria** row for the PurchaseType field, type Phone. In the **or** row just below the Criteria line in the PurchaseType field, type Online.

d. Click in the **Sort** row, and then select **Ascending** for the **PurchaseType** and **ProductDescription** fields.

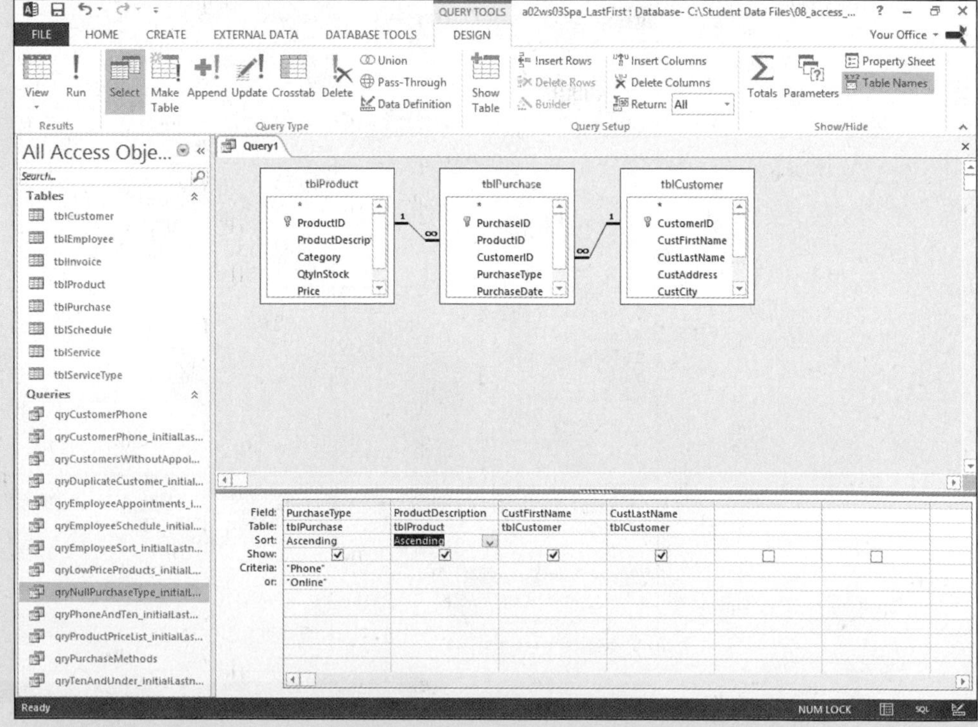

Figure 21 Or criteria for PurchaseType

e. In the Results group, click **Run** to run the query. The results should show 12 records, all with Phone or Online as the purchase type sorted by purchase type and product description.

f. Click **Save** on the Quick Access Toolbar, name the query qryPhoneOrOnline_initialLastname using your first initial and last name, and then click **OK**. **Close** the query.

Combining the AND and OR Logical Operators

There may be times when you want to use two logical operators, AND and OR, at the same time. Depending on the desired results, you may have to use one or both Criteria rows. If you use both Criteria rows for criteria for two fields, then Access treats it like two AND logical operators with one OR logical operator.

For this project, the manager wants you to find all phone purchase types for products over $20 as well as all online purchase types for products over $15. Phone and greater than 20 are one AND criteria. Online and greater than $15 are the other AND criteria. You want all purchases that are one OR the other of the two AND combinations. Access moves left to right on the first criteria so it will treat "Phone" and >20 as AND criteria and then move to the next row, which it will consider OR criteria. To see how this works, you will step through the query one criteria at a time.

A03.21

To Combine the AND and the OR Logical Operator

a. Click the **CREATE** tab, and then in the Queries group, click **Query Design**, and then double-click **tblProduct**, **tblPurchase**, and **tblCustomer** to add the tables to the query. Click **Close** to close the Show Table dialog box.

b. Double-click **PurchaseType** from tblPurchase, double-click **ProductDescription** and **Price** from tblProduct, and then double-click **CustFirstName** and **CustLastName** from tblCustomer in that order to add them to the query design grid.

c. Click in the **Sort** row, and then select **Ascending** for the **PurchaseType** and **Price** fields.

d. Click in the **Criteria** row for the PurchaseType field, and then type Phone. Click **Run** to run the query.

   Notice that five orders are shown. Why do you see these orders? Access has found all records that are Phone orders.

e. Switch to **Design** view. In the same Criteria row for the Price field, type >20. Click **Run** to run the query.

   Notice that two orders are shown. Why do you see these orders? They are both phone orders and both have prices of over $20. Access has found all records that are Phone AND >20.

f. Switch to **Design** view. In the **or** row below the Criteria row, type Online for the **PurchaseType** field. Click **Run** to run the query.

   Notice that nine orders are shown. Why do you see those orders? You still see the two phone orders with prices of over $20. You also see all online orders. Access has found all records that are Phone AND >20 OR orders that are Online.

g. Switch to **Design** view. In the same **or** row as Online, type >15 for the Price field.

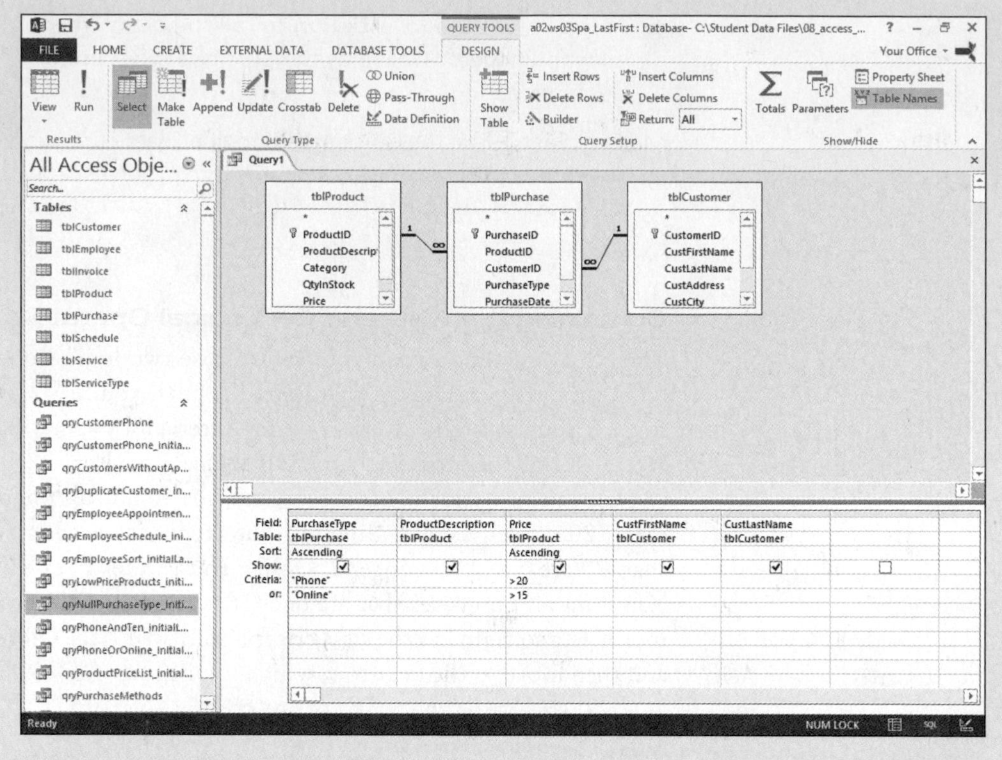

Figure 22 Two criteria rows added for PurchaseType and Price

h. Click **Run** to run the query.

Notice that six orders are shown. Why these six orders? You still see the two phone orders with prices of over $20. You also see four online orders with prices of over $15. Access has found all records that are Phone AND >20 OR orders that are Online AND >15.

Access moved left to right on the first criteria so it will treat "Phone" and >20 as AND criteria and then move to the next row, where it will consider "Online" and >15 as OR criteria.

i. Click **Save** on the Quick Access Toolbar, name the query qryPhoneAndOnline_initialLastname using your first initial and last name, and then click **OK**. **Close** the query.

Combining Multiple AND and OR Logical Operators

You cannot always use two rows for the OR criteria when you combine both logical operators. In cases like this, the word "or" can be used for two criteria used in the same field and the same Criteria row. For this project, the manager of the spa wants you to find all phone and online purchase types for products over $10. If you put the purchase type criteria on two rows and the price of >10 in one row, your results will show all records with phone purchase types over $10 or Online purchase types of any amount. Remember, Access moved left to right on the first criteria so it will treat "Phone" and >10 as AND criteria and then move to the next row, which it will consider OR criteria.

A03.22

To Combine Multiple AND and OR Logical Operators

a. Click the **CREATE** tab, and then in the Queries group, click **Query Design**. Double-click **tblProduct**, **tblPurchase**, and **tblCustomer** to add the tables to the query. Click **Close** to close the Show Table dialog box.

b. In the following order, double-click **PurchaseType** from tblPurchase, **ProductDescription** and **Price** from tblProduct, and **CustFirstName** and **CustLastName** from tblCustomer to add them to the query design grid.

c. Click in the **Criteria** row for the PurchaseType field, type Phone, and then in the **Criteria** row for the Price field, type >10. In the **or** row for the PurchaseType field, type Online.

d. Click in the **Sort** row, and then select **Ascending** for the **PurchaseType** and **Price** fields.

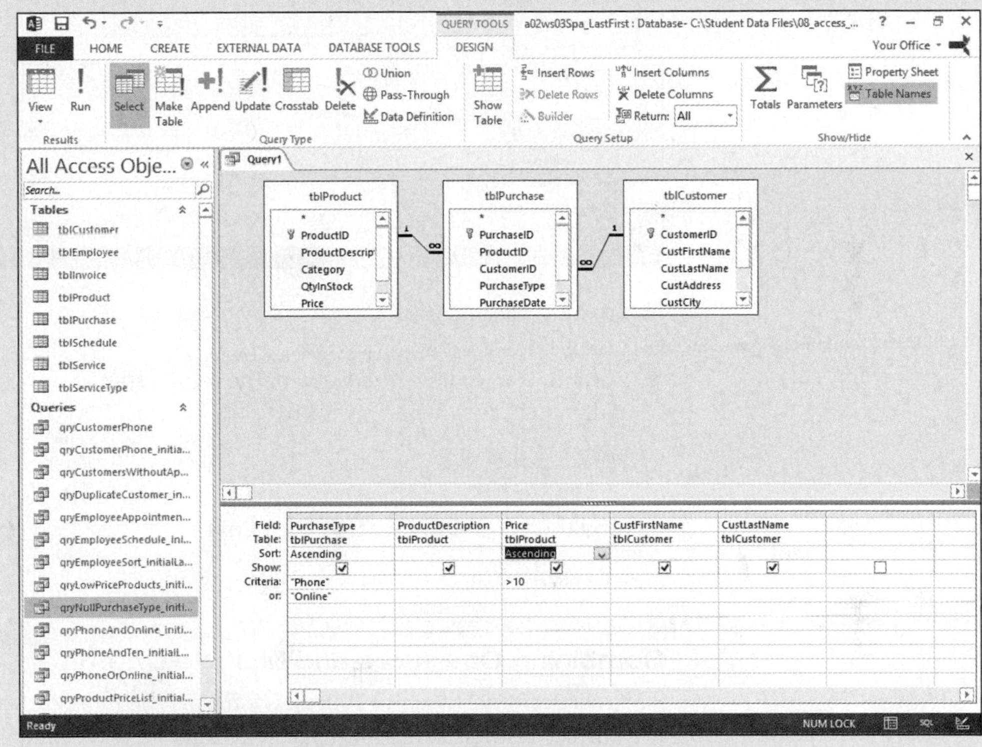

Figure 23 AND and OR criteria added to the query design grid

e. Click **Run** to run the query.
Notice the results are all Phone purchase types with prices over $10 or all Online purchase types, regardless of the price. The manager wants to see Phone or Online purchase types over $10, so this is not correct.

f. Switch to **Design** view. In the **or** row for the PurchaseType field, delete "Online." Click in the **Criteria** row for the PurchaseType field, and then change the criteria to Phone or Online.

SIDE NOTE
Access Puts in Quotes
You can leave the quotation marks around "Phone" or remove them. Access will add them for Short Text fields.

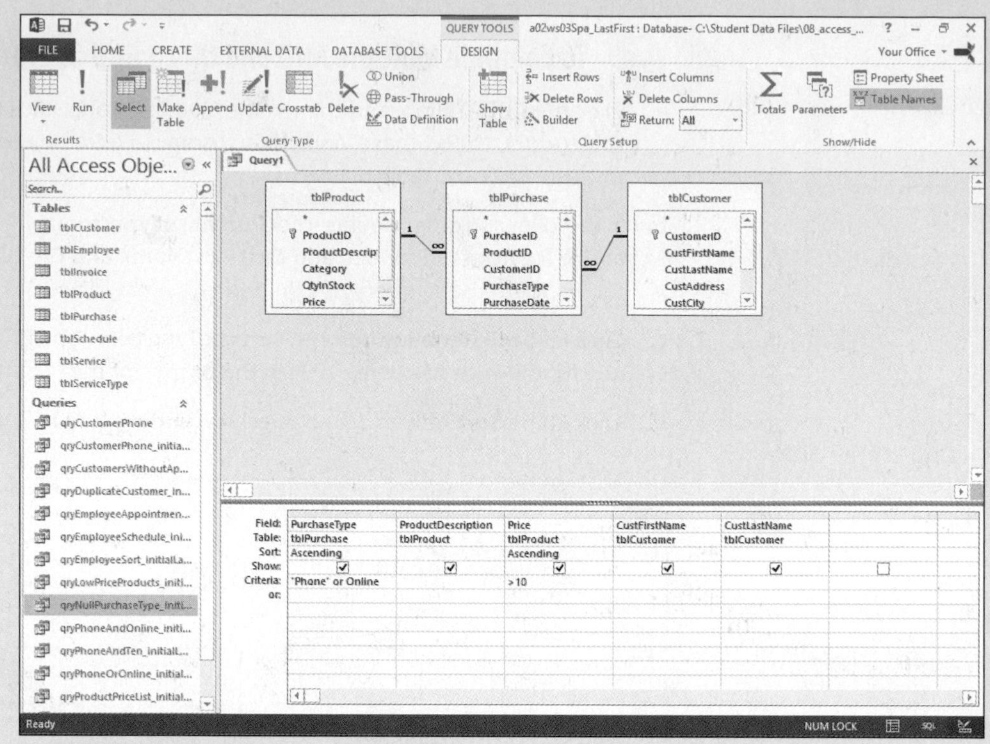

Figure 24 OR criteria in one row with AND criteria

g. Click **Run** to run the query again. The results should now show the 10 Phone or Online purchase types that are over $10.

h. Click **Save** on the Quick Access Toolbar, under Query Name type qryPhoneOrOnlineOverTen_initialLastname using your first initial and last name, and then click **OK**. **Close** the query.

Combining Operators and Multiple Criteria

The more criteria added to your query means the more difficult it will be to see if you have the correct results. With multiple criteria, it is good practice to add one criteria, run the query to make sure you are getting the correct results, and then continue adding criteria one at a time.

For this project, the spa manager would like to see all of her high-end services listed by price and then service type, and she would like to break down the criteria as follows: Hands & Feet or Body Massage services $50 or more, Facial or Microdermabrasion services over $55, Beauty or Waxing services over $45, and all Botanical Hair & Scalp Therapy services.

MODULE 2

A03.23

To Combine Operators and Multiple Criteria

a. Click the **CREATE** tab, and then in the Queries group, click **Query Design**, and double-click **tblService** to add the table to the query window. Click **Close** to close the Show Table dialog box.

b. In the following order, double-click **Fee**, **Type**, and **ServiceName** to add the fields to the query design grid.

c. Click in the **Criteria** row for the Fee field, type >55, and then in the **Criteria** row for the Type field type Facial or Microdermabrasion.

d. Click in the **Sort** row, and then select **Ascending** for the **Fee**, **Type**, and **ServiceName** fields.

e. Click **Run** to run the query. The results should show six records with Facial or Microdermabrasion for the Type field, and all values in the Fee field should be greater than $55.

f. Switch to **Design** view. In the **or** row for the Fee field, type >=50, and for the **or** row for the Type field type "Hands & Feet" or Body Massage. Click **Run** to run the query again.

The query results should show 19 records with types Facial or Microdermabrasion that have fees greater than $55, and records with types Hands & Feet or Body Massage that have fees greater than or equal to $50.

SIDE NOTE
Wider Columns
You can widen the columns in the query design grid by double-clicking the right border of the column selector bar.

Troubleshooting
If you only get 16 records in the results, you did not put the quotation marks around "Hands & Feet". Access will add those quotation marks for you. In this case, Access evaluates the ampersand character (&) as separating two values, so it will put the quotation marks around the word "Hands" and around the word "Feet" so it will look like "Hands" & "Feet". This is different than having the quotations around the whole phrase, which is what you want it to look like. In this case you should put the quotation marks around the phrase in order for it to appear as "Hands & Feet".

g. Switch to **Design** view. Click in the **second or** row for the Fee field, type >45, and then in the **Criteria** row for the Type field, type Beauty or Waxing. Click **Run** to run the query again.

The results should show 23 records with types Facial or Microdermabrasion that have fees greater than $55, and records with types Hands & Feet or Body Massage that have fees greater than or equal to $50, and records with types Beauty or Waxing that have fees greater than $45.

h. Switch to **Design** view. Click in the **third or** row for the Type field, and then type "Botanical Hair & Scalp Therapy".

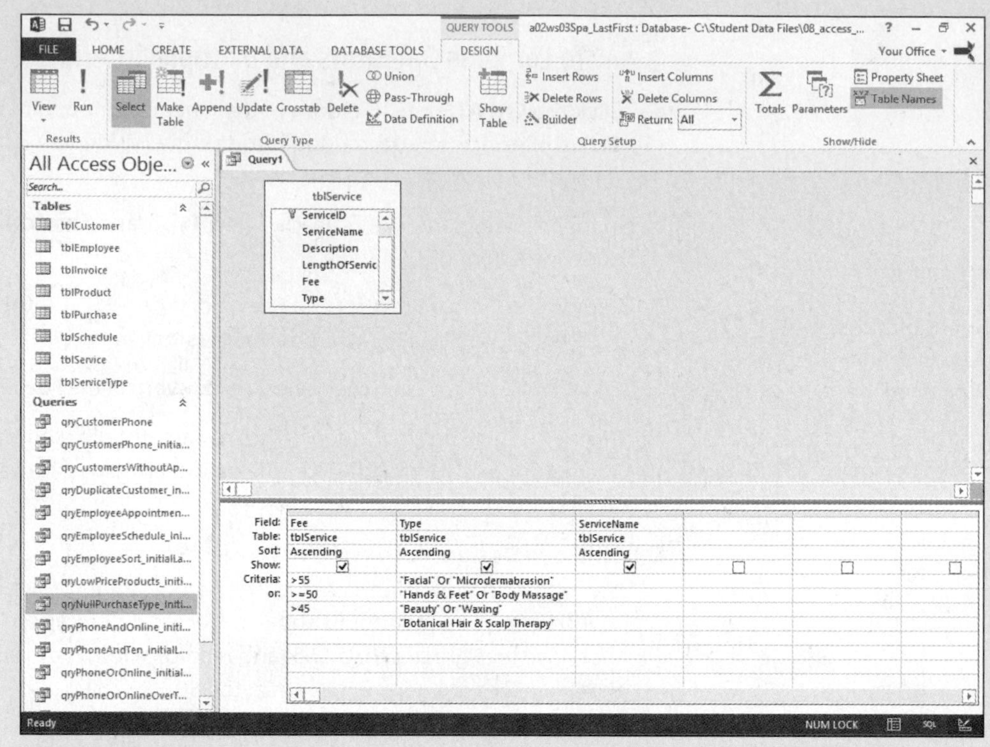

Figure 25 All criteria added to query design grid

i. Click **Run** to run the query again.

The results should show 25 records with types Facial or Microdermabrasion that have fees greater than $55, records with types Hands & Feet or Body Massage that have fees greater than or equal to $50, records with types Beauty or Waxing that have fees greater than $45, and all Botanical Hair & Scalp Therapy types.

> **Troubleshooting**
>
> If you still see 23 records, check to see that you put the quotation marks around "Botanical Hair & Scalp Therapy" and that you spelled the type correctly.

j. Click **Save** on the Quick Access Toolbar, name the query qryHighEndServices_initialLastname using your first initial and last name, and then click **OK**. **Close** the query.

Using Special Operators and Date Criteria

Special operators, as shown in Table 5, are used to compare text values using wildcards (LIKE), to determine whether values are between a range of values (BETWEEN), or in a set of values (IN).

Operator	Description
LIKE	Matches text values by using wildcards. These are the same wildcards that are shown in Table 1.
BETWEEN	Determines if a number or date is within a range.
IN	Determines if a value is found within a set of values.

Table 5 Special operators

For this project, the manager of the spa would like you to find all services scheduled for February 2015, along with the customer who is scheduled for those services. The Between special operator will return results that include and fall between the criteria you enter. If you recall, when working with dates as criteria, a # in front of and at the end of each date are required to identify the numbers as dates and not a string of text. You will use the Between special operator.

A03.24

To Use the Between Special Operator with a Date Criteria

a. Click the **CREATE** tab, and then in the Queries group, click **Query Design**. Double-click **tblSchedule** and **tblCustomer** to add the tables to the query. Click **Close** to close the Show Table dialog box.

b. Double-click **DateOfAppt**, **Service**, and **Employee**, from tblSchedule, and then double-click **CustFirstName** and **CustLastName** from tblCustomer in that order to add them to the query design grid.

c. Click in the **Sort** row, and then select **Ascending** for the **DateOfAppt**, **Service**, and **Employee** fields.

d. Click in the **Criteria** row for the DateOfAppt field, and then type **Between 2/1/15 and 2/29/15.**

e. Click **Run** to run the query.

Notice that the results do not show services in February. They show services in January. Access is misinterpreting your query criteria.

f. Switch to **Design** view to check the criteria. Move your pointer to the **border** between DateOfAppt and Service until it becomes ↔. Double-click to see the full criteria.

Notice that since there is no leap day in 2015, Access interpreted the 2/29/15 as 2/29/2012, the last leap day that occurred, and the /15 as a division. This is not what you wanted. This example shows why it is so important to check your results to see if they make sense.

SIDE NOTE
Formatting Criteria
Access will add pound signs around dates and quotation marks around text. However, if the criteria are ambiguous, you should put them in.

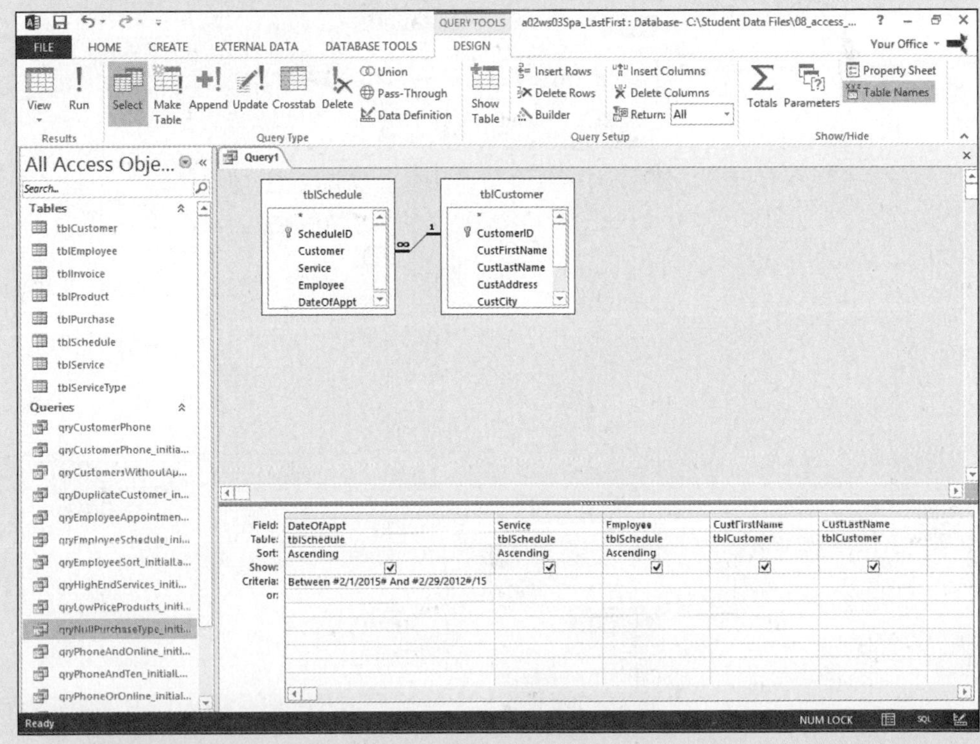

Figure 26 Misinterpreted criteria for DateOfAppt

g. Change the criteria to Between 2/1/15 and 2/28/15. Click **Run** to run the query. This time the results are as expected and show 47 appointments in February.

h. Click **Save** on the Quick Access Toolbar, under Query Name type qryFebruaryServices_initialLastname using your first initial and last name, and then click **OK**. **Close** the query.

Combining Special Operators and Logical Operators

Special operators can be combined with logical operators. As your criteria get more complex, you need to carefully check how Access interprets your criteria and your results.

For this project, the manager of the spa would like you to find all services scheduled for months other than February 2015, along with the customer who is scheduled for that service. You will use the LIKE special operator and combine it with the NOT logical operator. This query is very similar to the one you just created so you will open that query and modify it.

A03.25

To Use Combine Logical and Special Operators

a. Right-click **qryFebruaryServices_initialLastname**, and then select **Copy**. Right-click the **Navigation Pane**, and then select **Paste**. In the Query Name box type qryNotFebruaryServices_initialLastname. Click **OK**.

b. Double-click **qryNotFebruaryServices_initialLastname** to open it.

c. Switch to **Design** view. Click in the **Criteria** row for the DateOfAppt field, and then replace the current criteria with Like 2/*/2015. Remember that the asterisk (*) is a wildcard that will select all dates that have a month of 2 and a year of 2015.

d. Click **Run** to run the query. Notice that the results show 47 February service appointments.

e. Switch to **Design** view. Type Not before the current criteria so it reads **Not Like "2/*/2015"**.

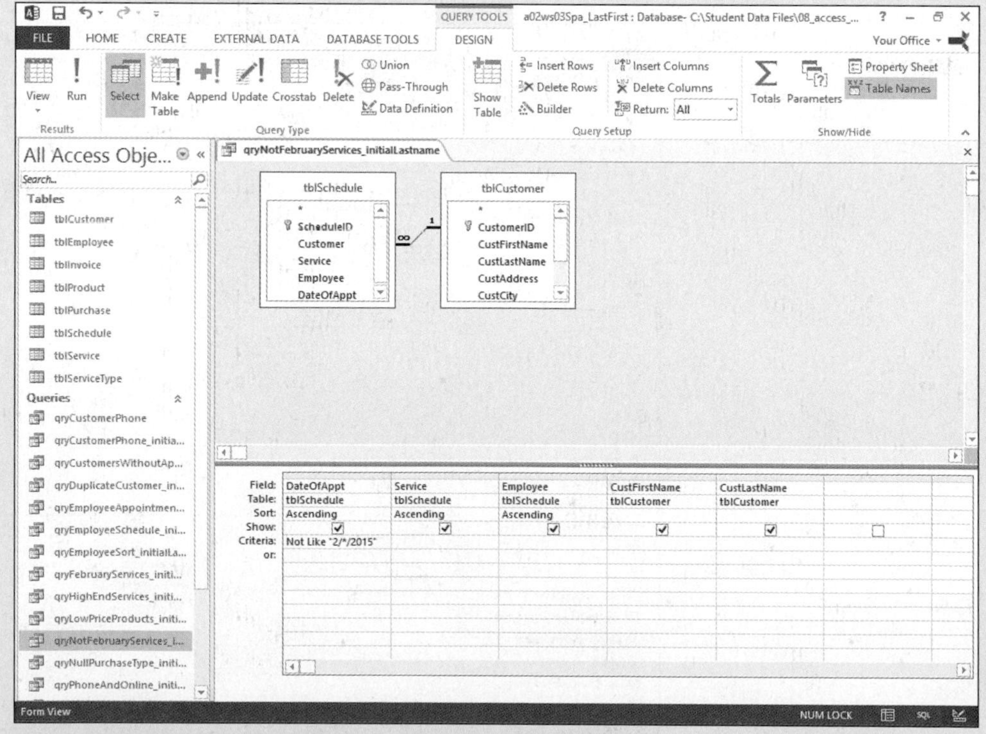

Figure 27 Combined Not and Like operators

f. Click **Run** to run the query. Notice that the results now show the six service appointments not in February.

g. **Save** and **close** your query.

Create Aggregate Functions

Aggregate functions perform arithmetic operations, such as calculating averages and totals, on records displayed in a table or query. An aggregate function can be used in Datasheet view by adding a total row to a table, or it can be used in a query on records that meet certain criteria.

QUICK REFERENCE	Commonly Used Aggregate Functions

There are a number of different aggregate functions that can be used depending on the type of calculation you want to perform.

1. **Sum**—Calculates the total value for selected records
2. **Average**—Calculates the average value for selected records
3. **Count**—Displays the number of records retrieved
4. **Minimum**—Displays the smallest value from the selected records
5. **Maximum**—Displays the largest value from the selected records

Adding a Total Row

If you need to see a quick snapshot of statistics for a table or query, you can use the **total row**. The total row is a special row that appears at the end of a datasheet that enables you to show aggregate functions for one or more fields. For this project, you will help the manager quickly find a total for all unpaid invoices listed in the invoices table and a count of the number of invoices in the table. The invoice table has a Yes/No field, so you will show her how to define criteria for Yes/No.

A03.26

To Add a Total Row to a Query That Uses Yes/No Criteria

a. Double-click **tblInvoice** to open it. Notice that the Paid field is a check box. Switch to **Design** view and see that the Data Type is Yes/No. Click the **Data Type** and see that the Format is Yes/No. **Close** the table.

b. Click the **CREATE** tab, and then in the Queries group, click **Query Design**. Double-click **tblInvoice** and **tblCustomer** to add the tables to the query. Click **Close** to close the Show Table dialog box.

c. Double-click **InvoiceDate**, **InvoiceTotal**, and **Paid** from tblInvoice, and then double-click **CustFirstName** and **CustLastName** from tblCustomer in that order to add them to the query design grid.

d. Click in the **Sort** row, and then select **Ascending** for **InvoiceDate**.

e. Click in the **Criteria** row for the **Paid** field, and then type No.

f. Click **Run** to run the query. The six unpaid invoices are shown.

SIDE NOTE

Removing Totals

To remove the total row, on the Home tab, click Totals.

g. In the Records group, click **Totals** so that the Total row shows.

h. Click in the **Total row** under the InvoiceTotal field, click the arrow, and then select **Sum**. Click in the **Total row** under the First Name field, click the arrow, and then select **Count**.

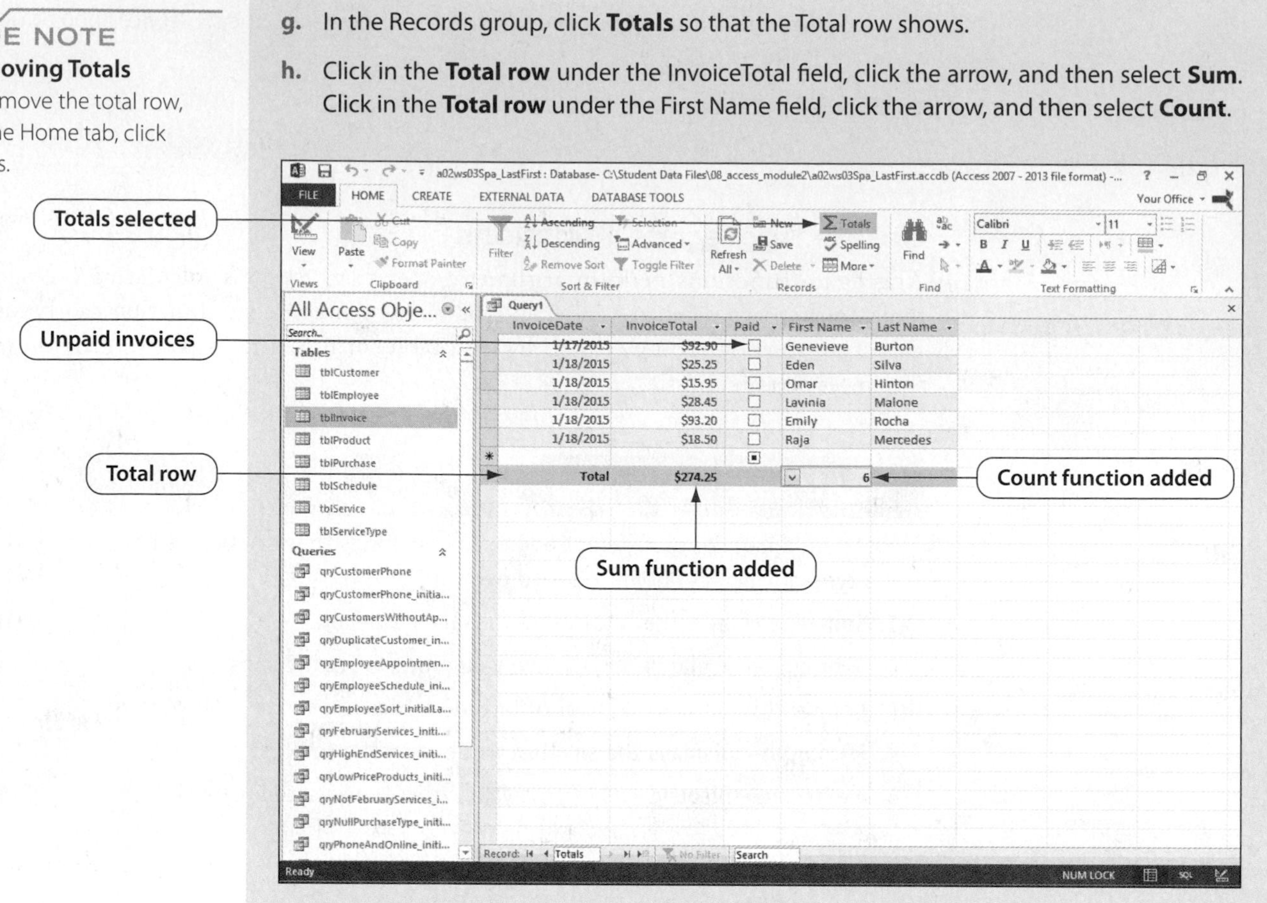

Figure 28 Sum and Count of Unpaid Invoices added to the Total row

i. Click **Save** on the Quick Access Toolbar, under **Query Name** type qryUnpaidInvoices_initialLastname using your first initial and last name, and then click **OK**. **Close** the query.

Using Aggregate Functions in a Query

Aggregate functions can be used in queries to perform calculations on selected fields and records. One advantage to using aggregate functions in queries, rather than just a total row, is that you can group criteria and then calculate the aggregate functions for a group of records. By default, the query design grid does not have a place to enter aggregate functions, so the total row must be added from the Query Tools Design tab. Each column or field can calculate only one aggregate function, so to calculate multiple functions on the same field, the field must be added to the grid multiple times.

For this project, you have been asked to provide a statistical summary of the spa's product prices. The manager would like to see how many products are offered, what the average product price is, and the minimum and maximum product prices.

A03.27

To Use Aggregate Functions in a Query

a. Click the **CREATE** tab, and then in the Queries group, click **Query Design**. Double-click **tblProduct** to add the table to the query. Click **Close** to close the Show Table dialog box.

b. Double-click **Price** four times to add the field four times to the query design grid.

c. In the Show/Hide group, click **Totals** to add a total row to the query design grid.

d. In the first Price column, click in the **Total** row, click the arrow, and then select **Count**. In the second Price column, click in the **Total** row, click the arrow, and then select **Avg**. Repeat for the next two **Price** columns selecting **Min** for the third column and **Max** for the last column.

SIDE NOTE

Pull Down Arrow

Alternatively, you can click the right side of the Total row and the pull down menu appears.

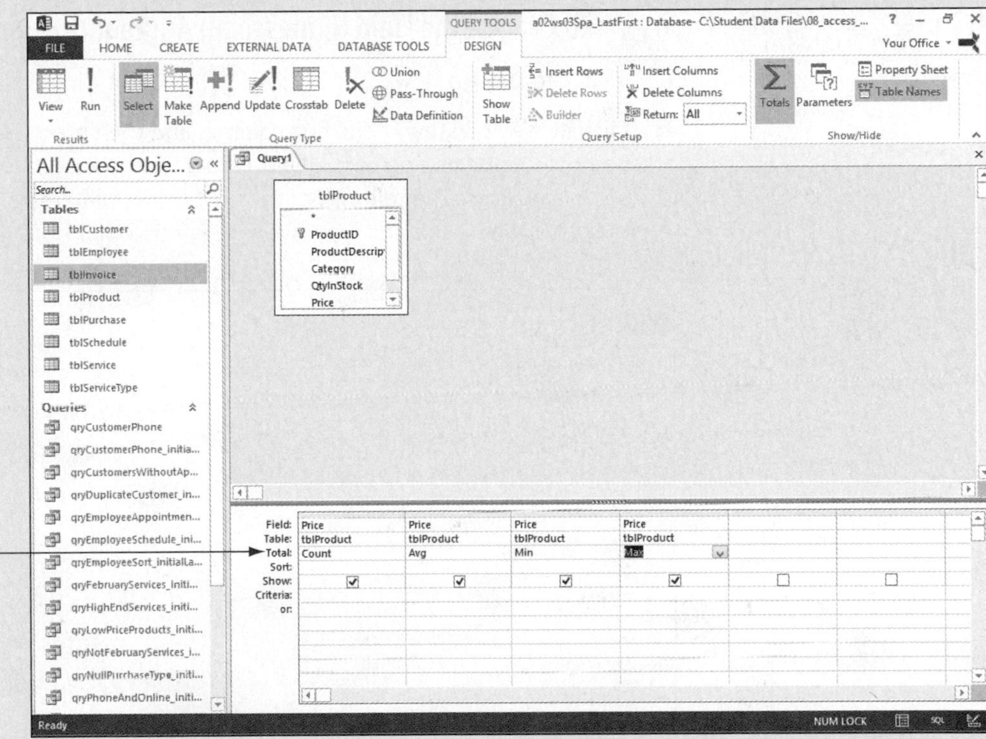

Figure 29 Aggregate functions selected for each column

e. Click **Run** to run the query. Because this is an aggregate query and you are calculating one statistic per column, there will only be one record in the results.

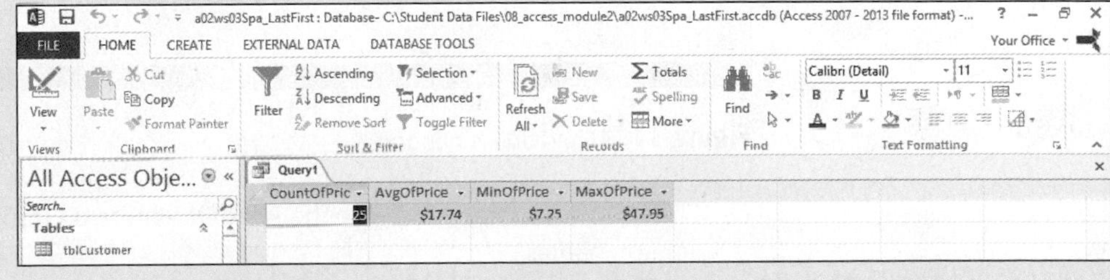

Figure 30 Aggregate query results

Changing Field Names

Field names in aggregate queries are a composite of the selected aggregate function and the table field name. For example, the Count function for Price is named CountOfPrice as shown in Figure 30. This is not particularly descriptive in what it actually shows is the number of products that have a price. The other functions are more descriptively named but still could have more useful names.

The field names assigned in an aggregate query can easily be changed either before or after the query is run. However, you must keep the original field name in the query design grid so Access knows what field to perform the calculation on. For this project, you will change the names of the fields in the aggregate query you just created.

A03.28

To Change the Field Names in an Aggregate Query

a. Switch to **Design** view.

b. Click in the **Field** row of the first column, and then press Home to move the insertion point to the beginning of the field name. Type Count of Products:. Do not delete the field name **Price**. The colon identifies the title as separate from the field name. Repeat for the other three fields and type Average Price:, Minimum Price:, and Maximum Price:.

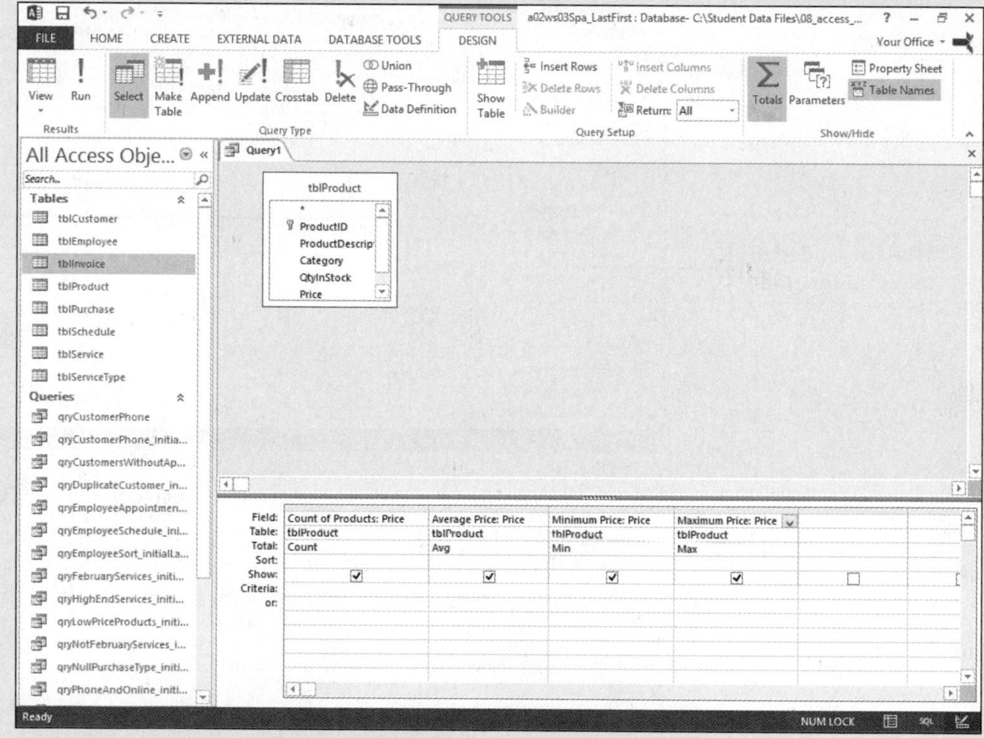

Figure 31 Field titles changed

c. Click **Run** to run the query. Use the **AutoFit** feature on the columns to see the complete column names.

d. Click **Save** on the Quick Access Toolbar, under Query name type qryProductStatistics_initialLastname using your first initial and last name, and then click **OK**. **Close** the query.

Creating Calculations for Groups of Records

Not only can you find statistical information on selected records using aggregate functions in a query, or for all records using the total row, you can also calculate statistics for groups of records. Creating a group to calculate statistics works the same way as an aggregate query but must include the field to group by. The additional field will not have a statistic selected for the total row, but instead it will have the default Group By entered in the total row.

For this exercise, you will help the spa manager find the same product price statistics you calculated above but this time grouped by product category.

A03.29

To Create a Group Calculation

a. Click the **CREATE** tab, and then in the Queries group, click **Query Design**, and then double-click **tblProduct** to add the table to the query. Click **Close** to close the Show Table dialog box.

b. Double-click **Category** to add it to the query design grid, and then double-click **Price** four times to add the field four times to the query design grid.

c. On the DESIGN tab, in the Show/Hide group, click **Totals** to add a total row to the query design grid.

d. In the first Price column, click in the **Total** row, click the **arrow**, and then select **Count**. In the second Price column, click in the **Total** row, click the **arrow**, and then select **Avg**. Repeat for the next two **Price** columns selecting **Min** for the third column and **Max** for the last column. Notice that the Category Total row displays Group By so the statistics will be grouped by each category type.

e. Click **Run** to run the query. Notice that there are five total lines, one for each category of product.

f. Switch to **Design** view.

g. Change the titles for the Price fields to the following: Number of Products, Average Price, Minimum Price, and Maximum Price remembering to put a colon between the name and the Price field name. **Run** the query again. Use the **AutoFit** feature on the columns to best fit the data.

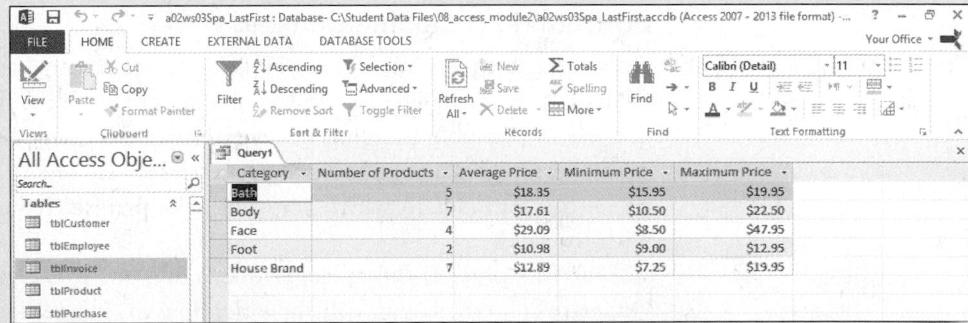

Figure 32 Query results with field titles changed

h. Click **Save** on the Quick Access Toolbar, under Query Name type qryPriceStatisticsByCategory_initialLastname using your first initial and last name, and then click **OK**. **Close** the query.

Troubleshooting an Aggregate Query

Caution should be used when using aggregate functions. Forgetting to add a function in the total row can cause a large number of records to be retrieved from the database, or a combination of records that do not make any sense. You must carefully select which field should have the Group By operator in the total row; many times only one field will use Group By. Combining search criteria and aggregate functions in a single query can make the query complex. It also makes troubleshooting more difficult if the query does not work. When in doubt, set all your criteria in one query and then use the aggregate functions in another query based on the query with the criteria. This way, you can first verify that your criteria worked and then concentrate on the aggregate function results.

For this exercise, the manager tried to create an aggregate query to calculate the total number of items and average number of items purchased by different methods—phone, online, and in person. The results made no sense, and she has asked you to help her figure out why.

A03.30

To Troubleshoot an Aggregate Query

a. Double-click **qryPurchaseMethods** to open the query. Notice the results in the second and third columns are exactly the same, when the intent was to have one column contain a total and the other column contain an average.

b. Switch to **Design** view. Look at the second column, **Quantity**, and notice the Total row shows the Group By operator instead of a function. Change this to **Sum**.

c. Rename the second and third column field titles to Total Quantity and Average Quantity, remembering to put a colon between the name and the Quantity field name.

d. Click **Run** to run the query. Use the **AutoFit** feature on the columns to best fit the data.

e. Click the **FILE** tab, select **Save As**, click **Save Object As**, and then click **Save As**. Under Save 'qryPurchaseMethods' to: type qryPurchaseMethods_initialLastname, using your first initial and last name, and then click **OK**.

Formatting a Calculated Field

An aggregate query may give you the correct results, but the formatting may not be what you expected. The fields used in a query that come from a table use the formatting defined in the table design. However, calculated query fields must be formatted in the query design grid using the Field properties sheet. The **Property Sheet** contains a list of properties for fields in which you can make precise changes to each property associated with the field.

For this project, the manager does not want to see decimal places for the Average Quantity column, so you will show her how to change the formatting of that field.

A03.31

To Change the Formatting of a Calculated Field

a. Switch to **Design** view.

b. Click the **Average Quantity: Quantity** column. On the DESIGN tab, in the Show/Hide group, click **Property Sheet**.

c. In the Property Sheet pane, on the General tab, click the **Format** box, click the **arrow**, and then select **Fixed**. Click the **Decimal Places** box, and then type 0.

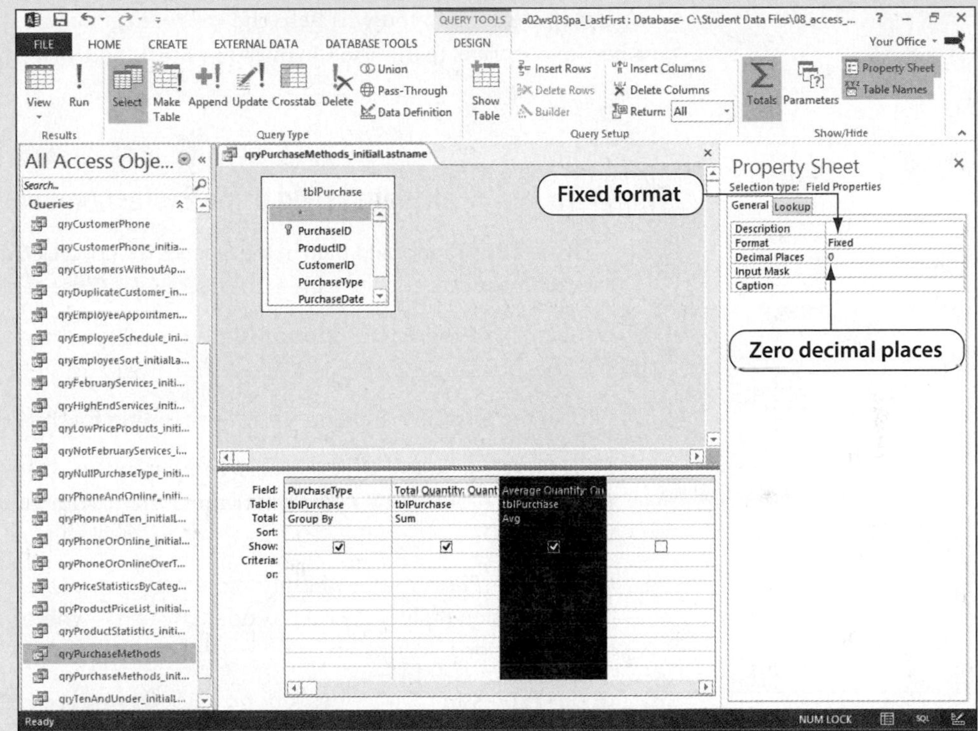

Figure 33 Property sheet open with changes

d. **Close** [X] the Property Sheet pane, and then **run** the query again. The results should be formatted with no decimal places.

e. **Save** and **close** [X] the query.

CONSIDER THIS | **How Many Decimal Places?**

Would having many decimal places for an average field give you a more accurate average? Why would you choose to show no decimal places on an average quantity field?

Create Calculated Fields

In addition to statistical calculations using aggregate functions, you can also perform an arithmetic calculation within a row of a query to create a new field. The result of the calculated field is displayed each time you run the query. However, this new field is not part of any other table.

A calculated field can be added to a query using the fields in the query or even fields in another table or query in the database. The calculation can use a combination of numbers and field values, which allows you flexibility in how you perform the calculation. For example, you can multiply a product price stored in the table by a sales tax rate that you enter into the calculation.

Building a Calculated Field Using Expression Builder

Expression Builder is a tool in Access that can help you format your calculated fields correctly. The Builder provides a list of expression elements, operators, and built-in functions. The capabilities of Expression Builder range from simple to complex.

For this exercise, you will help the spa manager create a query to show what the value of her inventory is using the Quantity in Stock and Price fields for each product.

A03.32

To Add a Calculated Field Using Expression Builder

a. Click the **CREATE** tab, and then in the Queries group, click **Query Design**, and then double-click **tblProduct** to add the table to the query. Click **Close** to close the Show Table dialog box.

b. Double-click **ProductDescription**, **Category**, **QtyInStock**, and **Price** to add the fields to the query design grid.

c. Click in the **Sort** row, and then select **Ascending** for the **ProductDescription** field.

d. Click **Save** on the Quick Access Toolbar, under **Query Name**, type qryProductInventory_initialLastName using your first initial and last name, and then click **OK**.

e. Click in the **Field** row in the fifth column, in the Query Setup group, click **Builder**. The Expression Builder dialog box opens, which is where you will build your formula for the calculation.

f. Under Expression Categories, double-click **QtyInStock** to add the field to the expression box, type * for multiplication, and then under Expression Categories double-click **Price**. Move the insertion point to the beginning of the expression, and then type Total Inventory:.

SIDE NOTE

Expression Box

When you use multiple tables in Expression Builder, the table name is put in front of the field name with an exclamation mark.

Troubleshooting

When you click Expression Builder to create a calculated field, and you do not see your field names listed in the Expression Categories box in the middle of the dialog box, it may be that the query has not been saved yet. If the query is not saved, then the field names will not appear and you will have to type them in the Expression Builder manually instead of clicking them to select them. It is good practice to save your query first, and then open the Expression Builder to create a calculated field.

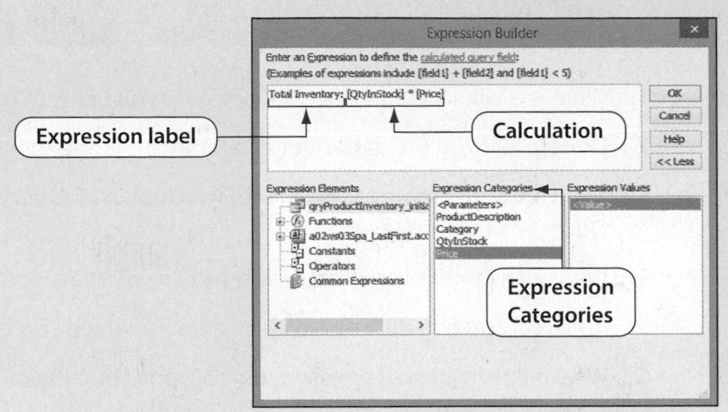

Figure 34 Expression Builder

g. Click **OK** to save the expression and add it to the query design grid. Use the **AutoFit** feature on all columns.

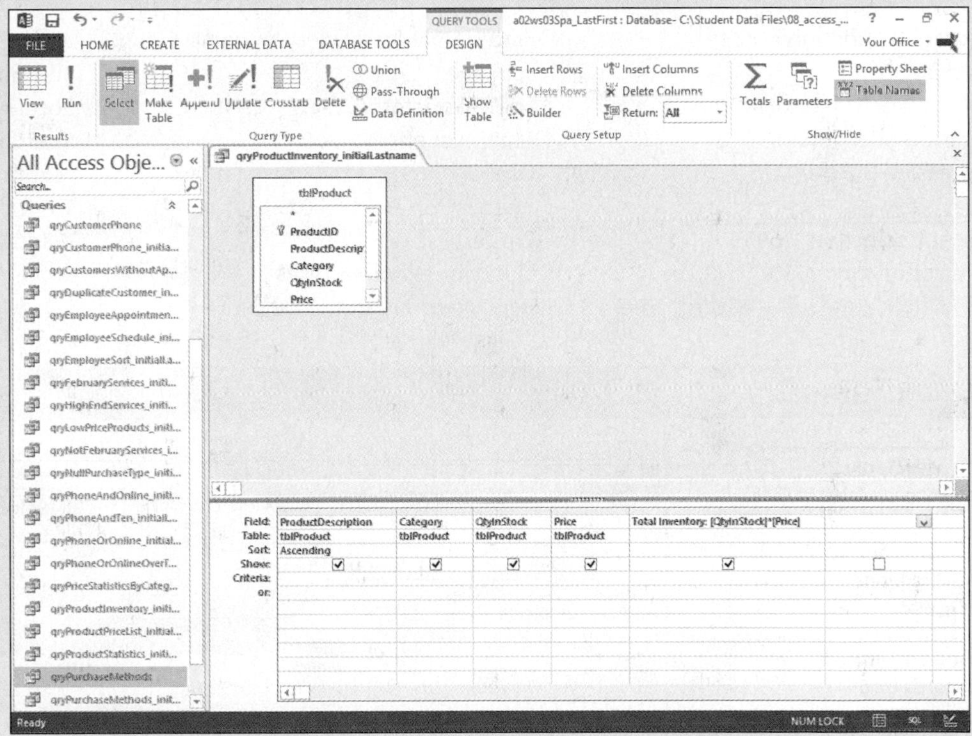

Figure 35 Design grid with calculated expression added

h. Click **Run** to run the query. Use the **AutoFit** feature on the Total Inventory column to best fit the data. The results should show 25 records with a new column titled **Total Inventory** that multiplies the QtyInStock and the Price fields.

i. **Close** [X] the query, and then click **Yes** when prompted to save changes. **Close** Access.

Concept Check

1. What is a wildcard character? How would you use it to find a record? p. 692–693
2. Does modifying the datasheet appearance change the data in your database? p. 695
3. What is the difference between the Find Duplicates Query Wizard and the Find Unmatched Query Wizard? p. 696–698
4. What is the multiplier effect, and how can you prevent it from happening? p. 702, 705
5. If you sort on two different fields in a query, which sort is done first? p. 707
6. What is the difference between using AND and OR as logical operators in a query? p. 712–714
7. What is an aggregate query? Why would you add the same field multiple times to an aggregate query? p. 723–724
8. How does a calculated field differ from an aggregate function? p. 729–730

Key Terms

Aggregate function 723
AutoFit 695
Comparison operator 708
Crosstab query 696
Expression Builder 730
Filter 693
Filter by selection 693
Find command 690
Find Duplicates Query Wizard 697
Find Unmatched Query Wizard 698
Join lines 702
Logical operator 712
Multiplier effect 702
Orphan 697
Primary sort field 707
Property sheet 728
Query by example 699
Replace command 690
Secondary sort field 707
Sort field 706
Sorting 706
Special operator 720
Text filter 694
Total row 723
Wildcard character 690

Visual Summary

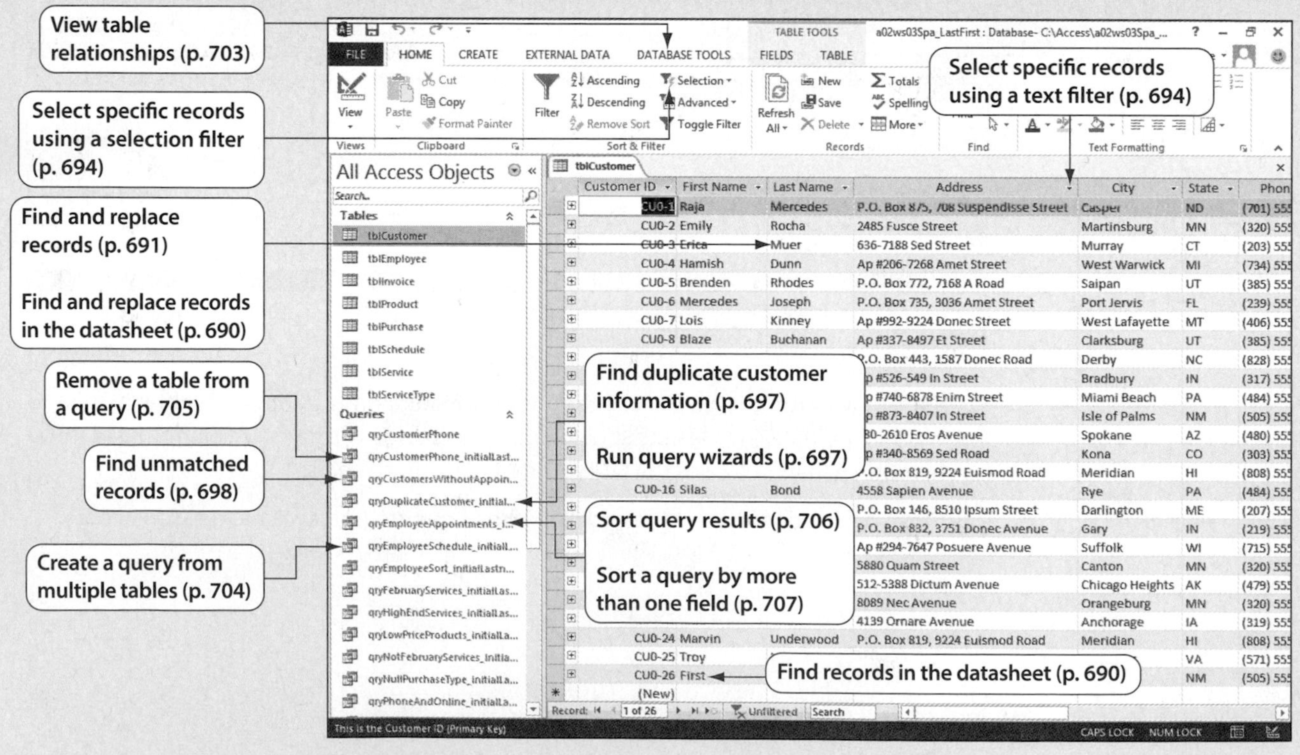

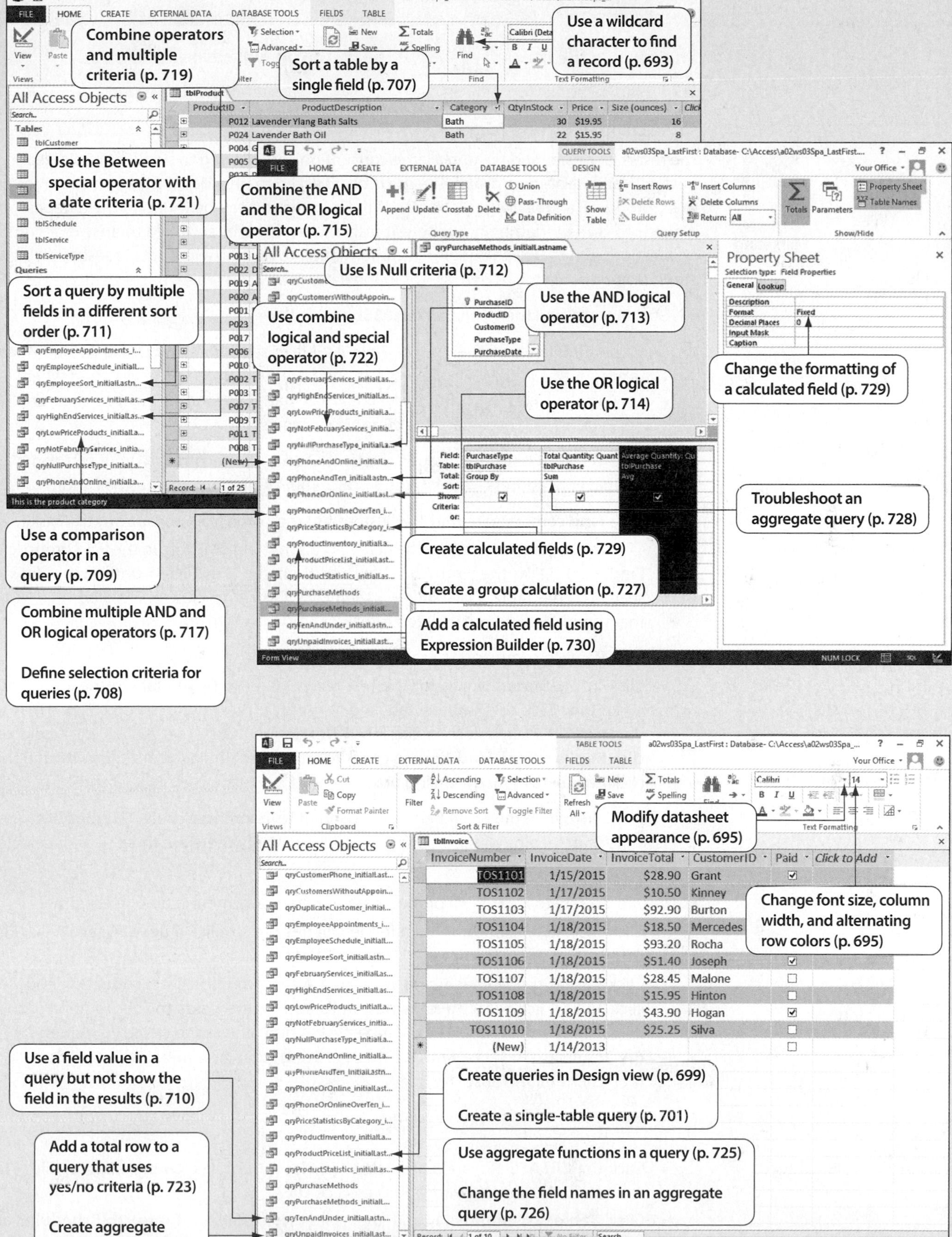
Combine operators and multiple criteria (p. 719)
Use a wildcard character to find a record (p. 693)
Sort a table by a single field (p. 707)
Use the Between special operator with a date criteria (p. 721)
Combine the AND and the OR logical operator (p. 715)
Use Is Null criteria (p. 712)
Sort a query by multiple fields in a different sort order (p. 711)
Use the AND logical operator (p. 713)
Use combine logical and special operator (p. 722)
Change the formatting of a calculated field (p. 729)
Use the OR logical operator (p. 714)
Troubleshoot an aggregate query (p. 728)
Use a comparison operator in a query (p. 709)
Create calculated fields (p. 729)
Create a group calculation (p. 727)
Combine multiple AND and OR logical operators (p. 717)
Define selection criteria for queries (p. 708)
Add a calculated field using Expression Builder (p. 730)
Modify datasheet appearance (p. 695)
Change font size, column width, and alternating row colors (p. 695)
Use a field value in a query but not show the field in the results (p. 710)
Create queries in Design view (p. 699)
Create a single-table query (p. 701)
Add a total row to a query that uses yes/no criteria (p. 723)
Use aggregate functions in a query (p. 725)
Change the field names in an aggregate query (p. 726)
Create aggregate functions (p. 723)

Figure 36 Turquoise Oasis Spa Data Management Final

Practice 1

Student data file needed:

 a02ws03Spa2.accdb

You will save your file as:

 a02ws03Spa2_LastFirst.accdb

Turquoise Oasis Spa

Sales & Marketing

The resort is considering hosting a large convention and is trying to sign a multiple-year contract with an out-of-town group. The spa is being asked to provide information about the services, products, and packages it offers. All the information can be found in the database, but it needs to come together in a coherent fashion. You have been asked to answer a number of questions about the spa and provide information to help answer those questions. You will also look for discrepancies or mistakes in the data, and correct them as necessary.

a. Start **Access**, and then open **a02ws03Spa2**.

b. Click the **FILE** tab, and then select **Save As**. Make sure **Save Database As** and **Access Database** are selected. Click **Save As**. In the Save As dialog box, navigate to where you are saving your files, and then type a02ws03Spa2_LastFirst, using your first and last name. Click **Save**. If necessary, click **Enable Content**.

c. Double-click **tblCustomer** to open the table. Add a new record with your first name and last name, your address, your city, your state, your phone, and your e-mail address.

d. Use the **Find** command to find spa customers who come from as far away as Alaska.
   - Click in the **State** column for the first record. On the HOME tab, in the Find group, click **Find**. Type AK in the Find What box, and then click **Find Next** until Access finishes searching the table. Click **OK**, and then click **Cancel** to close the dialog box. Notice that the Alaska address selected is really a city in Hawaii.

e. Use the Replace command to replace **AK** with HI in the table.
   - Click in the **State** column for the first record. On the HOME tab, in the Find group, click **Find**. Click the **Replace** tab, and type AK in the Find What box. Type HI in the Replace With box, and then click **Find Next**. When Customer ID CU0-21 is selected, click **Replace**. Click **Find Next** to check for any more similar errors. Click **OK**, and then click **Cancel** to close the dialog box.

f. Click the **arrow** on the **State** field column, point to **Text Filters**, select **Begins With**, type H in the State begins with box, and then click **OK**. Verify there are three records selected. Save and close the table.

g. Create a query to find which products are purchased by more than one customer.
   - Click the **CREATE** tab, and then in the Queries group, click **Query Wizard**. Click **Find Duplicates Query Wizard**, and then click **OK**.
   - Click **Table: tblPurchase**, and then click **Next**. Double-click **ProductID**, and then click **Next**. Click the **All Fields** button to add all the fields to the Additional query fields box, and then click **Next**. Under "What do you want to name your query?" type qryDuplicateProducts_initialLastname using your first initial and last name, and then click **Finish**. Close the query.

h. Create a query to find out which employees currently do not have any customer appointments at the spa.
   - Click the **CREATE** tab, and then in the Queries group, click **Query Wizard**. Click **Find Unmatched Query Wizard**, and then click **OK**.
   - Click **Table: tblEmployee**, and then click **Next**. Select **Table: tblSchedule**, and then click **Next**. Verify that Matching fields shows **EmployeeID <=> Employee**, and then click **Next**. Click the **All Fields** button to add all the fields to the Selected fields column, and then click **Next**.

- Name the query qryEmployeesWithoutAppointments_initialLastname, using your first initial and last name, and then click **Finish**.
- Switch to **Design** view. Click the **Sort** row for the EmpLastName field, click the **sort** arrow, and then click **Ascending** to sort the query in ascending order by Last Name. On the DESIGN tab, in the Results group, click **Run** to run the query. Close the query, and then click **Yes** when prompted to save the changes.

i. Create a query to list any customers who are not from New Mexico who have purchased bath products.
   - Click the **CREATE** tab, and then in the Queries group, click **Query Design**. Double-click **tblCustomer**, **tblPurchase**, and **tblProduct** to add the tables to the query window. Click **Close** to close the Show Table dialog box.
   - In the following order, from tblCustomer double-click **CustLastName**, **CustFirstName**, **CustState**; from tblPurchase double-click **PurchaseDate**; from tblProduct, double-click **ProductDescription**; and from tblPurchase, double-click **Quantity** to add the fields to the query design grid. Click the **Sort** row for the CustLastName and CustFirstName fields, and then select **Ascending**.
   - In the **Criteria** row for **CustState**, type Not NM. In the same Criteria row for **ProductDescription**, type Like *Bath*.
   - On the DESIGN tab, in the Results group, click **Run** to run the query.
   - Click **Save** on the Quick Access Toolbar, name the query qryBathProductsNotNM_initialLastname using your first initial and last name, and then close the query.

j. Create a query to list the spa's services by Type, Name, LengthOfService, and Fee.
   - On the **CREATE** tab, in the Queries group, click **Query Design**. Double-click **tblService** and **tblServiceType** to add the tables to the query window. Click **Close** to close the Show Table dialog box.
   - In the following order, from tblServiceType double-click **Type**, and from tblService double-click **ServiceName**, **LengthOfService**, and **Fee** to add the fields to the query design grid. Click the **Sort** row for the Type field, select **Ascending**, and then for the Fee field, select **Descending**. On the DESIGN tab, in the Results group, click **Run** to run the query.
   - Use the **AutoFit** feature on all columns. Click **Save** on the Quick Access Toolbar, name the query qryServicesAndFees_initialLastname using your first initial and last name, and then close the query.

k. Create a query to find how much each customer spent on their product purchase, including 8% sales tax, but only if the purchase was a quantity greater than 1.
   - Click the **CREATE** tab, and then in the Queries group, click **Query Design**. Add **tblProduct**, **tblPurchase**, and **tblCustomer** to the query window. Click **Close** to close the Show Table dialog box. From tblProduct, double-click **ProductDescription** and **Price**; from tblPurchase, double-click **Quantity**; and from tblCustomer, double-click **CustFirstName** and **CustLastName** in that order to add the fields to the query design grid.
   - Click in the **Criteria** row for Quantity, and then type >1. Click **Save** on the Quick Access Toolbar, name the query qryTotalPurchase_initialLastname using your first initial and last name, and then click **OK**.
   - In the sixth column, click in the **Field** row, and then on the DESIGN tab, in the Query Setup group, click **Builder**. Double-click **Price** to add it to the expression, type *, double-click **Quantity** to add it to the expression, type *, and then type 1.08. Click at the beginning of the expression, type Total Purchase with tax:, and then click **OK**.
   - Click the **Sort** row for the Quantity field, click the **arrow**, and then click **Ascending**. In the Results group, click **Run** to run the query.
   - Switch to **Design** view. Click the **Total Purchase with tax** field, on the DESIGN tab, in the Show/Hide group, click **Property Sheet**. On the Property Sheet's General tab, click the **Format** arrow, and then select **Currency**. Click the **Decimal Places**

arrow, and then select **2**. Close the Property Sheet, and then on the DESIGN tab, in the Results group, click **Run** to run the query. The Total Purchase with tax field should be formatted with currency and two decimal places.
- Use the **AutoFit** feature on all the columns.
- Close the query, and then click **Yes** when prompted to save the changes.

l. Create an aggregate query to find the average, minimum, and maximum fee for each type of service the spa offers.
   - Click the **CREATE** tab, and then in the Queries group, click **Query Design**. Add **tblService** to the query window. Click **Close** to close the Show Table dialog box. Double-click **Type** one time, and then double-click **Fee** three times in that order to add the fields to the query design grid. In the Show/Hide group, click **Totals** to add the Total row to the query design grid.
   - Click in the **Total** row, for the first Fee column, click the **arrow**, and then click **Avg**. For the second Fee column select **Min**, and for the third Fee column select **Max**. Click in the **Sort** row in the Type field, click the **arrow**, and then select **Ascending**. In the Results group, click **Run** to run the query.
   - Switch to **Design** view. Change the names of the three Fee columns to Average Fee, Minimum Fee, and Maximum Fee in that order, remembering to put a colon before the Fee field name. In the **Results** group, click **Run** to run the query.
   - Use the **AutoFit** feature on all the columns.
   - Click **Save** on the Quick Access Toolbar, name the query qryFeeStatistics_initialLastname using your first initial and last name, and then click **OK**. Close the query.

m. Close Access. Submit your file as directed by your instructor.

Problem Solve 1

Student data file needed:

You will save your file as:

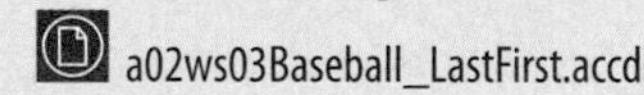

Baseball Academy

Production & Operations

Matt Davis is a retired baseball player who runs the Baseball Academy, an indoor baseball facility for middle school, high school, and college players. He offers lessons as well as practice times for individuals and teams. Due to his growing clientele and increased record keeping needs, Matt wants all his records in a database. While he has already set up a database, he now needs to take the database to the next level of performance by improving his ability to get specific data from the database. He has hired you to create the queries he will need to get this information.

a. Start **Access**, and then open **a02ws03Baseball**. Click the **FILE** tab, and save the file as an **Access Database** in the location where you store your files with the name a02ws03Baseball_LastFirst using your first and last name. If necessary, enable the content.

b. Open **tblMember**, and then add a new record with your first name, last name, address, city, state, zip code of 87594, and phone. Create a filter to show only those members who have a zip code of **87594**. Save and close the table.

c. Modify **tblPayments** so the font type is **Arial** and the font size is **14**. Adjust the column widths appropriately. Save and close the table.

d. Create a Find Duplicates Query that will show members who have the same address. Show all the fields in the query results. Name the query qryDupAddresses_initialLastname and then close the query.

e. Create an Unmatched Query that will return the last name, first name, address, city, state, zip code, and phone of anyone who is listed as a member in **tblMember** but has not made a payment matching on MemberID. Name the query qryNonPayment_initialLastname. Sort by last name and first name, and then save and close the query.

f. Create a query that will return the **member last name**, **first name**, **amount**, and **payment date**. Sort the query in ascending order first by last name then by first name. Name the query qryPayments_initialLastname.
   - Add a total row to show the sum of total payments made. Save and close the query.

g. Create a query that returns all the employees that have **Instructor** in their position. Include employee **first name**, **last name**, and **position**. Sort them by salary—highest to lowest but do not show the salary in the result. Name the query qryInstructors_initialLastname. Save and close the query.

h. Create a query to calculate employee salaries with a 3% raise. Include the employee's **last name**, **first name**, and **salary**. Name the query qryRaises_initialLastname.
   - The new calculated field is salary * 1.03 and should be called SalaryWithRaise. Format the new field as **Currency** with **Auto** decimal places, and then sort the results by SalaryWithRaise from highest salary to lowest.
   - Adjust the column widths as necessary. Include total payroll before and after the raises at the bottom of the datasheet. Save and close the query.

i. Create a query that returns the sum, average, minimum, and maximum of all the employee salaries. Name the fields Total Salary, Average Salary, Minimum Salary, and Maximum Salary. Adjust the column widths to fit. Name the query qrySalaryStats_initialLastname. Save and close the query.

j. Create a query that includes the member's **last name**, **first name**, **scheduled date**, and **fee** for any lesson between June 1 and June 30, 2015, which is greater than or equal to $250. Sort by last name and first name. Name the query qryBigJuneFees_initialLastname. Save and close the query.

k. Save and close the database. Submit your file as directed by your instructor.

Perform 1: Perform in Your Career

Student data file needed:	You will save your file as:
 a02ws03Roadhouse.accdb	 a02ws03Roadhouse_LastFirst.accdb

Beverage Database at The Roadhouse Bar and Grill

Production & Operations

You are the bar manager at The Roadhouse Bar and Grill, a local restaurant that specializes in home-cooked meals for breakfast, lunch, and dinner. You have developed a database for managing the inventory of beverage items.

You will expand the database by creating queries to help you manage the database. You have loaded a few sample transactions to help you develop these queries. For each query, choose which fields you need and which sort order makes sense.

a. Start **Access**, open **a02ws03Roadhouse**, and then save it as a02ws03Roadhouse_LastFirst.

b. Open **tblSuppliers**, and then change the name of the first supplier to your full name.

c. Open each table and familiarize yourself with the fields. Open the relationships window and note how the tables are related.

d. Change **tblSales** to have a larger font and alternating row colors.

e. Create a query that shows sales of beverages from suppliers in Maryland. Show the **Supplier Name** and **State**, the **Sales Date**, and beverage fields that make sense. Sort by fields that make sense. Save the query as qryMarylandSupplierSales_initialLastname.

f. Create a query to see if there are any Suppliers that are not supplying you with any beverages. Hint: this is a Find Unmatched Query. Save the query as qrySuppliersWithoutBeverages_initialLastname.

g. Create a query that shows beverages that have soda in their name, their size, the container type, and the suppliers that supply them. Sort by fields that make sense. Save the query as qrySodaSuppliers_initialLastname.

h. Create a query that shows all juices that were sold in February 2015. Sort by fields that make sense. Save the query as qryFebruaryJuiceSales_initialLastname.

i. Create a query that shows all root beer or cola sold in a bottle with the sale date. Sort by fields that make sense. Save the query as qryBottleSales_initialLastname.

j. Create an aggregate query that shows the average price, minimum price, and maximum price for each beverage serving. Hint: Group by beverage. Sort by fields that make sense. Save the query as qryBeveragePriceStatistics_initialLastname.

k. Create a query that calculates for each beverage the number of servings per container—container size divided by serving size. Sort by fields that make sense. Save the query as qryBeverageServings_initialLastname.

l. Create another query that you would find useful in your job.

m. Submit your file as directed by your instructor.

Additional Cases

Additional Workshop Cases are available on the companion website and in the instructor resources.

WORKSHOP 4 | ACCESS INFORMATION FROM AN ACCESS DATABASE

OBJECTIVES

1. Navigate in datasheets and forms p. 740
2. Update table records using forms p. 748
3. Create a form using the Form Wizard p. 751
4. Modify a form's design p. 756
5. Create a report using the Report Wizard p. 762
6. Customize a report p. 770
7. Save a report as a PDF file p. 777

Prepare Case

Turquoise Oasis Spa's New Database

Production & Operations

The Turquoise Oasis Spa has a database with customer, employee, product, and service information for easier scheduling and access. An intern created the database, and the manager and staff members are struggling to use the database to its fullest capacity. You have recently been hired to work in the office of the spa and you have knowledge of Access, so the manager has asked for your help in maintaining the records and creating forms and reports to help better use the data in the database.

Zadorozhnyi Viktor / Shutterstock

REAL WORLD SUCCESS

"After I started using Access for entering my data and running reports, my supervisor asked if I could set up a database for my coworker to use for her job. She didn't know Access so I created forms for her data entry. She just enters today's data and runs her daily reports."

- Elaine, marketing analyst and alumnus

Student data files needed for this workshop:

 a02ws04Spa.accdb

 a02ws04Spa.thmx

 a02ws04Spa.jpg

You will save your files as:

 a02ws04Spa_LastFirst.accdb

 a02ws04SpaEmployeeSchedule_LastFirst.pdf

Creating Customized Forms

Recall that forms are the objects in Access that are used to enter, edit, or view records in a table. Data can be entered, edited, or viewed directly in the table or in a form. Each option offers advantages and disadvantages.

In Datasheet view, data may be updated directly in the table where it is stored. When updating data in a table, you will be in Datasheet view. Datasheet view shows all the fields and records at one time, which provides all the information you need to update your data, unlike in a form or query, where some of the fields or records may not be in view. This section starts by describing how to navigate in datasheets and forms, continues to editing data in a table, and then finishes by discussing how to edit data in a form.

Navigate in Datasheets and Forms

As you may recall, you can navigate from record to record or field to field in a database using the Navigation bar, or in Navigation mode by using [Tab], [Enter], [Home], [End], [↑], [↓], [←], and [→]. **Navigation mode** allows you to move from record to record and field to field using keystrokes. To update data in a table, you must be in Edit mode. **Edit mode** allows you to edit, or change, the contents of a field. To switch between Navigation mode and Edit mode, press [F2].

If you can see the blinking insertion point in a field, you are in Edit mode. When the text of a field is selected and highlighted, you are in Navigation mode.

QUICK REFERENCE | **Keystrokes Used in Navigation Mode and Edit Mode**

Keystroke	Navigation Mode	Edit Mode
[→] and [←]	Move from field to field	Move from character to character
[↑] and [↓]	Move from record to record	Switch to Navigation mode and move from record to record
[Home]	Moves to the first field in the record	Moves to the first character in the field
[End]	Moves to the last field in the record	Moves to the last character in the field
[Tab] and [Enter]	Move one field at a time	Switch to Navigation mode and move from field to field
[Ctrl] + [Home]	Moves to the first field of the first record	Moves to the first character in the field, same as [Home]
[Ctrl] + [End]	Moves to the last field of the last record	Moves to the last character in the field, same as [End]

Opening the Starting File

The spa collects data about customers, employees, products, and services and uses them for scheduling. You will open the spa database to get started.

A04.00

To Open the a02ws04Spa Database

a. Start **Access**, and then open the student data file **a02ws04Spa**.

b. On the **FILE** tab, save the file as an **Access Database** in the location designated by your instructor with the name a02ws04Spa_LastFirst using your first and last name. If necessary, enable the content.

Editing a Table in Datasheet View

Datasheet view shows all the records and fields at one time, which is one advantage to using it to update your records. Another advantage is the ability to see all the records in the table, which gives you a perspective on the data you are entering. For this exercise, the staff has received a note from a customer who has changed his phone number. You will show the spa staff how to change that customer's record in the Customer table.

MyITLab®
Workshop 4 Training

A04.01

To Edit a Record in a Table in Datasheet View

a. In the Navigation Pane, double-click **tblCustomer** to open the table.

b. Locate the customer with the Customer ID **CU0-12** and the last name **Hinton**.

c. Click in the **CustomerID** field, and then press Tab. You are now in Navigation mode, and the First Name field should be highlighted.

SIDE NOTE
Prefix for Key
When you click CustomerID, the "CU0" disappears. The key is defined as numeric but has a prefix identifying the table it is key to.

First Name highlighted in navigation mode

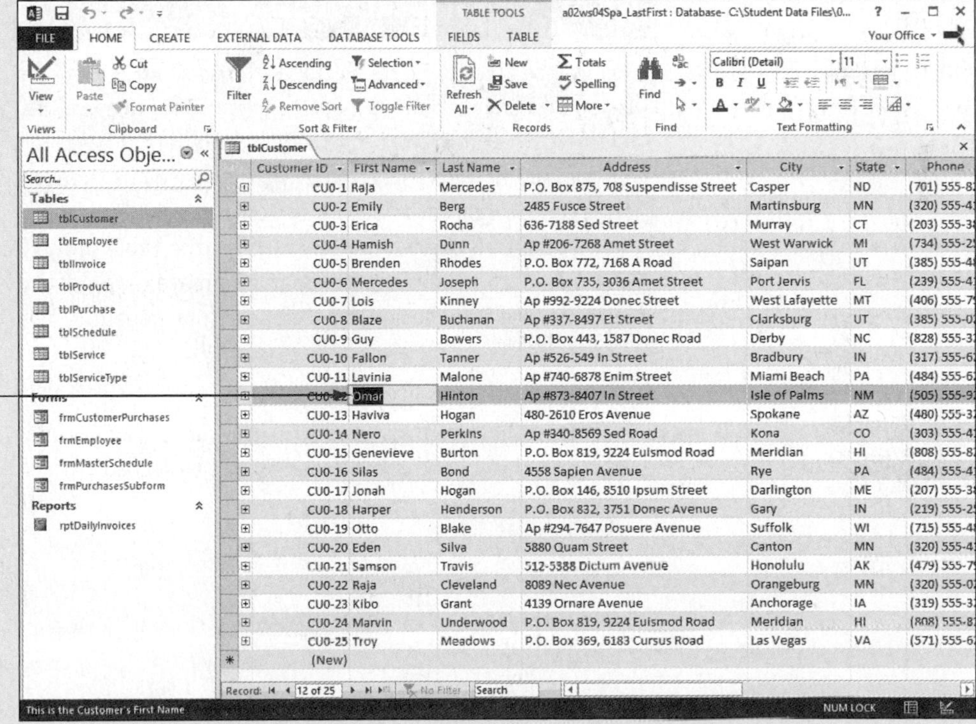

Figure 1 Table in navigation mode

d. Continue pressing [Tab] until the **Phone** field is highlighted. Press [F2] to switch from Navigation mode to Edit mode. Notice the insertion point is at the beginning of the Phone field and the first character is highlighted. Type **5055552923** to enter the new phone number. Because the field is already formatted as a phone number, it is not necessary to enter parentheses or dashes.

e. Press [Tab] to switch to Navigation mode and move to the next field.

f. **Close**  the table.

CONSIDER THIS | Why Put a Prefix Before a Primary Key?

CustomerID, the primary key for tblCustomer, is defined as AutoNumber but formatted to have the prefix "CU0-" (0 is a zero) before the number field. Similarly, EmployeeID, the key for tblEmployee, is formatted to have "EMP-" as a prefix before the number field. What is the advantage of putting a prefix before the primary key to a table? Are there disadvantages? Why were these two prefixes chosen?

Navigating Forms and Subforms

A form is an object in Access that you can use to enter, edit, or view records in a table. A simple form allows you to see records one at a time rather than as a group in Datasheet view.

REAL WORLD ADVICE | Data Overload!

You may be asked to create a database for someone else that is not familiar with how a database works or even how the computer works. Your role is to make their job as easy as possible so they can get their work done with as few errors as possible.

Looking at a database table with hundreds or thousands of records in Datasheet view can be very intimidating to some people. Trying to keep track of the record or field you are in can be more difficult as the table grows larger and larger. Often seeing one record at a time in a form can eliminate data entry errors and allow the user to focus on the information for that particular record.

You navigate records in a form the same way you navigate a table, using buttons on the Navigation bar to move from record to record.

MODULE 2

QUICK REFERENCE — **Navigation Buttons on the Navigation Bar**

Button	Description	What it does
[First]	First record	Moves to the first record in the table
[Last]	Last record	Moves to the last record in the table
[Previous]	Previous record	Moves to the record just before the current record
[Next]	Next record	Moves to the record just after the current record
[New]	New (blank) record	Moves to a new row to enter a new record

When you create a form from two tables that have a one-to-many relationship, the first table selected becomes the **main form** and the second table you select becomes the **subform**. A form with a subform allows you to see one record at a time from the main form and multiple records in Datasheet view from the other related table. Because you only see one record at a time or one record and a datasheet, navigation tools become important when you are working with forms as you cannot see all the records at one time.

Navigating a Main Form

Within each record, you can use a combination of Tab, Home, Enter, and End, as well as ↓, ↑, ←, →, to move from field to field as shown in the Quick Reference Box.

QUICK REFERENCE — **Navigating Forms**

Navigating a main form

Keystroke	What it does
Tab	Moves from field to field within a record; at the last field in a record, it moves you to the first field in the next record.
Home	Moves to the first field of the current record.
Ctrl + Home	Moves to the first field of the first record of the table.
End	Moves to the last field of the current record.
Ctrl + End	Moves to the last field of the last record of the table.
↓, ↑, ←, →	Move up or down a field of the current record.

(Continued)

QUICK REFERENCE	Navigating Forms *(Continued)*

Navigating a form with a subform

Keystroke	What it does
Tab	Moves from field to field within a main record. At the last field in a record, it moves to the first field in the subform. At the last record in the subform, it moves to the first field in the next record of the main form.
Home	From the main form, moves to the first field of the current record. From the subform, moves to the first field of the current record in the subform.
Ctrl + Home	From the main form, moves to the first field of the first record. From the subform, moves to the first field of the first record in the subform.
End	From the main form, moves to the last field of the current record in the subform. From the subform, moves to the last field of the current record in the subform.
Ctrl + End	From the main form, moves to the last field of the last record of the subform. From the subform, moves to the last field of the current record of the subform.
↓, ↑, ←, →	Move up or down a field in the current record in either the form or subform.

For this exercise, you will show the spa staff how to navigate the form frmEmployee, which is a list of all employees, one record at a time.

A04.02

To Navigate a Single-Table Form

a. On the Navigation Pane, double-click **frmEmployee** to open the form.

b. Click **Last record** ▸| to go to the last record of the table.

c. Click **First record** |◂ to return to the first record in the table.

d. Click **Next record** ▸ to go to the next record in the table.

e. Click **Previous record** ◂ to go back to the previous record in the table.

f. **Close** ✕ the form.

Navigating a Form with a Subform

When navigating forms with a subform, the Navigation bar buttons at the bottom of the main window are used to navigate the records in the main form, and a second Navigation bar at the bottom of the subform datasheet is used to navigate the records in the subform.

The same navigation keystrokes are used; however, they work a little differently when a subform is included.

For this exercise, you will show the spa staff members how to navigate the form frmCustomerPurchases, which shows one customer at a time with all their recent product purchases.

A04.03

To Navigate a Multiple-Table Form with a Subform

a. On the Navigation Pane, double-click **frmCustomerPurchases** to open the form.

Notice that the form has two parts. At the top is the main form that shows information about the customer. The lower part is the subform that shows all the purchases made by the customer. There are also two navigation bars, one for the main form and one for the subform.

Main form Last Record button on the Navigation bar

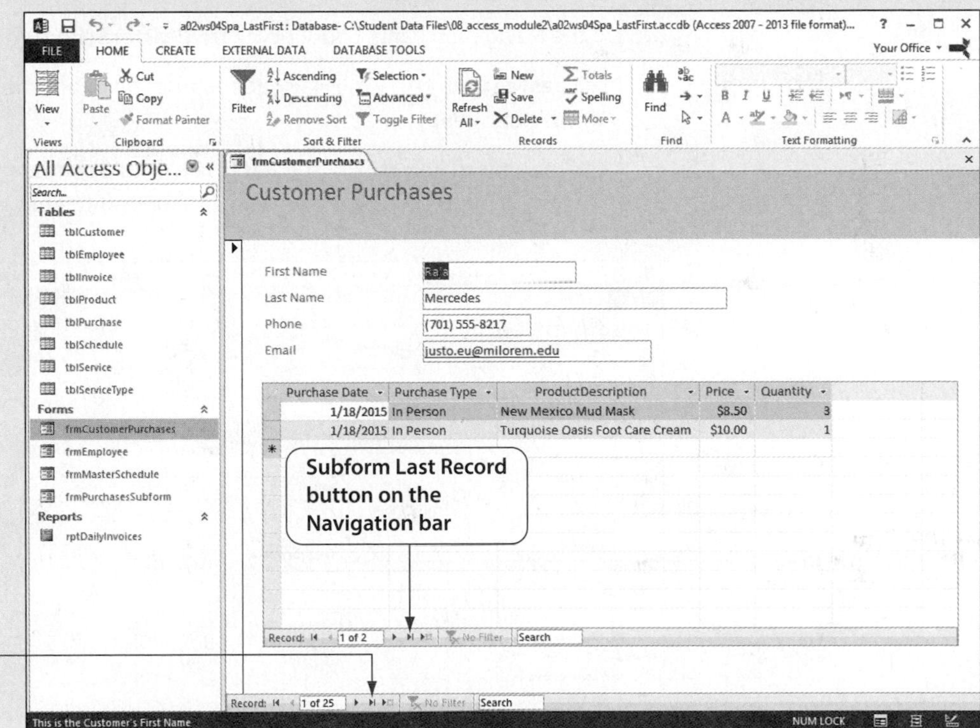

Figure 2 Form with a subform in Datasheet view

b. Click **Last record** [⏭] on the subform Navigation bar to highlight the last record in the subform.

c. Click **Last record** [⏭] on the main form Navigation bar to go to the last record in the table.

d. Click **Previous record** [◀] repeatedly to go to record 20 with the customer name Eden Silva.

e. Click **Next record** [▶] in the subform to go to the next record in the subform.

f. **Close** [X] the form.

Navigating a Split Form

A split form is a form created from one table, but it has a Form view and a Datasheet view in the same window. You can view one record at a time at the top of the window, and see the whole table in Datasheet view at the bottom of the window. This kind of form is helpful when you want to work with one record at a time and still see the big picture in the main table. In a split form, there are buttons on the Navigation bar to move only from record to record, and each record shown at the top is the record highlighted in the datasheet at the same time. You cannot highlight a different record in the form part and the datasheet part at the same time.

For this exercise, you will show the spa staff how to navigate the form frmMasterSchedule, which shows the schedule as a form and a datasheet in the same window.

A04.04

To Navigate a Split Form

a. On the Navigation Pane, double-click **frmMasterSchedule** to open the form.

b. Click **Last record** on the Navigation bar to highlight the last record in both the form and the datasheet.

c. Click the **record selector** in the datasheet with **Schedule ID S046**. The record will be highlighted in the datasheet and also be shown at the top in Form view.

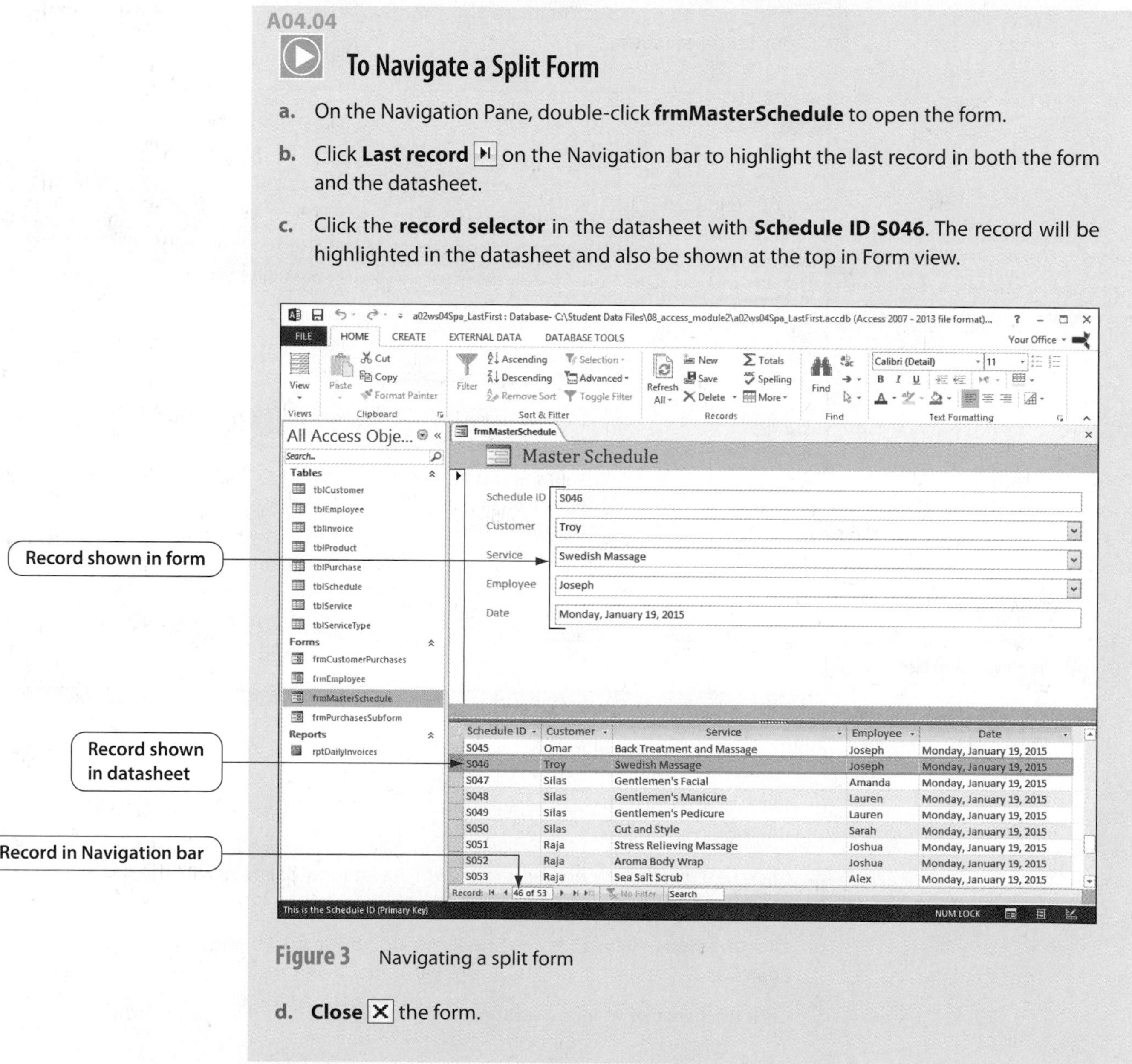

Figure 3 Navigating a split form

d. **Close** the form.

REAL WORLD ADVICE Using Tabs

People have become accustomed to using tabs in browsers, and they tend to have many tabs open at one time. In fact, it makes work more efficient because you do not have to keep opening and closing those windows. Unfortunately, Access does not work the same way. Every time you open an object in Access it opens in a new window with a tab. Those tabs, however, do not work the same way as tabs in your browser. While websites can be updated when they are open in a tab on your desktop, Access objects cannot be updated when they are open. It is therefore a good idea to close an object when you are done working with it, and then reopen it again later when you need it.

Using the Find Command in a Form

Finding data in a form is similar to finding data in a datasheet—you use the Find command. Because you only see one record at a time with a form, using Find can be a quick way to find a record with a specific value in a field and prevents you from having to scroll through all the records in the table one at a time in Form view.

When you are looking for a specific value in a field, you are looking for an exact match. For this exercise, a staff member has asked you to search the employee table to find any employees who may live in Las Vegas so they can try to set up a carpool with them. You will show the staff member how to use a form to look for that information.

A04.05

To Use the Find Command in a Form

a. On the Navigation Pane, double-click **frmEmployee** to open the form. Press Tab to move to the **City** field in the first record.

b. On the HOME tab, in the Find group, click **Find** to open the Find and Replace dialog box.

c. In the **Find What** box, type Las Vegas. Verify that the Look In text box is Current field, and then click **Find Next**.

Move the Find and Replace dialog box to see all the fields for the current record. The first record with Las Vegas as a value in the City field will be shown.

Troubleshooting

If you get the message that the search item was not found, make sure that you spelled "Las Vegas" correctly.

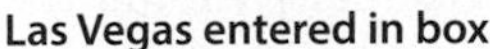

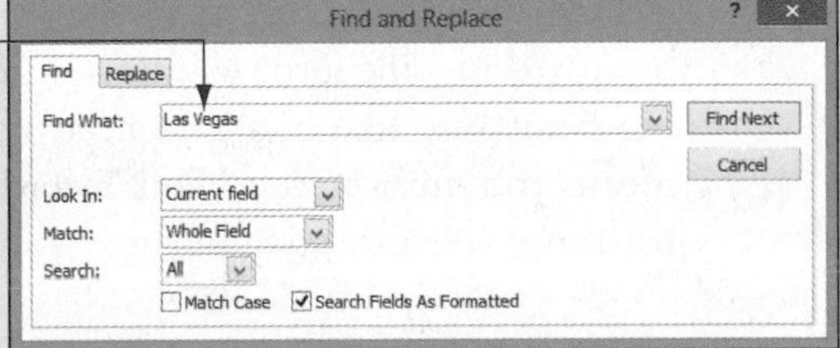

Figure 4 Find and Replace dialog box

d. Continue to click **Find Next** until Access gives you the message "Microsoft Access finished searching the records. The search item was not found." Click **OK**, and then click **Cancel** to close the Find and Replace dialog box.

Update Table Records Using Forms

Just as you can update data in a datasheet, you can also update data in a form. Remember, a form is just another way to view the data in the table, so when you see a record, you are seeing the record that is actually stored in the table. Nothing is actually stored in the form.

To make changes to data in a form, you must be viewing the form in Form view. You can also add a record to a table using the form. Using the Navigation bar, you can go directly to a new record.

QUICK REFERENCE | **Updating Tables**

Data can be edited in tables, queries, or forms. There are advantages and disadvantages to each method. The table below will help you decide the most appropriate place to edit data.

Method	Advantages	Disadvantages	Typical Situation to Use
Tables	All the records and fields are visible in the datasheet.	The number of records and/or fields in the datasheet can be overwhelming.	A user familiar with Access needs to add a record quickly to a smaller table.
Queries	There may be fewer records and/or fields in the datasheet making the data more manageable. A form can be based on a query rather than a table.	Not being able to see all the records and/or fields, you may inadvertently change related data in the fields you can see. Not all queries are editable, such as aggregate queries.	A user familiar with Access needs to see and modify appointments booked for a particular day.
Forms	Being able to view one record at a time can make the data seem more manageable.	Not all fields may be included in a form. If fields are missing, some data may mistakenly be left out of a record. Provides view of only one record at a time.	A user unfamiliar with Access needs to add data to a large table with many records.

Adding Records

When you add a record to a form, you are actually adding the record to the table it will be stored in. The form will open in Form view, which is the view that allows you to edit the data. Just like in a datasheet, new records are added at the end of the table, which means you must go to a blank record to enter new data. For this exercise, you will use the frmEmployee form to add your name to the list of employees in the tblEmployee table.

To Add a New Record in a Form

a. On the Navigation bar, click **New (blank) record** .

New (blank) record button

Figure 5 frmEmployee Navigation bar

b. Type your first name, last name, address, city, state, and phone in the new record. **Close** the form.

c. On the Navigation Pane, double-click **tblEmployee** to open the table, and then click **Last record** to see that your record was added. **Close** the table.

Editing Records

When you edit a record in a form, you are actually editing the record in the table it is stored in. Changes to data are saved automatically but can be undone while the table or form is open by using the Undo button or by pressing Esc just after the change is made while still in Edit mode.

For this exercise, you are asked to update the tblEmployee table with recent changes. Mary Murphy has recently changed her phone number, but it has not been changed in the table yet. You will show the staff how to find her record using a form and update her phone number.

A04.07

To Edit Records Using a Form

a. On the Navigation Pane, double-click **frmEmployee** to open the form. Press Tab to move to the **Last Name** field. On the HOME tab, in the Find group, click **Find** and then in the **Find What** box, type Murphy. Click **Find Next**.

b. When the record for Mary Murphy is displayed, click **Cancel** to close the Find and Replace dialog box, and then press Tab to move to the **Phone** field. Change Mary's phone number to 5055551289.

c. **Close** the form.

Deleting Records

Records can be deleted from a single table without additional steps if the table is not part of a relationship. If the table is part of a relationship, referential integrity has been enforced, and the cascade delete option has not been chosen, a record cannot be deleted if there are related records in another table until those records have also been deleted. For example, if you want to delete a customer from tblCustomer, and that customer has appointments in tblSchedule, then the appointments for the customer have to be deleted from the tblSchedule before the customer can be deleted from the tblCustomer. This prevents leaving a customer scheduled in one table without the corresponding customer information in another table.

For this exercise, the spa manager would like you to remove Peter Klein from tblEmployee because he has taken a new job and is leaving the spa. You explain to her that if he has any appointments scheduled in tblSchedule that those will have to be removed first. She tells you that rather than removing those records she would like to give those appointments to Alex instead. By changing the name to Alex, those appointments will no longer be linked to Peter, and Peter will be able to be deleted from tblEmployee.

CONSIDER THIS | Delete with Caution

Deleting records in a table is permanent. Once you confirm a deletion, you cannot use the Undo button. This is very different than programs like Excel or Word. Can you think of ways you could safeguard your data from accidental deletion?

A04.08

To Delete a Record with a Form

a. On the Navigation Pane, double-click **frmEmployee** to open the form. In the **Find** group, click **Find**, and then in the Find What box type Peter. Click **Find Next**, and then click **Cancel** to close the Find and Replace dialog box.

b. On the HOME tab, in the Records group, click the **Delete** arrow, and then click **Delete Record**. Access displays a message saying, "The record cannot be deleted or changed because table 'tblSchedule' included related records." Click **OK**.

Troubleshooting

If Access blanks out the First Name field, you chose Delete rather than Delete Record. Press [Esc] to undo the deletion, and then choose Delete Record.

c. On the Navigation Pane, double-click **tblSchedule** to open the table. Press [Tab] to move to the Employee field for the first record. Click the arrow next to **Peter**, and then click **Alex**.

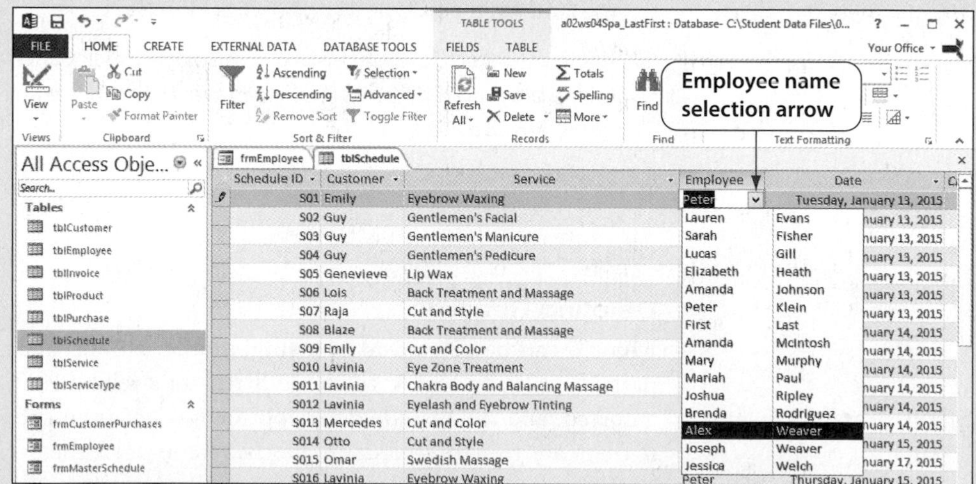

Figure 6 Replacing employee name using the selection arrow

d. On the HOME tab, in the Find group, click **Find**, and then in the **Find What** box, type Peter. Click **Find Next**. Click the **arrow** next to the name, and then click **Alex**. Click **Find Next**, and then repeat for all three records that have **Peter** listed as the Employee. Click **Cancel** to close the Find and Replace box.

e. **Close** [X] the table. On the form, make sure the record showing is for **Peter**. On the HOME tab, in the Records group, click the **Delete** arrow, and then select **Delete Record**. Click **Yes** to confirm the deletion.

f. **Close** [X] the form.

Create a Form Using the Form Wizard

Recall that the Query Wizard walks you through the steps in order to create a query, asking you questions and using your answers to build a query that you can then make changes to if necessary. The Form Wizard works in a similar fashion, walking you through step-by-step to create a form from one or more tables in your database.

Unlike creating a simple form using the Form button on the Create tab, when you create a form using the wizard, it opens automatically in Form view ready for you to enter or edit your records. To make changes to the form, you have to switch to either Layout view or Design view.

Exploring Form Views

Form view is only for viewing and changing data, so to make any changes to the form you need to switch to either Layout view or Design view. Layout view allows you to make changes to the form while viewing the data the same time. The effects of your changes can be viewed right away. Design view is a more advanced view that allows you to change the properties or structure of the form. Data is not shown while you are in Design view.

Both Layout view and Design view work with controls, as shown in Figure 7. A **control** is a part of a form or report that you use to enter, edit, or display data. There are three major kinds of controls: bound, unbound, and calculated. A **bound control** is a control whose data source is a field in the table such as the customer name. An **unbound control** is a control that does not have a source of data such as the title of the form. A **calculated control** is a control whose data source is a calculated expression that you create. Every field from the table is made up of two controls: a label and a text box. A **label control** may be the name of the field or some other text you manually enter and is an unbound control. A **text box control** represents the actual value of a field and is a bound control. When you add a text box to a form, the label is automatically added as well. However, a label can be added independently from a text box.

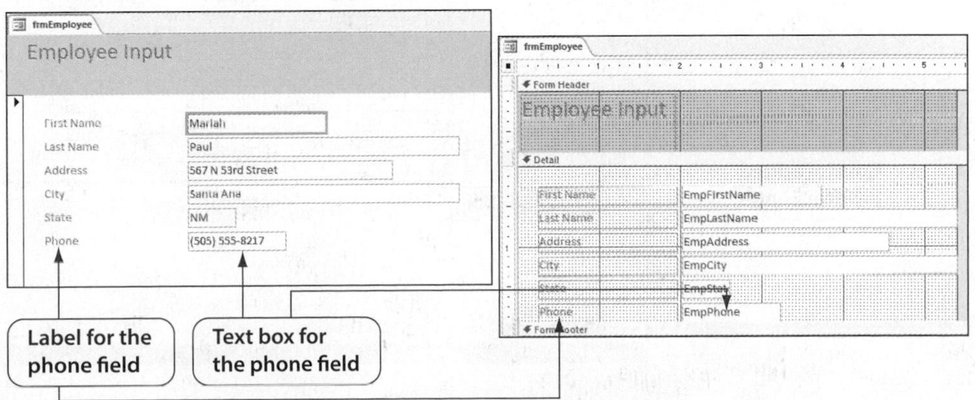

Figure 7 Text box and label controls in Layout view and Design view

For this exercise, the manager of the spa wants the staff to be able to enter and update customer information easily. She thinks it would be much easier to enter data in a form rather than in Datasheet view. You agree with her and offer to help set up the form.

A04.09

To Create a Single-Table Form in Design View

a. Click the **CREATE** tab, and then in the Forms group, click **Form Wizard**. The Form Wizard dialog box opens.

b. Click the **Table/Queries** arrow, and select **Table: tblCustomer**. Click the **All Fields** button >> to add all the available fields to the Selected Fields box, and then click **Next**.

c. Verify that **Columnar** is selected as the form layout, and then click **Next**.

d. Under **"What title do you want for your form?"** type frmCustomerInput_initialLastname using your first initial and last name. Verify that the **Open the form to view or enter information** option is selected, and then click **Finish**.

The form opens in Form view so you can immediately start adding or editing records. The form name is also displayed in the Navigation Pane under forms.

e. Switch to **Design** view. Notice the Form Footer at the bottom of the form window. On the DESIGN tab, in the Controls group, click **Label** Aa. Point to the Form Footer area, and then when your pointer changes to +A, drag your pointer to draw a label control about 2.5" wide in the top-left corner of the Form Footer section. In the new label, type Created by initial Lastname using your first initial and last name.

SIDE NOTE

Alternative Methods to Expand Footer

You can expand the footer and then add the label or you can add the label and the footer will automatically expand to fit what you add.

Troubleshooting

If the Field List pane opens, close it.

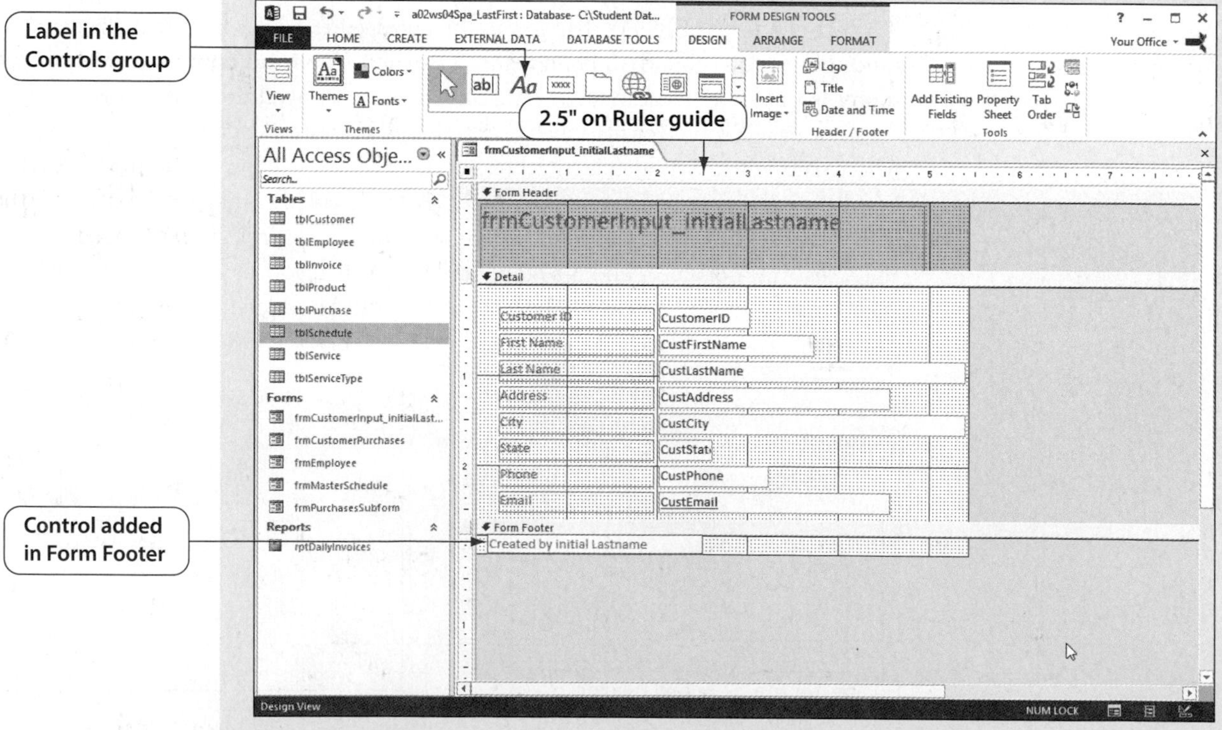

Figure 8 Form in Design view

f. Switch to **Form** view. Verify that your label has been entered in the bottom-left corner of the form.

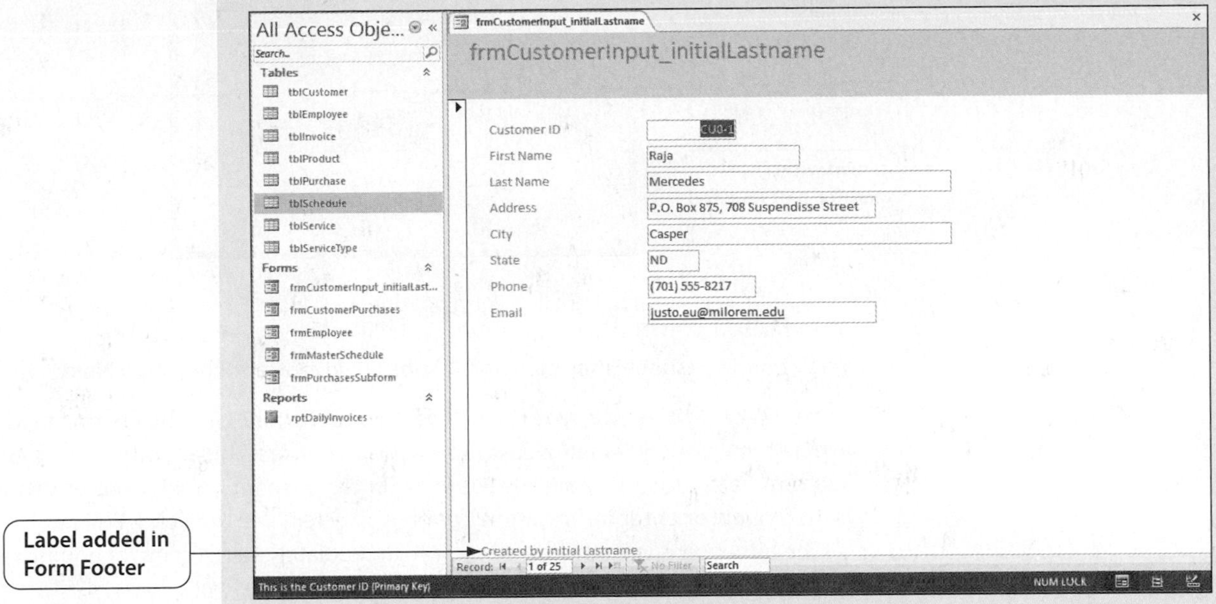

Label added in Form Footer

Figure 9 Form with footer added

g. **Close** [X] the form, and then click **Yes** to save the changes.

Creating Subforms (Multiple-Table Forms)

There may be times when you want to create a form using two tables. Before you can use two tables in a form, you must make sure there is a one-to-many relationship between the tables. Access will automatically use the common field between the tables to create the form.

The main form will display the first table one record at a time just like a single-table form. This is the "one" record in the one-to-many relationship. The subform will be displayed as a datasheet below the main form record. This will display the "many" records in the one-to-many relationship.

For this project, you will help the staff create another form that shows each customer in the main form and the customer's scheduled appointments in the subform.

A04.10

To Create a Subform

a. Click the **CREATE** tab, and then in the Forms group, click **Form Wizard**. The Form Wizard dialog box opens.

b. Click the **Table/Queries** arrow, and then select **Table: tblCustomer**. Click the **All Fields** button [>>] to add all the available fields to the Selected Fields list.

c. Click the **Tables/Queries** arrow, and then select **Table: tblSchedule**. Click the **All Fields** button [>>] to add all the available fields to the Selected Fields list, and then click **Next**.

d. Verify that **by tblCustomer** is selected and that **Form with subform(s)** is selected, and then click **Next**.

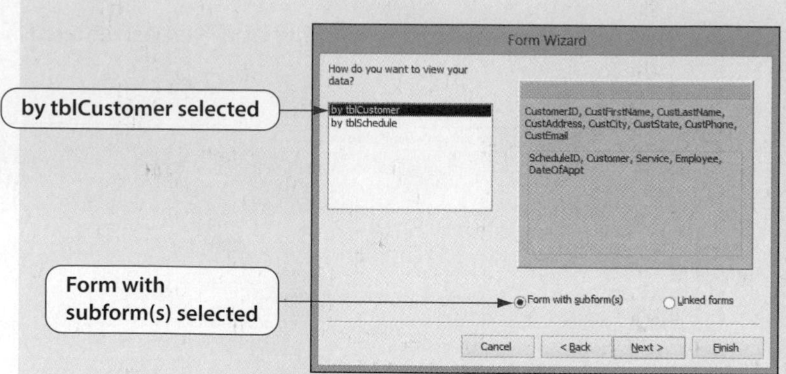

Figure 10 Form options are selected

e. Verify that **Datasheet** is selected as the subform layout, and then click **Next**.

f. Under **What titles do you want for your forms?** in the Form field, type frmCustomerSchedule_initialLastname, using your first initial and last name. In the Subform field, type frmCustomerSubform_initialLastname. Verify that the **Open the form to view or enter information** option is selected, and then click **Finish**.

The form opens in Form view so you can immediately start adding or editing records. The form and subform names are shown in the Navigation Pane.

g. Switch to **Design** view. Scroll to the bottom of the form to see the Form Footer at the base of the main form. On the DESIGN tab, in the Controls group, click **Label** Aa. When your pointer changes to +A, drag your pointer to draw a label control about 2.5" wide in the top-left corner of the Form Footer section. In the new label, type Created by initial Lastname using your initial and last name.

Troubleshooting

If the Field List pane shows and blocks parts of the form you need to see, close the Field List pane.

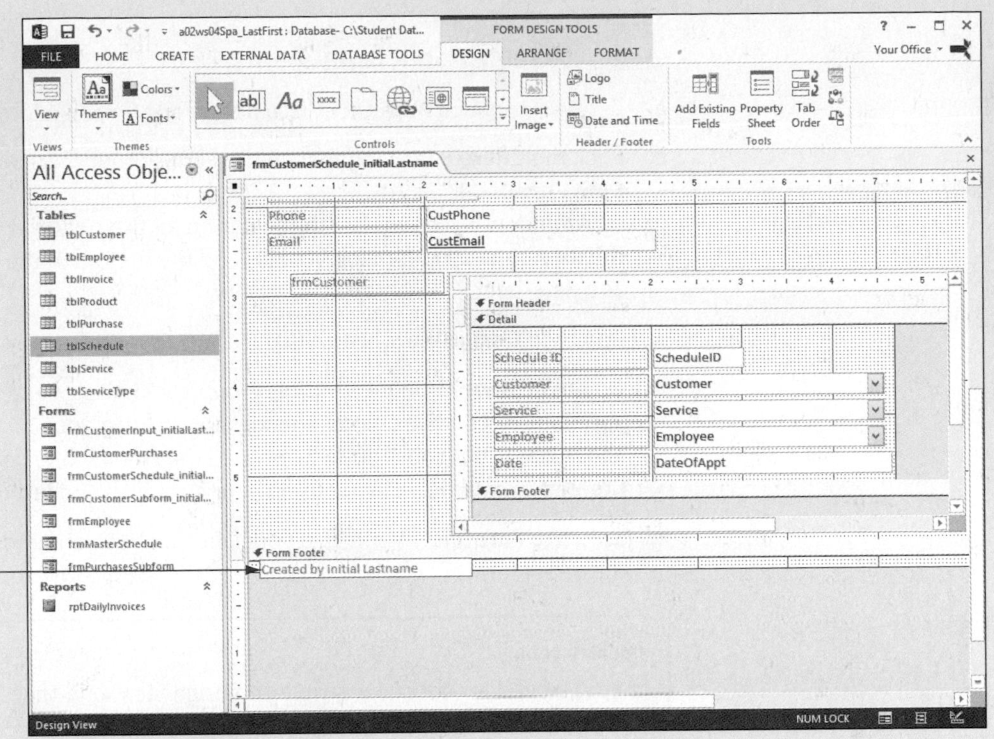

Figure 11 Add footer to main form

h. Switch to **Form** view. Verify that your label has been entered in the bottom-left corner of the form.

i. **Close**  the form, and then click **Yes** to save the changes.

CONSIDER THIS | **Include the Subform?**

When two tables are in a one-to-many relationship and you use the Form button to create a form for the table on the "one" side of the relationship, the wizard automatically adds a subform for the table on the "many" side. If you create the form using Form Wizard, you can choose whether to include the subform. When would you want to include the subform? When would you not want to include the subform?

Creating a Split Form

A split form is created from one table and displays each record individually at the top of the window and then again as part of the whole table datasheet in the bottom of the window. This type of form gives you the advantage of seeing each record and the whole table in one place.

For this exercise, the manager would like to see each customer's record individually along with all the records from the customer table. You will show her how to create a split form from the customer table.

A04.11

To Create a Split Form

a. On the Navigation Pane, click **tblCustomer** one time to select the table, but do not open it.

b. Click the **CREATE** tab, and then in the Forms group, click **More Forms**, and then select **Split Form**.

A window will open with the split form for the customer table. Notice that the top of the form shows a record individually and the bottom of the form shows the whole table as a datasheet.

c. Switch to **Design** view. Notice that Design view shows only the top of the split form.

d. On the DESIGN tab, in the Controls group, click **Label** [Aa], point to the Form Footer area, and then when your pointer changes to [+A], drag your pointer to draw a label control about 2.5" wide in the top-left corner of the Form Footer section. In the new label, type Created by initial Lastname using your first initial and last name.

e. Switch to **Form** view. Verify that your label has been entered in the bottom-left corner of the upper form.

Troubleshooting

If your label does not show, switch to Design view, and then switch back to Form view.

f. Click **Save** on the Quick Access Toolbar, under **Form Name** type frmCustomerSplit_initialLastname using your first initial and last name, and then click **OK. Close** [X] the form.

Modify a Form's Design

While creating a form using the wizard is quick and efficient, there may be times you will want to change how the form looks or add things to the form after you have created it. Formatting, like colors and fonts, can easily be changed. Controls can also be added to a form to include additional fields or labels with text. Pictures and other objects can also be added to a form to make the form more visually appealing.

Oftentimes, forms are customized to match company or group color themes, or other forms and reports already created by a user. Customizing forms can make them more personal and sometimes easier to use.

Colors, font types, and font sizes are just a few of the formatting changes you can make to an existing form.

Changing the Form Theme

By default, Access uses the Office theme when you create a form using the Form Wizard. Even though there is not a step in the wizard to select a different theme, you can change it once the form has been created. A **theme** is a built-in combination of colors and fonts. By default, a theme will be applied to all objects in a database: forms, reports, tables, and queries. However, you can select to apply a theme to only the object you are working with or to all matching objects. You can also select a theme to be the default theme instead of Office.

Because the form is displayed in Form view, once it is created, the first step is to switch to Layout view to make changes to the form itself. Changing the theme will not only change the colors of the form but also the font type and size and any border colors or object colors added to the form. Once a theme is applied to the form, the colors and fonts can be changed independently of the theme, so you can combine the colors of one theme and a font of another.

For this exercise, the manager of the spa would like to make the customer input form look more like the colors in the spa. The resort has a set of themes that she wants to apply to the selected form.

You will show her how to change the theme and the fonts for the form. The theme will be applied to all objects is the database. The font change will be applied to this form only.

A04.12

To Change the Theme of a Form

a. On the Navigation Pane, double-click **frmCustomerInput_initialLastname** to open the form. Switch to **Layout** view.

b. On the DESIGN tab, in the Themes group, click **Themes** to open the Themes gallery. Click **Browse for Themes**, navigate to where you stored your data files, click **a02ws04Spa**, and then click **Open**. This applies the spa theme to all objects.

c. On the DESIGN tab, in the Themes group, click **Fonts**. Scroll down, right-click the Font theme **Corbel**, and then click **Apply Font Theme to This Object Only**.

d. Double-click the **form title**, select the existing **text**, which by default is the name of the form, and then type Customer Input. Press Enter.

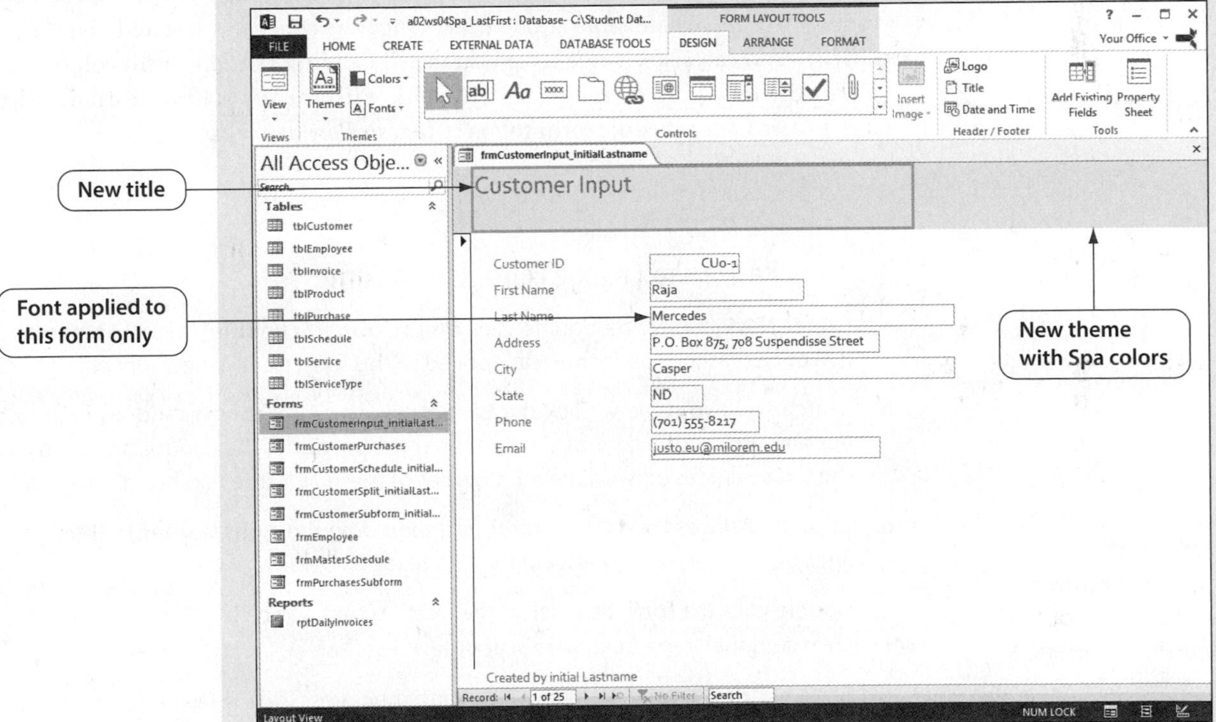

Figure 12 Form with theme, font, and title changed

e. Click **Save** on the Quick Access Toolbar to save the form. **Close** the form.

REAL WORLD ADVICE **Saving Custom Themes**

By default, all themes are saved in the Document Themes folder (C:\Users\username\AppData\Roaming\Microsoft\Templates\Document Themes). If you save a custom theme in the default folder, it will appear as a custom theme in the Themes gallery. If you save the theme in a different folder, you can select Browse for Themes and look for the saved theme in your Documents folder. You can change where you save the theme, but if another person wants to use that theme for one of their documents, they may not be able to find it if it is saved somewhere other than the default folder. One purpose of saving themes is to have them available for a unified look among various documents, and because you may not be the person creating all the documents, you may want to save the theme somewhere that everyone can find it.

Resizing and Changing Controls

Controls can be resized to make the form more user friendly. When you create a form using the wizard, the order that you choose the fields in the wizard step is the order the fields are added to the form. Once the form is created, you may decide the fields should be in a different order. When you click a control in Layout view, an orange border appears around the control. When you select a subform control, an orange border appears around the control and a layout selector appears in the top-left corner. The **layout selector** allows you to move the whole table at one time. Once the control is selected you can move it or resize it. You can also change its appearance by adding borders or fill color.

For the following exercise, you will work with the spa staff to rearrange the controls on the Customer Schedule form to make it easier for data entry.

A04.13

To Resize and Change Controls on a Form

a. On the Navigation Pane, double-click **frmCustomerSchedule_initialLastname** to open it. Notice that the spa theme was applied to this form but the new font was not.

b. Switch to **Layout** view. Click the **Last Name** text box control, and an orange border appears around the control. Point to the **right border** of the control, and then drag it to the left so it lines up with the right border of the First Name text box above.

c. Click the **Address** text box control, and then drag the **right border** to the right until it lines up with the right border of the City text box below.

d. Double-click the **form title**, select the existing **text**, which by default is the name of the form, and then type Customer Schedule. Press Enter.

e. Click the **frmCustomer** subform label, and then press Delete to delete it from the form.

f. Use the AutoFit feature on each column of the subform to best fit the data. Use the scroll bar on the Navigation bar of the subform to scroll to the right to see all the fields. Drag the **left border** of the subform to the left so that all fields are visible without scrolling.

g. In the main form, click the **Customer ID** label control, press and hold Shift, and then click the **CustomerID** text box control to select both controls.

SIDE NOTE
Selecting Controls
Each field has two controls—a label and a text box. The field name shows in the label, while the field value shows in the text box.

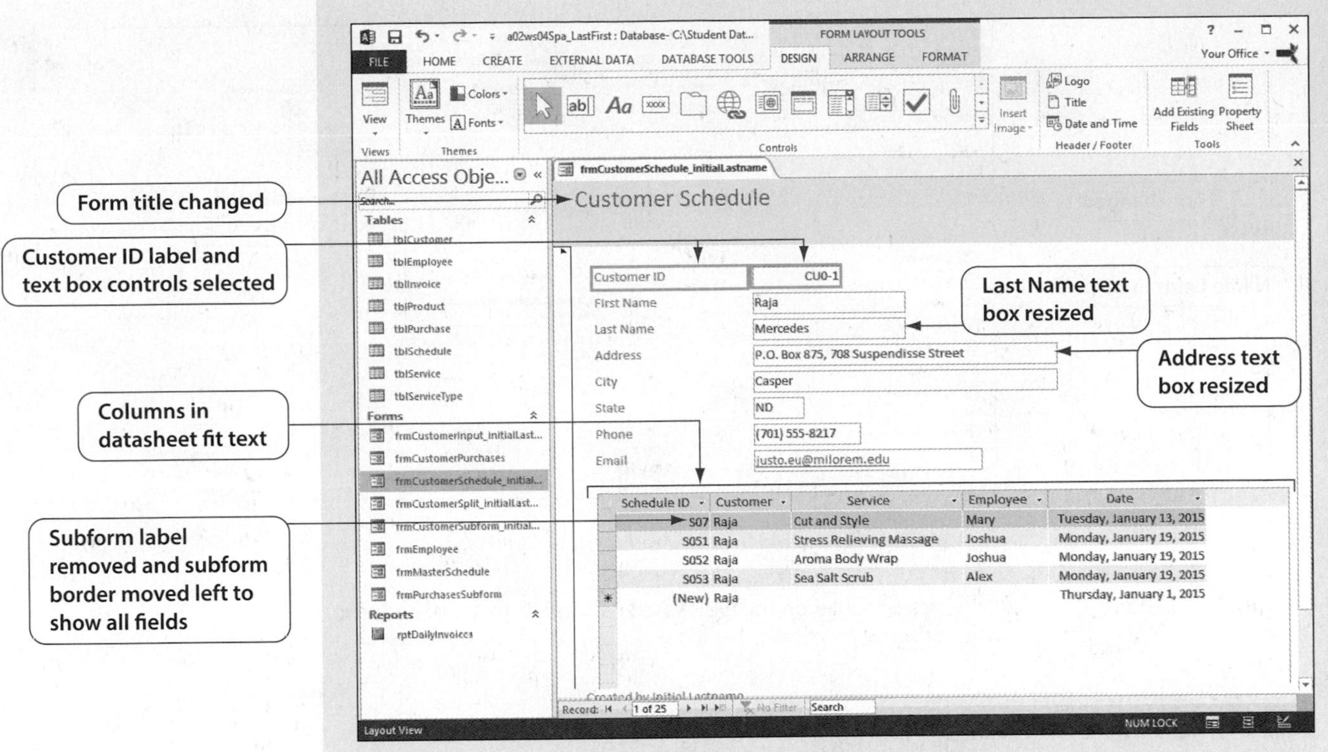

Figure 13 Select both label and name control to delete

h. Press [Delete] to delete both controls from the form.

i. Click the **Phone** label, hold down [Shift], and then click the **Phone** text box, the **Email** label, and the **Email** text box controls.

j. Point to any of the **selected controls**. When the pointer changes to [move icon], drag all four controls up and to the right until they are right next to the **First Name** and **Last Name** controls.

> **Troubleshooting**
> If when you release the pointer, the fields do not line up, repeat Step j, and then adjust the placement.

SIDE NOTE
Limited Visibility
If you cannot see the whole subform, use the scroll arrow on the right side of the window to scroll down the form.

k. Click the **subform** datasheet to select it. Click the **Layout Selector** [layout selector icon], and then drag it up and to the left so it is just under the State control.

l. Click the **title** of the form to select it. On the **HOME** tab, in the Text Formatting group, click **Bold** [B], click the **Font size** arrow [11], and then select **28**.

m. Click the **First Name** text box control, hold down [Shift], and then click the **Last Name** text box control. On the HOME tab, in the Text Formatting group, Click **Bold** [B].

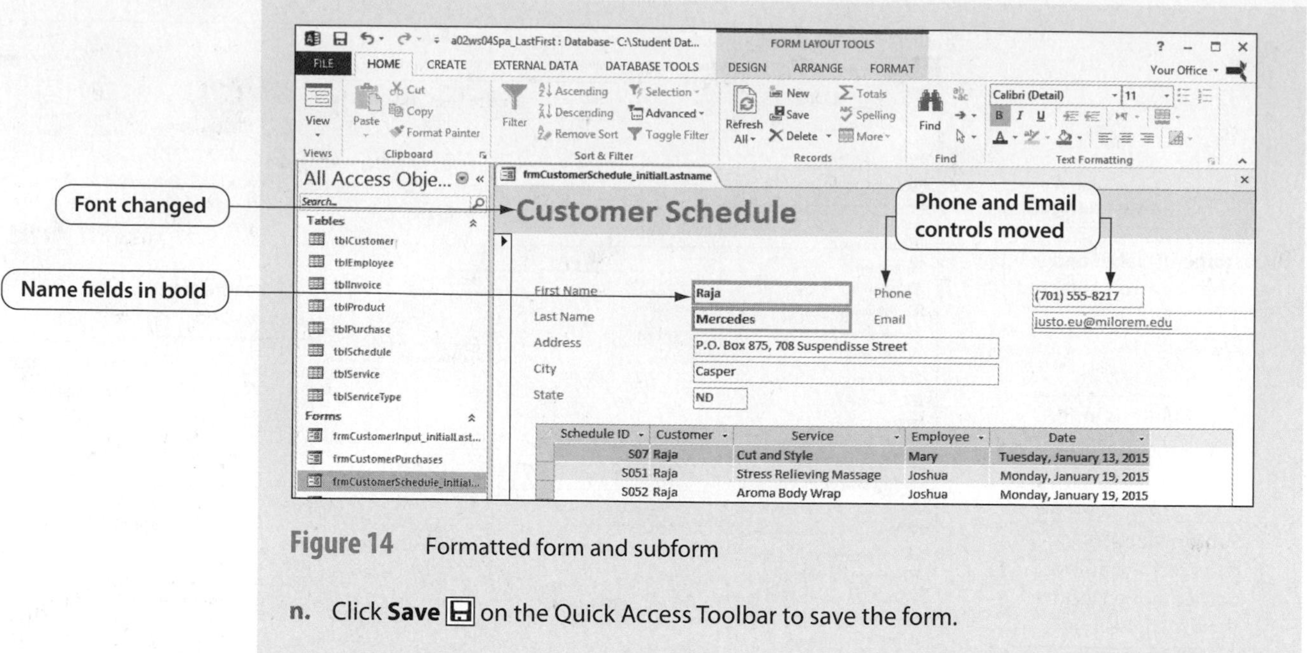

Figure 14 Formatted form and subform

n. Click **Save** on the Quick Access Toolbar to save the form.

Adding a Picture to the Form

Pictures can be added to forms to make them more appealing. When a picture is added to a form, then the same picture will appear for every record in the table. A different picture cannot be added for each record. A picture can be inserted in the header, footer, or the Detail area of the form where the record values are shown. For this exercise you will insert the spa's logo in the Detail area of the form to make it more personal for the spa.

A04.14

To Add a Picture on the Form

a. Click in the **Detail area** of the form to select it. If a text box or label is selected, then the Insert Image button will not be available to use.

b. On the DESIGN tab, in the Controls group, click **Insert Image**, and then click **Browse....**

c. In the Insert Picture dialog box, navigate to where your student files are located, click **a02ws04Spa,** and then click **OK**. With the image control pointer, click in the **form detail** to insert the picture. Move your pointer to the **top-left corner** of the picture until it becomes a diagonal resize pointer. Drag the corner until the picture is small enough to fit under **Email** and above the subform.

d. Click the **layout selector** and move the picture under the **Email** text box. Use the diagonal resize pointer to make the picture smaller until the picture fits between the **Email** text box and the subform.

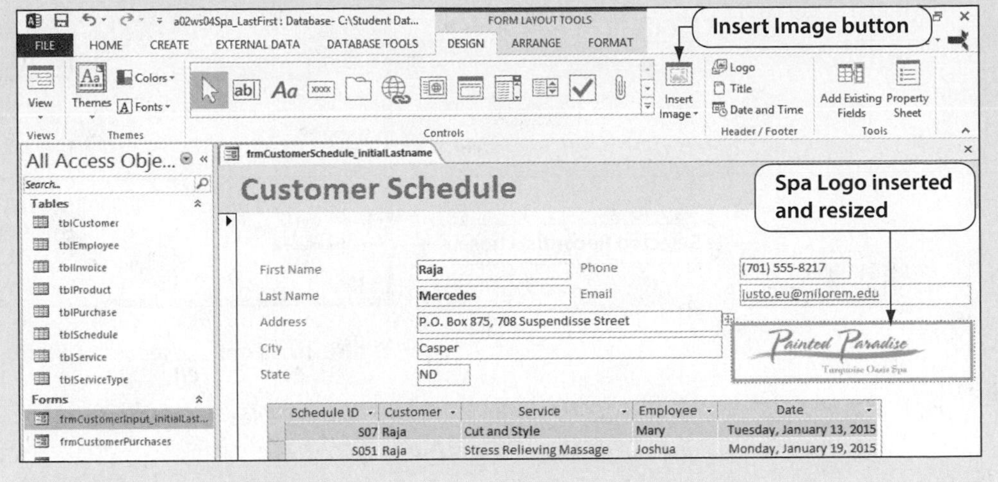

Figure 15 Logo inserted in form

e. **Close** [X] the form, and then click **Yes** to save the changes.

Printing a Record from a Form

Not only can you see one record at a time using a form, but you can also print one record at a time. Printing a form can be useful if you need only one record's information, or if you want to use a form for other people to manually fill in the information.

For this project, the spa manager would like you to print a record for a particular customer from the customer form. You will show her how to preview the form first, select one record, and then send it to the printer.

A04.15

To Preview and Print a Record from a Form

a. On the Navigation Pane, double-click **frmCustomerInput_initialLastname** to open it, and then switch to **Layout** view.

b. Click the **Address** text box control, and then drag the **right border** to the right until it is lined up with the Last Name and City text box controls.

c. Click the **FILE** tab, click **Print**, and then click **Print Preview**. Notice all the records will print in Form view.

d. Click **Last Page** [▸|] on the Navigation bar to go to the last record. Notice in the Navigation bar that the number of pages for the printed report will be seven.

e. On the PRINT PREVIEW tab, in the Close Preview group, click **Close Print Preview**.

f. Using the Navigation bar, advance through the customer records to find the record for **Jonah Hogan**.

g. Click the **FILE** tab, click **Print**, and then click **Print**. In the Print dialog box, in the Print Range section, click **Selected Record(s)**. Click **OK** to print the record if requested by your instructor.

When you view all the records in Print Preview, you cannot choose Selected Record(s) in the Print dialog box. To choose Selected Record(s) you must have one record showing in Form view when you click Print.

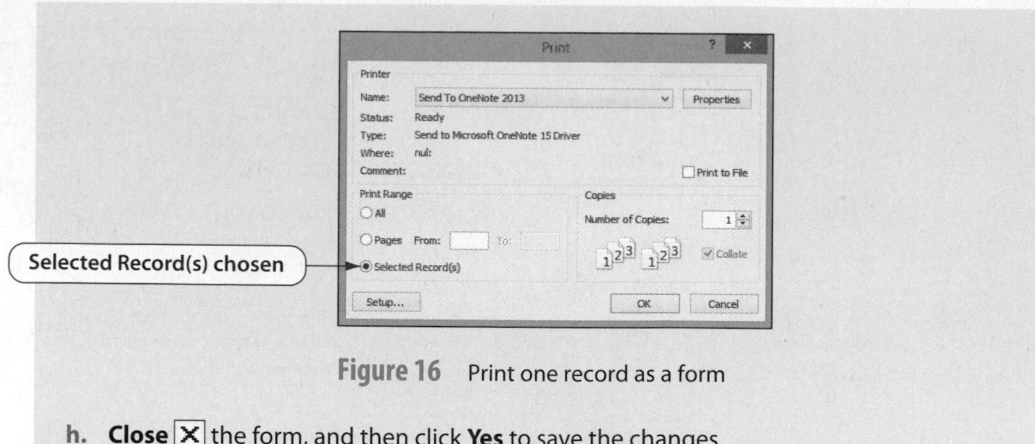

Figure 16 Print one record as a form

h. **Close** [X] the form, and then click **Yes** to save the changes.

Creating Customized Reports

While a report and a form may look similar, a form is a method for data entry and a report is a formatted printout of that data. A report can be created from either a table or query. Reports may be based on multiple tables in a one-to-many relationship using a common field to match the records. The "one" record from the first table in the relationship will be shown first—similar to a main form, while the "many" records from the second table will be displayed as detailed records in the **subreport**—similar to a subform. In this section, you will create a report using the report wizard and then make changes to the report in design and layout views.

Create a Report Using the Report Wizard

The Report Wizard will walk you step by step through the process of building your report. You will choose the table or query to base the report on, and choose the fields to include in the report. You will have the option to group the data in your report. A **group** is a collection of records along with introductory and summary information about the records. Grouping allows you to separate related records for the purpose of creating a visual summary of the data. Groups can be created with data from individual tables or from multiple tables.

For example, a report grouped by the primary table containing customer records would show all the selected fields for a customer, and then would list that customer's individual appointments from the secondary table below the customer's record.

Within a report you can also sort using up to four fields in either ascending or descending order. Once a report is created using the wizard, it will open in Print Preview. Print Preview provides a view of the report representing how it will look when it is actually printed and provides you with printing options such as orientation, margins, and size. The current date and page numbers are added, and you can navigate the report in this view using the Navigation bar. To make any changes to the report, you can switch to Layout view.

Creating a Single-Table Report

A report can be created using one table or multiple tables. A single-table report is a report created from one table. Any or all of the fields can be selected, and the report can be created from a table or query.

For this project, the spa manager would like to have a report to help the staff with scheduling. The report will be a list of employee names and phone numbers so the staff can contact each other if necessary.

A04.16

To Create a Single-Table Report Using Report Wizard

a. Click the **CREATE** tab, and then in the Reports group, click **Report Wizard**.

b. Click the **Tables/Queries** arrow, and then select **tblEmployee**.

c. Double-click **EmpFirstName**, **EmpLastName**, and **EmpPhone** from the Available Fields list. Click **Next**.

SIDE NOTE

Field Order

The order you add the fields in the Report Wizard is the order the fields will appear on the report.

d. You will not add any grouping levels to this report, so click **Next**.

e. Click the **1 Sort** arrow, select **EmpLastName**, click the **2 Sort** arrow, select **EmpFirstName**, and then click **Next**.

f. Verify that **Tabular** layout and **Portrait** orientation are selected, as well as **Adjust the field width so all fields fit on a page**. Click **Next**.

g. Under **What title do you want for your report?**, type rptEmployeeList_initialLastname using your first initial and last name, and then click **Finish**.

h. Switch to **Design** view. If necessary, **close** [X] the Field List pane. On the REPORT DESIGN TOOLS DESIGN tab, in the Controls group, click **Label** [Aa], point to the **Report Footer** area, and then when your pointer changes to [+A], drag your pointer to draw a label control about 2.5" wide in the top-left corner of the Report Footer section. In the new label, type Created by initial Lastname using your first initial and last name.

> **Troubleshooting**
> If the Label control is not visible, in the Controls group, click the More button to display the gallery, and then click Label.

i. Switch to **Report** view. Verify that your label is fully shown in the bottom-left corner of the report.

j. Switch to **Layout** view. Double-click the **form title**, select the existing text, type Employee List and then press [Enter].

In Layout view, you should also check that all the report column headers and data show fully. On this report they do, so there are no further changes necessary.

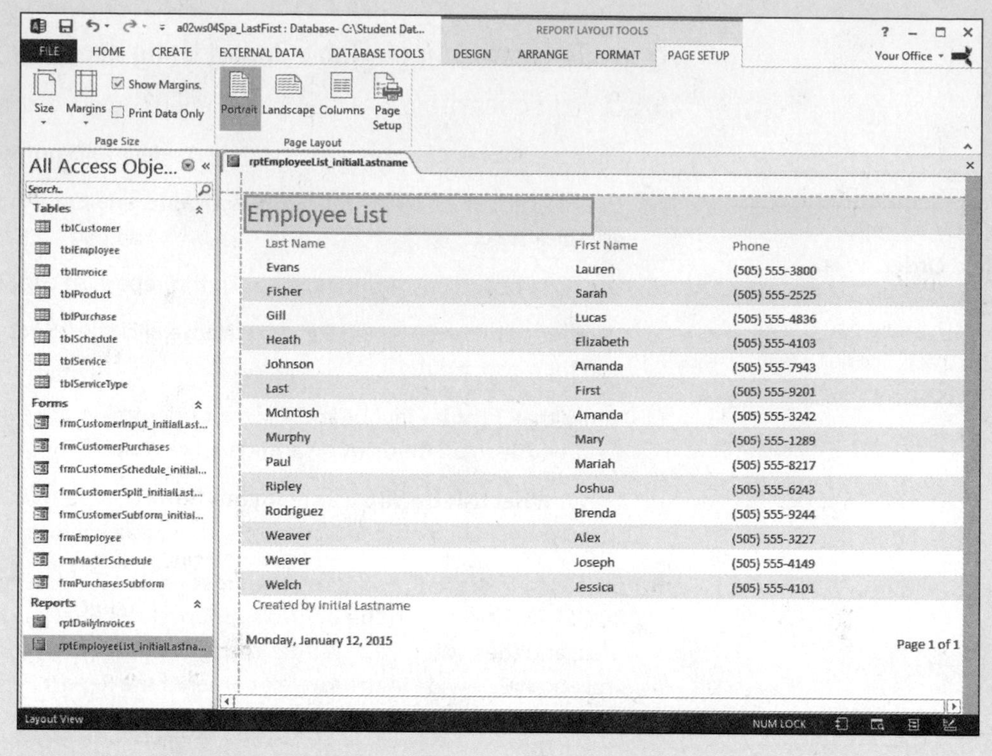

Figure 17 Completed Employee List report

k. **Close** [X] the report, and then click **Yes** to save the changes.

Creating a Multiple-Table Report

Similar to other objects created using more than one table, a multiple-table report must use tables that have a common field. The first table chosen for the report becomes the primary table, and the next and subsequent tables chosen become the secondary tables.

An employee has a one-to-many relationship with scheduled appointments. Each employee may have more than one appointment, and each appointment is with just one employee. Thus tblEmployee will be the primary table, and tblSchedule will be a secondary table.

In this exercise, the manager would like a report that will show each employee name and their upcoming appointments. This way the staff members can help coordinate their services for a guest who may be seeing more than one staff member in a day.

A04.17

To Create a Multiple-Table Report Using the Report Wizard

a. Click the **CREATE** tab, and then in the Reports group, click **Report Wizard**.

b. Click the **Tables/Queries** arrow, and then select **Table: tblEmployee**. Double-click **EmpFirstName** and **EmpLastName** in the Available Fields list.

c. Click the **Tables/Queries** arrow, and then select **Table: tblSchedule**. Double-click **Service**, **DateOfAppt**, and **Customer** from the Available Fields list, and then click **Next**.

d. Verify that **by tblEmployee** is highlighted to view the data by Employee, and then click **Next**.
   Notice that Access defaults to viewing the data by primary table, tblEmployee.

e. Double-click **DateOfAppt** to group by the date. Click **Grouping Options...**, click the **Grouping intervals** arrow, select **Normal**, and then click **OK**.
   Access defaults to grouping dates by Month. Normal groups by date value.

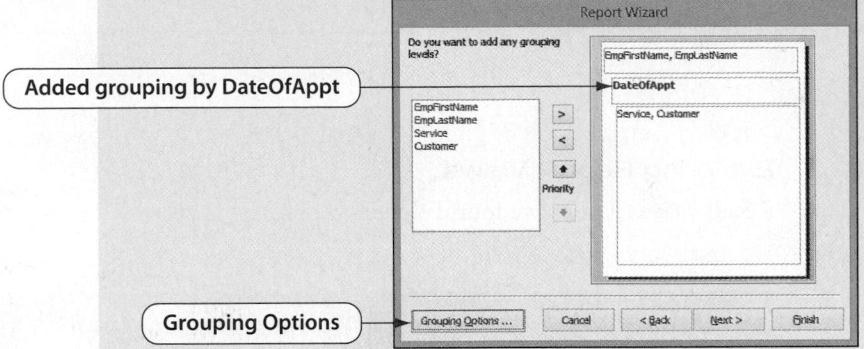

Figure 18 Report Wizard grouping step

f. Click **Next**.

g. Click the **1 Sort** arrow, select **Customer**, and then click **Next**.

h. Verify that **Stepped** is selected under Layout, and then under Orientation, click **Landscape**. Verify that **Adjust the field width so all fields fit on a page** is checked. Click **Next**.

i. Under **What title do you want for your report?**, type rptEmployeeSchedule_initialLastname, using your first initial and last name, and then click **Finish**. The report will open in Print Preview.

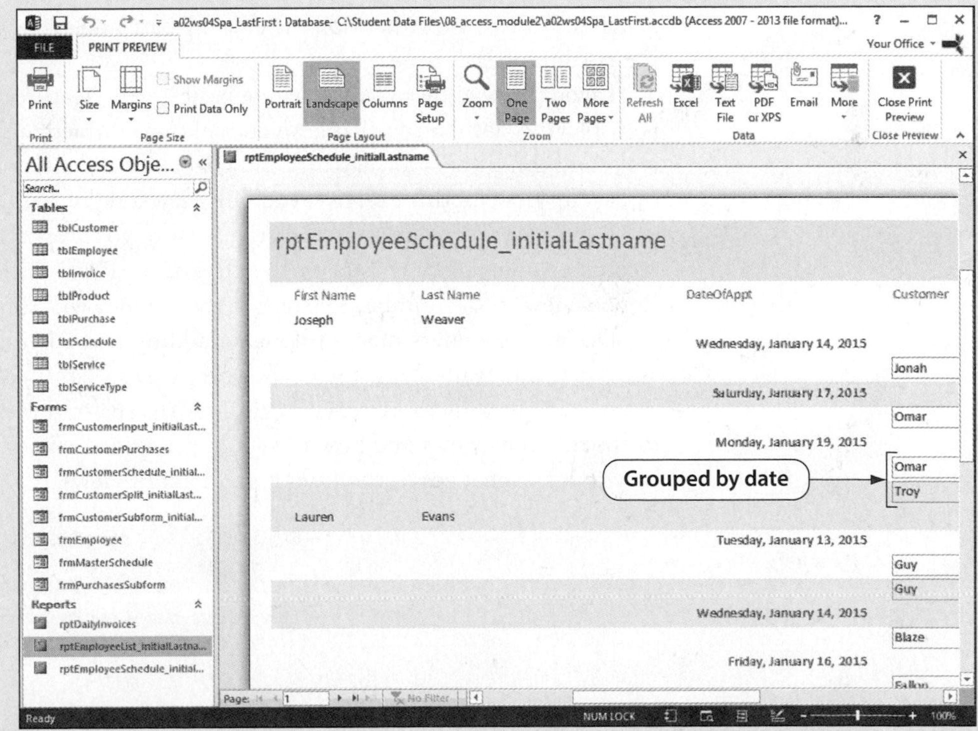

Figure 19 Report in Print Preview

Notice that the appointments are grouped by date. Your date column may not be wide enough to see the dates, but you will fix that in Layout view. Additionally, notice that in Print Preview view, at the bottom of each page of the report is today's date and the page number.

j. Click **Close Print Preview**.

Exploring Report Views

Recall that reports have four different views. Each type of view has its own features.

QUICK REFERENCE | **Different View Options for a Report**

View Name	What the View Is Used For
Print Preview	Shows what the printed report will look like
Layout view	Allows you to modify the report while seeing the data
Report view	Allows you to filter data or copy parts of the report to the Clipboard
Design view	Allows you to change more details of the report design or add other controls that are only available in Design view

When the Report Wizard is done creating the report, it shows you the report in Print Preview, which is the view that shows you exactly what the report will look like when it is printed. Print Preview adds the current date and page numbers in the page footer at the bottom of each page.

Layout view allows you to change basic design features of the report while the report is displaying data so the changes you make are immediately visible. You can resize controls, add conditional formatting, and change or add titles and other objects to the report in Layout view. In this exercise, you will view a report in Layout view.

Report view provides an interactive view of your report. In Report view, you can filter records or you can copy data to the clipboard. There will be no page breaks shown in Report view so the number of pages at the bottom will show Page 1 of 1.

Design view offers more options for adding and editing controls on a report, as well as options not available in any of the other views.

In the following exercise, you will show the spa staff members what a report looks like in the different views and how to switch from one view to another. You will show them how to make changes in the Layout and Design views.

A04.18

To Explore Report Views

a. Switch to **Layout** view.

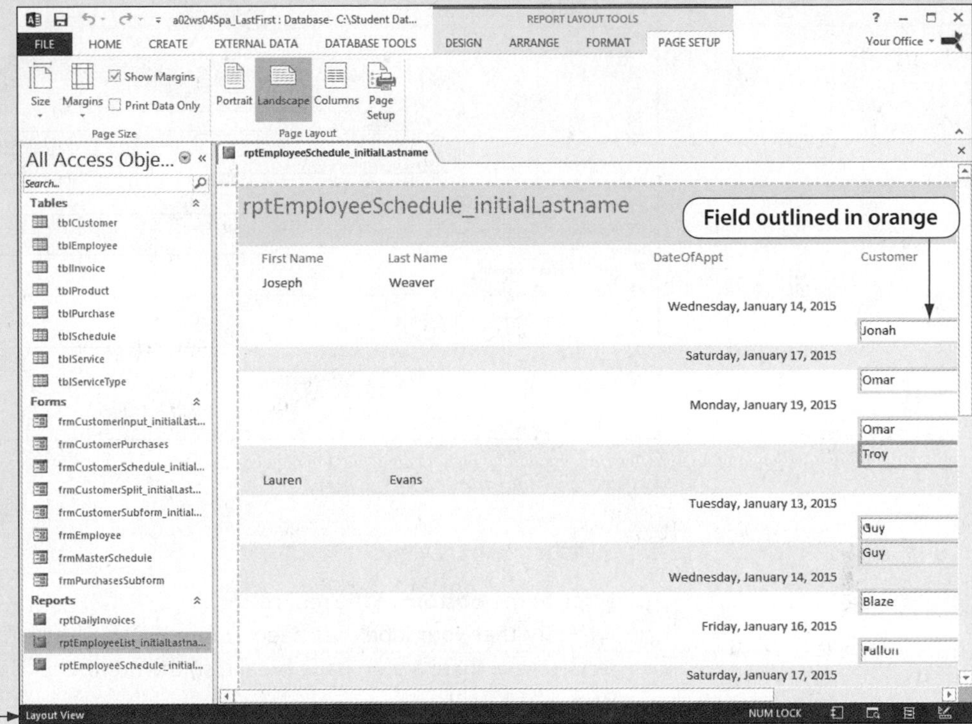

Layout view

Figure 20 Report in Layout view

Notice the orange border around the first Customer field. Customer is the active field. You can make changes such as making a column wider in Layout view.

b. If your dates are not visible, click the **DateOfAppt** column header, press and hold Shift, and then click the **DateOfAppt** text box. Use your pointer to drag the left border of the column to the left so that the date is fully shown.

c. Scroll to the **bottom right** of the report.

Notice there is the date and page number in the page footer, but the page number shows page 1 of 1. The actual number of pages will not be calculated until you switch to Print Preview.

d. Switch to **Design** view. Data in Design view is not visible, only the controls in each section of the report are.

e. On the DESIGN tab, in the Controls group, click **Label** Aa, point to the Report Footer area, and then when your pointer changes to +A, drag your pointer to draw a label control about 2.5" wide in the top-left corner of the Report Footer section. In the new label, type Created by initial Lastname using your first initial and last name.

SIDE NOTE
Two Footers
Be sure to put your label in the Report Footer, not the Page Footer.

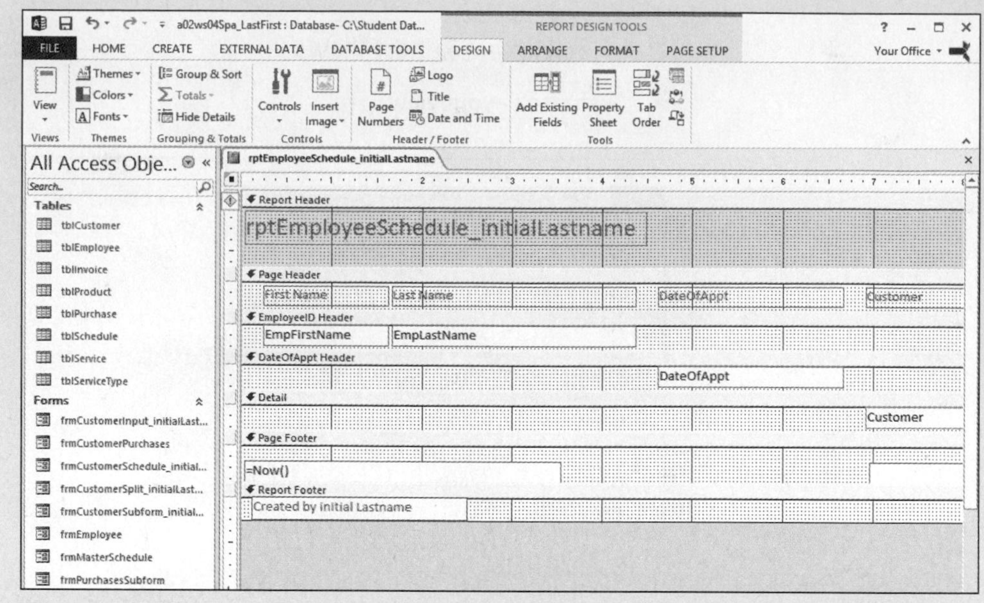

Figure 21 Report in Design view

f. Switch to **Report** view.

g. Scroll to the **bottom** of the report.

Verify that your label has been entered in the bottom-left corner of the report. In report view, there are no page breaks, so the number of pages at the bottom will show Page 1 of 1.

h. **Save** and **close** your report.

Creating Totals Using the Report Wizard

When you report on numeric data, you have the option to ask Access to calculate sums, averages, minimums, and maximums of the numeric data. The **grand total** calculates the total for all records. **Subtotals** calculate totals for smaller groups of records. In this exercise, you will use the wizard to request these totals. Later, you will add totals to an already created report.

The spa manager asks you to create a report showing the invoices collected each day. You will show her how to provide a daily total as well as a grand total using the Report Wizard.

A04.19

To Create Report Totals Using the Report Wizard

a. Click the **CREATE** tab, and then in the Reports group, click **Report Wizard**.

b. Click the **Tables/Queries** arrow, and then select **Table: tblInvoice**. Double-click **InvoiceDate** and **InvoiceTotal** in the Available Fields list. Click **Next**.

c. Double-click **InvoiceDate** to group by the date. Click **Grouping Options...**, click the **Grouping intervals** arrow, and select **Day**.

d. Click **OK**, and then click **Next**.

e. Click the **1 Sort** arrow, and then select **InvoiceDate**.

f. Click **Summary Options...**, and then click the **Sum** check box.

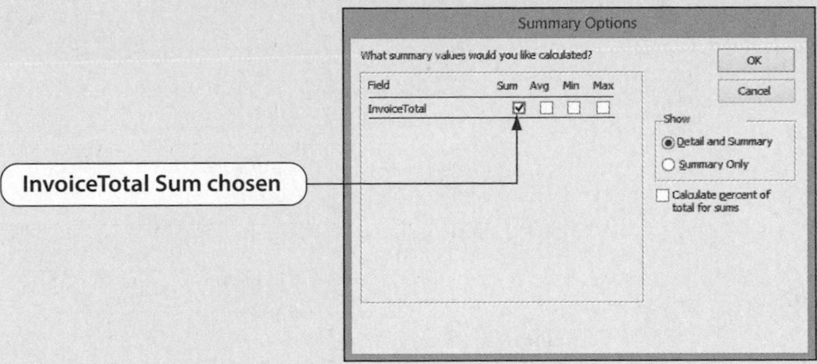

Figure 22 Report Summary Options

g. Click **OK**, and then click **Next**. Verify that **Stepped** and **Portrait** are selected, and then click **Next**.

h. Under **What title do you want for your report?**, type rptInvoiceTotals_initialLastname, using your first initial and last name, and then click **Finish**. The report will open in Print Preview. If necessary, scroll down to see the grand total.

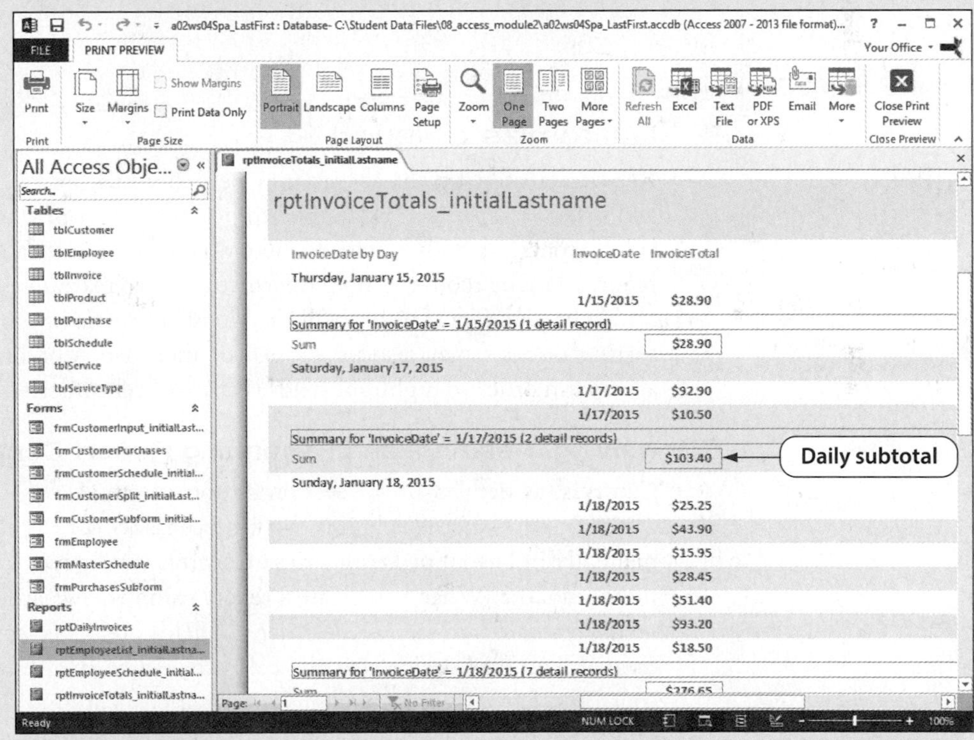

Figure 23 Report with daily subtotals and a grand total

Notice that there is a sum for each day and a grand total of all invoices for all days.

i. Switch to **Design** view. There is a new footer for InvoiceDate where the sum for each day is shown. There is also a Report Footer where the GrandTotal is shown.

j. On the DESIGN tab, in the Controls group, select **Label** *Aa*, move your pointer to the **Report Footer** just below the existing **Grand Total** label, and then when your pointer changes to +A drag your pointer to draw a label control about 2.5" wide in the Report Footer section. In the new label, type Created by initial Lastname using your first initial and last name.

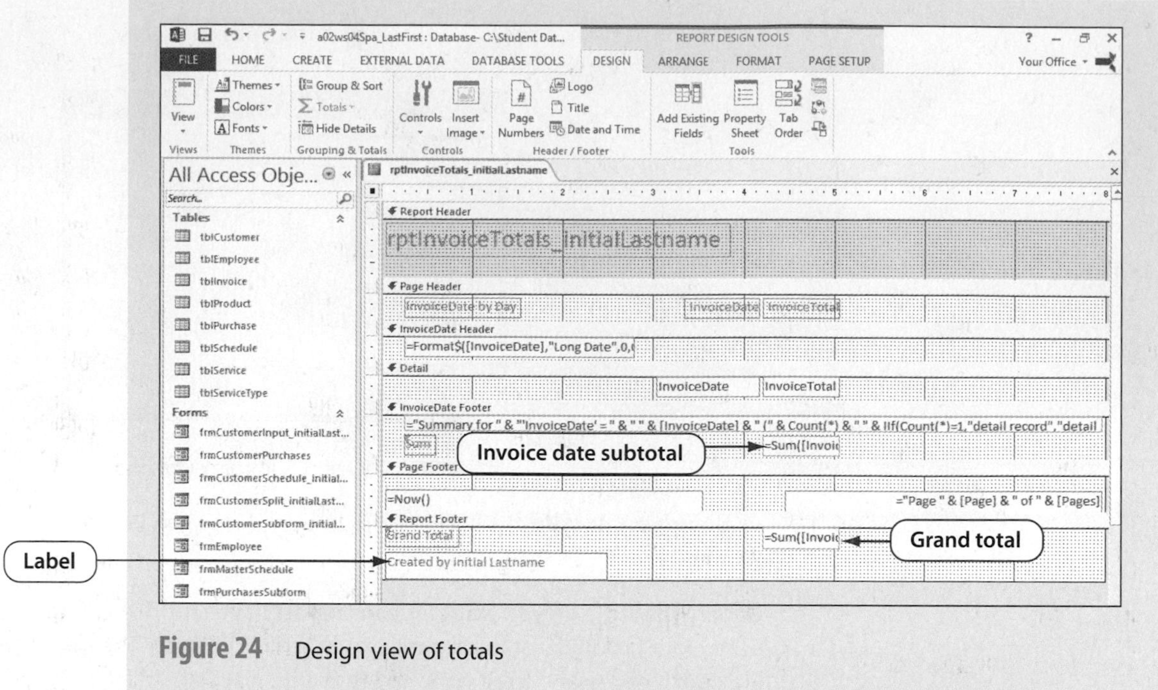

Figure 24 Design view of totals

k. Switch to **Print Preview** to check your label. **Save** and **close** your report.

Customize a Report

Reports created by the wizard can be easily customized after they have been created and saved. Themes can be applied to just the report or the whole database to change the colors, fonts, or both. Controls, bound and unbound, can be added or modified on the report to make room for more information or to rearrange the information already there.

To break a report into smaller sections, subtotals or groups may be added. Additional sorting options may also be applied or modified. Conditional formatting may also be applied in order to highlight fields that meet certain criteria.

Moving, Resizing, and Formatting Report Controls

Controls, as defined in the section on forms, are also used in reports. A control can be a text box, or another object that has been added to the form either by the wizard or manually in Layout or Design view. Controls can be moved or resized to make the report more readable. When you create a report using the wizard, the order that you choose the fields in the wizard step is the order the fields are added to the report. Once the report is created, you may decide that the fields should be in a different order. When you click a control in Layout view, an orange border appears around the control. Once the control is selected you can move it or resize it. You can also change its appearance by adding borders or fill color.

For this exercise, you will change the rptEmployeeSchedule schedule report to make it look more like what the manager expected. You will move the date, service, and customer name fields below the employee name, change the heading, and change the formatting to match the resort theme.

A04.20

To Move, Resize, and Format a Report Control

a. On the Navigation Pane, right-click **rptEmployeeSchedule_initialLastname**, and then click **Layout View**.

b. Click the **DateOfAppt** text box control to select it, and then drag the field to the left so it is just slightly indented under the employee first name.

c. Click the **First Name** label control—the column header, press and hold Shift, click the **Last Name** and the **DateofAppt** label controls, and then press Delete.

d. Click the **Customer** label control, press and hold Shift, and then click the **Customer** text box, the **Service** label, and the **Service** text box controls. Point to and click any field to drag all the controls to the left, just next to the date field.

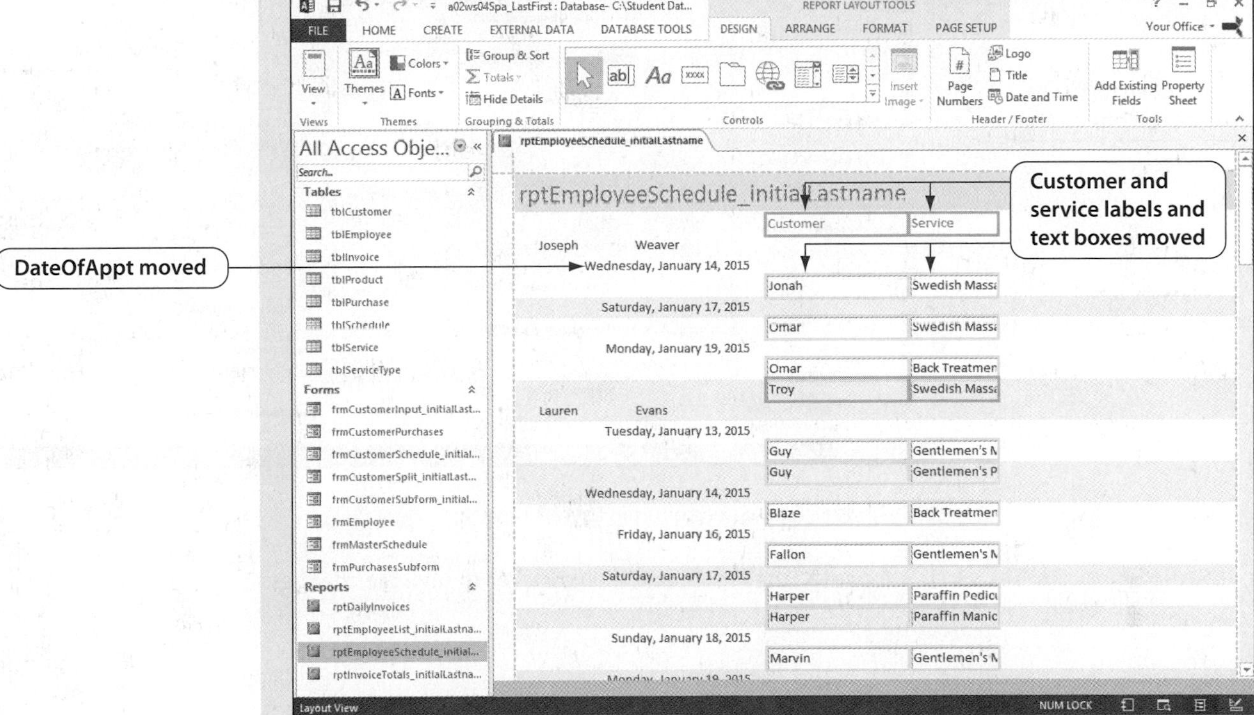

Figure 25 Fields moved

> **Troubleshooting**
>
> If you drag the controls too far to the left, reselect them, and then drag them back to the right.

e. Click the **Service** text box control. Drag the **right border** of the box to the right to fit all the service description. Scroll down to check **Chakra Body and Balancing Massage** to make sure the description is fully shown. If not, drag the border to make the field wider.

f. Scroll up, click the **Service** label control, and then press Delete.

g. Click the **Service** text box control, press and hold Shift, and then click the **Customer** text box control. On the FORMAT tab, in the Control Formatting group, click **Shape Outline**, and then select **Transparent**.

h. Click the employee's **First Name** text box control, press and hold Shift, and then click the **Last Name** text box control. On the FORMAT tab, in the Control Formatting group, click **Shape Fill**, and then select **Dark Teal Accent 2 Lighter 80%** in the second row of the sixth column under Theme colors. In the Font group, click **Bold** B.

i. Double-click the **title**, select the **text**, type Employee Schedule, and then press Enter.

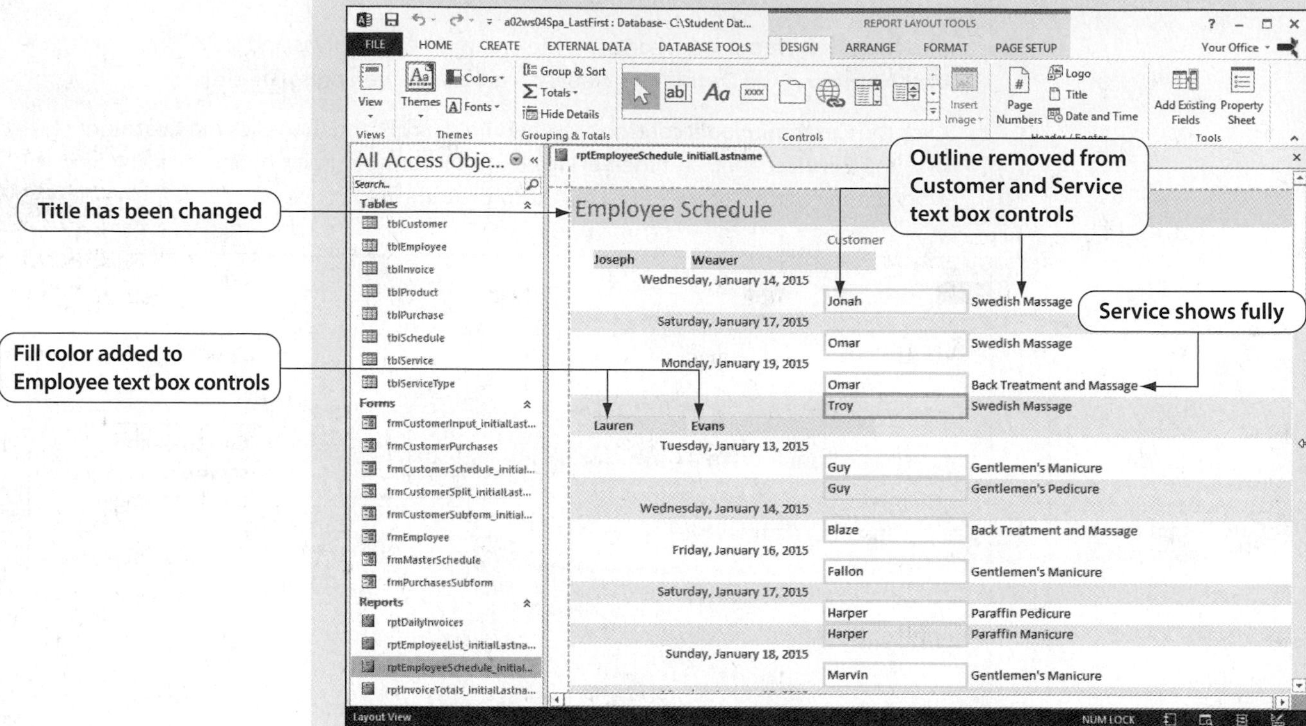

Figure 26 Formatted report in Layout view

j. **Close** X the report, and then click **Yes** to save the changes.

Enhancing a Report with Conditional Formatting

In the previous section, you changed the colors and fonts of fields. You can also change the fonts and colors of fields only when certain conditions are met in the field. This is called **conditional formatting**. If a field value meets the conditions you specify, then the formatting will be applied. This is a useful tool to automatically highlight sales numbers on a report if they meet a certain threshold, or to highlight students' grades when they exceed a certain limit.

To apply conditional formatting, you must select the field value in the field to which you want the formatting applied. You can select a different font color and font effects for the formatting.

For this exercise, the spa manager would like you to create a report and apply conditional formatting to all services currently scheduled that are over $100. These customers usually get some special treatments like complimentary coffee and tea, and the staff would like to be able to easily see which customers will get this service.

A04.21

To Apply Conditional Formatting to a Report Field

a. Click the **CREATE** tab, and then in the Reports group, click **Report Wizard**.

b. Click the **Tables/Queries** arrow, and then select **Table: tblSchedule**. Double-click **DateOfAppt**, **Customer**, and **Service** in the Available Fields list. Click the **Tables/Queries** arrow, and then select **Table: tblService**. On the Available Fields list, double-click **Fee**, and then click **Next**.

c. Verify that **by tblSchedule** is highlighted, and then click **Next**. You will not add any grouping to this report, so click **Next**.

d. Click the **1 Sort** arrow, click **DateofAppt**, and then click **Next**. Verify that **Tabular** is selected under Layout and **Portrait** is selected under Orientation. Verify that **Adjust the field width so all fields fit on a page** is checked. Click **Next**.

e. Under **What title do you want for your report?**, type rptHighFees_initialLastname using your first initial and last name, and then click **Finish**. The report will open in Print Preview. Switch to **Layout** view. If necessary, **close** the Field List pane.

f. Double-click the **title**, select the **text**, type High Service Customers, and then press Enter.

g. Click in the **Fee** text box control, and then, on the FORMAT tab, in the Control Formatting group, click **Conditional Formatting**.

h. In the Conditional Formatting Rules Manager dialog box, click **New Rule**. Verify that **Check values in the current record or use an expression** is highlighted. Find the three condition text boxes. The first should display **Field Value Is**. Click in the second condition box, and then select **greater than**. In the third condition text box, type 100.

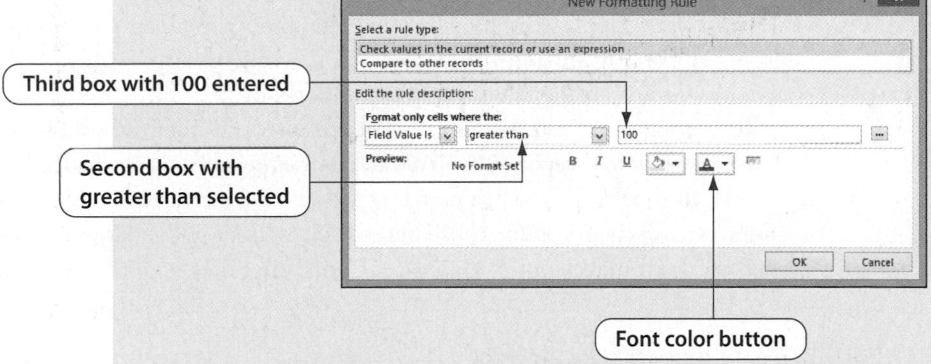

Figure 27 New Formatting Rule dialog box

i. Below the condition text boxes, click **Bold** B, click the **Font color** arrow, and then click **Dark Red**. Click **OK**, verify that your rule states **Value >100**, and then click **OK**.

All values greater than $100 in the Fee field should be highlighted in dark red and bold.

j. Switch to **Design** view. On the REPORT DESIGN TOOLS DESIGN tab, in the Controls group, select **Label** Aa, move your pointer to the **Report Footer**, and then when your pointer changes to +A drag your pointer to draw a label control about 2.5" wide in the top-left corner of the Report Footer section. In the new label, type Created by initial Lastname using your first initial and last name.

k. Switch to **Report** view. Verify that your label has been entered in the bottom-left corner of the report.

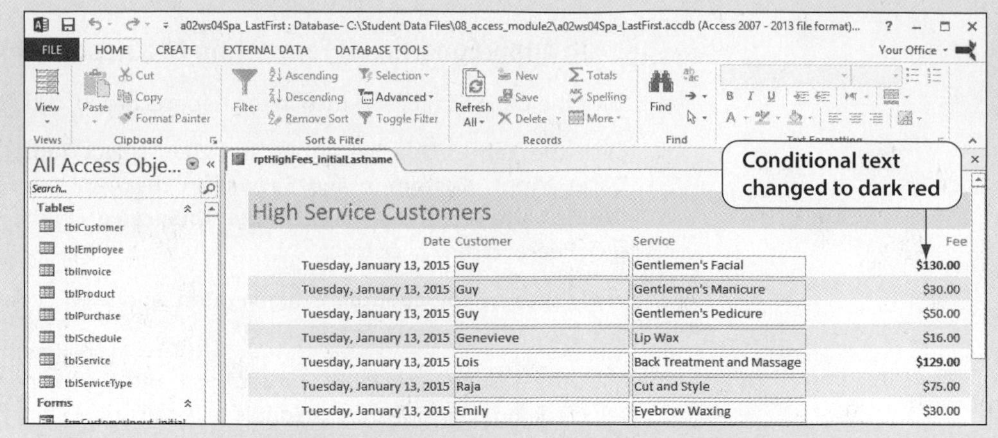

Figure 28 Report with conditional formatting applied

l. **Close** [X] the report, and then click **Yes** to save the changes.

To delete a conditional formatting rule, click the Format tab in Layout view, click the field that has the conditional formatting applied, in the Control Formatting group, click Conditional Formatting, click the rule you wish to delete, and then click Delete Rule.

Applying Grouping and Sorting

The Report Wizard gives you the opportunity to sort and group records, but sometimes seeing the report changes your mind about what and how to group and sort. You can change the sorting and grouping options from either Layout or Design view. Groups are added to a section of the report called the **group header**. Calculations performed on a group in a report are added to a section called the **group footer**. A report may have one or more Group Headers, Group Footers, both, or neither.

In Layout view, you will use the Group, Sort, and Total pane to select the sort fields and grouping fields for a report. This is done after the report has been created by the Report Wizard.

For this exercise, the spa manager would like a report that shows appointment dates and services scheduled for those dates. You will show her how to create the report, and then you will make some changes to it until she likes how the information is presented.

A04.22

To Add Group and Sort Fields to a New Report

a. Click the **CREATE** tab, and then in the Reports group, click **Report Wizard**.

b. Click the **Tables/Queries** arrow, and then select **Table: tblSchedule**. Double-click **DateOfAppt**, **Service**, **Customer**, and **Employee** from the Available Fields list. Click **Next**.

c. Click the **One Field Back** button [<] to remove the Service grouping level. Click **DateOfAppt**, and then click the **One Field** button [>] to add the date as a grouping level. Click **Grouping Options...**, click the **Grouping intervals** arrow, and then click **Normal**. Click **OK**, and then click **Next**.

d. Click the **1 Sort** arrow, select **Service**, and then click **Next**.

e. Verify **Stepped** layout and **Portrait** orientation are selected. Verify that **Adjust the field width so all fields fit on a page** is selected. Click **Next**.

MODULE 2

f. Under **What title do you want for your report?**, type rptAppointments_initialLastname using your first initial and last name, and then click **Finish**.

g. Switch to **Design** view. On the DESIGN tab, in the Controls group, select **Label** [Aa], move your pointer to the **Report Footer**, and then when your pointer changes to [+A] drag your pointer to draw a label control about 2.5" wide in the top-left corner of the Report Footer section. In the new label, type Created by initial Lastname using your first initial and last name.

h. Switch to **Layout** view. Verify that your label has been entered in the bottom-left corner of the report.

i. Click the **DateOfAppt** text box control, on the FORMAT tab, in the Font group, click **Align Text Left** [≡]. Drag the right border of the DateOfAppt text box to line up with the left border of the Service text box. All the date values should be visible.

j. Click the **Service** text box control, and then drag the left border to the left to make the control wider so all the text can be displayed. Scroll down to the appointments scheduled on January 18, and then confirm that the **Microdermabrasion Treatment (6 sessions)** is showing.

k. Double-click the **title**, select the **text**, and then type Daily Appointments. Press [Enter].

l. On the DESIGN tab, in the Grouping & Totals group, click **Group & Sort**, and then notice the Group, Sort, and Total pane that opens at the bottom of the report.

m. Click the line that displays **Sort by Service**, and then click **Delete** [X] on the far right of the line. This will delete the sort that was added in the Report Wizard.

n. Click **Add a group** in the Group, Sort, and Total pane, and then select **Employee**.

o. Click the **Employee** text box control, and then drag it to the left until it is under the date. Click the **Employee** label control, press and hold [Shift], click the **DateOfAppt** label control, and then press [Delete].

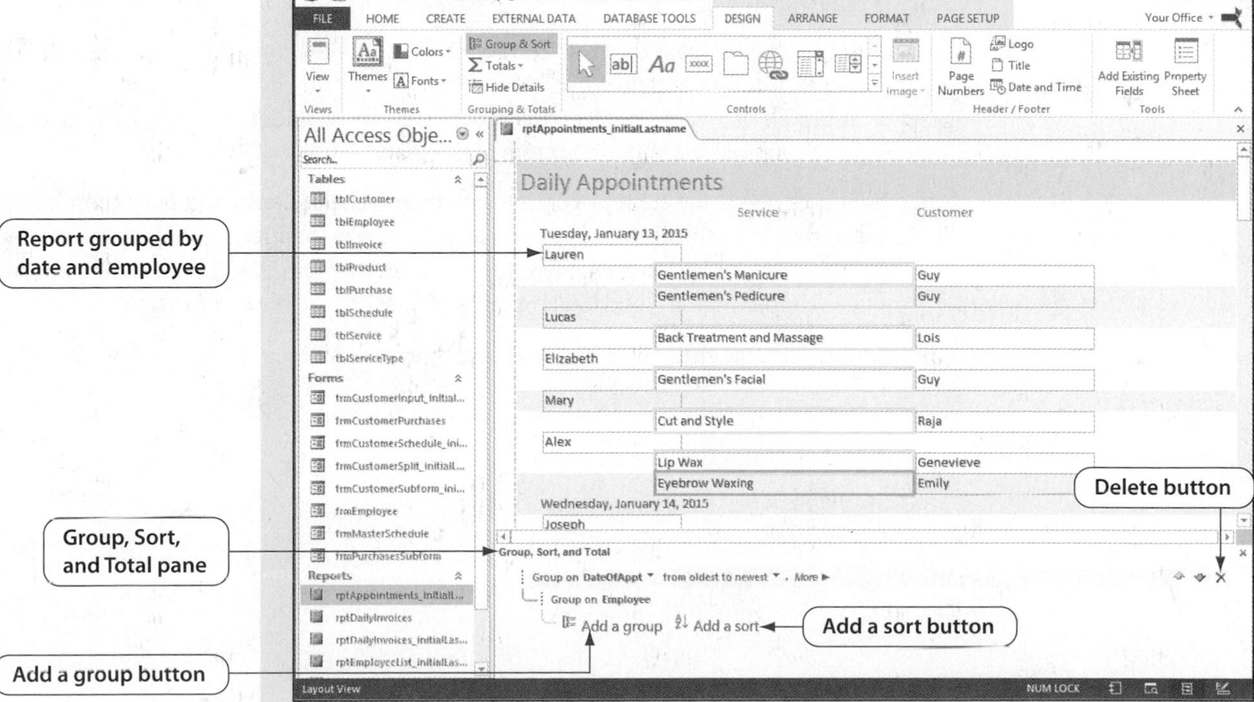

Figure 29 New grouping added to report

p. **Close** [X] the Group, Sort, and Total pane being careful that you are clicking Close and not the Delete button. **Close** [X] the report, and then click **Yes** to save the changes.

Adding Subtotals

Earlier, you added subtotals when you created the report using the wizard. However, sometimes seeing the report makes you realize that subtotals would be useful. You can add them in Layout view, using the Group, Sort, and Total pane when you are selecting or modifying groups and sorts for the reports.

For this exercise, the spa manager would like to add subtotals to a report that shows all invoices grouped by date.

A04.23

To Add Subtotals to a Report

a. In the Navigation Pane, right-click rptDailyInvoices, and then select **Copy**. Right-click in the **Navigation Pane**, and then select **Paste**. In the Paste As dialog box, in the **Report Name:** box, type rptDailyInvoices_initialLastname using your first initial and last name. Click **OK**.

b. In the Navigation Pane, double-click **rptDailyInvoices_initialLastname** to open the report. Notice the report shows all invoices by day but has no totals.

c. Switch to **Design** view. On the DESIGN tab, in the Controls group, click **Label** [Aa]. Move your pointer to the **Report Footer**, and then when your pointer changes to [+A] drag your pointer to draw a label control about 2.5" wide in the top-left corner of the Report Footer section. In the new label control, type Created by initial Lastname using your first initial and last name.

d. Switch to **Layout** view. Verify that your label has been entered in the bottom-left corner of the report.

e. Scroll right, click the **Invoice Total** label control, press and hold [Shift], click the **Invoice Total** text box control, and then drag the **right border** to the left so that it is to the right of the dotted line. Drag the **left border** to the right so the field is narrower but the column heading still shows.

f. Click the **InvoiceTotal** text box control. On the DESIGN tab, in the Grouping & Totals group, click **Totals**, and then click **Sum**.

   Subtotals for each InvoiceDate group will show under the InvoiceTotal details. A grand total will show at the bottom of the report.

g. Right-click one of the subtotal controls, and then click **Set Caption**. A label control will be added next to each subtotal amount that says "InvoiceTotal Total". Double-click the **label** control, select the **text**, and then type Invoice Subtotal. Press [Enter]. Repeat the same steps to set a caption for the grand total control, and then change the text to Invoice Total.

h. Double-click the **title**, select the **text**, and then type Invoice Amounts. Press [Enter].

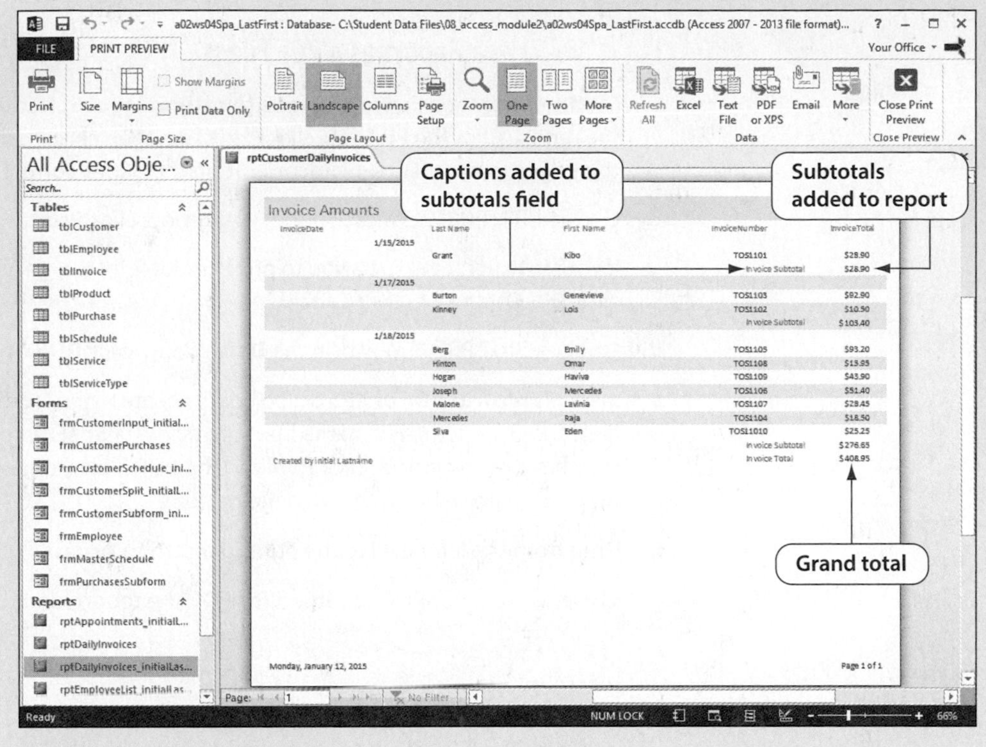

Figure 30 Report with subtotals added

i. **Close** [X] the report, and then click **Yes** to save the changes.

Save a Report as a PDF File

Reports are formatted printable documents of your data, so the final result of a report will usually be a printout. If not printed, then the report may be shared with other people electronically. When you send a report to someone electronically, they have to have the same program in which the report was created in order to open the report. To avoid this problem, you can save a report as a PDF file, which can be read by Adobe Reader, a free program that you can download from the Internet, or by Word 2013.

To print a report, you use the Print dialog box on the File tab to select your printing options. Before you print, it is always a good idea to view the report in Print Preview to make sure it looks the way you want. Viewing the report in Layout view and Report view does not show you page breaks and other features of the report as it will look when actually printed. In Print Preview, you have many options to make design changes to your report before you send it to the printer. You can change the margins and orientation, and you can select how many pages, if not all, you want to print.

Creating a PDF File

If you need to distribute the report electronically, you also have the option to save the report as an Adobe PDF file. An **Adobe PDF file** is usually smaller than the original document, is easy to send through e-mail, and preserves the original document look and feel so you know exactly what it will look like when the recipient opens it. The correct terminology for saving a report as a PDF file format is to "publish" the report. When you are saving the report as a PDF you will see the option to Publish, not to Save or Print.

For this exercise, you will show the staff how to print and publish a PDF file of the employee schedule so it can easily be e-mailed to the staff each week.

A04.24

To Save a Report as a PDF File

a. On the Navigation Pane, double-click **rptEmployeeSchedule_initialLastname** to open the report. Click the **FILE** tab, click **Print**, and then click **Print Preview**. Navigate through the pages to make sure the records fit on the pages correctly.

b. On the PRINT PREVIEW tab, in the Print group, click **Print**.

c. If your instructor instructs you to print, under Print Range, verify **All** is selected, and then click **OK**. Otherwise, click **Cancel**.

d. On the PRINT PREVIEW tab, in the **Data** group, click **PDF or XPS**.

e. In the **Publish as PDF or XPS** dialog box, navigate to the location where you are saving your files, and then in the **File name** box type a02ws04SpaEmployeeSchedule_LastFirst using your first and last name. Click **Publish**. The PDF file automatically opens. To close the file, drag down from the top bezel to the bottom.

f. Drag from the left bezel to the right to return to **Access**.

g. **Close** the Export - PDF window. **Close** [X] the report, and then **close** [X] Access.

Concept Check

1. What is the difference between Navigation and Edit modes? How can you tell you are in each mode? p. 740–742
2. When you add, change, or delete a record in a form, how does it affect the underlying table? Why? p. 748–749
3. What are controls? What is the difference between a label control and a text box control? Which is bound, and which is unbound? p. 751
4. What is a theme? What is the difference between applying a theme to an entire database and to a single object? p. 756–757
5. What view will you see when the Report Wizard is done creating a report? What is the difference between Report view, Layout view, Design view, and Print Preview when you are creating a report? Which view will show you the most accurate picture of what your printed report will look like? In which views do you see the data? p. 766
6. What is conditional formatting, and when would you use it? p. 772
7. What is a PDF file, and why would you want to save your report as a PDF? p. 777

Key Terms

Adobe PDF file 777
Bound control 751
Calculated control 751
Conditional formatting 772
Control 751
Edit mode 740
Grand total 768
Group 762
Group footer 774
Group header 774
Label control 751
Layout selector 758
Main form 743
Navigation mode 740
Split form 746
Subform 743
Subreport 762
Subtotals 768
Text box control 751
Theme 756
Unbound control 751

Visual Summary

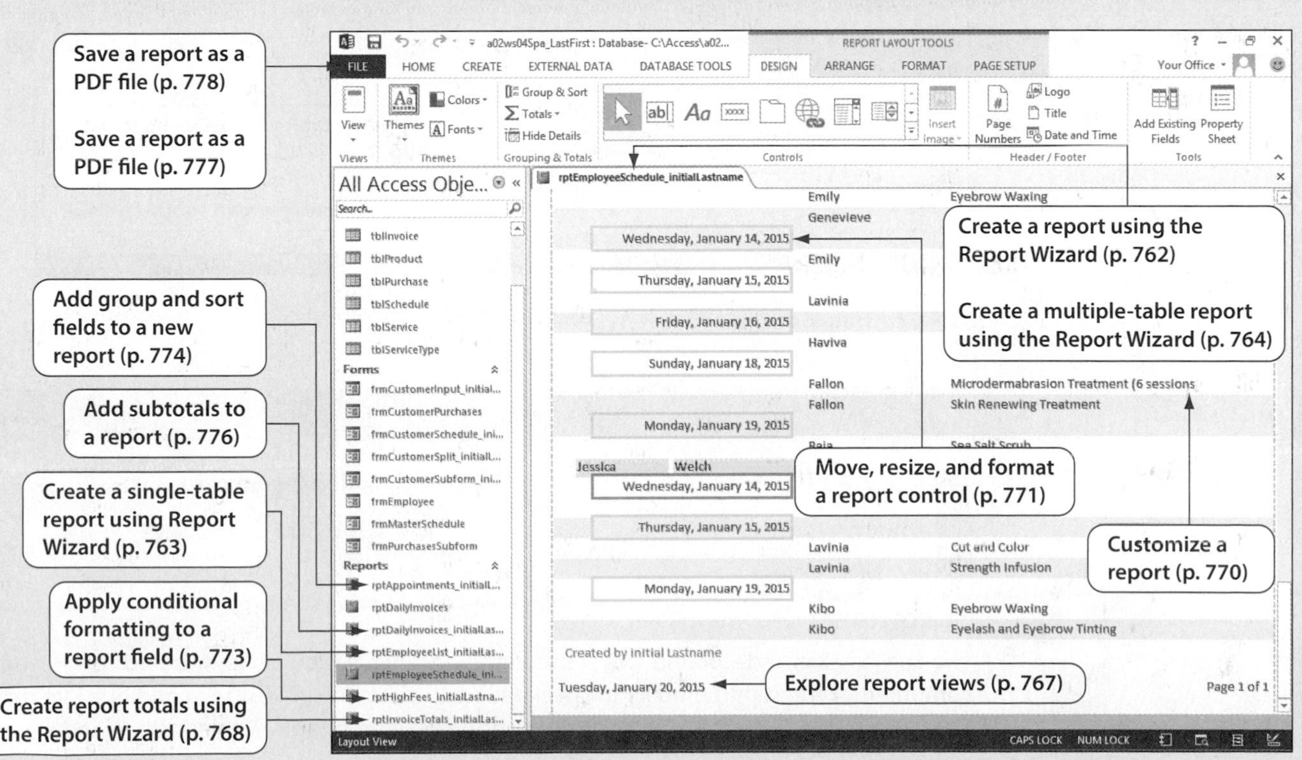

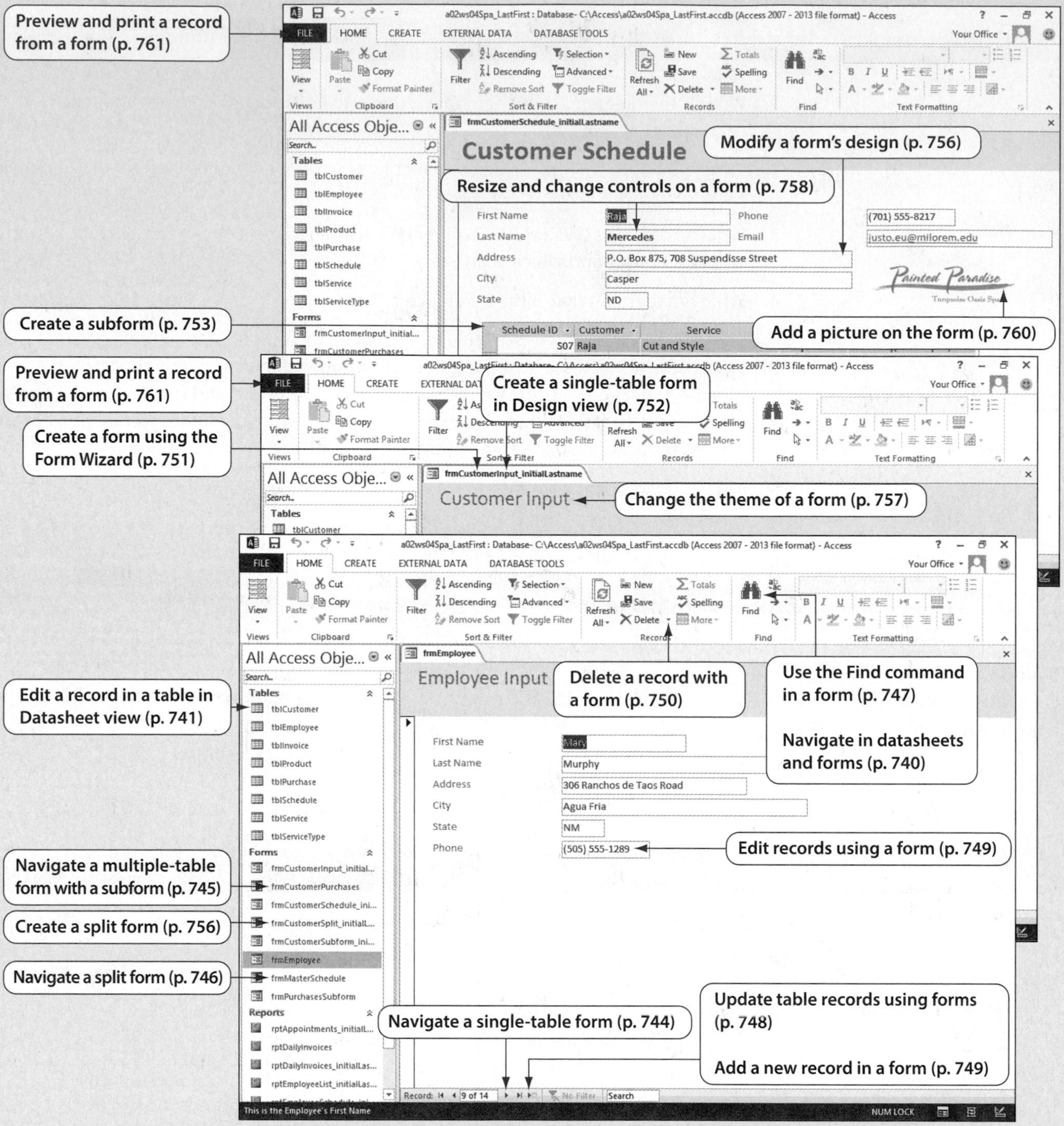

Preview and print a record from a form (p. 761)
Modify a form's design (p. 756)
Resize and change controls on a form (p. 758)
Create a subform (p. 753)
Add a picture on the form (p. 760)
Preview and print a record from a form (p. 761)
Create a single-table form in Design view (p. 752)
Create a form using the Form Wizard (p. 751)
Change the theme of a form (p. 757)
Delete a record with a form (p. 750)
Use the Find command in a form (p. 747)
Navigate in datasheets and forms (p. 740)
Edit a record in a table in Datasheet view (p. 741)
Edit records using a form (p. 749)
Navigate a multiple-table form with a subform (p. 745)
Create a split form (p. 756)
Navigate a split form (p. 746)
Navigate a single-table form (p. 744)
Update table records using forms (p. 748)
Add a new record in a form (p. 749)

Figure 31 Turquoise Oasis Spa's New Database

Practice 1

Student data file needed:

a02ws04Spa2.accdb

a02ws04Spa.thmx

You will save your file as:

a02ws04Spa2_LastFirst.accdb

Human Resources

Turquoise Oasis Spa

The spa has just redecorated the staff lounge and has added bulletin boards and even a computer for the staff members to check their appointments and sign in and out. The manager would like to create reports to post on the bulletin boards with schedule and service information, as well as make the database as easy to use as possible. You will help create some of the reports as well as forms to make the database easy for data entry and maintenance.

a. Start **Access**, and then open **a02ws04Spa2**.

b. Click the **FILE** tab, click **Save As**. Verify **Save Database As** and **Access Database** are selected. Click **Save As**. In the Save As dialog box, navigate to where you are saving your files and then type a02ws04Spa2_LastFirst, using your first and last name. Click **Save**. If necessary, in the Security Warning, click **Enable Content**.

c. Create a form that will allow employees to edit their personal information as well as their upcoming appointments:
   - Click the **CREATE** tab, and then in the Forms group, click **Form Wizard**.
   - In the Form Wizard dialog box, click the **Tables/Queries** arrow, and then select **Table: tblEmployee**. Click the **All Fields** button to add all the fields to the Selected Fields list.
   - Click the **Tables/Queries** arrow, and then select **Table: tblSchedule**. Double-click **Customer**, **Service**, **Employee**, and **DateOfAppt** to add the fields to the Selected Fields list. Click **Next**.
   - Verify that the data will be viewed **by tblEmployee**, and then click **Next**.
   - Verify that **Datasheet** is selected as the layout for the subform, and then click **Next**.
   - Name the form frmEmployeeSchedule_initialLastname using your first initial and last name, name the subform frmSubform_initialLastname, and then click **Finish**.
   - Switch to **Form** view. On the main form Navigation bar, click **New (blank) record**, and then add your first name, last name, address, city, state, and phone number. On the Navigation bar, click **First record** to return to the first record in the table, and then click in the **Last Name** field.
   - Click the **HOME** tab, in the Find group, click **Find**. In the **Find What** text box, type Rodriguez and then click **Find Next**. When you find the record for Brenda Rodriguez, click **Cancel**.
   - On the HOME tab, in the Records group, click the **Delete** arrow, and then click **Delete Record**. Click **Yes** when prompted to delete the record.
   - Switch to **Layout** view. Double-click the **title**, select the **text**, and then type Employee Schedule.
   - Click the **Last Name** text box control, and then drag the **right border** of the text box to line up with the right border of the First Name text box.
   - Click the **subform label**, and then press Delete to delete the control. Click the **Subform**, and then using the layout selector, drag it to the left so it is right below the Phone label. Use the AutoFit feature on all the columns to best fit the data.
   - Click the **Employee** label in the subform datasheet, and then press Delete to delete the label. Click the **subform** control, and then drag the **right border** to the right until you can see all the fields in the subform. Click the **Date** heading in the subform datasheet, and then drag it to the left of the Customer field.
   - On the DESIGN tab, in the Themes group, click the **Themes** arrow, click **Browse for Themes**, browse to where you stored data files, click **a02ws04Spa**, and then click **Open**.
   - Switch to **Design** view, on the DESIGN tab, in the Controls group, select **Label**, move your pointer to the **Report Footer**, and then draw a label control about 2.5" wide in the top-left corner of the Report Footer section. In the new label control, type Created by initial Lastname using your first initial and last name.
   - Close the form, and then click **Yes** when prompted to save the changes.

d. Create a report to show a list of customers and their purchases.
   - Click the **CREATE** tab, and then in the Reports group, click **Report Wizard**. In the Report Wizard dialog box, click the **Tables/Queries** arrow, and then select **Table: tblCustomer**. Double-click **CustFirstName**, **CustLastName**, **CustState**, and **CustPhone** to add the fields to the Selected Fields list.

- Click the **Tables/Queries** arrow, and then select **Table: tblProduct**. Double-click **ProductDescription** to add the field to the Selected Fields list.
- Click the **Tables/Queries** arrow, and then select **Table: tblPurchase**. Double-click **PurchaseType**, **PurchaseDate**, and **Quantity** to add the fields to the Selected Fields list. Click **Next**.
- Verify that the data will be viewed by **tblCustomer**, and then click **Next**.
- Double-click **ProductDescription** to add it as a grouping level, and then click **Next**.
- Click the **1 Sort** arrow, click **PurchaseDate**, and then click **Next**. Select a **Stepped** layout and **Portrait** orientation, and then click **Next**.
- Name the report rptCustomerPurchases_initialLastname using your first initial and last name, and then click **Finish**.

e. Customize the report's appearance.
   - Switch to **Layout** view.
   - Click the **Date** text box control, and then drag the **left border** to the left until the date is visible. Move the **Date** text box control to the left until it lines up under the First Name field.
   - Click the **ProductDescription** label control, press and hold Shift, click the **PurchaseDate** label control, click the **PurchaseType** label control, and then press Delete to delete the controls.
   - Click the **Phone** text box control, and then drag the **right border** so the whole field is visible. Click the **ProductDescription** text box control, and then drag the **right border** to the right until the whole field is visible.
   - Double-click the **title**, select the **text**, and then type Customer Purchases.
   - **Save** the report.

f. Add totals and subtotals.
   - On the DESIGN tab, in the Grouping & Totals group, click **Group & Sort** to open the Group, Sort, and Total pane. Click **Group on ProductDescription**, and then click **Delete** to delete the group.
   - In the Group, Sort, and Total pane, click **Add a group**, and then select **PurchaseType**. Click the **PurchaseType** text box control—on the far right of report, and then drag it just below the customer's first name and just above the date.
   - In the Group, Sort, and Total pane, click **Add a sort**, and then select **ProductDescription**. Close the Group, Sort, and Total pane.
   - Click the **PurchaseType** text box. On the FORMAT tab, in the Control Formatting group, click **Conditional Formatting**, and then click **New Rule**. In the second box, select **equal to**, and then in the third text box type Online. Click **Font color**, and then select **Purple**. Click **OK** twice.
   - Click the **PurchaseType** text box control. On the DESIGN tab, in the Grouping & Totals group, click **Totals**, and then select **Count Records**. Click the **PurchaseType** text box control, press and hold Shift, and then click the **subtotal** text box control. On the FORMAT tab, in the Control Formatting group, click **Shape Outline**, and then select **Transparent**.
   - Right-click the **Subtotal** text box control, and then select **Set Caption**. Replace the text in the caption box with Orders.
   - Scroll to the bottom of the report. Click the **Grand Total** text box control, and then move it under the product description. Right-click the **Grand Total** text box control, and then click **Set Caption**. Replace the text in the caption box with Total orders.
   - Switch to **Design** view. On the DESIGN tab, in the Controls group, select **Label**, move your pointer to the **Report Footer**, and then when your pointer changes drag your pointer to draw a label control about 2.5" wide on the left side of the Report Footer. In the new label control, type Created by initial Lastname using your first initial and last name.

g. Close the report, and then click **Yes** when prompted to save the changes.

h. Close your database. Submit your files as directed by your instructor.

Problem Solve 1

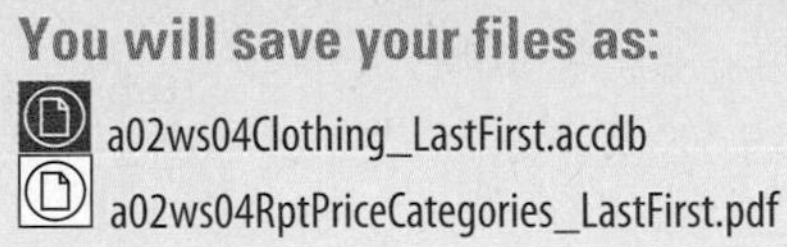

Student data file needed:

a02ws04Clothing.accdb

You will save your files as:

a02ws04Clothing_LastFirst.accdb

a02ws04RptPriceCategories_LastFirst.pdf

Clothing Sales

Sales & Marketing

Wanda Robinson runs a home business selling designer clothing and has started using an Access database to keep her records. The database has been created and is now able to retain data. Wanda wants to have some forms and reports created to make dealing with the data easier. She has hired you to develop the necessary forms and reports.

a. Start **Access**, and then open the student data file **a02ws04Clothing**. Click the **FILE** tab, and then save the file as an **Access Database** in the location where you store your data files with the name a02ws04Clothing_LastFirst using your first and last name. If necessary, enable the content.

b. Open **tblCustomer** and add a record with CustomerID 16, your last name, first name, address, city, state, and zip code.

c. Create a **split form** to show all the product information from **tblProduct**.
   - Save the form as frmProductInfo_initialLastname.
   - Apply the theme **Ion** to all objects in the database. Hint: The themes are listed alphabetically.
   - Add Created by initial Lastname to the Form Footer. Save and close the form.

d. Use the **Form Wizard** to create a form that will display in the main form the customer's **LastName**, **FirstName**, and display **Product Description**, **Price**, **Size**, and **Color** in the subform. Keep all other default options. Name the form frmCustOrders_initialLastname and the subform frmProductSubform_initialLastname.
   - Remove the subform label. Move the subform to line up with the FirstName label control.
   - Resize the columns in the subform so all the product information fits. Resize the form to fit the columns.
   - Change the title of the form to Customer Orders.
   - Add Created by initial Lastname to the main form's Form Footer. Save and close the form.

e. Use the **Report Wizard** to create a report to summarize each customer's purchases. Include **LastName**, **FirstName**, **ProductDescription**, **Price**, and **Quantity**. Hint: this information will come from three different tables. Accept the grouping options, sort by **ProductDescription,** use a format of **Stepped** and **Landscape**, and save the report as rptCustSummary_initialLastname.
   - Add the **sum of the quantities** for each customer. Add a caption of Total Products.
   - Apply conditional formatting to make any sum of quantities greater than 3 bold and red.
   - Add Created by initial Lastname to the Report Footer.
   - Change the title of the report to Customer Summary. Save and close the report.

f. Use the **Report Wizard** to create a report that includes all product fields except ProductID. Group products by **category** and then **price**, sort by **ProductDescription** and then **Size**. Use **Summary Options** in the wizard to show the **sum** of **QuantityInStock**. Change the setting to **Landscape**. Name the report rptPriceCategories_initialLastname.
   - Use the AutoFit feature, and then move the fields as necessary for the best fit.
   - Add Created by initial Lastname to the Report Footer.
   - Change the title of the report to Products by Category and Price. Save and close the report.
   - Create a PDF file from the rptPriceCategories. Save the file as a02ws04RptPriceCategories_LastFirst.

g. Close your database. Submit your files as directed by your instructor.

Perform 1: Perform in Your Career

Student data file needed:

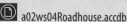

a02ws04Roadhouse.accdb

You will save your file as:

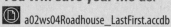

a02ws04Roadhouse_LastFirst.accdb

Beverage Database at the Roadhouse Bar and Grill

Production & Operations

You are the bar manager at the Roadhouse Bar and Grill, a local restaurant that specializes in home-cooked meals for breakfast, lunch, and dinner. You have developed a database for managing the inventory of beverage items.

You will expand the database by creating forms and reports to help you manage the database. You have loaded a few sample transactions to help you develop these forms and reports. For each report, choose which fields you need and which sort order makes sense. Choose appropriate titles and attractive formatting for all forms and reports. Add a Created by label to each report and form.

a. Start Access, open the student data file **a02ws04Roadhouse**, and then save it as a02ws04Roadhouse_LastFirst.

b. Open each table and familiarize yourself with the fields. Open the relationships window and note how the tables are related.

c. Create a split form to add a supplier to the database. Name the form frmSupplier_initialLastname. Use your form to change the name of the first supplier to be your full name. Pick an attractive theme, and then apply it to the entire database.

d. Create a form showing suppliers and the beverages they sell. Name the main form frmSupplierBeverage_initialLastname and the subform frmBeverageSubform_initialLastname. Use the form to add Ginger Ale to the canned beverages that you sell.

e. Create a report that shows the supplier, the beverages they sold, and the sales date of the sales. Name it rptSalesBySupplier_initialLastname.

f. Create a report that shows suppliers, the container types, container sizes, serving sizes, and price. Add a subtotal with average prices. Name the report rptAveragePrice_initialLastname.

g. Create a report showing daily sales of beverages, count the number of sales per day of beverages, and then name the report rptDailySales_initialLastname.

h. Create a report with conditional formatting to highlight something that you think is interesting.

i. Create another report that would be useful for your job.

j. Close your database. Submit your files as directed by your instructor. Close your database.

Additional Cases

Additional Workshop Cases are available on the companion website and in the instructor resources.

MODULE CAPSTONE

More Practice 1

Student data files needed:

a02mpRecipes.accdb

a02mpIndigo5.jpg

You will save your files as:

a02mpRecipes_LastFirst.accdb

a02mpRecipesPDF_LastFirst.pdf

Indigo5 Restaurant

Production & Operations

Robin Sanchez, the chef of the resort's restaurant, Indigo 5, has started a database to keep track of the recipes and ingredients that the restaurant includes. Right now there are no forms, queries, or reports created for this database, so the information available is very limited. You will help create some queries as well as forms for data entry and reports for the daily management of the food preparation.

a. Start **Access**, and then open **a02mpRecipes**. Click the **FILE** tab, and then save the file as an **Access Database** with the name a02mpRecipes_LastFirst using your last and first name. If necessary, in the Security Warning, click **Enable Content**.

b. Click the **CREATE** tab, and then in the Forms group, click **Form Wizard**. Add all of the fields from **Table: tblRecipes**. From **Table: tblRecipeIngredients**, and then double-click **IngredientID**, **Quantity**, and **Measurement**. View the form **by tblRecipes**, show the subform as a **Datasheet**. Save the form as frmRecipe_initialLastname and the subform as frmRecipeSubform_initialLastname, using your first initial and last name. Switch to **Design** view. On the DESIGN tab, in the Controls group, click **Label**, and then add a label to the form footer that says Created by initial Lastname.

c. Switch to **Layout** view. Click the **DESIGN** tab, in the Themes group, click **Themes**. Click the **Ion Boardroom** theme to apply it to all objects in the database.

d. Change the title of the form to Recipe Input. On the FORMAT tab, in the Font group, change the title font size to **28**, and then apply **Bold**.

e. On the DESIGN tab, in the Themes group, click **Fonts**, and then click **Office Calibri Light** to apply it to all objects.

f. Go to the recipe for **REC006**, **Pueblo Green Chili Stew**. Delete the subform label, and then move the subform to the left under the Instructions label. AutoFit the subform fields **Quantity** and **Measurement** to size them appropriately. Move the **right** border of the subform to the left to fit the subform columns.

g. Click in the form **body**. On the DESIGN tab, in the Controls group, click **Insert Image**, click **Browse**, navigate to your student data files, and then locate **a02mpIndigo5**. Insert the **image** to the right of the Recipe information. Resize the **image** as necessary to fit above the Instructions text box.

h. Switch to **Form** view. Click the **Recipe Name** text box. On the HOME tab, in the Find group, click **Find**, and then in the Find What box, type Pasta Napolitana, and then click **Find Next**. Click **Cancel**. Change the Quantity for the **IngredientID Honey** to 1.

i. Click the **New (blank) record** button on the main form Navigation bar, and then enter the following data into frmRecipe_initialLastname:

Recipe Name	Food Category ID	Subcategory	Prep Time (minutes)	Servings	Instructions
Avocado Salsa	Appetizer	Vegetarian	10	6	Peel and mash avocados. Add cayenne pepper, salt, chopped onion, and chopped tomato. Add lime juice and mix well. Refrigerate for at least 4 hours.

Enter the following data into the subform:

IngredientID	Quantity	Measurement
Avocado	2	whole
Tomato	1	cup
Cayenne pepper	.5	teaspoon
Salt	.5	teaspoon
Onions	1	cup
Lime juice	3	tablespoons

Save and close the form.

j. Click the **CREATE** tab, in the Queries group, click **Query Design**, and then add **tblRecipes**, **tblRecipeIngredients**, and **tblIngredients**. Include **RecipeName**, **Ingredient**, and **Quantity** in the results. In the **Ingredient Criteria**, type cumin or paprika. Sort in **Ascending** order by **Quantity**. Run the query, and then use the AutoFit feature on the query columns. Save your query as qryCuminOrPaprika_initialLastname. Close the query.

k. Create a query to show all ingredients not used in any recipe. Click the **CREATE** tab, and then in the Queries group, click **Query Wizard**, click **Find Unmatched Query Wizard**, and then click **OK**. Click **Table: tblIngredients**, and then click **Next**. Click **tblRecipeIngredients**, and then click **Next**. IngredientID will be the common field between the tables. Click **Next**, and then include all the available fields. Click **Next**. Save the query as qryUnusedIngredients_initialLastname. Click **Finish**. Switch to **Design** view, sort **IngredientID** in **Ascending** order. Save and close the query.

l. Click the **CREATE** tab, in the Queries group, click **Query Design**, and then add **tblRecipes** and **tblFoodCategories**. Include **RecipeName**, **TimeToPrepare**, and **FoodCategory** in the results. Add criteria < 30 to the **TimetoPrepare** field to find all recipes that take less than 30 minutes to prepare. Add criteria soup or pizza to the **FoodCategory** field. The results should show all recipes that take less than 30 minutes to prepare and are listed with the category of soup or pizza. Sort **TimeToPrepare** in **Ascending** order. **Run** the query. Use AutoFit on each column. Save the query as qryTimeAndCategory_initialLastname and then close the query.

m. Click the **CREATE** tab, in the Queries group, click **Query Design**, and then add **tblRecipes**, **tblRecipeIngredients**, and **tblIngredients**. Include **RecipeName**, **Ingredient**, **Quantity**, **Measurement**, and **RecipeID** from tblRecipeIngredients in the results, in that order. Sort **RecipeID** in **Ascending** order. **Run** the query. Use AutoFit on each column. Save the query as qryRecipeIngredients_initialLastname and then close the query.

n. Click the **CREATE** tab, in the Reports group, click **Report Wizard**, and then from **Table: tblRecipes** add the fields **RecipeName**, **Instructions**, **TimeToPrepare**, and **Servings**. From **Query: qryRecipeIngredients_initialLastname** add the fields **Ingredient**,

Quantity, and **Measurement** in that order. View your report **by tblRecipes**. Group by **RecipeName**. Sort in **Ascending** order by Ingredient. Accept all other default settings, and then name the report rptRecipes_initialLastname.

- Switch to **Layout** view, and then move the **Ingredient**, **Quantity**, and **Measurement** text boxes to the left under the Instructions field. Delete the Ingredient, Quantity, and Measurement labels. Move the **Servings text box** and **label** to the right. Make the **Prep Time (minutes)** and **Servings** labels wider so the text is visible. Double-click the report **title**, and then change it to Recipes.
- Click the **Recipe Name** text field. On the FORMAT tab, in the Font group, click **Bold**. Move the right border for the **Recipe Name** text box to make it wide enough to fit all the text for every record. Scroll down to **Gambas al Ajillo (Shrimp with Garlic)** to make sure the field is wide enough.
- Click the **Quantity** text box, and then move the **left** border to the right to make the field narrower. Click the **Ingredient** text box, and then move the **right** border to the right to make the field completely visible. Scroll down to see **Corn (whole kernel)** to make sure the field is wide enough.
- Click the **Prep Time** text box, and then in the Control Formatting group, click **Conditional Formatting**. Click **New Rule**, select **greater than** in the second box, and then type 15 in the third box. Click **Bold** and change the font color to **Red**, and then click **OK**. Click **OK** again.
- Switch to **Design** view. On the DESIGN tab, in the Controls group, click **Label**, and then add a label saying Created by initial Lastname to the Report Footer.
- Save the report, switch to **Report** view to check your report, and then close the report.
- Right-click **rptRecipes initialLastname**. Select **Export**, and then select **PDF or XPS**. Navigate to the folder where you are saving your files, type a02mpRecipesPDF_initialLastname, in the **Open after publishing** box, clear the check box, click **Publish**, and then click close.

o. Click the **CREATE** tab, in the Reports group, click **Report Wizard**, and then from **Table:tblRecipeIngredients** add the fields **IngredientID**, **Quantity**, and **Measurement**. From **Table: tblRecipes** add **RecipeName**. Click **Next**, check to make sure you view your data **by tblRecipeIngredients**, click **Next**, and then double-click **RecipeName** to add grouping. Accept all other default options, and then name your report rptIngredientCount_initialLastname.

- Switch to **Design** view. On the DESIGN tab, and then in the Controls group, click **Label**, and then add a label saying Created by initial Lastname to the Report Footer.
- Switch to **Layout** view. On the DESIGN tab, in the Grouping & Totals group, click **Group & Sort**, and then delete the grouping by RecipeName. Click **Add a group**, and then group by **IngredientID**. Move the **IngredientID** text box to the left margin, under the RecipeName label. Click the **IngredientID** text box, and then on the **FORMAT** tab, in the Font group, click **Align Left**. Delete the **RecipeName**, **IngredientID**, **Quantity**, and **Measurement** labels.
- Change the title to Ingredient List. Click the **IngredientID** text box, click **Shape Outline**, and then click **Transparent**. Click **Shape Fill**, and then under Theme Colors, click **Dark Purple, Text 2, Lighter 60%**.
- Click the **Quantity** text box. Click the **DESIGN** tab, in the Grouping & Totals group, click **Totals**, and then click **Sum** to add subtotals. Right-click the **subtotal** text box, select **Set Caption**, and then change the text to Total. Click the **subtotal** text box, and then on the **FORMAT** tab, in the Font group, click **Align Right** to change the alignment. Scroll down to the bottom of the report to find the grand total text box (value 84.5), click the text box and then press **Delete**. Make the **RecipeName** text box wide enough to fit all the text for every record (scroll to find **Gambas al Ajillo (Shrimp with Garlic)** to check the width.
- Close the Group, Sort, and Total pane. Close the report, and then save your changes.

p. Close Access. Submit your file as directed by your instructor.

Problem Solve 1

Student data files needed:

 a02ps1Hotel.accdb

 a02ps1Paradise.jpg

 a02ps1Paradise.thmx

You will save your files as:

 a02ps1Hotel_LastFirst.accdb

a02ps1PdfCharges_LastFirst.pdf

Hotel Reservations

Production & Operations

A database has been started to keep track of the hotel reservations with guest information, reservation information, and additional room charge information. There are no reports, forms, or queries built yet, so the staff feels like the database is not easy to use. You will create reports, forms, and queries to help the staff better manage the data in the database. Complete the following tasks:

a. Start **Access**, and then open the student data file **a02ps1Hotel**. Click the **FILE** tab, and then save the file as an **Access Database** with the name a02ps1Hotel_LastFirst using your last and first name. If necessary, enable the content.

b. Open **tblGuests**, and then add a new record with your last name, first name, address, city, state, zip code, and phone. Close the table.

c. Create a query using **tblReservations** to calculate the average room rate, the minimum room rate, and the maximum room rate for each **DiscountType** of the rooms that are currently reserved. Rename the fields Average Rate, Minimum Rate, and Maximum Rate. Sort the query in **Descending** order by DiscountType. Resize the columns to best fit the data. Save the query as qryDiscountTypeStatistics_initialLastname. Close the query.

d. Use the **Form Wizard** to create a form to enter guest information as well as reservation information. Add all fields from both tables EXCEPT **GuestID** (from either table) and **ReservationID**. The data should be viewed by **Guest information** first, and the subform should be in **Datasheet** layout. Accept all other default options, and then name the form frmGuestReservations_initialLastname and the subform frmGuestSubform_initialLastname.

- Change the form **title** to Guest Reservations. Make the title font size **28** and **bold**.
- Apply the theme **a02ps1Paradise** to all objects in your database. Insert and resize the image **a02ps1Paradise** in your form to the right of the guest fields.
- Resize the **phone number** text field so the entire phone number is fully visible.
- Delete the subform label. Move the **subform** to the left to line up with the labels for the guest fields. Resize the **column widths** in the subform datasheet, and then resize the object so all columns are visible. If necessary, collapse the navigation pane so you see the entire subform.
- Add Created by initial Last name to the form footer. Save the form.

e. Find the record for Elaine Foley. Add a new reservation from the information below.

CheckInDate	1/25/2015
Nights Stay	3
# of Guests	2
Crib	No
Handicapped	No
RoomType	Double (1 king bed)
RoomRate	$289
DiscountType	None

Close the form.

f. Create a query to find all guests who do not have matching reservations. Include the fields **GuestLastName**, **GuestFirstName**, **Address**, **City**, **State**, and **ZipCode**. Sort the query by **GuestLastName** and **GuestFirstName** in **Ascending** order. Save the query as qryGuestsWithoutReservations_initialLastname.
   - Change the font size of the query results to **14**, change the **Alternate Row Color** to theme color **Red, Accent 4, Lighter 60%**, and use AutoFit on all the columns. Close the query, and then save the changes.

g. Create a query that will calculate the total due for each guest based on the number of nights they have stayed and the room rate for each guest. The results should show the **GuestFirstName**, **GuestLastName**, **NightsStay**, and **RoomRate** in that order. Select only guests who checked in between December 1, 2014 and December 31, 2014 but do not show CheckInDate in your results. Save the query as qryDecemberRoomCharges_initialLastname.
   - Name the new field TotalRoomCharge. Use AutoFit on the new column.
   - Sort the query in **Ascending** order by **GuestLastName**. Close the query, and then save the changes.

h. Use the **Report Wizard** to create a report to show all room charges incurred for each guest (not including the charge for their room). Add the **GuestFirstName**, **GuestLastName**, **ChargeCategory**, and **ChargeAmount** to the report. View the report by **tblGuests**. Sort by **ChargeAmount** in Ascending order. Accept all other default options, and then save the report as rptRoomCharges_initialLastname.
   - Add a subtotal to the **Amount** field, set a caption, and then type Total Charges. Add conditional formatting to the subtotal text box to highlight in **Red** and **Bold** all subtotals that are over $200.
   - Add a caption of Grand Total for the grand total.
   - Change the title to say Room Charges by Guest.
   - Add Created by initial Last name to the report footer. Save and close the report.

i. Save the report as a PDF file and then name it a02ps1PdfCharges_LastFirst.

j. Create a split form from **tblReservations**. Name the form frmReservationSplit_initialLastname. Change the title to Reservations and then bold the title. Add Created by initialLastname to the form footer. Save the form.

k. Close the form, and then exit Access. Submit your file as directed by your instructor.

Problem Solve 2

Student data files needed:

 a02ps2Giftshop.accdb

 a02ps2Giftshop.jpg

 a02ps2Giftshop.thmx

You will save your file as:

 a02ps2Giftshop_LastFirst.accdb

Painted Treasures

Sales & Marketing

The Painted Treasures Gift Shop sells many products for the resort patrons including jewelry, clothing, and spa products. A database has been started to keep track of the customers, purchases, and products. There are no reports, forms, or queries built yet, so the staff feels like the database is not easy to use. You will create reports, forms and queries to help the staff better manage the data in the database. Complete the following tasks:

a. Start **Access**, and open the student data file **a02ps2Giftshop**. Click the **FILE** tab, and then save the file as an **Access Database** with the name a02ps2Giftshop_LastFirst using your last and first name. If necessary, enable the content.

b. Use the **Report Wizard** to create a report showing customers and their purchases. Include **LastName**, **FirstName**, **PurchaseDate**, **Quantity**, **ProductDescription**, **Category**, and **Price**. Accept the default view, and then add no additional grouping. Sort by **Category** and **Product Description**. Save the report as rptCustomerPurchases_initialLastname. Adjust the fields and titles so they are fully visible.
   - Add Created by initial Lastname to the report footer.
   - Change the report title to Customer Purchases.
   - Apply the theme **a02ps2Giftshop** to all objects in the database.

c. Use the Form Wizard to create a form for inputting customers. Select all fields from **tblCustomer**, and then accept all defaults. Name the form frmCustomerInput_initialLastname.
   - Add Created by initial Lastname to the form footer.
   - Change the form title to Customer Input.
   - Click the **label** and **text box** for CustomerID and delete them.
   - Adjust the right margin of **LastName** to be as narrow as FirstName. Adjust the right margin of **StreetAddress** to be as narrow as City.
   - Change the Shape Fill for **LastName** and **FirstName** to be **Red, Accent 2, Lighter 80%**.
   - Insert the image **a02ps2PaintedTreasures** into the form. Resize it, and then move it so the top lines up with **LastName** and it fits in the form.
   - Use the form to change the first record to have your last name and first name.

d. Create a query to see which customers made multiple purchases (Hint: This is a Find Duplicates Query). Show all fields available. Save the query as qryMultiplePurchases_initialLastname. Sort in **Ascending** order by CustomerID and PurchaseID.

e. Create a query to see if any customers have made no purchases. Show **LastName**, **FirstName** and **ResortHotelRoom**. Save the query as qryCustomerWithoutPurchase_initialLastname.

f. Create a query to find customers who made purchases but who have no ResortHotelRoom. Show **LastName**, **FirstName**, **PurchaseDate**. Do not show ResortHotelRoom. Sort in **Ascending** order by LastName and FirstName. Adjust the fields so that all fields are fully visible. Save the query as qryNonGuestPurchases_initialLastname.

g. Create a query to show customers who have purchased **Indigo5** or **Spa** category products in January 2015. Show **LastName**, **FirstName**, **PurchaseDate**, and **Category**. Sort in **Ascending** order by LastName and FirstName. Use AutoFit on the fields. Save the query as qrySpaIndigoJanuary_initialLastname.

h. Create a query to calculate the extended amount for each product purchased. Include **PurchaseID**, **PurchaseDate**, **PurchaseLine**, **Quantity**, **ProductDescription**, and **Price**. Save the query as qryExtendedAmount_initialLastname.
   - Add a new calculated field to the query to calculate each product's extended amount due based on the quantity and the price. Name the new field ExtendedAmount. Sort in **Ascending** order by PurchaseID. Use AutoFit on all fields. Save the changes, and then close the query.

i. Use the **Report Wizard** to create a report showing a complete purchase. Include all the fields from **qryExtendedAmount_initialLastName**. Group by **PurchaseID**. Sort in **Ascending** order by PurchaseLine. Change orientation to **Landscape**, accept all other default options, and then name the report as rptPurchases_initialLastname.
   - Add Created by initial Lastname to the report footer.
   - Change the title to Purchase Report.
   - Click on **ExtendedAmount**, and then add a sum. Open the Property Sheet pane, and then change the format to **Currency**. Add a caption, and then change it to read Total

Purchase. Repeat for the grand total, and then change the caption to read Grand Total Purchases.

- Change the subtotal **Total Purchase** caption and text box to bold with a Shape Fill of **Red, Accent 2, Lighter 80%**.
- Change the grand total **caption** and text box to bold with a Shape Fill of **Red, Accent 2, Lighter 60%**,
- Save and close the report, and then close Access. Submit your file as directed by your instructor.

Perform 1: Perform in Your Life

Student data file needed:

Blank Access database

You will save your file as:

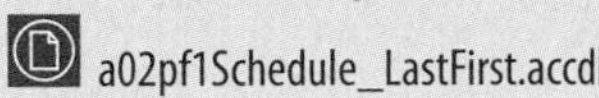

Class Schedule

One way to stay organized during the semester is to keep track of your schedule. You will create a database of all your classes and grades. The database should track the class information, your personal schedule, and the location of the class. To use this for more than one semester, you will keep each of the data in separate tables.

Once the tables are created, you will set up forms to make data entry easier, run queries to get more information, and create reports to help you manage your schedule. For each report, query, or form, make the object attractive and meaningful. You will start by adding data from your current schedule.

a. Start **Access**, and then click the **Blank desktop database**. Save the database as a02pf1Schedule_LastFirst.

b. To keep track of class information, design a table that includes fields for at least the class number, class description, credits offered, and professor name. Assign an appropriate primary key, and then save the table as tblClasses.

c. Add the class information for your classes from last semester, or fictitious classes, if necessary. Add at least six classes to the table. Use AutoFit on the columns so all text is visible.

d. To keep track of your class locations, design a table that includes fields for the building number, building name, and campus the building is located on. Assign an appropriate primary key, and then save the table as tblBuilding.

e. Add the location of the classes you entered in Step c. Include at least three different locations. Use AutoFit on the columns so all text is visible.

f. To keep track of your schedule, design a table that includes fields for the class number, semester, meeting days, meeting time, location, midterm grade (as a number), and Final Grade (as a number). Use AutoFit on the columns so all text is visible. Assign an appropriate primary key, and then save the table as tblSchedule.

g. Enter last semester's schedule, or a fictitious one, that includes at least six classes in at least three different locations. The classes and locations should be the ones entered in tblClasses and tblBuildings.

h. Create relationships as appropriate for tblSchedule, tblClasses, and tblBuilding.

i. You would like to be able to enter all your class and schedule information at one time. Create one form that will allow you to enter all the information. Save the form as frmSchedule_initialLastname.

j. Use the form to enter a new record for this semester. You should enter all the information except your grade. Add a new theme to the form, change the title to something more meaningful than the form name, add Created by initial Lastname to the form footer. Save and close the form.

k. You would like to see each class individually as well as all the class records at once. Create a form that will show you this view of the data. Change the form title to something meaningful. Save the form as frmClasses_initialLastname.

l. You want to find out what your average midterm grade and average final grade was each semester. Even though grades are only entered for one semester, create a query to perform this calculation.
   - Rename the fields to something more meaningful, and then format the fields to show only two decimal places. Sort the query by Semester in **Descending** order. Save the query as qryAverageGrades_initialLastname.

m. You want a schedule of last semester's classes only. Create a query that will show you last semester's classes, the instructor, and where and when it occurred. Save the query as qrySchedule_initialLastname.

n. Create a report that will show you last semester's schedule organized by each day. Sort it in order of class time.
   - Make sure all the fields print on one page of the report and that all the fields are visible. Add Created by initial Lastname to the report footer. Save the report as rptSchedule_initialLastname.

o. You want to know how to schedule your weekends. Create a query to see if you have classes after 9 a.m. on Friday. Save the query as qryFridayClasses_initialLastname.

p. You also want to know your average grade for your classes between midterm and final. Create a query to calculate the average grade in each class. Sort the query by an appropriate field. Save the query as qryGrades_initialLastname.

q. You want to print a report to show your parents your grades by class for the semester, including the average grade. Create a report that shows the class number, description, credits, midterm, final, and average grade for each class. Sort by an appropriate field. Resize all labels so all the text is visible. Change the title to something more appropriate. Save the report as rptGrades_initialLastname.
   - Add Created by initial Lastname to the report footer. Highlight all average grades over 90. Save and close the report.

r. Close Access. Submit your file as directed by your instructor.

Perform 2: Perform in Your Career

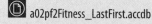

Student data file needed:

a02pf2Fitness.accdb

You will save your file as:

 a02pf2Fitness_LastFirst.accdb

Fitness Center

Production & Operations

A new fitness center has opened and is developing a database for keeping track of members. So far the fitness center has two tables for Membership information and Member information, and another table with Roster Information. It has no queries, forms, or reports created, so the center has asked you to help answer some questions with queries, make data entry easier with forms, and print some reports for reference. For each report, query, or form, make the object attractive and meaningful.

a. Start **Access**, and open the student data file **a02pf2Fitness**. Save the database as a02pf2Fitness_LastFirst.

b. Open each table, and then familiarize yourself with the fields. Open the **Relationships** window, and then note how the tables are related.

c. The staff wants to be able to enter all new member and roster information in the database at one time. Create a form that will allow them to enter the member records and the related membership records for a new member. Give the form a meaningful name. Add **Created by initial Lastname** to the report footer. Save the form as **frmMemberInput_initialLastname**.

d. Using frmMemberInput, enter yourself as a member. Use your actual name and address; all other information can be fictitious. Join the club today and have your membership end a year from now.

e. The staff wants to know how old each member is (in whole numbers) as of the date they joined the club. This will help them plan age-appropriate activities. Create a query to calculate the age of each member as of the date they joined the club. (Hint: When you subtract one date from the other, you get a total number of days, not years.) Save the query as **qryMemberAge_initialLastname**.

f. The manager wants to know which membership types are creating the most revenue and are the most popular. Create a query to calculate the total number of each membership type and the total fees collected for each membership type. Format the query so the manager will understand exactly what each field represents. Save the query as **qryMembershipStatistics_initialLastname**.

g. The manager would like to know if any membership types have not been applied for. Find any membership types that are not assigned to a current member. Save the query as **qryMembershipTypesUnused_initialLastname**.

h. The staff likes to celebrate birthdays at the club. Assume the current year is 2014. Everyone born in 1974 will turn 40 this year, and the staff would like a list of all those members along with their actual birthdays so they can quickly see who is celebrating a birthday each day. Save the query as **qry1974Birthdays_initialLastname**.

i. The staff likes to see each member's data as an individual record while still being able to view the whole table of data. Create a form that will allow the staff to view the data this way. Add **Created by initial Lastname** to the form footer. Give the form a meaningful name. Save the form as **frmMemberRecords_initialLastname**.

j. The staff needs a master list of members with their membership information. Create a report that will show the relevant information so the staff knows who is a current member and what kinds of membership each person has. Save the report as **rptExpirationDates_initialLastname**.
   - Add **Created by initial Lastname** to the report footer. Change the report title to something meaningful.
   - Modify rptExpirationDates_initialLastname so the records are grouped by the month of the expiration date. Highlight the expiration date field with a color so it stands out from the other fields.

k. The staff needs a list of members with the facilities their membership gives them access to. Create a report so the staff can quickly locate a member's name and determine which facilities they are allowed to access. Save the report as **rptFacilities_initialLastname**.
   - Add **Created by initial Lastname** to the report footer.
   - Change the report theme, change the report title to something other than the name of the report, and save the report.

l. Close Access. Submit your file as directed by your instructor.

Perform 3: Perform in Your Team

Student data file needed:

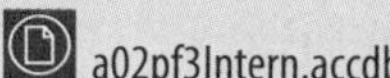

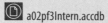

a02pf3Intern.accdb

You will save your files as:

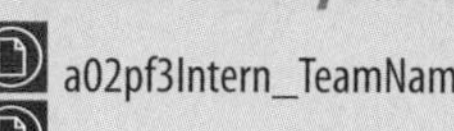

a02pf3Intern_TeamName.accdb

a02pf3InternPlan_TeamName.docx

Internships Coordination

Human Resources

You take a job with an organization that matches students from Indiana schools to internship opportunities. The database you use keeps track of the companies that offer internships, the potential intern's information, and interview information dates for the interns. You are often called upon to add new records to the table, find information for a company or intern, and provide reports for your staff. Currently there are no reports, forms, or queries, so you will have to build them from the existing data. For all reports, queries, and forms, use meaningful names, and make the objects attractive.

Because databases can only be opened and edited by one person at a time, it is a good idea to plan ahead. You will use a Word document to plan your database and to plan which team member will do what. You will use SkyDrive to store your Word document and Access database.

a. Select one team member to set up the Word document and Access database by completing Steps b–e.

b. Open your browser, navigate to **https://www.skydrive.live.com**, create a new folder, and name it a02pf3Intern_TeamName using the name assigned to your team by your instructor.

c. Start **Access**, and open the student data file **a02pf3Interns**. Save the database as a02pf3Intern_TeamName replacing TeamName with the name assigned to your team by your instructor. If necessary, enable the content.

d. Upload the **a02pf3Intern_TeamName** database to the a02pf3InternshipsFolder_TeamName folder, and then share the folder with the other members of your team. Make sure that the other team members have permission to edit the contents of the shared folder and that they are required to log in to SkyDrive to access it.

e. Create a new Word document in the assignment folder in SkyDrive, and then name it a02pf3InternPlan_TeamName using the name assigned to your team by your instructor.

f. In the Word document, each team member must list his or her first and last name as well as a summary of their planned contributions. As work is completed on the database, this document should be updated with the specifics of each team member's contributions.

g. Open each table, and then familiarize yourself with the fields. Open the Relationships window, and then note how the tables are related.

h. Create a form to enter data for new interns and their upcoming interviews. Pick a theme to apply to all objects in the database. Save the form as frmInterns and the subform as frmInternSubform.

i. Each team member should add his or her name as a new intern with one interview date and company of your choice.

j. You are scheduling for January and March and need to know which students already have interviews scheduled for those months, as well as the interview date and company the interview is with. Create a query, and then save it as qryJanuaryOrMarch.

k. Indiana University Purdue University Indianapolis (IUPUI) would like to know which of its students have interviews with Del Monte Foods Company or MMI Marketing and when those interviews are scheduled. Create a query, and then save it as qryIUPUI.

l. Your boss wants to know the total number of interns in the database from each university. Create a **query** with descriptive field names, and then sort appropriately to provide this information. Save the query as qrySchoolCount.

m. In the past, there have been problems with interns being scheduled more than once with the same company or scheduled for interviews on the same day. You need to find all students who have multiple interviews scheduled to check for conflicts. Create a query, and then save it as qryMultipleInterviews.

n. Your boss has asked for a master list of all interns who have interviews scheduled. He would like to be able to look up a student in the report to see when their interview is and who the interview is with. Save the report as rptInterviewsScheduled.

o. You need a report that counts and highlights how many interviews are scheduled each month. The report should also show the interview date and intern information. Save the report as rptInterviewDates.

p. When a company comes to interview, you need to quickly find who the interview is with. Create a report that will provide a master list of interviews that allows you to quickly see who is interviewing with each company. Save the report as rptCompanySchedule.

q. You would like to stay one step ahead of your boss. Create two more queries that may be helpful in analyzing the database information. Name the queries something descriptive so your boss will know what information is provided.

r. Once the assignment is complete, share the **a02pf3InternFolder_TeamName** folder with your instructor. Make sure that your instructor has permission to edit the contents of the folder.

Perform 4: How Others Perform

Student data file needed:

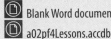

Blank Word document

a02pf4Lessons.accdb

You will save your file as:

a02pf4Answers_LastFirst.docx

Music Lessons

Production & Operations

You have just taken a new job in a music store, and one of your responsibilities is to manage the music instructors and their students. A database has been created, but as you run the queries you notice they are either missing data or have wrong results. Answer the following questions about each of the objects as completely as possible:

a. Start **Access**, and open the student data file **a02pf4Lessons**.

b. Create a Word document a02pf4Answers_LastFirst where you will answer the questions.

c. Open rptListOfTeachers. Why is the image repeated after each record? How could the image have been added to the report so it would not repeat like that?

d. Open qryGuitarPianoAndBeginners. The query is supposed to show all teachers who are teaching piano or guitar and are taking new students. Why are other records in the results? Switch to **Design** view, and then explain how you would correct the query criteria to show the correct results.

e. Open qryLessonTimes. The query is supposed to show the average lesson length for each teacher. Instead, the query shows different lesson times for each teacher. What is wrong with this query, and how can you fix it to show the average lesson length for each teacher?

f. Open rptLessonList. Can you tell what the report is grouped by and sorted by without looking at the Group, Sort, and Total pane? Describe how you would change the grouping to group by Instrument.

g. Open qryInstrumentList. The query was supposed to find all teacher names, student names, and the instrument the student plays. Instead there are over 200 records. What happened, and why did this happen? How can you fix the query so it will provide the information you really want?

h. Open frmStudents. This form was created to see only one student at a time. Why is it showing one student and the whole student table? How was this form created? How would you create the form with only one student record at a time?

i. Submit your file as directed by your instructor.

Microsoft Office PowerPoint 2013
Module 1
Understanding the Art of Presentation

WORKSHOP 1 | PRESENTATION FUNDAMENTALS

OBJECTIVES

1. Plan your presentation with a purpose for an intended outcome p. 798
2. Define the purpose, scope, and audience of a presentation p. 799
3. Plan the presentation content p. 803
4. Work with the PowerPoint window and views p. 807
5. Navigate in Slide Show view and Outline view p. 811
6. Understand the difference between a theme and a template p. 815
7. Create a presentation from a template p. 820
8. Add and delete slides, change slide layouts, and rearrange slides p. 825
9. Edit slides and move slide content p. 829
10. Replace words using the Research pane p. 831
11. Save a presentation p. 832
12. Preview and print a presentation p. 833

Prepare Case

The Red Bluff Golf Course & Pro Shop Putts for Paws Golf Tournament Presentation

Sales & Marketing

The Red Bluff Golf Course & Pro Shop hosts a tournament each year to benefit the Santa Fe Animal Center. Golf pro John Schilling speaks at community meetings, such as the Community Club and Women's Business Council, to gather sponsors and golfers. He asked you to assist him with the Putts for Paws tournament this year. Your first assignment is to review and update the PowerPoint presentation he uses during his speeches. This is a persuasive presentation, but it also provides basic information, such as the time, date, and cost of the tournament, sponsorship opportunities, and special events.

sattahipbeach / Shutterstock.com

REAL WORLD SUCCESS

"I was in a job interview for a major investment banking firm. After they had asked me all the basic skills questions about spreadsheets and databases, they asked me if I had any design experience, which was not included in the original job description. I was able to tell them that I had training in presentation design for target audiences. They were pleasantly surprised, and they offered me the job."

- Tanya, recent graduate

Student data files needed for this workshop:

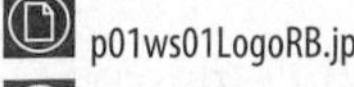

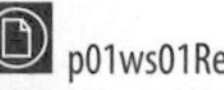

p01ws01LogoRB.jpg
p01ws01RedBluff.potx
p01ws01RedBluffBG.jpg
p01ws01Sponsor.pptx
p01ws01SponsorOLD.pptx
p01ws01SponsorStory.docx

You will save your files as:

p01ws01Sponsor_LastFirst.pptx
p01ws01Sponsor2_LastFirst.pptx
p01ws01SponsorPDF_LastFirst.pdf
p01ws01SponsorShow_LastFirst.ppsx

Understanding the Purpose of PowerPoint

Microsoft Office PowerPoint 2013 is a software application that enables you to efficiently build professional quality presentations that allow your audience to see what you are saying. PowerPoint is a visual and emotive aid used by a presenter. Adding a visual component to your presentation adds impact and helps make your presentation memorable. That is the primary reason to use presentation software. Unfortunately, many people use PowerPoint when they have nothing to say, pretending the slide show will do all the work for them. You have probably seen many presentations and may have even developed some of your own. Visual aids such as marks on a whiteboard or chalkboard, a test tube full of bubbling liquid, or a computer slide show support the speaker, but they cannot stand on their own; you must have a message that is compelling enough to ask for the attention of others.

Presentations are typically displayed on large screens for audiences; however, there are many creative ways to use PowerPoint. Kiosks, for example, are common in public locations such as malls, banks, hotels, zoos, or museums, and can display self-running PowerPoint presentations that provide information or display advertisements. PowerPoint is a versatile tool that can help you vividly communicate your message. In this section, you will explore PowerPoint and get a sense of how it can be used to enhance your presentation.

Plan Your Presentation with a Purpose for an Intended Outcome

PowerPoint presentations can help you communicate with your audience. Slides add interest and variety to your presentation. Because of the visual nature of the slides, your audience is able to grasp more information. Well-built presentations organize thoughts, stimulate interest, clarify and substantiate your message, reinforce what you say, and often motivate your audience to take some form of action.

SS REAL WORLD ADVICE | **Defining Your Target Audience**

Defining your **target audience** is important to effectively plan your presentation. Asking yourself a few starting questions can help identify your audience.

- Why were you invited to speak?
- Why is the topic important to the audience?
- What do they know about the topic? How will they use the information?
- How large is the audience? What is the physical layout of the presentation room?
- How long are you expected to speak?

Informing Your Audience

Generally, the purpose of your presentations will fall into one of three major categories. The first, an informational presentation, provides facts and figures to your audience. A fiscal report in business is an example of an informational presentation. The slides in a financial report may show business income and expense, perhaps employing charts and tables for the audience. Another example of an informational presentation is a museum kiosk, giving information about artists, their methods, and the history of the artwork. Yet another example is a class lecture, where objectives, concepts, examples, and questions for discussion are organized. When you provide information to your audience, you need to know what they already know about the topic and how you can support their needs.

Persuading Your Audience

The second purpose of a presentation is to persuade your audience. While this type of presentation may contain elements such as facts and figures, your main objective will be to appeal to members of the audience to persuade them to agree with you. Sales and political presentations are examples of persuasive presentations. Whenever you try to generate support for an idea, fund a proposal, or get people to change their beliefs about something, you are making a persuasive presentation. For this type of audience you need to know their expectations, biases for or against the topic, and how you relate to them on a personal level. You will need to address what your audience is resisting with regard to your position, address what the risks are, and how they will be rewarded for taking such risks.

MODULE 1

Preparing Your Audience

The third purpose of a presentation is to prepare your audience. In this case you may be preparing them for bad times, such as layoffs, or you may be preparing them for good times by cross-training them to do a different type of job. You will include important information and also help them to understand the circumstances they will encounter. When you prepare your audience, you need to know what their expectations are, and what they know about the topic.

CONSIDER THIS | Are There Mixed Purposes?

Can a presentation have a mixture of purposes? Or, if you begin with the purpose of persuading an audience, is it possible to also inform them? What role do your biases have in the purpose? Can an informational presentation really be devoid of persuasion? If you are preparing an audience, are you also informing them?

Telling a Story

Universally, your audience is concerned about "What is in it for me?" Your presentation should focus on answering this question while addressing what you want them to know. PowerPoint expert Cliff Atkinson, author of "Beyond Bullet Points" says, "Your audience doesn't care as much about your company history as they do about whether you can help them solve the specific problems they face. Write a script for your presentation that makes the audience the protagonist, or the main character, who faces a problem that you will help to solve."

Good presenters are often great story tellers and a pleasure to listen to. Good stories create a sense of tension that is somehow resolved. Chip and Dan Heath, authors of the bestseller "Made to Stick: Why Some Ideas Die and Others Survive," encourage presenters to generate unexpected "sticky" ideas: to "break patterns, create mystery, build unique stories, and find knowledge gaps." Give them something unexpected. Make them think. Stir up controversy, challenge their beliefs. Darrell Zahorsky, former About.com Guide, says to use these techniques as a method to "wake them up." Do not do what everybody else does. Your job is to stand out.

Define the Purpose, Scope, and Audience of a Presentation

Every presentation begins with planning. According to David A. Peoples, author of "Presentations Plus," "Ninety-five percent of how well your presentation is going to go is determined before you even start." Start by defining the purpose of your presentation. Be specific, and use action words as you list objectives. Determine the outcome you expect from the audience. Allow approximately four hours of planning time for each hour of presentation time. Clear thinking about what your objectives are, the type of content you will include, and the composition of the audience will assist you in creating a slide show that truly serves your purpose. In this section you will prepare a presentation using tools to help you develop your content.

As you define your objectives for the presentation, be specific. Ask such questions as:

- What is your purpose? To persuade? Inform? Prepare?
- Why is the topic important?

- Why should the audience be interested?
- What is in it for the audience?
- What do you expect the audience to do after your presentation?

Use paper sticky notes to brainstorm the possible main ideas for your presentation. Do not try to edit these ideas in the early stages; just generate ideas. When you reach a point where no more ideas come to mind, then begin eliminating some of the ideas. Your goal is to focus your presentation on two to five main ideas. Translate these ideas into action verb objectives, such as "update our computer systems," or "increase workflow by 15%." The objectives will determine the **content** of the presentation, determine the scope or level of detail, and enable you to give an effective presentation.

With the objectives clearly stated, continue to add sticky notes to develop the subtopics of the presentation. These subtopics will likely become the titles on your slides and will make the content of your presentation meaningful because they directly relate to the objectives. Consider the order of the subtopics, and try to provide organization so you can lead your audience through the presentation and achieve the purpose you have defined. You must understand and be clear about what needs to be communicated. If you are unsure, your audience will be, too.

Opening PowerPoint

In this section you will open the file for the Red Bluff Putts for Paws Golf Tournament, look at the beginning of a presentation, and review the objectives for the presentation.

P01.00

To Open a Presentation

a. From the Start screen or desktop, point to the **bottom-right** corner of the screen. The Charms will be displayed on the right side of the screen. Note the labels underneath each of the charms. Click the **Search** charm. Click inside the **search** box at the top of the page. Type PowerPoint.

b. Click **PowerPoint 2013** in the search results. The PowerPoint Start screen displays.

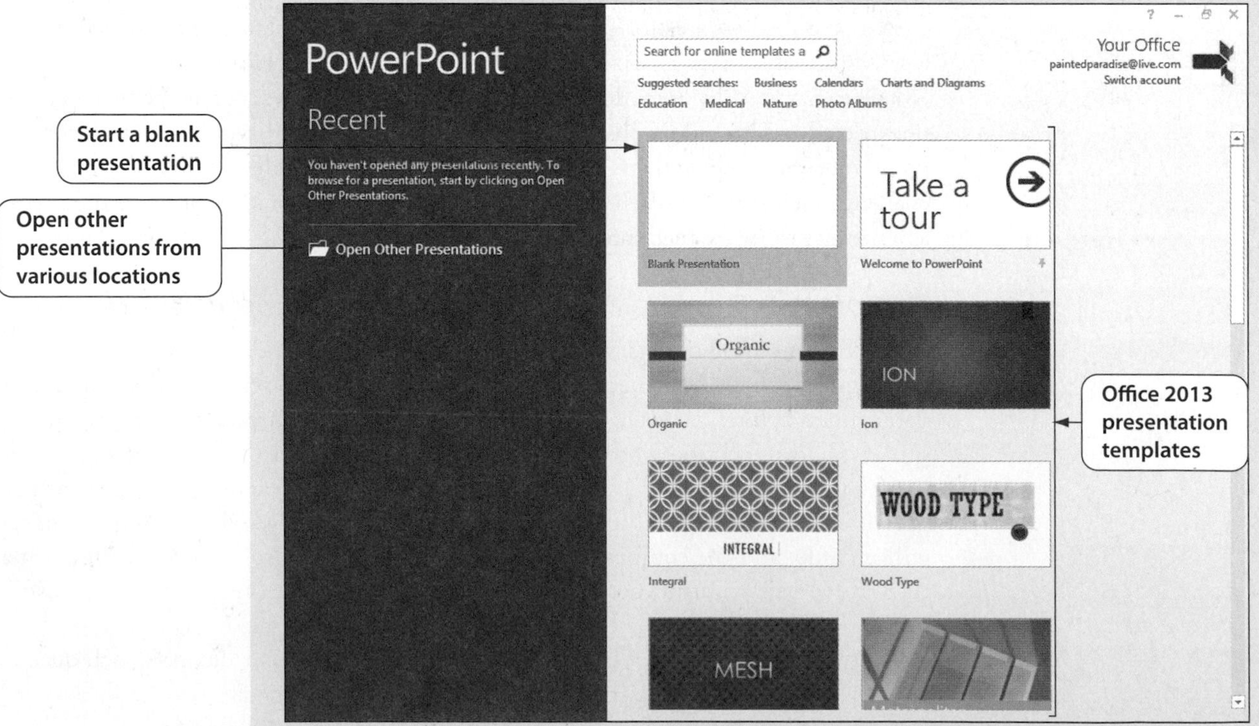

Figure 1 PowerPoint Start Screen

MODULE 1

c. Click **Open Other Presentations**. Under Open, click **Computer**.

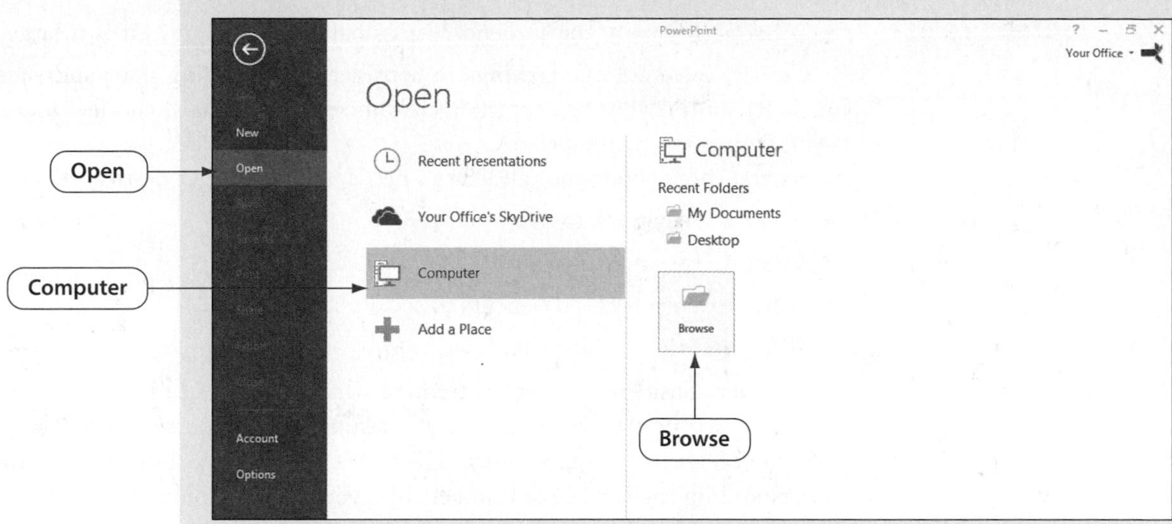

Figure 2 PowerPoint Backstage view

d. Under Computer, click **Browse**. Navigate to where your student data files are located, click **p01ws01Sponsor**, and then click **Open**.

e. Click the **FILE** tab, and save the file in the location where you are saving your files with the name p01ws01Sponsor_LastFirst, using your last and first name.

SIDE NOTE
Saving Files
Save the file with a new name so you will have the original in case you need to start over. Save often.

REAL WORLD ADVICE — Pecha Kucha Presentations

Pecha Kucha, pronounced *"pe-CHALK-cha,"* is a unique format for presentations, first used in Tokyo, Japan, in 2003. This type of presentation automatically displays 20 slides, for 20 seconds each, during which the presenter speaks. While this trend in presentations began with architects, it has spread worldwide, and now Pecha Kucha nights cover topics such as travels, artwork, business, and research. Practicing a Pecha Kucha presentation can help you become a better presenter by being more concise and clear in a short period of time. To give effective short presentations such as Pecha Kucha you must start early while planning! Think about how Pecha Kucha relates to various online videos you have seen and how it relates to presentation planning.

Considering the Target Audience and Their Needs

Figuring out the characteristics of an audience enables you to produce a presentation that is worthwhile to the audience and achieves your objectives. Many characteristics can help you to shape your presentation. Consider these questions:

- Why are they listening to your presentation?
- What are the attitudes they have about your topic?
- What do they know about the topic?
- What are the constraints? Are they political? Financial? Knowledge based?
- How will they use the information you present?

- What are the demographics of the audience? Number of people? Location of the presentation? What technical equipment is available? Will you have a microphone? Computer? Projector?
- What is the size of the audience? Is it small and intimate? Or is it large and formal?

Clearly, there are many things to consider, but knowing your audience will enable you to streamline your presentation, customize the materials, and feel more comfortable as you deliver the presentation.

As you think about your audience's needs, answer these questions:

- What do they want to hear?
- What do they need to know?
- What are the potential benefits to the audience?
- What questions might they have?

Another consideration is to determine what the audience members are doing before and after your presentation. Are they listening to another speaker? Are they about to go home or return to their desks? Have they had lunch? Put yourself in their shoes. Understanding their frame of mind enables you to better prepare to meet their needs.

CONSIDER THIS | How Many Audiences Do You Really Have?

Will you have only one target audience or multiple audiences in your presentation? Should you plan your presentation around all the different potential audiences or just your main target audience?

Understanding Commonality with Your Audience

Understanding the relationships you have with the audience and the relationships they have with each other helps you to set the tone for your presentation. You may find yourself making a presentation to your superiors, in which case you will want to make suggestions related to the topic so they can make an informed decision. Another audience might be made up of your peers or team members. You will want to engage these audience members by having them share their experiences or expertise. Use "we" language, such as "We can improve our customer service by responding to calls within 1 minute." Special interest groups expect you to focus on their concerns as they relate to your topic.

Anticipating Audience Expectations

Audiences anticipate that you have expertise in your topic area. This may call for concentrated study so you have a complete knowledge of the subject matter. This additional study can add significant time to your preparation for the presentation. The audience will ask you questions. Anticipating their questions and adding them to the planning of the presentation helps the audience to understand your topic more clearly.

An audience that is interested in your topic is concerned with what additional information you can provide. For this kind of presentation you can focus on teaching them about your topic. Another audience may not be quite as interested and may need to be involved in some way with your presentation. Group work or discussions are often the key in this situation. Still another audience will be uninterested in your presentation but forced to attend. With this group, strive to include them, too, maybe even directly, but if you have not established a common ground then this may backfire. Stay true to the purpose and objectives of your presentation.

Understanding Your Audience's Interaction with the Presentation

The expectation of most audiences is that your topic will be presented with few surprises, cover points A through D, and end on time. Planning for interaction should extend well beyond the standard question-and-answer period. Creatively develop activities that draw the audience into the presentation. Use a variety of visual aids, including PowerPoint slide shows, to explain concepts. Bring in a object that everyone can hold. Pass out specially made fortune cookies with questions about your topic for the audience to consider. Keep in mind that people remember much more when visual aids are used in the presentation.

As you plan for organization in your presentation, begin by telling the audience what you are going to discuss. Remember that first impressions do count. Capture the attention of the audience by establishing common ground. Often, presentations outline the objectives or major topic areas first. Next, follow through and talk about each item you said you would discuss in the same order. Finally, review what you have discussed as a summary of the presentation. Finish strong with a call to action or an appeal that supports your purpose for the presentation.

REAL WORLD ADVICE — Everyone Needs a Road Map

You can help to organize the thinking of your audience by providing a road map of your presentation. Set the tone early to draw them in to listening to you during the presentation instead of reading a lot of text; consider sharing a picture or graphic that invokes the tone of the presentation. The bulleted list you had in mind can be given to them verbally. The road map should be a part of the beginning of the presentation, and then you can do a short recap at the end to remind the audience of the important parts in the presentation.

Plan the Presentation Content

Once you have your script, you can begin to visualize your ideas. Developed by the Walt Disney Studio during the 1930s, storyboards are often used in business today to plan ad campaigns, web sites, and interactive user interfaces. Storyboards are conceptual drawings of your story, much like a comic book. Using a storyboard can enable you to plan and visualize how everything comes together in a scene or sequence of shots, to use the film industry analogy. Being an artist is not a prerequisite to using storyboards to plan your presentations. Quick drawings suffice and remind you of elements you want to include. Importantly, the best presentations are visual and not all text on the screen. Storyboarding also takes your concentration away from typing on the keyboard back to the visual the audience will see. Remember, PowerPoint presentations are not your notes but rather visual aids.

Using a Storyboard

Typically, storyboards are composed of three panels situated left to right: content, layout or action, and audio/visual elements, but this is not a rule. Storyboards should include information about your script, props or visual aids, backgrounds, and transitions. In this section, you will review a storyboard for the Red Bluff Putts for Paws Golf Tournament and review the objectives in this presentation.

MyITLab®
Workshop 1 Training

P01.01

To Review a Storyboard

a. Point to the **bottom-right** corner of the Start screen. On the Charms bar, click the **Search** charm. Click inside the **search** box at the top of the page and type Word.

b. Click **Word 2013**.

c. Click **Open Other Documents**. Then under Open, click **Computer**.

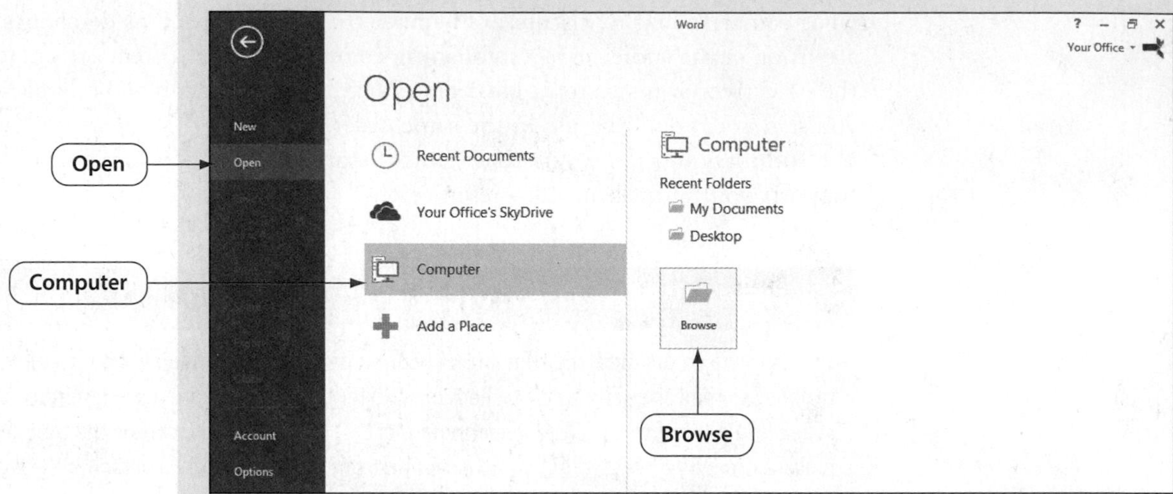

Figure 3 Word Backstage view

d. Under Computer, click **Browse**. Navigate to where your student data files are located, click **p01ws01SponsorStory**, and then click **Open**.

e. Scroll through the document, making note of the content, layout, and visual elements planned for each slide. Notice the progression from opening material about logistics, to the golfer incentives, corporate incentives, and contact information.

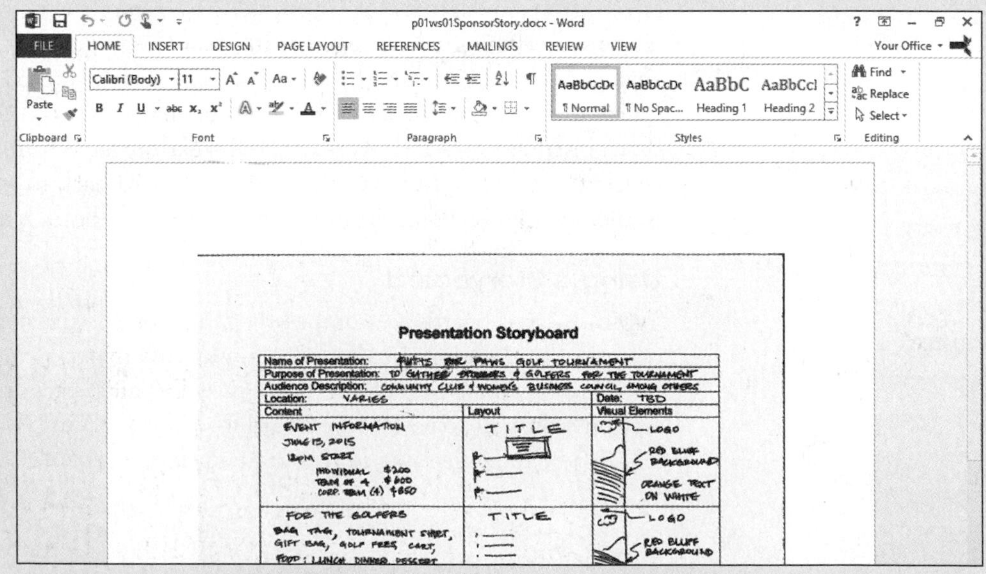

Figure 4 Sponsors Storyboard

f. **Close** ☒ Word.

As you build your story, keep in mind that you are the focus of the audience. The presentation text and graphics will assist the audience in seeing what you are communicating. People cannot listen and read at the same time. Thus, any text should be minimal and thoroughly edited to include only the main points or key terms. Complete sentences, with the exception of quotations, should be avoided as slide content. When complete sentences are used, the presenter must allow silence during the presentation to give the audience time to read before listening to the presenter. Think like a headline writer, distilling the content down to the essence of the topic. You want the audience to read and understand your slide in less than 10 seconds. People also like numbers in presentation content, such as "Four Hot Tips" or "Three Steps to Success." This helps you to organize content in a way that the audience will recall.

You have probably heard a picture is worth a thousand words, and in fact, media elements such as photographs, video, audio, charts, and graphics should be the bulk of your presentation. Media can be used to summarize, demonstrate, inject humor, clarify, and reinforce what has been said. As often as possible use pictures to replace words. Instead, keep it modern with well-chosen, professional-quality photos.

Using Anecdotes and Quotations

Anecdotes and quotations support your message and can be used either as an opening or closing statement. They give your presentation credibility. They can convey a startling fact or statistic. Anecdotes, such as stories in the news or experiences you have had, help you connect to your audience by explaining a situation. Quotations that relate to the subject can add humor to your presentation. Be sure to attribute the quotation to the proper person.

Encouraging Audience Participation

One of the reasons why people enjoy giving presentations is to make a connection with the members of the audience. Encouraging audience participation is an important part of your planning. This is one place where the evaluation of the audience comes into play. In a large group environment, you will use different strategies than in a conference room meeting. Remarkably, games are very engaging, and audience members become very active when a simple prize is offered, if appropriate. Asking questions of your audience helps to keep them on their toes and gives you feedback. Be sure to not put someone on the spot or make them feel uncomfortable. Small group discussions are effective if your presentation is educational in nature, or when debate or argument is necessary to make a decision. As with everything else involved with presenting, planning is the key in successful audience participation.

Including Quantitative and Statistical Content

When presenting data, you should resist the urge to put all of the numbers on the screen. If it is necessary for the audience to have all of the numbers, provide handouts. Just as you edited the text content of your presentation, critically review the numerical data and pull out the important numbers, such as the totals, for your slide.

Converting the numbers into a graph often enhances your slide show. It provides information related to trends or quantitative information. The graph can organize the information in a new way. The picture will last longer in the minds of the audience members. A rich visualization will add interest and color to your presentation and can often make a point more clearly than words.

As you create graphs for your presentation, make sure they convey the information in a way the audience can comprehend. Critically view the graphs and determine if the point you wish to make is evident. As you select the type of chart, consider these characteristics:

- **Pie chart**—Parts make up a whole; usually contains percentages
- **Bar** or **column chart**—Compares items in rank or changes over a period of time
- **Line chart**—Changes over time, frequency, or relationship between items

Using Appropriate Media

Good media choices, including graphics, audio, and video, stimulate interest, help you clarify important points, and reinforce what has been said. Poor media choices confuse the audience and distract them from your purposes.

Cliff Atkinson says, "When you overload your audience, you shut down the dialogue that is an important part of decision making." Pointing to research by educational psychologists, he says, "When you remove interesting but irrelevant words and pictures from a screen, you can increase the audience's ability to remember the information by 189% and the ability to apply the information by 109%."

As you select media consider the length of your presentation and the technology available in the presentation room:

- Does the media element completely support your objectives?
- Is the media element clear enough to see and understand?
- Will you have a good Internet connection for loading a web page or a YouTube video?
- Do you want to devote 3–8 minutes to a video?

Be ready to engage the audience regardless of the technology that is available. If the technology does not work as expected, how would you compensate?

Respecting Copyrights

As you select the content for your presentation, it is important to respect copyrights. Copyrights include the rights to reproduce, distribute, create derivative works, perform, and display intellectual property. Many people believe that everything on the Internet is copyright free, but it is not. Works that you create, such as photographs, poems and other writing, music, and video, are copyrighted to you automatically as soon as they are in a fixed format. You have the right to post them on the Internet, sell the work to another party, or display them in any way you see fit. If someone uses your materials without your permission, you have a legal path to follow if you want to protect your copyrights.

Copyright law and the Digital Millennium Copyright Act of 1998 address many aspects of how media elements are protected. A good rule of thumb is to seek permission before using copyrighted elements in your PowerPoint slide shows. Using the Internet, it is easy to research and request permission to use these elements. Often permission to use the elements is granted without cost or restriction, and sometimes you make a direct connection with the person that created the item. In some cases, the copyright holder will request a citation or attribution recognizing their contribution.

REAL WORLD ADVICE | **Citing Sources**

Depending on the presentation's purpose and audience, you should consider citing the sources you used in creating your presentation. Citation formats, such as APA (American Psychological Association), MLA (Modern Language Association), or the *Chicago Manual of Style*, may be recommended by your instructor or supervisor. You can learn more about the formats on the websites for each:

- **APA**—www.apa.org
- **MLA**—www.mla.org
- ***The Chicago Manual of Style***—www.chicagomanualofstyle.org

Work with the PowerPoint Window and Views

PowerPoint allows you to view the presentation from various perspectives. **Normal** view is the default view shown in Figure 5 below and provides the basic layout for presentation preparation. **Outline View** is a view that allows the presentation creator to focus on the content. In the early stages of presentation development, you should first focus on the quality and brevity of content in the presentation.

PowerPoint also has several panes for editing the presentation. On the left side, the **left hand pane** allows you to select a slide. In the middle, the **Slide pane** allows you to edit the text, images, and other objects on the slide. On the bottom, the **Notes pane** allows you to add speaker notes that the audience will not see.

As the tournament manager working with the golf pro at the Red Bluff Golf Course & Pro Shop, you will modify a persuasive presentation previously created for the Red Bluff Golf Course & Pro Shop Putts for Paws Golf Tournament. This presentation will be given by the golf pro to civic groups in the community with the purpose of soliciting financial sponsorship for the tournament, a benefit for the Santa Fe Animal Center. Also, golfers will be encouraged to register for the event. The golf pro has asked you to update the slides for the current year. You begin by reviewing the slide show from the previous year.

P01.02

To Explore PowerPoint and Add Notes

a. Using the file **p01w01Sponsor_LastFirst**, notice PowerPoint is divided into three main areas: the Slide pane, left hand pane, and Notes pane. The Ribbon is across the top of the window. The orange Status bar is across the bottom.

   Click through each slide in the **left hand** pane. Notice the progression from introductory material, to the incentives, to a call to action.

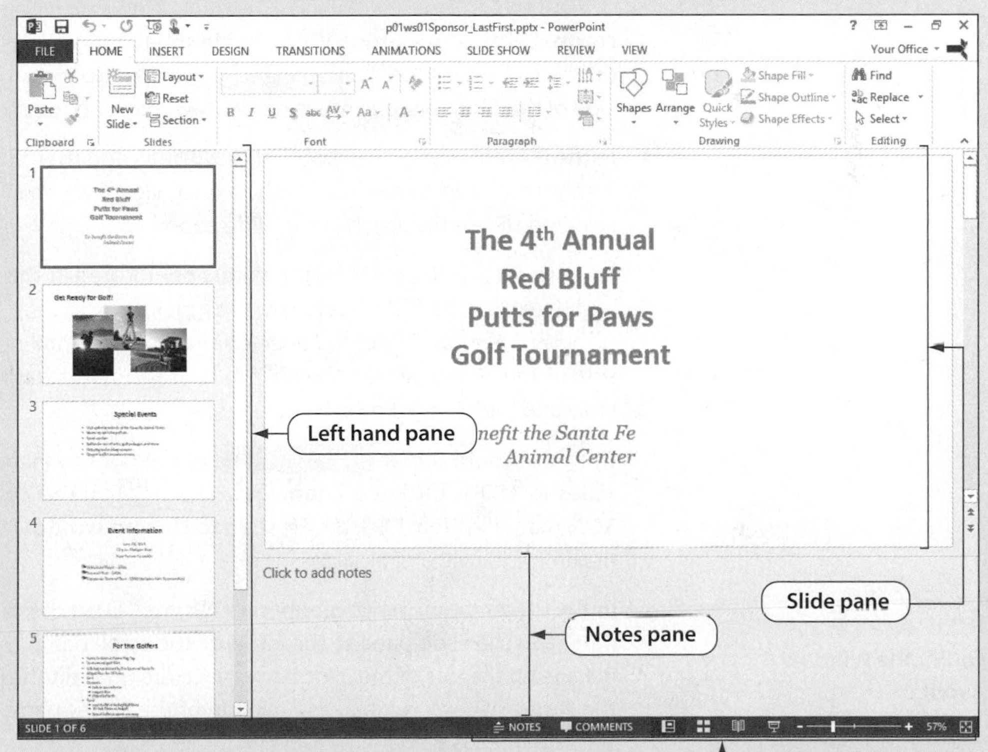

Figure 5 PowerPoint default, Normal View

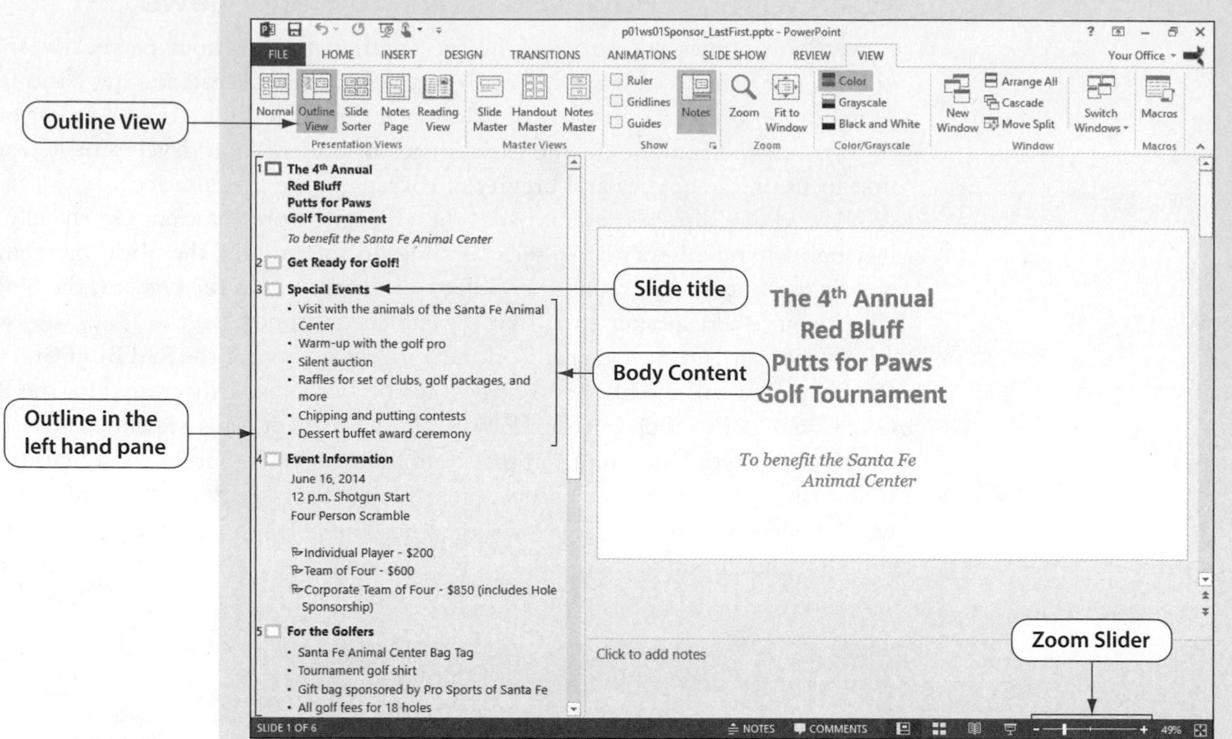

Figure 6 Outline view

b. Click the **VIEW** tab, and then in the Presentation Views group, click **Outline View**. Notice how the left hand pane changes. Outline view enables you to concentrate only on the text content of the slide presentation.

c. **Normal View** and **Outline View** enable you to move quickly between slides by clicking on the slide in the left hand pane that you want to view. Use the scroll bar on the right side of the **Slide** pane to move up or down through the slides.

d. In the Presentation Views group, click **Normal**, and then click the thumbnail for **Slide 2**.
The left hand pane displays thumbnail views of the slides in the presentation. The selected slide is displayed in the Slide pane.

e. Point to each of the areas on the **status bar** located at the bottom-right of the window, and then click the **Slide Sorter** button.
Notice, the number of the selected slide and the total number of slides are on the left side of the status bar. On the right side of the status bar are buttons for changing the view and look of the PowerPoint window.

f. Drag the **Zoom Slider** to the right to increase the magnification of the slides to **150%**. Click the **Zoom Out** button on the Zoom Slider until the slide is at **30%** magnification. Click the **Fit slide to current window** button in the status bar to maximize the view of all slides.

g. In the Presentation Views group, click **Normal**. Drag the **divider** between the left hand pane and the Slide pane to the left until the scroll bar in the left hand pane disappears, increasing the size of the Slide pane. Next, drag the **divider** between the Slide pane and the Notes pane up to increase the size of the Notes pane until the **Zoom level** on the status bar reads **33%**.

h. With **Slide 2** selected in the Slide pane, click the **Notes** pane, and then type Introduction - Name and job title. Press Enter to move to the next line, and then type Purpose - Introduce you to the opportunities for sponsorship of the Putts for Paws Golf

SIDE NOTE

Modify the Window Layout

If you need more room to view and work on the notes, you can drag the dividers to produce more space.

Tournament and to advocate for the needs of the animals and those who care for them at the Santa Fe Animal Center.

The Notes pane contains the speaker's notes for each slide in the presentation. These notes are not seen by the audience when the presentation is displayed. As the presenter, you can print the notes with the slides or use them in the new Presenter view when two displays exist.

i. **Save** the presentation.

Displaying the Presentation in Various Views

PowerPoint can display slides in a variety of views. Each view has a purpose, and the available tools change as you switch between views. Normal view is used to edit the slides. **Slide Sorter view** provides options for rearranging slides and reviewing slide transitions. In Slide Sorter view, you see thumbnails of each of the slides. **Reading view** displays the slides one at a time, offering tools such as the title bar Minimize, Maximize/Restore, and Close buttons, and navigation buttons for moving between slides. **Slide Show view** is used to display the presentation to an audience. The views are accessed using the View tab or the view buttons on the status bar.

P01.03

To Zoom and Display a Presentation in Various Views

a. Click the **Slide Sorter** button on the status bar.

Slide 2 is highlighted with an orange border because it was the slide selected in the previous view. Thumbnails of all six slides in the presentation are displayed.

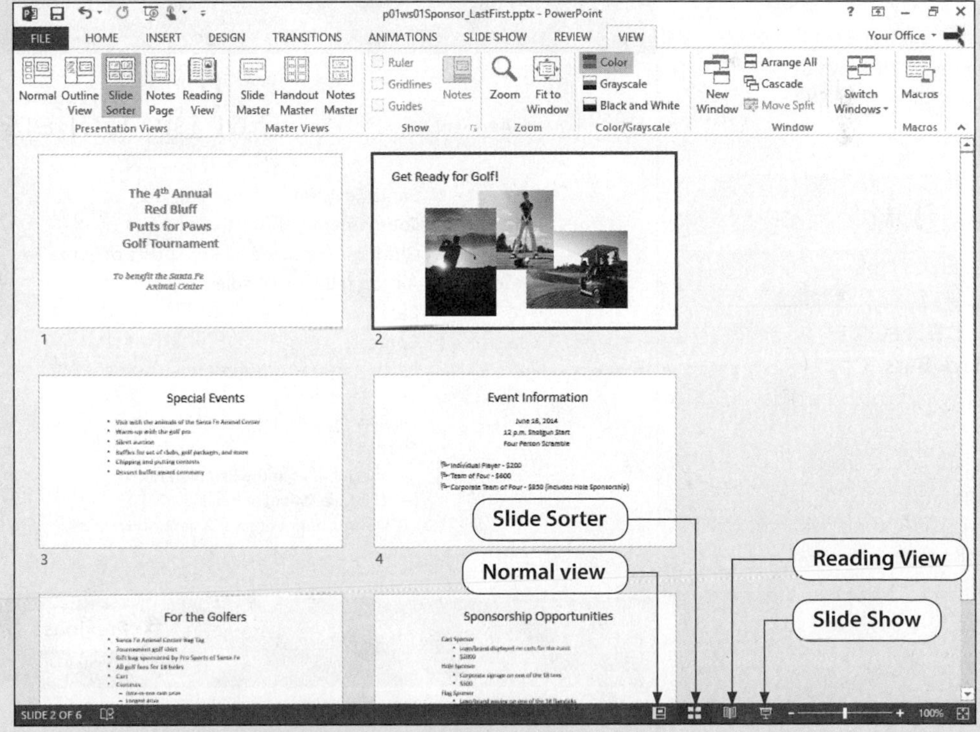

Figure 7 PowerPoint view buttons

b. On the VIEW tab, in the Zoom group, click **Zoom**, and select **50%**.

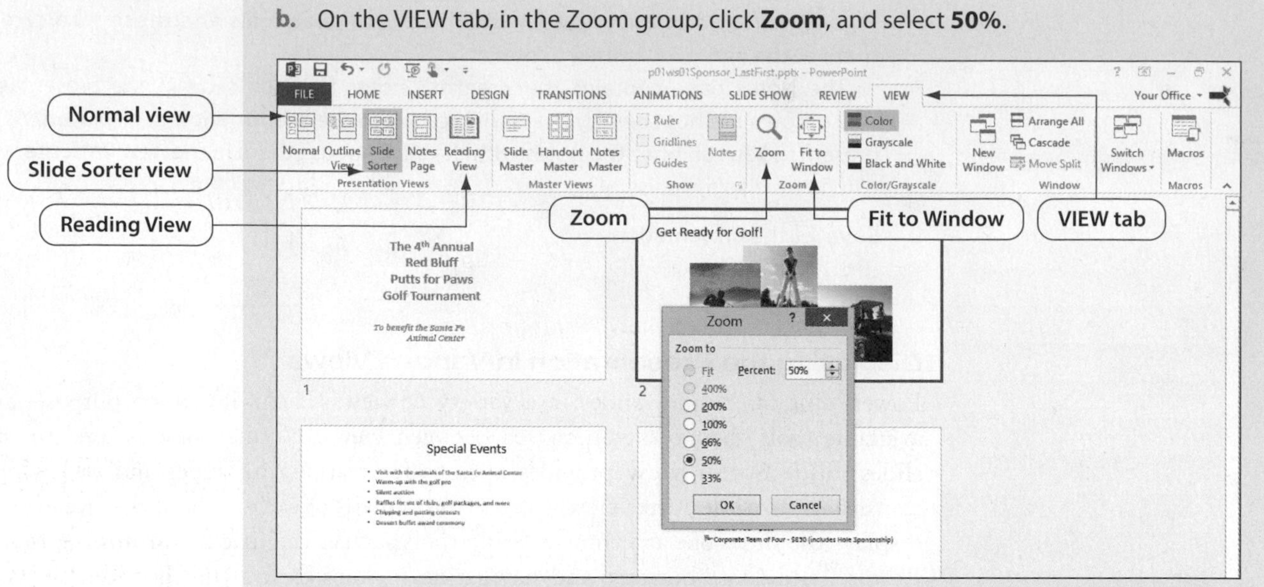

Figure 8 Slide Sorter view

c. Click **OK**. The thumbnails become smaller, which is useful for displaying more slides in a large slide show.

d. In the Zoom group, click **Fit to Window**. This causes the slides to be displayed as large as possible in this Slide Sorter view.

e. Click **Slide 5**, and then click **Reading View** on the status bar. Slide 5 is displayed in a view designed for reading on the screen.

SIDE NOTE

Reading View

Reading View on the View tab displays the first slide, but Reading View on the status bar displays the active slide.

PowerPoint Slide Show - [p01ws01Sponsor_LastFirst.pptx] - PowerPoint

For the Golfers

- Santa Fe Animal Center Bag Tag
- Tournament golf shirt
- Gift bag sponsored by Pro Sports of Santa Fe
- All golf fees for 18 holes
- Cart
- Contests
  - Hole-in-one cash prize
  - Longest drive
  - Closest to the pin
- Food
  - Lunch buffet at the Red Bluff Bistro
  - 19th hole Dinner at Indigo5
  - Dessert buffet at awards ceremony

Next

Previous

SLIDE 5 OF 6

Menu

Reading View

Figure 9 Reading view

SIDE NOTE

Black Bars

In PowerPoint 2013, slides size to Widescreen by default. Widescreen slides displayed on a Standard screen create black bars at the top and bottom—like the figures shown here.

f. Click the **Next** button on the status bar to view Slide 6. The Next and Previous buttons on the status bar make it easy to navigate through the slide show in this view.

g. Click **Menu** on the status bar, and then click **Edit Slides**. You return to Slide Sorter view.

SIDE NOTE
Using the Menu
The Reading View menu enables you to navigate through the slides, preview, print, copy, edit, and end a show.

h. In Slide Sorter view, click **Slide 2**, and then click **Slide Show** on the status bar. Slide 2 fills the primary screen. If a different slide was selected, then that slide would have been displayed. If you have two displays, you will also see the Presenter View. The Presenter View is not displayed to the audience and is new to Office 2013. Keep the slide show open as you move to the next section.

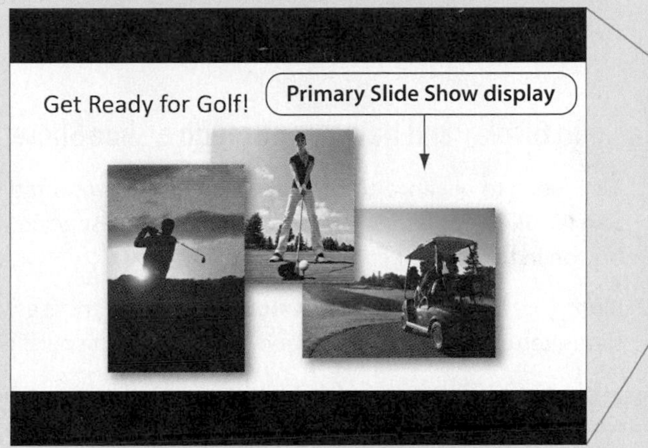

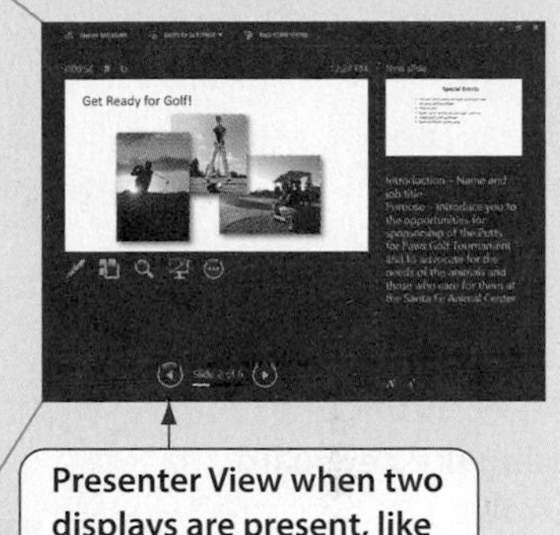

Figure 10 Slide Show displays

REAL WORLD ADVICE | **Widescreen versus Standard Screens**

New to PowerPoint 2013 is a default layout to widescreen size—16:9 ratio. However, if you open a file first started in a prior version of PowerPoint, the file will be in standard screen size—4:3 ratio. You can easily change the screen size by going to the Design tab and clicking the Slide Size button. The size of slide will change what your slide looks like and where you want to place text, objects, and pictures. If you have a standard screen size and a widescreen slide size, you will see black bars at the top and bottom similar to some of the screen shots in this workshop.

So, how do you know which one to use? You want to use the same size as the projector for the presentation. Thus, make sure you know what size the projector is in the room where the actual presentation will take place.

Navigate in Slide Show View and Outline View

Most often, when you give a presentation, you will display the slide show in Slide Show view, advancing each slide after you have spoken about the contents of the slide. PowerPoint offers many methods for advancing the slides and returning to previous slides. Some people prefer to use the mouse to move between the slides, yet others like to use the keyboard. Windows 8 enables you to gesture on touch devices to navigate. A presenter remote control can also free you from standing close to your computer while giving your presentation.

REAL WORLD ADVICE | **Presentation Remote Controls Free You from the Computer**

Consider using a remote control when presenting; it gives you the flexibility to move around. You can use a wireless mouse, connected via USB to your host PC, or a mobile app on your smartphone. Senstic makes an app called i-Clickr Remote, which controls the host PC from your smartphone or tablet. With this app, you can instantly broadcast annotations made on your device while you present. Using a new technology can be empowering, but make sure you always practice using it before you present.

Navigating the Presentation in Various Views

In this section you will practice various methods to navigate through a slide show.

P01.04

To Display and Navigate Through a Slide Show

a. Click once to advance to the next slide in the presentation. Right-click, and then click **See All Slides**. This view enables you to select a specific slide to display. Click the **Back** button in the top-left corner of the screen.

b. Right-click, and then click **Previous**. Using the mouse you can advance through the slides, return to previously viewed slides, or select specific slides to display.

SIDE NOTE
Using the Keyboard Arrows
↑ and ← return to the previous slide, and ↓ and → move to the next slide.

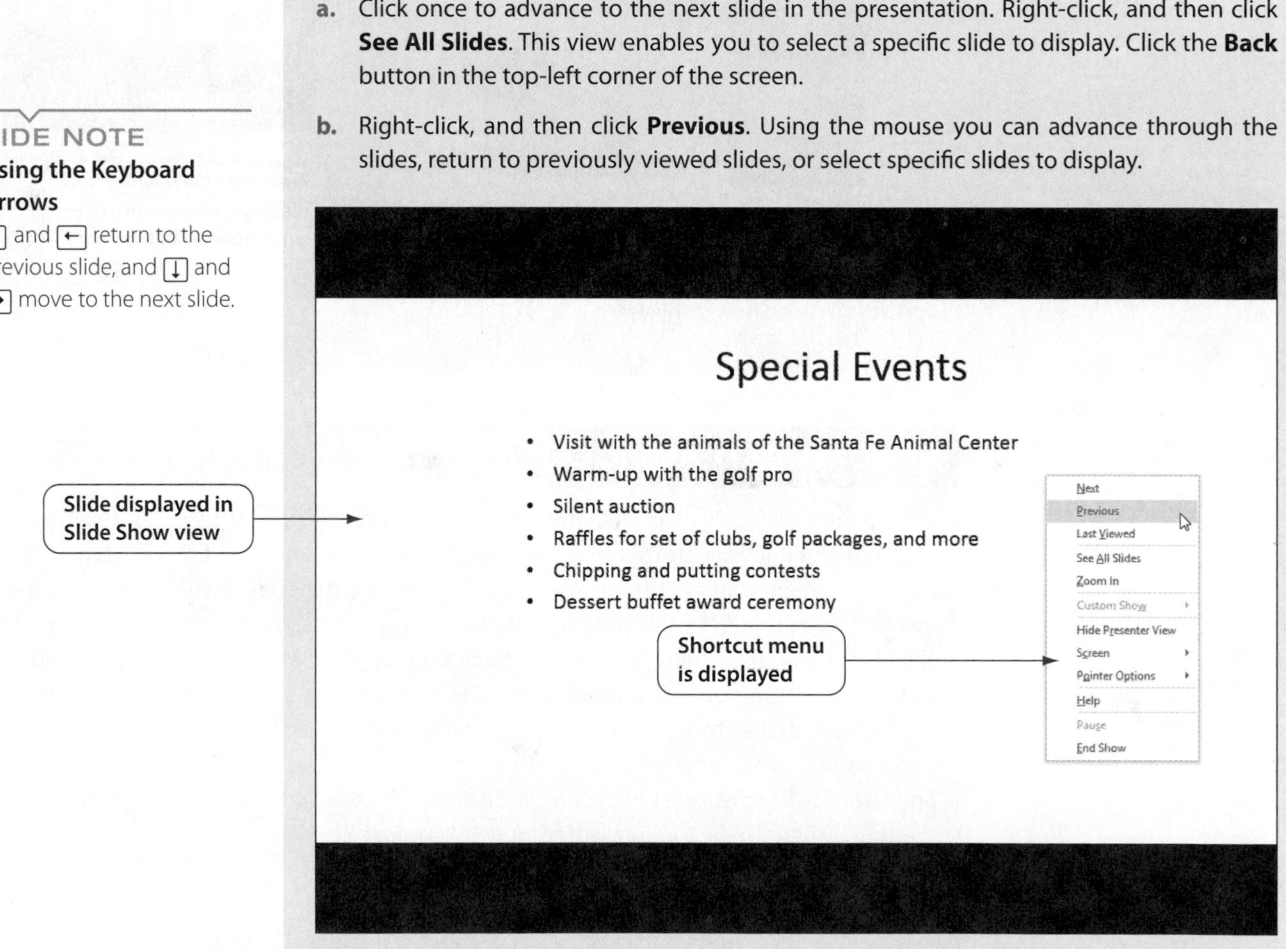

Figure 11 Slide Show view

c. Press Spacebar to display Slide 3, Special Events, again. Many people like to use the spacebar to advance through their presentations because it is a large key that is easy to find in a darkened room.

d. Use your favorite method to advance to the end of the presentation. When you advance the slides beyond the last slide, a black screen alerts you that the slide show is over. While the black screen is showing, any of the methods for moving to the next slide will return you to the view and slide from before you started the Slide Show. On the VIEW tab, in the Presentation Views group, click **Normal**.

Troubleshooting

To exit a presentation while it is displayed in Slide Show view, press Esc. This returns you to the previous view.

QUICK REFERENCE **Navigating the Slide Show**

There are many options for navigating through the slide show:

1. To advance to the next slide, either type an N, or press Enter, Page Down, →, ↓, or Spacebar. On a touch-enabled surface, swipe forward.
2. To return to a previous slide, either type a P, or press Page Up, ←, ↑, or Backspace. On a touch-enabled surface, swipe backward.
3. To view all slides, type a G, or zoom all the way out. To view a specific slide, press the number of the slide, and then press Enter.
4. To zoom in, either type a + (a plus sign) or stretch or double-tap on a touch-enabled surface.
5. To zoom out, either type a - (a minus sign) or pinch or double-tap on a touch-enabled surface.
6. To display a blank black screen, type a B or a . (a period). To return to the display, type a B or a . again.
7. To display a blank screen, type a W or a , (a comma). To return to the display, type a W or a , again.
8. Using the mouse, click the transparent icons in the lower-left corner of the slide in the Slide Show view.
9. To end the slide show, press Esc.

Promoting, Demoting, and Moving Text in Outline View

Outline view displays the titles and bullet points of the slides in the presentation. It is easy to add, modify, and delete text content in this view. You can also move the slides by dragging them to new positions in Outline view. Promoting outline text moves it up a level, and demoting outline text moves it down a level. In this next step, you will promote and demote text.

Some of the slides might appear to be blank in Outline view, when in fact they are not blank. Outline text is drawn from the title and content placeholders. **Placeholders** are objects in PowerPoint that hold different types of content for the presentation. Slides that do not contain text in these placeholders will appear to be blank in Outline view. To make modifications to these slides, you use Normal view.

In this next exercise, you will update the golf tournament presentation in Outline view.

P01.05

To Use Outline View

a. Click **Slide 6**. On the VIEW tab, in the Presentation Views group, click **Outline View**. If necessary, drag the **border** between the outline in the left hand pane and the Slide pane to increase the amount of text you can see in the outline.

Minimizing the size of the slide in the Slide pane enables you to focus more on the outline content.

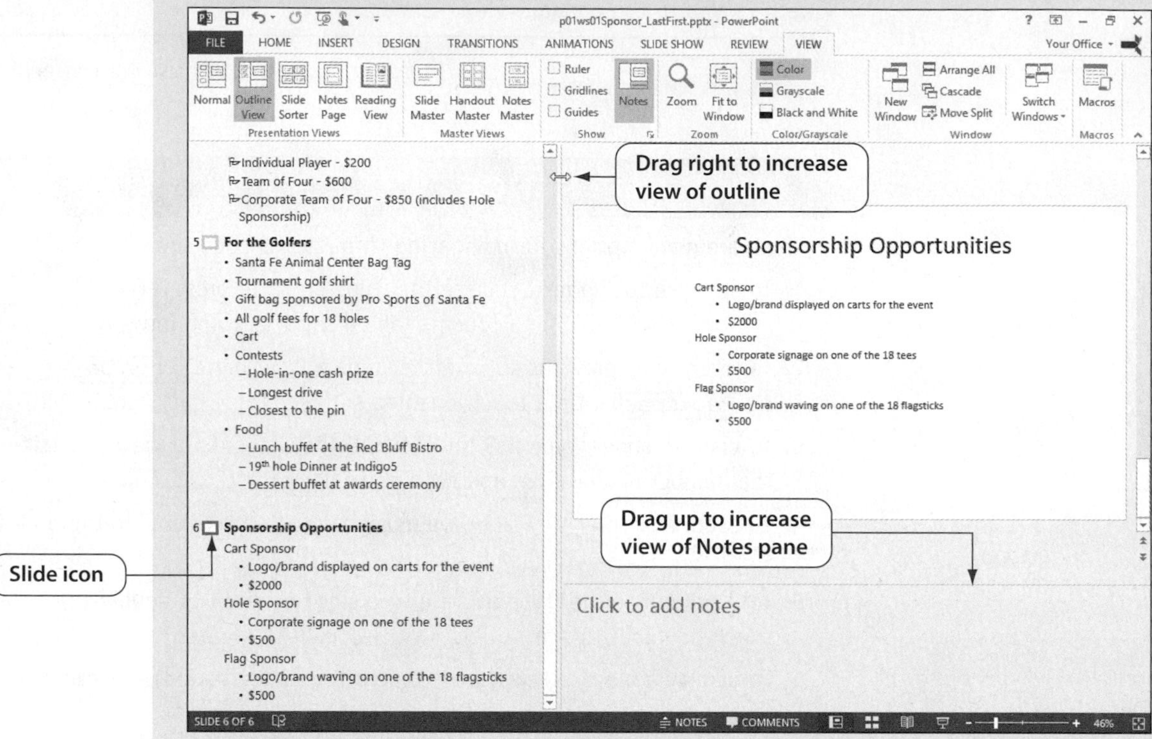

Figure 12 Using Outline view

b. On **Slide 6** in the outline on the left hand pane, position your cursor at the very end of the **bulleted text** right after $500, and then press Enter. Type the following, pressing Enter after each line:

- **Program Sponsor**
- **Logo/brand on program materials**
- **$200**

c. Place your cursor anywhere in the text **Program Sponsor**, click the **HOME** tab, and then in the Paragraph group, click **Decrease List Level**.

The text has been promoted in the outline. You will change the bullet and font size later.

d. On **Slide 5** in the outline on the left hand pane, click and drag to select the text for the sixth bullet beginning with the word **Contests** and ending with the word **pin**. On the HOME tab, in the Clipboard group, click **Cut** to remove the text and copy it to the Clipboard. On Slide 3 click to place your insertion point in front of the word **Chipping** in the fifth bullet, and then in the Clipboard group, click **Paste**.

e. Select the four bullet points in the outline on the left hand pane, beginning with the text **Hole-in-one** and ending with **putting contests**, and then in the **Paragraph** group, click **Increase List Level**.

SIDE NOTE

Pressing Tab in Outlines

Use Tab to increase the list level in the outline, and Shift + Tab to decrease it.

The text has been demoted in the outline. Pasting left inconsistent formating, you will change the bullets and font size later.

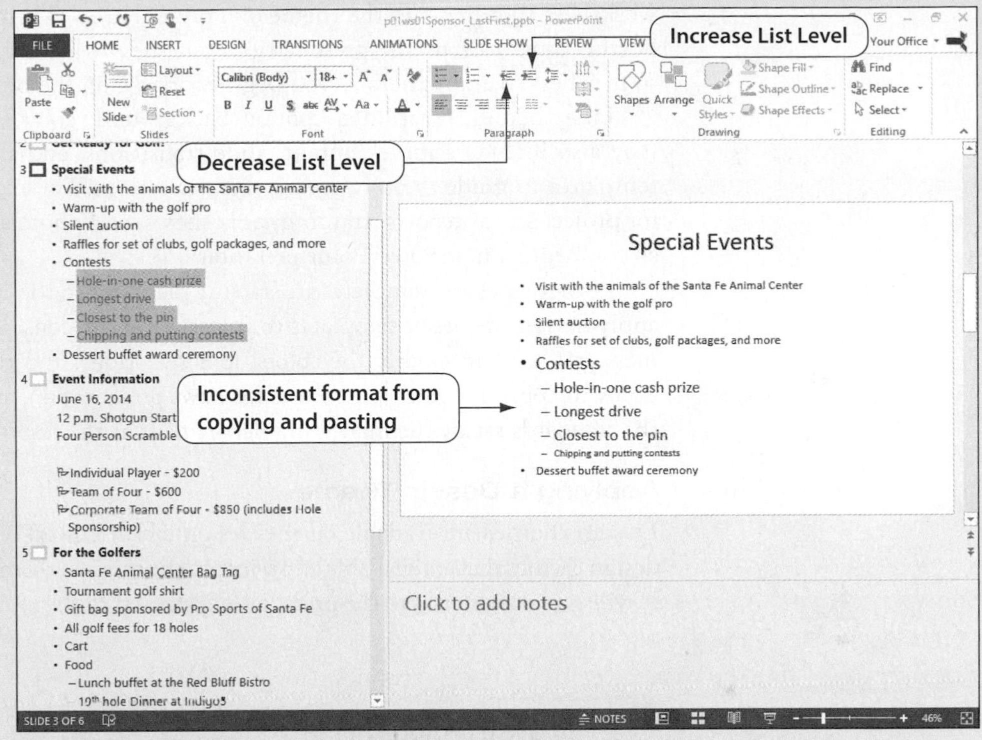

Figure 13 Demoting text

REAL WORLD ADVICE **Amount of Text on a Slide**

Audience members cannot read and listen well at the same time. Text on the screen should be as minimal as possible without sacrificing the message. Some use the 6x6 rule to help guide the amount of text. This rule limits the number of bullets to six and the number of words per bullet to six. Ideally, each slide would have even less text than 6x6. However, sometimes the message necessitates more text than 6x6. Your presentation will be at its best when you minimize text. How exciting was the last PowerPoint presentation that you saw with text heavy slides?

Understanding Effective Communication

You will want to develop your presentation with an eye toward what your audience will see as well as what they will hear. Effective communicators are good storytellers. They have a keen sense about designing imagery to generate interest and about using emotion to create tension. In this section, you will use effective communication techniques to help firmly implant your message into the minds of your audience.

Understand the Difference Between a Theme and a Template

PowerPoint enables you to concentrate on the message you are trying to convey to your audience and build your presentation around that message. Design themes and templates add visual interest to your message. Background, color, and font selections are included as part of the design themes that can easily be applied to your slide show. PowerPoint has at least 10 built-in themes, with more available online at Office.com. In some cases, you may want to build your own theme. Many businesses have a standard corporate theme that makes their presentations recognizable and professional. Themes can be used in the various Microsoft applications, so you can apply a theme to a Word document or Excel worksheet that matches the theme of a presentation. Themes can be applied at any time during your work on the presentation, but they will override other formatting changes, so it is best to apply them as you begin working on the presentation.

Like themes, **templates** contain background, color, and font selections, but they may also include sample content, slide transitions, and slide layouts. Many people use templates to guide them in creating presentations. For example, templates are available for project status reports, training, quiz shows, and photo albums. Templates are selected as you begin a new PowerPoint presentation.

Both themes and templates are starting places for the design of your presentation. As you apply design themes or templates to your slide show, consider your purpose, audience, and message. You can modify the colors, font selections, and theme effects to fit your needs. You will apply a theme to the Putts for Paws presentation, and then modify it according to the standards set by the marketing department at the resort for the golf courses.

Applying a Design Theme

Design themes are available on the Design tab in PowerPoint. You will briefly look at the design themes that are available and select an appropriate theme for the Red Bluff Golf Course. It will give consistency to the presentation and add to the visual appeal of the presentation.

P01.06

To Use a Design Theme

a. Click the **DESIGN** tab.

b. In the Themes group, point to the individual **theme thumbnails**, pausing momentarily so Live Preview displays the theme on the slide in the Slide pane.

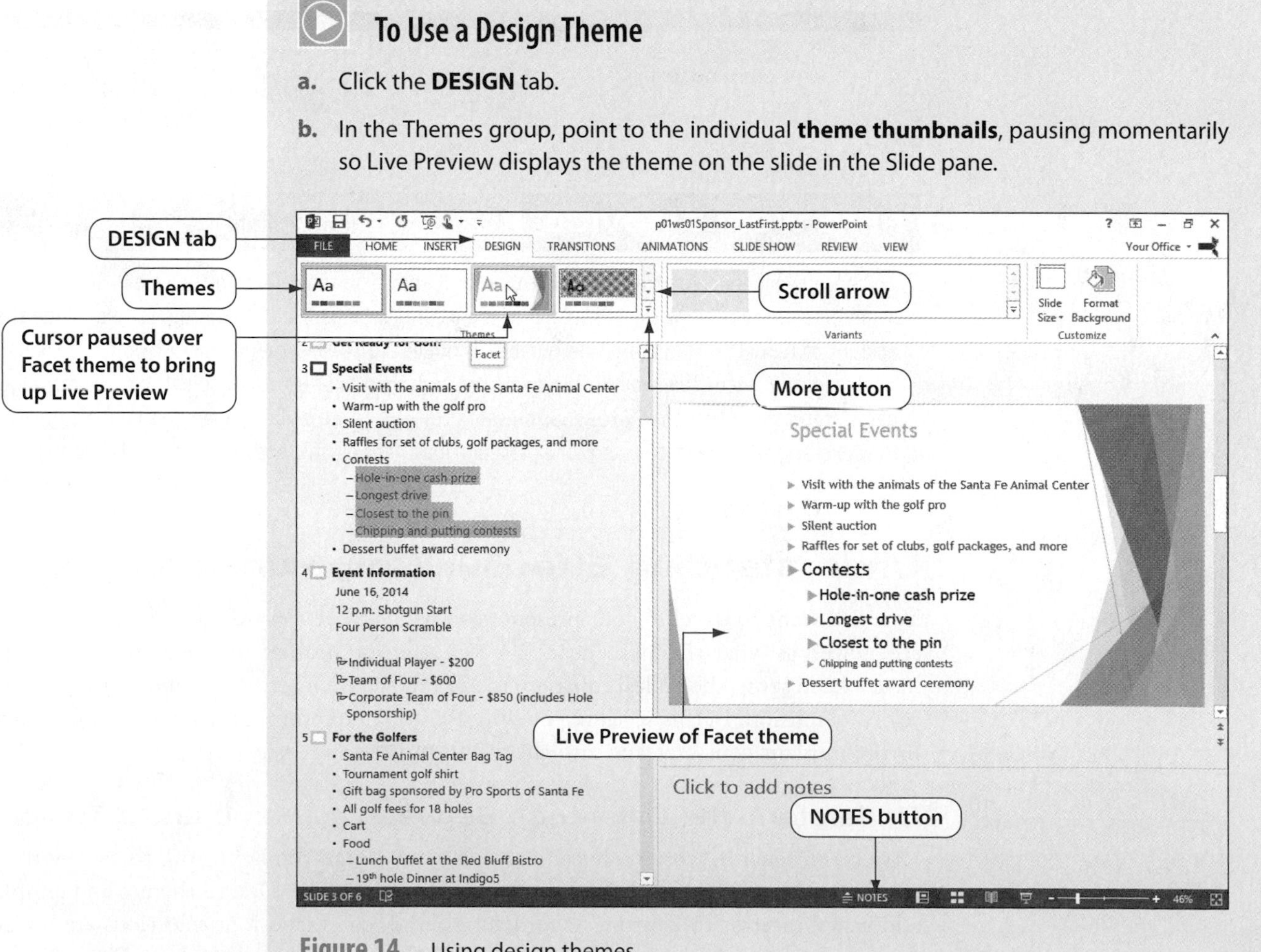

Figure 14 Using design themes

c. In the Themes group, click **More** [▾], and then preview additional themes.

d. Select the **Wisp** theme. The theme is applied to all slides in the presentation and on the DESIGN tab the Variants group populates with available variations—do not change the variant default.

e. Click the **VIEW** tab, and then in the Presentation Views group, click **Normal**. Zoom to **66%** in the Slide pane. On the status bar, click **NOTES** to toggle off the Notes pane and provide more space for the slide. Click through each of the **slides** in the left hand pane to review the changes made by applying the theme.

f. **Save** [💾] the presentation.

REAL WORLD ADVICE **Break the Pattern for Emphasis**

One way to generate a paper sticky note idea, explained earlier, is to break up the pattern established by the template. Perhaps to emphasize a point in the flow of your story, insert a picture that takes up an entire slide.

Modifying a Theme

There are times when you will not be able to find a design theme that fits your preferences. In this case, you can select a theme and then modify it. You can change the theme colors, fonts, and effects. When you change the theme elements, the changes can affect the entire presentation. This saves you time and effort over changing elements individually on each slide. For example, creating a **font group** for themes will enable you to apply a predetermined font family to Heading fonts and Body fonts simultaneously.

You see the presentation theme fonts do not comply with the resort font standards. The text you entered earlier on Slide 6 is not consistently sized with the surrounding text, and neither is the text you pasted into Slide 3.

P01.07

To Modify Theme Fonts

a. Click **Slide 1** in the left hand pane, if necessary, to display it in the Slide pane.

b. On the VIEW tab, in the Master Views group, click **Slide Master** and then scroll up in the left hand pane so the first slide—the Master Slide—appears. In the Background group, click the **Fonts** button, and then point to a few **fonts** on the list to view the preview of the title slide. As you view each font group, notice the change to the fonts on the title slide.

SIDE NOTE
Exploring Font Groups
Theme fonts are grouped so applying them for Heading fonts and Body fonts is simultaneous, quick, and easy.

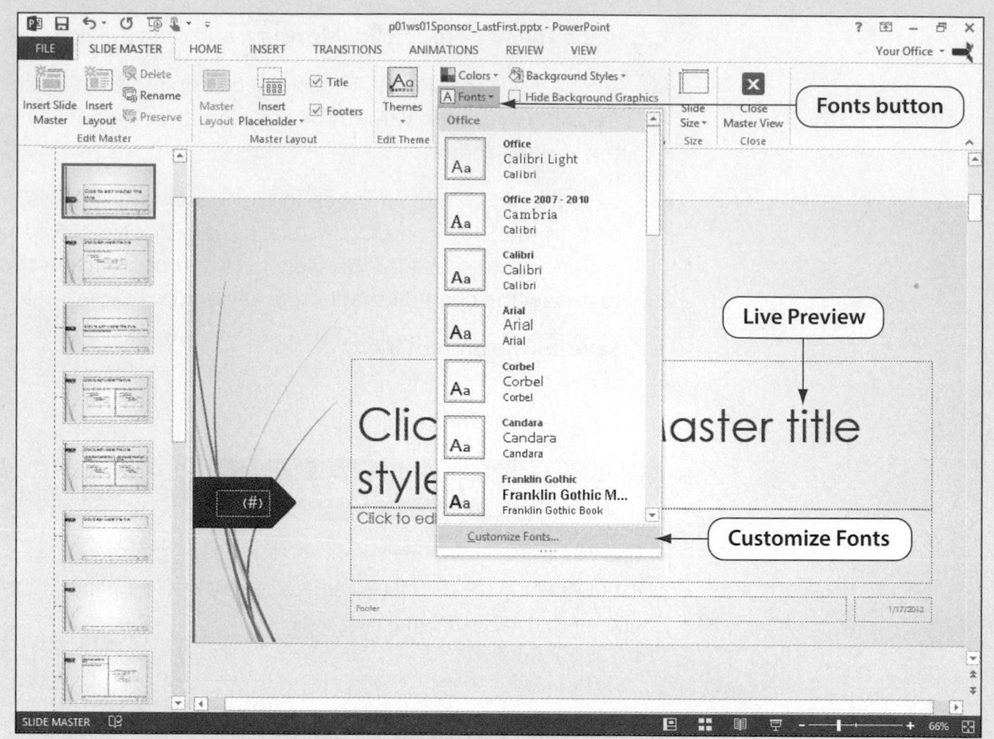

Figure 15 Modifying theme fonts

c. Click **Customize Fonts** at the bottom of the Fonts gallery.

d. Click the **Heading font** arrow, and then scroll to and click **Times New Roman**.

e. Click the **Body font** arrow, and then scroll to and click **Times New Roman**.

f. Select the text in the **Name** box, and then type Red Bluff LastFirst, using your last and first name.

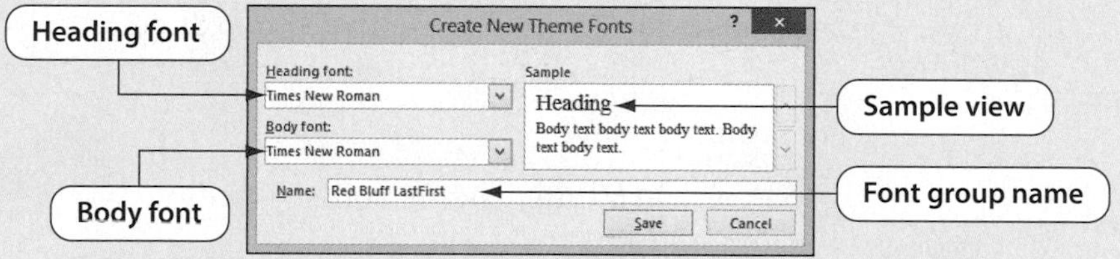

Figure 16 Creating New Theme Fonts

g. Click **Save**, and then in the Close group, click **Close Master View**.

h. Click **Slide 6**, then select the text **Program Sponsor**. Click the **HOME** tab, and then in the Font group, in the Font Size box, type 19, and then press Enter. In the Paragraph group, click **Bullets** to deselect it. The bullet has been removed.

i. Click **Slide 3**, and then select the three lines of text beginning with **Hole-in-one** and ending with **Closest to the pin**. On the HOME tab, in the Font group, in the Font Size box, type 17, and then press Enter. In the Font group, click **Font Color** arrow, and then select **Black, Text 1, Lighter 25%** the second color in the fourth row. All of the second level bullets on Slide 3 automatically resize to 18pt font.

j. Select the fifth bullet text **Contests**. On the HOME tab, in the Font group, in the Font Size box, type 22, and then press Enter. In the Font group, click **Font Color** arrow, and then select **Black, Text 1, Lighter 25%**.

k. **Save** the presentation.

Using Color Strategically

There are many aspects to consider when using color in a presentation. Color can be used to emphasize important elements and to organize the message. Colors are also associated with emotions or qualities, with different colors suggesting various things in different parts of the world. For instance, in the American culture, black is associated with death, but in the Chinese culture, the color associated with death is white. Business presentations are often clean and crisp, while presentations to children are often colorful and whimsical. Carefully consider your audience, objectives, and message as you make your selections for color in your presentation.

REAL WORLD ADVICE **Color Associations**

When using color in presentations, consider the psychology of common color associations. People may associate feelings of danger or excitement when using red colors. Blue can invoke calm and tranquility, and yellow can invoke cheer or optimism.

As you select the colors for the presentation, it is best to choose the background color first, and then place high contrast colors on top of it. Be careful the colors do not clash. For instance, a medium blue background and red text almost vibrates because the colors clash. Select a maximum of four colors to use in a presentation, and keep the colors consistent throughout the presentation. Use the brightest colors as accents in areas needing the most attention. Focus on design, and not decoration.

You will change the color of the title and subtitle text to coordinate with the color scheme of the theme.

P01.08

To Modify Theme Colors

a. Click **Slide 1** on the left hand pane, and then click the **HOME** tab. Select the title text **The 4th Annual Red Bluff Putts for Paws Golf Tournament.**

You will only change the color of the font on this one slide, so you select just the text you want to change.

b. On the HOME tab, in the Font group, click the **Font Color** arrow , and then click **More Colors** in the gallery.

c. In the Colors dialog box, click the **Custom** tab, and then modify the color numbers at the bottom of the dialog box as follows:

- Red: 190
- Green: 30
- Blue: 45

The color created is a color matching the Painted Paradise Resort and Spa logo.

SIDE NOTE

Custom Colors

For precise image matching colors, the eye dropper tool under Font Color can sample the image for the color. Image editing software can also provide RGB numbers.

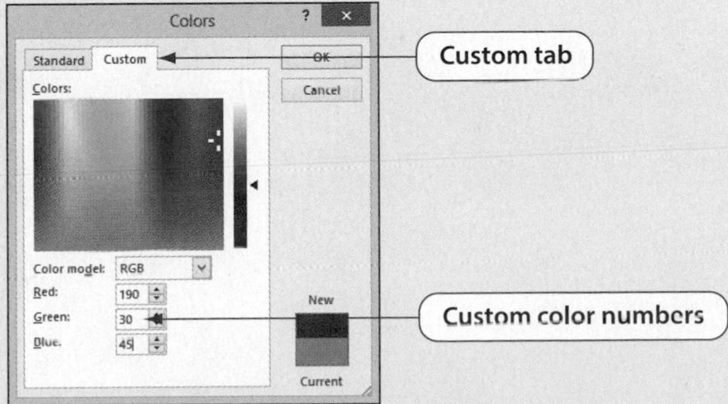

Figure 17 Selecting font colors

d. Click **OK**, and then click outside of the text placeholder. The color of the title text has changed to red.

e. Select the subtitle text, **To benefit the Santa Fe Animal Center**, click the **Font Color** arrow, and then click **Red** in the Recent Colors section of the gallery.

f. **Save** and **close** the presentation, but leave PowerPoint open for the next exercise.

Create a Presentation from a Template

PowerPoint templates enable you to focus on the content of your presentation by providing professional-looking designs. Additional templates can be downloaded for free from Office.com. You can also find free templates by completing an Internet search for "free PowerPoint templates." Templates, like themes, contain slide backgrounds, color schemes, and font selections. In some cases, templates also contain sample content or unique slide layouts. Templates are applied to new slide shows and can be modified as needed.

You will work on the Red Bluff Golf Club & Pro Shop tournament presentation by selecting a template recently developed by your marketing department, and then reusing your slides in the template.

Using a Template to Create a New Presentation

The tournament template you will use is based on the Red Bluff Golf Club & Pro Shop theme designed by the resort's marketing department and available in the student data files folder.

P01.09

To Create a Presentation with a Template

a. Click the **FILE** tab, and then click the **New** tab. On this tab, you can start a new presentation from blank slides with or without a theme applied. You can also search for and use an Office template.

b. Click **Open**, click **Computer**, and then click **Browse**. Navigate to where your student data files are located, and then open the file **p01ws01RedBluff**.

c. Click the **VIEW** tab, and then in the Master Views group, click **Slide Master**. Click each of the **slides** in the left hand pane. Scroll to the top of the left hand pane until you see the top slide, the Slide Master.

If you point to a slide, the ScreenTip indicates the type of layout used on that slide. You will work with slide layouts later in the workshop.

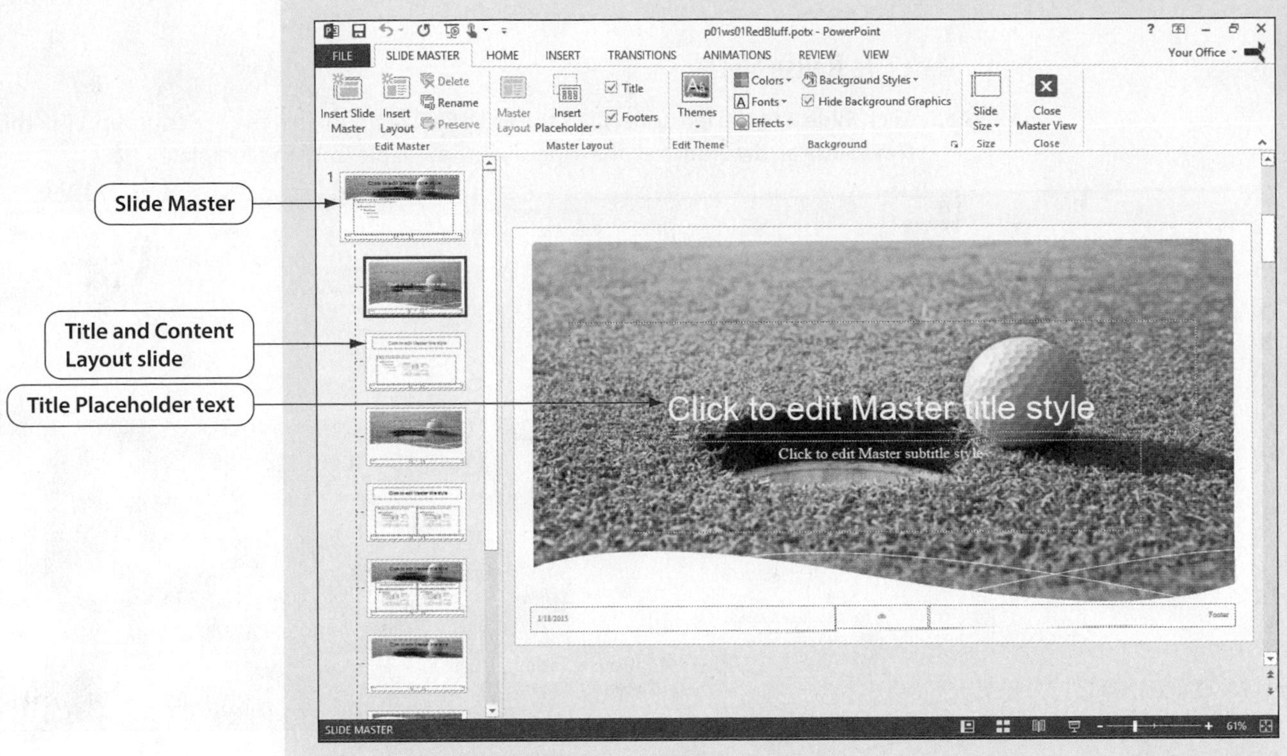

Figure 18 The Red Bluff template

d. In **Slide Master** view, click the **Title and Content Layout** slide, which is the third slide in the left hand pane. In the Slide pane, in the slide title select the text **Click to edit Master title style**. Release the mouse button to display the Mini toolbar. On the Mini toolbar, click **Font Color** arrow, to display the Theme Colors, and select **Red, Text 1**—top row, second from left. In the Close group, click **Close Master View** to return to Normal view.

e. Click the **FILE** tab, and then click **Save As**. Click **Computer** and then click **Browse**. Navigate to the location where you are saving your files. In the **File name** box, type p01ws01Sponsor2_LastFirst, using your last and first name. In the **Save as type** box, select **PowerPoint Presentation**, and then click **Save**.

SIDE NOTE
Save Often
Save at different intervals. If something goes wrong, you can open the previous file and recover most of your work.

Reusing Slides

Slides from other slide shows can be imported into your current slide show. Reusing slides saves you time. You can reuse the slides that you currently have available on your computer, or use Slide Libraries that are stored on a server. People with access to the server can share the slides in Slide Libraries, which is a more efficient and accurate way to build content.

The presentation given to you by the golf pro contains the information needed for the tournament presentation. You will reuse slides from that presentation in your current presentation.

P01.10

To Reuse Slides

a. Click **Slide 1** in the left pane. Click the **HOME** tab, and then in the Slides group, click the **New Slide** arrow. Notice all the slide layouts available from the template.

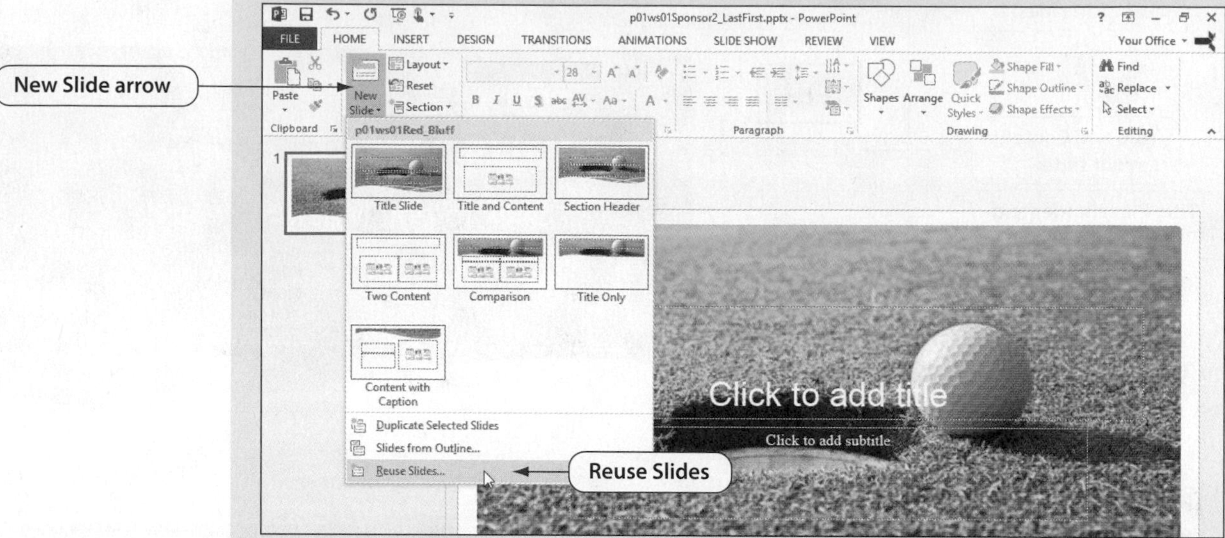

Figure 19 Reusing Slides

b. Click **Reuse Slides**. The Reuse Slides pane opens on the right side of the window.

c. Click **Browse**, and then click **Browse File**. Navigate to where you saved your solution file, click **p01ws01Sponsor_LastFirst**, and then click **Open**.

Slide thumbnails are displayed in the Reuse Slides pane. The title of each slide is listed beside the thumbnail.

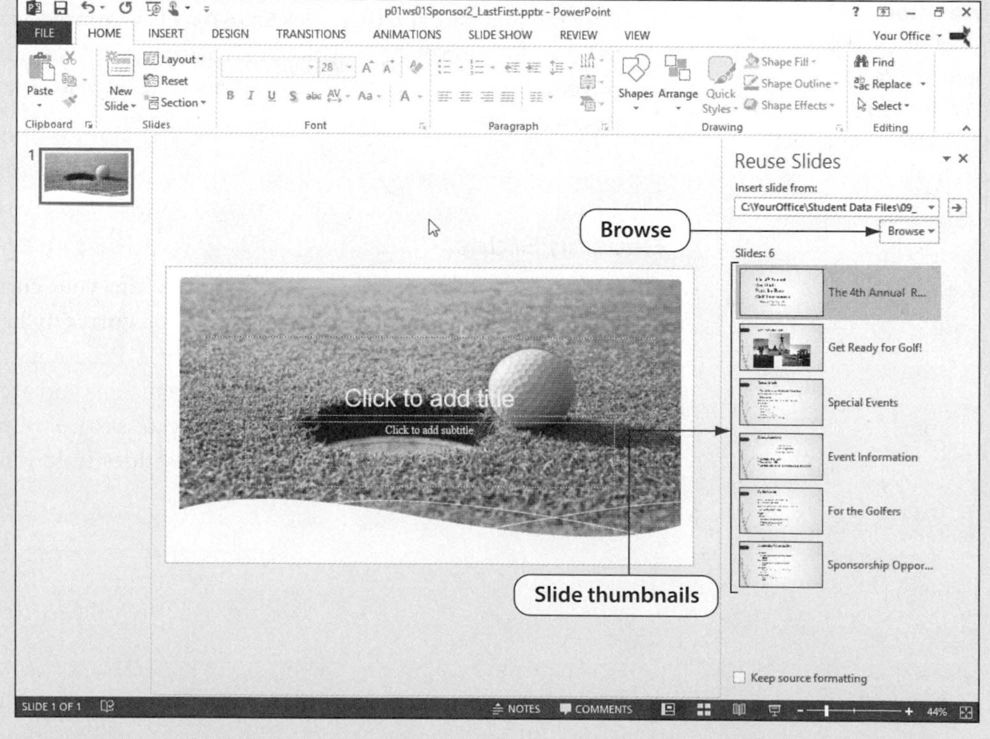

Figure 20 Reuse Slides pane

d. In the Reuse Slides pane, click the first slide thumbnail titled **The 4th Annual R....** The slide is inserted into the current Golf tournament presentation as Slide 2. However, it inherited the characteristics of the new slide show created with the new template. Now, there are two titles slides in the presentation. The first one is a blank slide remaining from the template. The blank slide will be deleted later in this workshop.

e. In the Reuse Slides pane, click each of the remaining **slides** to insert them into the presentation.

> **Troubleshooting**
> If you accidentally get the slides out of order, select a slide in the left hand pane. When inserting a slide from the Reuse Slides pane, it will be inserted after the slide you have selected in your presentation. You can also click and drag slides in the left hand pane to reorder them.

f. On the Reuse Slides pane, click close ☒. **Save** 🖫 the presentation.

Inserting Footers

Custom **slide footers** can be displayed on slides. Footers often contain the name of the company, the company slogan, dates, name of the presenter, or copyright notices. Slide numbers can also be displayed in the footer of slides.

The footer in this presentation needs to have slide numbers and the tournament name, Putts for Paws Golf Tournament. You will modify the presentation by placing footers on the content slides but not the title slide.

P01.11

To Add Slide Footers

a. Click **Slide 3**, click the **INSERT** tab, and then in the Text group, click **Header & Footer**.
The Header and Footer dialog box opens. There are two tabs in this dialog box, Slide and Notes and Handouts. You will focus on the Slide tab.

b. In the Include on slide section, click the **Slide number** check box, and then click the **Footer** check box. In the **Footer** box type Putts for Paws Golf Tournament. This footer text will appear in the bottom-right portion of the slide.

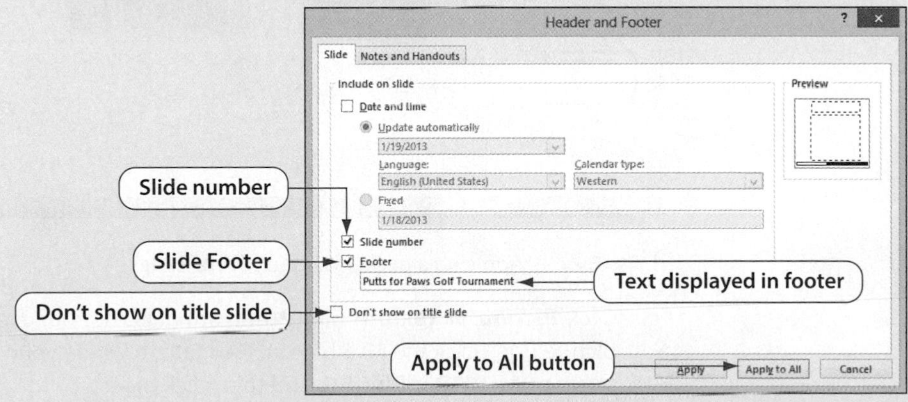

Figure 21 Applying slide footers

c. Click the **Don't show on title slide** check box, and then click **Apply to All** at the bottom of the dialog box.

The footer is applied to all but the title slide. The title slide will contain the name of the golf club, and a footer would detract from the overall design of the title slide.

d. **Save**  the presentation.

While templates and design themes often include background images, you can apply your own image to the background of a slide. It is important to remember that text on top of the background must still be easy to read.

Modifying the Slide Background

You will remove the background picture in the presentation and apply an appropriate picture to the background of a slide.

P01.12

To Modify a Background

a. Click **Slide 3**, hold down the Shift key, and then click **Slide 7** to select all but the first two slides.

b. Click the **DESIGN** tab, and then in the Customize group, click **Format Background**. The Format Background pane will open on the right.

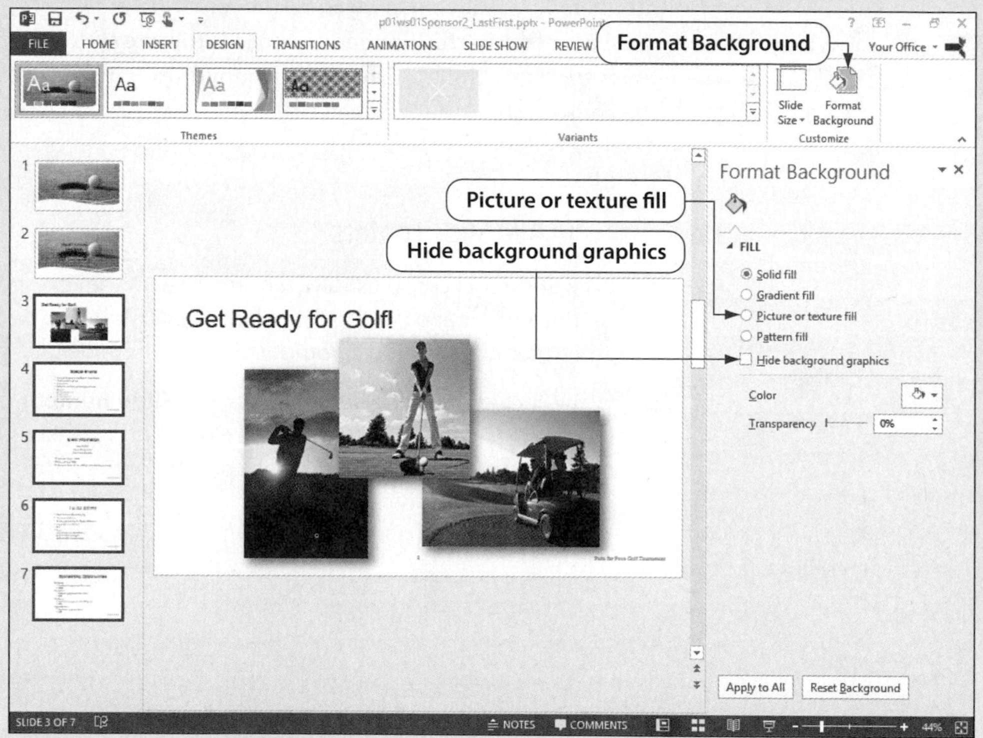

Figure 22 Applying a background to several slides

c. Click **Picture or texture fill** in the Format Background pane, and then under Insert picture from, click the **FILE** button. Navigate to where your student data files are located, select **p01ws01RedBluffBG**, and then click **Insert**.

d. Move the **Transparency** slider to **20%**, and set the **Offset right** box to **80%**. Ensure the remaining offsets are set to **0%**.

The background adjusts to fill the background of the slide, but because it is a narrow image, it was stretched across the screen. Offsetting it from the right kept the entire image on the left of the slides.

e. In the Format Background pane, click the **Hide background graphics** check box.

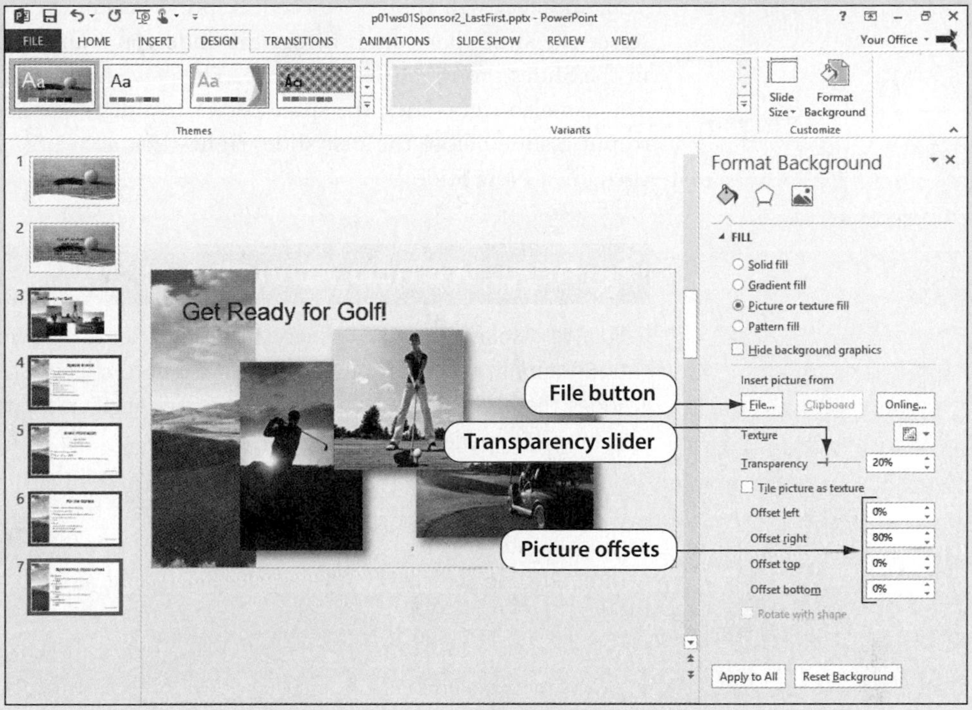

Figure 23 Background image setting applied

f. Click **Slide 2** so the slides are no longer selected together, and then **Close** [X] the Format Background pane.

g. **Save** [Save icon] the presentation.

Add and Delete Slides, Change Slide Layouts, and Rearrange Slides

PowerPoint includes tools that make it easy to add, modify, and delete content on the slides. It goes further by providing tools that enable you to manipulate the slides themselves. You can add new slides at any point in the presentation. The layout of the slides can be changed to provide better balance. You can delete unwanted slides. In addition, moving slides from one position in the presentation to another is as simple as a drag-and-drop operation.

You may have noticed some problems with the Putts for Paws presentation, such as no contact information. In addition, one slide does not have a real purpose in the presentation, and the organization of the slide show does not convey the most important information at the beginning of the presentation.

SS REAL WORLD ADVICE | **Provide Contact Information**

It is always a good idea to have contact information at the end of the presentation. Audience members will contact you to learn more about your topic and suggest that others, with similar interests, contact you.

Adding a New Slide

You can add slides anywhere in the presentation, but they should always be intentional. Your audience will appreciate a concise presentation with a clear message. To insert a slide, select the slide that comes before the slide you want to insert. Then on the Home tab, in the Slides group, click New Slide. The new slide is added after the slide you selected. You can also right-click the space between slides and then click New Slide. If you want to put a slide before the first slide, right-click above Slide 1 on the left hand pane, and then click New Slide.

SS REAL WORLD ADVICE **Planning the Number of Slides**

Plan to display a new slide every 2 to 3 minutes during your presentation. In a 20 to 30 minute presentation, this is a total of 10 slides. Be minimalist. The fewer the slides the better. Slides are aides and not a replacement for the presenter or speaker notes. This guideline keeps you on track with timing your presentation as you plan for and deliver your speech. Make sure you prepare for your presentation rather than relying on slides to guide you. How did you feel the last time a presenter either read slides to you in lieu of discussion? How did you feel the last time a presenter flipped through slides quicker than you could read—not alone listen?

With the exception of the title slide at the beginning of the presentation, every time you insert a new slide using the New Slide button, it will default to the layout of the previous slide. Most of the time this will be what you want, but in some cases you may want to use a different layout. To add a slide different than the last, click the New Slide arrow, and then select your slide layout.

P01.13

To Add Slides

a. Click **Slide 7** on the left hand pane, click the **HOME** tab, and then in the Slides group, click the **New Slide** arrow and then select **Title and Content**. The thumbnail slide appears at the bottom of the left hand pane as Slide 8, and the slide with empty placeholders is displayed in the Slide pane.

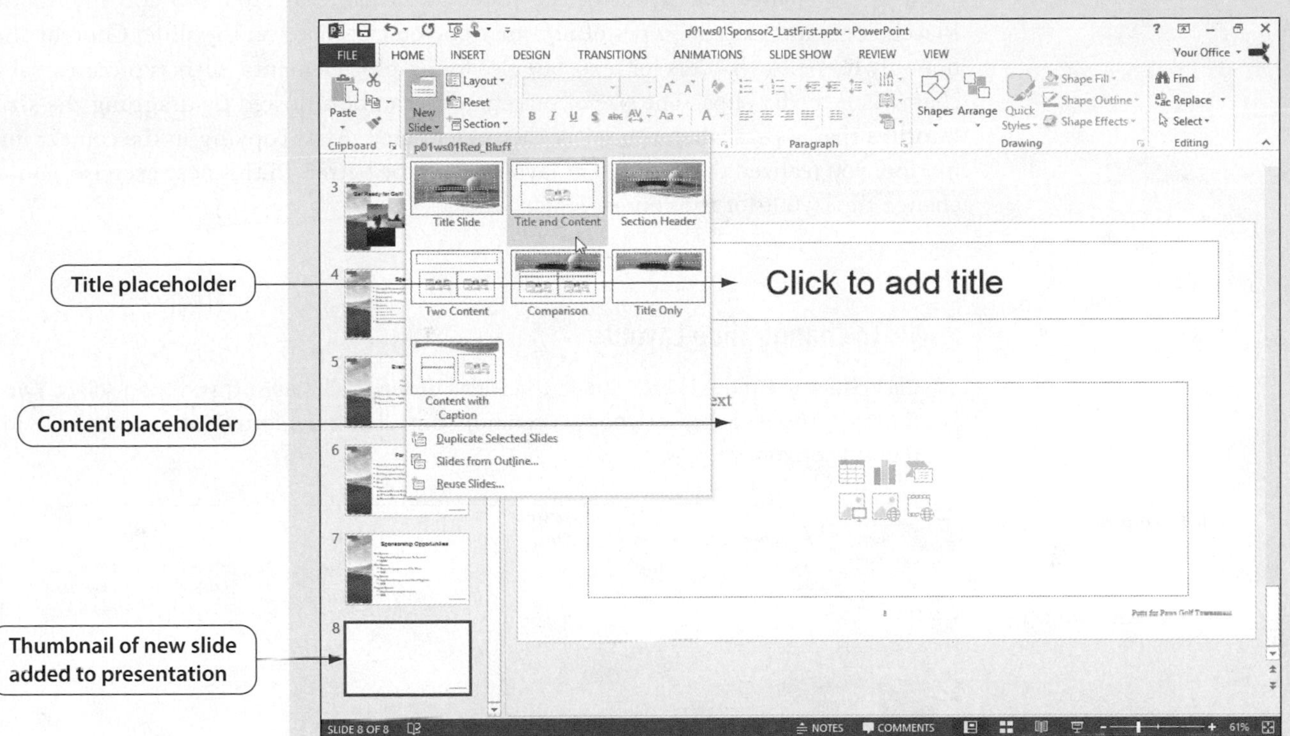

Figure 24 Adding a slide

b. Click **Slide 8** in the left hand pane, and then click the title placeholder text. Click to add title, and then type Contact Us.

c. You will need to insert the contact information from an old presentation. Click the **FILE** tab, and then click **Open**. Browse to your student data files folder, and then open the file **p01ws01SponsorOLD**. Click **Slide 1**, and then right-click the border of the content placeholder text box below the words **Contact Us**. Click **Copy**.

> **Troubleshooting**
> To make sure you have selected the box and not the text inside of the box, the border of the box will appear as a solid line instead of a dashed line.

d. Point to the **PowerPoint** program icon on the taskbar, and then select the file **p01ws01Sponsor2_LastFirst** from the open files. Select **Slide 8**, and then right-click the content placeholder text below the words **Contact Us**. On the shortcut menu, under Paste Options, click **Use Destination Theme**. **Save** the presentation.

e. Point to the **PowerPoint** program icon on the taskbar, and then select **p01ws01SponsorOLD** from the open files, and then **close** p01ws01SponsorOLD.

Changing the Slide Layout

Changing the layout of a slide can improve its readability. You can group similar information together. For example, you have listed yourself and John Schilling on the slide, but by changing the layout, you can be sure that your audience understands why to contact either of you.

The **slide layouts** are provided as part of the template and theme used for the presentation. The Putts for Paws presentation currently uses a template that provides slide layouts. Some templates offer more, some less. Most contain a title slide and a slide for title and content. Often you will find a blank slide that enables you to place elements where you wish.

You can change the layout of the slide either before or after you add information. Placeholders indicate the types of information you can place on the slide. Content slides not only have placeholders for text, but also for graphic elements, such as pictures, tables, charts, and media clips. The size of placeholders can be adjusted by dragging the **sizing handles** that appear when you select the content area. After copying in the contact information, you realized that a different layout would be better. In this next exercise, you will change the layout for the contact slide.

P01.14

To Change Slide Layouts

a. Click **Slide 8**. On the HOME tab, in the Slides group, click **Layout**, and then select **Two Content**. This layout gives you two columns, but all of the information you copied is in the first column.

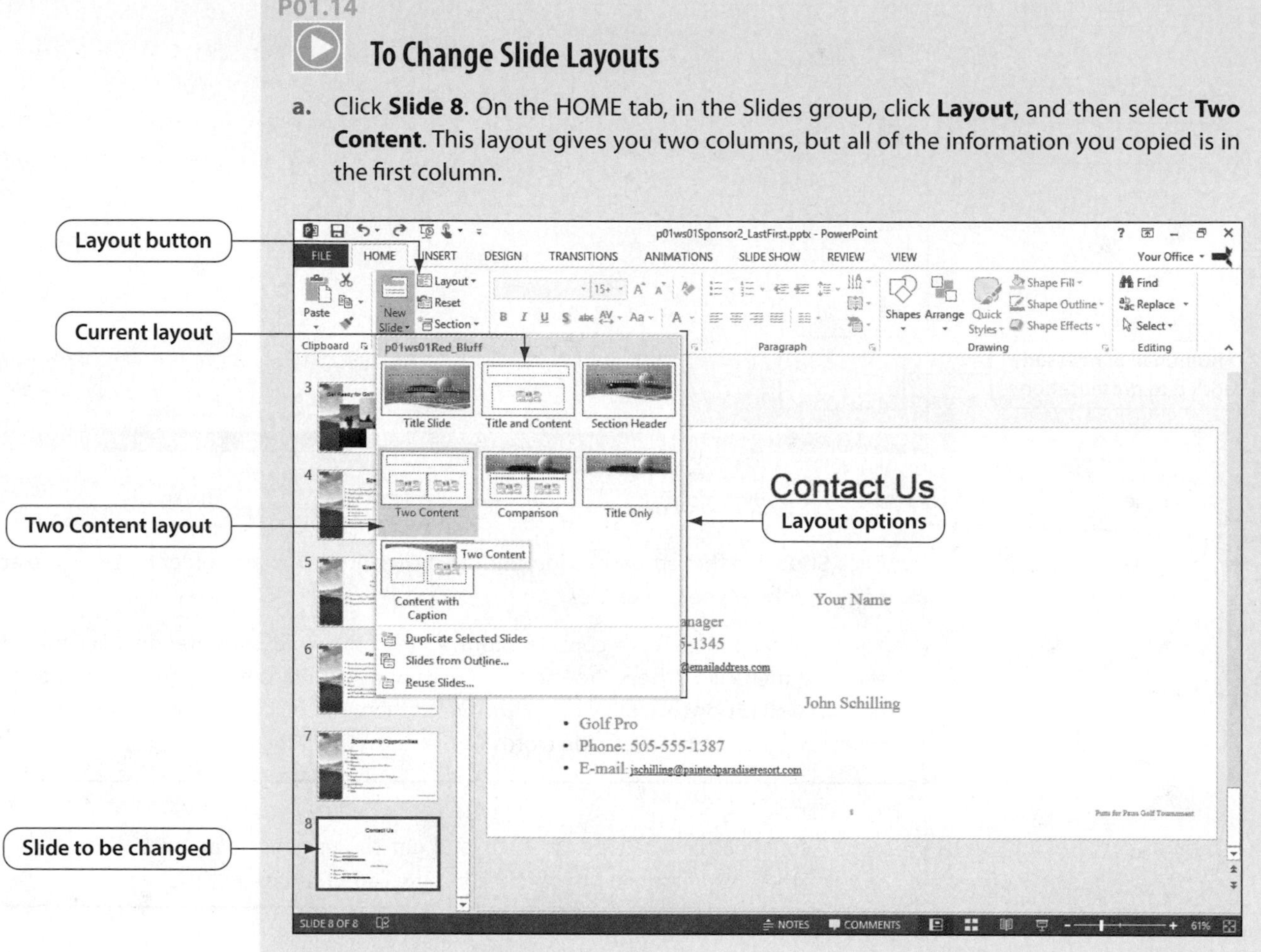

Figure 25 Selecting a layout

b. Select **John Schilling's** information, and then drag it to the text box in the right column.

c. Select **John's** name, and then in the Font group, click **Increase Font Size**. The font size is increased to 28. Repeat these steps for the text **Your Name** in the other text box. Replace the text **Your Name** using your first and last name. Change the email address to your email address.

d. **Save** the presentation.

Deleting Slides

On occasion you will delete unneeded slides from your presentation. The slide or slides you want to delete are selected in the left hand pane, and then you press Delete. If you delete a slide by mistake, click Undo to return it to the presentation in the original position. In this next exercise, you will delete the first, blank slide that remains from the template.

P01.15

To Delete Slides

a. Click **Slide 1** in the left hand pane. The slide is displayed in the Slide pane.

b. Press Delete. The next slide in the sequence is displayed in the Slide pane. You should now have seven slides in your presentation. **Save** the presentation.

Moving Slides in the Left Hand Pane

Even after the best planning, you may realize that the organization of the presentation would benefit from moving some slides. In PowerPoint there are two ways to do this. You can use the left hand pane, or you can use Slide Sorter view to drag slides to new positions.

The flow of the Putts for Paws presentation can be improved by moving the Special Events slide into position after the Event Information slide.

P01.16

To Rearrange Slides in the Left Hand Pane

a. Click **Slide 3** on the left hand pane, and then drag **Slide 3** on the left hand pane downward between Slide 4 and Slide 5. The Event Information slide will move up to the Slide 3 position. Release the mouse button and the Event Information slide is moved.

b. You should now have the title slide, Get Ready for Golf, Event Information, Special Events, For the Golfers, Sponsorship Opportunities, and Contact Us slides shown in this order in the left hand pane.

c. **Save** the presentation.

SIDE NOTE

Rearrange Slides in the Slide Sorter

You can also use Slide Sorter view to rearrange slides and then you can view more slides at one time.

Edit Slides and Move Slide Content

Your presentations can be quickly updated and modified, recycled, and personalized for the current audience. For instance, your sales presentation may have the basic information about your products, but for each customer you visit, you may wish to update the slide show to include the customer name and date. You may also want to move the slides around so the most relevant products are at the beginning of the presentation. In this section, you will edit the slides.

Editing Slides

As you continue with the Red Bluff Putts for Paws Golf Tournament presentation, you will modify last year's slide show to reflect a new date and add text to a slide.

P01.17

To Modify a Slide Show

a. Click **Slide 1** on the left hand pane to display it in the Slide pane.

b. Select the text **4**, and then type 5, indicating the years the tournament has been running.

c. Click **Slide 3**. Select the **date**, and then type June 13, 2015.

d. **Save** the presentation.

Various design principles apply to slides and serve as useful guidelines as you make adjustments to your presentations. Keep it short and simple. In most cases your presentation will benefit from simplicity to focus attention on the topic. Your audience should be able to read and understand your slide in less than 10 seconds. This means that they can quickly read the displayed slide and turn their attention back to you.

Aim to design slides with a path the eye can follow naturally. Keep in mind that people who read English are used to beginning at the top left of the page and reading to the lower right. While it may be interesting to place the titles of the slides in the bottom-right corner, it may also be very confusing to your audience without some additional clues such as font size, emphasis, or color changes.

Strive to make some important element on each slide dominant while achieving a sense of balance with the remaining elements on the slide. The dominant element can be the title, a quotation, or a graphic. Look at the slides in your presentation, and think about the purpose of each slide. The dominant element should reflect the purpose of the slide.

White space, which is not always white, is space on the slide without text or graphics. It serves as a resting place for the eye. It helps to provide organization to your slides. You can use white space to divide your slides in interesting ways to keep your audience involved.

Moving Slide Content

Slide placeholders, the containers for text and graphic elements, can be moved and resized to improve the use of the white space on your slides. You can also manipulate the placeholders to suggest a relationship between items on the slide. Placeholder adjustments can help to move the eye around the slide.

You notice that the Red Bluff Golf Club & Pro Shop logo is nowhere in the presentation, so you will add it. Additionally, you notice that the title slide text isn't readable. In this next exercise, you will fix these issues.

P01.18

To Move Slide Content

a. Click **Slide 7**, and then click the **INSERT** tab, and then in the Images group, click **Pictures**. Navigate to your student data files, select **p01ws01LogoRB**, and then click **Insert**.

b. Click the **FORMAT** tab, and then in the Size group, click in the **Shape Width** box and type 4.5", and then press Enter. Drag the picture into the lower-left corner of the slide. You can make small adjustments using the arrow keys if necessary.

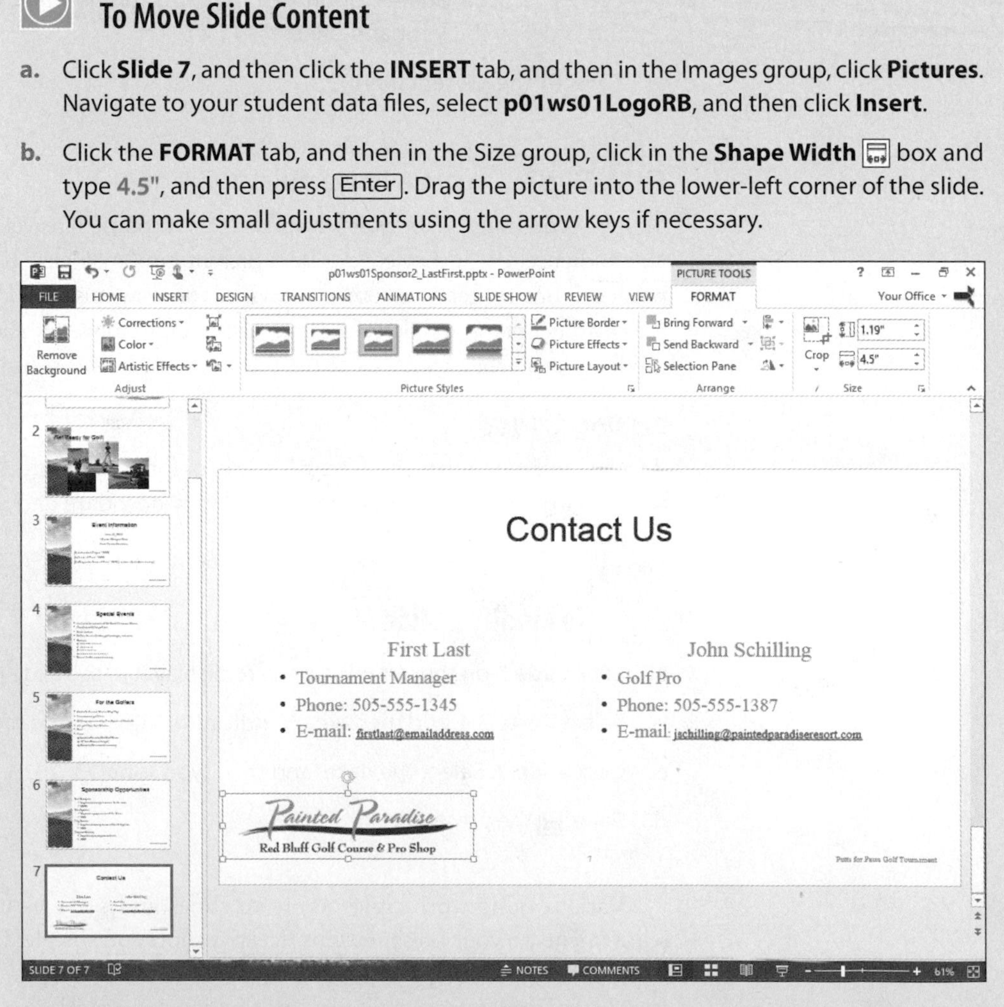

Figure 26 Moving slide content

c. Click **Slide 1**, click on the **title**, and then click the **border** to select the title object. On the FORMAT tab, in the WordArt Styles group, click **Text Outline** arrow and select **White, background 1**—the first color in the upper left hand corner.

d. With the title shape still selected, on the FORMAT tab, in the Arrange group, click the **Align Objects** arrow and select **Align Left**. Click the **HOME** tab, and then in the Paragraph group, click the **Align Text** arrow and select **Top**.

e. Click on the **subtitle**, and then click the **border** of the subtitle object. On the FORMAT tab, in the Arrange group, click the **Align Objects** arrow and select **Align Left**. Again, click the Align Objects arrow and select **Align Bottom**. Click the **HOME** tab, and then in the Paragraph group, click the **Align Text** arrow and select **Bottom**.

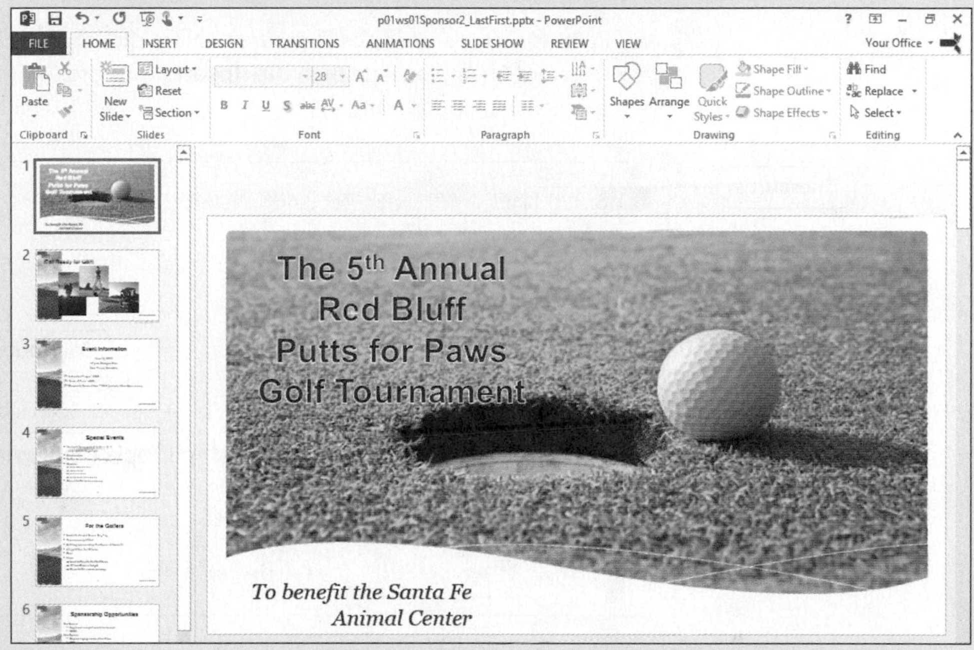

Figure 27 Finished Slide 1

f. **Save** the presentation.

Replace Words Using the Research Pane

PowerPoint provides access to other tools that can help you as you prepare presentations. The Research pane, opened by clicking Research in the Proofing group on the Review tab, provides access to a variety of reference books, research websites, and business and financial sites. You can use this pane to find and review information posted on the Internet by the Santa Fe Chamber of Commerce.

One of the reference books available on the Research pane is a **Thesaurus**. You notice that the word "sponsor" is used four times on Slide 4, and you would like to view other words that have a similar meaning.

P01.19

To Use the Thesaurus

a. Click **Slide 6** on the left hand pane, select the word **Sponsor** in the Cart Sponsor heading, click the **REVIEW** tab, and then in the **Proofing** group, click **Thesaurus**.

> **Troubleshooting**
> When selecting text for the Thesaurus, be careful not to select the space after the word "Sponsor". If you do, the end-of-line marker will be replaced, and the next bullet point will merge with the first line. Press Enter after the word "Sponsor" to resolve the problem.

b. Point to **Champion** in the Thesaurus listing, click the **arrow** that appears to the right of the word Champion, and then click **Insert**. The word **Champion** is applied to the largest sponsorship opportunity.

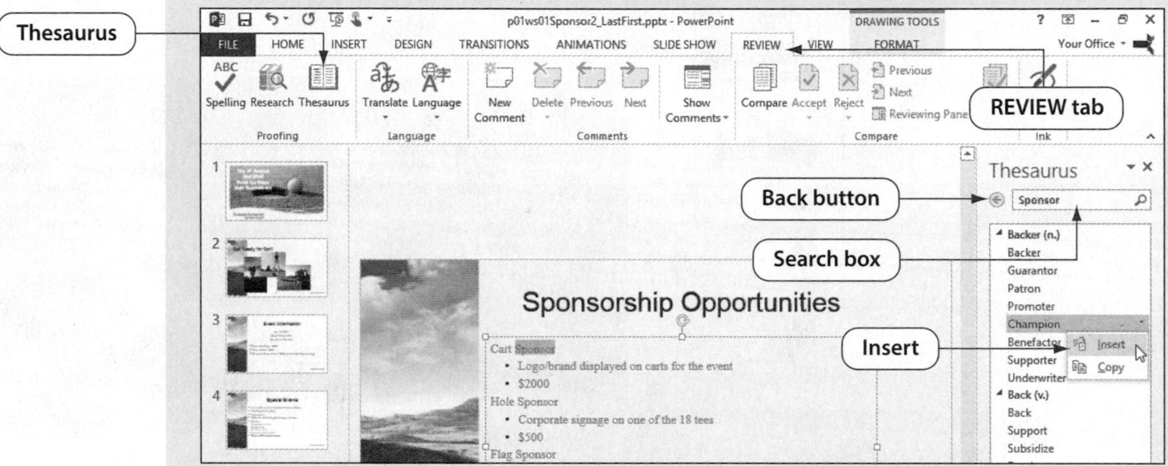

Figure 28 Using the Research pane

c. **Close** the Thesaurus pane. **Save** the presentation.

Saving and Printing a Presentation

PowerPoint has many options for saving a presentation to fit different needs. So far you have been saving your presentation in a format that can only be opened with PowerPoint 2007 or later. Because not everyone has the most recent version of the software, some options include saving the presentation so it is compatible with a previous PowerPoint version, in an OpenDocument format, or in a Portable Document Format (PDF). In this section, you will explore saving a presentation.

Save a Presentation

Sometimes it is appropriate to save the file so it opens directly in Slide Show view. **PowerPoint Show** is convenient because you do not have to open the software and then click the Slide Show button. It looks more professional to start the presentation without fumbling with additional clicks. This method also works well if you want to keep others from editing your slide content, because when you have displayed all of the slides, the application closes automatically.

Another option you have is to save the file for distribution on a website, via **PDF** (Portable Document Format). When a file is saved as a PDF file it does not open in PowerPoint but rather in a PDF Reader application. This means that you can not use PowerPoint to update a PDF file. Be sure to always save the file in PowerPoint format too so you have the latest version of your presentation in an editable format.

Saving Your Presentation in Different Formats

You will save the Putts for Paws presentation as a PowerPoint Show and as a PDF file. Each one will be named differently so you can observe the differences between them.

P01.20

To Save in Different File Formats

a. Click the **FILE** tab, and then click **Save As**.

b. Click **Computer**, and then click **Browse** on the bottom right. Click the **Save as type** arrow, and then click **PowerPoint Show**.

c. Click in the **File name** box, and then change the file name to p01ws01SponsorShow_LastFirst, using your first and last name.

d. Click **Save**.
The file is saved in PowerPoint Show format, and the Normal PowerPoint view is displayed.

e. Click the **FILE** tab, and then click **Save As**. Click **Computer**, then click **Browse**.

f. Click **Save as type**, and then click **PDF**.

g. Click **File name**, and then change the file name to p01ws01SponsorPDF_LastFirst.

h. Click **Save**. The file is published in PDF format. Close the **PDF** and return to PowerPoint.

i. Close your **PowerPoint Show**, but keep PowerPoint open. Open the folder where you store your PowerPoint projects. You should now see the several different files saved as a result of this exercise and you can explore opening the various file types.

Preview and Print a Presentation

Many audiences will request a copy of your presentation for future reference. Many speakers make the PDF version available on a website as an eco-friendly option, but more importantly, it is a universal format that anyone can read with a free reader. Other speakers will make hard copies of the most important slides in the presentation to distribute after the presentation. For other audiences, handouts with thumbnail versions of the slides are appropriate. The presentation can also be printed in outline format, so the audience has the text from the presentation but not the slide graphics, tables, or pictures. You can print the presentation as Notes Pages, which prints the slides and the notes in the Notes pane, so you can have a copy to use as your speaker notes. The decision to print or not depends upon the audience description and the purpose of the presentation.

CONSIDER THIS | When Should You Pass Out the Handouts?

Should you pass out the handouts before you begin the presentation or at the end? Describe a situation where it would be good to hand them out before the presentation. Is there any reason why it may be distracting for the audience to have printed versions of the slides during a presentation? List some reasons for waiting until the end of the presentation to distribute handouts.

The rule of thumb for printing is to print as few sheets as possible to conserve resources. It is important to use the preview function of PowerPoint to review the potential printout prior to printing the slide show. Keep in mind that it is more economical to print in black and white than color or gray scale, especially if you are planning to use a copier to make additional copies.

Printing Slides

Printing each slide individually is time consuming and not generally necessary. At times, one or two slides may contain information that is important. You will print Slides 3 through 7 from the presentation to share with the marketing director.

P01.21

To Print Selected Slides

a. Open the file **p01ws01Sponsor2_LastFirst** file, click the **FILE** tab, and then click **Print**.

b. Select the **printer name** as directed by your instructor.

c. Click the **Print All Slides** arrow, and then select **Custom Range**.

d. Type 3-7 in the **Slides** box. Be sure to include the dash.

e. Click **Color**, and then click **Pure Black and White**.

f. If your instructor directs you to submit a printed copy, click **Print** after reviewing the Preview pane.

g. Click the **Back** button to return to the presentation in Normal view.

Printing Handouts

As you print handouts for your audience, you have many style choices to make. You can print one to nine slides per page, determining whether they are sequential either horizontally or vertically. You can choose to frame the slides, scale them to fit the paper, and select high-quality printing.

You will print a copy of your entire presentation to use in a discussion you will have with the golf pro, John Schilling. He will give the presentation at various times during the next month and should review the slides. You will preview a few options before printing the final document.

P01.22

To Print Handouts

SIDE NOTE

Print Handouts with Note Lines

The 3 Slides handout is ideal to take notes during the presentation. Print on both sides.

a. Click the **FILE** tab, and then click **Print**. Click **Custom Range**, and then click **Print All Slides**.

b. Under **Settings**, click **Full Page Slides**, and then click **6 Slides Horizontal** in the Handouts section. The slides are displayed on a single sheet of paper, with Slide 2 next to Slide 1, and so on down the page.

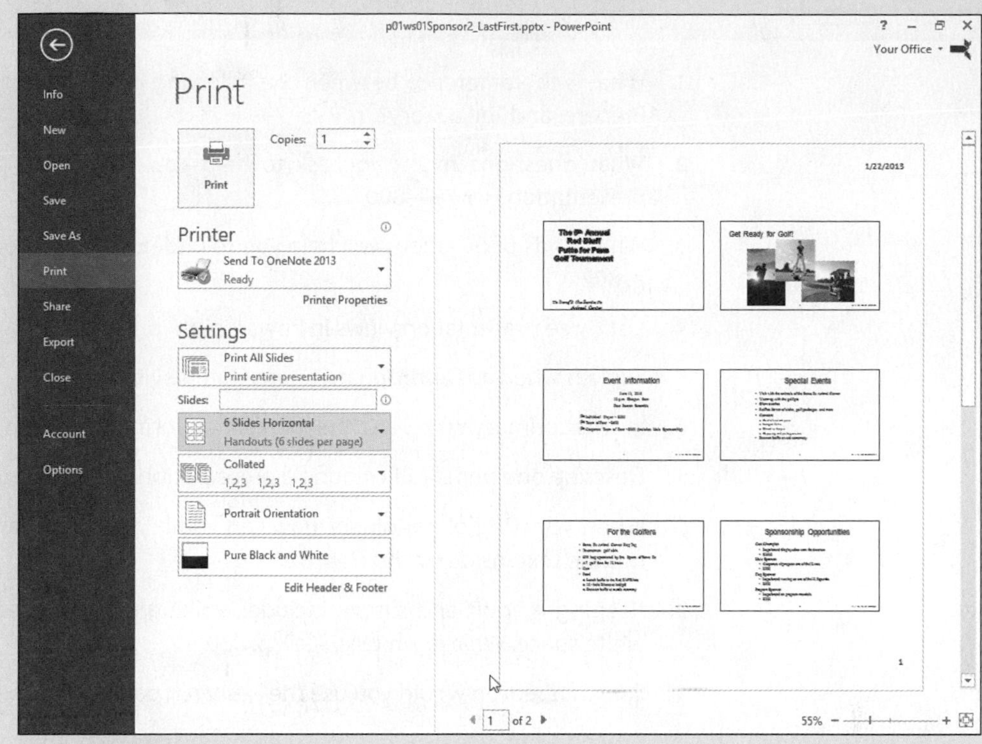

Figure 29 Printing handouts

c. If your instructor directs you to submit a copy of the document, click **Print**.

d. Click the **Back** button to return to Normal view.

Printing the Outline

For some audiences, an outline of the presentation is sufficient. The outline displays the headings and body text on the slides, but not the graphics. You will print an outline to use as a reminder sheet when you talk to potential sponsors and players. You want to accurately discuss the perks for the golfers, describe the special events, and recall the costs for participation.

P01.23

To Print an Outline

a. Click the **FILE** tab, and then click **Print**.

b. Click the **Print Layout** arrow, and then click **Outline**.
The content of the slides is displayed on two pages. You decide that you do not need to have the title slide information or the Contact Us slide, so you will set a range for the Slide numbers 2 to 6.

c. Type 2-6 in the Slides box, and then click the **Next Page** button, if necessary, to view the outline. Review the document preview.

d. Click **Print** if your instructor directs you to submit a copy of the document.

e. On the FILE tab, click **Close**. Exit **PowerPoint**, and then submit your files as directed by your instructor.

Concept Check

1. What is the difference between the following presentation purposes: Inform, Persuade, Prepare, and Tell a Story? p. 798–799
2. What questions might you ask to help you define the purpose and scope of your presentation? p. 799–800
3. What kinds of questions will help you to understand the needs of your target audience? p. 802
4. List three presentation views in PowerPoint. p. 809
5. Explain when it is appropriate to use Outline view. p. 813
6. In what primary way is a template distinct from a theme? pp. 815–816
7. Describe one benefit of creating a presentation from a template. p. 820
8. When selecting placeholders, how can you know if you have selected the text box and not the text inside the box? p. 827
9. Keeping it short and simple includes striking a balance between visual elements and white space. What is white space? p. 830
10. For what reason would you use the Research pane? p. 831
11. Explain when you would save a slide show as a PowerPoint Show versus a PDF. p. 832
12. List three options for printing a presentation. p. 833

Key Terms

Visual Summary

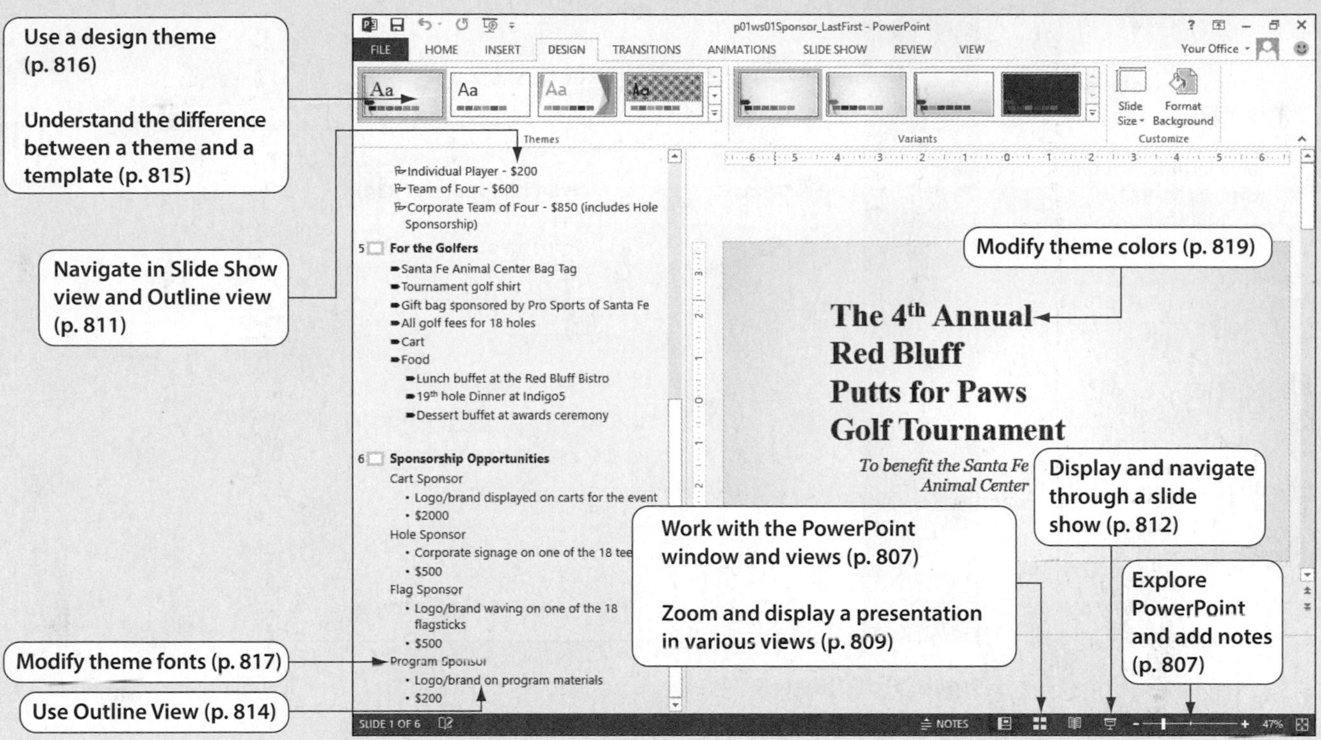
Use a design theme (p. 816)
Understand the difference between a theme and a template (p. 815)
Navigate in Slide Show view and Outline view (p. 811)
Modify theme colors (p. 819)
The 4th Annual Red Bluff Putts for Paws Golf Tournament
To benefit the Santa Fe Animal Center
Display and navigate through a slide show (p. 812)
Work with the PowerPoint window and views (p. 807)
Zoom and display a presentation in various views (p. 809)
Explore PowerPoint and add notes (p. 807)
Modify theme fonts (p. 817)
Use Outline View (p. 814)

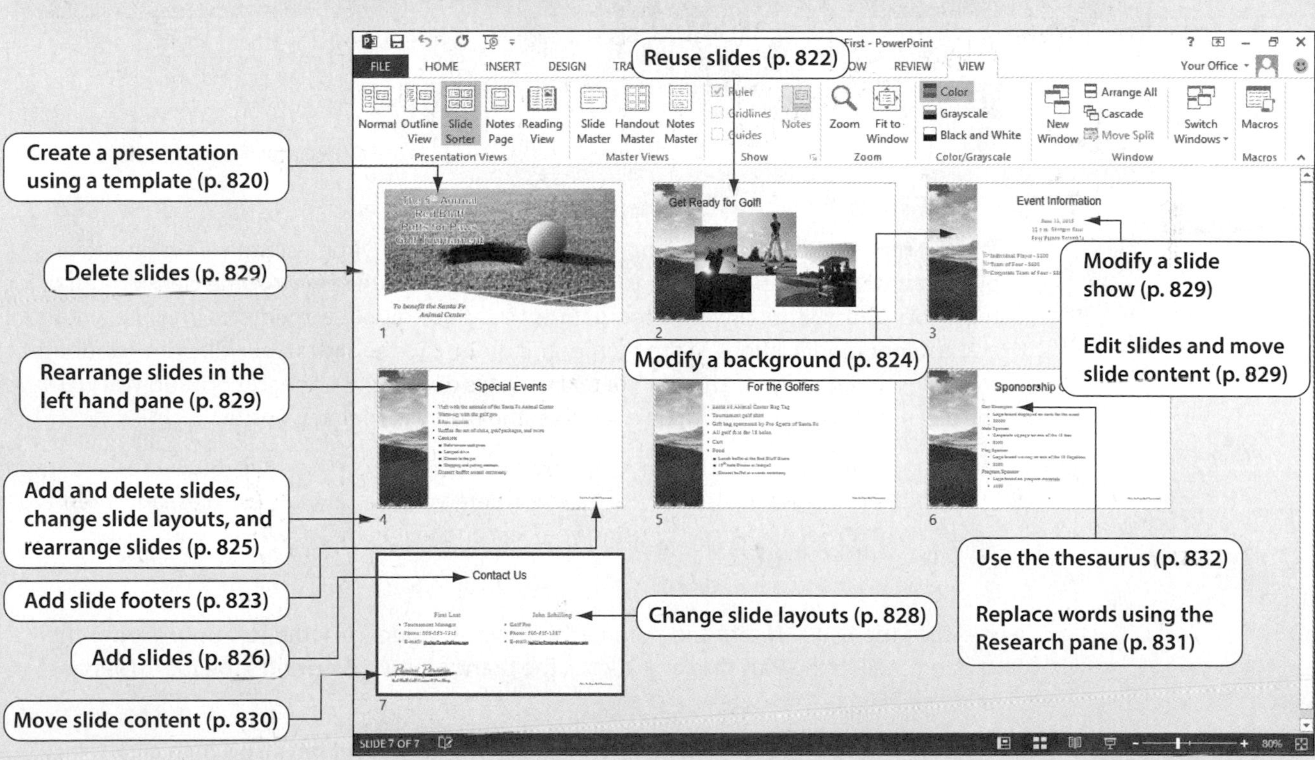
Reuse slides (p. 822)
Create a presentation using a template (p. 820)
Delete slides (p. 829)
Modify a slide show (p. 829)
Edit slides and move slide content (p. 829)
Modify a background (p. 824)
Rearrange slides in the left hand pane (p. 829)
Add and delete slides, change slide layouts, and rearrange slides (p. 825)
Add slide footers (p. 823)
Add slides (p. 826)
Move slide content (p. 830)
Change slide layouts (p. 828)
Use the thesaurus (p. 832)
Replace words using the Research pane (p. 831)

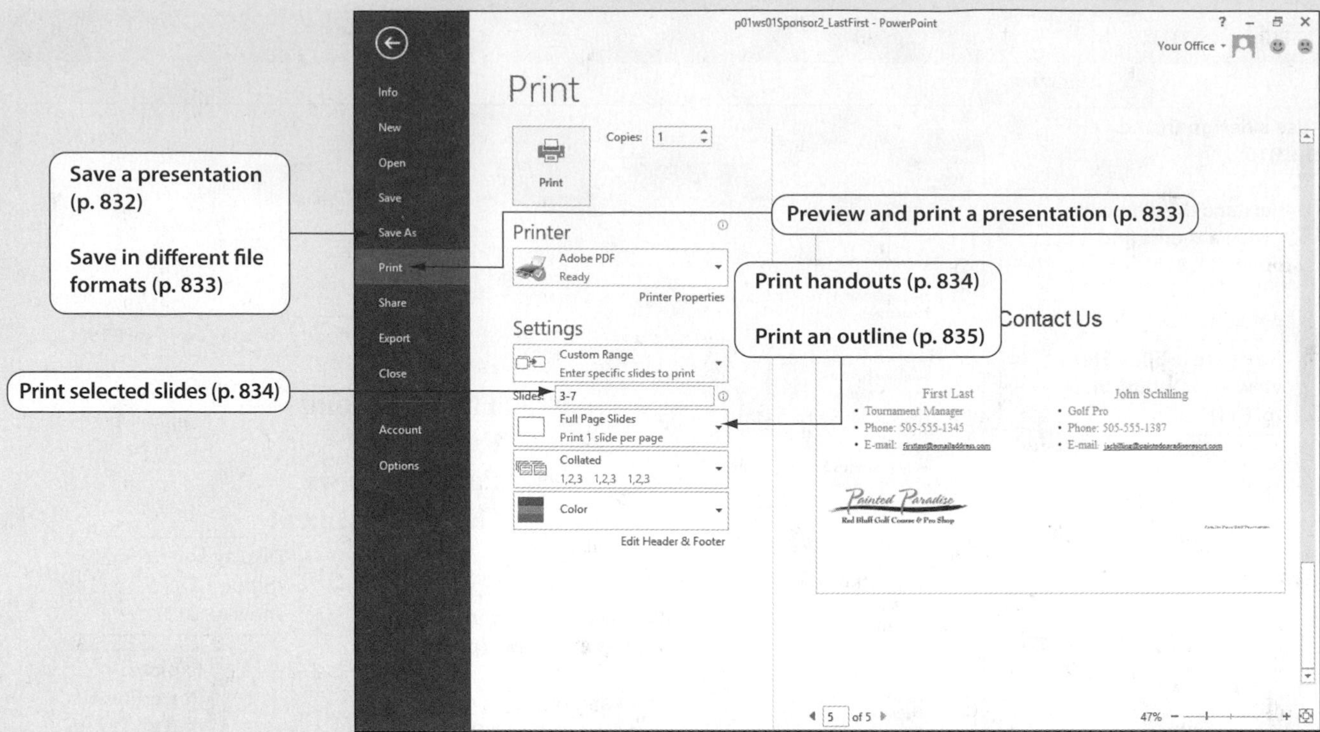

Figure 30 The Red Bluff Golf Course & Pro Shop Putts for Paws Golf Tournament Presentation Final

Practice 1

Student data files needed:

p01ws01Products.pptx

p01ws01LogoPT.jpg

You will save your files as:

p01ws01Products_LastFirst.pptx

p01ws01ProductsPDF_LastFirst.pdf

Gift Shop Product Line Presentation

The Painted Treasures gift shop manager requested your assistance in improving a presentation that she will make to the staff to introduce them to some new products for the shop. You will modify and reorganize the slides, apply a theme to the presentation, make minor modifications to the theme, and proofread the slides. You will print handouts of the slides to distribute to the staff for taking notes during the presentation, and you will save the file in PDF format so it can be posted on the resort's training website.

a. Start **PowerPoint**, and then open **p01ws01Products**. Click the **FILE** tab, and then click **Save As**. Navigate to the location where you are saving your files, and then type p01ws01Products_LastFirst, using your last and first name.

b. In the left hand pane, click **Slide 1**.

c. Click the **DESIGN** tab, and then in the Themes group, click the **Ion Boardroom** theme, and then in the **Variants** group, click the orange/brown **Variant**—the fourth variant.

d. You decide you will change the fonts. Click the **VIEW** tab, and then in the Master Views group, click **Slide Master**. In the Background group, click **Fonts**, and then click **Office**.

e. In the Background group, click **Colors**, and then click **Customize Colors**. Click the **Text/ Background - Dark 2** arrow, and then select **More Colors**. Click the **Custom** tab, and then type 241 in the **Red** box, 90 in the **Green** box, and 41 in the **Blue** box. Click **OK**.

f. Click the **Accent 5** arrow, and then select **More Colors**. On the Custom tab, type 40 in the **Red** box, 83 in the **Green** box, and 160 in the **Blue** box. Click **OK**, and then click **Save**. Click **Close Master View**.

g. Click **Slide 1**, click the **INSERT** tab, and then in the Images group, click **Pictures**. Browse to your data files, select **p01ws01LogoPT**, and then click **Insert**.

h. Right-click the **image**, and then click **Size and Position**. In the Format Picture pane, click the **POSITION** arrow, and type 1.5″ in the **Vertical position** box. Close the Format Picture pane.

i. Click the **FORMAT** tab, and then in the Picture Styles group, click **Drop Shadow Rectangle**, the fourth from left.

j. Right-click the image again, and then click **Copy**. Click the **VIEW** tab, in the Master Views group, click **Slide Master**. Scroll up to the **Ion Boardroom Slide Master** slide, right-click the slide, and then click **Paste, Use Destination Theme**.

k. Right-click the image again, and then click **Size and Position**. Click the **SIZE** arrow, and then type 2 in the Width box. Click the **POSITION** arrow. Type 0.1″ in the Horizontal position box, and then type 0.1″ in the Vertical position box.

l. Close the Format Picture pane, and then return to **Normal** view. With **Slide 1** selected, click the **DESIGN** tab, and then in the Customize group, click **Format Background**. Check **Hide background graphics**. Select the image on Slide 1, and then set it to **Align Center**.

m. Insert the following text in the footer, **Copyright 2015, Painted Paradise Resort and Spa** on all slides except the Title Slide.

n. Click the **HOME** tab, and then in the Slides group, click the **New Slide** arrow, and then click **Title and Content**. In the title placeholder of the new slide, type **Our Goals**. In the body placeholder type the following.

   - **Introduce our new product lines**
   - **Increase sales by 18%**
   - **Have fun!**

   Select the text you just typed, and change the **font size** to **24**.

o. On **Slide 1**, select the **subtitle text**, and then click **Increase Font Size** to **24**.

p. Display **Slide 5**. Select the second line of body text, press and hold Ctrl, and then select the **fourth** and **sixth line**. In the Paragraph group, click **Increase List Level**. Select all of the body text, and then set the font size to **20**.

q. Display **Slide 4**, and select the **Content Placeholder**, displaying the text **Comfort**, **Beauty**, and **Style**. Move the placeholder down until the there is no background behind the text. It is okay if some of the placeholder overlaps the picture.

r. On **Slide 4**, click the **top sizing handle** of the **Content Placeholder** beginning with **Cashmere Blankets** and drag it down until it aligns with the top of the picture on the left.

s. Click **Slide 6**. Select the **jewelry items**, including the bulleted items under each type of jewelry, and then set the **font size** to **20**. Drag the **top sizing handle** down until the placeholder aligns to the bottom of the title placeholder background.

t. On **Slide 7**, change the **font size** of the body text placeholder to **24**.

u. Click **Slide 3**, and then in the Slides group, click **Layout**, and then select **Two Content**. Select the text beginning with **Ask** and continuing through **Suggest additional items based on purchase**, and then drag the text to the placeholder on the right. In the Font group, click **Increase Font Size** once to change the font to size **20**.

v. Drag the **top sizing handle** of the left placeholder down to visually balance the text, and so that the first bullet of the text box on the left aligns with the one on the right. Click **Increase Font Size** once to change the font to size **20**.

w. Drag **Slide 3** on the Slide pane to the end of the slide show. Click **Slide 4** on the Slide pane, and drag it to the Slide 3 position. Delete **Slide 7**, "Contact Us."

x. Click the **Slide Show** button in the status bar, and hold the left and right mouse buttons down at the same time for two seconds to begin at the first slide. Press Enter to advance through the slides.

y. Click the **FILE** tab, and then click **Save As**. Click **Browse**, navigate to where you are saving your files, click the **Save as type** arrow, and then click **PDF**. Type p01ws01ProductsPDF_LastFirst, using your last and first name, and then click **Save**.

z. On the FILE tab, click **Print**, click the **Full Page Slides** arrow, and then click **3 Slides** in the Handouts group. Click the **Color** arrow, and then click **Grayscale**. If your instructor directs you to submit a printed copy, click **Print**. Save the presentation, close the presentation, and then exit PowerPoint.

Problem Solve 1

Student data file needed:

You will save your files as:

 p01ws01Wonders_LastFirst.pptx

 p01ws01WondersShow_LastFirst.ppsx

Your World Travel Presentation

Sales & Marketing

100 million votes were cast through the Internet or by telephone for a project conducted by the New7Wonders Foundation. On July 7, 2007, the 7 New Wonders of the World were announced at a ceremony in Lisbon, Portugal. Claire Alexander, owner of Your World Travel Agency, would like to encourage clients to visit these 7 Wonders. Each month she holds an open house at her agency and would like to use a presentation featuring the 7 New Wonders to generate interest in both individual and group tours. Claire has already created a presentation with basic information and pictures. Your job is to add a theme and to format the slides attractively. You will also save the file in PowerPoint Show format so it can be shared.

a. Start **PowerPoint**, open **p01ws01Wonders**, and then save the presentation as p01ws01Wonders_LastFirst. Review the information on the slides.

b. Apply the **Integral** theme.

c. Create a new **Theme** color. Click the **Accent 2** color, and then select **Dark Red** under Standard Colors. Type LastFirst New Integral in the Name box, and then click **Save**.

d. After Slide 1, add a new slide with the **Title and Content** layout. In the title placeholder, type New 7 Wonders of the World. In the body placeholder, type:

- Elected by more than 100 million votes from around the world
- Represents global heritage throughout history
- Announced at ceremony in Lisbon on 07-07-07
- Pyramids in Egypt were granted an honorary status as the only remaining Ancient Wonder

e. Insert a footer, Copyright 2015, Your World Travel. Have it appear on every slide except the title slide.

f. Select the **footer** placeholder, and change the font color to **Dark Red**.

g. On Slide 1, click after **Wonders** in the title, and add the words of the World.

h. On Slide 2, select the text **Cuzco Region, Peru (1460-1470 CE)** and apply bold formatting. Apply the same formatting to the first line of body text on Slide 4 through Slide 9.

i. On Slide 10, right-align the **title**. For the three lines of body text, increase the font size to **28**. Drag the **top sizing handle** down so the body text is the same distance from the bottom of the placeholder as it is from the top.

j. Change to **Slide Sorter** view. Change the Zoom to **100%**, if necessary. You should be able to see the dates on the first line of body text for Slides 3 to 9. You will arrange these slides in the order in which the sites were built. Drag **Slide 5**, The Great Wall of China, so it becomes Slide 3. Arrange the remaining slides in chronological order so that BCE dates come before CE dates. When a beginning date and ending date are given together, use the beginning date.

k. Return to **Normal** view. On **Slide 3**, format the background as **Picture or texture fill** using the image in your data files folder that matches the image on the slide. Make the background 80% transparent. Do this for the remaining slides with their respective background pictures.

l. On **Slide 8**, format the foreground picture with the Picture Style **Reflected Bevel, White**. Repeat this format for the remaining slides.

m. On **Slide 4**, drag the **right sizing handle** of the body text placeholder so that it aligns with the left edge of the foreground image. Repeat this for **Slide 9**.

n. View the slide show from the beginning, and then save the presentation.

o. Save the presentation as a PowerPoint Show as p01ws01WondersShow_LastFirst.

p. Close the presentation. Exit PowerPoint, and then submit your files as directed by your instructor.

Perform 1: Perform in Your Career

Student data files needed:

Blank PowerPoint presentation

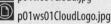

p01ws01Cloud.jpg

p01ws01CloudLogo.jpg

You will save your files as:

p01ws01Cloud_LastFirst.pptx

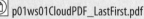

p01ws01CloudPDF_LastFirst.pdf

Cloud Storage Presentation

Information Technology

You have been asked to present options for cloud-based file storage at your company. You will create a presentation with five competing storage options and discuss the pros and cons of each, recommending your top pick at the end of the presentation. You will apply a theme to the presentation, make minor modifications to the theme, and include a logo in the top-left corner of each slide. You will print handouts of the slides to distribute for taking notes during the presentation, and then you will save the file in PDF format so it can be shared with remote attendees.

a. Create a new **presentation** from a template using available options. You may use an Office.com template in place of a built-in template if you prefer.

b. Modify your template by replacing the **background** of the title slide with the image **p01ws01Cloud**. Be sure to set an appropriate level of transparency so the title text is easy to read.

c. Your title text should read Cloud Storage Alternatives.

d. Your presentation should include a title slide, an agenda slide, one slide for each of the five alternatives presented, and a recommendation slide.

e. Make use of at least two different layout styles, in addition to the title slide.

f. On each slide presenting an alternative cloud storage service, be sure to include the following relevant facts: the name of the service, storage capacity, desktop and browser and mobile client support. Be sure to also include at least one positive and one negative evaluation for each about, for example, performance, file sync and versioning, security, or file and folder sharing and collaboration.

g. Insert your logo, **p01ws01CloudLogo**, in the top-left corner of every slide except the title slide. It should be sized appropriately and have a picture style applied from the available choices.

h. Save the presentation as **p01ws01Cloud_LastFirst**, print handouts with three slides to a page, and then save the presentation as a PDF, using the file name **p01ws01CloudPDF_LastFirst**. Submit your files as directed by your instructor.

Additional Cases

Additional Workshop Cases are available on the companion website and in the instructor resources.

WORKSHOP 2 | TEXT AND GRAPHICS

OBJECTIVES

Prepare Case

The Red Bluff Caddy School Presentation

Human Resources

The Red Bluff Golf Course & Pro Shop is sponsoring a caddy school. You will create the first-day presentation for training. The audience will be people 18–25 years old who are interested in learning about golf and who want to be caddies at the golf club. You will modify a presentation and add appropriate graphics before passing it along to John Schilling, the golf pro, for final approval.

Patricia Homeester / Shutterstock.com

REAL WORLD SUCCESS

"I remember how cluttered, confusing, and boring the vendor's presentation was. Then the presenter said, 'I think I'm putting Clark to sleep here.' That's when I woke up. It was embarrassing, but I was on the client team and unimpressed. His company did not win our business that day, and I learned a valuable lesson about how important a good presentation really is. The text and graphics have to come alive, and that's usually left to the presenter."

- Clark, client executive

Student data files needed for this workshop:

 p01ws02Caddy.pptx
 p01ws02ProShop.jpg
 p01ws02Pink.jpg
 p01ws02Caddy.jpg
 p01ws02GolfGirl.jpg
 p01ws02Blue.jpg
 p01ws02GolfBall.jpg
 p01ws02Green.jpg
 p01ws02Bullet.png

You will save your file as:

 p01ws02Caddy_LastFirst.pptx

Using Text Effectively

The content of your presentation, especially the text, is a very important element of your slide show. You must ensure the accuracy of your words. People remember and believe more of what they see on the screen than what they hear. In this section, you will review your content carefully because making retractions or corrections after a presentation is difficult.

Modify Text

As you use PowerPoint, you will make a lot of decisions. You will decide how to group content items. You will select fonts for the text elements. You will align the text and organize it on the slide. You will edit your content to improve the layout of slides.

After a discussion on font selections, you will continue to modify the Caddy School presentation to improve the readability of the slides. You will also align the text to better organize the information.

Understanding Print-Friendly and Screen-Friendly Fonts

Typography, the art of selecting and arranging text on a page, is an interesting topic for in-depth study. Understanding some basic concepts enables you to produce slides that are easy to read. People read printed pages and screen pages differently, which affects the choices you make for the fonts in your slide show.

REAL WORLD ADVICE **Readability Is Key!**

Readability is the most important aspect of a presentation. If possible, project your slides and stand at the far back of the room. Can you still read everything easily? What if you had vision problems? Anything that is too small to read should be adjusted prior to displaying the slide show to your audience. A common occurrence in the business world is a presentation that contains financial information or other numbers that are small and hard to read. A solution to the problem is to summarize the numbers on the slides and provide the complete data in handouts.

Printer-friendly fonts have characteristics that make them easy to read on paper, as shown in Figure 1. They are usually printed in black ink on a white page giving them high contrast, which improves the readability of the text. Serif fonts are considered formal, business-like, and powerful. Often, **serif fonts**, such as Times New Roman, are used for large blocks of text. The serifs, or small lines at the ends of the letters, provide guidelines for the eye to follow as the text is read. These fonts move the eye quickly across the page. Black-and-white printing is also less expensive than printing with color.

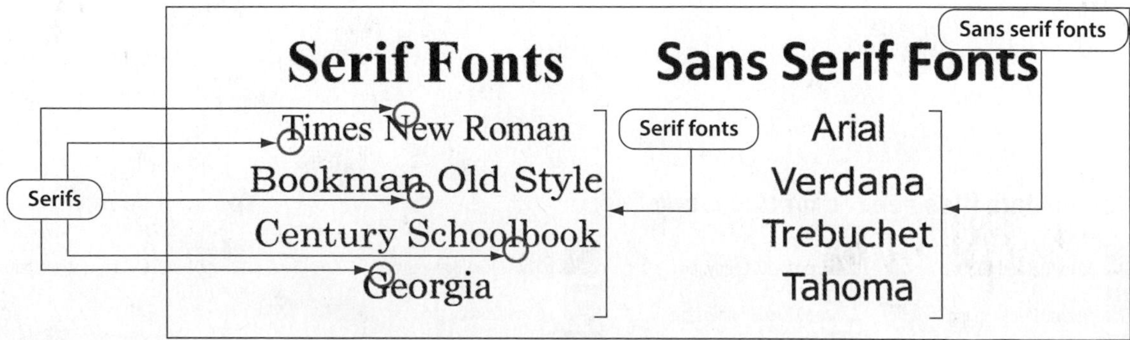

Figure 1 Serif and sans serif fonts

MODULE 1

Screen-friendly fonts are easy to read on the screen, help protect the eyes, and reduce stress. Because of the resolution of the text on displayed slides, fonts on slides must maintain their integrity at great size. **Sans serif fonts**, such as Verdana and Trebuchet, were designed specifically for screens. "Sans" means "without" in Latin, so sans serif fonts do not have small lines at the ends of the letters. Sans serif fonts give the text a casual, modern feel. The serif font Georgia is also a good screen-friendly font. You will often find the title of slides displayed in a serif font, while the content of the slide is set to a sans serif font. Screen-friendly fonts have an additional perk: you can use color without additional expense. Be aware that you must still select colors that have a good amount of contrast to make the text easy to read. Avoid color combinations that are hard on the eyes, such as a red background with turquoise text. Select two or three colors to use consistently throughout your presentation. Later you will learn about PowerPoint themes that enable you to use colors consistently. Remember that your goal is to have people read your slides.

CONSIDER THIS | Selecting Color for Accessibility

Did you know that about 8 percent of males and .5 percent of females are color-blind? How could you accommodate these individuals as you select colors and format important concepts and information? Are you limited to black and white?

Making Font Selections

Generally, you will design slides with a sans serif font for the majority of the text, occasionally using a serif font for emphasis. Text should be a mixture of upper and lowercase characters, even for headings. It is more difficult to read text that is written in all capitals. You should avoid hyphenation of words on your slides when possible. Tracking between the parts of hyphenated words is difficult when the slide is projected. It is a good idea to use bold for emphasis. Italic text is hard to read and underlined text can be confused with hyperlinks.

Importantly, you must also decide the font size. Your goal is to have your slides read. Text that is too small frustrates the audience. Slide titles are set in a larger font than the body of the slide. The minimum font size you should use for the body text is 18 point. Of course, larger is better!

Providing an Appropriate Amount of Text on a Slide

As you create content for your slides, think like a headline writer, striving for the fewest words possible to convey your point. For instance, replace "Our goal is to increase sales by 55% in the coming year," with "Goal—Increase sales 55%. "Use bullet points rather than complete sentences. Remove repetitive words, replacing them with a heading. Rather than placing a number-rich table on a slide, summarize the numbers. Focus your audience on your purpose by covering one major point or concept per slide.

A worthwhile rule of thumb is the **rule of six**—also known as the 6×6 rule. This rule calls for a maximum of six lines per slide and six words per line, not including the title. The rule helps to ensure that your slides are readable. Do not worry if you occasionally have more words on a line. This is a guideline. Your goal is to put the absolute essence of your message on your slides. You want the audience to interact with you—not spend all of their time reading the screen. Remember that the slide show is a visual aid, meant to support your presentation.

P02.00

To Open and Save a File

a. Point to the **bottom-right** corner of the Start screen. On the Charms bar, click the **Search** charm. In the search box at the top of the page, type PowerPoint.

b. Click **PowerPoint 2013**.

c. Click **Open Other Presentations**, then under Open, click **Computer**, and under Computer, click **Browse**. Navigate to where your student data files are located, click **p01ws02Caddy**, and then click **Open**.

d. Save the file as p01ws02Caddy_LastFirst using your last and first name.

Modifying Fonts in a Presentation

In this exercise, you will modify presentation slides for the Red Bluff Golf Course & Pro Shop Caddy School.

MyITLab®
Workshop 2 Training

P02.01

To Make Font Adjustments

a. Click **Slide 1**, and then select the text **Red Bluff Golf Course & Pro Shop Caddy School**. On the HOME tab, in the Font group, click the **Font** arrow, and then select **Calibri**. Notice that the words are in small caps.

b. In the Font group, click the **Font Dialog Box Launcher**. In the Font dialog box, uncheck **Small Caps**, and then click **OK**.

The words "Caddy School" appear on the same line as the rest of the title. Because these words are not related to the Red Bluff Golf Course & Pro Shop, it is best to separate them.

c. Click to position the insertion point before the word **Caddy**, and then press Enter.

d. Select the **title** placeholder—or border—so that you see a solid line instead of a dotted line. In the **Font** group, click the **Font Size** arrow, and then select **40**.

e. Click the **VIEW** tab, and then in the Show group, click **Ruler** to display the ruler. Click the **title text** placeholder and then drag the left **sizing handle** to the **4"** mark to the left of **0** on the horizontal ruler. The title text should fit in the placeholder.

SIDE NOTE
Display the Ruler
To display the ruler, click the View tab, and in the Show group, click Ruler.

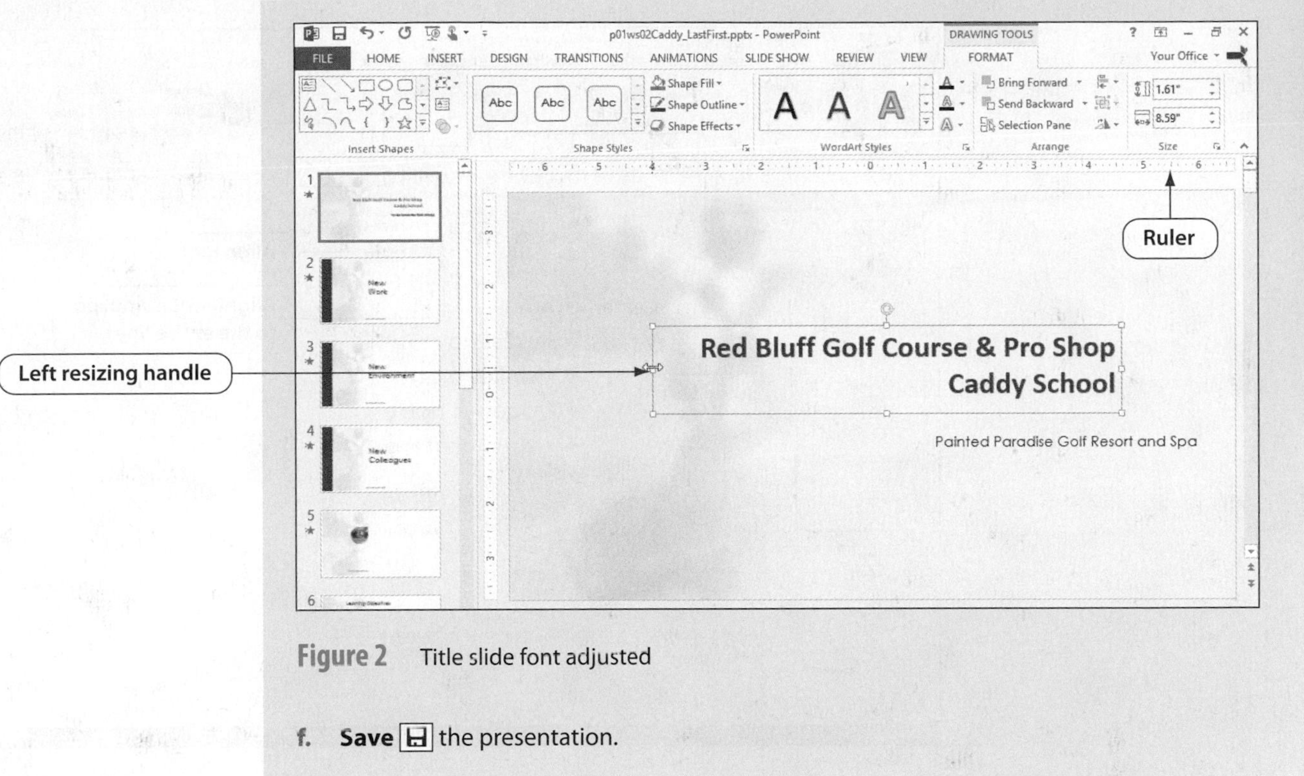

Figure 2 Title slide font adjusted

f. **Save** the presentation.

Aligning Text

Proper text alignment provides organization to the text and enables your audience to read the material more easily. On the Home tab, the Paragraph group contains options to Align Left, Center, Align Right, and Justify text. Most of the body text you type on slides should be left-aligned. People begin reading at the left side of the page and are comfortable with this alignment. Center alignment is sometimes used in titles. It is difficult to read large amounts of text that is centered, so it is a good idea not to center the slide body text. Right alignment is used for emphasis or artistic reasons, and with limited amounts of text. Often right alignment is a solution to placing captions close to photographs that are on the right side of the slide. Justified alignment produces a block with both the left and right margins aligned. Extra spaces are automatically added between the words to achieve the alignment of the margins. This works well for quotations that are longer than one line. In this exercise, you will change the alignment in the presentation.

P02.02

To Align Text

a. Select **Slide 14** from the thumbnails in the left pane.

b. On **Slide 14**, click anywhere in the title text of **Case Study**. On the HOME tab, in the Paragraph group, click **Align Left**. Alignment is applied to the entire line when you place the insertion point in the line.

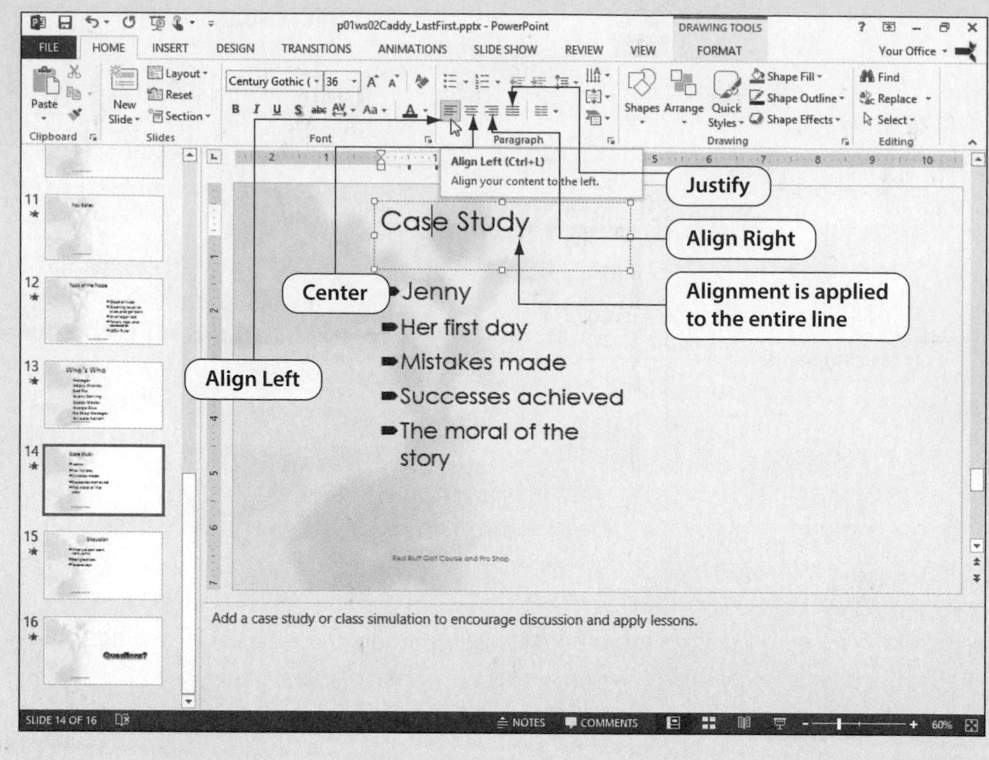

Figure 3 Aligning text

c. Click **Slide 15**. Select the **title text** placeholder. On the HOME tab, in the Paragraph group, click **Align Left**. The alignment is applied to the text within the placeholder.

d. **Save** the presentation.

Use Text Hierarchy to Convey Organization

As you develop the content of your presentation, you will quickly see that there are relationships between the pieces of information. You will want to group information together and perhaps provide a title so your audience sees the information in an organized way. This helps them to remember your key points.

List hierarchy can be shown using bullets or numbers. Bullets are used to group unordered items into a list. In PowerPoint, you can select different bullet symbols using the Bullets arrow in the Paragraph group. You can even customize the bullet symbol by changing the color or size. Many people select custom bullet symbols from the Wingdings font because of the graphic nature of the symbols. Numbers are used for **ordered lists**—sequential steps that need to appear in a specific order. The format of numbers can be Roman numerals, Arabic numerals, or letters. The color and size of the numbers can also be adjusted. You can also change the starting number for the list.

Using Lists

List hierarchy also includes indenting subitems on a slide. The first bulleted point may have three or four characteristics, which are indented and have a different bullet character. The Paragraph group contains the commands to increase and decrease the indention of the items. In this next exercise, you will add a picture bullet to the list of employees helping with the caddy school.

P02.03

To Apply Text Hierarchy and Bullets

a. Click **Slide 14** on the left hand pane, and select the text of the four bullets below the text "Jenny". On the HOME tab, in the Paragraph group, click **Increase List Level**.

b. Click **Slide 13**, and then click in the text **Barry Cheney**. On the HOME tab, in the Paragraph group, click the **Bullets** arrow.

c. Click **Bullets and Numbering**.

d. In the Bullets and Numbering dialog box, click **Picture**, and then next to From a file, click **Browse**. Navigate to where your student data files are located, select the file **p01ws02Bullet**, and then click **Insert**. The bullet has been updated to a custom bullet point.

e. In the Paragraph group, click the **Bullets** arrow, click **Bullets and Numbering**, set the **Size** to 150 % of text, and then click **OK**. You will apply the new bullet to the other names in the next exercise.

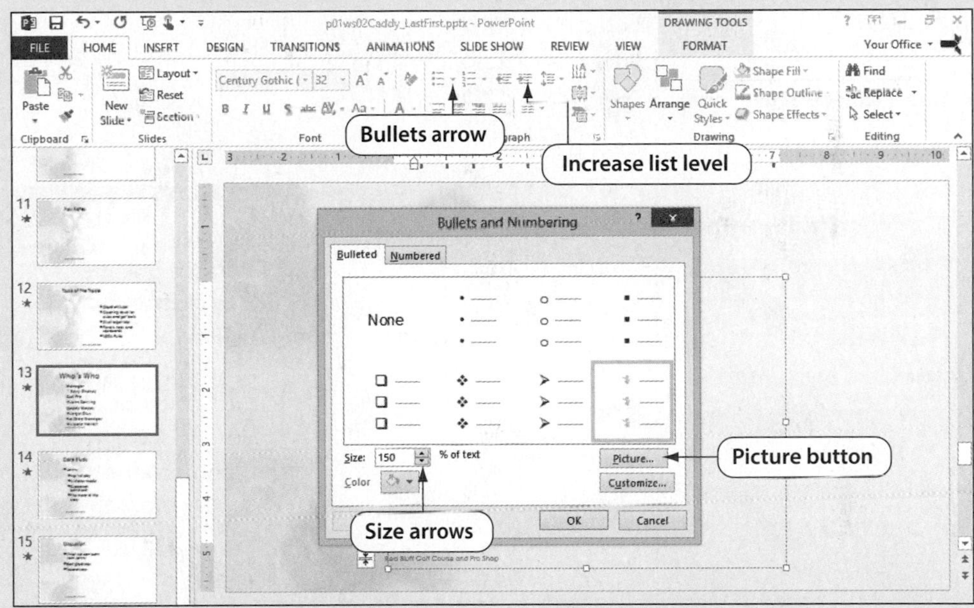

Figure 4 Bullets and Numbering dialog box

f. **Save** the presentation.

Reuse Formats

The **Format Painter** enables you to select the format of something and apply it to something else within the presentation. This is done quickly by touching the paintbrush to whatever has the format you need, and then touching the thing that needs it—like copy and paste, but with a paintbrush. To use Format Painter for multiple instances, such as applying the format to different slides, select the text you want to copy, and double-click Format Painter. When you have finished formatting, click Format Painter again to turn it off.

Using the Format Painter

Previously, you created a custom bullet on Slide 13. You will now use the format painter to apply the new bullet to the other names on the slide.

P02.04

To Use the Format Painter

a. Click **Slide 13**. The second, third, and fourth bullets on this slide need to be the same as the first bullet. Select the bullet text **Barry Cheney**.

b. On the HOME tab, in the Clipboard group, double-click **Format Painter** . As you move the insertion pointer onto the slide, you will notice a paintbrush icon on the pointer to indicate that the Format Painter is active.

> **Troubleshooting**
>
> The Format Painter icon will stay toggled after first use to indicate that you can use the format again. If it does not stay toggled on, try double-clicking faster.

c. Drag the pointer across the text **John Schilling**. The custom bullet was applied. Repeat for **Jorge Cruz** and **Aleeta Herriott**.

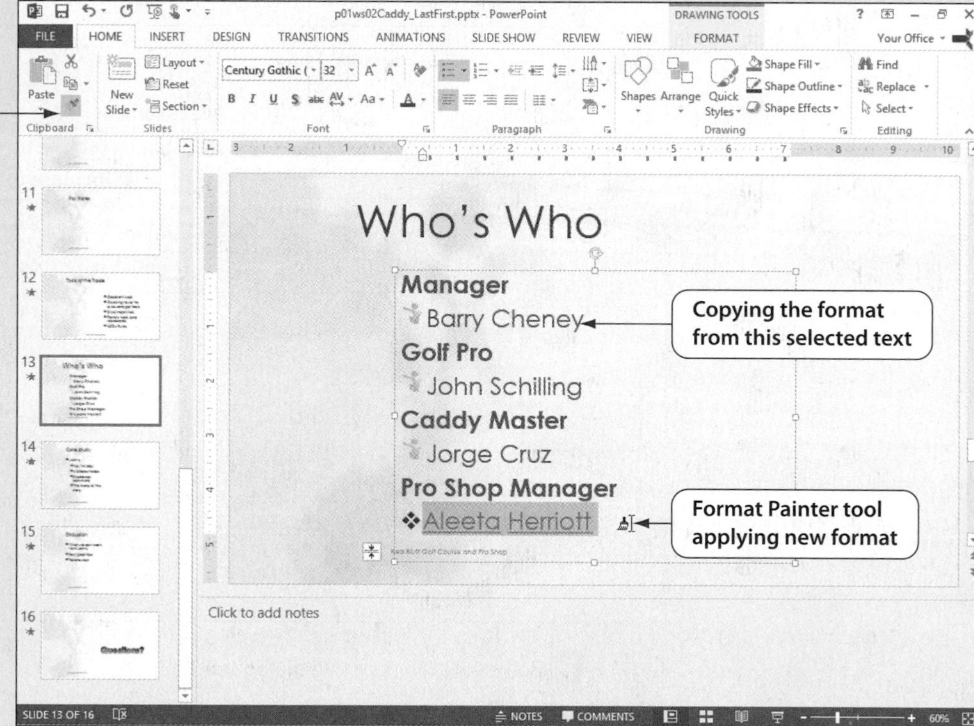

Figure 5 Format Painter

d. In the Clipboard group, click **Format Painter** to return to the normal pointer.

e. **Save** the presentation.

> SIDE NOTE
>
> **Finished with Format Painter?**
>
> When applying formats to multiple instances, you can also turn Format Painter off by pressing the Esc button.

Use Special Symbols

Special **symbols**, from various fonts, are characters not available on a standard keyboard that can be inserted into text placeholders in PowerPoint. The Symbol button on the Insert tab enables you to add these special symbols to your presentation. A common inserted character is the copyright symbol. Other characters include the trademark symbol, currency signs for different countries, and accents and letters from languages. For instance, the acute accent strokes over the "e" letters in the word "résumé" are in the Symbol dialog box.

Using the Symbol Dialog Box

The Symbol dialog box displays the special characters available for the selected font. Symbols you have used recently are displayed at the bottom of the dialog box, and you can click these to reuse the symbols in your current presentation. The character code is the unique number given to the symbol and can be typed into the box.

You will update the title slide of the Caddy School presentation to include a new title, your name, and a copyright notification.

P02.05

To Insert a Symbol

a. Click **Slide 1**, and then click to place the insertion point before the text **Painted Paradise**. Press Enter.

b. On the newly inserted line, type Barry Cheney.

c. Position the insertion point before the text **Painted Paradise**. Click the **INSERT** tab, and then in the Symbols group, click **Symbol**.

d. Click the **Font** box arrow and select (**normal text**). Scroll until you see the © copyright symbol, and then click the © copyright symbol—character code 00A9, click **Insert**, and then click **Close**. The symbol is placed at the insertion point. You will complete the copyright statement.

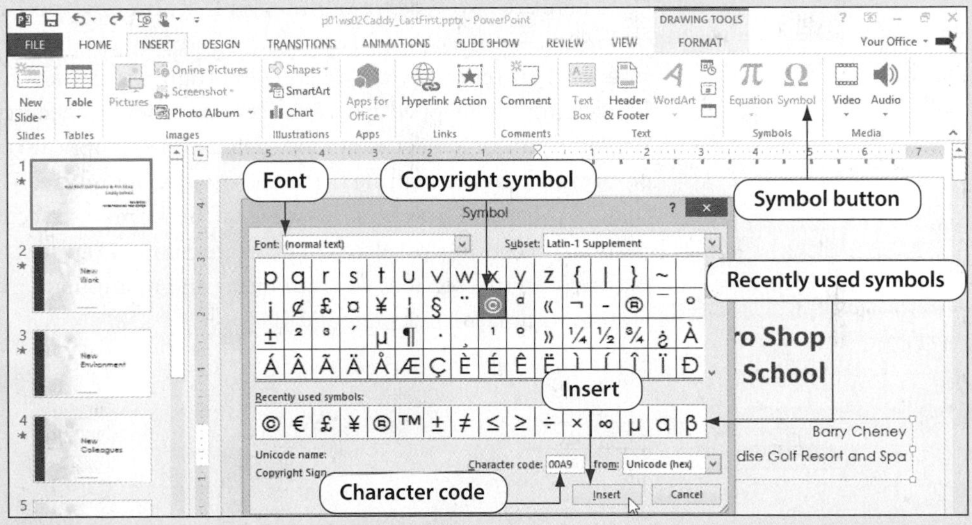

Figure 6 Adding a symbol

e. Type the current year and then press the Spacebar.

f. **Save** the presentation.

Selecting and Using Appropriate Graphics

Graphics, in the form of photographs, charts, graphs, and SmartArt, are valuable assets in presentations. Graphics convey information visually and can evoke a greater understanding of a concept. They add interest to the presentation.

There are some basic ground rules you should consider when selecting graphics. Foremost, the graphics must support your message; otherwise, they will distract and confuse your audience. The graphics should be clear and consistent in design with your presentation and the expectations of your audience. For instance, a business audience attending your presentation on policy changes would not appreciate the use of cartoon art. Likewise, complex charts and graphs would be incomprehensible to most audiences.

CONSIDER THIS | Selecting Graphics

Graphics add more than just interest to your presentation; they add information, both explicit and implicit. What forms of explicit information can graphics take? What forms of implicit information? Your graphic selections can have unanticipated meanings. Can you recall a time where the presenter's graphic selections were inappropriate or distracting?

SIDE NOTE
Online Content
Accessing Office.com content requires an Internet connection, and the content changes over time.

Graphics can come from a variety of sources. PowerPoint accesses Office.com to provide high-quality art and photographs. You can even find animated art that provides movement to the graphic. The Internet is a rich resource for graphics, but keep **copyright** laws in mind. Of course, photographs that you have taken and other artwork that you produce can be downloaded onto a computer and used in PowerPoint presentations. Large graphics and videos can load very slowly, dragging the presentation response and making it impossible to e-mail and otherwise difficult to share your presentation with others.

There are two types of digital graphics, **bit-mapped** and **vector graphics**, as shown in Figure 7. Bit-mapped images are stored as pixels, individual dots of color arranged in a grid to represent the image. Photographs are an example of bit-mapped images. Up-scaling bit-mapped images or resizing them larger than their stored size, results in a pixilated image: object edges lose definition and appear rough. Vector graphics are made of formulas that determine the shapes used in an image. They are often smaller in file size than bit-mapped graphics. Because of the formulas, vector graphics can also be resized without becoming pixelated. For more about graphics, see the quick reference below Figure 7. In this section, you will insert and manipulate images to balance text and visual representation in your presentation.

Pixelation

Bit-mapped graphic

Vector graphic

Figure 7 Vector and bit-mapped graphics

QUICK REFERENCE | **Graphic File Formats**

Common graphic file types are:

- JPEG—**J**oint **P**hotographic **E**xperts **G**roup. Compressed file format for raster—pixmap—data. Commonly used for web-based photographs saved as 24-bit RGB data. The higher the compression, the more data is lost, and is therefore a "lossy" type. Also known as JPG.
- GIF—**G**raphic **I**mage **F**ile format. Uses a color lookup table and supports up to 256 colors per image. For flat, solid colors, GIF is your best option. GIFs use lossless compression, which translates to larger file sizes than JPEG.
- TIFF—**T**agged **I**mage **F**ile **F**ormat. Uncompressed, very large files typically used in photo software or page layout software. Have the most flexibility in terms of grayscale, colors for print or web media, including content layers for transparency. Also known as TIF.
- PNG—**P**ortable **N**etwork **G**raphics. Substitute for GIFs and more features than JPEG. Allows for multibit transparency, a full range of color—16 million colors, and better compression.

Work with Images and Art

In his 1797 book *Remarks on Rural Scenery*, John Thomas Smith explains an idea of Sir Joshua Reynolds about balancing light and dark in paintings. He refers to his revolutionary notion as a "**rule of thirds**," discussing proportions of two-thirds to one-third, in particular reference to landscapes. For example, a picture could be framed two-thirds of one element—water—to one-third of another— land. Further, this picture could be framed in a larger scene, so that it occupies one-third while the sky, for example, occupies the upper two-thirds. Finally, Smith concluded that this general proportion of two and one was "the most picturesque medium in all cases of breaking or otherwise qualifying straight lines and masses and groups."

Today, the rule of thirds is used in photography, graphic design, art, composition, and landscape design. Horizontal and vertical guides are overlaid on a scene, and then the scene is manipulated until it is in balance. Some cameras today place a digital grid overlay in view of the photographer so the scene can be optimized specifically with this rule in mind.

In the grid, two equidistant vertical lines slice the scene into thirds vertically, and two equidistant horizontal lines do the same horizontally. The idea is that the most interesting parts of the scene should fall along these lines, or preferably, at the intersections. The intersections are where the most visual impact, or power, is derived, as shown in Figure 8. In some industries, the intersections are called "**power points**."

Figure 8 Rule of thirds

While PowerPoint does not tile this visual grid overlay in thirds automatically, you can add multiple visual guides manually. In this way, you will be able to see if your artwork, or your entire slide, is in balance.

Adding Guides

In this section, you will add guides to your slides. The guides will not show in your presentation, but they are an overlay for you to use while designing your presentation. The idea is to put the most important things at the guide intersections, or the power points, as discussed earlier. Depending on your use of power points, they may provide more impact than a bulleted list. The **vertical guide** spans the top and bottom of the slide and is used to align objects horizontally, while the **horizontal guide** spans the left and right of the slide and is used to align objects vertically.

P02.06

To Add Guides

a. Click **Slide 1**, click the **VIEW** tab, and then in the Show group, click **Guides**. Make sure **Ruler** is also checked.

The vertical and horizontal guides will be displayed at the zero mark on both the horizontal ruler above the slide and the vertical ruler to the left of the slide in the Slide pane.

b. Drag the **Vertical Guide** to the right until it reaches **2.25** to the right of **0** on the horizontal ruler.

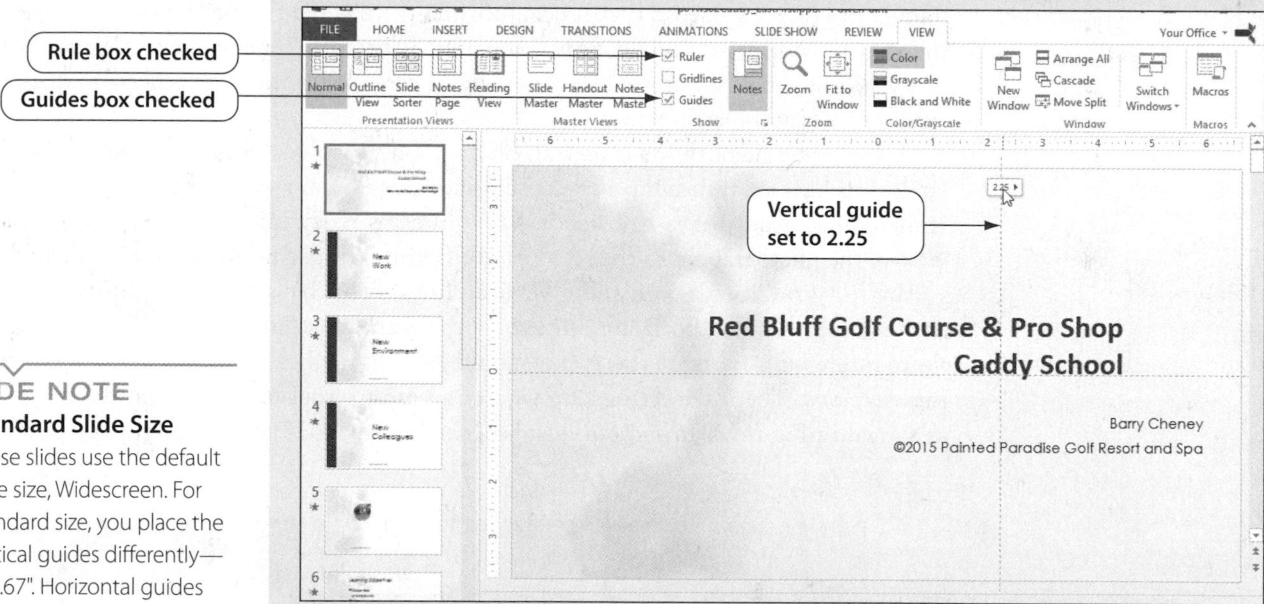

Figure 9 Positioning guides

SIDE NOTE

Standard Slide Size

These slides use the default slide size, Widescreen. For Standard size, you place the vertical guides differently—at 1.67". Horizontal guides are always at 1.25".

c. Right-click the **slide** in an area free of text, point to **Grid and Guides** on the shortcut menu, and then click **Add Vertical Guide**. Drag this guide to the left until it reaches **2.25** to the left of **0** on the horizontal ruler.

SIDE NOTE

Additional Guides

New guides are always positioned at the zero mark.

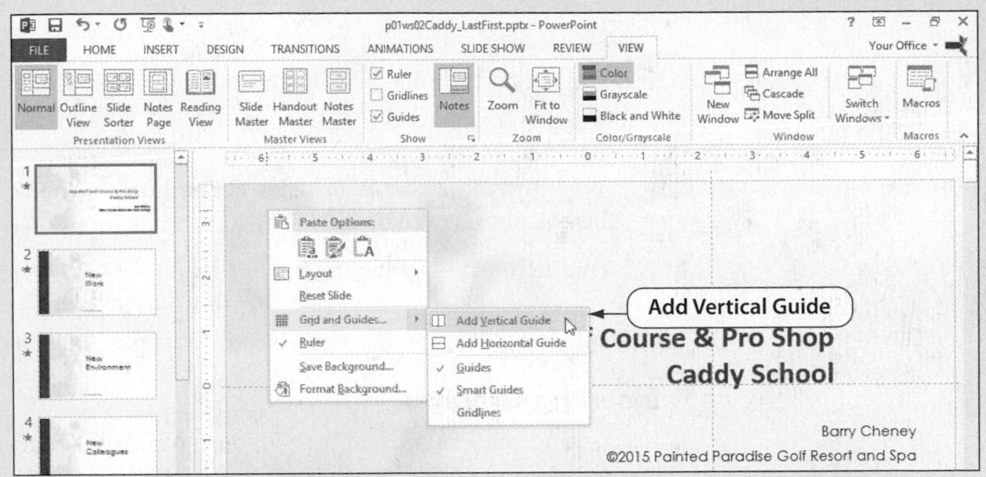

Figure 10 Adding guides

> **Troubleshooting**
> If your mouse pointer is blocking your view of the white box that indicates your exact position on the ruler, move your mouse pointer up to the ruler and you should be able to see the position indicator.

d. Drag the **Horizontal Guide** down until it reaches **1.25** below **0** on the vertical ruler. Because you want to divide the slide into thirds vertically, you only need to draw two equidistant horizontal guides.

e. Right-click the **slide** in an area free of text, point to **Grid and Guides** on the shortcut menu, and then click **Add Horizontal Guide**. Drag this guide up until it reaches **1.25** above **0** on the vertical ruler.

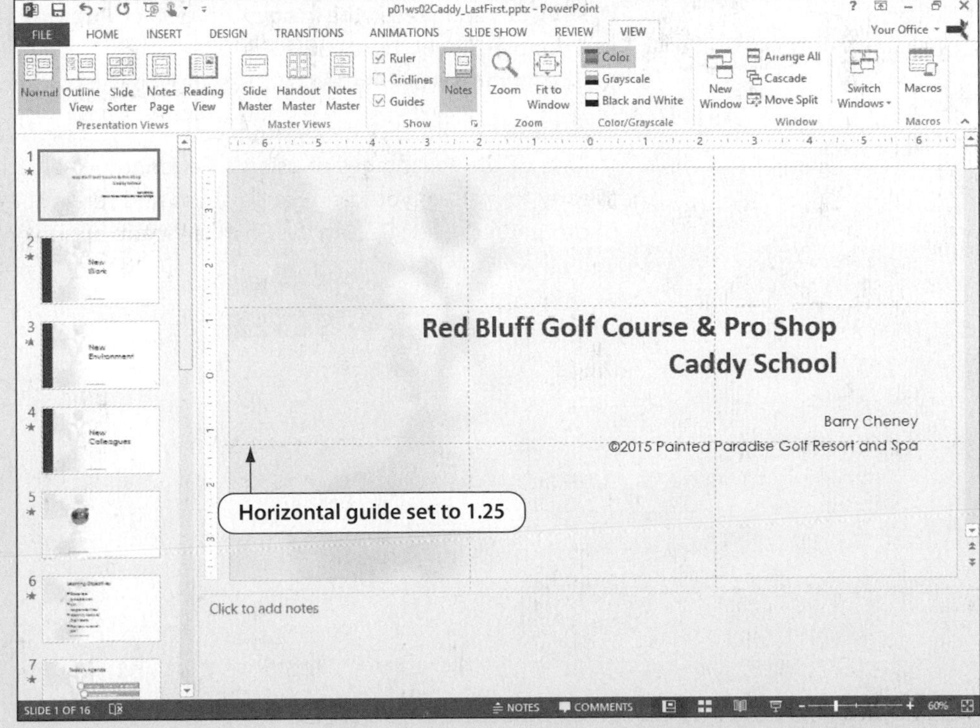

Figure 11 Guides set for Rule of Thirds and power point intersections

> **Troubleshooting**
> If you accidentally add more guides than you want or need, you can right-click a guide, and then click Delete.

f. Scroll through a couple of slides to see how the guides reveal the balance, or lack thereof, in the layout of these slides.

g. **Save** the presentation.

Inserting Graphics

By clicking the graphic icons shown on the **content placeholders** of PowerPoint slides, you will launch shortcuts to elments such as pictures, tables, charts, SmartArt graphics, online pictures, or video. You can also use commands on the Insert tab to place graphics on the slides. In the following sections, you will add graphics, a table, a chart, and SmartArt to your presentation.

P02.07

To Insert a Photograph

a. Click **Slide 12**. The content placeholder, with multimedia icons, is displayed on the left of the slide.

b. Click **Pictures** in the content placeholder. Navigate to where your student data files are located, click **p01ws02Caddy**, and then click **Insert**. The photograph appears on the slide, replacing the placeholder. Notice the image covers two of the guide intersections.

> SIDE NOTE
> **Inserting Images**
> You can also double-click the content file name to insert the image.

c. Click **Slide 6**. Because there is no content placeholder, to insert an image, click the **INSERT** tab, and then in the Images group, click **Pictures**. Locate your student data files, and double-click **p01ws02GolfGirl**.
   The image will be inserted on the slide. You will size and crop it later.

d. Click **Slide 5**. Right-click the **photograph**.
   One of the advantages of using an existing presentation is that if the pictures are already formatted, you can change them and retain the effects. You will change the photograph on Slide 5 using the Change Picture option on the shortcut menu.

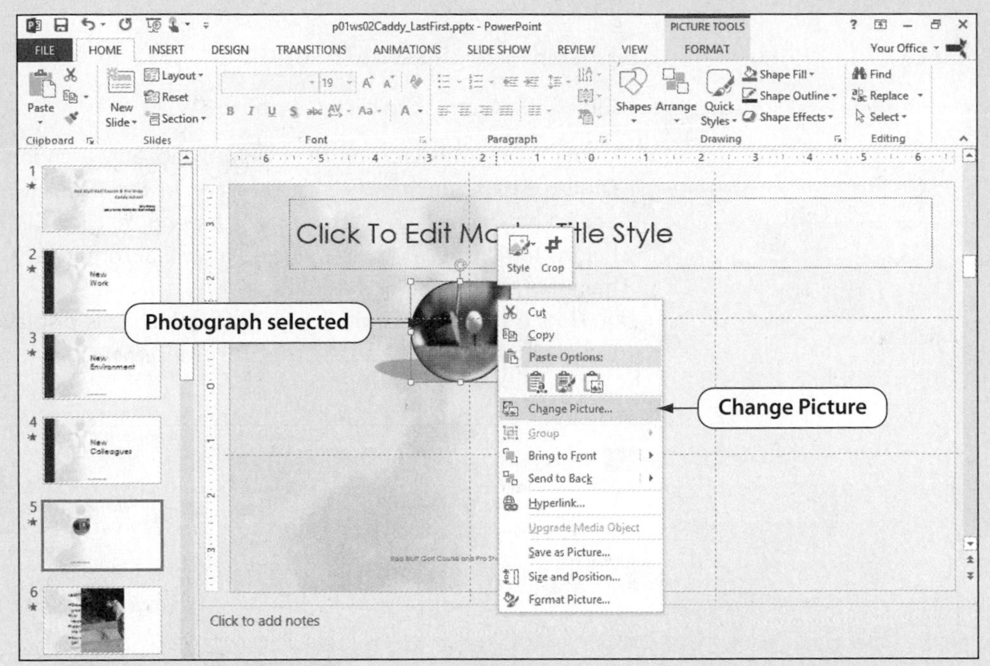

Figure 12 Change picture

e. Click **Change Picture**, browse to your student files, click **p01ws02Green**, and then click **Insert**. The photograph automatically adjusts, replacing the previous photograph.

f. Click **Slide 14**, click the **INSERT** tab, and then in the Images group, click **Pictures**. Navigate to your student data files, click **p01ws02Pink**, and then click **Insert**. The photograph appears on the slide. You will resize it later.

g. **Save** the presentation.

Resizing and Cropping Graphics

Graphics, such as photographs, are easily manipulated using PowerPoint tools. You can resize an object, making it fit into a placeholder; crop unwanted portions from photographs; and rotate or flip images to improve the design of the slide.

Sizing handles, displayed around a selected graphic, enable you to resize the graphic and move it around the slide. The corner sizing handles increase or decrease the size of the graphic when dragged, while retaining the proportions of the graphic. The side sizing handles increase or decrease the width or height of the graphic. Be careful not to distort the graphic when using the side handles. When pointing to a handle to perform a sizing action, the pointer will change to a two-pointed arrow. Point anywhere else on the object, and a four-pointed arrow pointer indicates that you can drag the graphic to a new location on the slide.

In this portion of the workshop, you will improve the graphics. You will resize and crop a photograph.

P02.08

To Resize and Crop Graphics

a. Click **Slide 6**, and then click the **photo**.

b. Under PICTURE TOOLS, on the FORMAT tab, and then in the Size group, click the **Size Dialog Box Launcher** . If necessary, in the **Format Picture** pane, click the **Lock aspect ratio** check box to select it. Under Size, click the **Height** arrow to change the height to **4"**. The width of the graphic will automatically change in proportion to the height of the object.

   Notice that the size of the graphic in inches is displayed in the Size group on the FORMAT tab. You can also use the Size group to resize the graphic.

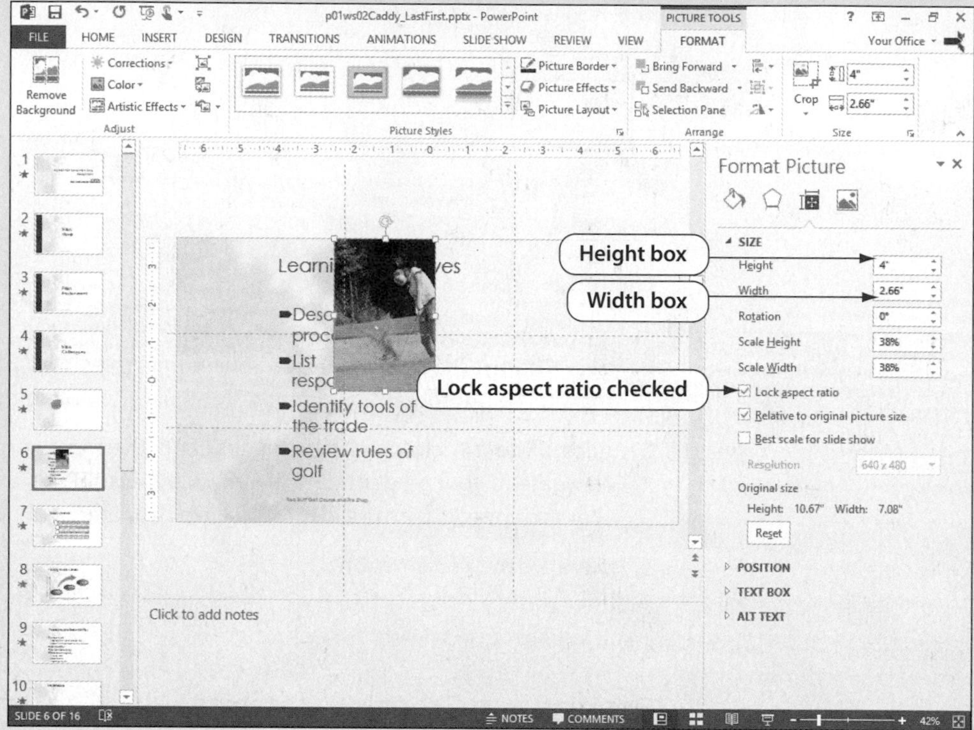

Figure 13 Resizing a picture

> **Troubleshooting**
> If you make an error in sizing the photograph and want to return to the original size, click Reset in the Format Picture pane.

c. Drag the **image** to the right until the face of the model is under the right vertical guide.

   You may notice special alignment guides show up momentarily on the slide, near the image. The guides are red. In this case, they indicate the position of the image relative to the other elements on the slide.

d. In the Format Picture pane, click the **Position** arrow. You can modify the placement of the graphic on the slide using this area of the pane.

e. Click the **Vertical position** arrow, and then set it to **2.1"**. Make sure the From box is set to **Top Left Corner**. Click **Close** [X] to close the Format Picture pane. Notice the image is now over two of the guide intersections.

f. Click **Slide 12**, and then click the **photograph**. You will crop some of the grass in the foreground of the photograph.

g. On the FORMAT tab, and then in the Size group, click the **Crop** button and then click **Crop**. **Cropping handles** appear at the edges of the photograph to enable you to cut away portions of the graphic that you do not need.

The corner cropping handles crop the vertical and horizontal sides of the photograph at one time. The side cropping handles enable you to crop from one direction.

h. Drag the **bottom-middle cropping handle** up until the handle is just below the feet of the caddy. The gray area below the cropping handle will be deleted from the image.

SIDE NOTE

Cropping

The cropped portion is removed permanently when you save the presentation.

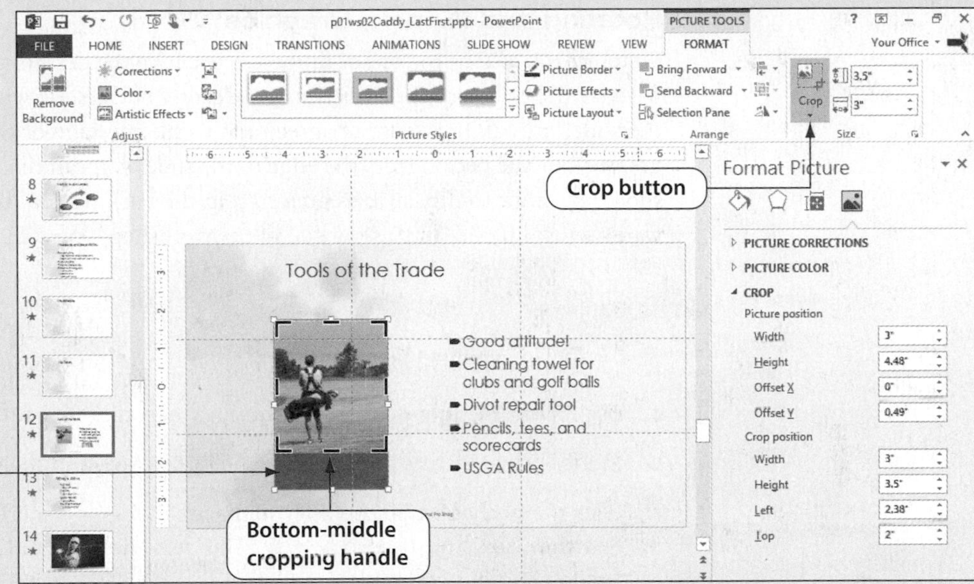

Figure 14 Cropping photos

i. Under PICTURE TOOLS, on the FORMAT tab, and then in the Size group, click the **Size Dialog Box Launcher**. In the Format Picture pane, click **Picture**, and then select **Crop**. Click the Crop position **Height** arrow toward the bottom of the list to change the position to **3.5"**. Notice, the Format Picture pane allows you to make more precise crops.

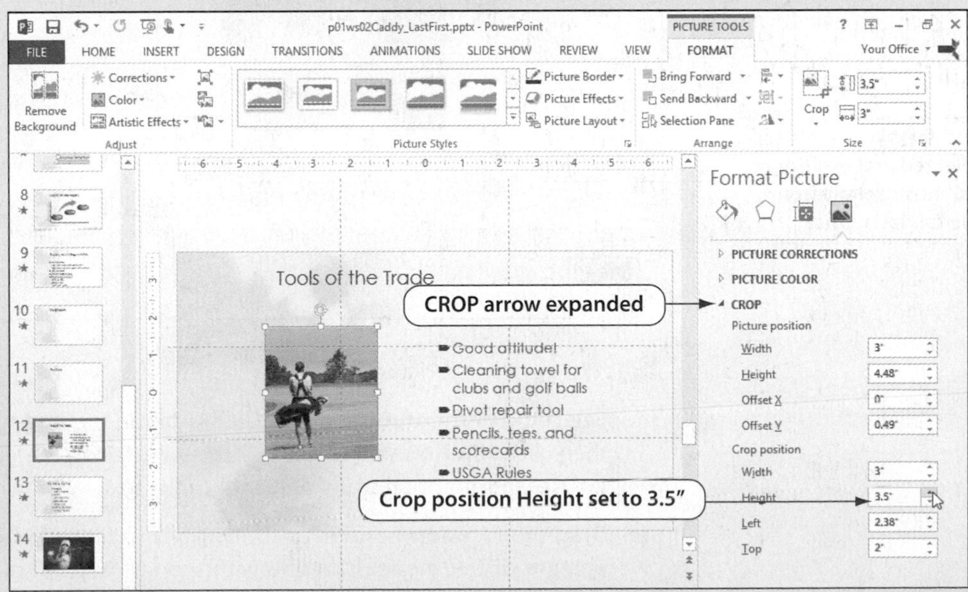

Figure 15 Cropping a photograph via the Format Picture pane

j. Click **Size & Properties** at the top of the Format Picture pane. In the Size section, click the **Scale Width** arrow to increase the scale of the picture to **120%**, click **Close** to close the Format Picture pane, and then click anywhere on the slide outside of the photograph. Using the Scale options, you can modify the size of the image by percentages.

k. **Save** the presentation.

Rotating and Flipping Graphics

Graphics can also be rotated or flipped to improve the design of the slide. For example, photos with faces should face the audience or the center of the slide whenever possible. This reinforces the slide, providing a sense of agreement to the message of the slide. If you find the perfect graphic but the person faces the edge of the slide, you can flip the image. Beware of words on slides you want to flip, such as on a sign in the background, because these will display backwards when flipped. In this portion of the workshop, you will rotate and flip a graphic.

P02.09

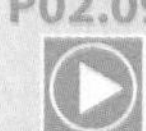

To Rotate and Flip Graphics

a. Click **Slide 14**, right-click the **image**, and then click **Size and Position**.

b. In the Format Picture pane, click in the **Width** box, and then type 6".

c. Click the **body text** placeholder so that its border is a solid line. Click in the **Horizontal Position** box, and then type 6.6". This sets the placeholder body text 6.6" from the top-left corner of the slide.

Body text placeholder selected and positioned 6.6" horizontally from the top left corner

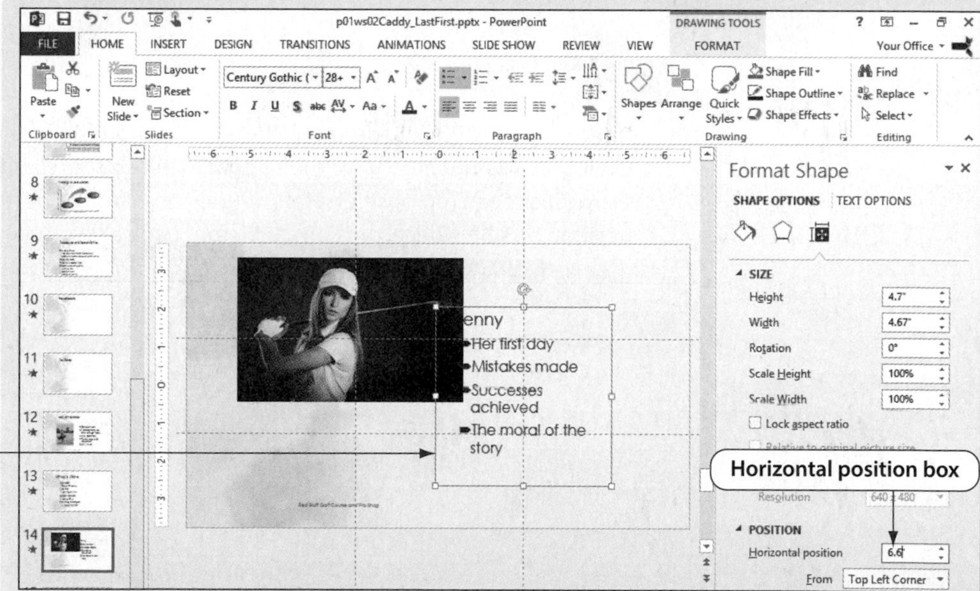

Figure 16 Format Picture pane

d. Select the **photograph**. On the FORMAT tab, in the Arrange group, click **Rotate**, and then click **Flip Horizontal**. The golfer is now facing the direction of the content, which focuses the attention of the audience to the text.

e. Drag the **rotation handle** to the right to tilt the photograph so that the vertical posture of the model is in line with the left vertical guide. It is okay if the top-left corner of the photograph is off the slide. Images arranged in unusual ways can add interest to the slide.

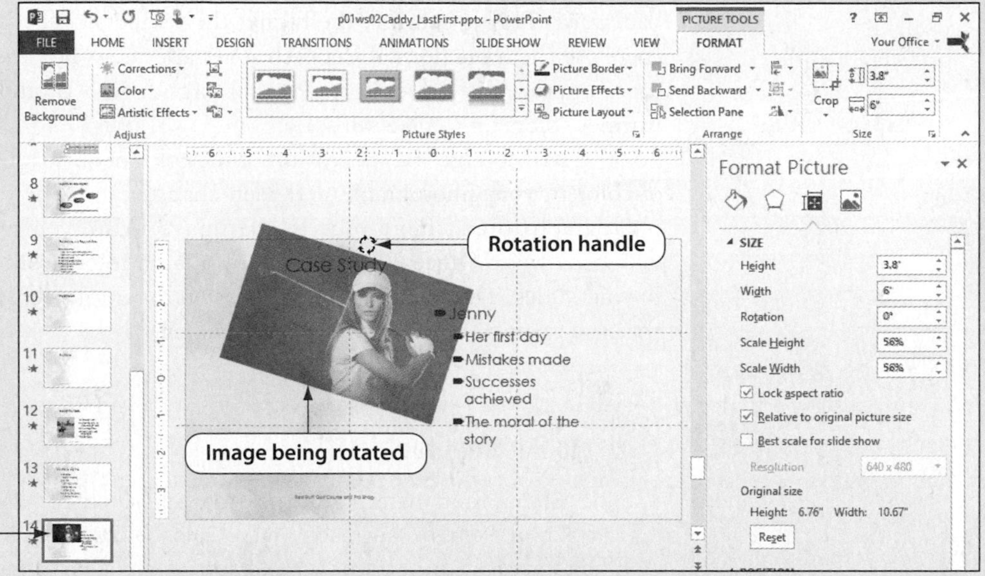

Figure 17 Rotating a graphic

f. Right-click the **image**, and then click **Size and Position**. In the Format Picture pane, click the **Horizontal position box**, and then type 0.7". Click the **Vertical position box**, and then type 1.3". The model's face is now behind the top-left power point and the upper right corner of the image covers the first bullet.

g. **Close** the Format Picture pane.

h. Right-click the **photograph**, point to **Send to Back**, and then click **Send to Back**. This moves the photograph behind the placeholder text on the right and you can now see the first bullet over the image.

i. Right-click the **photograph**, and then select **Copy**. Right-click **Slide 15** in the left hand pane, and then under Paste Options, click **Use Destination Theme**.

j. On the FORMAT tab, in the Arrange group, click **Rotate**, and then click **Flip Horizontal**. With the image selected, press → multiple times to move the picture to the right so the model's face is to the right of the right **Vertical Guide** and you can see all of the text. Click outside of the photograph. Since you used the arrow keys, you maintained the exact same Vertical placement as the photo on Slide 14.

k. **Save** the presentation.

Changing the Color of Graphics

PowerPoint contains sophisticated tools for modifying images. Using the Corrections tool on the Format tab under Picture Tools, you can improve the brightness, contrast, and sharpness of images. The Color tool enables you to change the color of a picture to better match your presentation's color scheme or to improve the quality of the image. Artistic Effects can make the picture appear as if it were sketched or painted. You can also **recolor** an image by altering the colors of the image to create a monochromatic effect.

The **Kelvin scale** describes a standard color temperature of light sources. For example, in photographs the lower numbers on the scale represent the warmer colors of yellow, red, and orange, such as candlelight, and the higher numbers, over 5,000K, representing blue or cooler colors. Regular daylight color temperature, as you would see outdoors on a clear day, is 5,500 on the Kelvin scale. Light source in this sense is measured between 1,000K and 25,000K.

In PowerPoint, changing the color tone or temperature of an image seems to work backward. This is because, the higher the temperature, the more daylight is added, and therefore the more normal the flesh tones appear. When the temperature drops, the flesh tones appear blue in color, such as at night, even though the temperature represents warmer colors on the Kelvin scale.

You will change the **saturation** of the color of one of your photographs—the amount of color in your photograph, and then change the **color tone**, or the temperature, of a photograph to add more blue to the image. Also, you will use the **Eyedropper tool** which is new to Office 2013 to precisely match colors from graphics to create uniformity in your slides. The dropper tool enables you to sample a color and drop it onto an element that you want to match to the sampled color.

P02.10

To Recolor Graphics

a. Click **Slide 6**, and then click the **photograph**. On the FORMAT tab, in the Adjust group, click **Color**. Point to the images in the Color Saturation gallery and preview the choices, and then click **Saturation: 200%** to apply more color to the image.

   The color scheme selected for the template or design theme affects the colors presented in the gallery. In the Recolor gallery, for example, Light and dark accent colors from the scheme appear with various black-and-white, sepia, and washout options.

b. In the Adjust group, click **Color**. Point to the images in the **Color Tone** gallery, and then observe that as the Temperature in Kelvin goes down, more blue is apparent in the photograph. As the temperature is increased, the yellow tones are enhanced as more daylight is added.

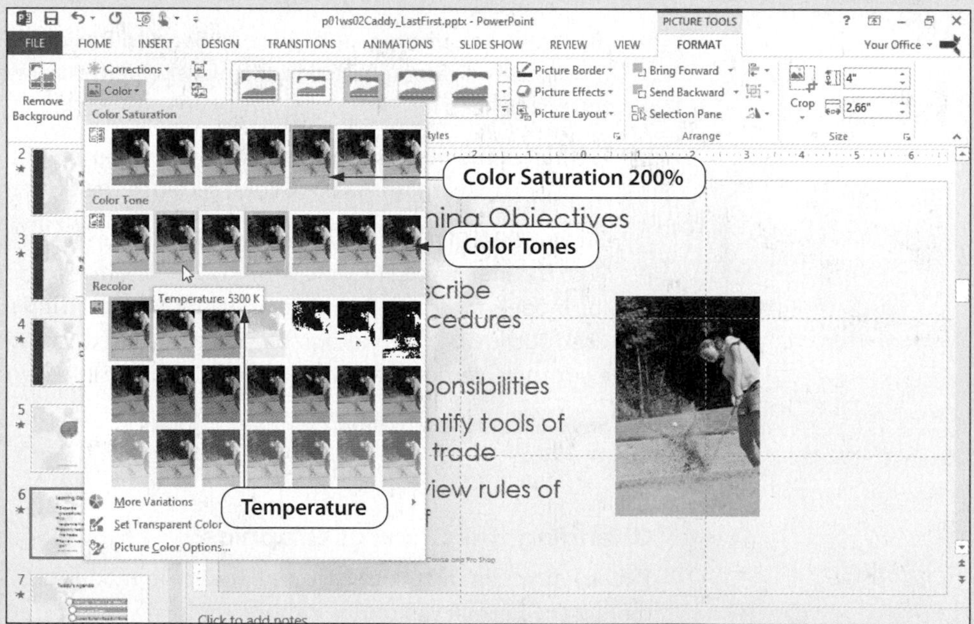

Figure 18 Color galleries

c. Click the thumbnail for **Temperature: 5300 K**.

d. To precisely match color from your photographs to other elements in your presentation, you first need to sample the color. You will use the Eyedropper tool to do this. Right-click the photograph on **Slide 6**, click **Format Picture**, and then in the Format Picture pane, click **Fill & Line**.

e. Click **Fill**, and then select **Solid fill**. Click the **Fill Color** arrow, and then click **Eyedropper**.

f. Now, you are ready to sample a color from the photograph. Notice when you point to the photograph, the pointer changes to an **Eyedropper**. Select and click a **color** from the model's shirt, from somewhere bright blue. The sampled color is now available to use and is shown in the pane in the bucket.

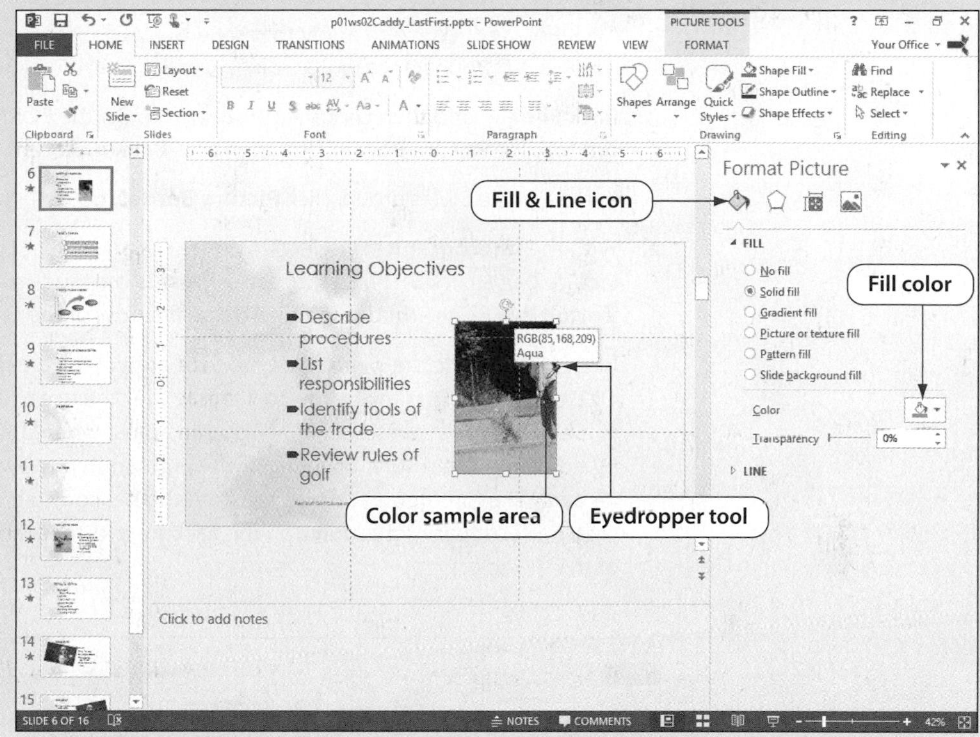

Figure 19 Eyedropper tool

g. Click the placeholder **text** to the left of the photograph, then in the **Format Shape** pane, click **Fill & Line** [icon], and then click **Solid fill**. The sampled color has been applied to the placeholder.

h. Under **Fill** in the **Format Shape** pane, drag the **Transparency** slider to **90%**. **Close** [X] the Format Shape pane.

Transparency allows some of the slide background to be visible through the placeholder background. The higher the transparency percentage, the more the background is visible.

i. Click the **photograph**. Drag the **top-right sizing handle** of the photograph until the top edge of the picture is the same height as the placeholder box.

j. **Save** [icon] the presentation.

Modifying the Picture Style of Graphics

Picture Styles enable you to add preset effects to your graphics. Options include frames, shadows, and unusual shapes. Too many styles in the same presentation will detract from the presentation, so you will explore only a few.

You will use Picture Styles to frame a photograph in the Caddy School presentation, change the border color in another, and add depth to a third.

P02.11

To Apply a Picture Style

a. Click **Slide 12**, and then click the **photograph**. On the FORMAT tab, in the Picture Styles group, click **More** [▾], and then point to the **style thumbnails** shown in the gallery and observe Live Preview. The name of the style appears as you point to each thumbnail.

b. Click **Rotated, White** to apply that style to the photograph. This style gives the photograph a 3-D appearance.

c. Click **Slide 6**, and then click the **photograph**. On the FORMAT tab, in the Picture Styles group, click **Picture Border**, and then click **Brown, Accent 3, Darker 25%**.

d. In the Picture Styles group, click **Picture Border**, point to **Weight**, and then click **3 pt**.

e. With the **photograph** still selected, right-click and select **Format Picture**. In the Format Picture pane, click **SHADOW**, click the **Presets** button, and then select **Offset Diagonal Bottom Left**—the third thumbnail in the first row of the Outer group.

f. In the Format Picture pane, click the **Size** arrow to increase the size of the shadow to **102%**. Click the **Distance** arrow to increase the distance to **10**.

Shadows are the result of light. You can adjust where the light source is coming from by adjusting the Angle, how bright the light source is by adjusting the Blur, and how far away the foreground objects are from the background by adjusting the Distance. To create a secondary light source on the background, for example, adjust the Transparency of the shadow.

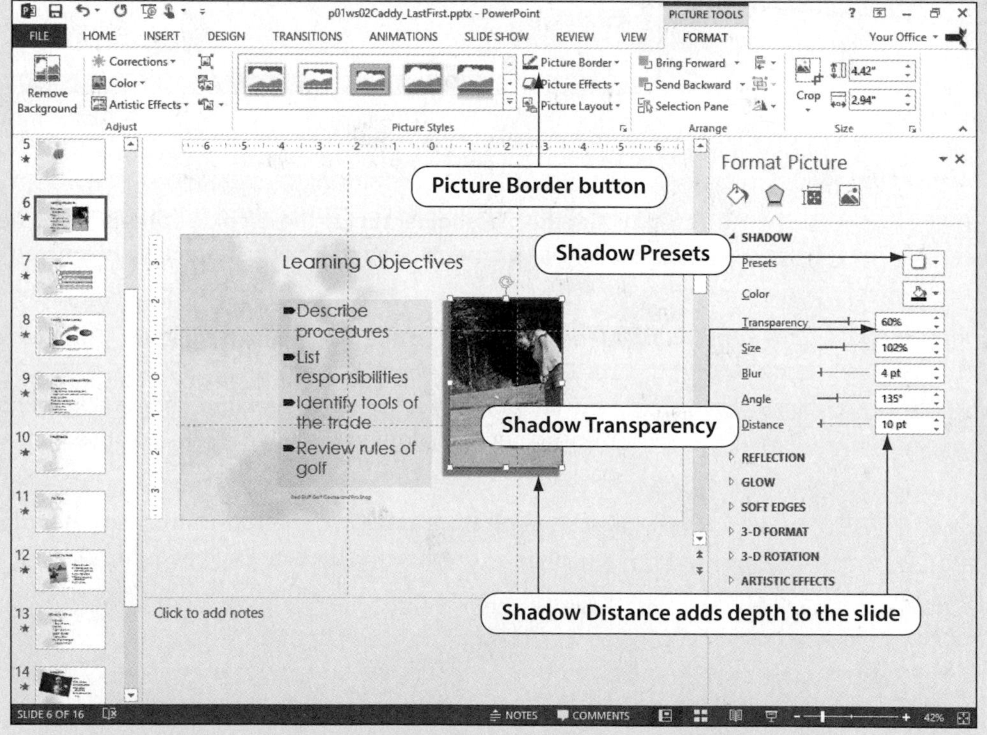

Figure 20 Applying a border

g. In the Format Picture pane, click **Close** [X] and then **save** [💾] the presentation.

MODULE 1

Work with Shape and Line Graphics

Lines and shapes increase understanding of your slides by creating focal points and explaining concepts. Add an arrow to a slide, and the audience will look where it is pointing. Lines and shapes also add color and interest. Boxes, also considered shapes, enable you to label objects. As you add shapes to your slides, keep in mind that the objects should remain consistent with the other graphics and colors in the presentation.

Applying Line Gradients

Gradients can give an illusion of depth to objects. Changing the angle of a gradient fill can indicate a light source. In this section, you will work with both.

P02.12

To Apply a Gradient Line

a. Click **Slide 8**, and then click the **left oval**. Press and hold Shift while you click once on the other **two ovals**. All three ovals are now selected. Release Shift.

b. On the FORMAT tab, in the Size group, click the **Size Dialog Box Launcher**. Under **SHAPE OPTIONS**, click **Fill & Line**.

c. Scroll down the Format Shape pane, click **LINE**, and then select **Gradient Line**.

d. Scroll down, and then click the **Width** arrow until the width of the line is **4 pt**.

e. Click the **Type** arrow, and then select **Radial**. Click the **Direction** arrow, and then select **From Top Right Corner**.

f. Under Gradient stops, notice the **markers** on the gradient line. Click **Stop 1 of 4**, which should be at position 0%. Click the **Color** arrow, and then select **White, Background 1**. This will be the first stop on the radius and will give you the spotlight effect from the top-right corner.

g. Click the **Position** arrow until the stop is at **25%**. Notice how the white spotlight effect has moved around the radius.

h. Under Gradient stops, click **Stop 2 of 4**. Click the **Color** arrow, and then select **Light Green, Background 2, Darker 50%**. Click the **Position** arrow until the stop is at **40%**.

i. Under Gradient stops, click **Stop 3 of 4**. Click the **Color** arrow, and then select **Light Green, Background 2, Darker 75%**. Click the **Position** arrow until the stop is at **75%**. This stop gives the most volume to the shape.

j. Under Gradient stops, click **Stop 4 of 4**. Click the **Color** arrow, and then select **Light Green, Background 2, Darker 25%**. If necessary, click the **Position** arrow until the stop is at **100%**. Using a lighter color at stop 4 gives the illusion of a secondary light source just off the screen and to the left, rounding out the volume of the shape.

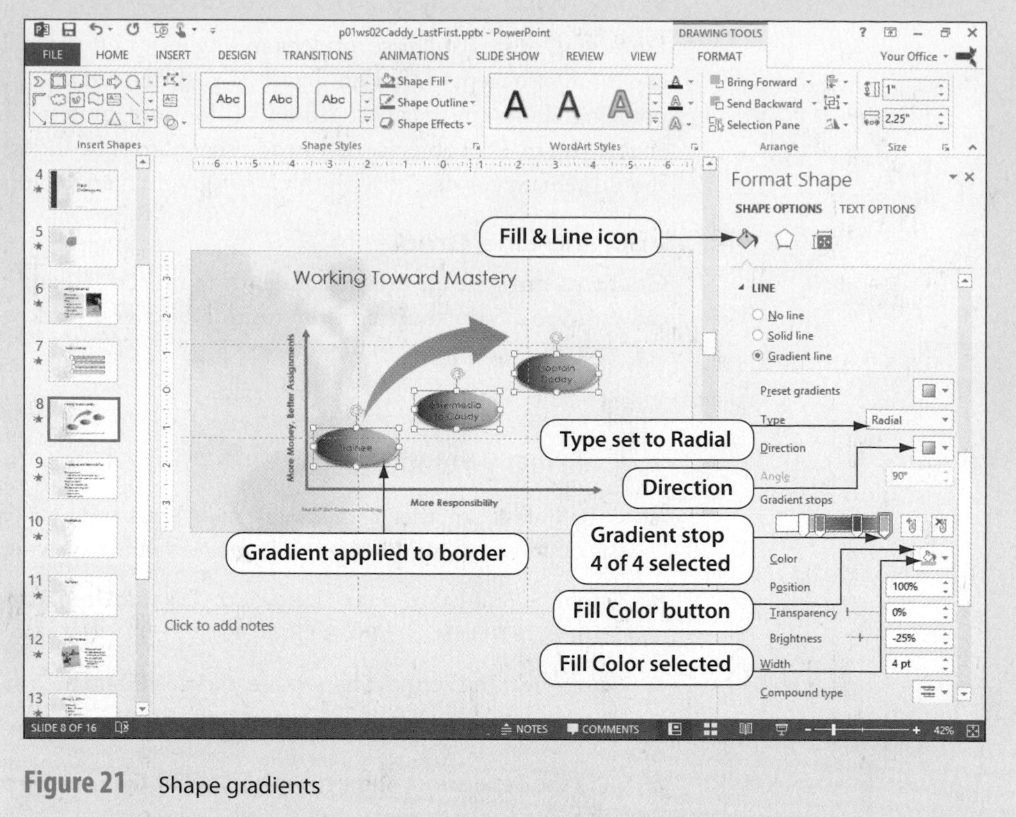

Figure 21 Shape gradients

k. **Close** [X] the Format Shape pane, and then **Save** [Save] the presentation.

Applying Shape Gradients

Gradients can give an illusion of volume. Changing the angle of a gradient fill can indicate a light source. In the last section, you worked with gradient lines. Now, you will apply a gradient fill to a shape to give it volume.

P02.13

To Apply a Shape Fill Gradient

a. On **Slide 8**, make sure that **all three ovals** are still selected. On the FORMAT tab, in the Size group, click the **Size Dialog Box Launcher** [icon]. Under SHAPE OPTIONS, click **Fill & Line** [icon]. Ensure that you have scrolled to the top of the Format Shape pane. In the FILL options, select **Gradient fill**.

> **Troubleshooting**
>
> If all three ovals are no longer selected, click on one of the ovals to select it. Next, press and hold Shift and then click each of the other two ovals once. Last, release Shift.

b. Under Gradient stops, click **Stop 1 of 4**. Click the **Color** arrow, and then select **White, Background 1**. Click the **Position** arrow until the stop is at **25%**. This stop gives the most spotlight to the shape.

c. Under Gradient stops, click **Stop 2 of 4**. Click the **Color** arrow, and then select **Light Green, Background 2, Darker 50%**. Click the **Position** arrow until the stop is at **60%**. This stop gives the most volume to the shape.

d. Under Gradient stops, click **Stop 3 of 4**. Click the **Color** arrow, and then select **Light Green, Background 2, Darker 75%**. Click the **Position** arrow until the stop is at **95%**. This stop rounds out the left side of the shape.

e. Under Gradient stops, click **Stop 4 of 4**. Click the **Color** arrow, and then select **Light Green, Background 2, Darker 25%**. Click the **Position** arrow until the stop is at **100%**. This stop completes the curve of the shape.

f. **Close** [X] the Format Shape pane. On the FORMAT tab, in the Size group, click in the **Shape Width** box and type 2.8".

g. Click the **HOME** tab. In the Font group, click **Bold** [B].

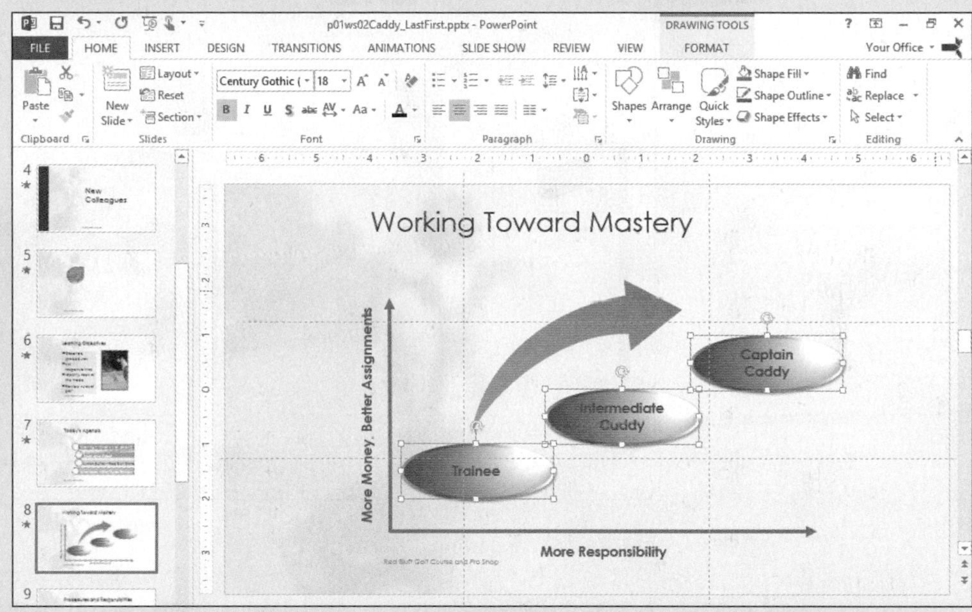

Figure 22 Finished shape fill gradients

h. **Save** [H] the presentation.

Applying Shape Styles

PowerPoint contains a wide range of shapes in the Illustrations group on the Insert tab. When you select a shape from the gallery, a crosshair pointer enables you to draw the shape on the slide. Sizing handles appear on selected shapes so you can change the shape or rotation of the object you have drawn, similar to sizing handles on images. Shapes can be filled, stacked, aligned, grouped, and merged.

Add a drop shadow behind shape elements to give them a light source. This makes them appear as if they are hovering on the slide. Images with drop shadows that overlap, however, will cast shadows from above onto the objects beneath. To avoid this, design a shape identical to the one you want to overlap, apply a drop shadow to it, insert it exactly behind the image you want to shadow, and then send it to the back of the objects. This gives the illusion that the shapes are closely stacked. Also, lines or a border around shapes helps to separate them visually.

You will modify the shapes on a slide in the Caddy School presentation to better suit your message. The objects you create will add visual interest to a few of the plainer slides.

P02.14

To Insert and Apply Styles to Shapes

a. Click **Slide 2**.

b. Click the **INSERT** tab. In the Illustrations group, click **Shapes**, and then in the Stars and Banners, select **Wave**. Position the insertion point at approximately 2.5" to the left of the horizontal 0" and 2.5" above the vertical 0". Click and drag to approximately 4" to the right of the horizontal 0" and 2.5" below the vertical 0".

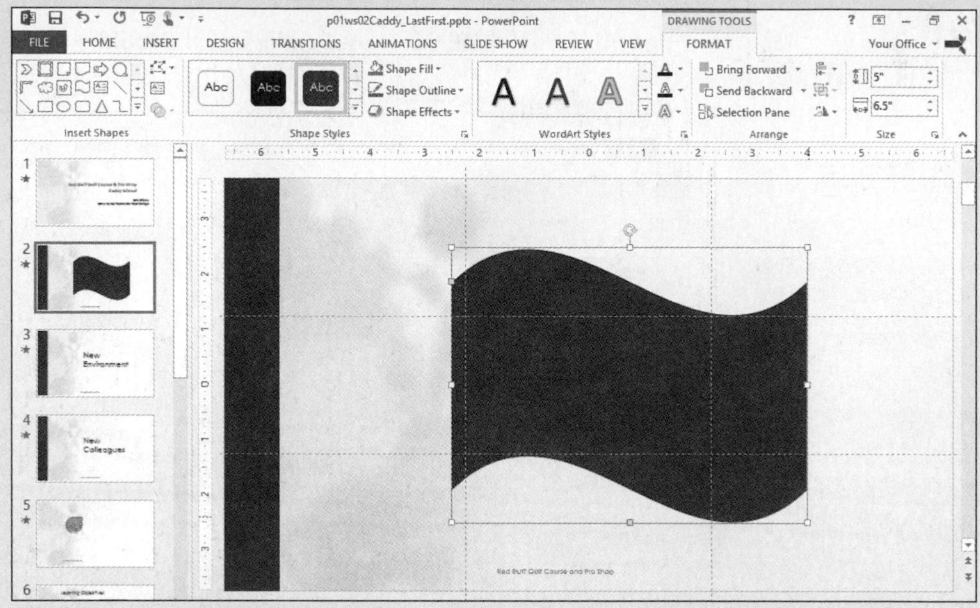

Figure 23 Inserting a wave shape

c. On the FORMAT tab, in the Shape Styles group, click on the **Shape Effects** arrow. Then, point your insertion point over **Preset** and select **Preset 8**. Click anywhere off of the shape to deselect it.

d. Click the **INSERT** tab. In the Illustrations group, click on the **Shapes** arrow. Under Lines, click **Line**.

e. Place your insertion point at the **top left corner** of the wave shape. Press and hold [Shift] while you click and drag to the **bottom** of the slide. Release [Shift]. Notice, [Shift] ensures that the line stays straight.

f. With the line still selected, on the FORMAT tab, in the Shape Styles group, click the **Shape Outline** arrow. Place your insertion point over **Weight** and select **6 pt**. Notice, the text looks like it is on a flag.

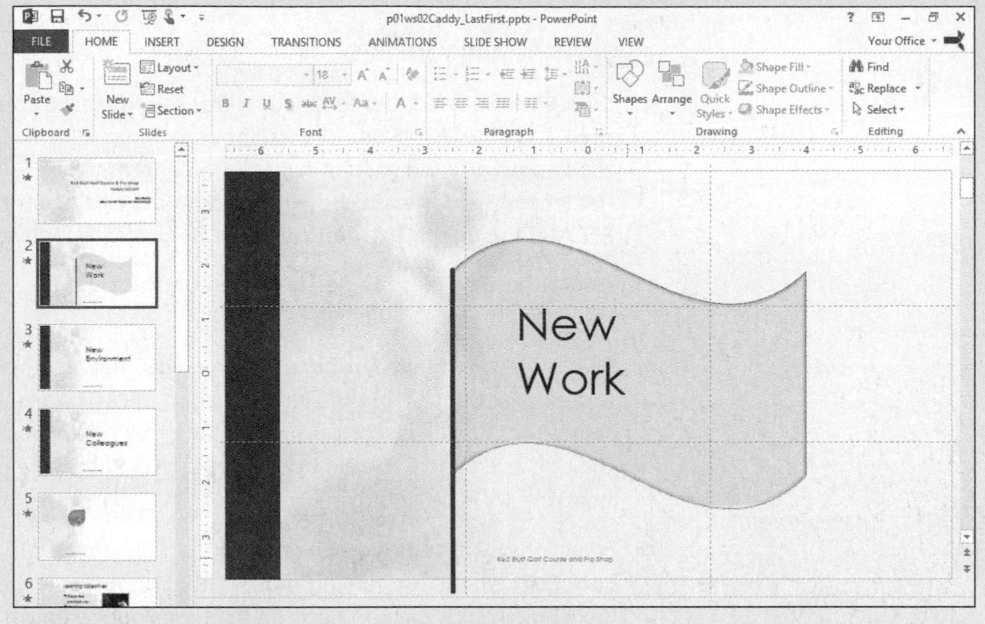

Figure 24 Finished line and wave shape forming a flag

g. **Save** the presentation.

Duplicating Shapes

After you have spent so much time formatting a shape just the way you like it, there is no need to re-create it all over again. In this section, you will duplicate the shapes on a slide in the Caddy School presentation.

P02.15

To Duplicate Shapes

a. Click **Slide 2**. Click the **wave** shape to select it. Press and hold Shift. Click the **line** shape. Release Shift. The line and wave shapes should both be selected.

b. Right-click one of the borders and select **Copy**. Right-click **Slide 3** in the left hand pane. Under Paste Options, select **Use Destination Theme**. Repeat this for **Slide 4**.

c. **Save** the presentation.

Arranging Shapes

PowerPoint has tools that enable you to precisely arrange the shapes you create. You can reorder items that are stacked to bring other shapes forward or send them backward. You can group objects so they are treated as one object.

You will make four boxes for the text on the Procedures and Responsibilities slide. You will begin by moving the text into their respective placeholders to prepare to move the text over the four power points.

P02.16

To Arrange Shapes

a. Click **Slide 9**. Select the text beginning with **Preserve course quality** and ending with **divots**. On the HOME tab, in the Clipboard group, click **Cut**. In the **Slides** group, click the **Layout** arrow, and then select **Two Content**. Click inside the top of the right placeholder box, and then in the Clipboard group, click **Paste** to insert the cut text. On the FORMAT tab, in the Size group, set the **Height** of the box to **3"**.

b. Select the **title** placeholder, and then on the FORMAT tab, in the Size group, set the **Height** of the box to **0.8"**.

c. Select the text **Maintain pace of play**, and then on the HOME tab, in the Clipboard group, click **Cut**. In the Drawing group, click **Shapes**, and then under Basic Shapes select **Text Box**. Click any part of the **slide** that does not contain a placeholder to insert the box, and then in the Clipboard group, click **Paste**. The text was inserted into the new box. You will move it into place later.

d. Select the text **Look your best**, and then on the HOME tab, in the Clipboard group, click **Cut**. In the Drawing group, click **Shapes**, and then under Basic Shapes, select **Text Box**. Click a part of the **slide** that does not contain a placeholder, and then in the Clipboard group, click **Paste**. The text was inserted into the new box. You will move it into place later.

e. Select the text **Arrive on time**, and then in the Clipboard group, double-click **Format Painter**. Drag the pointer over the text **Maintain pace of play** and the text **Look your best**. In the Clipboard group, click **Format Painter** to turn it off.

f. **Save** the presentation.

Aligning Shapes

PowerPoint has new smart tools in Office 2013 that enable you to make precision alignments to your shapes and elements in your presentation. You can align two or more shapes in relation to each other using red **Smart alignment guides** that assist you in aligning elements with other elements on your slide. Some Smart alignment guides assist with equidistance, too. The **Equidistant guides** assist you in placing one or more selected objects within equal distance of at least two other slide elements. This is not the same as Distribute Horizontally or Distribute Vertically, which attempt to distribute the space between the middle object or objects of three or more elements in a set between the outer elements.

In this section, you will align the text over the four power points.

P02.17

To Align Shapes

a. On **Slide 9**, drag the box with the text **Maintain pace of play** until it is positioned under the box beginning with **Preserve course quality**. Smart Alignment guides will appear to assist you in left-aligning this box with the one above it. Drag the **right sizing handle** until the Smart Alignment guide appears indicating that the widths of the two boxes are the same.

SIDE NOTE
Distribute Shapes
To distribute shapes vertically or horizontally on the slide, you need to select at least three shapes.

b. Drag the box with the text **Look your best** until it is positioned under the box beginning with **Arrive on time**. Use the Smart Alignment guides to assist you in aligning the **left bullet point** with the one above. Drag the **right sizing handle** until the Smart Alignment guide appears indicating that the widths and the top of this box with the top of the bottom box on the right.

c. Edit the text **30–40 minutes before shotgun starts** to read 30 – 40 m before shotgun. Edit the text **20 minutes before scheduled normal rounds** to read 20 m before normal rounds. Edit the text **Repair any divots** to read Repair divots.

d. Select the box beginning with **Arrive on time**, and then drag the **bottom sizing handle** until a red horizontal Smart Alignment guide appears indicating that it is the same height as the top box on the right.

e. Click any one of the **boxes**, press and hold Shift, and then click **each box** to select all four content boxes. Slowly drag the group of boxes upward until two multiple sets of Smart Alignment guides appear with equidistant guides above and below the group.

Arrows will appear between the guides indicating that the distances between the objects are the same. If you have trouble getting the equidistant guides to appear, position the boxes as shown below.

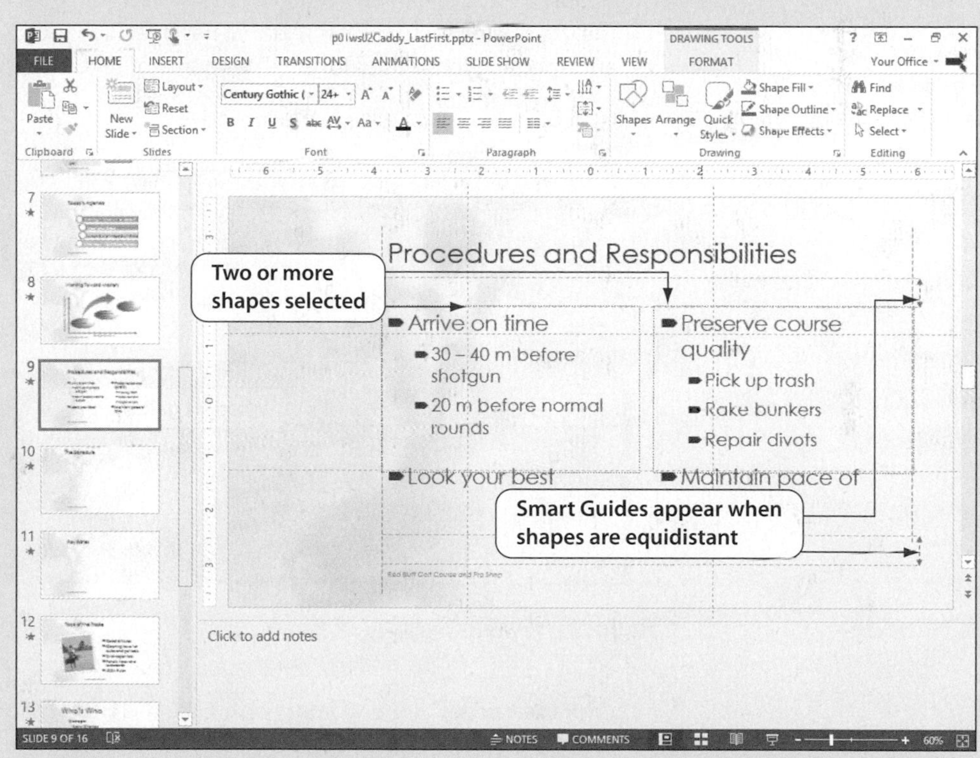

Figure 25 Aligning shapes

f. **Save** the presentation.

Merging Shapes

Sometimes to get the perfect shape, you need to customize what is available. Using the Merge Shapes feature in PowerPoint, you can create custom shapes from one or more built-in shapes. Such variations include union—taking the sum of two or more shapes; combine—the sum of two or more shapes, less their overlapping parts; or intersect—the overlap between two or more shapes. Other variations include fragment—breaking shapes into smaller parts along their overlapping lines; and subtract—removing whole parts of a shape using the outline of another shape. In this section, you will create a Welcome slide and merge a WordArt shape with an image.

P02.18

To Merge Shapes

a. Click **Slide 5**. Click the **INSERT** tab, and then in the Images group, click **Pictures**. Navigate to your student data files, select the file **p01ws02ProShop**, and then click **Insert**. Move the picture down so that the bottom edge of the picture is touching the bottom of the slide.

b. On the INSERT tab, in the Text group, click **WordArt**. Click **Fill - White, Outline - Accent 1, Shadow**—the fourth option in the first row. Type Welcome in the box. The size of the box expands to accommodate the word.

Just as shapes can be filled in and modified with effects, text can be enhanced with the use of **WordArt**, which is text that has been enhanced with color, outlines, shadows, and special effects. Used for small amounts of text, WordArt adds color and interest to your presentation.

SIDE NOTE
Keep It Short and Simple
Maintain balance on the slide. White space should be balanced with the number and size of shapes.

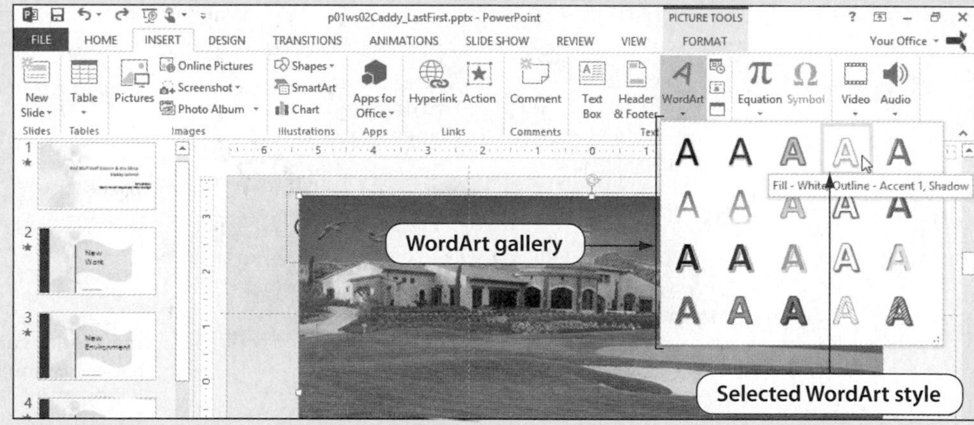

Figure 26 WordArt gallery

c. Click the **border** of the WordArt box. Click the **HOME** tab, and then in the Font group, change the **Font Size** to **80**. Drag the box up toward the sky in the image and to the right. The word welcome should be horizontally centered over the **right vertical guide** and vertically centered over the **edge** between the mountain and sky.

d. Click the picture to select it, press and hold Shift, and then click the **WordArt** box. Both objects should be selected. On the DRAWING TOOLS FORMAT tab, in the Insert Shapes group, click the **Merge Shapes** arrow, and then click **Intersect**. The shapes will now be merged.

Troubleshooting
If the Merge Shapes feature is not working properly, be sure to select the image first, and then select the WordArt box second.

Figure 27 Merging shapes

e. Drag the **merged shape** down and to the right until it is centered over the lower right power point. The top and bottom sizing handles should be centered on the vertical alignment guide.

f. **Save** the presentation.

MODULE 1

Using Elements to Communicate Information

Your presentation will likely include many elements: text elements such as those you have been working on in this workshop; graphic elements designed to communicate information, such as tables, charts, and SmartArt graphics; and elements that are designed to communicate or invoke emotion, such as pictures and other media. In this section, you will use a table, a chart, and SmartArt to convey information.

Create a Table

Tables, which are organized grids of information arranged in rows and columns, relate information together in a way that is meaningful to audiences. Short phrases, single words, and numbers can be placed in the table. You can even place graphics, such as photographs or clip art, in the cells. The table can be created as a media object directly from the icon on the content placeholder, or the Insert tab can be used to develop the table. Once you have created the table you can change the style, apply table effects, and change the layout. Table cells can be split or merged.

REAL WORLD ADVICE Using an Excel Worksheet as a Source

Often the data you need to convey in a presentation is already available in an Excel worksheet. You can copy the information from Excel and paste it onto a PowerPoint slide. Options you have for pasting include the following:

- Using the styles of the slide
- Keeping the source formatting from the worksheet
- Linking the information so changes in the worksheet will be reflected in the presentation
- Inserting the information as a picture
- Keeping the text only, and eliminating the worksheet grid
- Creating the table in PowerPoint, and then pasting the information from the worksheet into the table

Inserting a Table

You will create a table to explain the weekly golf schedule in the Caddy School presentation. To create a table, you can drag across cells on the Insert tab's Table grid, select Insert Table to use a dialog box, click Draw Table to draw the table cells, or click Insert Table in the content placeholder on the slide. In this section, you will insert and modify a table to fit your needs.

P02.19

To Insert a Table

a. Click **Slide 10**. Click the **INSERT** tab, and then in the Tables group, click **Table**. Click **Insert Table** below the table grid. The Insert Table dialog box is displayed.

b. Increase the Number of columns to **8**, increase the Number of rows to **5**, and then click **OK**.

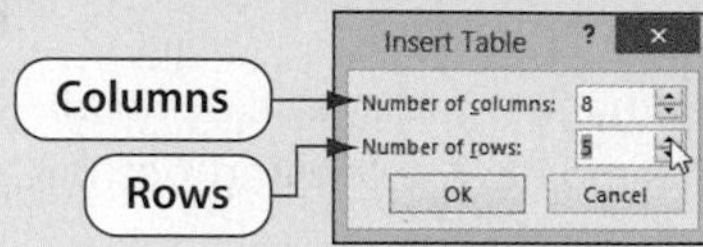

Figure 28 Insert table dialog box

c. Type Caddy in the first cell, press Tab to move to the next cell, and then type the abbreviations for the days of the week, beginning with Mon for Monday, in each of the cells on the top row of the table.

d. Click before the word **Caddy**. Under TABLE TOOLS, click the **LAYOUT** tab, and then in the Table group, click **Select**, and then click **Select Row**. In the **Alignment** group, click **Center** .

e. In the second cell of the first column, type Captain. In the third cell of the first column, type Intermediate, and then in the fourth cell of the first column, type Trainee.

Some of the words are broken in the middle so the words fit the cell. Do not worry about that at this time.

f. Continue to fill in the table as follows—the last row will remain blank for now.

Caddy	Mon	Tues	Wed	Thurs	Fri	Sat	Sun
Captain	8 AM	10 AM	8 AM	10 AM	8 AM	7 AM	7 AM
Intermediate	Noon	8 AM	Noon	8 AM	Noon	8 AM	8 AM
Trainee	8 AM	Noon	8 AM	Noon	8 AM	9 AM	9 AM

g. **Save** the presentation.

SIDE NOTE

Navigate a Table

Use arrow keys on the keyboard, or press Tab to move left to right and Shift + Tab to move right to left.

Changing the Table Style and Applying Table Effects

Table Styles provide options for color in the table. The Table Style Options, on the Table Tools Design tab, enable you to specify treatment for the various rows and columns in the table. The Header Row command affects the first row of the table where the column headers appear by applying a stronger color to the background of the cells and displaying the words in a bold font. banded rows or banded columns highlight the rows or columns with different colors. This assists your audience as they read the information in the table. You can apply styles to the total row, first column, and last column to highlight totaled information in your table. You can also change the color of individual cells on the table after applying a table style by using the Shading tool. You will continue to work with the schedule to enhance its appearance.

Table Effects further enhance a table by providing visual effects such as cell bevels, table shadows, and reflections. Cell bevel effects can make the cells appear in 3-D. Often you will see cell bevels applied to the column or row headers to differentiate them from the rest of the table. Apply simple table effects in a way that improves the table. The shadow and reflection effects are applied to the entire table when selected. You will update the Caddy School Schedule table with Table Effects.

P02.20

To Modify a Table Style and Effects

a. Click **Slide 10**. Click anywhere on the table. Under TABLE TOOLS, click the **DESIGN** tab, and then in the Table Styles group, click **More**. Point to the **thumbnails** in the gallery to see a live preview of the slide, and then under Best Match for Document, click **Themed Style 1 - Accent 3** in the top row.

The brown colors of the table coordinate with the colors of the background graphic. You will continue to modify the table design by applying a fill color to the caddy rank cells.

b. Select the **cells** containing the caddy ranks: **Captain**, **Intermediate**, and **Trainee**. In the Table Styles group, click the **Shading** arrow, and then click **Brown, Accent 3, Lighter 60%**.

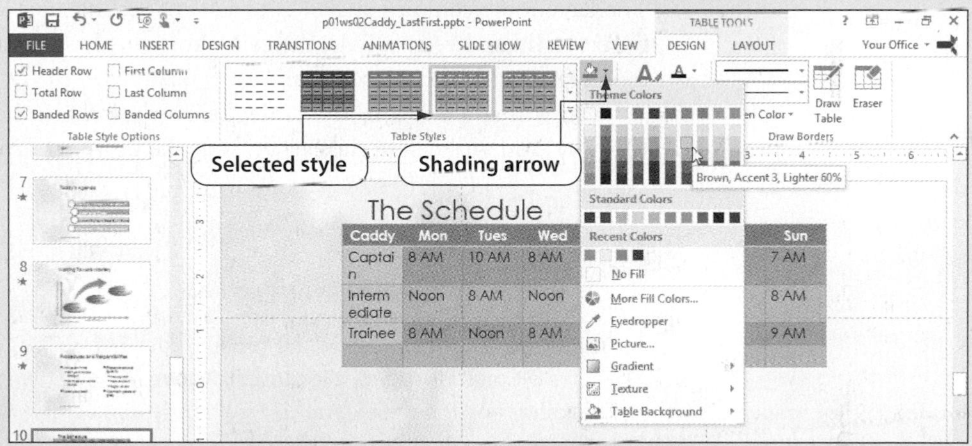

Figure 29 Modifying the table style

c. Select all of the **cells** in the top row of the table. Under TABLE TOOLS, on the DESIGN tab, in the Table Styles group, click **Effects**, and then point to **Cell Bevel**. Click **Soft Round** after pointing to the thumbnails to view Live Preview. This adds dimension to the cells, making the table more interesting.

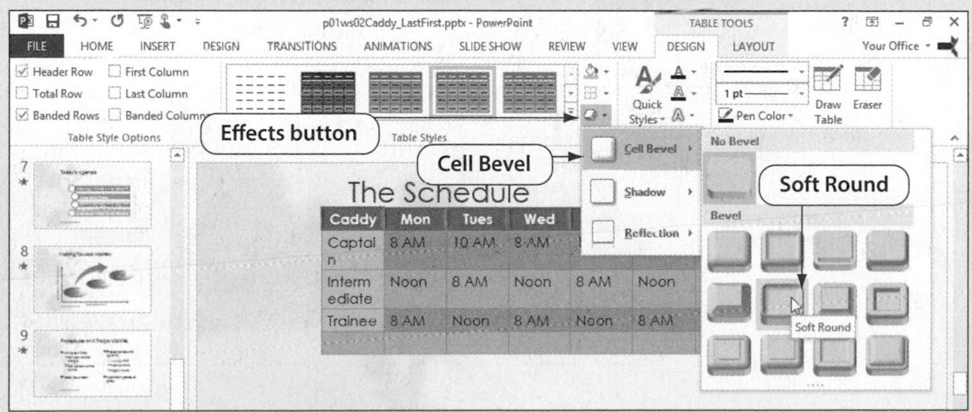

Figure 30 Selecting table effects

d. Select the **cells** containing the caddy ranks. In the Table Styles group, click **Effects**, point to **Cell Bevel**, and then click **Soft Round**. This effect mimics the effect of the column heading cells.

e. Select the **data in the second through fourth rows** of the table. Under TABLE TOOLS, on the DESIGN tab, in the Table Styles group, click the **Borders** arrow, and then select **All Borders**. Adding a border to the cells in the table enables your audience to differentiate between the cells of the table.

f. Click a **cell** in the table. In the Table Styles group, click **Effects**, point to **Shadow**, and then select **Offset Diagonal Bottom Left**. The shadow is applied to the entire table and helps maintain consistency with the other graphics in the presentation.

g. **Save** the presentation.

Changing the Table Layout

The Layout tab on the Table Tools tab enables you to make changes such as adding rows and columns to the table. You can also delete unnecessary rows or columns. Cells of the table can be merged into a single cell, and a single cell can be split into multiple cells. The Layout tab contains alignment tools that enable you to align the contents of the cells horizontally and vertically in the cells. You can also change the direction of the text and modify the width of the cell margins.

You will add a row to the table, below the column heading row, and merge cells in this row. You will delete the extra row at the bottom of the table.

P02.21

To Modify a Table Layout

a. Click in the **Captain** cell in the table. Under TABLE TOOLS, on the LAYOUT tab, in the Rows & Columns group, click **Insert Above**. A new row is placed between the column headings and the table data.

b. Select the **cells** under **Mon** through **Thurs** on the second row of the table. In the Merge group, click **Merge Cells**, and then type Weekday Rates in the merged cell. In the Alignment group, click **Center**. The cells are merged to show that the cells below are all related to the weekday rates.

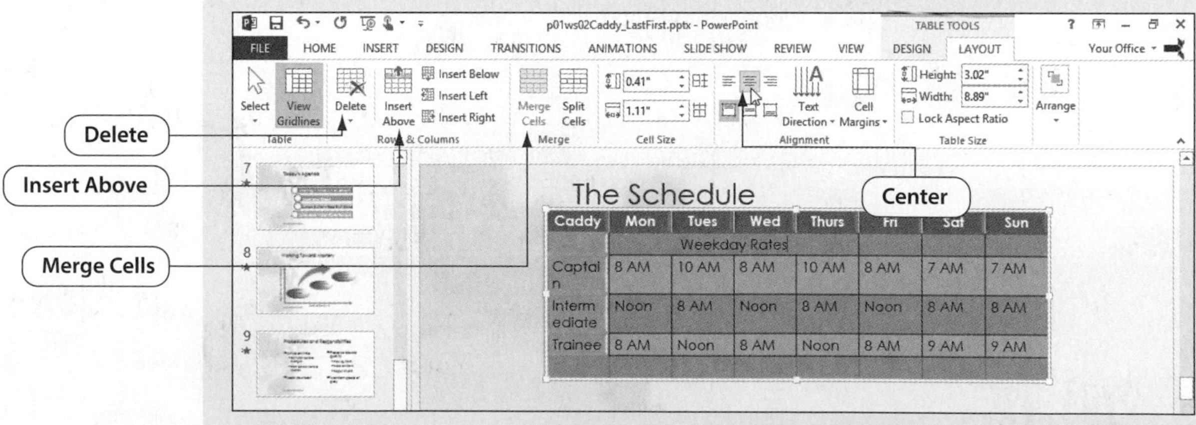

Figure 31 Modifying the table layout

SIDE NOTE

Delete Key or Delete Tool?

Delete removes data from cells but leaves the cell. The Delete tools remove the entire row or column.

c. Select the **cells** under **Fri** through **Sun** on the second row of the table. In the Merge group, click **Merge Cells**, and then type Weekend Rates. In the Alignment group, click **Center**.

d. Click a **cell** in the last row of the table. In the Rows & Columns group, click **Delete**, and then click **Delete Rows**. The extra row of the table is not needed.

e. Click the cell containing the **Intermediate** caddy rank. In the Cell Size group, click the **Table Column Width** arrow to increase the size until the word **Intermediate** fits on a single line. The width should be **1.8"**.

f. Select the **column headers** for the days of the week. In the Cell Size group, click in the **Table Column Width** box, type 1, and then press Enter.

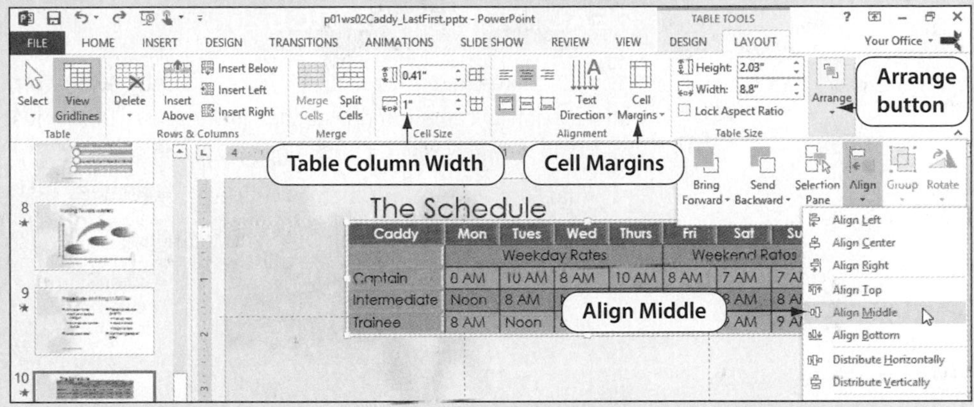

Figure 32 Modifying column width

g. With any cell selected, under TABLE TOOLS, on the LAYOUT tab, click **Arrange**, click **Align**, and then click **Align Center**. Click **Arrange** again, click **Align**, and then click **Align Middle**. Notice, the table is now centered both horizontally and vertically on the slide.

h. Select the entire **top row** of the table. In the **Alignment** group, click **Cell Margins**, and then click **Wide**. The size of the cells containing the headers seems to have increased, but in reality a wider margin was put around the words.

i. Select the word **Caddy** in the table, and then drag it to the first cell of the second row. This improves the balance of the table. With the word **Caddy** selected, on the **HOME** tab, in the **Font** group, click **Font Color**, and then click **White, Background 1**.

Troubleshooting

If the cell seems extra tall, you may have included the paragraph mark in the selection of the word. Click after the word "Caddy," and press Delete to remove the paragraph break.

j. **Save** the presentation.

Create and Insert Charts

Just as pictures can tell a story in your presentations, **charts** of numeric data assist your audience in grasping your message. Charts can be persuasive tools in presentations, giving your audience the essence of the problem and the solution. Large amounts of numbers are often difficult to read on the screen, but they can be distilled into charts that describe the real meaning of the data. The message of the chart should stand out as a single statement.

PowerPoint has tools that enable you to enter the data into a worksheet window and then create a chart. A wide variety of chart types are available. After the chart is created, you can edit the data and modify the characteristics of the chart including the design, layout, and format.

REAL WORLD ADVICE | **Critically Evaluate Your Charts**

As you create charts, it is important to critically evaluate them to ensure that the information is correct and that they make sense. Often, just switching the data in the rows and columns gives a whole new meaning to the chart. Ask yourself these questions:

- What is the one thing I am trying to convey with this chart?
- What is the core information to be included?
- Does the chart add to the message of the slide? Is it easy to read?
- Does the chart ethically represent the data and not misrepresent it?

Inserting a Chart

You create a chart by first selecting the type of chart to insert onto a slide. The type of chart relates to the type of data you have. For instance, pie charts are used to show the relationship of each part to the whole, and a line chart shows trends over a period of time. A column or bar chart shows the item relates to another item.

After selecting the chart type, a worksheet table window opens and displays default data. You replace the default data with your own, and the chart appears on the slide in Live Preview. You will create a stacked column chart to show the pay rate information in the Caddy School presentation.

P02.22

To Insert a Chart

a. Click **Slide 11**, and then click **Insert Chart**  in the content placeholder. In the Insert Chart dialog box, click the **Column** type in the left pane, and then click **Stacked Column**, and then click **OK**.

   The worksheet opens showing the Live Preview of the default data. The categories represent the columns, and the series provide the numeric data.

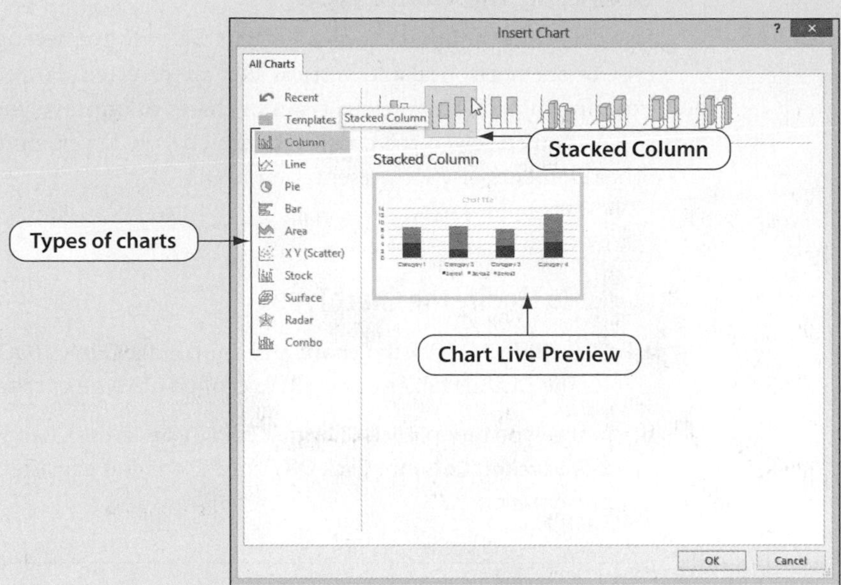

Figure 33 Inserting a chart

b. Type the following information into the worksheet, over the existing data:

	Base	Average Tips
Trainee	10	8
Intermediate	12.5	13
Captain	15	20

As you type, you should notice that the PowerPoint slide is updated in Live Preview. The final row and last column of the default worksheet are unneeded, so you will delete them.

c. Drag the **bottom-right corner** of the range—the blue square—up and to the left so only the data used—columns A-C and rows 1-4—are selected. Close [X] the worksheet window. Review the chart to ensure that the data is correct.

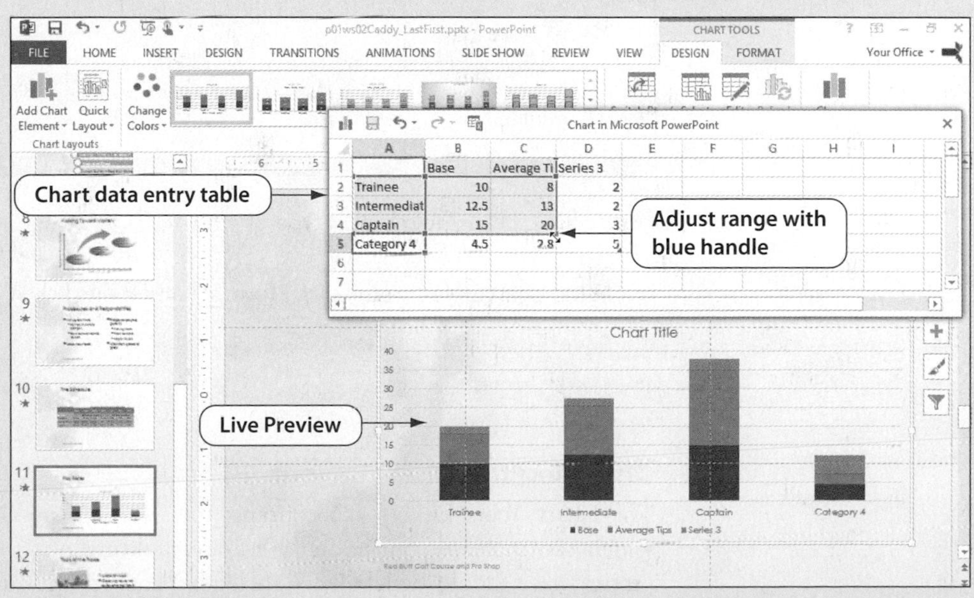

Figure 34 Inserting chart data

d. **Save** [Save icon] the presentation.

Changing the Chart Type

Usually, confusion with a chart occurs because the wrong choice was made for a chart type or the horizontal and vertical axes are reversed. PowerPoint makes it easy for you to experiment with the various types of charts to improve your message.

As you reviewed the chart, you noticed a 3-D version of the chart would fit with the other elements of your presentation better.

P02.23

To Modify the Chart Type

a. Click **Slide 11**. Click the **chart**, and then under CHART TOOLS, click the **DESIGN** tab.
   The DESIGN tab enables you to change the type of chart, the layouts, and the styles.

b. In the Type group, click **Change Chart Type**. In the Change Chart Type dialog box, click **3-D Stacked Column**. Click **OK**. The 3-D effect is consistent with other graphics in your presentation.

SIDE NOTE
Viewing Chart Names
Do not forget you can hover your mouse pointer over each chart type to see the name of each chart.

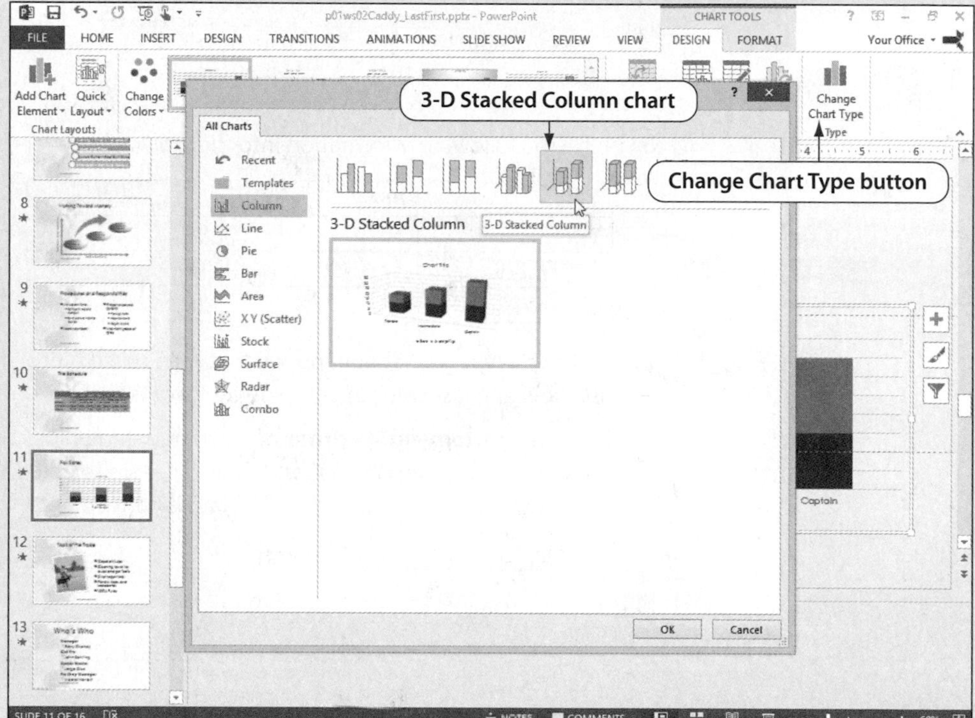

Figure 35 Changing the chart type

c. In the Chart Styles group, click **More**, and then click **Style 6**.

d. **Save** the presentation.

Changing the Chart Layout

The Chart Tools Design tab contains tools for adding descriptive labels to the chart, which can increase your audience's understanding of the material. The horizontal and vertical axes should be labeled. The legend enables the audience to match the bars with the caddy ranks. Data labels enable you to show the value of each of the bars on the table. This is beneficial if you do not use the gridlines in your chart. You can also display the data that you used to place the numeric data into the chart if necessary.

In this next exercise, you will change the layout and location of the legend.

P02.24

To Modify the Chart Layout

a. Click **Slide 11**. Click the **chart** to select it. Under CHART TOOLS, on the DESIGN tab, in the Chart Layouts group, click **Quick Layout**, and then click **Layout 1**.

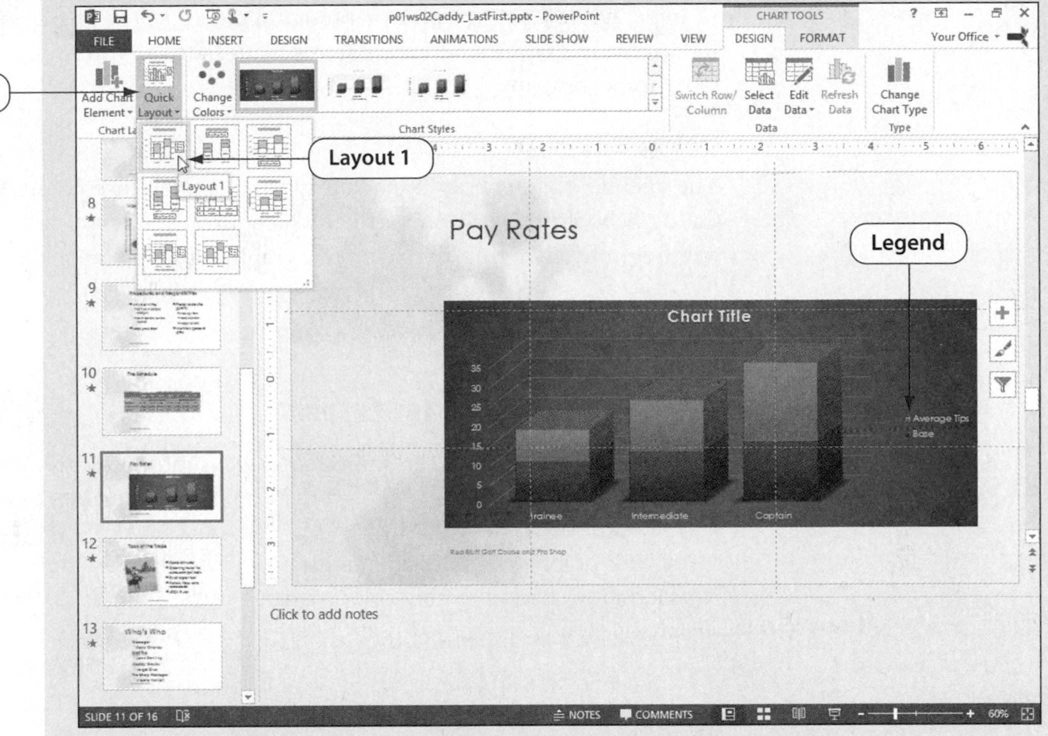

Figure 36 Modifying the chart layout

b. **Save** the presentation.

Changing Chart Elements

Individual elements on the chart, such as the title, series bars, axes, legend, and gridlines can be selected and modified using the Format tab under the Chart Tools tab. You can change the Shape Styles, and manipulate the shape fill colors, outline colors, and shape effects.

You still need to add a title to this chart. In this excerise, you will add a descriptive title.

P02.25

To Change Chart Elements

a. Click **Slide 11**. Click the **chart**, if necessary, to select it. Click **Chart Title** to select the title placeholder. Select the text **Chart Title**.

b. Type Pay per Hour, in Dollars. This will remove the words Chart Title and give a proper title.

c. **Save** the presentation.

Create a SmartArt Graphic

SmartArt graphics add color, shape, and emphasis to the text in your presentations. Specialty graphics such as list, hierarchy, process, pyramid, and cycle charts are preformatted using your color scheme for use in your slide shows. The gallery contains a number of versions for each chart type. As you review the different SmartArt graphics, you will see a wide range of graphic types. For instance, Process graphics show a sequence of steps, while Cycle graphics represent a circular flow of stages or tasks. Hierarchy and Relationship graphics show how items relate, such as you might find on an organizational chart for a company.

Using SmartArt

The agenda gives you an opportunity to effectively use SmartArt. You will modify the Caddy School presentation agenda, which already includes a SmartArt illustration. You will begin by changing the SmartArt graphic style using the SmartArt Styles gallery.

P02.26

To Modify a SmartArt Graphic

a. Click **Slide 7** and then click the SmartArt illustration **border**. Under SMARTART TOOLS, on the DESIGN tab, in the SmartArt Styles group, click **More** [▾], and then under 3-D, click **Sunset Scene**.

This graphic provides an interesting change from the normal bullet points used on slides. It will also be more colorful than a bullet point list. The SMARTART TOOLS tabs provide many options for modifying the design or format of the graphic.

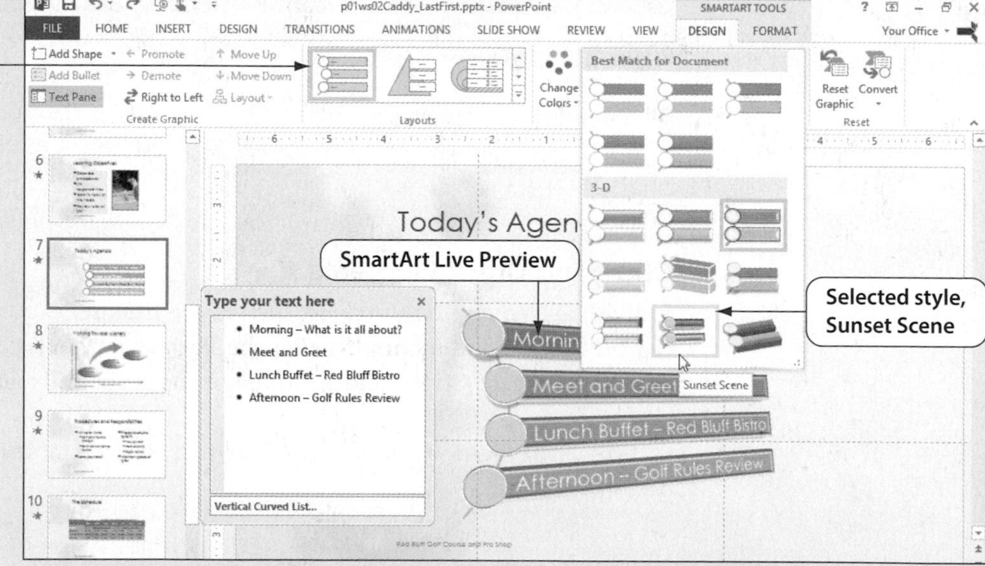

Figure 37 SmartArt Styles gallery

> **Troubleshooting**
> You can reset the graphic to the original version at any time. To do so, under SMARTART TOOLS, on the DESIGN tab, in the Reset group, click Reset Graphic.

b. Under SMARTART TOOLS, on the DESIGN tab, in the Create Graphic group, make sure **Text Pane** is toggled on and then **Type your text here** pane is visible. You will use the Text pane to quickly edit the information on the SmartArt graphic.

Similar to Outline view, the SmartArt Text pane enables you to concentrate on content without the visualizations. You can add additional bullet points at the end of the graphic by clicking after the last bullet point and pressing Enter. Use the arrow keys or click the bullet points to move within the Text pane. You can move the bullet text up and down on the graphic using tools on the DESIGN tab, and promote or demote text as needed.

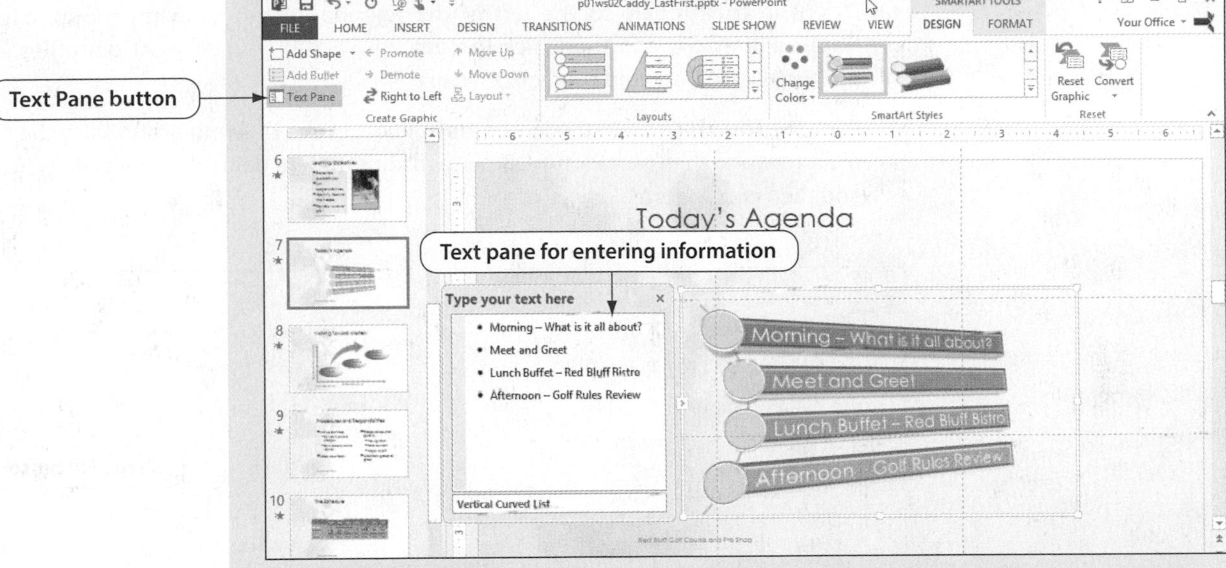

Figure 38 Adding text to a SmartArt graphic

c. In the Text pane, replace the text **Morning—What is it all about?** with the text Welcome, Caddy Overview.

d. Press ↓ twice to move to the bullet point **Lunch Buffet** in the Text pane, and then delete the text **Buffet**. In the next bullet point, delete the text **Afternoon –**, leaving only the words **Golf Rules Review**. Close the Text pane by clicking **Close** ✕ in the Text pane.

e. **Save** the presentation.

Customizing SmartArt

SmartArt can be customized by adding images. Also, the colors used in SmartArt graphics are based on the colors in the theme or template used for the presentation. Choices for coloring the graphics include Primary Theme Colors, Colorful combinations, and Accent color options. You can also recolor the individual shapes using the Shape Fill and Shape Outline tools on the Format tab. Shape effects, such as shadows and bevels, can be applied to the individual shapes. In this section, you will add relevant images for each agenda item.

P02.27

To Customize SmartArt

a. Click **Slide 7**. On the SmartArt graphic, click the **top tan-colored circle** to the left of the first agenda item. Click the **HOME** tab, and then in the Drawing group, click the **Shape Fill** arrow, and then click **Picture**. Browse to your student data files, select **p01ws02GolfBall**, and then click **Insert**.

b. Click the **second circle** to the left of the agenda. On the HOME tab, in the Drawing group, click the **Shape Fill** arrow, and then click **Picture**. Browse to your student data files, select **p01ws02Blue**, and then click **Insert**.

c. Click the **third circle** to the left of the agenda. In the Drawing group, click the **Shape Fill** arrow, and then click **Picture**. Browse to your student data files, select **p01ws02ProShop**, and then click **Insert**.

d. Click the **fourth circle** to the left of the agenda. In the Drawing group, click the **Shape Fill** arrow, and then click **Picture**. Browse to your student data files, select **p01ws02Pink**, and then click **Insert**.

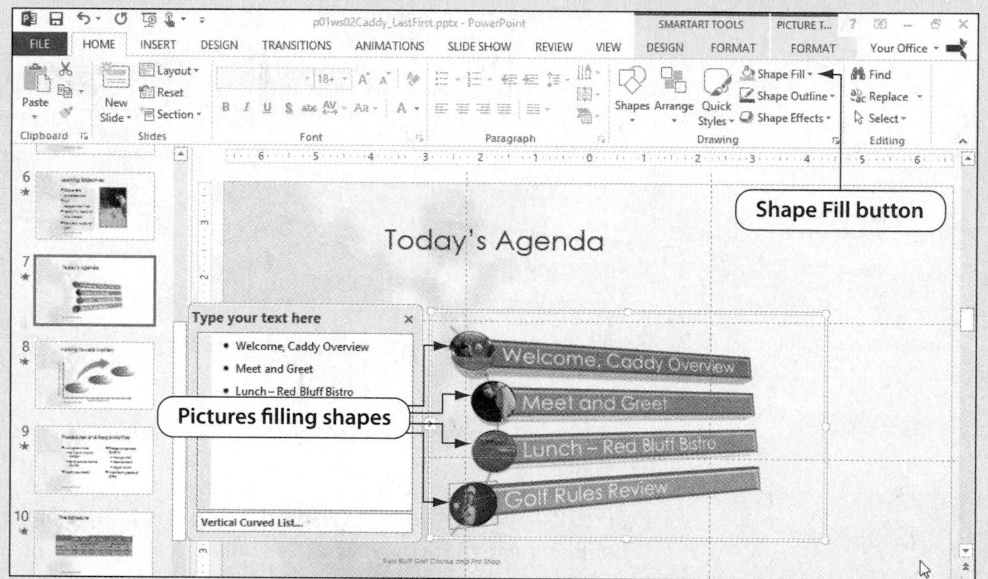

Figure 39 Modifying SmartArt

e. View the presentation in Slide Show view.

f. **Save** the presentation, and then **close** PowerPoint. Submit your file as directed by your instructor.

MODULE 1

Concept Check

1. Explain the rule of six. p. 845
2. When would you use numbered lists instead of bulleted lists? p. 848
3. Describe the usefulness of the Format Painter tool. p. 849
4. Explain what special symbols are. p. 850–851
5. Explain the rule of thirds. p. 853
6. List two things that gradients do for shapes when applied appropriately. p. 865
7. Tables organize information into columns and rows in a way that is meaningful to the audience. List three things you can do to tables to make them more visually understandable. p. 873–877
8. Explain when using a chart is beneficial to your presentation. p. 878
9. List three benefits of using SmartArt graphics. p. 882

Key Terms

Bit-mapped graphic 852
Chart 878
Color tone 862
Content Placeholder 856
Copyright 852
Cropping handles 859
Equidistant guides 870
Eyedropper tool 862
Format Painter 849
Horizontal guide 854
Kelvin scale 861
List hierarchy 848
Ordered List 848
Picture Style 863
Power points 853
Printer-friendly fonts 844
Recolor 861
Rule of six 845
Rule of thirds 853
Sans serif fonts 845
Saturation 862
Screen-friendly fonts 845
Serif fonts 844
Smart Alignment guides 870
SmartArt graphic 882
Symbols 850
Table 873
Transparency 863
Vector graphic 852
Vertical guide 854
WordArt 872

Visual Summary

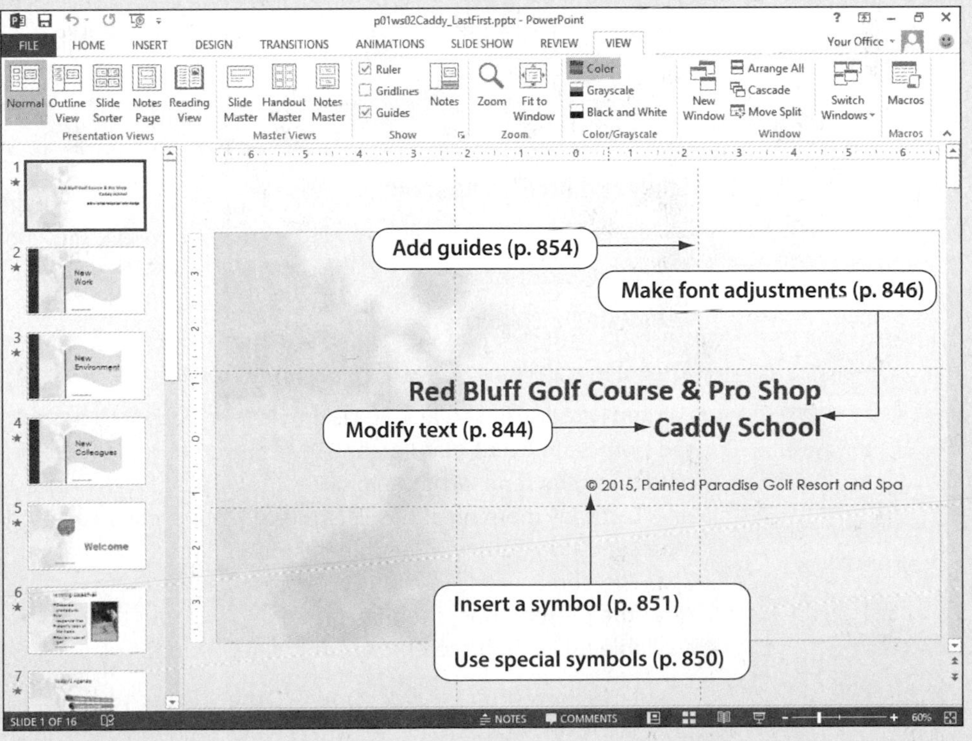

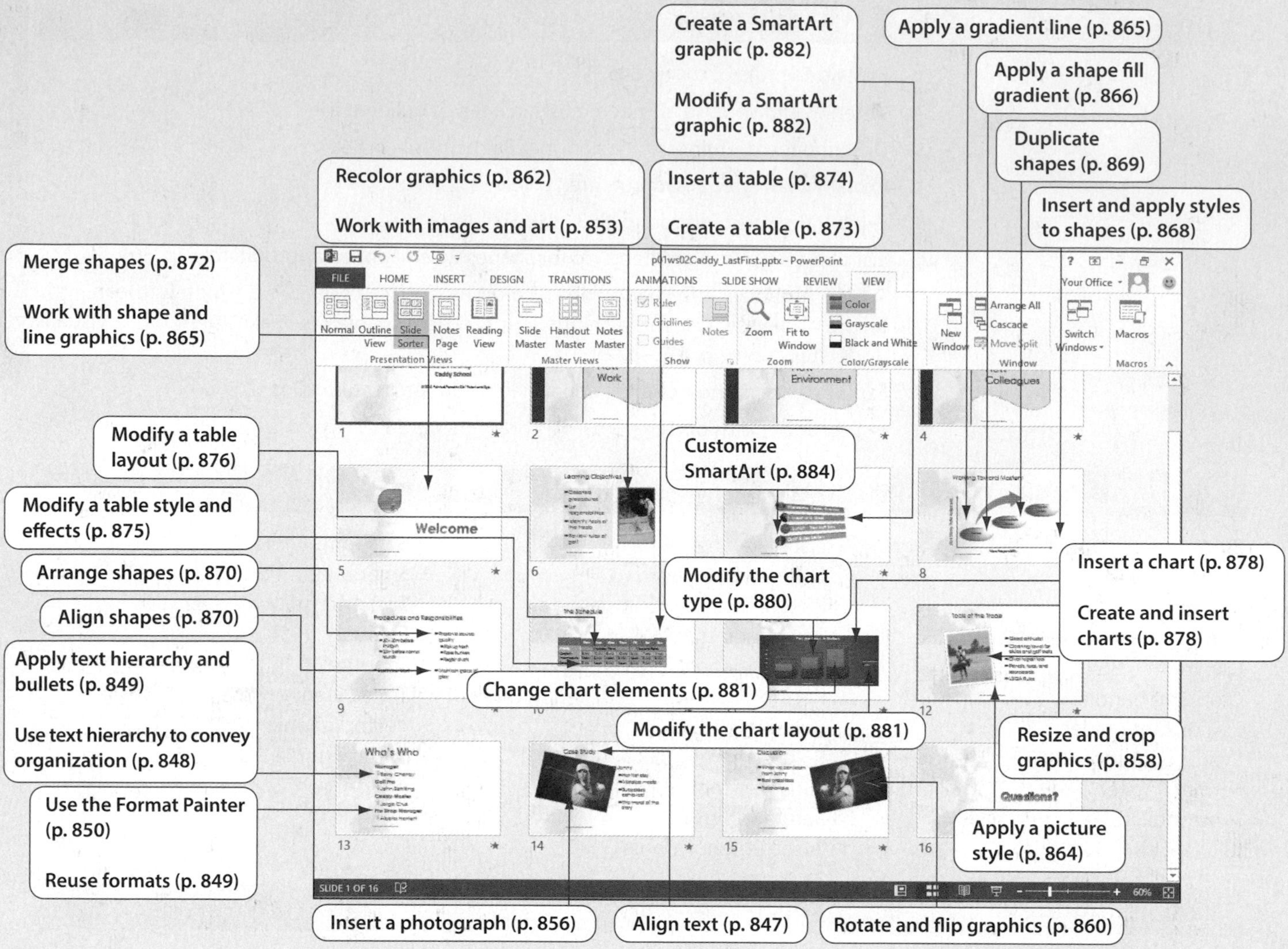

Create a SmartArt graphic (p. 882)

Modify a SmartArt graphic (p. 882)

Apply a gradient line (p. 865)

Apply a shape fill gradient (p. 866)

Duplicate shapes (p. 869)

Recolor graphics (p. 862)

Work with images and art (p. 853)

Insert a table (p. 874)

Create a table (p. 873)

Insert and apply styles to shapes (p. 868)

Merge shapes (p. 872)

Work with shape and line graphics (p. 865)

Modify a table layout (p. 876)

Customize SmartArt (p. 884)

Modify a table style and effects (p. 875)

Arrange shapes (p. 870)

Modify the chart type (p. 880)

Insert a chart (p. 878)

Create and insert charts (p. 878)

Align shapes (p. 870)

Apply text hierarchy and bullets (p. 849)

Change chart elements (p. 881)

Use text hierarchy to convey organization (p. 848)

Modify the chart layout (p. 881)

Resize and crop graphics (p. 858)

Use the Format Painter (p. 850)

Reuse formats (p. 849)

Apply a picture style (p. 864)

Insert a photograph (p. 856)

Align text (p. 847)

Rotate and flip graphics (p. 860)

Figure 40 Red Bluff Golf Course & Pro Shop Caddy School Final Presentation

Practice 1

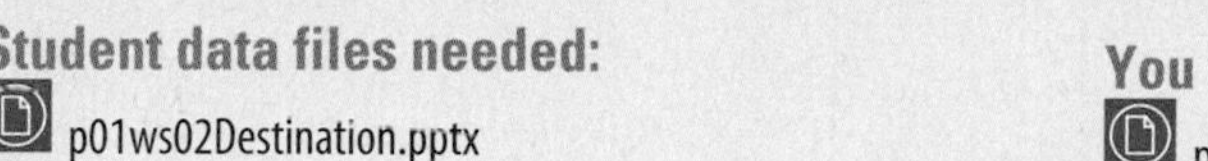

Student data files needed:

p01ws02Destination.pptx

p01ws02DestAlbum.pptx

p01ws02DestBouquet.jpg

You will save your file as:

p01ws02Destination_LastFirst.pptx

Planning Your Destination Wedding Seminar

Sales & Marketing

Painted Paradise Resort and Spa is the perfect place for a destination wedding. Patti Rochelle, the Corporate event planner, has several wedding planners on her staff. She would like to hold quarterly seminars to help brides-to-be plan for their special day. Seminars will be held on a Saturday morning and will feature a continental breakfast. Each seminar will begin with a presentation outlining the benefits of holding a wedding at Painted Paradise Resort and Spa. The audience also will include prospective grooms as well as parents of the couples. After the presentation, everyone attending will tour the resort to look at the various venues available for both the ceremony and the reception.

a. Start **PowerPoint**, click **Open Other Presentations**, and then click **Computer**. Click **Browse**, navigate to where your student data files are located, and then click **p01ws02Destination**. Click **Open**. Save the presentation as p01ws02Destination_LastFirst using your last and first name.

MODULE 1

b. On **Slide 1,** click the **title** placeholder, and then type Planning Your Destination Wedding. Type Painted Paradise Golf Resort and Spa in the **subtitle** placeholder, select the **text**, and then change the font size to **28**.

c. Click **Slide 3**. Click the **INSERT** tab, and then in the Images group, click **Pictures**. Navigate to the location of your student data files. Click **p01ws02DestBouquet**, and then click **Insert**.

d. Under PICTURE TOOLS, on the FORMAT tab, in the Size group, click the **Size Dialog Box Launcher**. In the Format Picture pane, click **Lock aspect ratio** to select it, if necessary, and then decrease the Scale Height to **75%**. Click **Close**. In the Pictures Styles group, click **Soft Edge Rectangle**. Drag the **picture** to the bottom-right corner of the slide.

e. Click **Slide 4**, and then click **Insert Table** in the content placeholder. Change the number of columns to **3**, the number of rows to **4**, and then click **OK**. Type the following in the table:

Wedding Type	Guests	Room
Small	Up to 50	Pueblo Room
Medium	50 to 250	Eldorado Room
Large	250 to 500	Musica Room

f. On **Slide 4**, click a cell in the table. Under TABLE TOOLS, on the DESIGN tab, in the Table Styles group, click **More**, and then click the **Themed Style 2 – Accent 4** Table Style. In the Table Style Options group, click the **Banded Rows** check box to remove the banded row formatting.

g. Under TABLE TOOLS, on the LAYOUT tab, in the Table Size group, change the Table Size Height to **4"**. Select all of the **cells** in the table, and then in the Alignment group, click **Center**. With the text selected, click **Center Vertically** in the Alignment group.

h. Click the **HOME** tab, and then in the Font group, increase the font size to **24**. Drag the table down so the top edge is in line with the bottom of the picture in the top-right corner.

i. Click **Slide 5**, and then click the **chart**. Under CHART TOOLS, on the DESIGN tab, in the Data group, click **Edit Data**. Add the following data to the worksheet, beginning with the cell immediately below the text **Groom's Attire**:

Photography	2,000
Miscellaneous	1,300

j. Close the chart worksheet. Under CHART TOOLS, on the DESIGN tab, in the Chart Layouts group, click **Quick Layout**, and then click **Layout 6**. In the Chart Layouts group, click **Add Chart Element**, point to **Chart Title**, and then click **None**.

k. Click **Slide 6**, and then click the **SmartArt graphic**. Under SMARTART TOOLS, on the DESIGN tab, in the Layouts group, click **More**, and then click **Circle Arrow Process**.

l. Under SMARTART TOOLS, on the DESIGN tab, in the SmartArt Styles group, click **Change Colors**, and then click **Transparent Gradient Range - Accent 4**. In the SmartArt Styles group, click **More**, and then under 3-D, click **Polished**.

m. Set **vertical guides** to **2.25** to the right and left of **0** on the horizontal ruler. Set **horizontal guides** to **1.25** above and below **0** on the vertical ruler. Click the **border** of the first box to the right of the rings so it has a solid border. Press and hold Shift, then click the three remaining boxes. Drag the **right sizing handle** of the top box until the red alignment guide is at **2.5"** to the right of **0** on the horizontal ruler.

n. Drag the boxes until the **center sizing handle** of the top box is behind the right vertical alignment guide. Click the **HOME** tab, and then in the Font group, increase the font size to **16**.

o. On the HOME tab, in the Slides group, click the **New Slide** arrow, and then click **Reuse Slides**. In the Reuse Slides pane, click **Browse**, and then click **Browse File**. Select **p01ws02DestAlbum**, and then click **Open**. In the Reuse Slides pane, click **Slides 2** to **7** in succession. In the left pane, select the slides you just added. On the DESIGN tab, in the Customize group, click **Format Background**. In the Format Background pane, click **Hide Background Graphics** to remove the image in the upper-right corner.

p. Close the Reuse Slides pane and the Format Background pane. Delete **Slide 13**. Click **Slide 1**, and then click the **photograph**. Under PICTURE TOOLS, on the FORMAT tab, in the Size group, click the **Crop** arrow, and then click **Fill**. Click in a blank area to deselect the photograph.

q. Click the **SLIDE SHOW** tab, and then in the Start Slide Show group, click **From Beginning**. Review the slides. Save the presentation, and then close PowerPoint. Submit your file as directed by your instructor.

Problem Solve 1

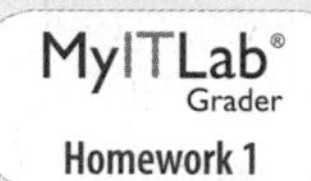

Student data files needed:

p01ws02Camp.pptx
p01ws02Camp1.jpg
p01ws02CampBall.jpg
p01ws02CampAlbum.pptx

You will save your file as:

p01ws02Camp_LastFirst.pptx

Golf and Swim Camp

Sales & Marketing

The Red Bluff Golf Club sponsors a Golf and Swim Camp for teens, aged 13–16. The teens learn about golf rules, play nine holes each day, compete for prizes, and swim at the Painted Paradise Water Park. After the six-week camp, a Teen Tournament and a Luncheon Awards Ceremony are held. You will create a presentation that gives the details about the camp, intended for the parents of the teens. You are creating a persuasive presentation to encourage them to send their children to the camp.

a. Start **PowerPoint**, and open **p01ws02Camp** from your student data files. Save the file as p01ws02Camp_LastFirst.

b. On **Slide 1**, after **Red Bluff Golf Club** add the text & Pro Shop. Change the font size of the subtitle to **20**.

c. Set vertical guides to **2.25** to the right and left of **0** on the horizontal ruler. Set horizontal guides to **1.25** above and below **0** on the vertical ruler.

d. Move the title text placeholder to align with the top horizontal guide so the guide is between the lines of text.

e. On **Slide 2**, fill the teardrop shape with the photo **p01ws02CampBall**.

f. Set the **Shape Height** to **2"**. Apply the Picture Effect Shadow **Perspective Diagonal Lower Left**. Drag the picture until it is centered over the bottom-right power point.

g. Delete one of the question marks on **Slide 3**.

h. On **Slide 4**, insert **p01ws02Camp1**, and then apply the Picture Style **Relaxed Perspective, White**. Drag the picture until the golf ball is centered behind the bottom-right power point.

i. On **Slide 5**, change the chart type to **3-D Pie**, apply chart **Style 8**, and then apply **Layout 6**. Remove the chart title, add **Data Callout** Data Labels, and then delete the Legend.

j. On **Slide 6**, remove the bullets from the text **Things to Bring**, and also from the text **Things to Wear**. Set the width of both placeholders to **4.5"**, and make sure they are centered over the vertical guides.

k. On **Slide 7**, change the SmartArt graphic to **Segmented Cycle**. Apply the **Polished** style, and then select colors **Colorful Range - Accent Colors 2 to 3**.

l. On **Slide 8**, apply table style **Themed Style 2 – Accent 1**. Align the left of the **table** with the left vertical guide. Drag the center vertical line of the table to **0.5"** to the left of **0** on the horizontal ruler. Drag the right edge of the table until is aligns with **4.0"** to the right of **0** on the horizontal ruler.

m. Select **Slide 5**. Insert **Slides 2–6** from **p01ws02CampAlbum** using the **Reuse Slides** option. Be sure to insert the slides in order.

n. On **Slide 6**, for both images, on the FORMAT tab, in the Adjust group, click **Reset Picture**. Apply the **Drop Shadow Rectangle** Picture Style to these images. For the remaining images through Slide 10, discard all formatting by resetting the pictures, and then apply the **Drop Shadow Rectangle** Picture Style.

o. Review the slides in Slide Show view. Save the presentation, and then close PowerPoint. Submit your file as directed by your instructor.

Perform 1: Perform in Your Career

Student data files needed:

p01ws02Money.pptx

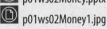

p01ws02Money1.jpg

You will save your file as:

p01ws02Money_LastFirst.pptx

Saving Money Workshops

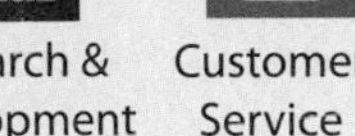

Research & Development   Customer Service

You have been interning at the local utility company that provides both electricity and water to area residents. Recently, there have been many inquiries about how to cut the high cost of utility bills. Charles Thomas, your supervisor, would like to hold a series of free workshops at branch libraries addressing these concerns. He has asked you to create a presentation that will show people how they can save money on energy and water as well as in other areas of daily living. Charles would also like to address the importance of increasing recycling. You will start with the presentation he has given you.

a. Start **PowerPoint**, and then open **p01ws02Money**. Save the presentation as p01ws02Money_LastFirst.

b. Apply a theme to the presentation. Insert a **footer** that appears on all slides except the title slide.

c. On one of the slides, add a chart to adequately represent the following data.

	Usage
Heating/Cooling	60
Water Heating	15
Refrigeration	13
Everything Else	12

d. Apply a chart layout and style with no chart title to the chart. Move any labels as necessary so they are visible.

e. On one of the slides, insert a table with 3 columns and 7 rows. Apply a table style. Merge the first row of cells and insert a title with an appropriate font size. Complete the table as follows:

Country	Amount (millions KWh)	Year
United States	3,892,000	2007
China	2,859,000	2006
Russia	895,200	2007
Japan	982,500	2006
Germany	549,100	2006

f. Set column widths and cell alignment. Fit the table to the slide.

g. On Slide 9, insert a Cycle SmartArt with the text: Recycle, Reuse, and Renew. Apply colors and style to the graphic.

h. On Slide 10, apply a layout, removing bullets and choosing a font size. Insert **p01ws02Money1**, and then choose a height and picture style. Use equidistant guides for placement.

i. On one of the slides, insert WordArt text Go Green! Apply a gradient, and then choose a font size. Correct any misspelled words, and then proofread the slide show.

j. View the slide show from the beginning. Review the slides. Submit your file as directed by your instructor.

Additional Cases

Additional Workshop Cases are available on the companion website and in the instructor resources.

MODULE CAPSTONE

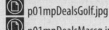

More Practice 1

Student data files needed:

- p01mpDeals.pptx
- p01mpDealsCont.pptx
- p01mpDealsGolf.jpg
- p01mpDealsMassg.jpg
- p01mpDealsRes.jpg
- p01mpDealsTheme.thmx

You will save your files as:

- p01mpDeals_LastFirst.pptx
- p01mpDealsPDF_LastFirst.pdf

Painted Paradise Golf Resort and Spa Special Deals

Sales & Marketing

The Painted Paradise Golf Resort and Spa along with the Red Bluff Golf Club offer special deals to families and couples. The special deals include various services such as golf, spa treatments, lodging, and meals. They are designed to persuade people to come to the resort and enjoy a perfect getaway. The deals are described in PowerPoint presentations that are sent via e-mail or shared online.

You will create a graphic-rich presentation to feature the Last Minute Deal, the Two Perfect Days Deal (for couples), and the Girls' Camp (for grown-ups). You will use a theme, modify the colors and font of the theme, and reuse slides. You will make use of WordArt, a table to detail the Girl's Camp options, special symbols, and a custom footer.

You might notice that there is more text than you might normally use in a slide show. This is because you will not be "delivering" this presentation. Instead, your audience will read it online. You will carefully check the spelling and proofread the document before saving the file as a PowerPoint PDF file.

a. Start **PowerPoint**, open **p01mpDeals**, and then save it as p01mpDeals_LastFirst, using your first and last name. Type your name in the slide title placeholder, then type today's date after the colon in the content area of the first slide.

b. Click the **DESIGN** tab, and then in the Themes group, click **More**, and then click **Browse for Themes**. Navigate to your student data files, and then apply the **p01mpDealsTheme** theme. In Slide Master view, change the theme fonts to **Corbel**, and then close this view.

c. Insert a **title slide layout** as Slide 2, and then type Special Deals for You from the Painted Paradise Golf Resort and Spa as the presentation title. Change the font size to **44**. Add A passion for helping people relax as the subtitle. Modify the subtitle font to italic and align the text to the right.

d. On **Slide 2**, add a **Rectangle** shape, **2"** in height and **5"** in width, to the top-right area of the slide. Make the following changes to the shape.

- Type The time to relax is when you don't have time for it in the shape. Press Enter, and then type Sidney J. Harris.
- Select the **quotation text**, apply the WordArt style **Fill - White, Outline - Accent 1, Shadow**, and then increase the size of the font to **32**.
- Insert the Wingdings symbol with a character code of **122** in front of the name **Sidney**. Align the author's name to the right.
- Add an **Offset Diagonal Bottom Left** shadow to the shape.

e. Create a new theme colors palette by changing the theme color Text/Background - Light 2 setting to **Blue, Text 2, Darker 50%**. Save the Theme Colors as Special Deals Colors LastFirst, using your last and first name.

f. Reuse all slides from the **p01mpDealsCont** file, adding them to the end of the current presentation. On the INSERT tab, apply **Date and time** footers to all of the slides except the title slide, click **Fixed**, and then replace the default date with Offers good through August 30. Click **Footer**, and then type Reserve now at www.paintedparadiseresort.com.

g. Using Outline view, make the following modifications.
   - Delete the Resort Special Deals slide (Slide 4).
   - Drag **Slide 7** to position **5**.
   - Drag **Slide 8** to position **7**.
   - On **Slide 9**, select the **Wine and appetizer buffet** line, and drag it below the Lunch line. Add Poppable Pastries and coffee in-room breakfast at the bottom of the feature list on **Slide 9**. Drag the **Poppable Pastries** line into position above the Lunch line.

h. In Normal view, on **Slide 3**, edit the graphic boxes to highlight each of the deals: Last Minute Deals, Two Perfect Days, and Girl's Camp.

i. Add a new **Title and Content** slide after Slide 4. Type Savings Highlights in the title placeholder. Insert a **3-D Stacked Column** chart, and then complete the worksheet as follows:

	Normal Pricing	Last Minute Deal 1	Last Minute Deal 2
Room	575	500	500
Spa Treatment	230	200	0
Golf	250	0	215
Meals	120	104	104

j. Under CHART TOOLS, on the DESIGN tab, in the Data group, click **Select Data**, and then switch the rows and columns in the chart. In the **Chart Layouts** group, click **Add Chart Element**, point to **Legend**, and then click **Top**. Click **Add Chart Element** again, point to **Chart Title**, and then click **None**. Edit the data by adding the following column to the end of the worksheet, and then close the chart data sheet.

Last Minute Deal 3
500
200
215
104

k. Change the layout of **Slide 4** to **Two Content**. Add the photograph from the student data files named **p01mpDealsMassg**. Modify the photograph as follows.
   - Resize the photograph to a height of **2.9"**.
   - Drag it into position at the bottom-right side of the white space of the slide. Remember, white space is empty space and no matter what the actual background color. Thus, the images may overlap with the orange color on the right of the slide.
   - Apply the **Drop Shadow Rectangle** picture style.

l. On **Slide 4**, to insert the photograph of a woman with a golf club, from the student data files, select **p01mpDealsGolf**. Modify the photograph as follows.
   - Resize the photograph to a height of **2.9"**.
   - Drag it above the massage photograph.
   - Apply the **Drop Shadow Rectangle** picture style.

m. On **Slide 4**, select the **body text** placeholder and right-click. Select **Format Shape**. In the Format Shape pane, under Text Options and then Text Box, set the Vertical alignment to the middle of the placeholder. If the right column content text placeholder is visible, delete it.

n. On **Slide 6**, drag the **right sizing** handle of the body text placeholder to the left until it is at the left edge of the photograph. On **Slide 7**, modify the photograph as follows.
   - Alter the color to **Red, Accent color 1 Light**.
   - Resize the photograph to a height of **5.9"**.
   - Drag the **photograph** to the left side of the slide.
   - Apply the **Soft Edge Oval** picture style.
   - Drag the **left sizing** handle of the body text placeholder to place the text to the right of the photograph.

o. On **Slide 8**, modify the photograph of the couple dancing by setting the **Color Tone** to **Temperature: 4700 K**. Apply the **Soft Edge Rectangle** picture style to the **couple dining** photograph. Use the **Format Painter** to apply the style to the other two photographs, and then select **all three photographs** and distribute them horizontally.

p. On **Slide 9**, select the photograph, and then modify it as follows.
   - Resize the photograph to a height of **3.5"**.
   - Align the photograph to the **Center** and then to the **Bottom**.
   - Change the Color Saturation to **200%**.
   - On the FORMAT tab, in the Arrange group, click the **Send Backward** arrow, then click **Send to Back**.

q. On **Slide 10**, insert the **Registered Sign** symbol after the word **Poppable**. This symbol is an "R" inside a circle. Modify the symbol's font effect to **Superscript**. Change the text **Poppable® Pastries** to the font color **Red, Accent 1, Darker 25%** and change the font style to **italic**.

r. Add a new **Title and Content** slide after Slide 10. **Type** The Girls' Camp Deal in the title placeholder. Add a table to the slide with **2 columns** and **6 rows**. Type the following information in the table.

Number of Guests	Cost per Guest
2	$500
3	$450
4	$400
5	$350
6	$300

s. Modify the table on **Slide 11** as follows.
   - Resize the table to a height of **4.5"** and a width of **4.5"**.
   - Center the text, and then in the Alignment group, click **Center Vertically**.
   - Apply the **Medium Style 3 - Accent 1** style to the table.
   - On the LAYOUT tab, in the Arrange group, click **Align**, and then click **Align Center**.

t. On **Slide 12**, insert the photograph **p01mpDealsRes** and resize it to a height of **3.8"**. Drag the **photograph** to the bottom-center on the slide, until the Smart Guides appear at the bottom center of the photograph. Apply the picture style **Simple Frame, White**.

u. Review the slides, carefully proofreading each item and making necessary corrections. Check the spelling, and then save the presentation. Save the file in PDF format, give it the name p01mpDealsPDF_LastFirst, and use the **Minimum size** button above **Publish**. Close the presentation, and then submit your files as requested by your instructor.

Problem Solve 1

Student data files needed:

- p01ps1Restaurant.pptx
- p01ps1ReBurger.jpg
- p01ps1ReFork.jpg
- p01ps1ReIndigo.jpg
- p01ps1ReSilver.jpg
- p01ps1ReSilver2.jpg
- p01ps1ReTea.jpg
- p01ps1ReTea2.jpg
- p01ps1ReTempl.potx
- p01ps1ReTerra.jpg

You will save your files as:

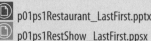

- p01ps1Restaurant_LastFirst.pptx
- p01ps1RestShow_LastFirst.ppsx

Restaurant Choices at the Painted Paradise Golf Resort and Spa

Sales & Marketing

There are many choices the guests can make for meals and snacks on the grounds of the Painted Paradise Golf Resort and Spa. You will create a presentation that describes the options. The presentation will be shown on flat panel displays throughout the resort, in places such as elevators and waiting areas. The presentation will also be a part of the in-room advertising via the resort's local TV channel. You can expect the audience to view the presentation for just a short amount of time, so the content will be minimal. You will use a template that has the timing already set up for advancing the slides every five seconds.

a. Open **p01ps1ReTempl**. Save the presentation as p01ps1Restaurant_LastFirst, making sure the file type is a **PowerPoint Presentation** and not a template. Switch to Normal view, if necessary, and then review and delete the notes on the title slide. To help you adhere to the rule of thirds, add vertical and horizontal guides at **1.67** and **1.25** respectively.

b. On **Slide 1**, replace the background with the file **p01ps1ReFork**. Change the background of the placeholder to **50%** transparent, color **Black, Background 1**. Resize the placeholder so that it fills the width of the slide and covers the top third. In the placeholder, type Painted Paradise Golf Resort and Spa Restaurants.

c. After Slide 1, add a new **Title and Content** slide, and then type Indigo5 in the title placeholder. Bring the title placeholder to the front, rotate it to horizontal, and then stretch it the width of the slide. Position the top of the title placeholder on the bottom horizontal guide, and then apply a **35%** transparent black background fill to it. Insert the photograph **p01ps1ReIndigo** into the content placeholder, and then resize it to fill the entire slide, but do not change the aspect ratio. It is okay if it is larger than the slide.

d. Reuse all six slides from **p01ps1Restaurant**, and then place them at the end of the presentation.

e. On **Slide 3**, apply customized bullets to the list, using the Wingdings font and the character code **157**. Change the height of the image to **6.5"**, and vertically align the picture on the slide using the Smart Guides. Align the **picture** horizontally under the left vertical guide, and then add a **black** solid border to the graphic.

f. Copy the title placeholder and text from Slide 2 and paste it onto **Slide 3**, moving it to the top edge of the slide. Change the height of the right placeholder to **5"**. Place it along the right edge of the slide, and then drag it down until the equidistant Smart Guides appear, aligning it between the title placeholder and the footer.

g. Add a new **Title and Content** slide after Slide 3, and delete the content placeholder. Enter the text Red Bluff Bistro in the title placeholder, and stretch it to fill the height of the slide, but leave it in place horizontally. Apply a **black** fill with a **35%** transparent background. Insert **p01ps1ReBurger** as the slide background. Using the Format Background pane, click **Picture**, then click **PICTURE COLOR**, and then set the Saturation to **400%** and the Color Tone to **6,500K**, if necessary.

h. On **Slide 5**, delete Red Bluff Bistro from the text placeholder. Copy and paste the title placeholder from Slide 4 to **Slide 5**, rotate it **180** degrees, and then set its right edge **4.5"** to the right of 0 on the horizontal ruler. Change the height of the graphic to **6.42"**, and then place its right edge on the right edge of the title placeholder. Center the image vertically. Change the height of the content placeholder to **4.37"**, and then center it horizontally and vertically under the left vertical guide. Apply customized bullets to the list, using the Wingdings font and the character code **157**. Add a **black** solid border to the graphic.

i. Add a new **Title and Content** slide after Slide 5, and then delete the content placeholder. Type Terra Cotta Brew in the title placeholder. Rotate the title placeholder to horizontal, stretch it the width of the slide, and align the top edge with the bottom horizontal guide. Fill it with a **50%** transparent black background. Fill the slide background with the image **p01ps1ReTerra**.

j. On **Slide 7**, apply custom bullets using the Wingdings font with the character code **155**. Increase the font size to **32**. Resize the box to be **4.4"** high by **3"** wide. Drag it to the right until the bullets are aligned under the right vertical guide and the Smart Guides appear. Position it vertically, 1" from the top-left corner. Insert the **Registered Sign** symbol after the word **Poppable**, and then make it **superscript**.

k. Continuing on **Slide 7**, use the **Format Painter** to copy the style of the title placeholder from Slide 6 to the title placeholder on **Slide 7**. Click in the **title text** of Slide 7 to apply the format. Rotate the placeholder to horizontal, and then stretch it the width of the slide. Drag the placeholder down until the Smart Guides show it is equidistant between the content placeholder and the footer. Bring the **title** placeholder to the front.

l. Continuing on **Slide 7**, resize the image to be **5.25"** tall by **3.5"** wide, and then drag it left of the vertical alignment until the equidistant guides appear. Move the **image** down behind the title placeholder until it is centered vertically with the content placeholder. Drag the **content** placeholder up until its top edge aligns with the top of the image. Add a **black** solid border to the graphic.

m. Add a new **Title and Content** layout slide after Slide 7. Type Silver Moon Lounge in the title placeholder, and then delete the content placeholder. Fill the background with image **p01ps1ReSilver**. Change the color saturation to **33%** and the color tone to **5,300K**. Stretch the title placeholder to the height of the slide, and fill it with a **70%** transparent black background. Leave it in place horizontally.

n. On **Slide 9**, use the **Format Painter** to copy the **title** placeholder from Slide 8 to the title placeholder on Slide 9, and then stretch it to the top and bottom of the slide. Rotate it **180** degrees, move its horizontal position to **5.7"** from the top-left corner, and then bring it to the front. Replace the picture with the file **p01ps1ReSilver2**, and then set the horizontal and vertical positions to **2.4"** and **0.25"** respectively. Resize the photo to **5.18"** square. Place a solid black border around the image. Center the content placeholder below the image, and then make it equidistant from the image and the footer.

o. Add a new **Title and Content** slide after Slide 9. Type Turquoise Oasis Spa in the title placeholder, and then delete the content placeholder. Rotate the **title** placeholder to horizontal, stretch it the width of the slide, and then fill it with a **35%** transparent black background. Drag the **placeholder** down until its top edge is aligned with the bottom Horizontal Guide. Fill the background of the slide with the image **p01ps1ReTea**. Change the Color Saturation to **200%** and the Color Tone to **4,700K**.

p. Copy the **title** placeholder from Slide 10, and then paste it onto **Slide 11**. Delete the original vertical title placeholder and default title text placeholder from Slide 11. On **Slide 11**, insert **p01ps1ReTea2** in the content placeholder, change the height of the image to **4.5"**, and add a black border. Position the image **2.74"** horizontally and **0.75"** vertically from the top-left corner. Apply custom bullets to the list using the Wingdings font and character code **155**.

q. Continuing with **Slide 11**, drag the **content** placeholder to the left until its left border aligns with the left edge of the slide. Drag the **right sizing** handle of the content placeholder to the left until it aligns with the left edge of the image. Drag the **placeholder** up until it is the same distance from the title placeholder as the title placeholder is from the footer.

r. On **Slide 12**, change the height of the image to **5"**, and then center it behind the left vertical guide. Drag the image up until the Smart Guide appears just below the title placeholder. Fill the **title** placeholder with a **35%** transparent black background, bring it to the front, and then stretch it to fill the top third of the slide. Edit the table by adding the two restaurants to the first column below **Terra Cotta Brew** as follows.

Restaurant
Silver Moon Lounge
Turquoise Oasis Spa

s. Increase the height of the table size to **3.5"**, and then align the **table** to the right of the slide, between the right edge of the slide and the image, and aligned with the bottom of the photo. Apply the **Medium Style 3** style to the table.

t. Review the slides, checking the spelling. View the slide show. The slides change automatically, so you do not have to click between slides. Save the presentation.

u. Save the presentation again as a **PowerPoint Show**, with the file name p01ps1RestShow_LastFirst. Close the presentation, and then submit your files as requested by your instructor.

Problem Solve 2

Student data files needed:

p01ps2MenuItems.pptx

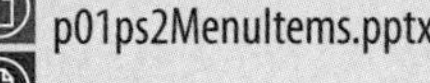

You will save your file as:

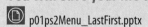

p01ps2Menu_LastFirst.pptx

Wait Staff Training

Human Resources

Chef Robin Sanchez has created some great new recipes for the Indigo5 restaurant at the Painted Paradise Resort and Spa. You have been asked to create a PowerPoint presentation that introduces the wait staff to the new menu items and reviews some important practices for the servers. The new dishes will be pictured on the slides along with information about the ingredients, and a table will show the name of the item, the cost, and additional wine or food pairings for each menu item.

The chef has prepared some slides for you to use in your presentation, but he has also requested that you create additional slides with guest service information. The chef also requested that handouts are made available so the staff can have the information for future reference.

a. Start **PowerPoint**, open **p01ps2Menu**, and then save it as p01ps2Menu_LastFirst. Type today's date after the colon in the body text placeholder. Apply the **Facet** theme, and then make the following changes to the theme colors.
   - Change the Text/Background - Light 2 to **Blue-Gray, Background 2, Lighter 80%**
   - Change the Accent 2 color to **Gold, Accent 3, Darker 50%**
   - Name the new Theme Colors LastFirst Menu, using your last and first name.

b. After Slide 1, insert a **Title Slide** layout, and then type the title New Menus and More with a subtitle of Autumn Season Training. Center both the **title** and the **subtitle**.

c. After Slide 6, reuse **Slides 2–5** from **p01ps2MenuItems**.

d. In Outline view, increase the list level of the ingredients listed on **Slide 7**, titled **Apple and Cheese Javelina Baguette**. Change the bullets for the ingredients to **Filled Round Bullets**. Repeat this step with the ingredient lists for **Slides 8–9**. Repeat this step on **Slide 10** for the three restaurants where Poppable Pastries are available.

e. On **Slide 7**, insert the **p01ps2MenuApples** picture, and then resize the picture to **3"** in height. Resize the text block to **3.13"** in width. Use vertical guides to align the picture and the text block to the power points on each slide. For the following slides, resize the pictures and text blocks as shown, and then align them to the power points on each slide.

Slide Number	Picture Height	Text block width
Slide 8	**3.1"**	**3.33"**
Slide 9	**2.9"**	**3.33"**
Slide 10	**3"**	**3"**

f. Move **Slides 4–6** to the end of the slide show. Move **Slide 3** (Our New Items) before Slide 8.

g. Add a new slide, with the **Title and Content** layout, after Slide 2. Type James Beard said... in the title placeholder. Type Food is our common ground, a universal experience. in the body placeholder. Include the punctuation. Remove the bullet, and then change the font style to **italic**. Increase the font size of the quotation to **36**, and then apply the **Fill - Dark Yellow, Accent 2, Outline - Accent 2** WordArt style to the quotation.

h. On **Slide 7**, insert the **Registered Sign** symbol immediately after the word **Poppable**, with no space between the word and the symbol. Alter the font of the symbol to **superscript**.

i. On **Slide 8**, modify the table by inserting a row at the bottom with the following information:

Item	Price	Up-sell Item
Poppable Pastries	$1 or 3 for $2.50	Freshly brewed coffee

j. Continuing with the table on **Slide 8**, make the following changes to the table.
   - Resize the table to **9.0"** in width. Align the **table** in the center of the slide.
   - Change the Table Style to **Medium Style 1 - Accent 4**.
   - Change the Table Style Options from Banded Rows to **First Column**.

k. On **Slide 11** add the SmartArt graphic **Circle Process** to the body content. For each shape, type the following:

Shape	Text
1	Be of Service
2	Do Offer World Class Care
3	Have Happy Customers

Alter the SmartArt graphic as follows.

- Change the colors to **Colorful Range - Accent Colors 3** to **4**.
- Change the SmartArt Style to **Polished**.

l. Edit the pie chart data on **Slide 9**, by adding the following information into the chart worksheet.

	%
Atmosphere	5
Not Sure	20

Make the following changes to the chart.

- Change the Chart Layout to **Layout 1**.
- Remove the chart title.
- Move the labels for **Atmosphere** and **Price** away from the chart and to the left to reveal the chart leader lines. Position the labels appropriately.
- Add a text box to the bottom-left corner of the chart, **0.4"** in height and **2.5"** in width, and then type Source: Restaurant Survey 2011.

m. Move **Slide 11** into position **9**.

n. Review the spelling of the presentation. Review each slide. Save the presentation. Print only **Slide 8** (Our New Items) as a **Full Page Slide**. Close the presentation, and then exit PowerPoint. Submit your files as requested by your instructor.

Perform 1: Perform in Your Life

Student data files needed:

 Blank PowerPoint presentation

p01pf1FamStory.docx

You will save your files as:

 p01pf1Family_LastFirst.pptx

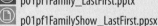

 p01pf1FamilyShow_LastFirst.ppsx

My Family Presentation

Information Technology

In this project, you will create a slide show based on your family using the skills you have learned in this module. You have many options on the organization of this presentation. You could focus on each member of your family on individual slides. You could highlight past generations of your family. This would be great to show at a family reunion. Plan to include between 7 and 10 slides. Use the file p01pf1FamStory document to draw some thumbnails and plan the content of your slides.

Select an appropriate template, changing the colors or fonts. Create an outline with the titles and body content for your slides. Change the slide layouts as needed to accommodate the information on the slides. Slide footers should include your name and the slide number. Pay attention to the graphic details of this presentation, selecting appropriate digital photographs you may have, and shapes to assist you in telling your family story. Use SmartArt creatively, perhaps to develop a family tree. Use a chart in your presentation, as well as a table.

You will print an outline of the presentation, so you will know what is on each slide as you speak to the audience. You will save the presentation in PowerPoint Show format so it is easy to start.

a. Open and print **p01pf1FamStory** to plan the content of your slides. Start **PowerPoint**, select a template, and then save the presentation as p01pf1Family_LastFirst.

b. Modify the colors or fonts of the template appropriately.

c. Create 7–10 slides, with titles and body content.

d. Modify the layouts of the slides appropriately. Add footers to every slide, except the title slide, that contains your name and the slide number.

e. On the title slide, include your name and a copyright notice with the copyright symbol.

f. Add photographs and shapes to slides in the presentation. Use vertical and horizontal guides to observe the rule of thirds.

g. Create a SmartArt graphic on a slide.

h. Create a table on a slide to describe some aspect of your family.

i. Create a chart on a slide.

j. Check the spelling throughout the presentation. Ignore the spelling of proper names, and correct any other misspelled words. Review each slide in Slide Show view.

k. Save the presentation. Save the presentation again as a PowerPoint Show named p01pf1FamilyShow_LastFirst. Print an outline of your presentation. Close the presentation, and then exit PowerPoint.

Perform 2: Perform in Your Career

Student data files needed:

 Blank PowerPoint presentation

 p01pf2HealthStor.docx

You will save your files as:

 p01pf2Health_LastFirst.pptx

p01pf2HealthShow_LastFirst.ppsx

Career Day

Human Resources

As the administrative manager of the American Health Group, you have been asked to discuss health care careers during the Fall Career Expo at the local high school. Your audience will be mainly 9th and 10th graders who are deciding what careers they wish to pursue. Your presentation will discuss at least five options in the health care field. Consider nurses, doctors, therapists, medical records personnel, phlebotomists, EMT workers, psychologists, optometrists, dentists, chiropractors, and other health care careers as you prepare the presentation. You will deliver the presentation to about 30 people at one time in a classroom situation. You will need to do enough research to adequately present the material.

a. Open and print **p01pf2HealthStor** to plan the content of your slides. Start **PowerPoint**, select a theme, and then save the presentation as p01pf2Health_LastFirst.

b. Modify the colors or fonts of the template appropriately.

c. Create 7–12 slides, with titles and body content.

d. Modify the layouts of the slides appropriately. Add a footer to every slide, except the title slide, that contains your name, the slide number, and the current date.

e. On the title slide, include your name and a copyright notice with the copyright symbol.

f. Add photographs and shapes to slides in the presentation. Use vertical and horizontal guides to observe the rule of thirds.

g. Create a SmartArt graphic on a slide.

h. Create a table on a slide, to either describe each career path or to show local training programs for each career.

i. Create a chart on a slide.

j. Type notes in the Notes pane that reflect your research for this project.

k. Check the spelling throughout the presentation. Ignore the spelling of proper names, while correcting any other misspelled words. Review each slide in Slide Show view.

l. Save the presentation. Save the presentation again as a PowerPoint Show named p01pf2HealthShow_LastFirst. Print an outline of your presentation, close the presentation, and then exit PowerPoint.

Perform 3: Perform in Your Team

Student data files needed:

Blank PowerPoint presentation

p01pf3Garden.pptx

You will save your files as:

p01pf3Garden_TeamName.pptx

p01pf3GardenShow_TeamName.ppsx

p01pf3GardenPDF_TeamName.pdf

Organizing a Community Garden

Customer Service

As active volunteers in your community, you have been working with the manager of Hilltop Community Gardens, which provides gardening plots for citizens in your community to grow fruits and vegetables. You coordinate three gardens. Each year, in the spring, you visit civic groups to encourage their members to get involved with the gardens, whether as gardeners or as sponsors. You talk to groups as small as 15 people and as large as 100 people. You will update a PowerPoint slide show to support you as you give your presentation.

a. Select one team member to set up the presentation by completing Steps b–e.

b. Open your browser, and then navigate to either **https://www.skydrive.live.com**, **https://www.drive.google.com**, or any other instructor assigned site. Be sure all members of the team have an account on the chosen site—a Microsoft or Google account.

c. Start a new presentation, with a title slide labeled Team Members. List the names of each of the team members in the subtitle. Include any additional information on this slide required by your instructor.

d. Save the presentation as p01pf3Garden_TeamName. Replace "Name" with the name assigned to your team by your instructor.

e. Share the presentation with the other members of your team. Make sure that each team member has the appropriate permission to edit the presentation.

f. Open the shared presentation, reuse all the slides from **p01pf3Garden**, and then review the slide show. Select an appropriate theme for the presentation. Custom Colors should be named Team Name Garden Colors. Insert an appropriate footer.

g. The slide show should be between 7 and 12 slides. Insert slides as appropriate. Change images, and then reformat the pictures. Use WordArt creatively. Observe the rule of thirds.

h. Observe the rule of six throughout your presentation. Use a background image on at least one slide. Adjust the transparency, and then hide background graphics if necessary.

i. The chart should be easily readable, the colors discernible, and it should appropriately characterize the information.

j. The table should be formatted and attractively display the information.

k. Choose a more appropriate SmartArt graphic.

l. Apply at least one background fill. Set appropriate gradient stops on the background fill and the border.

m. Review the slide show. Check the spelling throughout the presentation. Save the presentation. Save the presentation as a PowerPoint Show named p01pf3GardenShow_TeamName. Save it again as a PDF presentation for publishing online, named p01pf3GardenPDF_TeamName.

n. Once the assignment is complete, share the presentation with your instructor or submit it as your instructor directs. Make sure that your instructor has permission to edit the contents of the folder.

Perform 4: How Others Perform

Student data file needed:

p01pf4PuppyU.pptx

You will save your files as:

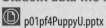

p01pf4PuppyU_LastFirst.pptx

p01pf4PuppyUShow_LastFirst.ppsx

Puppy U

Human Resources

Recently you have been in charge of supervising the veterinary technicians at the Pet Care Clinic. Josie Yancey, an experienced vet tech, is planning a puppy training course that she is calling Puppy U. She prepared a PowerPoint presentation to show at the orientation class. She asked you to review the presentation and improve it. The audience will be families, some with children as young as 7. The puppies will not be there the night of the orientation. The basic commands, procedures, and equipment are discussed in the slide show. This presentation is informational so the families are prepared when they bring their puppies to class.

a. Open **p01pf4PuppyU**, review the presentation, and then save the presentation as p01pf4PuppyU_LastFirst.

b. Consider the theme, color scheme, and font. What changes would you recommend? Update the presentation to reflect your thinking.

c. Apply the rule of six to the slides, and then adjust the information accordingly while preserving the message and intent.

d. What other topics make sense to include? Could any of the slides be deleted? Add or remove slides, but carefully plan to cover the same content or add additional content.

e. How could you make this presentation more attractive to people? Add items that will enhance the presentation, including SmartArt, WordArt, and personal digital photographs if you happen to have a dog. Evaluate the content of the presentation to determine if you can display the same information in a chart or table. Adhere to the rule of thirds.

f. Review the slide show. Check the spelling throughout the presentation. Save the presentation. Save the presentation again as a PowerPoint Show named p01pf4PuppyUShow_LastFirst. Print the presentation with four slides per page for handouts.

WORKSHOP 3 | MULTIMEDIA AND MOTION

OBJECTIVES

1. Use transitions and animations p. 904
2. Create hyperlinks within a presentation p. 912
3. Apply and modify multimedia in presentations p. 919
4. Create a PowerPoint photo album p. 925
5. Create a custom slide show p. 933
6. Save a presentation in multiple formats p. 936

Prepare Case

Sales & Marketing

The Turquoise Oasis Spa Presentation for Marketing

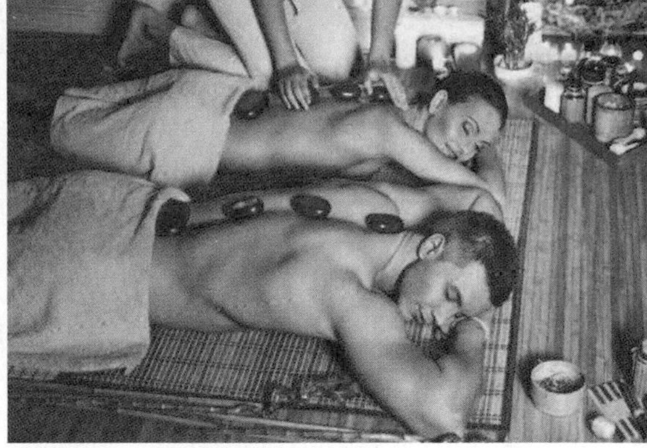

Gennadiy Poznyakov / Fotolia

The Turquoise Oasis Spa manager, Meda Rodate, asked you to create a presentation to send to people who make inquiries about the spa. This presentation is to introduce people to the spa by showing photographs of the spa, detailing the treatments, and giving other useful information for first-time spa guests. The presentation will be distributed on CD or via a PDF as an e-mail attachment. Custom slide shows will be developed from the presentation for specific clients, such as brides, who want to enjoy the spa prior to their wedding.

REAL WORLD SUCCESS

"Learning how to use PowerPoint as a way to reinforce my presentations, not be the presentations, has helped me throughout my entire college experience. Many of my classes require one or more presentations, and my classmates are always coming to me for advice!"

- Benjamin, current student

Student data files needed for this workshop:

- p02ws03Spa.pptx
- p02ws03Reflexology.mpg
- p02ws03Spa3.jpg
- p02ws03Spa6.jpg
- p02ws03SpaMeda.jpg
- p02ws03Greeting.wav
- p02ws03Spa1.jpg
- p02ws03Spa4.jpg
- p02ws03Spa7.jpg
- p02ws03PaintBrush.jpg
- p02ws03Music.mp3
- p02ws03Spa2.jpg
- p02ws03Spa5.jpg
- p02ws03SpaTheme.thmx

You will save your files as:

- p02ws03Spa_LastFirst.pptx
- p02ws03SpaAlbum_LastFirst.pptx
- p02ws03SpaCustom_LastFirst.pptx
- p02ws03SpaVideo_LastFirst.mp4
- p02ws03SpaCD_LastFirst folder
- p02ws03SpaHandouts_LastFirst.docx

Using Motion and Multimedia in a Presentation

Motion, like transitions and animations, along with multimedia elements, such as audio and video, can enhance presentations. Motion and animation can invoke emotion in the audience, multimedia can break up a presentation, and is often used to explain concepts in a way that appeals to people with different learning styles. Multimedia can also add entertainment value to your presentation while maintaining a professional appearance.

CONSIDER THIS | Beyond Presentations

With the help of multimedia, a PowerPoint presentation can be used as a marketing tool. Have you seen a PowerPoint presentation used in a nontraditional way outside the classroom? Describe the situation and the way the presentation was used.

Multimedia objects are applied in a variety of ways in PowerPoint. Simple transitions and animations of the slides and content can engage the audience. Hyperlinks enable you to move through the presentation in nonsequential slide order or to use the resources of the Internet. Buttons and triggers enable you to start multimedia actions. Sounds and recorded narrations enhance slide shows that are self-playing in kiosks or on CDs. Movies can be embedded into presentations to engage your audience.

As always, use caution when applying multimedia to your slide shows. Remember that you are the focus of the presentation, and the multimedia should support you and your message. Too much multimedia also tires your audience. Remember the KISS principle: Keep It Short and Simple!

In this section, you will apply a variety of multimedia features to your presentation to support the marketing message of the spa.

Use Transitions and Animations

PowerPoint 2013 has some incredibly powerful tools for creating transitions and animations within a presentation. **Transitions** are defined as the visual and audio elements that occur as the slides change. When used effectively, transitions can add a very professional quality to your presentations. **Animations** refer to the movement of elements, such as text and graphics, on a slide.

Transitions and animations have many settings, with opportunities to apply multiple actions to a slide. Consider the purpose of the slide, and select the elements that support the message. It is important that you maintain consistency with the transitions and animations within the presentation. Suppose you want to build interest in a product. You may decide to list the individual components of the product, one by one, and then make the big reveal at the end of the slide. This animation method works well if you want to focus the attention of the audience on one bullet point at a time.

Transitions can also be used to automatically advance the slides after a set amount of time. As you know, most of the time, slides are advanced by a person clicking the mouse button, remote slide presenter, or by pressing a key on the keyboard. Slides that you want to play on a **kiosk**—which is a computer system that provides information to people in nontraditional places such as museums, grocery stores, or banks—should have automatic transitions. You have the option to make each of the slides advance after a set amount of time, as indicated on the Transitions tab.

REAL WORLD ADVICE **Recording Slide Advancement Timings**

You have the option to record timings on the Slide Show tab. To record the timings, the slide is shown full screen in Slide Show view, and when you advance the slide, the length of time spent on the slide is recorded. Some presenters use this feature by viewing each page and reading the slide out loud before advancing to the next slide. You probably will not want to use this method to advance the slides if you are personally giving the presentation, because it is hard to maintain the same rhythm, and you may want to speed up or slow down based on audience reaction. You do not want your presentation jumping ahead of you or lagging behind!

Opening the Starting File

The people at the Turquoise Oasis Spa have put together a basic PowerPoint presentation. You have been asked to enhance it by adding effective transitions, animations, and other multimedia objects.

P03.00

To Get Started

a. Start **PowerPoint**, and then open **p02ws03Spa** from the student data files.

b. Click the **FILE** tab, click **Save As**, and save the file to the folder or location designated by your instructor with the name p02ws03Spa_LastFirst using your last and first name.

Applying Effective Transitions

Slide transitions can take many different forms in a presentation. The Transitions tab contains the options that are applied to the slides and are divided into three categories of transition types: Subtle, Exciting, and Dynamic Content. Sounds can be applied to the transitions. You can modify the length of time it takes for the transition to occur and also determine the action, such as a mouse click, that causes it to occur. If you want to have a self-playing presentation, such as one that might be displayed in a kiosk, you use the Transitions tab to set up the changing of the slides.

The presentation meets the minimum requirements that Meda Rodate asked for, but in order to be an effective marketing tool, it needs to engage the recipient and invoke a desire to come to the spa. In this exercise you will begin the process of improving the presentation by adding transitions.

MyITLab®
Workshop 3 Training

P03.01

To Apply Transitions

a. Click **Slide 2**, and then on the TRANSITIONS tab, in the Transitions to This Slide group, click **More** to reveal all of the available transitions. Notice the organization of the transitions into the three categories: Subtle, Exciting, and Dynamic Content.

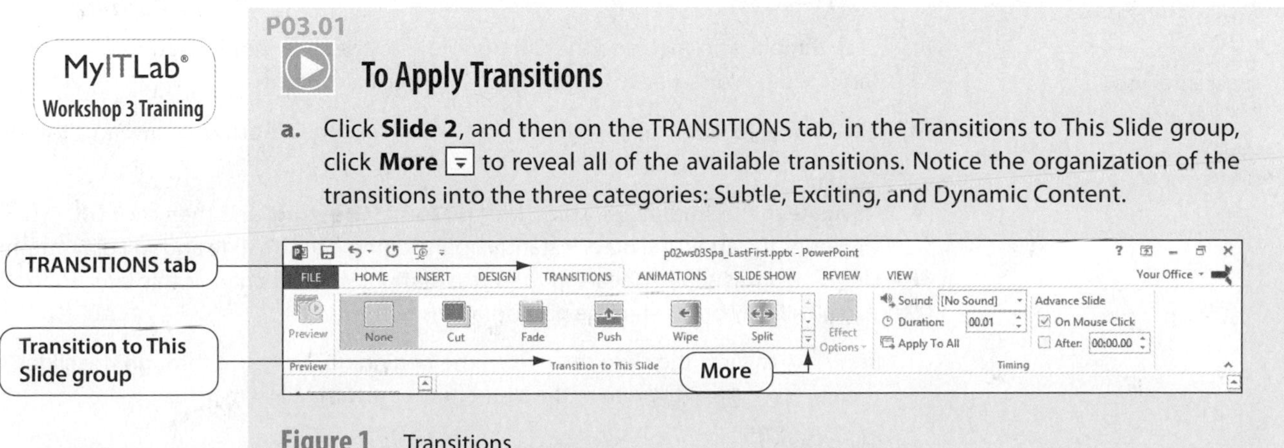

Figure 1 Transitions

b. Explore some of the various transitions and think about what kind of emotion they may invoke.

SIDE NOTE
Select Multiple Slides
You can select multiple slides by clicking the first slide in the range, and then pressing and holding [Shift] while clicking the last slide in the range.

c. Click the **TRANSITIONS** tab, and then in the Transitions to This Slide group, click the **Reveal** transition. This transition brings with it a feeling of calm relaxation, perfect for a relaxing day at the spa.

d. Select **Slides 3** through **13**, and then in the Transitions to This Slide group, click **Reveal** to apply this transition to all the slides except for the title slide.

e. Select **Slides 2** through **8**. In the Transition to This Slide group, click **Effect Options**, and then click **Smoothly From Left**. Slides 9–12 will use the default effect option of Smoothly From Right.

SIDE NOTE
Select Nonadjacent Slides
You can select nonadjacent slides by pressing and holding [Ctrl] while clicking on slides you want to select.

f. Click **Slide 13**. In the Transition to This Slide group, click **Effect Options**, and then select **Through Black From Right**. This change in transition effect will help to signify the end of the presentation.

g. Select **Slides 2** through **13**. On the TRANSITIONS tab, in the Timing group, click in the **Duration** text box, type 2.3 and then press [Enter] to reduce the duration of the Reveal transition.

h. Press [F5] to view the slide show from the beginning. Navigate through the slides, and then exit the presentation when you have reviewed each transition.

i. Click **Save** [Save icon].

Editing Transitions

As you work with transitions, you may want to change settings you have made. For instance, in the project you are working on, you may decide that the transitions need to occur more quickly, or you could modify the effects applied to the individual slides.

Keep in mind that you should have some consistency in the way the transitions occur. In your project, you selected a single transition type, but then you applied different effect options to the transitions on different slides. You will modify the speed of the transitions and add a sound to some of the slide transitions.

P03.02

To Modify Transitions

a. Click **Slide 2**. On the TRANSITIONS tab, in the Timing group, click the **Sound** arrow, and then select **Chime** from the list of available sounds.

SIDE NOTE
Audio Effects
You will need access to speakers or headphones to be able to hear the audio effects. If you do not, please continue with the exercise.

b. In the Preview group, click **Preview** to preview the gentle chime sound along with the transition.

c. Click **Slide 6**, and then add the **Chime** sound to the slide. Adding a transition sound to select slides is one way to add emphasis to specific content.

d. Click **Slide 13**, and then in the Timing group, click the **Sound** arrow, and then click **Other Sound**.

e. Navigate to the student data files, click **p02ws03Greeting**, and then click **OK**.
Notice the audio file plays instantly upon adding it to the slide and will play automatically when this slide appears in the presentation. You will change this later so that the audio will play only when the photograph is clicked.

f. Press [F5] to view the slide show from the beginning. Navigate through the slides, and then press [Esc] at the end of the slide show to return to Normal view.

g. Click **Save** [Save icon].

MODULE 2

Animating Objects for Emphasis

Animations affect the individual objects on the slide. Bullet points, other text, and graphics can be timed to appear on the slide in different ways. The three major animation groups are Entrance, Emphasis, and Exit. In the **Entrance animation** the action happens as the object enters the slide, and in the **Exit animation** the action occurs as the object leaves the slide. The **Emphasis action** is applied to the object after it is displayed on the slide. Another animation option is to set up a motion path to move the object. This is useful if you want to move a single object, such as a car or plane, across the screen.

Animations can be started in one of three ways. You can start the animation by clicking the mouse. The animation can be set up to play with any previous action on the slide. You can also set up the animation to play after another animation. You can set the **duration**, or length of time an animation effect takes to play, in parts of a second. You can also **delay** the action causing it to play after a certain number of seconds. When you select a content placeholder, you have the choice to apply the effect to the text as One Object, All at Once, or By Paragraph. The One Object option treats all of the text in the text box as a single animation. The All at Once animation may appear to be the same as the One Object animation, but with different animation types, such as the Fly In, it will be more evident. The By Paragraph animation applies the action to elements of the placeholder object one at a time.

CONSIDER THIS | Appropriate Animations

Using animations that support your presentation is a skill that is developed over time. Can you describe a presentation where you have seen appropriate, engaging animations used? Can you describe a situation where animations were overdone or poorly done?

You can combine animations so an element has an entry, emphasis, and exit animation, but this can be very distracting to the audience and slow down the flow of the presentation. Select the animations carefully, while keeping in mind the important points being made by the slide. Emphasize those points.

You will apply animations to the tour slides, making the photographs appear one after the other. This will give the feeling of walking through the spa.

P03.03

To Animate Objects

a. Click **Slide 2**. Click the **Reception Area** photograph, press and hold Shift, and then click the **Reception Area** text box to select both objects. On the ANIMATIONS tab, and in the Animation group, click **Fade** to apply the Fade animation to both selected objects.

Notice the two small numbered boxes next to the objects. The same number indicates that the animations applied to the objects will occur simultaneously.

Troubleshooting

If the Fade animation is not visible, click More, and then in the Entrance group, click Fade.

b. Select the **photo** and **text box** again. In the Timing group, click the **Start** arrow. Click **With Previous**, click the **Duration** text box, type 1.30 and then press Enter. In the Preview group, click **Preview** to view the animation. Notice that changing the start from On Click to With Previous has changed the animation sequence number from 1 to 0 on the photo and associated text box.

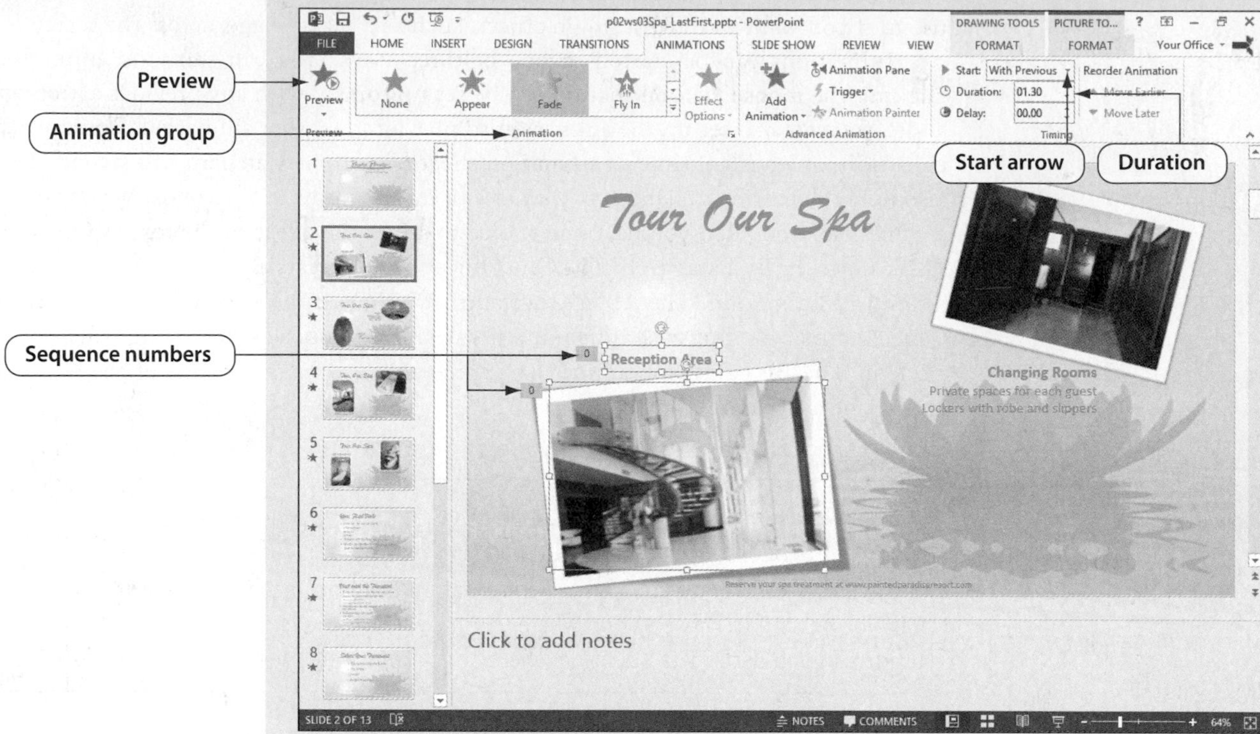

Figure 2 Animations tab

c. Click the **Changing Rooms** photograph, press and hold Shift, and then click the **Changing Rooms** text box. In the Animation group, click **Fade**.

d. Select the **photo** and **text box** again. In the Timing group, click the **Start** arrow, and then click **With Previous**. Click the **Duration** text box, type 1.30 and then press Enter. Click the **Delay** text box, type 1.30 and then press Enter.

Notice the numbers next to all the objects are zero, indicating that their animations are triggered by the display of the slide. After a 1.30 second delay, the Changing Rooms objects will appear with the same Fade animation.

e. Click the **Reception Area** photograph. In the Advanced Animation group, double-click **Animation Painter** to copy the animation settings so they can be applied to multiple objects.

f. Complete the following to use the Animation Painter to apply the animations to other objects.

- Click **Slide 3**, and then click the **Showers** photograph to apply the animation formatting to the image.
- Click **Slide 4**. Click the **Couples Massage Room** photograph, and then click the **Couples Massage Room** text.
- Click **Slide 5**, click the **Facial Treatment Room** photograph, and then click the **Facial Treatment Room** text box.
- Click the **Animation Painter** to return the mouse pointer to normal.

Troubleshooting

If the Animation Painter is not an active button on the ribbon, press Esc to return the mouse pointer to normal.

g. Click **Slide 2**. Click the **Changing Rooms** photograph, and in the Advanced Animation group, double-click **Animation Painter**.

h. Complete the following to use the Animation Painter to apply the animations to other objects.
   - Click **Slide 3**, and then apply the animation to the **Sauna** photograph.
   - Click **Slide 4**, and then apply the animation to the **Private Jacuzzi** photograph and text.
   - Click **Slide 5**, and then apply the animation to the **Pedicure Treatment Room** photograph and text. Click the **Animation Painter** to return the mouse pointer to normal.

i. Click **Slide 3**. Select the text **Showers**, **Private**, and **Wheelchair accessible** in the text box, and in the Animation group, click **Fade**.

   Notice the animation sequence applied to the text is 1, which means the text will appear after both images.

j. In the Advanced Animation group, click **Animation Pane**.

   The Animation Pane provides a roadmap of the order and duration in which the animations occur. The numbers indicate the order, and the bars indicate the duration.

k. In the Animation Pane, click the **Up** arrow to reorder the text animation to occur before the Sauna photograph (Picture 4) but after the Showers photograph (Picture 5).

l. In the Timing group, click the **Start** arrow, and then click **With Previous** so that the Showers text appears with the Showers photograph. In the Timing group, click in the **Duration** text box, type 1.30 and then press Enter.

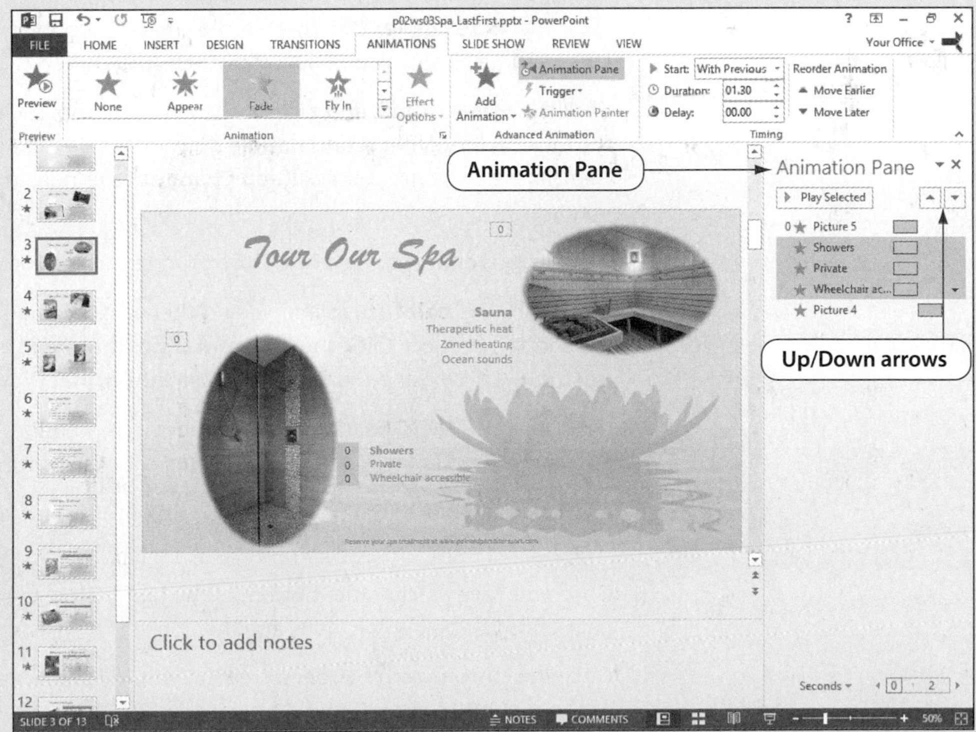

Figure 3 Animation Pane

m. Select the text **Sauna**, **Therapeutic heat**, **Zoned heating**, and **Ocean sounds**. On the ANIMATIONS tab, in the Animations group, click **Fade**. After the animation preview occurs, reselect the text, click the **Start** arrow, and then click **With Previous** so the Sauna text appears with the Sauna photograph. Click in the **Duration** text box, type 1.30 and then press Enter.

n. Close ✕ the Animation Pane, press F5 to view the slide show from the beginning, and then click through the first five slides to review the animations and transitions. Press Esc to return to Normal view.

o. Click **Save**.

Adding Motion Paths

Creating a motion path animation is another simple way to engage your audience. PowerPoint 2013 provides several basic motion paths including lines, arcs, turns, loops, and even custom paths that you design. The object simply follows the motion path that you define with the same options for when to start, duration, and delay that other animations have.

In this exercise, you will add an image of a paintbrush to Slide 11, apply a custom motion path to the image, and adjust the settings to create the illusion of the paintbrush painting the pricing table. This simple combination of animation can draw the audience's attention to the content on the slide.

P03.04

To Add a Motion Path

a. Click **Slide 11**.

b. Click the **INSERT** tab, and then in the Images group, click **Pictures**. Browse to your student data files, click **p02ws03PaintBrush**, and then click **Insert**.

c. Click the **FORMAT** tab, and then in the Adjust group, click **Remove Background**. Drag the lower right-corner **sizing handle** down to include the entire paintbrush handle, and then, in the Close group, click **Keep Changes** to remove the background color from the image.

d. In the Size group, click the **Shape Width** text box, type 6.0 and then press Enter.

e. Right-click the **paintbrush** image, and then click **Size and Position**. Click **Position** to expand the section. Click the **Horizontal position** text box, type 4, click the **Vertical position** text box, and then type .5. Close the **Format Picture** pane.

f. Click the **ANIMATIONS** tab, and then in the Animation group, click **More**, scroll down, and then in the Motion Paths group, click **Custom Path**.

g. Drag a **zigzag** pattern, starting from the tip of the paintbrush to the top right-corner of the pricing table, and then zig back and forth as you work your way down the table.

h. Once you have reached the bottom of the table, drag one more line so that the custom path ends just below the table, and then press Enter to create the custom path.

i. Once the custom path has been created, you will see a green arrow indicating the start of the motion path and a red arrow indicating the end of the motion path. Make any adjustments necessary so that the motion path end point does not block any of the information in the pricing table.

> **Troubleshooting**
> Once the custom path is created you may see that PowerPoint shifts the path to the right of the table. Using the Preview button is the best way to see the custom path in action.

j. In the Preview group, click **Preview** to see the custom path in action. The default duration of the custom path is too fast for the painting effect you are trying to create.

k. Click the **paintbrush** picture, and then in the Timing group, click in the **Duration** text box, type 4.25 and then press Enter.

l. In the Timing group, click the **Start** arrow, and then click **With Previous**. Now that the paintbrush has a custom path animation, you will now add an animation to the pricing table, giving it an effect of being painted by the paintbrush.

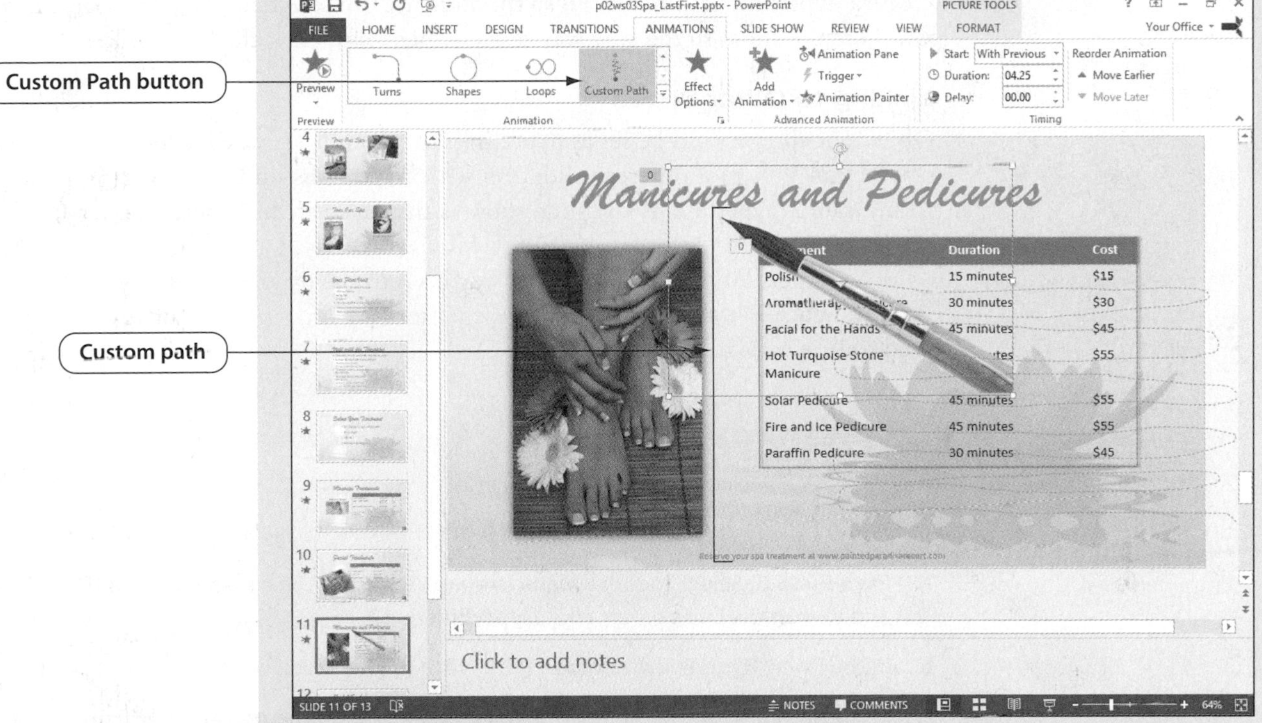

Figure 4 Custom motion path

m. Click the **pricing table**. In the Animation group, click **Wipe** to apply the Wipe animation to the photograph.

n. In the Animation group, click **Effect Options**, and then select **From Top**. In the Timing group, click the **Start** arrow, and then select **With Previous**. Click in the **Duration** text box, type 3.50, and then press Enter. Click the **Delay** text box, type .50 and then press Enter.

The .50-second delay will allow the paintbrush animation to begin moving before the pricing table animation begins.

> **Troubleshooting**
> Depending on how long your zigzag custom path is, you may need to adjust the animation durations and delay for the effect to look good.

o. Click **Slide Show** on the status bar to view the slide in presentation mode.

p. Click **Save**.

Create Hyperlinks Within a Presentation

Hyperlinks are objects, such as text or graphics, that provide a path to additional resources. Hyperlinks serve two purposes in PowerPoint. You can hyperlink to slides that are not in the normal progression of the slides. You can also provide hyperlinks to Internet resources, such as e-mail and the web. With a presentation distributed on CD or as a PDF, this gives the audience an opportunity to interact with the presentation.

You will begin by setting links from Slide 8, where the treatments are listed, to the slides later in the presentation that contain the appropriate information. You will also create a hyperlink back to Slide 8 so the audience can select another treatment. Later you will hide the slides so the only way to view them is to click the hyperlink.

Linking to Other Slides

Objects of all types can be set as hyperlinks in the slide show. This means that a graphic or text can link to a different slide. As with hyperlinks on the web, a  is displayed to indicate a hyperlink as the slide show is displayed if the mouse pointer hovers over the link.

It is important that you provide a way back to the original slide so you do not leave your audience at a dead end in the presentation. Again, a graphic or text object can be used to link back to the original slide.

P03.05

To Create Hyperlinks to other Slides

a. Click **Slide 8**. Select the text **Manicure and Pedicure**, and then click the **INSERT** tab, and then in the Links group, click **Hyperlink**.

b. In the Insert Hyperlink dialog box, click **Place in This Document** on the left.

c. In the Select a place in this document list, select **11. Manicures and Pedicures**.

d. Click **ScreenTip**, located in the top-right corner of the Insert Hyperlink dialog box. In the ScreenTip text box, type **Check out our manicure and pedicure offerings.**

SIDE NOTE

Insert Hyperlink Dialog Box

If you close the Insert Hyperlink dialog box too soon, you can right-click the text, and then click Edit Hyperlink in the shortcut menu to return to the dialog box.

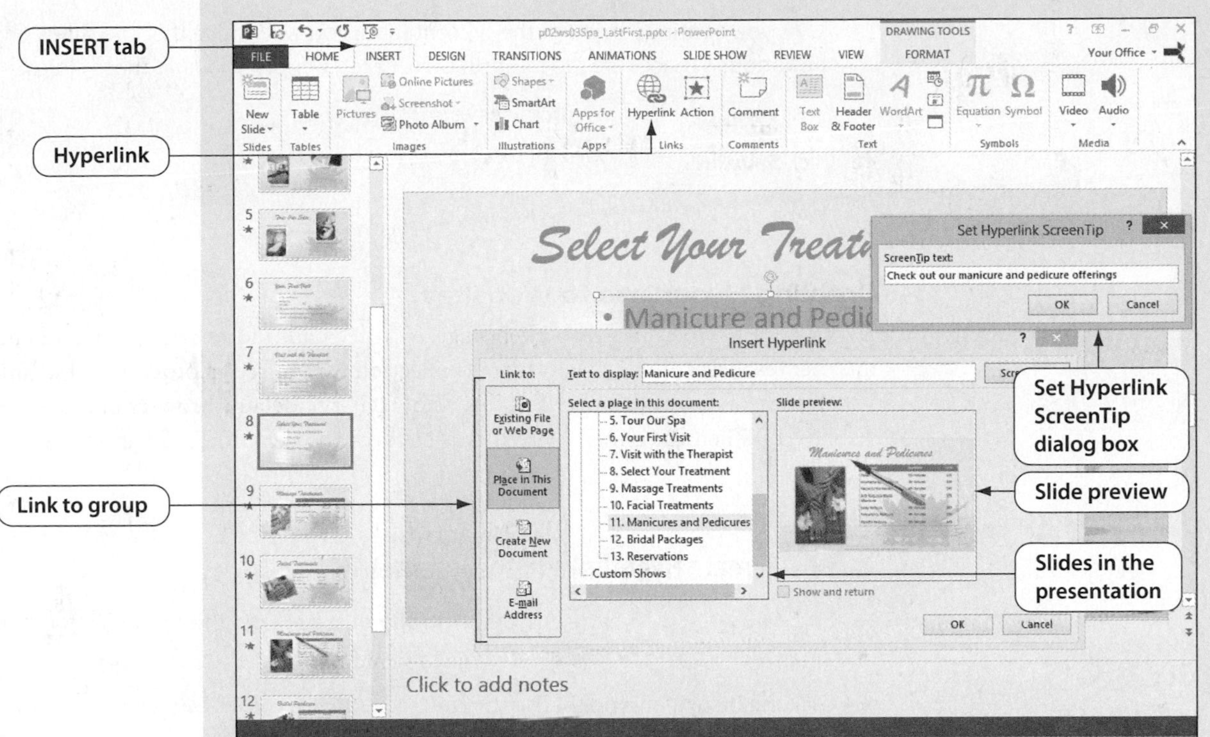

Figure 5 Creating hyperlinks in a presentation

e. Click **OK**, and then click **OK** again.

f. Click **Slide Show** on the status bar to view the slide in presentation mode.

Notice that if you hover your pointer over the Manicure and Pedicure text, the ScreenTip text appears. And if you click the text, the slide transitions to Slide 11.

g. Press Esc to return to Normal view.

h. Click **Slide 8**, and then complete the following to create a hyperlink to the Massage Treatments slide.
   - Select the text **Massage**, and then on the INSERT tab, in the Links group, click **Hyperlink**.
   - In the Select a place in this document list, select **9. Massage Treatments**.
   - Click **ScreenTip**. The Set Hyperlink ScreenTip dialog box opens. In the ScreenTip text box, type Relax with a professional massage, click **OK**, and then click **OK** again.

i. Complete the following to create another hyperlink to the Facial Treatments slide.
   - Select the text **Facial**, and then in the Links group, click **Hyperlink**.
   - In the Select a place in this document list, select **10. Facial Treatments**.
   - Click **ScreenTip**. The Set Hyperlink ScreenTip dialog box opens. In the ScreenTip text box, type Look years younger with our facial treatments, click **OK**, and then click **OK** again.

j. Complete the following to create another hyperlink to the Bridal Packages slide.
   - Select the text **Bridal Packages**, and then click **Hyperlink**.
   - In the Select a place in this document list, select **12. Bridal Packages**.
   - Click **ScreenTip**. The Set Hyperlink ScreenTip Dialog Box opens. In the ScreenTip text box, type Options for the bride and groom, click **OK**, and then click **OK** again.

k. Press F5 to view the slide show from the beginning. As you view the slides, check each hyperlink to verify that it goes to the correct slide. You can right-click the slide, and then click **Last Viewed** to return to Slide 8 after checking each hyperlink.

As you continue through the presentation, you will notice that the slides promoting the various services are repeated. In a later exercise, you will hide those slides.

l. Press Esc to return to Normal view.

m. Click **Save**.

Creating Hyperlinks to Websites

Two types of hyperlinks, to a web page or an e-mail address, link the audience to these Internet resources. An active Internet connection is required in order for these links to work. When someone clicks a hyperlink to a web page, the default browser opens and the page is displayed. When the e-mail hyperlink is clicked, the default e-mail application opens.

P03.06

To Create Hyperlinks to the Internet

a. Click **Slide 13**. Click at the end of the **phone number**, and then press Enter to move to the next line. Type E-mail: and then press Enter.

b. Click the **Insert** tab, and then in the Links group, click **Hyperlink**, and then under Link to, click **E-mail Address**.

c. In the **Text to display** text box, type mrodate@paintedparadiseresort.com. In the **E-mail address** text box, type mrodate@paintedparadiseresort.com again. Notice that PowerPoint automatically adds the words **mailto:** before the e-mail address.

d. In the **Subject** text box, type Important request from presentation. Providing an automatic subject line gives Meda or her staff a way to recognize that the e-mail came from this link in the presentation.

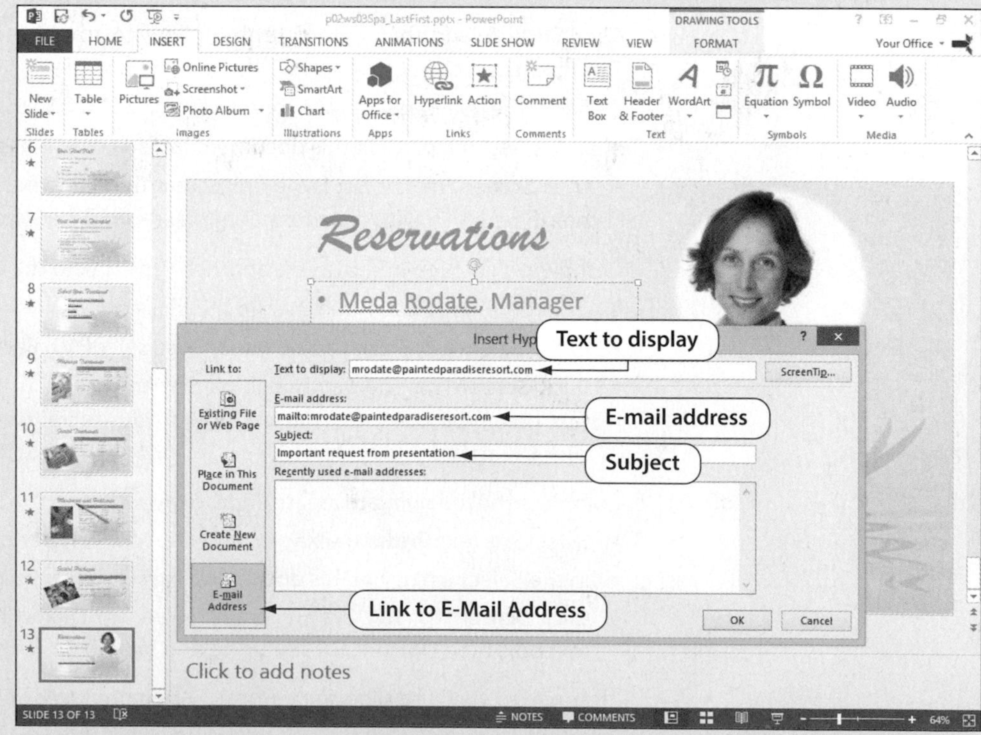

Figure 6 Setting up an e-mail hyperlink

SIDE NOTE
Hyperlinks
Hyperlinks should always appear on a single line. If the URL does not need to be viewed create descriptive text to use instead.

e. Click **OK**. Select the **e-mail address text**, click the **HOME** tab, and then in the Font group, click in the **Font Size** text box, type 24, and then press Enter.

f. Click the slide text placeholder, and then in the Paragraph group, click **Bullets** to remove the bullets. The e-mail address should now fit on one line.

g. Click at the end of the **e-mail address text**, and then press Enter twice. Click the **INSERT** tab, and then in the **Links** group, click **Hyperlink**, and then under Link to, click **Existing File or Web Page**.

h. In the **Address** text box, type www.paintedparadiseresort.com. Notice that PowerPoint adds " http://" before the typed URL and automatically copies the URL into the Text to display text box.

i. Click **ScreenTip**. The Set Hyperlink ScreenTip dialog box opens. Click in the **ScreenTip** text box, and then type Visit our website, click **OK**, and then click **OK** again.

j. Select all the **text** in the slide text placeholder. Click the **HOME** tab, and then in the Paragraph group, click **Center** to center the text.

k. Click the **ANIMATIONS** tab, and then in the Animation group, click **Fade**. Select all of the text in the slide text placeholder again, and then in the Timing group, click the **Start** arrow, and then click **With Previous**. Click in the **Duration** text box, type 2.0 and then press Enter.

l. Click **Slide Show** on the status bar to view the slide in presentation mode. Confirm that the hyperlinks start the correct Internet resource—the default browser or e-mail application.

m. Close each application after it opens. Press Esc to return to Normal view.

n. Click **Save**.

Adding Action Buttons

Action buttons are special shapes, predefined to include actions that help you navigate through slides. The buttons are available on the Insert tab in the Shapes gallery. If the shape you wish to use is not available in the Shapes gallery, then you can either modify an existing shape or combine shapes together to make new shapes. The actions include moving to a previous slide or the next slide, skipping to the first or last slide of the presentation, playing a sound or movie, opening a document, or opening a Help feature.

You will add Action buttons to your presentation to return to Slide 8 from each of the treatment slides. You will modify the shape by changing the colors to better blend with your presentation.

P03.07

To Add and Modify Action Buttons

a. Click **Slide 9**. Click the **INSERT** tab, and then in the Illustrations group, click **Shapes**. In the Action Buttons group, click **Action Button: Back or Previous**. Click the bottom-right corner of the **slide** to place the graphic.

b. In the Action Settings dialog box, click the **Hyperlink to** arrow, select **Last Slide Viewed**, and then click **OK**. Selecting Last Slide Viewed will return the presentation to Slide 8.

c. With the Back or Previous shape selected, click the **FORMAT** tab, and then in the Size group, click the **Shape Height** text box, type 0.5, and press Enter. Click the **Shape Width** box, type 0.5, and then press Enter.

d. In the Arrange group, click **Align Objects**, click **Align Right**, click **Align Objects** again, and then click **Align Bottom**.

   The shape is now aligned to the bottom-right corner of the slide.

e. In the Shapes Styles group, click the **Shape Fill** arrow, and then select **Aqua, Accent 5, Lighter 80%** located in the second row of the second column from the right.

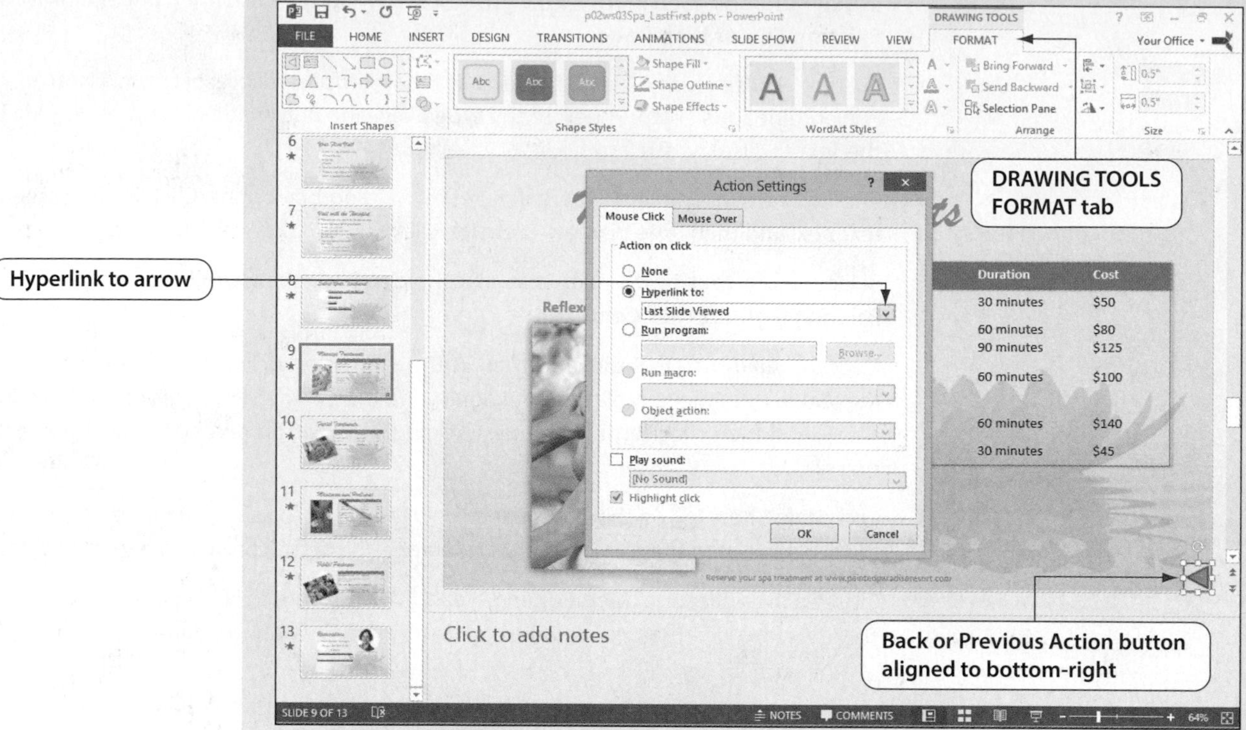

Figure 7 Action buttons

f. Right-click the **Action Button: Back or Previous** shape and then select **Copy**. Click **Slide 10**, right-click the slide, and then under Paste Options, select **Use Destination Theme**. Repeat the pasting of the **Action Button: Back or Previous** shape on **Slide 11** and **Slide 12**.

g. Click **Slide 8**, and then click **Slide Show** on the status bar. Click each **link**, and then click the **Action** buttons on the resulting slides to ensure they work correctly. Press Esc to return to Normal view.

h. Click **Save**.

Hiding Slides

There are a number of reasons why you might want to hide slides in a presentation. In this project, you want to hide the treatment detail slides unless the person viewing the presentation clicks on a hyperlink. In other cases, you may want to anticipate questions your audience might have and place some hidden slides within your presentation to reveal if they ask these questions.

You will hide Slides 9–12 in the presentation. They will open only if someone clicks a link on Slide 8. With the Back buttons you set up, they can return to Slide 8 to view other treatments.

P03.08

To Hide Selected Slides

a. Select **Slides 9** through **12**.

b. Click the **SLIDE SHOW** tab, and then in the Set Up group, click **Hide Slide** to hide slides 9–12 from the presentation. Notice the slide images fade and slashes are placed through the slide numbers.

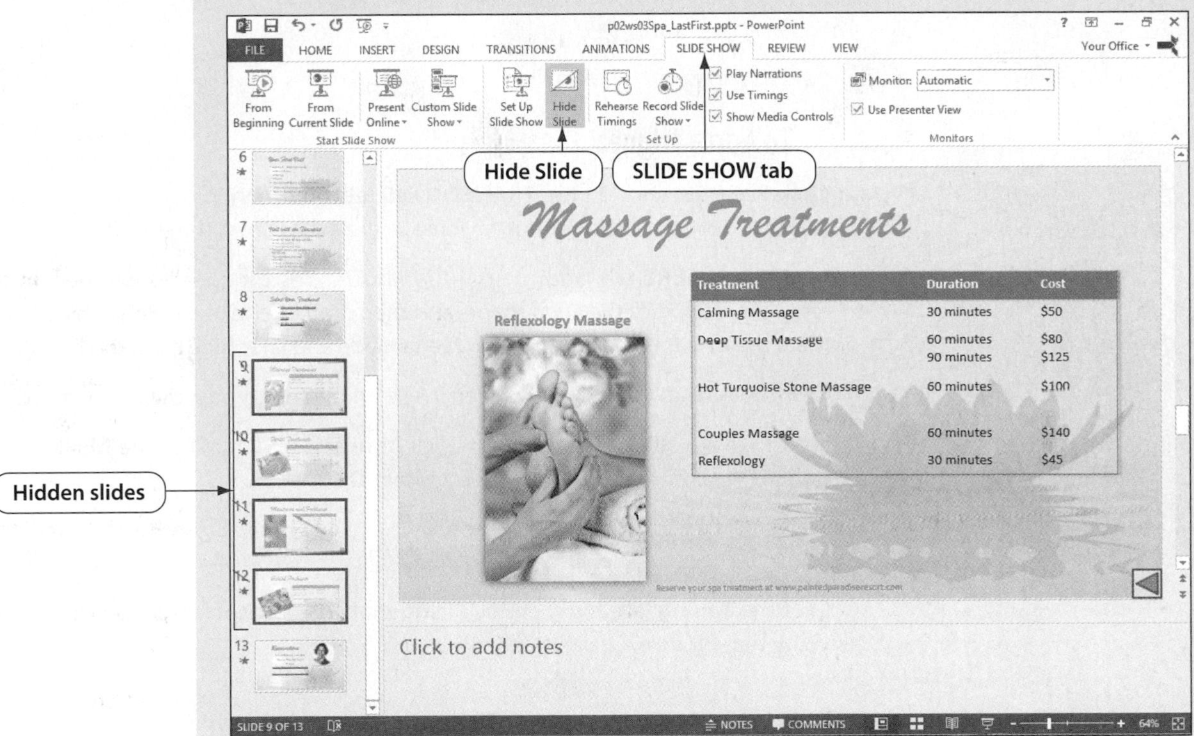

Figure 8 Hiding slides

c. Click **Slide 8**, and then click **Slide Show** on the status bar to view the presentation from the current slide. Click each **link**, and then click the **Back or Previous Action** button to return to Slide 8.

d. Press Enter to advance to the next visible slide.

   Notice the next visible slide is Slide 13 with Meda Rodate. Hidden slides are only accessible via links or using the See All Slides command when you right-click a slide during a slide show.

e. Press Esc to return to Normal view, and then click **Save**.

Adding a Trigger

Triggers are set on objects that already contain animation; this enables you to create movement, reveal additional objects, play a sound or movie, or emphasize objects. The trigger object can be a graphic or text, and it must be clicked in order for the animation to occur.

In your project, Meda begins speaking as soon as Slide 13 is displayed. This can be disconcerting for people to suddenly hear someone speaking when they did not expect it. You will change the transition and apply a trigger to Meda's photograph to play her recorded message when someone clicks the photograph.

REAL WORLD ADVICE Making Sound Choices

When working on a slide show, consider the audience as you add audio to your presentation. Will they view your presentation in a quiet location where sound would not be appreciated, such as in the office or library? Also consider the likelihood they will have speakers, or a headset, and that the sound will be turned up so they can hear your sounds. If you are making the presentation in person, make sure the sounds you select add to the value of the presentation.

P03.09

To Add a Trigger

a. Click **Slide 13**. Click on the **TRANSITIONS** tab, and then in the Timing group, click the **Sound** arrow. Click **[No Sound]** to remove the sound from the transition.

b. Click the **INSERT** tab, and then in the Illustrations group, click **Shapes**. In the Basic Shapes group, click the **Oval** shape, and then drag an oval over Meda's face. You will animate the oval to play the recording Meda made and later hide it behind her photograph.

c. Click the **ANIMATIONS** tab, and then in the Animations group, click **Appear**.

d. In the Advanced Animation group, click **Animation Pane**. Click the **black** arrow to the right of the oval name, and then click **Effect Options**.

e. In the Appear dialog box, on the Effect tab, click the **Sound** arrow, and then click **p02ws03Greeting**.

f. Click the **Timing** tab, and then click **Triggers**. Click the **Start effect on click of**, and then verify that **Picture 4** is selected.

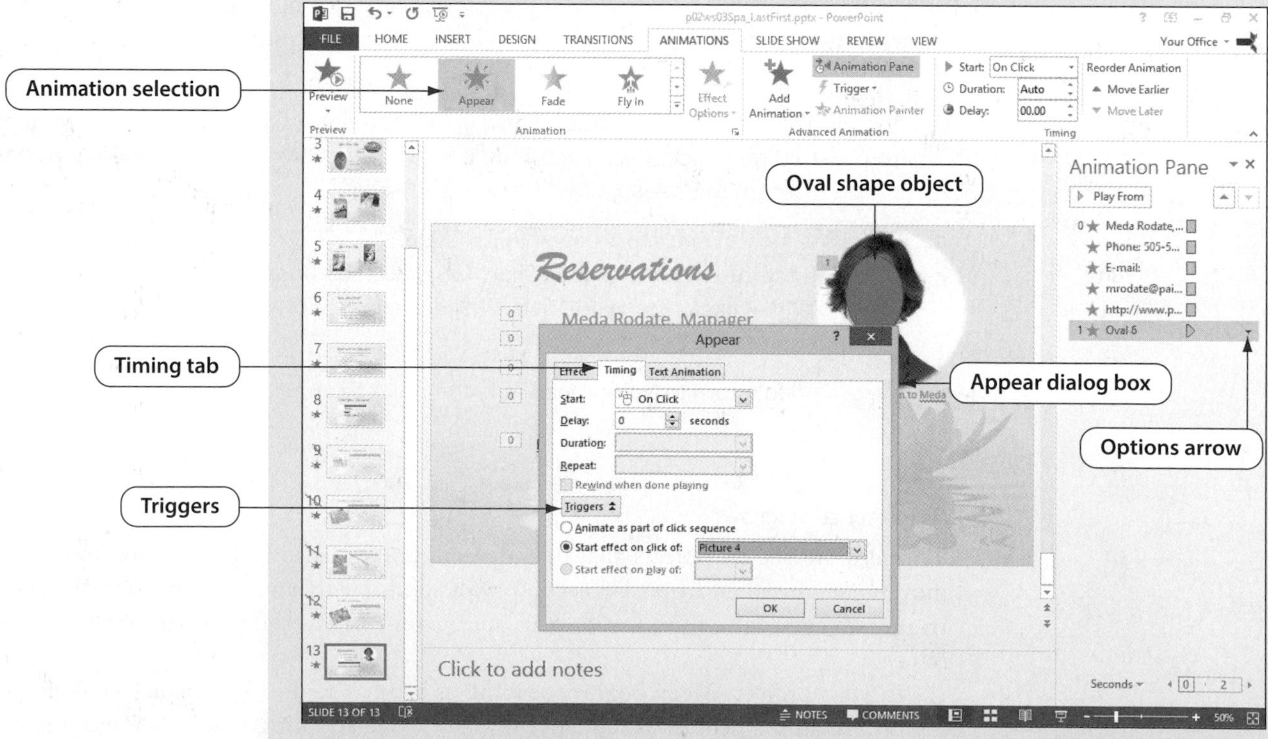

Figure 9 Adding a trigger

g. Click **OK**. The recording begins to play as a preview of the animation.

h. Click the **oval** to select it. Click the **FORMAT** tab, and then in the **Arrange** group, click the **Send Backward** arrow, and then click **Send to Back**. Notice the oval is no longer visible as it is behind the photograph of Meda Rodate.

i. Click the **ANIMATIONS** tab, in the Advanced Animation group, click **Animation Pane** to close the Animation Pane, and then click **Save**.

j. Click **Slide Show** on the status bar. Click **Meda's photograph** to listen to her message, press Esc to return to Normal view.

Apply and Modify Multimedia in Presentations

As with other elements you add to your presentation, sounds and videos are inserted using the Insert tab. Sounds can be found and added from Office.com Clip Art, or audio files, such as MP3 or WAV files. As the audio is added, a player with a Play button is automatically added to the slide. With the player selected, you can modify the way the sound is played, either having it play automatically when the slide is displayed, or when the Play button is clicked. You can also set the audio to play across slides so a background song continues to play as the user advances the slides. Audio can be looped so it continues to play until it is stopped. The audio file can be set to fade in at the beginning of the playback and fade out at the end. If the file is too long, it can be trimmed.

PowerPoint 2013 supports a wide variety of multimedia formats and includes more built-in codecs than ever before so you do not have to install them on your computer for certain file formats to work.

QUICK REFERENCE | **Supported Audio File Formats**

File Format	Extension
AIFF audio file	.aiff
AU audio file	.au
MIDI file	.midi or .mid
MP3 audio file	.mp3
Advanced Audio Coding—MPEG-4 audio file	.m4a or .mp4
Windows audio file	.wav
Windows Media audio file	.wma

In some cases, video is the only way to explain a concept to your audience. At other times, you may want to use video to emphasize something on the slide. Videos can come from a variety of sources. You can embed a video file that you have on your disk drive, SkyDrive online storage, or show a Bing video. YouTube videos can also be embedded into a presentation by using the Embed code under the Share option for a particular video.

QUICK REFERENCE	Supported Video File Formats
File Format	**Extension**
Windows Media file	.asf
Windows video file	.avi
MP4 video file	.mp4, .m4v, or .mov
Movie file	.mpg or .mpeg
Adobe Flash media	.swf
Windows Media video file	.wmv

PowerPoint allows you to add bookmarks to both audio and video files. Bookmarks enable you to mark sections of the file so you can jump to a certain point in the file before starting the playback. This is useful if you want to focus on a part of the audio file during a presentation as a sound bite but also have the entire file available if you decide to play the complete file for the audience.

REAL WORLD ADVICE | **Embedding or Linking to Video**

Audience engagement is the key to a successful presentation. Using a video, game, or other activity to break up a presentation can help to keep your audience engaged. If you cannot insert a video due to the large file size, consider placing a hyperlink to the video source on the web. Make sure you have an Internet connection in your presentation environment if you are linking to the web.

Keep in mind that when you add video to your presentation, you are significantly adding to the size of the file. You may also notice that the slide is slow to display if a large file is embedded.

REAL WORLD ADVICE | **Compressing Media in a Presentation**

Multimedia objects such as animations, transitions, audio, and video can result in presentations being very large in size. Large presentations are often difficult to share with others or store when storage space is limited. PowerPoint 2013 has the ability to compress the media in a presentation to various levels of quality. Presentation Quality should be used when possible to maintain the overall quality while still saving some storage space; however, if file sharing via e-mail is necessary, Low Quality should be used.

Inserting Audio Files

To set the mood for the spa presentation, you will play a short musical file on the first slide. It will start automatically and not require a player. You will trim the file to create a smaller presentation file. You will also adjust the volume, so it is a gentle, soft musical interlude.

P03.10

To Add an Audio File to a Presentation

a. Click **Slide 1**. Click the **INSERT** tab, and then in the **Media** group, click the **Audio** arrow, and then click **Audio on My PC**.

b. If necessary, navigate to your student files, click **p02ws03Music**, and then click **Insert**. On the player controls, click **Play/Pause** to listen to the song.

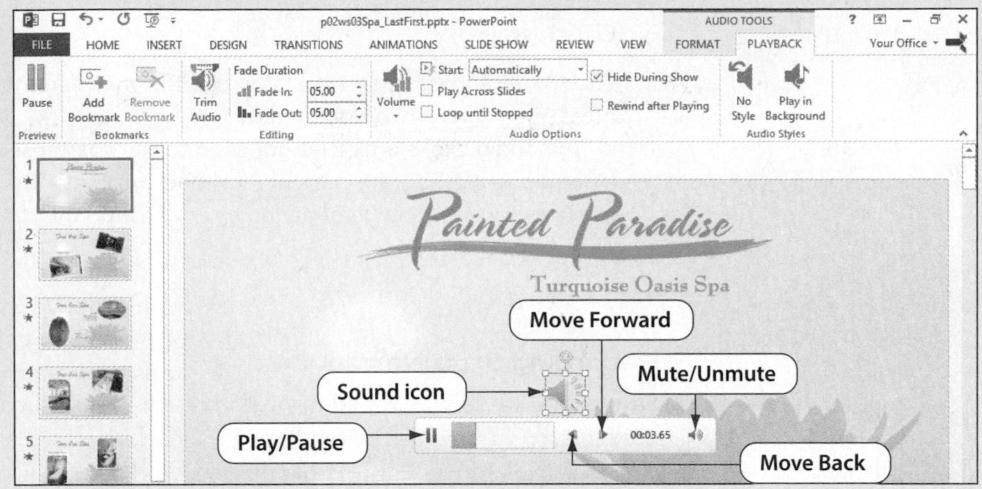

Figure 10 Adding audio and the player controls

c. Click the **AUDIO TOOLS PLAYBACK** tab, and then in the Editing group, click **Trim Audio.** In the **End Time** box, select the numbers, type 15.5 and then press Enter.

d. Click the **AUDIO TOOLS PLAYBACK** tab, and then in the Editing group, click the **Fade In** box, type 5.0 and then press Enter. Click the **Fade Out** box, type 5.0 and then press Enter.

e. In the Audio Options group, click the **Volume** arrow, and then click **Medium**. Click **Play/Pause** ▶ to listen to the edited song.

f. In the Audio Options group, click the **Start** arrow, select **Automatically**, and then click **Hide During Show**.

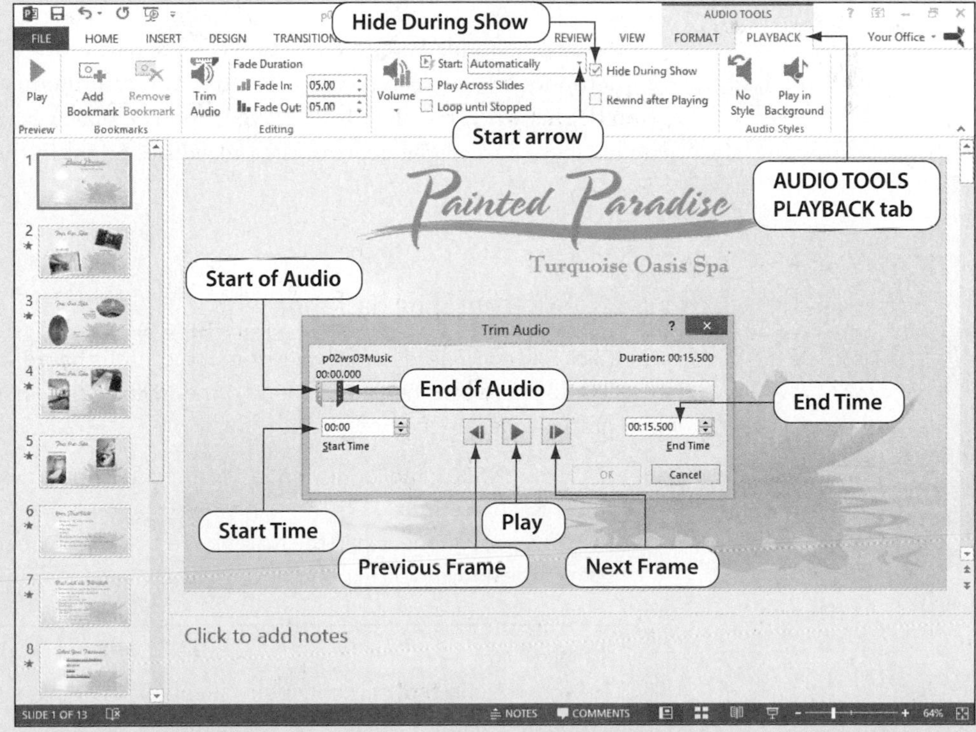

Figure 11 Trimming audio

g. Click **Save** [Save icon].

h. Click **Slide Show** [Slide Show icon] on the status bar. You may continue through the slide show or press Esc to return to Normal view.

The audio clip is a nice introduction to the spa presentation by setting the mood. If someone viewing the presentation does not have the volume turned up, they do not lose any important information by not hearing the clip.

Recording Slide Narration

Slide narration is a useful addition to presentations where you will not be making the presentation in person. You can record the narration as you view the slides using a simple recorder available in PowerPoint, or you can record the narration in a different sound software application, such as Audacity, and add the narration to the slides as a part of the transitions or animations as you did with the audio files earlier.

REAL WORLD ADVICE | **Recording Narration and Slide Advances**

The Slide Show tab contains options for setting up the slide show with timed advancement of the slides as well as recorded narration. If you will not be giving the presentation in person, this method works well. The slides are displayed full screen as you record your presentation. You record the narration and advance each slide. When you have reached the end of the slide show, you will be asked if you want to retain the timings. This method of preparing a presentation works well for distance learning, sales presentations, and kiosks.

Slide 6 contains notes for you to record as narration. The computer you use will need a microphone so you can record the notes. You will modify the sound object so the narration begins when the slide is displayed, and the player does not show on the slide. If you do not have a microphone, read the procedure, but skip the steps.

P03.11

To Record Slide Narration

a. Click **Slide 6**. If necessary, click Notes in the status bar to show the slide notes. Drag the **border** between the Slide pane and the Notes pane up, until you can see both paragraphs of text in the Notes pane.

b. Click the **INSERT** tab, and then in the Media group, click the **Audio** arrow, and then select **Record Audio**.

Read through the text in the Notes pane before you begin to record. This will save you some time and let you experiment with the inflections of your voice.

Troubleshooting

The Record Audio tool will only be available if you have a built-in or plugged in microphone. Skip the Record Narration steps if you do not have a microphone available.

c. If necessary, drag the **Record Sound dialog** box up so you can see the notes. Click the **Record** button, and then begin reading the notes into the microphone. Click the stop button when you have completed the reading. Click **Play** to review the recording.

> **Troubleshooting**
> If you would like to re-record the audio, click Cancel, and then repeat Steps b and c.

d. In the Name text box, type Slide 6 Recording.

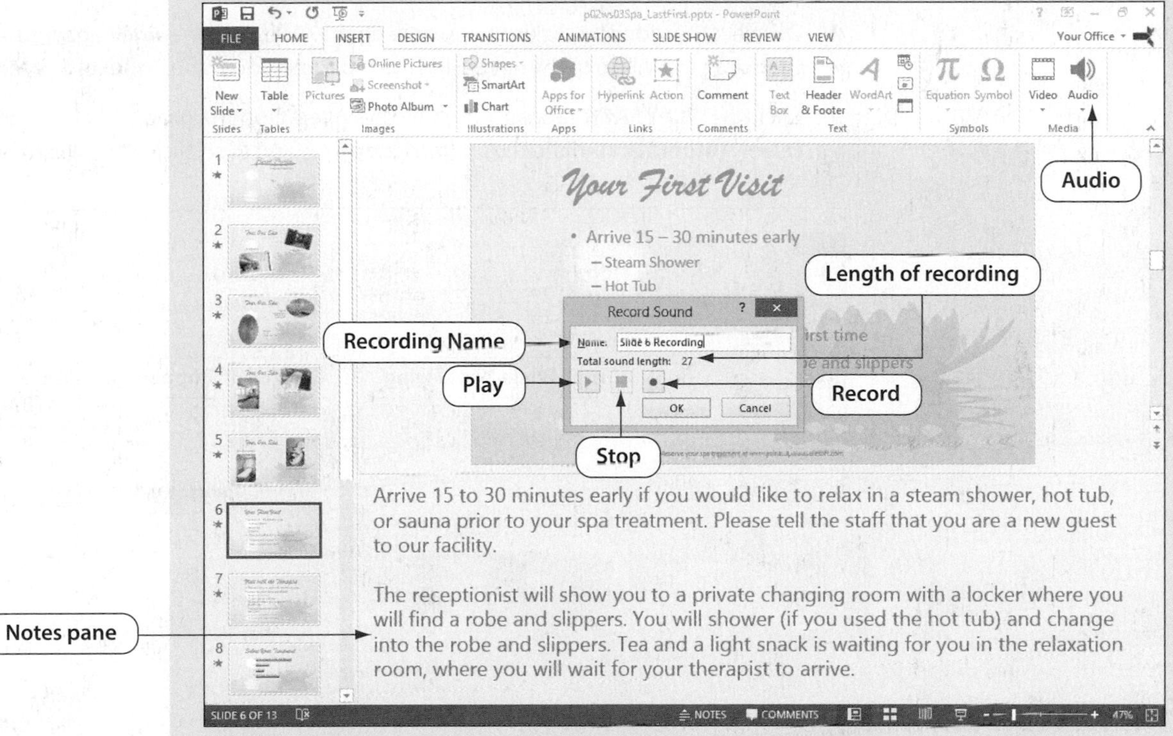

Figure 12 Recording slide narration

e. Click **OK** to save the recording to the slide.

f. Click the **Speaker** that appears in the center of the slide, and then click the **PLAYBACK** tab.

g. In the Audio Options group, click the **Start** arrow, select **Automatically**, and then click **Hide During Show**.

h. Click **Save**.

i. Click **Slide Show** on the status bar. Review **Slide 6**, and then press Esc to return to Normal view. Readjust the Notes pane so it takes up less space.

Inserting Video Files

Video clips are engaging to the audience. They provide movement on the screen. They can be used to show live action of a procedure, as you might do in training. You can creatively use video to introduce products, provide support to your sales staff, and present customer testimonials.

In this exercise you will replace the Reflexology Massage photograph on Slide 9 with a short video.

P03.12

To Add Video to a Presentation

a. Click **Slide 9**, click the **reflexology** photograph, and then press Delete.

b. Click the **INSERT** tab, and then in the Media group, click the **Video** arrow, and then select **Video on My PC**. Navigate to your student files, click **p02ws03Reflexology**, and then click **Insert**.

c. Click the **FORMAT** tab, and then in the Size group, click the **Video Width** text box, type 3.5 and then press Enter. In the Size group, click **Crop**, and then drag the **middle-right sizing handle** in slightly to remove the green bar on the right side of the video.

d. Deselect the video by clicking anywhere on the slide, click the video again to select it, and then drag the **video** to the left beside the table and under the **Reflexology Massage** box.

e. Click the **PLAYBACK** tab, and then in the Video Options group, click the **Start arrow**, select **Automatically**, click **Loop until Stopped**, and then click **Hide While Not Playing**.

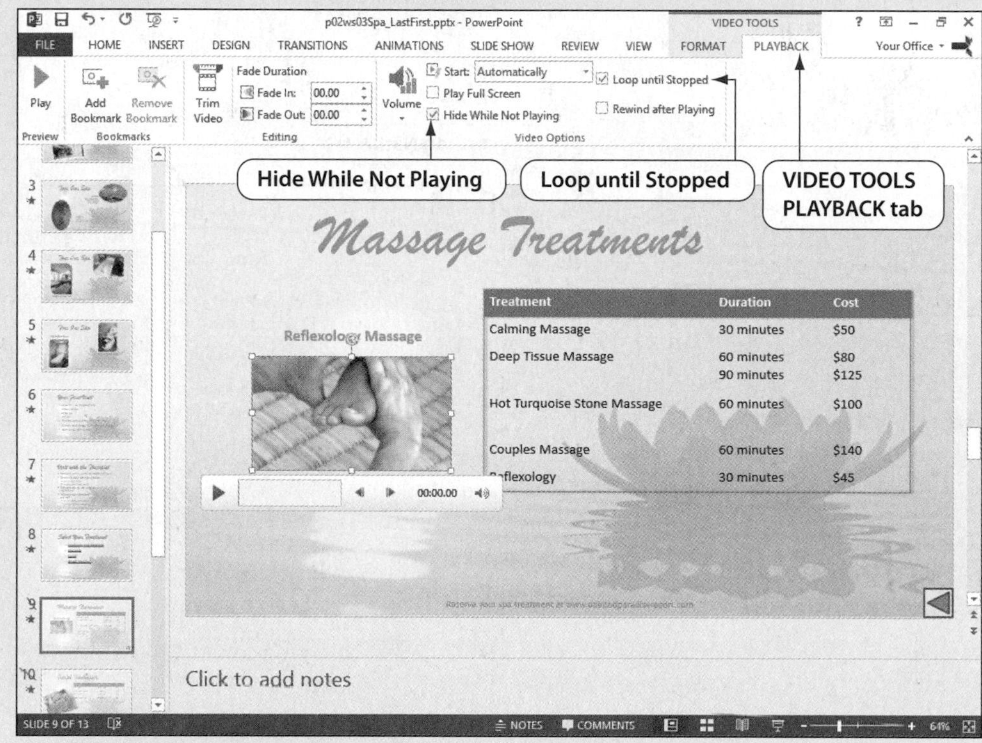

Figure 13 Video embedded

f. Click **Save**.

g. Click **Slide Show** on the status bar, and then review the slide. Press Esc twice when you have finished watching the video.

Creating Useful Photo Albums

The **Photo Album** feature of PowerPoint is an efficient way to insert a large number of photographs into a slide show just by selecting the photographs you want to include in the presentation. You do not have to individually insert, resize, or arrange the pictures on the slides. This saves you time and effort, and produces a professional looking album of photographs.

It is important to note that when you use the Photo Album feature in PowerPoint, a new file will be generated. The photo album is not added into the current open presentation. Once the album has been created, the slides can be reused in other slide shows. In this section, you will create and modify a photo album.

REAL WORLD ADVICE | **Using a Photo Album in Business**

Most people turn to PowerPoint's Photo Album feature when they have a lot of vacation or family photos to make into a presentation, but photo albums also have uses in the business world. Consider these ideas:

- Product catalog, showing the items and a short description
- Project history album, showing photographs of different stages towards completion of a project, such as a building project
- Owner's manual, showing photographs of important parts of the machinery
- Training manual, showing a group of figures with comments
- Testimonials from satisfied customers with photographs of them enjoying the product
- Meet the staff album, showing photographs of everyone on the staff with their names and other important information

Create a PowerPoint Photo Album

Available on the Insert tab, the Photo Album button opens a dialog box that enables you to select the photographs from a storage location, such as a disk drive or USB drive. Once the photographs are in the album, you can preview them in the dialog box and change the rotation, brightness, and contrast. You can change the order of the photographs. Text can be added to the slide at this stage or added with boxes after the presentation has been created. You can modify the layout of the pictures on the page, specify the shape of the frames around the photographs, and apply a theme.

Continuing with the spa workshop, you will create a photo album that will introduce members of the spa staff. You will later combine these album slides with the slides from the spa presentation.

Selecting Photographs

The most efficient way to select the photographs for the album is to group all of the pictures in a single folder. It makes it easier to select the ones you need. For instance, in the photo album you will create in this workshop, the photographs you will use begin with the same code and name, p02ws03SpaS. If necessary, later you can update a photo album and add more photographs, using the Edit Photo Album feature.

CONSIDER THIS | **Using Social Networking Photographs**

Given the popularity of social networking sites, such as Facebook, what pictures could be found of you on the Internet? Is it ethical to use a picture from one of these sites without permission? Are there times where it would be illegal?

In this exercise you will create a small photo album with photographs of the members of the staff. It will be added to the spa presentation later.

P03.13

To Create a Photo Album in PowerPoint

a. Click the **INSERT** tab, and then in the Images group, click **Photo Album**, and then click **New Photo Album**.

b. In the Photo Album dialog box, click **File/Disk**, and then navigate to your student files. Select all seven of the files beginning with **p02ws03Spa1** through **p02ws03Spa7**, and then click **Insert**.

> **Troubleshooting**
> You can select multiple files at once by clicking the first file name, pressing Shift, and then clicking the last file name, or you can select nonadjacent files by pressing Ctrl, while clicking each file name.

c. Click each **file name** in the Pictures in album box to see a preview of each file.
The files are not in the correct order. You will arrange them in a later part of the project. One of the photos is displayed sideways. You will correct that in the next part of the project as well.

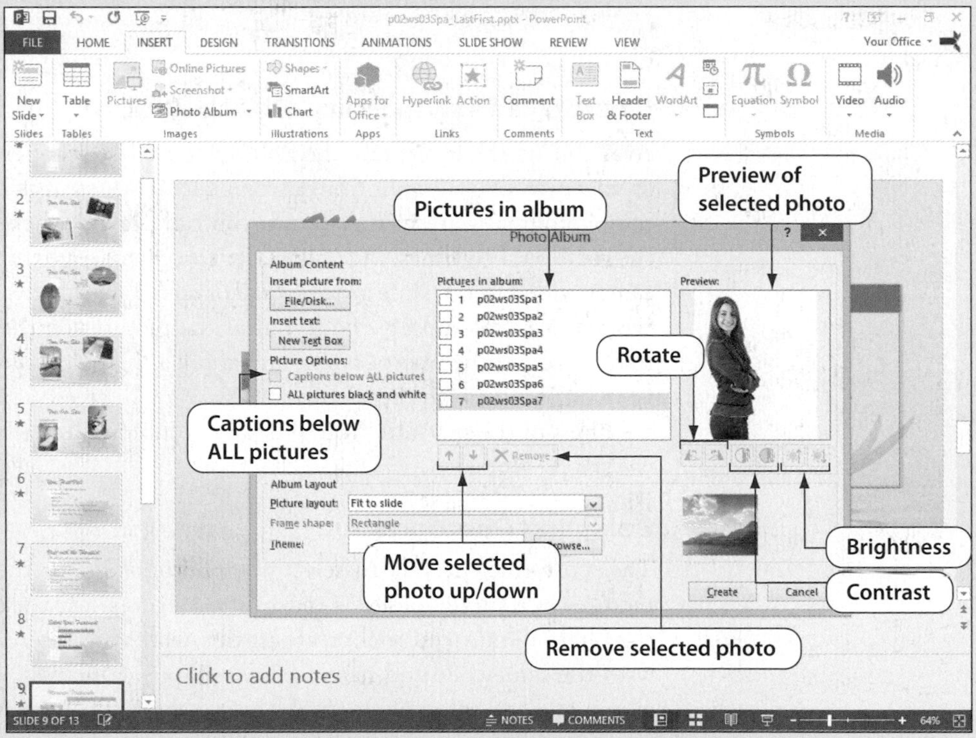

> SIDE NOTE
> **Preview Pictures**
> Alternatively, to preview all pictures, click the first picture and then use the arrow keys.

Figure 14 Creating a photo album

Modifying Photographs

Once imported into a photo album, photographs can be modified with some simple tools. They can be rotated in 90-degree increments, either clockwise or counterclockwise. The contrast and brightness of the photographs can be adjusted in the Photo Album dialog box. You can also specify that all pictures be converted to black-and-white in the photo album without changing the original picture color.

MODULE 2

When the photo album is created, you will be able to make more sophisticated adjustments, such as altering the color temperature and color tone. You will adjust the brightness and contrast of a photograph and rotate one of the photographs.

P03.14

To Modify the Photographs with the Photo Album Tools

a. Select **p02ws03Spa5** in the Pictures in album box by clicking the box next to the name, and then click **Rotate 90 degrees Clockwise** once. Deselect **p02ws03Spa5**.

Troubleshooting

If you clicked the wrong button and the woman is now displayed upside down, continue clicking the button until she is in the correct orientation.

b. Select **p02ws03Spa3** in the Pictures in album box, click **Decrease Brightness** twice, and then click **Increase Contrast** twice. Deselect **p02ws03Spa3**.

Arranging Photographs

There are a number of layouts to select from when creating a photo album in PowerPoint. A picture can fill the slide, be placed in the middle of the slide, or you can have two or four pictures per slide. There is an option to place a title on each of the slide pages, regardless of the number of photographs on the slide. You can also choose from seven frame shapes that will hold the photographs.

Photographs can be moved in the photo album with the arrow buttons at the bottom of the Pictures in album box. If you will be placing two or more photographs on a slide, you can also control which photograph appears on the right or left by the order in which you place the file names.

You have decided to display four photographs per slide, with a title. You will specify a rounded rectangle for the frame shape. You will move the files into the correct order.

P03.15

To Alter the Arrangement of Photographs in the Photo Album

a. Under Album Layout, click the **Picture layout** arrow, and then select **4 pictures with title**.

b. Click the **Frame shape** arrow, and then select **Rounded Rectangle**.

c. Select **p02ws03Spa5**, and then click **Up** to move the photograph into position 1. Deselect **p02ws03Spa5**.

d. Select **p02ws03Spa7**, and then click **Up** to move the photograph into position 3. Deselect **p02ws03Spa7**.

e. Select **p02ws03Spa2** and **p02ws03Spa3**, and then click **Down** to move these two files to the end of the list. Deselect **p02ws03Spa2** and **p02ws03Spa3**.

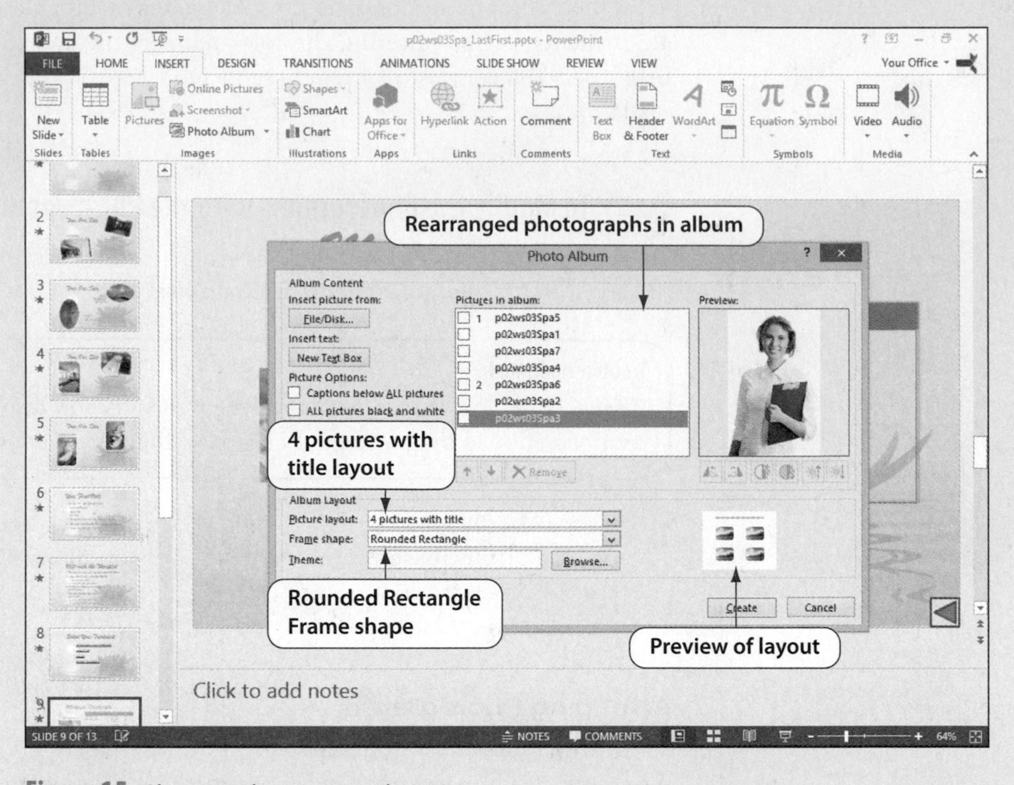

Figure 15 Photographs rearranged

Inserting Text

Text can be added to slides in two ways from the Photo Album dialog box. You can add boxes that you will later fill with text or you can add **captions**, which are boxes that describe the photographs. The default captions will be the names of the files and not something you want the audience to see, so do not forget to update the captions if you use them. If you later decide you do not want to use the boxes, they can be replaced with other objects or deleted.

In this exercise, you will add captions to all of the pictures, and you will add boxes to a few of the slides.

P03.16

To Add Text to a Photo Album

a. Click **New Text Box**. The box appears in the list under the photograph file name that was highlighted. Select **Text Box**, and then click **Up** [↑] to move the box to the first position in the album. Deselect **Text Box**.

b. Select **p02ws03Spa7** in the Pictures in album list, and then click **New Text Box** under the Insert text heading. Deselect **p02ws03Spa7**.

c. Select **p02ws03Spa3** in the Pictures in album list, and then click **New Text Box** under the Insert text heading. Deselect **p02ws03Spa3**.

d. Under Picture Options, click **Captions below ALL pictures**.

Selecting a Theme

Just as you can add themes to a presentation, you can add a theme to a photo album. The Microsoft Office themes that are stored on your computer during the installation of Office 2013 are available. You can also use themes that you have created.

The theme for the Introduction to the Spa presentation is available in your student data files. You will apply the theme to your photo album to maintain consistency with the spa presentation, because you will be reusing slides from the album in the spa presentation.

P03.17

To Add a Theme to a Photo Album

a. In the Photo Album dialog box, under Album Layout, click **Browse**. Navigate to your student files, click **p02ws03SpaTheme**, and then click **Select**.

b. Click **Create**, and then press F5 to view the slide show from the beginning. Review the slides in the Photo Album presentation, and then press Esc to return to Normal view.

   Notice the first slide of the photo album contains a title and the name of the person logged on the computer. The subsequent slides contain the photographs of the staff members with text boxes for adding content to the slides. All of the photographs are formatted with the rounded rectangle frame shape.

c. Click the **FILE** tab, click **Save As**, and then navigate to where you are saving your files. Type p02ws03SpaAlbum_LastFirst using your last and first name, and then click **Save**.

Editing a Photo Album

As you can see, it is quick work to select photographs and place them on slides using the Photo Album feature of PowerPoint. Depending on selections you make, you may need to edit the slides. Once the photo album has been created, the slides can be modified using the normal PowerPoint tools. You can resize and move the photographs, modify the appearance of the photographs, and add text.

After reviewing the slides, you realize that you did not include Meda Rodate in the staff photo album. You will return to the Photo Album dialog box to add her photograph. You will also add text to the presentation in Normal view.

P03.18

To Add Text and Edit the Photo Album

a. Click the **INSERT** tab, and then in the Images group, click the **Photo Album** arrow, and then select **Edit Photo Album** to open the Edit Photo Album dialog box.

b. Click **File/Disk**, click **p02ws03SpaMeda**, and then click **Insert**.

c. Select **p02ws03SpaMeda**, click the **Down** arrow ↓ to move the photograph into position **4**. Deselect **p02ws03SpaMeda**.

d. Select the last two boxes under **Pictures in album**, and then click **Remove** so that only one text box appears at the end of the third group of pictures.

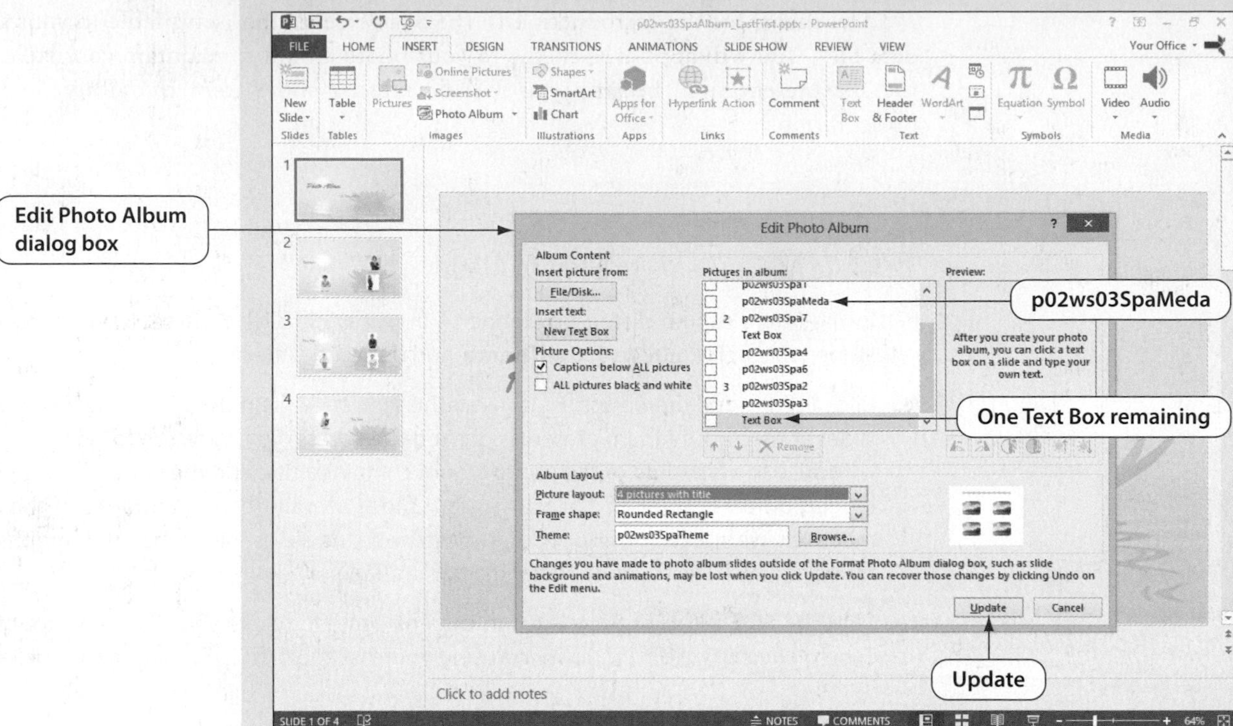

Figure 16 Editing a photo album

e. Click **Update** to display the revised photo album.

f. Click **Slide 2**, select the file name **p02ws03Spa1**, and then type Kelly Masters, Receptionist. Select the file name **p02ws03Spa5**, and then type Irene Kai, Manager. Select the file name **p02ws03SpaMeda**, and then type Meda Rodate, Manager.

g. Click the title placeholder, and then type What Our Guests Say:. Select the words **Text Box**, and type "... the receptionist made me feel very welcome and helped me to relax before my day of beauty." Press Enter twice, leaving a blank line before typing the next testimonial. Type "The manager helped me to plan a wonderful girls' spa day prior to my wedding. We felt really pampered."

h. Click **Kelly's photograph** to select it.

i. On the PICTURE TOOLS FORMAT tab, in the Size group, click the **Shape Height** box, type 3.1 and then press Enter. Move the photograph up so that it fits on the slide.

j. Click **Irene's photograph**, and then click it again, to select only the photograph, and not the box.

k. On the PICTURE TOOLS FORMAT tab, in the Size group, click **Crop**. Drag the **top cropping handle** down on Irene's photograph until it is just above her hair. Click **Crop** again to hide the cropping handles. Click away from the photograph, and then click it again, displaying only the outer sizing handles. Click the **Shape Height** box, type 3.1 and then press Enter. Drag **Irene's photograph** up on the slide until the outer sizing handles are just above Meda Rodate's photograph.

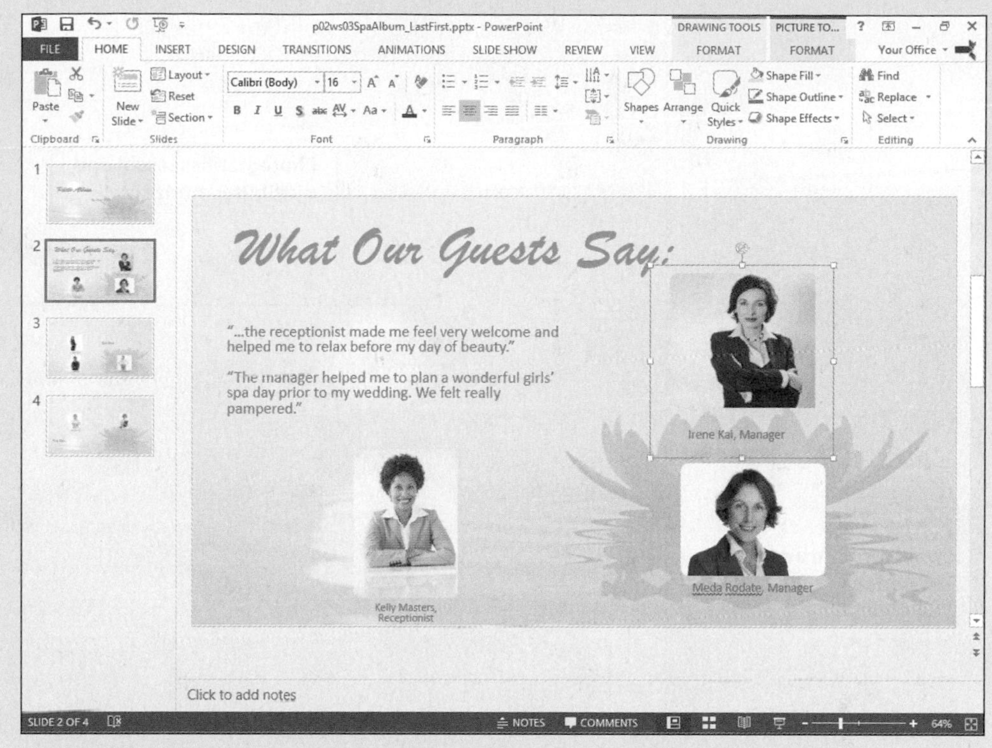

Figure 17 Slide 2 of a photo album

l. Click **Slide 3**, click the **title** placeholder, and then type Our Amazing Therapists:. Select the text **p02ws03Spa7**, and then type Christy Istas. Select the text **p02ws03Spa4**, and then type Jason Niese. Select the text **p02ws03Spa6**, and type Kendra Mault. Select the words **Text Box**, and type "Kendra was a wonderful massage therapist!" Press Enter twice, leaving a blank line before typing the next testimonial. Type "Christy helped release the stress in my back so I could enjoy my wedding day." Press Enter twice, and then type "Jason made me feel so relaxed with a hot stone massage."

Now that the text objects are on Slide 3, you will align the objects on the slide. You will place the photographs in a line under the title, and move the text below the photographs. You will then increase the size of the text placeholder to modify the size of the text.

SIDE NOTE

Select Multiple Objects

You can select multiple objects on a slide by holding the left mouse button and dragging a rectangle around the objects.

m. Drag **Kendra's photograph** to the left of Christy's photograph. Drag the **text** placeholder down toward the bottom of the slide. Drag **Jason's photograph** to the right of Christy's. Select all **three photographs**. On the PICTURE TOOLS FORMAT tab, in the Size group, click the **Shape Height** box, type 3.5 and then press Enter.

n. In the Arrange group, click **Align Objects**, and then select **Align to Slide**. Click **Align Objects** again, and then select **Distribute Horizontally**. Click **Aligns** again, and then select **Align Middle**. Click the slide text placeholder, and then drag the **right sizing handle** to the right edge of the slide. Drag the **left sizing handle** to the left edge of the slide. Click the **DRAWING TOOLS FORMAT** tab, and then in the Arrange group, select **Align Objects**, and then select **Align Bottom**. Click the **HOME** tab, and then in the Paragraph group, click **Center**. The objects are now nicely balanced.

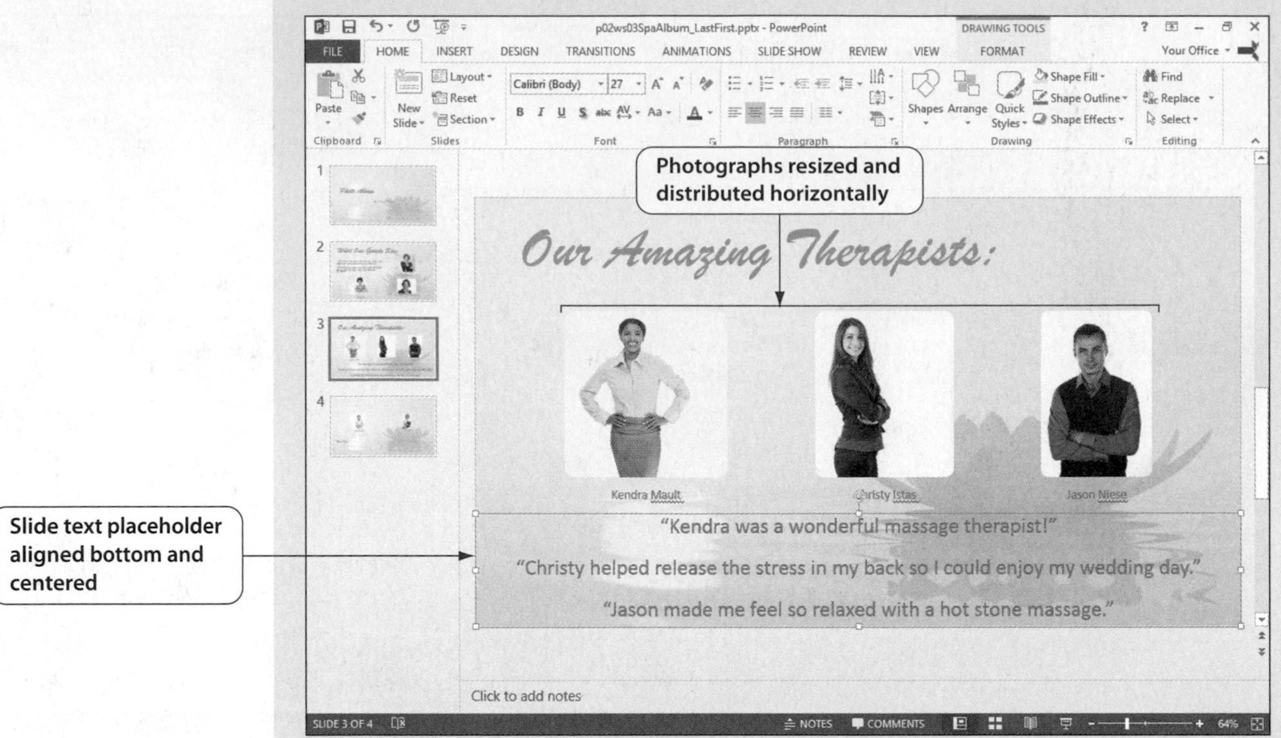

Figure 18 Slide 3 of a photo album

o. Click **Slide 4**, click the **title** placeholder, and type What Our Guests Say:. Select the **p02ws03Spa2** text, and then type Leslie Dixon. Select the **p02ws03Spa3** text, and then type Susan Hemmerly. Select the words **Text Box**, and then type "...my hands were beautiful as Mike slipped the wedding ring on my finger." Press Enter twice, leaving a blank line before typing the next testimonial. Type "The girls in my wedding loved the manicure/pedicure as part of the bachelorette party. What a great idea!"

p. Select **Leslie's photograph**. Click the **PICTURE TOOLS FORMAT** tab, and then in the Size group, click the **Shape Height** box, type 3.5 and then press Enter.

q. Select **Susan's photograph**. In the Size group, click the **Shape Height** box, type 3.5 and then press Enter.

r. Drag **Susan's photograph** up until the outside sizing handles align with the top of the slide to make room, and then drag **Leslie's photograph** under Susan's. Select **Leslie** and **Susan's photographs**. On the PICTURE TOOLS FORMAT tab, in the Arrange group, click **Align**, and then select **Align Selected Objects**. Click **Align** again, and then select **Align Left**. Click the **testimonials** box. Drag the **top-center sizing handle** up to just below the title text. Drag the **right sizing handle** in the box to the edge of the photographs.

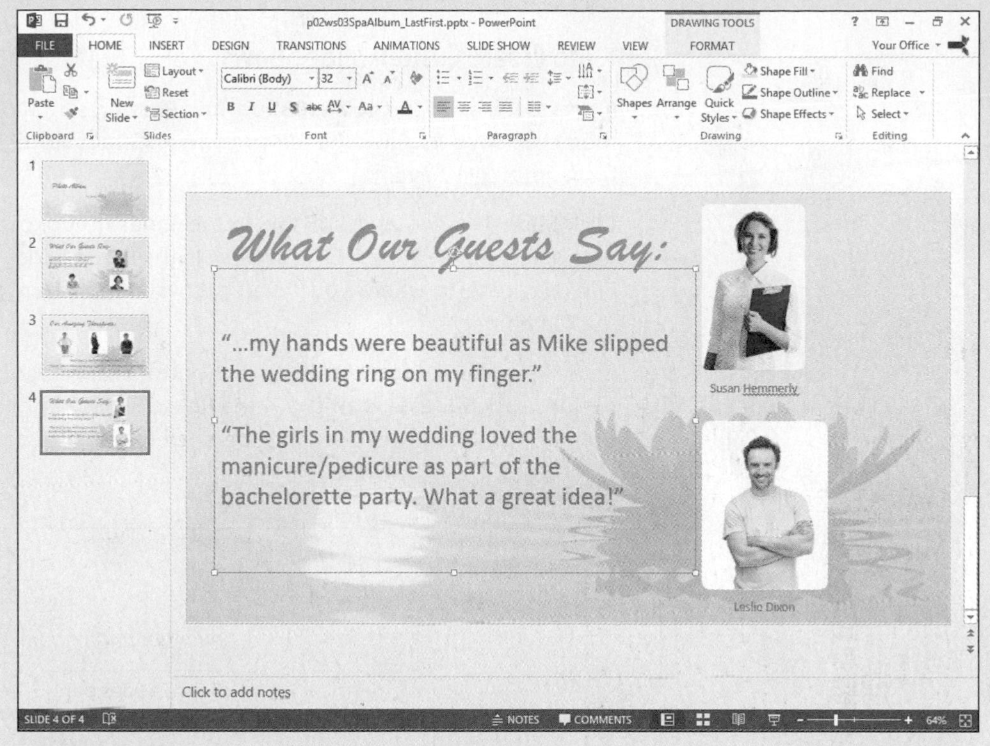

Figure 19 Slide 4 of a photo album

s. Click **Save** , and then close the presentation.

The photo album was modified to create a testimonial slide presentation to include with the Introduction to the Spa presentation. Later, you will reuse the slides in the photo album in the Introduction to the Spa slide show and create a customized presentation that will be distributed to wedding couples.

Create a Custom Slide Show

A **custom slide show** is a subset of slides in a larger presentation. Perhaps you do not need all of the slides in a presentation because your audience has different characteristics or needs. Using the Custom Slide Show feature, you can select just the slides you want to display. Another advantage of creating custom slide shows is that you can display the slides in a different order than in the original slide show.

Customizing a Slide Show

All of the slides that you will need in a custom slide show must be in the same slide presentation. You cannot select slides from different presentations. Because you want to use slides from both the photo album and the Introduction to the Spa presentation, you will save the spa presentation with a new name, and reuse the slides from the photo album.

Once the slides are combined into the same presentation, you will build the custom show. Only certain slides will be selected. You will also modify some parts of the new spa presentation so it functions more efficiently.

P03.19

To Create Custom Slide Shows

a. If necessary, open the **p02ws03Spa_LastFirst** presentation file. Click the **FILE** tab, and then click **Save As**. Save the file as p02ws03SpaCustom_LastFirst using your last and first name. Click **Save**.

b. Click **Slide 12**. On the HOME tab, in the Slides group, click the **New Slide** arrow, and then select **Reuse Slides**. Click **Browse** in the Reuse Slides pane, and then click **Browse File**. Navigate to where you saved **p02ws03SpaAlbum_LastFirst**, and double-click the **file name**.

c. Click **Keep source formatting** at the bottom of the Reuse Slides pane to select this option. Click **Slides 2**, **3**, and **4** in the Reuse Slides pane to add them to the presentation. Be sure to only click each slide once to avoid inserting multiple slides into the presentation.

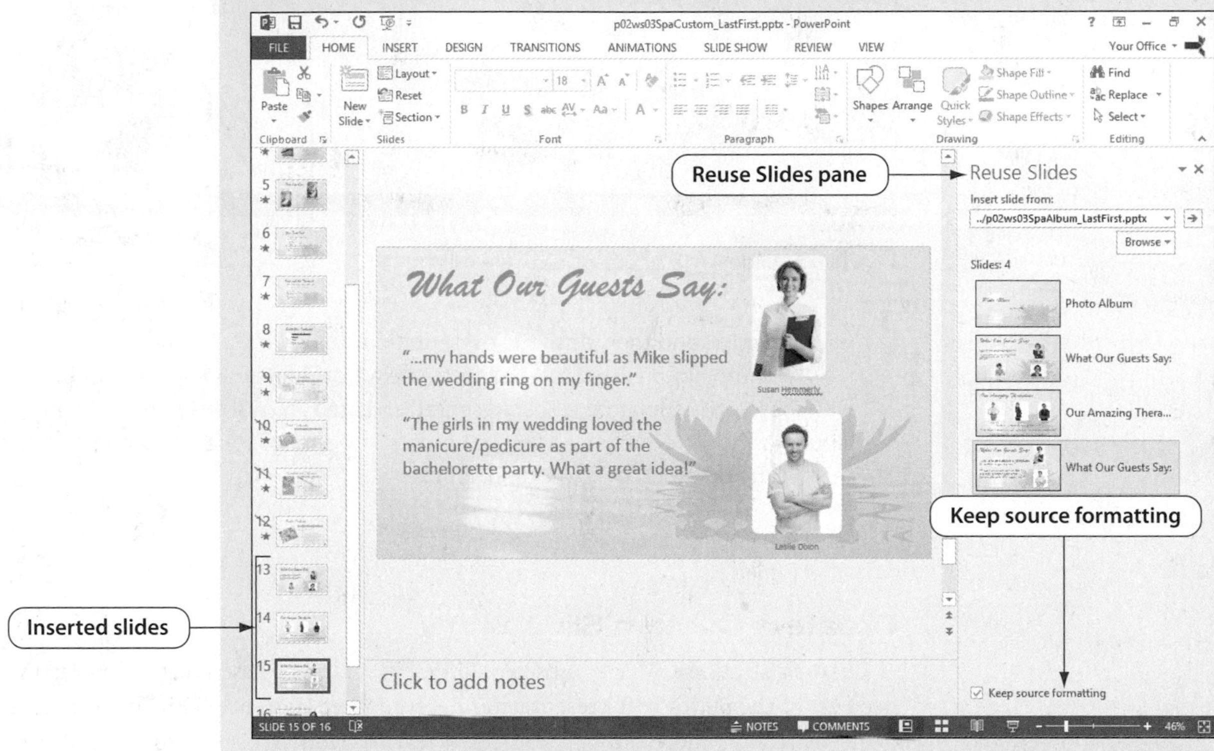

Figure 20 Reuse Slides pane

d. **Close** [X] the Reuse Slides pane.

e. Click the **SLIDE SHOW** tab, and then in the Start Slide Show group, click **Custom Slide Show**, and then select **Custom Shows**. In the Custom Shows dialog box, click **New**. Select the **Custom Show 1** text, and then in the Slide show name text box, type Bridal Presentation.

f. Under Slides in presentation, select **1. Slide 1** through **7. Visit with the Therapist**.

g. Select **[11] Manicure and Pedicures** through **16. Reservations**, and then click **Add**.

SIDE NOTE

Brackets Around Slide Numbers

The brackets around slides 9 through slide 12 indicate those slides are currently hidden from the main slide show.

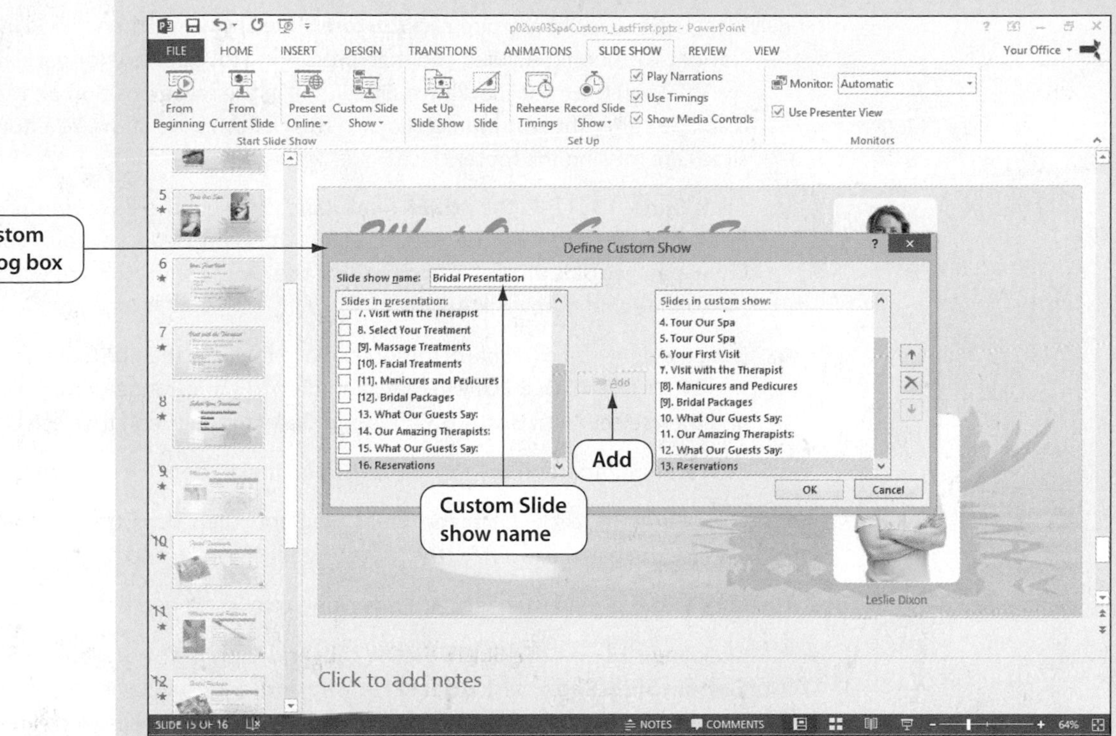

Figure 21 Creating a custom slide show

h. Click **OK**, and then click **Close**. **Save** the presentation. You have created the presentation, and you will now display it as a custom slide show.

i. Click the **Slide Show** tab, click the **Custom Slide Show** arrow, and then select **Bridal Presentation**. Navigate through the presentation, noting that the slide with the prices for the bridal packages does not show and that there are no transitions on the slides that were reused from the photo album.

Because you created a new presentation for the custom Bridal Presentation show, you can make changes to the slides. You will add transitions to Slides 13, 14, and 15. You will also unhide Slide 12.

j. Click **Slide 13**, press and hold Shift, and then click **Slide 15** to select the three slides. Click the **TRANSITIONS** tab, and then in the Transitions to This Slide group, click **Reveal**. Click **Effect Options**, and then select **Smoothly From Right**. Adjust the duration of the transition to 2.30.

k. Right-click **Slide 12**, and then select **Hide Slide**. This reverses the hiding of the slide so it will be viewable in the regular progression of the slides.

l. Click the **SLIDE SHOW** tab, and then in the Start Slide Show group, click **Custom Slide Show**. Click **Bridal Presentation**, and then review each slide. Press Esc to return to Normal view.

Did you notice the Previous button on the Bridal Packages slide? If you clicked it, it returns to the Visit with the Therapist slide. You decide to move a slide in the custom slide show to improve the flow of information.

m. In the Start Slide Show group, click **Custom Slide Show**, and then click **Custom Shows**. The Bridal Presentation is selected because it is the only show. Click **Edit**.

n. Click **9. Bridal Packages** in the Slides in custom show box. Click the **Down** arrow in the dialog box to move the slide into position 12. The Bridal Packages slide will be displayed right before the slide with information on reservations. Click **OK**, and then click **Close**.

o. In the Start Slide Show group, click **Custom Slide Show**, and then click **Bridal Presentation**. Navigate through the slides, and then press Esc to return to Normal view.

Although the Bridal Packages slide is still in the same position on the Slide pane, it is displayed after the testimonial slides in the custom slide show. You notice that the new slides are missing the footer.

p. Click **Slide 13**. Click the **INSERT** tab, and then in the Text group, click **Header & Footer**, and then click **Footer** to select it. Type Reserve your spa treatment at www.paintedparadiseresort.com. Click the **Don't show on title slide** check box to deselect it, and then click **Apply**.

q. Drag the right-sizing handle of the footer placeholder so that the footer fits on one line. Click the **DRAWING TOOLS FORMAT** tab, and then in the Arrange group, click **Align Objects**, and then select **Align Bottom**. Click **Align Objects** again, and then select **Align Center**.

r. Move the photograph of Kelly Masters up to make room for the footer.

s. Click **Slide 14**, click the **testimonial** box, and then drag the **bottom-middle sizing handle** up to make room for the footer. Repeat Steps p and q.

t. Click **Slide 15**, and then repeat Steps p and q to insert and position the footer.

u. Click **Save** . On the **SLIDE SHOW** tab, and then in the Start Slide Show group, click **Custom Slide Show**, click **Bridal Presentation**, and then review each of the slides in the presentation. Press Esc to return to Normal view. You will now create another custom slide show to focus on the facilities and staff at the Turquoise Oasis Spa.

v. If necessary, click the **SLIDE SHOW** tab, and then in the Start Slide Show group, click **Custom Slide Show**, and then select **Custom Shows**. Click **New**, select the **Custom Show 1** text, then type Facilities-Staff Presentation in the **Slide show name** box. Select **1. Slide 1** through **7. Visit with the Therapist** in the Slides in presentation box. Select **13. What Our Guests Say:** through **16.Reservations**. Click **Add**, click **OK**, and then click **Close**.

w. In the Start Slide Show group, click **Custom Slide Show**, and then select **Facilities-Staff Presentation** to view the newly created custom slide show. Press Esc to return to Normal view. You will now create one more custom slide show, this time just focusing on the facilities.

x. In the Start Slide Show group, click **Custom Slide Show**, and then select **Custom Shows**. Click **New**, select the **Custom Show 1** text, and then type Spa Facilities. Select **1. Slide 1** through **5. Tour Our Spa**. Select **16. Reservations**, click **Add**, click **OK**, and then click **Close**.

y. In the Start Slide Show group, click **Custom Slide Show**, and then select **Spa Facilities**. Review each slide, and then press Esc to return to Normal view.

z. Click **Save** , and then **close** the presentation.

Now, with a single presentation, you have three customized presentations to share with different audiences. The presentation can be used with guests who are new to the spa. Meda can also use the presentation when she wants to introduce people to the spa but not discuss the cost of the treatments. The Spa Facilities custom show can be used for guests who have visited a spa before but who have not been to the Turquoise Oasis Spa.

Save a Presentation in Multiple Formats

PowerPoint can save your presentation files in a variety of formats and allows you to easily share your presentation with others. Using the Share tab on the File tab you can share your presentation files in a variety of ways, depending on whether or not your presentation file is saved locally, on a SharePoint site, or on SkyDrive. Using the Invite People option, you can invite people to view or collaborate with you on your presentation, generate a link to share with others, and give them view or edit permissions. You can post your presentation to various social networks like Facebook, Twitter, and LinkedIn.

Using the E-mail option, you can send a presentation via an e-mail as either a PowerPoint, PDF, or XPS attachment, or as a link. Using the Present Online option, you can set up the presentation to be broadcast to remote viewers by sending them a link so they can view the slides on the web in real time as you display them. Slides can also be published to a slide library or SharePoint site so other people can access and update the presentation.

Using the Export tab on the File tab, you can also save the presentation in different types of file formats. You can create a PDF/XPS document. These file formats retain the fonts, formatting, and images exactly as you created them in PowerPoint, and the content cannot be easily changed. You can export the presentation as a video with automatic timings to advance the slides to be displayed on computer monitors, projectors, mobile devices, or DVDs. You can also export one or more presentations as part of a package that can be copied to a CD so they can be viewed on most computers with or without PowerPoint installed.

The Export tab also has the option to Create Handouts. Handouts allow you to create Word documents with the slides and notes. This enables you to make modifications in layout and format to the handouts. You can also add additional content to the handouts. When you use this option to create the handouts, changes you make to the slide presentation will automatically update the handout.

Saving and Sending a Presentation via E-Mail

You have a number of options to select from when you use the E-mail option on the Share tab. You can attach the PowerPoint file in its native format (.pptx) to an e-mail message. You can e-mail a link to a shared location on a server so others can view it and make modifications. The file can be saved in PDF format and attached to an e-mail message. You can do the same for an XPS file. The file can also be sent as an Internet fax if you have a fax service provider.

In this exercise you will share the Spa presentation via e-mail as a PDF attachment to yourself so you can see the result. Keep in mind that the various formats create files of different sizes. Generally a PDF file is smaller than an XPS file. Both of these types are smaller than the PowerPoint format of .pptx. Consider the content of the presentation as you select the file type. PDF and XPS files do not enable internal hyperlinks to other slides, play audio or video, or display slide transitions or animations. If these things are necessary for your presentation, you need to send the file in PowerPoint format.

P03.20

To Send the Presentation as a PDF

a. Open **PowerPoint**, under Recent, double-click **p02ws03Spa_LastFirst**. If the file is not available under Recent, click **Open Other Presentations**, navigate to the location where you store your completed PowerPoint files, and then double-click **p02ws03Spa_LastFirst**.

b. Click the **FILE** tab, and then click **Share**.

c. Click **Email**, and then click **Send as PDF**. PowerPoint will now publish the slides as a PDF and attempt to launch your default desktop e-mail program.

Troubleshooting
If you do not have a desktop e-mail client configured, you may not be able to complete these steps. Ask your instructor for additional information.

d. Type your e-mail address in the To field. Type your instructor's e-mail address in the Cc field. Select the **Subject** text, which is the file name, and then type **Enjoy this introduction to the Spa from Firstname Lastname** using your first and last name. Click in the **Message** box, and then type **I am sending you this file in PDF format. It is a smaller file, but you will not be able to hear the audio or see the animations.** Press Enter, and then type **Enjoy!** Press Enter again, and then type your first and last name.

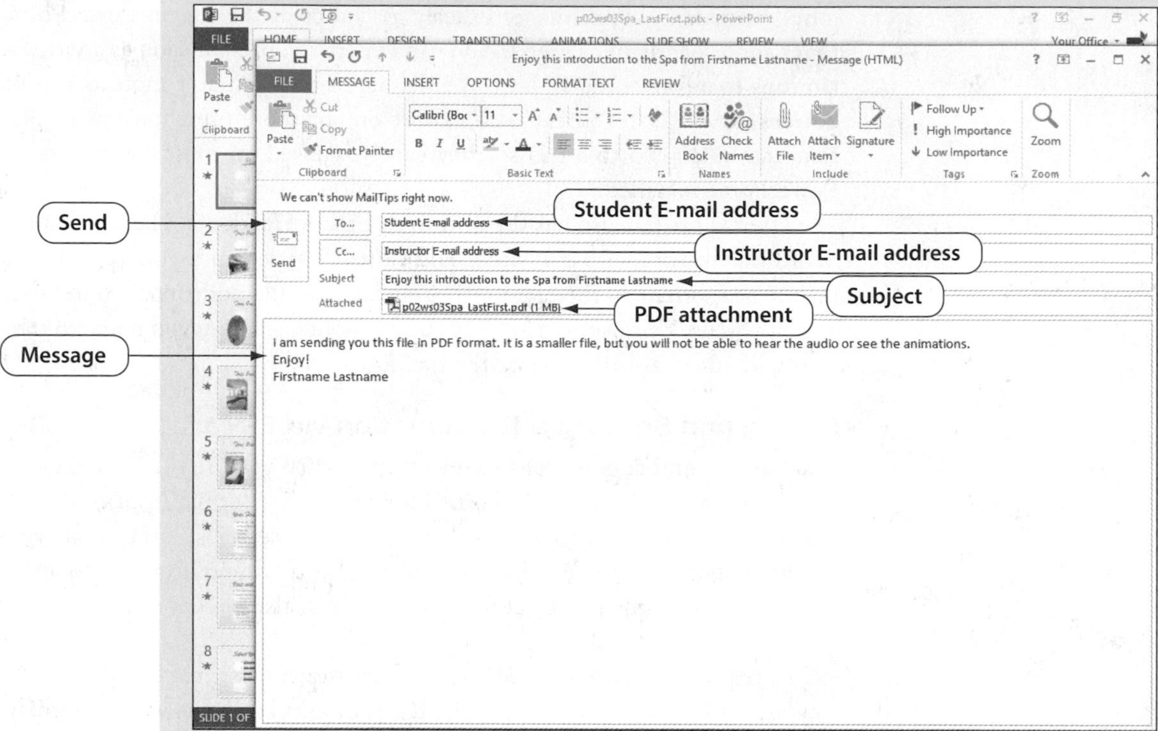

Figure 22 Sending a presentation as a PDF

e. Click **Send**. Navigate to your inbox to which the e-mail was sent. Open the message when it arrives, and then click the **attachment link**. Your default PDF reader opens the file and the presentation is displayed in PDF format.

f. Scroll through the PDF to advance the slides. Notice the speaker icon replaces audio. There are no transitions. On the Select Your Treatment slide, click a **hyperlink**. It will not link to the hidden slides because those slides were not saved as part of the PDF file. Click the **e-mail hyperlink** for Meda and an e-mail message window opens. Close the window without sending a message to Meda.

g. Close the **PDF**.

Saving a PowerPoint Presentation as a Video

PowerPoint videos display the slides with all of the features that you build into the slide. The animations, transitions, audio, and video work as they do in the normal Slide Show view. Be aware that hidden slides are not part of the video and that hyperlinks do not work. Once you have created the video, it can be distributed via DVD, the Internet, or e-mail.

Saving a presentation as a video provides an opportunity to create the presentation one of three different formats and with different overall file sizes. You can create the video for computers and high-definition (HD) displays, such as you might find in the resort waiting areas. Video for computers and high-definition monitors is displayed at 960 × 720 pixels and requires the most storage space. For the Internet or DVD video, the file is displayed at 640 × 480 pixels, which is a commonly used size for a web page. The file is saved as an MPEG-4 Video (mp4) and can be played using Windows Media Player, iTunes, or any other desktop video player. The smallest format is 320 × 240 pixels, for display on any portable device capable of playing .mp4 files. In the smallest format, it may be difficult to read the text on the screen, so plan accordingly and bump up the size of the font in the presentation.

In this exercise, you will compress the media in the presentation to low quality to minimize storage space and then create a video for Internet and a DVD. Because the slides were not set up to automatically advance, you will use the timings provided on the Create a Video pane to advance the slides.

P03.21

To Export a PowerPoint as a Video

a. Click the **FILE** tab, and then on the Info tab, click **Compress Media**, and then select **Low Quality**, and then click **Close**.

b. Click **Export**, and then click **Create a Video**.

c. Click the **Computer & HD Displays** arrow, and then select **Internet & DVD**.

SIDE NOTE
Compress Media Option
The Compress Media button will only appear in presentations that have audio and/or video embedded.

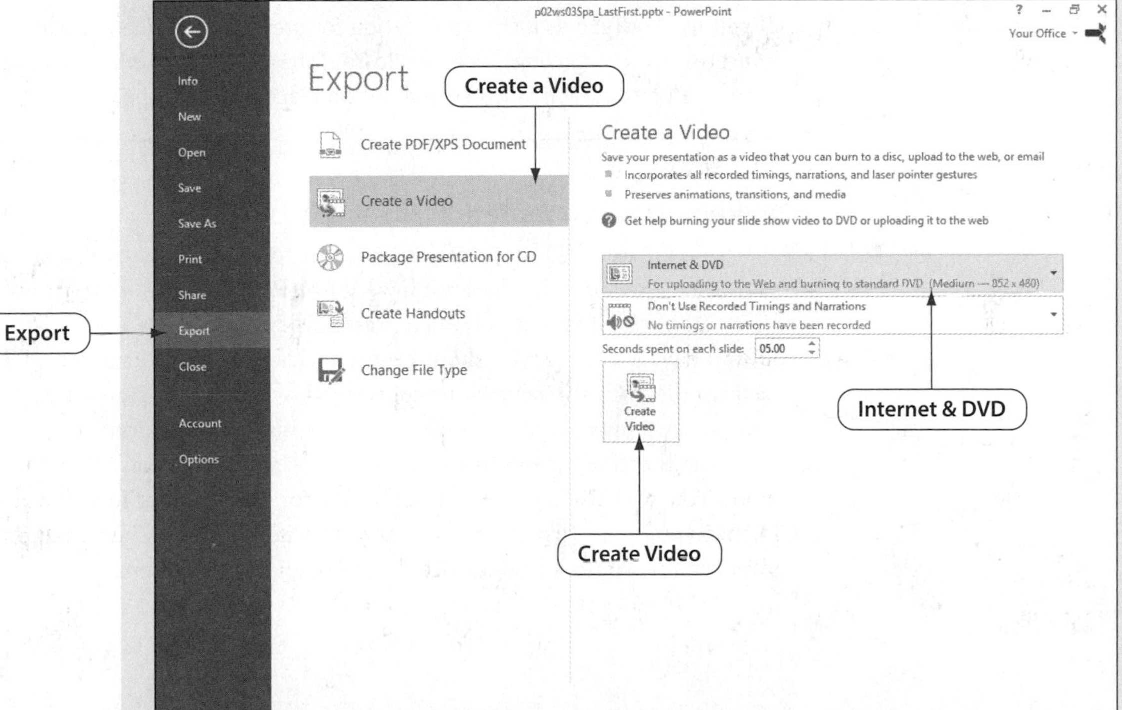

Figure 23 Exporting a presentation as a video

d. Click **Create Video**. The Save As dialog box will open. Save your file as p02ws03SpaVideo_LastFirst using your last and first name and then click **Save**.

The video will be processed and stored in the location where you save your project files. This process can take quite a bit of time. Notice the status bar at the bottom of the window reports that it is creating a video. Wait until it is finished before proceeding to the next step.

e. Navigate to where you are storing your completed files, and then open **p02ws03SpaVideo_LastFirst** to play it.

Notice the slides advance automatically after five seconds of display. If media elements are on the slide, such as the music on the first slide, those elements will completely play before the five-second counter begins. If you have slides with a lot of text, you may have to increase the time the slides are displayed before creating the video so people can read the whole slide before it advances.

f. Close the media player, and then return to the **p02ws03Spa** presentation.

REAL WORLD ADVICE | **Video Considerations**

As you consider the size limitations that some people have on their e-mail inbox, you may turn to YouTube or your SkyDrive as alternative storage locations for the video. You could then provide a link to the video in the e-mail message that you send to your intended audience.

CONSIDER THIS | **YouTube Privacy**

If you use YouTube as a storage location for presentation video, privacy can become a concern. In what circumstances would YouTube be an appropriate storage location? What type of a presentation video should not be placed on YouTube?

Packaging a Presentation for a CD

When you create a CD presentation, you put together a player and the presentation. This means that someone who does not have PowerPoint can still play your presentation on his or her computer. If you are giving a presentation where you are not sure of the equipment you will have available, you should burn a package presentation on a CD so you will have a backup plan. CD presentations contain all of the slides, transitions, animations, media elements, and hyperlinks that are in the original presentation.

You will create a new directory on your storage location for the CD package presentation. You will package the presentation for a CD. This folder would be placed on a CD that you could distribute to your potential clients. When they put the CD in their computers, it would automatically begin playing the presentation.

P03.22

To Create a CD Presentation

a. Click the **FILE** tab, click **Export**, and then select **Package Presentation for CD.**

b. Click **Package for CD**. The Package for CD dialog box opens.

c. Select the **Presentation CD** text, and then type Spa Presentation in the Name the CD box on the Package for CD dialog box. Click **Copy to Folder**.

d. In the Folder name box, select the **Spa Presentation text**, and then in the Copy to Folder dialog box, type p02ws03SpaCD_LastFirst. Click **Browse**, navigate to the location where you are saving your files, and then click **Select**. Click **OK**. When asked if you want to include linked files in your package, click **Yes**. An additional message indicating that comments, revisions, and ink annotations will not be included in the package may appear and disappear. If necessary, click **Continue** if you see the message and it does not disappear automatically.

The folder opens with three files: the PowerPoint presentation, an AUTORUN.INF application, and a PresentationPackage folder. You would copy the entire folder you created to a CD so all of the necessary elements are available.

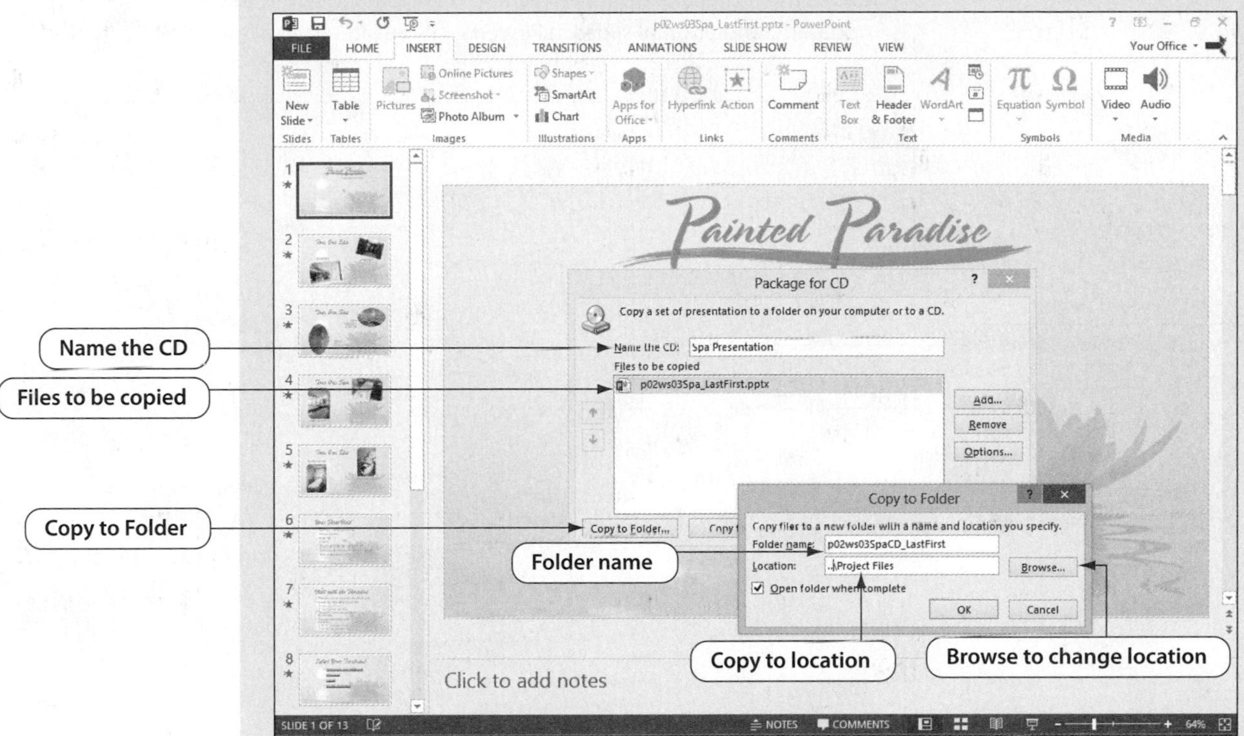

Figure 24 Exporting a package presentation for a CD

e. **Close** the folder window, and then click **Close** on the Package for CD dialog box.

Creating Handouts in Word Format

PowerPoint creates handouts by showing the slides in full-slide format or thumbnail format. There are times when you might want to have the handouts in Word format so you can manipulate them using Word. For instance, you may want to add additional content to the handouts or change the layout. You could also use this document as a beginning point for creating training materials, with details of procedures, for the audience to take with them after viewing a presentation.

You will create a Word document that contains thumbnails of the slides and the notes. You will add your name and today's date to the first page of the document. Do not print the document unless directed by your instructor.

P03.23

To Create Handouts

a. Click the **FILE** tab, and then click **Export**. Click **Create Handouts**, and then click **Create Handouts**.

The Send to Microsoft Word dialog box shows five options. You can place notes or blank lines next to the slides or below them. You can also send only the outline to Word. In this dialog box, you have the option to paste the slides into the Word document or to use the Paste Link option, which creates linked slides in the Word document that are updated if the original slides in PowerPoint are altered at a later time.

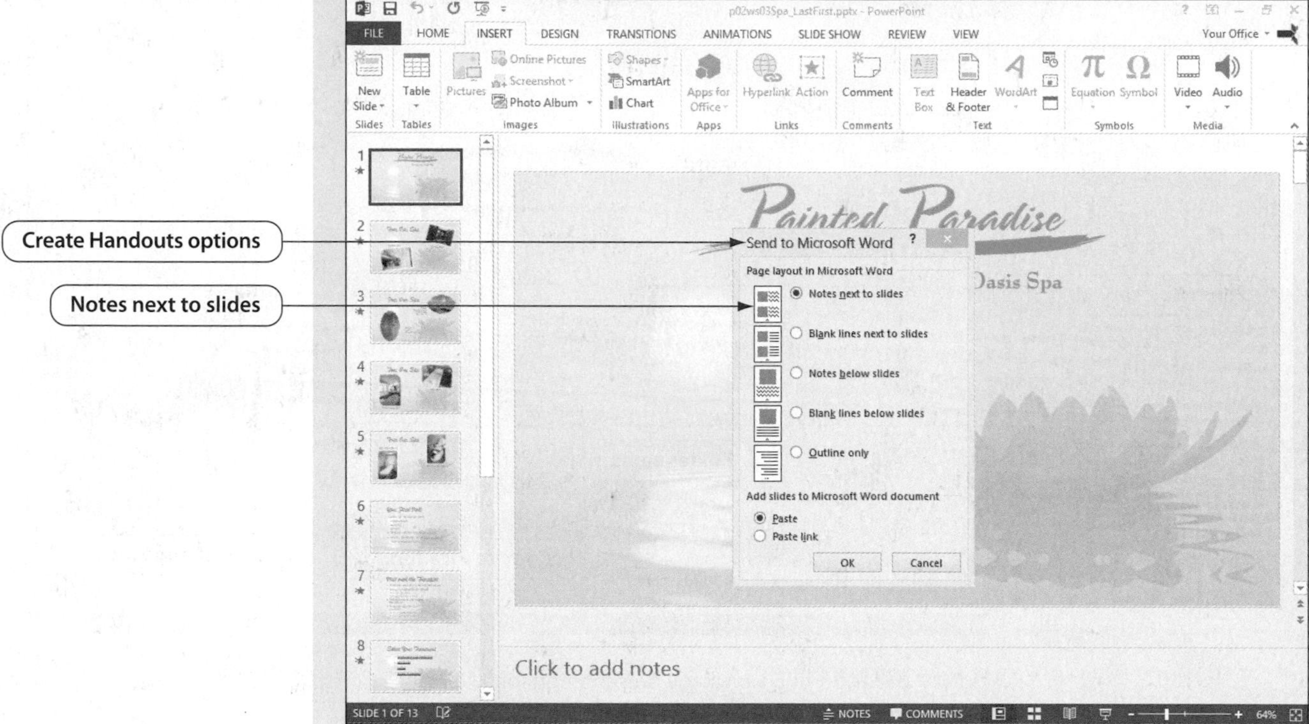

Figure 25 Exporting a presentation to print handouts

b. The first option, with Notes next to slides is already selected, click **OK**.

A new Word document will open on your desktop. You may have to click the application on the taskbar to view the file. It will take a little time for the document to completely render. The first several slides do not have notes. Notice that the hidden slides are also shown in the Word document.

c. Scroll down the document until you see **Slide 6**. Notes were on that slide as well as Slide 7. Scroll back to the top of the document. Click in front of **Slide 1**, and then type your first and last name and today's date. Press Enter.

d. In the Word document, click the **FILE** tab, and then click **Save As**. Navigate to the location where you save your project files, and then save the file as p02ws03SpaHandouts_LastFirst using your last and first name. Click **Save**, close **Word**, and then close **PowerPoint**.

Concept Check

1. Your supervisor, Larry Houck, has asked you to add some pizzazz to a quarterly report presentation that he created. His intended audience for the presentation includes his boss and the upper management of the company. What types of transitions or animations might you use to engage this audience? Discuss your reasons. p. 904-910
2. Larry, your supervisor, asked you to create a presentation comparing three laptop computers that the department is considering purchasing. You have decided to add hyperlinks to the websites of the three companies on which you have focused your research. What are some key points to keep in mind for using these hyperlinks? What kind of internal hyperlinks—to slides within the presentation—might you use? p. 912–915
3. As a volunteer at a local animal shelter, you decide you want to add some audio to a presentation you have created. What kinds of sounds would you use? How would this audio improve the delivery of your message? Would this change your distribution plans? If so, how? p. 919–920
4. Continuing with your work on the animal shelter presentation, you have decided to photograph all of the animals that are up for adoption and create a presentation to persuade people to support the shelter by adopting or making donations. Describe how you would use the Photo Album feature of PowerPoint to create the presentation. How would you distribute the presentation to people who might adopt or make a donation? p. 924–926
5. PowerPoint allows for the creation of custom slide shows. Discuss some of the uses and benefits of creating custom slide shows from a presentation. p. 933–936
6. A PowerPoint presentation can be exported into several different formats. Discuss the benefits and limits of a PDF and video export. p. 936–942

Key Terms

Action buttons 915
Animation 904
Caption 928
Custom slide show 933
Delay 907
Duration 907
Emphasis action 907
Entrance animation 907
Exit animation 907
Hyperlink 912
Kiosk 904
Photo Album 924
Transition 904
Trigger 917

Visual Summary

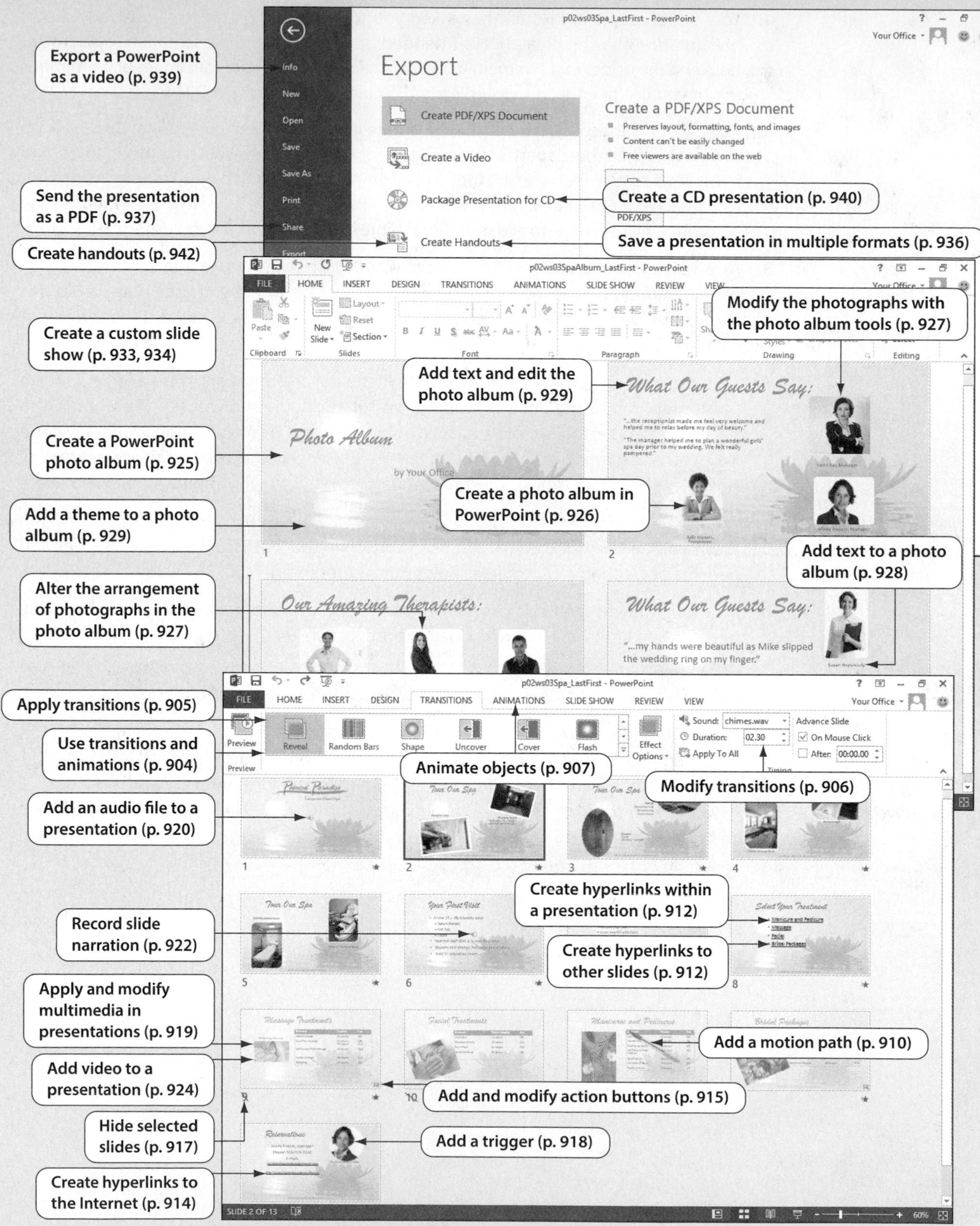

Figure 26 The Turquoise Oasis Spa Final Marketing Presentation

Practice 1

Student data files needed:

- Blank PowerPoint presentation
- p02ws03ProductsTheme.thmx
- p02ws03ProductsLogo.png
- p02ws03SpaProducts1.jpg
- p02ws03SpaProducts2.jpg
- p02ws03SpaProducts3.jpg
- p02ws03SpaProducts4.jpg
- p02ws03SpaProducts5.jpg
- p02ws03SpaProducts6.jpg
- p02ws03SpaProducts7.jpg
- p02ws03SpaProducts8.jpg
- p02ws03SpaProducts9.jpg

You will save your file as:

- p02ws03Products_LastFirst.pptx

Spa Product Album

Sales & Marketing

The marketing team at the Spa would like to promote a few of their products that are available for purchase. In this exercise you will create a PowerPoint Photo Album featuring images of these products.

a. Start **PowerPoint 2013**, and then in the PowerPoint Start screen, click **Blank Presentation**.

b. Click the **INSERT** tab, and then in the Images group, click the **Photo Album** arrow, and then select **New Photo Album**.

c. In the Photo Album dialog box, click **File/Disk**. Navigate to where you are storing your student files, select all nine files beginning with **p02ws03SpaProducts1** through **p02ws03SpaProducts9**, and then click **Insert**.

d. Make the following changes in the Photo Album dialog box.
   - Select **p02ws03SpaProducts5**, and then click **Rotate 90 degrees counter-clockwise** once. Deselect **p02ws03SpaProducts5**.
   - Select **p02ws03SpaProducts9**, click **Increase Brightness** twice, and then click **Increase Contrast** twice. Deselect **p02ws03SpaProducts9**.
   - Select **p02ws03SpaProducts1** through **p02ws03SpaProducts3**, and then click **Down** to move the three images into positions 7, 8, and 9. Deselect **p02ws03SpaProducts1** through **p02ws03SpaProducts3**.
   - Select **p02ws03SpaProducts4**, and then click **New Text Box**. Deselect **p02ws03SpaProducts4**.
   - Select **Text Box**, and then click **Up** to move it into position 1. Deselect **Text Box**.
   - Select **p02ws03SpaProducts6**, and then click **New Text Box**. Deselect **p02ws03SpaProducts6**.
   - Click **p02ws03SpaProducts9**, and then click **New Text Box**.
   - Under Album Layout, click the **Picture layout** arrow, and then click **4 pictures with title**.
   - Under Album Layout, click the **Frame shape** arrow, and then click **Center Shadow Rectangle**.
   - Under Picture Options, click **Captions below ALL pictures**.
   - Under Album Layout, to the right of Theme box click **Browse**. Navigate to your student files, click **p02ws03ProductsTheme**, and then click **Select**.
   - Click **Create**.

e. Click the **FILE** tab, and then click **Save**. Browse to where you are saving your files, and then save your file as p02ws03Products_LastFirst using your last and first name, and then click **Save**.

f. Click **Slide 1**, click the **INSERT** tab, and then in the Images group, click **Pictures**. Navigate to your student files, click **p02ws03ProductsLogo**, and then click **Insert**.

g. In the Arrange group, click **Align Objects**, and then click **Align Top**.

h. Select the **Photo Album** text, and then type Product Catalog. Select the **Product Catalog** text. In the **Font** group click the **Font** arrow, and then select **Cambria** from the list of fonts. With the text selected, right-click the text, and then click **Font**. Under Effects, click **Small Caps**, and then click **OK**.

i. In the subtitle placeholder, select the **text**, and then type Featured Products for Sale at the Turquoise Oasis Spa.

j. Select **Slides 1** through **4**. Click the **TRANSITIONS** tab, and then in the Transition to This Slide group, click **Reveal**. In the **Timing** group, click the **Duration** text box, type 2.5 and then press Enter.

k. Click **Slide 2** and make the following changes.
   - Click the **Title** placeholder, and then type Nail Care Products.
   - Select the words **Text Box**, and then type Enjoy beautifully manicured hands any time. Click the **p02ws03SpaProducts5** image. Click the **ANIMATIONS** tab, and then in the Animation group, click **More**, and then click **Wheel**.
   - Select the file name **p02ws03SpaProducts5**, and then type Hundreds of Colors.
   - Click the **p02ws03SpaProducts4** image. Click the **ANIMATIONS** tab, and then in the Animation group, click **More**, and then click **Wheel**.
   - Select the file name **p02ws03SpaProducts4**, and then type Dry Your Nails Fast.
   - Click the **p02ws03SpaProducts6** image, and then on the PICTURE TOOLS FORMAT tab, in the Size group, click the **Shape Width** box, type 1.6 and then press Enter.
   - On the ANIMATIONS tab, in the Animation group, click **More**, and then click **Wheel**.
   - Select the file name **p02ws03SpaProducts6**, and then type Professional Tools.

l. Click **Slide 3** and make the following changes.
   - Click the **Title** placeholder, and then type Home Facial Products.
   - Select the words **Text Box**, and then type High Quality Products to Help You Stay Beautiful.
   - Click the **p02ws03SpaProducts8** image. Click the **ANIMATIONS** tab, and then in the Animation group, click **More**, and then click **Wheel**.
   - Select the file name **p02ws03SpaProducts8**, and then type Cucumber Anti-Aging Cream.
   - Click the **p02ws03SpaProducts7** image. Click the **ANIMATIONS** tab, and then in the Animation group, click **More**, and then click **Wheel**.
   - Select the file name **p02ws03SpaProducts7**, and then type All Natural Face Mask.
   - Click the **p02ws03SpaProducts9** image. Click the **ANIMATIONS** tab, and then in the Animation group, click **More**, and then click **Wheel**.
   - Select the file name **p02ws03SpaProducts9**, and then type Natural Mineral Makeup.

m. Click **Slide 4** and make the following changes.
   - Click the **Title** placeholder, and then type Luxury Bath Products.
   - Select the words **Text Box**, and then type Enjoy a Soothing and Relaxing Spa Experience at Home.
   - Click the **p02ws03SpaProducts2** image. Click the **ANIMATIONS** tab, and then in the Animation group, click **More**, and then click **Wheel**.
   - Select the file name **p02ws03SpaProducts2**, and then type Homemade Soaps.
   - Click the **p02ws03SpaProducts1** image. Click the **ANIMATIONS** tab, and then in the Animation group, click **More**, and then click **Wheel**.
   - Select the file name **p02ws03SpaProducts1**, and then type Relaxing Bath Salts.

- Click the **p02ws03SpaProducts3** image. Click the **ANIMATIONS** tab, and then in the Animation group, click **More**, and then click **Wheel**.
- Select the file name **p02ws03SpaProducts3**, and then type Aromatic Bath Oils.

n. Save your presentation, and then close PowerPoint. Submit your file as requested by your instructor.

Problem Solve 1

Student data file needed:

You will save your files as:

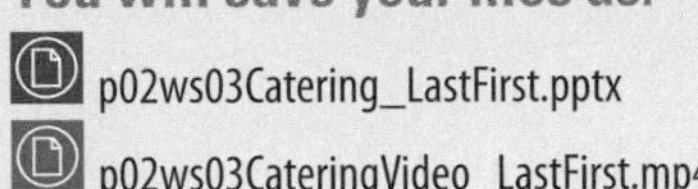

Terry's Banquet Hall and Catering Promotional Video

Sales & Marketing

Terry's Banquet Hall and Catering is a new business in town. They are looking to create a low-cost promotional video using PowerPoint 2013 and have requested your expertise. In this exercise you will create a presentation using the photographs provided, to emphasize the company's professional staff, beautiful facilities and furnishings, and the excellent food. You will then export the presentation as a video to be played at various kiosks around town.

a. Start **PowerPoint 2013**. Open the file **p02ws03Catering**, and then save the presentation as p02ws03Catering_LastFirst.

b. On **Slide 1**, on the TRANSITIONS tab, in the Transition to This Slide group, click **More**. In the **Exciting** group, click **Curtains**.

c. In the Timing group, click the **Duration** box, type 3 and then press Enter.

d. Select **Slides 2** through **8**, apply the **Uncover** transition, and then adjust the duration of the transitions to 1.50.

e. Make the following changes to **Slide 2**.
   - Click **Slide 2**. Apply the **Shape** animation to the Weddings text.
   - Modify the animation to occur after previous with a .25 second delay.
   - Apply the **Shape** animation to each of the bullets below the Weddings text.
   - Modify each bullet to occur **After Previous** with a .25 second delay.
   - Apply the same animations and settings to the Parties text and each of the bullets below it.

f. Make the following changes to **Slide 3**.
   - Apply a **Fly In** animation to the first photograph. Adjust the effect options so it flies in **From Bottom-Left**.
   - Apply a **Fly In** animation to the second photograph. Adjust the timing of the animation to occur after the previous animation has completed.
   - Apply a **Fly In** animation to the third photograph. Adjust the effect options so it flies in **From Bottom-Right**. Adjust the timing of the animation to occur after the previous animation has completed.

g. Make the following changes to **Slide 4**.
   - Apply a **Fade** animation to the first photograph. Adjust the **Duration** of the animation to 1.00.
   - Apply a **Fade** animation to the second photograph. Adjust the **Duration** of the animation to 1.00. Adjust the timing of the animation to occur after the previous animation has completed.
   - Apply a **Fade** animation to the third photograph. Adjust the **Duration** of the animation to 1.00. Adjust the timing of the animation to occur after the previous animation has completed.

h. Make the following changes to **Slide 5.**
   - Apply a **Float In** animation to the first photograph.
   - Apply a **Float In** animation to the second photograph. Adjust the timing of the animation to occur after the previous animation has completed.
   - Apply a **Float In** animation to the third photograph. Adjust the timing of the animation to occur after the previous animation has completed.

i. Make the following changes to **Slide 6**.
   - Insert three oval callout shapes. Using the Format Shape pane, position the first oval callout shape with a Horizontal position of 0.1" from the Top Left Corner and a Vertical position of 2.28" from the Top Left Corner. Adjust the Shape Width to be 4.50" and the Shape Height to 3.0".
   - Position the second oval callout shape with a Horizontal position of 4.54" from the Top Left Corner and a Vertical position of 3.22" from the Top Left Corner. Adjust the Shape Width to be 4" and the Shape Height to 3".
   - Position the third oval callout shape with a Horizontal position of 8.64" from the Top Left Corner and a Vertical position of 2.15" from the Top Left Corner. Adjust the Shape Width to be 4.5" and the Shape Height to 3". Type the following testimonial inside the oval callout shape on the left: **"The food was fabulous and, as always, it was simply a pleasure working with you and your entire staff."** Press Enter, and then type Mary.
   - Type the following testimonial inside the oval callout shape in the middle: **"Our holiday party last night was great, and the staff and food were fantastic as always!"** Press Enter, and then type Amber.
   - Type the following testimonial inside the oval callout shape on the right: **"We were totally satisfied. Everything went well and we heard nothing but good things from those who attended."** Press Enter, and then type Harold and Brenda.
   - Apply the **Subtle Effect – Blue, Accent 3** shape style and the Split animation to each of the three oval callout shapes. Adjust the duration of the split animation to 1 second for each of the three oval callout shapes. Adjust the timing of oval callout shapes in the middle and on the right to occur after the previous animation has finished with a 1 second delay.

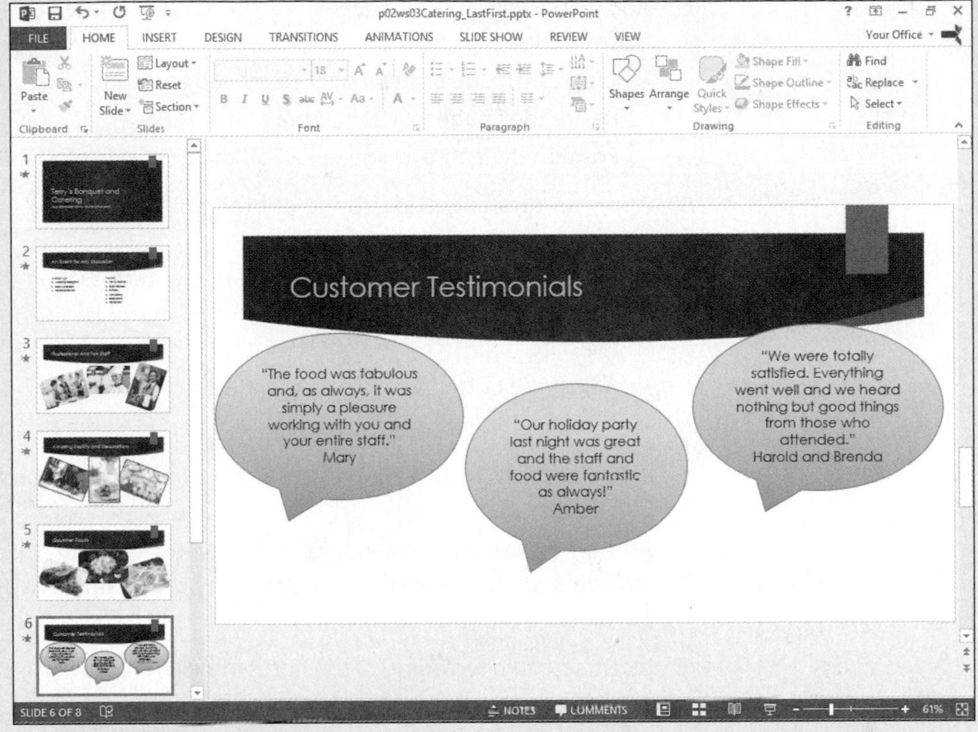

Figure 27

j. Click **Slide 7**. Apply a **Wheel** animation to the table.

k. Make the following changes to **Slide 8**.
   - Insert an E-mail link next to the E-mail text prochelle@terryscatering.com. Add the following text to the Subject box: Re: Terry's catering presentation.

l. Save the presentation.

m. Export the presentation as a Video for **Internet & DVD**. Save the video as p02ws03CateringVideo_LastFirst.

n. Exit **PowerPoint**. Submit your files as requested by your instructor.

Perform 1: Perform in Your Career

Student data file needed:

 p02ws03Job.pptx

You will save your file as:

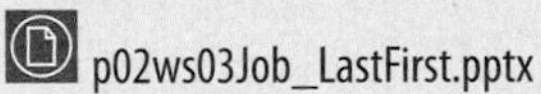 p02ws03Job_LastFirst.pptx

Job Qualifications Presentation

Human Resources

You are seeking an internship position at a local business. In addition to a traditional resume and cover letter you would also like to prepare a PowerPoint presentation summarizing your qualifications for the position. In this exercise you will create a PowerPoint presentation, using the file provided, outlining your qualifications.

a. Start **PowerPoint 2013**, navigate to your student files, and then open **p02ws03Job**. Save the presentation as p02ws03Job_LastFirst.

b. On Slide 1, type your first and last name in the title placeholder, and type Summary of Qualifications in the subtitle placeholder.

c. Add a photograph of yourself to the picture placeholder and make the following adjustments:
   - Crop the image to show only your head and shoulders.
   - Resize the image to a 2" height.
   - Position the entire image to just off the right side of the slide.

d. Apply an Arcs animation to the photograph, reverse the path direction so that it arcs toward the slide.
   - Adjust the starting path so that the image starts just off the right side of the slide.
   - Adjust the ending path so that the image ends inside the upper-right corner of the slide.
   - Adjust the bottom-middle sizing handle of the arc patch to increase the arc.
   - Modify the timing of the animation to start with the previous animation.

e. Add a text box below the photo in its final position that reads **Click photo to hear my statement**.

f. Add an introduction statement to the Notes pane of Slide 1. This statement should include your name and a sentence or two explaining why you are qualified for the position.

g. Insert an audio recording of the notes into Slide 1.
   - Use the Animation Pane to adjust the timing of the recording to occur when the photograph is clicked.
   - Ensure that the audio player is hidden during the presentation.

h. On Slide 2 type any work experience you have.
   - Apply entrance animations to each bullet point. Be sure your animations bring attention to the bullets and do not distract from their content.
   - Each animation should automatically follow the preceding one with a 1-second delay.

i. On Slide 3 type your education background including when you graduated high school, expected graduation date from college, along with your major(s), minor(s), and/or relevant course work.
   - Apply entrance animations to each bullet point. Be sure your animations bring attention to the bullets and do not distract from their content.
   - Each animation should automatically follow the preceding one with a 1-second delay.

j. On Slide 4 type any awards received or accomplishments such as honor roll, dean's list, school elections, or competitions.
   - Apply entrance animations to each bullet point. Be sure your animations bring attention to the bullets and do not distract from their content.
   - Each animation should automatically follow the preceding one with a 1-second delay.

k. Apply a transition to Slide 1 that is appropriate for the message you are trying to convey.

l. Apply a transition to each of the remaining slides. The chosen transition should be the same for the remaining slides but different from Slide 1.

m. Add a footer to all the slides with your e-mail address and current date.

n. Submit your file as requested by your instructor.

Additional Cases

Additional Workshop Cases are available on the companion website and in the instructor resources.

Microsoft Office PowerPoint 2013

Module 2

Collaborating and Invoking Emotion with the Audience

WORKSHOP 4 | CUSTOMIZATION AND COLLABORATION

OBJECTIVES

1. Create a custom template using the slide master p. 952
2. Customize the notes master, and customize the handouts master p. 959, 961
3. Develop a presentation from a custom template and an outline p. 965
4. Use slide sections and proofing tools to organize and prepare a presentation p. 966
5. Create comments, and navigate comments p. 969, 970
6. Create and use speaker notes p. 972
7. Mark presentations as final and apply password protection p. 974
8. Develop skills in delivering presentations p. 976

Prepare Case

Corporate Identity Template

Sales & Marketing

Andreka / Shutterstock

The management of the Painted Paradise Turquoise Oasis Spa understands the importance of developing a corporate identity recognizable by employees and the public. You have been asked to create a professional PowerPoint template that will be used in the Turquoise Oasis Spa as the beginning point for slide shows. The specifications from management include developing a color theme, font theme, custom page layouts, and a copyright notice in the footer. The color scheme will work to create a branding for the spa. Many of the things you already know about developing slides will be used as you create the template. Once the template is finished, you will collaborate with the spa manager, Irene Kai, to create a quarterly report using the template. You will assist her in creating speaker notes and develop a template for handouts. You will also work with Irene to prepare her for the actual presentation to the board of directors, giving her advice on overcoming presentation nervousness, being prepared, and engaging the audience.

REAL WORLD SUCCESS

"I interned for a small business last summer, and their sales team was continually creating presentations for various events where they would have an opportunity to inform people about their products. I noticed that each presentation had a completely different look and feel to it as if each presentation was from a completely different company. I took the initiative to create a custom template that incorporated colors and themes from their company's logo, and it was a big hit!"

- Blake, recent graduate

Student data files needed for this workshop:

 Blank PowerPoint presentation

 p02ws04Outline.docx

 p02ws04Comments.pptx

You will save your files as:

 p02ws04Template_LastFirst.potx

 p02ws04Presentation_LastFirst.pptx

 p02ws04Update_LastFirst.pptx

 p02ws04Notes_LastFirst.docx

 p02ws04Delivery_LastFirst.pptx

Creating a Corporate Identity with a Custom Template

Corporations throughout the world take pride in their **corporate identity**. Visual identities are carefully crafted to make products recognizable. Logos, color schemes, and fonts are used for years to ensure that customers identify with the product. Think about how you can recognize one soft drink can from another just by looking at the colors on the can. People visiting foreign countries are often surprised to recognize the golden arches of McDonald's.

Corporate identities are normally developed by the marketing group of a company. They conduct market research, costs analysis, and other studies to build the identity. They hire professional designers to produce pieces of the overall identity, such as the logo, with guidance from studies. They develop guidelines for the use of the corporate materials, often specifying the exact placement of the logo on a page, or the exact color numbers for the colors used in advertising. Each branch of the organization is expected to use the identity to create consistency and present a unified public view of the company. In this section you will work toward creating a custom template for the Turquoise Oasis Spa using custom colors, fonts, and layouts.

Create a Custom Template Using the Slide Master

Templates begin on the **slide master**. The slide master is a special template slide that details fonts, placement of footers, background colors, and other characteristics for the presentation. The slide master also contains layouts for the template. You can add new layouts, delete layouts, and modify the existing layouts. For instance, if you wanted the title of the slides to appear along the bottom of the slides, you would move the title placeholder to the location on the slide master.

The slide master tools are available on the View tab. While you are working on the slide master, all of the other PowerPoint tools are available. When you have completed your work with the slide master, it is very important that you close Slide Master view before you begin to populate your presentation with information. Otherwise, the information you add to the slides becomes a part of the template.

Opening the Starting File

This workshop focuses on building a template for a presentation. The template can be reused so an identity emerges over time. A template is also somewhat secure because most casual PowerPoint users do not know how to modify a template. In this section, you will modify a slide master, the handout master, and the notes master.

P04.00

To Get Started

a. Start **PowerPoint**, and then on the Start screen, click **Blank Presentation**.

b. Click the **FILE** tab, and then click **Save As**. Click **Computer**, click **Browse**, click **Save as type**, click **PowerPoint Template**, browse to where you are storing your files, type p02ws04Template_LastFirst as the file name using your last and first name, and then click **Save**.

Troubleshooting

Once you change the Save As file type to PowerPoint Template (*.potx), the Save As dialog box will direct you to a Custom Office Template directory. Be sure to change the storage location so the file is saved with your project files.

Modifying the Slide Master Theme

A theme adds color and font consistency to a normal presentation. By setting up the colors and fonts in Slide Master view, you customize the template. You can add background colors, textures, or pictures to all of the slide layouts or to individual slide layouts. It is easier to set up the background for all of the slides using the slide master, but keep in mind that anything you put on the slide master is locked in the slide layouts and cannot be changed without changing the slide master. For instance, if you put a shape on the slide master, it will appear in the same location on every slide layout.

You will begin this project by opening the slide master and adding background colors to the slide master.

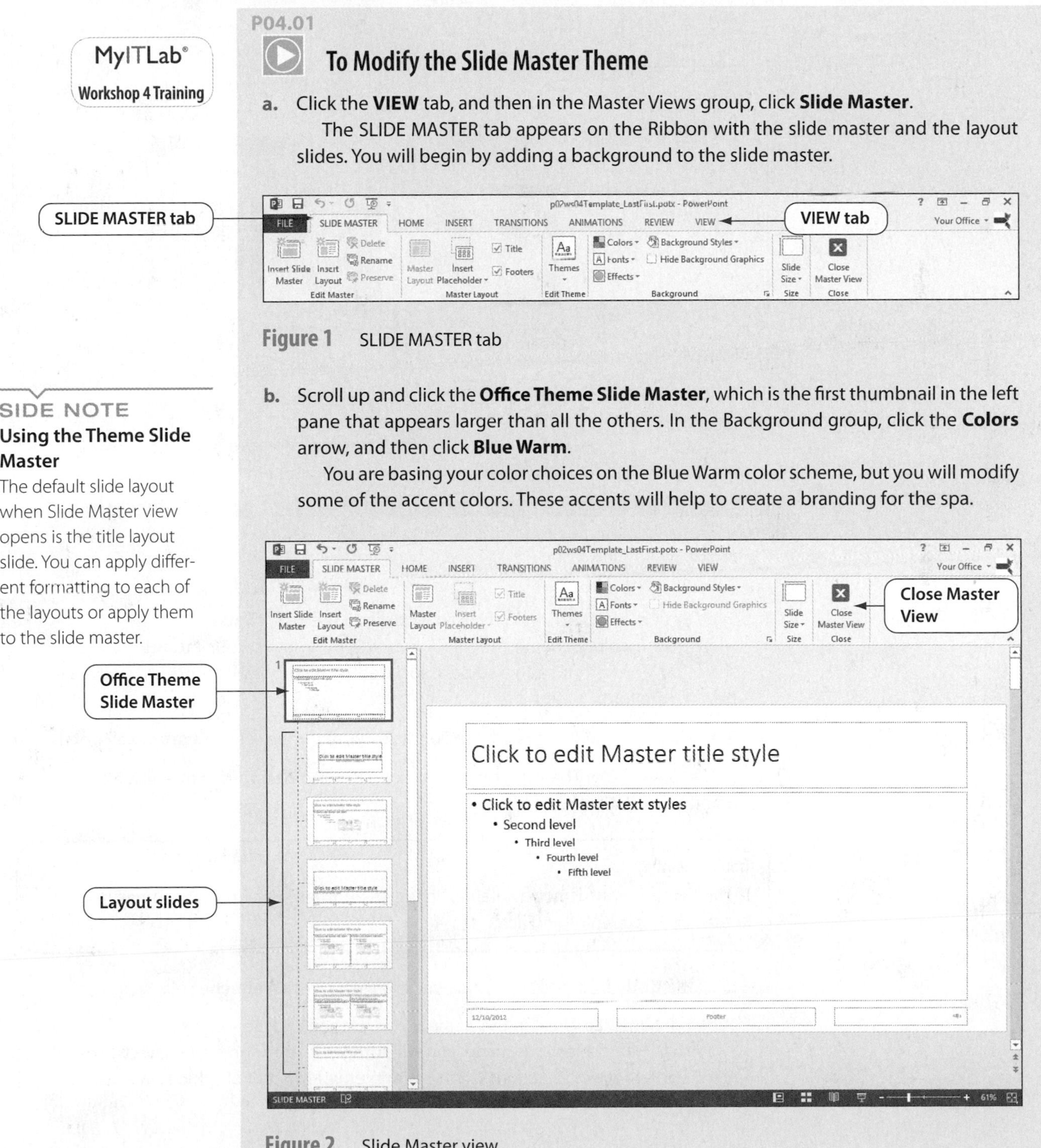

P04.01

MyITLab®

Workshop 4 Training

To Modify the Slide Master Theme

a. Click the **VIEW** tab, and then in the Master Views group, click **Slide Master**.

The SLIDE MASTER tab appears on the Ribbon with the slide master and the layout slides. You will begin by adding a background to the slide master.

Figure 1 SLIDE MASTER tab

b. Scroll up and click the **Office Theme Slide Master**, which is the first thumbnail in the left pane that appears larger than all the others. In the Background group, click the **Colors** arrow, and then click **Blue Warm**.

You are basing your color choices on the Blue Warm color scheme, but you will modify some of the accent colors. These accents will help to create a branding for the spa.

SIDE NOTE

Using the Theme Slide Master

The default slide layout when Slide Master view opens is the title layout slide. You can apply different formatting to each of the layouts or apply them to the slide master.

Figure 2 Slide Master view

c. In the **Background** group, click **Colors**, and then select **Customize Colors**. In the Create New Theme Colors dialog box, click the **Accent 1** arrow, and then select **More Colors**. On the Custom tab, type 0 for **Red**, 167 for **Green**, 157 for **Blue**, and then click **OK**.

d. Click the **Accent 2** arrow, and then click **More Colors**. Type 238 for **Red**, 192 for **Green**, 146 for **Blue**, and then click **OK**.

e. Click the **Accent 5** arrow, and then click **More Colors**. Type 253 for **Red**, 114 for **Green**, 9 for **Blue**, and then click **OK**.

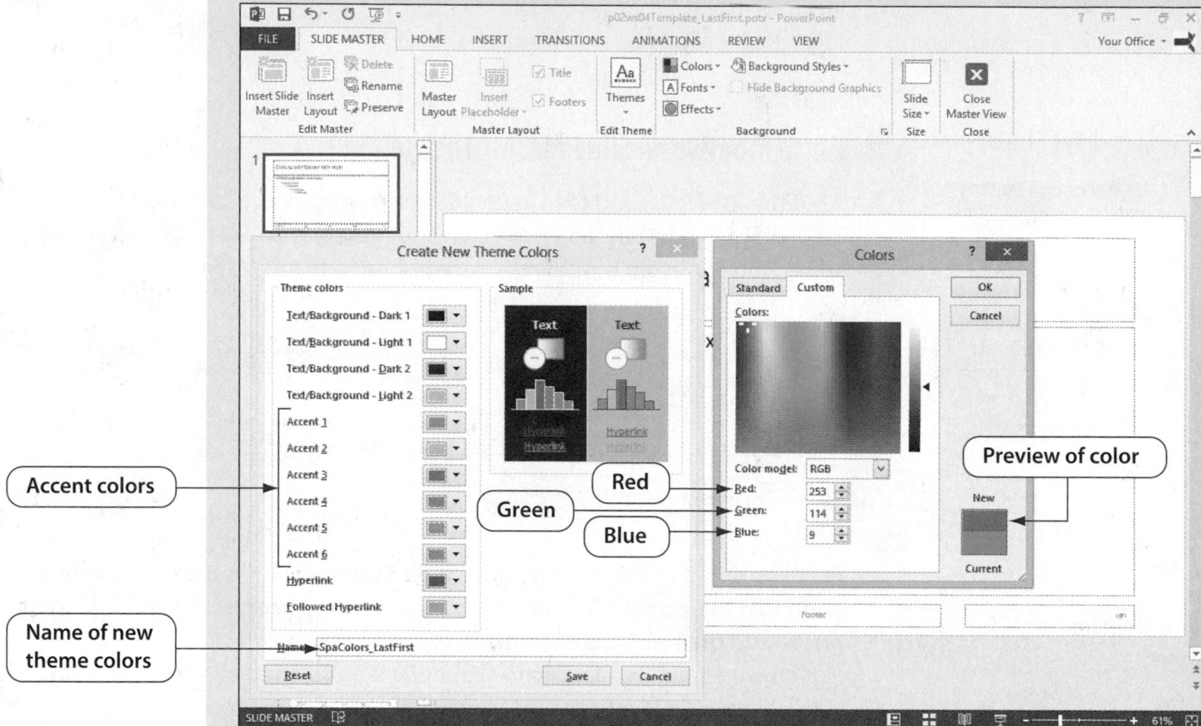

Figure 3 Edit theme colors

f. Type SpaColors_LastFirst in the Name box, and then click **Save**.

With the color scheme modified, you will now focus your attention on the font selection. Font groups can also be associated with corporate identities. You will select new theme fonts.

g. In the Background group, click the **Fonts** arrow, and then select **Customize Fonts**.

h. In the Create New Theme Fonts dialog box, click the **Heading font** arrow, scroll down, and then click **Cambria**.

> **Troubleshooting**
>
> If the Cambria font is not available, then use another serif font, like Times New Roman or Baskerville Old Face.

i. Click the **Body font** arrow, scroll down, and then select **Trebuchet MS**.

j. Type SpaFonts_LastFirst in the Name box, and then click **Save**.

With the font selections made, you will turn your attention to the effects. The effects enable you to make selections that determine the format of graphic elements.

k. In the Background group, click the **Effects** arrow, and then select **Smokey Glass**.

Now you have set the theme properties. You will modify the master title text style to be shadowed.

l. Select the text **Click to edit Master title style**, click the **FORMAT** tab, and then in the WordArt Styles group, click **Fill-Black, Text 1, Shadow**.

m. On the SLIDE MASTER tab, in the Background group, click **Background Styles**, and then select **Format Background**. Select **Gradient fill**, click the **Type** arrow, and then select **Shade from title**. Click **Apply to All**, and then close the Format Background pane.

n. Click **Save** [save icon].

SIDE NOTE
Format Background with a Picture
The Format Background pane also allows for pictures, textures, and patterns to be used as a background for one or all slides.

Customizing Slide Master Layouts

By default Master Slide view provides you with 11 different layouts that can be used in a presentation. You can edit or delete existing layouts or create new ones that fit the needs of the organization or presenter.

In the next few exercises you will further customize the template by deleting unnecessary layouts, editing the title layout, customizing the slide footers, and creating a new slide layout.

P04.02

To Customize Slide Master Layouts

a. Scroll to the bottom of the slide master layouts in the left pane, click **Vertical Title and Text Layout**, and then on the SLIDE MASTER tab, in the Edit Master group, click **Delete**.

The slide layout is removed and the previous slide (Title and Vertical Text Layout) in the pane is selected. You will delete this layout next.

SIDE NOTE
Deleting Slide Layouts
Alternatively you can select the slide layout you wish to delete and press Delete.

> **Troubleshooting**
> Point to the slide layout in the left pane to view the names of the layouts.

b. Press Delete to delete the **Title and Vertical Text Layout**. Continue deleting the following layouts:

- Picture with Caption Layout
- Content with Caption Layout
- Blank Layout
- Title Only Layout
- Comparison Layout
- Section Header Layout

This leaves four slides in the left pane: the Office Theme Slide Master, Title Slide Layout, Title and Content Layout, and Two Content Layout.

c. Click the **Office Theme Slide Master** thumbnail. Click the **slide number footer** placeholder on the right side of the slide, and then press Delete to delete the entire placeholder. Do this for all of the slide layouts.

d. Click the **Office Theme Slide Master** thumbnail. Click the **center footer**, click the **DRAWING TOOLS FORMAT** tab, and then in the Arrange group, type 5.0" in the Shape Width [icon] box. In the Arrange group, click **Align Objects**, and then select **Align Right**.

SIDE NOTE
Modifying Slide Footers
When working with footers in Slide Master view, you are setting up the formats not the actual footer text.

e. Click the **left footer**. In the Size group, type 4.5" in the Shape Width box. In the Arrange group, click **Align**, and then select **Align Left**.

f. Click the **Title Slide Layout** in the left pane. Click the title placeholder, and then on the DRAWING TOOLS FORMAT tab, in the WordArt Styles group, click the **Text Effects** arrow, point to **Reflection**, and then select **Tight Reflection, touching**.

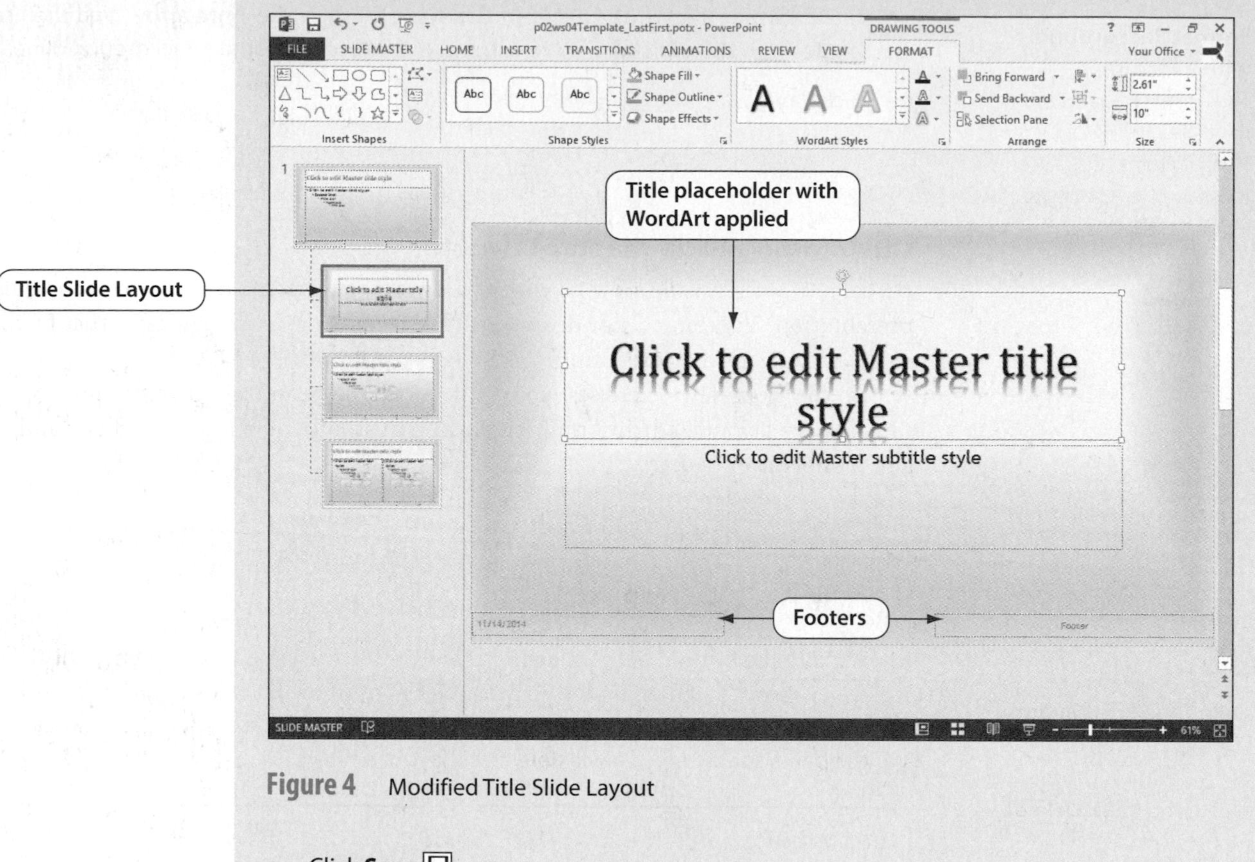

Figure 4 Modified Title Slide Layout

g. Click **Save**.

Adding a New Slide Layout

Just as slides can be added to regular slide shows, you can insert additional slide layouts into the template. You have decided to add a layout that will contain Irene's contact information, since you know that she always uses this type of slide in her presentations.

P04.03

To Add Slide Master Layouts

a. If necessary to view the master slide layout, click the **VIEW** tab, and then in the Master Views group, click **Slide Master**. On the SLIDE MASTER tab, in the Edit Master group, click **Insert Layout**.

b. In the Edit Master group, click **Rename**, select the **text** in the Rename Layout dialog box, and then type Contact Information. Click **Rename**.
The slide appears with just a title placeholder. You decide to create a similar shape object to hold the contact information.

c. Click the **INSERT** tab, and then in the Illustrations group, click **Shapes**. In the Rectangles group, select the **Round Diagonal Corner Rectangle**.

d. Drag a **large rectangle** shape under the title placeholder, and then make the following modifications to the shape:

- Click the **DRAWING TOOLS FORMAT** tab, and then in the Shape Styles group, click **More**, and then select **Subtle Effect - Dark Teal, Accent 1**.
- Click the **Shape Outline** arrow, and then select **No Outline**.
- Click the **Shape Effects** arrow, point to **Shadow**, and then in the **Outer** group, select **Offset Center**.
- In the Arrange group, click the **Send Backward** arrow, and then select **Send to Back**.
- In the **Size** group, type 4.7" in the Shape Height box and 11.5" in the Shape Width box. In the Arrange group, click **Align Objects**, and then click **Align Center**.

e. Click the **SLIDE MASTER** tab, and then in the Master Layout group, click the **Insert Placeholder** arrow, and then select **Text**. Drag a **rectangle** under the title placeholder that fills most of the rectangle shape.

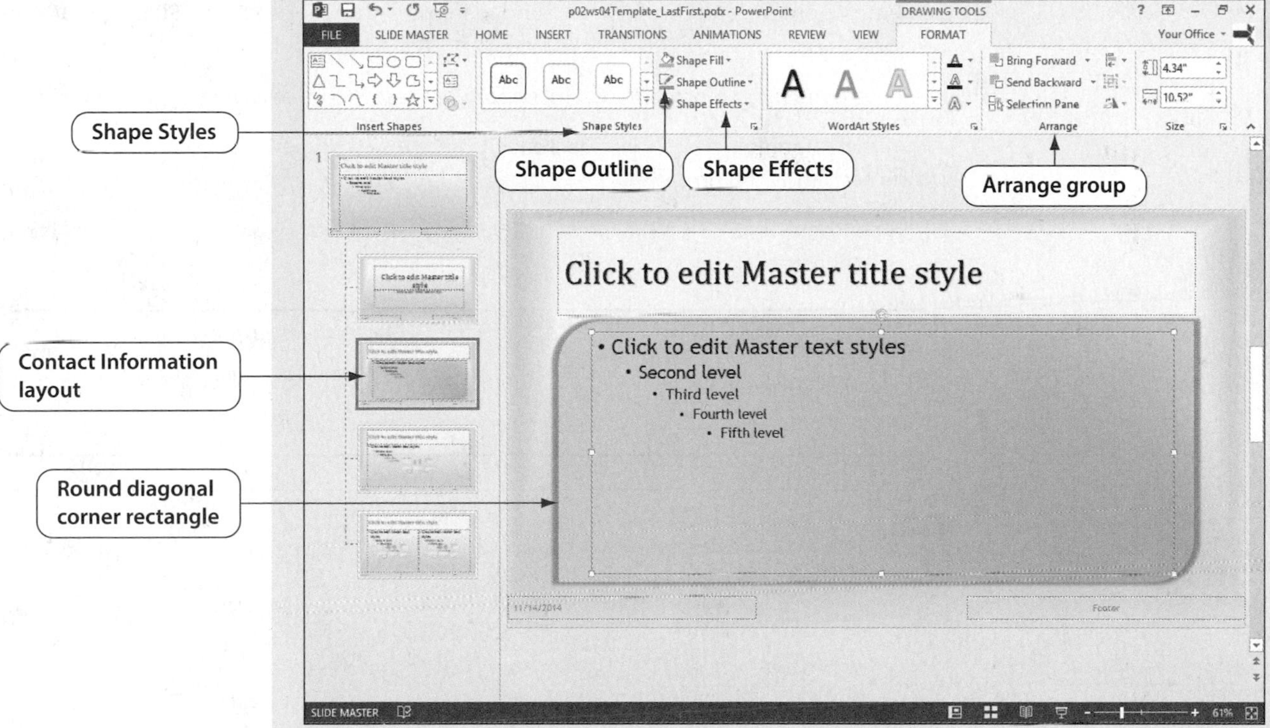

Figure 5 Contact Information layout

f. Click **Save**.

You may notice that your Contact Information layout is in a different place on the left pane than pictured above. It does not matter where this layout is shown, because you will apply the layouts to slides that are in the correct order.

Placing Text on the Slide

In some cases, the text that will appear on slides will be consistent between presentations. For instance, the template you have been working on will always be used by Irene Kai for presentations related to the spa. To save time, you can place and format text in the template that will always be displayed when the template is opened. It is important to note that this must be done with Slide Master view closed; otherwise, the text that you add will be placeholder text that will not be displayed on the slide.

You will add the name of the spa and the slogan to the title slide. You will make some minor adjustments to the fonts.

P04.04

To Add Text to a Slide Layout

a. Click the **SLIDE MASTER** tab, and then in the Close group, click **Close Master View**.

b. Click the title placeholder text on **Slide 1**, and then type Turquoise Oasis Spa. Select the **text** you just typed, and then click **Increase Font Size** [A] twice, to increase the font size to **72**.

c. Click the subtitle placeholder text, press [Enter] to create more space below the title, and then type A Passion for Relaxation. Select the **text** you just typed, and then click **Italic** [I].

d. Click the **HOME** tab, in the Slides group, click the **New Slide** arrow, and then select **Contact Information**. Click the title placeholder, and then type Contact Information.

e. Click the **text** placeholder, press [Backspace] to remove the bullet point, and then type Irene Kai, Spa Manager. Press [Enter]. In the Paragraph group, click **Bullets** [☰▾].

f. Type Appointments, press [Enter], and then press [Tab]. Type Phone: 505 555-7329 and then press [Enter].

g. Type E-mail: appointments@paintedparadiseresort.com and then press [Enter].

h. In the Paragraph group, click **Decrease List Level** [⇤], type Questions/Concerns, press [Enter], and then press [Tab].

i. Type Phone: 505 555-7328, press [Enter], type E-mail: ikai@paintedparadiseresort.com and then press [Enter].

> **Troubleshooting**
>
> If the appointments e-mail address is on a line by itself, click after the word "E-mail" and press [Shift]+[Enter].

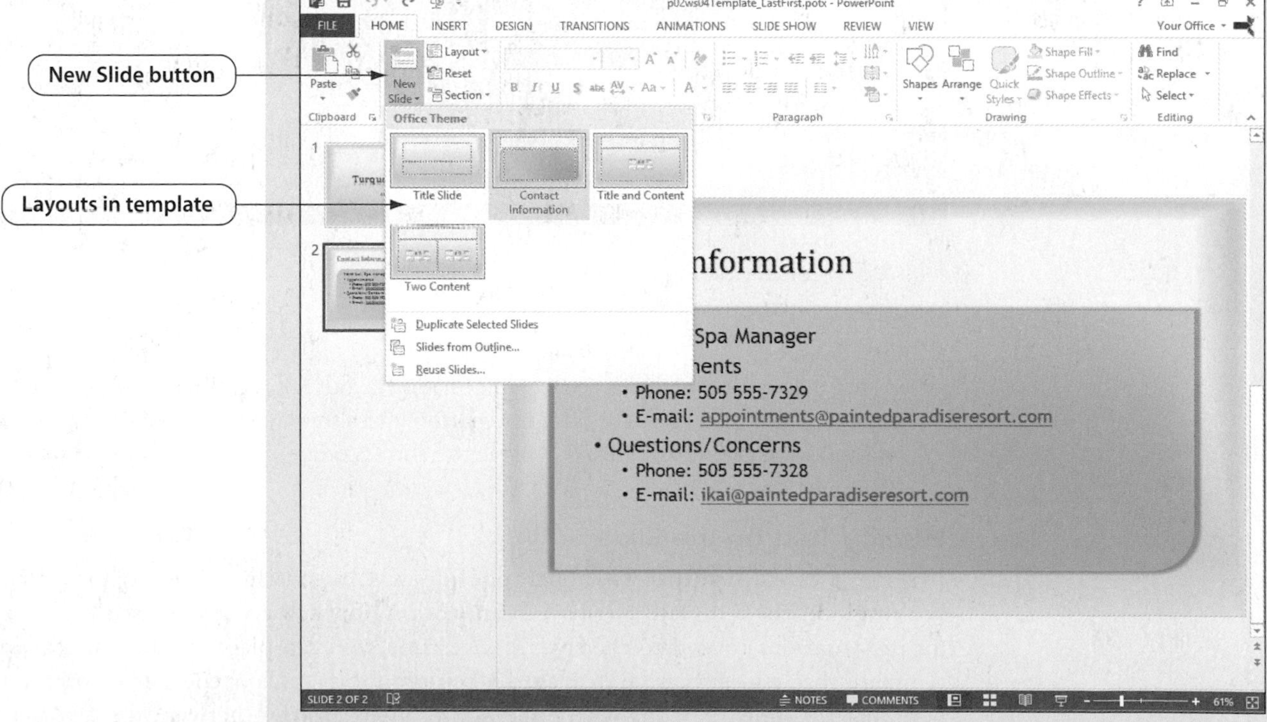

Figure 6 Contact Information layout with text

j. Click **Save** [💾].

MODULE 2

When creating PowerPoint templates, you must remember to close Slide Master view before finalizing any changes made to the template and closing PowerPoint. If you open a .potx template file by double-clicking the file name, PowerPoint will create a new Presentation with the template applied. If you need to make any changes to the template itself, then you will need to Save As a .potx file type and replace the previous version. If you use the Open command within PowerPoint, or click the file name in the Recent files list, it will open as a .potx file.

Customize the Notes Master

Many corporations, businesses, and organizations have guidelines for materials that are printed. They may require things such as a copyright notice or privacy statement. Others will expect you to use a standard format for all documents. The speaker notes can be customized so certain things will appear on the printed document in the **notes master**. The notes master determines the layout of elements, such as the slide thumbnail and note placeholder, on the speaker notes pages.

By default, the notes printed from PowerPoint contain headers and footers. They include a space for a customized header, along with the current date at the top of the page, a space for a customized footer, and the page number at the bottom. The default items can be removed from the notes or modified in placement and text. A graphic of the slide appears above the notes in standard layout, but that can be modified as needed. The size of the text can be increased or decreased, and fonts can be edited on the notes pages.

Modifying Headers and Footers

You modify the headers and footers through the View tab, using Notes Master view. Using Notes Master view, you have access to the other tabs within PowerPoint so you can modify fonts, for example.

You will modify the header and footer on the notes master to customize the areas for the Turquoise Oasis Spa. You will do this on the template, so the customization is available in each presentation that Irene creates using the template. Later you will apply the template to the presentation in order to update it.

P04.05

To Customize the Notes Master Header and Footer

a. Click the **VIEW** tab, and then in the Master Views group, click **Notes Master**.

b. Click the **Header** box, type Turquoise Oasis Spa and then press Enter. Type Irene Kai, manager.

c. Click the **Footer** box, and then type Confidential, All Rights Reserved. Type a space, and then type the current year. Select the **footer text**, click the **HOME** tab, and then in the Font group, click the **Font Size** arrow 20, and then change the font size to **14**.

d. Click in front of the **page number** symbol in the bottom-right placeholder, and then type Slide. Leave a blank space in between the word and the page number symbol. Select the **text** in the slide number footer, and then change the font size to **24**.

This footer will print the number of the slide. The larger font will enable Irene to more easily keep track of where she is in the presentation.

NOTES MASTER tab

Headers

Footer

Slide number footer

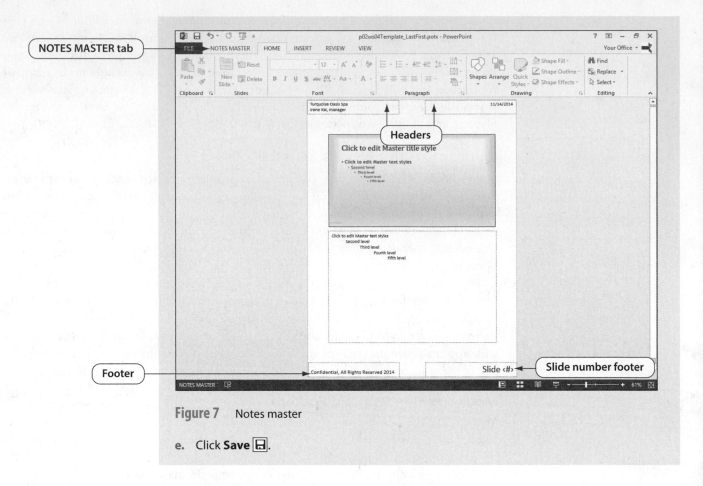

Figure 7 Notes master

e. Click **Save**.

Modifying Slide and Notes Placeholders

Many people do not realize that you can change the slide image and the notes placeholder of the notes page. If you make the image smaller, there is more room for notes. You can also change the font size in the notes placeholder, so the text is easier to read as a presenter. If you like your pages in landscape orientation, you can change the orientation on the notes master.

P04.06

To Customize the Notes Master Layout and Notes Placeholders

a. Click the **NOTES MASTER** tab, and then in the Page Setup group, click **Notes Page Orientation** arrow, and then select **Landscape**.

b. Click the **slide image**. Click the **DRAWING TOOLS FORMAT** tab, and then in the Size group, in the Shape Height box, type 2.2.

c. In the Arrange group, click **Align**, and then select **Align Left**.

d. Click the **border** of the notes placeholder, and then drag the **center-top sizing handle** up to just below the slide image. In the Arrange group, click **Align**, and then select **Align Left**. Drag the **center-right sizing handle** to the right to expand the notes placeholder to the right edge of the slide.

e. Select **all the text** in the notes placeholder, and then increase the font size to **16** to make reading the notes easier.

f. Click the **INSERT** tab, and then in the Illustrations group, click **Shapes**, and in the Lines group, click **Line**. Hold Shift, and then drag a horizontal line to the right of the slide image that ends near the right edge of the notes page.

MODULE 2

- Right-click the **line**, and then select **Copy**. Right-click the **line**, and then under Paste Options, select **Use Destination Theme** . Paste the line four times so there are a total of five lines.
- If necessary, drag the **lines** onto the page, and then place them roughly next to the slide image, spaced equally apart from each other.
- Select all of the **lines**. Click the **DRAWING TOOLS FORMAT** tab, and then in the Arrange group, click **Align**, and then select **Distribute Vertically**.
- Click **Align** again, and then select **Align Right**.

These lines will be used for last minute notes that Irene might want to write on the printouts. She may want to note the name of the contact person for the presentation or list pertinent information that she wants to work into the presentation. For instance, she may talk to someone in the audience prior to the presentation and want to include his or her name and a short story about that person.

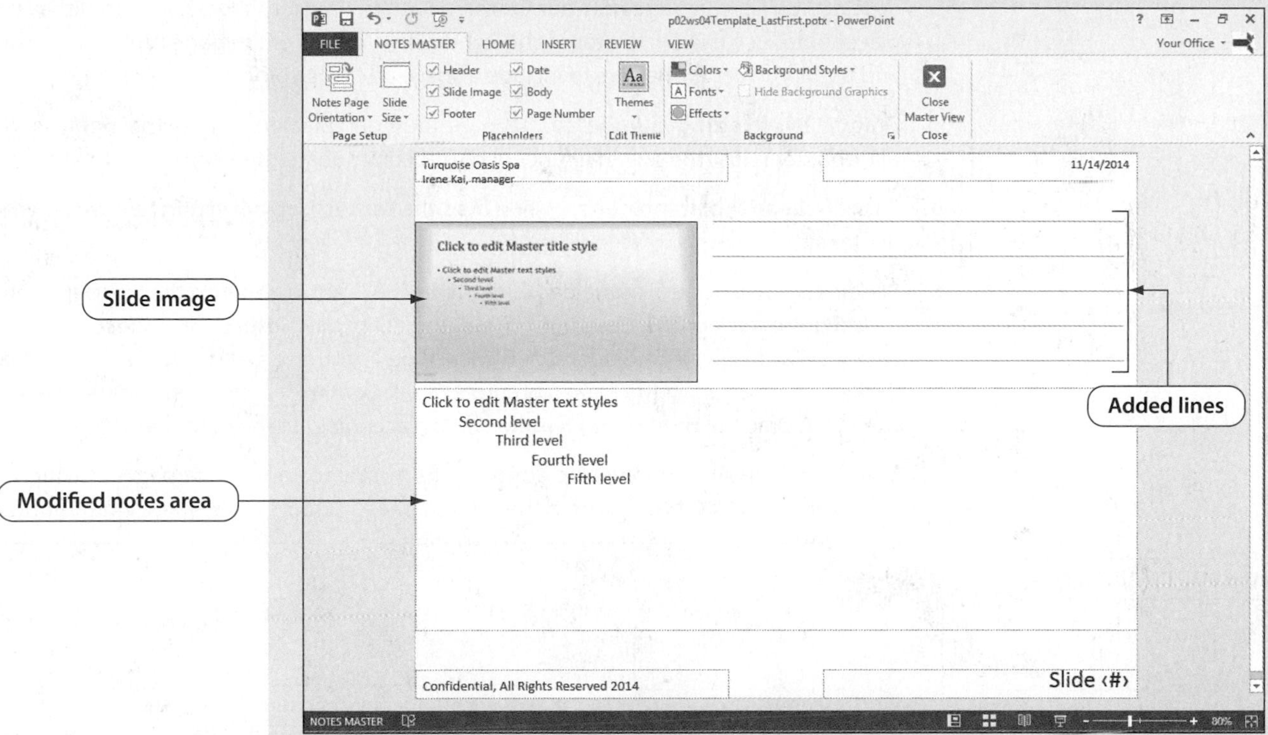

Figure 8 Modifying notes placeholders

g. Click the **NOTES MASTER** tab, and then in the Close group, click **Close Master View**, and then click **Save** .

Customize the Handout Master

Just as you can customize the notes master, you can make changes to the **handout master**, which determines the layout of elements, such as the header and footer, on the handout pages. In this case, the corporate office may be even more vigilant about changing the printouts as these are handed directly to audience members.

Handouts pages are good places to list contact and company information. You might also be required to place a copyright notice on the page. Using Handout Master view you can specify whether the handouts will be printed in portrait or landscape orientation. It is interesting to note that you cannot move or modify the slide placeholders in a handout master.

Modifying the Headers and Footers

You will add Irene's contact information to the header and place a standard copyright notice on the handouts. You will also move the page number to the top of the slide and include the word "Page" next to it. You will remove the date placeholder.

P04.07

To Customize the Handout Master Headers and Footers

a. Click the **VIEW** tab, and then in the Master Views group, click **Handout Master**.

b. Click the **Header** placeholder, type Irene Kai, Turquoise Oasis Spa, and then press Enter. Type ikai@paintedparadiseresort.com. Select the **header text**. Click the **HOME** tab, and then in the Font group, click the **Font** arrow Trebuchet MS (Headings), select **Trebuchet MS**, click the **Font Size** arrow 20, and then select **14**.

c. Click the **HANDOUT MASTER** tab, and then in the Placeholders group, click **Date** to deselect it. Click the **page number footer**, and then drag it to the position that the Date placeholder occupied in the top-right corner. Click in front of the **page number symbol**, and then type Page: . Be sure to include a space after the colon.

d. Drag the **left sizing handle** of the page number placeholder to the right so the placeholder is just the size that is needed to accommodate the text.

e. Click the **header** placeholder, and then drag the **center-bottom sizing handle** down so the text fits within the placeholder.

f. Click inside the **Footer** placeholder. Click the **INSERT** tab, and then in the Symbols group, click **Symbol**, select the **Copyright Sign**, and then click **Insert**. Click **Close**. Type the current year followed by a space, and then type Turquoise Oasis Spa. Select the **text**. Click the **HOME** tab, in the Paragraph group, click **Center**, and then increase the font size to **14**. Drag the **right sizing handle** of the placeholder to the right side of the page.

g. Move the footer placeholder up about .5" from the bottom of the page. Moving the footer up will allow it to fit within the default page margins of the page when printed.

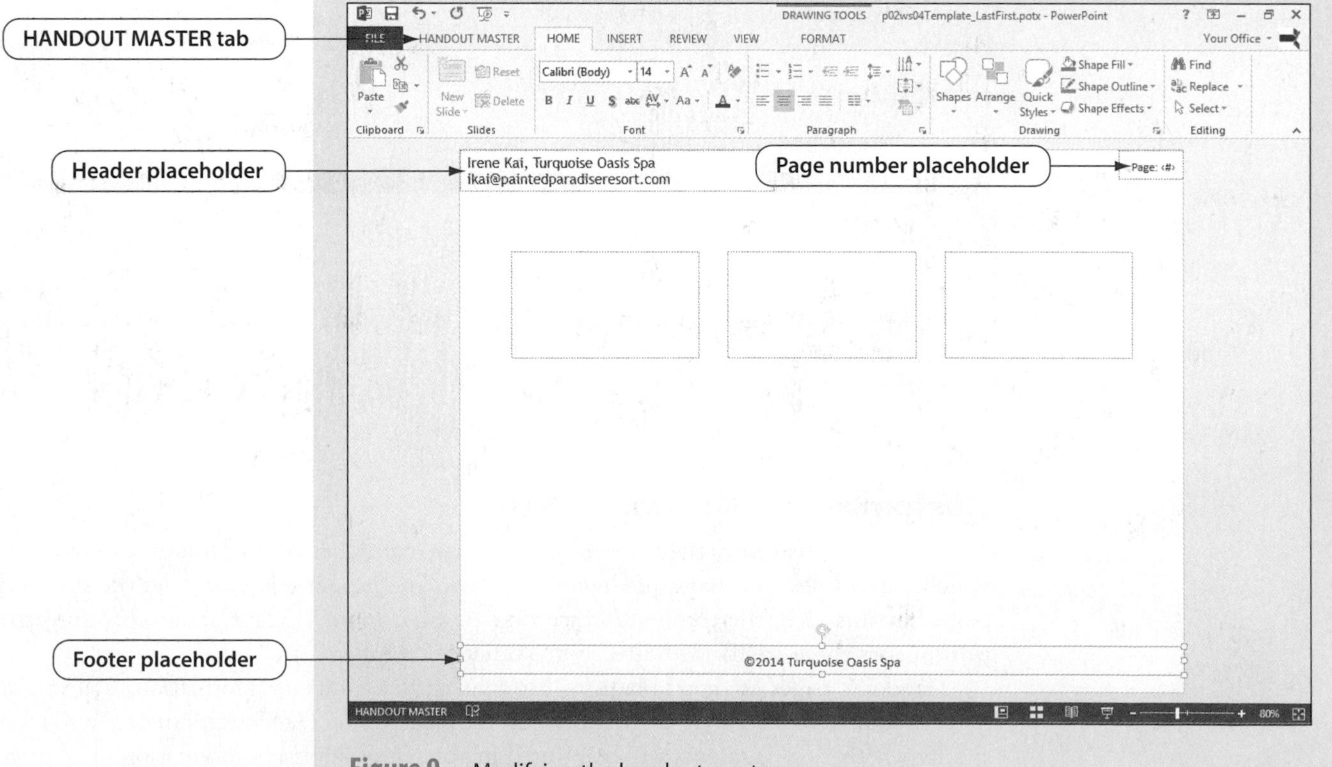

Figure 9 Modifying the handout master

h. Click the **HANDOUT MASTER** tab, and then in the Page Setup group, click **Slides Per Page**, and then click each of the **slide numbers** to review each of the layouts and make sure that none of the header or footer text conflicts with the slides. After confirming that the header and footer text does not conflict with any of the layouts change the Slides Per Page to 6 Slides.

i. Click **Save**.

Setting Up the Page

Some people prefer to see handout pages in a landscape orientation, while others prefer portrait. You can change the orientation of the pages as well as the slide images. Since PowerPoint 2013 has been optimized for wide screen monitors and tablets, slides are typically displayed in a 16:9 ratio, making them wider than they are tall. For this reason, you will generally display the slides in landscape orientation to avoid distorting them. Selecting a portrait or landscape handout orientation makes no difference in the size or shape of the slide images, so it becomes a matter of personal preference.

REAL WORLD ADVICE | **Printing Handouts**

When using handouts for your presentation, it is important to have a good idea of how they will supplement your message. Of course, you want to print handouts that are valuable tools for the audience, and you probably want to avoid printing those that do not contribute information. This helps you to be more environmentally conscious because you are not using printing resources, such as paper and ink, for unnecessary handouts. You should also consider when to distribute the handouts. Do you want the audience members to use them for supplemental notes during your presentation? Are you distracted by people turning the pages or rustling the paper? There are many considerations you should make before printing handouts.

In this exercise you will print a sample handouts and notes page using the two slides that were added to the template.

To Print Handouts and Notes

a. Click the **HANDOUT MASTER** tab, and then in the Close group, click **Close Master View**.

b. Click the **FILE** tab, click **Print**, and then click **Full Page Slides**. In the Handouts group, click **2 Slides**.

c. Review the preview of the handout page, and then click **Print** if your instructor requests a copy of the printout.

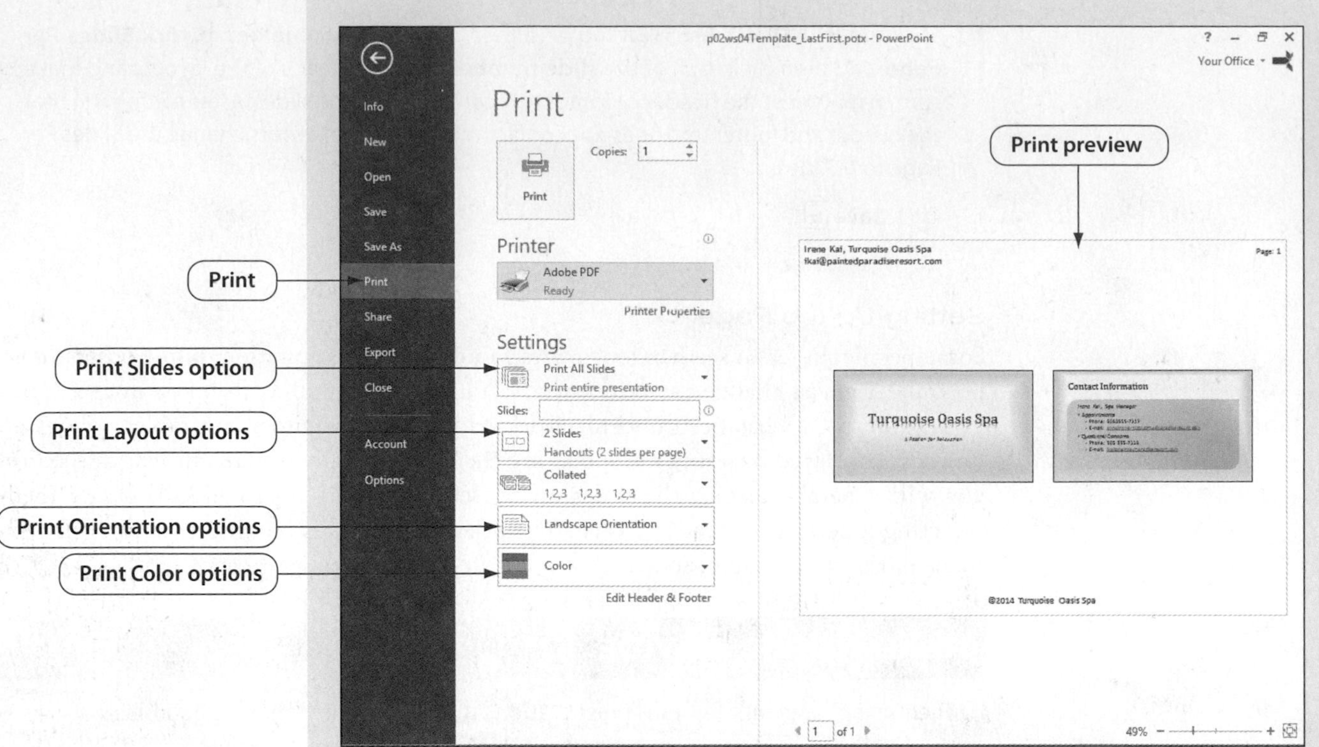

Figure 10 Printing handouts

d. If you printed the handouts in Step c, click the **FILE** tab if necessary, and then click **Print**.

e. Click **2 Slides**, and then in the Print Layout group, click **Notes Pages**. Click the **Next Page** and **Previous Page** arrows at the bottom of the Preview pane to review the Notes Pages print layout. Click **Print** if your instructor requests a copy of the printout.

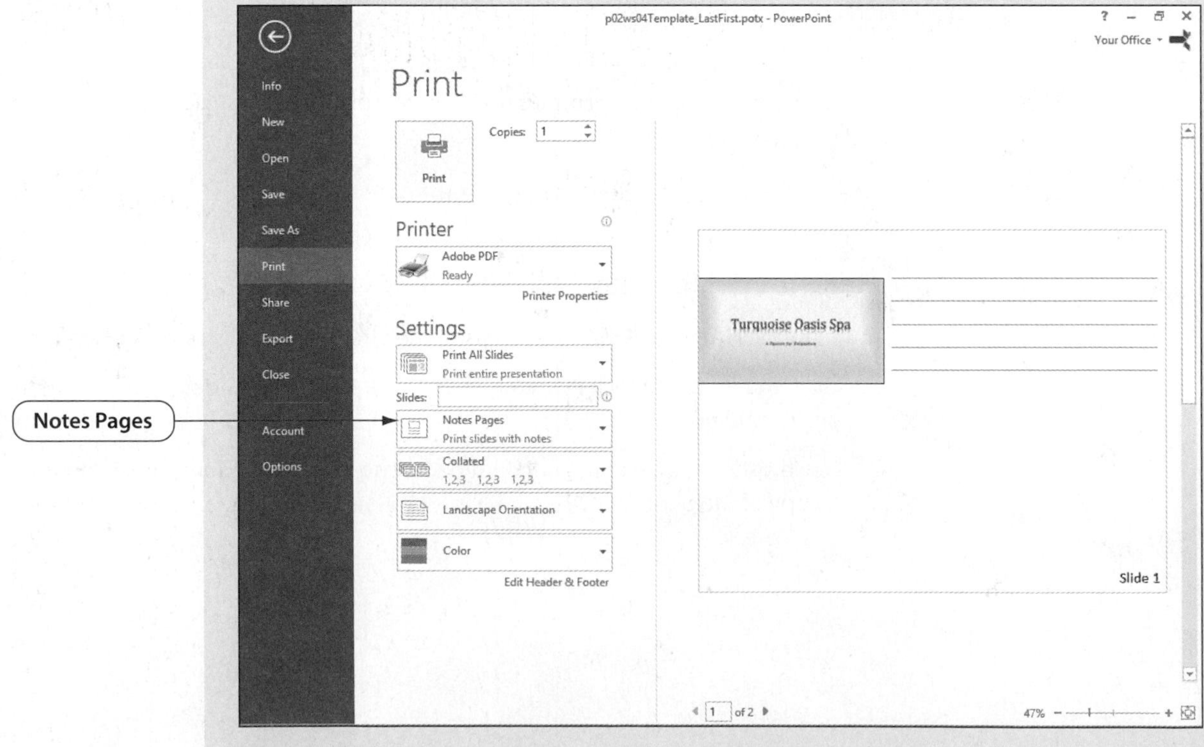

Figure 11 Printing notes

f. Click **Save** [icon].

g. **Close** [X] PowerPoint.

Develop a Presentation from a Custom Template and an Outline

Custom templates are accessed in the same way that you use other templates. Begin a new PowerPoint presentation, and select the template. As you add slides, the layouts that are a part of the template are available on the Home tab.

Sometimes it is more convenient to add content to a slide show by importing it from a file created in another application such as Word or Notepad as opposed to starting from scratch. If the outline was created using heading styles, the slides will be created with the hierarchy of data reflected in the outline. If the outline does not have heading styles applied, each item on the outline will appear on a different slide. Content created on the Outline tab of Word flows into the PowerPoint slides very well.

Using a Custom Template

In this exercise, you will create a new presentation using the spa template.

P04.09

To Create a Presentation Based on a Template

a. Navigate to the location where your project files are stored, and then open **p02ws04Template_LastFirst**. PowerPoint opens the file as a new presentation using the template.

b. Click the **FILE** tab, click **Save As**, and then navigate to the location where you are storing your project files. Type p02ws04Presentation_LastFirst as the file name using your last and first name, and then click **Save**.

Importing an Outline into a Presentation

Irene created an outline in Word that she would like for you to include in the presentation. You will import the outline and set the layout for each slide. You will make modifications to the imported text to improve the consistency with the PowerPoint presentation.

P04.10

To Import a Word Outline

a. On **Slide 1**, on the HOME tab, in the Slides group, click the **New Slide** arrow, and then select **Slides from Outline**.

b. Navigate to the location of your student data files, click **p02ws04Outline**, and then click **Insert**.

The slides flow into the presentation but do not have the same corporate branding that the spa is looking to incorporate into the presentations. Since the slides were imported from an external source, layouts and font colors are not applied.

SIDE NOTE

Outlines in Different Formats

Outline file formats suitable for importing into a PowerPoint presentation include .docx, .txt, .rtf, and others.

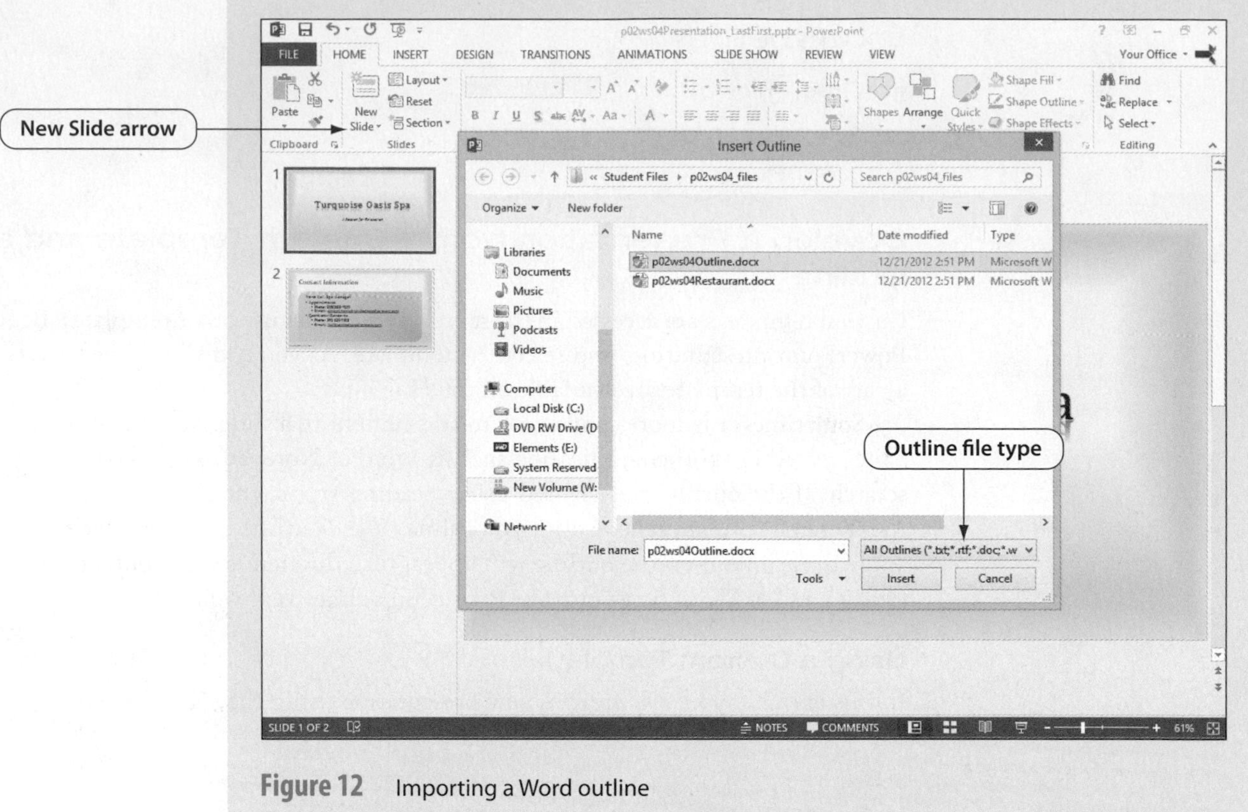

Figure 12 Importing a Word outline

c. Select **Slides 2** through **10**, and then in the **Slides** group, click **Reset**. This restores all the imported fonts, font styles, and font colors on the selected slides to the default settings of the template.

d. Click **Slide 8**, click inside the **text** placeholder, and then on the HOME tab, in the Paragraph group, click **Bullets** to remove the bullet from the quotation.

e. Click **Slide 9**, click inside the **text** placeholder, and on the HOME tab, in the Paragraph group, click **Bullets** to remove the bullet from the quotation.

f. Click **Save**.

Use Slide Sections and Proofing Tools to Organize and Prepare a Presentation

Slide sections are organizational tools for use on the Slides tab. You can place section titles between groups of slides and then collapse or expand the sections. This means that you can see sections you want to work with, while minimizing sections you do not need to see. This is very beneficial on large slide shows, saving you time as you search for a slide.

Proofing documents, especially for spelling, is one of the most important final steps in the preparation of your presentation. Small errors look a whole lot worse when displayed on a giant screen. PowerPoint provides three **proofing tools**: Spelling, Research, and Thesaurus.

Using Slide Sections

In this exercise you will assign sections to the slides and experiment with collapsing or expanding the sections.

P04.11

To Assign Slides to Sections

a. Click the gap between **Slide 2** and **Slide 3**. On the HOME tab, in the Slides group, click the **Section** arrow, and then select **Add Section**.

Notice the section was created and all subsequent slides 3–10 were placed in the section. You will now rename the section.

b. Click **Section**, and then select **Rename Section**. In the Rename Section dialog box, type Solutions as the Section name, and then click **Rename**.

c. Right-click between **Slide 5** and **Slide 6**, and then click **Add Section**. Right-click **Untitled Section**, select **Rename Section**, and then type Inspire Employees. Click **Rename**.

d. Right-click between **Slide 6** and **Slide 7**, and then click **Add Section**. Right-click **Untitled Section**, select **Rename Section**, and then type Financial Success. Click **Rename**.

e. Add a section entitled Feedback between **Slide 7** and **Slide 8**.

f. Add a section entitled Future between **Slide 9** and **Slide 10**.

g. Right-click the first section entitled **Default Section**, and then rename it Introduction.

h. In the Slides group, click the **Section** arrow, and then click **Collapse All**. Click **arrow** ▷ next to the Solutions section to expand it.

Notice that when the sections are collapsed, you see the section name along with the number of slides that belong to that section. With the section expanded, you see three slides in the Solutions section.

i. Click the ◢ next to the **Solutions** section to collapse it. Click the ▷ next to the **Feedback** section to expand it.

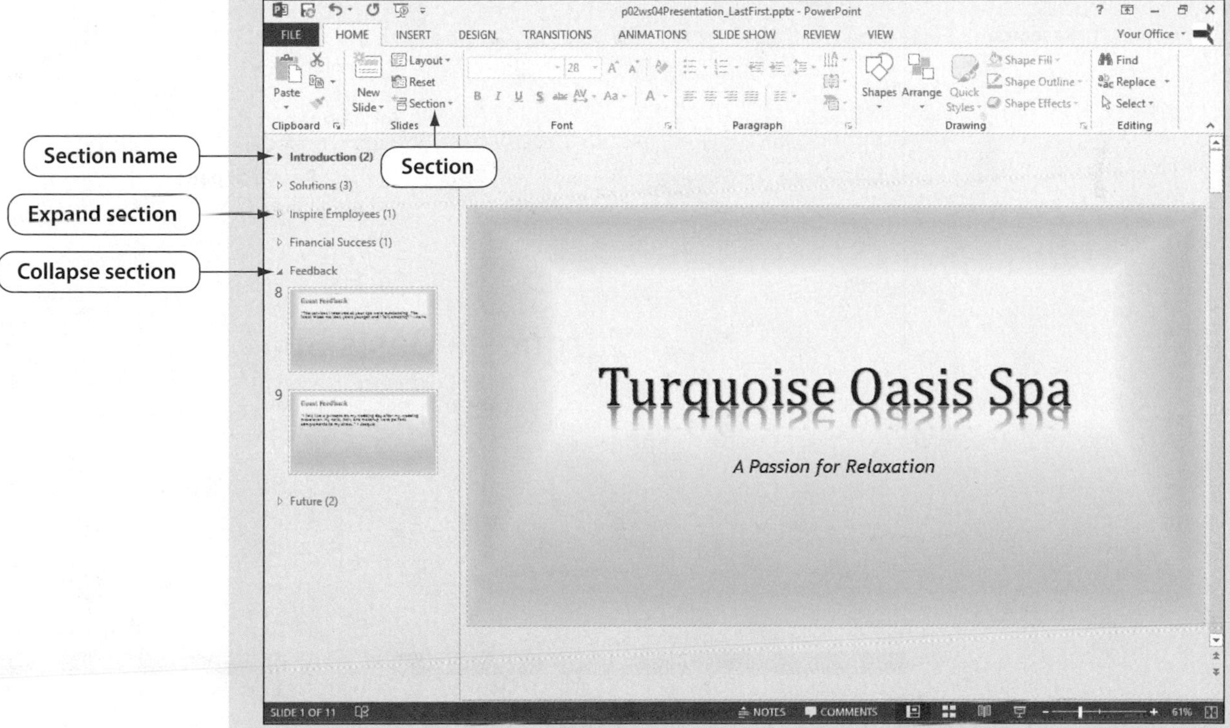

Figure 13 Slide sections

j. In the Slides group, click the **Section** arrow, and then click **Expand All**.

k. Click **Save** 🖫.

Using Proofing Tools

You are already aware of the interactive spelling checker—squiggly red lines under misspelled words that appear as you type on slides. However, some words that are flagged are spelled correctly. When you are completing the project, it is a good idea to use the spelling checker to check the entire document. Sometimes you miss the flag of the interactive spelling check, so a final run through will help you find any problems.

The Thesaurus pane provides you with alternative word choices. As you read each slide, think about whether you are using a particular word or phrase too much. Select the word in the content area, and click Thesaurus to display words with similar meanings.

The Research tool enables you to check facts and develop your ideas for the presentation. References available on the Research pane include the Encarta Dictionary; English, French, and Spanish Thesauruses; Internet research sites, such as Bing; and business and financial websites. For your project, you decide to research some ways to inspire employees, as outlined on Slide 6.

P04.12

To Use the Research Pane

a. Click the **REVIEW** tab, and then in the Proofing group, click **Research**.

b. In the Research pane, type Inspire Employees in the Search for box. Click the **arrow** next to the word Bing, and then select **All Research Sites**.

A large number of results are returned that contain the words "Inspire Employees". You will view one site to get some ideas.

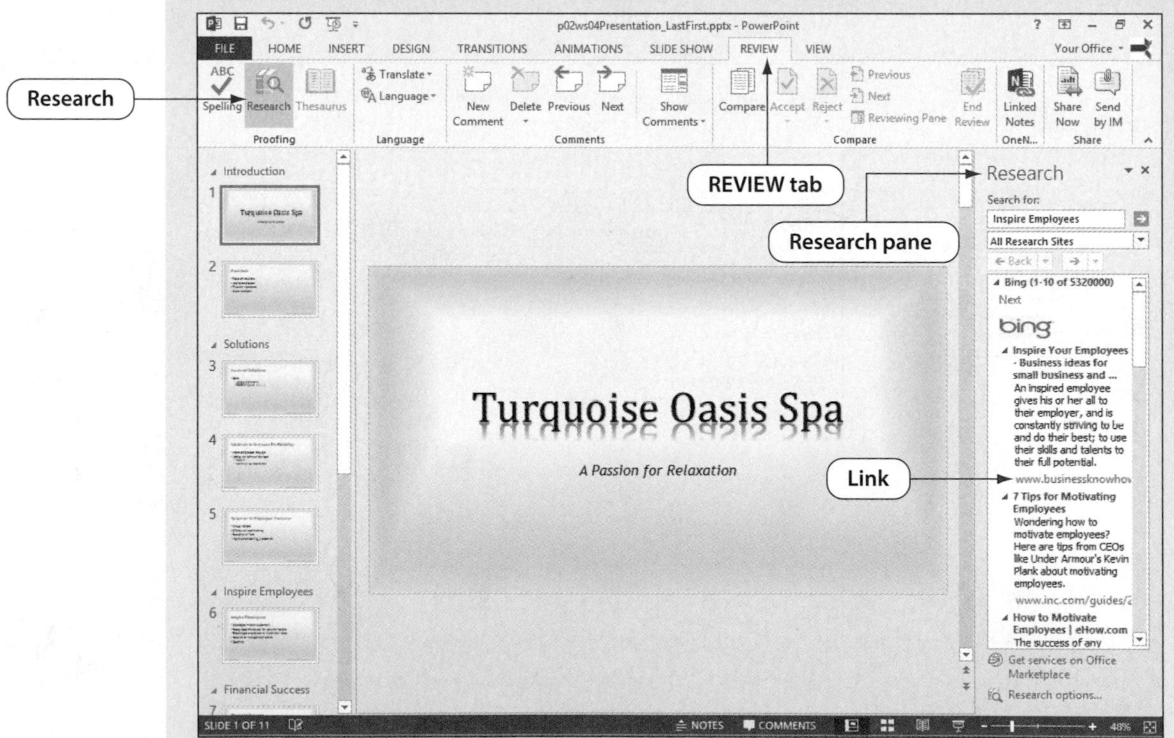

Figure 14 Using the Research pane

c. Click the **link** for the first site listed in the results. Review the information, and then **close** the browser window.

d. **Close** the Research pane, and then click **Save**.

Collaborating and Presenting

In business, collaborating effectively with your coworkers is a valuable skill. Microsoft provides many methods for collaboration through its Office applications and SkyDrive. With Microsoft's SkyDrive and PowerPoint Web App you can share your presentation and collaborate with anyone on virtually any device even if he or she does not have PowerPoint installed. With the PowerPoint application itself you can add comments to explain to the others your thoughts on a particular topic and even keep track of changes that others have made or suggested. The comments are not displayed during the Slide Show. In this section, you will learn to use comments effectively.

MODULE 2

CONSIDER THIS | Working in a Team

Teamwork is common in today's corporate world. You may collaborate on a presentation as a team member. What challenges would you anticipate while working on a presentation in a team? How could you overcome those challenges?

REAL WORLD ADVICE | Restrict Access

Sharing your presentation with others from a shared folder can lead to unauthorized changes made to your presentation. It is a good idea to use the PowerPoint Restrict Access feature. It is located on the File tab, in the Info section, under Protect Presentation. To use this feature, your computer will need to be set up for Information Rights Management though Microsoft Office.

Create Comments

Comments are short notes explaining your thoughts. They appear in comment boxes that look like speech callouts you might see near a person's mouth in a comic strip. When the speech callout icon is clicked, a Comments pane is displayed, showing the names of the commenters along with their messages, when the comment was made, and possibly their photo if they were logged in to a Microsoft Account.

In this exercise, you will add comments to the presentation, asking Irene for some additional content.

P04.13

To Add Comments to a Presentation

a. Click **Slide 2**. Click the **REVIEW** tab, and then in the Comments group, click **New Comment**, type This slide could use a nice photograph of some of your employees and then press Enter.

   Notice that below your comment is a section for Reply. In PowerPoint 2013 the comments have been redesigned so they mimic a conversation and are not just isolated comments.

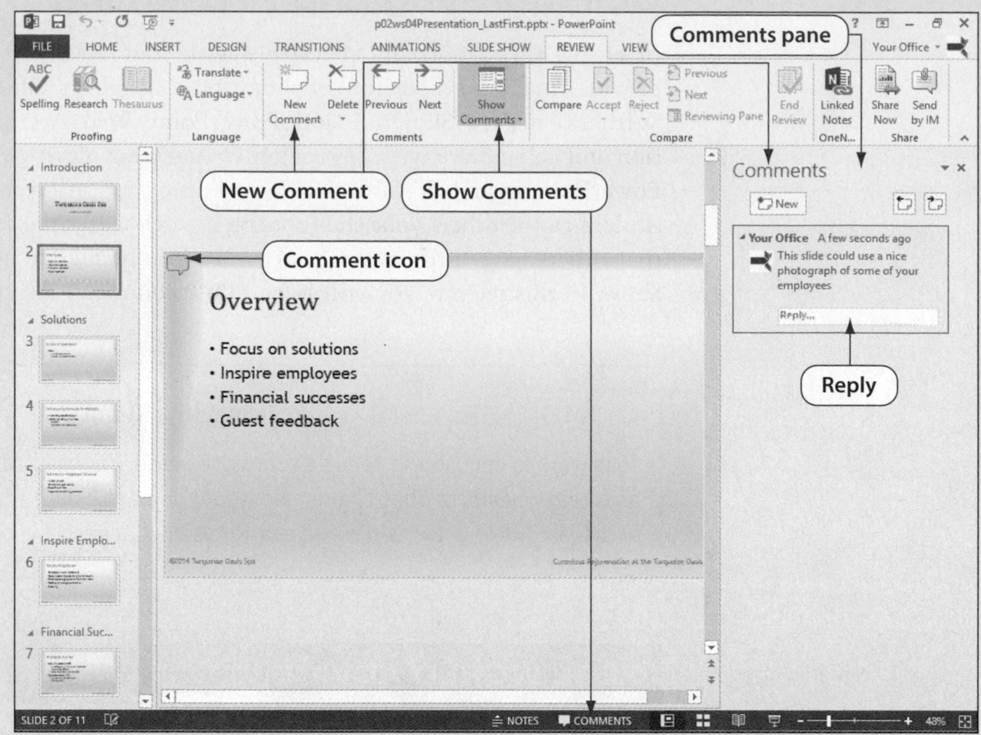

Figure 15 Creating comments

b. Click **Slide 9**, and then in the Comments group, click **New Comment**. Type Irene, can we get a photograph from Jacquie's wedding? Close the Comments pane. You will update the presentation to include the actual footer text before sending the presentation to Irene.

c. Click the **INSERT** tab, and then in the Text group, click **Header & Footer**. Click the **Date and time** check box to select it, and then click **Fixed**. You will replace the contents of this box. Type the current year followed by a space. Continue by typing Turquoise Oasis Spa. Click the **Footer** to select it, and then type Conscious Rejuvenation at the Turquoise Oasis Spa. Click **Don't show on title slide** to select it, and then click **Apply to All**.

   You may have noticed that you cannot access the symbols while viewing the Header & Footer dialog box. You will modify the footer, return to the Header & Footer dialog box, and then apply the modification to all slides.

d. Click in front of the year on the footer. On the INSERT tab, in the Symbols group, click **Symbol**, and then click the **copyright symbol**—character code **00A9** in the normal text font. Click **Insert**, click **Close**, and then click **Header & Footer** again. Notice the copyright symbol is now in front of the date in the footer in the dialog box. Click **Apply to All**.

e. **Save** and **close** the presentation.

Navigate Comments

When a file is returned to you with comments, the comment icons will appear on the slides. You can click each slide in the presentation and search for the icons, but this takes time. Instead, you can use the Comments group on the Review tab to move to the next comment or the previous comment. You can also edit comments and delete comments in this group.

You sent the file to Irene for her review. She sent it back to you with her comments. You will review the changes she made to the file and the comments she added.

P04.14

To View and Delete Comments

a. Start **PowerPoint**. On the Start screen, click **Open Other Presentations**. Navigate to the location of the student data files, click **p02ws04Comments**, and then click **Open**.

b. Click the **FILE** tab, and then click **Save As**. Navigate to the location of your project files, and then type p02ws04Update_LastFirst. Click **Save**.

The presentation that Irene has modified is displayed. She added some photographs, added new comments, and replied to some of yours.

c. Click the **REVIEW** tab, and then in the Comments group, click **Show Comments**.

The Comments pane opens to the right, and Irene's comment on Slide 1 is displayed.

SIDE NOTE

Showing Comments

Alternatively you can click COMMENTS in the status bar at the bottom to open the Comments pane.

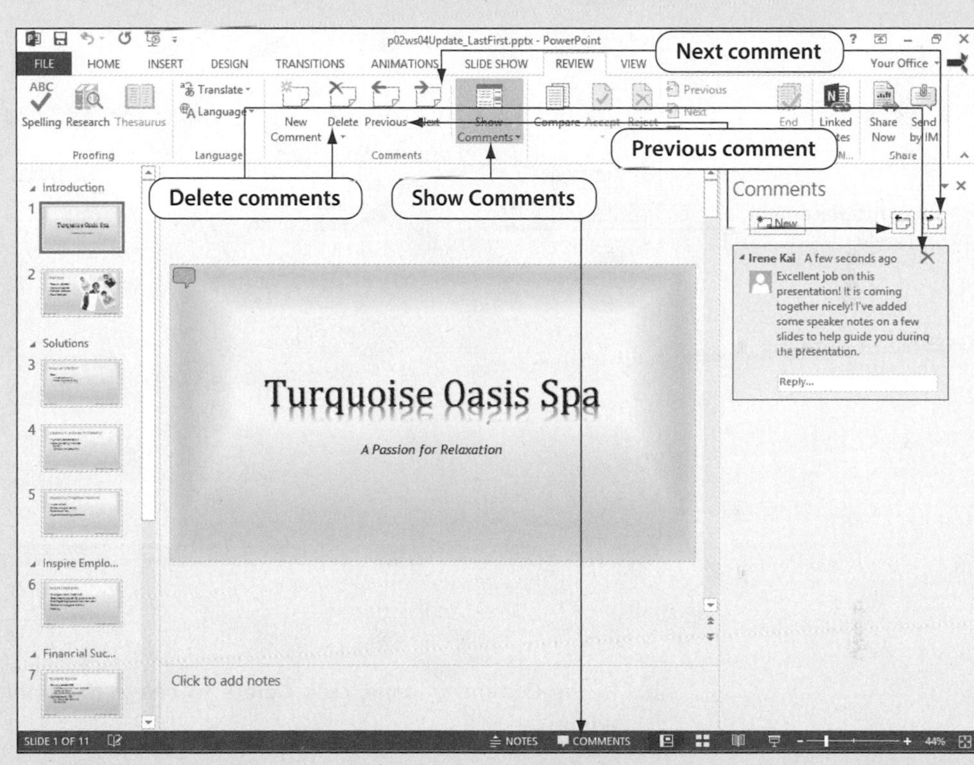

Figure 16 Reviewing comments

d. On the REVIEW tab, in the Comments group, click **Next** to view the next comment. Notice on Slide 2 Irene has replied to your comment.

e. Continue clicking **Next** to review the other comments.

f. Click **Slide 1**, in the Comments pane, click the **comment**. On the REVIEW tab, in the Comments group, click **Delete** to delete the comment. Click **Slide 2**, click the **comment**, and then click **Delete** to delete the comment thread since it has been addressed.

g. Click **Slide 3**, click the **INSERT** tab, and then in the Illustrations group, click **SmartArt**. Click **Relationship** on the left, click the **Opposing Arrows** SmartArt illustration, and then click **OK**.

- In the **top text** placeholder type Increase Profitability.
- Select the **text** you just typed, and then reduce the font size to **36**.
- Click the **bottom text** placeholder, and then type Reduce Employee Turnover.
- Select the **text** you just typed, and then reduce the font size to **36**.

- Delete the **bulleted list** behind the SmartArt illustration, and then delete the **text placeholder**.
- Click the **SmartArt illustration**, and then click the **SMARTART TOOLS DESIGN** tab. In the SmartArt Styles group, click the **Intense Effect**.
- Adjust the size of the **SmartArt** placeholder so it fits below the slide title.

You have finished the suggested changes made by Irene, so you will now delete all remaining comments.

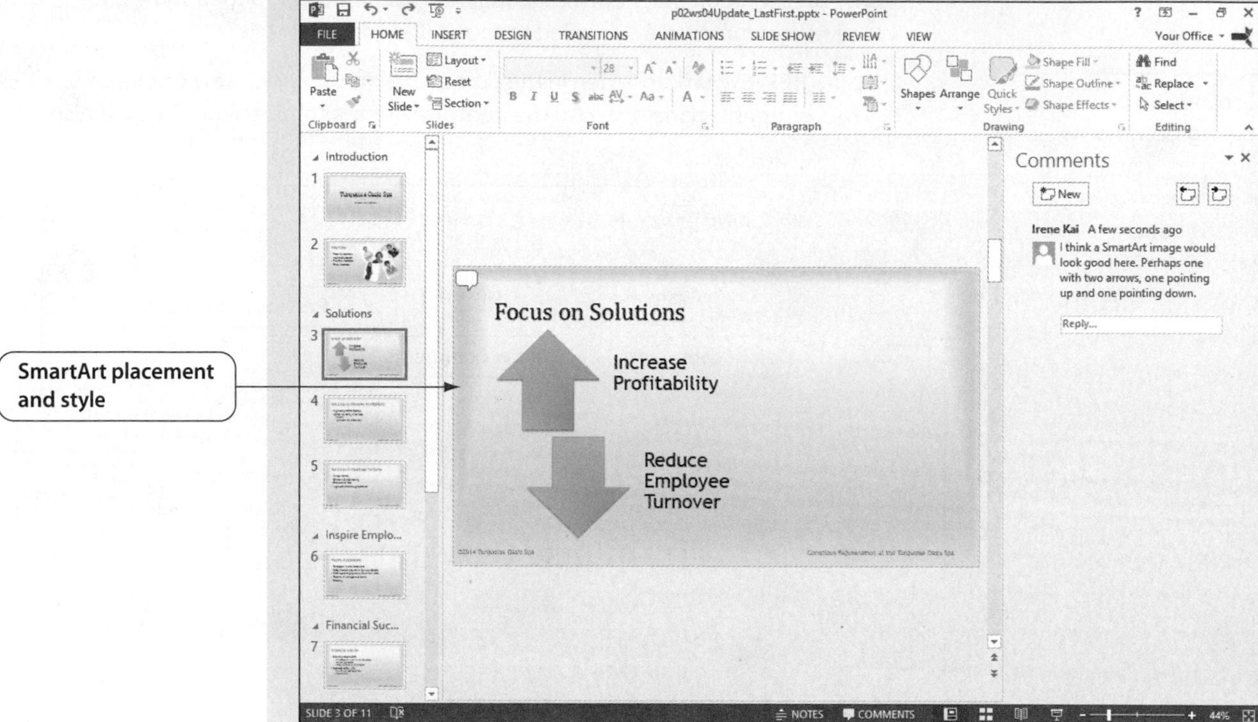

Figure 17 SmartArt illustration

h. In the Comments pane, click **Delete** to delete the comment since it has now been addressed.

i. Click **Slide 8**, and then in the Comments pane, click **Delete** to delete the comment.

j. Click **Slide 9**, and then in the Comments pane, click **Delete** to delete the comment thread.

k. **Close** the Comments pane, and then click **Save**.

Create and Use Speaker Notes

Speaker notes, displayed in the Notes pane of the PowerPoint window, enable you to write the words you will say during the presentation and store them with the actual presentation. You can later print the notes for reference during the presentation, or if you are using a dual display screen system, or are projecting your presentation, you can show the audience the slides, while you view the notes in Presenter view.

There are some tips you should consider while creating speaker notes. Avoid writing complete sentences. This will help keep you from reading word for word from the notes. Organize the notes with numbers or letters in outline format. Use the Export feature on the File tab to create handouts in Microsoft Word, in order to see notes on the side or below the slide pictures. Having a picture of the slide on the notes enables you to stay on track during the presentation. By converting the presentation file to Word, you can then modify the font size of the notes, making it larger and easier to read in a darkened room.

While Irene was reviewing the presentation and adding comments, she also added some speaker notes to a few of the slides. In this exercise you will create some additional speaker notes in the presentation. You will then create a Word document with the notes.

P04.15

To Add and Print Speaker Notes

a. Click **Slide 1**. Click **Notes** in the status bar, and then drag the **border** between the Slide pane and the Notes pane upward, so you have more room to type notes. The slide becomes smaller but is still clear enough for you to read.

b. Click the **Notes** pane, and then type Introduce yourself. Press Enter. Click the **HOME** tab, and then in the Paragraph group, click **Increase List Level**. Type Name and then press Enter. Type Spa Manager and then press Enter. Click **Decrease List Level**, and then type Quarterly report on the successes of the spa.

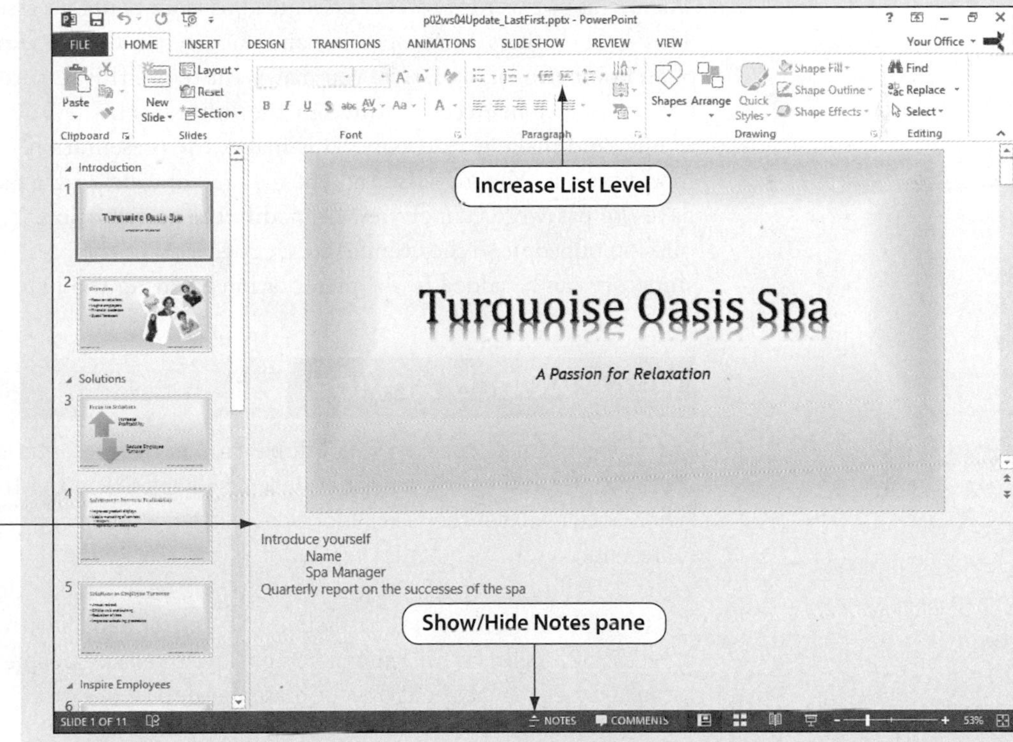

Figure 18 Speaker notes

c. Browse through the presentation, and then examine the notes on **Slides 3**, **5**, **7**, and **10**.

d. Continue adding speaker notes to the Notes pane of each slide noted below:

Slide 4	Product display makeover Mobile marketing extremely successful On low-booked days—increased walk-ins by 25%

Slide 6	Worked to develop the employees
	    Recognized
	    Encouraged
	    Offered hands-on management training
	    One-on-one coaching

e. **Save** the presentation, click the **FILE** tab, click **Export**, click **Create Handouts**, and then click **Create Handouts**.

f. Leave **Notes next to slides** selected, and then click **OK**. Click the **Word application** when it appears on the taskbar.

g. Select the **Notes** column in the Word document by clicking above the Slide 1 Notes column when the ↓ is displayed. On the HOME tab, in the Font group, click **Increase Font** once to make the notes easier to read.

h. Click **Save** in the Word document, browse to where you are saving your student files, type p02ws04Notes_LastFirst as the file name using your last and first name, and then click **Save**.

i. **Close** the Word document.

Mark Presentations as Final and Apply Password Protection

The use of passwords protects presentations from being accessed by unauthorized people. This keeps others from opening and modifying the documents. On a shared server, SharePoint site, or SkyDrive, you may want to use this feature when you have completed the presentation. Accessed through the Info tab on the File tab, you can mark the file as final and make it read-only. This makes the presentation viewable but does not allow modifications. You may also encrypt the presentation with a password. People who do not have the password cannot view or modify the presentation. You can also restrict the permission of people so they cannot edit, copy, or print the presentation. An invisible digital signature can be added to the presentation ensuring the integrity of the document.

REAL WORLD ADVICE **Before Marking a Presentation as Final**

It is important to consider who will be viewing the presentation and what version of PowerPoint they will be using. Under the File tab, on the Info tab, you will find options under the Check for Issues button. If people may be viewing your presentation with an earlier version of PowerPoint, you will want to check for any compatibility issues. If you will be publishing your presentation to the web you will also want to check for any accessibility issues for people with visual impairments. The Accessibility Checker will inform you of ways to ensure people with visual impairments can still get the most out of your presentation.

In this exercise you will protect the presentation with a password and then mark the presentation as final.

P04.16

To Encrypt a Presentation with a Password and Mark as Final

a. In the **p02ws04Update_LastFirst** presentation, click the **FILE** tab, click the **Info** tab, click **Protect Presentation**, and then click **Encrypt with Password**.

Notice the Caution message in the Encrypt Document dialog box. PowerPoint does not provide a password recovery system so if you lose your password you will not be able to access the presentation.

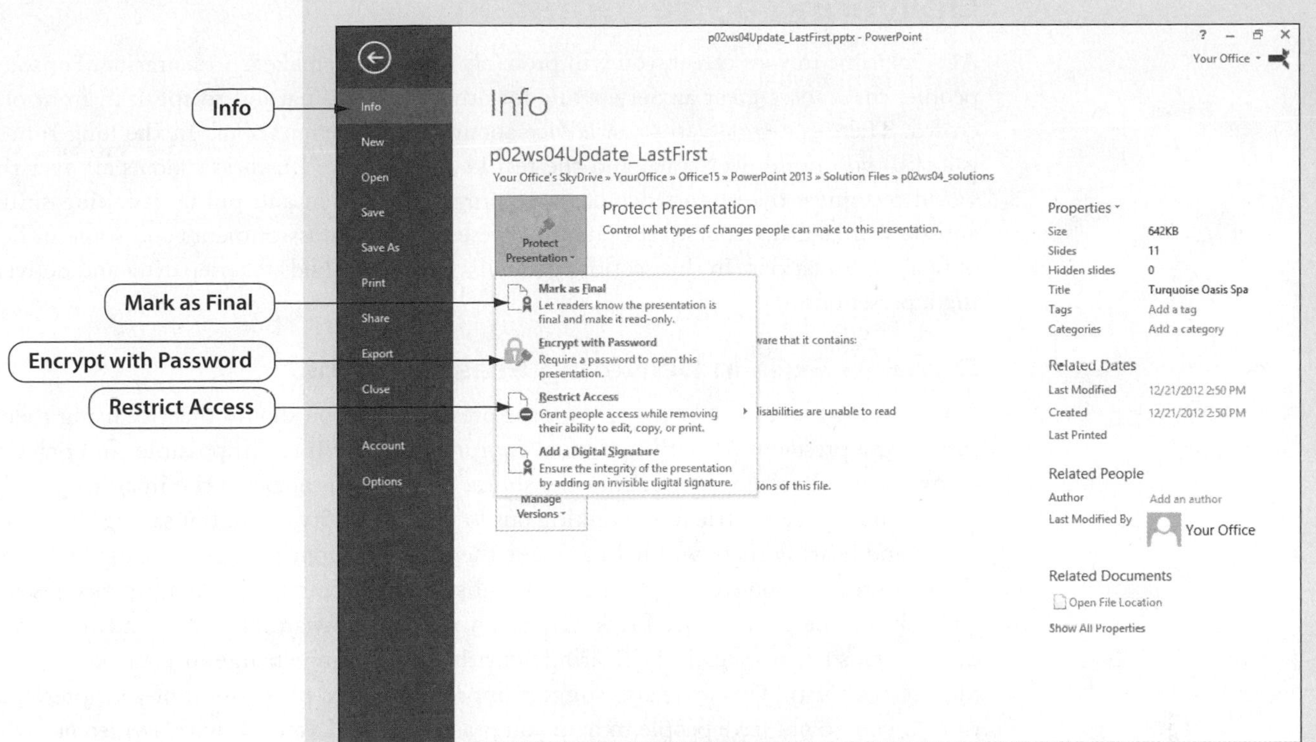

Figure 19 Protecting presentations

b. Type SpaPresentation for the password, and then click **OK**. Type the same password again to confirm, and then click **OK**.

c. Click the **arrow** on the Start screen to return to the presentation. **Save** and **Close** the presentation.

d. Double-click the **p02ws04Update_LastFirst** presentation file to open it. Type SpaPresentation as the password, and then click **OK**.

   The presentation opens, and you can make edits to the slides. You will need to share the password with anyone who will be editing, viewing, or presenting the presentation.

e. Click the **REVIEW** tab, and then in the Proofing section, click **Spelling** to check the spelling before marking the presentation as final. Ignore any names that the spelling checker marks as misspelled and correct any typos.

> SIDE NOTE
> **Spelling Checker**
> The spelling checker will check for incorrectly spelled words in the presentation, SmartArt figures, and speaker notes.

f. Click the **FILE** tab, click the **Info** tab, click **Protect Presentation**, and then click **Mark as Final**.

g. Read the warning message, and then click **OK**.

h. Read the information message that is displayed, and then click **OK**.

   Notice the yellow bar across the top of the window. Notice the Ribbon is not visible above the yellow bar. The file has been marked as final, but edits are still possible if someone ignores the warning and clicks Edit Anyway.

i. **Close** the presentation and exit **PowerPoint**.

Delivering a Presentation

At some time in your career, you will probably be asked to make a presentation. For some people, this causes great anxiety, while for others it seems natural to speak in front of a crowd. There is a wide variety of advice about giving presentations. In the long run, it is a skill you build over time, and the real key is practice. Business schools all over the world recognize the importance of developing presentation and public speaking skills, and they offer many courses that require presentations for assignments and some in lieu of final examinations. In this section, you will explore methods for preparing and delivering a presentation.

Develop Skills in Delivering Presentations

Once you have completed the slides for the presentation, you should practice using them. Project the presentation with the actual equipment you will use, if possible, and practice using the speaker notes, advancing the slides, and looking out into the imaginary audience. You may feel a little funny talking out loud to an empty room, but saying the actual words and hearing them will help to make them flow off your tongue more easily during the real presentation. It is a good idea to enlist a few people to watch a practice session and ask for their honest feedback. They can make you aware of verbal and nonverbal distracters, such as excessively clearing your throat, jingling change in your pocket, and talking too softly. They may also suggest improvements to the content of your presentation. If you do not have people to help you practice, record yourself with a video or audio recorder so you can review the practice session.

Overcoming Presentation Nervousness

Rest assured, even the most accomplished presenter occasionally suffers from presentation nervousness. Most people are nervous in the few minutes leading up to being introduced and in the minutes just after the presentation has begun. There are many things you can do to lessen the effects of the anxiety. Remember to breathe. Take full breaths, filling your lungs and breathing out through your mouth. Even during your presentation, taking a full breath gives you time to straighten out your thoughts, relax, and give the audience a little break. It is like adding white space to your presentation. Smile at your audience. Nod your head. Use hand gestures. These physical movements help to relax your body and reassure your mind that you are in control.

Remind yourself that you are prepared. You have your materials at hand. Your speech has been polished through practice. For the most part, audiences want you to succeed and will support you if you make a genuine effort.

REAL WORLD ADVICE **Memorizing Your Presentation**

You may have observed presenters who do not seem to have any notes at all. They may have given the speech so many times it comes to mind naturally, or they may have memorized what they want to say. There is a difference between memorizing the presentation and memorizing the outline. If you are comfortable with the material, memorizing the outline will not only help keep you on track during the presentation but also enable you to choose the actual language you use on the fly. If specific things need to be said during a presentation, then memorizing it is the best way to deliver all of the parts. This takes some time and practice to accomplish, and in some cases, the delivery may seem "canned."

Last minute changes or accidents add stress to the presentation. As you prepare, think about the possible problems and try to frame emergency actions. You will be ready for the unexpected if you have previously thought about it. If something unexpected does happen, evaluate whether you can do anything about it. If you can, do it. If you cannot, do not overreact to the situation. The audience may not even know that the widget you were supposed to hold up did not arrive on time or that you are wearing your travel clothes because your luggage went to a different city. Good presenters do not let internal or external forces ruin their presentations.

P04.17

To Review Speaking Fears

a. Open **PowerPoint 2013**, and then on the Start screen click **Blank Presentation.** On **Slide 1** in the title placeholder, type Presentation Delivery. In the subtitle placeholder, type your name.

b. Insert a **Title and Content slide** as **Slide 2**, in the title placeholder, type **Five Fears People Have** and then in the content placeholder list five fears that people might have about presenting in front of an audience.

c. Classify each of the fears as Internal or External.

d. Develop one or two methods of minimizing each of the fears.

e. Save the document where you are storing your project files with the file name p02ws04Delivery_LastFirst.

Being Prepared

From bandages to extension cords to multiple versions of your presentation saved on a USB flash drive, computer hard drive, SkyDrive, and CD/DVD, you can never be too prepared for a presentation. As discussed in the previous section, practice is the best way to arrive prepared for your speech. Arrive 15 minutes to an hour prior to the presentation. If at all possible, you should check the seating arrangements, lighting, audio equipment, handouts, laser pointers, and the projection equipment prior to the presentation. If you bring your own presentation equipment, make sure you have all of the cords to plug the projector into your computer and into the wall. Be sure you have the cord for the computer, even if you have a fully charged battery. You might need a long extension cord. It is a good idea to bring an extra bulb for the projector. A book light might be a handy tool to use for reading your notes if the room will be darkened. Another consideration is what you have on the background of your desktop because the audience may see this displayed on the screen at some point. Be sure that the background is appropriate for a public view.

Walking around the room prior to the presentation gives you a feel for how you might be able to move and engage the audience during the speech. Find out where the light switch is and how to work the microphone if you will be using one. Decide where you will place your computer, the projector, other visual aids, and handouts. If possible, place the projector, focus it on the screen, and test it prior to the audience arrival. Better yet, open your presentation and have it queued to the first slide, so the audience does not see you fumble through your directories looking for the PowerPoint file. This gets you off to on a running start and adds professionalism to your presentation.

REAL WORLD ADVICE | **Displaying a Presentation**

If at all possible, avoid displaying your presentation from a USB flash drive. These devices slow down animations, crash easier, and introduce other problems. If possible, copy the presentation from the USB flash drive onto the desktop computer, and launch the desktop version before your speech. Remember to delete the desktop version after your speech if you are using someone else's computer.

Presenters are a little like airline flight attendants. They need to know where the emergency exits are, the location of the restrooms, and where the refreshments are served. They need to know when the presentation should begin and end. The presenter is viewed as the leader during a speech, so take charge.

Another aspect of being prepared centers around your appearance. You will be more confident if you are comfortable in your clothing. Do not wear a hat during your presentation unless it is part of the speech, and then remove it as soon as your point is made. For instance, you might be playing the role of a coach, complete with a ball cap and whistle. As soon as you have blown the whistle, catching the attention of the audience, remove the cap for a more professional appearance. Make a last minute stop in front of a mirror before your presentation. Check your smile. No spinach between your teeth? Check your hair. Check to make sure all zippers are secured. Give yourself a thumbs-up, and head out to meet the audience.

P04.18

To Create a Preparedness Checklist

a. Insert a **Title and Content** slide as **Slide 3** into the presentation.

b. In the title placeholder, type Presentation Checklist.

c. In the content placeholder type a list of 10 to 12 items that you should have when you arrive at a presentation. If necessary, apply **Bullets** to the list.

d. Insert three additional **Title and Content slides** for Slide 4 through Slide 6. In the title placeholder for Slide 4 through Slide 6 type Scenario Reactions.

e. React to the following scenarios by listing what you would do if they happened during your presentation. Insert your answer to the first question on Slide 4, your answer to the second question on Slide 5, and your answer to the third question on Slide 6. Apply Numbering to each answer as 1., 2., and 3..

   1. You are about four minutes into delivering your presentation. The bulb on the projector burns out. What would you do?
   2. During the luncheon prior to your speech, you spilled coffee on your clothing. What would you do?
   3. As you were coming to the stage, you heard thunder in the distance. About 10 minutes after you began your speech, the lights went out. What would you do?

f. Click **Save**.

Engaging Your Audience

From shaking hands and introducing yourself to audience members prior to the presentation until you have completed your speech, you should strive to engage your audience and make a connection. Your enthusiasm for the topic should draw the audience into your presentation. You should speak with confidence and humility.

Make eye contact with audience members. If possible, look directly at the person who introduced you or arranged for you to speak, and mention his or her name in the first few sentences you speak. Then, turn your head to the other side of the audience, make eye contact with someone else, and continue speaking. You should maintain eye contact for one to three seconds per person. Do not focus on just the front row, but also look to the middle and back of the crowd. It is important that you do not face the projection screen and give your presentation with your back to the audience. Avoid standing in front of the screen, where you will be blinded by the projector light and mask the presentation content from the audience. Use a laser pointer or the annotation tools in PowerPoint to focus the attention of the audience on specific parts of the slide.

REAL WORLD ADVICE **Do Not Be Afraid of Silence**

If one of your slides is filled with a lot of text, do not be afraid of a little silence in order to give the audience members time to read it. It is extremely difficult to retain what you have read while you are trying to actively listen to the presenter and vice versa.

If at all possible, leave the lights on in the presentation room. This enables you to see the audience, discourages dozing, and increases the interactivity. If the projector is not powerful enough to use with all of the lights on, try to shut off just the lights closest to the projector.

Use natural gestures during your speech. Avoid putting your hands in your pockets or behind your back, crossing your arms, or wringing your hands. If possible, move toward the audience during your presentation. Occasionally take a step to one side or the other, but avoid pacing. Do not look at your feet.

REAL WORLD ADVICE **Break Up the Presentation**

Depending on the age of your audience and the degree of interest in your topic, the average attention span ranges from 10 to 20 minutes. If you are giving a long presentation, be prepared with a few appropriate distractions, such as a short video, a joke, or an engaging animation if you notice your audience is losing interest. This can easily grab their attention for a few more slides and make the overall presentation memorable and engaging.

Your voice is a tool during the presentation. Be interested enough in what you are saying that you do not use a monotone voice to deliver the message. If you find yourself falling into a monotone voice, take a deep breath. Also, many speakers have problems with the speed at which they speak. Presentation nerves make them talk faster. When giving a presentation, slow down. This helps your voice to take on a lower pitch, which projects authority and power. The volume of your speech is something you can check during your presentation preparations, or you can ask your audience if they can hear you. Practice helps you learn how to project your voice so it is clear. You might want to take a bottle of water with you to the podium to moisten your throat during nonspeaking portions of your presentation when others are talking.

CONSIDER THIS | Using a Microphone

Most people hesitate to use a microphone, but some people cannot project their voices well enough to be heard. What are some situations where you should use a microphone if you have that option?

Another aspect of engaging your audience is the question-and-answer portion of the presentation. Many speeches end with "Are there any questions?" It is more advisable to ask "What questions can I answer?" Make the assumption that people in the audience will have questions. As an audience member asks a question, make eye contact and listen to the full question. Rephrase the question to help clarify it and to give you some time to frame your response. This also makes sure the audience heard the question you are about to answer. Be honest and sincere in your reply, and try to involve the whole audience with your response. It helps to think about possible questions your audience might ask prior to the presentation, so you have an answer in mind.

P04.19

To Practice Your Presentation Skills

a. Use the **Presentation Delivery** slides you developed in the last two exercises and practice presenting the material while looking in a mirror. Do you seem friendly? Sincere? Knowledgeable?

b. If possible, record your voice while practicing the presentation, and then review the recording, evaluating whether you have nervous habits, such as clearing your throat or saying, "um," that need to be addressed.

c. Practice the speech one more time in front of a mirror, or if possible, use a video camera to record your practice. Evaluate your performance. Were you speaking clearly? Did you need to use the notes in order to explain or expand on the points made on the slides?

d. After Slide 6, insert a **Title and Content** slide to the presentation, and then title it Evaluation. Write a short evaluation of your practice sessions, and then , if necessary, apply **Bullets** for each comment.

e. Click **Save**.

Introducing and Providing a Road Map for Your Audience

As you begin your presentation, you should let the audience know your purpose and provide them with an overview of your presentation. You may have a slide or two that lays out the points you will make at the beginning of your presentation. You should prepare the audience for any unusual activities you have planned, such as group work or a game.

Your initial comments should focus on gaining the attention of the audience members. People have many distractions from their own life or job that they bring to your presentation, such as a difficult meeting they had with their boss. You need to draw them into your agenda. Have a clear preview sentence memorized so it is easy to state. For instance, you might say, "I would like to tell you why sales are down this quarter, and propose a plan for improvement."

Your road map might be organized in a variety of ways. You may break up the topic into patterns such as past, present, and future. You might present your topic as steps that need completion before the next step occurs. You might use a pro-and-con approach with the topic. It is easier to keep the attention of audience members if they have some idea of where they are in the presentation and where you are going to take them.

Another approach to presentations that can be used in place or alongside the road map method is making sure that the "destination" is well known before you begin taking them down the road. For example, if you are about to begin a section of your presentation that explains how profits had increased by 25% then start off with, "Profits are up 25% and here is why!" This will grab the audience member's attention and provide them with a reason to keep listening if they already know where they are going and are excited about it. This method is often implemented by using the title of a slide or the top bullet point to present the "destination". This way it is known from the start why the slide(s) are of significance.

P04.20

To Create an Introduction

a. After Slide 7, insert a **Title and Content** slide to the presentation, and then title it Attention Getters. List four ways that you could gain the attention of your audience at the beginning of your presentation, and then, if necessary, apply **Bullets** to each new thought.

b. After Slide 8, insert three additional **Title and Content** slides to the presentation, and then title them Road Maps. Consider the following three topics, and then develop a general road map plan for each.

   1. The spa is rolling out a new customer relationship management electronic system. This system records past treatments and products the customer has purchased and provides additional information about the customer, such as phone number, e-mail address, and how often he or she visits the spa.
   2. The spa is reorganizing, hiring new management, and undergoing construction for a new area.
   3. The lead massage therapist is retiring, and you have been asked to speak about the person at the retirement luncheon.

c. Click **Save**, and then **close** the presentation.

Annotating Slides

As you make your presentation, you may want to emphasize certain points on your slides. You have probably seen presenters use laser pointers for this purpose. If you decide to use a laser pointer, keep in mind that "dancing" the pointer all over the screen is very distracting. Try to point to the area you want to emphasize, and then turn off the pointer, rather than move it back and forth over the area. Generally your audience will see the location and focus on it very quickly.

PowerPoint goes one step better by enabling you to **annotate**, or make notations or marks on the slides during your presentation. You can use an arrow to point to objects or a pen or highlighter to make long-lasting notations on the slides. You can even select the color of the ink or highlighter. When you close PowerPoint, a warning message will ask whether you want to save the annotations with the file or not. Just like so many other things, it is important to practice using the mouse to draw on the slides prior to using the tool in front of an audience.

P04.21

To Use Annotation Tools

a. Start **PowerPoint**. On the Start screen, click **Open Other Presentations**, browse to the location of your project files, click **p02ws04Update_LastFirst**, and then click **Open**.

b. Type SpaPresentation when the Password dialog box appears, click **OK**, and then click **Edit Anyway** in the yellow bar at the top.

c. Press F5 to start the presentation from the beginning. Right-click **Slide 1**, point to **Pointer Options**, point to **Ink Color**, and then select **Dark Blue**.

d. Drag an underline below the slogan **A Passion for Relaxation**.

SIDE NOTE
Recent Presentations
This presentation file may also be under the Recent heading on the Start screen.

SIDE NOTE
Pointer Options
Pointing to the lower-left corner of the slide will also bring up pointer options as an alternative to the right-click method.

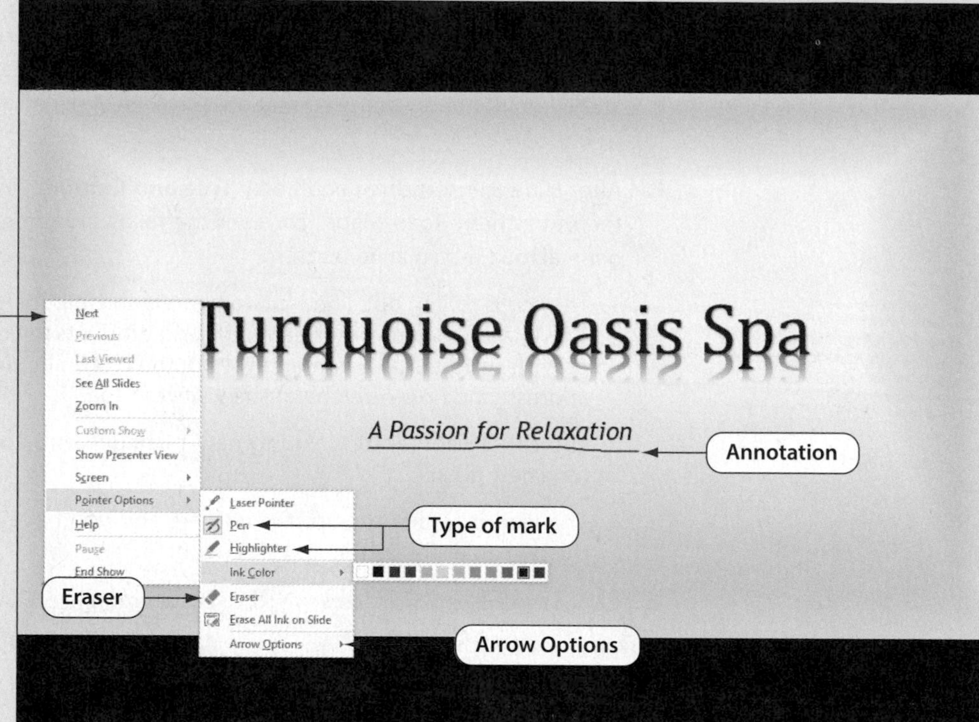

Figure 20 Annotating presentations

> **Troubleshooting**
> When the pen annotation tool is being used, the left mouse button no longer advances the slides. You can press Enter, the letter "N", or the arrow keys to navigate through the slides.

e. Press Enter to advance to the next slide. Right-click and point to **Pointer Options**, and then select **Highlighter**. Highlight the word **solutions**.

f. Right-click the **slide**, point to **Screen**, and then select **Show/Hide Ink Markup** to hide the markup on the slide. Repeat this step to display the markup again.

g. Press Esc to return to Normal view, and then click **Keep** when you see the warning **Want to keep your ink annotations?**. Click **Slide 1** on the Slides tab, and then confirm the ink is still visible.

h. Click the **ink annotation** on Slide 1 to select it, and then press Delete. Slide annotations that have been kept can be manipulated in Normal view.

i. **Save** and **close** the presentation. Open the file again, type the password SpaPresentation and then click **OK**. Click **Slide 2**, and then confirm the highlighting is still visible on the word **solutions**.

You can save annotations for future use or to distribute them with a slide show you are sending to others.

j. **Close** the presentation and exit **PowerPoint**.

Displaying the Presentation in Presenter View

If your computer can be attached to two monitors, PowerPoint can display the speaker notes on one monitor, usually the laptop, and the presentation slides on the second monitor while in **Presenter view**. As shown in Figure 21, the computer displays Presenter view, and speaker notes are displayed on the right. Information such as which slide you are currently on and how long the presentation has lasted are easily available. Icons on the window enable you to move forward and backward through the presentation. Annotation tools are easily accessed in the window. The next slide in the slide show is displayed so that you are reminded of what is next.

PowerPoint 2013 is automatically configured to display Presenter view if two displays are detected. However you can check by clicking Use Presenter View on the Slide Show tab in the Monitors group. Here, you can also select which monitor will display Presenter view. If you only have one monitor, you can still use Presenter view. While in Slide Show view, right-click a slide, and then click Show Presenter View.

In PowerPoint 2013 there have been many enhancements made to Presenter view. Presenter view now offers zooming onto a specific part of a slide and seeing all slides in a presentation at once, as well as more controls over presentation timing with Pause, Resume, and Restart buttons. Also, you now have easier access to the laser pointer tool.

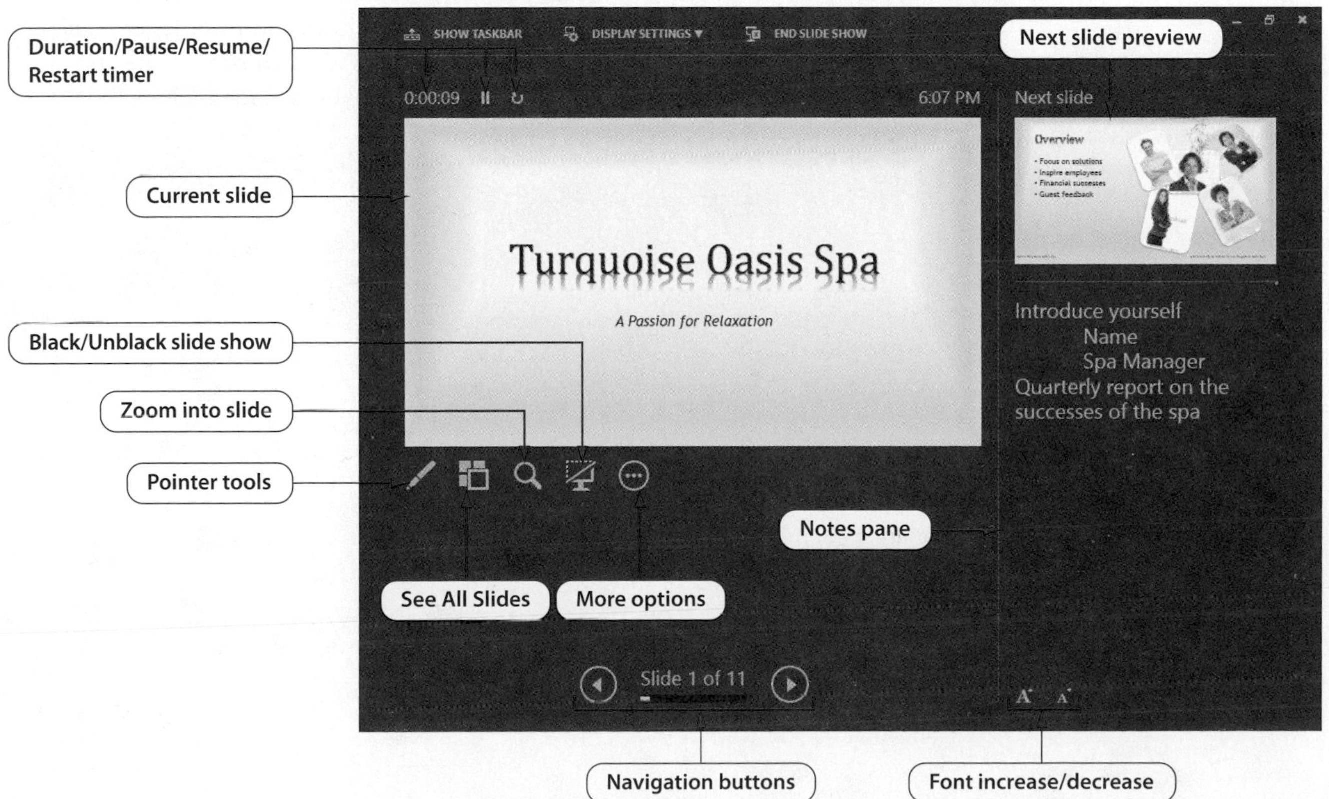

Figure 21 Presenter view

Concluding Your Presentation

The conclusion of the speech is one of the most important parts because you can encourage the audience to fulfill the purpose of your presentation. You should review the road map and remind the audience of the content. You can summarize the main points, or ask the audience what they have learned. You can tell a story that emphasizes the content. You can emphasize the importance of action and the benefits the audience members will gain.

In most cases, the conclusion of a presentation includes a question-and-answer period. You should set up some time limits so everyone knows when the Q&A will end. Be concise with your answers, and resist the urge to argue with the person who asks a question or challenges you. Admit if you cannot answer the question, and offer to get back to the person at a later time with the answer.

REAL WORLD ADVICE **When to Accept Questions**

Some presenters encourage audience members to participate in the presentation by asking questions or making comments as they think of them. Other presenters prefer to have the audience members hold their questions until the end of the presentation. The size of the audience and the environment of the presentation will help you decide which tactic to use. Keep in mind that questions during your presentation may distract you or the audience and keep you from making all of your points. Regardless of when you accept questions, be sure to repeat the question or paraphrase it so the audience can clearly hear what the question was. This also gives you a chance to frame your response.

When your time is up, thank the audience for its attention. If audience members applaud, acknowledge the response. Some presenters ask the audience to fill out an evaluation form. This can offer you valuable insight into the pluses and minuses of your presentation. After the presentation, be available to speak with members of the audience. Thank the people who arranged for you to speak. Reward yourself for a job well done.

Concept Check

MODULE 2

1. You have been working on a template for your company that will be used by all of the sales people when they visit customers in the field. The sales people want to create their own customized presentations so they can add the name of the customer and other information to the slide show. What kinds of information would you include on a template for this use? p. 952
2. What purpose do handouts and presentation notes have? What are some things to consider when creating handouts? p. 959–961
3. When creating a presentation from an outline in Word, what are some things to consider? p. 965
4. What are some benefits of using slide sections to organize a presentation? p. 966
5. Steve Michaels, the vice president of production at your company, requested your input on a presentation he plans to present to the board of directors. He wants feedback on the design of his slides, and he wants you to write some of the text of his presentation. What PowerPoint tools will you use to provide the feedback and text? p. 969–970
6. What benefits do speaker notes provide? What are some things to consider when creating speaker notes? p. 972
7. Why would you want or need to encrypt a presentation? Why would you want or need to mark a presentation as final? p. 974
8. The board of directors meeting is today, and Steve is in the hospital. You have been asked to make his presentation. You have never made a speech to the board, and you are becoming increasingly nervous. What would you do to control your nerves before the presentation? Once you get into the board room, how will you engage the members of the board and get them to agree to the proposal Steve was making? p. 976

Key Terms

Annotate 981
Comments 969
Corporate identity 952
Handout master 961
Notes master 959
Presenter view 983
Proofing tools 966
Slide master 952
Slide sections 966
Speaker notes 972
Template 952

Visual Summary

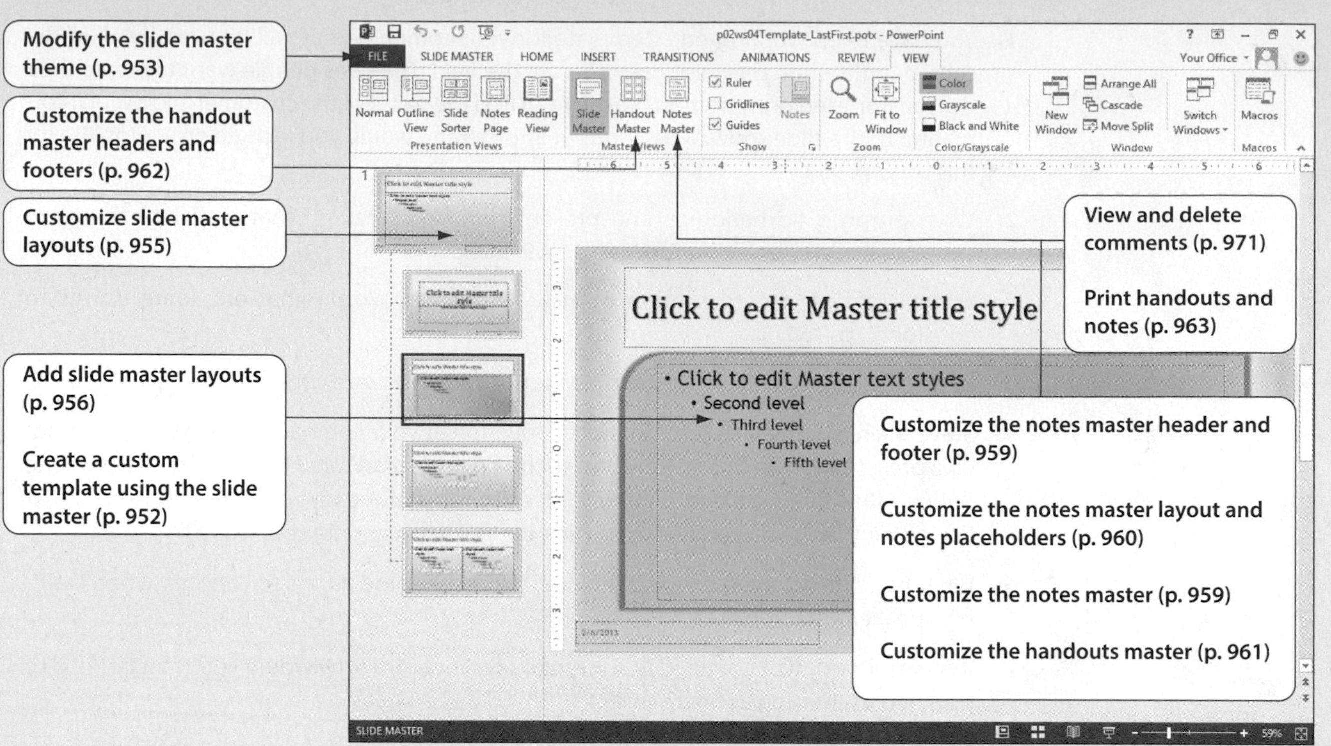
Modify the slide master theme (p. 953)
Customize the handout master headers and footers (p. 962)
Customize slide master layouts (p. 955)
Add slide master layouts (p. 956)
Create a custom template using the slide master (p. 952)
View and delete comments (p. 971)
Print handouts and notes (p. 963)
Customize the notes master header and footer (p. 959)
Customize the notes master layout and notes placeholders (p. 960)
Customize the notes master (p. 959)
Customize the handouts master (p. 961)
p02ws04Template_LastFirst.potx - PowerPoint
Click to edit Master title style
Click to edit Master text styles
Second level
Third level
Fourth level
Fifth level
SLIDE MASTER

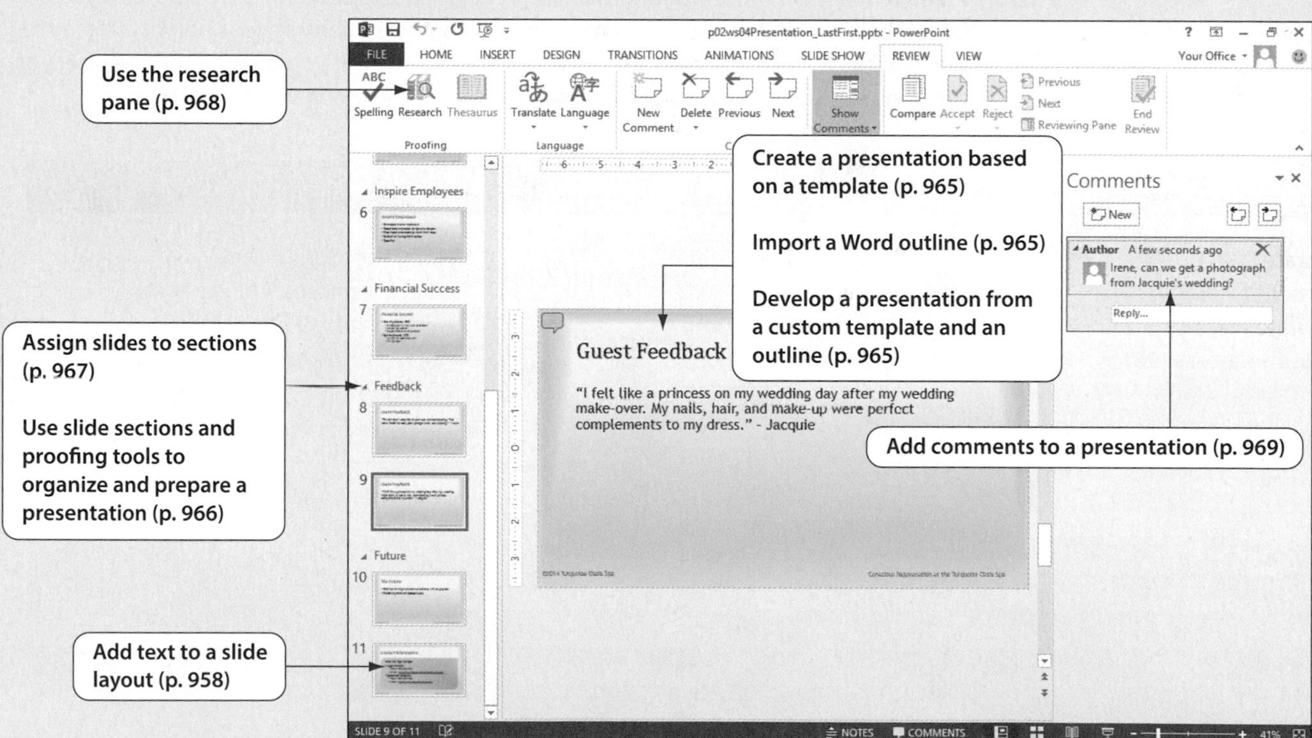
Use the research pane (p. 968)
Assign slides to sections (p. 967)
Use slide sections and proofing tools to organize and prepare a presentation (p. 966)
Add text to a slide layout (p. 958)
Create a presentation based on a template (p. 965)
Import a Word outline (p. 965)
Develop a presentation from a custom template and an outline (p. 965)
Add comments to a presentation (p. 969)
p02ws04Presentation_LastFirst.pptx - PowerPoint
Comments
Irene, can we get a photograph from Jacquie's wedding?
Guest Feedback
"I felt like a princess on my wedding day after my wedding make-over. My nails, hair, and make-up were perfect complements to my dress." - Jacquie
SLIDE 9 OF 11

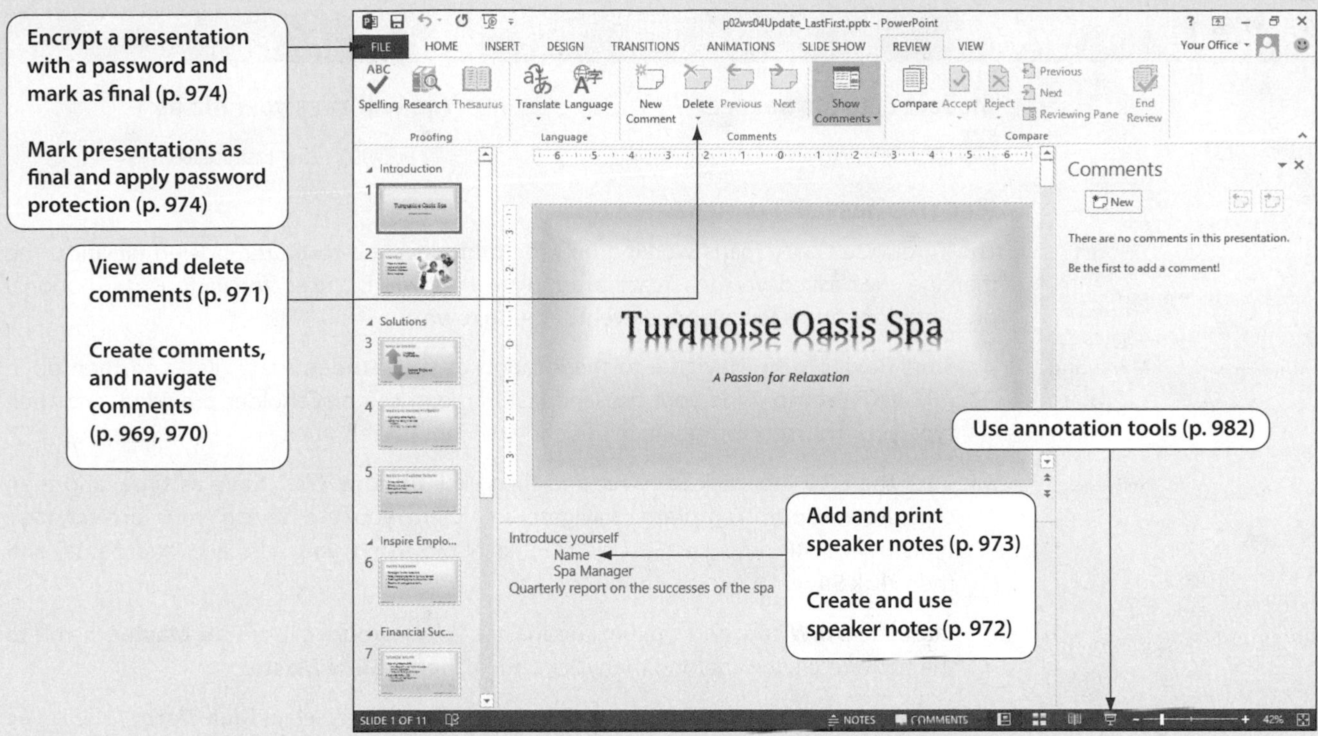

Encrypt a presentation with a password and mark as final (p. 974)
Mark presentations as final and apply password protection (p. 974)
View and delete comments (p. 971)
Create comments, and navigate comments (p. 969, 970)
Use annotation tools (p. 982)
Add and print speaker notes (p. 973)
Create and use speaker notes (p. 972)
p02ws04Update_LastFirst.pptx - PowerPoint
Turquoise Oasis Spa
A Passion for Relaxation
Comments
There are no comments in this presentation.
Be the first to add a comment!
Introduce yourself
Name
Spa Manager
Quarterly report on the successes of the spa

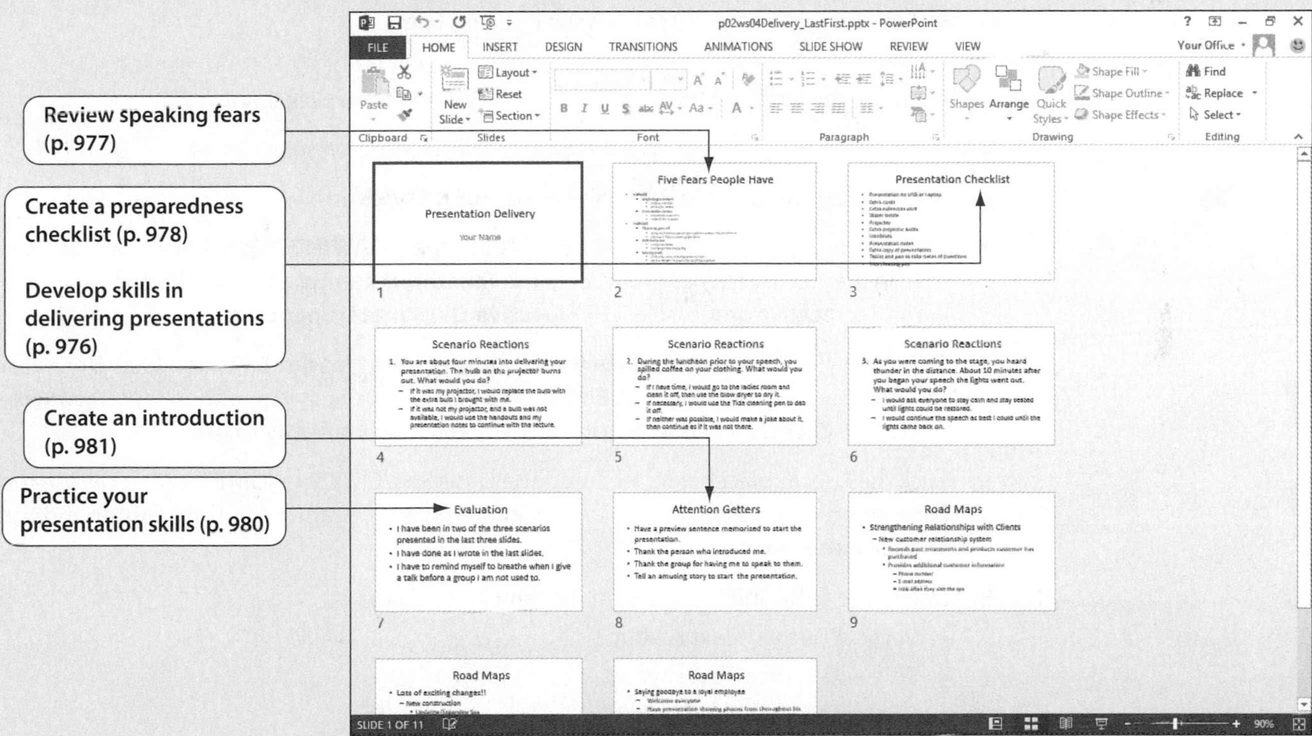

Review speaking fears (p. 977)
Create a preparedness checklist (p. 978)
Develop skills in delivering presentations (p. 976)
Create an introduction (p. 981)
Practice your presentation skills (p. 980)
p02ws04Delivery_LastFirst.pptx - PowerPoint
Presentation Delivery
Five Fears People Have
Presentation Checklist
Scenario Reactions
Evaluation
Attention Getters
Road Maps

Figure 22 Corporate Identity Template Final Document

Practice 1

Student data file needed:

You will save your file as:

Promotional Template

Sales & Marketing

The Turquoise Oasis Spa is working on promoting its soon-to-be remodeled facilities. The manager has asked you to create a template that will be used for various promotional presentations and a few planned events around town.

a. Start **PowerPoint**. Navigate to the location of your student data files, and then open **p02ws04Promo**. Type your first and last name in the placeholder provided, and then type your course information in the body content placeholder.

b. Click the **FILE** tab, click **Save As**, and then click **Browse**. Click **Save as type**, and then click **PowerPoint Template**. Navigate to where you are saving your project files, type p02ws04Promo_LastFirst as the file name using your last and first name, and then click **Save**.

c. Click the **VIEW** tab, and then in the Master Views group, click **Slide Master**. Scroll to the top of the left pane, and then click **Office Theme Slide Master**.

d. In the Background group, click the **Colors** arrow, and then select **Blue Warm**.

e. In the Background group, click the **Fonts** arrow, and then select **Customize Fonts**.
   - Select **Baskerville Old Face** as the Heading Font.
   - Select **Century** as the Body Font.
   - Name the custom font PromoFont_LastFirst and then click **Save**.

f. In the Background group, click the **Effects** arrow, and then select **Inset**.

g. In the Background group, click the **Background Styles** arrow, and then select **Style 10**.

h. Click the border of the title placeholder. Click the **DRAWING TOOLS FORMAT** tab, and then in the WordArt Styles group, click the **Text Effects** arrow, point to **Shadow**, and then in the Perspective group, select **Perspective Diagonal Upper Left**.

i. Click the **INSERT** tab, and then in the Text group, click **Header & Footer**. Click **Date and time** to select it, and then click **Fixed**. Click **Footer** to select it, and then type Turquoise Oasis Spa. Click **Don't show on title slide**, and then click **Apply to All**.

j. Click the **Footer** placeholder for Turquoise Oasis Spa. Click the **HOME** tab, and then in the Font group, change the font color to **Black, Text 1**. Repeat for the **Date footer** and the **Slide number footer**.

k. Delete the following layouts from the template:
   - Vertical Title and Text Layout
   - Title and Vertical Text Layout
   - Content with Caption Layout
   - Blank Layout
   - Title Only Layout
   - Comparison Layout
   - Section Header Layout

l. Click the **Title Slide Layout**. Click the **INSERT** tab, and then in the Illustrations group, click the **Shapes** arrow, and then in the **Stars and Banners** group, select **Horizontal Scroll**. Drag a scroll to cover the subtitle placeholder.
   - Click the **DRAWING TOOLS FORMAT** tab, and then in the Shape Styles group, click the **More** button, and then click **Light 1 Outline, Colored Fill - Blue-Gray, Accent 1**.
   - Click the **Shape Effects** arrow, point to **Shadow**, and in the Outer group, select **Offset Diagonal Top Left**.
   - In the **Size** group, type 1.8 in the Shape Height box, and then type 7.5 in the Shape Width box.
   - In the **Arrange** group, click the **Send Backward** arrow, and then select **Send to Back**.
   - Click **Align**, and then select **Align Center**.

m. Click the **SLIDE MASTER** tab, and then in the Close group, click **Close Master View**.
   - Click the **HOME** tab, and then in the Slides group, click the **New Slide** arrow, and then select **Title Slide** to insert a title slide.

n. Type Turquoise Oasis Spa in the title placeholder, and then type A Grand Reopening in the subtitle placeholder.

o. Save the presentation, making sure it is saved as a Presentation Template. Submit your file as directed by your instructor.

Problem Solve 1

Student data files needed:

Blank PowerPoint presentation

p02ws04Restaurant.docx

p02ws04Farm.jpg

You will save your file as:

p02ws04Training_LastFirst.pptx

Employee Training

Production & Operations

FARMhouse is a local restaurant that specializes in serving local, farm-fresh food at an affordable price. The managers are looking to hire some new staff to run a new location and would like you to help get them started by customizing a presentation for them to use. In this exercise, you will import an outline from a Word document and then customize the slide master and notes master.

a. Start **PowerPoint**, and then create a blank presentation. Save the presentation as p02ws04Training_LastFirst.

b. In the title placeholder, type FARMhouse, and then in the subtitle placeholder, type New Staff Training.

c. Import the outline file **p02ws04Restaurant**, located within your student data files, into the presentation.

d. Go to the slide master, and then make the following changes to the Office Theme Slide Master.
   - Change the Master title style font to **Times New Roman**, set the font size to **54**, and then change the character spacing to **Loose**.
   - Select **Orange Red** as the Theme Colors.
   - Make each of the three footer placeholders **bold** with a font color of **Orange, Accent 1**.
   - Format the Background to a **Solid fill** with the color **Brown, Accent 4** and a Transparency of **60%**. Apply to **all**.

e. Make the following changes to the **Title Slide Layout**.
   - Insert the **p02ws04Farm** as a picture background with a transparency of 79%. The default values for Offset top and Offset bottom should be **-39%**. If not, adjust both values.
   - Add a WordArt Style to the title of **Fill-Orange, Accent 1, Shadow**.
   - Apply a text effect to the title of a Glow Variation of **Brown, 5 pt glow, Accent color 3**.
   - Increase the font size of the subtitle to **28**.

f. Close Master View, and then reset Slides 2 through 6 so that the changes you have made are applied to the imported slides.

g. View the notes master and make the following changes.
   - Change the Notes Page Orientation to Landscape.
   - Change the size of the slide image to 3" in width.
   - Align the slide image to the left of the slide.
   - Adjust the size of the Notes pane to fill the width of the slide and end just under the slide image.
   - Increase the font size of the notes to **18**.
   - Clear the page number and date from the Notes.
   - Type FARMhouse Staff Training in the **Header** placeholder.
   - Type the current year followed by Training Notes in the **Footer** placeholder.

h. Close the notes master.

i. Save and close PowerPoint. Submit your file as directed by your instructor.

Perform 1: Perform in Your Life

Student data file needed:

Blank PowerPoint presentation

You will save your file as:

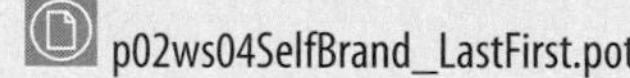

p02ws04SelfBrand_LastFirst.potx

Personal Branding

Sales & Marketing

You know the importance that many corporations place on branding themselves to their employees and the public. Personal branding is also important, and thinking about yourself as a brand can prove insightful. In this exercise you will create a PowerPoint template with custom colors, fonts, and a custom slide layout that will help to express your personal brand.

a. Start **PowerPoint**, and then create a blank PowerPoint template with the name p02ws04SelfBrand_LastFirst.

b. Create a customized set of Theme Colors for all slides, based on an existing theme of your choosing. Customize any two Accent colors. Name the custom theme colors BrandColors_LastFirst.

c. Create a customized Theme Font for all slides, with your choice of Heading and Body fonts. Name the custom theme fonts BrandFonts_LastFirst.

d. Create a custom background style of your choosing for all slides. You may choose any style that you feel represents your personal brand; however, it cannot be one of the preset background styles.

e. Apply any text effects to the master title style. Be sure the title is readable with the background style you chose.

f. If necessary, modify the font colors in the footer so they are easily visible.

g. Customize the Title Slide Layout to your liking. When customizing this layout, consider that the title slide's purpose is to introduce the presentation, or in this case, your brand. You must incorporate at least one shape illustration into the Title Slide Layout design.

h. Create a new custom layout that will be used to display your course information. Rename the custom layout to CourseInfo_LastFirst. You must incorporate at least one shape illustration into your custom layout.

i. Remove all layouts from the template except for the following:
   - Office Theme Slide Master
   - Title Slide Layout
   - Title and Content Layout
   - CourseInfo_LastFirst Layout

j. Close Master View, and then on **Slide 1** type your name as the slide title and Personal Brand Template as the subtitle.

k. Add the **CourseInfo_LastFirst** layout as **Slide 2**. Type Course Information as your slide title, and then add your first and last name, course name, course number, and today's date to the template.

l. Submit your file as directed by your instructor.

Additional Cases

Additional Workshop Cases are available on the companion website and in the instructor resources.

MODULE CAPSTONE

More Practice 1

Student data files needed:

- p02mpVacation.pptx
- p02mpLogo.jpg
- p02mpV1.jpg
- p02mpV2.jpg
- p02mpV3.jpg
- p02mpV4.jpg
- p02mpV5.jpg
- p02mpV6.jpg
- p02mpV7.jpg
- p02mpV8.jpg
- p02mpV9.jpg
- p02mpV10.jpg
- p02mpV11.jpg
- p02mpV12.jpg
- p02mpV13.jpg
- p02mpV14.jpg
- p02mpVCover.jpg

You will save your files as:

- p02mpVacation_LastFirst.pptx
- p02mpVTemplate_LastFirst.potx
- p02mpVAlbum_LastFirst.pptx
- p02mpVVideo_LastFirst.mp4
- p02mpVCDFolder_LastFirst

Family Vacation Presentation

Sales & Marketing

Production & Operations

Timothy Smith, the marketing manager of the Painted Paradise Resort and Spa, is interested in marketing to families who might want to spend a vacation at the resort. The recreational facilities, including the golf course, spa, water park, and nearby hiking trails, make this an attractive destination for all members of the family. The restaurants at the resort make it convenient and cost-effective to feed the family. Timothy asked you to create a template and develop a sample presentation to advertise the benefits of a Painted Paradise vacation. You will create a template that appeals to kids and parents. You will develop a template for handouts as a part of the main template. You will develop a photo album of photographs from around the resort. Hyperlinks will be added to a slide. You will add transitions and animations to the slides, along with audio. The presentation will be packaged as a CD because Timothy intends to mail out the full presentation along with other marketing pieces about the resort. In addition, because Timothy wants to post the presentation on the website, you will create a video of the presentation. He also requested that you deliver the presentation at his next staff meeting, so you will create some speaker notes and make some planning comments on the slides.

a. Start **PowerPoint**, navigate to the location of your student data files, and then open **p02mpVacation**. Click the **Title** placeholder, and then type your first and last name. Enter your course name, your course number, and today's date on the slide. Click the **FILE** tab, click **Save As**, and then double-click **Computer**. Change the **Save as type** to **PowerPoint Template**, and then navigate to the location where you are saving your project files. Change the file name to p02mpVTemplate_LastFirst, using your last and first name. Click **Save**.

b. Click the **VIEW** tab, and then in the Master Views group, click **Slide Master**. Scroll to the top of the left pane, click the **Office Theme Slide Master** thumbnail, and then in the Background group, click **Colors**. Scroll down, and then select the **Blue Green** theme colors. Click **Colors** again, and then select **Customize Colors**. Click the **Hyperlink** arrow, and then select **White, Text 1**. In the Name box, type VacationColors_LastFirst to create a new color group, using your last and first name. Click **Save**. In the Background group, click **Fonts**, scroll to the bottom and select the **TrebuchetMs** theme fonts. In the Background group, click **Background Styles**, and then select **Style 6**.

c. Select the **text** in the title placeholder. Click the **FORMAT** tab, and then in the WordArt Styles group, click **Text Effects**, point to **Shadow,** and then select **Perspective Diagonal Upper Left**. With the text still selected, increase the font size to **54**.

d. Delete the left footer placeholder, currently holding the date. Similarly, delete the right footer placeholder with the page number field. Click in the **center footer** placeholder, and change the font color to **Black, Text 1, Lighter 25%**. Click the **FORMAT** tab, and then in the Size group, change the value in the **Shape Width** box to 12". In the Arrange group, click **Align Objects**, and then select **Align Center** to center-align the box to the slide.

e. Click the **Title Slide Layout** thumbnail. In the Master Layout group, deselect **Footers**. Delete the title placeholder. Click in the **subtitle** placeholder. Click the **FORMAT** tab, and then in the Arrange group, click **Align Objects**, and then select **Align Bottom** to align the placeholder to the bottom of the slide. Select the text in the **subtitle** placeholder, apply **Italic**, and then set the font color to **Black, Text 1, Lighter 15%**.

f. Click the **INSERT** tab, and then in the Images group, click **Pictures**, and then insert the **p02mpLogo** picture from your student data files folder. On the FORMAT tab, in the Size group, change the value in the **Shape Width** box to 10". In the Arrange group, click **Align Objects**, select **Align Center**, click **Align Objects** again, and then select **Align Middle**. The logo is now aligned to the center and middle of the slide.

g. In the Adjust group, click **Color**, and then select **Set Transparent Color**. With the new pointer, point to the **white background** of the logo, and then click. In the Pictures Styles group, select the **Double Frame, Black** picture style.

h. With the logo still selected, click the **ANIMATIONS** tab, and then in the Animation group, click **More**, and then select **Grow & Turn**. In the Timing group, change the **Duration** to 2.50.

i. Click the **subtitle** placeholder. In the Animation group, apply the **Wipe** animation effect, click **Effect Options**, and then select **From Left**. In the Timing group, set the **Duration** to 1.50, click the **Start** arrow, and then select **After Previous**. In the Preview group, click **Preview** to view the result.

j. Click the **Section Header Layout** thumbnail, and then press Delete. Similarly, delete the following layouts.
   - Two Content Layout
   - Title Only Layout
   - Blank Layout
   - Picture with Caption Layout
   - Title and Vertical Text Layout
   - Vertical Title and Text Layout

k. Click the **VIEW** tab, and then in the Master Views group, click **Handout Master**. In the Background group, click **Background Styles**, and then select the **Style 9** background style. Select the **TrebuchetMs** theme fonts.

l. Delete the date placeholder. In the **Header** placeholder, type Painted Paradise Resort and Spa. Press Enter, and then type your first and last name. Click the **FORMAT** tab, and then in the Arrange group, click **Align Objects**, and then select **Align Center**. Select all the text in the header placeholder, click the **HOME** tab, and then in the Paragraph group, click **Center** to center the text within the placeholder.

m. In the **Footer** placeholder, type All Offers Subject to Availability. Place the insertion point in front of the page number symbol, type Page, and then press Spacebar. Click the **HANDOUT MASTER** tab, and then in the Close group, click **Close Master View**. Save and close the template. Exit PowerPoint.

n. Open **File Explorer**. Create a presentation based on the template by navigating to where you are saving your project files, and then opening the **p02mpVTemplate_LastFirst** file. Save the presentation as p02mpVacation_LastFirst.

o. On the HOME tab, in the Slides group, click the **New Slide** arrow, and then select **Title Slide**. In the **subtitle** placeholder, type The Destination for Your Next Vacation!

p. Click the **INSERT** tab, and then in the Images group, click the **Photo Album** arrow, and then select **New Photo Album**. Click **File/Disk**, navigate to the location of your student data files, select the following photographs, and then click **Insert**.

- p02mpV1
- p02mpV2
- p02mpV3
- p02mpV4
- p02mpV5
- p02mpV6
- p02mpV7
- p02mpV8
- p02mpV9
- p02mpV10
- p02mpV11
- p02mpV12
- p02mpV13
- p02mpV14

Click the **p02mpV4** check box to select picture 4. Click the **Up** arrow three times to move picture **4** to position **1**. Click the **p02mpV4** check box to deselect the picture. Using the same technique, move pictures **p02mpV5** and **p02mpV6** into positions **3** and **4**. Move pictures **p02mpV11**, **p02mpV12**, and **p02mpV13** into positions **6**, **7**, and **8**. Move picture **p02mpV14** to position **9**. Remove the pictures **p02mpV12** and **p02mpV13**. Click the **Picture layout** arrow, and then select **2 pictures with title**. Click the **Frame shape** arrow, and then select **Simple Frame, White**. Click **Create**, and then save the new album where you are saving your project files as p02mpVAlbum_LastFirst. Click the **FILE** tab, and then click **Close**.

q. With the **p02mpVacation_LastFirst** file open, click the **HOME** tab, and then in the Slides group, click the **New Slide** arrow, and then select **Reuse Slides**. In the Reuse Slides pane, click **Browse**, and then select **Browse File**. Navigate to where you are saving your project files, and then double-click **p02mpVAlbum_LastFirst**. In the Reuse Slides pane, click **Slide 2** to add it to the presentation. Similarly, click **Slides 3–7**, in that order, to add them to the presentation. Close the Reuse Slides pane.

r. Type the following titles on each of the following slides.

Slide number	Title
3	Whether You Bike or Hike
4	Golf with Family or Friends
5	Swim, Sun
6	Spa, or Just Laugh Together
7	Catch a Snack, or Dine
8	Suites or Queens

s. After **Slide 6**, add a new **Comparison** layout slide. Click in the top **title** placeholder, and then type Painted Paradise Deals! In the **left column heading** placeholder, type Family of 4 Deal - 3 Nights. In the **right column heading** placeholder, type Large Family Deal - 4 Nights. Type the following text in the body placeholders.

• Double-Queen Room • Round of Golf for 2 • Spa Package for 2 • Access to Water Park • Family Service Meal at Indigo5 • Breakfast at Red Bluff Bistro each morning • $595	• Family Suite-Sleeps 8 • Round of Golf for 4 • Spa Package for 4 • Access to Water Park • Family Service Meal at Indigo5 • Breakfast at Red Bluff Bistro each morning • $895

t. After **Slide 9**, add a new **Content with Caption** layout slide. Click the **Pictures** icon in the right body content placeholder, and then insert the **p02mpV13** photograph. On the FORMAT tab, in the Size group, increase the **Shape Height** of the photograph to 6". In the Arrange group, click **Align Objects**, and then select **Align Middle**. In the Picture Styles group, click **More**, and then select **Rounded Diagonal Corner, White**.

u. In the **title** placeholder, type Make Your Reservations Today!. Center the **text** within the placeholder.

v. In the **left content** placeholder, type www.paintedparadiseresort.com. Press Enter, and then notice that a hyperlink with a white font was automatically inserted. Type 505-555-1792. Press Enter twice, and then type Timothy Smith, Marketing Manager. Select all the **text** within the placeholder, and then center the text within the placeholder.

w. With the text still selected, change the font size to **28**. Change the **Shape Width** of the placeholder to 6", and then change the **Shape Height** to 4". Apply the **White, Background 1** font color to the phone number.

x. Select the text in the title placeholder, and then increase the font size to **44**. Change the **Shape Width** of the placeholder to 6", and then change the **Shape Height** to 1.5".

y. Click the dashed border of the title placeholder to make it a solid border, press Ctrl, and then click in the **left content** placeholder. With both boxes selected, on the FORMAT tab, in the Arrange group, click **Align Objects**, verify that **Align to Slide** is selected, and then select **Distribute Vertically**. The two text boxes are now aligned with the slide.

z. Select **Slides 2–10**. Click the **TRANSITIONS** tab, and then in the Transition to This Slide group, apply the **Uncover** transition, and then in the Timing group, set the duration of the transition to **1.00**.

aa. Apply animations to the slides as follows.

Slide Number	Element to Animate	Animation	Timing
3	Title	Zoom	Start With Previous, Duration 1.00
4	Title	Zoom	Start With Previous, Duration 1.00
5	Title	Zoom	Start With Previous, Duration 1.00
6	Title	Zoom	Start With Previous, Duration 1.00
7	Title	Split (Effect Options – Vertical Out)	Start With Previous, Duration 1.00
8	Title	Zoom	Start With Previous, Duration 1.00
9	Title	Zoom	Start With Previous, Duration 1.00

(Continued)

Slide Number	Element to Animate	Animation	Timing
9	Two photographs (select both pictures and then apply animation)	Split (Effect Options – Vertical Out)	Start With Previous, Duration 1.00, Delay 1.00
10	Title	Zoom	Start With Previous, Duration 1.00
10	Hyperlink	Grow & Turn	Start After Previous, Duration 1.00
10	Phone number	Grow & Turn	Start After Previous, Duration 1.00
10	Manager name and title	Grow & Turn	Start After Previous, Duration 1.00

bb. Click **Slide 2**. Click the **DESIGN** tab, and then in the Customize group, click **Format Background**. In the Format Background pane, click **Picture or texture fill**. Under Insert picture from, click **File**, navigate to your student data files, and then open the **p02mpVCover** file. Change the **Transparency** to 60%. Click the **Effects** icon at the top of the Format Background pane, click the **Artistic Effects** arrow, and then select **Glow Diffused**. Click the **Picture** icon at the top of the Format Background pane, click **PICTURE COLOR** to expand the section, and then change the **Saturation** to 50%. Close the Format Background pane. If you make a mistake and need to start over, click Reset Background at the bottom of the Format Background pane.

cc. While still on Slide 2, click the **INSERT** tab, and then in the Media group, click **Audio**, and then select **Online Audio**. Click in the **Office.com Clip Art** search box, and then type Xylo Beat. Press Enter. Insert the **Xylo Beat** audio. On the PLAYBACK tab, in the Audio Options group, click **Hide During Show** and **Loop until Stopped**. Click the **Start** arrow, select **Automatically**, and then click **Volume** and select **Low**. Save the presentation.

dd. On the INSERT tab, in the Text group, click **Header & Footer**. Insert a footer with the text http://www.paintedparadiseresort.com to all of the slides except the title slide.

ee. Click the **FILE** tab, click **EXPORT**, and then click **Create a Video**. Click **Computer & HD Displays**, and then select **Portable Devices**. Click **Create Video**. Save the video where you are saving your project files with the name p02mpVVideo_LastFirst.

ff. Click the **FILE** tab, click **Export**, click **Package Presentation for CD**, and then click **Package for CD**. Name the CD SpaVacation and then click **Copy to Folder**. Change the folder name to p02mpVCDFolder_LastFirst and then click **Browse**. Navigate to the location where you are saving your project files, click **Select**, and then click **OK**. Click **Yes** to include linked files. If necessary, close the folder window containing the packaged presentation. Close the Package for CD dialog box.

gg. Click **Slide 2**, click the **REVIEW** tab, and then in the Comments group, click **New Comment**. Type This presentation will be given to the marketing staff under the direction of Timothy Smith. Don't forget the computer, power supply, extension cords, and projector. Close the Comments pane.

hh. Type This slide can be updated as needed. as the speaker notes to **Slide 7**.

ii. Prepare to print Handouts with **2 Slides** per page. Review each page of the handout. Notice that page 2 contains the comment that was typed on Slide 2. Print the handout if directed by your instructor. Press Esc to return to the presentation.

jj. Click the **FILE** tab, click **Info**, click **Compress Media**, and then select **Low Quality**. Close the Compress Media dialog box. Save and close the presentation file, and then exit PowerPoint. Submit the files as directed by your instructor.

Problem Solve 1

Student data files needed:

- p02ps1BTemplate.potx
- p02ps1B1.jpg
- p02ps1B2.jpg
- p02ps1B3.jpg
- p02ps1B4.jpg
- p02ps1B5.jpg
- p02ps1B6.jpg
- p02ps1B7.jpg
- p02ps1B8.jpg
- p02ps1B9.jpg
- p02ps1B10.jpg
- p02ps1BCake.jpg
- p02ps1BOutline.docx
- p02ps1EventLogo.jpg

You will save your files as:

- p02ps1Bridal_LastFirst.pptx
- p02ps1BAlbum_LastFirst.pptx
- p02ps1BVideo_LastFirst.mp4

The Wedding Catering Presentation

Sales & Marketing

Ellie Gold, the wedding planner for the Painted Paradise Golf Resort and Spa, and Robin Sanchez, the chef for the resort, are participating in an upcoming Bridal Fair where brides shop for and plan their weddings. You will create a presentation that will be continuously displayed on a computer screen in a booth. The presentation's main audience will be brides, but a secondary audience of mothers, fiancés, and bridesmaids should be considered. You will create a presentation based on a template, you will update the Slide Master view, and then create and use a photo album to insert graphics into the presentation. An outline will provide some content. You will include transitions, animations, and audio to engage the audience in the presentation. A comment, placed on a slide, will remind Ellie and Robin of the equipment they will need. Because they plan to add this presentation to their website, you will create a video in a reduced-size format, so you can get approval for it before creating the larger video file.

a. Create a new presentation based on the template in your student data files **p02ps1BTemplate**. Type your first and last name, course name, course number, and today's date. Save the presentation as p02ps1Bridal_LastFirst.

b. View the slide master. Select the **Office Theme Slide Master** thumbnail. Customize the theme fonts and select **Brush Script MT** for the Heading font, and **Arial Narrow** for the Body font. Name the font group BridalFont_LastFirst.

c. Apply the **Style 6** background style.

d. Click to place the insertion point in the first bulleted line. Click the **HOME** tab, and then in the Paragraph group, click the **Bullets** arrow, and then select **Bullets and Numbering**. Click **Customize**, select the **Wingdings** font, type 152 in the Character code box, and then click **OK**. Click the **Color** arrow, and then select **Brown, Accent 5, Darker 25%**. Change the value in the **Size** box to 80 and then click **OK**. Similarly, change the second-level bullet to a **Wingdings** symbol with a character code of 153, **Brown, Accent 5, Darker 25%** color, and a **70%** size. Change the third-level bullet to a **Wingdings** symbol with a character code of 154, **Brown, Accent 5, Darker 25%** color, and a **60%** size.

e. Delete the following layouts.
   - Section Header Layout
   - Two Content Layout
   - Comparison Layout
   - Blank Layout

MODULE CAPSTONE

- Picture with Caption Layout
- Title and Vertical Text Layout
- Vertical Title and Text Layout
- Content with Caption Layout

f. Close the Master view. Create a new photo album with the following photographs.
   - p02ps1B1
   - p02ps1B2
   - p02ps1B3
   - p02ps1B4
   - p02ps1B5
   - p02ps1B6
   - p02ps1B7
   - p02ps1B8
   - p02ps1B9
   - p02ps1B10

   Move the photographs until they appear in this order in the Pictures in album box.
   - p02ps1B8
   - p02ps1B2
   - p02ps1B1
   - p02ps1B3
   - p02ps1B6
   - p02ps1B4
   - p02ps1B5
   - p02ps1B7
   - p02ps1B9
   - p02ps1B10

   Remove the photographs **p02ps1B3** and **p02ps1B8**. Select **1 picture with title** for the Picture layout, with a **Simple Frame, White** Frame. Create the album, and then save the photo album as p02ps1BAlbum_LastFirst. Close the album.

g. With the **p02ps1Bridal_LastFirst** file open, create new slides from the outline **p02ps1BOutline** located with your student data files. Reset Slide 2 and Slide 3.

h. Select **Slide 2**, and then create new slides by reusing the photograph content slides from the **p02ps1BAlbum_LastFirst** presentation. Insert **Slides 2–8**, in that order. Close the Reuse Slides pane.

i. Select **Slide 2**. Insert the photograph **p02ps1B8**. Change the height to 5". Apply the **Rotated, White** picture style to the photograph. With the picture still selected, on the FORMAT tab, in the Size group, click the **Dialog Box Launcher**. The Format Picture pane opens. Click **POSITION** to expand the section. Change the **Horizontal position** to 5 and the **Vertical position** value to 1.5.

j. Select the text **Food**, **Décor**, and **Custom Cakes**, and then apply **Bold**. With the text still selected, apply the **Zoom** animation with the **Object Center** effect option, starting **With Previous**, with the Duration of **2.0**.

k. Type the following titles on the following slides.

Slide Number	Title
3	Table Service for up to 500
4	Appetizer Service
5	Buffets
6	Custom Cakes with Fresh Flowers
7	Custom Cakes with Lace
8	Custom Cakes in Many Flavors

l. Delete Slide 9.

m. Select **Slide 9**. Select the text **Painted Paradise Golf Resort and Spa**, and then set a hyperlink to the URL/address http://www.paintedparadiseresort.com. Type Click here for the ScreenTip.

n. On Slide 9, insert a **Heart** shape (under Basic Shapes) measuring 6" in height by 5" in width. Remove the shape outline. Align the heart to the **right** and **bottom** of the slide. Fill the heart shape with the picture **p02ps1B10**. Under DRAWING TOOLS, on the FORMAT tab, in the Arrange group, click **Rotate Objects**, and then select **More Rotation Options**. In the Format Picture pane, change the **Rotation** value to -20. Close the Format Picture pane.

o. Insert a **footer** with the text http://www.paintedparadiseresort.com. The footer should appear on all slides except the title slide.

p. On **Slide 1**, insert the comment Don't forget the computer monitor, three extension cords, laptop, and presentation. Close the Comments pane.

q. Select **Slide 2**. Add a new section named Wedding Services. Similarly add a new section above Slide 3 named Food Service, and above Slide 9 named Contact Info.

r. Insert a **Title Slide** below Slide 1. Delete the title and subtitle placeholder. Insert the **p02ps1EventLogo** picture. Change the color of the logo to **Saturation: 33%**. Apply the **Drop Shadow Rectangle** picture style and the **Texturizer** Artistic Effect. Apply the **Grow & Turn** animation to the logo, with a **3.00** duration, starting **With Previous**. Change the width of the logo to 10". Align the logo to the center and middle of the slide.

s. Insert the **p02ps1BCake.jpg** as the background image. Change the transparency to **65%**.

t. Apply the transition **Reveal**, with a Duration of **04.00** to **Slides 2–10**. Advance the slides on a mouse click and after **2.00** seconds.

u. Apply the **Grow & Turn** animation, starting **With Previous**, with a **2.00** duration, to the photos on **Slides 3–10**. Click the **SLIDE SHOW** tab, and then in the Set Up group, click **Set Up Slide Show**, select **Loop continuously until 'Esc'**, and then click **OK**.

v. On **Slide 2**, insert an **Online Audio**. Type wedding in the Office.com search box, and then select the **Marriage** audio. Set the Audio Options to start playing the audio **Automatically**, **Hide During Show**, **Loop Until Stopped**, and **Play Across Slides**. Set the Volume to **Low**. With the audio still selected, open the **Animation Pane**, and then click the **Up** arrow once to move the audio to the first position. Close the Animation Pane.

w. **Compress Media**, with a **Low Quality** setting.

x. Save the presentation. Review the presentation in **Slide Show** view. Create a video for **Portable Devices**. Accept all the defaults. Save the video file as p02ps1BVideo_LastFirst. Wait until the movie has been rendered, review it, and then close the presentation. Submit the files as directed by your instructor.

Problem Solve 2

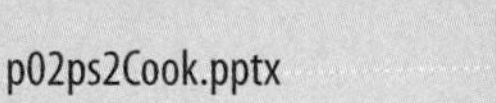

Student data files needed:

p02ps2Cook.pptx
p02ps2C1.jpg
p02ps2C2.jpg
p02ps2C3.jpg
p02ps2C4.jpg
p02ps2C5.jpg
p02ps2C6.jpg
p02ps2C7.jpg
p02ps2CFork.jpg
p02ps2COutline.docx

You will save your files as:

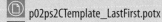

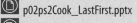

p02ps2CTemplate_LastFirst.potx
p02ps2Cook_LastFirst.pptx
p02ps2CAlbum_LastFirst.pptx

Indigo5 Cooking School

Sales & Marketing

Production & Operations

The chef, Robin Sanchez, along with sous chef, Matt Andretti, and pastry chef, Michael Benoit, decided to offer cooking classes on Tuesday afternoons in the Indigo5 kitchen. Guests of the resort, as well as local residents, will spend a few hours learning how to cook soup, pasta, fish, bread, and desserts. You will create the PowerPoint presentation the chef will deliver to various audiences. For the most part, the audiences will be viewing the presentation for entertainment, but Robin would like to also advertise the classes and persuade people to participate.

You will begin the project by creating a template. You will import an outline that the chef has provided. A photo album will provide an inside look at the Indigo5 kitchen. You will add transitions to the slides. Some slides will be hidden. Links between the slides will provide nonsequential viewing of the slides. A graphic will be used to return you to previous slides. A slide footer, added to the slide master, will contain the web address for the restaurant. You will customize the handout master, so it includes the contact information necessary to register for the courses. After completing the presentation, you will print selected slides as handouts.

a. Open **p02ps2Cook**, and then save the file as a PowerPoint Template with the name p02ps2CTemplate_LastFirst. (Hint: After you select PowerPoint Template as the file type you will have to navigate to where you are saving your project files.)

b. Open **Slide Master** view. Click the **Office Theme Slide Master** thumbnail. Set the background style to **Style 6** so the slides will appear to be stainless steel, the surface of much of the equipment in the Indigo5 kitchen.

c. Customize the theme colors and change the Hyperlink color to **Black, Background 1, Lighter 35%**. Change the **Followed Hyperlink** color to **Black, Background 1, Lighter 50%**. Save the new theme color group with the name CookColors_LastFirst, using your last and first name.

d. Change the theme fonts to **TrebuchetMs**.

e. Select the **title** placeholder, and then apply the **Tan, Background 2, Darker 10%** Shape Fill. Apply a **White, Background 1, Darker 50%** Shape Outline.

f. Customize the top-level bullet to a **Wingdings** symbol with a character code 117, with a size of **75%**, using the color **Black, Text 1, Lighter 50%**. Customize the second-level bullet to **Wingdings** character code 117 with a size of **65%**, using the color **Black, Text 1, Lighter 50%**.

g. Click the **Title Slide Layout** thumbnail. Select the text in the **subtitle** placeholder, and then change the Font Color to **White, Background 1**.

h. Close the Slide Master view, and then open the **Handout Master**. Remove the date placeholder. In the header placeholder, type Indigo5 Cooking School. Type your Firstname Lastname on the second line in the header placeholder, using your first and last name. Center-align the header placeholder on the page, and then center the text within the placeholder. In the **footer** placeholder, type rsanchez@paintedparadiseresort.com. Type 505-555-1964 on the second line in the footer placeholder, and then close the master view.

i. Save and close the template. Exit PowerPoint. Create a new presentation based on the template file you just created, and then save the presentation as p02ps2Cook_LastFirst.

j. Create a new photo album using the following photographs.

- p02ps2C1
- p02ps2C2
- p02ps2C3
- p02ps2C4
- p02ps2C5
- p02ps2C6
- p02ps2C7

Move **p02ps2C4** to position 1. Move **p02ps2C7** to position 6. Add a text box at position 2. Set the Picture layout to **2 pictures with title**, and then set the Frame shape to **Simple Frame, Black**. Create the **photo album**. Alter the slides in the Photo Album as follows.

- On **Slide 2**, click the **title** placeholder, and then type Meet Our Chefs. Click in the text box, remove any current text, and then type Chef Robin Sanchez. Type Pastry Chef Michael Benoit on the second line and Sous Chef Matt Andretti on the third line. Change the font size of all three lines to **24**, and then center the text within the box.
- On **Slide 3**, click in the **title** placeholder, and then type The Finest Ingredients. Select both pictures, and then change the height to 4.25". Click **Align Objects**, and then select **Align Top**.
- On **Slide 4**, click in the **title** placeholder, and then type Learn the Secrets.
- On **Slide 5**, click in the **title** placeholder, and then type Learn from Us!

k. Save the photo album with your project files with the name of p02ps2CAlbum_LastFirst. Close the photo album. With the **p02ps2Cook_LastFirst** file open, reuse the four photograph slides from the photo album you just created in the following order: Meet Our Chefs, The Finest Ingredients, Learn the Secrets, and Learn from Us!. Close the Reuse Slides pane.

l. Select **Slide 5**. Create new slides using the outline **p02ps2COutline**. Reset all the slides created from the outline.

m. Delete Slide 9. Move Slide 6 (Indigo5 Cooking School) to position **2**. Move Slide 7 (Classes this Month) to position **4**. Hide Slides 9, 10, and 11. Insert a **footer** with the text Firstname Lastname, using your first and last name. Apply the footer to all slides except the title slide.

n. On **Slide 4**, create a hyperlink on the text **Chop Chop** to **Slide 9**. Create a hyperlink for the **One Night Stand** text to **Slide 10**. Create a hyperlink for the **Santa Fe Secrets** text to **Slide 11**.

o. On **Slide 4**, insert the photograph **p02ps2CFork**. Increase the height of the photograph to 5.5". Apply the **Drop Shadow Rectangle** picture style. Change the Horizontal position to 6.5" and the Vertical position to 1.5".

p. On **Slide 9**, insert a **Left Arrow** shape (under Block Arrows). Adjust the shape to a height of 3" and a width of 4". Apply a **Subtle Effect – Black, Dark 1** shape style. Align the arrow to the bottom and right of the slide. With the graphic selected, insert a hyperlink back to **Slide 4**. Include a ScreenTip with the text Click to go back.

q. Copy the left arrow to **Slides 10** and **11**.

r. On **Slide 3**, apply the **Reflected Perspective Right** picture style to the photograph.

s. On **Slide 3**, apply the **Grow & Turn** animation to the photograph, starting **With Previous**. Select all the names, and then apply the **Wipe** animation. Select the **From Top** Effect Option, and then start **After Previous**.

t. Select **Slide 1**. Change the width of the logo to **10"**, and then align the logo to the center and middle of the slide. Change the Color to **Grayscale**. Apply the **Crisscross Etching** artistic effect and the **Metal Frame** picture style. Apply the **Tight Reflection, touching** picture effect. Apply the **Fade** animation, with a 3.00 duration, and start **With Previous**.

u. On **Slide 1**, delete the subtitle placeholder.

v. Select **Slides 1–11**, apply the **Gallery** transition to the slides, and then set the **Duration** to 1.75 seconds.

w. Add the following speaker notes to **Slide 7**.
   mbenoit@paintedparadiseresort.com
   rsanchez@paintedparadiseresort.com

x. Review the slide show testing each of the hyperlinks on **Slide 4** and returning to the slide using the graphic hyperlink.

y. Set up the print function for four slides per page (horizontal) handouts, printing only **Slides 3**, **5**, **8**, and **9**. Preview the print out, and then check it for the header and footers. Print the document if requested by your instructor. Save and close the presentation. Submit the files as directed by your instructor.

Perform 1: Perform in Your Life

Student data file needed:

 Blank PowerPoint presentation

You will save your files as:

 p02pf1Reunion_LastFirst.pptx

 p02pf1RVideo_LastFirst.mp4

High School Reunion Presentation

Sales & Marketing

Human Resources

As a member of the reunion planning committee for your high school class, you will be creating a PowerPoint presentation to show your classmates' current photographs. For this project, you are to create only a small number of slides to use as an example of how a presentation for your entire class would look. You want to share this idea with the committee before you spend a lot of time producing the presentation. You will use PowerPoint's Photo Album feature to quickly create a presentation with photographs and text. You will modify the colors to reflect your school colors. You will create the video in a small format so you can get approval for it, before creating the larger video file.

a. Start **PowerPoint**, and then create a blank presentation. Create a photo album based on a group of 10–20 photographs. Add **captions** to the slides. Apply a **design theme**, keeping in mind that you can alter the colors of the theme to reflect your school colors after you have created the photo album. Apply the **Center Shadow Rectangle** frame shape to all of the pictures. Adjust the size and position of the photos, if necessary. If necessary, you can search the Office.com clip art for pictures.

b. After creating the photo album, save it as p02pf1Reunion_LastFirst.

c. On the title slide, insert an appropriate title and subtitle, and then add a graphic or photograph that associates the presentation with your high school. The title slide should contain a copyright notice, with the copyright symbol, the four-digit year, a comma, and your name (©2015, Your Name). The high school website address/URL should appear somewhere on the title slide as a hyperlink.

d. If your computer has a microphone, record an audio to one slide.

e. Apply transitions to the slides.

f. Add animations to elements on the slides.

g. Modify the theme as needed for colors and fonts.

h. Insert text boxes as needed to provide brief information about the people on the slide. Insert the name of each person in the caption box.

i. Create speaker notes on each slide with the names of the people pictured and a short snippet of information about the person, such as where they live now and if they are married with children.

j. Save the presentation after you have made the modifications listed here.

k. Save the presentation as a video for Portable Devices as p02pf1RVideo_LastFirst.

l. Click **Compress the Media**, saving it as **Low Quality**. Save and close the presentation file, and then exit PowerPoint. Submit the files as directed by your instructor.

Perform 2: Perform in Your Career

Student data files needed:

- Blank PowerPoint presentation
- p02pf2G1.jpg
- p02pf2G2.jpg
- p02pf2G3.jpg
- p02pf2G4.jpg
- p02pf2G5.jpg
- p02pf2G6.jpg
- p02pf2G7.jpg
- p02pf2G8.jpg
- p02pf2G9.jpg
- p02pf2GOutline.docx

You will save your files as:

- p02pf2GAlbum_LastFirst.pptx
- p02pf2Garden_LastFirst.pptx
- p02pf2GHandout_LastFirst.docx

Let's Grow Community Garden Report to Board Presentation

Sales & Marketing

Research & Development

It has been a successful year for the Let's Grow Community Garden project, in which you have been participating. You need to make a report to the members of the executive board, and you plan to focus on the newest garden. There are six board members, but other people who are interested in the project will attend the meeting where you will give your presentation. The board is interested in the success of the North garden and is expecting to see some of the results. For this presentation, you will design a slide and handout master, import an outline, create a photo album, and apply transitions and animations to the slides. You will create an outline for this presentation.

a. Start **PowerPoint**, create a blank presentation, and then save the presentation file as p02pf2Garden_LastFirst.

b. Open Slide Master view. Apply an appropriate design theme. Use clip art to design a creative, but professional background. Use color, corrections, and effects on the clip art to create a subtle, but creative background.

c. Design the Title Slide Layout with a background image that is different from the other layout slide backgrounds. Incorporate clip art as part of the background. Only include layouts in the template that you think you will use in the presentation.

d. Create a handout master, delete the right footer, and then include the following information, in an appropriate font and size.
   - Left Header: **Let's Grow Community Gardens**
   - Right Header: **Your Name**
   - Left Footer: **Copyright symbol, the four-digit year, comma, and Let's Grow, Inc.**

e. Import the outline file **p02pf2GOutline**, and then select appropriate slide layouts for the information on the slides.

f. Create a photo album using the photographs provided and/or any personal photographs you might have that relate to the garden theme. Select a layout for the photo album that has two or more photographs per slide. Use text where appropriate. Save the photo album as **p02pf2GAlbum_LastFirst**.

g. Reuse the slides from the photo album in the original presentation. Make adjustments to the slides to integrate them into the message of the presentation.

h. Apply a motion path animation to one of the graphics.

i. Apply transitions to each of the slides, and then apply animations to the text elements on the slides so bullet points are introduced with a click.

j. Locate an audio file of birds chirping in the Office.com Clip Art, and then insert it on the title slide of the presentation. Hide the playback controls, and then have the audio file play until the slide is advanced (loop until stopped).

k. Using the Internet, research the topic of community gardens. Provide a slide with at least three website hyperlinks that would be useful to the audience.

l. Insert an online video that highlights a community garden. Keep the video as short as possible.

m. Create a custom slide show named **Let's Grow Board** that only includes the slides created by importing the outline and the photo album. In other words, the hyperlink slide and the video slide will not be visible in this custom slide show.

n. Create an Outline only handout, and then save it as **p02pf2GHandout_LastFirst**.

o. On the title slide, place a comment that lists all of the equipment and auxiliary items, such as a basket of produce from the garden that you might need for the presentation.

p. Compress the media, saving it as a low quality. Save the presentation, exit PowerPoint, and then submit the files as directed by your instructor.

Perform 3: Perform in Your Team

Student data file needed:

Blank PowerPoint presentation

You will save your files as:

 p02pf3HHS_TeamName.pptx

 p02pf3HTemplate_TeamName.potx

 p02pf3HVideo_TeamName.pptx

HHS Training

Production & Operations

You are one of the trainers for the U.S. Department of Health & Human Services. Your group is responsible for training the staff. You will create a presentation that reviews a topic covered on the **www.hhs.gov** website. You will create the presentation using either a Standard or Widescreen slide size. Examples of possible topics are the Health Insurance Portability & Accountability Act of 1996, MedlinePlus, prevention of diseases, and so on. Your audience will be medical workers and staff members such as receptionists, records managers, and insurance processors. You may have new employees as part of the audience, but for the most part, this is refresher training. Most of the time, the presentation will be given to groups of 10 to 12 people during coffee meetings that normally last about 15 minutes. In some cases, people will view the slides on their own time, so you will create a Portable Devices version for distribution to these people.

a. Select one team member to set up the documents by completing Steps b–d.

b. Open your browser and navigate to either **www.skydrive.live.com**, **www.drive.google.com**, or any other instructor-assigned tool. Be sure all members of the team have an account on the chosen system—Microsoft or Google account.

c. Start **PowerPoint**. Create a template. Have your team decide if they plan to use a Standard or Widescreen Slide Size, and then if necessary, make the Slide Size change in the template, from within Slide Master view. Save the file as p02pf3HTemplate_TeamName where TeamName is the name assigned to your team by your instructor.

d. Share the file with the other members of your team and make sure that each team member has the appropriate permissions to edit the document. Divide the work evenly among team members.

e. You should make adjustments to the template background, colors, fonts, and other design elements. Modify the handout master to include a header with your team name, the current date, and the text HHS. Save the template, and then close the template file.

f. Keep the rule of six in mind as you place content on the slides.

g. Begin a new presentation, using the template, based on your research. Name this file p02pf3HHS_TeamName. Be sure to provide an introduction and roadmap.

h. The title slide should contain a title and a list of the team members.

i. Add appropriate transitions to each of the slides.

j. Animate text elements on slides so they appear individually, allowing you to focus the attention of the audience on one major point at a time.

k. Create speaker notes for each slide.

l. Insert appropriate pictures or clip art.

m. In an appropriate location, include a hyperlink to the external website http://www.hhs.gov with the display U.S. Dept. of Health & Human Services.

n. Insert an appropriate online video related to your presentation. Make sure the video is under two minutes. Apply a video style. Adjust the start of the video to occur when the video is clicked.

o. The final slide of the presentation should contain a conclusion.

p. Add comments to the title slide describing how you would prepare for this presentation. Provide a checklist of items that you should remember to take with you to the presentation.

q. Add comments to the introduction/roadmap slide describing what you will do during the presentation to engage the audience. Save the presentation.

r. Create a custom slide show that does not contain the video slide. Type NoVideo in the Slide show name box.

s. Carefully proofread the presentation, and then save the presentation. Save the presentation as a video for Portable Devices, with the file name p02pf3HVideo_TeamName. Continue without including the media.

t. Once the assignment is complete, share the documents with your instructor or turn in as your instructor directs. Make sure that the instructor has permission to edit the file.

Perform 4: How Others Perform

Student data files needed:

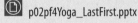

 p02pf4Yoga.pptx

 p02pf4YBackground.jpg

You will save your file as:

p02pf4Yoga_LastFirst.pptx

The Yoga for You Presentation

Sales & Marketing

The local yoga studio, 2 Yogis, wants to advertise to the community through a PowerPoint presentation to be shown at an upcoming fitness event. Maddie Wollman asked you to review the presentation that she created and comment on it. She worked hard to put this presentation together, using a template, animations, transitions, a photo album, and an interesting video. Her target audience includes people who are interested in being fit and reducing the stress in their lives. She expects the potential students to be in the age range of 15 to 50 years old. She knows they will only stop by her booth for a few moments, and she needs to quickly catch their attention and engage them.

a. Start **PowerPoint**, and then open the file **p02pf4Yoga**. Click **Enable Content**, and then save the file as p02pf4Yoga_LastFirst.

b. The presentation was created using a Standard slide size. You prefer using a Widescreen slide size. View the slide master, and then on the SLIDE MASTER tab, change the Slide Size to Widescreen. Review the presentation in Slide Show view. You may have to watch it multiple times to evaluate the content and design.

c. Place comments with ideas for improvement on the slides. Make comments regarding the slide content or design. You may also mention the positive elements on the slides.

d. Make changes to the fonts, WordArt, and color scheme in the slide master. Keep the font sizes and colors consistent. Make changes to the animations and transitions, making them more consistent, without having them become a distraction. Because you are now using a Widescreen slide size, you will have to adjust the size and position of the boxes and images.

e. Insert an online audio from the Office.com Clip Art containing soothing music. Place it on the title slide, have it start automatically, play it throughout all the slides in the presentation, and keep it hidden during the show.

f. Add at least one clip art or photo. Use the **p02pf4YBackground** photograph as a background for the title slide. Add more photos or clip art as necessary.

g. Remember, make sure you have a comment somewhere in the presentation for each change that you make. Similar changes can be grouped together in one comment.

h. Submit the file as directed by your instructor.

Integrated Projects

WORKSHOP 1 | WORD AND EXCEL INTEGRATION

OBJECTIVES

1. Link an object p. 1011
2. Update a linked object p. 1014
3. Embed an object p. 1019
4. Modify an embedded object p. 1021

Prepare Case

Updated Menu

Sales & Marketing

Blend Images / Shutterstock

Indigo5 is an upscale restaurant always striving to stay one step ahead of its clientele. Based on marketing and customer analysis over the past year, Alberto Dimas, restaurant manager, has decided to add new selections to the menu. He is writing a memo in Word to his staff to inform them of these new additions. He would like to include a chart he created in Excel. Alberto will also write a memo to William Mattingly, CEO of the Painted Paradise Golf Resort and Spa, informing him of customer trends for the past year. The memo will include a line chart to add visual impact. Your assignment is to practice linking and embedding the charts from Excel into the Word documents.

REAL WORLD SUCCESS

"I just started working for a travel agency that publishes a quarterly newsletter promoting upcoming tours. Travel information, including dates, length of tour, and price is kept in an Excel workbook. The newsletter is created using Word. I really impressed my new boss when I was able to show her how easy it is to link data from one document and have it updated in another. She was delighted to learn that it was not necessary to type everything twice."

- Elena, recent graduate

Student data files needed for this workshop:

 i01ws01IndigoMenu.docx

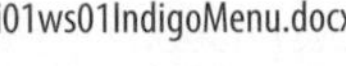 i01ws01IndigoMemo.docx

 i01ws01IndigoData.xlsx

 i01ws01IndigoReport.xlsx

You will save your files as:

 i01ws01IndigoMenu_LastFirst.docx

 i01ws01IndigoMemo_LastFirst.docx

 i01ws01IndigoData_LastFirst.xlsx

 i01ws01IndigoReport_LastFirst.xlsx

Object Linking and Embedding

An **object** is any item that can be selected and manipulated independently of surrounding text. Examples include pictures, shapes, charts, tables, sound clips, and videos. Using **OLE (Object Linking and Embedding)**—a feature in Microsoft Office—an object can be inserted into a file either as a linked object or an embedded object.

The program that creates the object is called the **source program**, and the file where the object is created is called the **source file**. The program that you insert the object into is called the **destination program**, and the file that you insert the object into is called the **destination file**.

A **linked object** is inserted into a document as a link that is still connected to the source file where it was originally created. When the object is updated in the source file, it will also be updated in the destination file. This is particularly useful if you have inserted the linked object into several different documents because they will all be updated automatically whenever changes are made to the source file. This means that you can make a change one time and the same change will be reflected in all objects that are linked to the source.

An **embedded object** is an object that is inserted into a document but is not connected to the file in which it was created. Changes made to the source of an embedded object will not be automatically updated in the embedded copy as they are with a link, and changes to the embedded object will not be reflected in the source. However, you can use the tools in the source program to update the embedded object in the destination file. There may be times when this is exactly what you want, since you can make changes in the destination file without changing the source file.

REAL WORLD ADVICE **To Link or Embed?**

Sometimes it is easier to copy and paste an object, but when you do, you lose the advantages that come with linking and embedding. The choice to link or embed is determined primarily by how you want to update your object. If you want to update the object in its original source program, then you would choose to link the object to the destination file. For example, you create a chart in Excel that has data that will change frequently. When you link the chart to a Word document, any changes you make to the chart in Excel will be reflected in Word. On the other hand, if you want the ability to update the chart in the destination file, you would choose to embed the chart. The advantages and disadvantages of linking and embedding are shown below in Table 1.

	Copy & Paste	Linking	Embedding
Where copied object is located	Destination file where it is pasted	Source file where it is created	Destination file where it is inserted
How copied object is updated	In the destination file with limited options	In the source file	In the destination file
Advantages	Simple way to create a copy of an object and paste it in another location	A single chart can be displayed in multiple files and only updated in the source file. Destination file size is reduced.	The destination file is a self-contained file not dependent on a source file
Disadvantages	Objects have to be updated in both the source and destination files	Must have access to source file to make changes	Objects may have to be updated in both the source and destination files. Destination file size is increased.

Table 1 Comparison of different methods of copying objects

Linking Objects

When an object is linked, information can be updated if the source file is modified. A linked object is stored in the source file. The destination file stores only the location of the source file, and it displays a representation of the linked object. Linking keeps the size of the destination document small. Use linked objects if the size of the destination file is a consideration. Linking is also useful when the data source is maintained by someone else and must be shared among many users. In this section, you will link an object, modify the object in the source file, and then update the object in the destination file.

Link an Object

Linking an object is advantageous because the data can be updated in the source file and the changes are reflected in the destination file. The data can be any object, including a chart, table, range of cells, or SmartArt graphic. An object can be linked to several documents, which will all be automatically updated when changes are made to the source file.

Linking an Excel Chart to a Word Document

When you link an Excel chart to a Word document, any changes you make to the Excel data will update the chart not only in Excel, but also in the linked Word document. The chart is still part of the source file, which is the Excel document, while the destination file, which is the Word document, contains the link file that is automatically updated. For this exercise, you will link an Excel chart to an existing Word document.

IP01.00

To Link an Excel Chart to a Word Document

a. Start **Word**, and then open **i01ws01IndigoMenu**. Maximize the Word window, if necessary.

b. Click the **FILE** tab, click **Save As**, and then navigate to the location where you are saving your files. Change the file name to i01ws01IndigoMenu_LastFirst using your last and first name. Click **Save**.

c. Insert a **left-aligned footer** with the file name, and then click **Save**. Click **Minimize** to minimize the Word window.

d. Start **Excel**, and then open **i01ws01IndigoData**. Maximize the Excel window, if necessary.

e. Click the **FILE** tab, click **Save As**, and then navigate to the location where you are saving your files. Change the file name to i01ws01IndigoData_LastFirst using your last and first name. Click **Save**.

f. Insert a **footer** with the file name in the left section, and then click **Save**.

g. Click the **Menu** worksheet tab, if necessary. Click the **chart border** once to select the pie chart. A border will appear around the edge of the object and the CHART TOOLS contextual tabs are displayed.

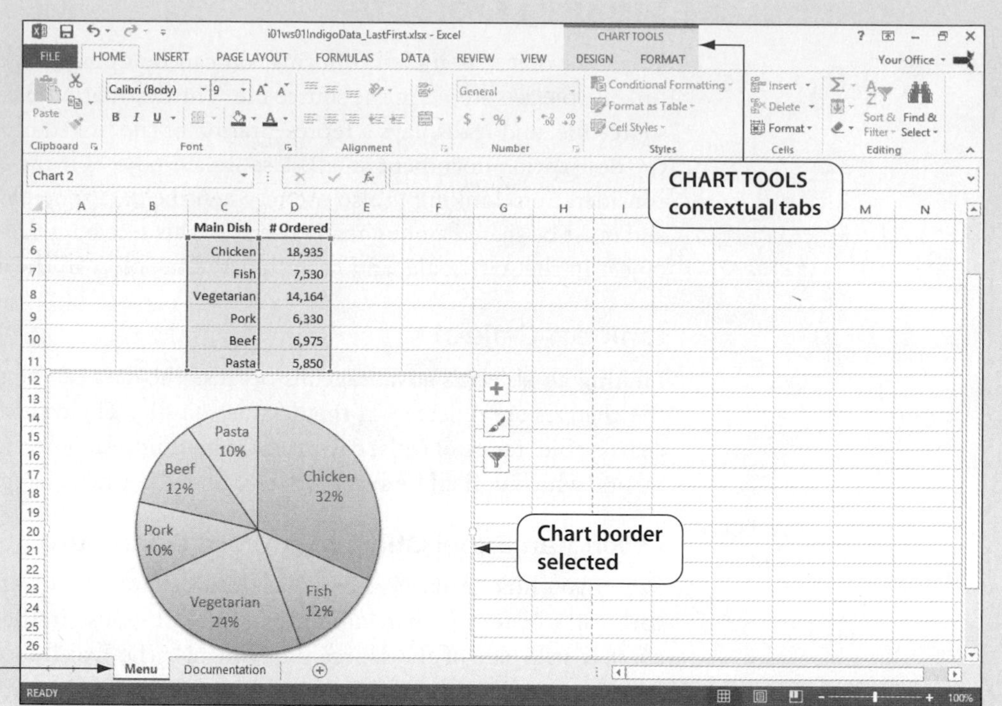

Figure 1 Chart selected in Excel

SIDE NOTE
Clipboard
Once on the Clipboard, an object can be pasted into any Office program.

h. On the HOME tab, in the Clipboard group, click **Copy** to copy the chart to the Clipboard.

i. Click **Word** on the taskbar to display the Word document. On the HOME tab, in the Paragraph group, click **Show/Hide** ¶ to show paragraph marks, and then click at the end of the second body paragraph after **vegetarian dishes**. Press Enter twice to insert a blank line and start a new paragraph.

SIDE NOTE
Paste Button
The choices you see on the Paste button menu change depending on the object you have selected to paste.

j. On the HOME tab, in the Clipboard group, click the **Paste** arrow, and then select **Paste Special**.

k. In the Paste Special dialog box, click the **Paste link** option, and then in the As box, select **Microsoft Excel Chart Object**.

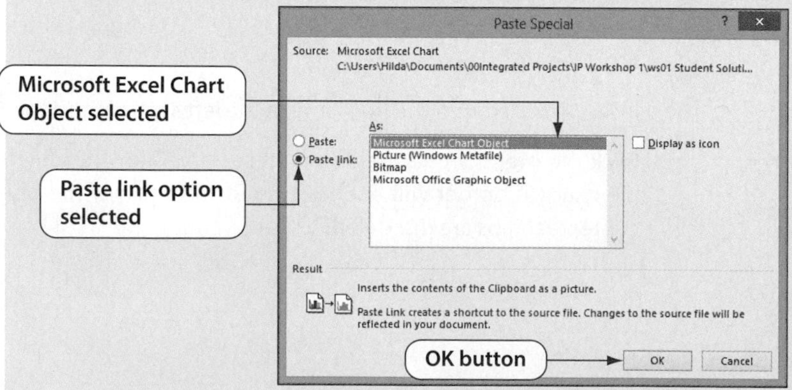

Figure 2 Paste Special dialog box with Paste link option selected

l. Click **OK**. The chart is pasted in the Word document as a linked object.

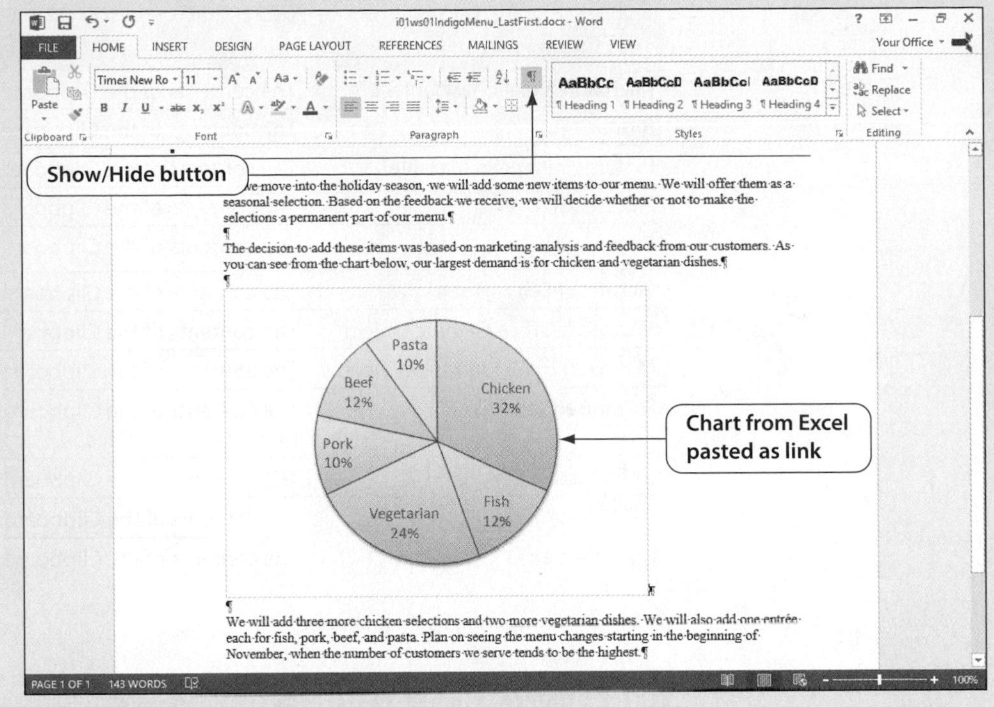

Figure 3 Word document with linked Excel chart

m. Click **Save** [Save], and then click **Minimize** [Minimize] to minimize the Word window.

REAL WORLD ADVICE Nonprinting Characters

To see things like spaces, paragraph marks, and other nonprinting characters, on the HOME tab, in the Paragraph group, click Show/Hide ¶. With this option turned on, you will see the paragraph marks and other hidden formatting symbols. It may be easier to see the end of a paragraph with this option turned on. To hide the marks and symbols, click Show/Hide ¶ again.

If the source file is in Excel and you choose Paste link As:	Depending on what has been copied, this will be inserted:
Microsoft Excel Chart Object	The contents of the Clipboard
Bitmap	The contents of the Clipboard as a bitmap picture
Picture (Enhanced Metafile)	The contents of the Clipboard as an enhanced metafile
Picture (GIF)	The contents of the Clipboard as a GIF picture
Picture (PNG)	The contents of the Clipboard as a PNG picture
Picture (JPEG)	The contents of the Clipboard as a JPEG picture
Microsoft Office Graphic Object	The contents of the Clipboard as shapes
Microsoft Excel Worksheet Object	The contents of the Clipboard
Formatted Text (RTF)	The contents of the Clipboard as text with font and table formatting
Unformatted Text	The contents of the Clipboard without any formatting
HTML Format	The contents of the Clipboard in HTML format
Unformatted Unicode Text	The contents of the Clipboard as text without any formatting

Table 2 Comparing Paste link options

REAL WORLD ADVICE **What Else Can Be Linked?**

Any time you want to maintain continuity between data in two programs like Excel and Word, consider linking the data so when the data is updated, it is updated in both places at the same time. You can link anything between Excel and Word—objects, text, charts, or tables. You can also link from Excel to Word or from Word to Excel using the Paste link option in the Paste Special dialog box. See Table 2 for the different Paste link options.

SIDE NOTE

A Link Is Not the Same as a Hyperlink

A link between a source and destination file is different than a hyperlink. A hyperlink is a navigation tool, a link is not.

Update a Linked Object

When both the source file and destination file are open and data is changed in the source file of a linked object, the data will only be updated in the destination file if you manually update the link for the object. This gives you control over when and how to update a link in the destination file.

When the destination file is closed and then opened, the linked object is automatically updated unless you turn off automatic updates in the Links options.

REAL WORLD ADVICE **Change Automatic Link Updates**

There may be times when you do not want the link to be automatically updated when the destination file is opened. If you are sharing a file with people who are unfamiliar with Word, it might confuse them or frustrate them if they do not know what to do when they get the dialog box asking to update the link. Instead, you can turn off the option to update links automatically and require a manual update of the link. This option can be set for a specific object or for all objects in Word.

- To turn off the automatic update option for all linked objects in Word, on the File tab, click Options, and select Advanced. Under General—you may have to scroll down—click Update automatic links at open to clear the check box.
- To turn off the automatic update option for a specific object in Word, right-click the object and point to Linked Worksheet Object. Click Links, and in the Links dialog box click Manual update. Click OK.

Updating a Linked Excel Chart in a Word Document

When data related to a chart is changed in Excel, the chart in Excel is automatically updated. However, the chart may or may not be automatically updated in the destination file depending on whether the destination file is open or closed. For this exercise, you will make changes to a chart in Excel, and then manually update the chart in the Word document, which is open.

IP01.01

To Update an Excel Chart

a. Click **Excel** on the taskbar to display the Excel workbook.

b. Click the **chart** to select it. Under CHART TOOLS, on the DESIGN tab, in the Type group, click **Change Chart Type**. Select **3-D Pie**, and then click **OK**.

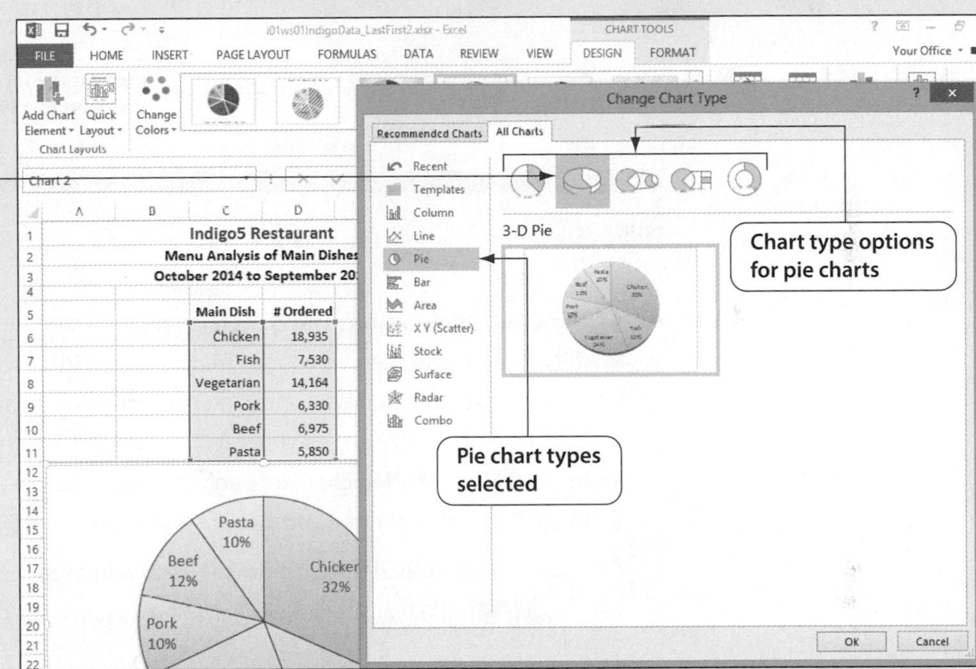

Figure 4 Change Chart Type options for Pie charts

c. In the Chart Layouts group, click the **Add Chart Element** arrow, point to **Chart Title**, and then select **Above Chart**. In the formula bar, type Main Dishes Ordered by Type and then press Enter. Click the **HOME** tab, and then in the Font group, click **Bold** B to apply bold to the title.

d. Click cell **D7**, type 9000 to change the number of Fish dishes ordered, and then press Enter. The percentage for Fish in the chart changes from 12% to 15% to reflect this change.

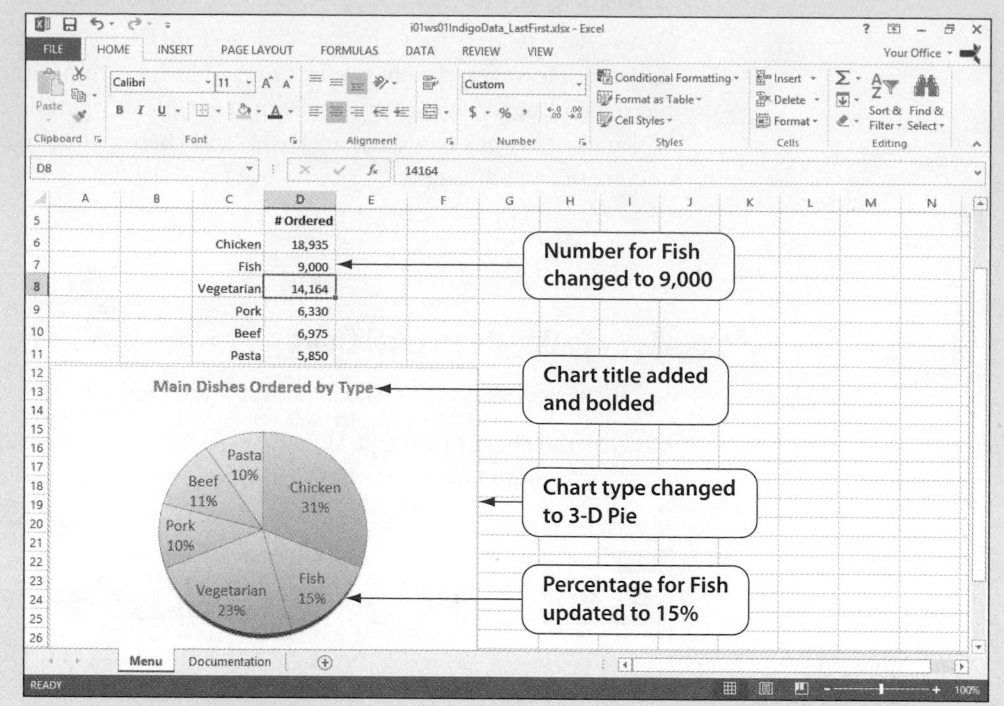

Figure 5 Chart type and data in Excel changed

e. Click the **Documentation** worksheet tab, and then complete the following:
   - Click cell **A8**, and then type today's date in mm/dd/yyyy format.
   - Click cell **B8**, and then type your name in last name, first name format.
   - Click cell **C8**, type Changed chart type to 3-D Pie and then press Enter.
   - In cell **C9**, type Added chart title and then press Enter.
   - In cell **C10**, type Changed number of Fish dishes in cell D7 to 9000 and then press Enter.

f. Click **Save**, and then click **Minimize** to minimize the Excel window.

g. Click **Word** on the taskbar to display the Word document.

h. Click the **chart** to select it, right-click the **chart**, and then on the shortcut menu, select **Update Link**. The chart is updated with the changes you made in Excel.

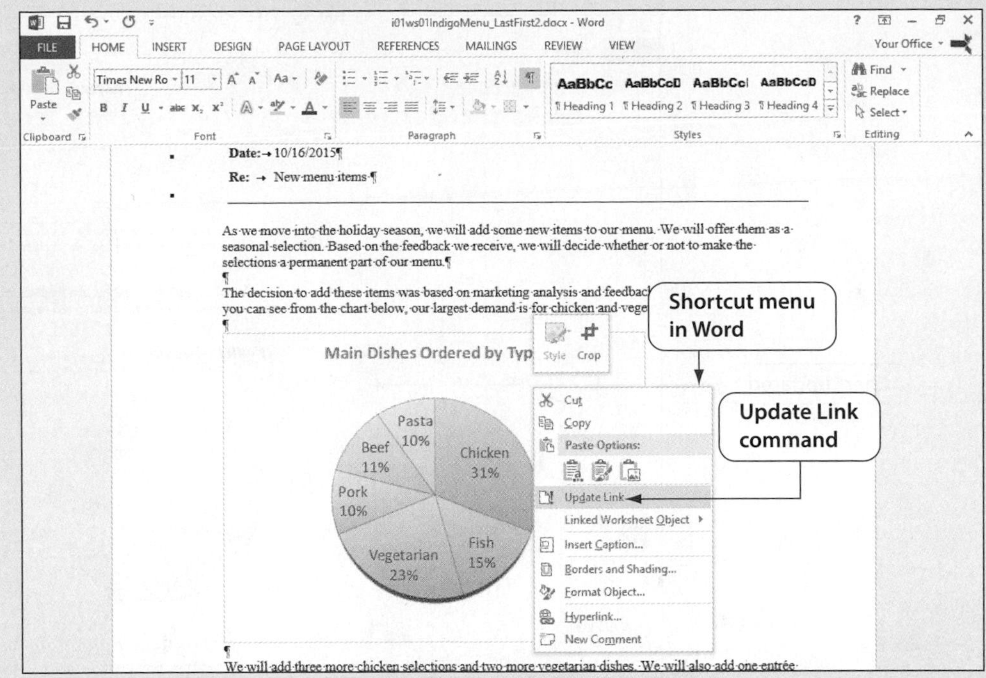

Figure 6 Shortcut menu with Update Link command

Troubleshooting

Did you get an error message? If you changed the name of the source file or moved the source file to a new folder, the update will not work. If Excel cannot find the source file in the same folder as the destination file, it will break the link with the destination file. To have the object linked again, you will have to open the Links dialog box and change the source file to the new location or new file name, or move the source file to the same folder as the destination file. To change the source file do the following:

1. Right-click the object in the destination file.
2. Point to Linked Worksheet Object, and then click Links.
3. Click Change Source, select the new location or name of the source file, and then click Open. Click OK.

i. On the HOME tab, in the Paragraph group, click **Center** to center the chart horizontally in the document. Click **Show/Hide** to hide paragraph marks.

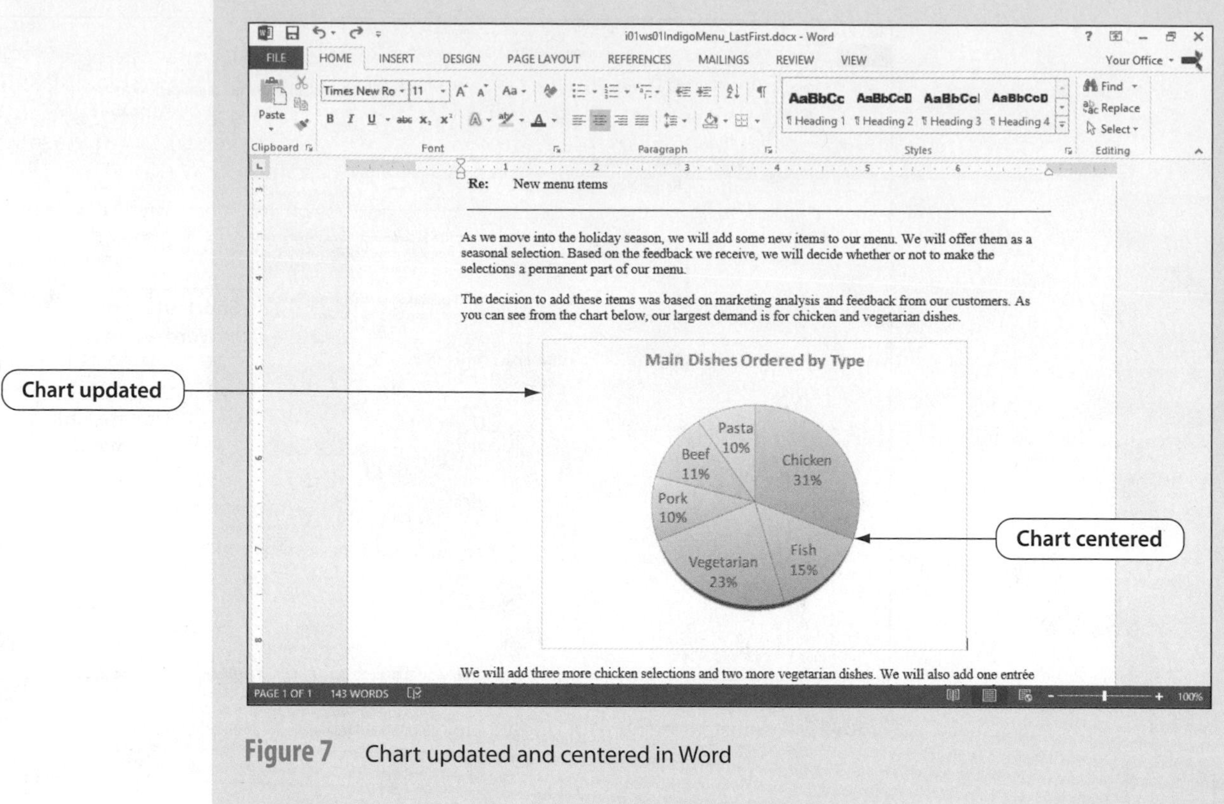

Figure 7 Chart updated and centered in Word

j. Click **Save** , and then click **Close** to close Word.

k. Click **Excel** on the taskbar to display the Excel workbook, and then close Excel.

CONSIDER THIS | **To Link or Not to Link?**

Teamwork is an important part of business. When sending files between team members, linking can easily cause errors because of the source file. Do you think when working in a team you should not use links? Why or why not?

REAL WORLD ADVICE | **Teamwork and Linking Files**

There are a number of options you can choose when setting up links to help preserve those links, especially when files are being shared by several people. Right-click a linked object, point to Linked Worksheet Object, then select Links to open the Links dialog box where you will find the options listed in Table 3.

Action	Effect	Advantages	Disadvantages
Manual Update	When the destination file opens, the user will not get a message about there being a linked object.	If the user of the destination file is unfamiliar with Word, the manual update will not cause any confusion over what to do.	The destination file object will not be automatically updated to reflect changes made in the source file.
Locked	The object will not be updated.	When someone else is given a file, you may want to have control over what data they see, so having an object that cannot be updated may be beneficial.	The link will not be updated even though it has not been broken.
Change Source	Changes the source file where the object is found.	If a source file has been renamed or moved, the source file for the object can be changed to the new name or location.	If the source file has been renamed or moved but you do not know the new name or where it has been moved, then this option will not help.
Break Link	The destination file and source file will no longer be linked by the object.	No need to worry about moving a source file or changing its name.	Changes made in the source file will no longer be reflected in the destination file.

Table 3 Links options

Embedding Objects

When you embed an object, the object is physically stored in the destination file along with all the information needed to manage the object. After embedded objects are inserted, they become part of the destination file and are not linked to the source file. A document containing embedded objects will be larger than one containing the same objects as links. Changes can be made to the object in the destination file. These changes will not be automatically reflected in the source file. If you also want to make changes in the source file, you will have to make those changes manually. In this section, you will embed an object and then modify it in the destination file using tools from the source program.

Embed an Object

For certain purposes, embedding offers several advantages over links. Users can transfer documents with embedded objects to other computers or other locations on the same computer, without breaking a link. Embedding can also be useful when you do not want changes to be reflected in the source file.

Embedding an Excel Chart in a Word Document

An Excel chart embedded in a Word document becomes part of the document and any changes made to the chart will remain in the document. Changes made to the chart in the Word document will not be reflected in the Excel worksheet. For this exercise, you will embed an Excel chart in a Word document.

IP01.02

To Embed an Excel Chart

a. Start **Word**, and then open **i01ws01IndigoMemo**. Maximize the Word window, if necessary.

b. Click the **FILE** tab, click **Save As**, and then navigate to the location where you are saving your files. Change the file name to i01ws01IndigoMemo_LastFirst using your last and first name. Click **Save**.

c. Insert a **left-aligned footer** with the file name, and then click **Save**. Click **Minimize** to minimize Word.

d. Start **Excel**, and then open **i01ws01IndigoReport**.

e. Click the **FILE** tab, click **Save As**, and then navigate to the location where you are saving your files. Change the file name to i01ws01IndigoReport_LastFirst using your last and first name. Click **Save**.

f. Insert the **file name** in the left section of the footer, and then click **Save**. Maximize the Excel window, if necessary.

g. Click the **Customers** worksheet tab, if necessary. Select the line chart by clicking the **chart border** once. A border appears around the edge of the object.

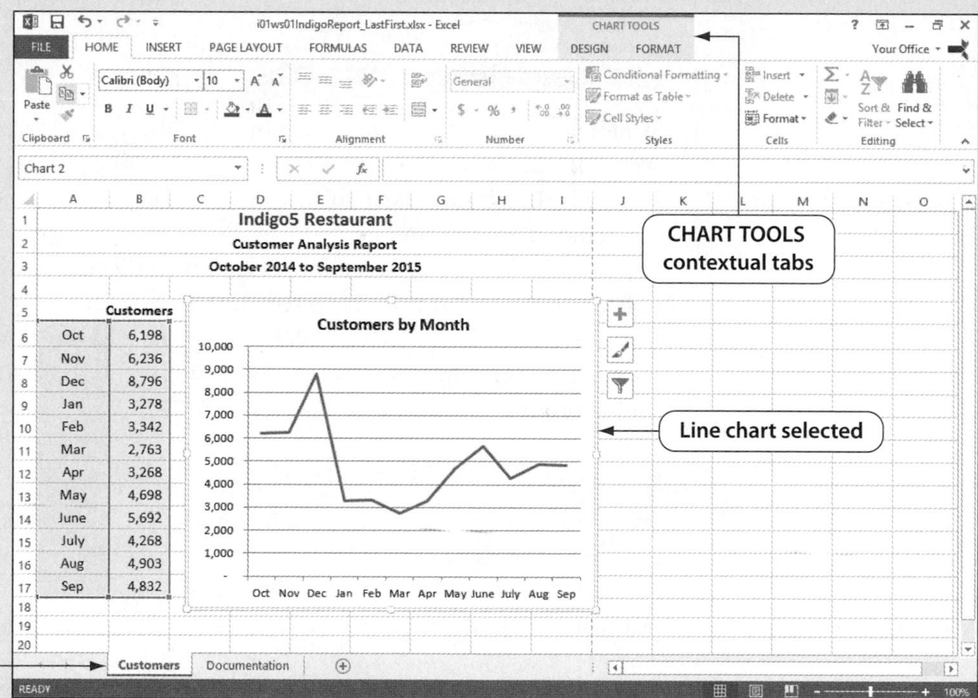

Figure 8 Excel worksheet with chart selected

h. On the HOME tab, in the Clipboard group, click **Copy** to copy the chart to the Clipboard. Click **Minimize** to minimize the Excel window.

i. Click **Word** on the taskbar. On the HOME tab, in the Paragraph group, click **Show/Hide** to show paragraph marks. Click at the end of the last sentence of the last paragraph. Press Enter twice to insert a blank line and start a new paragraph.

j. On the HOME tab, in the Clipboard group, click the **Paste** arrow, and then select **Paste Special**. In the Paste Special dialog box, click the **Paste** option, and then in the As box, select **Microsoft Excel Chart Object**.

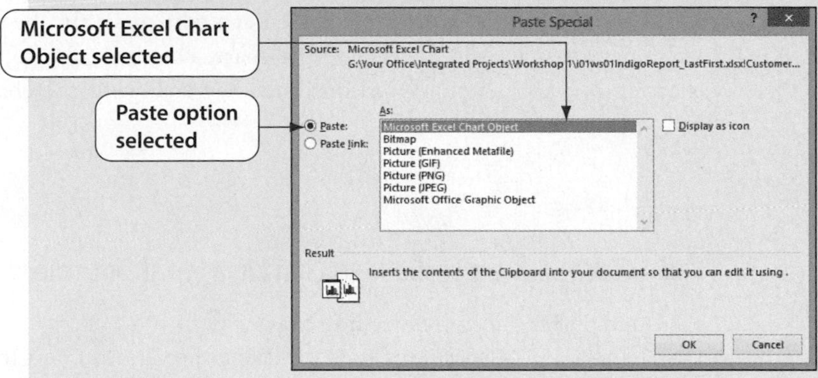

Figure 9 Paste Special dialog box with Paste option selected

k. Click **OK**. The chart is embedded in the Word document.

l. On the HOME tab, in the Paragraph group, click **Show/Hide** to hide paragraph marks, and then click **Save**.

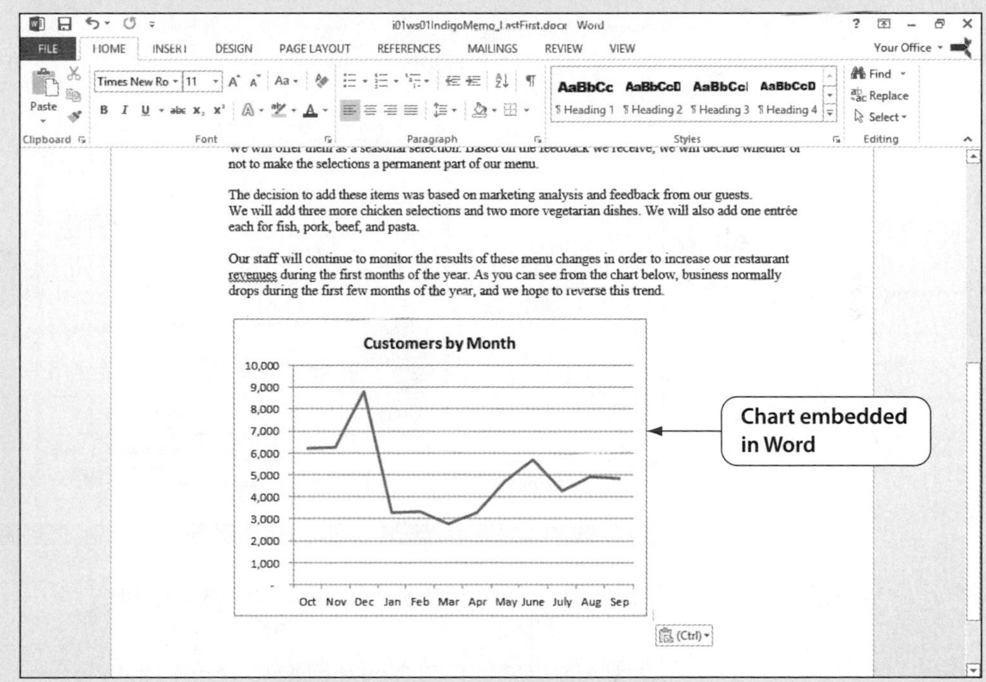

Figure 10 Word document with embedded Excel chart

Modify an Embedded Object

When you edit an embedded object in the destination file, the changes affect only the object in the destination file. This is what makes it different from linking or using a copy and paste command.

Modifying an Embedded Chart in a Word Document

Modifying an embedded chart in a Word document will change the chart in the document, but the chart in the Excel workbook will remain unchanged. Alternately, changing the chart in Excel will not change the chart in the Word document. However, the embedded chart can be edited using Excel tools in the Word document because it was embedded as a Microsoft Excel Chart Object. You can edit not only the chart options but also the Excel data that was used to create the chart. For this exercise, you will modify an Excel chart embedded in your Word document by changing the chart type, editing the title, and revising data.

IP01.03

To Modify an Embedded Chart in a Word Document

a. Double-click the embedded **line chart**.

The CHART TOOLS tabs appear, making the various Chart Tools from Excel available. The worksheet tabs in the original worksheet are also visible at the bottom of the object, with an additional tab for Chart 1.

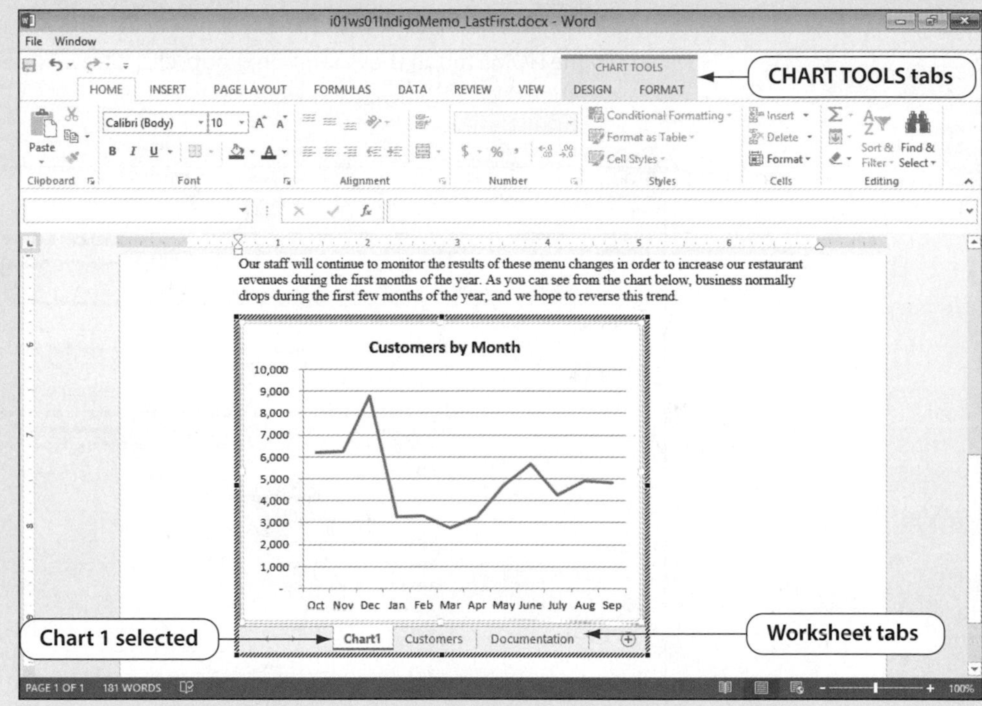

Figure 11 Chart Tools show editing options available

b. Under CHART TOOLS, on the DESIGN tab, in the Type group, click **Change Chart Type**. Select **Line with Markers**, the fourth option.

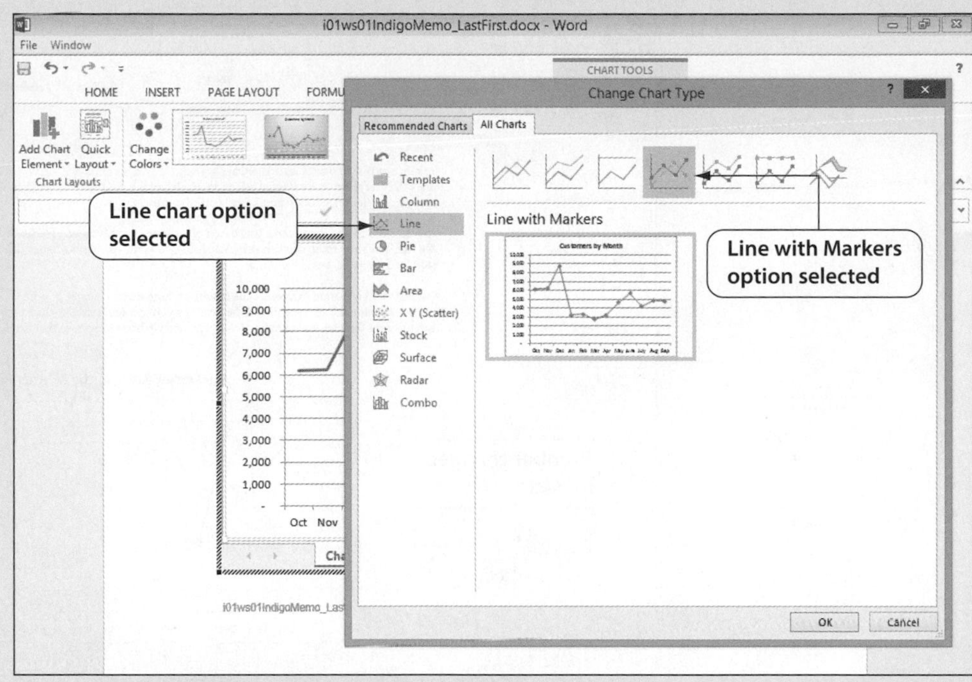

Figure 12 Change Chart Type options for Line charts

c. Click **OK**. The line chart in the Word document changes to add markers.

d. Click the **chart title** to select it, and then click the title again to place the insertion point within the placeholder. Change the title to read Customer Analysis by Month.

e. Click the **Customers** worksheet tab. Click cell **B6**, change the Oct Customers to 8000 and then press Enter. The chart is updated to show this change.

f. Click the **Chart 1** worksheet tab to see the change reflected in the chart. Click outside the chart to deselect it.

g. Click the **border** of the chart to select it. On the HOME tab, in the Paragraph group, click **Center** to center the chart horizontally in the document. Click outside the chart to deselect it.

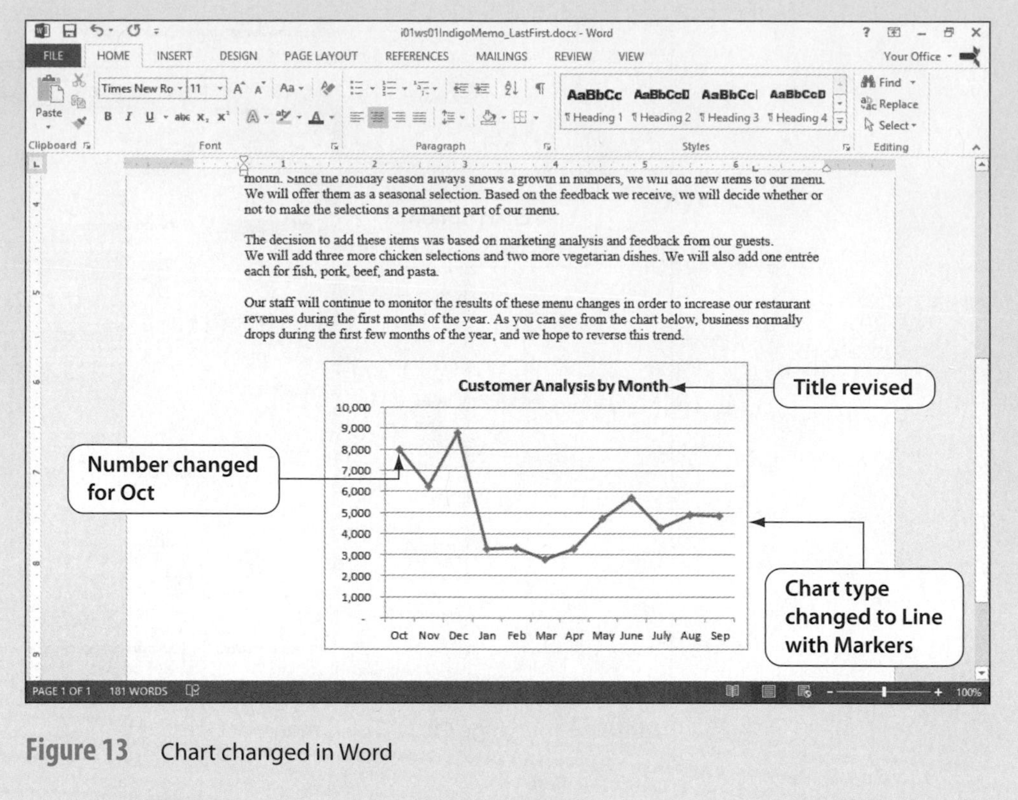

Figure 13 Chart changed in Word

h. Click **Save** [Save icon], and then click **Close** [Close icon] to close Word.

Modifying a Chart in an Excel Workbook

The chart and data in the Excel workbook have not changed. If you want to make sure that both documents reflect the changes made in the Word document, you will need to make the same changes manually in the Excel workbook. For this exercise, you will update the chart and data in the Excel workbook to correspond to the changes that you made to the chart and data in the Word document. Note that there may be times when you choose not to update the source document.

IP01.04

To Modify a Chart in an Excel Workbook

a. Click **Excel** [Excel icon] on the taskbar to display the Excel workbook.

b. Click the **chart border** to select the chart. The CHART TOOLS contextual tab appears, making the various Chart Tools available.

c. Under CHART TOOLS, on the DESIGN tab, in the Type group, click **Change Chart Type**, select **Line with Markers**, the fourth option, and then click **OK**.

d. Click the **chart title** to select it, and then click the placeholder again to place the insertion point within the title placeholder. Change the title to read Customer Analysis by Month and then click outside the chart.

e. Click cell **B6**, change the Oct Customers to 8000 and then press Enter.

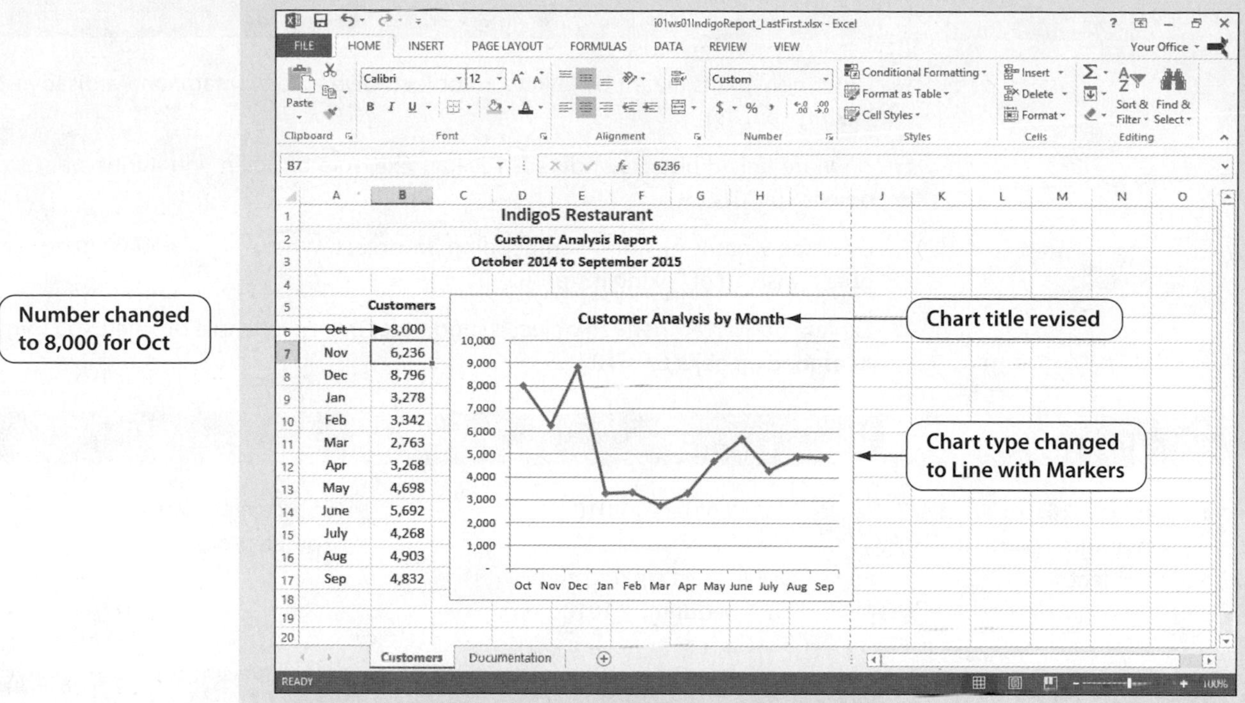

Figure 14 Chart changed in Excel

f. Click the **Documentation** worksheet tab, and then complete the following.
   - Click cell **A8**, and then type today's date in mm/dd/yyyy format.
   - Click cell **B8**, and then type your name in last name, first name format.
   - Click cell **C8**, type Changed chart type to Line with Markers and then press Enter.
   - In cell **C9**, type Revised chart title and then press Enter.
   - In cell **C10**, type Changed Oct Customers in cell B6 to 8000 and then press Enter.

g. Click **Save**, and then click **Close** to close Excel. Submit your files as directed by your instructor.

Concept Check

1. Describe what is meant by linking an object. Give an advantage and a disadvantage of linking. p. 1011
2. How are linked objects updated? Give an example of when you might want to link an object. p. 1014
3. Describe what is meant by embedding an object. When might you want to embed an object instead of linking it? p. 1019
4. Explain how an embedded object is modified. Give an example of when you might want to embed an object. p. 1021

Key Terms

Destination file 1010
Destination program 1010
Embedded object 1010
Linked object 1010
Object 1010
OLE (Object Linking and Embedding) 1010
Source file 1010
Source program 1010

Visual Summary

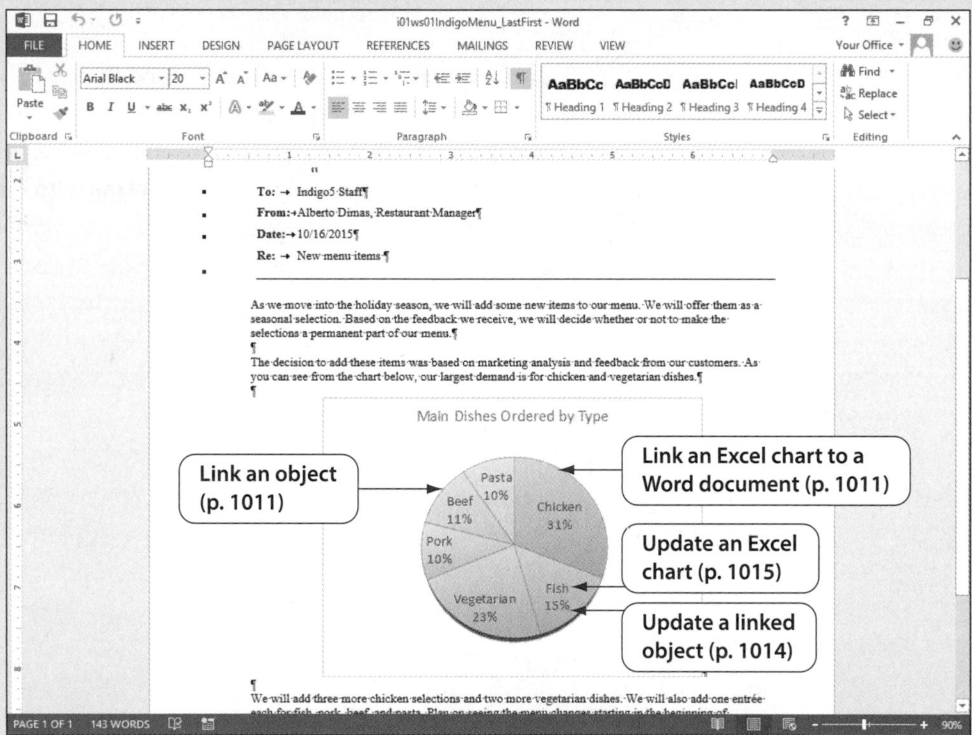

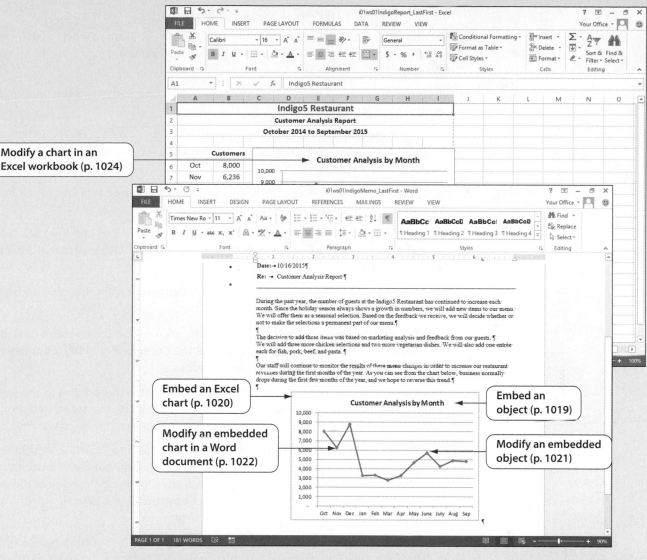

Modify a chart in an Excel workbook (p. 1024)

Embed an Excel chart (p. 1020)

Modify an embedded chart in a Word document (p. 1022)

Embed an object (p. 1019)

Modify an embedded object (p. 1021)

Figure 15 Object Linking and Embedding Final

Practice 1

Student data files needed:

- i01ws01WeddingPlan.docx
- i01ws01WeddingCost.xlsx

You will save your files as:

- i01ws01WeddingPlan_LastFirst.docx
- i01ws01WeddingCost_LastFirst.xlsx

Wedding Planning

Sales & Marketing

The staff in the Event Planning department would like to promote full-service weddings at the Painted Paradise Golf Resort and Spa. A full-service wedding includes all aspects of the planning and execution of the event. One staff member wrote a short description in Word promoting the service and another staff member put together a sample budget and time line in Excel. Your job is to link the budget and embed the time line in the Word document.

a. Start **Word**, and then open **i01ws01WeddingPlan**.

b. Click the **FILE** tab, click **Save As**, and then navigate to the location where you are saving your files. Save the file as i01ws01WeddingPlan_LastFirst using your last and first name. Click **Save**.

c. Insert a **left-aligned footer** with the file name, and then click **Save**. Click **Minimize** to minimize the Word window.

d. Start **Excel**, and then open **i01ws01WeddingCost**.

e. Click the **FILE** tab, click **Save As**, and then navigate to the location where you are saving your files. Save the file as i01ws01WeddingCost_LastFirst using your last and first name. Click **Save**.

f. Insert the **file name** in the left section of the footer, and then click **Save**. Maximize the Excel window, if necessary.

g. Click the **Budget** worksheet tab. Select the range of cells **A4:C17**. On the HOME tab, in the Clipboard group, click **Copy** to copy the data to the Clipboard. Click **Minimize** to minimize the Excel window.

h. Click **Word** on the taskbar to display the document. Click the blank line below **Budget Worksheet**, and then press Enter to go to a new line.

i. On the HOME tab, in the Clipboard group, click the **Paste** arrow, and then select **Paste Special**. Select the **Paste link** option button, and then select **Microsoft Excel Worksheet Object**. Click **OK**.

j. On the HOME tab, in the Paragraph group, click **Center** to center the table horizontally. Click **Save**, and then close Word.

k. Click **Excel** on the taskbar to display the workbook. Change the **Average Cost of the Coordinator** to 750 and the **Average Cost of the Ceremony** to 1500. Click **Save**, and then click **Minimize** to minimize the Excel window.

l. Start **Word**, and then open **i01ws01WeddingPlan_LastFirst**. Click **Yes** to the warning about updating links. If the data was not updated, right-click the **table**, and then click **Update Link**. Click **Save**, and then click **Minimize** to minimize the Word window.

m. Click **Excel** on the taskbar to display the workbook. Click the **Timeline** worksheet tab, click the **SmartArt graphic** to select it, and then click the **top border** to ensure that the entire SmartArt graphic is selected. A border will appear around the edge of the object. On the HOME tab, in the Clipboard group, click **Copy** to copy the SmartArt graphic to the Clipboard. Click **Minimize** to minimize the Excel window.

n. Click **Word** on the taskbar to display the document. Place the insertion point in front of the **Wedding Timeline** heading, and then press CTRL+Enter to insert a page break and move the heading to the top of page 2.

o. Click the blank line below **Wedding Timeline**. On the HOME tab, in the Clipboard group, click the **Paste** arrow, and then select **Paste Special**. Select the **Paste** option, and then select **Microsoft Office Graphic Object**. Click **OK**.

p. Click the embedded **SmartArt graphic**. Under SMARTART TOOLS, on the DESIGN tab, in the SmartArt Styles group, select **Change Colors**, and then change the color to **Accent 3 - Gradient Range - Accent 3**. Change the heading for **1 Month** to 1–2 Months. Click outside of the SmartArt graphic to deselect it. Click **Save**, and then close Word.

q. Click **Excel** on the taskbar to display the workbook. Click the **Timeline** worksheet tab. Change the heading for **1 Month** to 1–2 Months. Do not change colors.

r. Click the **Documentation** worksheet tab, and then complete the following:

- Click cell **A8**, and then type today's date in mm/dd/yyyy format.
- Click cell **B8**, and then type your name in last name, first name format.
- Click cell **C8**, type Changed the Average Cost of the Coordinator to 750 and then press Enter.

- In cell **C9**, type Changed the Average Cost of the Ceremony to 1500 and then press Enter.
- In cell **C10**, type Changed heading from 1 Month to 1–2 Months.

s. Click **Save**, and then close Excel. Submit your files as directed by your instructor.

Practice 2

Student data files needed:	You will save your files as:
i01ws01RaceFlyer.docx	i01ws01RaceFlyer_LastFirst.docx
i01ws01RaceBudget.xlsx	i01ws01RaceBudget_LastFirst.xlsx

Running Event

Customer Service

The Event Planning department is excited about organizing a new competitive 5k and 10k run/walk at the resort. The event is designed to bring families to the resort for the weekend and will include a cookout, prizes, and opportunities to tour the resort. The flyer for the event was created in Word and has some charts that would be nice to include in the financial report that was created in Excel. Your assignment is to link and embed the data from Word into Excel.

a. Start **Word**, and then open **i01ws01RaceFlyer**.

b. Click the **FILE** tab, click **Save As**, and then navigate to the location where you are saving your files. Change the file name to i01ws01RaceFlyer_LastFirst using your last and first name. Click **Save**.

c. Insert a **left-aligned footer** with the file name, and then click **Save**. Click **Minimize** to minimize the Word window.

d. Start **Excel**, and then open **i01ws01RaceBudget**.

e. Click the **FILE** tab, click **Save As**, and then navigate to the location where you are saving your files. Change the file name to i01ws01RaceBudget_LastFirst using your last and first name. Click **Save**.

f. Insert a **left-aligned footer** with the file name, and then click **Save**. Maximize the Excel window, if necessary.

g. Click **Word** on the taskbar to display the document. Select the **table** with the registration fees. On the HOME tab, in the Clipboard group, click **Copy** to copy the table to the Clipboard. Click **Minimize** to minimize the Word window.

h. Click **Excel** on the taskbar to display the workbook. Select cell **D3**. On the **HOME** tab, in the **Clipboard** group, click the **Paste** arrow, and then select **Paste Special**. Select the **Paste link** option, and then select **Microsoft Word Document Object**. Click **OK**. Click **Save**, and then close Excel.

i. Click **Word** on the taskbar to display the document. Change the **Day of Race** amounts for the **5k** to $35 and for the **10k** to $45. Click **Save**, and then click **Minimize** to minimize the Word window.

j. Start **Excel**, and then open **i01ws01RaceBudget_LastFirst**. Click **Enable Content** in the Security Warning bar. The Day of Race amounts are updated. Click **Save**, and then click **Minimize** to minimize the Excel window.

k. Click **Word** on the taskbar to display the document. Click the **SmartArt** graphic once to select it, and then click the **top border** to ensure that the entire SmartArt object is selected. A border will appear around the edge of the object. On the HOME tab, in the Clipboard group, click **Copy** to copy the SmartArt graphic to the Clipboard. Click **Minimize** to minimize the Word window.

l. Click **Excel** on the taskbar to display the workbook. Select cell **E12**. On the HOME tab, in the Clipboard group, click the **Paste** arrow, and then select **Paste Special**. Select the **Paste** option, and then select **Microsoft Office Drawing Object**. Click **OK**.

m. Click the embedded **SmartArt** graphic. Change the order of the text to read **Race Run Walk**. Click outside the SmartArt graphic to deselect it.

n. Click the **PAGE LAYOUT** tab, and then in the Page Setup group, click **Orientation**, and then select **Landscape**. In the **Scale to Fit** group, click the **Width** arrow, and then select **1 page** so the table and SmartArt graphic will print on the same page as the budget.

o. Click the **Documentation** worksheet tab, and then complete the following:

- Click cell **A8**, and then type today's date in mm/dd/yyyy format.
- Click cell **B8**, and then type your name in Last name, First name format.
- Click cell **C8**, type Inserted linked table in cell D3 and then press Enter.
- In cell **C9**, type Inserted embedded SmartArt graphic in cell E12 and then press Enter.
- In cell **C10**, type Changed order of text in SmartArt graphic and then press Enter.
- In cell **C11**, type Changed orientation to Landscape and to fit 1 page.

p. Click **Save**, and then close Excel.

q. Click **Word** on the taskbar to display the document. Click the embedded **SmartArt graphic**. Change the order of the text to read **Race Run Walk**. Click outside the SmartArt to deselect it. Click **Save**, and then close Word. Submit your files as directed by your instructor.

Problem Solve 1

Student data files needed:

i01ws01ShopReport.docx

i01ws01ShopAnalysis.xlsx

You will save your files as:

 i01ws01ShopReport_LastFirst.docx

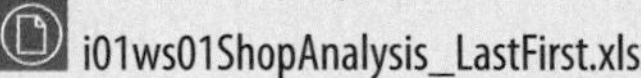

Gift Shop Update

Finance & Accounting

The gift shop, Painted Treasures, is reporting its revenue and staffing for the first quarter of the year. A short document has been created with a description of the analysis in Word, but the numbers, charts, and graphics are all in Excel. Your assignment is to link the chart created in Excel to the Word document, and embed the organization chart created in Excel in the Word document.

a. Start **Word**, open **i01ws01ShopReport**, and then save it as i01ws01ShopReport_LastFirst using your last and first name.

b. Start **Excel**, open **i01ws01ShopAnalysis**, and then save it as i01ws01ShopAnalysis_LastFirst using your last and first name.

c. Click the **Revenue** worksheet tab, copy the pie chart, and then paste it in the Word document after the first body paragraph as a linked Microsoft Excel Chart Object.

d. In the source file, add a **chart title** above the pie chart with the title Gift Shop Sales by Segment. In the Word document, update the link to reflect this change.

e. In the source file, on the **Staffing** worksheet tab, copy the **organization chart**, and then paste it in the Word document after the second body paragraph as an embedded Microsoft Office Graphic Object.

f. In the destination file, change the **Manager** name to First Last, using your first and last name.

g. Resize the pie chart and the SmartArt graphic so everything fits on one page, delete any blank pages, and then center the pie chart and SmartArt graphic horizontally on the page. Save the document and close Word.

h. In the source file, change the **Manager** name in the SmartArt graphic to your own name. If requested by your instructor, update the Documentation worksheet appropriately. Save the workbook and close Excel. Submit your files as directed by your instructor.

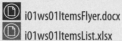

Problem Solve 2

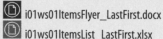

Student data files needed:	You will save your files as:
i01ws01ItemsFlyer.docx	i01ws01ItemsFlyer_LastFirst.docx
i01ws01ItemsList.xlsx	i01ws01ItemsList_LastFirst.xlsx

Gift Shop Preview

Sales & Marketing

People have been asking for articles with the Painted Paradise logo that can be purchased as souvenirs of their resort visit. Susan Brock, Painted Treasures Gift Shop manager, has decided to add some new, low-cost items to meet this need. She has created a worksheet with the names of new items, wholesale cost, and retail cost. Susan has asked you to create a flyer advertising a preview of the new items with just the item name and the retail cost. After embedding the data from the Excel worksheet in the Word document, you will format it attractively.

a. Start **Word**, open **i01ws01ItemsFlyer**, and then save it as i01ws01ItemsFlyer_LastFirst using your last and first name. Insert a **left-aligned footer** with the file name, and then save the flyer.

b. Start **Excel**, open **i01ws01ItemsList**, and then save it as i01ws01ItemsList_LastFirst using your first and last name. Click the **New Items** worksheet tab, and then insert a footer with the file name in the left section. Save the workbook.

c. Select cells **A4:C13**, and then click **Copy**.

d. Click **Word** on the taskbar, and then show paragraph marks and other hidden formatting symbols. Position the insertion point in front of the **second section break**. Paste the **table** as an embedded Microsoft Excel Worksheet Object.

e. Double-click the **embedded table**. Delete the middle column that lists wholesale prices.

f. Select cells **A4:B13**, and then increase the font size to 18. Increase the width of column **B** so the heading **Retail Price** is on one line, and then center the heading vertically. Click the **View** tab, and then in the Show group, deselect **Gridlines** to remove gridlines from the table.

g. Deselect the table, and then hide the paragraph marks. Save the document, and then close Word and Excel. Submit your files as directed by your instructor.

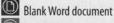

Perform 1: Perform in Your Career

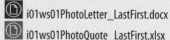

Student data files needed:	You will save your files as:
Blank Word document	i01ws01PhotoLetter_LastFirst.docx
Blank Excel worksheet	i01ws01PhotoQuote_LastFirst.xlsx

Photography Quotes for Potential Customers

Sales & Marketing

You are an independent photographer who specializes in small events and small groups, including families. You are constantly sending out quotes to potential clients. Your quote form is kept in Excel, but the letters you send out are in Word. You therefore need to link your workbook data with the letter you send to potential clients. Your quote must include the date of the event, customer name, a description of the job and its location, the approximate number of hours the job will take, extra travel time required, and any special requests. You need the flexibility to change the data in Excel and have it change in Word at the same time.

a. Start **Word**, and then create a letter to potential clients. Include a return address, date, greeting, and closing, and then save the letter as i01ws01PhotoLetter_LastFirst using your last and first name. Insert a left-aligned footer.

b. Start **Excel**, and then create a **quote sheet** for your services. Include a heading with your company information, headings for the date of the event, customer name, job location and description, number of hours required, extra travel time involved, any special requests, and the cost of the job. Save the file as i01pf1PhotoQuote_LastFirst using your last and first name. Insert a footer in the left section of the Excel workbook with the file name.

c. Complete the quote for a fictitious client. Copy the data for the quote, and then paste it into your Word document so it is linked to Excel. Save **i01pf1PhotoLetter_LastFirst** with the linked data.

d. Submit your files as directed by your instructor.

Perform 2: How Others Perform

Student data files needed:

i01ws01SurveyReview.docx

i01ws01SurveyData.xlsx

You will save your files as:

i01ws01SurveyReview_LastFirst.docx

i01ws01SurveyData_LastFirst.xlsx

Computer Students Survey

Information Technology

Your computer professor has surveyed 100 students to determine how comfortable they are with the four major Microsoft Office applications. A student assistant has compiled the survey results using Excel and has written a Word document summarizing the outcome. The professor plans to give the survey again at the end of the semester to assess how comfort levels have changed. She would like to enter new data results in the Excel worksheet and then automatically update both the table and chart in the Word document. So far, what the student assistant has done is not working properly. You have been asked to look at both documents and make any revisions necessary to link the data in the Excel file to the Word file, so changes made to the Excel data can be easily updated in the table and chart in the Word document.

a. Open **i01ws01SurveyReview**, and then save it as i01ws01SurveyReview_LastFirst. Insert a left-aligned footer with the file name, and save the workbook.

b. Determine how the objects were pasted into the document. Do you think the table was linked, embedded, or copied and pasted? What about the chart?

c. Open **i01ws01SurveyData**, and then save it as i01ws01SurveyData_LastFirst replacing Last and First with you own name. Insert a left-aligned footer with the file name, and then save the workbook.

d. In the Word document, make corrections to the table and chart, so that when changes are made to the data in Excel, those changes will be reflected in the Word document. Save the document.

e. In the Excel workbook, in cell D5, change the **Very Comfortable** value to 8, and then in cell **D8**, change the **Very Uncomfortable** value to 64. If requested by your instructor, update the Documentation worksheet appropriately. Save the workbook, and then close Excel.

f. In the Word document, update the table and the chart. Make sure the changes made in Excel are reflected in the Word document. Submit your files as directed by your instructor.

Additional Cases

Additional Workshop Cases are available on the companion website and in the instructor resources.

WORKSHOP 2 | WORD, EXCEL, AND ACCESS INTEGRATION

OBJECTIVES

Prepare Case

Coupon Mailing

Sales & Marketing

Andrey Armyagov / Shutterstock

Indigo5 is an upscale restaurant always looking for ways to promote good relationships with current customers. Over the past year, the restaurant has used comment cards to collect customer suggestions. Customers are promised a special treat if they indicate their birthday month. This information is maintained in an Excel workbook. Each month the restaurant sends out coupons for a free dessert to customers with birthdays in the following month. Your assignment is to import the Excel data into Access, query Access for all birthdays in April, and then use the Mail Merge feature in Word to create coupons based on the results of the Access query.

REAL WORLD SUCCESS

"My boss is a nationally recognized motivational speaker. She gives lectures and workshops all over the country. One of my many jobs is to create name tags for all the people registered to attend these workshops. As this involves hundreds of people, it was often difficult to get the name tags ready in time. We were already keeping information about the attendees in an Excel workbook. Once I learned how to import the names into Access and then use Word to perform a mail merge, creating the name tags was easy. What had once been an onerous task became extremely fast and stress free."

- Claire, recent graduate

Student data files needed for this workshop:

 i01ws02PromoNames.xlsx

 i01ws02PromoCoupon.docx

You will save your files as:

 i01ws02PromoNames_LastFirst.xlsx

 i01ws02Promo_LastFirst.accdb

 01ws02PromoMerge_LastFirst.docx

Use Excel Data in Access

Both Excel and Access can be used to collect, sort, and store data, but Access generally has more sophisticated tools to accomplish those tasks than Excel. However, Excel has capabilities such as formulas, functions, and charts that are lacking in Access. Deciding where to store your data depends on what kind of data you have and what you want to do with it, as summarized in Table 1.

	Excel	Access
How data is stored	In worksheets using rows and columns	In a relational structure of multiple tables
What it stores best	Numbers and formulas	Text, numbers, other objects
Advantages	What-if models and analysis PivotTables Charts and graphs Conditional formatting, color bars, and other visual displays	Generates reports Multiple users Data entry forms Connecting multiple databases Data extraction

Table 1 Storing data in Excel and Access

Data can be exchanged between Access and Excel in order to take advantage of the strengths of each program. There are multiple ways to exchange data between the two programs, as shown in Table 2.

Data from Access to Excel	Data from Excel to Access
Copy and paste	Copy and paste
Connect to Access database	Import data directly
Export data directly	Link to Excel worksheet

Table 2 Sharing data

Import has two different meanings when referring to Excel and Access. When data is imported into Excel from Access, a permanent connection is created. As the data in Access is updated, the data in Excel is also updated automatically.

When data is imported into Access from Excel, there are two options in the Get External Data dialog box. If you select the Import the source data into a new table in the current database option, changes made to the source data will not be reflected in the database. If you select the Link to the data source by creating a linked table option, Access will create a table that will maintain a link to the source data in Excel. Changes made to the source data in Excel will be reflected in the linked table. In this section, you will import Excel data into Access and export Access data to Word.

REAL WORLD ADVICE **No Need to Fear Access**

Most people in business are either very comfortable with Excel or have some familiarity with it. On the other hand, not as many people are familiar with Access, and some even avoid it. Excel is therefore used more for data collection purposes than is necessary or appropriate, since much of the process could be done more easily in Access. Having knowledge of both programs is critical so you can make decisions about which program is best to use for your purpose. You will also be able to move data between the two programs. For example, if your data in Access needs to be subtotaled and charted, you can import the data into Excel, apply subtotals, and then chart the data. On the other hand, if you do a lot of data entry, it would be beneficial to create a form in Access to make entering data more user-friendly.

Prepare Excel Data for Export to Access

Data in Excel can be easily imported into an Access table. Because all data is stored in tables in Access, the data in Excel must be in a list form. Examples may be an address book, a list of inventory, or a list of employees.

Preparing an Excel List for Export

Before data is imported into Access, you need to make sure the data is compatible. The data should have column headings that will become the field names in the Access table. The rows in Excel will become the records in the Access table, so there should be no blank rows in the data you are importing. In this project, you will edit a list of data in Excel so it can be imported easily into Access.

IP02.00

To Edit Excel Data for Exporting to Access

a. Start **Excel**, and then open **i01ws02PromoNames**. Maximize the Excel window, if necessary.

b. Click the **FILE** tab, click **Save As**, and then navigate to the location where you are saving your files. Change the file name to i01ws02PromoNames_LastFirst using your last and first name. Click **Save**.

c. Click the **Birthdays** worksheet tab, if necessary. Insert a **footer** with the file name in the left section, and then click **Save**.

d. Scroll through the list of names and notice the blank rows. Select row **257** by clicking on the row number. On the HOME tab, in the Cells group, click **Delete**. Repeat these steps to delete rows **75**, **19**, and **9**.

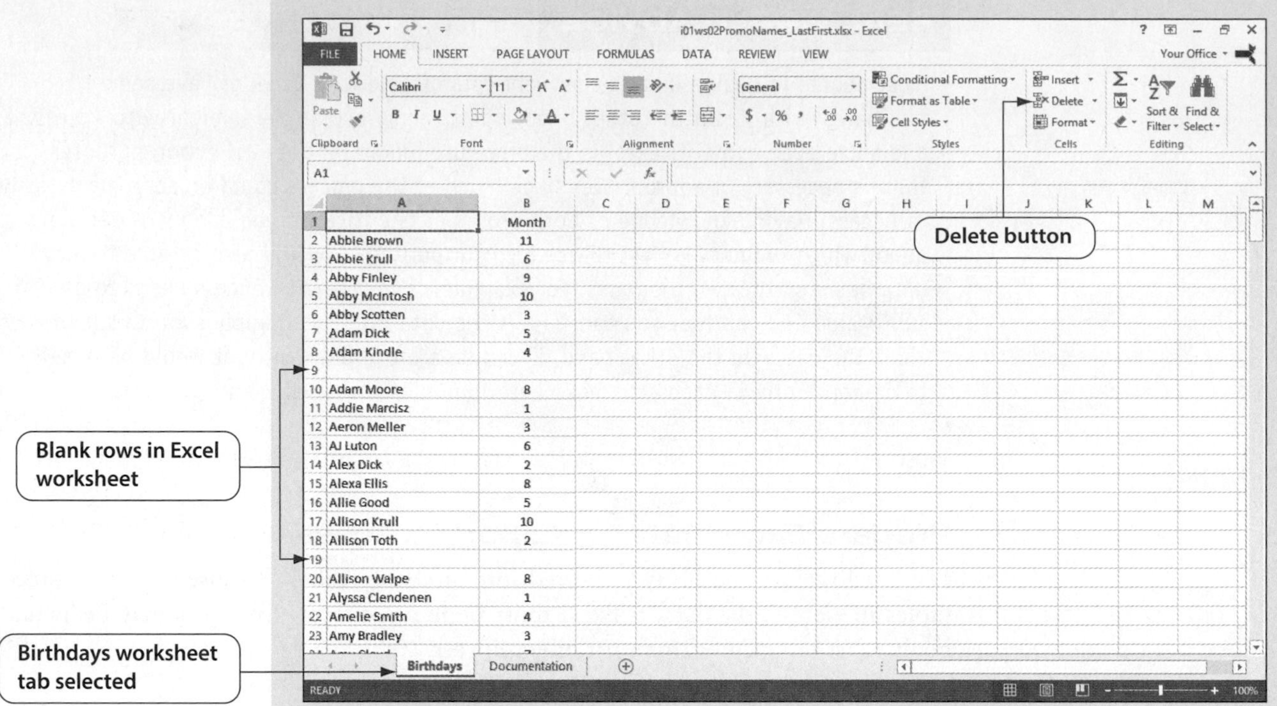

Figure 1 Blank rows in Excel worksheet

e. Press Ctrl + Home to return to cell A1. In cell **A1**, type Name, and then press Enter. In cell **A2**, using all lowercase letters, replace the existing name with your first and last name. Make sure that you do not capitalize your first and last name. You will learn the reason later in this exercise. In cell **B2**, change the Month to 4.

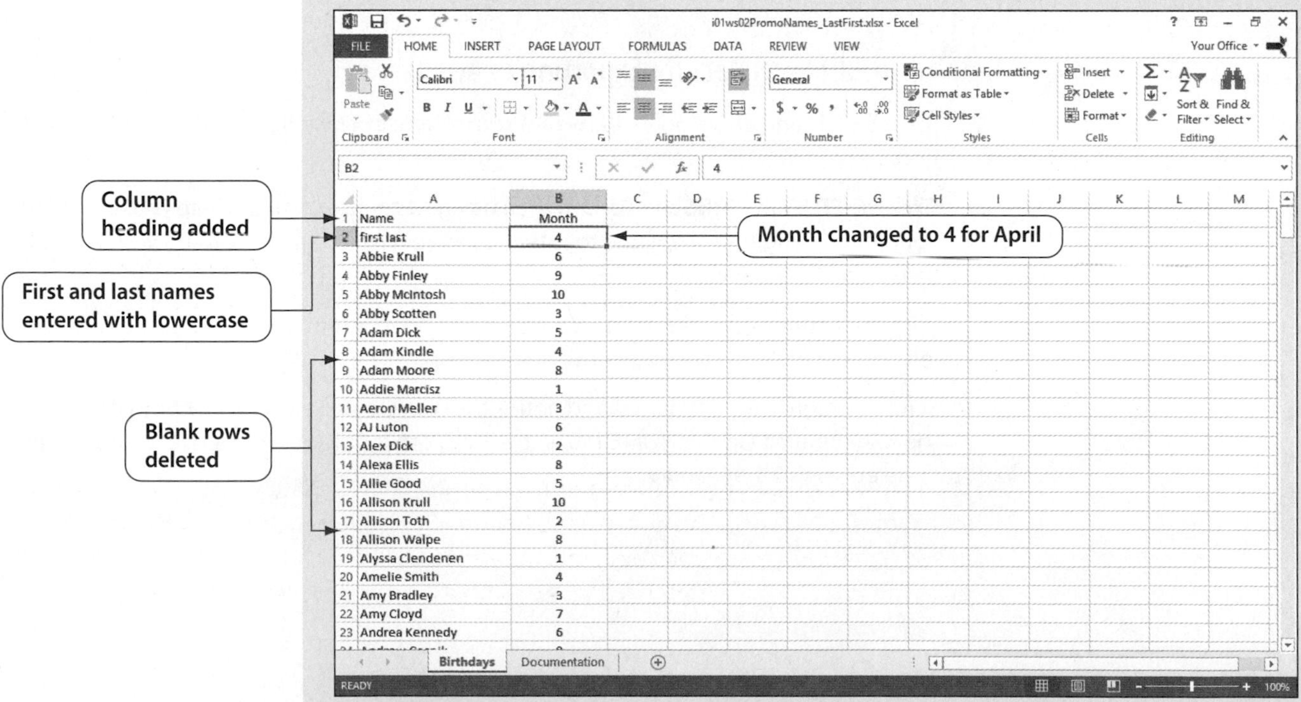

Figure 2 Excel worksheet edited for export to Access

f. Click the **Documentation** worksheet tab, and then complete the following:
   - Click cell **A8**, and then type today's date in mm/dd/yyyy format.
   - Click cell **B8**, and then type your name in Lastname, Firstname format.
   - Click cell **C8**, type Added column heading Name in cell A1 and then press Enter.
   - In cell **C9**, type Replaced name in cell A2 with first and last name and then press Enter.
   - In cell **C10**, type Changed month in cell B2 to 4 and then press Enter.

g. Click **Save**, and then click **Close** to close Excel.

Import Excel Data into Access

When you import data from Excel into Access, Access stores the data in a new or existing table without making changes to the data in Excel. You can only import one worksheet at a time, so if you have multiple worksheets, you will have to repeat the steps for each sheet. If your data is on a worksheet with other unwanted data, you can create a **named range**, which is a specific name you give to a range of cells other than the cell references, for the data in Excel. Then, in Access you can specify that you only want the data in your named range.

REAL WORLD ADVICE **Data in Two Places**

Once you import data from Excel into Access, the data is stored in two different places and may or may not be linked, depending on the option you selected in the Get External Data dialog box. If a change to a record is made in Excel, it will change the record in Access only if you selected the Link to the data source by creating a linked table option. However, data imported from Access into Excel may be updated. Trying to maintain the same records in two different programs is not good business practice. It is better to import or export data for a specific one-time purpose, like to query the data or create a chart from data.

CONSIDER THIS | **Creating Connections**

As you complete this project, you change the data in two places because a permanent connection does not exist. What recommendations might you make for processing comment cards and birthday data from the customer?

Importing an Excel List into an Access Table

The **Import Spreadsheet Wizard** will walk you through the steps to import your Excel data into an Access table. When you import data, the wizard provides three options: create a new table with the data, append the Excel data to an existing table, or created a linked table. For this exercise, you will import Excel data into a new Access table that will be called tblBirthdays.

IP02.01

To Import an Excel List into a New Access Table

a. Start **Access**, click **Blank desktop database**, and then in the File Name box type i01ws02Promo_LastFirst, using your last and first name.

b. Click **Browse**, navigate to the location where you are saving your files, click **OK**, and then click **Create**.

c. Click the **EXTERNAL DATA** tab, and then in the Import & Link group, click **Excel**. In the Get External Data - Excel Spreadsheet dialog box, click **Browse**, and then navigate to your student folder. Select **i01ws02PromoNames_LastFirst**, and then click **Open**.

d. Make sure **Import the source data into a new table in the current database** is selected.

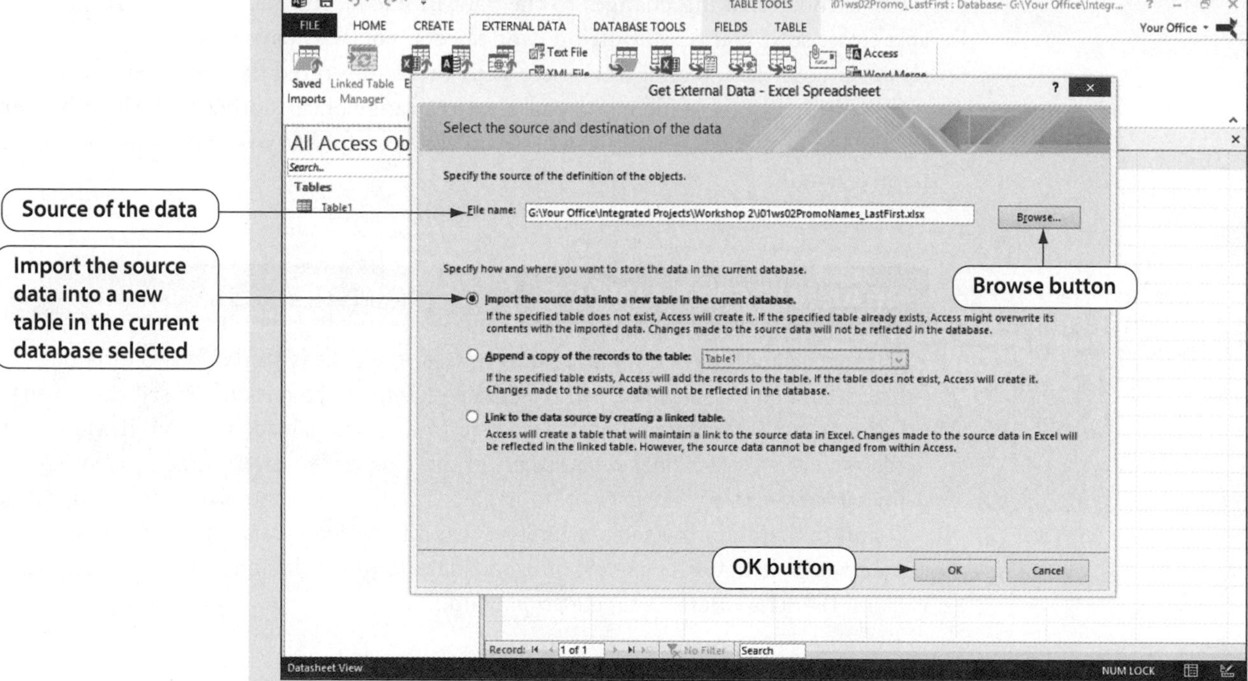

Figure 3 Get External Data - Excel Spreadsheet dialog box

e. Click **OK**. The Import Spreadsheet Wizard opens. In the Import Spreadsheet Wizard dialog box, make sure **Show Worksheets** is selected, and then select **Birthdays**. Click **Next**.

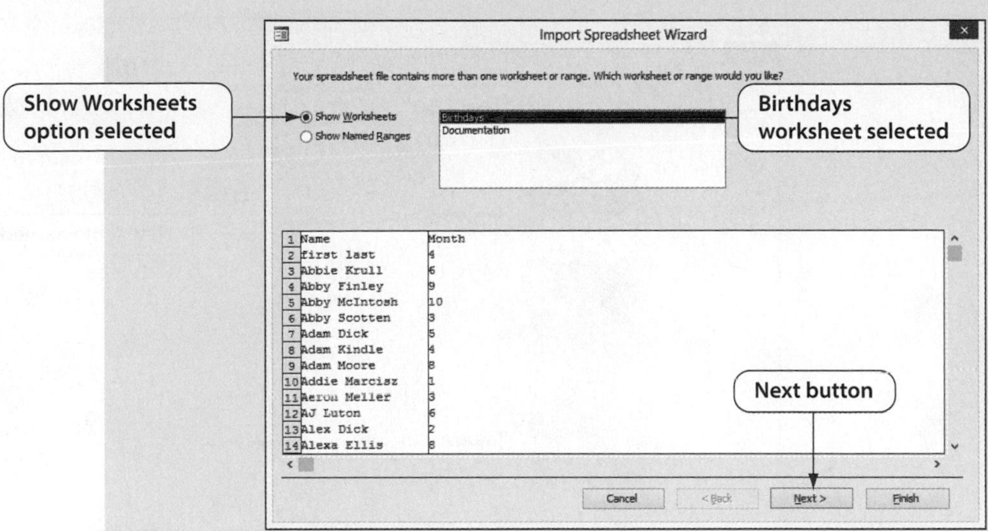

Figure 4 Import Spreadsheet Wizard

f. Select **First Row Contains Column Headings**.

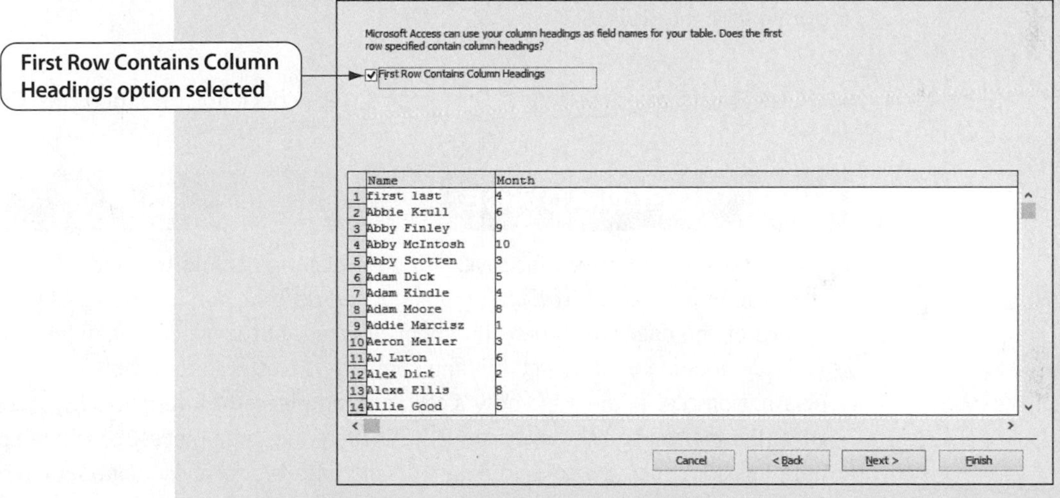

Figure 5 First Row Contains Column Headings

g. Click **Next**, and then click **Next** again. Make sure **Let Access add primary key** is selected, and then click **Next**.

h. In the Import to Table text box, type tblBirthdays for the name of the new table.

SIDE NOTE
Primary Key
In a well-designed database, a primary key is selected for every table. If you are importing a list that does not contain a field for a primary key, Access will assign one.

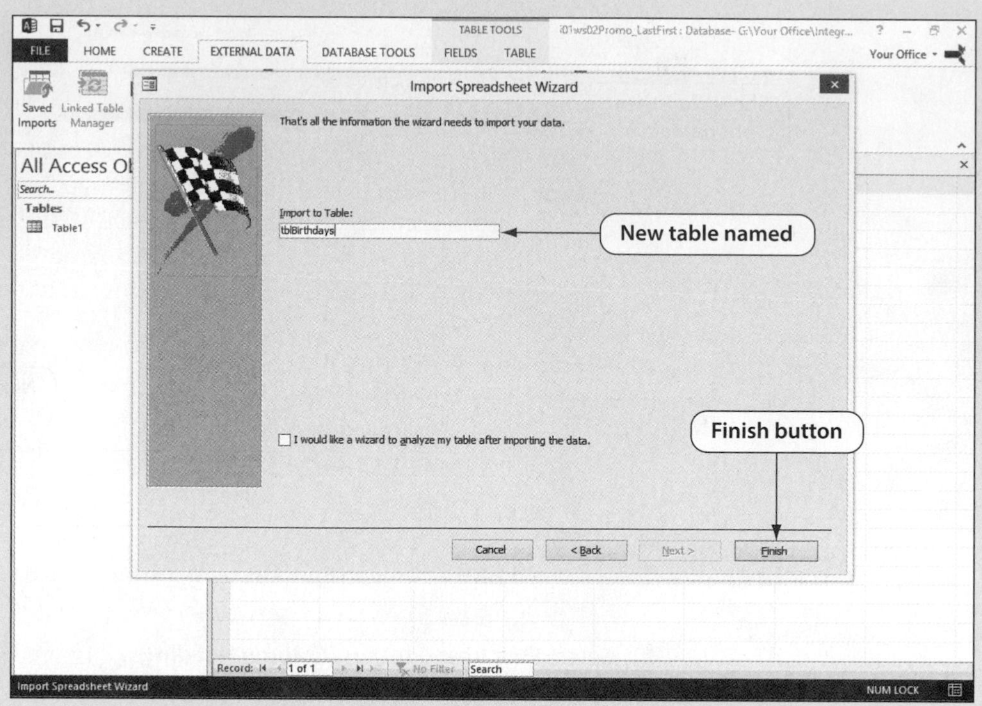

Figure 6 Name new table

i. Click **Finish**, do not select the Save import steps check box, and then click **Close**.

REAL WORLD ADVICE Error Importing File

Did you receive an error that says, "An error occurred trying to import file"? If so, then the import failed. If a dialog box opened up that prompts you to save the details of the operation, then the import worked, but some data may be missing. Start by opening your source file and compare it to the Access table—your destination file. If there are only a few missing pieces of information, you can add that information to the table manually. If there are large pieces, or whole columns of data missing, compare column headings and data types, revise your source data, and try to import again.

SIDE NOTE
Table 1
Table 1 is automatically created when another table is imported. Unless it is modified, it will automatically disappear once the file is closed and reopened.

j. In the Navigation Pane, double-click the **tblBirthdays** table to open it. Scroll down the list of names to make sure they were imported correctly. Click **Close** [X] to close the tblBirthdays table.

k. Click **Close** [X] to close the Table1 table, which is open by default. Leave the database and Access open.

REAL WORLD ADVICE Matching Fields

When you import data into a new table, Access will use the field names and data types of the imported data for the new table structure. If you import data into an existing table, the field names and data types of the imported data must exactly match the field names and data types of the existing Access table or you will get an error. The Import Spreadsheet Wizard gives you the option to change the field names and data types before you import the data. Successful importing takes a few extra planning steps in order for the import process to run successfully the first time.

Use Access Data in Word

Access data, whether it was entered in Access directly or imported from an Excel workbook, can be used in a Word document. One common example of using Access data in a Word document is to create a **mail merge**, which is a process that simplifies the task of preparing documents that contain identical formatting, layout, and text but where only certain portions of each document vary. In this section, you will create an Access query from an existing Access table, and then use the results to create a mail merge document in Word.

Prepare Access Data for a Mail Merge

Data for a mail merge in Word can come from either an Access table or query. If the data is coming from a query, then the query must be created first.

Querying Data in an Access Database

To find the customers with birthdays in a particular month, you need to query the birthday table with the birthday month as the criteria. For this exercise, you will create a query to find all customers with April birthdays.

IP02.02

To Create a Query in an Access Database

a. Click the **CREATE** tab, and then in the Queries group, click **Query Design**. In the Show Table dialog box, select **tblBirthdays**, and then click **Add** to add the tblBirthdays table to the query.

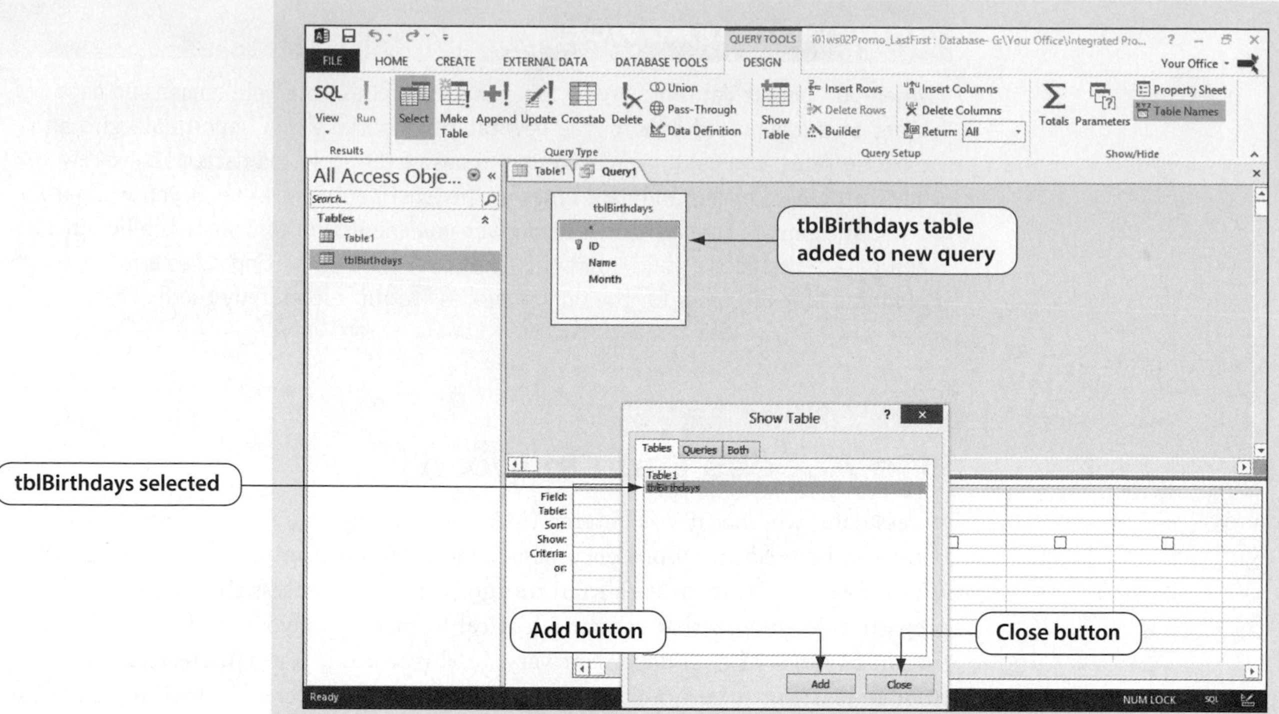

Figure 7 Table added to Query 1

b. Click **Close** [×] to close the Show Table dialog box. In the tblBirthdays table box, double-click **Name**, and then double-click **Month** to add the fields to the query design grid.

c. Click the **Show** check box under Month to hide this field. In the **Criteria** row for the Month field, type 4 to query for all birthdays in April.

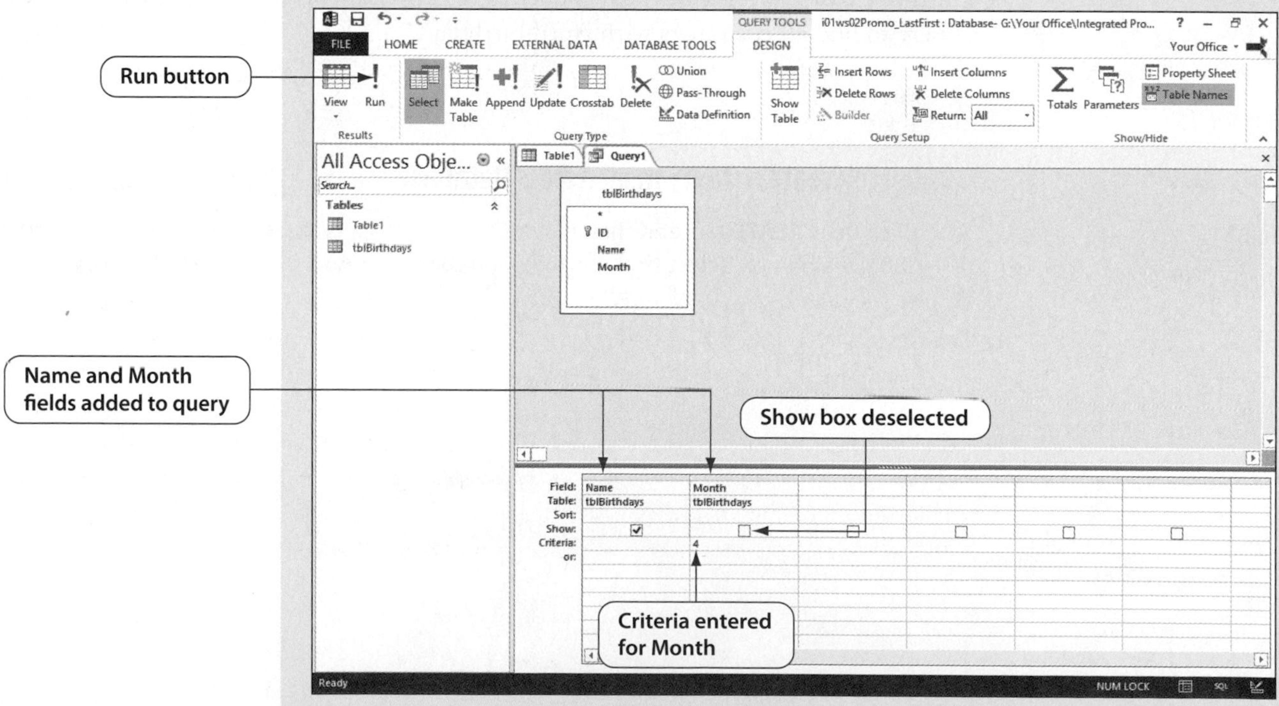

Figure 8 Query design grid for April birthdays

d. Click **Save** [Save]. In the Save As dialog box, type qryAprilBirthdays in the Query Name box, and then click **OK**.

e. On the DESIGN tab, in the Results group, click **Run** to run the query. This retrieves 20 records with the names of people with April birthdays. In the **Name** field, double-click the **right border** to automatically adjust the width of the column so all names are visible.

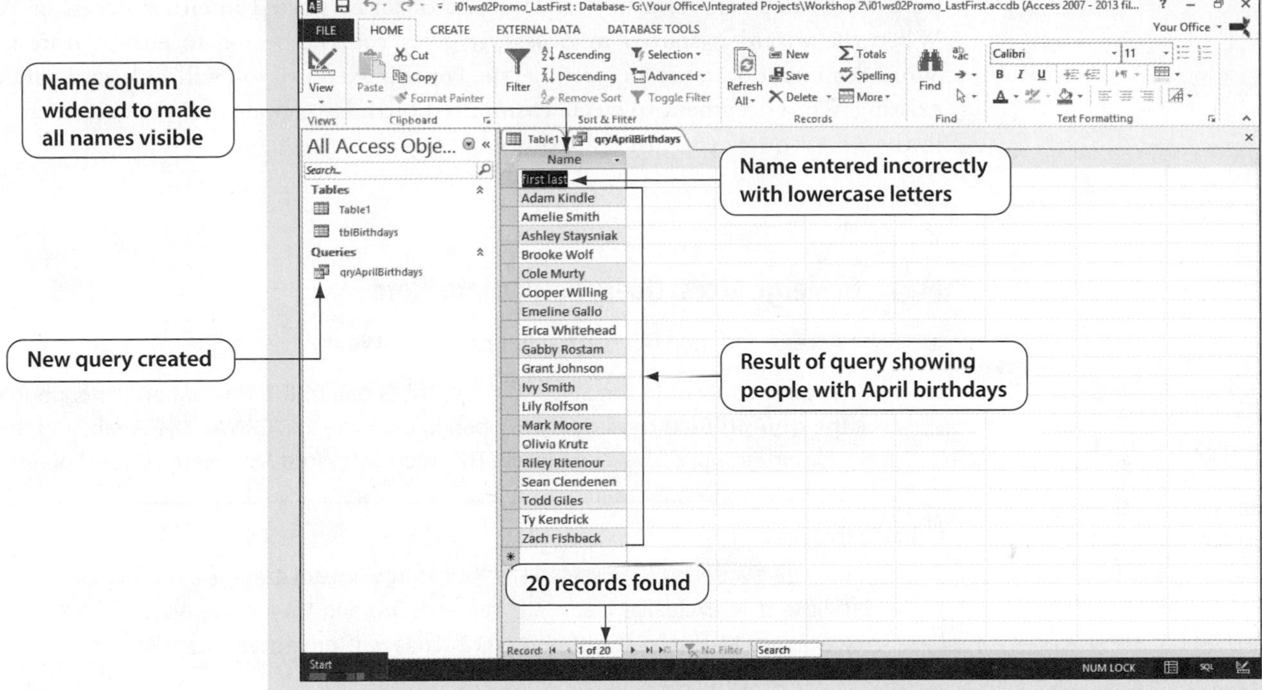

Figure 9 Result of running query

f. Click **Save** [Save], click **Close** [X] to close the qryAprilBirthdays query, close Table1, and then close Access.

Export Access Query Results to Word

Word has no import command to import data from Access, therefore the data must be exported from Access to be opened in Word. The exception to this is a mail merge, which will be discussed below. When you use the export command in Access to export the data in a form or datasheet, that data is exported as a **Rich Text Format (.RTF)** file, a format that retains the formatting of the original document. It is then stored in a new Word document. From the new Word document, you can copy and paste the object into another existing Word document. Alternatively, you can copy data from an Access table, query, form, or report and paste it into an existing document.

CONSIDER THIS | RTF Files

Exporting data to an RTF file to use in another document takes two steps: creating the RTF file and copying and pasting it into another file. Are there advantages to this method versus a direct copy and paste into a document?

If the data in Access is going to be used in a Word mail merge document, then the Mail Merge Wizard can be used to export the data and an RTF file is not necessary. You can use the results of an Access query or any other data stored in an Access table to merge into a Word document to create customized letters or labels.

Exporting Data for a Mail Merge

To export a list of data from Access to Word, the **Word Mail Merge Wizard** can be used to help create a new mail merge document or employ an existing mail merge document from which to create form letters. The wizard can be started in either Access or Word. When the wizard is started in Access, it gives you the option to either create a new Word document or to use an existing one. For this exercise, you will link your data to an existing Word document to create customized birthday coupons for the customers listed in the Access query you just created.

IP02.03

To Merge Access Query Results into Word

a. Start **Access**, and then open **i01ws02Promo_LastFirst**.

b. Click **Enable Content** in the SECURITY WARNING bar. In the Navigation Pane, double-click the **qryAprilBirthdays** query to open it. Click the **EXTERNAL DATA** tab, and then in the Export group, click **Word Merge**. The Microsoft Word Mail Merge Wizard opens.

SIDE NOTE

Security Warning

When you open a database, you will see a Security Warning bar just below the Ribbon. Microsoft disables certain features to maintain security and prevent viruses from entering your computer.

Troubleshooting

Did you receive an error that says, "The Mail Merge Wizard cannot continue because the database is in exclusive mode"? If so, click OK, and then close Access. Click Yes to save changes to the layout of qryApril Birthdays if prompted. Start Access, and open i01ws02Promo_LastFirst.

c. If necessary, select **Link your data to an existing Microsoft Word document**, and then click **OK**.

d. Navigate to the location of your student data files, select **i01ws02PromoCoupon**, and then click **Open**.

e. Click **Word** on the taskbar to display the birthday coupon. Maximize the Word window, if necessary. In the Mail Merge pane, under Selected recipients, make sure **Use an existing list** is selected. Note that [qryApril Birthdays] in "i01ws02Promo_LastFirst" is displayed under Use an existing list.

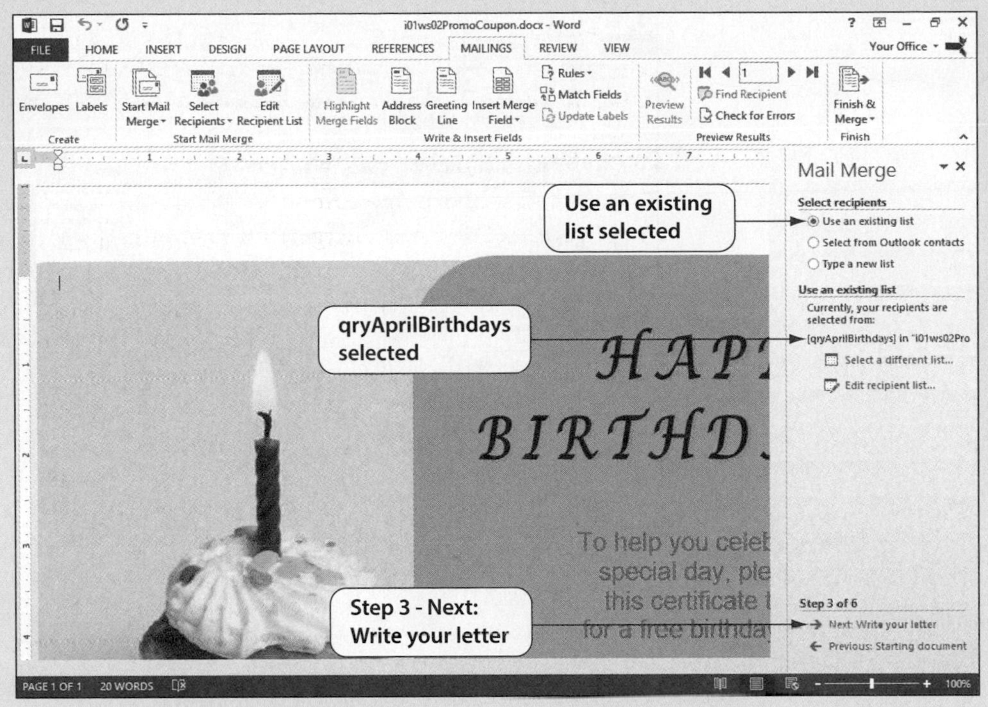

Figure 10 Mail Merge pane open in Word

f. Click **Next: Write your letter** at the bottom of the Mail Merge pane.

g. Click the **Happy Birthday coupon**, and then decrease the size so the entire coupon is displayed. Click before **To** on the coupon to place the insertion point.

h. In the Mail Merge pane, under **Write your letter**, click **More items**. In the Insert Merge Field dialog box, if necessary, select **Database Fields**, and then in the Fields box, make sure **Name** is selected. Click **Insert**, and then click **Close**.

i. Press Enter twice so there is a blank line after the field. Right-click **<<Name>>**, select **Edit Field** from the shortcut menu, and then in the Field dialog box, under Format, select **Title case**.

You have just added a **format field switch** that determines the use of uppercase and lowercase letters. By selecting Title case, you specify that the first letter of all names will be capitalized, even if the names were entered incorrectly in the Excel worksheet. Remember that you were asked to type your first and last names using lowercase letters earlier in this exercise. Without the format switch, your first and last names would not be capitalized on the birthday coupon. If you choose First capital, only the first name will be capitalized.

SIDE NOTE
Format Switches
You can select from the following format switches:
- Uppercase
- Lowercase
- First capital
- Title case

This assures that your final document will always appear the way you want.

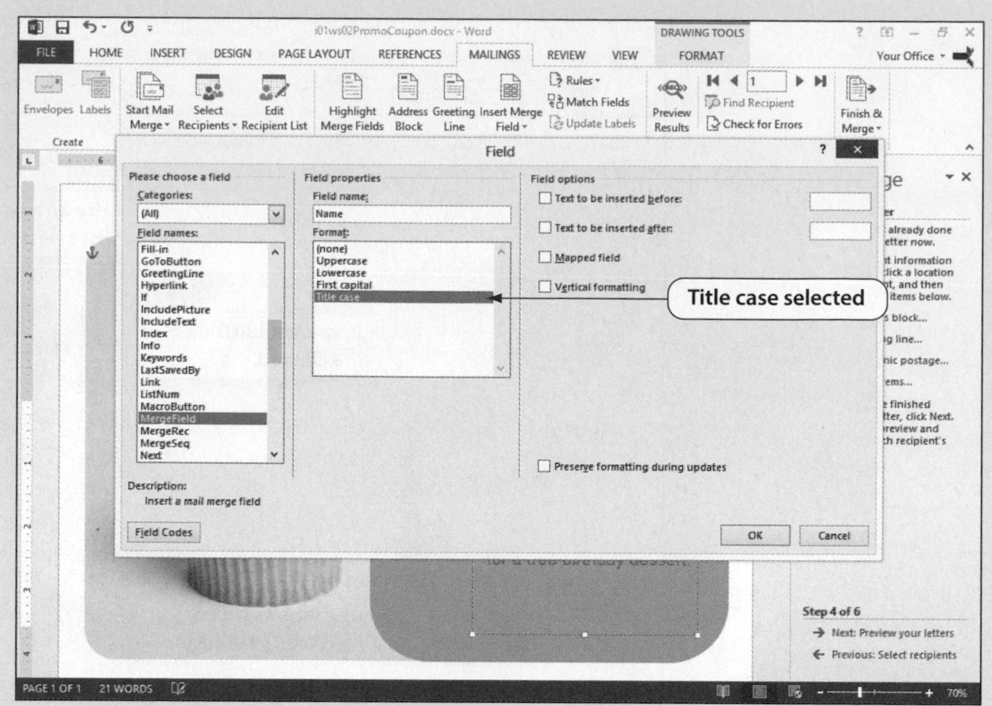

Figure 11 Edit MergeField to add format switch

j. Click **OK** to close the Field dialog box. Select **<<Name>>**. Click the **HOME** tab, in the **Font** group, click **Bold** B and then change the Font Size to **28**.

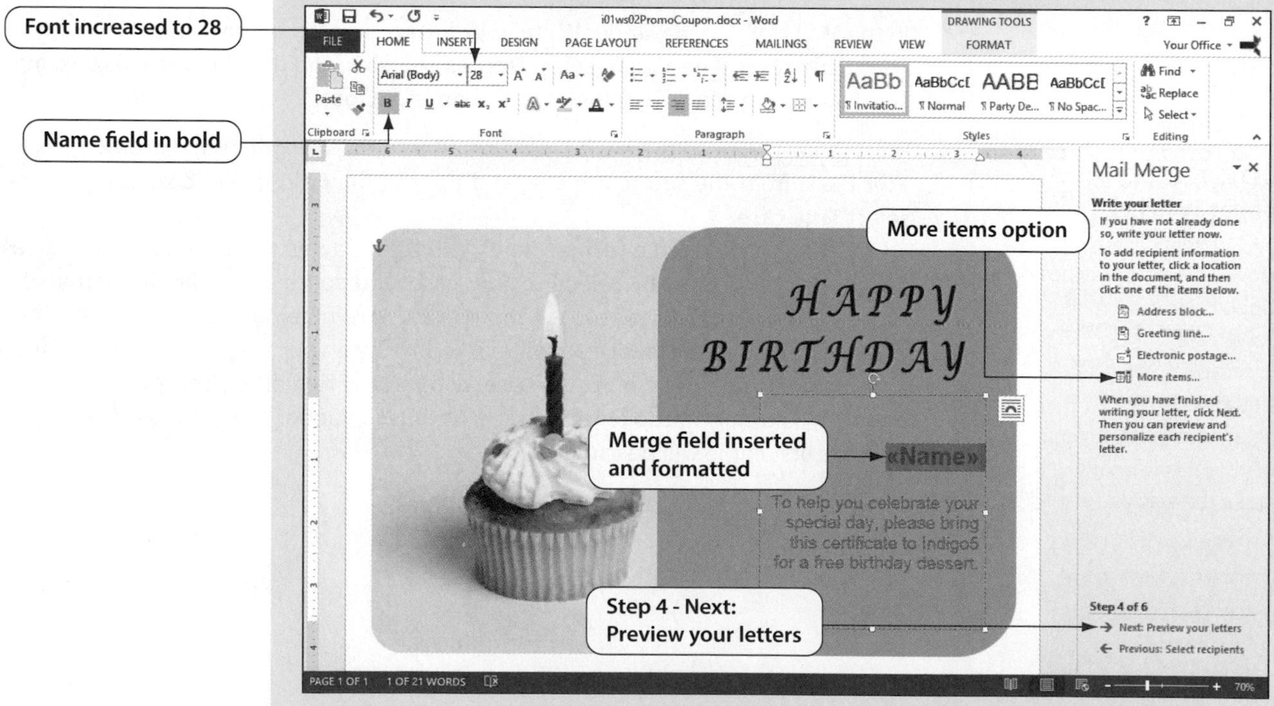

Figure 12 Name field inserted and formatted

k. In the Mail Merge pane, click **Next: Preview your letters**. The first certificate should display your first and last name with initial caps. Under **Preview your letters**, click the **double arrow** button to scroll through the names of several other recipients with April birthdays.

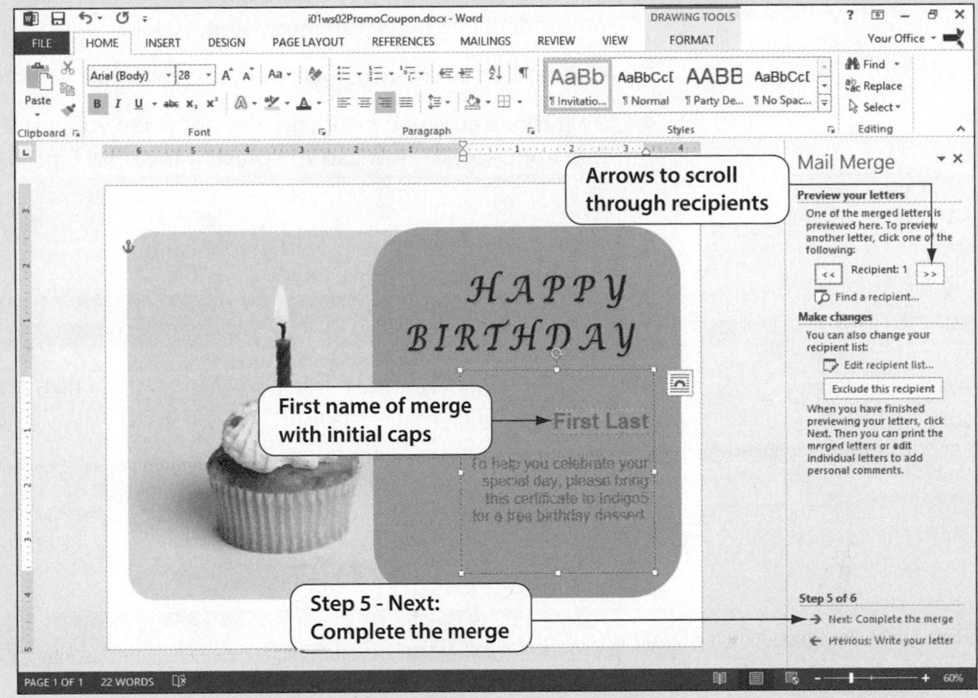

Figure 13 Completed merge with names inserted in coupons

l. Click **Next: Complete the merge**. Under Merge, click **Edit Individual letters** to merge the individual coupons in a new document.

m. In the Merge to New Document dialog box, if necessary, select **All**, and then click **OK**. A new document opens with one page for each coupon. Scroll through the document to examine several of the coupons.

n. Click the **FILE** tab, click **Save As**, and then navigate to the location where you are saving your files. Name this document i01ws02PromoMerge_LastFirst, and then click **Save**.

o. Click **Close** to close i01ws02PromoMerge_LastFirst. Click **Close** to close i01ws02PromoCoupon without saving the changes. Click **Close** to close Access.

SIDE NOTE
Saving Merged Files
If you are going to use the merged file just once, you do not need to save it. For this exercise, you could print the coupons and then close the document without saving it.

Concept Check

1. Why is it important to prepare your Excel data before importing it into Access? What kinds of things should you look for? p. 1035
2. Why would you want to import data into Access from Excel? Why would you want to import data into Excel from Access? p. 1037
3. Why would you create a query in Access to export to Word? Give an example. p. 1041
4. What is one common error you may get when you use the Mail Merge Wizard to export data from Access? How can you prevent this error? p. 1044

Key Terms

Format field switch 1045
Import 1034
Import Spreadsheet Wizard 1037
Mail merge 1041
Named range 1037
Rich Text Format (RTF) 1043
Word Mail Merge Wizard 1044

Visual Summary

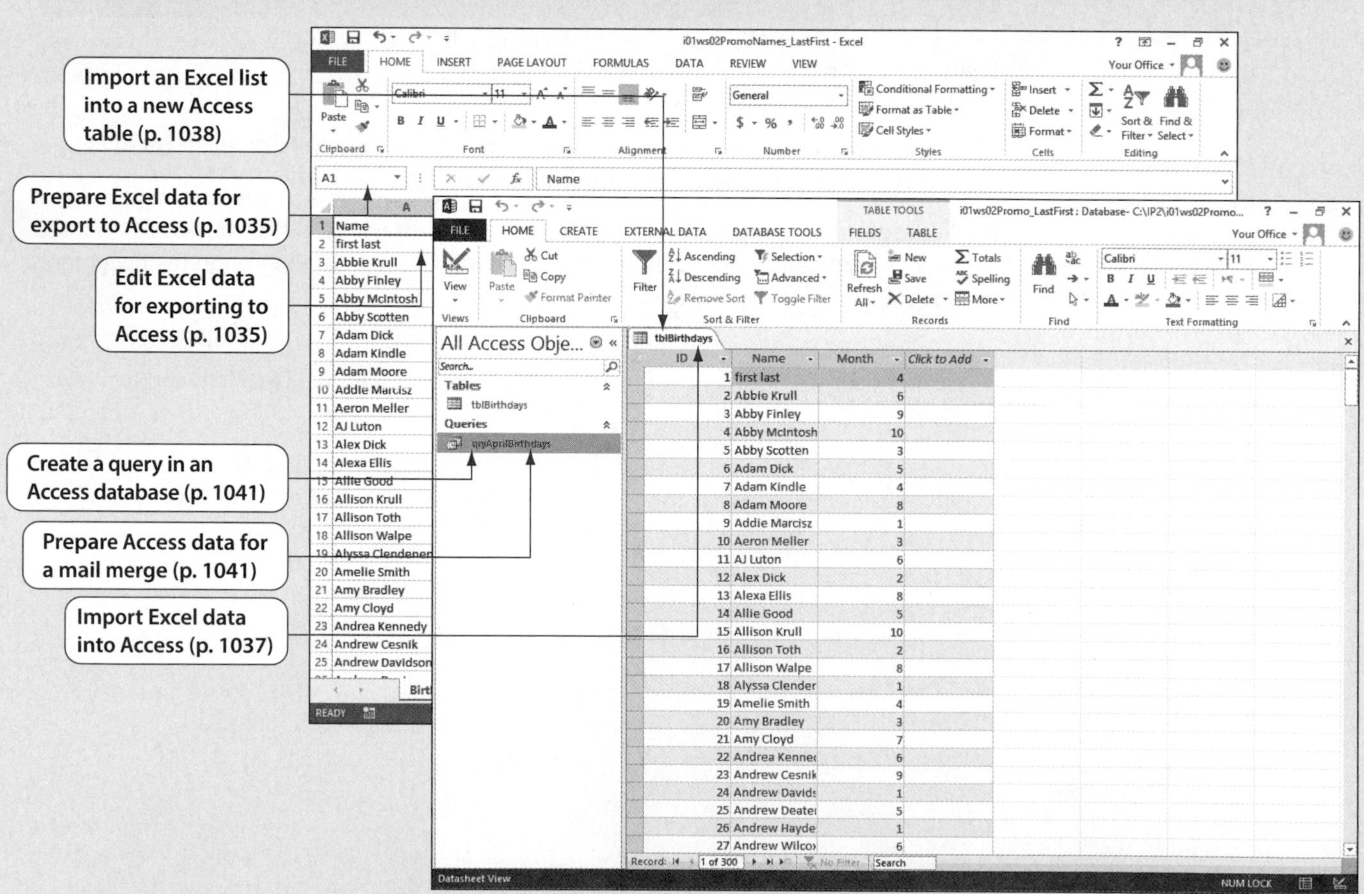

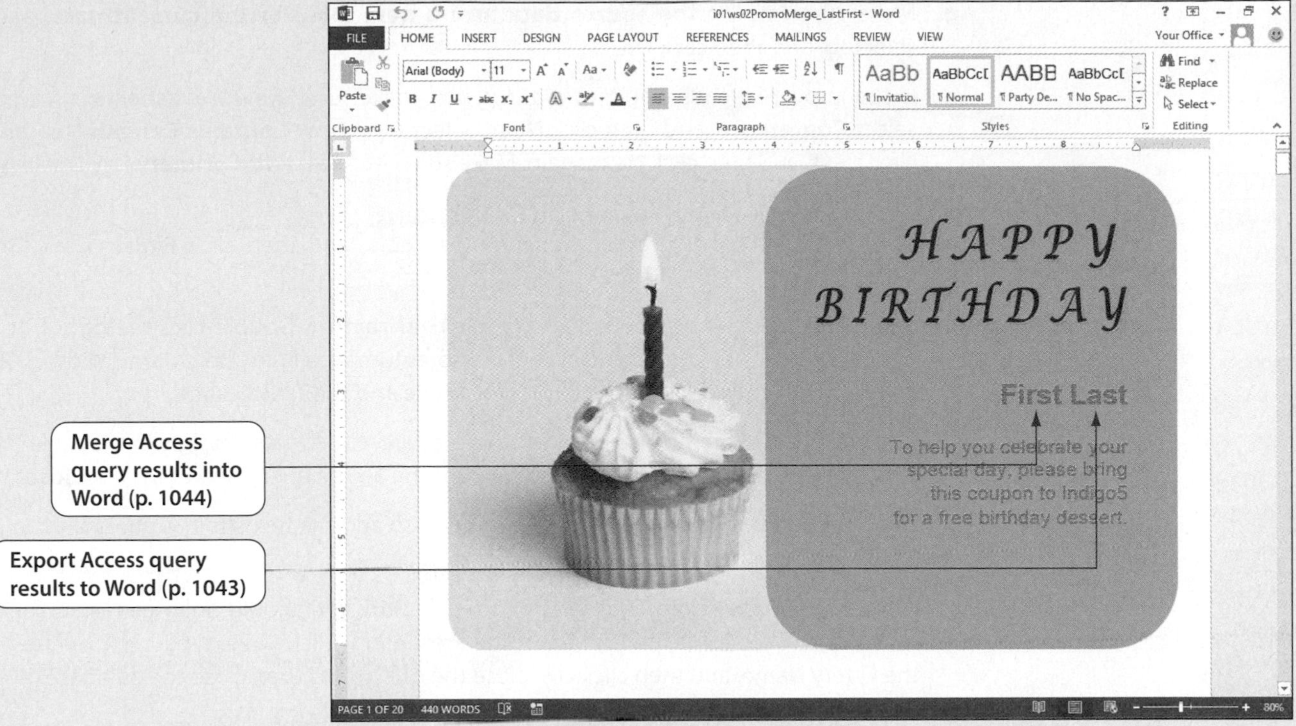

Figure 14 Importing and Exporting Data Final

Practice 1

Student data file needed:

i01ws02LibraryList.xlsx

You will save your files as:

i01ws02LibraryList_LastFirst.xlsx

i01ws02Library_LastFirst.accdb

i01ws02LibraryMerge_LastFirst.docx

Library Conference

Customer Service

Painted Paradise Resort Event Planning is getting ready for an onsite library conference. Library directors from all over the country will be attending. Some directors will be speaking or giving presentations. You have been assigned to create name tags for just the attendees, since presenters will have special badges. Information has been kept in an Excel workbook with the name of the library director, the name of the library, and the status indicating whether the director is an attendee or a presenter. You will have to import the Excel list into Access, and then use Word Merge to create name tags for all attendees.

a. Start **Excel**, and then open **i01ws02LibraryList**. Maximize the Excel window, if necessary.

b. Click the **FILE** tab, click **Save As**, and then navigate to the location where you are saving your files. Change the file name to i01ws02LibraryList_LastFirst.xlsx, using your last and first name. Click **Save**.

c. If necessary, click the **Conference** worksheet tab, and then select **row 42**. On the HOME tab, in the Cells group, click **Delete**. Repeat the same steps for **row 18**.

d. In cell **A2**, replace the existing name with your first name and last name, and then save the workbook. Close Excel.

e. Start **Access**, click **Blank desktop database**, and then in the File Name box, type i01ws02Library_LastFirst, using your last and first name. Click **Browse**, and then navigate to the location where you are saving your files. Click **OK**, and then click **Create**.

f. Click the **EXTERNAL DATA** tab, and then in the Import & Link group, click **Excel**. Click **Browse**, locate your student files, select **i01ws02LibraryList_LastFirst**, and then click **Open**.

g. Make sure **Import the source data into a new table in the current database** is selected, and then click **OK**.

h. In the Import Spreadsheet Wizard dialog box, make sure **Show Worksheets** is selected, select **Conference**, and then click **Next**. Select **First Row Contains Column Headings**, click **Next**, and then click **Next** again. Make sure **Let Access add primary key** is selected, and then click **Next**.

i. Type tblDirectors for the name of the new table, and then click **Finish**. Click **Close** without saving the import steps.

j. In the Navigation Pane, open the new table **tblDirectors**. Double-click the **right border** of the Director field and the Library field to automatically fit the column widths. Click **Save**, and then close both the tblDirectors table and the Table1 table.

k. Click the **CREATE** tab, and then in the Queries group, click **Query Design**. In the Show Table dialog box, click **Add** to add the **tblDirectors** table to the query, and then click **Close**.

l. Double-click **ID**, **Director**, **Library**, and **Status** to add the fields to the query grid. In the Criteria line for the Status field, type Attendee.

m. On the DESIGN tab, in the Results group, click **Run**. You should only see results for the Attendees of the conference and not the Presenters. Click **Save**, type qryAttendees for the Query Name, and then click **OK**. Close the query, and then close the database.

n. Open **i01ws02Library_LastFirst**. Click **Enable Content**, if necessary. Open the **qryAttendees** query. Click the **EXTERNAL DATA** tab, and then in the **Export** group, click **Word Merge**.

o. In the Microsoft Word Mail Merge Wizard dialog box, select **Create a new document and then link the data to it**, and then click **OK**.

p. Click **Word** on the taskbar, and then click **Maximize**, if necessary. In the Mail Merge pane, under Select document type, select **Labels**. Click **Next: Starting document**.

q. Under Change document layout, click **Label options**. In the Label Options dialog box, under Label information, select **Avery US Letter** for Label vendors, and then under Product number select **5390 Name Badges Insert Refills**. Click **OK**.

r. In the Mail Merge pane, click **Next: Select recipients**, and then click **Next: Arrange your labels**. Under Arrange your labels, click **More items**. In the Insert Merge Field dialog box, double-click **Director** and **Library**, and then click **Close**.

s. Resize the document so you can see the text on the nametag. Click between <<Director>> and <<Library>>, and then press Enter to place "Library" on a new line. Select both **<<Director>>** and **<<Library>>**. Click the **HOME** tab, and then in the Font group, increase the font size to **18**. Select only **<<Director>>**, and then in the Font group, click **Bold**.

t. In the Mail Merge pane, under Replicate labels, click **Update all labels**. Click the **Table Selector** in the top-left corner of the table to select all the records. Under TABLE TOOLS, on the LAYOUT tab, in the Alignment group, click **Align Center**.

u. With the table still selected, click the **HOME** tab, and then in the Paragraph group, click the **Borders** arrow, and then select **All Borders** to place borders around all labels.

v. In the Mail Merge pane, click **Next: Preview your labels**, and then click **Next: Complete the merge**. Under Merge, click **Edit individual labels**. In the Merge to New Document dialog box, under Merge records, select **All** if necessary, and then click **OK**.

w. Click **Save**, locate the folder where you are saving your files, and then name the file i01ws02LibraryMerge_LastFirst. Click **Save**, and then close the document. Close the mail merge document called Document1 without saving it. Close Access. Submit all files as directed by your instructor.

Practice 2

Student data files needed:

i01ws02EventPoster.docx

i01ws02EventList.xlsx

You will save your files as:

 i01ws02EventPoster_LastFirst.docx

 i01ws02EventList_LastFirst.xlsx

i01ws02Event_LastFirst.accdb

Corporate Challenge Event

Sales & Marketing

Painted Paradise Resort Event Planning is coordinating an upcoming corporate challenge event on the grounds of the resort. The events will include a 5K Race, a 100-Meter Sprint, a 400-Meter Track Relay, a Tug of War, and a Water Balloon Toss. Each event will need a poster with the name of the event and a list of participants. Your assignment is to create the poster for the 400-Meter Track Relay. The participant information is in an Excel list. You will import that list into Access, query for that particular event, and then export the list of participants to a poster in Word. You will also format the poster attractively.

a. Start **Word**, and then open **i01ws02EventPoster**. Maximize the Word window, if necessary.

b. Click the **FILE** tab, click **Save As**, and then navigate to the location where you are saving your files. Change the file name to i01ws02EventPoster_LastFirst, using your last and first name. Click **Save**.

c. Start **Excel**, and then open **i01ws02EventList**. Maximize the Excel window, if necessary.

d. Click the **FILE** tab, click **Save As**, and then navigate to the location where you are saving your files. Change the file name to i01ws02EventList_LastFirst, using your last and first name. Click **Save**.

e. Select **row 103**. On the HOME tab, in the Cells group, click **Delete**. Repeat these steps for **rows 59**, **36**, and **12**.

f. In cell **B1**, type Event for the column heading. In cell **A2**, replace the existing name with your first name and last name. In cell **B2**, change the event to 400-Meter Track Relay. Click **Save**, and then close Excel.

g. Start **Access**, click **Blank desktop database**, and then in the File Name box type i01ws02Event_LastFirst, using your last and first name. Click **Browse**, and then navigate to the location where you are saving your files. Click **OK**, and then click **Create**.

h. Click the **EXTERNAL DATA** tab, and then in the Import & Link group, click **Excel**. Make sure **Import the source data into a new table in the current database** is selected, and then click **Browse**. Navigate to the location where you are saving your files, select **i01ws02EventList_LastFirst**, and then click **Open**. Click **OK**.

i. In the Import Spreadsheet Wizard dialog box, make sure **Show Worksheets** is selected, and then if necessary, select **Participants**. Click **Next**. Select **First Row Contains Column Headings**, click **Next**, and then click **Next** again.

j. Make sure **Let Access add primary key** is selected, and then click **Next**. In the Import to Table box, type tblEvents, and then click **Finish**. Click **Close** without saving the import steps.

k. In the Navigation Pane, open the **tblEvents** table. Double-click the **right border** of the Name field and the Event field to automatically fit the column widths.

l. Click the **CREATE** tab, and then in the Queries group, click **Query Design**. In the Show Table dialog box, make sure **tblEvents** is selected, click **Add**, and then click **Close** to close the dialog box. Double-click the **Name** and **Event** fields to add them to the query grid.

m. Click **Show** under the Event field to hide this field. Click the **Criteria** line for the Event field, type 400-Meter Track Relay. Click **Save**, name the query qry400Meter, and then click OK.

n. On the DESIGN tab, in the Results group, click **Run**. Double-click the **right border** of the Name field to automatically widen the column. Click **Save**.

o. Click the **Select All** button in the upper left corner of qry400Meter, to select all the records. Click the **HOME** tab, and then in the Clipboard group, click **Copy**.

p. Click **Word** on the taskbar. In the Word document **i01ws02EventPoster_LastFirst**, on the HOME tab, in the Paragraph group, click **Show/Hide** to show paragraph marks. Click the first paragraph mark under the graphic, and then in the **Clipboard** group, click **Paste**.

q. Click the **Table Selector** to select the entire table, and then in the Paragraph group, click **Center**. Select the **first two rows**, and then delete them, leaving only the names. Click the **Table Selector** to select the table, and then in the Font group, increase the font size to **14**. Place the insertion point in front of your name, and drag to select the names—not the table, and then in the Paragraph group, click **Center**. In the Paragraph group, click the **Borders** arrow, and then select **No Border**. Click **Show/Hide** to turn off the paragraph marks. Click **Save**, and then close Word.

r. Close Access, and then select **Yes** to save all changes when asked. Submit all files as directed by your instructor.

Problem Solve 1

Student data file needed:

i01ws02ItemsList.xlsx

You will save your files as:

i01ws02ItemsList_LastFirst.xlsx

i01ws02Items_LastFirst.accdb

i01ws02ItemsMerge_LastFirst.docx

Merchandise Labels

Production & Operations

Painted Treasures Gift Shop staff would like to put merchandise labels on the different items they carry in order to quickly manage inventory and ring up sales based on the category of merchandise. The item list is in an Excel spreadsheet, and the labels are in Word. Your assignment is to import the Excel list into Access, then find the records for all items except those categorized as "Other." You will use Word Mail Merge to create labels for the queried data.

a. Start **Excel**, open **i01ws02ItemsList**, and then save it to your student files as i01ws02ItemsList_LastFirst. Insert the **file name** in the left section of the footer.

b. Prepare the list for importing into Access by deleting any blank rows, and then save the workbook. If requested by your instructor, update the **Documentation** worksheet to reflect the changes that have been made.

c. Import the data into a new Access database called i01ws02Items_LastFirst. Do not save the import steps. Save the new table and name it tblInventory.

d. Query the **tblInventory** table for records in all categories except Other. Show fields **Item** and **Category**. Save the new query as qryCategories.

e. Use Word Mail Merge to create labels in a new Word document using the records in the **qryCategories** query. For Label options, select **Avery US Letter** as the Label vendor and Product number **18160 Address Labels**.

f. Add the **Item** field on the first line of the label and the **Category** field on the second line of the label. Increase the font size, and then center the text so the information fits well on the label.

g. Complete the merge, and then save the new document as i01ws02ItemsMerge_LastFirst. Close the document, and then close all documents in Word without saving.

h. Close Access, and then close Excel. Submit all files as directed by your instructor.

Problem Solve 2

Student data files needed:

 i01ws02ArtList.xlsx

 i01ws02ArtNews.docx

You will save your files as:

 i01ws02ArtList_LastFirst.xlsx

 i01ws02Art_LastFirst.accdb

 i01ws02ArtMerge_LastFirst.docx

Art Sale Newsletter

Sales & Marketing

Susan Brock, manager of Painted Treasures Gift Shop, has just received an amazing shipment of African art. She would like to send out a newsletter to customers who live in the local area telling them of these new acquisitions. Susan has been keeping data about past customers in an Excel worksheet listing names and addresses. She has created a newsletter in Word, and she would like you to take over the task of merging the names of customers who will receive the newsletter. Your assignment is to import the Excel list into Access, and then find the names for all customers who live in New Mexico. You will use Word Mail Merge to create personalized newsletters addressed to each individual.

a. Start **Excel**, and then open **i01ws02ArtList**. Save it to your student files as i01ws02ArtList_LastFirst. Insert the **file name** in the left section of the footer, and then save the document. Prepare the list for exporting to Access by deleting any blank rows. Save the workbook.

b. Import the data into a new Access database called i01ws02Art_LastFirst. Do not save the import steps. Save the new table and name it tblAddresses.

c. Change the first name in the table to your own name. Query the **tblAddresses** table for records of all people who live in **NM**. Show fields **First Name** and **State**. Save the new query as qryNewMexico.

d. Use Word Merge to create newsletters that address each recipient by first name using **i01ws02ArtNews**. Add the **First Name** and **Last Name** fields after the word **DEAR:** at the top of the newsletter. Complete the merge, save the new document as i01ws02ArtMerge_LastFirst.docs, and then close the document.

e. Close all documents in Word without saving. Close Access, and then close Excel. Submit all files as directed by your instructor.

Perform 1: Perform in Your Career

Student data files needed:

 Blank Word document

 Blank Excel worksheet

 Blank Access database

You will save your files as:

 i01ws02BookAward_LastFirst.docx

 i01ws02BookList_LastFirst.xlsx

 i01ws02Book_LastFirst.accdb

 i01ws02BookMerge_LastFirst.docx

Book Award Certificates

Customer Service

You are a teacher and would like to reward your students for completing a reading program that lasted the entire school year. Students would choose a book to read each week. On Fridays, they would sit at a special table, have pizza for lunch, and discuss the book. Some children read just a few books, but others read almost one a week. You would like to print certificates for students who read 25 books or more. You have been tracking your students in Excel with the students' names and number of books read. You will need to import the data into Access, query the data for names of students who deserve the award, and then use the query results in a Word document that shows each student's name and the number of books read.

a. Start **Word**, and then create an award certificate for your students. You may use a template and modify it as necessary. Save the file as i01ws02BookAward_LastFirst and then close Word.

b. Open **Excel**, and create a list of names and number of books read for at least 40 students. The highest possible number of books read is 32. The first record should have your name as the student and 28 books read. Save the file as i01ws02BookList_Last First. If requested by your instructor, update the **Documentation** worksheet to reflect the changes that have been made.

c. Import the **Excel** list into an Access database called i01ws02Book_LastFirst. Name the new table tblBooksRead. Query the table for students who read 25 books or more. Save the query as qryStudents.

d. Use Word Mail Merge to create award certificates with the results of your query. Include the student's name and the number of books read. Save the merged document as i01ws02BookMerge_LastFirst. Close all documents without saving. Submit all files as directed by your instructor.

Perform 2: How Others Perform

Student data files needed:

 i01ws02SalesNews.docx

 i01ws02SalesData.xlsx

i01ws02SalesReps.accdb

You will save your files as:

 i01ws02SalesReps_LastFirst.accdb

i01ws02SalesMerge_LastFirst.docx

Quarterly Newsletter

Sales & Marketing

Barbie Fredericks makes unique one-of-a kind jewelry. Since this consumes a great deal of her time, she has hired five of her friends to help sell her jewelry. Each of the ladies hosts several parties during the month where she exhibits Barbie's latest creations and takes orders. To avoid conflicts, each lady covers a certain neighborhood in the city. You have been asked to create a newsletter to keep the women informed of sales during each quarterly period. Barbie hopes this will motivate her friends to increase sales. You have been asked to include a chart to illustrate sales visually and a table that ranks the sales staff for the quarter. Then you will need to personalize each newsletter with each person's name and area.

a. Start **Word**, open **i01ws02SalesNews**, and then save it as i01ws02SalesNews_LastFirst. Insert a left-aligned footer with the file name.

b. Start **Excel**, and then open **i01ws02SalesData**. Copy the column chart, and then paste it on the right side at the bottom of the newsletter. Copy the data for first quarter sales, and then paste it to the left of the chart. Adjust size as necessary and format attractively. Save the document.

c. Start Access, and then open **i01ws02SalesReps**. Change the name of the North area's sales rep to your own name. Save the file as i01ws02SalesReps_LastFirst.

d. Complete a mail merge to add each sales rep's name and area to the newsletter. Save the merged document as i01ws02SalesMerge_LastFirst. Close all documents without saving. Submit all files as directed by your instructor.

Additional Cases

Additional Workshop Cases are available on the companion website and in the instructor resources.

WORKSHOP 3 | WORD, EXCEL, ACCESS, AND POWERPOINT INTEGRATION

OBJECTIVES

1. Work in Outline view p. 1056
2. Create a PowerPoint presentation from a Word outline p. 1060
3. Insert Access data into a PowerPoint presentation p. 1062
4. Import Access data into Excel p. 1065

Prepare Case

Indigo5 Restaurant Training

Every quarter, Indigo5 requires that all staff members undergo extensive training on customer service in its determination to remain a top-rated restaurant. Alberto Dimas, restaurant manager, has written an outline in Word for the training seminar listing topics he wants to cover. Survey results ranking customers' satisfaction with food and service have been kept in an Access database for the past year. Your assignment is to complete a PowerPoint presentation using the Word outline. You will include a data table with satisfaction rankings from the previous quarter, and then import the Access data into Excel to create a chart that summarizes the survey results.

Golden Pixels LLC / Shutterstock

REAL WORLD SUCCESS

"I am a physical therapist, and I work only with young children who have developmental disabilities. When parents come to my clinic for the first time, they are often apprehensive and overwhelmed. I decided to create a PowerPoint presentation that could be shown to families of new patients explaining how our department functions. We keep statistics in Access that show there is a direct relationship between attending therapy sessions consistently and achieving the goals set for a patient. I was able to create charts in Excel emphasizing these outcomes. Once I started using this presentation, parents were motivated to bring their child to appointments more regularly, and we had fewer cancellations. Children were able to reach their goals in a shorter amount of time."

- Lisa, recent graduate

Student data files needed for this workshop:

 i01ws03ServeOutline.docx

 i01ws03ServeShow.pptx

 i01ws03ServeChart.xlsx

 i01ws03ServeSurvey.accdb

You will save your files as:

 i01ws03ServeOutline_LastFirst.docx

 i01ws03ServeChart_LastFirst.xlsx

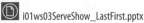

 i01ws03ServeShow_LastFirst.pptx

Integrating Word and PowerPoint

Text can easily be copied from Word to PowerPoint, but sometimes a copy and paste is not efficient or effective. Copying and pasting large amounts of text can be time consuming, and deciding how to split up text for different PowerPoint slides can often be overwhelming.

To efficiently use Word text in a PowerPoint presentation, a Word outline can be used. An **outline** is a hierarchical representation of paragraphs that are recognized by Word by nonprinting, end-of-paragraph marks. A paragraph can be a blank line, one or two words, or multiple sentences. When you type a paragraph into a document in **Outline view**, Word automatically assigns heading styles to each paragraph to create different levels. At the top of the hierarchy are **Level 1** paragraphs. Paragraphs at the next level are **Level 2**. These outlining levels correspond to the Heading styles available for formatting located on the Home tab, in the Styles group. Paragraphs already formatted with heading styles will appear at different levels in Outline view. Paragraphs that have not been formatted with heading styles will appear as **body text** in Outline view. In this section, you will create a PowerPoint presentation from a Word outline.

Work in Outline View

When Outline view is opened, a new Outlining tab is displayed on the Ribbon with tools available for formatting paragraphs. The Promote button and Demote button move paragraphs to different levels. When you **promote** a paragraph, you move it to a higher level in the outline. When you **demote** a paragraph, you move it to a lower level in the outline.

As your outline develops, it is often helpful to see only one level at a time. If a paragraph has levels below it, a plus sign appears at the beginning of the line. Double-clicking the plus sign temporarily hides all the lower levels below that paragraph. To redisplay all subheadings under a heading, double-click the plus sign again. You can also select text and use the **Expand** [+] and **Collapse** [−] buttons in the Outline Tools group to expand and collapse paragraphs.

If you select a heading that includes collapsed subordinate text, the collapsed text is also selected, even though it is not visible. Any changes you make to the heading, such as moving, copying, or deleting, also affect the collapsed text.

A minus sign at the beginning of the line is assigned to paragraphs with no lower levels below them. Paragraphs that have a simple bullet point, that is, no plus or minus sign, are body text and cannot be collapsed or expanded. You can click Show Level to choose which levels to view at one time. When you click Show Level and select Level 2, only Level 1 and Level 2 paragraphs will be visible. Table 1 below lists the outline tools and their functions.

Tool	Name	Function
←	Promote	Moves selected heading and subtext by promoting them—moving them up one level and to the left
→	Demote	Moves selected heading and subtext by demoting them—moving them down one level and to the right
«	Promote to Heading 1	Changes the selected paragraph(s) to Heading 1
»	Demote to Body Text	Changes the selected paragraph(s) to Body Text
▲	Move Up	Moves selected heading and subtext up
▼	Move Down	Moves selected heading and subtext down
+	Expand	Expands selected headings and subtext groups
−	Collapse	Collapses selected headings and subtext groups
Body Text	Outline Level	Shows the level where the insertion point is located

Table 1 Outline tools and their functions

Working with Levels in Outline View

You can view a Word document in Outline view at any time. When you switch to Outline view your paragraphs are displayed by levels. You can make changes to the levels of the paragraphs in either Print Layout view or directly in Outline view. For this exercise, you will open a Word document, view it in Outline view, and make changes to the paragraph levels in Outline view.

IP03.00

To Work with a Document in Outline View

a. Start **Word**, and then open **i01ws03ServeOutline**. Maximize the Word window, if necessary.

b. Click the **FILE** tab, click **Save As**, double-click **Computer**, and then navigate to the location where you are saving your files. Save the document as i01ws03ServeOutline_LastFirst using your last and first name. Click **Save**.

c. Insert a **left-aligned footer** with the file name, and then click **Save**. Double-click in the document, and then press Ctrl + Home to move the insertion point to the beginning of the document.

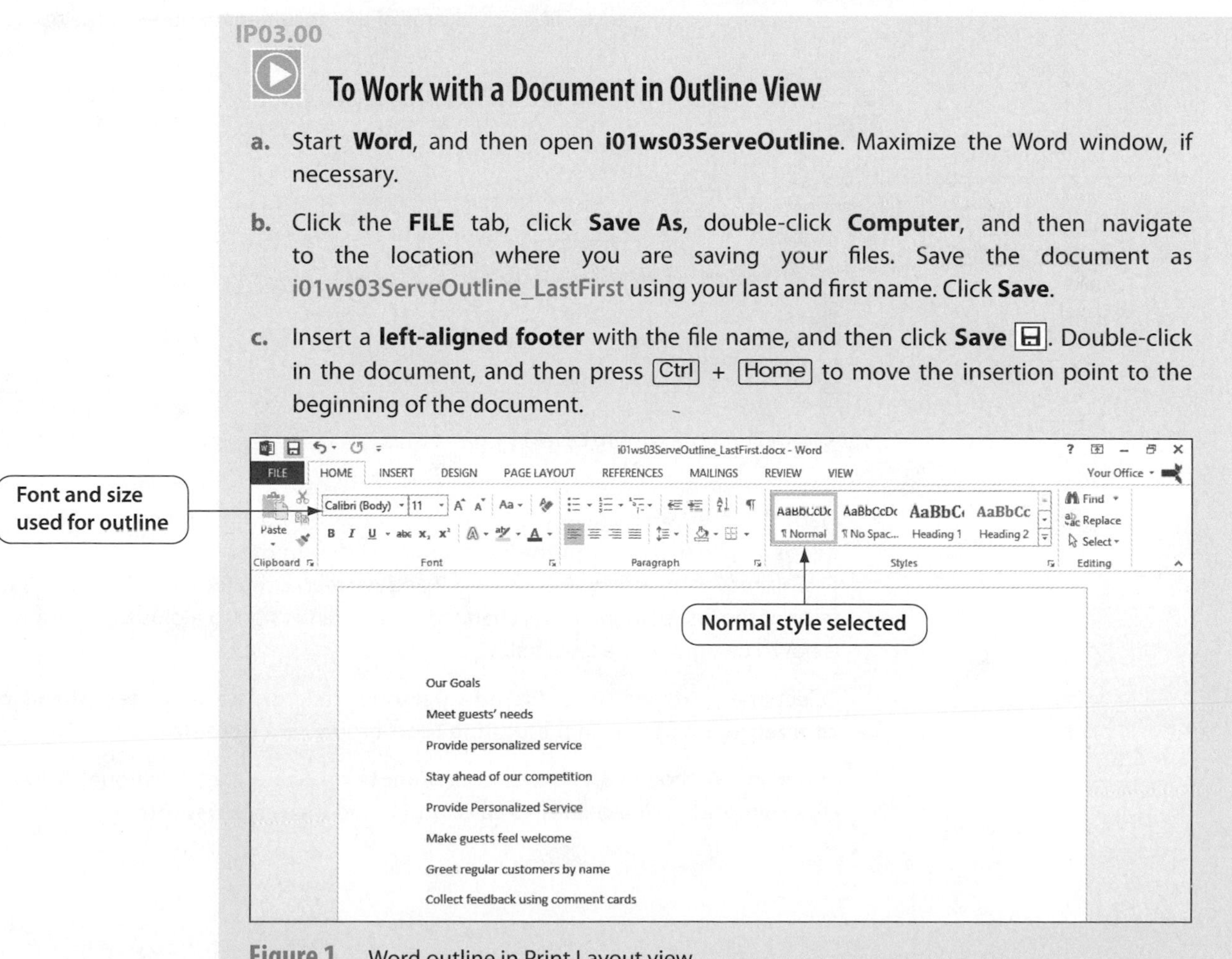

Figure 1 Word outline in Print Layout view

d. Click the **VIEW** tab, and then in the Views group, click **Outline**. Notice in the Outline Tools group, in the Outline Level box, that all paragraphs are considered Body Text.

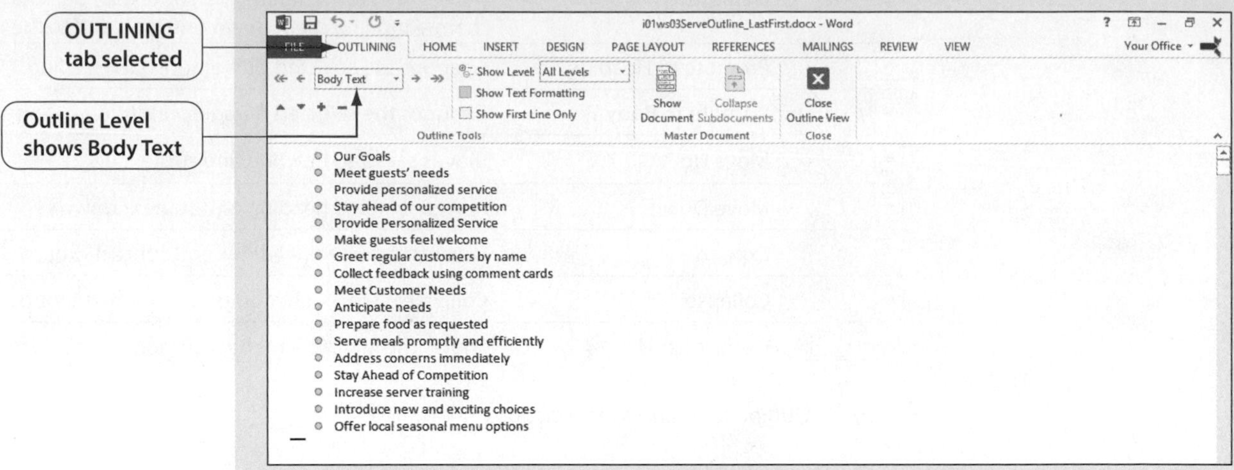

Figure 2 Word outline in Outline view

e. Press Ctrl + A to select all the lines of text. On the OUTLINING tab, in the Outline Tools group, click **Promote** ←.

All lines of text are promoted to Level 1. The font type and font size change, and a minus sign is displayed at the beginning of each line to visually show that the paragraphs are Level 1 and not body text. Click a blank area of the document to deselect the text.

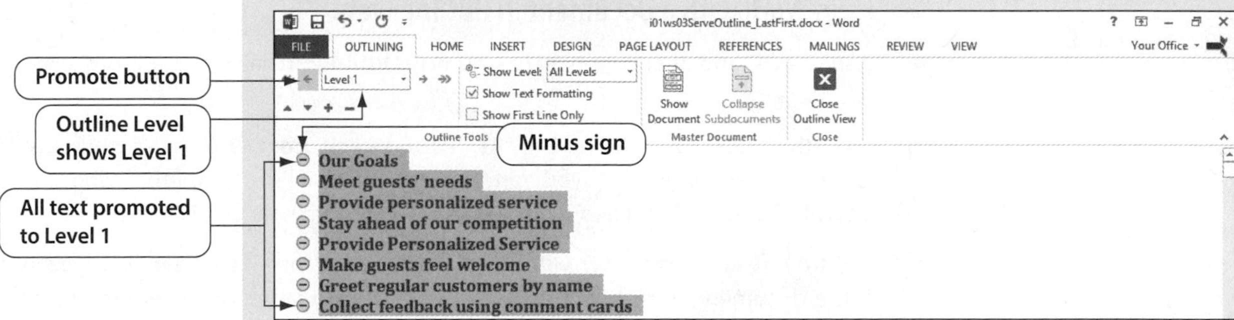

Figure 3 Text promoted to Level 1

f. Place the insertion point at the beginning of the second line, which says **Meet guests' needs**, and then in the **Outline Tools** group, click **Demote** →.

This moves the paragraph to Level 2 and decreases the font size. Note the button in front of the first paragraph has changed from a minus sign to a plus sign because there is now a paragraph at a level below.

g. Select the next two lines, **Provide personalized service** and **Stay ahead of our competition**, and then in the **Outline Tools** group, click **Demote** →.

h. Select lines **6** through **8**, and then click **Demote** →. Select lines **10** through **13**, and then click **Demote** →. Select lines **15** through **17**, and then click **Demote** →.

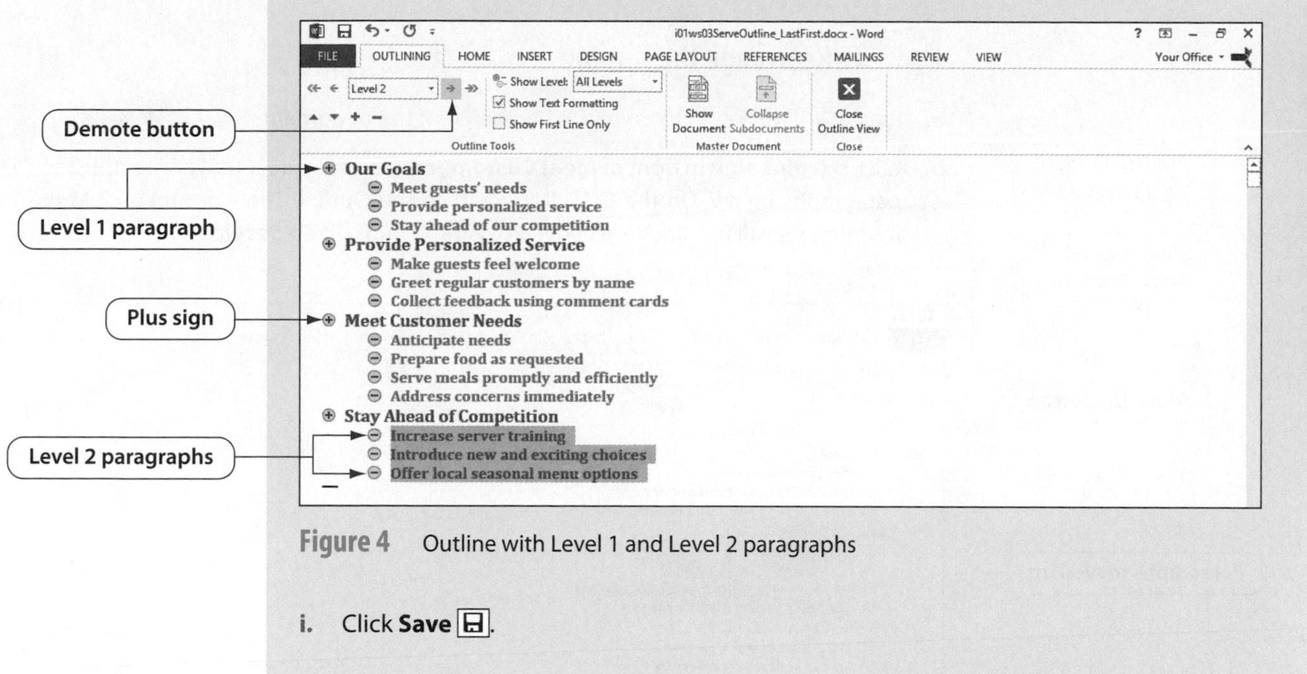

Figure 4 Outline with Level 1 and Level 2 paragraphs

i. Click **Save**.

REAL WORLD ADVICE **Optional Outlining Method**

You may want to use the Styles options on the Home tab to create your outline instead of using Outline view. Select a paragraph and then on the Home tab, in the Styles group, select a style—Heading 1, Heading 2, and so on—to create different levels of paragraphs. By using the Style method, you will see the different formatting of the text, but you will not see the plus and minus signs as you do in Outline view.

Rearranging a Word Outline

After you have created an outline, you can move paragraphs from one part of the outline to another without changing their levels. The Outlining tab has Move Up and Move Down buttons that will move selected lines up or down one or more lines at a time. This does not change the levels, only the position of the paragraphs within the outline. For this exercise, you will rearrange your paragraphs in Outline view.

IP03.01

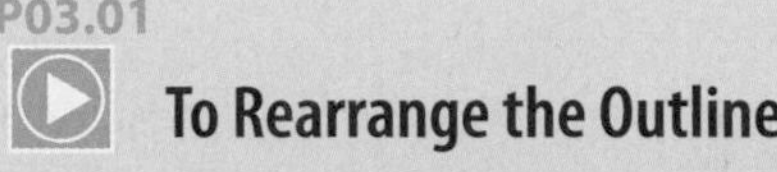

To Rearrange the Outline

a. Press Ctrl + Home to go to the beginning of the document.

b. Click the **plus sign** in front of **Meet Customers Needs** to select that paragraph and the four paragraphs below. On the OUTLINING tab, in the Outline Tools group, click **Move Up** four times so all five lines are above **Provide Personalized Service**.

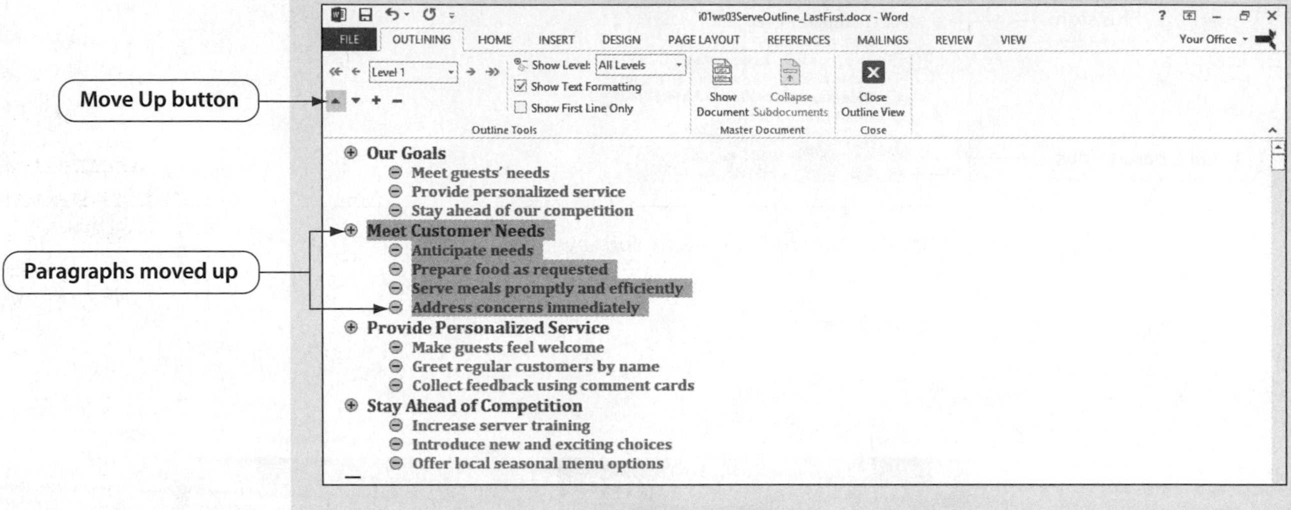

Figure 5 Paragraphs moved up

c. In the Close group, click **Close Outline View** to return to Print Layout view.

d. Click **Save**, and then click **Close** to close Word.

Create a PowerPoint Presentation from a Word Outline

It is easy to create slides for a PowerPoint presentation from a Word outline. PowerPoint automatically uses the highest level of paragraphs in the outline as slide titles on new slides and the lower-level text as bulleted text. Each level after the first-level slide text displays one level lower, using a bullet or number outline. Once the slides are created, you can modify them as necessary in PowerPoint by changing the formatting or the levels of text.

Creating PowerPoint Slides from a Word Outline

PowerPoint offers a command that allows you to import an outline. For this exercise you will open the PowerPoint presentation that Alberto Dimas has already created. Then you will use the Word outline to create new PowerPoint slides.

IP03.02

To Create PowerPoint Slides from a Word Outline

a. Start **PowerPoint**, and then open **i01ws03ServeShow**.

b. Click the **FILE** tab, click **Save As**, double-click **Computer**, and then navigate to the location where you are saving your files. Change the name of the presentation to i01ws03ServeShow_LastFirst using your last and first name. Click **Save**.

SIDE NOTE

No Outlining?

If your document has no heading styles, PowerPoint will create slides based on paragraphs only, and each paragraph will become a new slide.

c. On the HOME tab, in the Slides group, click the **New Slide** arrow, and then select **Slides from Outline**.

d. In the Insert Outline dialog box, navigate to the location where you are saving your files, select **i01ws03ServeOutline_LastFirst**, and then click **Insert**. Four new slides are inserted from the outline.

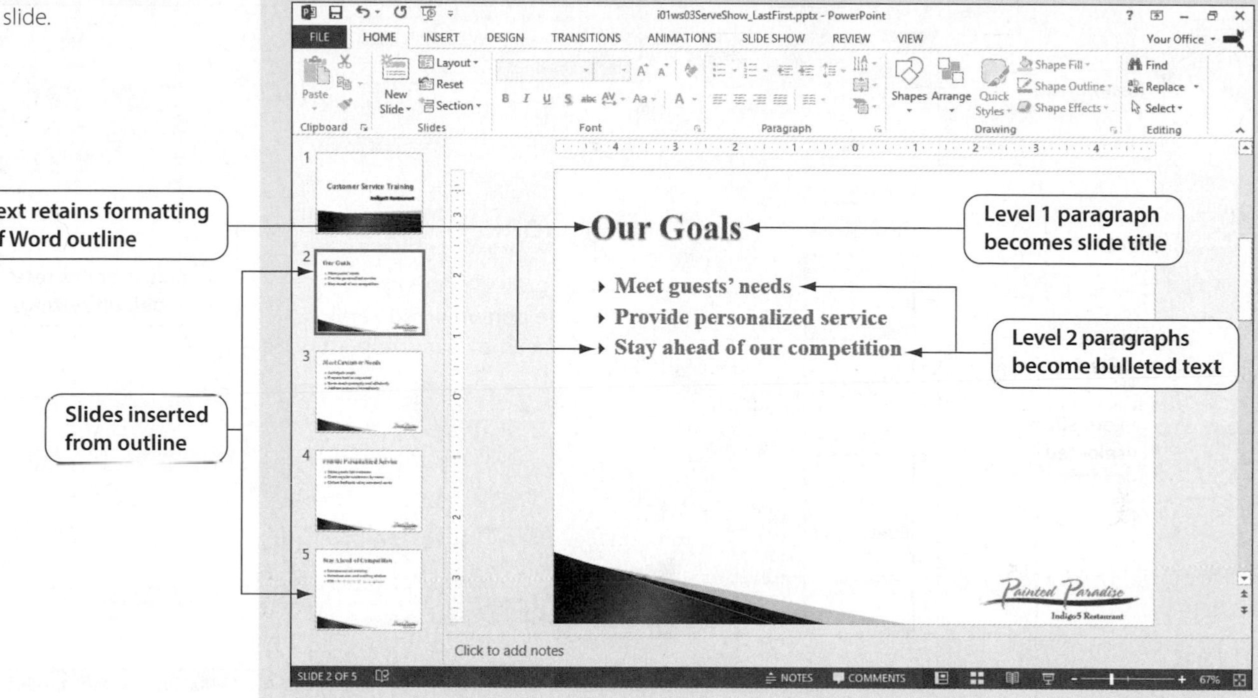

Figure 6 PowerPoint slides inserted from Word outline

> **Troubleshooting**
> PowerPoint cannot make slides from an open Word document. If you get an error message when you try to select a file, make sure the file is closed, and then try selecting the Slides from Outline command again.

Resetting Formatting of Slides Inserted from an Outline

When you insert slides into a PowerPoint presentation from an outline, the new slides retain some of the formatting from the Word document. Notice that the font on the new slides does not really match the font on the title slide. This would be even more noticeable if your presentation already contained several other slides before you inserted new ones. The title slide uses the Lucida Sans Unicode font, and the slides inserted from the outline use the Times New Roman font. The text on the new slides is formatted in shades of blue used for Heading 1 and Heading 2 styles. You would like the new slides to match the title slide. For this exercise you will **reset** the position, size, and formatting of slide placeholders to the default settings determined by the slide master.

IP03.03

To Reset Formatting of Slides Inserted from an Outline

SIDE NOTE

Another Way to Reset

You can also right-click a slide or group of selected slides, and then select Reset Slide from the shortcut menu.

a. In the left pane, with **Slide 2** already selected, hold down Shift, and then click **Slide 5**. The four slides you inserted are selected. On the HOME tab, in the Slides group, click **Reset**. The four slides now reflect the format determined by the slide master and match the title slide.

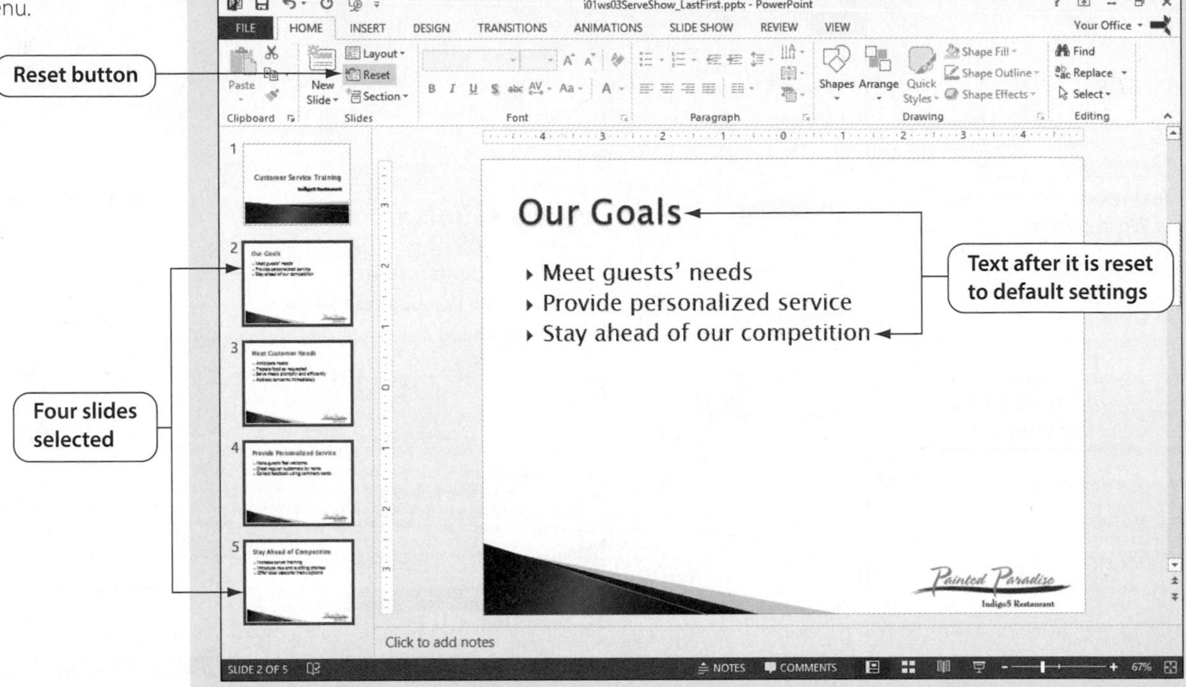

Figure 7 Slides reset to default settings

b. Click the **INSERT** tab, and then in the Text group, click **Header & Footer**. In the Header and Footer dialog box, click the **Notes and Handouts** tab. Click **Footer** to select it, and then type i01ws03ServeShow_LastFirst, using your last and first name. Click **Apply to All**.

c. Click **Save**. Click **Minimize** to minimize the PowerPoint window to the taskbar.

Integrating Access and PowerPoint

Data can be shared between PowerPoint and Access. Access tables and queries can be copied and pasted directly into a PowerPoint presentation. The data is therefore shared, but not linked, so any changes made to the data in Access will not be reflected in data that is copied and pasted in PowerPoint. In this section, you will practice copying data from Access and then pasting it to a PowerPoint slide.

Insert Access Data into a PowerPoint Presentation

Unlike exporting data in Access to Word or Excel, there is no import or export command for moving Access data to a PowerPoint presentation. Instead, simple copy and paste commands are used.

Copying and Pasting Access Data

Because data must be copied and pasted from Access to PowerPoint, any data from a table or query can easily be selected, copied, and pasted using the commands on the Clipboard. For this exercise, you will copy the results of a query in Access and paste it onto a slide in PowerPoint.

IP03.04

To Copy and Paste Access Query Results to a PowerPoint Slide

a. Start **Access**, and then open **i01ws03ServeSurvey**.

b. If necessary, click **Enable Content** in the SECURITY WARNING bar. In the Navigation Pane, double-click the query **qrySummary** to open it in Datasheet view.

c. Click **Select All** in the top-left of the query datasheet. This selects all the records in the query datasheet.

SIDE NOTE
Security Warning
Microsoft disables features to prevent malicious software from entering your computer through a database file. If you trust the contents, click Enable Content.

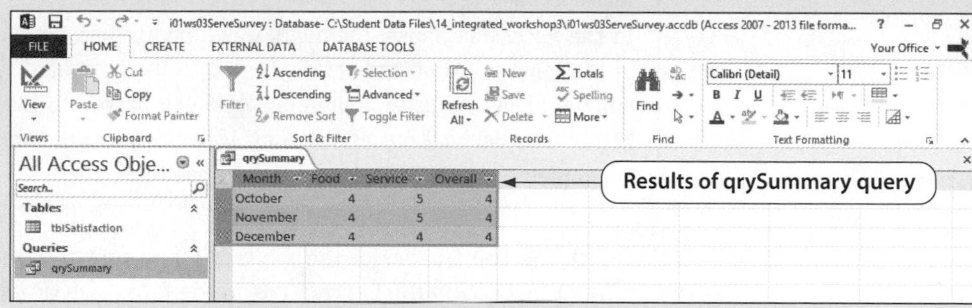

Figure 8 Query showing summary of customer satisfaction

d. On the HOME tab, in the Clipboard group, click **Copy**, and then close Access.

e. Click **PowerPoint** on the taskbar to display the PowerPoint window. With the **i01ws03ServeShow_LastFirst** presentation open, click **Slide 3** to select it.

f. Click the **HOME** tab, and then in the Clipboard group, click **Paste**. Point to the top of the table, and when your mouse pointer turns into a four-sided arrow, drag the **table** below the text.

SIDE NOTE
Queries and Tables
You opened and copied query results in Steps b through d. You can also open and copy a table the same way.

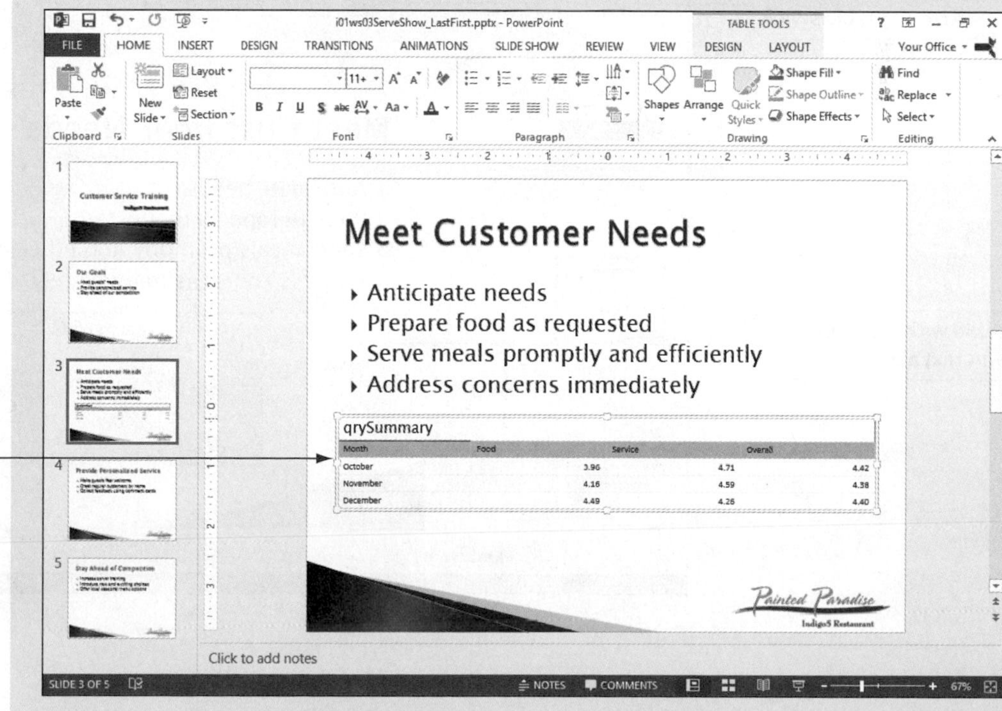

Figure 9 Table pasted from Access

g. With the table selected, on the HOME tab, in the Font group, click the **Font Size** arrow, and then select **18**. The font size for all text in the table is increased.

h. Select the title **qrySummary**, and then type Satisfaction Survey Results as the new title.

i. Resize the columns starting with the first column on the left. Point to the **line** between the Month and Food column headings, and then when your mouse pointer turns into a horizontal resize pointer, double-click to automatically fit the widest entry. Repeat for the other three columns.

> **Troubleshooting**
>
> In the Access database, the query was formatted so no decimal places were displayed in the number. When the data is copied to the Clipboard, the actual data is copied, not the displayed data. Therefore, when you paste the table into PowerPoint, there will be two decimal places showing. If necessary, you can type over the numbers that are copied and replace them with a rounded number.

j. Click the **top border** of the table to make sure the entire table is selected. Under TABLE TOOLS, on the LAYOUT tab, in the Table Size group, change the **Height** to 2.5" and the **Width** in to 4.5". In the **Alignment** group, click **Center** and **Center Vertically** to center all text horizontally and vertically within the cells of the table. In the **Arrange** group, click **Align**, and then select **Align Center** to center the table horizontally on the slide.

k. With the table selected, under TABLE TOOLS, on the DESIGN tab, in the Table Styles group, select the **Themed Style 1 - Accent 1** style to apply the style to the table.

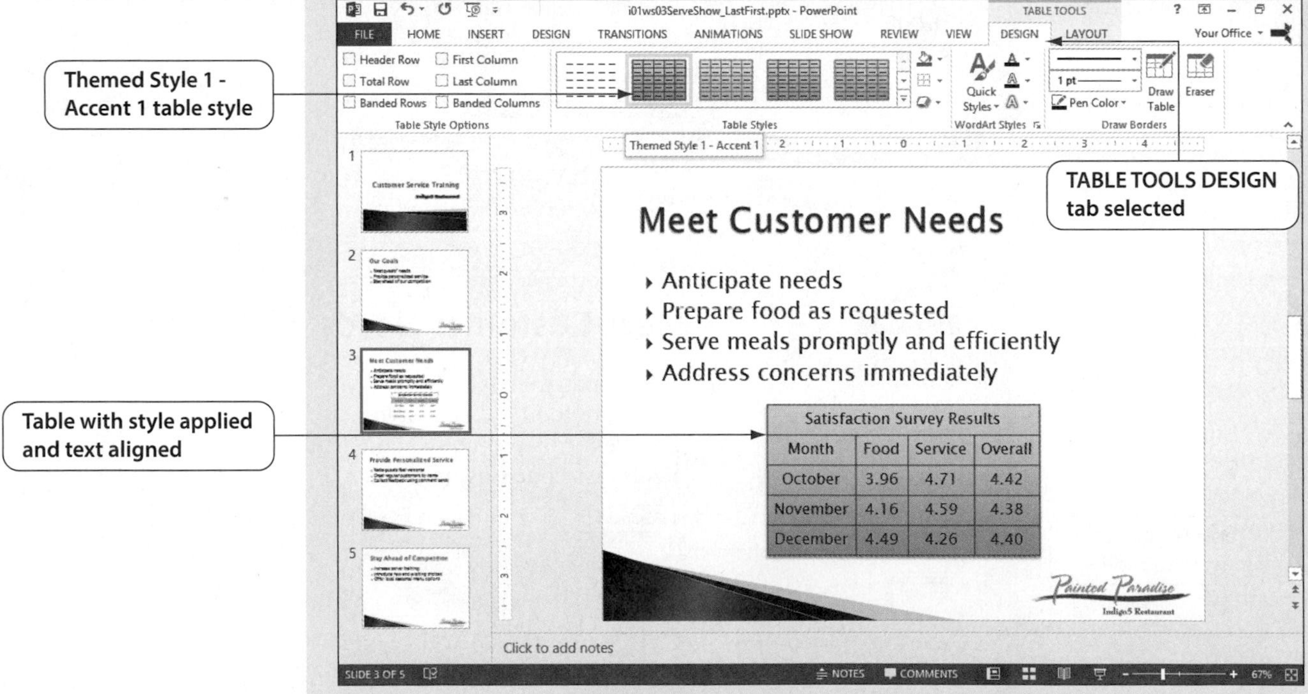

Figure 10 Table after formatting

l. Click **Save**, and then click **Minimize** to minimize PowerPoint on the taskbar.

CONSIDER THIS | Paste Options

You are performing a simple copy and paste with the data from Access. There are other options under Paste Special that you could have used. What are they? When would you want to use Paste Special rather than Paste?

Integrating Access, Excel, and PowerPoint

You can bring data into Excel from Access by using the copy and paste commands, by importing Access data into Excel, or by exporting Access data into the worksheet. The method you choose to use will determine whether the data is linked and can be automatically updated from one program to another. An import will create a permanent connection between Excel and Access, while a simple copy and paste will not. Table 2 shows the results of various methods of sharing data between Access and Excel. In this section, you will import data from Access into Excel, create a chart from the imported data, and then link the chart to a slide in PowerPoint.

Sharing Data Between Access and Excel	Type of Connection	Results
To bring data into Excel from Access:		
Copy and paste	None	No connection between Excel and Access after the copy and paste
Import Access data into Excel (in Excel)	Permanent	Can refresh the data in Excel when changes are made in Access
Export Access data into an Excel worksheet (in Access)	None	No connection between Excel and Access, but export steps can be saved for future use
To bring data into Access from Excel:		
Copy and paste	None	No connection between Access and Excel after the copy and paste
Import an Excel worksheet into an Access datasheet (in Access)	None	No connection between Access and Excel
Link to an Excel worksheet from an Access table (in Access)	Permanent	Can refresh the data in Access when changes are made in Excel

Table 2 Sharing data between Access and Excel

Import Access Data into Excel

When you import data from an Access database into an Excel worksheet, a permanent connection is created, and when data is changed in the database, the data can be refreshed in the worksheet. If you use the copy and paste commands or export the Access data, you create a copy of the data that cannot be updated.

Creating a Chart with Imported Access Data

There may be times when you have data in Access and realize that the data could be shown better as a chart. Access does not have charting capabilities. If the chart is a one-time project and will not need to be updated, then a copy and paste of the data will be sufficient. However, if the data will be frequently updated in Access and will therefore require the chart to be updated also, a link would be a better option. For this exercise you will import data from Access into Excel so when the data is changed in Access, the change is reflected in Excel.

IP03.05

To Import Access Data into Excel

a. Start **Excel**, and then open **i01ws03ServeChart**. Maximize the Excel window, if necessary.

b. Click the **FILE** tab, click **Save As**, double-click **Computer**, and then navigate to the location where you are saving your files. Save the document as i01ws03ServeChart_LastFirst using your first and last name. Click **Save**.

c. Make sure the **Satisfaction** worksheet tab is selected. Insert the **file name** in the left section of the footer, and then click **Save**.

d. Click cell **A3**. Click the **DATA** tab, and then in the Get External Data group, click **From Access**.

e. Navigate to the folder where your student data files are located, select **i01ws03ServeSurvey**, and then click **Open**.

f. In the Select Table dialog box, select **qrySummary** if necessary, and then click **OK**. This selects the Access query that has the data you want to import to create the desired chart.

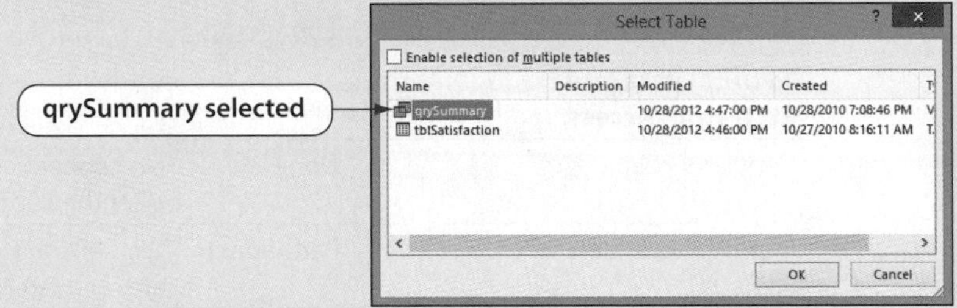

Figure 11 Select Table dialog box

g. In the Import Data dialog box, verify that **Table** is selected, and that the Existing worksheet text box contains **=$A$3**. This tells Excel where to put the data table in the worksheet.

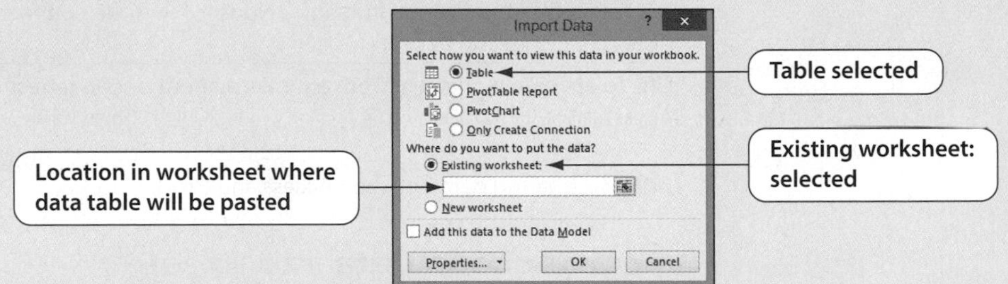

Figure 12 Import Data dialog box

h. Click **OK**. Select cells **B4:D6**. Click the **HOME** tab, and then in the Number group, click **Decrease Decimal** until the numbers are formatted with only two decimal places. Click **Save**.

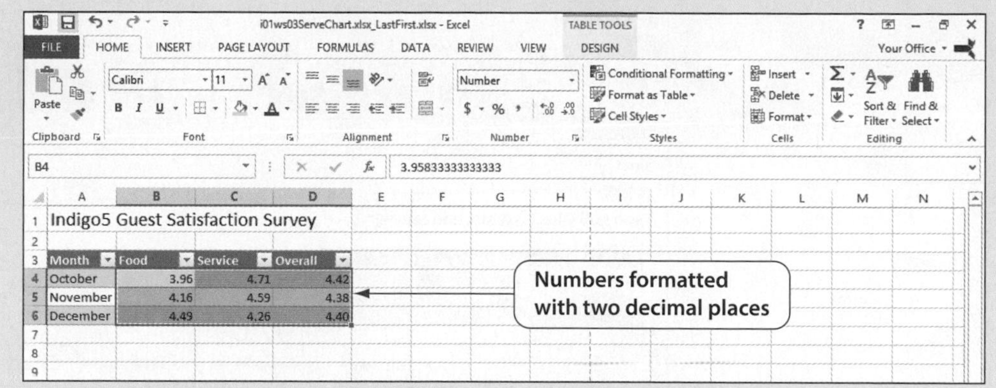

Figure 13 Datasheet from Access formatted in Excel

REAL WORLD ADVICE **Charting Access Data**

While it may seem redundant to copy data from Access into Excel, it can be a very useful exercise. Access is best used for storing, sorting, and reporting data, while Excel is best for charting and manipulating data. Rather than recreating data in Excel, it can be easier and more accurate to copy data from Access, whether from a table or a query, and then use Excel to create the chart.

Linking an Excel Chart to a PowerPoint Presentation

After you have created a chart in Excel with Access data, you can use that chart in another program like PowerPoint. If you link the chart to the presentation, then when the data is updated in Access, it can be refreshed in Excel and PowerPoint at the same time. For this exercise, you will link the Excel chart you create from the Access data to a slide in your PowerPoint presentation.

IP03.06

To Create an Excel Chart and Link it to a PowerPoint Slide

a. Select cells **A3:D6**. Click the **INSERT** tab, and then in the Charts group, click **Insert Column Chart** , and then select **3-D Clustered Column**.

b. Point to the **top-left edge** of the chart. When your mouse pointer changes to afour-sided arrow, drag the **chart** so the **top-left** corner is in cell **A8** and the **bottom-right** corner is in or close to cell **G22**.

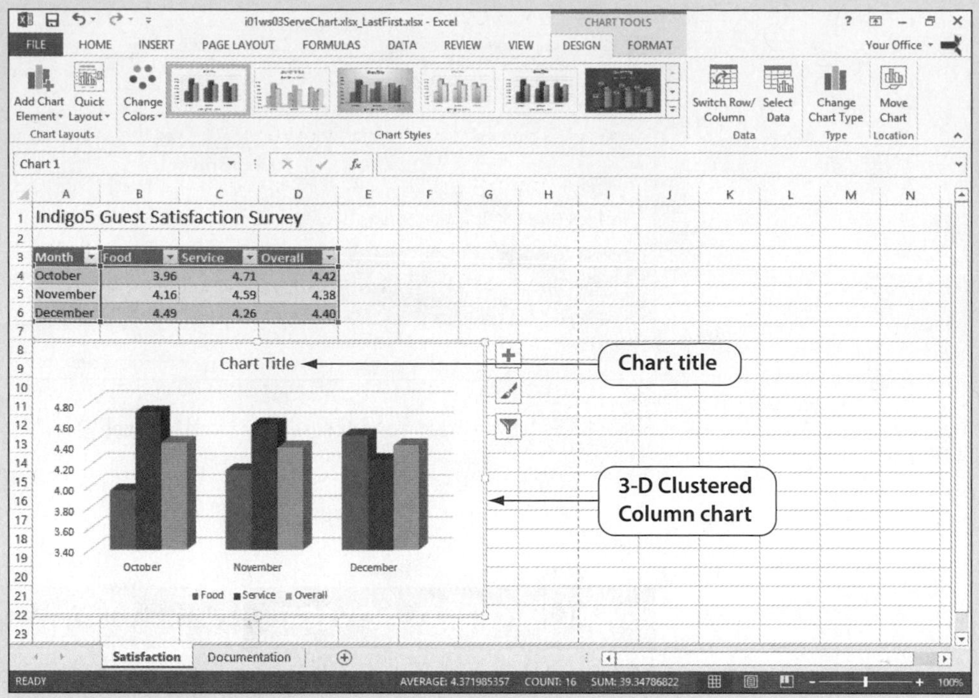

Figure 14 Column chart inserted

c. Click **Save** [Save icon]. With the chart still selected, click on the **HOME** tab, and then in the Clipboard group, click **Copy** [Copy icon] to copy the chart to the Clipboard.

d. Click **Minimize** [Minimize icon] to minimize the Excel window to the taskbar.

e. Click **PowerPoint** on the taskbar to restore the PowerPoint window. Click **Slide 4** to select it. On the HOME tab, in the Clipboard group, click the **Paste** arrow, and then select **Paste Special**. Select **Paste link**, choose **Microsoft Excel Chart Object**, and then click **OK**.

> **Troubleshooting**
>
> If you close Excel before you paste the chart in PowerPoint, then Paste Special will only give you the option to Paste but not Paste link. If you closed Excel before you pasted the chart, open Excel, copy the chart again, and keep Excel open while you paste it into PowerPoint.

f. Click **Excel** [Excel icon] on the taskbar to restore the Excel window. Select the **Chart Title** text, type Summary of Customer Surveys.

g. Click the **top border** of the chart to select it. Under CHART TOOLS, on the DESIGN tab, in the Chart Styles group, click **Change Colors**, and then under Colorful, select **Color 4**.

h. Click the **Documentation** worksheet tab, and then complete the following:
   - Click cell **A8**, and then type today's date in mm/dd/yyyy format.
   - Click cell **B8** and then type your name in Lastname, Firstname format.
   - Click cell **C8**, type Imported data from Access qrySummary to cell A3 and then press Enter.
   - In cell **C9**, type Formatted numbers in B4:D6 to two decimal places and then press Enter.
   - In cell **C10**, type Created 3-D Clustered Column chart from data in A3:D6 and then press Enter.

- In cell **C11**, type Edited chart title to Summary of Customer Surveys and then press Enter.
- In cell **C12**, type Changed chart color to Color 4 and then press Enter.

i. Click **Save**, and then click **Close** to close Excel.

j. Click **PowerPoint** on the taskbar to restore the PowerPoint window. Click **Slide 4**, if necessary. Note that the chart in the presentation now shows the chart title you added in Excel, as well as the color change. Move the **chart** below the text. With the chart selected, under DRAWING TOOLS, on the FORMAT tab, in the Arrange group, click **Align Objects**, and then click **Align Center**.

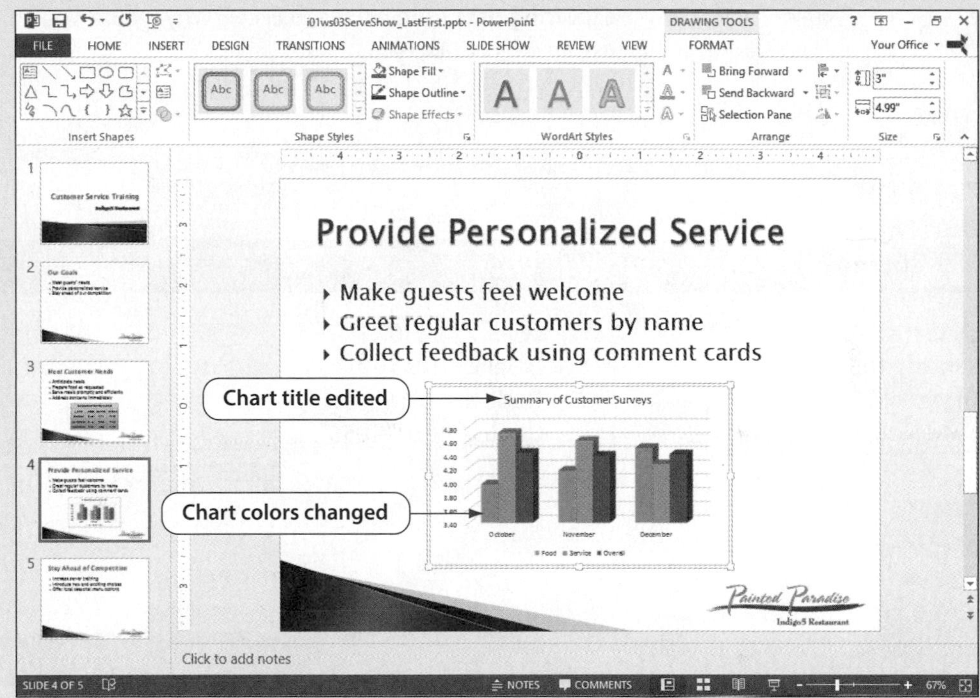

Figure 15 Chart updated in PowerPoint

k. Click **Save**, and then click **Close**.

REAL WORLD ADVICE Link, Embed, or Copy and Paste?

As you recall, the source file is the file that the original data comes from, and the destination file is where the data is copied to. When a chart is linked to an Excel worksheet, any changes in the worksheet are made to the linked chart as well. This is helpful if you are planning to change the data on a regular basis, such as a monthly or quarterly report. If you do not plan on changing the original data but would like the option to make changes to the chart in the destination file, then you can embed the chart. This allows you to change layout, design, and formatting options of the chart in either the destination or source file, but not both. If you do not need that kind of flexibility, then copying and pasting is the simplest method for copying the chart from one file to another.

Concept Check

1. How is working in Outline view in Word different from working in Print Layout view? What is the advantage to being able to expand and collapse the different-level paragraphs in an outline? p. 1056
2. How do you prepare a Word outline so it can be imported into PowerPoint as slides? p. 1060
3. Why would you want to export Access data to Excel before using it in another application, such as PowerPoint? p. 1062
4. What is the difference between copying and pasting data from Access to Excel and exporting data from Access to Excel? Why would you copy and paste? When would you use an export? p. 1065

Key Terms

Body text 1056
Collapse 1056
Demote 1056
Expand 1056
Level 1 1056
Level 2 1056
Outline 1056
Outline view 1056
Promote 1056
Reset 1061

Visual Summary

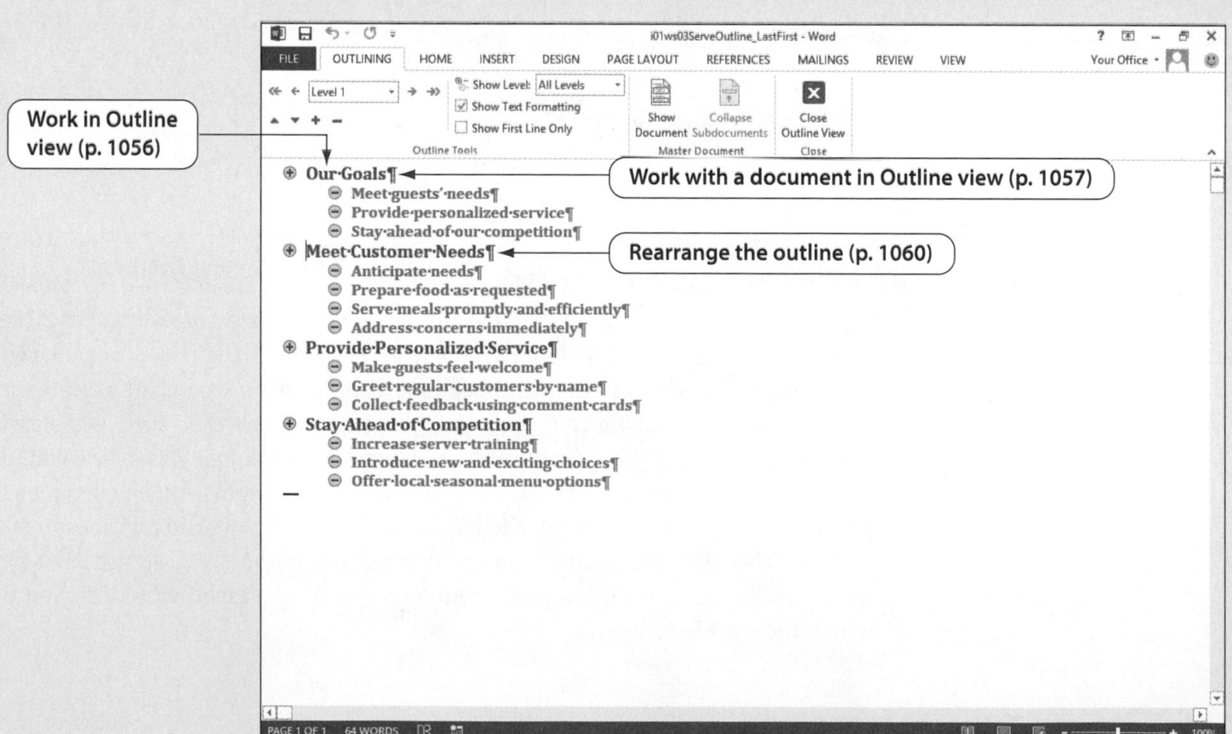

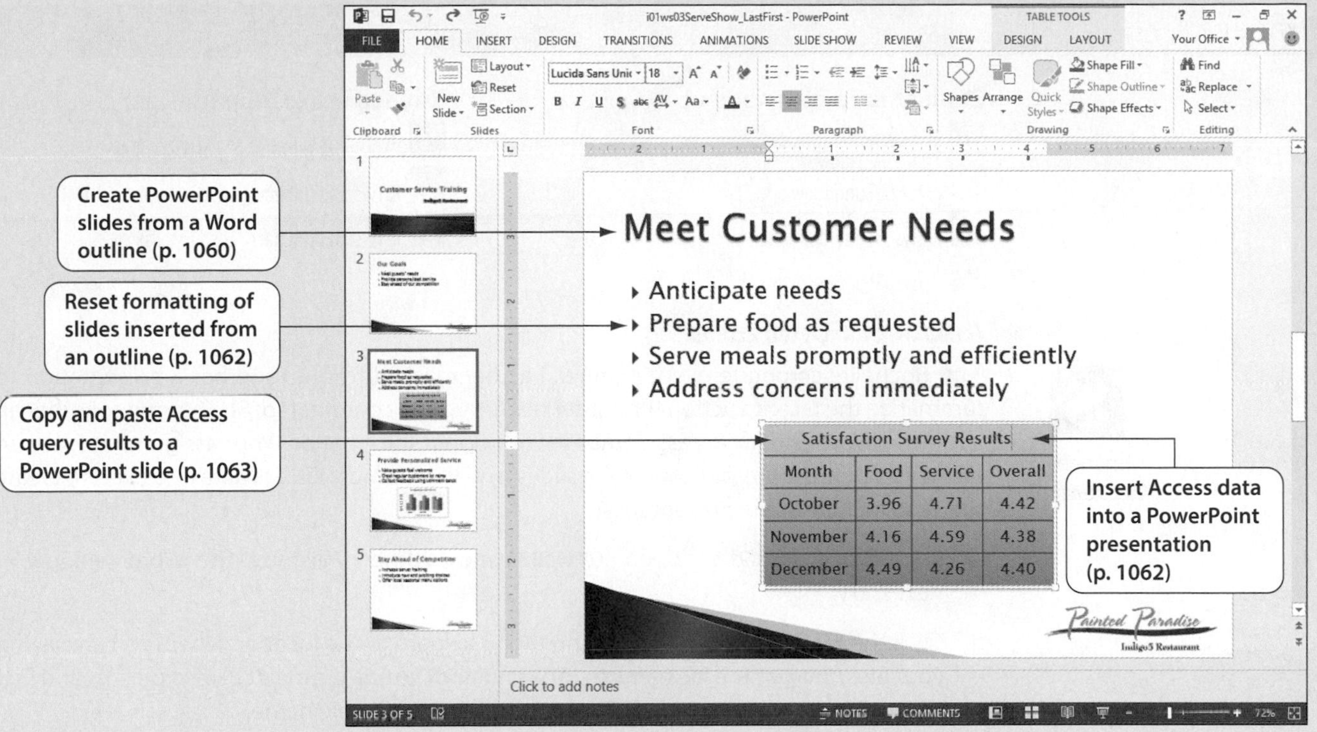

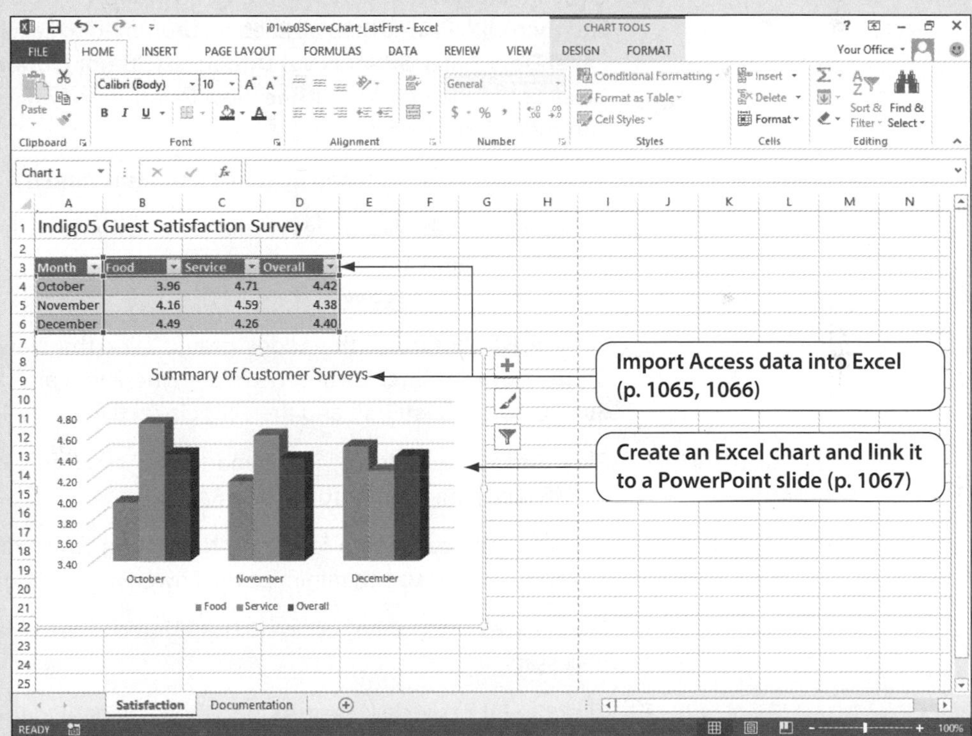

Figure 16 Customer Service Training Final

Practice 1

Student data files needed:

- i01ws03FundOutline.docx
- i01ws03FundShow.pptx
- i01ws03FundChart.xlsx
- i01ws03FundResult.accdb

You will save your files as:

- i01ws03FundOutline_LastFirst.docx
- i01ws03FundShow_LastFirst.pptx
- i01ws03FundChart_LastFirst.xlsx

Auction Fundraiser

Finance & Accounting

Patti Rochelle, corporate event planner, has been asked to put together a presentation to summarize the recent auction fundraiser her group has coordinated. She has put together an outline in Word and an Access database with donor information. Your assignment is to use the Word outline to create PowerPoint slides, and then import Access data into Excel to create charts to include in the presentation.

a. Start **Word**, and then open **i01ws03FundOutline**. Maximize the Word window, if necessary.

b. Click the **FILE** tab, click **Save As**, and then navigate to the location where you are saving your files. Change the file name to i01ws03FundOutline_LastFirst using your last and first name. Click **Save**. Insert a **left-aligned footer** with the file name.

c. Click the **VIEW** tab, and then in the Views group, click **Outline**. Select **all the lines of text**, and then click **Promote** so all lines are promoted to Level 1. Demote all lines except **Gold Level Donations**, **Silver Level Donations**, **Major Donors**, and **Donor Summary**. In the Close group, click **Close Outline View** to return to Print Layout view, save the document, and then close Word.

d. Start **PowerPoint**, and then open **i01ws03FundShow**.

e. Click the **FILE** tab, click **Save As**, and then navigate to the location where you are saving your files. Change the file name to i01ws03FundShow_LastFirst using your last and first name, and then click **Save**.

f. On the HOME tab, in the Slides group, click the **New Slide** arrow, and then select **Slides from Outline**. Locate the folder where you are saving your files, select **i01ws03 FundOutline_LastFirst**, and then click **Insert**.

g. Click **Slide 2**, hold down Shift, and then click **Slide 5** to select the four slides. On the HOME tab, in the Slides group, click **Reset**.

h. Insert the **file name** in a footer on **Notes and Handouts**, **apply to all**, and then click **Save**. Click **Minimize** to minimize the PowerPoint window to the taskbar.

i. Start **Excel**, and then open **i01ws03FundChart**. Maximize the Excel window, if necessary.

j. Click the **FILE** tab, click **Save As**, and then navigate to the location where you are saving your files. Change the file name to i01ws03FundChart_LastFirst using your last and first name. Click **Save**. Insert the **file name** in the left section of the footer.

k. Click cell **A4**. Click the **DATA** tab, and then in the Get External Data group, click **From Access**. Navigate to the location of your student data files, select **i01ws03FundResult**, and then click **Open**.

l. In the Select Table dialog box, select **qrySummary**, and then click **OK**. In the Import Data dialog box, verify that **Table** is selected, and that the Existing worksheet text box contains **=$A$4**. Click **OK**.

m. Select cells **B5:E7**. Click the **HOME** tab, and then in the Number group, click **Accounting** Number Format to format the numbers with a dollar sign and two decimal places.

n. Select cells **A4:B7**. Click the **INSERT** tab, and then in the Charts group, click **Insert Pie or Doughnut Chart**, and then under the 3-D Pie category, select **3-D Pie**. Move the chart so the **top-left** corner is in cell **A9** and the **bottom-right** corner is in or close to cell **E23**.

o. Select the **chart**, and then change the chart title to Summary of Donor Values. Under CHART TOOLS, on the DESIGN tab, in the Chart Styles group, click **Change Colors**, and then select **Color2**. In the Chart Layouts group, click the **Add Chart Elements** arrow, point to **Data Labels**, and then select **Best Fit**. Click **Save**.

p. If requested by your instructor, update the **Documentation** worksheet to reflect the changes that have been made, and then save the workbook.

q. Click the **Summary** worksheet tab, if necessary. Select the **chart**. Click the **HOME** tab, and then in the Clipboard group, click **Copy**. Close Excel.

r. Click **PowerPoint** on the taskbar to restore the PowerPoint window. Click **Slide 5** to select it. On the HOME tab, in the Slides group, click the **Layout** arrow, and then select **Title Only**. In the Clipboard group, click the **Paste** arrow, and then select **Paste Special**. Click **Paste link**, select **Microsoft Excel Chart Object**, and then click **OK**.

s. With the chart selected, under DRAWING TOOLS, on the FORMAT tab, in the Size group, increase the **Shape Height** to **4**. Align the chart so it is centered in the blank area on the slide. Save the presentation, and then close PowerPoint, saving changes if prompted. Submit all files as directed by your instructor.

Practice 2

Student data files needed:

 i01ws03GuestOutline.docx

 i01ws03GuestShow.pptx

i01ws03GuestList.accdb

You will save your files as:

 i01ws03GuestOutline_LastFirst.docx

 i01ws03GuestShow_LastFirst.pptx

Marriage Presentation

Customer Service

The staff in Event Planning has been asked to create a short PowerPoint presentation to celebrate an upcoming marriage. The bride and groom have given Patti Rochelle, corporate event planner, a Word outline listing topics they want in the presentation. The presentation will run continuously in an alcove during the reception. The guest list has been maintained in an Access database. Your assignment is to create a PowerPoint presentation from the Word outline and insert a query table into the presentation to show how many guests, by state, will be at the ceremony.

a. Start **Word**, and then open **i01ws03GuestOutline**. Maximize the Word window, if necessary.

b. Click the **FILE** tab, click **Save As**, and then navigate to the location where you are saving your files. Change the file name to i01ws03GuestOutline_LastFirst using your last and first name. Click **Save**. Insert a **left-aligned footer** with the file name.

c. Click the **VIEW** tab, and then in the Views group, click **Outline**. Select **all the lines of text**, and then click **Promote** so all the lines are promoted to Level 1. Demote all lines except **The Bride**, **The Groom**, **The Bridal Party**, and **Our Guests**. Click **Close Outline View** to return to Print Layout view. Click **Save**, and then close Word.

d. Start **PowerPoint**, and then open **i01ws03GuestShow**.

e. Click the **FILE** tab, click **Save As**, and then navigate to the location where you are saving your files. Change the file name to i01ws03GuestShow_LastFirst using your last and first name. Click **Save**.

f. On the HOME tab, in the Slides group, click the **New Slide** arrow, and then select **Slides from Outline**. Navigate to the location where you are saving your files, select **i01ws03GuestOutline_LastFirst**, and then click **Insert**.

g. Click **Slide 2**, hold down Shift, and then click **Slide 5** to select the four slides. On the HOME tab, in the Slides group, click **Reset**. With the slides still selected, click **Layout**, and then select **Title and Content**.

h. Insert the **file name** in a footer on **Notes and Handouts**, **apply to all**, and then click **Save**. Click **Minimize** to minimize the PowerPoint window to the taskbar.

i. Start **Access**, and then open **i01ws03GuestList**. If necessary, click **Enable Content** in the SECURITY WARNING bar.

j. In the Navigation Pane, double-click the query **qryStates** to open it in Datasheet view. Click **Select All** at the top left of the query datasheet to select all the records in the query datasheet. On the HOME tab, in the Clipboard group, click **Copy**. Close Access.

k. Click **PowerPoint** on the taskbar to restore the PowerPoint window. Click **Slide 5** to select it. On the HOME tab, in the Slides group, click the **Layout** arrow, and then select **Two Content**. Click the **right** placeholder, and then in the Clipboard group, click **Paste**.

l. With the table selected, on the HOME tab, in the Font group, click the **Font Size** arrow, and then select **14**. Replace the title **qryStates** with Home States of Guests and then increase the font size to **16**. Resize the columns starting with the column on the left. Center the title and column headings. Center the number of guests under the column **Guests**. Align the table so it is centered in the right area of the slide.

m. Select the **table**. Under TABLE TOOLS, on the DESIGN tab, in the Table Styles group, select the **Light Style 3 - Accent 3** style to apply the style to the table.

n. In the left placeholder, click in front of **Jill**, and then press Shift twice to add a blank line and move the names to a new line. On the HOME tab, in the Paragraph group, click **Bullets** to remove the bullet, and then in the Paragraph group, click **Align Right** to move the names to the right side of the placeholder. Save the presentation, and then close PowerPoint. Submit all files as directed by your instructor.

Problem Solve 1

Student data files needed:

- i01ws03BoardOutline.docx
- i01ws03BoardShow.pptx
- i01ws03BoardList.accdb

You will save your files as:

- i01ws03BoardOutline_LastFirst.docx
- i01ws03BoardShow_LastFirst.pptx
- i01ws03BoardChart_LastFirst.xlsx

Sales Presentation

Finance & Accounting

The manager of Painted Treasures Gift Shop needs to give a sales presentation to the resort board of directors each month. There is an existing Access database with information on items sold as well as a Word outline with the basic information for the presentation. Your assignment is to create a PowerPoint presentation from the Word outline, copy Access query results into the presentation, and finally, import the Access data into Excel to create a chart to include on one of the slides.

a. Start **Word**, and then open **i01ws03BoardOutline**. Save the file to your student folder as i01ws03BoardOutline_LastFirst. Insert a **left-aligned footer** with the file name.

b. In Outline view, promote and demote the paragraphs so **January Trends**, **January Sales by Category**, and **February Strategy** are all Level 1 paragraphs. The other paragraphs should all be Level 2. Close Outline view, save the file, and then close Word.

c. Start **PowerPoint**, and then open **i01ws03BoardShow**. Save the presentation as i01ws03BoardShow_LastFirst. Insert new slides using the file **i01ws03BoardOutline_LastFirst**. Reset the new slides that you inserted. Insert the **file name** in a footer on **Notes and Handouts**, **apply to all**, and then click **Save**. Save the presentation.

d. Start **Excel**, open a new blank workbook, and then save it to your student folder as i01ws03BoardChart_LastFirst. Insert the **file name** in the left section of the footer. Save the workbook.

e. Get external data from the query **qryJanuarySales** in the Access database **i01ws03BoardList**. Insert the table in cell **A1**, and then format cells **B2:B9** with the **Accounting** format. Create a **3-D Clustered Column** chart from the data table. Change the chart title to January Sales and then apply the **Style 3** chart style. Move the chart below the data table. Save the workbook.

f. Copy the **column chart** to the Clipboard. In the PowerPoint presentation, select **Slide 3**, and then paste the **Excel chart** as a link. Align the chart so it fits well on the slide and all text is visible. Save the presentation, and then minimize PowerPoint.

g. Start **Access**, open **i0ws03BoardList**, and then click **Enable Content**. Copy the **qryJanuarySales** query results to the Clipboard, and then close Access.

h. In the PowerPoint presentation, change the layout of **Slide 2** to **Two Content**. Paste the **table** on the right side of the slide. Increase the font size, replace the title, and then resize the columns. Apply a style to the table, and then make any formatting changes to improve the appearance of the table. Align the table so it fits well on the slide and all the text is visible. Save the presentation, and then close PowerPoint. Submit all files as directed by your instructor.

Problem Solve 2

Student data files needed:

i01ws03TrendOutline.docx

i01ws03TrendShow.pptx

i01ws03TrendData.accdb

You will save your files as:

i01ws03TrendOutline_LastFirst.docx

i01ws03TrendShow_LastFirst.pptx

i01ws03TrendCharts_LastFirst.xlsx

New Gift Items

Sales & Marketing

The manager and staff of the Painted Treasures Gift Shop have been brainstorming to find ways to expand inventory and increase sales. They have been researching trends in the gift shop industry and have developed several different possibilities. They want to create a presentation for Painted Paradise management detailing their ideas. Data has been kept in an Access database with information about potential new items, wholesale cost, and suggested sale price. There is also an outline in Word showing the topics they would like to cover. Your assignment is to create a PowerPoint presentation from the Word outline, import the Access data into Excel, and then create charts for the presentation.

a. Start **Word**, and then open **i01ws03TrendOutline**. Save the file to your student folder as i01ws03TrendOutline_LastFirst. Insert a **left-aligned footer** with the file name.

b. Using **Outline** view, promote and demote the paragraphs so **Luxuries and indulgences**, **Green Products**, and **Soft Goods** are all Level 1 paragraphs. The other paragraphs should all be Level 2. Close Outline view, save the file, and then close Word.

c. Start **PowerPoint**, and then open **i01ws03TrendShow**. Save the presentation as i01ws03TrendShow_LastFirst. Note that the manager has already created two slides. Click **Slide 2** to select it, and then insert new slides from **i01ws03TrendOutline_LastFirst**. Reset the new slides that you inserted. Insert the **file name** in a footer on **Notes and Handouts**, **apply to all**, and then click **Save**. Save the presentation, and then minimize PowerPoint.

d. Start **Excel**, open a new blank workbook, and then save it as i01ws03TrendCharts_LastFirst. Insert the **file name** in the left section of the footer.

e. Import data from the Access database **i01ws03TrendData** by importing the datasheets from the three queries: **qryLuxuries**, **qryGreenProducts**, and **qrySoftGoods**. Use a separate worksheet for each datasheet, and name the worksheet tabs appropriately.

f. Format numbers on all worksheets as **Currency**. Insert a line chart using the **Line with Markers** style on each worksheet showing the cost and retail price for each item in that category. Move the chart under the data. Change the chart titles to match the name of the categories, and then save the workbook.

g. If requested by your instructor, add the **Documentation** worksheet, and then complete it to reflect the changes that have been made. Save the workbook.

h. Copy each chart and paste it on the corresponding slide in the PowerPoint presentation. Move each chart so it fits well on the slide and all text is visible. Increase the font size on the charts if necessary. Save the presentation and then close PowerPoint. Close Excel. Submit all files as directed by your instructor.

Perform 1: Perform in Your Career

Student data files needed:

- Blank Word document
- Blank PowerPoint presentation
- Blank Access database
- Blank Excel worksheet

You will save your files as:

- i01ws03GrantOutline_LastFirst.docx
- i01ws03GrantShow_LastFirst.pptx
- i01ws03GrantRatio_LastFirst.accdb
- i01ws03GrantChart_LastFirst.xlsx

Grant Presentation

Information Technology

You are the director of a new and innovative high school and are looking for ways to increase the technology available to your students. You have learned of a grant that would pay for tablets for each student to use during the school year. You would like your school to become a leader in technology, and you have Access data that shows how most schools are lacking in this area. Along with writing the grant proposal, you need to create a presentation for the school board with the grant proposal information. The project name is Technology Grant Proposal. The grant presentation must include the following information:

- An introduction to your school with background information and a mission statement
- A problem statement that identifies the problems the project will address
- A comparison of student-to-computer ratios of area schools
- A project summary of what your school will need
- A list of key benefits the project will provide your school
- A budget for the project

a. Start **Word**, and then create a Word outline that will eventually become your PowerPoint slides. You must include the bulleted information above in your presentation. There should be Level 1 and Level 2 paragraphs for each slide. Save the document as i01ws03GrantOutline_LastFirst. Insert a left-aligned footer with the file name, save the document, and then close Word.

b. Start **PowerPoint**, and then create slides from the Word outline created in Step a. Add a title and subtitle to the presentation on Slide 1. Insert the file name in the footer of Notes and Handouts. Apply a theme to the presentation. Save the presentation as i01ws03GrantShow_LastFirst.

c. Start **Access**, and then create a new database called i01ws03GrantRatio_LastFirst. Add the following fields after the ID field: School Name, School Enrollment, and Computer Ratio. Add at least 12 records to fill in this table. The first record should have your first name and last name as the School Name, followed by HS. The records should show that the maximum Computer Ratio is 4:1. That is, all records should be 4:1, 5:1, or higher. Save the database.

d. Copy all the records in the Access table, and then paste the datasheet into the appropriate slide in your PowerPoint presentation. Resize the columns, apply a style to the table, and then save the presentation.

e. Start **Excel**, and then create a budget for the project. Assume there are 426 students. Include the cost of the tablet, the cost of any additional hardware or software, and the estimated cost of maintenance per student and for the total project. Create a chart for the data. Save the workbook as i01ws03GrantChart_LastFirst. Insert the file name in the left section of the footer.

f. If requested by your instructor, add the Documentation worksheet, and then complete it to reflect the changes that have been made.

g. Link the Excel data and the chart to a slide in your PowerPoint presentation. Save the workbook, and then close Excel.

h. Save the PowerPoint presentation. Close all applications. Submit all files as directed by your instructor.

Perform 2: How Others Perform

Student data files needed:

i01ws03ClassShow.pptpx

 i01ws03ClassOutline.docx

 i01ws03ClassList.accdb

You will save your files as:

 i01ws03ClassOutline_LastFirst.docx

 i01ws03ClassShow_LastFirst.pptx

 i01ws03ClassCharts_LastFirst.xlsx

Presentation Gone Wrong

Production & Operations

The local university offers specialized classes for people who are 50 years old or more. Some of the classes last only one day and others span several weeks. Various excursions are also offered that could be day trips or might extend over a weekend. Your friend works in the Continuing Education office and has put together a presentation to show how many students have signed up for these classes. He created an outline in Word and tried to create PowerPoint slides using the Slides from Outline feature, but he ended up with a slide for each class, instead of a slide for each type. The types of classes are One Day Classes, Multi-Week Courses, and Excursions. When students register, their data is entered in an Access database. Queries have been created to track the number of students in each class and in each type of class. Your friend would like to import this data into Excel to create charts, but he cannot do that until he corrects the presentation. He has asked for your help.

a. Start **PowerPoint**, and then open **i01ws03ClassShow**. Examine the way the slides were created from the Word outline. Close PowerPoint.

b. Start **Word**, and then open **i01ws03ClassOutline**. Save the file as i01ws03ClassOutline_LastFirst.

c. Edit the outline so the three types of classes will be the titles on three different slides and the class names will be the details on each slide. Insert a left-aligned footer with the file name, save the document, and then close Word.

d. Start **PowerPoint**, open a new presentation, and then save it as i01ws03ClassShow_LastFirst. Insert slides from the outline **i01ws03ClassOutline_LastFirst**. There should be a title slide and three slides from the Word outline. Add an appropriate title and subtitle to Slide 1. Insert a **Notes and Handout** footer with the file name. Save the presentation, and then minimize PowerPoint.

e. Start **Excel**, open a new workbook, and then save it as i01ws03ClassCharts_LastFirst. Change the orientation to **Landscape** and the width to **1 page**. Click the **OneDay** worksheet tab, if necessary, and then insert the file name in the left section of the footer. Save the workbook.

f. Import data from the Access database **i01ws03ClassList** by importing the datasheets from the three queries: qryOneDay, qryMultiWeek, and qryExcursions. Use a separate worksheet for each datasheet and name the worksheet tabs appropriately. Create a column chart on each worksheet showing the number of students enrolled for each type of class. Change the chart titles to match the names of the tables, and then save the workbook.

g. If requested by your instructor, add the Documentation worksheet, and then complete it to reflect the changes that have been made. Save the workbook.

h. Click **PowerPoint** on the taskbar to restore the PowerPoint window. Apply a Design theme that coordinates with the colors of the charts. Link each chart to the appropriate slide in the PowerPoint presentation. Move and size each chart, if necessary, so it fits attractively on the slide. Save the presentation, and then close PowerPoint. Close Excel. Submit all files as directed by your instructor.

Additional Cases

Additional Workshop Cases are available on the companion website and in the instructor resources.

Appendix

EFFICIENT INTERACTION WITH A TOUCHSCREEN

OBJECTIVES

1. Understand variations in tablets p. 1080
2. Understand methods for interacting with a tablet PC p. 1082
3. Use flick, touch, and bezel gestures p. 1086
4. Use Office 2013, and other, touch features p. 1091, 1092

Prepare Case

Painted Paradise Resort and Spa Works with Touch Features

IT
Information Technology

NAN / Fotolia

In his position as the CIO of Painted Paradise Resort and Spa, Aidan Matthews travels frequently. Traditionally, Aidan would take four devices with him—a laptop to work on Microsoft Office files, a Kindle to read, a Google tablet to watch videos, and an iPhone to make phone calls. He recently acquired a Windows 8 tablet PC and Windows 8 phone with Office 2013. This will allow him to only carry two devices and still complete all the same tasks. Aidan has asked you to teach him the most efficient ways to interact with his new Windows 8 tablet PC, a Surface Pro.

REAL WORLD SUCCESS

"As a business analyst for a large technology consulting company, I travel four days a week. Most of my colleagues carry four or more devices while traveling. I only carry my Windows 8 tablet PC and phone. I can do everything my colleagues can and more—with less hassle in the security line and more room in my luggage! My colleagues and clients have been quite impressed with the efficiency of the touch and pen integration."

- Dana, recent graduate

Interacting with a Windows 8 Tablet PC

Microsoft Windows 8 is the latest version of the Windows operating system. The **operating system** is system software, which controls and coordinates computer hardware operations so other programs can run efficiently. The operating system acts as an intermediary between **application software**—programs that help you perform specific tasks, such as word processing—and the computer hardware.

Like previous versions of Windows, Windows 8 uses a **graphical user interface (GUI)**, an interface that uses icons, which are small pictures representing commands, programs, and documents. However, Windows 8 introduces a number of new features that will leave even an experienced user in need of some retraining.

Windows 8 has moved away from the Start button and moved towards a touch-screen interface. Windows 8 also supports gesture recognition, which allows you to control the computer with gestures instead of mouse clicks, if you have a touch-screen device. Gestures allow you to perform actions like zooming and switching programs by performing certain movements. In this section, you will learn about the various ways to efficiently interact in the Windows 8 environment.

Understand Variations in Tablets

People use different devices for different purposes. You may use your tablet for information consumption and entertainment. Likewise, you may prefer your desktop computer to write a paper. These preferences account for the vast market diversity in devices. You may even know someone who regularly uses five or more devices. The capabilities of these devices can be quite divergent and cause consumer confusion. Further, some consumers—particularly cost-conscious consumers—seek to minimize the number of devices.

There are many types of tablet computers in terms of hardware, software, and size. Further, the types are constantly changing as new versions come out. Some of the most popular currently available devices are the Microsoft Surface, Apple iPad, and the Android tablet computer. Each device runs a different operating system and has different features and capabilities. Which tablet is the best for you depends on many questions.

- How much are you willing to spend?
- Do you need to use it for business production?
- Do you need to connect to specific hardware such as a camera or microphone?
- Do you want a high-quality display?
- How does the device feel when you hold it?
- Do you find the device easy to use?
- Do you need it to connect to a cellular network?

One major discriminator when answering these questions is the operating system it runs. Table 1 describes the capabilities of the various operating systems and the devices they are found on. Since technology is constantly changing, you should research any potential changes to the table that follows.

Operating System	Software It Runs	Types of Devices	Hardware Manufacturers	Office Capabilities
Macintosh	Runs software written for the Macintosh operating system	Laptops and desktops	Apple only	Mac Office versions such as Office 2011 and PC versions via dual boot or parallels
Windows 8	Runs software written for Windows 7 and above. Also, runs apps from the Windows store	Laptops, desktops, and some newer Intel chip-based tablets	Various: Microsoft, Lenovo, Dell, ASUS, and others	Full Office 2013
Windows 8 RT	Runs apps from the Windows store only	Arm chip-based tablets	Various: Microsoft, Lenovo, Dell, ASUS, and others	Office 2013 RT: Visually, the same as the full Office 2013 but lacks some sophisticated Office features
Android	Runs apps from the Google Play Store only	Smartphones and tablets	Various: Google, Samsung, ASUS, HTC, LG, and others	Some limited native capability to work with Office files
iOS	Runs apps from the Apple Store only	iPads and iPhones	Apple only	Very limited ability to work with Office files. Some capability with purchased third-party apps
Windows Phone	Runs apps from the Windows store only, including Office 2013 for Windows Phone	Smartphones	Various: Nokia, HTC, Samsung, and others	Office 2013 for Windows Phone: Visually different than the full Office 2013 but similar functionality to Office 2013 RT
Blackberry	Runs apps from BlackBerry App World only	Smartphones and tablets	Blackberry only	Very limited ability to work with Office files. Some capability with purchased third-party apps

Table 1 Operating system capabilities

Tablets can run one of two kinds of chips: an Intel-based or ARM-based chip. An **Advanced RISC Machine chip (ARM chip)** is designed for low-energy embedded systems, such as in an iPad. An **Intel chip** is a series of microprocessors made by the manufacturer Intel, for example the chip used in most traditional laptops or desktops.

In October 2012, Microsoft released the Surface tablet. This tablet comes in two versions, the Surface and Surface Pro—as seen in Figure 1. The Surface RT runs on an ARM chip device and contains substantively similar functionality for Word, PowerPoint, Excel, and OneNote as the Windows version of Office 2013. Visually, Windows RT even looks the same as the full Office 2013 for Windows. However, applications that run on Windows Phone and RT do not support some of the more sophisticated Office features or back-end Visual Basic programming.

The Surface Pro tablet runs Windows 8 Pro and is built with a more traditional Intel chip hardware that lets it perform like a traditional PC. Tablets capable of performing like a traditional PC are typically referred to as a **tablet PC**.

Aidan Matthews purchased a Surface Pro tablet PC because he can use it for personal, business, and mobile tasks. Thus, you need to learn about the touch interface for the full Windows 8 specifically—the same touch interface for any PC with any kind of touch screen.

Figure 1 Microsoft Surface

Understand Methods for Interacting with a Tablet PC

Users can interact with the tablet PC via several built-in ways: speech, keyboard, trackpad, digitizer pen, or touch screen. Windows 8 is smart enough to detect the method of input you are using and adapts the menus and options accordingly. To maximize your efficiency, you need to understand when to use which method of input.

Inputting Text with Speech Recognition

Speech recognition in Windows 8 is better than any prior version of Windows. Typically, whether speech recognition is desirable or efficient is highly dependent on voice, accent, and personal preference. Windows 8 has a built-in speech recognition app. By default, the app is not pinned to the Start screen. However, you can easily find it by doing a search as shown in Figure 2. While the Surface Pro includes a microphone, most users prefer and have better accuracy with a headset or desktop microphone—purchased separately.

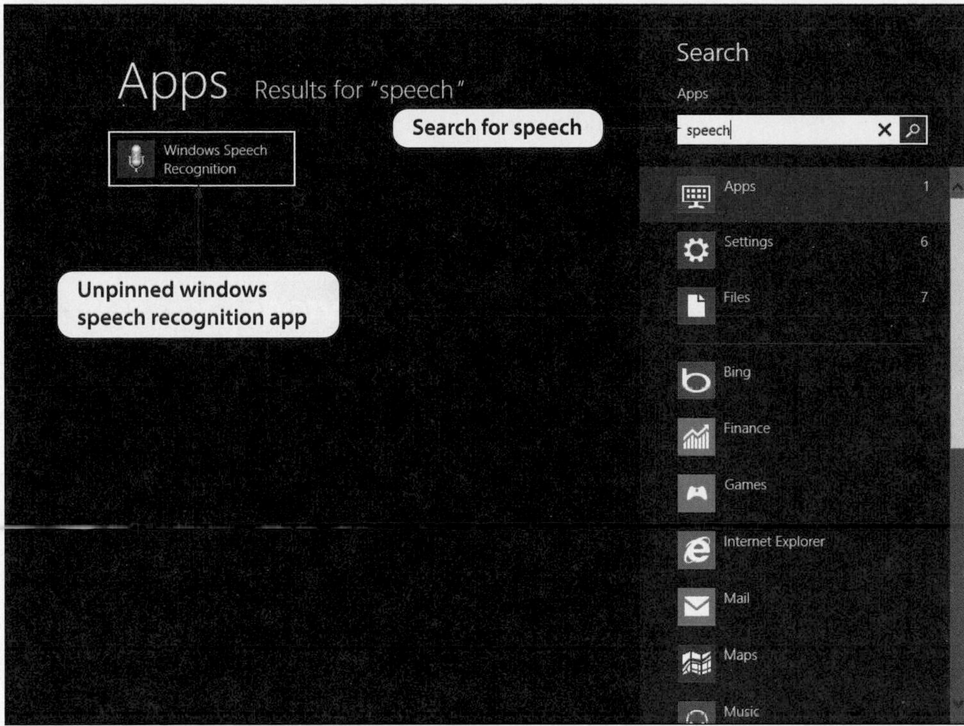

Figure 2 Search for speech recognition app

Using the Keyboard and Trackpad

The Surface comes with two types of covers: the touch cover and type cover as seen in Figure 3. The type cover provides a depression keyboard similar to traditional keyboards. Both keyboards have the same functionality except that only the type cover has the traditional F1–F12 keys. Thus, personal preference is the most important determinant on which is best. Even though Windows 8 has a touch keyboard, most users still find an actual keyboard preferable when needing more than a few words entered.

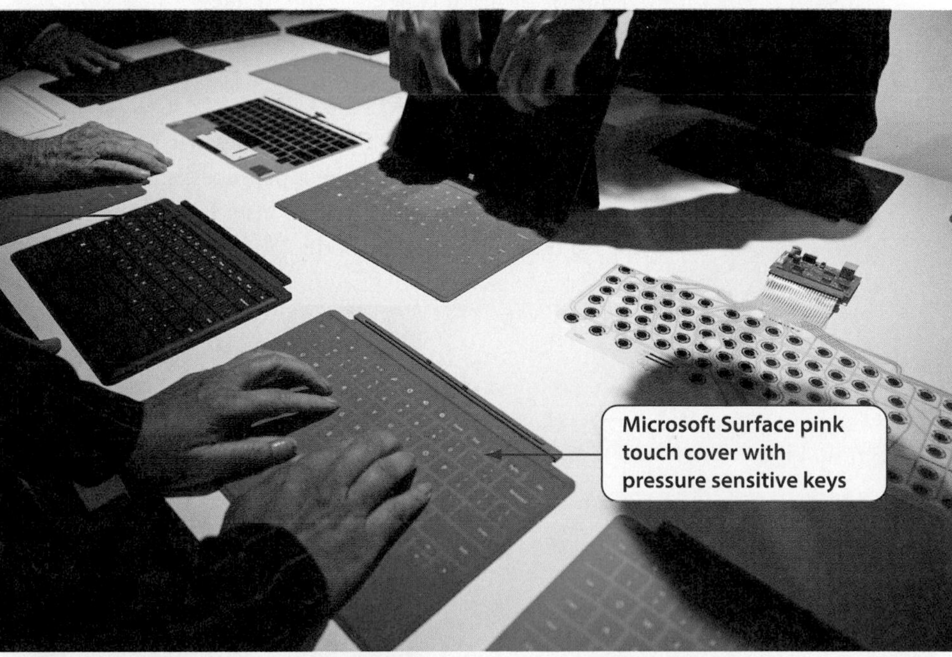

Figure 3 Microsoft Surface covers

The covers come with a built-in **trackpad**—a pad that works like a traditional mouse but uses touch. Trackpads are typically found on laptops and tablet PCs. Many users find a trackpad awkward when needing to drag. Thus, a user that drags a lot may want to consider purchasing a USB wireless mouse.

The touch interface can replace the need for a mouse in many situations. In fact, keyboard shortcuts can also cut down dramatically on the need for a mouse. Thus, keyboard shortcuts improve efficiency in Windows 8 more than any prior version of Windows.

REAL WORLD ADVICE | **Using Keyboard Shortcuts and KeyTips**

Keyboard shortcuts are extremely useful because they allow you to keep your hands on the keyboard instead of reaching for the mouse to make Ribbon selections. This can dramatically increase your efficiency and save you time.

Pressing the Alt key will display KeyTips—or keyboard shortcuts—for items on the Ribbon and Quick Access Toolbar. After displaying the KeyTips, you can press the letter or number corresponding to Ribbon items to request the action from the keyboard. Pressing Alt again will remove the KeyTips.

Many keyboard shortcuts are universal to all Windows programs. Keyboard shortcuts usually involve two or more keys, in which case you hold down the first key listed, and press the second key once.

QUICK REFERENCE | **Common Keyboard Shortcuts**

Press Ctrl and type C	Copy the selected item
Press Ctrl and type V	Paste a copied item
Press Ctrl and type A	Select all the items in a document or window
Press Ctrl and type B	Bold selected text
Press Ctrl and type Z	Undo an action
Press Ctrl + Home	Move to the top of the document
Press Ctrl + End	Move to the end of the document
Press F1	Microsoft Help
Press Ctrl and type S	Save a file

Using the Digitizer Pen

The Surface Pro tablet PC also comes with a **digitizer pen**—a device that allows you to write on a touch screen like a pen does on paper as shown in Figure 4. Windows 8 can recognize whether you use a mouse, finger, or digitizer pen. Apps may react differently based on your input method.

Figure 4 Surface digitizer pen

If you use the pen in Word, the Pens contextual Ribbon tab automatically appears for drawing options: Highlighter, Eraser, or Selection as seen in Figure 5. Word accepts only drawing input from the pen and cannot recognize handwritten text. Thus, best practice is to use the pen in Word to replace a mouse or to draw a picture.

If you want to take handwritten notes—for example in a meeting—best practice is to use OneNote. OneNote has excellent handwriting-to-text conversion capabilities using the Ink to Text button as shown in Figure 6. Thus, you gain efficiency by using the pen in situations where handwriting is most natural.

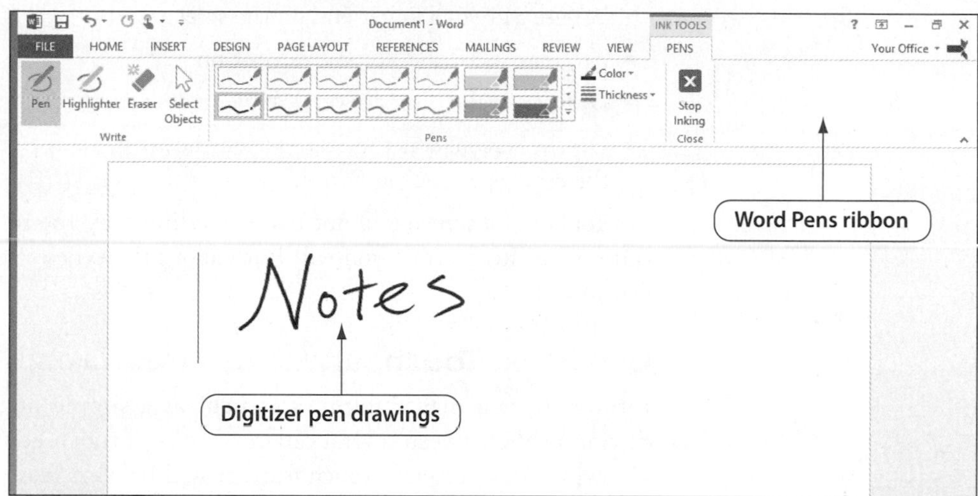

Figure 5 Pens Ribbon in Word

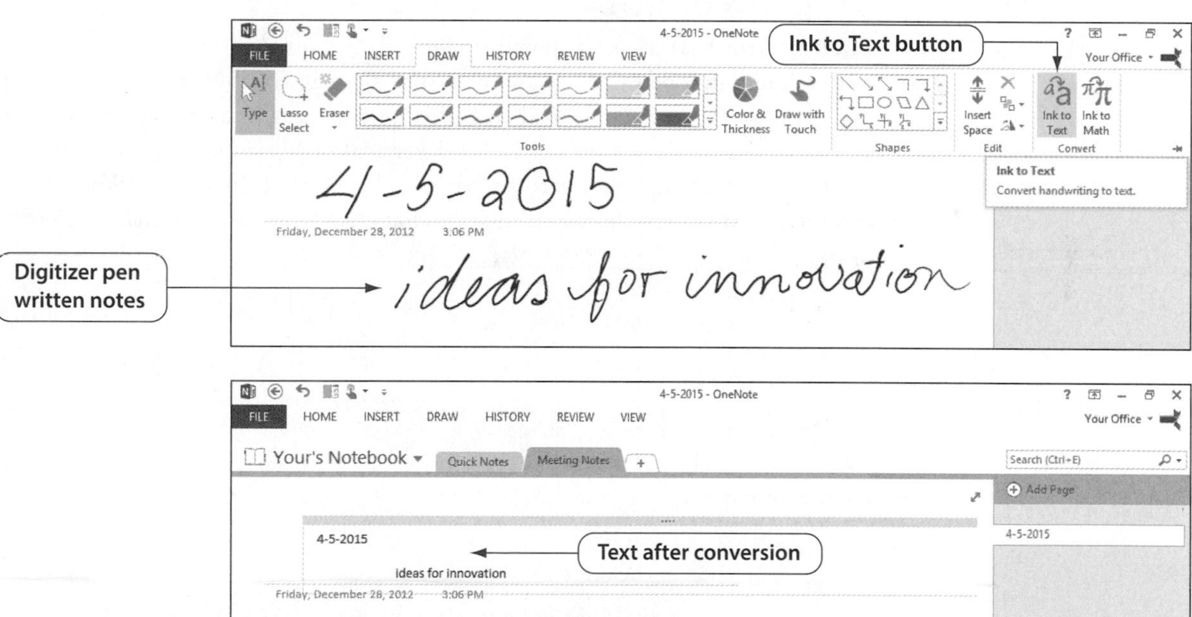

Figure 6 Handwriting in OneNote

Understanding When the Touch Interface Is Effective

Windows 8 and Office 2013 have fully integrated the touch environment. If you have a touch screen, you can manipulate Windows, Office, and other apps by just touching the screen. Fingers are larger than a mouse point. Thus, the app must be designed to be easy to use with a simple touch. One of Microsoft's main goals with the latest release of Windows and Office was to make it easier to use with touch. Touch increases efficiency and productivity when used while mobile, to replace traditional mouse movements, and to use apps specifically designed for touch.

Using the Touch-Screen Interface

One of the key features that sets Windows 8 apart from previous versions is the built-in touch-screen recognition. A **gesture** is a movement of the user's finger, fingers, or pen on a touch screen resulting in a particular action. Many gestures are available, and several factors determine the result.

- Are you using one or two fingers?
- Where did your finger start on the screen?
- Where did your finger end on the screen?
- At what speed did you move your finger?
- Did you make one or several movements together?
- On the screen, was the Start screen showing, an app running, or an app that runs on the desktop—such as Word?

Touching a screen and not understanding why the resulting action occurred is frustrating. In this section, you will learn about the types of touch and other touch-friendly features.

Use Flick, Touch, and Bezel Gestures

Intuitively, you may think of a "touch" as a simple finger tap. However, Windows 8 distinguishes between several different types of touch gestures—flicks, touch, and bezel. Knowing these different touch features will help decrease frustration, increase efficiency, and increase productivity.

Using Flick Gestures

Flick gestures (flicks), as shown in Table 2, are quick short gestures that can be made with a finger or a pen. Flicks cannot start at the edge of the screen—the **bezel**. There are two types of flicks, navigational and editing. **Navigational flicks** are enabled by default and are quick short gestures either in a vertical or horizontal direction that either scroll up and down or move forward or backward a page. **Editing flicks** are not enabled by default and are quick short gestures in a diagonal direction that either delete, copy, paste, or undo.

Flick Gesture	Result Action	Image
Up	Scroll up	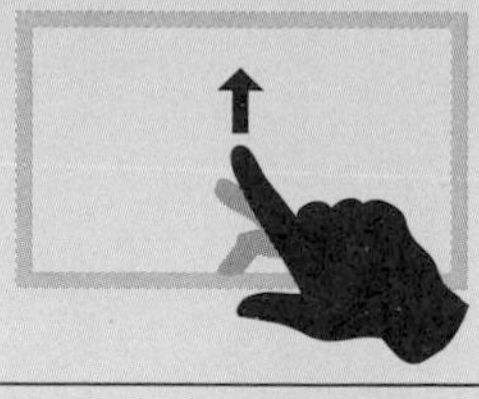
Down	Scroll down	
Right	Turn page to the right	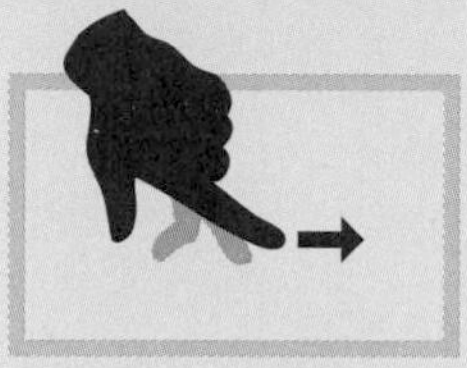
Left	Turn page to the left	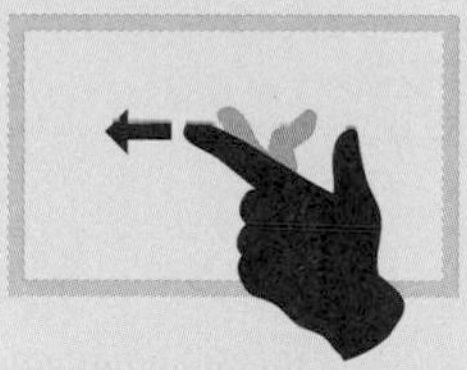
Diagonally to upper left	Delete	
Diagonally to upper right	Copy	
Diagonally to lower left	Undo	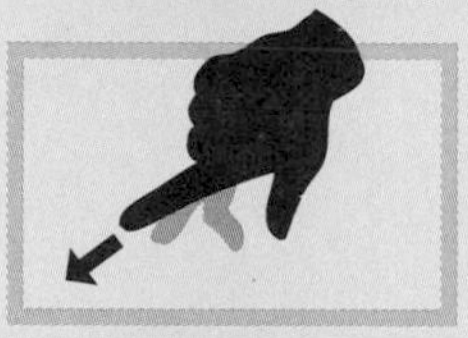
Diagonally to lower right	Paste	

Table 2 Flick gestures

You can adjust settings, modify sensitivity, enable editing flicks, turn flicks off, and practice flicks from the Pen and Touch dialog box. To modify these settings, search Windows settings for flicks as seen in Figures 7 and 8 shown here. In the same dialog box, you can also change settings and customize the pen and other touch actions.

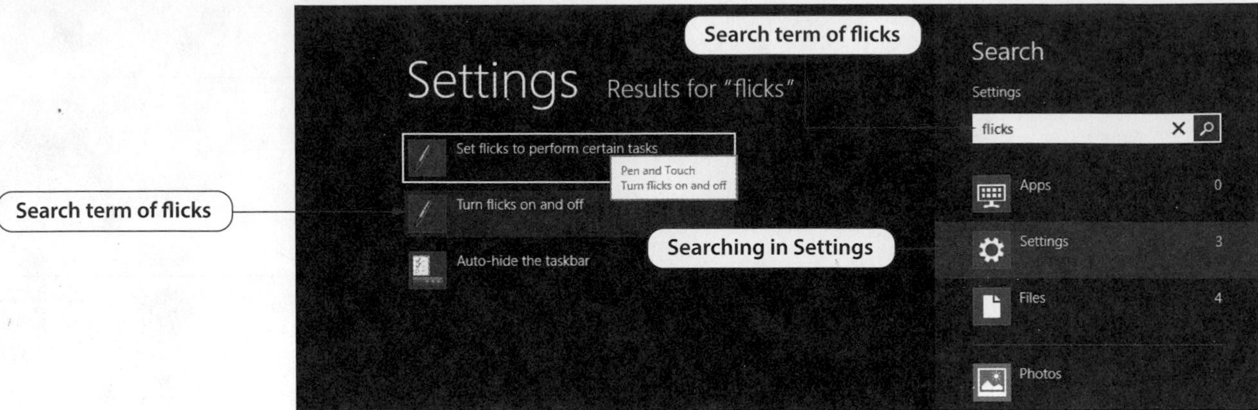

Figure 7 Search settings for flicks

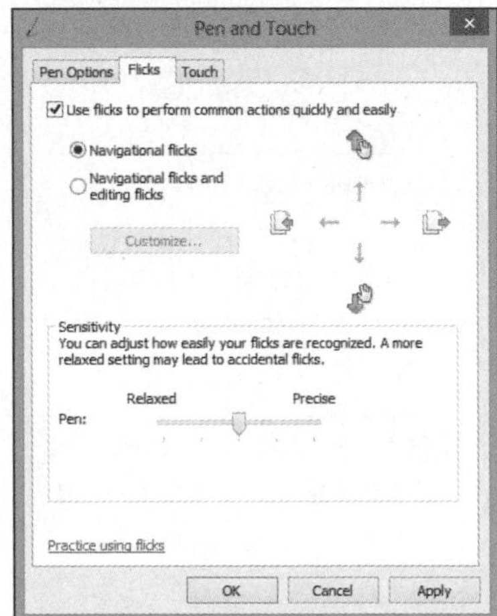

Figure 8 Pen and Tools dialog box

APPENDIX

Using Touch Gestures

Touch gestures are gestures made with a finger. Generally, these gestures cannot be completed with a pen—except pen actions set by default for tap, double-tap, and tap and hold. Touches can bring up additional menus and mimic traditional mouse actions such as double-clicking. Table 3 shows the available touch gestures.

Touch Gesture	Result Action	Image
Tap	Same action as a single mouse click	
Double-tap	Same action as a double-click on a mouse	
Tap and hold	Same action as a right-click on a mouse	
Slide	Pans or scrolls	
Pinch and stretch	Zoom in or out	
Rotate	Rotates the item that is selected	
Tap and swipe in the opposite direction as any scroll bars, not starting at a bezel	Selects the item and brings up additional menus	

Table 3 Touch gestures

Using Bezel Gestures

A **bezel gesture** is a gesture that starts and/or ends at the edge of the screen, as shown in Table 4. For example, a left bezel starts with your finger on the left edge—middle of the screen is the easiest—and swipes to the center of the screen. Some tablet cases can make these gestures difficult. These gestures are easiest when they start completely off screen.

Bezel Gesture	Result Action	Image
Left bezel	Switches to the last app that was used	
Right bezel	Opens the charms menu	
Top bezel	Brings up additional menus dependent on the currently open app. On the Start screen, it brings up menu to go to all apps. In Internet Explorer, it brings up a menu of all tabs.	
Bottom bezel	Brings up additional menus dependent on the currently open app; usually, a menu similar to the options given from a right-click on a mouse	
Left bezel and then back to left bezel again	Brings up a menu of all open apps	
Slow left bezel*	When multiple apps are open, snaps the current app to a docked position to view more than one app at the same time on the same screen	
Top bezel ending at the bottom bezel	Shows the app window shrinking and then closes the app when the bottom bezel is reached	
From title bar of a program window to the left or right bezel*	Snaps app to left or right portion of the screen docking it to view multiple apps on the same screen	

*Must have a screen resolution of at least 1366 * 768 to snap.

Table 4 Bezel gestures

Use Office 2013 Touch Gestures

Gestures can be combined or have different effects within different apps, including Office 2013. For example, the Mini toolbar is particularly helpful with the touch interface. When Office recognizes that you are using touch instead of a mouse or digitizer pen, it creates Mini toolbars that are larger and designed to work with fingers easier. To get the Mini toolbar in Excel, a combination of several gestures are needed.

1. Tap a cell.
2. Use the touch handles to select the desired cells.
3. Tap again anywhere but on the handle.

Figure 9 is an example of a touch Mini toolbar in Excel when using touch input.

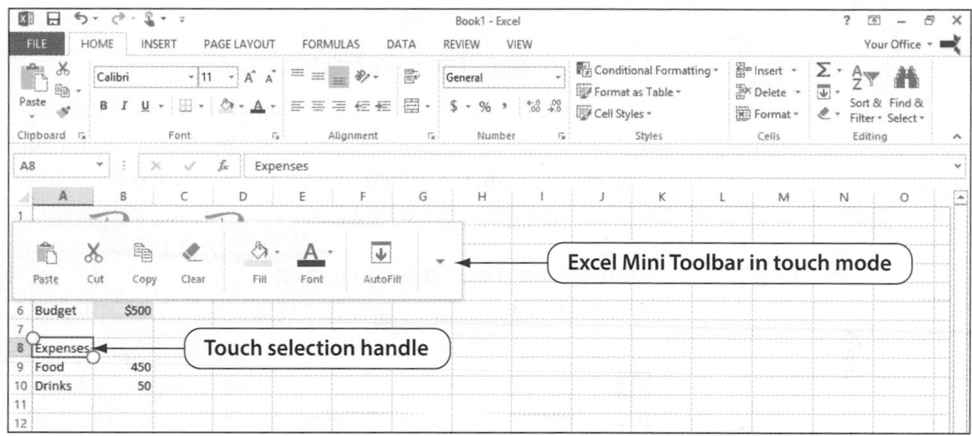

Figure 9 Excel Mini toolbar when using touch input

If you need to use Office by touch for an extended period of time, you can also use touch mode. **Touch mode** switches Office into a version that makes a touch screen easy to use, as shown in Table 5. Click the Touch Mode button on the Quick Access Toolbar, and the Ribbon spreads its icons further apart for easier access to fingers. When you toggle this display mode, the on-screen controls space out a bit from each other to make them more accessible to users via touch. Figure 10 displays the normal Word 2013 Ribbon. Figure 11 displays the Ribbon in touch mode.

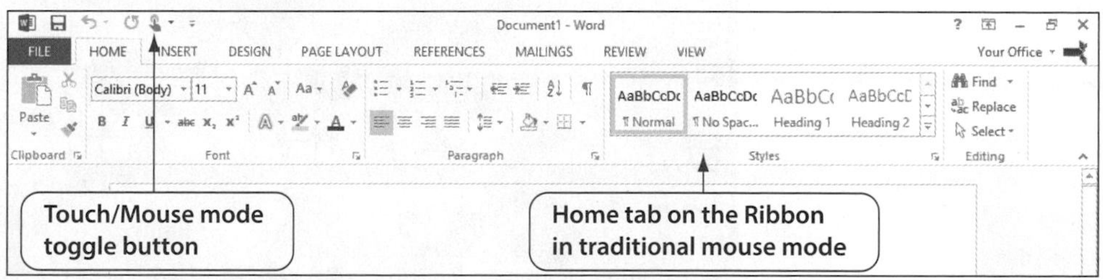

Figure 10 Normal Ribbon

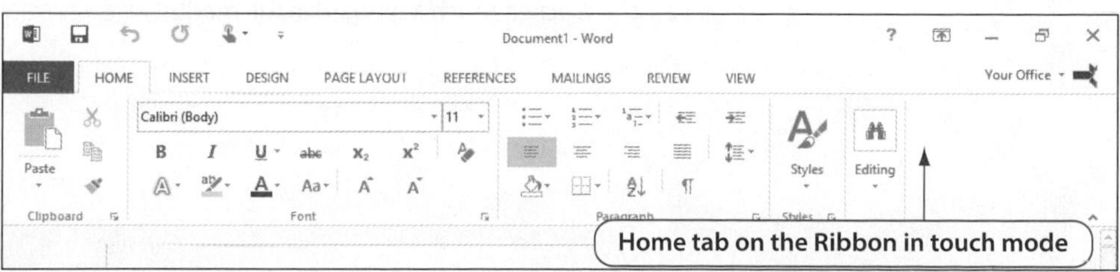

Figure 11 Touch mode Ribbon

To	Gestures Steps
Place the cursor insertion point	Tap the location for the cursor.
Select and format text	Tap the text, drag the selection handle to the desired selection, and tap the selection to show and use the Mini toolbar.
Edit an Excel cell	Double-tap.
Change PowerPoint slides in Normal view	A quick vertical flick
Customize the Quick Access Toolbar	Tab and hold any button on the Quick Access Toolbar.

Table 5 Common Office 2013 gestures

Use Other Touch Features

To make the touch experience as versatile and robust as possible, a few last touch-friendly features exist. When a keyboard is not available, a touch-screen keyboard can be used. Conversely, when a touch screen is not available, several options exist for accessing the same items achieved with touch.

Using the Touch Keyboard

If a keyboard is not available, Windows 8 provides an on-screen touch keyboard. You can access this keyboard by tapping Touch Keyboard in the taskbar. Tapping Dock will make the keyboard stay open. Tapping Undock will make the keyboard float allowing you to move it to various parts of the screen. Tapping Keyboard Mode allows you to switch between a full, thumbs, or pen handwriting mode as seen in Figures 12, 13, and 14.

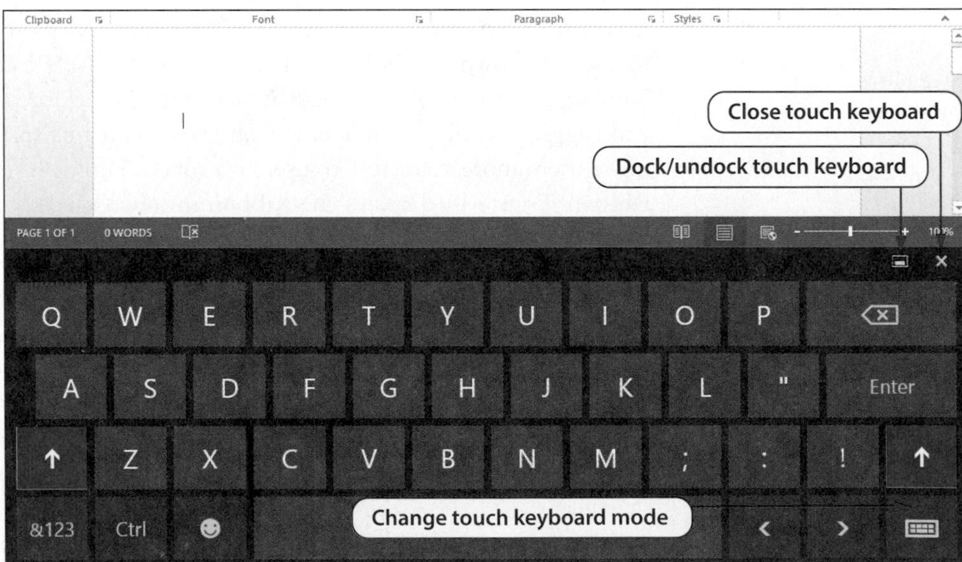

Figure 12 Docked touch keyboard in full mode

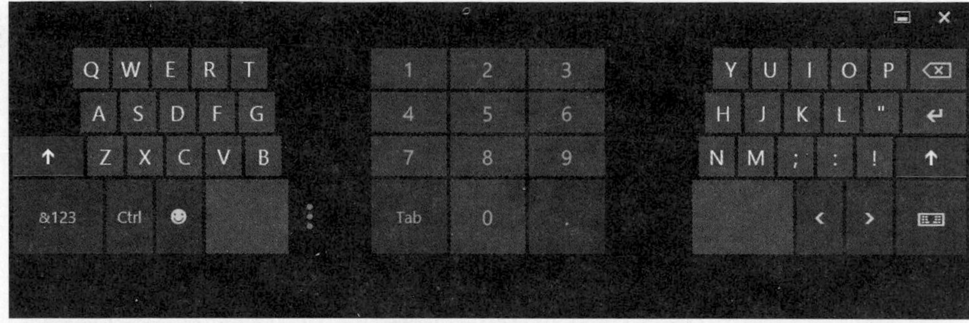

Figure 13 Docked touch keyboard in thumbs mode

Figure 14 Docked touch keyboard in pen handwriting mode

Using Alternatives to a Touch Screen

If a touch screen is not available, you have three choices. You can use a traditional mouse and point it in particular places to access the Start screen and charms menu as shown in Table 6. You can use gestures on your trackpad or Windows 8 mouse. Not all gestures work on the trackpad and may be slightly different than on a touch screen. However, device makers can add custom gestures accessible via the trackpad only. You should consult your touchpad or Windows 8 mouse manufacturer for specifics. Lastly, you can use keyboard shortcuts to access the most common bezel gestures as shown in Table 7.

Result Action	Mouse Equivalent
Start screen	Point mouse to edge of lower-left corner.
Charms menu	Point mouse to edge of lower-right or upper-right corner.

Table 6 Mouse alternatives for Windows 8

Result Action	Touch Gesture	Keyboard Shortcut
Charms menu	Right bezel	Press Windows and type C
Additional menus, similar to the right-click menus, when additional options exist	Bottom bezel	Press Windows and type Z
Switch between open apps	Left bezel swipe and then back to bezel	Press Windows + Tab or press Alt + Tab
Shrinks and then closes program	Top bezel to bottom bezel	Alt + F4

Table 7 Keyboard shortcut alternatives for bezel gestures

Concept Check

1. What is the difference between a tablet and a tablet PC? Provide an example of each. p. 1081
2. What is a digitizer pen, and when is it the most effective to use? p. 1084
3. What is the difference between a flick, touch, and bezel gesture? Provide an example of each. p. 1086–1090
4. Does touch differ at all inside of Office 2013? Explain. How could you use a tablet PC without a keyboard? How could you use a tablet PC without a touch screen? p. 1093

Key Terms

Advanced RISC Machine chip (ARM chip) 1081
Application software 1080
Bezel 1086
Bezel gesture 1090
Digitizer pen 1084
Editing flicks 1086
Flick gestures (flicks) 1086
Gesture 1086
Graphical user interface (GUI) 1080
Intel chip 1081
Navigational flicks 1086
Operating system 1080
Tablet PC 1081
Touch gestures 1089
Touch mode 1091
Trackpad 1084

Index

C

E

F

T